Concise History of
Western Music

FIFTH EDITION

Concise History of Western Music

FIFTH EDITION

Based on J. Peter Burkholder, Donald J. Grout, and Claude V. Palisca,
A History of Western Music, Ninth Edition

Barbara Russano Hanning

Professor Emeritus of The City College of New York
City University of New York

W. W. NORTON & COMPANY • NEW YORK • LONDON

W. W. Norton & Company has been independent since its founding in 1923, when William Warder Norton and Mary D. Herter Norton first published lectures delivered at the People's Institute, the adult education division of New York City's Cooper Union. The firm soon expanded its program beyond the Institute, publishing books by celebrated academics from America and abroad. By mid-century, the two major pillars of Norton's publishing program—trade books and college texts—were firmly established. In the 1950s, the Norton family transferred control of the company to its employees, and today—with a staff of four hundred and a comparable number of trade, college, and professional titles published each year—W. W. Norton & Company stands as the largest and oldest publishing house owned wholly by its employees.

Editor: Maribeth Payne
Manuscript and Project Editor: Justin Hoffman
Editorial Assistant: Michael Fauver
Electronic Media Editor: Steve Hoge
Electronic Media Assistants: Andrew Ralston and Stefani Wallace
Marketing Manager: Christopher J. Freitag
Designer: Chris Welch
Photograph Editor: Daniella Nilva
Director of Production, College: Jane Searle
Proofreader: Barbara Necol
Indexer: Marilyn Bliss
Composition by Jouve North America
Manufacturing by Courier Companies, Kendallville

Library of Congress Cataloguing-in-Publication Data
Hanning, Barbara Russano, 1940– author.
    Concise history of western music / Barbara Russano Hanning, emeritus of The City College of New York ; based on J. Peter Burkholder, Donald J. Grout, and Claude V. Palisca, A history of western music, ninth edition.—Fifth edition.
        pages cm
    Includes bibliographical references and index.
    ISBN 978-0-393-92066-6 (hardcover)
    1. Music—History and criticism.   I. Burkholder, J. Peter (James Peter). History of western music.   II. Title.
    ML160.H2827   2014
    780.9—dc23   2013046767

ISBN: 978-0-393- 92066-6

W. W. Norton & Company, Inc., 500 Fifth Avenue, New York, N.Y. 10110
wwnorton.com

W. W. Norton & Company, Ltd., Castle House, 75/76 Wells Street, London W1T 3QT

CONTENTS

PART FOUR

The Eighteenth Century

MAPS

GUIDE TO RECORDINGS

VOLUME 2: CLASSIC TO ROMANTIC

PREFACE

Like so many music students, I came to music history through performance. But it was my good fortune to have studied music history in college and beyond with instructors for whom music history was just one branch of the history of ideas, a reflection of broader movements of cultural history, the history of science, of art and literature, or religion and philosophy—in short, a record of human thought and creative activity.

From the beginning of my work on the first edition of *Concise History of Western Music*, I have striven to introduce performers and liberal arts students to the forces that shaped the works discussed in the text. In discovering how those forces played out in the works of successive generations of composers, I hope that students will be excited—as I was—to see how new discoveries, new ways of thinking, and conflicts and their resolutions influence human choices and values.

The fifth edition of *Concise History of Western Music* parallels the ninth edition of *A History of Western Music* (HWM) by J. Peter Burkholder, Donald J. Grout, and Claude V. Palisca, and matches the seventh edition of the *Norton Anthology of Western Music* (NAWM) by Burkholder and Palisca. The first fourteen chapters of *Concise*, organized into three parts that survey music from Antiquity and the Middle Ages, Renaissance music, and Baroque music through Bach and Handel, are intended for use with Volume I of NAWM; Chapters 15–22 of *Concise* (or Parts 4 and 5) discuss the Classic and Romantic repertories presented in Volume II of NAWM, including some music from the New World; and the final section of *Concise* (Part 6), now containing six chapters, 23–28, corresponds to NAWM Volume III, which is devoted to twentieth- and twenty-first-century music in Europe and the Americas and has been considerably expanded.

At the suggestion of some of the reviewers of the fourth edition, I have given the new text three more chapters than it had in the previous version. One of these is accounted for by the separation of a previously overstuffed Chapter 7 into two smaller chapters treating vocal and instrumental music of the Renaissance, respectively. The other new chapters appear in Part 6, where I have thoroughly revised, updated, and expanded coverage of the twentieth and twenty-first centuries. Reorganized chapters on the early twentieth century integrate American music into the narrative, showing the connections between European and American modernists. A new chapter on vernacular music clarifies the roles of jazz, musical theater, and other genres in twentieth-century culture. And the inclusion of new works—by Varèse, Saariaho, Villa-Lobos, Adams, and others—dramatically expands options for studying music from the recent past. Although many more works are included than can usually be covered in a given course, my aim is to provide a comprehensive background against which the instructor may undertake, with the help of the Norton Anthology, to foreground a limited number of pieces.

Pedagogical features

In order to emphasize the human choices and values that are central to music history, this text includes a number of features that place musical works in a memorable context:

At the Time boxes, new to this edition, bring the past to life, contextualizing musical work with details about contemporaneous political, cultural, and scientific developments.

At the Time

In 1913, at the time of the premiere in Paris of Igor Stravinsky's *Rite of Spring*, which provokes audiences to riot with its evocation of primitive ritual, shocking choreography, and compelling modernist score:

- The New York Armory show introduces Pablo Picasso's works to the American public.
- Charles Ives, a mature composer residing in New York, is writing his second String Quartet, in three movements titled "Discussions," "Arguments," and "The Call of the Mountains."
- Suffragettes demonstrate in London and Washington, D.C. for women's right to vote, not granted until 1920 (in the United States) and 1928 (in the United Kingdom).
- Hungarian pianist-composer Béla Bartók, disenchanted with the musical establishment in Budapest, collects folk songs among Romanians in Hungary and the Berbers in North Africa (in a region now in Algeria).
- Mohandes (Mahatma) K. Ghandi is arrested for leading Indian miners in a protest march in South Africa.
- The Ford Motor Company introduces a continuously moving assembly line to mass-produce its Model T, allowing each car to be manufactured in two hours and forty minutes.
- The Futurist Manifesto, *The Art of Noises*, published in Italy, declares that the modern world of machines calls for a new type of music based on noise (see Figure 25.15).
- A concert in Vienna, conducted by Arnold Schoenberg and featuring modernist works by Schoenberg, Anton Webern, Gustav Mahler, and Alban Berg, becomes a notorious event; the performance of Berg's new songs cause a riot of such proportions that the police are called in and the concert cannot be finished.
- Charlie Chaplin begins his film career at Keystone Studios, earning $150 per week.
- A Swedish immigrant in Hoboken, New Jersey, patents the zipper.

Figure 25.15 Music *(1911) by futurist painter Luigi Russolo, author of* The Art of Noises.
(Private collection. Photo: © DeA Picture Library/Art Resource, NY.)

In Performance sidebars highlight issues relevant to performers today, including ornamentation, continuo realization, tempo rubato, and improvisation.

In Performance Baroque Ornamentation

The word *ornament* now connotes something superficial, an added decoration that has no intrinsic merit; but for the Baroque musician, ornaments were the chief way of moving the affections. Musical ornamentation originated in improvisation—that is, it was applied spontaneously to make a performance more expressive; more wondrous; and, in the case of certain dissonant ornaments, to add a touch of spice that the notated music lacked. Even though it might later be written down or indicated with special symbols (as in Example 12.4 and Figure 12.18), ornamentation retained a degree of spontaneity.

Both vocalists and instrumentalists recognized two principal ways of ornamenting a melody. First, brief formulaic clusters of notes—such as trills, turns, appoggiaturas, and mordents—were added at certain points in the melody to highlight accents, emphasize some words

cadences and other signi
sometimes indicated the
below. Second, more ex
such as passages (*passag*

gios, and other types of flourishes—were added to create a free and elaborate paraphrase of the written line. This process—sometimes called division, diminution, or figuration—was especially appropriate for melodies in slow tempo, as in Figure 12.19. Performance practices relating to the interpretation and execution of ornaments varied from nation to nation and from one generation to another, but the tasteful and appropriate application of ornaments was always an essential part of the performer's training and skill. Although the task is complex and the results sometimes controversial, modern performers and scholars try to reconstruct these practices based on written treatises, descriptive accounts, and transcribed improvisations.

A number of "tutors," or practical treatises, were published in the seventeenth and eighteenth centuries. Most were written for a specific instrument

Innovations Recorded Sound and Its Impact

The advent of recording technology had the most significant impact on musical culture of any innovation since the printing press. It completely revolutionized the way we experience and share music as listeners, performers, or composers. When Thomas Edison made the first sound recording in his laboratory in Menlo Park, New Jersey, in 1877, using his tinfoil cylinder phonograph shown in Figure 24.6, he intended his new device as a dictation machine for offices. He had no idea that his invention would catapult some musicians to fame and fortune, deliver their product to huge audiences, and spawn a multibillion-dollar industry.

Early recordings featured famous artists, such as the great Italian tenor Enrico Caruso (1873–1921), who cut his first disc in 1902. Because he became one of the recording industry's earliest superstars, it has been said that "Caruso made the phonograph and it made him." His recordings also

preserved his performances beyond the grave. The new technology allowed performers to achieve for the first time the kind of immortality previously available only to composers.

Edison's phonograph recorded sound by a mechanical process. Mechanical recording was well suited for voices, but the limited range of frequencies that it could reproduce made orchestra music sound tinny. For years, the only symphony available was Beethoven's Fifth, recorded in 1913 by the Berlin Philharmonic for His Master's Voice (Figure 24.7). Because it was such a long piece, the company had to issue it on eight discs gathered into an "album," which became the standard format for longer works. In the 1920s, new methods of recording and reproduction using electricity—including the electric microphone—allowed a great increase in frequency range, dynamic variation, and fidelity, making the medium still more attractive to musicians and music lovers.

Figure 24.6 The design of Thomas Edison's first "talking machine," a cylinder phonograph built in 1877. To record, a person spoke into the mouthpiece while cranking the handle.
(Bridgeman Art Library.)

Innovations essays focus on musical innovations that fundamentally change how we create, disseminate, and consume music. Topics include music printing, the rise of star singers, the invention of the public concert, and the introduction of recorded sound.

In Context sidebars go beyond the narrative to contextualize musical works in broader cultural trends. Topics include nationalism, exoticism, and Expressionism.

A Closer Look sidebars unpack important genres, forms, and works. Topics include Palestrina's counterpoint, Wagner's use of Leitmotives, and serialism.

A Closer Look Leitmotives in the *Ring* Cycle

The relationship of leitmotives to one another and to drama can be illustrated by a few examples from *Das Rheingold*, the first of the operas in the *Ring* tetralogy. Near the beginning of the opera, when one of the Rhine maidens tells Alberich that whoever fashions the Rhine gold into a ring can gain limitless power, the motive under the bracket in Example 20.6a descends by thirds through a half-diminished seventh chord (E–C–A–F♯) and rises again. Its very contour suggests the circularity of a ring throughout the four-opera cycle.

The motive's identification with the ring is confirmed by several repetitions and, by the time it is recalled in the orchestral interlude between scenes one and two, in the new rhythmic form seen in Example 20.6b, the motive's identity is firmly established.

The Valhalla leitmotive, introduced at the beginning of scene two (Exa_____ _____)
with a diatonic variant of _____
linking the two in our mi_____
learn that their fates are i_____
will pay for the castle, whic_____
Alberich's curse on the ring.

Alberich's curse is prono_____
scene, after Wotan tricks hi_____
the ring. The curse motive r_____

the ring motive F♯–A–C–E), as if perverting its significance (Example 20.6d). At the same time the strong dissonances that are formed with the F♯ pedal tone rolling in the timpani intensify the threat and foreboding associated with the curse leitmotive.

The melodic relationships among the motives make the dramatic point that the ring, the castle, and the curse are bound up with each other. At the same time, they are part of a web of dozens of such leitmotives that permeate all four operas and link them to one another. In this way, the entire course of the plot is determined by the music, exemplifying Wagner's concept that the actual drama plays itself out in the music while the words, scenery, and stage action do their part to make it visible.

The elemental quality of some of Wagner's leitmotives and the fact that they draw on codes of _____

Example 20.6 Wagner, Das Rheingold, Leitmotives

a. The ring leitmotive's first appearance, as the Rhine maiden refers to the ring

Der Welt Er - be ge - wän-ne zu ei - gen, wer aus dem Rhein - gold schü-fe den Ring,

Inheritance of the world would be won as his own by he who from the Rhine gold could fashion the ring [that would endow him with limitless power].

b. The ring leitmotive in definitive form

c. Beginning of the Valhalla leitmotive

d. The first appearance of the curse leitmotive

Wie durch Fluch er mir ge - riet, ver - flucht sei die-ser Ring!

As through a curse it came to me, cursed be this ring!

Vignettes allow composers, performers, and patrons to speak in their own words with first-hand accounts of significant musical events.

Full-color illustrations throughout the volume illuminate music history by drawing connections to the visual arts.

Composer biographies introduce readers to major composers and include lists of major works.

Hildegard of Bingen (1098–1179)

Born to a noble family in the Rhine region of Germany, Hildegard at age eight was consecrated to the church by her parents. Six years later she took vows at the Benedictine monastery of Disibodenberg, and she became prioress of the attached convent in 1136. Led by a vision, she founded her own convent around 1150 at Rupertsberg, near Bingen, where she was abbess. Famous for her prophecies, Hildegard corresponded with emperors, kings, popes, and bishops and preached throughout Germany. Her many prose works include *Scivias* (Know the Ways, 1141–51), an account of twenty-six visions, and books on science and healing.

Hildegard wrote religious poems as well as prose, and by the 1140s she began setting them to music. Her songs are preserved in two manuscripts organized in a liturgical cycle, with indications that many were sung in her convents and nearby monasteries and churches. Her *Ordo virtutum* (The Virtues, ca. 1151) is the earliest surviving music drama not attached to the liturgy.

Hildegard exemplifies the flourishing musical culture of medieval women who, like their male counterparts, saw themselves as saving humanity through prayer. A letter she wrote near the end of her life reveals her view of music's profoundly spiritual nature:

so that mankind . . . be awakened to . . . the divine sweetness and the praise which Adam

Figure 2.13 Hildegard of Bingen with Volmar, a monk who assisted her in recording her visions, in an illustration from Scivias. *(Erich Lessing/Art Resource.)*

had enjoyed before his fall . . . holy prophets, taught by that Spirit which they had received, not only composed psalms and canticles, which were to be sung in order to kindle the devotion of those hearing them, but also invented diverse instruments of the musical art. . . . They did so for this reason: so that the listeners would . . . be educated in interior matters . . . while being urged on and prodded by exterior objects.[1]

Major works: *Ordo virtutum*, 43 antiphons, 18 responsories, 7 sequences, 4 hymns, 5 other chants

1. Hildegard of Bingen, Epistle 47: To the Prelates of Mainz, trans. James McKinnon; in Oliver Strunk, ed., *Source Readings in Music History*; rev. ed. by Leo Treitler (New York: Norton, 1998), vol. 2, p. 74.

Preludes and **postludes** at the beginning and end of each chapter provide overviews, summaries, retrospectives, and transitions that draw together the material presented in the text.

Total Access

Every new copy of this text includes **total access** to a full suite of media resources including:

- **Streaming recordings** of the entire *Norton Anthology of Western Music* repertoire (discussion of NAWM works throughout the book is highlighted by [Full] and [Concise] icons)
- Stunning **Metropolitan Opera video** of scenes from selected operas (availability of opera video is indicated by ▶ icons in the margin of the text)
- An **interactive ebook** that allows readers to take notes, highlight, and listen to audio examples at the click of a mouse
- **Listening quizzes** by Jessie Fillerup and Joanna Love that test students' understanding of NAWM works

To access these resources and more, go to wwnorton.com/studyspace and register with the code in the front of this book.

Accompanying Texts and Recordings

Although this book stands on its own as a narrative history, the reader's learning experience will be enriched by using it in tandem with the accompanying anthology, recordings, and study guide:

- The three-volume **Norton Anthology of Western Music (NAWM)**, seventh edition, by J. Peter Burkholder and Claude V. Palisca (Volume 1: *Ancient to Baroque;* Volume 2: *Classic to Romantic;* Volume 3: *The Twentieth Century and After*), provides a comprehensive collection of 220 scores illustrating the most significant musical composers, trends, and genres in the Western world from antiquity to the present. In the seventh edition of NAWM, 15% of the selections are new. The anthology now includes more complete works and more selections by major composers such as Bach. In addition, five selections from the past fifteen years offer unprecedented access to recent music. While almost every work appearing in the anthology is cited in the text of *Concise*, I have concentrated on the core repertoire in the *Concise Norton Recorded Anthology of Western Music*. My discussions of these works overlap with, but generally avoid repeating, the detailed musical essays that accompany them in the anthology volumes.
- The **Norton Recorded Anthology of Western Music** includes outstanding recordings of the entire NAWM repertory by some of the best ensembles performing today. It is available in a complete set of three mp3 discs and a single concise disc with selections from across the three volumes of NAWM. Streaming recordings of the complete NAWM repertoire are now included free with every new text.

For Instructors

A number of additional resources are available to adopters:

- The **Coursepack** enables students to access quizzes, recordings, and more via their campus learning management system.
- A **Test Bank** by Anthony Barone (University of Nevada–Las Vegas), Stephanie Schlagel (University of Cincinnati, College Conservatory of Music), and Laurel Zeiss (Baylor University) includes over 2,000 multiple-choice, true/false, short-answer, matching and essay questions.
- An **Instructor's Manual** by Roger Hickman (California State University–Long Beach) includes detailed teaching advice for new and experienced instructors alike.
- The **Instructor's Resource Disc** includes PowerPoint lecture outlines with eye-catching maps and illustrations from the text.

Acknowledgments

In preparing this Fifth Edition, I am indebted, first of all, to J. Peter Burkholder, whose broad knowledge and authoritative voice informs the ninth edition of *A History of Western Music* and from whose text I borrowed liberally for this revision. I have also profited enormously from comments about this new edition in all phases of its development by reviewers, including Michael Alan Anderson (Eastman School of Music), Daniel Beller-McKenna (University of New Hampshire), Keith E. Clifton (Central Michigan University), Charles Dill

(University of Wisconsin–Madison), Lars Helgert (Georgetown University), Sonya Lawson (Westfield State University), Claudia Macdonald (Oberlin College), Renee McCachren (Catawba College), Christina L. Reitz (Western Carolina University), and Marie Sumner Lott (Georgia State University). The staff at W. W. Norton has been an unfailing source of ideas, enthusiasm, and support. I am particularly grateful to Maribeth Payne, music editor, and Justin Hoffman, associate music editor, who guided the book through its many stages, provided useful advice during all of them, and cheerfully tolerated my occasional intransigence. Others at Norton have also earned my admiration and gratitude for their invaluable assistance, in particular Jane Searle, Chris Welch, and Daniella Nilva, who are largely responsible for the book's beautiful appearance. I am also deeply grateful to Barbara Necol for proofreading the text and Marilyn Bliss for preparing the index. Those involved in the preparation and editing of the electronic media, especially Steve Hoge, also deserve my thanks.

In addition, I have incurred many debts to people outside of the Norton family: Juilliard faculty member and CUNY Ph.D. Ed Klorman, who generously shared his knowledge of performance practice with me; those colleagues and former colleagues at The City College of New York who willingly answered my questions about jazz and other areas of contemporary music; my students, who constantly keep me on my toes in the classroom; and former students and instructors around the country who have used the book in its previous incarnations and offered valuable suggestions. My acknowledgments would be incomplete were they not to express my heartfelt gratitude to my husband Robert W. Hanning, an unfailing fount of information and endless encouragement; to my parents Helen and George Russano, the memory of whose love and support buoy me still; and to my mentor Claude V. Palisca, whose legacy is an ongoing source of inspiration. Finally, I dedicate this volume to my children, Rob and Amy Welsh Hanning, and Gina Hanning, and to my grandchildren Benjamin, Evan, and Noah, who will, I hope, continue to take great pleasure in music and be inspired to learn its secrets.

Barbara Russano Hanning
August 2013

Pitch Designations

In this book, a note referred to without regard to its octave register is designated by a capital letter (A). A note in a particular octave is designated in italics, using the following system:

WHY STUDY MUSIC HISTORY?

We study music history because in music, as in all other realms of human endeavor, the past influences and informs the present. Never in music history has this been more true than in our own time, when scholars have retrieved and restored so much music from the past, performers have brought it to life, and recordings, radio, television, and the Internet have disseminated it more widely than ever before. Generations ago, people had access only to music that was performed live by their parents, teachers, friends, and local entertainers. If they could read music and afford lessons, they might also have become acquainted with a few piano pieces by favorite composers or with the popular songs of Tin Pan Alley. In contrast, the technological revolution has made an overwhelming number of works available: ten centuries of written music as well as the (often unwritten) musical styles of cultures from around the globe.

Composers and musicians have always been influenced by the sounds around them, and today those sounds are almost infinite. Accessible sounds range from the folk music of various cultures and ethnic groups to popular music broadcast over the airwaves or via the Internet, even to the raw sounds of nature (such as whale songs) harnessed by modern technology. These influences are absorbed almost unconsciously and are either unintentionally or purposely incorporated into new works. Other influences are also evident as throughout history composers of one generation have engaged in a conscious and determined struggle to define themselves in opposition to, or in sympathy with, the sounds and styles of previous generations. Like children growing away from their parents, composers sometimes rebel and strike out on their own, only later to acknowledge and embrace or transform the ways of their predecessors. We find this tension—between rejecting the immediate past and accepting or reinterpreting it—in every era of music history. In fact, it mirrors a pattern we recognize in all fields of learning and the arts since the beginning of recorded history. In modern times, however, the restoration of works from the more remote past has complicated the issue for creative artists by providing an awesome array of additional models and stylistic possibilities.

In itself, the influence of a rich past may not offer enough reason to study music history. But if we want to understand *why* the music we hear was composed to sound the way it does, we look to music history for explanations. And in the process of pursuing these explanations, not only will we become better listeners, but our deepened understanding will also increase the pleasure we derive from hearing and performing the music that we do. Beyond that, it is important to recognize music's emotional power and its role in society, which has always been a forceful one but which has grown in direct proportion to its increased presence in our lives. A heightened awareness of the place that music occupies in our society will be gained by examining the role it has played in past eras. Whether heard in the concert hall or in sports and political arenas, whether used as an important element of religious services or as a strategic device in consumer and marketing services, its significance bears on every facet of our culture, and our knowledge to a certain extent determines our responses to it at every level. But there's something more we should be aware of. As violinist Christian Tetzlaff aptly stated during an interview published in *The New Yorker* (August 27, 2012):

> [Performing music] is the job that has most to do with the belief in the existence of a soul. I deal in Berg's soul, Brahms's soul—that's my job. . . . Trying to turn lead into gold is nothing compared to taking something mechanical like an instrument—a string and a bow—and using it to evoke a human soul, preserved through the centuries.

If performing music from the past is about conjuring souls, then surely the intelligent listener must be attuned to its message.

Concise History of
Western Music

FIFTH EDITION

PART ONE

The Ancient and Medieval Worlds

PART CONTENTS

From the beginning of human existence, singing has been a natural outlet for the expression of feelings. Probably even before the development of language, the utterances of the human voice gave vent to basic emotions—the wails of lament, the howls of pain, the giggles of joy, the quavering of fear. Once combined with language, singing became a powerful means of communicating not only generalized feelings, but also the most personal and subtle sentiments. By heightening and coloring the words, the singing voice can render their meaning with a force greater than they have when merely spoken.

In fact, vocal music dominates the first two parts of our history—antiquity through the Renaissance—but not because that is all there was. Rather, it constitutes most of what survives in written form. And that music, in turn, is almost exclusively a product of the elite and literate classes of society and only a tiny fraction of all the music that was made through these centuries. Nevertheless, since the advent of recorded history, attitudes toward singing have reflected the cultural and intellectual concerns peculiar to a given time and place. For example, the ancient Greeks stressed vocal music over instrumental music

Troubadour from a thirteenth-century manuscript.
(Gianni Dagli Orti/The Art Archive at Art Resource, NY.)

3

Musical Events

Musician with kithara

582 B.C.E.
Famous music-
festival competition
at Pythian games

ca. 500 C.E.
Boethius, *De
institutione musica*

Plato

Illuminated manuscript

9th cent.
Earliest notated
manuscript of
Gregorian chant

Historical Events

800 B.C.E.

800 B.C.E.
Rise of Greek city-states

753 B.C.E.
Rome founded

660 B.C.E.
Byzantium founded

ca. 500 B.C.E.
Roman Republic begins

ca. 380 B.C.E.
Plato, *Republic*

ca. 330 B.C.E.
Aristotle, *Politics*

ca. 33 C.E.
Crucifixion of Jesus

70
Destruction of the Second
Temple in Jerusalem

392
Christianity becomes official
Roman religion

400
Saint Augustine, *Confessions*

ca. 530
(Monastic) *Rule of Saint
Benedict*

590
Gregory I ("the Great")
elected pope

ca. 610–622
Founding of Islam by
Muhammad

800
Charlemagne crowned
emperor by pope

800–821
Rule of Saint Benedict
introduced in Frankish
lands

because they expected a distinctive character (ethos) from their arts that only words could impart to music. All ancient Christian music was vocal, but during the Middle Ages some church leaders were troubled by the sensuality of the voice in the performance of religious plainsong (or chant) and expressed concern about the potential distractions of song as an aid to worship (see Vignette, page 21). In the court cultures of sixteenth-century Italy, the art of singing was particularly significant: not only was it a marker for grace and nobility, but it was also believed to be the link that connected us to the entire cosmos, putting the individual in touch with the harmony of the universe.

Despite the lack of surviving musical pieces, scholars believe that the repertories of the ancient Near East (Babylonia, Mesopotamia, and other civilizations between the Mediterranean Sea and the Persian Gulf) were not very different from ours today: wedding songs, funeral dirges, military marches, work songs, nursery songs, dance music, tavern songs, banqueting music, devotional and ceremonial music, and stories sung to instrumental accompaniment—all functioning to comfort, edify, amuse, and celebrate. Although we can postulate

ca. 1180
Beginnings of
Notre Dame
polyphony

A rose window in the
cathedral of Chartres

ca. 1320
Beginning of
Ars Nova

1400

1000–1300
European population triples

ca. 1050
Watermills and windmills
boost production

ca. 1050
Romanesque style flourishes

1066
Norman Conquest of England

1095–1270
Crusades to reconquer the
Holy Land

1163
Cornerstone of Notre Dame of
Paris laid; Gothic style
flourishes in northern Europe

1264–1274
Saint Thomas Aquinas, *Summa
theologica*

ca. 1266–1337
Giotto (Florentine painter)

1309
Clement V moves papacy to
Avignon

1315–1317
Famine in northwestern Europe

1337–1453
Hundred Years' War

1347–1350
Plague kills one-third of
Europe

1353
Boccaccio, *Decameron*

1374
Petrarch dies

1378–1417
Papal Schism

1387–1400
Chaucer, *Canterbury Tales*

1431
Joan of Arc burned at the
stake

a vibrant musical life, without actual music to perform, it remains almost entirely silent.

Ancient Greece is the earliest civilization that offers us enough evidence to construct a well-rounded view of musical culture. From the myth of Orpheus, who overturned the laws of nature with his singing, we understand the power with which music was invested. In real life, the Greeks used musical magic to heal the body as well as the soul. Carefully chosen melodies could banish illness and restore order in society. Not for nothing did Plato, in the fourth century B.C.E., recommend that the ideal state be founded on suitable types of music and warn against the unsettling effects of musical innovation (see Figure I.1). Citizens of Sparta were alarmed when the contemporary musician Timotheus performed with four additional strings on his lyre, and the court ordered that they be snipped off. Lawlessness in art could lead to anarchy in society.

During the first millennium B.C.E., Rome rose from an insignificant settlement on the banks of the Tiber to perhaps the most successful empire in history. Around the time that Plato wrote his *Republic,* the actual republic of Rome, governed by a

Ancient Greece

Ancient Rome

Figure I.1 Giovanni Pisano, Plato, *ca. 1280.*
(Museo dell'Opera Metropolitana, Siena, Italy. Photo: Foto Lensini, Siena.)

The Christian Church

Church music

patrician or aristocratic class, was thriving on the Italian peninsula and absorbing many aspects of Greek culture. By the end of the first century c.e., Roman armies had conquered Greece and held sway over the entire Mediterranean world and western Europe, from Mesopotamia in the east to Spain in the west, and from Britain in the north to Egypt in the south (see Figure I.2). The musical culture they brought with them was basically that of the Greeks, which helps to explain why Greek theories became so pervasive and exerted so much influence on the various types of music and musical eras we study in this book.

Overview of the Early Middle Ages

Greek musical thought influenced medieval church music and music theory as it was transmitted to the West by Boethius (ca. 480–ca. 524; see Chapter 1), the most revered authority on music in the Middle Ages. This period in history, reckoned from the disintegration of the Roman Empire in the West during the fourth and fifth centuries to the middle of the fifteenth century, overlapping with the early Renaissance, saw the spread of the new religion, Christianity, and the establishment of many of the ideas and institutions of Western civilization, such as the university, trade guilds, and certain legal principles such as trial by jury. The term *Middle Ages* acknowledges the era's position in time between the ancient and modern worlds, or between the "classical" civilizations of Greece and Rome and the emergence of the new humanistic culture of the Renaissance. After the collapse of the Roman Empire, Christianity remained the strongest unifying force in medieval Europe. The papacy gradually gained secular authority; monastic communities, mostly following the Rule of Saint Benedict, preserved classical learning; and missionaries, sent to convert Germanic and other tribes, spread Latin civilization far and wide, including what became the first literate repertory of song—"Gregorian" chant (see Chapter 2).

As with music in any age, medieval music was shaped by currents in the larger society. Its history is particularly interwined with the history of the Christian Church, the dominant social institution for most of the Middle Ages. The Church was very much a part of the world, and the relationship between "church" and "world," or between ecclesiastical and secular leadership, advanced the causes of both sides. In the eighth century, Carolingian rulers made a concerted effort to create a new world order in which church and king worked together. This alliance was cemented in the year 800 when Charlemagne (742–814), ruler of the Frankish lands, went to Rome to be crowned emperor by the pope, thereby becoming the temporal ruler of the newly reconstituted Western Roman Empire anointed by the spritual ruler of Western Christendom (Figure I.3). One result of this political maneuver was the importation across the Alps from Italy of Roman chant, along with Roman art and architecture as well as manuscript production and illumination. Thus was Gregorian chant "imposed" on the Christian liturgy throughout Frankish lands, its repertory subsequently becoming stabilized and eventually singled out for preservation in written form.

Many aspects of Western music, from notation to polyphony, originated in church music. Those who were educated at all were educated in schools established by the Church, and most composers and theorists were trained there. We can study medieval church music today only because, unlike some other repertories, it survived. And it survived—the product of a very small number of people of wealth, leisure, and literacy, in the largest monasteries and cathedrals—only because church musicians invented notation sometime during the ninth century, and

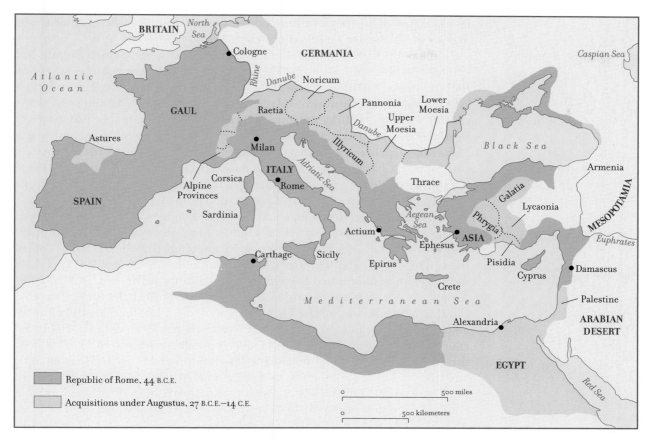

Figure I.2   The Roman Empire at the death of Augustus in 14 C.E.

*Figure I.3   Pope Leo III crowns Charlemagne emperor on Christmas day, 800, beginning
a tradition of Germanic kings being crowned by the pope, one that would last until the
fifteenth century.*
(Scala/Art Resource.)

followed it with a series of innovations in musical notation that enabled song to be written down with increasing accuracy.

Three empires

In the political arena, three principal successors to the Roman Empire had emerged by the ninth century. The most direct successor was the Byzantine Empire in Asia Minor and southeastern Europe. The strongest and most vibrant was the Arab world, which, from the founding of Islam early in the seventh century by Muhammad, rapidly expanded to dominate a vast territory from modern-day Pakistan through the Middle East, North Africa, and Spain. The weakest, poorest, and most fragmented of the three was western Europe. In this context, Charlemagne's coronation in 800 as emperor in Rome asserted to the world a continuity with the Roman past, independence from the Byzantine East, and the promise of a unified civilization in western Europe.

European culture owes much to all three empires. The Byzantines preserved Greek and Roman science, architecture, and culture. Most writings that survive from ancient Greece exist only because Byzantine scribes copied them. The Arabs extended Greek philosophy and science, fostered trade and industry, and contributed to medicine, chemistry, technology, and mathematics. Arab rulers were patrons of literature, architecture, and other arts. Charlemagne, as ruler of the Frankish kingdom and, after 800, Holy Roman emperor, also promoted learning and artistic achievement. He improved education, encouraging primary schools in monasteries and cathedral towns throughout his realm. By sponsoring scholarship and the arts, Charlemagne and his son Louis I the Pious (r. 814–43) made their courts into centers for intellectual and cultural life, setting a pattern for Western rulers that endured for a thousand years.

Political Change and Economic Development

European kings

After Louis's death, his empire was divided. Over the next few centuries the modern European nations began to emerge, although their boundaries changed frequently (see Figure I.4). The western part of the empire became France. Until about 1200, the French king was relatively weak, directly ruling only the area around Paris, while other regions were governed by nobles who owed nominal allegiance to the king but often acted independently. Their courts provided opportunities for poets and musicians, nurturing the troubadours and trouvères (see Chapter 2). In the eastern part of the empire, German kings claimed the title of emperor as Charlemagne's successors. Their realm, eventually known as the Holy Roman Empire, included non-German lands as well, from the Netherlands to northern Italy. The regional nobility in the empire competed for prestige by hiring the best singers, instrumentalists, and composers, which fueled the development of music until the nineteenth century. Outside the former Frankish lands, a centralized kingdom emerged in England in the late ninth century and continued after the Norman Conquest of England in 1066. Italy remained fragmented among several rulers, including the pope, and Spain was divided between Christian kingdoms in the north and Muslim lands in the south. The Crusades, a series of campaigns organized by both religious and secular leaders between 1095 and 1270 to retake Jerusalem from the Turks, ultimately failed but showed the growing confidence and military power of western Europe.

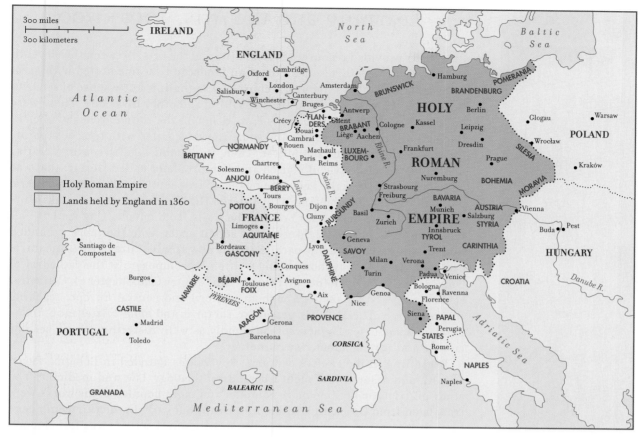

Figure I.4   Europe in the mid-fourteenth century.

These political developments went hand in hand with remarkable economic progress. Technological advances in agriculture and an expansion of cultivated lands led to great growth in production. An increasing food supply raised the standard of living and allowed the population to triple between 1000 and 1300. From about 1050 on, water-powered mills and windmills provided mechanical power for milling grain, manufacturing goods, and other uses, further boosting productivity. By 1300, western Europe had surpassed the Byzantine Empire and the Islamic world in economic strength.

The medieval economy was largely agricultural and the population mostly rural. Under feudalism (the dominant political and economic system of the Middle Ages), society was organized into three broad classes, as shown in Figure I.5: the nobility and knights, who controlled the land and fought the wars; priests, monks, and nuns, who studied and prayed; and peasants, the vast majority of the population, who worked the land and served the nobles. Peasants and serfs lived lives of oppression and drudgery, laboring from morning to night for the barest subsistence, which prompted occasional outbreaks of violent rebellion. By the twelfth century, trade in food and other products promoted the growth of markets, towns, and cities, although the largest centers were still small in modern terms: in 1300, Paris had about 200,000 residents; London about 70,000; and Venice, Milan, and Florence about 100,000 each. Music was enjoyed at all levels of society, but the nobility had the luxury of emphasizing its importance and preservation as a symbol of wealth, leisure, and status.

Economic progress

Classes of society

Learning and the Arts, 1050–1300

Prosperity provided resources for learning and the arts. Between the eleventh and thirteenth centuries, the European landscape became dotted with great cathedrals and abbeys (monastic churches), signaling a new sense of security throughout Europe after centuries of Viking and other invasions. These were built first in the Romanesque style, modeled on the round arches of ancient Roman buildings (Figure I.6) and sometimes decorated with frescoes (paintings on wet plaster) and sculptures. Then, in the mid-twelfth century, craftsmen created a new style of church architecture, later called Gothic, that was characterized by height and spaciousness, frequently with soaring towers, pointed arches, shimmering light filtered through large stained-glass windows, and flying buttresses bracing the walls from outside (Figure I.7)—all resulting in a sense of lightness that sets it apart from the more grounded Romanesque style. Roughly parallel to this new architectural style is the intricate and graceful polyphony being written by composers at the cathedral of Notre Dame in Paris in the early thirteenth century (see Chapter 3). Cathedral schools were established throughout western and central Europe, teaching future church officials Latin grammar, rhetoric, and music. After 1200, independent schools for laymen spread rapidly as well, fostering a more secular culture and a tremendous rise in literacy.

Beginning in the twelfth century, universities founded in Bologna, Paris, Oxford, and other cities taught liberal arts, theology, law, and medicine. The study of Aristotle became more common and more popular as his works were translated from Greek and Arabic into Latin. But early in the thirteenth century, the teaching of Aristotle's books about natural science was forbidden at the University of Paris. In the 1240s, the scientist Roger Bacon, who wrote commentaries on several of Aristotle's books, became the first to lecture formally on the Greek philosopher's works at the university, defending and "correcting" them after they were condemned. As the concept of university education took

Figure I.5 Fourteenth-century French manuscript illumination from a Latin translation of Aristotle's Politics, *illustrating the three estates, or classes of medieval society: the nobility, who governed and waged war; the clergy, who prayed; and the peasants, who worked the land controlled by the nobles.*
(Royal Library of Belgium.)

Figure I.6 The façade of the Romanesque church of Saint Sernin, Toulouse, France (ca. 1080–1120).
(Scala/Art Resource, NY.)

Figure I.7 The Gothic cathedral of Notre Dame (ca. 1163–1250) in Chartres, France soars over the city.
(Adam Woolfitt/Corbis.)

hold, a new kind of critical thinking known as Scholasticism emerged and dominated medieval universities from about 1100 to 1500. Scholastics (or schoolmen) developed a curriculum that attempted to reconcile the various authorities of Christian teaching, collectively known as the Church Fathers, with the classical philosophers of antiquity, especially Aristotle. Intellectuals within the Church such as Saint Thomas Aquinas articulated and defended orthodoxy by synthesizing Greek rationalism and Christian doctrine, thereby making new contributions to philosophy and theology.

Writers in vernacular languages produced a new literature of knighthood and chivalry in which courtly love was a major element. Courtly love literature presented a highly idealized image of love that contained elements common to all feudal relationships: the lover assumed a subordinate role to his beloved; he was her loyal "vassal" and, therefore, subject to her will. Much of the poetry of courtly love was sung, forming, along with chant, one of the two great monophonic repertories of medieval song.

Courtly love

Overview of the Fourteenth Century

In the fourteenth century, western Europe's economy and population declined, ravaged by famine, war, and plague. Power struggles and scandals afflicted the Church as a series of French popes maintained a splendid court in Avignon, notorious for luxury and corruption. Along with French cardinals, who functioned truly as princes of the Church, they dispensed liberal patronage to musicians, artists, and scholars, among whom was the Italian poet Petrarch, whose lyrics were to inspire composers of polyphonic song two centuries after his death. The crisis of the papacy reached its climax in the Papal Schism (1378–1417),

ARTS & IDEAS

One of the most influential philosophers in the history of Western civilization, Plato (ca. 427–347 B.C.E.) was convinced of the harmonious structure underlying the universe. The goal of his teachings was to show the rational relationship among the soul, the state, and the cosmos. His ideas about music, including its moral function in society, appear mainly in his dialogues, particularly *Republic, Laws,* and *Timaeus* (see Figure I.1).

The Greek philosopher Aristotle (384–322 B.C.E.), Plato's star pupil, relied on logic, analysis, and observation to discover what he thought were the universal truths about the world. His philosophy was often contrary to the religious doctrine of Christianity, prompting the development of Scholasticism, which tried to reconcile those ideas with religious beliefs. His views on music, expressed in *Politics* and *Poetics,* formed the basis for later theories about emotional responses to music (see vignette, page 19).

Saint Augustine (354–430 C.E.), still considered one of Christianity's most influential thinkers, was born in the Roman province of Numidia (modern-day Algeria) in north Africa and converted to Christianity in his early thirties. His *Confessions,* written when he was forty-five, tells of his spiritual journey from a worldly life to one devoted to religious thought (see vignette, page 21).

The founder of monasticism in the West, Saint Benedict (ca. 480–ca. 543) withdrew from a life of privilege in Rome to a cave outside the city, where he lived in solitude for three years before forming his own monastic community (the Benedictines) on a mountaintop in Monte Cassino, a town in central Italy. His book, *The Rule of Saint Benedict,* outlined his views on monastic life, in which music occupied a place of enormous importance (see Chapter 2 and Figure 2.3).

Born in Mecca on the Arabian peninsula, Muhammad (ca. 570–632) was the founder of Islam and the inspiration for a number of empires that dominated a large portion of the civilized world during the Middle Ages. Today there are more than 1 billion Muslims worldwide, fewer than one-fifth of whom are Arab. Muhammad's teachings were collected after his death as the Quran, the sacred text of Islam.

The English scientist Roger Bacon (1214–1292) probably studied at Oxford. He subsequently lectured on Aristotle at the University of Paris and introduced the study of light, integrating all known Greek and Islamic knowledge of the eye, vision, perspective, and optics. After joining the Franciscans, he came under suspicion by his superiors for the wealth of new ideas in his writings, the *Opus maius* (Major work), a vast encyclopedia of the arts and sciences, and of all the disciplines taught in universities at that time.

The works of Saint Thomas Aquinas (ca. 1225–1274) stand as the crowning achievement of medieval Scholastic philosophical theology. By synthesizing Aristotelian

---

during which there were two popes claiming legitimacy, one in Avignon and one in Rome (and, for a while, a third one in Pisa), with all of Europe being forced to take sides.

War   The Hundred Years' War (1337–1453), actually a series of intermittent sieges, raids, and battles, was part of the long and bitter rivalry between England and France that has surfaced periodically from the eleventh century until modern times. During its final phase, a French peasant girl who later became known as Joan of Arc, obeying voices she claimed to have heard, led an army of several thousand French forces to drive the English from French soil (Figure I.8). Although her expedition was successful, she was eventually captured, tried for heresy, and, still in her teens, burned at the stake in 1431.

Famine and plague   The worst period of famine Europe experienced during the Middle Ages occurred in the fourteenth century, from 1315 to 1317, when unusually heavy rains devastated crops and caused over 10 percent of the population to die of starvation. Later in the century, terrible epidemics of plague further decimated the population of cities like Florence so badly that they did not recover their

Science and technology   numbers until the late nineteenth century. The resulting desire to understand

thought and Christian beliefs, he elevated philosophy and theology in the minds of the learned for centuries. His greatest work, *Summa theologica* (a compendium of Christian doctrine), argued that reason and science are compatible with revelation and faith, then a radical position for a Christian theologian.

Italian sculptor and architect Giovanni Pisano (ca. 1250–1314), son of sculptor Nicola Pisano, apprenticed in his father's workshop. Together they initiated a new style of marble sculpture that culminated with Michelangelo in the Renaissance. Giovanni designed the façade of the cathedral in Siena and produced much of its sculptural decoration. Inspired by classical elements, his statuary is elegant and monumental as well as emotionally charged (see Figure I.1).

An Italian painter and designer, Giotto di Bondone (1266–1337) was the first artist since antiquity whose fame extended beyond his lifetime and native region (Florence). He led painting away from the highly formal, stylized poses of Byzantine and northern European painting and toward a more lifelike depiction of movement and expression. His justly famous fresco cycles of the lives of Jesus, Saint Francis, and the Virgin Mary drew on classical principles of form, which humanized the figures in a way that became characteristic of Renaissance art (see Figure I.9).

Petrarch (Francesco Petrarca, 1304–1374) was raised in Avignon and studied law in France and at the University of Bologna. An avid collector of ancient manuscripts, he eventually replaced law with literary studies and composed works that influenced learning and literature long after his death. He is best known for his *Rime sparse*, a collection of sonnets and other lyric poems that set the standard for Italian vernacular verse for centuries.

Italian poet and storyteller Giovanni Boccaccio (1313–1375) was educated by his father for a career in commerce and law, but, drawn instead to literature, he became a Latin and Greek scholar as well as a prolific author. His classic secular work, the *Decameron*, is a collection of one hundred witty and occasionally bawdy tales set against the somber background of the plague in Florence (see vignette, page 77).

Geoffrey Chaucer (ca. 1343–1400), the son of a prosperous London wine merchant, served two English kings (Edward III and Richard II) in a variety of governmental and civil service positions while creating a body of English poetry unequaled for its creative adaptation of French, Italian, and Latin sources. Its complex representation of interpersonal and social relationships includes *Troilus and Criseyde,* the magnificent story of a love affair tragically disrupted by the Trojan War, and *Canterbury Tales,* a collection of stories, varied in form, told by pilgrims on the road to Canterbury and featuring the celebrated and enigmatic "confessions" of the Wife of Bath and the Pardoner.

Figure I.8 A fifteenth-century German tapestry depicting Joan of Arc arriving at the Château de Marçay, Chinon, in March 1428. She is dressed in knight's armor and is being greeted by King Charles VII.
(Erich Lessing/Art Resource.)

and control disease and nature also spurred advances in science and technology. Theories of light and vision (the chief sense for the acquisition of knowledge) were highly refined, and theories of motion, explored at the universities of Paris and Oxford, provided the conceptual framework for Galileo's experiments three hundred years later.

An increasing interest in the natural world, the individual, and human nature led to a style in art and literature that was truer to life. During an outbreak of plague in Florence, Giovanni Boccaccio wrote his *Decameron*, based on the premise of ten travelers escaping to the countryside who amuse each other by telling stories. The pilgrims so imaginatively brought to life by Geoffrey Chaucer in his masterpiece, *Canterbury Tales*, engage in the same pastime on their way to the shrine of Saint Thomas Becket, the martyred archbishop of Canterbury, who was assassinated in the cathedral there in 1170. Italian artists, like the sculptor Giovanni Pisano and the painter Giotto, anticipated the Renaissance in their works by incorporating classical elements of symmetry and balance and depicting the human form with greater realism (Figures I.1 and I.9).

Figure I.9   Giotto, The Nativity, *detail, ca. 1305.*
(Cameraphoto Arte/Art Resource, NY.)

Art and literature   The elite music of the late Middle Ages reflects many of these trends. A preoccupation with structure and pleasure in certain genres surfaced for the first time, perhaps partly as a response to the disorder in society (Chapter 4). Composers in France and Italy extended the vernacular repertory of courtly love lyrics **Music** to the polyphonic realm, and the elaborate textures and rhythmic complications characteristic of the repertory at the end of the fourteenth century suggest the ostentatious pleasures of the court at Avignon (see Figure I.10). Polyphonic church music flourished, and not only in the cathedrals, as princes and patrons in every country supported musicians to write and perform music for their private chapels, both to adorn the liturgy and to foster a sense of their own importance.

Figure I.10   Scenes of Earthly Life, detail from a fresco by Andrea Bonaiuti da Firenze. The upper figures include a viella player, a falconer, a woman holding a monkey, and a merchant; below them is a group of dancers accompanied by a bagpiper. The context suggests they represent vice or overindulgence in worldly pastimes and pleasures.
(Photo courtesy of the author.)

Music in Ancient Greece and Early Christian Rome

PRELUDE

The history of Western music—that is, the art music of Europe and the Americas, as opposed to the musics of many Eastern and other cultures—begins with the ancient civilizations of the Near East and Mediterranean regions, particularly ancient Greece and Rome. Like many elements of European and American culture such as philosophy, literature, visual arts, and government, Western music has tangible connections to these early civilizations, links that go back more than three thousand years. We acknowledge these connections when we design our Supreme Court and other civic buildings to look like ancient Greek temples, when we talk about *platonic* love, and when we build bridges supported by Roman arches.

Unlike the surviving statues and architectural ruins of antiquity, however, the musical works themselves have vanished, except for about forty-five Greek songs and hymns (praise songs). But knowledge of Greco-Roman musical heritage was transmitted to modern civilization through written descriptions and through images that survived in painting or sculpture, on vases, buildings, tombs, and other artifacts from the ancient world. This evidence suggests that ancient Greek music has much in common with Western music. Then, as now, music was used in religious ceremonies, as popular entertainment, and as accompaniment to drama. Greek music theory—especially its ideas concerning pitch—was passed on to the Romans and became the basis for Western music theory. During the first and second centuries, when the Roman Empire was in its heyday, cultivated people were supposed to be educated in music, just as they were expected to know Greek and Latin. Many of the emperors were patrons of music, and one—Nero—even aspired to personal fame as a musician.

With the decline of the Roman Empire, the intellectual musical heritage of ancient Greece and Rome was transmitted to the West, if incompletely and imperfectly, through the early Christian Church, specifically in the writings of the Church Fathers and other scholars who studied and preserved this enormous body of information about music and other subjects. As the public rituals and musical practices of the early Church spread from Jerusalem to Asia Minor and westward into Africa and Europe, they picked up musical elements from different areas of the Mediterranean region. At first there was little standardization but as the prestige of the Roman emperor declined, the importance of the

Roman bishop (eventually, the pope) increased, and Christians began to acknowledge the authority of Rome in matters of faith and doctrine. This Roman dominance gradually led to the regulation and standardization of the Christian liturgy, or public worship service, and eventually (in the seventh and eighth centuries) fostered the organization of a repertory of melodies for singing sacred texts now known as Gregorian chant.

Music in Ancient Greek Life and Thought

In Greek mythology, music had a divine origin: its inventors and earliest practitioners were gods and demigods such as Apollo, Amphion, and Orpheus, and their music had magical powers. People thought it could heal sickness, purify the body and mind, and work miracles. In the Hebrew Scriptures, similar powers were attributed to music: we may recall the stories of David curing Saul's madness by playing the harp (1 Sam. 16:14–23) or of the trumpet blasts and shouting that toppled the walls of Jericho (Josh. 6:12–20).

Extant Greek music

Full 🔊   Concise 🔊

Most of the approximately forty-five surviving examples of ancient Greek music come from relatively late periods. Among them is the *Epitaph of Seikilos*, a brief song from about the first century C.E., inscribed on a tombstone (see Figure 1.1 and its transcription in NAWM 1). From this and similar examples, and from what was written about Greek music, we may deduce a close correspondence between theory and practice. Greek music was primarily monophonic—that is, melody without harmony or counterpoint—but instruments often embellished the melody while a soloist or an ensemble sang it, thus creating heterophony (simultaneous performance of a melody in different ways by two or more parts). Greek music, moreover, was almost entirely improvised. Its melody and rhythm were intimately linked to the sound and meter of Greek poetry.

Despite some similarities between Greek and early Christian musical practice, we have no evidence of any continuity in musical repertory from the earlier culture to the later one. By contrast, Greek philosophy and theory profoundly affected musical thought in western Europe in the Middle Ages. From the ancient writers, we know much more about Greek musical thought than about the music itself. Philosophers such as Plato and Aristotle wrote about the nature of music, its place in the cosmos, its effects on people, and its proper uses in human society. In both the philosophy and the science of music, the Greeks achieved insights and established principles that have survived to this day. Here we will discuss only those that were most characteristic of, and important for, the later history of Western music. We will also discover that the word *music* had a much wider meaning to the Greeks than it has today.

Figure 1.1   A tomb stele from Aydin, near Tralles, Asia Minor (now Turkey). It bears an epitaph, a kind of scolion, or drinking song, with pitch and rhythmic notation, identified in the first lines as being by Seikilos, probably first century C.E. See the transcription in NAWM 1.
(National Museum, Copenhagen, Department of Classical and Near Eastern Antiquities, Inventory No. 14897.)

The close union between music and poetry is one measure of the Greeks' broad conception of music. For them, the two were practically synonymous. Plato, for example, held that song (*melos*) was made up of speech, rhythm, and harmony (which he defined as an agreeable succession of pitches in a melody). "Lyric" poetry meant poetry sung to the lyre; the original Greek word for "tragedy" incorporates the noun *ōdē*, "the art of singing." Many other words that designated different kinds of poetry, such as *hymn*, were musical terms. In the *Epitaph of Seikilos*, the musical rhythms of each line of the poem follow the text rhythms very closely. And if we knew the correct pronunciation of the ancient

A Closer Look   Ancient Greek Music: Kithara and Aulos

From earliest times, music played an integral role in religious ceremonies. The lyre was associated with the cult of Apollo, god of light, prophecy, and the arts, especially music and poetry. It was used to accompany dancing, singing, or recitation of epic poetry such as Homer's *Iliad* and *Odyssey*; to provide music for weddings; and to play for recreation. The lyre and its larger counterpart, the kithara (Figure 1.2), had five to seven strings (later as many as eleven) that were plucked. Another instrument, the aulos, was characteristically used in the worship of Dionysus, god of fertility and wine; hence its presence in the drinking scene in Figure 1.3. A single- or double-reed instrument sometimes incorrectly identified as a flute, it often appears with twin pipes. It was also used in theatrical performances of the great Greek tragedies by Aeschylus, Sophocles, and Euripides created for the Dionysian festivals in Athens. These plays have choruses and other musical sections that combined or alternated with the sounds of the aulos.

From the sixth century B.C.E. or even earlier, both the lyre and the aulos were independent solo instruments. In fact, learning to play the lyre was a core element of the education of Athenian youth, both male and female. Contests of kithara and aulos players as well as festivals of instrumental and vocal music became increasingly popular. When instrumental music grew more independent, the number of virtuosos multiplied and the music itself turned more complex. Alarmed by this trend, the philosopher Aristotle warned against too much professional training in general music education. A reaction against technical virtuosity and musical complexity set in, and by the beginning of the Christian era Greek music as well as its theory were simplified.

Figure 1.2   A kitharode singing to his own accompaniment on the kithara. His left hand, which supports the instrument with a sling (not visible), is damping some of the strings, while his right hand has apparently just swept over all the strings with a plectrum. A professional musician like this one wore a long, flowing robe and a mantle. The Berlin Painter (?), detail from an Attic red-figured amphora, ca. 490 B.C.E. (Metropolitan Museum of Art, Fletcher Fund, 1056 (56.171.38).)

Figure 1.3   Woman playing the double aulos in a drinking scene. Usually a single-reed but sometimes a double-reed instrument, the aulos was typically played in pairs. Here the player seems to finger identical notes on both pipes. Oltos (?), Attic red-figured drinking cup, 525–500 B.C.E. (Archivo Fotográfico, Museo Arqueológico Nacional, Madrid.)

Greek verses, we might well discover that the contours of the melody match the rising and falling inflections of the words.

Music and ethos

Ethical

Greek philosophers believed that music could influence ethos, one's ethical character or way of being and behaving. In the Pythagorean view that the same mathematical laws governing music operate throughout the cosmos in both the visible and invisible world, even the human soul was a composite whose parts were kept in harmony by numerical relationships. Music, then, could penetrate the soul and restore (or shatter) its inner harmony in the same way that *harmonia* determined the orderly motion of the planets. And the legendary musicians of mythology, it was believed, owed their ability to sway human beings as well as nature to this transforming power of music.

Theory of imitation

Closely related to the concept of ethos is Aristotle's theory of imitation, which explains how music affects behavior (see Vignette, page 19). Music, he writes in the *Politics* (ca. 330 B.C.E.), imitates (that is, represents) the passions or states of the soul, such as gentleness, anger, courage, temperance, and their opposites. Music that imitates a certain passion also arouses that passion in the listener and thereby influences a person's ethos. Habitual listening to music that stirs up ignoble passions, for example, may warp a person's character, whereas the right kind of music tends to fashion a person of good character. Aristotle argues, for example, that those being trained to govern should avoid melodies expressing softness and indolence and should listen instead to melodies that imitate courage and similar virtues.

Music in education

Both Plato and Aristotle believed that a public system of education stressing gymnastics to discipline the body and music to discipline the mind could create the "right" kind of person. In his *Republic,* written about 380 B.C.E., Plato insists that these two educational components must be balanced: too much music makes a man effeminate or neurotic, while too much athletics makes him uncivilized, violent, and ignorant. Plato recommends the use of two modes (styles of melody)—Dorian and Phrygian—because they foster the passions of temperance and courage. He excludes other modes from his ideal republic and deplores current styles that rely on too many notes, on scales that are too complex, and on the mixing of incompatible genres, rhythms, and instruments. He disapproves of changing established musical conventions, saying that lawlessness in art and education inevitably leads to poor manners and anarchy in society. In contrast, Aristotle is less restrictive than Plato about particular modes and rhythms. He holds that music can be used for amusement and intellectual enjoyment as well as for education. But he also believes that music is powerful enough, especially in combination with drama, to arouse certain emotions (like pity and fear) in people and so relieve or purge them of those same emotions cathartically.

In limiting the kinds of music they would allow in the ideal society, Plato and Aristotle showed their appreciation of the great power music held over people's intellectual and emotional well-being. In later centuries, the Church Fathers also warned regularly against certain kinds of music. Nor is the issue dead. In more recent times, guardians of morality have expressed concern about the kinds of music (and pictures, lyrics, and performances) to which young people are exposed, and ragtime, jazz, rock, punk, rap, and hip-hop were all initially condemned for these very reasons.

Greek music theory

Our modern system of music theory and its vocabulary derives largely from ancient Greek musical thought. Greek theorists, from Pythagoras (ca. 580 – ca. 500 B.C.E.) to Aristides Quintilianus nine hundred years later, not only discovered numerical relationships among pitches, but also developed systematic descriptions of the elements of music and the patterns of musical composition.

Music and number

For Pythagoras and his followers, numbers were the key to the universe, and music was inseparable from numbers. Rhythms were ordered by numbers, as was poetic meter, because each note or syllable was some multiple of a primary duration. Pythagoras is credited with discovering that the octave, fifth, and fourth, long recognized as consonances, are generated by the simplest possible numeric ratios. For example, when a vibrating string is divided into segments, one twice as long as the other (expressed by the ratio 2:1), an octave results; 3:2 yields a fifth; and 4:3, a fourth.

The Greek discipline of harmonics, or the study of matters concerning pitch, laid the foundation for modern concepts such as notes, intervals, scales, and modes. These were first explored and defined by Greek writers, including Aristoxenus around 320 B.C.E. (*Harmonic Elements*) and Cleonides, who lived some five or six hundred years later. Intervals, such as tones, semitones, and ditones (thirds), were combined into scales. Certain intervals, such as the fourth, fifth, and octave, were recognized as consonant. The scale's principal building block was the tetrachord, made up of four notes spanning the interval of a fourth. Theorists recognized three kinds, or genera, of tetrachord: diatonic, chromatic, and enharmonic, the last involving intervals smaller than a semitone. Such variety allowed for a broad range of expression and many different nuances within melodies.

Harmonic Elements

Tetrachords

Because musical rhythms and sounds were ordered by numbers, they were thought to exemplify the general concept of *harmonia,* the unification of parts into an orderly whole. Through this concept—flexible enough to encompass

---

VIGNETTE Aristotle on the Doctrine of Imitation, Ethos, and Music in Education

Music's importance in ancient Greek culture is evident in contemporary books about society, such as Aristotle's Politics. *Aristotle believed that music could imitate and thus directly affect character and behavior, and, therefore, should play an important role in education.*

[Melodies] contain in themselves imitations of ethoses; and this is manifest, for even in the nature of the harmoniai [modes or styles of music] there are differences, so that people when hearing them are affected differently and have not the same feelings in regard to each of them, but listen to some in a more mournful and restrained state, for instance the so-called Mixolydian, and to others in a softer state of mind, for instance the relaxed harmoniai, but in a midway state and with the greatest composure to another, as the Dorian alone of the harmoniai seems to act, while the Phrygian makes men divinely suffused; for these

things are well stated by those who have studied this form of education, as they derive the evidence for their theories from the actual facts of experience. And the same holds good about the rhythms also, for some have a more stable and others a more emotional ethos, and of the latter some are more vulgar in their emotional effects and others more liberal. From these considerations therefore it is plain that music has the power of producing a certain effect on the ethos of the soul, and if it has the power to do this, it is clear that the young must be directed to music and must be educated in it. Also education in music is well adapted to the youthful nature; for the young owing to their youth cannot endure anything not sweetened by pleasure, and music is by nature a thing that has a pleasant sweetness.

Aristotle, *Politics* 8.5, trans. Harris Rackham; in Oliver Strunk, ed., *Source Readings in Music History,* rev. ed. by Leo Treitler (New York: Norton, 1998), vol. 1, p. 29.

mathematical proportions or the structure of society as well as musical intervals—Greek writers perceived music as a reflection of the order of the entire universe (see In Context, page 24).

Early Christian writers about music transmitted some of these Greek concepts to the Middle Ages in their original form. Other concepts were poorly understood and survived only after being adapted to the musical practice of Gregorian chant. Still others were forgotten altogether until their rediscovery by the great Renaissance humanist scholars of the fifteenth and sixteenth centuries (see Chapter 6).

Roman Music, 200 B.C.E.—500 C.E.

The Romans took much of their musical culture from Greece, especially after the Greek islands became a Roman province in 146 B.C.E. As in Greece, lyric poetry was often sung. Music was part of most public ceremonies and played an important role in religious rites, military events, theatrical performances, private entertainment, and education.

Rome's decline

During the great days of the Roman Empire in the first and second centuries C.E., art, architecture, music, philosophy, and other aspects of Greek culture were imported to Rome and other cities. Ancient writers tell of famous virtuosos, large choruses and orchestras, and grand music festivals and competitions. But with the economic decline of the empire in the third and fourth centuries, production of music on the large and expensive scale of earlier days ceased, leaving almost no traces on later European developments.

By the fifth century, the Roman Empire, which had for a time imposed peace on most of western Europe and on large parts of Africa and Asia as well, declined in wealth and strength. Unable to defend itself against invaders from the north and east, it was too large and weak to continue. The common civilization it had fostered throughout Europe splintered into fragments that would take many centuries to regroup and emerge as modern nations (compare maps, pages 33 and 112).

The Early Christian Church: Musical Thought

Church Fathers

As the Roman Empire declined, however, the Christian Church gained influence, becoming the main—and, often, the only—unifying force and channel of culture in Europe until the tenth century. With the help of the Church Fathers, highly influential Christian writers and scholars who interpreted the Bible and set down some guiding principles, the Church took over Rome's mission of civilizing and unifying the peoples under its sway. Writing in Greek (Clement of Alexandria, Origen, Saint Basil, and Saint John Chrysostom in the third and fourth centuries) or in Latin (Saint Ambrose, Saint Augustine, and Saint Jerome in the fourth and early fifth centuries), they saw in music the power to inspire divine thoughts and to influence, for good or evil, the character of its listeners (a version of the Greek concept of ethos). When the last Roman emperor finally left the throne in 476 C.E. after a terrible century of wars and invasions, the power of the papacy was already well established.

Philosophers and church leaders of the early Middle Ages disdained the idea that music might be enjoyed solely for its play of sounds, something we now take for granted. Without denying that the sound of music could be pleasurable, they held to the Platonic principle that beautiful things exist to remind us of divine and perfect beauty, not to inspire self-centered enjoyment or seduce our senses. This view forms the basis for many of the pronouncements against music made by some Church Fathers (and, later, by some theologians of the Protestant Reformation; see Chapter 8). Others, however, not only defended pagan art, literature, and music, but found themselves so deeply affected by these arts that they actually worried about taking pleasure in listening to music, even in church. Saint Augustine (354–430 c.e.) expresses this concern in a well-known passage from his *Confessions* (see Vignette, below).

The music theory and philosophy of the ancient world—or whatever could still be found after the collapse of the Roman Empire and the invasions from the north—were gathered, summarized, modified, and transmitted to the West during the early Christian era, most notably by the writers Martianus Capella and Boethius.

In his widely read treatise *The Marriage of Mercury and Philology* (early fifth century), Martianus described the seven liberal arts: grammar, dialectic (logic), rhetoric, geometry, arithmetic, astronomy, and harmonics (music). The first three, the verbal arts, came to be called the *trivium* (three paths), while the last four, the mathematical disciplines, were called the *quadrivium* (four paths) by Boethius. Music was part of the Quadrivium because its precise numeric relationships seemed to furnish the key to explaining the universe, the harmony of the entire cosmos.

Boethius (ca. 480–ca. 524), depicted in Figure 1.4, was the most revered authority on music in the Middle Ages: his *De institutione musica* (The Fundamentals of Music; see A Closer Look, page 22), widely copied and cited for the next thousand years, treats sounding music as a science of numbers because numerical relationships and proportions determine intervals, consonances, scales, and tuning. Boethius compiled the book from Greek sources, mainly a long treatise by Nicomachus and the first book of Ptolemy's *Harmonics*. Although medieval readers may not have realized how much Boethius borrowed from other authors (a standard practice at the time), they understood that his statements were based on Greek mathematics and music theory.

Dangers of music

Transmission of Greek music theory

Martianus Capella

Boethius

VIGNETTE Saint Augustine on the Benefits and Dangers of Music

Augustine is one of the most significant thinkers in the history of Christianity and Western philosophy. His Confessions are often considered the first modern autobiography. In the passage below, he expresses the tension between music's abilities to heighten devotion and to seduce with pleasure.

When I recall the tears that I shed at the song of the Church in the first days of my recovered faith, and even now as I am moved not by the song but by the things which are sung—when chanted with fluent voice and completely appropriate melody—I acknowledge the great benefit of this practice. Thus I waver between the peril of pleasure and the benefit of my experience; but I am inclined, while not maintaining an irrevocable position, to endorse the custom of singing in church so that weaker souls might rise to a state of devotion by indulging their ears. Yet when it happens that I am moved more by the song than by what is sung, I confess sinning grievously, and I would prefer not to hear the singer at such times. See now my condition!

Saint Augustine, *Confessions* 10:33, trans. James W. McKinnon, in Oliver Strunk, ed., *Source Readings in Music History*, rev. ed. by Leo Treitler (New York: Norton, 1998), vol. 2, p. 22.

A Closer Look Boethius's *Fundamentals*

In the opening chapters of *De institutione musica,* the most original part of the treatise, Boethius divides music into three types. The first is the inaudible *musica mundana* (cosmic music), the numerical relations controlling the movement of the planets, the changing of the seasons, and the combination of elements. The second is *musica humana,* which harmonizes and unifies the body and soul and their parts. Last is *musica instrumentalis,* audible music produced by instruments and voices, which exemplifies the same principles of order as the other types of music, especially in the numerical ratios of its musical intervals.

Because music could influence character and morals, Boethius assigned it an important place in the education of the young, both in its own right and as an introduction to more advanced philosophical studies. In placing *musica instrumentalis*—the art of music as we commonly understand it now—in the third and presumably lowest category, Boethius indicated that, like his predecessors, he saw music primarily as a science, the discipline of examining the diversity of high and low sounds by means of reason and the senses, and only secondarily as a practice. Therefore, the true musician is not the singer or someone who makes up songs by instinct without understanding the nature of the medium, but rather the theorist and critic, who can use reason to make discoveries and judgments about the essence and the art of music.

Figure 1.4   An early twelfth-century drawing with fanciful portrayals of Boethius and Pythagoras, above, and Plato and Nicomachus, below. Boethius measures out notes on a monochord, a string stretched over a long wooden box with a movable bridge to vary the sounding length of the string. Pythagoras strikes bells with hammers. The others were revered as authorities on music.

(By permission of the Syndics of Cambridge University Library, England.)

The Early Christian Church: Musical Practice

Greek legacy

During their first two or three centuries, Christian communities incorporated features of Greek music and the music of other cultures bordering on the eastern Mediterranean Sea into their observances. However, early church leaders saw music as the servant of religion, and they rejected the idea of cultivating music purely for enjoyment. They also disapproved of the forms and types of music connected with great public spectacles such as festivals, competitions, and dramatic performances, as well as the music of more intimate social occasions. It was not that they disliked music itself; rather, they wanted to wean converts away from anything associated with their pagan past. For this reason, the entire tradition of Christian music for over a thousand years was one of unaccompanied singing.

Christianity sprang from Jewish roots, and some elements of Christian observances derive from Jewish traditions, chiefly the chanting of Scripture and the singing of psalms, poems of praise from the Old Testament Book of Psalms. We find parallels between the Jewish temple service and the Christian Mass of later centuries (described in Chapter 2): both centered on sacrifice—in the temple, literally in the form of burnt offerings, and in the Mass, symbolically in the form of bread and wine as the body and blood of Christ. Both traditions relied on vocal music in worship services, the playing of musical instruments having been banned as a sign of mourning after the destruction of the Second Temple in 70 C.E. The Mass also commemorates the Last Supper that Jesus shared with his disciples and thus imitates the festive Jewish Passover Seder, which was accompanied by psalm-singing. Singing psalms assigned to certain days eventually became a central element in all Christian observances.

As the early Church spread from Jerusalem to Asia Minor, North Africa, and Europe, it absorbed other musical influences. For example, the monasteries and churches of Syria were important in the development of psalmsinging and the use of strophic devotional songs, or hymns. The singing of devotional songs was the earliest recorded musical activity of Jesus and his followers (Matthew 26:30; Mark 14:26). Both psalms and other types of praise songs traveled from Syria by way of Byzantium (in Asia Minor) to Milan (Italy) and other Western centers.

In 395 C.E. the political unity of the ancient world was formally divided into Eastern and Western Empires, with capitals at Byzantium and Rome, followed eventually by a theological rift between Eastern and Western churches. The Western church became the Roman Catholic Church and the bishop of Rome was known as the pope. The city of Byzantium (later Constantinople, now Istanbul), at the crossroads between Europe and Asia Minor, remained the capital of the Eastern Empire for more than a thousand years, until its capture by the Turks in 1453. During much of this time, Byzantium, located on the northern rim of the Mediterranean Sea, flourished as a cultural center that blended elements of Western, African, and Eastern civilizations. From the Byzantine church, ancestor of the present-day Orthodox churches, missionaries took their Greek rites north to the Slavs, resulting in the establishment of the Russian and other Slavic Orthodox churches. But in the absence of a strong central authority, the various Christian churches of the Eastern Empire developed different liturgies. Byzantine musical practices left their mark on Western chant, particularly in the classification of the repertory into eight modes, or melody types, and in a number of hymns borrowed by the West between the sixth and ninth centuries.

In the West, the diffusion of the Latin liturgy and its music occurred in the fifth and sixth centuries, with the texts remaining more stable than the melodies. As in the East, local churches were relatively independent at first. Although they shared a large area of common practice, each Western region probably received the Roman heritage, including the Latin liturgy, in a somewhat different form. These original differences, combined with local variations, eventually produced several distinct Western liturgies and bodies of liturgical music between the fifth and eighth centuries. Peoples who inhabited what is now Italy, France, and Germany developed their own repertory of melodies for singing sacred texts in Latin. We call these melodies chants, and the

In Context   Sounding and Silent Harmony: Music and Astronomy

Figure 1.5   Venus Playing a Psaltery, *folio 42v of the fourteenth-century astrological treatise* Liber astrologiae. *Seated on an elaborate throne, the goddess is plucking a psaltery. On the left is a fiddle, on the right a cittern.*
(From *Liber Astrologiae*. Courtesy The British Library, Sloane 3983, f.42v.)

For many thinkers of the ancient world, music was closely connected to astronomy because mathematics dominated the study of both subjects. In fact, Pythagoras (fl. 530 B.C.E.), who recognized the numerical relationships that govern musical intervals, is famous for his discovery of specific mathematical laws such as the familiar Pythagorean theorem. Ptolemy (second century C.E.), the most systematic of the ancient Greek theorists of music, was also the leading astronomer of antiquity. Numerical proportions were thought to underlie the systems both of musical intervals and of the heavenly bodies, and certain modes and notes were believed to correspond to particular planets, their distances from each other, and their movement in the heavens. Plato gave this idea poetic form in his myth of "the music of the spheres" (*Republic* 10.617), the unheard music produced by the harmonious relationships among the planets as they revolved around the earth.

In the Middle Ages, music was defined as the discipline that deals with numbers in their relationship to sounds. Medieval Christian philosophers from Saint Augustine (354–430 C.E.) to Saint Thomas Aquinas (ca. 1225–1274) believed that a knowledge of proportion and number was essential to understanding God's universe. Seen as one of the seven liberal arts, music was grouped with the mathematical and speculative sciences in the quadrivium, the path of learning that led to the contemplation of philosophy. In this curriculum, music had a place of honor next to astronomy because, through numerical analogies and ratios, it could help explain connections between things perceived by the senses (such as sound), things knowable only through reason and speculation (such as the movement of heavenly bodies), and things that could never be known because they belonged to the realm of the divine (such as the mysteries of the human soul). So the numerical relationships that regulated both music and astronomy provided the foundation for knowledge about the order and system of the entire universe.

Pythagorean and Platonic ideas about cosmic harmony and music of the spheres prevailed during the Renaissance and persist even into the modern era. Along the way, these ideas strongly influenced astronomers, physicians, architects, and poets, including Dante, Shakespeare, and Milton. In addition, astronomy and music had close ties to astrology, which has maintained considerable appeal since antiquity, despite arousing the suspicion of Christian philosophers and theologians through the ages and the derision of scientists and other rationalists today. Boethius's popular notions about *musica mundana* and *musica humana* (see A Closer Look, page 22), which affirmed Greek theories about the relationship between the music of the spheres and music's influence on human character and morals, left the door wide open for astrology in the Middle Ages; then, as now, astrologers interpreted the influence of the heavenly bodies on human affairs. In astrological symbolism, the planets Venus and Mercury hold particular sway over the musical attributes of humans; for this reason, medieval and Renaissance depictions of Venus often include musical instruments (see Figure 1.5).

TIMELINE Greece and Rome

Musical Events	**582 B.C.E.** Famous music festival competition at Pythian games	**ca. 320** Aristoxenus, *Harmonic Elements*	**ca. 1st cent. C.E.** *Epitaph of Seikilos* (NAWM 1)

1000 B.C.E.   **1 C.E.**

Historical Events	**800 B.C.E.** Rise of Greek city-states	**ca. 497** Pythagoras dies	**4 C.E.** Birth of Jesus
	753 Rome founded	**458** Aeschylus, *Agamemnon*	**ca. 33** Crucifixion of Jesus
	ca. 700 or earlier Homer, *Iliad* and *Odyssey*	**414** Euripides, *Iphigenia in Taurus*	**54** Nero becomes emperor of Rome
	660 Byzantium founded	**ca. 380** Plato, *Republic*	**70** Second Temple at Jerusalem destroyed
		ca. 330 Aristotle, *Politics*	
		46 B.C.E. Julius Caesar becomes dictator	
		29–19 Virgil, *Aeneid*	

different regional styles may be called dialects by analogy to language. Gaul (approximately the same area as modern France) had the Gallican chant; southern Italy, the Beneventan; Rome, the Old Roman chant; Spain, the Visigothic, or Mozarabic; and the area around Milan, the Ambrosian. Eventually, most of the local versions either disappeared or were absorbed into the single uniform practice under the central authority of the Roman Catholic church. From the thirteenth to the sixteenth centuries, the liturgy of the Western church became increasingly Romanized.

Rome's musical dominance

How did the thousands of chant melodies associated with Christian worship survive over so many centuries? During the ninth century, Frankish monks and nuns—from modern-day Switzerland, France, and western Germany—played a crucial role in their preservation, not only by learning to sing them, but also by laboriously notating the texts and melodies by hand into manuscripts that were housed in monastic libraries (see In Context, page 35). The repertory of melodies thus transmitted in writing, known as Gregorian chant, will be examined in the next chapter. Although its origins are still being unraveled by modern scholars, it testifies to the enduring power of music in medieval civilization and to its role in sustaining the faith of a people.

Gregorian chant

POSTLUDE

Although many details are uncertain, we know that in the ancient world (1) music consisted essentially of a single melodic line; (2) vocal melody was intimately linked with the rhythm and meter of words; (3) musical performances were memorized or improvised (not read from notation), in keeping with accepted conventions; (4) philosophers believed that music was both an orderly system interlocked with nature and a force in human thought and conduct; (5) a scientifically based acoustical theory was in the making; (6) scales were built up from tetrachords; and (7) musical terminology was well developed. The last three elements of this heritage were specifically Greek; the others were common also among other cultures in the ancient world.

This heritage was transmitted to the West, if incompletely and imperfectly, through the Christian Church, the writings of the Church Fathers, and early medieval scholarly treatises on music and other subjects. The awesome powers attributed to music by the ancient Greeks were still convincing 600 years later to Saint Augustine, who confessed his concern about the pleasure he experienced while listening to music. Boethius wrote an influential treatise based on the Greek view of music as a science of numerical ratios and an important educational force. In practice, early Christian church music absorbed elements from many cultures, and local variants of the liturgy and its chant existed throughout the Byzantine and Western Roman Empires. Eventually, the practices of the Roman church prevailed, and the body of melodies known as Gregorian chant became the established repertory in the West.

The church music we will examine in the next several chapters accounts for only a small part of the music-making in the Middle Ages. Popular and folk traditions, from games and dances to work-related activities, learned aurally and passed on from memory, were all accompanied by instrumental or vocal music of which we have no knowledge. From the necessarily limited survey contained within the pages of this book, therefore, it might be easy to conclude that in the West sacred music came before secular music, or that vocal music preceded instrumental music, or that Christian worship music was the only kind of ritual music in existence in Europe for the first thousand years of the Common Era. But such conclusions would be inaccurate. It is simply that, thanks to notation, the chant repertory of Western Christian worship is available to us for study, unlike the many other musical repertories that have not been so preserved.

Ⓢ Resources for study and review available at
wwnorton.com/studyspace

Chant and Secular Song in the Middle Ages

PRELUDE

Two distinct bodies of song, one sacred (religious) and the other secular (worldly), flourished side by side during the Middle Ages—the thousand-year period that began with the fall of the Roman Empire in the fifth century. The sacred repertory, known as plainchant (eventually, Gregorian chant), was created for ceremonial use and served as a principal element in the communal liturgy, or public worship service, of the Western Christian Church; it was essentially musical prayer (or, in the case of the psalms, praise), the devotional words heightened through melody and rhythm. Nonsacred songs—called *secular monody*—were of two types: courtly and elite or popular and traditional. Both types were intended mainly for entertainment or for communicating feelings. Like songs of any age, these gave voice to the celebration of heroes, the expression of protest, and, especially, the pain and pleasure of love. All three repertories—one sacred and two secular—were primarily monophonic, although for secular song instrumental accompaniments were probably improvised, especially for dancing, marching, exhorting to battle, and so on. All three originated in oral cultures, and their texts and melodies were initially performed from memory according to formulas handed down by older singers or invented by new poet-composers. Chants and courtly songs were transmitted this way for many centuries before they were eventually written down in a gradually evolving notation that was developed in order to preserve the music, more or less accurately, for future generations. But for most people, music was purely aural, and most of the secular and nonliturgical music they heard, sang, and played has vanished. The second half of this chapter, then, of necessity focuses on the written repertory of courtly or aristocratic song that flourished in France in the late Middle Ages.

Christianity sprang from Jewish roots and spread westward from Jerusalem throughout the Roman Empire (see Figure 2.1). As the Western Christian liturgy was disseminated with its music, it changed and expanded over time; while the texts were relatively stable (they were written down hundreds of years before the melodies), the repertory of chant was more fluid, and the process of variation and expansion continued even after the advent of notation. Another important factor in the transmission and preservation of these melodies was their classification into church modes. Learned theorists who interpreted (and sometimes misinterpreted) Boethius, as well as teachers responsible for training student

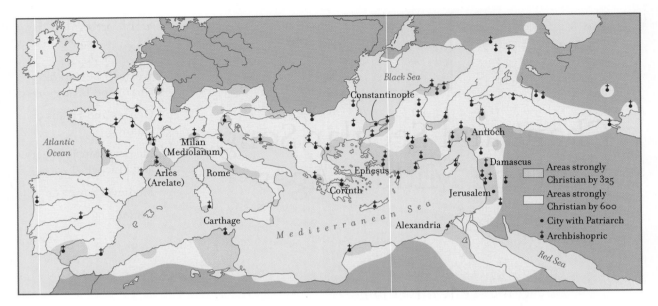

Figure 2.1 The diffusion of Christianity.

monks and nuns (who did not necessarily have any musical aptitude) to sing plainchant, created a system of medieval music theory and practice, at first based on practical considerations and then modified and elaborated from concepts inherited from the ancient Greek science of music. Other elements of this medieval system were newly invented—such as the syllables associated with sightsinging, which are still used in the classroom today.

Like plainchant, the repertory of medieval song outside the Church comprised many different types and forms that had distinct functions and differing conventions. One kind was intended for performances of medieval drama (on both religious and secular subjects), while another was epic or lyric in style. Among the most artful and refined were the songs of the twelfth- and thirteenth-century poet-composers—called troubadours and trouvères—who wrote their own lyrics in either of the two principal French dialects of the time. Some features of these medieval lyrics are echoed in nineteenth-century art song (see Chapter 18) and even in modern rap: they all often deal openly with sensual subject matter, use coded language, and address some sort of coterie—a group of aristocrats at court, a closed circle of friends, or a commercial audience of fans.

Western Christian Chant and Liturgy

The chants of the Christian Church rank among the great treasures of Western civilization. Like Romanesque architecture, they stand as a memorial to religious faith in the Middle Ages, embodying the sense of community and the aesthetic values of the time (see Figure 2.2). Not only does this body of plainchant include some of the noblest melodies to survive to modern times, it also served as the source and inspiration for later music in the Western art tradition, much of which bears its imprint. If we are to understand the various genres and forms of chant and how they were used in medieval ceremonial context, we need to know the basic elements of the Western Christian liturgy, especially the daily Mass.

Figure 2.2 *Interior view of the basilica of San Clemente, Rome, showing the choir stalls facing each other in front of the altar. As Christians grew in number, they met for worship in basilicas like this one, where sung words carried more clearly through the large, resonant space than did spoken words.*
(Corbis.)

Because plainchant is a melody that projects the sacred and devotional words of ritual, its shape cannot be separated from its verbal message or from its place in the worship service. Musically, it can be as simple as a recitation on a single pitch or as elaborate as a long, winding melody that requires a highly trained soloist to perform. The degree of musical elaboration depends on the function of the words in the ritual and on who is singing—a soloist, a trained choir, or the people. All of this is determined by the position of the chant in the liturgy.

Liturgy

The sacred worship service known as the liturgy is comprised of a body of texts and rites whose purpose is to glorify God and the saints, teach the Gospels—the life and works of Jesus—and exhort the worshippers along the path of salvation. At its core is a yearly cycle of readings from the Bible and a weekly cycle of readings from the Book of Psalms. The texts are prescibed according to the church calendar, a yearly cycle that determines which saints, events, and feast days are remembered in a given service, or which seasons of the church year (for example, the Advent season leading up to Christmas or the penitential Lenten season preparing for Easter) are being celebrated. Although much of each worship service is the same at every observance, other aspects change with the day or season.

The readings that make up the liturgy are at the core of the two principal types of service: the Office and the Mass. The Divine Office centers on the communal reading of the psalms. The Mass also includes readings and prayers, but is unique in its ritualistic commemoration of the last supper of Jesus and his disciples as recounted in the Gospels.

The Office, or Canonical Hours, first codified in the *Rule of Saint Benedict* (ca. 530; see Figure 2.3), consists of a series of eight prayer services observed at specified times around the

Figure 2.3 *Saint Benedict giving the* Rule *to a group of monks.*
(Granger Collection.)

The Mass was the focal point of medieval religious life. For the illiterate populace, it was the main source of instruction about the central tenets of their faith. It was also—and most essentially—the ritual reenactment of the last supper in the Eucharist, a sacrament or sign that at once symbolized and encouraged the communal life of Christians. Ideally, these fundamental elements were meant to engage and inspire, gripping not only the mind but also the heart.

The building where Mass was celebrated was designed to evoke awe. Whether a simple rural church or a grand cathedral, it was likely to be the tallest structure most people would ever enter. Its dome,

Figure 2.4   The Last Supper *in an anonymous manuscript illumination from ca. 1200.*
(Musée Condé, Chantilly, France/Giraudon/The Bridgeman Art Library.)

whether painted with simple stars or studded with gold mosaics, was a replica of heaven. Pillars and walls were adorned with sculptures, tapestries, or paintings depicting pious saints, the sufferings of Jesus, or the torments of hell, each image a visual sermon. In these resonant spaces, the spoken word was easily lost, but singing carried words clearly to all corners.

Medieval Christians, especially in central and northern Europe, were not long removed from old pagan customs of propitiating the gods to ensure good crops or prevent misfortune, and they looked to Christian observances to serve the same role. Life for most was hard, and with the constant threat of disease, famine, and war, average life expectancy was under thirty years. Worship in a well-appointed church afforded not only an interlude of beauty, but also a way to approach God and secure blessings in this life and the next.

In such a space, the Mass begins with the procession of the priest and his assistants to the altar, an action which invites those who gather to form an assembly of believers. The choir sings the Introit (a psalm, Latin for "he enters") and continues with the Kyrie, whose threefold invocations symbolize the Trinity of Father, Son, and Holy Spirit. The Greek words and text repetitions reflect the Kyrie's origins in Byzantine processional rituals. There follows the Gloria, a song of praise, and a collective prayer (the Collect), intoned by the priest on behalf of all those present.

The Liturgy of the Word focuses on Bible recitations (the Epistle and Gospel), florid chants (Grad-

clock by the members of a religious community. By calling a group of monks or nuns to pray collectively every few hours (see Figures 2.6 and 2.10), the Office provides the ritual around which life in a monastery or convent is structured. It consists of prayers, recitation of scriptural passages, and songs.

Every Office liturgy includes several psalms, each with an antiphon, a chant sung before and after the psalm; lessons (Bible readings) with musical responses called responsories, hymns, canticles (poetic biblical passages outside the Book of Psalms), and prayers. Over the course of a normal week, all 150 psalms are sung at least once. The principal Office services, liturgically and musically, are Matins and Vespers.

The Mass remains the most important service of the Catholic Church. In other Christian churches, the service is also known as the Eucharist, the Liturgy, Holy Communion, and the Lord's Supper, but all of them culminate in a symbolic reenactment of the last supper (Luke 22:19–20; 1 Corinthians 11:23–26) in which

ual, Alleluia, and Sequence), church teachings as summarized in the profession of faith called the Credo ("I believe"), and meditation on their message (the sermon). In the Liturgy of the Eucharist, the priest turns from words to actions as he prepares, consecrates, consumes, and distributes the bread and wine. The main sung portions of this part of the Mass include the Offertory, a florid chant on a psalm verse performed during the offering of bread and wine, the Sanctus (Holy, holy, holy), and the Agnus Dei (Lamb of God), which respectively exalt and petition the Lord. After communion is distributed the choir sings the Communion chant, based on a psalm. The priest concludes the service by singing Ite, missa est (Go, you are dismissed). From this phrase came the Latin name for the entire service, Missa, which became the English word *Mass*.

Throughout the Mass, the music serves both to convey the words and to engage the worshippers. As Saint Basil the Great (ca. 330–379), a father of the Eastern church, observed,

> When the Holy Spirit saw that mankind was ill-inclined toward virtue and that we were heedless of the righteous life because of our inclination to pleasure, what did he do? He blended the delight of melody with doctrine in order that through the pleasantness and softness of the sound we might unawares receive what was useful in the words.est (Go, you are dismissed). From this phrase came the Latin name for the entire service, Missa, which became the English word *Mass*.

	Proper	Ordinary
Introductory Section	Introit (a)	
		Kyrie (b)
		Gloria (c)
	Collect	
Liturgy of the Word	Epistle	
	Gradual (d)	
	Alleluia (or Tract) (e)	
	Sequence (on major feasts)	
	Gospel	
	Sermon (optional)	
		Credo (f)
Liturgy of the Eucharist	Offertory (g)	
		Prayers
	Secret	
	Preface	
		Sanctus (h)
		Canon
		Pater noster (Lord's Prayer)
		Agnus Dei (i)
	Communion (j)	
	Postcommunion	
		Ite, missa est (k)

Blue: Sung by choir   Red: Intoned   Green: Spoken

Figure 2.5   The outline of the Mass with the most important musical parts indicated by letters corresponding to their position in NAWM 3, the complete Mass for Christmas Day.

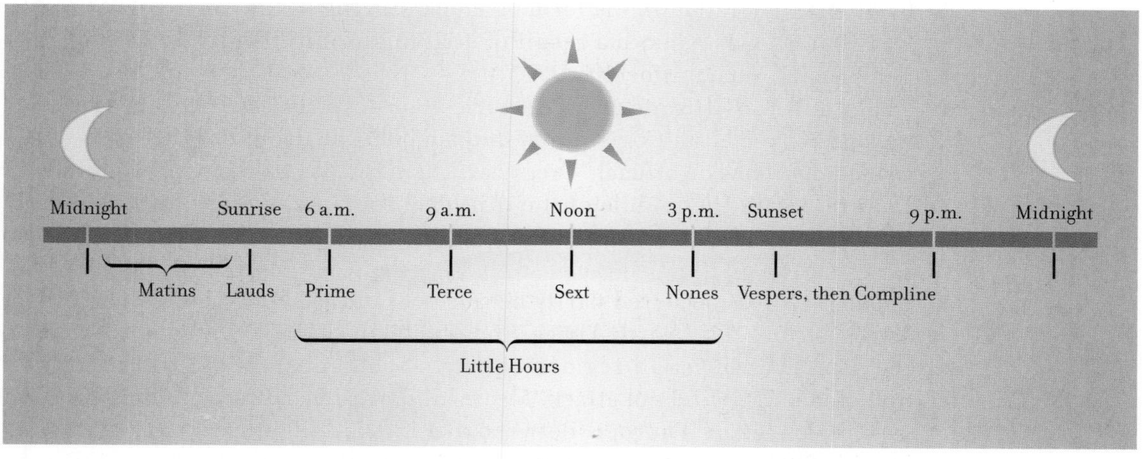

Midnight   Sunrise   6 a.m.   9 a.m.   Noon   3 p.m.   Sunset   9 p.m.   Midnight

Matins   Lauds   Prime   Terce   Sext   Nones   Vespers, then Compline

Little Hours

Figure 2.6   The Office.

Full 🔊   Concise 🔊

the celebrant blesses bread and wine and offers them to the faithful in memory of Jesus' sacrifice for the atonement of sin. An outline of the Catholic Mass, as it has been practiced since about 1200, appears in Figure 2.5, with letters next to the important musical items to indicate their position in NAWM 3, the complete Mass for Christmas Day.

The liturgy of the Mass falls into three successive parts: introductory prayers; the Liturgy of the Word, during which the congregation listens to passages intoned from the Hebrew Scriptures and from the apostles and Gospel writers of the New Testament; and the Liturgy of the Eucharist, during which the bread and wine are consecrated and distributed. Within these three stages, some texts remain the same from one day to the next while others change according to the season or the particular occasion being celebrated. The variable texts, called the Proper of the Mass, include the Introit, Collects, Epistle, Gradual, Alleluia, Gospel, Offertory, Communion, and others. The unchanging texts (each of which, however, may be sung to several different melodies throughout the year), called the Ordinary of the Mass, include the Kyrie, Gloria, Credo, Sanctus, Agnus Dei, and Ite, missa est.

Oral transmission

Initially, chant melodies were learned by hearing others sing them, a process called oral transmission, leaving no written traces. How chant melodies were created and transmitted without writing from the fourth to the eighth century has been the subject of much study and controversy. Some scholars suggest that many chants were improvised within strict conventions based on formulas such as those used by epic singers and storytellers. We can find evidence for such oral composition in the chants themselves, many of which share the same melodic contour or feature characteristic internal and cadential patterns. However, as long as this process depended on memory and learning by ear, melodies were subject to change and variation.

Notation of chant

Such variation was not suitable if the chants were to be performed in the same way each time in churches across a wide territory, as the pope and Frankish kings (Charlemagne and others) eventually came to require. In the late eighth and ninth centuries, therefore, rudimentary systems of musical notation were invented to standardize the performance of chant melodies. This coincided with a determined campaign by Frankish political leaders to promote a uniform liturgy and music in order to consolidate and increase their influence on worshippers throughout their lands. Trained "missionaries" traveled between Rome and the north to stabilize the repertory of tunes and suppress local variations. A persuasive tool of Frankish propaganda was the legend of Saint Gregory, who was reputed to have written down the chant melodies, guided by divine inspiration in the form of a dove singing in his ear (see Figure 2.9). Notation, then, was both a result of striving for uniformity and a means of perpetuating that uniformity.

Diffusion of chant

Between the fifth and ninth centuries, the peoples of western and northern Europe converted to Christianity and adopted the doctrines and rites of the Roman church. The official "Gregorian" chant was established in the Frankish Empire before the middle of the ninth century, and from then until nearly the close of the Middle Ages, all important developments in European music took place not in Rome, but north of the Alps (see Figure 2.7). This shift in musical centers occurred partly because of political conditions. The Muslim conquests of Syria, North Africa, and especially Spain, completed by 719, left the southern Christian regions either in the hands of occupying forces or under constant threat of attack. Meanwhile, various cultural centers arose in western and central Europe. Between the sixth and eighth centuries, missionaries from Irish and Scottish monasteries established schools in their own lands and abroad, especially in what is now Germany and Switzerland. An

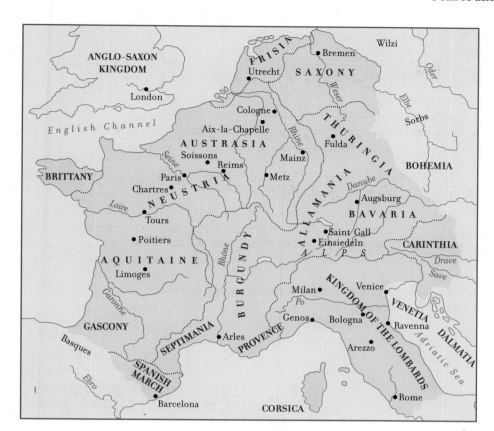

Figure 2.7 The Holy Roman Empire under Charlemagne around 800.

English monk, Alcuin of York, helped Emperor Charlemagne in his project to revive education throughout the Frankish Empire. One result of this eighth- and ninth-century renaissance was the development of important musical centers, including the famous monastery of Saint Gall in what is now Switzerland. Here, the northern, Frankish influence on plainchant is evident in melodic lines with more leaps, especially thirds, and in the introduction of both new melodies and new forms of chant such as tropes, sequences, and liturgical drama, all to be discussed below.

Genres and Forms of Chant

Chants are classified in different, overlapping ways: (1) by their texts, which may be biblical or nonbiblical, prose or poetry; (2) by their manner of performance, which may be antiphonal (sung by alternating choirs), responsorial (with a choir responding to a soloist), or direct (sung by one choir); and (3) by their musical style, which may be syllabic (one note per syllable of text) or melismatic (many notes per syllable). This last distinction is not always clear-cut, because chants that are mostly melismatic usually include some syllabic sections or phrases, and many syllabic chants have occasional syllables with prolonged melodic gestures of two to seven notes each, passages that are sometimes called neumatic (from *neume,* or "pitch symbol"; see Example 2.1 and Figure 2.8).

Most parts of the Mass and Office are chanted to recitation formulas, simple melodic outlines that can be used with many different texts. Some parts of the

Basic formulas

Example 2.1 *Antiphon:* Salve Regina

Hail, O Queen, Mother of mercy, our life, our sweetness and our hope! To thee do we cry, banished children of Eve; to thee do we send up our sighs, mourning and weeping in this vale of tears.

Figure 2.8   The opening phrases of the antiphon to the Blessed Virgin Mary, Salve Regina mater misericordiae *(Hail, O Queen, Mother of mercy) as notated in a modern book of the most frequently used chants of the Mass and Office, the* Liber usualis.

liturgy, however, are sung to fully formed melodies. The two are not entirely separate since even complex melodies may be elaborations of an underlying formula.

Text setting   Chant proclaims the text, sometimes straightforwardly and other times ornately. It follows that the musical contours of a chant generally reflect the way the Latin words were pronounced, with prominent syllables set to higher notes or to a melisma. But in florid chants, naturally occurring accents often take a backseat to the melodic curve, resulting in long melismas on weak syllables, such as the final "a" of "alleluia" or "e" of "Kyrie." In such cases, the most important words or syllables of a phrase are emphasized with syllabic treatment that makes them stand out against the rich ornamentation of the unstressed syllables. Plainchant calls for word repetition only where it exists in the text of the prayer itself (such as the phrase "Kyrie eleison"; see page 38). Melodies usually conform to the rhythm of the text and to the liturgical function of the chant. Rarely does a chant melody realize emotional or pictorial effects.

In Context In the Monastic Scriptorium

During the first millennium of Christianity, the preservation of liturgical texts and melodies in manuscripts—books laboriously written and copied by hand—became one of the great accomplishments of the monastic communities of the Middle Ages.

Manuscript production became a routine part of monastic life, and special places within the monastery were set aside as writing workshops, or scriptoria. The scriptorium also refers to the entire group of monks or nuns who were engaged in producing a manuscript, from those who prepared the ink and parchment or drew the lines on which the music was then notated, to the skilled workers who put the finishing touches on the book's covers. The bookmaking process extended beyond the scriptorium to the monks who toiled outside the monastery. An entire flock of sheep was needed to provide the parchment for a single book, and wild game such as deer and boar were hunted in order to furnish the leather used for binding the volumes.

But the copyist's job was paramount and required both manual dexterity and intellectual fortitude. Trainees first had to learn how to make the letters and notes conform exactly to the style of writing that was in use at the time; there was little room for individuality. As a result, the scribes throughout northwestern Europe produced works of incredible regularity and perfect legibility.

Straightforward copying of text and music was only one stage of the manuscript's production. Another was the exacting job of decorating the

Figure 2.9 Saint Gregory writing with scribes. Franco-German school, ivory, ca. 850–875.
(Kunsthistorisches Museum, Vienna/Bridgeman Art Library.)

more important books with elaborate initials and capital letters in gold leaf or colored paints, and illustrating them with miniature scenes or brightening up the text's margins with illuminated designs. Finally came the binding, which could be more or less elaborate. The most important books were encased in ornamental covers made by specialized craftsmen and enriched with metals and gems.

All this labor helped to keep alive a widespread appreciation for music manuscripts whose creation represented so much effort and expense. And for the monks themselves, copying a book was regarded like prayer and fasting—as a way to keep one's unruly passions in check. But the monks also saw in their painstaking work a means of spreading the word of God. The abbot of one important Benedictine monastery in the twelfth century has this to say about the solitary monk who devotes his life to the scriptorium (as opposed to the garden or vineyards):

He cannot take to the plow? Then let him take up the pen; it is much more useful. In the furrows he traces on the parchment, he will sow the seeds of the divine words. . . . He will preach without opening his mouth; . . . and without leaving his cloister, he will journey far over land and sea.[1]

1. Peter the Venerable, abbot of Cluny, France, quoted by Jean LeClercq, *The Love of Learning and the Desire for God: A Study of Monastic Culture*, trans. Catharine Misrahi (New York: Fordham University Press, 1961), p. 128.

Every chant melody is divided into phrases and periods corresponding to the phrases and periods of the text. Many phrases follow the curve of an arch, beginning low, rising to a higher pitch, perhaps remaining there for a while, then descending. This simple and natural design occurs in a great variety of subtle combinations—extending over two or more phrases, for example, or including many smaller arches within its span. A less common melodic design,

Melodic structure

Example 2.2 Outline of the psalmody of the Office

	Intonation Tenor	Mediant	Tenor	Termination
Tecum . . .				
1. Di-xit	Dominus	Do - mi - no me - o:	sede a	dex-tris me - is.
2.	Donec ponam ini -	mi - cos tu - os,	scabellum pe -	dum tu - o - rum.
3.	Virgam virtutis tuae emittet Domi-nus	ex Si - on:	dominare in medio inimico -	rum tu - o - rum.
. . .				
9.	Gloria	Pa - tri, et Fi - li - o,	et Spiri -	tu - i Sanc - to.
10.	Sicut erat in principio, et	nunc et sem - per,	et in saecula saecu -	lo - rum. A - men. *Tecum . . .*

characteristic of phrases beginning with an especially important word, starts on a high note and descends gradually to the end.

Chant forms

Full 🔊

We can distinguish three main forms in the chant repertory. One, exemplified in the psalm tone (one of eight melodies used for singing psalms), consists of two balanced phrases that correspond to the two halves of a typical psalm verse (see Example 2.2). In the second form—such as strophic form in hymns—the same melody is sung to several stanzas of text (as in NAWM 4b). A third is free form, which may be entirely original in its content or may incorporate a series of traditional melodic formulas into an otherwise original composition.

We will now look at the important types of chants used in the Mass and Office, beginning with syllabic and proceeding to more melismatic styles.

Chants of the Office

Psalm tones

Full 🔊   Concise 🔊

Doxology

The formulas for chanting the psalms, called psalm tones, are among the oldest chants of the liturgy. They are designed so they can be adapted to fit the words of any psalm. There is one tone (formula) for each of the eight church modes (discussed below; see Example 2.3) and an extra one called the *tonus peregrinus,* or "wandering tone." In the Office, a psalm is usually sung to the tone that matches the mode of its prescribed antiphon (see, for example, NAWM 4a).

A psalm tone consists of five separate melodic elements. It begins with an intonation (used only in the first verse of the psalm), which rises to a reciting tone, or tenor (a single, repeating note that is used for recitation); bends at the midpoint of the verse for a semicadence, or mediant; continues on the reciting tone (tenor) for the second half-verse; and concludes at the end of the verse by descending to a final cadence, or termination. This formula is repeated for each verse of the psalm. The final verse usually leads into the Lesser Doxology, an expression of praise to the Trinity, which is added to "christianize" the psalms, originally a body of Hebrew poetry inherited from the Jewish liturgy. The words of the Doxology, *Gloria Patri . . .* (Glory be to the Father . . .), are fitted to the same psalm tone as the psalm verses (here shown as verses 9 and 10). Every psalm in the Office is framed by a different antiphon, attached to it solely for one particular day of the calendar year. So, although all 150 psalms are sung in the course of a week's cycle of Canonical Hours, each will have a new antiphon the following week and thereafter throughout the year. A model for the chanting of antiphon and psalm in the Office is outlined in Example 2.2. (The full text of the antiphon *Tecum principium* [Thine shall be the dominion] and Psalm 109, *Dixit Dominus* [The Lord said], is found in NAWM 4a.)

Antiphonal psalmody

This kind of psalmodic singing is called antiphonal (from the Greek for "sounding against") because the half-verses alternate between two choirs or between a small choir and the full choir (see Figure 2.10). The practice, believed to imitate ancient Syrian models, was adopted early in the history of the Church.

In earliest times, the antiphon, a verse or sentence with its own melody, was probably repeated after every verse of a psalm, like the phrase "for his mercy endureth forever" in Latin Psalm 135 (English 136). Eventually, only the open-

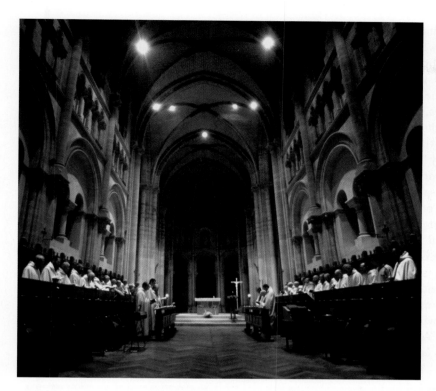

Figure 2.10 Monks at the Abbey of Notre-Dame de la Trappe in Soligny, France, singing an Office service. They are seated in front of the altar in two sets of choir stalls that face each other (compare with Figure 2.2).
(Jacques Pavlovsky/Sygma/ Corbis)

ing phrase of the antiphon was sung before the psalm, with the entire antiphon performed after the psalm.

Antiphons are more numerous than any other type of chant; about 1,250 appear in modern chant books. However, many antiphons employ the same melody, using only slight variations to accommodate the text. Since antiphons were originally intended to be sung by a group rather than a soloist, the older ones are usually syllabic or only slightly florid, with stepwise melodic movement, comparatively simple rhythm, and a limited melodic range.

Early Christians often sang psalms responsorially, with a soloist performing each verse and the congregation or choir responding with a brief refrain. This practice is reflected in the Office responsories, chants that begin with a choral section or respond, proceed with a single psalm verse sung by a soloist, and close with a full or partial repetition of the respond.

Chants of the Mass Proper

Like the Office, the Mass included antiphonal and responsorial psalmody. Among the antiphonal chants are the Introit and Communion, belonging to the Proper of the Mass. The Introit was originally a complete psalm with its antiphon, the many verses of which were used to accompany the entrance procession. Over time, this opening part of the service was shortened so that today the Introit consists only of the original antiphon, a single psalm verse with the customary Doxology (*Gloria Patri*), sung to a more elaborate variant of a psalm tone, and a repetition of the antiphon (NAWM 3a). The Communion, coming near the end of the Mass as a counterpart to the Introit at the beginning, is a short chant, often consisting of only one scriptural verse (NAWM 3j). Some of the more elaborate antiphons developed into independent chants, retaining only a single psalm verse or none at all.

Musically, the most highly developed chants of the Mass are the Gradual (from Latin *gradus*, "step," with the gospel book being carried in procession

Antiphons

Introit

Full 🔊 Concise 🔊

Full 🔊

Gradual and Alleluia

from altar to lectern) and Alleluia, probably because they occur at moments in the service that are more contemplative, when no ritual action occurs. These are responsorial chants, intended for choir and soloist in alternation (NAWM 3d and 3e). Each has only one psalm verse, usually sung to a more elaborate melody than the verses of antiphonal chants and introduced—or, in the case of the Alleluia, framed—by a separate melody and text known as a respond.

Graduals came to the Frankish churches (in what is now France) from Rome in a form that was already highly evolved. Their melodies and those of the Alleluia are very florid and have a similar structure. Certain melismatic formulas recur in different Graduals at similar points in the chant, such as intonations, internal cadences, and terminations. Some melodies consist almost entirely of such formulas, pointing to an earlier, prenotational time when singers had to rely on their memories; recurring patterns made performing much easier. In the Alleluias, the respond text is always the single word "Alleluia" (from the Hebrew *Hallelujah*, "Praise God") with the final syllable "-ia" receiving an effusive melisma called a jubilus (see NAWM 3e). The responsorial performance of the Alleluia proceeds as follows: the soloist (or solo group) sings the word "Alleluia" up to the asterisk; the chorus repeats it and continues with the jubilus; the soloist then sings the psalm verse, with the chorus joining on the last phrase marked by an asterisk; then the entire "Alleluia" is repeated by the soloist with the chorus joining in again at the jubilus (see Figure 2.11).

Responsorial performance

SOLOIST	CHORUS	SOLOIST	CHORUS	SOLOIST	CHORUS
Alleluia*	Allelu-ia...(jubilus)...	Ps. verse...*	...	Allelu-*	-ia (jubilus)

Figure 2.11   Responsorial performance of the Alleluia.

Many Alleluias sound carefully planned and composed rather than improvised. For example, they often include what might be termed "musical rhyme," in which matching phrases occur at the ends of sections. Alleluias were created throughout the Middle Ages and spawned important new forms, such as the sequence (see below).

Offertory

Offertories are as melismatic as Graduals but include the respond only (see NAWM 3g). In the Middle Ages, they were performed during the offering of bread and wine, with a choral respond and two or three very ornate verses sung by a soloist, each followed by the second half of the respond. When the ceremony was curtailed, the verses were dropped.

Later Developments of the Chant

Chants of the Ordinary

The chants for the Mass Ordinary probably started out as simple syllabic melodies sung by the congregation. After the ninth century, these were replaced by more ornate settings for choral performance. The syllabic style was retained for the Gloria and Credo, which have the longest texts. The Kyrie, Sanctus, and Agnus Dei, because of the repeating nature of their texts, have three-part sectional arrangements. The Kyrie, for example, suggests a setting in which the first and last sections are identical:

Kyrie

A   *Kyrie eleison, Kyrie eleison, Kyrie eleison*
B   *Christe eleison, Christe eleison, Christe eleison*
A   *Kyrie eleison, Kyrie eleison, Kyrie eleison*

The threefold repetition of each phrase of text may be reflected in a variety of musical forms, such as AAA BBB AAA′, AAA BBB CCC′ (as in NAWM 3b), or ABA CDC EFE′. The Kyrie is usually performed antiphonally, with half-choirs alternating statements. The final Kyrie is often extended by the insertion of an additional phrase, allowing each half-choir to sing a phrase before joining together for the last "eleison."

Many antiphons were composed for additional feasts introduced into the Church calendar between the ninth and thirteenth centuries. This same period produced a number of antiphons that were not attached to particular psalms, for use in processions and at special occasions. The four Marian antiphons—liturgically not antiphons at all, but independent compositions—are of comparatively late date (see, for example, the *Salve Regina,* Example 2.1).

A trope expanded an existing chant by adding one of three things: (1) new words and music before the chant and often between phrases; (2) melody only, extending melismas or adding new ones; or (3) text only, set to existing melismas. The first method of troping was by far the most common, used especially with Introits. All three types increased the solemnity of a chant by enlarging it, and all afforded musicians an outlet for creativity, paralleling the way medieval scribes embellished books with marginal decorations. Moreover, the added words provided a gloss (see Figure 3.1), interpreting the chant text and linking it more closely to the occasion. For example, the Introit antiphon for Christmas day (NAWM 3a) used a text from the Hebrew Scriptures, a passage Christians view as a prophecy of Jesus' birth (Isaiah 9:6). Prefacing it with a trope text (here in italics) made this interpretation explicit:

> *God the Father today sent his Son into the world, for which we say,*
> *rejoicing with the prophet:* A child is born to us, and a Son is given. . . .

Two other tropes to this same Introit appear in NAWM 6: a brief dialogue, *Quem queritis in presepe* (discussed below), and a textless melisma that embellishes the end of the antiphon.

Trope composition flourished especially in monasteries during the tenth and eleventh centuries. We know the name of at least one composer, Tuotilo (d. 915), who was a monk at Saint Gall. Tropes were eventually banned by the Council of Trent (1545–1563; see Chapter 8) in the interest of simplifying and standardizing the liturgy. But they testify vividly to the desire of medieval church musicians to embellish the chant repertory. This same impulse played an important role in the development of polyphony, as we shall see in the next chapter.

Sequences, so called because they "follow" the Alleluias, began as tropes in the ninth century, probably as text additions to the jubilus in Alleluias, but they quickly became independent compositions. Notker Balbulus (his name means "The Stammerer"; ca. 840–912), another Frankish monk of Saint Gall and the most famous early writer of sequence texts, describes how he learned to write text syllables under long melismas to help him memorize them. The sequence was an important creative outlet from the tenth to the thirteenth centuries and later. Popular sequences were even imitated and adapted for secular genres, both vocal and instrumental, in the late Middle Ages. Like tropes, most sequences were banned from the Catholic service by the liturgical reforms of the Council of Trent. The five that survive still hold vital places in the liturgy, such as the celebrated *Dies irae,* with its familiar melody, in the Requiem Mass (Mass for the Dead), and the Easter sequence *Victimae paschali laudes* (NAWM 5).

Full 🔊 Concise 🔊

Tropes

Full 🔊 Concise 🔊

Full 🔊

Sequences

Full 🔊 Concise 🔊

All are syllabic and are arranged in couplets, with the second line repeating the melody of the first.

Liturgical drama

Liturgical drama—a type of play that grew out of ritual and was performed on important holy days near the altar—also originated in troping. One of the earliest of these dramas, *Quem quaeritis in sepulchro* (Whom do you seek in the tomb?), took shape in the tenth century as a dialogue preceding the Introit for Easter Sunday Mass—in effect, a trope. In the dialogue, the three Marys come to the tomb of Jesus. The angel asks them, "Whom do you seek in the tomb?" They reply, "Jesus of Nazareth," to which the angel answers, "He is not here, He is risen as He said; go and proclaim that He has risen from the grave" (Mark 16:6–7). According to contemporary accounts, the dialogue was sung responsorially, and the scene was acted out. The Easter trope and a similar one for Christmas, *Quem queritis in presepe* (Whom do you seek in the manger? NAWM 6 and Figure 2.12), were performed all over Europe. Other plays survive from the twelfth century and later. The early thirteenth-century *Play of Daniel* from Beauvais and *The Play of Herod*, concerning the Slaughter of the Innocents, from Fleury, have become staples in the repertories of early-music ensembles. The music for these plays consists of a number of chants strung together, with processions and actions that approach theatrical representation. A few manuscripts give evidence that the works were staged, with scenery, costumes, and actors drawn from the clergy.

Hildegard of Bingen

Although most liturgical dramas from this period are anonymous, we have a unique, nonliturgical but sacred music drama by Hildegard of Bingen (1098–1179; see Biography, page 41). *Ordo virtutum* (The Virtues, ca. 1151) is Hildegard's most extended musical work, consisting of eighty-two songs for which she wrote both the melodies and the poetic verse (uncommon among authors of tropes and sequences). It is a morality play with allegorical characters such as the Prophets, the Virtues, the Happy Soul, the Unhappy Soul, and the Penitent Soul. All sing in plainchant except the Devil, who can only speak: the absence

Figure 2.12   The earliest surviving copy of the Christmas dramatic trope Quem queritis in presepe, *in a manuscript collection from Saint-Martial de Limoges. For a transcription, see NAWM 6.*

(Bibliothèque Nationale, Paris.)

of music symbolizes his separation from God. The final chorus of the Virtues (NAWM 7) is typical of Hildegard's expansive melodic style.

Full 🔊 Concise 🔊

Women were excluded from the priesthood, and as the choir took over the singing in services, they were also silenced in church. But in convents—separate communities of religious women (nuns)—they could hold positions of leadership and participate fully in singing the Office and Mass (which, however, was "said" by a priest). Here they also learned to read and write Latin and music, and had access to an intellectual life available to few outside convent walls. In this context, Hildegard achieved great success as prioress and abbess of her own convent and as a writer and composer. She claimed that her songs, like her prose writings, were divinely inspired. At a time when women were forbidden to instruct or supervise men, having a reputation for direct communication with God was one way she could be heard outside the convent. Her visions became famous, but her music was apparently known only locally. Although her writings were edited and published in the nineteenth century, her music was not

Hildegard of Bingen (1098–1179)

Born to a noble family in the Rhine region of Germany, Hildegard at age eight was consecrated to the church by her parents. Six years later she took vows at the Benedictine monastery of Disibodenberg, and she became prioress of the attached convent in 1136. Led by a vision, she founded her own convent around 1150 at Rupertsberg, near Bingen, where she was abbess. Famous for her prophecies, Hildegard corresponded with emperors, kings, popes, and bishops and preached throughout Germany. Her many prose works include *Scivias* (Know the Ways, 1141–51), an account of twenty-six visions, and books on science and healing.

Hildegard wrote religious poems as well as prose, and by the 1140s she began setting them to music. Her songs are preserved in two manuscripts organized in a liturgical cycle, with indications that many were sung in her convents and nearby monasteries and churches. Her *Ordo virtutum* (The Virtues, ca. 1151) is the earliest surviving music drama not attached to the liturgy.

Hildegard exemplifies the flourishing musical culture of medieval women who, like their male counterparts, saw themselves as saving humanity through prayer. A letter she wrote near the end of her life reveals her view of music's profoundly spiritual nature:

so that mankind . . . be awakened to . . . the divine sweetness and the praise which Adam

Figure 2.13 Hildegard of Bingen with Volmar, a monk who assisted her in recording her visions, in an illustration from Scivias. *(Erich Lessing/Art Resource.)*

had enjoyed before his fall . . . holy prophets, taught by that Spirit which they had received, not only composed psalms and canticles, which were to be sung in order to kindle the devotion of those hearing them, but also invented diverse instruments of the musical art. . . . They did so for this reason: so that the listeners would . . . be educated in interior matters . . . while being urged on and prodded by exterior objects.[1]

Major works: *Ordo virtutum,* 43 antiphons, 18 responsories, 7 sequences, 4 hymns, 5 other chants

1. Hildegard of Bingen, Epistle 47: To the Prelates of Mainz, trans. James McKinnon; in Oliver Strunk, ed., *Source Readings in Music History*; rev. ed. by Leo Treitler (New York: Norton, 1998), vol. 2, p. 74.

rediscovered until the late twentieth century in the search to reclaim the history of music by women. She quickly became the most recorded and best-known composer of sacred monophony.

Medieval Music Theory and Practice

Treatises in the age of Charlemagne and in the later Middle Ages reflected actual practice to a greater extent than the more speculative earlier writings. They always spoke of Boethius with reverence and passed along the mathematical fundamentals of scale building, intervals, and consonances that he transmitted from the Greeks. But reading Boethius did not help solve the immediate problems of singing intervals, memorizing chants, and, later, reading notes at sight. Theorists partially addressed these goals by establishing the system of eight modes, or *toni* ("tones"), as medieval writers called them.

Church modes   The medieval modal system developed gradually, achieving its complete form by the eleventh century. It encompassed eight modes, each defined by the sequence of whole tones and semitones in a diatonic octave built on a *finalis,* or final. In practice, this note was usually the last note in the melody. The modes were identified by numbers and grouped in pairs; the odd-numbered modes were called authentic, and the even-numbered modes plagal (collateral). Each pair of modes shared the same final (identified as bracketed whole notes in Example 2.3), but their melodies had different ranges: those belonging to the authentic modes rose above the final, and those in the plagal modes circled around or went further below the final. The authentic modal scales may be thought of as analogous to white-key octave scales on a modern keyboard rising from the notes D (mode 1), E (mode 3), F (mode 5), and G (mode 7), with their corresponding plagals (modes 2, 4, 6, and 8) a fourth lower. These notes, of course, do not stand for specific "absolute" pitches—a concept foreign to plainchant and to the Middle Ages in general; they are simply a convenient way to distinguish the interval patterns, which are unique to each pair of modes, as partially shown in the example. In addition to the final, each mode has a second characteristic note, called the tenor or reciting tone (shown in Example 2.3 as whole notes), as in the psalm tones. Although the finals of the paired plagal and authentic modes are the same, their tenors are higher or lower in keeping with their ranges. The church modes also had Greek names (as shown in the example), although these were a misapplication of the ancient

Example 2.3 The medieval church modes

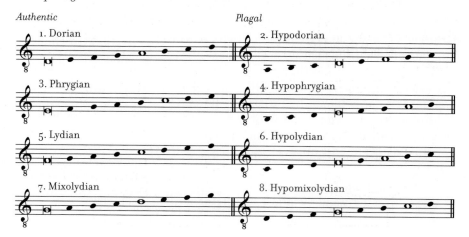

Greek scales. The modes became a primary means for classifying chants and arranging them in books for liturgical use. However, because many of the chants existed before the theory of modes evolved, their melodic characteristics do not always conform to modal theory.

For teaching sightsinging, the eleventh-century monk Guido of Arezzo (ca. 991–after 1033) proposed a set of syllables—*ut, re, mi, fa, sol, la*—to help singers remember the pattern of whole tones and semitone in the six steps (known as hexachords) that begin on C, G, or F. (This became known as solmization.) In this pattern (for example, C–D–E–F–G–A), a semitone falls between the third and fourth steps, and all other steps are whole tones. The syllables of solmization (also known as solfège or solfeggio) are still employed in teaching, except that in English we say *do* for *ut* and add a *ti* above *la*.

Followers of Guido developed a pedagogical visual aid called the "Guidonian hand" (Figure 2.14). Pupils were taught to sing intervals as the teacher pointed with the index finger of the right hand to the different joints of the open left hand. Each joint stood for one of the twenty notes that made up the musical system of the time; any other note, such as F♯ or E♭, was considered "outside the hand." No late medieval or Renaissance music textbook was complete without a drawing of this hand.

In earlier stages of musical notation, scribes placed the note symbols, or neumes, above the text, sometimes at varying heights to indicate the relative size as well as direction of intervals (as in Figure 2.12). Eventually, one scribe conceived the idea of scratching a horizontal line in the parchment corresponding to a particular note and oriented the neumes around that line. This was a revolutionary idea: a musical sign that did not represent a sound, but clarified the meaning of other signs. In the eleventh century, Guido suggested an arrangement of lines and spaces from which evolved the modern staff. Guido's scheme not only enabled scribes to notate (relative) pitches precisely, but also freed music from its dependence on oral transmission. The achievement proved to be as crucial for the history of Western music as the invention of writing was for literature.

Solmization

The Guidonian hand

The staff

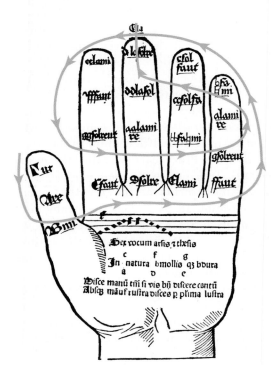

Figure 2.14 The "Guidonian hand," a visual mnemonic device used for locating the pitches of the system of hexachords by pointing to the joints of the left hand. Although credited to Guido, the hand was probably a later application of his solmization syllables. The notes are laid out in a counterclockwise spiral, beginning with the lowest note (gamma ut) at the tip of the thumb, moving down the thumb, across the base of each finger, up the little finger, across the tips, down the index finger, and around the middle joints.
(Wikimedia Commons.)

Medieval Song

Goliard songs

Music outside the church spawned many types and forms of song. A few of them will be described here. The oldest *written* specimens of secular music are songs with Latin texts, among them the goliard songs from the eleventh and twelfth centuries. Their poets and composers were students or clerics who exalted a libertine lifestyle, naming themselves after a fictitious and scurrilous patron, Bishop Goliath. The songs, preserved in numerous manuscript collections, celebrate three topics of interest to young men then, as now: wine, women, and satire. In most cases, however, the music does not survive in a notation precise enough to permit accurate modern transcriptions and performances.

The goliard songs, although written mostly in Latin, are early manifestations of literacy in the secular musical culture of western Europe. As the vernacular languages also gradually came to be written down, we begin to see glimpses of entire repertories—work songs, dance songs, lullabies, laments—that were lost over time. Among these are chansons de geste, praise songs that celebrate the deeds of past warriors and present rulers, and love songs, which became popular at the increasingly powerful courts of western Europe.

Jongleurs

The people who sang these and other secular songs in the Middle Ages were the jongleurs (from the same root as English *jugglers*), or minstrels (from the Latin *minister,* "servant"), who were either itinerants or in service to a particular lord, or sometimes both. Jongleurs traveled alone or in small groups from village to village and castle to castle, earning a precarious living by performing tricks, telling stories, and singing or playing instruments. Figure 2.15 shows a dancing bear accompanied by a jongleur playing a fiddle. Jongleurs especially were social outcasts, often denied the protection of the law and the sacraments of the Church. With the economic recovery of Europe in the eleventh and twelfth centuries, society became more stably organized, and towns sprang up. The minstrels' situation improved, though for a long time people continued to regard them with a mixture of fascination and revulsion. In the eleventh century, minstrels organized themselves into brotherhoods, which later developed into guilds of musicians offering professional training, much as a modern conservatory does.

Troubadours (male) and trobairitz (female, singular and plural) were poet-composers who flourished during the twelfth century in the south of France and spoke Provençal (also called the *langue d'oc* or Occitan). Trouvères were their equivalent in northern France. One theory is that the art of the troubadours took its inspiration in part from the Arabic love poetry cultivated in Moorish Spain and then spread quickly northward. The trouvères, who were active throughout the thirteenth century, spoke the *langue d'oïl,* the medieval French dialect that became modern French (*oïl = oui,* "yes"; *oc =* "yes" in Occitan).

Neither troubadours nor trouvères constituted a well-defined group. They flourished in castles and courts throughout France. Some were kings: others came from families of merchants, craftsmen, or even jongleurs but were accepted into aristocratic circles because of their accomplishments. Many of the poet-composers not only created their songs but sang them as well; those who did not

Figure 2.15 Jongleur playing a fiddle while accompanying a dancing bear. French painting on glass, ca. 1350, from the abbey of Jumièges, Normandy.

(Société Civile Immobilière.)

entrusted the performance to a minstrel. The songs are preserved in collections called *chansonniers* (songbooks). About 2,600 troubadour poems survive, only a tenth with melodies; by contrast, two-thirds of the 2,100 extant trouvère poems have music. No other surviving body of secular tunes and lyrics is as large.

The poetic and musical structures of the songs show great variety and ingenuity. Some are simple, others dramatic, suggesting two or more characters. Some of the dramatic ones were probably intended to be mimed; many obviously called for dancing. The dance songs may include a refrain sung by a chorus of dancers. An important structural feature of numerous trouvère (as opposed to troubadour) songs, the refrain is a line or two of poetry that returns with its own music from one stanza to another. The troubadours especially wrote complaints about love, the subject par excellence of their poetry. But they also wrote songs on political and moral topics, songs that tell stories, and songs whose texts debate or argue esoteric points of chivalric or courtly love. Among these are several particular genres, such as the alba (dawn song), canso (love song), and tenson (debate song).

Many old Occitan lyrics were openly sensual; others hid sensuality under a veil of *fine amour* or "refined love." The object of the passion they expressed was a real woman—usually another man's wife—but she was adored from a distance, with such discretion, respect, and humility that the lover is made to seem more like a worshipper content to suffer in the service of his ideal love. The lady herself is depicted as so lofty and unattainable that she would step out of character if she condescended to reward her faithful lover. By playing on common themes in fresh ways through artfully constructed lyrics, the poets demonstrate refinement and eloquence, two main requirements for success in aristocratic circles. Thus, the entire poetic genre was more fiction than fact, addressed as much to other men (patrons whose wives were being flattered) as to women, and rewarded not by love, but by social status.

Among the best preserved courtly songs is *Can vei la lauzeta mover* (When I see the lark beating, NAWM 8) by the troubadour Bernart de Ventadorn (ca. 1150–ca. 1180), one of the most popular poets of his time. Stories about his life assert that he was the son of a serf and baker in the castle of Ventadorn and rose to become the great lover of three noble ladies. Of the eight stanzas of *Can vei la lauzeta mover*, the second typifies the lover's complaints that are the main subject of this repertory.

Figure 2.16 Troubadour Jaufré Rudel and the countess of Tripoli in a miniature from a French manuscript of the thirteenth century. (Bibliothèque Nationale, Paris.)

Figure 2.17 Bernart de Ventadorn, as depicted in a thirteenth-century manuscript of troubadour songs. (Bibliothèque Nationale, Paris.)

Ai, las! tan cuidava saber	*Alas! I thought I knew so much*
d'amor, e tan petit en sai,	*of love, and I know so little;*
car eu d'amar no • m posc tener	*for I cannot help loving a lady*
celeis don ja pro non aurai.	*from whom I shall never obtain any favor.*
Tout m'a mo cor, e tout m'a me,	*She has taken away my heart and myself,*
e se mezeis e tot lo mon;	*and herself and the whole world;*
e can se • m tolc, no • m laisset re	*and when she left me, I had nothing left*
mas dezirer e cor volon.	*but desire and a yearning heart.*[1]

Like Bernart's song, or canso, the typical troubadour and trouvère text is strophic, with each stanza sung to the same melody. The settings are generally syllabic with an occasional short melismatic figure near the end of a line. Such a simple melody invites improvised ornaments and other variants as the singer

Typical song structure

---

1. Text and translation are from Hendrik van der Werf, *The Chansons of the Troubadours and Trouvères: A Study of the Melodies and Their Relation to the Poems* (Utrecht: A. Oosthoek, 1972), pp. 91–95, which presents versions of the melody from five different sources, showing surprising consistency of readings. The dot splitting two letters of a word, as in "no·m," stands for contraction.

Musical Events

386
Bishop Ambrose
introduces
responsorial
psalmody in Milan

ca. 500
Boethius, *De institutione musica*

300

Historical Events

313
Constantine I issues Edict of
Milan, proclaiming religious
freedom in the Roman Empire

330
Constantinople becomes new
capital of Roman Empire

395
Separation of eastern and
western Roman empires

397
Saint Augustine begins writing
his *Confessions*

ca. 530
(Monastic) *Rule of Saint
Benedict*; Benedictine order
founded

590
Gregory I ("the Great")
elected pope

600s
Muslim conquests in Asia,
North Africa, and southern
Europe (completed by 719)

768
Charlemagne becomes king of
the Franks with his brother

789
Charlemagne orders Roman
rite used throughout empire

moves from one stanza to the next. The range is narrow—a sixth, perhaps, or an octave. Because the songs have finals on C, D, and F, the entire body of works displays a certain coherence. The notation yields no clue to the rhythm of the songs: they might have been sung in a free, unmeasured style, or in long and short notes corresponding to the accented and unaccented syllables of the words. Most scholars now prefer to transcribe them as they do plainchant—in neutral note values without bar lines.

Each poetic line of a canso receives its own melodic phrase. The phrases join to make one long melody to accommodate a complete stanza of poetry. While Bernart's melody is arranged in this manner, a variety of formal patterns emerges through variation, contrast, and the repetition of short, distinctive musical phrases. Many of the troubadour and trouvère melodies repeat the opening phrases or section before proceeding in a free style—for example, AAB, or, in more detail, ab ab cdef. Phrases are modified on repetition, and elusive echoes of earlier phrases are heard; but the main impression is one of freedom, spontaneity, and simplicity, although in fact both the music and poetry are very skillfully crafted.

Some of these features are illustrated in another canso—the only song by a trobairitz to survive with music—composed by the Comtessa Beatriz de Día (d. ca. 1212). A *vida*, or biographical tale, written about a century later describes Beatriz as a "beautiful and good woman, the wife of Guillaume de Poitiers. And she was in love with Rambaud d'Orange and made about him many good and beautiful songs." In *A chantar* (To sing, NAWM 9) the countess berates her

Full 🔊

9th cent. Earliest notated manuscripts of Gregorian chant	**ca. 1025–1028** Guido proposes system of solmization	
	11th cent. Goliards flourish	**ca. 1180** Bernart de Ventadorn dies
10th cent. Monks at Saint Gall compose tropes (NAWM 6) and sequences (NAWM 5)	**ca. 1151** Hildegard, *Ordo virtutum* (NAWM 7)	**ca. 1212** Beatriz de Día dies

1300

800 Charlemagne crowned emperor by pope	**1095–1099** First Crusade	**1189–1192** Third Crusade
800–821 *Rule of Saint Benedict* introduced in Frankish lands	**ca. 1100** *Chanson de Roland*, French epic poem	**1347–1350** Plague devastates Europe
	1147–1149 Second Crusade	

unfaithful lover and reminds him of her own worthy qualities. The song uses four distinct melodic phrases arranged in the form ab ab cdb.

The troubadours served as the model for a German school of knightly poet-musicians, the Minnesinger, who flourished between the twelfth and fourteenth centuries. The love (*Minne*) of which they sang in their Minnelieder (love songs) was even more abstract than troubadour love and sometimes had a distinctly religious tinge. The music is correspondingly more sober. Some of the melodies are written in the church modes, while others sound as though they were built on major scales. Because of the rhythm of the texts, scholars think that the majority of the tunes were sung in triple meter. As in France, strophic songs were very common. Their tunes, however, were more tightly organized through melodic phrase repetition. A typical German poetic form called *bar* (AAB) inspired a common musical pattern: the melodic phrase A (called the Stollen) is sung twice for the stanza's first two units of text, while the remainder, B (the Abgesang), containing new melodic material, is longer and sung only once.

The Middle High German texts include loving depictions of the glow and freshness of spring. There are also dawn songs, like the French alba, sung by the faithful friend who stands guard and warns the illicit lovers that dawn is approaching. A new genre is the Crusade song, recounting the experiences of those who renounced worldly comfort to join the Crusades (Christian military expeditions to recover the Holy Land from the Muslims). A famous example is the *Palästinalied* (Palestine song, NAWM 11) by Walther von der Vogelweide (ca. 1170?–ca. 1230?).

Figure 2.18 Walther von der Vogelweide as depicted in a fourteenth-century Swiss manuscript. Vogelweide means "bird-meadow," and his shield, shown in the upper left, includes a caged bird. (Universitätsbibliothek, Universität Heidelberg.)

Figure 2.19   Illustrations from the Cantigas de Santa María
*(ca. 1250–1280) manuscript, showing musicians playing
(clockwise from upper left) transverse flutes, shawms, pipes
and tabors, and trumpets.*
(Oronoz, Madrid.)

One of the treasures of medieval song is the *Cantigas de Santa María,* a collection of over four hundred cantigas (songs) in Galician-Portuguese in honor of the Virgin Mary. The collection was prepared about 1270–1290 under the direction of King Alfonso el Sabio ("the Wise") of Castile and León (northwest Spain) and is preserved in four beautifully illuminated manuscripts. Whether Alfonso wrote some of the poems and melodies is uncertain. Most songs in the collection relate stories of miracles performed by the Virgin, who was increasingly venerated from the twelfth century on. Cantiga 159, *Non sofre Santa María* (NAWM 12), tells of a cut of meat, stolen from some pilgrims, that Mary caused to jump about, revealing where it was hidden by the perpetrators. All the songs have refrains, perhaps performed by a group alternating with a soloist who sang the verses. Songs with refrains were often associated with dancing, a possibility reinforced by illustrations of dancers in the *Cantigas* manuscripts and by the dancelike rhythm of many of the songs.

POSTLUDE

The spread and stabilization of the Roman rite through western Europe during the Middle Ages resulted in the creation of a repertory of Gregorian chant that survives to this day. This repertory includes many different types of chant, each with a distinct function within the liturgical celebrations of the Office and the Mass. It also contains many chronological layers, having evolved from early Christian times down to the sixteenth century, when some types of chant (new Offices, liturgical dramas, hymns, and sequences) were still being written. Chants were classified into eight church modes and written down in a notation that gradually evolved as a means of teaching and standardizing performance.

Secular songs also flourished. They were most sophisticated and virtuosic in the cultural centers and courts of the later Middle Ages. These songs, in a variety of strophic forms often including refrains, had many different uses, sometimes involving dance. Some were narrative or dramatic, others lyrical. The body of courtly love songs created by troubadours and trouvères as a monument to the sentiments and ideals of refined and courtly love remains unequaled for its sheer beauty and artfulness.

 Resources for study and review available at
wwnorton.com/studyspace

3

Polyphony through the Thirteenth Century

PRELUDE

The years 1050 to 1300 saw an increase in trading and commerce throughout western Europe, as its growing population began to build modern cities. The Normans (a warrior people originally from Scandinavia who settled Normandy in northern France) crossed the English Channel to capture England, while Spain was seeking to liberate itself from Muslim conquerors. The First Crusade (1095–1099) united Christian ruling families from all over Europe in a successful campaign to drive the "infidel" Turks out of Jerusalem. After centuries of political instability and limited literacy, Europe enjoyed a cultural revival, which included music and all the arts; we have seen some of its effects in the eloquent love songs of the troubadours and trouvères. Scholars translated important works from Greek antiquity and the Arab world into Latin, encouraging the development of music theory. Places of teaching and learning that eventually became universities sprang up in Paris, Oxford, and Bologna. Large Romanesque churches (see Figure I.6), built on the architectural principle of the round arch of the Roman basilica, began to dominate the landscape, just as Gregorian chant and the Roman rite had prevailed in the liturgy. Pious donors funded hundreds of new monasteries and convents, filled by rising numbers of men, women, and children seeking a religious life. As scholars revived ancient learning, Saint Anselm, Saint Thomas Aquinas, and others associated with the intellectual movement called Scholasticism sought to reconcile classical philosophy with Christian doctrine through commentary on authoritative texts (see Figure 3.1). The Romanesque style yielded to a new style of church architecture called Gothic, which emphasized height and spaciousness, with soaring vaults, pointed arches, slender columns, large stained-glass windows, and intricate carvings (see Figure 3.4). Some of these developments found parallels in the art of written polyphony, which blossomed in certain regions of France and England in the twelfth and thirteenth centuries. (see In Context, page 62.)

By polyphony, we mean music in which voices sing together in independent parts. At first, polyphony was a style of performance, a manner of accompanying chant with one or more added voices. This heightened the grandeur of chant and, thus, of the liturgy itself, just as art and architectural decoration ornamented the church and, thus, the service. The added voices elaborated the

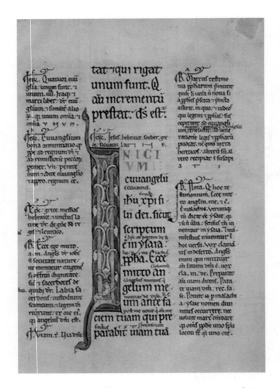

Figure 3.1   A leaf from a manuscript copy of the Gospel of Saint Mark. The central text is heavily glossed with commentary (akin to footnotes) between its lines and along both sides of the page in a process that illustrates the Scholastic method and also has parallels in troping and in the musical layering of early polyphony.
(The Morgan Library.)

authorized chants through a musical gloss or commentary, a process resembling troping; and, indeed, polyphony developed in the same regions and contexts as the monophonic tropes discussed in Chapter 2. Therefore, the kind of polyphony we associate with Notre Dame Cathedral in Paris has roots in a long prehistory of improvised polyphony, of which few written traces exist. We have good reason to believe that European musicians used polyphony in and outside of church long before it was first unmistakably described in a ninth-century treatise called *Musica enchiriadis* (Music Handbook).

When, in the ninth century, singers improvising on plainchant departed from simple parallel motion to give their parts some independence, they set the stage for counterpoint, the combination of multiple independent lines. The need for regulation of these simultaneous sounds led eventually to the precepts of harmony. As the parts were combined in more complex ways, refinements in notation permitted music to be written down and performed repeatedly. Written composition began to replace improvisation as a way of creating musical works, and notation began to replace memory as a means of preserving them. Consequently, the rise of written polyphony is of particular interest because it inaugurated four concepts that have distinguished Western music ever since: (1) counterpoint, the combination of multiple independent lines; (2) harmony, the regulation of simultaneous sounds; (3) the centrality of notation; and (4) the idea of composition as distinct from performance. These concepts changed over time, but their presence in this music links it to all that followed.

Such changes came about gradually during the eleventh, twelfth, and thirteenth centuries; there was no sudden break with the past. Monophony remained the principal medium of both performance and new composition. Indeed, some of the finest monophonic chants, including antiphons, hymns, and sequences, were produced after 1200, some as late as the sixteenth century. Musicians continued to improvise as well, and many stylistic details of the polyphonic music that remains in written form grew out of improvisational practice.

After developments traceable from the ninth century, several types of polyphony gained a secure place in the extant written repertories of France and England. We will study two of them in this chapter: organum and motet. Organum (pronounced *or'-ga-num;* Lat., pl. *or'-ga-na*) was, as we have suggested, a form of troping the chant. But now, instead of attaching a melodic trope to the beginning or end of an existing chant—a horizontal extension—organum offered the possibility of adding new layers of melody in a vertical dimension. This polyphonic elaboration of plainchant reached its most sophisticated level in Paris at the cathedral of Notre Dame, a church built in the soaring, new Gothic style of the twelfth century (see Figure 3.4). By creating different rates of motion among the voice parts, singers at Notre Dame forced a breakthrough in rhythmic notation, which until then had been vague at best. They also began creating other polyphonic genres, the most enduring among them being the motet, which also had its origins in the process of troping, as we shall see. The motet eventually became the dominant genre of both sacred and secular polyphonic music.

Early Organum

The anonymous author of *Musica enchiriadis* examines and illustrates two distinct kinds of "singing together," both designated by the term *organum*. In one species of this early organum, a plainchant melody in the principal voice (Latin, *vox principalis*) is duplicated a fourth or a fifth below by an organal voice (Latin, *vox organalis*). Example 3.1 shows parallel organum at the fifth below (NAWM 14.a). Either voice or both may be further duplicated at the octave to create an even richer sound (NAWM 14.b). Of course, singing in parallel fourths or fifths sometimes produces a harsh tritone (such as occurs between F and B), and the adjustments needed to avoid it led to organum that was not strictly parallel (Example 3.2 and NAWM 14.c). In this type, called oblique organum or organum with oblique motion, the added part was melodically different from the plainchant, and a wider variety of intervals, including dissonances, came into use.

In eleventh-century music, contrary and oblique motion predominated over parallel motion, and, as a consequence, the polyphonic voices grew increasingly independent and more like equal partners. Though the parts often cross, the organal voice shifted to a position above the chant, where it gained more rhythmic and melodic prominence, occasionally singing two notes against one of the principal voice. Consonant intervals—the unison, octave, fourth, and fifth—prevail, while others—including thirds, then understood as dissonant—occur only incidentally (Example 3.3). The rhythm is identical to the unmeasured flow of plainchant, which forms the basis for all these pieces.

In the eleventh century, polyphony was applied chiefly to the troped plainchant sections of the Mass Ordinary (such as the Kyrie and Gloria), to certain parts of the Proper (Tracts and Sequences), and to responsories of the Office and Mass (Graduals and Alleluias). Because polyphony demanded trained

Parallel organum

Full 🔊

Contrary and oblique motion

Example 3.1 Parallel organum at the fifth below, from Musica enchiriadis

You of the father are the everlasting son (from Te Deum laudamus*).*

Example 3.2 Mixed parallel and oblique organum, from Musica enchiriadis

King of Heaven, Lord of the roaring sea.

Example 3.3 Free organum, from Ad organum faciendum *(ca. 1100)*

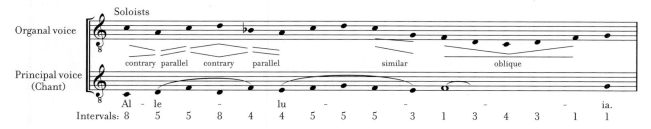

Full 🔊   Concise 🔊

Free and florid
organum

Figure 3.2   Master of the Platerias Portal, King David bowing a rebec, ca. 1100. Granite. South portal, cathedral of Santiago de Compostela, Spain. The decorative folds of David's garment have their counterpart in the florid melismas of the more elaborate melodies of the Mass and Office.
(Giraudon/Art Resource, NY.)

soloists who could follow rules of consonance while improvising or who could read the approximate notation, only the soloists' portions of the original chant were embellished polyphonically. In performance, then, polyphonic sections alternated with monophonic chant, which the full choir sang in unison. The solo sections from the *Alleluia Justus ut palma* (NAWM 15) are preserved in a set of instructions headed *Ad organum faciendum* (On making organum) and date from about 1100. The added voice proceeds mostly note-against-note above the chant, but toward the end of the opening "Alleluia" the performer sings a melismatic passage against a single note of the chant (Example 3.3). In this new style of organum, known today as free organum, the organal voice has more rhythmic and melodic independence.

A more florid style of free organum appeared early in the twelfth century in Aquitaine, a region in southwestern France. In Aquitanian organum, the lower voice, usually an existing chant but sometimes an original melody, sustains long notes while the upper (solo) voice sings decorative phrases of varying length. Pieces in this new style resulted in much longer organa, with a more prominent upper part that moved independently of the lower one. The chant, meanwhile, became elongated into a series of single-note "drones" that supported the melismatic elaborations above, thereby completely losing its character as a recognizable tune. The lower voice was called the tenor, from the Latin *tenere* ("to hold"), because it held the principal—that is, the first or original—melody. For the next 250 years, the word *tenor* designated the lowest part of a polyphonic composition.

Writers in the early twelfth century began distinguishing between two kinds of organum. For the style just described, in which the lower voice sustains long notes while the upper voice moves more melismatically, they reserved the terms *organum, organum duplum,* or *organum purum* ("double organum" and "pure organum," respectively), all of which we now associate with organum that is free or florid in style. The other kind, in which the movement is primarily note against note, they called *discantus* (discant). When the Notre Dame composer Leoninus was praised by a contemporary writer as *optimus organista,* he was not being called an excellent organist but the best singer or composer of organum (see Biography, page 59). The same writer described Perotinus, Leoninus's younger colleague, as the best *discantor,* or maker of discants. In both styles, the upper part elaborates an underlying note-against-note counterpoint with the tenor.

We can see a good example of florid Aquitanian organum and discant in the two-voice *Jubilemus, exultemus,* illustrated in Figure 3.3 and transcribed in Example 3.4 (see NAWM 16 for the complete version). The section in Example 3.4a uses the florid style of organum, with melismas of three to fifteen notes in the upper part for most notes in the tenor. Example 3.4b shows a passage in discant style, with fewer notes in the upper part for every tenor note until the penultimate syllable, which typically has a longer melisma. In both excerpts, contrary motion is more common than parallel, and most note groups in the upper voice begin on a perfect consonance with the tenor, although dissonances generously pepper the melismas. In the discant section, the composer seems to have chosen an occasional dissonance above the tenor note for variety and spice (as in "-ter-" of "eterna" and "-cu-" of "secula," as shown by the arrows). Phrases end on octaves or unisons, emphasizing closure.

When organum was written down (which ordinarily it was not), one part sat above the other, fairly well aligned as in a modern score, with the phrases marked off by short vertical strokes on the staff. Two singers, or one soloist and a small group, could not easily go astray. But when the rhythmic relation between the parts became complex, singers had to know exactly how long to hold each note. As we have seen, the late medieval notations of plainchant and

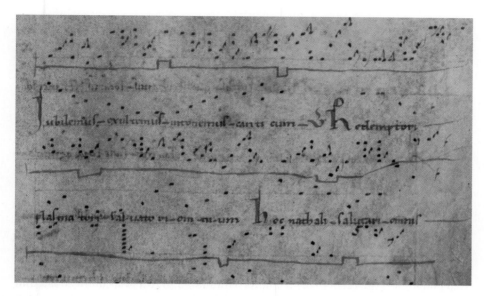

Figure 3.3 An example of two-voice Aquitanian organum, also known as free or florid organum, which may have been written as early as 1100. The solid lines separate the upper and lower voices. (For a partial transcription, see below and NAWM 16.)
(Bibliothèque Nationale, Paris, fonds Latin, MS 1139, fol. 41.)

Example 3.4 Aquitanian (florid) organum and discant in Jubilemus, exultemus

a. *Verse 2*

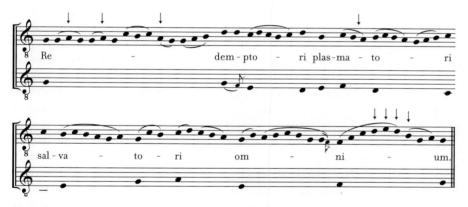

To the redeemer, savior of all.

b. *Verse 4*

Praise God and eternally applaud.

of troubadour and trouvère songs did not indicate duration. Indeed, no one felt a need to specify it, for the rhythm was either free or was communicated orally. Uncertainty about note duration was not a serious concern in solo or monophonic singing but could cause chaos when two or more melodies were sung simultaneously. Singers in northern France solved this problem by devising a system of rhythmic notation involving patterns of long and short notes known today as the rhythmic modes (see Innovations, page 56).

Notre Dame Polyphony

Leoninus

Musicians in Paris developed a still more ornate style of polyphony in the late twelfth and early thirteenth centuries. Two musicians associated with the new Cathedral of Notre Dame ("Our Lady," the Virgin Mary; see Figure 3.4) were Leoninus (fl. 1150s–ca. 1201), who was a priest and poet-musician, and Perotinus (fl. 1200–1230), who probably trained as a singer under Leoninus (see Biography, page 59). Both may have studied at the University of Paris, which was becoming a center of intellectual innovation; a typical classroom setting is shown in Figure 3.9. Leoninus was credited with having compiled a *Magnus liber organi* ("great book of polyphony"). This collection contained two-voice settings of the solo portions of the responsorial chants (Graduals and Alleluias of the Mass, and Office responsories) for the major feasts of the church year, some or all of which he himself composed. To undertake such a cycle shows a vision as grand as that of the builders of Notre Dame Cathedral. The *Magnus liber* offers different settings for the same passages of chant, including organa for two, three, and four voices, making them ideal for tracing the process of revision and substitution by which the repertory grew and the style evolved from one generation to the next. An ideal example is *Viderunt omnes*, the Gradual for Christmas Day.

Full 🔊   Concise 🔊

If we compare the setting ascribed to Leoninus of *Viderunt omnes* (NAWM 17) to the original chant (NAWM 3d), we see that polyphonic music is provided only for the sections of the chant performed by soloists, while the choir was expected to sing the rest of the melody in unison (see Figure 2.11). The responsorial chant by itself displays contrasts in form and sound in that some sections are syllabic and others are melismatic. The elaboration emphasizes these contrasts by featuring two different styles of polyphony, organum and discant (see Figure 3.5). In the opening section on "Viderunt," shown in Example 3.5, the organum extends the notes of the original melody into a series of drones, while the added voice spins expansive melismas above it. The original notation suggests a free, unmeasured rhythm; the fluid melody—loosely organized in a succession of unequal phrases often lingering on dissonances with the tenor—suggests improvisational practice. Then, as the choir enters after the word "omnes," this lengthy soloistic beginning reverts to plainchant (see Figure 3.5).

The next section of the Gradual was sung in two styles, moving from organum to discant on the

Figure 3.4   Part of the nave and transept of the Cathedral of Notre Dame in Paris, built ca. 1163–1250. Its great height and elaborate interior have parallels in the unprecedented length, intricacy, and carefully worked-out structure of the vocal music that singers collectively created to resound in its vast space.
(Laurent Lucuix/Alamy.)

Example 3.5 First section of Viderunt omnes, *in organum duplum*

Example 3.6 Discant clausula on "do-" of Viderunt omnes

SOLOISTS	CHORUS	SOLOISTS			CHORUS
Organum	Plainchant	Organum	Discant	Organum	Plainchant
Viderunt omnes	fines terra . . .	℣. Notum fecit	Do-[melisma]	minus salutare, etc.	justitiam suam

Figure 3.5   Performance textures of organum duplum, where sections of organum alternate with plainchant in the respond and with discant in the verse.

word "Dominus," where a long melisma had appeared in the original chant (compare Example 3.6 with Figure 3.5). Had the singers not quickened the pace of the tenor voice here, the result would have been a work of excessive length. But by singing occasional discant passages where the original chant was melismatic, and placing them alongside sections of plainchant and organum, Leoninus and his colleagues created a piece of manageable size within the context of the liturgy and offered the worshippers a variety of pleasing textures without changing a word or note of the original chant, although they occasionally repeat a phrase to provide structural support for their discant elaboration.

A section in discant style was called a clausula (plural, clausulae), the Latin word for a clause or phrase in a sentence. Discant clausulae are characteristically more consonant than organa and have relatively short phrases and more lively pacing because both voices move in modal rhythm, repeated patterns of long and short notes (see Innovations, page 56), creating contrast with the surrounding unmeasured sections of organa. Perotinus was credited with composing "very many better clausulae" as he and his contemporaries continued editing and updating the *Magnus liber*. Hundreds of separate clausulae appear in the same manuscripts as the organa themselves; because some may have been designed to replace the original setting of the same segment of chant, they are sometimes called, collectively, *substitute clausulae*. One manuscript includes ten clausulae on the word

Clausula

Perotinus

Substitute clausulae

Innovations Modal Rhythm

It is no coincidence that the earliest solution to the problem of notating rhythm is associated with Paris, particularly with its rising cathedral and its flourishing university (see p. 10). With the recovery of Aristotle's writings and the reliance on Aristotelian logic, Scholasticism, the dominant intellectual movement of the age, displayed a fascination with order. This fascination led to an interest in classifying rhythms. One significant source for classifying poetic meters, Saint Augustine's *De musica*, written in the fourth century, analyzes the motion of poetic meters according to their "music" or "sounding numbers." (Like Boethius, Augustine considered music to be one of the mathematical arts of the quadrivium.) Borrowing from ancient sources, music, Augustine says, is "the art of measuring well." The crystallizaion of the six rhythmic modes (shown in Figure 3.6), which correspond roughly to the arrangement of long and short syllables of ancient Latin verse, took place against this background.

Even though Latin poetry of the Middle Ages was no longer organized quantitatively (by the twelfth century, it was defined by stress rather than by syllable length), the theory of the rhythmic modes appears to derive from the principles underlying the measurement of classical poetic meter. It posits that music, like poetry, can be ordered or measured by units of time that have an exact numerical relationship with one another, the long note being twice or three times the duration of the short note, or breve (L and B, respectively, in Figure 3.6). In this way, the new musical practice at Notre Dame, which may have originated in rhythmic patterns to aid in the memorization of organa's long melismas, was reconciled with the University of Paris curriculum that considered music a branch of mathematics—the science of numbers as they relate to sound. This revolutionary new application of old principles is what allowed the repertory from Notre Dame to be preserved and disseminated across much of Europe, from Spain to Scotland. And from this innovation, the development of musical notation in the West unfolds.

1. LB   3. LBB   5. LL
2. BL   4. BBL   6. BBB

Figure 3.6   The six rhythmic modes

Figure 3.7   This tympanum over the main portal of the Romanesque church of Saint Pierre in Moissac, France (1125–1130), shows the medieval delight in small repetitive forms similar to the repeating patterns of modal rhythm. In this case, the module that repeats is one of the Twenty-four Elders of the Apocalypse. Each one holds an identical rebec or fiddle or perhaps a lutelike instrument and has stopped playing to look up in astonishment at Christ, whose Second Coming is depicted above their heads.
(Photo courtesy of the author.)

Example 3.7 Two substitute clausulae on "Dominus" from Viderunt omnes

a.

b.

Full 🔊

"Dominus" from *Viderunt omnes,* any one of which could have been used at Christmas Mass. The openings of two of them are shown in Example 3.7 (NAWM 18).

Both clausulae exhibit a common trait of discant in Perotinus's generation: the tenor repeats a rhythmic motive based on one of the rhythmic modes. Because these rhythmic patterns use shorter notes than earlier discant, the tenor melodies were often repeated, though over a longer span of time than the rhythmic pattern itself. These repetitive motives create a sense of coherence for an extended passage, and both types of repetition in the tenor—of rhythm and of melody—gained significance in the motet of the thirteenth and fourteenth centuries (see below and Chapter 4).

Perotinus "the Great" and his contemporaries expanded organum's dimensions by increasing the number of voice parts to three and (in two instances) to four. Since the second voice was called the duplum, by analogy the third was called the triplum and the fourth the quadruplum. These same terms also designated the composition as a whole: a three-voice organum came to be called an organum triplum, or simply triplum, and a four-voice organum a quadruplum. One of the two astonishing examples of four-voice organum—which stretches out the first word of the chant to extraordinary melismatic lengths—is the setting ascribed to Perotinus of *Viderunt omnes* (NAWM 19). Like other works of its kind, it begins in a style of organum with patterned clusters of notes in modal rhythm in the upper voices above very long, unmeasured notes in the tenor (see Figure 3.8 and its partial transcription in Example 3.8). As in the two-voice setting, such passages alternate with sections of discant, of which the longest is again on "Dominus" (not shown here).

The repertory created at Notre Dame was sung for more than a century, from the late twelfth century through the thirteenth. Music historians have long regarded it as the first polyphony to be primarily composed in writing and read from notation rather than improvised or orally composed. But, according to recent research, it was more likely a repertory developing from orality to literacy, or a fluid body of polyphony created by

Triple and quadruple organum

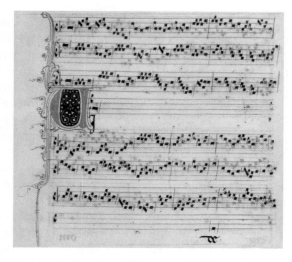

Figure 3.8   Opening of the setting of Viderunt omnes *in organum quadruplum. The upper three voices are in modal rhythm over a sustained tenor note. (For a transcription, see Example 3.8 and NAWM 19.)* (Biblioteca Medica-Laurenziana, Florence.)

Example 3.8 Perotinus, Viderunt omnes, *opening, with repeating elements indicated by letter*

singers and preserved in memory before it was written down. How such a vast and complex repertory was remembered, and how it was written down, are aspects that make this music especially significant in music history.

The Motet

A clausula, cut loose from its larger setting, could enjoy a second life as a separate piece, a little independent composition in melismatic polyphony. When Latin or French words were added to the upper voice, a new type of work, originating like earlier troped genres, was created: the motet (from the French *mot,* meaning "word"). The Latin form, *motetus,* also designates the second voice—the original duplum, now sporting its own text. In three- and four-part motets, the third and fourth voices carry the same names—triplum and quadruplum—that they had in organum.

Origins   The motet originated, then, when musicians at Notre Dame troped the repertory of clausulae preserved in the *Magnus Liber.* These clausulae, having earlier belonged to the genre of organum, themselves featured newly created melodies layered above old chants. Thus, a defining characteristic of the motet was its use of borrowed chant material in the tenor. Such a tenor was known as **Cantus firmus** the *cantus firmus* (Latin, plain chant; plural, *cantus firmi*). Just as new clausulae were produced using the same favorite cantus firmi, so, too, were motets throughout France and western Europe during the thirteenth century derived from a common stock of motet melodies—both tenors and upper parts—and transformed into new works.

Some motets were intended for nonliturgical use, and their upper voices could have vernacular texts while the tenor may have been played on instruments or vocalized wordlessly. After 1250, it was customary to use different but topically related texts in as many as two upper voices. These motets are identified by a compound title made up of the incipit (the first word or words) of each voice part, beginning with the highest.

Early motets   A typical early motet is *Factum est salutare/Dominus* (NAWM 21a), shown in Example 3.9 and based on one of the substitute clausulae from the *Magnus liber* **Full 🔊** (Example 3.7a). Like many early Latin motets based on clausulae, this text is a trope on the original chant text, elaborating its meaning and drawing on its words or sounds. The poem ends with the word "Dominus" ("Lord"), to which the tenor melody was originally sung, and incorporates several other words from the chant (underlined in the example), some of which are echoed in subsequent

Leoninus (fl. 1150–ca. 1201)
Perotinus (fl. 1200–1230)

Leoninus served at the cathedral of Paris in many capacities, beginning in the 1150s, before construction started on the Cathedral of Notre Dame. His title (Magister, or Master; see below) suggests that he earned a Master of Arts degree, presumably at the University of Paris, and eventually became a priest and then canon at Notre Dame. As a poet, he wrote a paraphrase, in verse, of the first eight books of the Bible as well as several shorter works.

Less is known about Perotinus. He, too, possibly, had a Master of Arts and must have held an important position at Notre Dame.

Virtually all we know about the musical activities of Leoninus and Perotinus is contained in an anonymous treatise from about 1275. The writer makes a pointed comparison between the two:

> And note that Master Leoninus was an excellent *organista* [singer or composer of organum], so it is said, who made the great book of organum [*magnus liber organi*] on the gradual and antiphonary to enrich the Divine Service. It was in use up to the time of Perotinus the Great, who edited it and made many better clausulae or puncta, being an excellent *discantor* [singer or composer of discant], and better [at discant] than Leoninus was. (This, however, is not to be asserted regarding the subtlety of organum, etc.)
>
> Now, this same Master Perotinus made the best *quadrupla* [four-voice organa], such as *Viderunt* and *Sederunt*, with an abundance of musical *colores* [melodic formulas]; likewise, the noblest *tripla* [three-voice organa], such as *Alleluia Posui adiutorium* and [*Alleluia*] *Nativitas*, etc. He also made three-voice conductus, such as *Salvatoris hodie*, and

Figure 3.9   We have no images of Leoninus or Perotinus. This illumination from an early fourteenth-century French manuscript shows a class at the University of Paris from their era.
(British Library.)

two-voice conductus, such as *Dum sigillum summi patris*, and also, among many others, monophonic conductus, such as *Beata viscera*, etc. The book or, rather, books of Master Perotinus were in use up to the time of Master Robertus de Sabilone in the choir of the Paris cathedral of the Blessed Virgin [Notre Dame], and from his time up to the present day.[1]

Like the Scholastic theologians who glossed and commented on the Scriptures, adding their own layers of interpretation to those of previous scholars. Leoninus and Protinus expanded the musical dimensions of the liturgy by "glossing" the preexisting chant. Their newly composed voices sung in counterpoint to the Gregorian melody were like the marginal commentaries surrounding a central authoritative text.

1. Translation adapted from Edward H. Roesner, "Who 'Made' the *Magnus liber*?," *Early Music History* 20 (2001): 227–28.

Example 3.9 Factum est salutare/Dominus

Salvation was made known in the sight of the Gentiles.

rhymes. The original discant clausula, a musical decoration of a word, is here embellished by the addition of words, like a gloss upon a gloss. The resulting motet is an ingenious composite artwork with multiple layers of borrowing and of meaning. In an eccesiastical culture that treasured commentary, allegory, and new ways of reworking traditional themes, such pieces must have been highly esteemed for their many allusions.

Versatility of motet

Musicians soon regarded the motet as a genre independent of church performance. In the process, the tenor lost its connection as a melody to a specific place in the liturgy and became raw material for a new piece, a firm foundation for the upper voice or voices. This change in the role of motets raised new possibilities that encouraged musicians to rework existing motets in several ways: (1) writing a different text for the duplum, in Latin or French, that was no longer necessarily linked to the chant text and was often on a secular topic; (2) adding a third voice to those already present; and (3) giving the additional parts words of their own to create a double motet (one with two texts above the tenor). Motets were also devised from scratch, with one of the tenor melodies from the Notre Dame clausula repertory being laid out in a new rhythmic pattern and new voices being added above it.

The two motets in Examples 3.10 and 3.11 illustrate some of these characteristics. *Fole acostumance/Dominus* (Example 3.10 and NAWM 21b) employs the same tenor as Example 3.9 but states it twice and substitutes a new, more quickly-moving duplum for the original one. The doubled length and faster motion accommodate a much longer text, a secular French poem complaining that envy, hypocrisy, and deception have ruined France. The composer of *Super te*

Example 3.10 Fole acostumance/Dominus

It is only a crazy habit that makes me sing.

Example 3.11 Super te Ierusalem/Sed fulsit virginitas/Dominus

Triplum: *For you, Jerusalem, from a virgin mother, was born in [Bethlehem] . . .*
Duplum: *But her virginity glowed with the Spirit's breath. Therefore, pious . . .*

Ierusalem/Sed fulsit virginitas/Dominus (Example 3.11 and NAWM 21c) began with a portion of the same chant melisma on "Dominus" but imposed a different modal rhythmic pattern. The two upper voices set the first and second halves respectively of a Latin poem about the birth of Jesus, thereby confirming the motet's connection to the feast of Christmas on which the tenor melody was originally sung and making it appropriate to be performed during that season, either in private devotions or as an addition to the church service. As in most motets with more than two voices, the upper parts rarely rest together or with the tenor, so that the music moves forward in an unbroken stream. A composite of Examples 3.9, 10, and 11, all on the same cantus firmus, may be seen in Example 3.12.

Figure 3.10 Detail of the Twenty-four Elders and their instruments from the Pórtico de la Gloria, cathedral of Santiago de Compostela, ca. 1158 (compare Figure 3.7). (Bridgeman Art Library.)

In the earlier motets, all the upper parts were written in one melodic and rhythmic style. Later composers distinguished the upper voices from each other as well as from the tenor, achieving more rhythmic freedom and variety both among and within voices. In this new kind of motet, called Franconian (after Franco of Cologne, a composer and theorist who was active from about 1250 to 1280), the triplum bears a longer text than the motetus and features a fastermoving melody with many short notes. The result is the kind of layered texture seen, for example, in the motet by Adam de la Halle (ca. 1240–1288?), *De ma dame vient/Dieus, comment porroie/Omnes* (NAWM 22). Here, rhythmic differences between the voices reinforce the contrast of texts, the triplum voicing the complaints of a man separated from his sweetheart and the duplum (motetus) the woman's thoughts of him. Below them, the slowest-moving part, the tenor, repeats the melody for "omnes," from the Gradual *Viderunt omnes*, twelve times.

Full 🔊

Example 3.12 A composite of Examples 3.9, 3.10, and 3.11, all on the same tenor or cantus firmus, "Dominus"

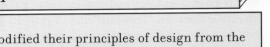

In Context The Motet as Gothic Cathedral

A distinctive feature of music is its movement through time. But to understand time, we must be able to measure it. The makers of polyphony in the twelfth and thirteenth centuries devised a way of measuring musical time so that it could be manipulated and controlled. By the late thirteenth century, the motet, wholly a creation of French musicians, illustrates this accomplishment better than any other genre of the era.

Each voice of a motet moves within its own rhythmic framework yet is perfectly compatible with every other voice. In the case of a three-voice motet, for example, the tenor measures the passage of time in long note values while the middle voice superimposes its own rhythmic design, consisting of shorter values, on the support created by the tenor. Meanwhile, the highest voice relates to time differently from its two partners, usually in notes that move even more quickly than those of the middle voice and with phrases that coincide with (or sometimes overlap) the ends of the phrases below. The result is a three-tiered structure in which each level is independent of, yet completely coordinated with, the other two levels.

If we look at the interior space of a typical Gothic cathedral that was created by French architects during the very period in which the medieval motet flourished (see Figure 3.11), we see a formal design remarkably similar to the structure just described. Along either side of the nave, or central aisle of the church, is an arcade of huge columns that have been placed at regular intervals to define the length of the cathedral and support its soaring height. Along the next higher storey are the paired arches of the gallery, measuring the same regular spaces by smaller distances, in effect quickening the rhythm. Superimposed atop this layer, just below the level at which walls give way to windows, is a third tier of still smaller, triple arches (the triforium), ornamental rather than functional, independent of and yet perfectly harmonized with the lower levels.

The similarities described here are not accidental: the architects of the Gothic style codified their principles of design from the same mathematical laws that the creators of modal rhythm and the composers of motets used in establishing their theories of proportion and measure. The results of their efforts are, on the one hand, a glorious edifice in which we can "hear" a kind of silent music and, on the other, a genre of polyphonic composition that allows us to "see" the harmonious plan of its underlying structure.

Neo-Gothic churches are still being built in our day. The chapel at West Point; Princeton University Chapel; Saint Thomas Church, Saint Patrick's Cathedral, and the huge cathedral of Saint John the Divine in New York City; the National Cathedral in Washington, D.C.; Saint Paul's Anglican Church in Toronto; Montreal's Notre-Dame Basilica; and more than a hundred other North American churches all testify to the inspiring grandeur of the Gothic style.

Triforium

Gallery

Arcade

Figure 3.11 *The nave of Notre Dame de Laon, looking west. This Gothic cathedral was built from about 1165 to 1215.*
(Anthony Scibilia/Art Resource, NY.)

The motet in France had an astonishing career in its first century. What began as a work of poetry more than a composition, fitting a new text to an existing piece of music, developed into the leading polyphonic genre, home to the most complex interplay of simultaneous and independent lines yet conceived. In their texts and structure, motets of the late thirteenth century mirrored both the century's intellectual delight in complication and its architectural triumph of the Gothic cathedral (see In Context, page 62).

Role of motet

The Polyphonic Conductus

The Notre Dame composers and others in France, England, and elsewhere also wrote polyphonic conductus. These were settings for two to four voices of rhymed, metrical, strophic poems in Latin, rarely taken from the liturgy though usually on a sacred or serious topic. Typical is *Ave virgo virginum* (NAWM 20), which addresses the Virgin Mary and was perhaps used in special devotions and processions.

Full 🔊

The conductus differs from other Notre Dame polyphony in musical features as well as text. First, the tenor was newly composed rather than taken from chant. Second, all voices sing the text together in essentially the same rhythm. The nearly homorhythmic quality of the conductus has been called *conductus style* when used for other genres. Third, the words are set syllabically for the most part, although (unlike *Ave virgo virginum*) many feature melismatic passages, called caudae ("tails") at the beginning or end, or before important cadences.

Figure 3.12   The Last Supper, *depicted under the tympanum arch of a mid-twelfth-century church in Charlieu, in the Loire district of France. The modular, multilayered structure of the arch's sculptural elements is typical of Romanesque and Gothic church portals and resembles the layered texture of a medieval motet.*

(Alinari/Art Resource, NY.)

TIMELINE The Ninth through the Thirteenth Centuries

Musical Events				**early 13th cent.** Early motets (NAWM 21)
		12th cent. Aquitanian polyphony (NAWM 16)		**ca. 1200–ca. 1238** Perotinus at Notre Dame
	9th cent. *Musica enchiriadis* (NAWM 14)	**ca. 1150–ca. 1180** Flourishing of Bernart de Ventadorn	**1163–1190** Leoninus at Notre Dame Cathedral, Paris	**late 13th cent.** Franconian motets (NAWM 22)
800				**1200**
Historical Events	**11th cent.** Romanesque churches and monasteries	**12th cent.** Universities of Bologna, Oxford, and Paris established	**1163** Cornerstone laid for Gothic cathedral of Notre Dame, Paris; Gothic style flourishes in northern Europe	**1209** Saint Francis of Assisi founds Franciscan order
	1054 Final split between Roman and Byzantine churches	**1100** Cult of the Virgin Mary flourishes		**1264–1274** St. Thomas Aquinas, *Summa theological*
	1066 Norman Conquest of England	**1147–1149** Second Crusade	**1189** Richard Coeur de Lion, king of England	
	1095–1099 First Crusade		**1189–1192** Third Crusade	

POSTLUDE

The rise of polyphony in the Middle Ages parallels in many ways the development of monophonic song, including plainchant. It began as a manner of performance, became a practice of oral composition, and developed into a written tradition. Much of its history is hidden from view and can only be reconstructed partially from the traces that remain—chiefly descriptions in treatises and notated examples. But what was written down was only a small part of the polyphony that was sung.

The Notre Dame repertory gradually expanded through the process of troping, whereby combinations of new melodies and texts were added to, or layered above, the original monophonic lines. By the late twelfth and early thirteenth centuries, organum and motet were well-established genres in which musicians elaborated on chant tenors. Organum evolved from parallel types (where added voices merely duplicated the contour of the chant melody) to more florid pieces (where the added voices assumed greater melodic and rhythmic independence from the cantus firmus). Sections of discant-style organa, called clausulae, became separate works and, with added texts, gave rise to the motet, a new genre that dominated the polyphonic scene in France by the mid-thirteenth century.

These genres and conventions were soon to be outmoded, however, because of newer motet styles. The rhythmic modes gradually became obsolete, and the chant tenor was relegated to a purely formal function, elevating the triplum to the status of a solo voice against the accompanying lower parts. The road was open to a new musical style, a new way of composing (Ars Nova), in an age that looked back on the music of the latter half of the thirteenth century as the antique, outdated way (Ars Antiqua).

 Resources for study and review available at wwnorton.com/studyspace

French and Italian Music in the Fourteenth Century

PRELUDE

After the comparative stability of the thirteenth century, the fourteenth century experienced terror and turmoil. The Hundred Years' War (1337–1453) between France and England disrupted agriculture, manufacturing, and trade, and prolonged an economic decline initially caused by bad weather, famine, and floods. From 1348 to 1350, the Great Plague (also known as the Black Death) marched across Europe, wiping out a third of the population; almost everyone who became infected died in agony within days, while others fled the cities and towns to escape illness. Poverty, war, taxes, and political grievances combined to spark peasant and urban rebellions in France, England, Flanders (modern-day Belgium), Germany, Italy, and Spain.

The church was also in crisis. In the thirteenth century, Europeans viewed the church as the supreme authority not only in matters of faith, but also in intellectual and political affairs; now its authority, and especially the supremacy of the pope, was widely questioned. Early in the century, King Philip IV ("the Fair") of France had engineered the election of a French pope, who never went to Rome because of the hostility there to foreigners. Instead, from 1309 until 1378, the popes resided in Avignon, in southeastern France, under the virtual control of the French king. The papacy in Avignon was more like a princely court than a religious community, and it is not surprising that the surviving music from this period is almost entirely secular. The political situation became even more complicated when Italian factions elected their own pope and, between 1378 and 1417, there were two—and sometimes three—rival claimants to the papal throne. This state of affairs, known as the Papal Schism, was compounded by the often corrupt life of the clergy and drew sharp criticism, expressed in polemical writings, in motet texts of the time, and in the rise of popular heretical movements. When the papacy finally moved back from Avignon to Rome, it brought French music with it.

Europeans in the thirteenth century could generally reconcile revelation and reason, the divine and the human, the claims of the kingdom of God and those of the political powers of this world. But in the fourteenth century, people began to separate science from religion and to see different roles for church and state, notions still held today. Philosophers distinguished between divine revelation and human reason, each prevailing only in its own sphere. In other words, the church cared for people's souls while the state looked out for their earthly concerns. Without denying the claims of religion, this view spurred advances in science and technology; and an increasing interest in the world, the individual, and human nature made way for a growing secular culture.

The fourteenth century was also a period of remarkable creativity. The growth of literacy among the populace encouraged authors to write in the vernacular. Dante's *Divine Comedy* (1307), Boccaccio's *Decameron* (1353), and Chaucer's *Canterbury Tales* (1387–1400) are the great literary landmarks of the century, the latter two reflecting daily life and portraying people of all classes more realistically than earlier literature had done. The Florentine painter Giotto (ca. 1266–1337) broke away from the formalized Byzantine style and achieved more naturalistic representation, as seen in the facial expressions, posture, and garments of his figures (see Figure 4.1). Although there was no decline in the production of sacred music, the best-known composers of the time, Guillaume de Machaut and Francesco Landini, focused on secular music.

A treatise called *Ars Nova* (New Art or New Method; early 1320s) is attributed to Philippe de Vitry (1291–1361), French

Figure 4.1   Giotto (ca. 1266–1337), The Wedding Procession. This fresco is one of a series on the life of the Virgin Mary painted around 1305 in the Arena Chapel in Padua, Italy, also known as the Scrovegni Chapel after the banker Enrico Scrovegni, who built the chapel and commissioned the frescoes. Mary (with halo) leads a group of virgins, while a vielle player and two brass players provide music. Giotto created a sense of depth by placing the figures on different planes of the picture. (Cameraphoto Arte/Art Resource, NY.)

musician, poet, and bishop of Meaux. Modern scholars use the term *Ars Nova* to denote the French musical style during his lifetime—that is, the first half of the fourteenth century. The stylistic and technical innovations of the Ars Nova in France centered on rhythm and its notation, areas that became the playground of the fourteenth-century French composer, who sometimes carried them to extremes that delighted the intellect but could not be perceived by the ear (see Figure 4.13; Innovations, pages 72–73). A hotly contested issue of the new style was whether a duple, or "imperfect," division of note values should be allowed alongside the traditional triple, or "perfect," division. One theorist of the time, Jacques de Liège, argued against the duple division and syncopation (see Vignette, page 68). Although the motet, in which many of these experiments occurred, continued to be a favorite French genre of composition, its topics became less amorous and more political. It also became structurally more complex than it had been in the thirteenth century, evident in the rhythmic and melodic patterning known as isorhythm, a new feature of the genre and one that privileged abstract construction over the faculty of hearing. Earlier advances in polyphony had generally been associated with sacred music, but the most important new genre of the fourteenth century was now the polyphonic art song. Indeed, the two musical giants of the era, Guillaume de Machaut in France and Francesco Landini in Italy, concentrated on writing love lyrics in the traditional refrain forms of the trouvères, creating both monophonic and polyphonic settings.

VIGNETTE Jacques de Liège Rails against the Ars Nova

Jacques de Liège (ca. 1260–after 1330) was probably a native of Liège, in modern Belgium, and studied at the University of Paris. His Speculum musicae *(The Mirror of Music, ca. 1330) is the longest surviving medieval treatise on music. In the last of its seven books, he argued that the old style of the thirteenth century was more pleasing and "more perfect" than the new art of the younger generation.*

In a certain company in which some able singers and judicious laymen were assembled, and where new motets in the modern manner and some old ones were sung, I observed that even the laymen were better pleased with the ancient motets and the ancient manner than with the new. And even if the new manner pleased when it was a novelty, it does so no longer, but begins to displease many. So let the ancient music and the ancient manner of singing be brought back to their native land; let them come back into use; let the rational art flourish once more. It has been in exile, along with its manner of singing; they have been cast out from the fellowship of singers with near violence, but violence should not be perpetual.

Wherein does this lasciviousness in singing so greatly please, this excessive refinement, by which, as some think, the words are lost, the harmony of consonances is diminished, the value of the notes is changed, perfection is brought low, imperfection is exalted, and measure is confused?

Jacques de Liège, *Speculum musicae* 7.48, trans. Oliver Strunk and James McKinnon; in Oliver Strunk, ed., *Source Readings in Music History*, rev. ed. by Leo Treitler (New York: Norton, 1998), vol. 2, pp. 167–168.

The Ars Nova in France

Roman de Fauvel

The flavor of the times is captured in the *Roman de Fauvel*, a narrative poem satirizing political corruption both secular and ecclesiastical, apparently written as a warning to the king of France and enjoyed in political circles and at court. Fauvel, a jackass who rises from the stable to a powerful position, symbolizes a world turned upside down. His name is an acrostic for the sins he personifies: Flattery, Avarice, Villainy (*U* and *V* were interchangeable), Variété ("Fickleness"), Envy, and Lâcheté ("Baseness"). He ultimately marries and produces little Fauvels, who destroy the world. A beautifully illuminated manuscript from around 1317 (see Figure 4.2) has 169 pieces of music interpolated within the poem. These constitute a veritable anthology of works from the thirteenth and early fourteenth centuries, some written for this collection, others chosen for their relevance to the poem's message. Most are monophonic, from Latin chants to secular songs. But 34 are motets, many with texts that denounce the lax morals of the clergy or refer to political events. Among these motets in the *Roman de Fauvel* are the first examples of the new style known as the Ars Nova.

Philippe de Vitry

Isorhythm

Philippe de Vitry, associated with the *Ars Nova* treatise, may have written at least five of the motets in the *Roman de Fauvel*, and their tenors provide the earliest examples of a musically unifying device called isorhythm ("equal rhythm"). These tenors are laid out in segments of identical rhythm, which might recur as many as ten times in one piece, thus producing an isorhythmic motet. We have already seen this principle at work in the repertory that grew out of Notre Dame clausulae (see Example 3.11). But now, all this takes place on a much larger scale. The tenor is longer, the rhythms are more complex, and the whole line moves so slowly in comparison to the upper voices that it is heard less as a melody than as a foundation for the entire polyphonic structure.

Figure 4.2   A charivari, or noisy serenade, awakens Fauvel and Vaine Gloire after their wedding in the Roman de Fauvel *(1310–1314), a poem by Gervais du Bus with many musical interpolations. Fauvel, an allegorical ass, embodies the sins represented by the letters of his name.*
(Bibliothèque Nationale, Paris, MS Fr. 146.)

Theorists of the time recognized two recurring elements in motet tenors, rhythmic and melodic. They called the repeating rhythmic unit the *talea* and the recurring segment of melody the *color*. In an isorhythmic motet by Vitry from the *Roman de Fauvel* (NAWM 25) the tenor, shown in Example 4.1, has a talea (indicated with Roman numerals) that sounds three times before running through all the notes of the color (labeled A in the example). At the fourth statement of the talea, the notes of the color begin again (B IV). The color and talea could be the same length, always beginning and ending together, but most often the color extended over two, three, or more taleae, as in Example 4.1. In some motets, the endings of the color and talea do not coincide, so that repetitions of the color begin in the middle of a talea. Upper voices could also be organized isorhythmically, featuring repeating rhythmic units to emphasize the recurring rhythmic patterns in the tenor. Isorhythm was occasionally applied to compositions in other genres, as illustrated by the movement of Machaut's Mass (NAWM 26a) discussed below.

Isorhythmic designs helped not only composers at every stage of composition, but also singers who, seeing the repeating patterns in the original notation, could more easily grasp the shape of the music and commit it to memory.

Talea and color

Full 🔊   Concise 🔊

Full 🔊   Concise 🔊

Example 4.1 Philippe de Vitry, *Cum statua/Hugo, Hugo/Magister invidie*

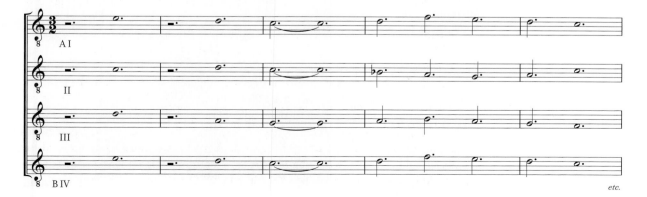

etc.

Guillaume de Machaut

The leading composer and poet of the Ars Nova in France, Guillaume de Machaut (ca. 1300–1377), was fully involved in the political, intellectual, and ecclesiastical worlds of his time (see Biography, page 74). He composed in most of the genres then current, from motets to secular songs, and a survey of his music also serves to introduce the main types of Ars Nova composition.

Machaut's Motets   Most of Machaut's twenty-three motets date from relatively early in his career. They employ the traditional texture in which a borrowed tenor supports two upper voices with different texts. Like other motets of the time, Machaut's are longer and more rhythmically complex than earlier examples. Nineteen are isorhythmic, and in some cases the isorhythmic structure involves all three voices. Machaut frequently emphasized the talea's recurrences by clever use of a technique called hocket, which also animates the polyphonic texture. In *Hocket* hocket (French *hoquet,* "hiccup"), two voices alternate in rapid succession, one resting while the other sings. Although Machaut did not invent the technique, he used it to great effect.

During the thirteenth century, chants from the Mass Proper were set polyphonically much more often than Ordinary chants. But in the fourteenth century, there are numerous settings of Ordinary texts by French, English, and Italian composers, some written for the papal chapel at Avignon, others for Masses celebrated on special occasions warranting added solemnity. Most were set as individual pieces that could be combined with others in a service, and a few were gathered into anonymous cycles, forming a complete set of Ordinary *Machaut's Mass* texts. Machaut's *Messe de Nostre Dame* (Mass of Our Lady) builds on this polyphonic tradition but treats the six texts of the Ordinary as one composition

Figure 4.3   Reims Cathedral, site of the coronation of French kings and of Machaut's activities as cleric, poet, and composer. The alternating grounded columns and elaborately carved arches recall the solid pillars of sound and lively rhythms that animate the texture of an isorhythmic motet or mass.
(SEF/Art Resource, NY.)

rather than as separate pieces. Machaut likely intended it to be performed with one singer on each part, like most polyphony of the time. He apparently composed the work in the early 1360s for performance at a Mass for the Virgin Mary celebrated every Saturday at an altar of the cathedral in Reims (Figure 4.3). After his death, an oration for Machaut's soul was added to the service, and his mass continued to be performed there well into the fifteenth century.

The six movements of Machaut's four-voice mass are linked together by similarities of style and approach and by some recurring motives and cadence tones. The Kyrie, Sanctus, Agnus Dei, and Ite, missa est are in motet style, each using a different cantus firmus that is organized isorhythmically. The Gloria and Credo, having longer texts, are written in discant style—that is, essentially syllabic and largely homorhythmic, although both movements end with elaborate isorhythmic "Amens."

The Kyrie (NAWM 26a) is typical of the isorhythmic movements. The tenor cantus firmus is the melody of a Kyrie chant, divided into taleae of different lengths for each section of the setting. A second supporting voice, called the contratenor ("against the tenor") and sharing the same range as the tenor, is also isorhythmic but has its own talea. Together they form the harmonic foundation of the four-part texture. Example 4.2 shows the opening of the Christe, including the first two statements of the seven-measure talea, marked by

Kyrie

Full 🔊   Concise 🔊

Example 4.2 *Guillaume de Machaut,* Messe de Nostre Dame, *beginning of Christe*

Innovations   Writing Rhythm

The new musical style of the Ars Nova was made possible by a set of innovations in notating rhythm, innovations that underlie our modern system of note values. The new notation required a rethinking of musical time. Composers of the Notre Dame school had conceived of musical rhythm in terms of repeating patterns of longs and shorts (the rhythmic modes; see Chapter 3). Their system was based on a unit of time that could be subdivided in only certain ways: long–breve (2:1), or breve–long (1:2), or breve–breve–breve (three shorts). The result was that any mode could be combined with any other, but the effect was a series of building blocks or modules always based on triple groupings. As long as theorists conceived of musical time in this limited way—a succession of perfections, as the modules were called—many rhythms could not be written, including anything in duple meter.

As with the innovations at Notre Dame, it was again the French theorists and composers who created the new system of measured music (mensuration). Instead of relying on the limited modules of the old way (the Ars Antiqua), they conceived of using a specific note form, the breve (■), as the basic building block of rhythm. The breve could be divided into either two or three notes of the next smaller value, the semibreve (♦), as shown in Figure 4.4; and semibreves, in turn, could be subdivided into two or three minims (♩), a new note form whose name means "least" in Latin. The division of the breve was called time (*tempus*) and that of the semibreve, prolation (*prolatio*). Division was perfect or major ("greater") if triple, imperfect or minor ("lesser") if duple.

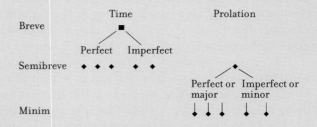

Figure 4.4   The relationship of time and prolation.

The four possible combinations of time and prolation, shown in Figure 4.5, produce four different meters, comparable to four in use today. Later in the century, time and prolation were specified by mensuration signs that are the ancestors of modern time signatures. A circle indicated perfect time and an incomplete circle imperfect time; the presence or absence of a dot signaled major or minor prolation. The incomplete circle with no dot (◖) has come down to us as a signature for $\frac{4}{4}$ time (equivalent to imperfect time, minor prolation), linking these four Ars Nova groupings to modern conceptions of meter.

Unlike the old system, based on modules, the new system of notation indicated particular durations whose measurement or value resided in the note's shape, not in its relationship to the module or pattern of which it was a part. This made it possible for the first time to notate syncopation, a prominent feature in melodies by composers from the fourteenth century on. Indeed, one theorist wrote of the new system, "Whatever can be sung can be written down." That was certainly not true

Roman numerals. The upper two voices move more rapidly, with syncopation typical of Machaut. They are also partly isorhythmic, which makes the recurring talea in the lower parts more evident, as does the placement of sustained notes on the first and fifth measures of each talea. (See the red and blue boxes in Example 4.2, which show isorhythmic patterns in the upper voices.) To generate rhythmic activity, Machaut often relies on repeated figuration. For example, the descending figure in the second measure of the triplum, echoed later in both duplum and triplum, recurs frequently throughout the mass, serving less as a unifying motive than as a way to create movement.

Machaut the songwriter   Machaut was both the leading practitioner of the Ars Nova in France and the last great poet-composer of monophonic courtly lyrics in the trouvère tradition. His songs were performed as entertainment in the courts and elite circles in which he moved. He wrote his monophonic pieces in the standard poetic forms of rhythmic notation in the thirteenth century, when what could be written down greatly limited what could be composed. Moreover, notation was now so specific that, for the first time, a piece of music could be written down in one city, carried to another, and performed there exactly as the composer had intended by singers who had nothing but the manuscript. Such a piece could be as fixed and permanent as a poem, and likely for that reason composers began to attach their names to their works and take pride in their authorship, as poets had been doing for centuries.

The new notation of the Ars Nova, then, accomplished several breakthroughs. It allowed for the notation of both triple and duple subdivisions of longer notes; it introduced new note shapes to indicate shorter durations than had previously been used; and it made possible a greater variety of rhythmic combinations and a more flexible flow of longer and shorter values, including syncopations. Indeed, we see French composers exploring and exploiting all of these innovations, especially in the music of the latter part of the century. They also employed other notational devices, such as dotted and "colored" notes, for more complicated effects. White notes, or open noteheads, replaced black notation about 1425; black was reserved for special usage. Renaissance composers added still shorter note values (the equivalent of our eighths and sixteenths). And with the addition of barlines in the seventeenth century, rhythmic notation had evolved from its first manifestations to its modern form in little more than four hundred years.

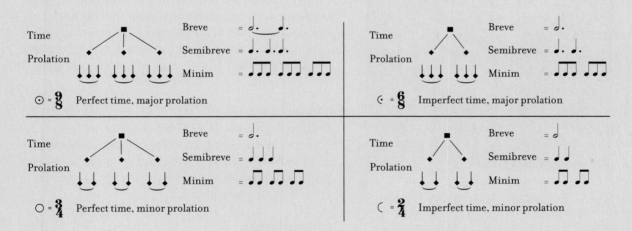

Figure 4.5   The four combinations of time and prolation with modern equivalents.

(*formes fixes*; see A Closer Look, page 75) cultivated by his predecessors, including the lai, a twelfth-century form akin to the sequence, and virelai, a type of song with refrain that had its heyday in the thirteenth and fourteenth centuries.

All of the *formes fixes* were derived from genres associated with dancing, as is evident by their use of refrains. Machaut's monophonic virelais could still be danced: Figure 4.7 shows an illumination from a manuscript of his works in which a singer (perhaps Machaut himself) performs a monophonic virelai while he and several companions dance in a circle. Machaut's monophonic virelai *Douce dame jolie* (Sweet lovely lady, NAWM 27) has a text replete with images and lists the many ways in which the poet wishes to pay homage to his beloved. Although the genre belongs to a tradition that predates the composer by a couple of centuries, he gives it a new spin by using the innovative rhythms and supple syncopations made possible by Ars Nova notation. In *Douce dame,*

Machaut's virelais

Full | Concise

Guillaume de Machaut (ca. 1300–1377)

Machaut was the most important composer and poet in fourteenth-century France. His reputation as a poet exceeded that of Chaucer, on whom Machaut exercised a profound influence, and his music has come to typify the French Ars Nova.

Much of what we know of Machaut's life and career derives from his own narrative poems. He was born in the province of Champagne in northeastern France, probably to a middle-class family, was educated as a cleric, probably in Reims, and later took Holy Orders. Around 1323, he entered the service of John of Luxembourg, king of Bohemia, eventually becoming the king's secretary. In

Figure 4.6   In this miniature from the last manuscript of Guillaume de Machaut's works prepared during his lifetime (ca. 1372), the elderly Machaut is visited in his study by Love, who introduces his three children—Sweet Thoughts, Pleasure, and Hope. (Bibliothèque Nationale, Paris.)

that role, he accompanied John on his travels and military campaigns across Europe, describing these exploits in poetry. From 1340 until his death in 1377, Machaut resided in Reims as a canon of the cathedral, an office whose liturgical duties left ample time for poetry and composition. He had close ties to royalty all his life, always moving in courtly circles, a fact which helps to account for the large amount of secular music and occasional motets he produced. His poetry and music reflect an idealized vision of his audience and their pursuits. Other patrons included John of Luxembourg's daughter Bonne, the kings of Navarre and France, and the dukes of Berry and Burgundy.

Machaut was the first composer to compile his complete works, a sign of his self-awareness as an artist. His patrons gave him the resources to supervise the preparation of several illuminated manuscripts containing his works, but the choice to do so seems to have been a conscious one, inspired by a sense of his own worth and a desire to preserve his music and poetry for future generations.

Major musical works: *Messe de Nostre Dame* (Mass of Our Lady), *Hoquetus David* (hocket), 23 motets (19 isorhythmic), 42 ballades (1 monophonic), 22 rondeaux, 33 virelais (25 monophonic), 19 lais (15 monophonic), 1 complainte, and 1 chanson royale (both monophonic)

Poetic works: *Remède de Fortune* (Remedy of Fortune), *Le livre du voir dit* (A True Story, actually a satirical autobiography), numerous other narrative poems, over 280 lyric poems.

Machaut uses the new imperfect time with minor prolation and calls attention to its novelty with a brief, syncopated melisma on the word *jolie* (lovely) and its rhymes.

That Machaut also created polyphonic chansons (French for "songs") in the standard poetic refrain forms is not surprising. His polyphonic settings reveal a new kind of lyricism, a treble-dominated style in which the upper voice (the treble or cantus) carries the text, supported by a slower-moving tenor without text. To this essential two-voice framework may be added one or two other untexted voices: a contratenor in the same range as the tenor or, less often, a fast-moving triplum in the treble range. This is the texture of his *Rose, liz, printemps, verdure* (Rose, lily, springtime, foliage, NAWM 28), composed in another of the

Treble-dominated style

Full 🔊   Concise 🔊

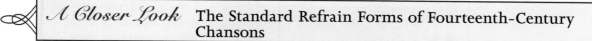

A Closer Look   **The Standard Refrain Forms of Fourteenth-Century Chansons**

Avcounting All fourteenth-century chansons have two sections of music and a refrain (a phrase or section that repeats both words and music). What differs from one form to another is the arrangement of the two musical sections and the position of the refrain. By convention, the repetition of both text and music in the refrains is shown in capital letters, and the repetition of music with new words is represented by lowercase letters. The number of lines of poetry for each section of music may vary.

Virelai   Characteristic of the virelai is the form AbbaA in which A stands for the refrain, b for a musical phrase used twice at the beginning of each stanza, and a for the last part of the stanza, which uses the music of the refrain but with new words. The typical virelai has three stanzas, with the refrain linking them together: A bba A bba A bba A. The form of the virelai is given here. (For an example, see *Douce dame jolie* in NAWM 27.)

REFRAIN	STANZA			REFRAIN
Sections of poetry: 1	2	3	4	1
Sections of music: A	b	b	a	A

Ballade   The form of Machaut's ballades, inherited in part from the trouvères, consists of three or four stanzas, each sung to the same music and each ending with the same line of poetry, which serves as a refrain. Within each stanza, the first two lines (or pairs of lines) have the same music (a a), although often with different endings (a^1 a^2); the remaining lines and the refrain have a different melody, whose close might echo that of the first section. One possible scheme for the ballade, used in Du Fay's *Resvellies vous* (NAWM 36), is represented here (where C stands for a refrain that reappears only in successive strophes):

STANZA				REFRAIN
Lines of poetry: 1 2	3 4	5 6 7		8
Sections of music: a	a	b		C

Rondeau   Like the virelai, the rondeau has a strophic structure organized around a refrain; unlike the other *formes fixes*, however, the rondeau refrain always has two sections, one of which returns halfway through the piece. The form, AB a A ab AB, shows at a glance that the refrain itself contains all the music for the entire piece. The following diagram matches Machaut's four-part rondeau, *Rose, liz* (NAWM 28):

REFRAIN			HALF REFRAIN			REFRAIN		
Lines of poetry: 1 2 3	4 5		6(1)	7(2)	8 9 10	11(1)	12(2)	13(3)
Sections of music: A	B	a	A		a	b	A	B

Rose, liz

"fixed forms," the rondeau—one that eventually surpassed the virelai in popularity and continued to be written well into the fifteenth century. (On the performance of the polyphonic chansons, see In Performance, pages 82–83.) *Rose, liz* is unusual in its four-voice texture but is typical of Machaut's lyric style, with its long melismas, occupying as many as four measures, that enhance the appeal of the melody. Although Machaut's polyphonic chansons do indulge in the rhythmic sophistication of the Ars Nova, they do not employ isorhythmic techniques; since the poetic forms determine their musical design in every case, no further structural organization was necessary.

Machaut's ballades

Judging by the number of chansons Machaut wrote in each of the *formes fixes*, his favorite was clearly the ballade, whose popularity, however, was to wane after 1400. Of the three types, the ballade was the most serious, appropriate for philosophical or historical themes or for celebrating a political event or person. It was also possibly the most challenging from a compositional point of view because it contained the least amount of musical repetition relative to the text (see diagram, page 75). Machaut wrote more than forty ballades for two, three, and four parts; his typical settings were for high tenor solo with two lower parts. Those few ballades for two upper parts (as opposed to one), each having its own text, are called double ballades.

Italian Trecento Music

The 1300s in Italy were known as the Trecento (short for *mille trecento*, or "1300"). Italy's prominent place in the Mediterranean world, with its diverse cultures and distinctive local traditions, accounts for many characteristics of its native art. The tension that existed in Mediterranean cultures between popular and learned traditions, and between oral and literate practices, helps to explain, for example, the continued preference in Italy for improvised solo singing accompanied by a bowed or plucked string instrument long after written polyphony became widespread in northern France. But while France had a monarchy with increasingly centralized power and stability, Italy was a collection of isolated city-states, each with its own political, cultural, and linguistic traditions that perpetuated long-established performance practices. Yet we learn from writings of the time that music accompanied nearly every aspect of Italian social life. In Boccaccio's *Decameron,* for example, a group of friends who have retreated to the country from plague-ridden Florence pass the time by telling stories, dancing, singing, and playing instruments (see Vignette, below). But most Italian music from this time was never written down. Even sacred music, though it used spare polyphonic textures, was still largely improvised in fourteenth-century Italian churches. At the courts, Italian *trovatori* of the thirteenth and fourteenth centuries followed in the footsteps of the troubadours, singing their solo songs from memory. The only music of the people to survive in written form are monophonic laude, or processional songs that were devotional in nature.

Composers of Italian secular music cultivated the short, lyrical, monophonic forms typical of Italy's native poets and musicians, who did not always write them down. The first impetus for secular polyphonic composition may have come from Naples, where a French king presided in the early fourteenth century over the only royal court on the Italian peninsula. From there, the cultivation of polyphonic song probably spread northward to university towns in central and northern Italy, where they were performed as refined entertainment in elite circles for wealthy patrons. Florence, the home of the literary giants Dante and Boccaccio, was a particularly important cultural center from the fourteenth through the sixteenth centuries. Francesco Landini, the most famous Italian musician of the Trecento, was also Florentine and, like many of his fellow composers, an organist who worked in ecclesiastic circles. Such musicians composed and performed polyphony for their own pleasure rather than for aristocratic patrons.

The most copious source of Italian Trecento polyphony is the magnificent Squarcialupi Codex, named for its former owner, the Florentine organist Antonio Squarcialupi (1416–1480). This is a retrospective anthology, copied about 1410–1415, which contains 354 pieces, mostly for two and three voices, by twelve composers of the Trecento and early Quattrocento (1400s). A miniature portrait of each composer appears at the beginning of the section containing his works, as shown in Figure 4.8. Three types of secular Italian composition are represented in the codex and in other manuscripts of the period: madrigal, caccia, and ballata (see Figure 4.9).

Madrigals were idyllic, pastoral, satirical, or love poems usually set for two voices. Jacopo da Bologna's *Non al suo amante* (NAWM 30), setting a poem by the great Italian lyric poet Francesco Petrarca (1304–1374), is a typical example of

Secular songs

Squarcialupi Codex

Madrigal

Full 🔊

VIGNETTE Giovanni Boccaccio, from the *Decameron*

Giovanni Boccaccio (1313–1375) was one of the great fourteenth-century writers whose use of the local dialect of Tuscany, around Florence, made that dialect into the national literary language of Italy. His masterpiece is the Decameron *(1348–1353), a collection of one hundred witty, sometimes ribald stories, told over a ten-day period by ten friends who have fled to the country to avoid the Black Death ravaging Florence. The evening before the first day of storytelling, they enjoy dinner, dancing, and music.*

The tables having been cleared away, the queen commanded that instruments be brought in,

for all the ladies knew how to do the round dance, and the young men too, and some of them could play and sing very well. Upon her request, Dioneo took a lute and Fiammetta a viol, and began sweetly to play a dance. Then the queen together with other ladies and two young men chose a carol and struck up a round dance with a slow pace—while the servants were sent out to eat. When this was finished, they began to sing charming and merry songs. They continued in this way for a long time, until the queen thought it was time to go to sleep.

Giovanni Boccaccio, *Decameron*, Day One, Introduction.

Figure 4.8   A page from the richly illustrated Squarcialupi Codex, an early fifteenth-century manuscript named for its fifteenth-century owner, Antonio Squarcialupi, showing Francesco Landini wearing a laurel crown and playing a portative organ. The portrait is set inside the initial letter M of Landini's madrigal Musica son *(I am music). The decorative border depicts (counterclockwise from the upper left) a lute, vielle, cittern or citole, harp, psaltery, three recorders, a portative organ, and three shawms.*
(Biblioteca Medicea-Laurenziana, Florence, Italy.)

this Trecento form and of the early Trecento style, characterized by rhythmic variety and fluidity. Its texture differs from a French chanson in that the two voices are relatively equal in melodic and rhythmic style and occasionally echo one another. Typical of the Italian style are the long melismas carefully placed on the last accented syllable of each line of poetry; these are more florid in the upper voice but are entirely without the syncopations so characteristic of French music at this time.

Ballata   The polyphonic ballata became popular later than the madrigal and betrays the influence of the treble-dominated French chanson. The word *ballata* (from *ballare,* "to dance") originally meant "a song to accompany dancing." Thirteenth-century ballate (of which no musical examples are known today) were monophonic dance songs with choral refrains, and in Boccaccio's *Decameron* the ballata was still associated with dancing. Although a few early fourteenth-century monophonic examples have survived, most of the ballate in the manuscripts are for two or three voices and date from after 1365. Their form, as outlined in Figure 4.9, resembles a single stanza of the French virelai.

Francesco Landini

The leading composer of the Trecento, Francesco Landini (ca. 1325–1397; see Biography, page 80; and Figure 4.8) wrote 140 ballate (and likely their texts as well), many of which are for two voices singing the same text, like the earlier

Madrigal

	Stanza		Stanza			Ritornello	
Sections of music:	a		a			b	
Lines of poetry:	1	2	3	4	5	6	7	8

Ballata

	Ripresa			Stanza (2 piedi)				Volta			Ripresa		
Sections of music:	A			b		b		a			A		
Lines of poetry:	1	2	3	4	5	6	7	8	9	10	1	2	3

Figure 4.9 Fourteenth-century Italian song forms.

madrigal. Others, evidently later works, have three parts in a treble-dominated style, featuring solo voice with two untexted accompanying parts that were most likely sung, as in Machaut's chansons. Landini's ballata *Non avrà ma' pietà* (She will never have mercy, NAWM 32) typifies this genre's form and style. Melismatic passages decorate the ends and sometimes the beginnings of lines but never interrupt the middle of a verse, showing an early concern for text declamation—a characteristic feature of Italian music. The end of every line, and often a structurally important internal point as well, is marked by a cadence, which in the later works is usually of a type now known as the under-third or Landini cadence. Here, the progression from the major sixth to the octave is ornamented by a lower neighbor leaping up a third in the top voice (see the boxed notes in Example 4.3, which shows the first line of the refrain). A great appeal of Landini's music, in addition to its graceful vocal melody, lies in the sweetness of its harmonies. Sonorities containing both the intervals of

Landini cadences

Example 4.3 Francesco Landini, beginning of Non avrà ma' pietà

She will never have mercy, this lady of mine . . . /Perhaps by her [the flames] would be extinguished . . .

Francesco Landini (ca. 1325–1397)

Landini was born in northern Italy, probably in Florence or nearby Fiesole. The son of a painter, he was blinded by smallpox during childhood and turned to music, becoming an esteemed performer, composer, and poet. A master of many instruments, he was especially known for his skill at the organetto, a small portative organ.

Landini was organist at the monastery of Santa Trinità in 1361–1365, then became a chaplain at the church of San Lorenzo, where he remained until his death. Although he may have improvised organ music in church, he apparently wrote no sacred music and is best known for his ballate. Landini is a principal character in Giovanni da Prato's *Paradiso degli Alberti*, a narrative poem from around 1425 that records scenes and conversations in Florence from the year 1389. Giovanni includes a legendary incident that testifies to Landini's skill as a performer:

Figure 4.10 The tombstone of Francesco Landini. The composer, depicted with hollowed eye sockets, plays a portative organ, accompanied by two angel-musicians above his head.
(Art Resource, NY.)

Now the sun rose higher and the heat of the day increased. The whole company remained in the pleasant shade, as a thousand birds sang among the verdant branches. Someone asked Francesco [Landini] to play the organ a little, to see whether the sound would make the birds increase or diminish their song. He did so at once, and a great wonder followed. When the sound began many of the birds fell silent and gathered around as if in amazement, listening for a long time. Then they resumed their song and redoubled it, showing inconceivable delight, and especially one nightingale, who came and perched above the organ on a branch over Francesco's head.

The Latin inscription around Landini's marble effigy (Figure 4.10), still housed in the church of San Lorenzo in Florence, reads:

Francesco, who was deprived of sight but whose mind was skillful at [composing] songs and [playing] melodies on the organ, whom alone Music brought to birth for all the world, has left his ashes here on earth, but his soul beyond the stars.

Major works: 140 ballate, 12 madrigals, 1 caccia, 1 virelai.

---

the third and fifth or of the third and sixth are plentiful, though they never begin or end a section or piece.

Caccia

Full 🔊

Another type of Italian song, the caccia, parallels the French chace, in which a strict canon is set to lively, graphically descriptive words. The song's name in each language means "hunt," referring to the pursuit of one voice by another. In some cases, it also applies to the subject matter of the text, as in Landini's caccia *Cosi pensoso* (NAWM 31), which actually evokes a fishing scene. The musical imitations of companions shouting encouragement to one another as they attempt to catch their prey are both high-spirited and comic, especially when treated in canon. Unlike its French and Spanish counterparts, the caccia usually has a free, untexted tenor in slower motion below.

At the Time

In **1397,** at the time of Francesco Landini's death in Florence, Italy,

- Two popes have been elected by rival factions; Pope Boniface IX is enthroned in Rome, backed by Germany and England, and Pope Benedict XIII is seated in Avignon, supported by the French.
- England and France are still fighting the Hundred Years' War. About 70,000 people live in the city of London. The population of Paris, having been reduced by war, plague, and famine, is about 200,000.
- Many people believe the earth is flat.
- As much as 60% of the population of Europe has been killed in the Great Plague, carried by flea-infested rats on ships returning from the ports of Asia; it spreads quickly due to poor sanitary conditions.
- The Gothic cathedral of Notre Dame in Paris has been completed (Figure 3.4).
- Giotto's fresco paintings adorn the walls of several churches in northern Italy (Figure 4.1).
- Music (what we would now call music theory), a subject in the quadrivium, is being taught as part of the Scholastic curriculum at the universities of Paris and Oxford.
- Chaucer is still writing or revising *The Canterbury Tales.*
- Most men carry knives for self-protection and use them to cut meat or spear food at dinner. Spoons made from wood or horn may be supplied by one's host; but forks are rarely used except in Italy.
- Machaut's complete works, including several hundred compositions and poems, have been collected and copied by hand into manuscripts (Figures 4.6 and 4.7). The printing press will not be invented until the next century.

Figure 4.11   Flagellants in Tournai scourge themselves in an attempt to stop the bubonic plague.
(HIP/Art Resource, NY.)

Figure 4.12 Tapestry from the Low Countries (ca. 1420) showing a man in courtly dress singing from a manuscript. He is accompanied by a woman playing a positive organ, which is portable but must be placed on a table to be played, rather than resting on a lap like the portative organ played by Landini in Figure 4.8. A boy stands behind the organ, pumping the bellows to force air through the pipes and produce the sounds. (Bridgeman-Giraudon/Art Resource, NY.)

The most common texture of a fourteenth- or fifteenth-century chanson was three parts, with only the cantus or uppermost part having the complete text for the first stanza laid out under the notes. The supporting parts typically had only the first few words written at the opening of their music. We know from pictorial and literary sources of the time that polyphonic music was usually performed by a small vocal or instrumental ensemble or a combination of the two, with only one voice or instrument to a part. But there was—and still is—no uniform way of performing any particular piece. Some modern performing groups sing the text in all parts, assuming that the scribe meant the incipit, or opening words, as an abbreviation for the entire stanza and simply spared himself the effort of writing it out fully. Others, because of the lack of words, assign instruments to the untexted lines.

Some scholarship suggests that Machaut and his contemporaries intended all the parts to be sung, with the lack of words in the supporting voices making the cantus stand out in relief. But in that case, might some or all of the parts have also been played on instruments? If the presence of a text does not mean that the part was always sung, or the absence of words that it was necessarily instrumental, we can say only that performances probably varied according to circumstances, depending on tastes and preferences and on the singers and players who happened to be on hand.

Manuscripts never specified instruments, leaving the choice of forces to the performers, guided by habit and tradition. One prevalent tradition had to do with sound quality. In the fourteenth through sixteenth centuries, instruments were grouped into two categories—haut (French for "high") and bas ("low")—based on their relative volume rather than pitch. The most common soft, or bas, instruments—bowed and plucked strings, woodwinds, portative organs—were used for indoor dancing and background music. The

French influence

Like their French counterparts, Italian composers of the Trecento wrote music in several genres, including settings of Mass Ordinary chants for two to four voices or for keyboard, along with some other liturgical settings and motets. In the late 1300s, with the increased contact between native Italian composers and northern musicians in the retinues of the several simultaneously reigning popes, the music of Italian composers began to lose its specific national characteristics and to absorb the contemporary French style. The trend was especially noticeable after the papal court moved from Avignon—where it had been for most of the century—back to Rome in 1377. Italians wrote songs to French texts in French genres, and their works recorded in late fourteenth-century manuscripts often appear in French notation. The loud, or haut, instruments—shawms (ancestor of the oboe), trumpets, trombones—were associated with outdoor and ceremonial music, and with dancing and processions (see Figure 4.1).

Recently, scholars have argued that the contratenors in some fifteenth-century chansons were written for a plucked string instrument. Three kinds of evidence support their arguments: contratenor parts are melodically angular, with more large leaps than other parts, making them harder to sing; sustained notes in these parts create dissonances and other problems in counterpoint that disappear if the part is played on a plucked instrument (whose sounds decay rapidly) rather than being sung by a voice; and some contratenors are notated with more than one note sounding at once, impossible for a voice but suitable for a harp or lute. If this is confirmed for chansons in the fifteenth century, could it also be true for fourteenth-century chansons? Stray dissonances in the contratenor of Philippus de Caserta's ballade *En remirant* (NAWM 29) suggest it might.

Just as the choice of instruments was normally left to the performers, so was the use of certain chromatic alterations known as *musica ficta* ("false music" or "feigned music"). This practice gave a special flavor to fourteenth-century French and Italian music and continued in use through much of the sixteenth century. Performers raised or lowered notes by a semitone (without benefit of written accidentals) to avoid the tritone F–B in a melody, to make a smoother melodic line, or to avoid sounding an augmented fourth or dimin-

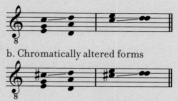

Example 4.4 Alteration at cadences

a. Strict modal forms

b. Chromatically altered forms

c. Form with double leading tones

ished fifth against the lowest note of the texture. Such alterations were also common at cadences, in order to make them sound sweeter and more emphatic (see Example 4.4). Cadences of the type shown in Example 4.4b would have both upper notes of the penultimate chord raised to avoid the tritone, resulting in a double leading-tone cadence (Example 4.4c), one of the most distinctive sonorities of the period.

Musica ficta would present no difficulty to modern performers if composers and scribes had written the sharps, flats, and naturals in the manuscript. But they often did not, or they did so inconsistently. In view of these factors, conscientious modern editors include only those accidentals found in the original sources and indicate in some way (usually above or below the staff) those that they believe should be additionally supplied by the performers.

influence was reciprocated in the fifteenth century, however, when composers from France and other northern countries took up positions in Italy and their music was unquestionably affected by what they heard and learned there.

The Ars Subtilior

French and Italian music of the late fourteenth century became ever more refined and complex, catering to the extravagant tastes of increasingly polished performers and the educated, courtly elite of society. In a paradox typical of the

Later fourteenth century

century, the papal court at Avignon was one of the main patrons of secular music. There and at other courts across southern France and northern Italy, a brilliant chivalric and ecclesiastical society allowed composers to flourish. Their music consisted chiefly of polyphonic ballades, rondeaux, and virelais, continuing the *formes fixes*. These chansons, mostly love songs, were intended for a highbrow audience—aristocrats and connoisseurs who esteemed this music because it developed every possibility of melody, rhythm, counterpoint, and notation. The composers' fascination with technical possibilities and their willingness to take a given procedure to new extremes have led music historians to term this repertory Ars Subtilior ("the subtler art"), a phrase derived from a treatise on notation attributed to Philippus de Caserta (fl. 1370s), a theorist and composer at the Avignon court. The flamboyantly elevated style of these songs is matched by their sumptuous appearance in manuscripts, including fanciful decorations, intermingled red and black notes, ingenious notation, and occasional caprices that include a love song written in the shape of a heart or a canon in the shape of a circle.

Rhythmic complexity

Some songs from this period feature remarkable rhythmic complexities, reaching a level not seen again until the twentieth century. Voices move in contrasting meters and conflicting groupings; beats are subdivided in many different ways; phrases are broken by rests or suspended through chains of syncopations; and harmonies are purposely blurred through rhythmic disjunction. Whatever the notation allowed, someone would try. Caserta's ballade *En remirant vo douce pourtraiture* (While I gazed at your sweet portrait; NAWM 29) exemplifies the virtuosity of the Ars Subtilior. The original notation, with its numerous tails, flags, dots, and red notes, appears in Figure 4.13.

Full 🔊

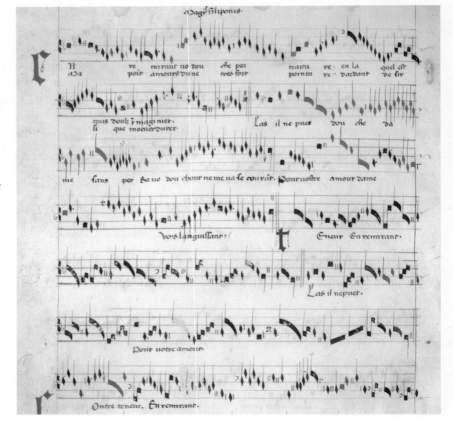

Figure 4.13 Philippus de Caserta's En remirant vo douce pourtraiture *in a manuscript from ca. 1410. The texted cantus (staves 1–4) is followed by the textless tenor (starting middle of the fourth staff) and contratenor (staves 7–9, though 8 and 9 are not visible). The red notation indicates changes from triple to duple subdivision, such as from a dotted quarter to a quarter. Changes of meter and proportion are indicated by mensuration signs—small circles or partial circles with or without dots between the staff lines.*

(Biblioteca Estense Universitaria a.M.5.24, fol. 35v.)

English Polyphony

English polyphony, sometimes called descant, was abundant in the fourteenth century, particularly in the sacred genres. It had a distinctive sound and other qualities that signaled its independence of musical trends on the Continent (not surprising considering England's cultural insularity). But its very distinctiveness was to have an enormous impact on Continental developments in the next century, as we shall discover in Chapter 5.

POSTLUDE

The musical landscape of the fourteenth century presents a variety of new forms and practices. Ars Nova musicians developed a sophisticated system for rhythmic notation that, in turn, allowed for greater freedom and flexibility of rhythmic play. At the same time, French composers created the structural device of isorhythm to control and organize their seemingly unlimited choices. Thus, the emphasis on structure and rhythmic play in fourteenth-century music was in part a response to the new freedom of Ars Nova notation and in part, perhaps, a reaction to the forces of disorder and discontent in society at large.

The principal types of polyphonic composition in France were the polyphonic Mass Ordinary movement and cycle; the isorhythmic motet, which had an elusive structure and a complicated, layered texture; and the secular love songs in the fixed poetic forms inherited from the trouvères, which had very obvious structures involving refrains and simpler, songlike textures. These chanson types—chief among them the virelai, ballade, and rondeau—made use of a more ingratiating idiom as composers aimed for a sensuously appealing sound. New genres of composition (mass, motet, and refrain song) emerged in Italy as well, some probably derived from popular musical practice. Italian smoothness of melody and clarity of declamation and the growing use in both French and Italian traditions of prominent harmonic thirds and sixths all contributed to the new style of the fifteenth century.

Two very different composers of equally great renown dominated the scene in their respective countries: Machaut in France and Landini in Italy. By the year 1400, however, the French and Italian musical styles, formerly distinct, had started to merge and move toward a more international style. As we will see in the next chapter, this new style became diversified in the fifteenth century by influences from other sources—chiefly England and the Low Countries.

 Resources for study and review available at
wwnorton.com/studyspace

PART TWO

The Age of the Renaissance

PART CONTENTS

The fifteenth and sixteenth centuries were a period of great change for European culture, literature, art, and music. To some, it seemed that the arts had been reborn after a period of stagnation. In his 1855 *Histoire de France*, Jules Michelet crystalized this notion by coining the term *Renaissance* (French for "rebirth") to designate the historical period after the Middle Ages. The idea of rebirth captures the aims of scholars and artists to restore the learning, ideals, and values of ancient Greece and Rome. But scholarship, literature, art, and music did far more than revive the old. Currents already strong in the late Middle Ages continued, and the introduction of new technologies, from oil painting to the printing press, brought radical changes. In many cases, classical antiquity provided the inspiration for something really new, including new ways to read and understand the Bible, literature in vernacular languages, and realism and perspective in painting.

Page from a manuscript of chansons and motets, copied for Duchess Marguerite of Austria between 1516 and 1523.

(Culture-images/Lebrecht.)

TIMELINE The Age of the Renaissance

Musical Events

Master of Female Half-Lengths, *The Lute Player*

ca. 1450s
Du Fay, *Missa Se la face ay pale* (NAWM 38)

1453
Dunstable dies

1474
Du Fay dies

ca. 1484–1489
Josquin employed in Italy

1497
Ockeghem dies

1501
Petrucci publishes *Odhecaton A*

1521
Josquin dies

1528
Attaingnant publishes first collection of chansons in Paris

1400

Historical Events

1415
English under Henry V defeat French at Agincourt

1417
End of Papal Schism

1431
Joan of Arc executed

ca. 1440
Donatello, *David*

1453
End of Hundred Years' War

1454
Feast of the Oath of the Pheasant in Lille

1492
First voyage of Columbus to America

Donatello, *David*

1504
Michelangelo, *David* (Figure III.3)

1517
Martin Luther, ninety-five theses

1527
Sack of Rome

1528
Castiglione, *The Book of the Courtier*

The beginning of the Renaissance has been debated ever since the term *Renaissance* was introduced. No single event or generation inaugurated the Renaissance; it continued on political and economic paths established by the late Middle Ages rather than breaking with medieval traditions. Considering the Renaissance primarily as a movement in scholarship and the arts, some aspects are apparent already in the 1300s, while others emerged only in the 1500s, and many continued into the 1600s. In letters and the visual arts, the Renaissance began in Italy and spread north; in music, as we will see, northern composers played the leading role in the fifteenth century, Italians in the sixteenth. Here, we will define the span of the Renaissance as the fifteenth and sixteenth centuries, while recognizing that its characteristics developed over time.

Europe in the Renaissance

Several important political events occurred in the fifteenth and sixteenth centuries, including the end of the Hundred Years' War between the French and English in 1453; the fall of Constantinople to the Ottoman Turks that same year, ending the Byzantine Empire; and the rise of Western Europe as a world power.

1539
Arcadelt, first
book of four-part
madrigals

1558
Zarlino, *Le istitutioni
harmoniche*

William Byrd in an engraving
by Van der Gucht

1567
Palestrina, *Pope
Marcellus Mass*
(NAWM 51)
published

1572
William Byrd
appointed to
Chapel Royal

1588
Yonge, *Musica
transalpina*

1597
Dowland, *First
Booke of Songes or
Ayres*

1605
Monteverdi
publishes *Fifth Book
of Madrigals*

1611
Thomás Luis de
Victoria dies

1600

1532
Henry VIII breaks
with pope

1535
Execution of Sir
Thomas More

1543
Copernicus, *On the
Revolutions of the
Heavenly Spheres*

1545–1563
Council of Trent

1553–1558
Mary I restores
Latin rite and link to
Rome

1558
Elizabeth becomes
queen of England
and restores
Church of England

1564
Calvin dies

1586
El Greco, *Burial of
the Count of Orgaz*
(Figure 9.7)

1594
Shakespeare,
Romeo and Juliet

ca. 1595
Caravaggio, *The
Lute Player*
(Figure 7.7)

top left: Bildarchiv
Preussischer
Kulturbesitz/Art
Resource, NY.
top right: Colouroser
AL/Lebrecht.
bottom: Museo
Nazionale del
Bargello, Florence,
Italy. Photo:
Nimatallah/Art
Resource, NY.

Larger ships, better navigational aids, and more powerful artillery helped
Europeans expand their influence beyond the Mediterranean and northern
Atlantic into the New World.

After the economic turmoil of the fourteenth century, the European economy stabilized around 1400 and began to grow. Regions specialized in different
agricultural and manufactured products, and traded with each other across
great distances. Towns and cities prospered from trade, and many city dwellers
accumulated wealth through commerce, banking, and crafts. Merchants, arti-
sans, doctors, and lawyers continued to increase in number, influence, and
economic importance, seeking prosperity for their families, property and
prestigious art for themselves, and education for their children. Rulers sought
to glorify themselves and their communities by erecting impressive palaces
and country houses decorated with new artworks, by hosting lavish entertainments, and by supporting talented musicians. These conditions, strongest in
Italy but gaining strength throughout western Europe during the fifteenth and
sixteenth centuries, laid the economic and social foundations for the
Renaissance.

Why did the Renaissance begin in Italy? One reason was geography: Italy was
close to, or even at the very source of, the learning and art that inspired the
movement. Another reason was Italy's commercial dominance: its trade with
Byzantium, its wealthy families (like the Medici, who were bankers), and its

Economy and society

Why Italy?

Figure II.1 Botticelli's Adoration of the Magi, *ca. 1475. In this treatment of the traditional religious subject, not only does the artist portray himself (standing apart on the extreme right, looking boldly out at the viewer), but he also replaces the three Magi (Wise Men) with several members of the Medici family—his patrons—dressed in elegant princely attire.* (Uffizi Gallery, Florence/ Scala/Art Resource, NY.)

profusion of secular princes all spurred the growth of a worldly culture alongside the ecclesiastical culture fostered by the great monasteries and cathedrals of northern Europe. The Italian peninsula in the fifteenth century was made up of a collection of city-states and small principalities that were often at war with each other. The rulers, many of whom had gained their positions by force, sought to glorify themselves and magnify their city's reputation by erecting palaces decorated with newly commissioned artworks and recently unearthed artifacts from ancient civilizations; by employing talented singers and gifted instrumentalists; and by entertaining neighboring potentates. Meanwhile, the citizenry—no longer in feudal service to a lord and free of military duties (wars were fought mostly by mercenaries)—accumulated wealth through commerce, banking, and crafts. Although they prayed and attended church, these people gave priority to earthly matters. Personal fulfillment through learning, public service, and accomplishment motivated their individual lives as well as their social contacts and institutions.

Rediscovery of ancient texts

Renaissance thinkers had broader access to the classics of Greek and Roman literature and philosophy than their medieval predecessors. Ottoman attacks on Constantinople beginning in 1396 led many Byzantine scholars to flee to Italy, taking with them numerous ancient Greek writings. They taught the Greek language to Italian scholars, some of whom traveled to the East. Soon the Greek classics were translated into Latin, making most of Plato and the Greek plays accessible to Western Europeans for the first time. Scholars rediscovered complete copies of works on rhetoric by Cicero and Quintilian, and, later, other texts from Roman antiquity.

Humanism

The increasing availability of ancient writings was complemented by new ways of approaching them. The strongest intellectual movement of the Renaissance was humanism, the study of the humanities and things pertaining to human knowledge. Humanists sought to revive ancient learning, emphasizing the study of grammar, rhetoric, poetry, history, and moral philosophy in classical Latin and Greek writings. They believed these subjects developed the individual's mind, spirit, and ethics and prepared students for lives of virtue

Figure II.2 Idealized View of the City, *ca. 1480, by a painter from the school of Piero della Francesca, in the Ducal Palace in Urbino, northern Italy. The scene looks realistic because of attention paid to lighting and the use of perspective. All the lines that in three-dimensional reality would be parallel to each other, like the lines in the pavement or on the sides of buildings, converge toward a single vanishing point, just under the top of the doorway of the center building. Objects farther away from the viewer look smaller in exact mathematical proportion to their distance.*

(Galleria della Marche, Urbino, Italy. Photo: Erich Lessing/Art Resource, NY.)

and service through greater reliance on independent reasoning and empirical evidence. Gradually, humanistic studies replaced medieval Scholasticism, with its emphasis on logic and authority as the center of intellectual life. At the same time, a humanist education allowed the rich to move in a world that acknowledged values other than Christian morals. The role of the Church was not diminished; rather, the Church borrowed from classical sources, sponsored classical studies, and supported thinkers, artists, and musicians.

Renaissance Art and Architecture

Renaissance art shows striking contrasts with medieval art and several parallels with new developments in scholarship and music.

The revival of classical antiquity in new guise is embodied in the bronze statue of David by Donatello (ca. 1386–1466), seen in the Timeline (page 88), the first freestanding nude since Roman times. Nakedness in the Middle Ages implied shame, as in depictions of the expulsion of Adam and Eve from the Garden of Eden. Here, nudity shows the beauty of the human figure, as in the Greek and Roman sculptures Donatello used as models. The work's naturalism—its attempt to reproduce nature realistically—is in tune with humanists' endeavors to see the world as it really is.

Donatello's statue also betrays Renaissance artists' new interest in the individual. David strikes a swaggering pose, fresh from his victory over Goliath; Botticelli (1445–1510) portrays himself and his patrons in his *Adoration of the Magi* (Figure II.1); and the unknown courtier in Figure 7.1 radiates a convincing air of self-importance.

Italian painters had been pursuing greater realism since Giotto in the early fourteenth century (see Figure 4.1), but far more naturalistic representations were made possible in the early 1400s through the use of perspective, a method for representing three-dimensional space on a flat surface, creating a sense of depth. Figure II.2, a late fifteenth-century painting of an "ideal" city, shows the

Figure II.3 Detail from The Effects of Good and Bad Government in the Town and in the Country *(1337–1391), a fresco by Ambrogio Lorenzetti painted in the Palazzo Pubblico (public palace) in Siena, a city in Tuscany. The subject of the painting illustrates the new humanist concern with government and civic virtues, yet the technique is still medieval in many respects. While objects farther away are depicted as behind others and smaller than those closer to the viewer, there is no true perspective.*

(Scala/Art Resource, NY.)

use of perspective, in which all parallel lines converge to a single vanishing point and objects of the same size appear smaller in exact proportion as they grow more distant. This reflects what we might actually see, and creates the illusion of real space, in contrast to the fourteenth-century cityscape in Figure II.3, where the buildings seem heaped on top of one another, their distance from the viewer unclear.

The later picture is also more orderly, with clean lines, symmetry, and little clutter. This preference for clarity, typical of Renaissance architecture, contrasts markedly with Gothic decoration, such as the ornate carving on the façade of Reims cathedral in Figure 4.3. The use of columns with capitals on the center and leftmost buildings in the ideal city shows the Renaissance interest in imitating ancient architecture.

Musical parallels

Like the ideals of beauty and naturalism discussed above, clarity, depth, and interest in the individual also have parallels in music. Renaissance composers expanded the range of their pieces to include lower and higher pitches than before, and they coordinated the separate lines of their polyphonic textures through points of imitation. In this way, their musical structures, especially in the sixteenth century, took on the clarity of line and function characteristic of Renaissance architecture and perspective in painting. Some composers set tunes that pay tribute to individuals, but even more important is the rising significance of composers as individual artists, as celebrated in their sphere as Donatello was in his.

Figure II.4 Music portrayed as a liberal art, probably from the 1470s by Justus of Ghent, a Netherlandish painter who was also active in Italy. The unidentified kneeling gentleman illustrates the new respect accorded the science of music in the Renaissance.
(National Gallery, London/Bridgeman Art Library.)

The Musical Culture of the Renaissance

In addition to providing a new intellectual climate to the Renaissance, humanism had a very practical outcome in music: a rebirth of interest in music theory's Greek past. As early as 1424 at the court of Mantua, students were reading the musical treatise of Boethius (see Chapter 1) as a classical text rather than as a basis for professional training (see Figure II.4). Over the next half century, Greeks emigrating from Byzantium as well as Italian manuscript hunters brought the principal Greek treatises on music to the West. Among these were the theoretical works of Aristides Quintilianus, Claudius Ptolemy, Cleonides, and Euclid. Also newly available were passages by Plato and Aristotle on music (see Chapter 1). By the end of the fifteenth century, all of these treatises were translated into Latin.

The rediscovery of the ancient Greek philosophers and their theory of musical modes—especially their belief that the choice of mode could affect the listener's emotions—led to renewed interest in the Greek modal system (see Vignette, page 93). Both Plato and Aristotle had insisted that various modes had different ethical effects (see Vignette, page 19). Like their medieval predecessors, however, Renaissance theorists and composers mistakenly assumed that the old Greek modes

VIGNETTE Bernardino Cirillo on Reviving Ancient Music

Bernardino Cirillo (1500–1575), rector of the famous shrine and pilgrimage destination the Santa Casa of Loreto, was a prominent churchman in mid-sixteenth-century Rome. Here, in a letter published during his lifetime (1549), he allies himself with the humanists by finding modern polyphony wanting in expression and urges a revival of the Greek doctrine of ethos and a restoration of the ancient modes.

Music among the ancients was the most splendid of all the fine arts. With it they created powerful effects that we nowadays cannot produce either with rhetoric or with oratory in moving the passions and affections of the soul. . . . By means of the power of song [using the correct modes], a slow and lazy man becomes lively and active; an angry man is calmed; . . . a miserable man becomes happy; and thus music governs human affections and has the power to alter them as need be. Now, where has this led?

I should like, in short, when a mass is to be sung in church, the music to be framed to the fundamental meaning of the words, in certain intervals and numbers apt to move our affections to religion and piety. . . . Each mode should be adapted to its subject, and when one has a lullaby to sing, or a plaintive song, one should do likewise. Thus the musicians of today should endeavor in their profession to do what the sculptors, painters, and architects of our time have done, who have recovered the art of the ancients; and the writers, who have reclaimed literature from the hell to which it was banished by corrupt ages; and as the sciences have been explained and given in their purity to our times. Thus the musicians should seek to recover the styles and modes, and the power of the Phrygian, Lydian, Dorian, and Mixolydian compositions, with which they would be able to do what they wish.

Bernardino Cirillo, letter to Ugolino Gualteruzzi, trans. Lewis Lockwood; in Oliver Strunk. ed., *Source Readings in Music History*, rev. ed. by Leo Treitler (New York, Norton, 1998), vol. 3, pp. 91–93.

were identical to the similarly named church modes and that the legendary powers of the former could be attributed to the latter although they disagreed about which affects were associated with each mode. The Swiss theorist Heinrich Glarean (1488–1563), in his book *Dodekachordon* (The Twelve-String Lyre, 1547), added four new modes to the traditional eight: the Aeolian and Hypoaeolian with the final on A, and the Ionian and Hypoionian with the final on C. With these additions, he tried to reconcile the theory of the modes with the practice of composers, who frequently employed tonal centers on A and C. In using something borrowed from ancient culture to modify medieval theory, Glarean was typical of his age.

In keeping with the ancient Greek view of music and poetry as virtually inseparable, humanists believed that music and words could strengthen each other. The image of the ancient poet, singer, and accompanist united in a single person inspired both poets and composers of the Renaissance to seek a common expressive goal. Authors became more concerned with the sound of their verses, and composers with matching and projecting that sound. The

Figure II.5 Miniature by Jean Le Tavernier, ca. 1457–1467. Philip the Good, duke of Burgundy, at Mass. Philip is in the center, his chapel singers at the lower right. (Royal Library of Belgium.)

Called "the Maid of Orleans," Joan of Arc (ca. 1412–1431) was a French national heroine who raised an army to drive the English from French soil during the Hundred Years' War. More a spiritual than a military leader, she interpreted the "voices" she heard as direct inspiration from God. She was captured by the English, tried by French clerics for heresy and witchcraft, and burned at the stake in Rouen. She was elevated to sainthood only in 1920.

Sandro Botticelli (1445–1510), Florentine painter in the Medici orbit (see Figure II.1), combined sharp contours and sinuous line with a lyrical intensity that make his works seem like visual poetry (*La Primavera, Birth of Venus*).

The most wide-ranging genius of the age, Leonardo da Vinci (1452–1519) practiced all the arts of the Renaissance, including music, painting, sculpture, architecture, astronomy, optics, mechanical engineering, and natural science. A native of Florence, he left to work for the Sforza dynasty in Milan and the French king Francis I. Best known for his painting called the *Mona Lisa,* he ushered in the modern age of the individual, socially mobile artist and epitomized the artist's new role in society as not merely a craftsman but also a thinker and theorist.

The Polish astronomer Nicolaus Copernicus (1473–1543) articulated the first modern European theory of planetary motion around the sun, contradicting the ancient Ptolemaic system, which had placed the Earth at the center of the universe. His treatise *On the Revolutions of the Heavenly Spheres* was completed by 1530 but not published until he was on his deathbed.

Isabella d'Este (1474–1539), intellectually gifted and supremely well educated, was one of the most celebrated women of the Italian Renaissance. A daughter of the duke of Ferrara, she married into the Gonzaga family of Mantua and became a major cultural and political figure. Admired for her knowledge of history and languages, she was also a talented singer and lutenist as well as a leader in fashion and an important patron of the arts (see Figure II.7).

In service to the Este family of his native Ferrara, Ludovico Ariosto (1474–1533) wrote the classic romantic epic *Orlando furioso* (1516), a fusion of French and English romance traditions centering on Charlemagne and King Arthur, with humanist echoes of the Latin and Italian poets Virgil and Petrarch. He was also a pioneer in Renaissance drama.

Michelangelo Buonarroti (1475–1564), Florentine sculptor and protégé of the Medici, was also a painter (Sistine chapel ceiling in Rome), architect (Medici tombs and the Laurentian Library), and poet (sonnets). More than any other Renaissance artist, his works illustrate the tension between classical and Christian subject matter, and reveal an awesome power that led him to be called "divine." Perhaps his most famous work is the huge figure

Music and words   grammatical structure of a text guided the composer in shaping its musical setting and in placing cadences (of greater or less finality) according to the text's punctuation. Inspired by the poet's message and images, composers tried new ways to express the content of the text. They were increasingly careful to follow the rhythm of speech and the natural accentuation of syllables, whether in Latin or the vernacular. Where singers had previously been responsible for matching syllables with the notated pitches and rhythms, composers now took greater care in aligning words with music, although they had no control over copyists and rarely had the opportunity to correct proofs of their printed works.

Music printing   In fact, the development of the printing press in the mid-fifteenth century had a huge impact on the musical culture of the Renaissance—first, by producing books and treatises that helped spread the ideas of antiquity, and, in the next century, by putting music in the hands of far more people than the few who could afford to own even the simplest hand-copied *chansonnier* earlier (see Innovations, pages 118–119). It is no exaggeration to say that the invention of music printing caused changes that were as revolutionary for musical culture in the Renaissance as the development of notation and music literacy had been for the Middle Ages or as the advent of sound recording was to be for music in the nineteenth and twentieth centuries.

of David (1504; see page 173), the virtuous fighter for freedom against superior odds and a favorite hero of the Florentines.

An English statesman and author, Sir (Saint) Thomas More (1478–1535) described in his *Utopia* (1516) an ideal state founded entirely on reason. He opposed Henry VIII's divorce from Catherine of Aragon and refused to subscribe to the Act of Supremacy, which made the king head of the English church. Imprisoned in the Tower of London in 1534, he was tried and beheaded for treason, and is celebrated as a martyr by the Roman Catholic Church.

Baldassare Castiglione (1478–1529) was a diplomat and author of *The Book of the Courtier* (see Vignette, page 126), both an idealized portrait of the court at Urbino and a skillful popularization of the ideas of humanist philosophers. His ruling precept, that all of the courtier's accomplishments in arms, letters, art, sport, music, or conversation should be marked by *sprezzatura* — an unforced quality of effortless superiority — became the trademark of the perfect gentleman in European society and remained so for centuries.

Martin Luther (1483–1546), the German leader of the Protestant Reformation, was ordained a priest in 1507, then became a professor at the University of Wittenberg. Shocked by the spiritual laxity in ecclesiastical Rome, he

began his protest in 1517 by posting his historic ninety-five theses on the door of the castle church in Wittenberg.

Titian (ca. 1488–1576) is considered by many the greatest painter of the Venetian school in the sixteenth century. He forged a new style, evident in *Venus and Adonis* (Figure 7.2), characterized by his use of broader brush strokes, more layered colors, and less defined outlines than earlier Renaissance artists, thereby influencing some painters of the next century.

John Calvin (1509–1564), the French Protestant theologian of the Reformation, preached the virtues of thrift, hard work, sobriety, and responsibility. Opposed to elaborate sacred polyphony, he condoned as service music only the congregational singing of the psalms. His influence spread throughout western Europe and, via his English followers, the Puritans, to North America.

Although originally from Greece, the painter El Greco (Domenicus Theotokopoulos; ca. 1541–1614) was active in Spain and Italy during the time of Victoria and Palestrina. Except for some portraits, two views of Toledo, and a mythological painting, his work — like theirs — deals almost exclusively with religious subjects. His highly subjective and dynamic style, exemplified by his *Burial of the Count of Orgaz* (Figure 9.7), is suggestive of the religious fervor of the Counter-Reformation.

The careers of musicians—their training, employment, and mobility—changed radically during this period. New musical institutions and support for musicians led to an unprecedented flowering of professional music-making. Rulers all over Europe established their own court chapels and hired musicians and clerics to staff them. Members of the chapel served as performers, composers, and scribes, furnishing music for church services as well as for secular entertainments (see Figure II.5). Most fifteenth- and sixteenth-century composers were trained as choirboys and hired as singers, even though their reputations rested primarily on their compositions. In some cathedrals and chapels, choir schools taught not only singing, but also music theory, grammar, mathematics, and other subjects. Cities such as Cambrai, Bruges, Antwerp, Paris, Dijon, and Lyon, shown in Figure II.6, most renowned for their musical training in the fifteenth century, were later joined by Rome, Venice, and other Italian cities. This helps to explain why the most prominent composers of the fifteenth and early sixteenth centuries came from Flanders, the Netherlands, and northern France, while Italians became more prominent from the mid-sixteenth century on. Because only male children were admitted into choirs, women did not have this educational opportunity or the chance to make careers in public churches and princely courts, although nuns and novices in convents did receive musical instruction, and a few

Increased support for music

Training of musicians

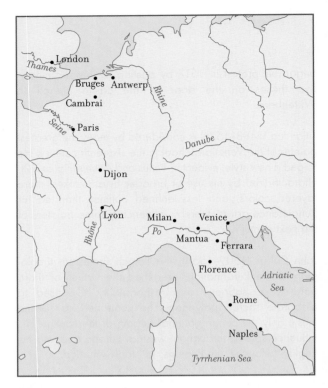

Figure II.6 Major centers for training musicians in the Renaissance.

distinguished themselves as composers. Courts also employed instrumentalists, who typically were trained in the apprentice system and often were less musically literate than singers. Guilds protected the rights of instrumentalists; because their music was regarded as a "trade secret," it was closely guarded and scarcely notated. Consequently, we know much less about the training of instrumentalists than we do about the education of singers.

Many rulers avidly supported music and competed with each other for the best composers and singers who had been trained in the magnificent northern cathedrals and chapels. Like fine clothes and impressive pageantry, excellent music was both enjoyable in itself and valuable as a way of displaying wealth and power. The Medici, the leading family in Florence during most of this period, sponsored Franco-Flemish musicians such as Henricus (or Heinrich) Isaac (ca. 1450–1517) and Jacques Arcadelt (ca. 1507–1568) as well as native Italian painters and sculptors like Donatello, Botticelli (see Figure II.1), and Michelangelo (1475–1564). The Sforza, who ruled Milan from the 1450s, employed for a time Josquin des Prez (ca. 1450–1521), the leading composer of his generation, and Leonardo da Vinci, the leading artist. The court of Ferrara under the Este family hosted Josquin and his colleague Jacob Obrecht (1457/8–1505). Isabella d'Este (see Figure II.7), who presided at her husband's court in Mantua, attracted many artists, poets, and musicians. Popes and cardinals from the Medici, Este, Sforza, and other families were as committed as secular princes to supporting cultural activity.

In the early fifteenth century many northern musicians had come to Italy with leading figures of the Church who attended the several Councils in northern Italy in an effort to resolve the Papal Schism. The presence at courts of musicians from different lands allowed composers and performers to learn styles and genres current in other regions. Many composers changed their place of service, exposing themselves to various types of music. The exchange of national traditions, genres, and ideas fostered the development of an international style in the fifteenth century, synthesizing elements from English, French, Burgundian, and Italian traditions. As new national styles of vernacular song emerged in the sixteenth century (see Chapter 7), the cosmopolitan careers of some composers prepared them to write songs in Italian, French, German, and Spanish with equal flair.

The Renaissance had a profound and enduring effect on music in subsequent centuries. The growing European economy, patronage for musicians, and the advent of music printing laid the economic foundation for an increase in musical activity that continued into later centuries. Humanism and the rediscovery of ancient texts fostered a reexamination of what music is and what it should do. Forged in this period were new musical styles that focused on consonance, clarity, direct appeal to the listener, natural declamation of words, and emotional expressivity. The musical language of the Renaissance lasted for generations and undergirds the treatment of dissonance, consonance, voice-leading, and text setting in most later styles.

Figure II.7 Titian's portrait of Isabella d'Este, noblewoman of Mantua, whose virtues were lauded by poets, scholars, popes, and statesmen.
(Kunsthistorisches Museum/Wikimedia commons.)

5

England, France, and Burgundy in the Fifteenth Century

PRELUDE

nglish victories during the Hundred Years' War, such as the Battle of Agincourt in 1415, left a strong English presence in France. The conquerors brought with them not only governmental and military personnel, but also composers and musicians to sing the Mass and provide secular entertainment. English music and its influence spread throughout the Continent, and many British works were copied into Continental manuscripts during the first half of the fifteenth century. The music made quite an impression on the French, particularly the distinctive sound of its "lively consonances." A French poem of the early 1440s enthusiastically describes this new *contenance angloise* ("English quality"), citing especially the "marvelous pleasingness" that made English music so "joyous and remarkable" (see Vignette, page 100).

Toward the middle of the century, music in the Burgundian lands—the parts of France and the Low Countries (Belgium and the Netherlands), ruled by the dukes of Burgundy—became the chief conduit for a new style that assimilated Italian, French, and English elements. Although the Burgundian dukes were nominally vassals of the kings of France, they virtually equaled them in power and influence. During the second half of the 1300s and the early 1400s, the ruling dukes acquired vast territories—adding to their original area of Burgundy, in east central France, most of the present-day Netherlands, Belgium, northeastern France, Luxembourg, and Lorraine—and presided over the whole until 1477 as though it were an independent kingdom (see Figure 5.1). Nearly all the leading composers active during the late fifteenth century came from these regions, and a number of them had some connection with the Burgundian court and chapel.

Chapels were musical establishments with salaried composers, singers, and sometimes instrumentalists who furnished music for church services and court entertainment. These ensembles might include as many as thirty professionals and members of the court. The court and chapel of Philip the Good, duke of Burgundy (r. 1419–1467), and his successor, Charles the Bold (r. 1467–1477), were the most resplendent in fifteenth-century Europe (see Figure 5.2 and In Context, page 107). Most of their musicians came from northern France, Flanders, and the Low Countries. In addition to his chapel, Philip the Good

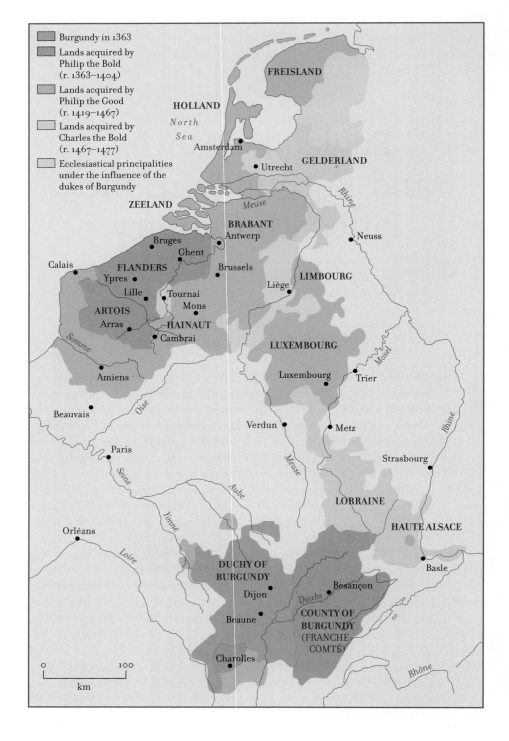

Figure 5.1 The growth of Burgundian possessions, 1363–1477.

maintained a band of minstrels—trumpeters, drummers, viellists, lutenists, harpists, organists, and players of bagpipes and shawms—that included musicians from France, Italy, Germany, and Portugal.

Cosmopolitan musicians

The presence of many foreign musicians contributed to the cosmopolitan atmosphere of the Burgundian court. Also, members of the chapel themselves were continually moving from one court to another as better job opportunities arose. Inevitably, these circumstances fostered a cosmopolitan musical style. At the same time, the Burgundian court enjoyed such great prestige that its music influenced other European musical centers. A Flemish theorist writing about 1475 tells how the honor and riches offered to prominent musicians stimulated the growth of talent so much that music in his day seemed like "a new art, the source of which was among the English, with Dunstable at their head, and, contemporary with him in France, Du Fay and Binchois." These are the very composers who will be introduced in this chapter.

English Music and Its Influence

From earliest times, England's sacred and secular art music, like northern Europe's generally, kept close connections with folk styles, with their penchant for imperfect consonances, often in parallel motion. This may be seen in the most famous medieval canon or round, *Sumer is icumen in* (NAWM 24), from about 1250, also called a rota (from the Latin for "wheel"), presumably because of the way the voices rotate through the texture. Then, too, English carols (songs in strophic forms with refrains) reveal a new stylistic feature: successions of simultaneous thirds and sixths in parallel motion (see NAWM 33). Such writing, which reflected the English taste for bright, harmonious sounds, appeared as early as the thirteenth century and played an important role on the Continent, two hundred years later.

Figure 5.2 *An outdoor entertainment at the court of Philip the Good (1396–1467), duke of Burgundy. In the gardens of the Château de Hesdin, musicians play for the duke (center) and his company. In the foreground couples dance, while in the background hunters are chasing game. Detail from a sixteenth-century copy of an anonymous fifteenth-century painting,* The Garden of Love at the Court of Philippe le Bon. *(Réunion des Musées Nationaux/Art Resource.)*

John Dunstable (also known as Dunstaple, ca. 1390–1453), named in Martin Le Franc's poem (see Vignette, page 100), was the leading English composer of his time. He may have spent part of his career in France with the English duke of Bedford, who was regent of France from 1422 to 1435 and commander of the English armies that Joan of Arc tried to drive off French land. Among Dunstable's sixty or so known compositions, we find examples of all the principal types and styles of polyphony that existed in his lifetime: isorhythmic motets, Mass Ordinary settings, secular songs, and three-part settings of miscellaneous liturgical texts. His twelve isorhythmic motets show that this old form was still in fashion. Some of the mass sections, which make up about one-third of Dunstable's surviving works, also use isorhythm. We know of only a few secular songs attributed to Dunstable; several of these illustrate the expressive lyrical melodies and clear harmonic profile common to the English music of his time.

Dunstable

Historically, Dunstable's three-voice sacred pieces—settings of antiphons, hymns, Mass movements, and other liturgical or biblical texts—remain his most important works. Some use a cantus firmus in the tenor or an ornamented chant melody in the treble. Others have florid treble lines and borrowed melodies in the middle voice, with the tenor moving mostly in thirds and sixths below. Still others, like the antiphon *Quam pulchra es* (How beautiful you are, NAWM 34), are not based on an existing melody.

Dunstable's motets

Full 🔊   Concise 🔊

Some features of *Quam pulchra es* are exceptional even in Dunstable's output. Its three voices are similar in character and nearly equal in importance. They move mostly in the same rhythm and usually pronounce the same syllables together in syllabic fashion. The brief melisma at the end of the word "Alleluia" animates the conclusion. The vertical sonorities are consonant, except for the brief suspensions at cadences, yet show considerable variety. Dunstable chose not to restrict himself to a cantus firmus or an isorhythmic scheme; instead, he molded the phrases to the rhythm of the words. Compared to the French-style motets of the time, this composition, with its parallel thirds, sixths, and tenths, sounds astonishingly fresh, revealing even greater melodic and harmonic suavity than some of the secular songs of the day, and its attention to text declamation allies it to the musical Renaissance. Only the double-leading-tone cadences recall the medieval style.

Types of motet   *Quam pulchra es* is usually classified as a motet, even though it has no borrowed tenor. The term *motet*, coined in the thirteenth century for pieces that added text to the upper part of a discant clausula, gradually broadened its meaning to include any work with texted upper voices above a cantus firmus, regardless of whether the text was sacred or secular. By the early fifteenth century, the isorhythmic motet, which had been an Ars Nova invention, was considered old-fashioned, and

---

VIGNETTE "The Contenance Angloise" (The English Quality)

Martin Le Franc (ca. 1410–1461) was a poet, cleric, and secretary at the court of Savoy, where Guillaume Du Fay periodically worked as chapelmaster. At the wedding of the duke's son in 1434, both had occasion to meet Binchois, who was in the retinue of the visiting duke of Burgundy. In his poem Le Champion des dames *(1440–1442; The Champion of Women), dedicated to Philip the Good, Le Franc praised the music of Du Fay and Binchois (soon to be discussed) in terms that have shaped our view of fifteenth-century music history.*

Tapissier, Carmen, Cesaris	Tapissier, Carmen, Cesaris
Na pas longtemps si bien chanterrent	not long ago sang so well
Quilz esbahirent tout paris	that they astonished all Paris
Et tous ceulx qui les frequenterrent;	and all who came to hear them.
Mais oncques jour ne deschanterrent	But the day came when they did not discant
En melodie de tels chois	such finely wrought melody—
Ce mont dit qui les hanterrent	so those who heard them told me—
Que G. Du Fay et Binchois.	as G. Du Fay and Binchois.
Car ilz ont nouvelle pratique	For they have a new practice
De faire frisque concordance	of making lively consonance
En haulte et en basse musique	both in loud and soft music,[1]
En fainte, en pause, et en muance	in feigning,[2] in rests, and in mutations.[3]
Et ont prins de la contenance	They took on the guise
Angloise et ensuy Dunstable	of the English and follow Dunstable
Pour quoy merveilleuse plaisance	and thereby a marvelous pleasingness
Rend leur chant joyeux et notable.	makes their music joyous and remarkable.

French text in Charles van den Borren, *Guillaume Dufay: Son importance dans l'évolution de la musique au XVe siècle* (Brussels, 1926), pp. 53–54.

1. This distinction was explored in Chapter 4, pp. 82–83.
2. The word refers to the application of musica ficta; see Chapter 4, p. 83.
3. A reference to shifting from one set of six scale steps (hexachord) to another in the solmization system devised by Guido; see Chapter 2, p. 43.

Motet	
1. early 1200s	Polyphonic piece derived from discant clausula, with words added to the upper voice
2. 1200s–1300s	Polyphonic piece with one or more upper voices, each with sacred or secular text in Latin or French, above a borrowed chant or other tenor
3. ca. 1310–1450	Isorhythmic motet: distinguished by a borrowed tenor structured by isorhythm
4. 1400s on	Polyphonic setting of a Latin, especially sacred, text other than the Mass Ordinary

Figure 5.3 The changing meanings of motet.

by 1450 it disappeared. Meanwhile, the term was applied to settings of sacred texts in the newer musical styles of the time, whether or not the settings were based on a chant melody. The term *motet* came to designate almost any polyphonic composition on a Latin text, including settings of texts from the Mass Proper and the Office. The erotic poetry of Dunstable's *Quam pulchra es* was nevertheless sacred, having been adapted by the Church from the Old Testament Song of Songs as an allegory of Christ's love for the individual soul. For a summary of the changing meanings of *motet,* see Figure 5.3.

Renaissance Music Theory

Consonance

The new emphasis on thirds and sixths, evident in Dunstable's music, posed a challenge to music theorists, who had defined only the octave, fifth, and fourth as consonant in the Middle Ages because these were generated by the simple ratios that Pythagoras had discovered. Moreover, although the imperfect consonances sounded rough to the ear and out of tune, fourths and fifths were perfectly consonant in the tuning system of the Middle Ages and were, therefore, along with the octave, the only permissible cadential sonorities until the sixteenth century.

Tinctoris

The most up-to-date instruction book on counterpoint in the late fifteenth century was the *Liber de arte contrapuncti* (A Book on the Art of Counterpoint, 1477) by Johannes Tinctoris (ca. 1435–1511), a Flemish composer who settled at the court in Naples in the early 1470s. He deplored the works of the "older composers in which there were more dissonances than consonances" and proclaimed that nothing written before the 1430s was worth hearing. Tinctoris shows his humanism by referencing numerous Greek and Roman writers; but lacking examples of ancient music, he claims only the composers of the last two generations, starting with Dunstable, as models worth imitating. Drawing on the practices of the composers he names, he relied on empirical evidence based on sensory perception, a methodology deeply mistrusted by Scholastics but embraced by humanists. In his counterpoint treatise, Tinctoris defined consonances based on their degree of sweetness and devised strict rules for introducing dissonances, limiting them to passing and neighbor tones on unstressed beats and to syncopated passages (or what we call suspensions) at cadences. These rules were further refined in later treatises by Italian authors and finally synthesized in Gioseffo Zarlino's massive treatise *Le istitutioni harmoniche* (Harmonic Foundations) of 1558.

Music in Burgundian Lands

Figure 5.4 Guillaume Du Fay next to a portative organ and Binchois holding a harp, in a miniature from Martin Le Franc's poem Le Champion des dames *(1440–1442). Du Fay, Binchois, and Le Franc were together at Savoy in 1434 when Du Fay was in the service of the duke of Savoy, and the two composers may have met on other occasions as well.*
(Bibliothèque Nationale, Paris, MS Fr. 12476, f.98r.)

The foremost composers of music in the dominant, so-called Burgundian style of the fifteenth century were Guillaume Du Fay (ca. 1397–1474) and Gilles de Bins (more often called Binchois, ca. 1400–1460). The two are shown conversing in the miniature illuminating Martin le Franc's poem (see Figure 5.4). It may be significant that the painter depicted Du Fay standing next to an organ and Binchois holding a harp because, although both composers wrote in all the main genres of the day, Du Fay was particularly esteemed for his contributions to sacred music and Binchois for his secular songs or chansons.

Most of the polyphonic compositions of the early to mid-fifteenth century were of four basic types: secular chansons with French texts, motets, Magnificats and hymn settings for the daily Offices, and settings of the Mass Ordinary. Most pieces were for three voices, in a texture resembling the fourteenth-century French chanson or Italian ballata, with the cantus spanning up to a tenth and the tenor and contratenor sharing a narrower range about a sixth below. As in some fourteenth-century secular songs, each line has a distinct role, with the main melody in the cantus, contrapuntal support in the tenor, and harmonic filler in the contratenor.

Binchois

Binchois flourished at the center of musical life in the Burgundian court, serving in the chapel of Duke Philip the Good from the 1420s until 1453. He did not travel widely and remained in his post for three decades, which may help to explain the consistent quality of his style. But prior experience in the service of the earl of Suffolk, who was with the English forces occupying France, gave him direct knowledge of English musicians and made him a central figure in the creation of a Burgundian style that embraced the *contenance angloise.*

Binchois's chansons

Binchois composed more than fifty chansons, among them some of the greatest hits of the fifteenth century, when the term *chanson* denoted any polyphonic setting of a French secular poem. Chansons most often set stylized love poems in the courtly tradition of *fine amour* (see Chapter 2), and most followed the form of the rondeau (AB aA ab AB). Binchois's well-known rondeau *De plus en plus* (NAWM 35), from around 1425, illustrates his style and provides an example of a typical Burgundian chanson. One measure of its popularity is that a later composer, Jean de Ockeghem, used it as the basis for a setting of the Mass Ordinary.

 Full 🔊   Concise 🔊

De plus en plus (More and more [renews again . . . my wish to see you]) reflects English influence in its upbeat opening; its relatively full, consonant harmonies; and its basically triadic melody (Example 5.1). Binchois

Example 5.1 Binchois. De plus en plus, *opening phrase*

More and more renews again, . . .

continued the treble-dominated style of the fourteenth century, but his gracefully arched melodic contours and fluid,
lilting rhythms enlivened by dotted figures and subtle syncopations are much less intricate than in chansons by Machaut or
Ars Subtilior composers. The end of the first phrase (boxed in
Example 5.1) illustrates a newer version of the cadence formula
used in the fourteenth century (compare Example 4.4). The
major sixth between cantus and tenor still expands to an
octave, often with the so-called "Landini" embellishment in
the cantus, but the contratenor leaps up an octave to sound the
fifth above the tenor's final note; the result sounds like a V–I
cadence.

Guillaume Du Fay was the most famous composer of his time.
His many travels (see Biography, page 105) exposed him to a wide
variety of music, from his French and Italian predecessors to his
English and Burgundian contemporaries, and he absorbed many
of their musical traits into his own works, sometimes combining
contrasting styles in a single piece. His music represents well the
cosmopolitan style of the mid-fifteenth century.

Du Fay's assimilation of national traits can be traced in his
chansons. While serving at the Malatesta court in Italy, he wrote
Resvellies vous (Awake and be merry, NAWM 36) in 1423 to celebrate his patron's wedding. French characteristics are suggested
by the ballade form itself (aabC), some rhythmic complications
including persistent syncopation, and some dissonant ornamental notes. Italian elements are evident in the relatively smooth
vocal melodies and virtuosic vocal melismas on the last accented
syllable of each line of text. *Se la face ay pale* (If my face is pale,
NAWM 38a), a chanson that Du Fay wrote about ten years later
while at the court of Savoy, shows the strong influence of English
music, with its short, tuneful, clearly marked phrases and its
consonant harmonies.

Du Fay wrote sacred music in a variety of styles. Many of his
motets and Office pieces were in three voices with a texture
resembling the chanson: the main melody in the cantus supported by tenor and contratenor. The cantus might be newly
composed, but often it was an embellished version of a chant. Du
Fay's setting of the hymn *Christe, redemptor omnium* (Christ,
Redeemer of the world, NAWM 37) paraphrases the chant in the
treble part and uses a technique called fauxbourdon, which was
inspired by the bright consonances of music imported from England. Under the melody, the tenor moves mostly in parallel sixths
while the middle voice, unwritten, parallels the melody a fourth
below. The effect is a stream of $\frac{6}{3}$ sonorities between cadences,
which always arrive on an open fifth and octave.

In addition to motets in the modern chanson style, Du Fay and his contemporaries still wrote "occasional" isorhythmic motets for solemn public
events, following the convention that a conservative musical style was
more fitting for ceremonial and state occasions. Du Fay's monumental
Nuper rosarum flores (Roses recently [bloomed]) was such a work; it was
performed at the dedication of Filippo Brunelleschi's magnificent dome
for the church of Santa Maria del Fiore (the "Duomo") in Florence in 1436
(see Figure 5.8).

*Figure 5.5 Among the painters who enjoyed
the patronage of the dukes of Burgundy was
Jan van Eyck (1390–1441), whose depiction of
the angels' instruments in his Ghent
Altarpiece is so vivid that modern instrument
makers have used them as models for recon-
struction. Shown here are a positive (or
chamber) organ, a harp, and a vielle (or tenor
fiddle), all belonging to the category of soft
(bas) instruments, discussed on pages 82–83.*
(Altarpiece: Church of Saint Bavon, Ghent. Photo:
Scala/Art Resource, NY.)

Figure 5.6 *Chansonnier of Tournai. Pages illustrated with miniatures. Note the eyes weeping tears into a bucket in the lower right-hand corner.*

(Royal Library of Belgium, Robert Wangermee, *Flemish Music and Society in the Fifteenth and Sixteenth Centuries* © 1968 Frederick A. Praeger, Publishers.)

Masses

Masses eventually replaced the "occasional" motet to commemorate important events. Like their English colleagues, composers on the Continent wrote polyphonic settings of Mass Ordinary texts in increasing numbers during the late fourteenth and early fifteenth centuries. Until about 1420, the various sections of the Ordinary were nearly always composed as separate pieces (Machaut's mass and a few others excepted), although occasionally the compiler of a manuscript would group separate items together. In the course of the fifteenth century, it became standard practice for composers to set the Ordinary as a musically unified whole, or a polyphonic mass cycle. Writing a mass became the best way for a composer to showcase his creative ingenuity, much as designing a chapel or painting an altarpiece was for an artist of the time. Just as those works were usually ordered and paid for by a particular institution or private patron, settings of the Mass Ordinary were sometimes commissioned for specific occasions or devotional services by individuals or families for whose benefit the mass was then performed, as in Du Fay's *Missa Se la face ay pale* (see below), linked to his Savoy patrons. Similarly, the long tradition of composing masses on the *L'Homme armé* tune (The Armed Man—a title with obvious military connotations) may be connected to the Order of the Golden Fleece, an association of noblemen from all over Europe instituted by Charles the Good of Burgundy, and linked to calls for a new Crusade (see In Context, page 107).

Cyclic masses   Composers in the fifteenth century devised a variety of means to link the separate sections of a mass to each other. Some musical unity resulted simply from composing all five parts of the Ordinary in the same general style, whether freely composed or based on paraphrased chants in the upper voice or on a cantus firmus in the tenor. Unity, then, initially derived from two factors: liturgical association (all movements were part of the cycle of prayers constituting the Mass Ordinary) and compositional procedure. Composers soon achieved a more perceptible and effective musical interconnection by using the same thematic material in all sections of the mass. At first, this connection

Guillaume Du Fay (Dufay) (ca. 1397–1474)

Du Fay was addressed in a letter from the Florentine organist Antonio Squarcialupi as "the greatest ornament of our age." Surely the most cosmopolitan composer of his time, he excelled in every genre, and his music was known and sung throughout Europe.

The illegitimate son of an unknown man and a single woman, Du Fay was born in modern-day Belgium, near Brussels. He studied music and grammar in the cathedral school of Cambrai, in northeastern France, where he became a choirboy in 1409. As a young man, he worked as a singer and composer at various Italian courts and chapels, including the papal chapel, and in Savoy (a region that comprised parts of Italy, Switzerland, and France). At age thirty, probably while he was in Italy, he was ordained a priest. From at least 1439 until 1474, Du Fay's home base was his native Cambrai, by then under Burgundian control, where he served as an administrator at the cathedral and probably enjoyed an honorary appointment to the chapel of Duke Philip the Good. After another period as choirmaster in Savoy, he spent his last years at Cambrai as a canon of the cathedral, occupied by administrative tasks but still active as a composer, living in his own house, and enjoying considerable wealth.

Du Fay's music survives in almost one hundred manuscripts copied between the 1420s and the

Figure 5.7 Du Fay's funeral monument, showing the composer kneeling in prayer at the left.
(Art Resource, NY.)

early sixteenth century in regions from Spain to Poland and from Italy to Scotland, attesting to his popularity and fame as a composer.

Major works: at least 6 masses, 35 independent mass movements, 4 Magnificats, 60 hymns and other chant settings, 24 motets (13 isorhythmic, 11 freely composed), 34 plainchant melodies, 60 rondeaux, 8 ballades, 13 other secular songs.

Figure 5.8 The great dome of the cathedral of Santa Maria del Fiore rises above the city of Florence. Du Fay wrote the isorhythmic motet Nuper rosarum flores *for its consecration in 1436.*
(Art Resource, NY.)

Motto mass

consisted only of beginning each movement with the same melodic motive, usually in the treble. Because the Ordinary sections do not follow one another in unbroken succession, a mass that uses such a "head motive," or "motto," signals to the listener that a particular section belongs with the other sections of the Ordinary.

The motto technique was soon superseded by, or combined with, another: constructing each movement around the same borrowed melody or cantus firmus, normally placed in the tenor. The resulting cyclical form is known as a cantus firmus mass, or tenor mass. English composers wrote the earliest cantus firmus masses, but the practice was soon adopted on the Continent, and by the second half of the fifteenth century it had become the principal type of mass setting.

Cantus firmus or tenor mass

Placing the borrowed melody in the tenor followed the medieval-motet tradition, essentially a Scholastic one in that it relied on abstract mathematical principles and featured the use of an "authoritative" preexistent melody, sacred or not, which virtually dictated the work's structure. But this created compositional problems. The sound-ideal of the fifteenth century needed the lowest voice to function as a harmonic foundation, particularly at cadences. Letting the lowest voice carry a preexistent melody limited the composer's ability to provide such a foundation. The solution was to add a part below the tenor, first called *contratenor bassus* ("low contratenor") and later simply *bassus*. A second contratenor called *contratenor altus* ("high contratenor"), later *altus*, sounded above the tenor. The highest part was the treble, called variously the *cantus* ("melody"), *discantus* ("discant"), or *superius* ("highest part"). These four voice parts became standard by the mid-1400s and remain so today.

Four-voice texture

Compositional techniques

The practice of writing the tenor cantus firmus in long notes was a holdover from the medieval motet. When the chosen melody was a plainchant, a rhythmic pattern was imposed on it and repeated, if the melody was repeated. When the borrowed melody was a secular tune, the song's original rhythm was retained; but in successive appearances, the pattern could be made faster or slower in relation to the other voices. As in the isorhythmic motet, the identity of the borrowed tune might, therefore, be thoroughly disguised, the more so now that it lay in an inner voice, but obscuring the cantus firmus in this way did not diminish its power to unify the five divisions of the mass. Borrowed chant melodies came from the Proper or the Office, secular ones most often from the tenors of chansons; in neither case did they have any liturgical connection with the Ordinary. But the mass usually owed its name to the borrowed melody, as in Du Fay's *Missa Ave regina caelorum*, based on the Marian antiphon; such a connection would also have made this particular setting suitable for performance at any mass in honor of the Blessed Virgin.

Missa Se la face ay pale

One of the most celebrated tenor masses is Du Fay's *Missa Se la face ay pale*, based on the tenor of his own ballade *Se la face ay pale*. The practice of using one's own (presumably popular) love song as the basis for a liturgical composition may seem inappropriate to us today. But in the fifteenth century, when court and chapel composers were one and the same, it may have been motivated at least in part by pride of authorship, a humanist trait—the desire of composers to assert their individuality by marking works as their own so that they would be unmistakable to their employer and other listeners. Similarly, using a cantus firmus borrowed from another's song may have been a way of paying tribute to a colleague, as with Ockeghem's mass based on Binchois's chanson *De plus en plus*, or,

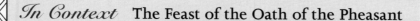

In Context   The Feast of the Oath of the Pheasant

When Constantinople, the last Christian stronghold in the East, fell to Turkish Muslims in 1453, reactions at the other end of Europe were immediate and profound. The leading composer of the time, Guillaume Du Fay, wrote a lament, a motet for which he chose a cantus firmus from a Latin chant with these words from the Lamentations of Jeremiah: "All her friends have dealt treacherously with her, among all her lovers she hath none to comfort her." Philip the Good, duke of Burgundy, was so troubled that he determined to launch a new crusade to rescue the Eastern church. Although the crusade never materialized, Philip created quite a stir. As leader of the wealthiest and most cultured court of Europe, he assembled hundreds of noble lords and vassals and their ladies at a huge banquet, where they took a solemn oath to come to the aid of the captive church.

The Feast of the Oath of the Pheasant, as it is known, took place in Lille on June 17, 1454. Court chroniclers described the event in ways that suggest that every detail was designed to enhance the theme, which was to mobilize Christian nobles to retake Constantinople. The tables were decorated with enormous constructions that came alive as people and animals emerged from them during interludes performed between courses. During the first interlude, a church bell rang loudly, then three choirboys and a tenor sang a song. At other moments, minstrels sang and played on portative organs, bagpipes, lutes, krummhorns, flutes, fiddles, harps, and drums. There were pantomime tableaux, each punctuated by trumpet fanfares, involving knights on horseback, a falcon slaying a heron, and scenes from the adventures of Jason, heroic patron of the Knights of the Order of the Golden Fleece.

At the climax of the banquet, the interlude that symbolized the reason for the entire feast was staged. Into the huge hall a giant Arab led an elephant bearing on its back a miniature castle; within its tower was imprisoned a woman personifying Mother Church. After chanting a *complainte* (lament) about the fall of Constantinople,

she begged the Burgundian nobles to take up her cause. At that point, the chronicles explain, it was the custom to present a live pheasant decorated with pearls and precious gems to the assembled noblemen "in order that they make useful and worthy vows." After the tables were taken out, the final episode was a joyous ballet.

The magnificence of the occasion reveals something about the extravagant lifestyle of the Burgundian court, where refinement mingled with vulgarity and chivalric ideals combined with religious sentiment. But it also shows that ceremonial music and theater were purposefully linked to meaningful action in life.

Figure 5.9 Philip the Good, *by Rogier van der Weyden (1400–1464). Philip wears the chain of the Order of the Golden Fleece, of which he was grand master.*
(Erich Lessing/Art Resource, NY.)

TIMELINE Fifteenth-Century England and Burgundy

Musical Events

1422–1435
Dunstable possibly
in France

1423
Du Fay, *Resvellies
vous* (NAWM 36)

ca. 1425
Binchois, *De plus en
plus* (NAWM 35)

ca. 1427–1453
Binchois at
Burgundian court

1430s
Du Fay, *Se la
face ay pale*
(NAWM 38a)

1436
Du Fay, *Nuper
rosarum flores*

ca. 1450s
Du Fay, *Missa Se
la face ay pale*
(NAWM 38b)

1453
Death of Dunstable

1460
Binchois dies

1474
Du Fay dies

1477
Tinctoris, *Liber de
arte contrapuncti*

1400   **1500**

Historical Events

1415
English under Henry V defeat
French at Agincourt

1417
End of Papal Schism

1419
Philip III (the Good) begins his
reign as duke of Burgundy

1431
Joan of Arc executed

1453
Turks conquer Constantinople

1453
French defeat English, ending
Hundred Years' War

1454
Feast of the Oath of the
Pheasant in Lille

1467
Charles the Bold of Burgundy
succeeds Philip III (the Good)

1477
Charles the Bold dies in battle;
France absorbs duchy of
Burgundy

perhaps, of acknowledging the influence of a teacher. It is also possible in Du Fay's case that the "pale face" of the chanson was reinterpreted as the face appearing on the most famous relic of the time—the Shroud of Turin, the linen cloth believed by some to bear the image of the crucified Christ. In any case, in the growing humanistic environment of the time composers were prized for their ability to create something new from borrowed material.

In the Kyrie, Sanctus, and Agnus Dei of Du Fay's *Missa Se la face ay pale*, the value of each note of the ballade's tenor melody is doubled. In the Gloria (NAWM 38b) and Credo, the cantus firmus is heard three times, first in notes that are triple their normal values, then in doubled note values, and finally at their original note values, so that the melody becomes easily recognizable only at the third hearing. In this way, Du Fay applied the principles of the isorhythmic motet on a larger scale. In Example 5.2a, we see the first phrase of the song in very long notes in the tenor at "Adoramus te," its first appearance in the Gloria. (For ease of comparison, the notes of the borrowed melody have been numbered.) The next time this opening phrase occurs, at "Qui tollis peccata mundi" (Example 5.2b), the tenor sings the tune in smaller note values to the words "miserere nobis." The third time, at "Cum sancto spiritu" (Example 5.2c), the song is heard at its normal tempo. By speeding up the tenor's cantus firmus and imitating some of its motives in the other parts, Du Fay built momentum toward the closing "Amen."

Example 5.2 Guillaume Du Fay, Missa Se la face ay pale, *Gloria*

a. Cantus firmus in the tenor at three times its original duration

We adore thee. We glorify thee.

b. Cantus firmus in the tenor at twice its original duration

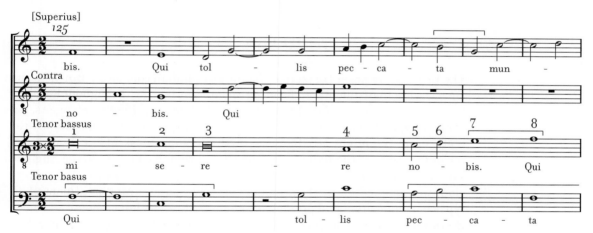

Have mercy upon us. Thou who takest away the sins of the world.

c. Cantus firmus in the tenor at its original duration.

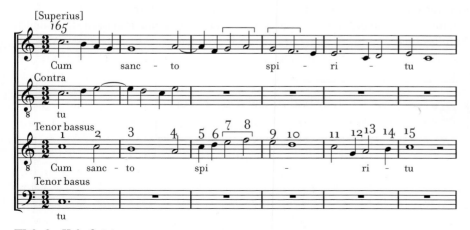

With the Holy Spirit

Layered texture in
Du Fay's masses

The diverse characters of the voices in Du Fay's mass nearly overshadow the unity achieved by the threefold statement of the chanson melody in the tenor. As in the old-fashioned French motet, each voice exists as an independent layer, having its own melodic and rhythmic logic and function. The top two voices—the superius and the contratenor altus—maintain smooth melodic contours and occasionally exchange motives, while the contratenor bassus, more angular in shape though still sung, provides a harmonic foundation. This texture also prevails in other masses by Du Fay.

Consonance and
dissonance in
Du Fay's masses

Consonance and dissonance are carefully controlled rather than used haphazardly. The stronger dissonances appear as suspensions and resolve downward by step; this treatment of dissonance became standard and was considered "proper" practice in the sixteenth century. Other dissonances, mainly between beats, pass quickly. Otherwise, Du Fay favors thirds and sixths sounding with octaves, fifths, and fourths, producing many different qualities of triads on the beats.

Du Fay's four-part cantus firmus (or tenor) masses are late works, dating mostly from after 1450. Their structural procedures distinguish them from the earlier chansons and chansonlike motets and masses. As opposed to the pleasing qualities of the Burgundian chanson, some of their new features reflect an extremely artful or learned musical style, one that rose to prominence after the middle of the century.

POSTLUDE

The English composer Dunstable and the Burgundian composers Binchois and Du Fay were instrumental in forming and disseminating throughout Europe a new musical language fused from French, Italian, and English elements. An overly simple description of the new style—but one that does not distort the truth entirely—might attribute its rhythmic suppleness to the French, its melodic suavity to the Italians, and its clear, bright harmonies to the English. The full consonant sound of sixths and thirds, sometimes in parallel succession, was adopted on the Continent. This new sound strongly influenced all types of composition and prompted composers to write homophonic or homorhythmic textures that emphasized the similarity among the parts rather than their differences. After about 1430, then, certain characteristic features of the new style emerged in the Burgundian orbit: predominantly consonant sonorities, including parallel $\frac{6}{3}$ chords; control of dissonances; equal importance of the voices; greater melodic and rhythmic identity of lines; four-part textures; and occasional use of imitation. These features represented a departure from the musical style of the late Middle Ages and became hallmarks of the musical Renaissance.

 Resources for study and review available at
wwnorton.com/studyspace

6

Music of Franco-Flemish Composers, 1450–1520

PRELUDE

People of the fifteenth and sixteenth centuries could see and emulate the rediscovered architectural monuments, sculptures, plays, and poems of antiquity, but they could not actually hear ancient music. Although the revival of the arts and architecture of ancient Greece and Rome was in full swing by 1450, the music of antiquity could be understood only through the writings of classical philosophers, poets, essayists, and music theorists that were becoming available in translation. "Moderns" learned about the power of ancient music to move the listener and wondered why their own music did not have the same effect. The influential religious leader Bernardino Cirillo (see Vignette, page 93) expressed disappointment with the artful polyphonic music of his time, and he urged musicians to follow the example of the other arts and to reclaim the power of classical musical styles and modes.

We may think of the musical Renaissance more as a general cultural movement and state of mind than as a specific set of musical techniques. Furthermore, music changed so rapidly during these centuries—though at different rates in different countries—that we cannot identify one uniform Renaissance style. Nevertheless, with the expansion of Burgundian territories and influence, the musical Renaissance spread chiefly from the Low Countries to other areas of western Europe. In this chapter, we will explore the music of northern composers, who are referred to variously as French, Franco-Flemish, or Netherlandish, depending on where they were born. Each new generation built on the musical accomplishments of the previous one, and composers of the same generation competed with one another in writing masses, motets, and chansons.

The chapter will close with a discussion of Josquin des Prez (ca. 1450–1521) and his contemporaries. Of the large number of first-rank composers active around 1500, Josquin was surely the greatest. Few musicians have enjoyed higher renown while they lived or exercised more profound and lasting influence. One of his contemporaries, Martin Luther, acknowledged Josquin's complete technical and expressive control of his art by calling him "master of the notes." Others hailed him as "the best of the composers of our time" and the "father of musicians." Florentine diplomat and humanist Cosimo Bartoli wrote in 1567 that Josquin had been without peer in music, on a par with Michelangelo in architecture, painting, and sculpture: "Both opened the eyes of all those who now take pleasure in these arts and shall find delight in the future."

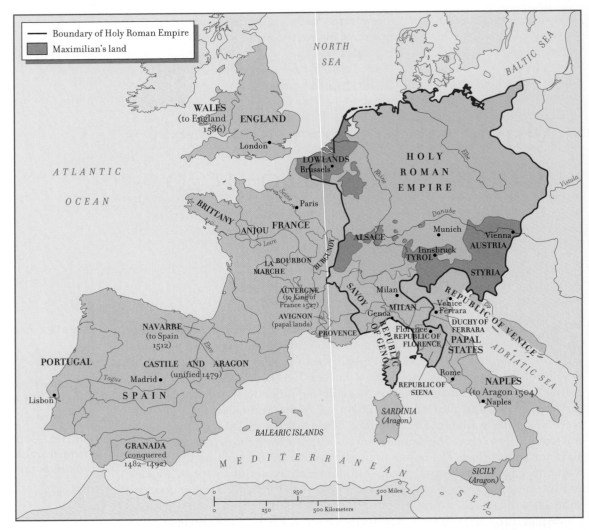

Figure 6.1 Western Europe about 1500. By this time, the Spanish rulers Isabella and Ferdinand had united Spain; the kings of France controlled several former quasi-independent fiefdoms within their borders, including Burgundy, Anjou, Brittany, and Provence; and Maximilian I, king of Germany and Holy Roman emperor, ruled directly over Austria, Alsace, and the Low Countries.

Northern Composers: The Generation after Du Fay

Ockeghem

Although the migration of musical talent across the Alps to Italy had already begun in the fifteenth century (and was to continue for another three hundred years), Jean de Ockeghem (ca. 1420–1497) was one northern composer who was known in Italy only by reputation (see Biography, page 113, and Figure 6.3). More than half a century after Ockeghem's death, the Italian humanist Cosimo Bartoli paid him a tribute comparable to the one he gave to Josquin des Prez: "I know well that Ockeghem was, so to speak, the first who in these times rediscovered music, which had almost entirely died out—not in other wise than Donatello, who in his time rediscovered sculpture."

Most of Ockeghem's thirteen masses resemble each other in their general sonority: four voices of similar character interact in a contrapuntal texture of independent melodic lines. He extended the bass, which before 1450 rarely moved below c, downward to G, F, and even C in special combinations of low voices. Ockeghem achieved a full, thick texture that gives his works a darker and more homogeneous sonority than we find, for example, in Du Fay's masses.

Some of Ockeghem's masses, like Du Fay's *Missa Se la face ay pale*, are tenor masses, which are built on a single cantus firmus that is used as the basis for every movement. For example, the *Missa De plus en plus* takes as its cantus firmus the tenor part of the chanson by Binchois (NAWM 35), with whom Ockeghem may have studied. This work can also be considered a cyclic mass because its movements are unified musically: in this case, the Kyrie, Gloria, Credo, Sanctus, and Agnus Dei are all based on the same borrowed tenor line; though not as attractive and recognizable as the top voice, it nevertheless makes a firm

Ockeghem's Masses

Tenor mass

Full 🔊   Concise 🔊

Cyclic mass

Jean de Ockeghem (Johannes Okeghem) (ca. 1420–1497)

Ockeghem was celebrated as a singer (he is said to have had a fine bass voice), as a composer, and as the model and perhaps mentor of many leading composers of the next generation, including Josquin, who set to music the French words of a moving lament on his death:

> Nymphs of the woods, goddesses of the
>   fountains,
> Skilled singers of all nations,
> Change your voices so clear and proud
> To sharp cries and lamentations.
> For Death, terrible despot,
> Has trapped your Ockeghem . . .

The poem goes on to portray Ockeghem as the "good father" of several younger composers.

He was born and trained in the province of Hainaut in northeastern France, served briefly in Antwerp, and spent several years in France with the chapel of Charles I, duke of Bourbon. He is most closely identified with the French royal court, where he served three kings over a span of more than four decades. He was a member of the royal chapel from 1451 on, led the chapel as First Chaplain from 1454, and became master of the chapel in 1465. He was also treasurer at the royal church of Saint Martin of Tours from 1458 and became a priest around 1464. He returned to his native region on occasion, where he was in touch with Du Fay, Binchois, and Busnoys, and traveled to Spain on a diplomatic mission for King Louis XI around 1470. But he seems never to have gone to Italy, and his music shows little Italian influence.

Figure 6.2 Relief portrait of Jean de Ockeghem, created by twentieth-century medalist Pierre Turin.
(Photo by Arn Dekker, Cambridge, England.)

In fact, both his career and his music are notably less cosmopolitan than those of Du Fay.

Ockeghem's known output was relatively small for a composer of his renown, although many of his works may have been lost or destroyed by fire, war, or other devastations. Most of his works cannot be dated with any certainty. In some respects, his music continues in the style of previous generations; in others, it typifies his time; but in certain ways, it is unique, perhaps because his long service in one place encouraged the development of an individual idiom.

Major works: 13 masses, Requiem Mass, at least 5 motets, 21 chansons.

foundation for the composition. Ockeghem follows custom by placing the cantus firmus in the tenor, but freely changes the rhythm and adds notes.

In the fifteenth and sixteenth centuries, masses without a cantus firmus sometimes took their titles from the mode in which they were written (for example, *Missa quinti toni*—Mass in mode 5). Ockeghem's *Missa mi-mi* derives its name from the first two notes of the bass voice, e–A, both of which in solmization were sung to the syllable *mi*. Because the opening of each movement quotes this two-note motive, the *Missa mi-mi* is known as a motto mass. Some masses are named for a structural feature, such as Ockeghem's *Missa prolationum* (a canon) and *Missa cuiusvis toni* (in any mode). A mass having neither a cantus firmus nor any other identifying peculiarity was often called a *Missa sine nomine* (mass without a name—the musical equivalent of "Untitled" in modern art).

The word *canon* (Latin for rule) has two musical meanings: the compositional technique of deriving two or more voices from a single notated voice, as Ockeghem does in *Missa prolationum* (NAWM 40), and the instruction or rule by which these parts were derived. The rule might instruct the second voice to sing the same melody starting after a certain number of beats have elapsed and at the same or a different pitch, as in the kind of canon most familiar today; alternatively, the second voice might be instructed to invert the original melody or sing it backward, resulting in an inversion or retrograde canon. The type of canon used in *Missa prolationum*, in which the voices move at different rates of speed, is known as a mensuration canon. Each movement of this work is also a double canon—that is, two canons sung or played simultaneously. Musicians valued such puzzle canons for the ingenuity and skill they displayed, but they have more in common with the structural complexities of medieval Scholasticism than with the text-based ideals of humanism; nor do they exemplify the new cosmopolitan style discussed in the preceding chapter.

Ockeghem's *Missa prolationum* shows exceptional compositional virtuosity: the mass is notated in two voices but sung in four, using the four prolations of mensural notation (see Chapter 4). Example 6.1a shows the original notation and 6.1b the transcription for the opening of the second Kyrie (the full Kyrie is in NAWM 40). Each of the two written parts has two clefs and two mensuration signs, so each of the four singers observes the pertinent symbols. The soprano sings the notes of the superius part in the C clef placed on the lowest staff line in imperfect time, minor prolation (the mensuration encoded by the semicircle in the first space), while the alto reads the same notes using the C clef placed on the second staff line in perfect time, minor prolation (the mensuration indicated by the circle) to produce the two top lines in Example 6.1b. The tenor and bass read the contra part in a similar fashion to produce the two bottom lines of the transcription.

In prestige and craft, writing secular music did not lag far behind composing masses. Chansons from 1460 to 1480 show more and more use of imitative counterpoint, at first between the superius and tenor voices and later among all three parts. Most of Ockeghem's chansons, as well as those of his equally famous contemporary Antoine Busnoys (ca. 1430–1492), made use of the traditional *formes fixes* of courtly poetry. Of these, the rondeau's popularity endured until the end of the century, whereas that of the ballade and virelai declined. Certain chansons by Ockeghem, Busnoys, and their successors were enormous hits: some favorites appear again and again in manuscripts and prints from many different regions of western Europe. Composers freely altered their own and others' chansons, rearranged them, and transcribed them for instruments. Above all, the chansons provided an inexhaustible supply of material for masses.

Some medieval traits still common in the music of Ockeghem and Busnoys, such as the *formes fixes* and reliance on a repeating tenor for structure, disappear in the next generation. Others, such as the use of a cantus firmus, continue

Figure 6.3 This miniature, from a French manuscript of about 1530, shows a singer thought to be Ockeghem and eight other chapel musicians singing a Gloria in the usual fashion of the time—from a large manuscript choir book on a lectern.

(Bibliothèque Nationale, Paris. MS F.1587, fol. 58.)

Example 6.1 Ockeghem, opening of Kyrie II from Missa prolationum

a. Original notation

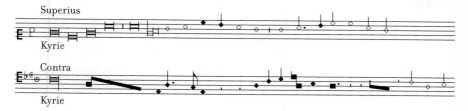

b. Transcription with lines showing the canon (the text has been omitted from the upper voices)

but become less prominent. The newer elements, including greater equality of voices, more use of imitation, and expansion of range, were extended by their successors and became characteristic of sixteenth-century musical style.

The Next Generation: Josquin and His Contemporaries

Many of the next generation of Franco-Flemish composers modeled their works on those of Ockeghem. Among the most eminent figures were Jacob Obrecht (1457/8–1505; see Figure 6.4), Henricus (Heinrich) Isaac (ca. 1450–1517), and Josquin des Prez (ca. 1450–1521; see Biography, page 120). Each was born around the middle of the century, each received his earliest musical training and experience in the Low Countries, and each traveled widely, working in various courts and churches in different parts of Europe, including Italy. Consequently, the

Ockeghem's pupils

Figure 6.4 Jacob Obrecht in a portrait from 1496 by an anonymous Flemish painter.
(Kimball Art Museum.)

careers of each illustrate the lively musical interchange between northern and southern Europe—that is, between the Franco-Flemish centers and those of Italy and Spain. Obrecht, from the Dutch town of Bergen op Zoom, died in Italy of the plague while working as a member of the ducal chapel in Ferrara, where Josquin was also employed for a time. Isaac, Flemish by birth, also ended his years in Italy, serving the Medici rulers of Florence. It is no surprise, then, that their music mixes and even combines northern and southern elements: the serious tone, formal structure, intricate polyphony, and subtly flowing rhythms of the north; and the spontaneity, simpler structure, homophonic texture, dancelike rhythms, and more clearly articulated phrases of the south. Isaac's tender song *Innsbruck, ich muss dich lassen* (Innsbruck, I must leave you, NAWM 41), with its appealing melody, sweet harmonies, and clear phrase structure, is a good example of the Italian style even though its text is in German.

The *Odhecaton*, the first printed anthology of chansons (see Innovations, pages 118–119), illustrates how deeply northern music penetrated into Italy. It contains works dating from about 1470 to 1500 by composers from the late Burgundian era to the generation of Obrecht, Isaac, and Josquin. In Petrucci's title *Harmonice musices odhecaton A*, the letter "A" indicates that the volume was planned as the first in a series. In fact, two more chanson volumes followed in short order. Over the next half-century, Petrucci and other Italian music printers issued a great number of such anthologies by French and Franco-Flemish composers, attesting to the popularity and longevity of their songs.

Chansons in the Odecaton

More than half of the chansons in the *Odhecaton* are for three voices and written primarily in the older styles. In the four-voice chansons, however, we see the genre developing toward a fuller texture, a more completely imitative counterpoint, clearer harmonic structure, and greater equality of voices. Duple meter replaced the more common triple meter of the Burgundian period. Many of these pieces, like the masses of the time, were based either on a popular tune or on a single voice from some earlier chanson.

Josquin des Prez

Of all the composers we have studied since Du Fay, none enjoyed higher renown or exercised greater influence than Josquin des Prez. Composers from his own time through the late sixteenth century emulated and reworked his compositions. His music, privileged by Petrucci's printing press, continued to be recopied, published, and performed for almost a century after his death, a rare honor at a time when most music more than a few decades old was deemed unworthy of performance. Josquin was so esteemed and popular that publishers and copyists often attributed works by other composers to him as a marketing device; historians are still having difficulty sorting out which pieces are truly his.

Josquin's chansons

By contrast with Ockeghem, Josquin virtually abandoned the *formes fixes*, choosing instead strophic texts and simple four- or five-line poems. The polyphonic fabric of his chansons is not formed from independent layers, like Ockeghem's, but is unified and interwoven with imitation, the most important new compositional device of the sixteenth century. Instead of the cantus-tenor voice pair providing the scaffolding of the texture, with the other voices filling in, all the parts are now structurally equal.

Mille regretz

Mille regretz (A thousand regrets, NAWM 43), a chanson attributed to Josquin though perhaps not by him, illustrates the style of about 1520. In contrast to the chansons of Du Fay and Ockeghem, the voices are more alike, yielding a homogeneous texture that alternates between homophony and imitation, as well as between all four voices and ever-changing combinations of two or three voices. Each phrase of text receives its own treatment, a lesson that Josquin learned well from the Italian humanists.

The high proportion of motets in Josquin's output is also noteworthy. In his day, the mass was still the form that composers turned to in order to demonstrate mastery of their craft. But the mass's liturgical formality, unvarying text, and established musical conventions placed as much emphasis on structure as on expression. Motets, on the other hand, could be written on a wide range of relatively unfamiliar texts that offered interesting new possibilities for word-music relationships. For a composer of Josquin's inclination, the motet became the genre of sacred composition that invited the most attention to expressive details.

In keeping with humanist ideals, Josquin and his contemporaries tried to make the music communicate the meaning of the text. They carefully fit the musical stress to the accentuation of the words, whether Latin or vernacular, and wanted the words to be heard and understood. The highly florid lines of Ockeghem and other Franco-Flemish composers gave way to more direct syllabic settings in which a phrase of text was presented as an uninterrupted thought. Composers turned to the chanson and the Italian popular genres as models for their vocal writing.

We see Josquin's typical approach to motet writing in *Ave Maria . . . virgo serena* (Hail Mary . . . serene Virgin, NAWM 44), probably from about 1485, one of his best-known pieces. The music is perfectly crafted to fit the words. Josquin calls attention to the text by giving each segment a unique musical treatment and a concluding cadence on C. Although the texture varies, its main method of construction is imitation—that is, each voice takes up the same motivic idea, or "point of imitation," one after the other (Example 6.2). This equalizes and unifies the voices, bringing the lines of the texture into a more congruous whole and creating an effect similar to that of perspective in painting. Before the last voice has finished its musical phrase, a different voice begins the next phrase of text with a new subject. By having the voices overlap in this way, Josquin avoids a cadence until the first full grammatical stop at "serena," where all the parts sing together for the first time, building with increasing rhythmic activity to the first simultaneous cadence. The words are declaimed naturally, the accented syllables being given longer and higher notes in most cases, and their meaning is occasionally reinforced by a particularly suitable musical gesture.

Not all of Josquin's work is so forward-looking. As we might expect, he employs conservative styles most conspicuously in his masses, which abound in technical ingenuity. Most use a secular tune as a cantus firmus. In *Missa L'homme armé super voces musicales*, Josquin transposes the familiar tune,

Josquin's Motets

Text and music

Ave Maria . . . virgo serena

Full 🔊 | Concise 🔊

Cantus firmus masses

Example 6.2 Josquin des Prez, motet: Ave Maria . . . virgo serena

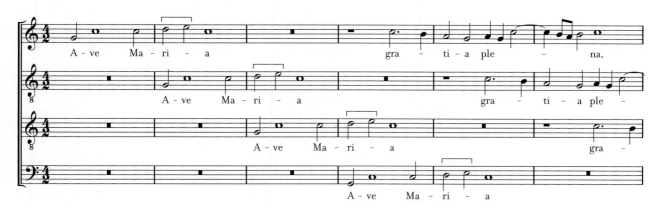

Hail Mary, full of grace

A great number of gentlemen and merchants of good account . . . [were entertained] by the exercise of music daily used in my house, and by furnishing them with [printed] books of that kind yearly sent me out of Italy and other places.

So wrote Nicholas Yonge, a London clerk with enough means and social position to support an active amateur musical life, in the dedication to his 1588 collection of madrigals, *Musica transalpina* (see Chapter 7). His words reveal how the music-printing and music-publishing business changed the way people used and enjoyed notated music during the Renaissance, allowing it to be cultivated not only in noble courts and churches, but also in ordinary households as recreation.

Printing from movable type, known in China for centuries and perfected in Europe by Johannes Gutenberg around 1450, was first used for music in the 1470s in liturgical books with chant notation. The application of movable type meant that notes could be assembled in any order, rearranged, and reused. This method proved much more practical than other procedures, such as carving music into wood blocks.

In 1501 in Venice, Ottaviano Petrucci (1466–1539) produced the first collection of polyphonic music printed entirely from movable type, the *Harmonice musices odhecaton A* (One hundred songs of harmonic music [polyphony]—it actually contained only ninety-six). Figure 6.5, a page from this collection, shows the elegance of his work.

Petrucci used a triple-impression process in which each sheet went through the press three times: once to print the staff lines, another to print the words, and a third to print the notes and the florid initials. His method was time-consuming, labor-intensive, and costly, but his results were models of clarity and accuracy. The high survival rate of Petrucci's beautiful prints perhaps betrays the fact that they were purchased and collected as luxury items.

Petrucci was no less clever a businessman than he was a craftsman. Before setting up shop, he had procured a patent on his process and a "privilege" that effectively guaranteed a monopoly on music printing in Venice for twenty years. After sizing up the market, he decided to make his first volume (the *Odhecaton*) an anthology of secular song, including what he judged to be among the best tunes of his own and the preceding generations. These were short pieces for three or four parts that could easily be performed at home or in the company of friends. Two more song collections followed—*Canti B* in 1502 and *Canti C* in 1504,—allowing Petrucci to corner the market for the most up-to-date and popular secular music of the day. By 1523, he had published fifty-nine volumes (including reprints) of vocal and instrumental music.

Printing from a single impression—using pieces of type that printed staff, notes, and text together in one operation—was apparently first practiced by John Rastell in London about 1520 and first applied on a large scale in 1528 by Pierre Attaingnant (ca. 1494–1551/2) in Paris. Although more efficient and less costly than Petrucci's triple-impression method, the process produced results that were much less elegant because the staff lines were no longer continuous but part of each piece of type; inevitably, the lines were imperfectly joined and appeared broken or wavy on the page, as seen in Figure 6.6. Nevertheless, the practicality of the method ensured its commercial success. Attaingnant's process set the standard for all printed music until copperplate engraving became popular in the late seventeenth century.

Most ensemble music published in the sixteenth century was printed in

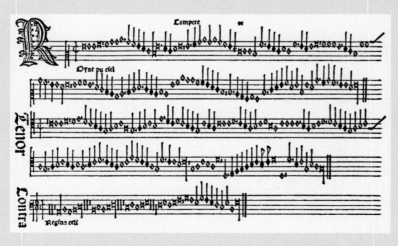

Figure 6.5 Loyset Compère's chanson Royne de ciel, *from* Harmonice musices odhecaton A, *published by Ottaviano Petrucci in 1501. The incipit of the text appears under the cantus part.*

Figure 6.6 First portion of the superius part for the motet Laudate Dominum *by Pierre de Manchicourt, as printed in Pierre Attaingnant's* Liber decimus quartus XIX musicas cantiones continet *(Paris, 1539). Attaingnant printed with a single-impression process, using type in which each note, rest, clef, or other sign includes the staff lines on which it sits.*

the form of rectangular part-books, each volume containing the music for a particular voice so that a complete set was needed to perform the piece. Part-books were intended for use at home or in social gatherings (see Figure 6.7), and most church choirs continued to use the large handwritten choirbooks (see Figures 6.3 and 6.9). Because there was not enough demand for these large books to make printing them economical, new ones were still being hand-copied in the sixteenth century even as printed collections began appearing.

In general, the existence of printed copies meant that both sacred and secular works would become known more widely and would be preserved for performance and study by later generations. This, in turn, stimulated awareness of individual influence and achievement. Josquin des Prez was the first composer whose widespread renown and lasting impact was assured by the printing press when Petrucci devoted three volumes to the publication of Josquin's masses during the composer's lifetime but no more than one volume to the works of any other composer.

The economics of supply and demand for printed music grew in ever widening circles: printing stimulated the desire for music books and increased their affordability, which, in turn, spurred the further development of music printing and competition among publishers. Printing became a reliably profitable business in the last third of the sixteenth century, and by the end of the century, Rome, Nuremberg, Lyon, Louvain, Antwerp, and London had joined Venice and Paris as centers of music publishing. Printed music had become an indispensable part of musical life.

Figure 6.7 A vocal quartet reading from partbooks. The rich costumes suggest that these are aristocratic amateurs performing for their own pleasure in the privacy of an idyllic island. Detail from an anonymous sixteenth-century painting.
(Erich Lessing/Art Resource, NY.)

Josquin des Prez (Josquin Lebloitte, dit Desprez) (ca. 1450–1521)

Josquin's motets, masses, and songs were widely sung, praised, and emulated in his lifetime and for decades after his death. He was known by his given name because "des Prez" was a nickname.

Josquin's biography has been clarified by recent research, but there are still gaps. Historians only recently discovered his family name—Lebloitte—from a will leaving him a house and land in Condé-sur-l'Escaut in Hainaut, now in Belgium. His early life is undocumented, but he was probably born and trained in or near Saint-Quentin in northern France, about halfway between Paris and Brussels. He served in the chapel of René, duke of Anjou, at Aix-en-Provence in the late 1470s. After René's death in 1480, his singers transferred to the service of King Louis XI in Paris, and Josquin may have been among them.

Josquin spent much of his career in Italy, serving the Sforza family, rulers of Milan (ca. 1484–1489), and in the Sistine Chapel in Rome (1489–1495 or later). Josquin may have been in France at the court of King Louis XII from 1501 to

Figure 6.8 *Josquin des Prez, in a woodcut from Petrus Opmeer,* Opus chronographicum *(Antwerp, 1611). Opmeer based his portrait on an oil painting that once stood in Saint Gudule Church in Brussels but was destroyed in the 1570s.* (Bettmann/Corbis.)

1503. He was appointed maestro di cappella to Duke Ercole I d'Este in Ferrara in 1503, commanding the highest salary in the history of that chapel. A recruiter for the duke had recommended Isaac instead, "because he is of a better nature among his companions and will compose new works more often. It is true that Josquin composes better, but he composes when he wants to, and not when one wants him to, and he is asking 200 ducats in salary while Isaac will come for 120." The duke hired the temperamental Josquin anyway, no doubt aware of the prestige to be gained by employing the best musician available. Josquin left after a year, apparently to escape the plague. From 1504 until his death in 1521, he resided at Condé-sur-l'Escaut, where he was provost at the church of Notre Dame.

Major works: about 18 masses, over 55 motets and liturgical works, about 65 chansons (about 10 for instruments), and over 70 doubtful and misattributed works.

L'homme armé, to successive degrees (or musical syllables—*voces musicales*) of the scale—C for the Kyrie, D for the Gloria, and so on—and includes a mensuration canon in the Agnus Dei.

For *Missa Hercules dux Ferrariae*, written to honor Ercole (Hercules) I, who was duke of Ferrara from 1471 to 1505 and Josquin's employer at one point in his career, Josquin used as a cantus firmus a *soggetto cavato dalle vocali*, a "subject drawn from the vowels" of the duke's name and title, by letting each vowel indicate a corresponding scale syllable, thus:

Her	cu	les	dux	Fer	ra	ri	e
re	ut	re	ut	re	fa	mi	re

Paraphase mass

Full 🔊   Concise 🔊

Missa Pange lingua (excerpted in NAWM 45; see Example 6.3), one of the last masses that Josquin composed, represents another new type of work: the paraphrase mass. It is based on the plainchant hymn *Pange lingua gloriosi* (Sing, tongue, of the glorious), but instead of using the hymn melody as a cantus firmus in the

Example 6.3 Pange lingua

a. Hymn

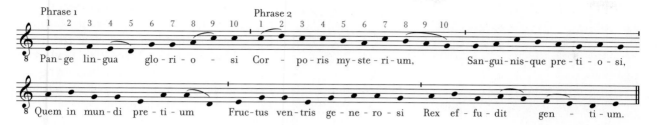

Sing, tongue, of the glorious body's mystery

b. Josquin des Prez, Missa Pange lingua: *Kyrie*

Lord, have mercy

Figure 6.9 Kyrie of the Missa Ave maris stella *by Josquin; one of two facing pages of the manuscript, showing two of the four voice parts.*
(Royal Library of Belgium, Robert Wangermee, *Flemish Music and Society in the Fifteenth and Sixteenth Centuries* © 1968 Frederick A. Praeger, Publishers.)

tenor, Josquin paraphrases it in all four voices, in whole or in part, in each movement. Phrases from the hymn melody are adapted as motives that are treated in points of imitation, or occasionally declaimed homophonically. Example 6.3a gives the first two phrases of the hymn with their notes numbered (ten pitches in each). Example 6.3b shows how Josquin begins by using the first phrase, *Pange lingua gloriosi*, as the basis for the opening section of the Kyrie. The tenor quotes the first six pitches literally and is then imitated by the bassus, superius, and altus in succession. The remaining pitches (7–9) are dissolved by the paraphrase process into shorter note values that follow only the contour of the hymn tune before coming to rest on pitch 10. Then, at measure nine, the bassus anticipates the melody of the hymn's second phrase (*corporis mysterium*), the new pitches of which are again clearly stated by the tenor before the tune is obscured by the melismatic activity leading to the cadence. Toward the end of this section, the contour of the second phrase remains clearest in the superius (measures 13–16) as the texture thickens for the close in all four voices. Josquin similarly employs the next two phrases of the hymn in the Christe section, and the final pair of phrases as the melodic material for the last Kyrie.

Josquin's *Missa Malheur me bat* illustrates the newer approach of basing a mass on an existing polyphonic work. Instead of using one voice as a cantus firmus, the composer borrows extensively from all voices of the

Type	Cantus firmus mass	Paraphrase mass	Parody or Imitation Mass
Example	Du Fay, *Missa Se la face ay pale*	Josquin, *Missa Pange lingua*	Josquin, *Missa Malheur me bat*
Borrowed material	Chant or other melody	Chant or other melody	All voices from polyphonic work
Where is it used?	Tenor of mass	All voices of mass	All voices of mass
How is it used?	In long notes, as structural cantus firmus	Paraphrased and with notes added	Motives, points of imitation, or other elements reworked
Main texture	Layered, with tenor as structural voice	Imitative, with some homophonic passages	Imitative, with some homophonic passages

Figure 6.10 Types of cyclic masses based on borrowed material.

TIMELINE   The Age of the Renaissance: Franco-Flemish Composers

Musical Events

1451–97
Ockeghem at French royal chapel

1474
Du Fay dies

ca. 1484–1495
Josquin employed in Italy

1497
Ockeghem dies

1501
Petrucci publishes *Odhecaton A*

1502
Petrucci publishes first volume of Josquin masses

1503–4
Josquin in Ferrara

ca. 1515
Josquin, *Missa Pange lingua* (NAWM 45)

1521
Josquin dies

1450   **1515**

Historical Events

1453
France defeats England in Hundred Years' War

1477
France absorbs duchy of Burgundy

1485–1603
Tudor dynasty in England

1492
First voyage of Columbus to America

1493–1519
Maximilian I reigns as Holy Roman Emperor

1495
Leonardo da Vinci, *The Last Supper*

1504
Michelangelo, *David* (Figure III.3)

1509
Henry VIII becomes king of England

1519
Charles V becomes Holy Roman Emperor

---

model, reworking the latter's characteristic motives, points of imitation, and general structure in each movement of the mass. This approach is especially successful when the model is a motet or chanson in the new, predominantly imitative or homophonic styles of the sixteenth century because in such works the tenor is not the main structural voice and no voice would function well as a cantus firmus. Typically, the resemblance to the model is strongest at the beginning and end of each movement, and the composer's skill is demonstrated by the new combinations and variations he can achieve within the borrowed material. A mass composed in this manner is called a parody (or imitation) mass because it reworks material from another polyphonic work. As with the paraphrase mass, the new technique still results in a cyclic mass because the same basic material underlies each movement, tying all the movements together.

Although composers continued to write cantus firmus masses in the sixteenth century, around 1520 paraphrase and parody techniques became dominant over the structurally confining cantus firmus technique, which came to be seen as archaic. The source material was likely chosen for the same reasons as before: to suit a particular religious holiday or saint; to honor a patron; to convey meaning by alluding to the original words of the chanson or motet (which would not be heard, but perhaps remembered, by the listener); or, in the case of a parody mass, to pay homage to another composer through emulation. Figure 6.10 provides a comparison of the various types of mass settings based on borrowed material that are discusssed in Chapters 5 and 6.

POSTLUDE

The Renaissance was an era of rediscovery and rapid change that affected the way educated people lived and thought about their own era and culture. It had far-reaching consequences in all the arts and, with the help of the printing press, brought about new attitudes toward the creation, consumption, and reception of music. The international style that had begun to emerge from the variety of compositional techniques practiced in England and on the Continent during the 1400s now spread to Italy and throughout the Holy Roman Empire.

The Renaissance produced a number of specific musical styles and influenced many features of European art music. More and more, composers let the structure of the text determine the structure of the music, relying less and less on the intellectual and abstract principles of construction that prevailed with Scholasticism. Rather than being woven into a complex layered texture, polyphonic parts were unified through imitation and became nearly equal in importance. The quest by composers for full harmonies, singable melodies, and motivic relationships between the voices influenced the texture of sacred as well as secular pieces. Borrowed melodies, whether sacred or secular, were still used to unify large compositions, but the borrowed material was often distributed among the voices rather than confined to the tenor. Although the tenor remained a key voice in the structure, the bass began to assume its modern role as the foundation of the harmony. Final cadences continued to close in perfect consonances, but elsewhere composers strove for full triadic sonorities. Simplification and standardization of rhythm favored duple measure organized by the value of the breve (alla breve). The preferred sacred genres were the cyclical mass and the motet. The chanson, breaking out of the *formes fixes*, was cast in new shapes, and its texture was gradually pervaded by imitation. Hidden and esoteric structural devices, such as isorhythm and mensuration canon, gave way to transparent textures, principally that of overlapping imitative sections, relieved occasionally by homophonic ones. These trends provided composers more compositional choices than they had had earlier and, aided by the success of music printing, more opportunity to communicate with a wider audience. Many of the trends discussed in this chapter continued throughout the sixteenth century.

 Resources for study and review available at wwnorton.com/studyspace

Secular Song and National Styles in the Sixteenth Century

PRELUDE

If fifteenth-century composers forged an international idiom, sixteenth-century musicians participated in a new flowering of national styles, especially in secular vocal music. Poets, writing in the vernacular, and composers in different regions naturally developed distinctive genres and forms. Music printing made possible the dissemination of music in the vernacular for amateurs to sing for their own pleasure, further encouraging the growth of national styles.

The development of music printing in 1501 (see Innovations, pp. 118–119) changed the economics of music. Prior to this, a musical composition was preeminently a performance—a service provided by musicians. Now, for the first time in printed form, it could be sold as a commodity. The new supply of printed music dovetailed with a growing demand for notated music that amateurs could perform for their own enjoyment. People have always made music to entertain themselves and their friends, but for most of human history they did so without using notation. When notation was invented, it was used for church music and secular music of the aristocracy, as we have seen, leaving few written traces of the general populace's music-making. In the sixteenth century, the ability to read notation and to perform from printed music became an expected social grace first among the upper classes and then among the literate urban middle classes. In Baldassare Castiglione's influential *Book of the Courtier* (1528), several speakers praise those who can sing and play from notation (see Vignette, page 126). Many paintings from the time, such as Figures 6.7 and 7.4, show singers or instrumentalists reading from published music, usually in the form of partbooks. In such settings, music served as a kind of social glue, an activity that friends and family could enjoy together.

Amateur vocalists were most interested in singing in their own language, reinforcing an already evident trend toward diverse national genres and styles. Among the significant national genres of the sixteenth century were the Spanish villancico, the Italian frottola, and a new kind of French chanson, all simple, strophic, mostly syllabic and homophonic, easily singable, and thus ideally suited for amateur performers. The genre that proved most significant historically was the Italian madrigal, in which Renaissance poets and composers brought to a peak their intense interests in humanism, in the individual, and in realizing in music the accents, images, and emotions of the text. Besides influencing later French chansons, madrigals gained fashion in England and were joined around the end of the century by the lute song. Through the madrigal, Italians became the leading forces in European music for the first time, a role they would maintain for much of the seventeenth century.

The Rise of National Styles: Italy and Spain

Frottola and lauda

In Italy, two types of native song prevailed when the northerners arrived, and other types developed during the sixteenth century. The two earlier types, the frottola and lauda (plural: frottole and laude), were both strophic, four-part homophonic songs with refrains, with the melody in the upper voice, simple diatonic harmonies, and words set syllabically to catchy rhythmic patterns that repeat from one line to the next. Frottole, composed and sung for entertainment in the sophisticated Italian courts of Ferrara and Mantua, were more highbrow versions of earthy, satirical street music. Laude, performed at semi-public gatherings of the faithful, were religious and devotional. Neither bore any resemblance to the intricate Franco-Flemish polyphony. Petrucci, the great Venetian music printer, published thirteen collections of these highly popular tunes (eleven of frottole and two of laude) within a span of ten years in the early sixteenth century (for an example of the frottola, see NAWM 55). The frottola may also have influenced the emerging new French chanson (see page 134).

Full 🔊

Villanella and villancico

Later in the century, composers in Italy cultivated other types of light secular song. The canzon villanesca (peasant song), or villanella for three voices, was a lively little homophonic strophic piece that flourished chiefly in the Neapolitan area and sometimes mimicked the more sophisticated madrigal. The canzonetta (little song) and the balletto also gained prominence. The balletto, as the name suggests, was intended for dancing as well as singing or playing, and its

---

Baldassare Castiglione (1478–1529) was a courtier, ambassador, and poet. His most influential work was The Book of the Courtier *(1528), a manual on proper behavior at court in the guise of conversations at the ducal palace in Urbino. The ability to sing and play from notation was expected.*

The Count began again: "Gentlemen, you must know that I am not satisfied with our Courtier unless he be also a musician, and unless, besides understanding and being able to read music, he can play various instruments. For, if we rightly consider, no rest from toil and no medicine for ailing spirits can be found more decorous or praiseworthy in time of leisure than this; and especially in courts where, besides the release from vexations which music gives to all, many things are done to please the ladies, whose tender and delicate spirits are readily penetrated with harmony and filled with sweetness. Hence, it is no wonder that in both ancient and modern times they have always been particularly fond of musicians, finding music a most welcome food for the spirit."

Baldassare Castiglione, *The Book of the Courtier,* trans. Charles S. Singleton (Garden City, N.Y.: Doubleday, 1959), p. 74.

typical "Fa-la-la" refrains later made their way into English songs. In fact, German and English composers imitated both canzonette and balletti in the late sixteenth century.

In Spain, in the late fifteenth century, during Ferdinand and Isabella's campaign to unify and invigorate their lands, Ferdinand and others at the Aragonese court encouraged the development of a traditional and uniquely Spanish music. They especially cultivated the villancico, which became the most important form of secular polyphonic song in Renaissance Spain. Although the name is a diminutive of *villano* ("peasant") and the texts are usually on rustic or popular subjects, villancicos were composed for the aristocracy. Short, strophic, syllabic, and mostly homophonic, they reflect a growing preference for simplicity and for what were considered more authentic representations of Spanish culture than the Spanish songs written in imitation of the polyphonic French chanson.

Juan del Encina (1468–1529), the first Spanish playwright, was a leading composer of villancicos. His *Oy comamos y bebamos* (Today let's eat and drink, NAWM 54) is typical of the genre. In language befitting the rustic nature of the play from which it comes, the text exhorts listeners to feast and be merry on the day preceding Lent, a season of fasting. The music, melodically simple, has focused harmonic progressions and dancelike rhythms marked by frequent metrical shifts between $\frac{3}{4}$ and $\frac{6}{8}$.

Figure 7.1 Bronzino (1503–1572), portrait of a courtier, 1530s. The subject radiates an air of self-importance and accomplishment (what Castiglione calls "sprezzatura"), and the portrait, along with many others by Renaissance artists, demonstrates a new interest in the individual. (The Metropolitan Museum of Art/Art Resource, NY.)

The Italian Madrigal

Native Italian song was naturally and intimately bound up with native Italian poetry. Early in the century, a renewed appreciation for the great fourteenth-century Italian poet Petrarch (who had been crowned poet laureate in Rome in 1341) sparked a movement during which the poet's sonnets and other poems were analyzed, discussed, edited, and imitated. One admirer, Pietro Bembo, praised Petrarch for his combination of *piacevolezza* ("pleasantness") and *gravità* ("seriousness") and for his remarkable ability to match the sound qualities of his verses to their meanings. For example, harsh sentiments were expressed with words containing gruff consonants, while tender thoughts were couched in phrases that used soothing vowels and liquid consonants. The Petrarchan movement soon attracted the attention of composers, who found inspiration in the sound qualities of Petrarch's poetry. Many of the early madrigalists turned to Petrarch for their texts. So even though the madrigal arose in part from the merger of native and foreign musical styles, it owes its elevated tone and serious subject matter to the Petrarchan movement.

The popularity of the Italian madrigal, which dominated secular music in the sixteenth century, allowed Italy to assume a leading role in European music for the first time. Unlike the trecento madrigal—which employed fixed patterns of poetic and musical repetition—the sixteenth-century madrigal was a through-composed setting of a short poem. The term *through-composed* says it all: every line of poetry received a different musical setting reflecting the rhythm and sense of the words. In contrast to the poetry of the frottola, madrigal poetry was more artful and elevated in tone, and borrowed its amorous situations from the

VIGNETTE Women's Vocal Ensembles

Vincenzo Giustiniani (1564–1637) was a well-to-do musical amateur who described contemporary musical life in Discorso sopra la musica de' suoi tempi *(Discourse on the music of his times, 1628). His account of the women's vocal ensembles at Ferrara and Mantua in the 1570s reveals their manner of performance and some of the reasons they were so greatly esteemed.*

[The dukes of Ferrara and Mantua] took the greatest delight in the art, especially in having many noble ladies and gentlemen learn to sing and play superbly, so that they spent entire days in some rooms designed especially for this purpose and beautifully decorated with paintings. The ladies of Mantua and Ferrara were highly competent, and vied with each other not only in regard to the timbre and training of their voices but also in the design of exquisite passages of embellishment delivered at opportune points, but not in excess. Furthermore, they moderated or increased their voices, loud or soft, heavy or light, according to the demands of the piece they were singing; now slow, breaking off with sometimes a gentle sigh, now

singing long passages legato or detached, now *gruppi*, now leaps, now with long trills, now with short, and again with sweet running passages sung softly, to which sometimes one heard an echo answer unexpectedly. They accompanied the music and the sentiment with appropriate facial expressions, glances, and gestures with no awkward movements of the mouth or hand or body that might not express the feeling of the song. They made the words clear in such a way that one could hear even the last syllable of every word, which was never interrupted or suppressed by passages and other embellishment. They used many other particular devices that will be known to persons more experienced than I. And under these favorable circumstances the abovementioned musicians made every effort to win fame and the favor of the Princes their patrons, who were their principal support.

Vincenzo Giustiniani, *Discorso sopra la musica de' suoi tempi* (1628), in Angelo Solerti, *Le origini del melodramma: Testimonianze dei contemporanei* (Turin: Fratelli Bocca, 1903), pp. 107–108; trans. Carol MacClintock, Musicological Studies and Documents IX (Rome: American Institute of Musicology, 1962), pp. 69–70.

---

pastoral genre, which was all the rage in the sixteenth century. Many madrigal texts were taken from works by major poets, including Ludovico Ariosto (1474–1533), Torquato Tasso (1544–1595), and Giovanni Battista Guarini (1538–1612); others were written in imitation of Petrarch. Their subject matter was either heroic or sentimental, and the poems became more and more sensual—even erotic—as the century progressed. Madrigal composers dealt attentively with the poetry, using a variety of homophonic and contrapuntal textures in a series of overlapping sections, each based on a single phrase of text, with all voices playing essentially equal roles. In these respects, madrigals resemble motets of the same era. Most important, madrigalists aimed to match the seriousness or playfulness of the poetry with the elegance or wit of their music in order to communicate the poem's ideas, images, and emotions.

Social settings   The singing of madrigals held a privileged position in the cultural life of Renaissance Italy. Initially composed chiefly for the enjoyment of the singers themselves, the pieces were performed in mixed groups of women and men at social gatherings, after meals, and at meetings of academies (societies organized to study and discuss literary, scientific, or artistic matters). The demand for madrigals was great: counting reprints and new editions, some two thousand collections were published between 1530 and 1600, and their popularity continued well into the seventeenth century.

In addition to amateur performances, by 1570 some princely patrons began to cultivate specialized singers to perform madrigals for audiences at court. Virtuoso singing ensembles formed, encouraging composers to write more difficult music demanding the execution of florid runs, trills, and turns and the application of a variety of attacks, dynamics, and vocal colors. In 1580, Alfonso d'Este, duke of Ferrara, established the most famous of these ensembles—the *concerto delle donne* (ensemble of ladies), a trio of trained singers (Laura Peverara, Anna Guarini, and Livia d'Arco) appointed as ladies-in-waiting to his music-loving wife, Margherita Gonzaga.

Concerto delle donne

The *concerto delle donne* instilled in listeners an insatiable appetite for high voices, one that was to prevail in the following centuries. There were other consequences as well. Talented women moved swiftly from a position of relative cultural obscurity to one of exceptional opportunity and influence. The increasing separation between performer and audience, resulting from the development of a class of highly trained performers, encouraged composers to address their works to members of the listening audience rather than exclusively to the enjoyment of the singers themselves. By dramatizing and projecting the words by means of contrast and other bold effects written into the music—effects that could readily be perceived by the ear—they hoped to lead the listener to understand and delight in the madrigal poetry's overt as well as covert meanings, as the performers had long been able to do. As a result, the madrigal became an increasingly dramatic and extrovert genre toward the end of the century. We may observe this trend in the madrigals chosen here to represent this genre in the sixteenth century.

The leading composers of the Italian madrigal, initially emigrants from the north, also worked as church musicians and transferred their skills in sacred polyphony to the writing of secular madrigals. The northerner Jacques Arcadelt (ca. 1505–1568) sang in the pope's chapel for a time and later joined the royal chapel in Paris. Arcadelt's madrigal *Il bianco e dolce cigno* (The white and sweet swan, NAWM 56), from about 1538, is justifiably among the most famous of the early madrigals. The poet cleverly contrasts the swan's literal death with his own figurative death (a metaphor for sexual climax, known in the sixteenth century as "the little death"), "death that in dying fills me with complete joy and desire." The antitheses are further developed: the swan dies disconsolate, though singing—the traditionally mute creature supposedly emits a "swan song" just before its death—while the poet, though weeping, would be content to die "a thousand deaths a day." Arcadelt's setting plays with these poetic conceits in many ways, but principally it contrasts a sweet, homophonic texture that suggests contentment with the multiple imitative entrances of the phrase "a thousand deaths a day" and its sexual connotations (see Example 7.1).

Arcadelt

Full 🔊   Concise 🔊

Example 7.1 Jacques Arcadelt, Il bianco e dolce cigno

With a thousand deaths a day I would be content.

Rore

The madrigal continued to thrive at midcentury, particularly in the works of Cipriano de Rore (1516–1565). Flemish by birth, Rore worked in Italy, chiefly in Ferrara and Parma, and briefly succeeded his teacher, Adrian Willaert, as music director at Saint Mark's in Venice. He became the madrigalist most admired by composers later in the century; Monteverdi in particular proudly claimed that he was following in Rore's footsteps (see Chapter 10).

Full 🔊 Concise 🔊

In his madrigal *Da le belle contrade d'oriente* (From the fair regions of the East, NAWM 57) of about 1560–1565, Rore imbued every detail of the music with the sense and feeling of the poem, a sonnet modeled on Petrarch. The expanded range of five voices suits this text particularly well since it allowed Rore to divide the ensemble into higher and lower groupings to distinguish subtly between the lovers' voices as they are about to part. As may be seen in Example 7.2, Rore gives each phrase of text a distinct musical profile, choosing intervals associated with sadness especially for the woman's utterances, which also imitate natural speech inflections: rising semitones for "T'en vai" (You go); falling minor thirds, semitones, and minor seventh for "haimè!" (alas!); and descending intervals on "Adio!" (Farewell!). At the words "Sola mi lasci" (You're leaving

Example 7.2 Cipriano de Rore, Da le belle contrade d'oriente

[Hope of my heart,] sweet desire,
you go, alas! You're leaving me alone! Farewell!
What will [become of me, gloomy and sad?]

me alone), the lower voices drop out, leaving the soprano to sing a plaintive solo phrase, which ascends chromatically, A–B♭–B♮, to convey her anxiety and sadness. In a famous contemporary painting by Titian, the lovers Venus and Adonis find themselves in a similar situation (see Figure 7.2).

As part of the humanistic revival of ancient Greek musical thought, theorists in the mid-sixteenth century embraced chromaticism, pointing to the chromatic and enharmonic tetrachords discussed by Greek writers (see Chapter 1 and NAWM 2). Without advocating chromaticism, Zarlino devoted an entire chapter of his book *Le istitutioni harmoniche* (Harmonic Foundations, 1558) to instructing composers on how to set words to music, and suggested that motion "through the semitone" was effective in expressing sorrow (see Vignette, page 132). Rore frequently introduces notes outside the mode, sometimes to the point where all twelve notes of the chromatic scale appear in the course of just a few phrases, as in Example 7.2. But such harmonic adventures were not tonal in the modern sense; rather, they were motivated by local expressive goals.

Toward the end of the century, the leading madrigalists were native Italians, not the northerners who first dominated the field. Luca Marenzio (1553–1599), who spent most of his career in Rome in the service of several cardinals, depicted contrasting ideas and images in his music with complete artistry and dazzling virtuosity. Like other madrigal composers of the late sixteenth century, Marenzio favored pastoral poetry, but he was by far the most prolific, publishing more than four hundred madrigals over a period of only two decades. One of his most celebrated is a setting of Petrarch's sonnet *Solo e pensoso* (Alone and pensive, NAWM 58). It is replete with examples of the typically clever "word painting" devices, later called madrigalisms, which evoke the

Chromaticism

[Full 🔊]

Marenzio

[Full 🔊]

Figure 7.2 Titian, Venus and Adonis, *1553. A contemporary of Cipriano da Rore, Titian (ca. 1488–1576) was the foremost Venetian painter of his time. This work depicts the lovers' separation in a scene that parallels the words of Rore's madrigal (NAWM 57 and Example 7.2), showing Venus clinging to Adonis and begging him not to leave her for the hunt, where he is eventually killed.*
(Bridgeman Art Library.)

VIGNETTE Suiting the Music to the Words

Le istitutioni harmoniche (The Harmonic Founda-
tions) by Gioseffo Zarlino (1517–1590) was the most
respected treatise of the mid-sixteenth century. His
advice to composers on how to express emotions corre-
sponds almost exactly to the practice of the prominent
madrigal composers of his generation.

When a composer wishes to express harshness, bitterness, and similar things, he
will do best to arrange the parts of the composition so that they proceed with movements that are
without the semitone, such as those of the whole
tone and ditone [major third]. He should allow the
major sixth and major thirteenth, which by nature
are somewhat harsh, to be heard above the lowest
note of the concentus [interval], and should use
the suspension of the fourth or the eleventh above
the lowest part, along with somewhat slow movements, among which the suspension of the seventh may also be used. But when a composer
wishes to express effects of grief and sorrow, he
should (observing the rules given) use movements which proceed through the semitone, the
semiditone [minor third], and similar intervals,
often using minor sixths or minor thirteenths
above the lowest note of the composition, these
being by nature sweet and soft, especially when
combined in the right way and with discretion and
judgment.

It should be noted, however, that the cause of
the various effects is attributed not only to the
consonances named, used in the ways described
above, but also the movements which the parts
make in singing. These are two sorts, namely,
natural and accidental. Natural movements are
those made between the natural notes of a composition, where no sign or accidental note inter-
venes. Accidental movements are those made by
means of the accidental notes, which are indicated
by the signs ♯ and ♭. The natural movements have
more virility than the accidental movements,
which are somewhat languid. . . . For this reason
the former movements can serve to express effects
of harshness and bitterness, and the latter movements can serve for effects of grief and sorrow.

Gioseffo Zarlino, *Le istitutioni harmoniche* (1558) III.31, trans.
Vered Cohen; in Gioseffo Zarlino, *On the Modes,* ed. Claude V.
Palisca (New Haven: Yale University Press, 1983), p. 95.

meaning of individual words or phrases with a musical image: long note values
for "deliberate and slow" steps, quickly moving figures in close imitation for
"flee," quarter notes alternating between two pitches a whole step apart for
"footstep(s)." Of these devices Marenzio was an acknowledged master. But the
opening of the madrigal goes well beyond word painting to create an extraordinary soundscape of loneliness and alienation, rendered by a painfully slow,
ascending, chromatic scale in the soprano that rises through a ninth before
reversing direction, moving all the while in stark rhythmic and melodic contrast to the other voices.

Vincentino and Luzzaschi

Ferrara, the city renowned as the home of the original *concerto delle donne,*
also boasted several important madrigal composers, all Italians. Nicola Vicentino (1511–ca. 1576) explored chromatic passages in his madrigals, inspired by
chromatic and enharmonic Greek tetrachords. To promote his theories, Vicentino not only published a treatise, *L'antica musica ridotta alla moderna prattica*
(Ancient Music Adapted to Modern Practice, 1555), but also designed a specially
constructed harpsichord and organ (an *arcicembalo* and *arciorgano*) that
divided the scale into quarter tones on which to perform his experimental
music. Another composer of the Ferrarese "avant-garde" was the madrigalist
Luzzasco Luzzaschi (ca. 1545–1607), who became a master at improvising on
Vicentino's chromatic-enharmonic keyboards. Luzzaschi, in turn, influenced
the madrigal composer most associated with chromaticism at the end of the

Gesualdo

century—Carlo Gesualdo, prince of Venosa (ca. 1561–1613; see Figure 7.3).

One of the most colorful figures in music history, Gesualdo was an aristocratic amateur who nevertheless sought publication for his unconventional music, unusual for nobility at the time. He was also a murderer: when he discovered his wife in bed with her lover, he killed them both on the spot—not so unusual among the nobility at the time—and then fled to his hilltop village near Naples. Gesualdo survived the scandal to marry Eleanora d'Este, niece of Alfonso II, duke of Ferrara, in 1594.

In his imaginative madrigals, which often dwell on themes of torment and death, Gesualdo dramatizes and intensifies the antitheses in the poetry through sudden contrasts between diatonic and chromatic passages, dissonance and consonance, chordal and imitative textures, and slow- and fast-moving rhythmic motives. These contrasts may be seen in *"Io parto" e non più dissi* ("I am leaving," and I said no more, NAWM 59), published in his last book of madrigals in 1611. In the dialogue between the lovers, the woman's tearful pleas are conveyed by slow, chromatic, mostly chordal music touched with dissonance; the man's return to life ("vivo son") after his symbolic, sexual death prompts a turn to faster, diatonic, imitative figures (Example 7.3). Although these devices tend to fragment the sense of the poetry, Gesualdo achieved continuity by avoiding conventional cadences, and despite the prevalent chromaticism in many of his madrigals, he also provided tonal coherence by emphasizing the main steps of the mode at important moments.

Figure 7.3 Detail from Giovanni Balducci, The Penitence of Gesualdo, *1604. The composer commissioned this painting of the Last Judgement showing himself (in black) kneeling at the mouth of Hell while his uncle, St. Carlo Borromeo, intercedes with Heaven on his behalf.*

(Lebrecht Music & Arts Photo Library/Colouriser AL.)

The madrigal had a special place in the career of Claudio Monteverdi (1567–1643), whose biography will be considered in Chapter 9, but whose compositions

Monteverdi

Example 7.3 Don Carlo Gesualdo, "Io parto" e non più dissi, measures 26–31

[" . . . Ah, may I never
cease to pine away] in sad laments."
Dead I was, now I am alive, [for my spent spirits
returned to life at the sound of such pitiable accents.]

made a crucial stylistic transition in this genre—from the polyphonic vocal ensemble to the instrumentally accompanied song for duet or larger ensembles.

Of Monteverdi's eight books of madrigals, the first five, published between 1587 and 1605, are monuments in the history of the polyphonic madrigal. Without going to such extremes as Gesualdo, Monteverdi demonstrated remarkable expressive power through his smooth combination of homophonic and contrapuntal part writing, his sensitivity to the sound and meaning of the text, and his free use of chromaticism and dissonance. But certain features—only suggested in the music of his contemporaries—indicate that Monteverdi was moving swiftly and confidently toward a new idiom. For example, many of his musical motives are not melodic, but declamatory in the manner of the later style known as recitative; the texture often departs from the medium of five equal voices and becomes a duet over a harmonically supportive (vocal) bass; and ornamental dissonances and embellishments that previously would have occurred only in improvisation are written into the score.

Full 🔊   Concise 🔊

Cruda Amarilli (Cruel Amaryllis, NAWM 71) exemplifies the flexible and lively style of Monteverdi's polyphonic madrigals. The sound is rich in musical invention, humorous yet weighty, and audacious yet perfectly logical in its harmonies (see the more detailed discussion in Chapter 9).

Figure 7.4 Three Musicians (*or* The Concert), *by the Master of the Female Half-Lengths, shows the ways in which sixteenth-century part-songs could be performed. The music is Sermisy's Parisian chanson* Joyssance vous donneray. *The flutist reads from the soprano partbook, the singer performs the tenor part, and the lutenist adds the other voices from memory or perhaps improvises an accompaniment.*

(Harris Collection, Schloss Rohrau, Vienna/Art Resource.)

The Rise of National Styles: France and England

During the long reign of Francis I (1515–1547), composers in France developed a new type of chanson that was light, fast, strongly rhythmic, and in four parts. Favored subjects were playful, amorous situations that allow for double meanings, although more serious texts were occasionally chosen. The text was set syllabically with many repeated notes, usually in duple meter. The principal melody was in the highest voice, the musical texture largely homophonic with occasional short points of imitation. Most pieces were divided into short sections arranged in a simple pattern, such as aabc or abca. The strophic, repetitive forms did not allow word painting, and composers focused on tuneful melodies and pleasing rhythms rather than profound expression of the text. Nevertheless, the French chanson exerted some influence on the Italian madrigal, which was developing at the same time in the hands of northern composers.

The new French chansons were satisfying to sing and ideally suited to amateur performance. Between 1528 and 1552, Pierre Attaingnant (ca. 1494–1551/2), the first French music printer, brought out more than fifty collections of such chansons—about 1,500 pieces altogether—and other publishers soon followed. The great number of chansons of this type printed in the sixteenth century, including hundreds of arrangements for voice and lute or for lute alone, testifies to their popularity.

Example 7.4 Claudin de Sermisy, Tant que vivray, *measures 1–8*

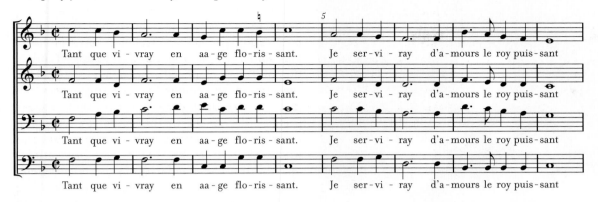

Tant que vi - vray en aa - ge flo - ris - sant. Je ser - vi - ray d'a - mours le roy puis - sant

Tant que vi - vray en aa - ge flo - ris - sant. Je ser - vi - ray d'a - mours le roy puis - sant

Tant que vi - vray en aa - ge flo - ris - sant. Je ser - vi - ray d'a - mours le roy puis - sant

Tant que vi - vray en aa - ge flo - ris - sant. Je ser - vi - ray d'a - mours le roy puis - sant

As long as I am able-bodied,
I shall serve the potent king of love.

The two principal composers in Attaingnant's early chanson collections were Claudin de Sermisy (ca. 1490–1562) and Clément Janequin (ca. 1485–ca. 1560). Sermisy's *Tant que vivray* (NAWM 60), shown in Example 7.4, is typical. The text is a lighthearted and optimistic love poem, far removed from the old tradition of courtly love. As in a frottola or villancico, the melody is in the top voice, and the harmony consists of thirds and fifths with only an occasional sixth above the bass. The voices declaim the text mostly together. One result is that accented dissonances appear where earlier chansons would have featured a syncopated suspension before a cadence, as on the third quarter note of measure 3 in the top voice. The opening long-short-short rhythm is common. The end of each line of text is marked by a relatively long note or repeated notes, emphasizing the form of the poetry. Several of Sermisy's chansons were so popular that they were reprinted for decades and adapted into many new forms, from dance melodies to psalm tunes. Some even showed up in paintings, as in Figure 7.4.

Janequin wrote more than 250 chansons, some of which were extremely popular, as evinced by Attaingnant's four printed volumes of Janequin's music, including lyrical love songs, narrative songs, and bawdy songs. He was particularly celebrated for turning birdsong, street cries, battle sounds, and the like into descriptive chansons for four voices, using onomatopoeic syllables to imitate the sounds of a fanfare, a hunting party, or the chatter of women.

Traditions mix in the chansons of Orlande de Lassus, reflecting his cosmopolitan background (see Chapter 10). While some are in the new homophonic style, others show the influence of the Italian madrigal or grow from the Franco-Flemish tradition, using a tight polyphonic texture with close imitation and sudden changes of pace. His range of subject matter was equally wide; no one was more accomplished at writing humorous and even bawdy chansons, but he also wrote songs of impressive seriousness. Lassus was always acutely attuned to the text and made sure that the music fit its rhythm, reflected its imagery, and conveyed the appropriate feelings. In his setting of *La nuict froide et sombre* (NAWM 61), he captured the overall mood—contrasting somber night and sweet sleep to the shining day that brings activity and varied colors—and depicted vivid images in the poem, from the contrast of earth and sky to the weaving of a tapestry of light.

The late sixteenth century brought a fashion for Italian culture, art, and music to England. Many of Shakespeare's plays are set in Italy; and while

Sermisy

Full 🔊 | Concise 🔊

Janequin

Lassus

Full 🔊 | Concise 🔊

Figure 7.5 A copy (1600) of the lost Coronation Portrait *of Elizabeth I (r. 1558–1603).*
(National Portrait Gallery, London.)

Triumphes of Oriana

Full 🔊   Concise 🔊

Lute songs

everything from manners to clothing was affected, music was in the vanguard. Italian madrigals had begun to circulate in England in the 1560s, but the publication in 1588 of Nicholas Yonge's *Musica transalpina* (Music from across the Alps), a collection of Italian madrigals translated into English, accelerated the vogue for singing madrigals that was already underway. According to Yonge's preface, the pieces in the anthology were part of a repertory sung by gentlemen and merchants who met daily at his home (see Innovations, pp. 118–119). The popularity of this and other collections spurred native composers to cash in on the trend by writing their own compositions in the Italian manner. Leading English madrigal composers include Thomas Morley (1557/8–1602) and Thomas Weelkes (ca. 1573–1623).

Morley, the earliest and most prolific, wrote canzonets and balletts as well as madrigals, all based on Italian models. He composed his ballett *My bonny lass she smileth* (NAWM 63) in imitation of a specific balletto by Giovanni Giacomo Gastoldi, borrowing its dancelike meter and aspects of its text, rhythm, melody, and harmony. Like most balletts, it is strophic, with each stanza comprising two repeated sections of music (AABB). These are set homophonically with the melody in the top voice, and each concludes with a refrain, sung to the syllables "Fa-la-la," that is more contrapuntal, with some imitation between the parts. The distinctive rhythms, varied textures, and occasional contrapuntal challenges make Morley's "Fa-las" particularly satisfying to sing.

In 1601, Morley published a collection of twenty-five English madrigals by different composers modeled after a similar Italian anthology called *Il trionfo di Dori* (1592). He called his *The Triumphes of Oriana*, possibly in honor of Queen Elizabeth I (r. 1558–1603; see Figure 7.5). Each madrigal in Morley's collection ends with the words "Long live fair Oriana," a name sometimes applied to Elizabeth.

One of the most famous madrigals in the collection is Weelkes's *As Vesta was* (NAWM 64), on his own poem. Elizabeth, who never married, was called the Virgin Queen, and the poem invokes both Diana, Roman goddess of virginity, and Vesta, Roman goddess of fire, hearth, and home, an unmarried sister of Jupiter. Since word painting was a strong tradition in the madrigal, Weelkes as poet provided numerous opportunities for musical depiction, and Weelkes as composer capitalized on all of them. Most striking—and less conventional—is Weelkes's treatment of the final phrase. "Long live fair Oriana" is set to a motive that enters almost fifty times in all voices and all transpositions possible in the mode, suggesting the acclamation of a vast people. The effect is both virtuosic and meaningful, exemplifying the mixture of wit, wordplay, sentiment, contrapuntal skill, melodiousness, and sheer pleasure for the singers that characterizes the best madrigals, English or Italian.

In the early 1600s, the solo song with accompaniment became more prominent, especially the lute song (or air). The leading composers of lute songs were

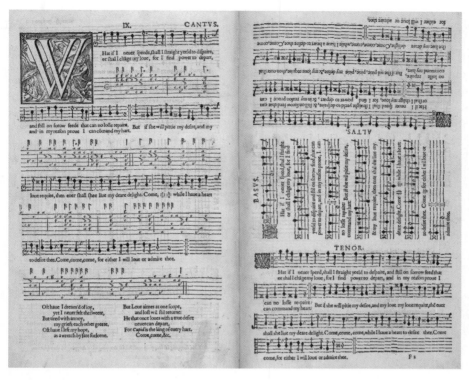

Figure 7.6   John Dowland's song What if I never speede *as printed in his* Third and Last Book of Songs or Ayres *(London, 1603). The song may be performed as a solo with lute accompaniment, reading from the left-hand page, or as a four-part vocal arrangement, with or without lute accompaniment, or by viols, with or without a singer. The altus, tenor, and bassus parts are arranged on the page to accommodate the performers' varying perspectives.*
(British Library, London.)

John Dowland (1563–1626) and Thomas Campion (1567–1620). The lute song was a more personal genre than the madrigal, with none of the latter's aura of social play. The music generally reflects the overall mood, with much less word painting than is typical of madrigals. The lute accompaniments, always subordinate to the vocal melody, have some rhythmic and melodic independence. Unlike madrigal collections, which were issued in partbooks, lute songs were printed in one book, with voice and lute part in vertical alignment on the same page. This format allowed singers to accompany themselves. In some collections, the songs appear both this way and in an alternative version, with three additional vocal parts so arranged on the page that performers sitting around a table could read all their parts from the same book (see Figure 7.6). The alternative four-part version, which sometimes resembled a madrigal, could be performed with voices, instruments, or both. The lute part is in tablature, a notational system that tells the player which strings to pluck and where to place the fingers on the strings, rather than indicating which pitches will result.

Dowland's remarkable *Flow, my tears* from his *Second Book of Ayres* (1600); (NAWM 65)—perhaps Elizabethan England's best-known air—spawned over two hundred variations and arrangements. It is in the form of a pavane, a sixteenth-century Italian processional dance, with three repeated sections of music, or strains. A performer sings the first two stanzas of the poem to the first strain, the next two to the second, and the final stanza twice to the third strain, resulting in the musical pattern aabbCC. Even though the repeats

Dowland's air

Full 🔊   Concise 🔊

In Performance   Vocal Chamber Music or Accompanied Song?

Frottole, as well as French chansons and madrigals dating from about 1520 to 1550, were written for four voice parts; after the middle of the century, five voices became the rule for the madrigal, and settings for six or more voices were not unusual. The word *voices* should be taken literally: by definition, these were vocal chamber works with one singer to a part (see Figure 6.7). Throughout the sixteenth century, however, instruments sometimes doubled the voices or replaced some or all of the parts. This was particularly true of the frottola, which was presumably sung either a cappella (although Petrucci usually supplied the text only for the cantus) or as a song for solo voice with lute accompaniment, in which case the solo voice took the top part, the lutenist played the tenor and bass parts, and the alto was omitted altogether. Evidence of this practice exists in some arrangements published by lutenists early in the sixteenth century. Although we should be wary of taking iconographical evidence too literally—artists often imbued the theme of music with allegorical meaning—images like the one in Figure 7.4 suggest that French chansons were also subjected to similar arrangements or ad hoc instrumental performances.

Toward the end of the century, something similar took place in the madrigal repertory as well. Certain pieces published early in the century became so popular that they had a long afterlife in just such a performance tradition, one that allowed for spontaneous substitutions of instruments for voices or more formal transformations into instrumental transcriptions or variations. Vincenzo Giustiniani, a Roman nobleman and the same author who described the *concerto delle donne* in Ferrara (see Vignette, page 128), also wrote about a new style of singing that appeared in the last quarter of the sixteenth century, "chiefly in the manner of one voice singing with accompaniment." We have independent testimony of this vogue in the painting by Caravaggio known as *The Lute Player* (see Figure 7.7), in which the youth is both playing and singing. Scholars have identified the open music book in the painting as a madrigal collection published by Jacques Arcadelt more than fifty years earlier. Indeed, the painting captures the yellowing condition of the book's pages. Although the music's style was by then

old-fashioned compared to more recent examples of this rapidly changing genre, the fact that only the bass part is visible reflects the up-to-date performance practice of the end of the century: the performer would have sung the highest part and its text from memory, perhaps adding ornaments to enhance the melody's expressivity, while rendering on the lute a simple accompaniment improvised from the bass line. This type of performance was undoubtedly intended for more intimate settings in the privacy of one's own chamber or in the company of a few friends.

Caravaggio painted this work in the 1590s when the fashion of singing polyphonic madrigals as solo songs with instrumental accompaniment was in full swing. It was also the decade during which the composer Giulio Caccini was writing a new breed of madrigal expressly for solo voice with instrumental accompaniment (see Chapter 10) and forging the new "monodic" style of the early seventeenth century. Decorative, accompanied singing, then, as practiced by the ladies in Ferrara and as depicted by Caravaggio's *Lute Player*, was an important link between the Renaissance and the Baroque.

Figure 7.7 The Lute Player *(1590s), one of several paintings on musical subjects by Michelangelo Merisi da Caravaggio (1571–1610). The youth is simultaneously playing and singing an Italian madrigal from the early sixteenth century, rendering it as a solo song with lute accompaniment. Solo singing became newly fashionable toward the end of the Renaissance, when Caravaggio was working in Rome.*
(Geoffrey Clements/Corbis.)

TIMELINE   The Age of the Renaissance: Secular Song

Musical Events

1496
Encina publishes *Cancionero* (NAWM 54)

1501
Petrucci publishes *Odhecaton A*

1504–1514
Petrucci issues thirteen frottola collections

1521
Josquin dies

1528
Attaingnant publishes first collection of chansons

1538
Arcadelt publishes *Il bianco e dolce cigno* (NAWM 56)

1558
Zarlino, *Le istituzioni harmoniche*

1566
Rore publishes *Da le belle contrade d'oriente* (NAWM 57)

1580
Concerto delle donne established

1588
Yonge, *Musica transalpina*

1595
Morley publishes *My bonny lass she smileth* (NAWM 63)

1597
Dowland publishes *First Booke of Songes or Ayres*

1599
Marenzio publishes *Solo e pensoso* (NAWM 58)

1601
Morley issues *Triumphes of Oriana*

1605
Monteverdi publishes *Cruda Amarilli* (NAWM 71)

1611
Gesualdo publishes *Io parto* (NAWM 59)

1500 —— **1600**

Historical Events

1504
Michelangelo, *David*

1519–1556
Charles V, Holy Roman emperor

1528
Castiglione, *The Book of the Courtier*

1532
Henry VIII breaks with pope

1543
Copernicus, *On the Revolutions of the Heavenly Spheres*

1558
Elizabeth I becomes queen of England

1590
Spenser, *The Faerie Queene*, Books 1–3

1594
Shakespeare, *Romeo and Juliet*

ca. 1595
Caravaggio, *The Lute Player* (Figure 7.7)

---

prevent any concrete expression of individual words and phrases, Dowland's music matches the dark mood of the poetry.

A great deal of vocal music was performed instrumentally, and instruments had participated with voices in polyphonic textures since the Middle Ages. Throughout the sixteenth century, much instrumental music remained closely associated, in both style and performance, with vocal music. Instruments sometimes doubled or replaced voices in secular and sacred polyphonic compositions. For example, the lowest parts of a madrigal or chanson were often reduced for lute or keyboard, becoming an accompaniment to the melody performed by a solo voice (see In Performance, page 138). Portions of a hymn or sections of the mass (especially the Kyrie and Gloria) alternated with short organ pieces that substituted for the passages normally sung (such as one of the threefold Kyrie or Christe acclamations), incorporating some or all of the chant melody that they replaced. These and other types of instrumental music will be discussed in the next chapter.

Instrumental participation

POSTLUDE

Developments in the sixteenth century included the emergence of new secular genres—madrigal, chanson, and villancico—as the sophisticated Franco-Flemish style encountered native traditions in Italy, France, and Spain. Among the composers in the generation after Josquin, Arcadelt and others in Italy were driven by the spirit of humanism to seek a close rapport between music and text. In both sacred and secular compositions, they shaped the music to follow the sound and syntax of the words and to represent musically the essence of a text's message. Yet they remained faithful to the Renaissance ideal of modal, diatonic counterpoint, equality and independence of voices, full harmony, controlled dissonance, and clarity of form.

Midcentury composers such as Rore sought an even closer bond between music and text, but they tilted the balance—at least in the madrigal—toward the expression of a poem's contrasting feelings and images, sacrificing a certain musical coherence and unity of style. At the same time, the madrigal became more extroverted and declamatory as composers attempted to project the sentiments of the text to a *listening* audience—that is, a social group other than the performers themselves. During the last decades of the century, composers found new ways to express intense passions and the clever conceits of modern poetry. Gesualdo and others explored chromaticism, while Monteverdi (as we shall see) experimented with dissonance, new textures, and speechlike rhythms that led him, in the first decade of the seventeenth century, to write for the rising genre of opera. Because the Italian madrigal was the most forward-looking and innovative of the new sixteenth-century genres, these developments allowed Italian music to dominate in the seventeenth century and made Italy the leader in European music for the first time.

In France, chanson composers turned from writing serious motetlike polyphony to cultivating light, tuneful, homophonic songs. A number of English composers enthusiastically took up the new Italian trends, but the most characteristic genre to emerge from the widespread interest in vocal chamber music in the British Isles was the lute song, or air.

During this same period, instrumental music began to emerge from the long shadow cast by vocal music. In the next chapter we will shed some light on the various categories of instrumental music that became prominent in the sixteenth century.

 Resources for study and review available at wwnorton.com/studyspace

8

The Rise of Instrumental Music

PRELUDE

Why has our history so far been silent about instrumental music? From about 1450 to 1550, distinct styles, genres, and forms of instrumental music were emerging, and publications of instrumental works began to proliferate after about 1550. Yet, because almost all the composers we have studied were trained principally as singers (most were choirboys), they channeled their talents to contribute innovatively to the body of vocal music sung in churches and courts. As adults, even those who made their reputations as composers of secular music aspired to the position of chapelmaster or, in modern terms, choir director—the most prestigious appointment any musician could have from about the twelfth century.

During the Middle Ages, distinct class and educational differences separated singers and composers from instrumentalists, who were less apt to be literate and often were expected to perform in situations in which improvisation was the norm—dancing or ceremonial fanfare for instance. Since performers of instrumental music either improvised or played from memory, their music has not survived or has survived in only an approximate state. What seems like a greater emphasis on instrumental music after 1450 is, perhaps, an illusion: it may be only that more of it was written down once instrumentalists began performing polyphonic works that required coordination of parts. Even so, only a small portion of the instrumental music appearing in manuscripts and printed books during the Renaissance exists today.

Two different tendencies governed the rise of instrumental music in the Renaissance: (1) the exploitation of compositional styles and genres peculiar or idiomatic to the instruments themselves and functioning independently of vocal music; (2) the reliance on preexisting vocal genres, including mere substitution of instruments for voices, instrumental transcriptions and arrangements of vocal compositions, and newly composed instrumental works either based on or otherwise inspired by vocal models.

We can divide the emerging types of instrumental music into five broad categories, which organize this chapter:

· dance music
· arrangements of vocal music

Figure 8.1 Detail from Albrecht Dürer's Jabach Altarpiece (ca. 1504), of two musicians—a shawm player and a drummer. Note that no written music is in evidence.

(Wallraf-Richartz Museum, Cologne. Lebrecht Music & Arts Photo Library.)

- settings of existing melodies
- variations
- abstract instrumental works

Dance Music

Social dancing was widespread and highly valued beginning in the Renaissance, and well-bred people were expected to be accomplished dancers (see In Context, page 143). Performers frequently improvised dance music or played dance tunes from memory, as in earlier times, but with the advent of music printing, many dance pieces were published in collections issued by Petrucci, Attaingnant, and other publishers, for ensemble, lute, or keyboard.

These published dances show that dance music served two very different purposes in the Renaissance. On the one hand, dances for ensemble were functional music, suitable for accompanying dancers. In these pieces, the principal melody is typically in the uppermost part, sometimes highly ornamented but often left plain, allowing the performer to add embellishments. The other parts are mostly homophonic, with little or no contrapuntal interplay. Most dance pieces for solo lute or keyboard, on the other hand, are stylized, intended for the enjoyment of the player or listeners rather than for dancing; these often include more elaborate counterpoint or written-out decoration. This type of dance music was probably the earliest to gain independence from vocal music because it drew attention to the instrument itself. The use of social dance music for solitary music-making is interesting; perhaps the pleasure of solo performance was enhanced by incorporating the familiar

Figure 8.2 Apollo and the Muses was painted by Maerten de Vos (1532–1603) on the underside of a harpsichord lid, a common practice at the time that served to individualize the instrument and enhance its value. In fact, the spinet or virginal within this painting has just such an elaborate scene painted on its lid. Apollo, crowned in laurel, plays a kithara; two of the Muses sing from partbooks while one of them holds a trumpet; others play lutes, virginal, fiddle, tambourine, cornett, and harp.

(Musées Royaux des Beaux-Arts de Belgique, Brussels.)

In Context Social Dance

Dancing is essential in a well-ordered society, because it allows males and females to mingle and observe one another. How else does a lady decide whom to marry? Through dancing, she can tell whether someone is shapely and fit or unattractive and lame, whether he is in good health or has unpleasant breath, and whether he is graceful and attentive or clumsy and awkward.

So writes the dancing master Thoinot Arbeau (pen name for the astronomer Jehan Tabourot) in his *Orchésographie* (1589), the best-known dance treatise of the Renaissance. He offers these views to a young man who has just returned home from a big city where he devoted many years to studying law but where, as he confesses with some regret, he did not make time to learn to dance. Belatedly, the young man has realized that, far from being a frivolous pastime, dancing is a pleasant and profitable activity, one that confers and preserves health provided it is practiced in moderation at suitable times and in appropriate places. It is especially recommended for those who lead sedentary lives, such as students intent upon their books and young women who spend long hours at knitting and needlework.

Most dances of the sixteenth and seventeenth centuries were performed by couples who arranged themselves in rows or circles. Some dances, like the pavane, were elegant and dignified, involving a series of gliding steps as in a stately procession. Others, like the various branles, were executed with sideways or swaying motions. Still others, like the galliard, required such nimble steps and leaps that sometimes the man had to hoist his partner in the air. (With the ladies dressed in the elaborate costumes that we see in Figure 8.3, it is no wonder the women needed help getting off the ground.)

As the dancing master went on to suggest to his new pupil, dancing is also a kind of mute rhetoric by which persons, through movement, can make themselves understood and persuade onlookers that they are gallant or comely and worthy to be acclaimed, admired, and loved. Such attitudes help to explain the importance of social dance in the musical culture of the past. And although the steps may be different, the value and uses of dance in society today remain remarkably unchanged.

Figure 8.3 Ball at the court of Henri III, ca. 1581 (oil on panel) by an anonymous French painter. Three lute players perform at the right while another couple at the left seem about to join the dancers in the center.
(Giraudon/Bridgeman Art Library.)

Figure 8.4 Musicians, *a painting by Reinhold Timm, dated ca. 1620, portrays four musicians playing bass viol, harp, lute, and transverse flute. These instruments are listed in the inventory of the royal chapel of Denmark, where King Christian IV employed a number of virtuosos, one of whom—the famous Irish harpist Darby Scott—may be portrayed here.*
(Musikhistorisk Museum, Copenhagen, Denmark. Carl Clausius Collection.)

rhythms of dance, which carried associations with social interaction or with the physical motions of dancing. Whatever the reason, from the Renaissance to the present, many instrumental works are stylized dances.

Each dance follows a particular meter, tempo, rhythmic pattern, and form, all of which are reflected in pieces composed for it. This particularity of rhythm and form distinguishes each type of dance from the others. Dance pieces feature distinct sections, usually repeated, with two, three, or more sections depending on the dance. Usually the phrase structure is clear and predictable, often in four-measure groups, so that dancers can follow it easily.

These features may be seen in Tielman Susato's *Danserye* (excerpts in NAWM 66), published in Antwerp in 1551. *La morisque* (The Moor, NAWM 66a) is a *basse danse* ("low dance"), a stately couple's dance marked by gracefully raising and lowering the body. The music consists of two sections, each repeated. This structure, called binary form, became standard for dances in the seventeenth and eighteenth centuries.

Susato's print does not specify which instruments should play which parts; the choice was up to the performers. Not until the seventeenth century, when instrumental music began to develop characteristic idioms peculiar to one type of instrument or another, did composers name instruments in their scores. Most wind and string instruments were built in sets or families, covering the

Figure 8.5 Title page of Silvestro Ganassi's instruction book on recorder playing, Opera intitulata Fontegara *(1535). A recorder consort and two singers perform from printed partbooks. In the foreground are two cornetti, and on the wall hang three viols and a lute.*
(Österreichische Nationalbibliotek, Vienna.)

Figure 8.6 Three couples dance a stately pavane at a party in the court of Duke Albrecht IV in Munich. The dancers are accompanied by a flute and drum visible in the left balcony, while the right balcony holds a kettledrum player and two trumpeters, whose instruments are hung up. In the background, the duke and a lady play cards. Engraving by Matthäus Zasinger, ca. 1500.
(Kupferstichkabinett, Dresden.)

Figure 8.7 A couple dancing a galliard, accompanied by pipe and drum, fiddle, and what appears to be a viol.
(Bayerisches Staatsbibliothek, Munich.)

entire range from soprano to bass, so that any of the *Danserye* could theoretically be played entirely by recorders or viols, for example. In England, an ensemble comprised of members of the same family of instruments was known as a consort (see Figure 8.5). More common later in the sixteenth century were mixed ensembles, called in English "broken" consorts, that used instruments from different families (see Figure 8.6). Toward the end of the sixteenth century, however, contrasting sounds became the rule in instrumental music, and the combination of bowed and plucked strings seen in Figure 8.4 became the foundation of the opera orchestra and other ensembles that supported solo-voice textures (see Chapter 10).

Consorts

Renaissance musicians often grouped dances in pairs or threes. A favorite combination was a slow dance in duple meter followed by a fast one in triple meter on the same tune, the music of the second dance being a variation of the first. One such pair, the pavane (or pavan) and galliard, a favorite in sixteenth-century France and England, may be seen in Susato's *Danserye* (NAWM 66b and c). The pavane was a stately dance in three repeated strains (AABBCC), and the more lively galliard followed the same form with a variant of the same melody. Figure 8.6 shows three couples dancing a pavane, clearly more reserved and less vigorous than the galliard shown in Figure 8.7. A similar pairing of dances in slow duple and fast triple meter was the passamezzo and saltarello, popular in Italy and elsewhere.

Pavane and galliard

Full 🔊   Concise 🔊

Arrangements of Vocal Music

Another major source for instrumental music was, paradoxically, vocal music. Instruments frequently doubled or replaced voices in polyphonic compositions. Instrumental ensembles often played vocal works, reading from the

Sources for instrumental music

vocal parts and adding their own embellishments. We have seen that the first book of music published from movable type, Petrucci's *Odhecaton* was primarily a collection of vocal works without their texts, presumably adaptable for instrumental performance. Indeed, vocal music, printed in great quantities and often labeled "for singing and playing." represented the bulk of what instrumentalists played when they were not improvising or accompanying singers or dancers.

Intabulations

Lutenists and keyboard players made arrangements of vocal pieces, either improvised or written down. These arrangements were often written in tablature, so they became known as intabulations. Great numbers of intabulations were published during the sixteenth century, testifying to their popularity. Since the sounds of plucked instruments suffer rapid decay, arrangers had to recast the original work in a manner idiomatic to the instrument. The intabulations by Spanish composer Luys de Narváez (fl. 1526–49) demonstrate that such works are much closer to inventive variations than to simple transcriptions, making intabulations yet another instance of the Renaissance tendency to rework existing music. In his version of Josquin's *Mille regretz* (NAWM 68a), published in 1538, Narváez preserves the four-voice texture of the original (NAWM 43) but introduces runs, turns, and other figures, called "divisions" or "diminutions" in the terminology of the time, that enliven the rhythm and sustain the listener's interest. This figural style became characteristic of the lute and other plucked string instruments, including some keyboards, as a means of sustaining the melodic and rhythmic motion of their tones.

Settings of Existing Melodies

Instrumental music, like vocal music, sometimes incorporated existing melodies. Composers in the late fifteenth and early sixteenth centuries wrote many instrumental settings of chanson melodies; these pieces, among the first written chamber music, could be played as background music for other activities or by amateurs for their own pleasure. Church organists often improvised or composed settings of Gregorian chant or other liturgical melodies for use in services, replacing portions that were normally sung.

Chant settings and organ masses

In Catholic services, chants traditionally performed by two half-choirs alternating segments or verses, such as psalms, could instead alternate between the choir singing chant and the organ playing a cantus-firmus setting or paraphrase. Such settings of short segments of chant were called *organ verses* or *versets*. Example 8.1 shows the beginning of a Kyrie by organist-composer

Example 8.1 Cavazzoni, opening of Kyrie I from Missa Apostolorum

Full   Concise

Girolamo Cavazzoni with the chant melody (from NAWM 3b) paraphrased in the upper voice; later other voices carry phrases of the chant as well. This Kyrie is part of an organ mass, a compilation of all the sections of the mass for which the organ would play. Its texture, more contrapuntal than figural, betrays the fact that, unlike plucked instruments, the organ could better reproduce the complex polyphonic lines of vocal music because its sound did not decay.

In Lutheran churches, verses of hymns could alternate between the congregation singing in unison and a polyphonic setting for choir or organ. Organists typically improvised settings for their verses, but from the 1570s on, collections of hymn settings for organ appeared. These pieces varied in style, from harmonizations to more elaborate cantus-firmus settings or embellished paraphrases. More will be said about this genre of instrumental music in Chapter 9.

Hymn settings for organ

Variations

Improvising on a tune to accompany dancing has ancient roots, but the compositional structure known as variation form is a sixteenth-century invention, used for independent instrumental pieces rather than as accompaniment for dance. Variations combine change with repetition, taking a given element—an existing or newly composed tune, bass line, harmonic plan, melody with accompaniment, or other musical subject—and presenting an uninterrupted series of variants on that element. The goal was to showcase the variety that could be achieved by embellishing a basic idea and, often, to provide a technical challenge as the figuration becomes increasingly complex. The result, however, was a very practical solution to the problem of how to achieve length and coherence in a piece without words. For this reason, perhaps, variation became the formal structure most favored by composers of instrumental music in the early seventeenth century.

Some of the earliest books of printed music include variations on dance tunes written specifically for the lute. Pavane variations, for example, featured either a varied repetition of each strain (AA'BB'CC') or several variations of a single strain. The lute, shown in Figure 7.7, was the most popular household instrument in the sixteenth century and continued to be a mainstay of the basso-continuo ensemble in the seventeenth century. The standard lute had a pear-shaped body with a rounded back, and a long neck with a flat fingerboard at the end of which a pegbox (where the strings attached to tuning pegs) turned back at a right angle. It had one single and five double strings, usually tuned G–c–f–a–d'–g', which were plucked with the fingers. Frets, made of strips of leather wound around the neck, marked where the player stopped the string with the fingers of the left hand to raise the pitch one or more semitones. A skilled player could produce a great variety of effects, from melodies, runs, and ornaments of all kinds to chords and counterpoint. The instrument played a variety of roles: lutenists accompanied singing, played in ensembles, and performed solos.

The lute

By the sixteenth century, the lute, introduced by the Arabs into Spain, had been known in Europe for almost five hundred years. Its very name was derived from the Arabic al-'ud. Perhaps because of its non-European origins, much of the lute's solo repertory developed independently of mainstream vocal music and became the first to harbor a style that was idiomatic to the instrument; what

Example 8.2 Luys de Narváez, "Guárdame las vacas," structural outline of melody and bass

Vihuela

sounded and felt "natural" on the lute could not easily be played or imitated on another instrument and was certainly out of the realm of the voice. This is evident even from its special type of notation, based not on pitch, as vocal notation is, but rather on touch. Closely related to the lute was the Spanish vihuela, which had a flat back and guitar-shaped body.

Full 🔊   Concise 🔊

Lute performers and composers also created sets of variations on standard airs for singing poetry, such as the Italian romanesca and Ruggiero, or the Spanish tune *Guárdame las vacas* (see Example 8.2), which feature a spare melodic outline over a standard bass progression. The 1538 collection of works for vihuela by Spanish composer Luys de Narváez, *Los seys libros del Delphin* (The Six Books of the Dauphin), contains the first published sets of variations (called *diferencias* in Spanish), including "*Guárdame las vacas*" (NAWM 68b). In the first examples of the genre, ideas that were to characterize variation form for the next five centuries are already in place: each variation preserves the phrase structure, harmonic plan, and cadences of the theme while recasting the melody with a new figuration that distinguishes it from the other variations.

The variation enjoyed an extraordinary flowering in the late sixteenth and early seventeenth centuries among a group of English keyboard composers known as the English virginalists, after the name of their instrument, which was a member of the harpsichord family. (As such, its robust sound was produced by using the keys to activate quills that plucked the strings.) The English virginalists typically used dances or familiar songs of the time as themes for variation. Their interest in varying melodies distinguishes the English from earlier Spanish and Italian composers, who focused more on bass patterns and bare melodic outlines. The songs used were generally short, simple, and regular in phrasing as in *John come kiss me now*, a tune used by the leading English composer William Byrd (ca. 1540–1623; see Biography, page 149) as the basis for a set of variations. In Byrd's imaginative treatment (NAWM 69) the melody is presented intact in every variation, but passes from the upper to the lower register, from the right to the left hand, and even changes from duple to triple meter at one point. Sometimes it is broken up by decorative figuration, so that its original profile disappears only to reemerge before the closing cadence. As in most variation sets, each presentation of the tune uses only one type of figuration, but the rhythmic animation increases as the work progresses, as does the virtuosity demanded of the player, until, typically, the composer puts on the brakes in order to end the set with a slower, final variation. Byrd is credited with having founded the English virginal school of composition and bringing a new flexibility and subtlety to the variation form. Some of his stylized dance variations appear in the first published collection of music for virginal, *Parthenia* (1613), shown in Figure 8.8. Byrd was an extremely innovative and versatile musician; in Chapter 9 we will encounter him again as a composer of sacred vocal music.

Figure 8.8 Title page of Parthenia; or, The Maydenhead, *a collection of music for virginal by William Byrd and other English keyboard composers presented to Princess Elizabeth on her wedding in 1613. Parthenia were Greek maidens' choral dances, so both the title and subtitle allude whimsically to the bride, the keyboard instrument's name, and the fact that this was the first such collection ever printed.*

(Wikimedia Commons.)

Figure 8.9. Engraving after Hendrik Goltzius (1558–1617) of Saint Cecilia playing the organ in the company of two singing angels. The association between young women and keyboard playing was affirmed by images of the newly popular Saint Cecilia, a fifth-century virgin martyr who became the patron saint of music. Depictions such as this engraving, which obviously inspired the title page of Parthenia *(Figure 8.8), proliferated during the seventeenth century as both the saint's stature and the status of instrumental music grew. (See also Figure 12.11, a later painting by Poussin.)*
(Bibliothèque Nationale, Paris.)

William Byrd (ca. 1540–1623)

The most important among the many keyboard composers active in England in the late sixteenth and early seventeenth centuries, William Byrd probably learned music as a choirboy in the royal chapel in London, his native city, during the reign of Catholic Queen Mary ("Bloody Mary"). He began writing music in his teens and was appointed organist and choirmaster of Lincoln Cathedral in 1563. About ten years later, he moved back to London after being named a Gentleman of the Chapel Royal, a post he held for the rest of his life despite his remaining Catholic during the long Protestant reign of Elizabeth I, when disloyalty to the established religion was tantamount to treason. His musical career reflected the political and religious controversies of the time in that he wrote a large amount of both Anglican church music and Latin masses and motets for the Roman rite (see Chapter 9).

In 1575, Byrd and his former teacher, Thomas Tallis, were granted a monopoly for music printing in England, which Byrd continued to control after Tallis's death. Byrd left his position at court in 1593 and moved with his family to a small town in Essex, where he spent the remaining thirty years of his life composing sacred and secular music in almost every medium. But he managed to retain his membership in the royal chapel and its benefits even from a distance, probably an indication of the high

Figure 8.10 William Byrd in an engraving by Van der Gucht.
(Colouriser AL/Lebrecht.)

esteem in which he was held. One modern scholar praises Byrd in exuberant terms as a composer of keyboard music: "He kindled English virginal music from the driest of dry wood to a splendid blaze that crackled on [in his successors] and even lit some sparks on the Continent."[1]

Major works: Pavanes, Galliards, and other types of variations for keyboard; three fantasias and other works for instrumental consort; Anglican church music, including a Great Service, three Short Services, and many anthems; three Latin masses; 109 settings of items from the Mass Proper (*Gradualia*); dozens of madrigals and songs, both secular and sacred.

1. Joseph Kerman, "William Byrd," *Grove Music Online* (New York: Oxford University Press, 2013)

Abstract Instrumental Works

The instrumental genres we have seen so far are all based on dance patterns or derived from song, the two traditional wellsprings of music. The remaining instrumental genres may be viewed as abstract because they cultivated several types of music that were truly independent of dance rhythms or borrowed tunes. Most of these developed from habits of improvising figuration on polyphonic instruments such as lute or keyboard, while others drew on imitative textures derived from vocal music. Such pieces could be played or listened to for their own sake, and improvisers and composers frequently employed unusual or highly expressive effects to attract listeners' attention.

Introductory and improvisatory pieces

Performers on keyboard and lute often had reason to improvise: to introduce a song, to fill time during a church service, to establish the mode of a subsequent chant or hymn, to test the tuning of a lute, or to help quiet audiences before an event. Compositions that resemble such improvisations rank among the earliest examples of solo instrumental music and became mainstays of the repertory for solo players. Such pieces were given a variety of names, including toccata, prelude, fantasia, and ricercare. Not based on any preexisting melody, they unfold freely, with varying textures and musical ideas. They served the same function as an introduction to a speech, preparing the listener and establishing the tonality for what followed. Examples of these genres will be explored in Chapter 11.

Canzona

The Italian canzona or canzon became one of the leading genres of contrapuntal instrumental music in the late sixteenth century, alongside the fantasia and ricercare, but had a different origin. The earliest pieces called canzonas were transcriptions of French chansons, after which the canzona was named. By midcentury, composers were writing canzonas that thoroughly reworked chansons rather than simply embellishing them. Newly composed canzonas in the style of an imitative French chanson appeared by 1580, first for ensemble and then for organ. Canzonas were light, fast-moving, and strongly rhythmic, with a fairly simple contrapuntal texture. From the chanson, composers adopted the typical opening rhythmic figure that occurs in most canzonas: long–short–short. Like chansons, canzonas often feature a series of themes that differ from one another in melodic outline and rhythm. Each serves as the basis of its own section, resulting in a series of contrasting sections.

Ensemble canzonas

The most celebrated composer of ensemble canzonas was Giovanni Gabrieli (ca. 1555–1612), organist and supervisor of instrumental music at Saint Mark's church in Venice (see In Context, page 151). His splendid polychoral motets (to be discussed in Chapter 11), with their *cori spezzati* ("divided choirs"), and his innovative instrumental works, both shaped by the rich musical environment of Venice, employed all the resources available at the church, which had a long tradition of organ and instrumental music.

Full 🔊

Gabrieli and other Venetian composers applied the idea of divided choirs to their instrumental works. The *Canzon septimi toni a 8* (Canzona in Mode 7 in Eight Parts, NAWM 70) from Gabrieli's *Sacrae symphoniae* (Sacred Symphonies, 1597) resembles a double-chorus motet for two groups of four instruments, with organ accompaniment. Like other canzonas, it presents a series of contrasting sections, some imitative, others more homophonic. The two instrumental groups alternate long passages, engage in more rapid dialogue, and sometimes play together, especially at the end. The canzona had no standard form; in this case, its form is defined by a repeating section that occurs three times.

In Context Venice and Saint Mark's Church

Venice, the second most important Italian city after Rome, was an independent state with its own empire of extensive territories on the Italian peninsula. Nominally a republic, it was actually an oligarchy run by several important families, with an elected leader called the doge (Venetian for "duke"). Because Venice was a city of merchants and the chief port for trade with the East, it had accumulated enormous wealth, power, and splendor by the fifteenth century. Despite wars and other misfortunes in the sixteenth century, the government still had plenty of money and spent lavishly on public spectacle, music, and art; this type of cultural propaganda was meant to project Venice's lingering glory, rally the public behind the state, and intimidate potential enemies at home and abroad.

The center of Venetian musical culture was the great eleventh-century Church of St. Mark, whose Byzantine domes, spacious interior, bright gold mosaics, and ostentatious altarpiece of solid gold and precious jewels proclaimed the city's wealth and close links to the East. Although San Marco was the private chapel of the doge, many civic and religious ceremonies took place each month in the church and in the vast piazza in front of it, like the procession depicted in Figure 8.11. On each occasion, Mass and Vespers were celebrated with great pomp and elaborate music.

One of the special features of the church's interior was that it had not one but three organs, separated spatially: two were located in lofts on either side of the altar, and another in the nave at ground level. Renowned performers, chosen after stringent examination, served as organists, including Andrea Gabrieli (ca. 1532–1585) and his nephew Giovanni Gabrieli (ca. 1555–1612). Beginning in 1568, a first-rate permanent ensemble of instrumentalists was assembled, centering on brass instruments such as cornets and sackbuts (earlier versions of trumpets and trombones), which were especially appropriate for processions and other outdoor ceremonial music, but also including violin and bassoon. Additional players were hired on major feast days, when as many as two dozen instrumentalists performed, alone or together with the choir of twenty to thirty voices. No wonder the position of music director (choirmaster)—held by Willaert, Rore, Zarlino, and Andrea Gabrieli in the sixteenth century, and Giovanni Gabrieli from 1585 until his death in 1612—was the most coveted musical post in all Italy!

Figure 8.11 Procession in Piazza San Marco (1496) *by Gentile Bellini, which includes singers and instruments, with Saint Mark's church in the background.*
(Erich Lessing/Art Resource, NY.)

TIMELINE The Renaissance: The Rise of Instrumental Music

Musical Events

1501
Petrucci, *Odhecaton A*

ca. 1538
Luys de Narváez, *Los seys Libros del Delphin* (NAWM 68)

ca. 1551
Tielman Susato, *Danserye* (NAWM 66)

1558
Zarlino, *Le istitutioni harmoniche*

1585–1612
Giovanni Gabrieli at Saint Mark's, Venice

1589
Thoinot Arbeau, *Orchésographie*

1597
Gabrieli, *Sacrae symphoniae* (NAWM 70)

1613
William Byrd, *John come kiss me now* (NAWM 69)

1500		1600

Historical Events

1504
Michelangelo, David

1528
Castiglione, *The Book of the Courtier*

1532
Henry VIII breaks with pope

1543
Copernicus, *On the Revolution of the Heavenly Spheres*

1553–58
Reign of Mary I of England restores Catholicism

1558
Elizabeth I becomes queen of England

1594
Shakespeare, *Romeo and Juliet*

ca. 1595
Caravaggio, *The Lute Player* (Figure 7.6)

POSTLUDE

Instrumental music came into its own during the Renaissance. By the mid-sixteenth century, independent genres of written instrumental music could be distinguished by their functions and formal procedures—dance, variations, and others. Some composers such as Narváez specialized in writing instrumental music, particularly for vihuela and lute, but composers of vocal music such as Byrd and Gabrieli also wrote important works for solo or ensemble instruments. Around 1600, English lute and keyboard composers would take the lead in instrumental writing until a new generation of Italian composers appeared in the seventeenth century who devoted their attention for the first time completely to writing instrumental music.

 Resources for study and review available at wwnorton.com/studyspace

Sacred Music in the Era of the Reformation

PRELUDE

Begun as a theological dispute, the Reformation was set in motion by Martin Luther in 1517 and mushroomed into a rebellion against the authority of the Catholic Church and the spiritual leadership of Rome, the center of Western Christianity. The liturgical changes that eventually ensued naturally brought about musical changes, which differed from country to country according to the degree of reform advocated by the various Protestant leaders: Luther in Germany; Jean Calvin and his followers in France, the Low Countries, and Switzerland; and King Henry VIII in England.

At first, the music of the Reformation in Germany, written by Lutheran composers, remained very close to the traditional Catholic sources and styles of plainsong and polyphony. Some music retained the original Latin texts, other works used German translations, and still others had new German texts fitted to old melodies; these works were called contrafacta (sing. contrafactum). The Lutheran Church's most distinctive and important musical innovation became the strophic hymn—called Choral or Kirchenlied (church song) in German and chorale in English—intended for congregational singing in unison. Just as plainchant was the basis for musical expansion and elaboration for Catholic composers, so, too, the repertory of chorales became a foundational treasury for a great deal of Lutheran church music from the sixteenth century until the time of Johann Sebastian Bach (1685–1750) and beyond.

Reformation church music outside Germany developed along similar lines, except that Calvin and leaders of other Protestant sects opposed certain elements of Catholic ceremony much more strongly than Luther had. They distrusted the allure of art in places of worship and in services, and prohibited singing of texts not found in the Bible. As a result, the only notable contributions to music from the Calvinist churches were their Psalters—rhymed metrical translations of the Book of Psalms set to newly composed melodies or, in many cases, to tunes of popular origin or plainchant. Since the Calvinists discouraged liturgical elaboration in general, they seldom expanded the Psalter tunes into larger vocal or instrumental forms. In England, under Henry VIII, the Anglican Church's separation from Rome in 1534 occurred more for political than for religious reasons, so English church music was less affected and remained closer to Catholic musical traditions (except that English replaced Latin in the liturgy).

The Catholic Church met the defection of the Protestant reformers by starting its own program of internal reform, known as the Catholic Reformation. This movement not only resulted in many liturgical reforms, it also reaffirmed the power of music to affect the hearts and minds of the faithful through an appropriate style of sacred polyphony. At the same time, a broader movement, known as the Counter-Reformation, attempted to win back those who had left the Catholic Church, appealing to their senses through the sheer beauty of its liturgy, religious art, and ceremonial music. Among all the Catholic composers of sacred music to succeed in this strategy, the Roman Giovanni Pierluigi da Palestrina (1525/6–1594) was the most important. Not only did he capture the essence of the musical Counter-Reformation, but his style became a model for church-music composition—one that has served teachers and students of counterpoint to this day.

The Music of the Reformation in Germany

Luther's views

The instigator of the Reformation was Martin Luther, a priest and professor of biblical theology at the University of Wittenberg. His approach to theology was influenced by his humanistic education, which taught him to rely on reason, on direct experience, and on his own reading of Scripture rather than on received authority. Study of the Bible led Luther to conclude that God's justice consists not in rewarding people for good deeds or punishing them for sins, but in offering salvation through faith alone. His views contradicted Catholic doctrine, which held that religious rituals, penance, and good works were necessary for the absolution of sin. Luther also insisted that religious authority was derived from Scripture alone, so that if a belief or practice had no basis in the Bible it could not be true. This notion challenged the authority of the Church, which had developed a rich tapestry of teachings and practices that rested on tradition rather than Scripture.

Lutheran church music

The central position of music in the Lutheran Church reflects Luther's own convictions. He was a singer, a composer of some skill, and a great admirer of Franco-Flemish polyphony, especially the works of Josquin des Prez. Like Plato and Aristotle, he believed strongly in the educational and ethical power of music and wanted the entire congregation to participate in the text and music of the services in order for them to experience their faith through direct contact with Scripture. Although he altered the words of the liturgy to conform to his own views on certain theological points, he kept much of the Catholic liturgy, some in German translation and some in Latin, a language he considered valuable for educating the young.

German Mass

In applying Luther's beliefs to local conditions, congregations all over Germany developed a number of usages. Large churches with trained choirs kept much of the Latin liturgy and its polyphonic music. Smaller congregations adopted a German Mass (*Deudsche Messe*), published by Luther in 1526, which followed the main outline of the Roman Mass but differed from it in many details and replaced most elements of the Proper and Ordinary with German hymns or chorales (from *Choral*, German for "chant").

Chorale

Just as most Catholic church music developed from plainsong enriched by harmony and counterpoint and reworked into larger musical forms, so Lutheran church music largely grew out of the chorale. As in plainsong, the chorale originally consisted of only two elements—a text and a tune. The congregation learned the tenets of their faith and celebrated the yearly cycle of religious holidays by singing these easily memorized hymns, comprised of simple, metrical tunes and rhyming verses. Many chorales were newly composed; Luther himself wrote many texts and some melodies. The best known is *Ein feste Burg ist unser Gott* (A mighty fortress is our God, 1529, NAWM 46c), shown in Example 9.1, which became the anthem of the Reformation. Adaptations of secular and devotional songs or Latin chants supplied an even larger number of chorale tunes. Thus, the Easter sequence *Victimae paschali laudes* (NAWM 5), for example, provided the model for *Christ lag in Todesbanden* (Christ lay in the bonds of death).

Luther and his colleagues used many well-known secular tunes for chorales, substituting religious words. The resulting compositions, called contrafacta (Latin for "counterfeits"), often had wholly new texts but sometimes included clever reworkings of the existing poems. The most famous contrafactum (but not by Luther) is *O Welt, ich muss dich lassen* (O world, I must leave you), based on the Lied *Innsbruck, ich muss dich lassen* (NAWM 41).

Lutheran composers soon began to write polyphonic settings of chorales, using a variety of approaches borrowed from existing genres. Some composers used the older technique of the German Lied, placing the unaltered chorale tune in long notes in the tenor and surrounding it with three or more free-flowing parts, as in the setting by Luther's collaborator Johann Walter (1496–1570; see NAWM 46d). Others developed each phrase of the chorale imitatively in all voices in the manner of Franco-Flemish motets. Still others wrote in a simple, almost chordal style, with the tune in the soprano instead of the tenor; this became the preferred arrangement.

The choir, sometimes doubled by instruments, commonly alternated chorale stanzas sung in four parts with the congregation, which sang in unison without accompaniment. After 1600, it became customary to have all the parts played on the organ, while the congregation sang all the verses of the tune. This style of harmonization and performance has continued to the present and is evident in almost all Protestant hymnbooks. More elaborate treatments of the chorale—for example, for organ solo or for trained choir—also became part of the Lutheran church-music repertory in Germany. By the end of the sixteenth century, some Protestant composers created chorale motets or free polyphonic compositions around the traditional melodies, incorporating personal interpretations and pictorial details in the manner of the Latin motet. Others used chorale tunes as the basis for organ improvisations. Both traditions culminated more than a hundred years later in the keyboard chorale preludes and vocal chorale fantasias of J. S. Bach.

Polyphonic chorale settings

Example 9.1 Martin Luther, Ein feste Burg

A mighty fortress is our God, a good defense and weapon. He helps us free from all afflictions that have now befallen us. The old, evil enemy now means to deal with us seriously; great power and much cunning are his cruel armaments; on Earth is not his equal.

Reformation Church Music outside Germany

Calvin's views

Outside Germany and Scandinavia, Protestantism took different forms. The largest branch was led by Jean Calvin who, like Luther, rejected papal authority and embraced justification through faith alone. But Calvin believed that some people are predestined for salvation, others for damnation. He also held that all aspects of life should fall under God's law as given in the Bible, requiring of his followers lives of constant piety, uprightness, and work. From his center at Geneva, missionaries spread Calvinism across Switzerland and to other lands, establishing the Dutch Reformed Church in the Netherlands, the Presbyterian Church in Scotland, the Puritans in England, and the Huguenots in France.

Seeking to focus worship on God alone, Calvin stripped churches and services of everything that might distract worshipers with worldly pleasures, including decorations, paintings, stained-glass windows, vestments, colorful ceremony, incense, organs and other musical instruments, and elaborate polyphony. Figure 9.1 shows how spare Calvinist churches were. Consequently, the only music heard in the Calvinists' worship service was the singing of psalms to monophonic tunes published in collections called Psalters. (See Vignette, page 157.) The principal French Psalter was published in 1562, with all 150 psalm texts translated into strophic, rhyming, and metrical verse, and set to melodies selected or composed by Loys Bourgeois (ca. 1510–ca. 1561). The melodies move mostly by step, giving them an austere simplicity. The best known is the tune for Psalm 134 (NAWM 47a), shown in Example 9.2. Because it was used in English Psalters for Psalm 100, it became known as "Old Hundredth."

French Psalter

Full 🔊

Like Lutherans, Calvinists originally sang at church services only in unaccompanied unison. For devotional use at home, they availed themselves of settings in four or more parts, with the tune in either the tenor or the soprano, sometimes in simple chordal style and sometimes in fairly elaborate motetlike arrangements.

The most prominent French composers of psalm settings were Claude Goudimel (ca. 1520–1572) and Claude Le Jeune (ca. 1528–1600); the leading Netherlandish composer was Jan Pieterszoon Sweelinck (1562–1621). Translations of the French Psalter appeared in Germany, Holland, England, and Scotland, and the Reformed Churches in those countries took over many of the French tunes. The Germans adapted Psalter melodies for use as chorales. The French model also influenced the most important English Psalter of the sixteenth century; and the Psalter brought by the Pilgrims to New England in 1620 was a combination of the English and the French-Dutch traditions.

Example 9.2 Original melody from the French Psalter of 1562, with a later adaptation

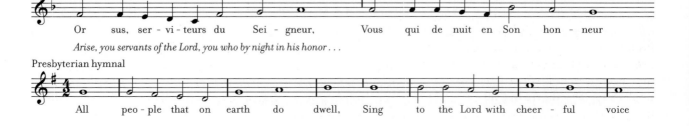

Psalm 134

Or sus, ser - vi - teurs du Sei - gneur, Vous qui de nuit en Son hon - neur

Arise, you servants of the Lord, you who by night in his honor . . .

Presbyterian hymnal

All peo - ple that on earth do dwell, Sing to the Lord with cheer - ful voice

VIGNETTE Jean Calvin on Singing Psalms

In his preface to the psalter published at Geneva in 1542, Calvin detailed his views for how music should be used in services, and why only psalms sung by the entire congregation were appropriate.

We know by experience that song has great force and vigor to move and inflame people's hearts to invoke and praise God with a more vehement and ardent zeal. Care must always be taken that the song be not light and frivolous but have weight and majesty, as Saint Augustine says, and there is likewise a great difference between the music one makes to entertain people at table and in their homes, and the psalms that are sung in the Church in the presence of God and the angels. . . .

It is true that, as Saint Paul says, every evil word corrupts good manners, but when it has the melody with it, it pierces the heart much more strongly and enters within; as wine is poured into the cask with

a funnel, so venom and corruption are distilled to the very depths of the heart by melody. Now what is there to do? The solution is to have songs not merely honest but also holy, which will be like spurs to incite us to pray and praise God, and to meditate on God's works in order to love, fear, honor, and glorify God. Now what Saint Augustine says is true—that we cannot sing songs worthy of God save what we have received from God. Wherefore, although we look far and wide and search in every land, we will not find better songs nor songs better suited to that end than the Psalms of David, which the Holy Spirit made and uttered through him. And for this reason, when we sing them we may be certain that God puts the words in our mouths as if God sang in us to exalt God's glory.

Jean Calvin, "Epistle to the Reader," in the Geneva Psalter (1542). Adapted from the translation by Oliver Strunk, in *Source Readings in Music History*, rev. ed. by Leo Treitler (New York: Norton, 1998), vol. 3, pp. 87–89.

The third major branch of Protestantism in the sixteenth century was the Church of England, whose origins lay more in politics than in doctrine. King Henry VIII (r. 1509–1547; see Figure 9.2) was married to Catherine of Aragon, daughter of Ferdinand and Isabella of Spain. Henry needed a male heir, but their only surviving child was a daughter, Mary. With Catherine past childbearing age, in 1527 Henry sought an annulment so he could marry Anne Boleyn. The pope could not grant this without offending Catherine's nephew, Emperor Charles V, so in 1534 Henry persuaded Parliament to separate from Rome and name Henry head of the Church of England.

The Church of England remained Catholic in doctrine under Henry. But during the brief reign of Edward VI (r. 1547–1553), Henry's son by his third wife, Jane Seymour, the Church adopted Protestant doctrines, reflecting Edward's Protestant upbringing and the views of the regents who governed in his name. English replaced Latin in the service, and in 1549 the *Book of Common Prayer* was

Figure 9.1 The Calvinist Temple at Lyon in a 1564 painting that shows the austerity of Calvinist churches. The preacher wears no elaborate vestments, there is no choir or altar, the focus is on the pulpit, and the only decorations are coats of arms in the windows and above the pulpit. (Bibliothèque Publique et Universaire, Geneva. Erich Lessing/Art Resource, NY.)

*Figure 9.2 Henry VIII, in a portrait by
Hans Holbein the Younger.*
(National Trust/Art Resource, NY.)

adopted as the only prayerbook permitted for public use. Edward's early death at the age of fifteen brought to the throne his half sister, Mary (r. 1553–1558). Loyal to her mother, Catherine, and to the pope, she restored Catholicism, but met considerable resistance. She was succeeded by Elizabeth I (r. 1558–1603; see Figure 7.5), Henry's daughter by Anne Boleyn, who again broke from the papacy and brought back the liturgical reforms instituted under Edward, yet tolerated Catholicism so long as its adherents conducted their services in private and remained loyal to her as queen. She sought to steer a middle course, compromising enough on doctrine to make the Church of England hospitable to some Catholics as well as Protestants. The present-day Anglican Church (including the Episcopal Church in the United States) continues to blend Catholic and Protestant elements in theology, ritual, and music.

All these events had repercussions for church music. New forms were created for services in English, but Latin motets and masses were composed during the reigns of Henry, Mary, and even Elizabeth, because the tradition of Latin sacred polyphony was valued for its links to the past and its musical splendors.

Even though English composers were aware of developments in Continental music, they worked in relative isolation, only gradually adopting the prevailing international style of imitative counterpoint. Consequently, many works illustrate the English preference for full textures, display a strong feeling for the harmonic dimension of music, and achieve textural variety through the use of contrasting voice groups. Long melismas executed simultaneously in all voices often resulted in passages of extraordinary beauty and expressiveness.

Tallis

Toward the middle of the century, the leading English composer was Thomas Tallis (ca. 1505–1585), whose career reflects the religious upheavals and bewildering political changes that influenced English church music in this period. Historians have disagreed about Tallis's religious conviction, but his long association with William Byrd, who never relinquished his Catholic faith, suggests that he remained Catholic. However, Tallis's output implies that he was simply a pragmatist who avoided religious controversy: under Henry VIII, Tallis wrote Latin masses (including one parody mass) and motets. Under Edward VI, he composed music for the Anglican service and motets to English texts (such as *If ye love me*, c. 1546–1549, NAWM 48). During the reign of Catholic Queen Mary, he wrote a number of Latin hymns, and his large seven-voice mass *Puer nobis* probably also dates to those years. Under Queen Elizabeth, Tallis composed music to both Latin and English words. His late works include two sets of Lamentations, among the most eloquent surviving settings of these verses from the Hebrew Scriptures used as responsories in the Office of Holy Week. One remarkable feature of all his compositions (and of much sixteenth-century English music) is the obvious vocal quality of the melodies. So closely is the melodic curve wedded to the natural inflection of speech and so imaginatively does it project the content of the words, they strike the listener not as an interplay of abstract musical lines, but as a profusion of human voices.

Full 🔊

Anglican Church music

The principal forms of Anglican music are the Service and the anthem (from the Latin "antiphon"). A complete Service consists of the music for fixed portions of Morning and Evening Prayer (corresponding to the Catholic Matins and Vespers) and for Holy Communion (which corresponds to the Mass). Music for a Great Service is contrapuntal and melismatic, for a Short Service, chordal and syllabic—but there is no difference in content between the two. One of the finest examples of Anglican church music remains the Great Service of William Byrd (see page 149).

The Counter-Reformation

In the wake of the Protestant Reformation and the capture and sack of Rome by Charles V's imperial forces and an army of mainly Lutheran soldiers (1527), advocates of internal reform came to power in the Catholic Church. Their main tool of change was the Council of Trent, which met intermittently in Trent (a city in northern Italy) between 1545 and 1563 to find ways to purge the Church of abuses and laxities. In the discussions of liturgical reform, church music took up only a small part of the council's time, but it was the subject of serious complaints. Some contended that the Mass was profaned when its music was based on secular cantus firmi or chansons. Others argued that complicated polyphony made it impossible to understand the words, even if they were pronounced correctly—and often they were not. Musicians were accused of using instruments inappropriately, of being careless in their duties, and of having an irreverent attitude. Despite these charges, the Council of Trent's final pronouncement on church music was extremely general. Neither polyphony nor the imitation of secular models was specifically forbidden. The council merely banished from the Church everything "lascivious or impure" and left the task of implementing the directive to the local bishops.

Meanwhile, in those countries that remained Catholic, music was changed relatively little by the religious turbulence of the sixteenth century and even less by the Council of Trent. The Renaissance was still in full swing, and Flemish composers remained in prominent positions all over Europe. Among the best known was Adrian Willaert (ca. 1490–1562; see Figure 9.3), whose career took him to Rome, Ferrara, Milan, and finally Venice, where he was director of music at the principal church, Saint Mark's, for thirty-five years. There he trained many eminent Italian musicians, including the theorist Gioseffo Zarlino and influenced composers such as Cipriano de Rore and Nicola Vicentino (see Chapter 7). With his long career in Italy, Willaert was most affected by the humanist movement and the attention it paid to the relationship between music and words. Like the Italian madrigalists who followed in his footsteps, he carefully molded his music to the pronunciation of the words by matching long notes to accented syllables, and planned his compositions to suit the structure and meaning of the text in every detail. For example, he never allowed a rest to interrupt a word or thought within a phrase, and he brought the voices to a cadence only at the end of a unit of text. Willaert was also one of the first composers to insist that his printer place the syllables exactly under their corresponding notes rather than spread them anywhere within the phrase.

Palestrina

Although the concern for the intelligibility of words in polyphonic music was long-standing among humanists and churchmen alike (see Vignette, page 93), it now became linked to Giovanni Pierluigi da Palestrina (1525/6–1594; see Biography, page 160), the premier Italian composer of church music in the sixteenth century. According to a legend already circulating soon after his death, Palestrina saved

Council of Trent

Willaert

Figure 9.3 Woodcut portrait of the aged composer Adrian Willaert, published as the frontispiece to the collection of his motets and madrigals, Musica Nova, *issued in 1559.* (Bibliothèque Royale de Belgique.)

Giovanni Pierluigi da Palestrina (1525/6–1594)

Palestrina's name is legendary among church musicians for his almost exclusive concentration on sacred music and for his lifelong loyalty to Rome and the goals of the Counter-Reformation. As a result, the "Palestrina style" became the standard for polyphonic church music in later ages.

Born near Rome in the small town of Palestrina, he served as a choirboy and received his musical education at the church of Santa Maria Maggiore in Rome. After seven years as organist and choirmaster in Palestrina (1544–1551), he returned to Rome under the patronage of Pope Julius III and became choirmaster of the Julian Chapel at Saint Peter's (1551–1555). In 1555, he was briefly a singer in the Sistine Chapel choir but had to relinquish the honor because he was married. He spent the remaining forty years of his career in Rome as choirmaster at two important churches: Saint John Lateran (1555–1560) and Santa Maria Maggiore (1561–1566). He also taught music at the new Jesuit seminary and eventually returned to his position at the Julian Chapel (1571–1594).

Palestrina composed more masses than any other composer. In the dedication to his *Second Book of Masses* (1567), Palestrina claimed:

> "I . . . have considered it my task . . . to bend all my knowledge, effort, and industry . . . to adorn the holy sacrifice of the Mass in a new manner. I have, therefore, worked out these masses with the greatest possible care, to do honor to the worship of almighty God. . . ."[1]

Figure 9.4 Giovanni Pierluigi da Palestrina in a contemporary painting, 1594. (Istituto dei Padri dell'Oratorio, Rome. Scala/Art Resource, NY.)

His main secular works are madrigals. Late in life, he confessed that he "blushed and grieved" to have written music for love poems.

After the Council of Trent ordered changes in the liturgy, Palestrina and a colleague were commissioned to revise the official chant books to conform to the new liturgy and purge the chants of "barbarisms, obscurities, contrarieties, and superfluities." The revised edition, which arbitrarily eliminated melismatic passages, was completed by others after Palestrina's death and published in 1614. It remained in use until the early twentieth century, when Benedictine monks produced new editions based on surviving early manuscripts.

Palestrina married Lucrezia Gori in 1547, and they had three sons. After he lost two of them in the 1570s to the plague, followed by Lucrezia in 1580, Palestrina considered becoming a priest. Instead, in 1581 he married Virginia Dormoli, an affluent widow whose financial resources allowed him to publish his own music. His reputation as a composer, already high in his lifetime, grew exponentially after his death, and he eventually became known as "the Prince of Music."

Major works: 104 masses, over 300 motets, 35 Magnificats, about 70 hymns, many other liturgical compositions, about 50 spiritual madrigals with Italian texts, and 94 secular madrigals

1. Quoted in *Source Readings in Music History*, trans. Oliver Strunk, rev. ed. by Leo Treitler (New York: Norton, 1988), vol. 3, pp. 95–96.

Full 🔊 Concise 🔊

polyphony from being condemned by the Council of Trent by composing a six-voice mass that was both reverent in spirit and attentive to the words. The work in question was the *Missa Papae Marcelli* (Pope Marcellus Mass; NAWM 51), published in Palestrina's *Second Book of Masses* in 1567. While the legend is probably inaccurate and was embellished over time, Palestrina did note in his dedication to the collection that the masses it contained were written "in a new manner," no doubt responding to the desire of some for greater clarity in presenting the text.

Figure 9.5 Title page of the first published collection of works by Palestrina (Rome: Valerio and Luigi Dorico, 1554). The composer is shown presenting his music to Pope Julius III.
(Staatsbibliothek zu Berlin, Bildarchiv Preussischer Kulturbesitz, Musikabteilung.)

Palestrina's style was the first in the history of Western music to have been consciously preserved, isolated, and imitated as a model for sacred polyphony. Few composers before Bach are as well known today, and perhaps no other composer's technique has received closer scrutiny. Better than any of his contemporaries, he captured the essence of the sober, conservative, yet elegantly expressive style of the Counter-Reformation.

Palestrina studied the works of the Franco-Flemish composers and completely mastered their craft. Half of his masses are parody masses, many based on polyphonic models by leading contrapuntists of previous generations or on his own motets. Palestrina used the old-fashioned cantus-firmus method for a few of his masses (including the first of two he wrote on the traditional *L'homme armé* melody), but generally he preferred to paraphrase the chant in all the parts rather than confine it to the tenor voice. Also reminiscent of the older Flemish tradition are a small number of canonic masses. Six masses, including the *Pope Marcellus Mass*, are free, using neither canons nor borrowed material.

Palestrina's melodies share qualities with plainchant: their curve often describes an arch, and the motion is mostly stepwise with few repeated notes. In the first Agnus Dei from the famous *Pope Marcellus Mass* (Example 9.3 and NAWM 51b), for example, we observe long, gracefully shaped phrases, easily singable and staying for the most part within the range of a ninth. The few leaps greater than a third are immediately filled in by notes that reverse the direction of the skip and smooth the contour. The rhythmic units vary in length without ever creating extreme contrasts of motion. The flowing melodies remain in the diatonic modes; Palestrina studiously avoided chromaticism, admitting only those alterations demanded by the conventions of musica ficta (see Chapter 4).

Pope Marcellus Mass

Full 🔊   Concise 🔊

Example 9.3 Giovanni Pierluigi da Palestrina, Pope Marcellus Mass: *Agnus Dei I*

Lamb of God

Musical unity

This same Agnus Dei also illustrates how Palestrina unifies a composition by purely musical means. Each phrase of the text has its own musical motive, and the contrapuntal development of each motive through imitation overlaps at a cadence with the next phrase. But there is more connection between motives than mere succession; Palestrina achieves a certain clarity and logic through systematic repetition of phrases and by carefully placing cadences only on those scale degrees that define the mode. (For a discussion of his treatment of dissonance, see A Closer Look, page 163.)

Text declamation

Full 🔊

Palestrina composed the *Pope Marcellus Mass* in the 1560s, when the Council of Trent's *Canon on Music to Be Used in the Mass* urged that "the words be clearly understood by all." His attention to text setting is particularly evident in the Credo (NAWM 51a), where the voices often pronounce a given phrase simultaneously rather than in the staggered manner of imitative polyphony. To achieve variety, Palestrina divided

A Closer Look   Palestrina's Counterpoint

Palestrina's counterpoint conforms in most details to the precepts of Willaert's style as transmitted by Zarlino in *Le istituzioni harmoniche*. The music is written almost entirely in the alla breve measure of ¢, which in the original editions (as in Example 9.4) consists of a downbeat and upbeat of one semibreve each (or a half note in the transcription of Example 9.3). The independent lines are expected to meet in a full triad on each beat. This convention is broken for suspensions—a contrapuntal device in which a voice, consonant with the other parts on the upbeat, is held through the downbeat while one or more of the other parts forms a dissonance against it; then the suspended voice resolves into a consonance by moving downward by step. More than the recurrence of accented syllables, this alternation of tension and relaxation—strong dissonance on the downbeat and sweet consonance on the upbeat—endows the music with a pendulum-like pulse (indicated by the vertical arrows in Example 9.4). Dissonances between beats may occur if the voice that is moving does so in stepwise fashion. Palestrina's only exception to this rule is his use of the cambiata, in which a voice leaps a third down from a dissonance to a consonance and then ascends by step. (The term *cambiata* means "exchanged"—that is, a dissonance is exchanged for a consonance.)

Example 9.4 Contrapuntal analysis of Example 9.3, measures 10–15, Tenors I, II, Basses I, II

The alternation of consonance and dissonance is clearly evident in Example 9.4, which gives the lowest four voices of Example 9.3, measures 10–15, in their original values. P stands for passing note, S for suspension, and C for cambiata; numbers indicate the dissonant intervals and their resolutions.

The smooth diatonic lines and the discreet handling of dissonance give Palestrina's music a consistent serenity and transparency. Another positive quality of his counterpoint lies in the vertical combination of voices. Because the voice groupings and spacings are so varied, the same harmony produces a large number of subtle shadings and sonorities.

---

the six-voice choir into various smaller groups, each with its particular sonorous color, and reserved the full six voices for climactic or particularly significant words, such as "Et incarnatus est" (and [He] was made incarnate [became flesh]).

Palestrina's Contemporaries

In addition to Palestrina, the most illustrious composers of sacred music at the end of the sixteenth century were the Spanish priest Tomás Luis de Victoria (1548–1611), the cosmopolitan Orlande de Lassus (1532–1594; see also Chapter 7), and the Englishman William Byrd (ca. 1540–1623; see Chapter 8), who remained a lifelong Catholic even though he worked for the Anglican Church and English monarchy. Their compositions—all products of the international musical language of the late Renaissance—share characteristics of Palestrina's polished style, yet each composer is different enough to warrant separate attention here.

Victoria

Throughout the sixteenth century, Spanish and Roman composers were closely connected. Victoria spent two decades in Rome, where he almost certainly knew Palestrina and may have studied with him. Returning to Spain about 1587, he became chaplain to the Empress Maria, for whose funeral services he wrote a famous Requiem Mass in 1603. In the spirit of the Counter-Reformation, he composed sacred music exclusively. Although his style resembles Palestrina's, Victoria infused his music with greater expressive intensity, comparable to that of the contemporary Spanish painter El Greco (see Figure 9.7), and he utilized more notes outside the diatonic modes. For example, in his mass *O magnum mysterium* (O great mystery, NAWM 52b), which is in the transposed first mode, the sixth degree is often lowered and the seventh raised, as in the later minor mode.

Full 🔊   Concise 🔊

Victoria's motet and mass

Like most of Victoria's masses, this one is a parody or imitation mass based on his own motet, *O magnum mysterium* (Example 9.5 and NAWM 52a), in which the opening motive, with its stark falling and rising fifth imitated downward throughout the entire musical space, conveys the magnitude, wonder, and mystery of Christ's birth. Although this is a more dramatic gesture than any

Full 🔊   Concise 🔊

Example 9.5 Tomás Luis de Victoria, motet: O magnum mysterium

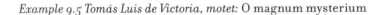

O great mystery, and wondrous sacrament . . .

Palestrina would have used, Victoria achieved the same melodic and rhythmic smoothness and suave triadic harmonies as his Roman contemporary.

Orlande de Lassus was the last in the long line of sixteenth-century Franco-Flemish composers and perhaps the most international in terms of his career and his compositions. In his youth, he served Italian patrons in Mantua, Sicily, Rome, and elsewhere, allowing him to become completely familiar with Italian styles. In 1556, he entered the service of Duke Albrecht V of Bavaria. He became director for the ducal chapel in Munich and remained in that post until his death in 1594 (see Figure 9.6), although he traveled often and kept abreast of developments in Flanders, France, and Italy. Unlike Palestrina and Victoria, he wrote many secular works. By the age of twenty-four, Lassus had already published books of madrigals, chansons, and motets, and his total production eventually amounted to over two thousand works. Yet he ranks with Palestrina as one of the great composers of sacred music in the late sixteenth century. Whereas Palestrina became a model of the restrained church style and of strict counterpoint, Lassus was equally influential as an advocate of text expression, even in sacred music.

In each of his seven hundred motets, Lassus's rhetorical, pictorial, and dramatic interpretation of the text determines both the overall form and the details. Especially vivid is the six-voice motet *Cum essem parvulus* (NAWM 53), composed in 1579 to words from St. Paul's first epistle to the Corinthians (1 Corinthians 13:11–13). Lassus set the opening words "When I was a child" as a duet between the two highest voice parts, representing the child through the thin texture and the high vocal range sung by the boys in the choir, alternating with phrases in the four lower voices, representing Paul speaking as an adult. Lassus sets the text "Now we see as if through a mirror in riddles" with enigmatic, nonimitative counterpoint full of suspensions and a brief mirror figure between the bassus and other voices; but then we will see "face to face," a moment of revelation that Lassus portrays with the only fully homophonic passage in the motet, as all six voices declaim the words together in rhythmic unison. Throughout, the words prompt every gesture in the music, from changes of texture and the placement of cadences to the rhythm, accents, and contours of the musical motives.

More fully than any other sixteenth-century composer, Lassus synthesized the achievement of an epoch. He was so versatile that we cannot properly speak of a "Lassus style." He was a master of Flemish, French, Italian, and German styles and of every genre from lofty church music to the bawdy secular song. His motets were especially influential, particularly on German Protestant composers. Lassus's creative use of musical devices to convey the emotions and depict the images of his texts led to a strong tradition of such expressive and pictorial motives among German composers, as we will see with Heinrich Schütz (Chapter 11) and Johann Sebastian Bach (Chapter 14).

William Byrd (see Biography, page 149) was the most important English composer since Dunstable and the first to absorb imitative techniques from the Continent so thoroughly that he could apply them imaginatively and without constraint. In his *Sing joyfully unto God* (NAWM 49), an energetic and vivid full anthem for six voices, points of imitation succeed one another, occasionally interspersed with more homophonic declamation. The imitation is handled freely, often with changes of interval and rhythm.

Byrd's Latin masses and motets are his best-known vocal compositions. He probably intended his earlier Latin motets for private devotional gatherings

Figure 9.6 Orlande de Lassus at the keyboard
(a virginal) leading his chamber ensemble in Saint George's Hall at the Munich court of Albrecht V, duke of Bavaria. Shown are three choirboys (in the middle of the group by the virginal, to Lassus's left), about twenty singers, and fifteen instrumentalists. Miniature by Hans Mielich, in a manuscript of Lassus's Penitential Psalms.
(Bayerisches Staatsbibliothek, Munich.)

Lassus's influence

Byrd

Full 🔊   Concise 🔊

At the Time

In **1594,** at the time of Palestrina's death in Rome,

- Martin Luther has been dead for almost 50 years and Jean Calvin for 30, but Protestantism has taken root and is thriving in northern Europe. Music printing helps to disseminate Protestant psalm settings and Lutheran chorales across western Europe. (NAWM 46 and 47.)
- Pope Clement VIII is head of the Roman Catholic Church and the last pontiff to serve during the Counter-Reformation, an era of spiritual reform that arose largely in response to the Protestant Reformation. It fosters an intensely pious and fervent style in art and music that may be seen in the paintings of El Greco (Figure 9.7) and heard in the entirely sacred musical output of Victoria, a Spanish priest (NAWM 52).
- In 1594 the southern Italian composer Don Carlo Gesualdo, Prince of Venosa (Figure 7.3), after the gruesome end of his first marriage some years earlier, travels to the glittering Ferrarese court for his wedding to Eleanora d'Este, cousin to the duke of Ferrara. His new bride is more fortunate if no happier than his first wife: she outlives him by two dozen years. (NAWM 59.)
- The New World is still being explored and its ownership contested. In 1594 an English seaman, Richard Hawkins, is wounded in a battle with Spanish warships off the coast of Peru, taken prisoner, and held for ransom in Spain.
- Queen Elizabeth I (Figure 7.5) rules England, her powerful navy having recently defeated the Spanish Armada. In 1594 English authorities arrest, torture, and execute the queen's personal physician, originally a Portuguese Jew, on charges that he colluded with Phillip II of Spain and Portuguese agents in a plot to poison the queen. As a lover of music and patron of the arts, Elizabeth is the subject of praise and homage in many printed madrigals and other music books dedicated to her (NAWM 64).
- The French Wars of Religion abate when Henry IV, a Huguenot (French Protestant), converts to Catholicism and is crowned king of France in Chartres cathedral. He will later marry Marie de Medici, for whose wedding the first opera was to be composed and performed in Florence in 1600.
- The young Caravaggio starts selling his paintings in Rome, where his practice of painting from life is to make an enormous impact on the art world (Figure 7.7).
- Shakespeare's *Romeo and Juliet* is first performed in London. On stage, in a hall in Capulet's house, "music plays and they dance." Juliet's father says, "Nay sit, good cousin Capulet;/For you and I are past our dancing days."
- Tulips bloom for the first time in the Low Countries, where they continue to flourish as nowhere else in the world.

Figure 9.7 El Greco, Burial of the Count of Orgaz, *1586–1588. A contemporary of Victoria, El Greco (1541–1614) was also active in Italy and Spain in the late sixteenth century. His religious paintings are associated with an intensely expressive and visionary style, as in this large canvas, where the burial scene below, with its relatively naturalistic array of contemporary citizens of Toledo, is crowned by a fantastic one, filled with divine elements.* (Santo Tomé, Toledo. Scala/Art Resource, NY.)

of secret Catholics, or recusants, but he designed the later ones, published in two collections (*Gradualia* 1605, 1607), for liturgical use. In the dedication of the first collection, he praised the power of scriptural texts to inspire a composer's imagination:

> I have found there is such a power hidden away and stored up in those words [of Scripture] that—I know not how—to one who meditates on divine things, pondering them with detailed concentration, all the most fitting melodies come as it were of themselves, and freely present themselves when the mind is alert and eager.

This passage also serves as an eloquent reminder that most Renaissance composers relied on the text as their starting point for musical invention.

Although Byrd was in trouble from time to time for his Catholic practices, the fact that he and his predecessor Tallis avoided a worse fate is a sign of how valuable their music was to the Anglican Church and to the state. Indeed, the first Queen Elizabeth understood that Byrd was the chief adornment of her chapel and used his reputation as a composer to raise hers as a monarch and that of England as a cultured nation.

POSTLUDE

Renaissance, Reformation, Counter-Reformation—these terms have been used to suggest different aspects of sixteenth-century musical styles and practices. Yet their meanings overlap, and more than one term may be applicable to the same composer. Certainly, their qualities outlived the chronological boundary of the year 1600, which is the convenient but artificial limit usually assigned to the Renaissance period. Although our discussion of Renaissance music officially ends with this chapter, the musical characteristics connoted by the word *Renaissance* persisted well into the next century, when Palestrina's style continued to be revered by some as the "absolute perfection" of church music. In the next century, Palestrina's style became known as the *stile antico*, the "old style," shared by Victoria, Lassus, Byrd, and earlier Renaissance composers such as Josquin and Willaert.

The new musical practices of the Reformation—especially those involving the chorale—had far-reaching consequences for music history: among other things, they resulted in Bach's glorious church cantatas and his superb chorale harmonizations, which still serve as a bible for students of harmony. Finally, the goal of the Counter-Reformation—which had idealized sacred polyphony as a vehicle for drawing "the hearts of the listeners . . . to desire of heavenly harmonies"[1]—was to reconquer the minds and souls of the faithful, bringing them back into the papal fold. This Counter-Reformation attitude, intent on manipulating the senses and the emotions, influenced the new Baroque musical aesthetic, which we will explore next.

 Resources for study and review available at
wwnorton.com/studyspace

---

1. From a draft of the Council of Trent's recommendation on church music.

PART THREE

The Long Seventeenth Century

PART CONTENTS

I n music history, we invoke the term *Baroque* to describe the period between 1600 and 1750. While the word is sometimes still used in its original, negative sense —"abnormal," "bizarre," "exaggerated," "grotesque"—art critics of the nineteenth century gave it a more positive spin. For them, *Baroque* summed up the delightfully flamboyant, theatrical, and expressive tendencies of seventeenth-century art and architecture. Eventually, the word also embraced poetry and drama, and, finally, music historians followed suit and adopted it in the twentieth century to describe the music of the age. Although we now recognize that a single adjective cannot adequately suggest the many different musical styles in use during these years, there are certainly traits that early seventeenth-century composers share with those in the first half of the eighteenth century. In the following chapters, we will discover common elements in the music of Monteverdi and Bach, who flourished

Lully's Armide *performed at the Palais-Royal. Watercolor by Gabriel de Saint-Aubin (1724–1780).*

(Wikimedia Commons)

at the beginning and end of the period, respectively, as well as in the music of the generations of composers who lived between them. The idea of a "long" seventeenth century, then—one that expands the normal chronological boundaries of a single century-long time period—may be appropriately applied to the Baroque era.

Europe in the Seventeenth Century

The scientific revolution

Around the year 1600, Europe was in the midst of a scientific revolution, led by a new breed of investigators who relied on mathematics, observation, and practical experiments, not on traditional opinion. Johannes Kepler showed in 1609 that the planets, including the earth, move around the sun in elliptical orbits at speeds that vary according to their distance from the sun. During the following decade, Galileo Galilei demonstrated the laws of motion and used the newly invented telescope to discover sunspots and moons orbiting Jupiter. René Descartes posited a deductive approach to philosophy that explained the world through mathematics, logic, and reasoning from first principles. These two strands joined in the work of Sir Isaac Newton, whose law of gravitation, developed in the 1660s, combined acute observation with mathematical elegance and set the pattern for scientific methods for centuries to come. The same interest in what is useful and effective, rather than what is hallowed by tradition, is apparent in seventeenth-century music and lay at the heart of the new styles in art and music around 1600, including the "second practice" and opera (see page 184).

Politics, religion, and war

The seventeenth century also saw new thinking about politics, ranging from those who advocated democracy in England to those who supported absolute monarchy in France. Religious strife between German Protestants and Catholics precipitated the Thirty Years' War (1618–1648), which later included political rivalries among France, Sweden, and Denmark on the one hand, and the Holy Roman Empire and Spain on the other (see Figure III.1). Actually a series of wars, this conflict devastated Germany, reducing the population in some areas by more than half. The English Civil War (1642–1649), primarily a battle for power between the king and Parliament, also had religious aspects. It culminated in the execution of King Charles I (r. 1625–1649) during the Puritan Revolution, led by Oliver Cromwell (1599–1658), who in effect presided over a military dictatorship until the monarchy was restored with the coronation of Charles II in 1660.

Colonialism

Meanwhile, Europeans were expanding overseas. During the seventeenth century, the British, French, and Dutch established colonies in North America, the Caribbean, Africa, and Asia in competition with Spain and Portugal. Especially lucrative imports were sugar and tobacco, new luxury items for Europe, grown on plantations in the Americas. These crops required intensive labor provided by the cruel trade in human life that brought Africans to the New World as slaves. Europeans who settled in the Western Hemisphere brought their traditions with them, including Catholic service music and villancicos to the Spanish colonies and Protestant psalm and hymn singing to British North America (see Chapter 15).

Capitalism

Britain, the Netherlands, and northern Italy prospered from capitalism, a system in which individuals invested their own money (capital) in businesses designed to return a profit. An important innovation was the joint stock company, which pooled the wealth of many individuals while limiting their risk. These companies were formed to finance opera houses in Hamburg, London,

Figure III.1 Europe, about 1610.

and other cities. By putting money in the hands of individuals to invest or spend locally, capitalism boosted the economy. Among the effects on music were the rise of public opera and public concerts, and an increased demand from the upper and middle classes for published music, musical instruments, and music lessons. Consequently, instrumental music came of age during the seventeenth century (see Chapter 12), and new genres of vocal and instrumental chamber music flourished.

Musicians continued to depend on patronage from courts, churches, and cities, and the types of music that won support varied from region to region. Musicians were best off in Italy, which was wealthy from trade yet still dominated by a combination of princely courts: the Spanish presence in the south, Papal States around Rome, and independent states in the north

Patronage

(see the map in Figure 12.13). Rulers, cities, and leading families supported music and the arts as a way of competing for prestige. Aristocrats in Florence sponsored a brilliant series of musical and theatrical innovations around 1600, spawning similar efforts by the dukes of Mantua, churchmen in Rome, and the government and citizens of Venice (see Chapter 10). Their support continued Italy's reign as the dominant influence in European music through the mid-eighteenth century.

In France, power and wealth were increasingly concentrated in the monarchy. Louis XIV (r. 1643–1715) controlled the arts, including music, and used them to assert his glory. During the seventeenth century, France replaced Spain as the predominant power on the Continent; partly as a result, French music was widely imitated, while the music of Spain had little presence beyond its borders. Civil war and parliamentary prerogative limited the wealth of the English royalty, but their patronage strongly influenced national tastes. The calamity of the Thirty Years' War sapped treasuries throughout the Holy Roman Empire, but after midcentury, German courts and free city-states built up their musical establishments, influenced by both Italy and France. The Church continued to support music, although its role was less important than it had been in previous centuries.

Along with aristocratic, civic, and ecclesiastical patronage, many cities had "academies," private associations that, among other functions, sponsored musical activities. Public opera houses were established in many cities, beginning in Venice in 1637. Public concerts to which one subscribed or paid admission first occurred in England in 1672, but the practice did not become widespread in Europe until the later 1700s.

From Renaissance to Baroque

Figure III.2 Saint Peter's Square and Basilica at the Vatican in Rome, designed by Gian Lorenzo Bernini in 1657.
(Aerocentro Varesino SRL, Italy.)

The seventeenth century was the golden age of European drama, beginning with William Shakespeare (1564–1616) and ending with the great French tragedian Jean Racine (1639–1699). But it was also an age in which the collaboration of theater, painting, and music culminated in the invention of opera, a new theatrical genre that became the art form par excellence of Baroque Europe. At the same time, painting and sculpture became intensely and explicitly theatrical in their own right; along with music, they shared in the theater's immediacy, attempting to function as a kind of show, a *rappresentazione*, designed to move and impress an audience. Even the literature of the time often had theatrical qualities, and dramatic scenes in the epic *Paradise Lost* by John Milton and the novel *Don Quixote* by Miguel de Cervantes at times assume the power of a staged performance.

In art and architecture, as in music, the Baroque began in Italy. Rome provided the stage for Gian Lorenzo Bernini, the outstanding sculptor of the century. In addition to Saint Peter's Basilica (Figure III.2) and fountains,

Figure III.3 (left)
Michelangelo's David
*(1501–1504), which evokes
ancient Greek statuary
and illustrates the ideals
of Renaissance human-
ism, including nobility,
balance, and calm.*
(Museo Nazionale del Bargello,
Florence, Italy. Photo:
Nimatallah/Art Resource, NY.)

Figure III.4 (right)
Bernini's David
*(1623–1624), embodying
the dramatic and Baroque
qualities of dynamic
motion and emotion.*
(Galleria Borghese, Rome. Art
Resource, NY.)

piazzas, and sculpture all over the city, he designed a stunning chapel for one of his Roman patrons, for which he fashioned a sculptural group of Saint Teresa in Ecstasy, positioning it as though it were a theatrical performance (see In Context, page 206). Contrasting Michelangelo's famous statue of David from the early sixteenth century (Figure III.3) with Bernini's *David* of about 1620 (Figure III.4) shows the difference between Renaissance and Baroque artistic goals. Michelangelo evoked ancient Greek statuary with his standing nude, celebrated the nobility and beauty of the human figure through balance and proportion, and portrayed his hero as contemplative and still, with only a furrowed brow to suggest the coming battle with Goliath. Bernini captures David as he winds up to sling the stone, his body expressing dynamic action, his muscles tense, his lips and face distorted with exertion. The effect is dramatic, making the viewer respond emotionally rather than with detached admiration.

Expressing emotion was at the core of the Baroque aesthetic, and emotion was a function of motion. The dynamic movement so characteristic of the art of the seventeenth century and the active bass lines so typical of its music are closely linked to the theory of the affections, a concept that empowered all the arts of this period. The affections—emotions such as sadness, joy, anger, love, fear, excitement, or wonder—were thought of as relatively stable states of the soul, each caused by a certain combination of spirits, or "humors," in the body. According to Descartes, once these spirits were set in motion by external stimuli via the senses, they conveyed their motions to the soul, thus bringing about specific emotions. His treatise *The Passions of the Soul* (1645–46), an attempt to analyze and catalogue the affections, posited a simple mechanical theory to explain their cause: for every motion stimulating the senses there is a specific emotion evoked in the soul.

All the arts of this period sought to move the emotions and conjure the passions, or affections, in the soul. In an essay on expression in painting, French painter and designer Charles Le Brun (1619–1690) portrayed and labeled an entire gallery of

The affections

Figure III.5 Charles Le Brun (1619–1690), who dominated seventeenth-century French painting as head of the Royal Academy of Painting and Sculpture, drew these facial expressions illustrating various emotional reactions such as alarm, fear, anger, hope, sorrow, and so forth. They were published at the end of the century as "Method for Learning How to Draw the Passions" in his Conférence . . . sur l'expression générale et particulière *(Amsterdam and Paris, 1698). Writers about music made similar attempts to isolate and catalogue the passions.*

(From *Traité des Passions*, 1698.)

emotions and their corresponding facial gestures (excerpted in Figure III.5) to serve as examples for artists. In similar fashion, composers of opera displayed a musical gallery of emotions by writing a series of arias for every act, each aria seeking to render a psychological portrait of a character aroused by a certain emotion. By imitating the emotion in musical gestures—such as melodic and rhythmic motives, harmonic motion, bass line activity, meter, and figuration—the composer expected to create the corresponding affection in the listener.

Such theories were reinforced by the scientific discoveries of the era. Galileo's observations through the telescope and his experiments with the laws of motion had demonstrated that the senses as well as reason were instruments of learning. Placed in the service of human knowledge, then, the eyes and ears could be conduits for influencing emotions and behavior. This new respect for the senses helps to explain the seemingly trivial debates that raged in the seventeenth century over such matters as whether design (drawing) or color in painting was the more important element in representing a subject convincingly, or whether composers were justified in using dissonance more freely than their predecessors in order to express the words more forcefully (see below). These were meaningful issues if the goal of stirring the affections was to be achieved.

Like the sculptor Bernini, painters of the period frequently concentrated on subjects involving physical action and psychological reaction. For example, Artemisia Gentileschi's powerful work *Judith Slaying Holofernes* (Figure III.6, ca. 1620) depicts the biblical heroine *in the act* of decapitating her victim at the same time as she *reacts* emotionally by recoiling in disgust from his gushing blood. The first operas were also about a single significant action—often

Figure III.6 Artemisia Gentileschi, Judith Slaying Holofernes, *ca. 1620. The painting, a depiction of both violent action and psychological reaction, reveals the essential theatricality of Baroque art.*

(Galeria degli Uffizi, Florence. Alinari/Art Resource, NY.)

merely narrated—and the reaction it prompted, such as Orpheus's response to the death of Eurydice. In music, a motion intended to represent and ultimately stimulate an emotion could be encoded in many ways, the most obvious being by means of rhythm. This was the principle behind Monteverdi's *concitato genere* ("excited style"; see page 202) and the relentless motion of a Baroque ostinato bass pattern, such as the doleful descending tetrachord that eloquently imitates the drooping gesture of sorrow (see page 203 and the laments presented in NAWM 65, 77, 80b, and 89b).

In seeking to move the affections, painting in the Baroque period did not always aspire to be beautiful. Among the many artists influenced by the kind of naturalism characteristic of Bernini and Gentileschi was the court painter Diego Velázquez. He not only produced intimate portraits of the Spanish royal family but also, like some of his Dutch contemporaries, chronicled a subheroic world of vernacular experience, of humble subjects pursuing ordinary activities (Figure III.9). In the seventeenth century, Dutch painting experienced a golden age; for the sheer power of his naturalistic detail, Rembrandt van Rijn stands out among his peers. Just as in music Monteverdi broke the rules of counterpoint in order to make certain dissonances acceptable for expressive purposes, disturbing the smooth surface of the texture with crude "imperfections" (see below), so, too, Rembrandt—by choosing models from among the most ordinary and coarse specimens of humanity and daring to show them as they were, sometimes marred by warts and wrinkles (as in his own self-portrait on page 177)—made physical imperfection acceptable in art.

Naturalism

Figure III.7 Nicolas Poussin (1594–1665), The Rape of the Sabine Women, *ca. 1635–1640. An advocate of drawing and formal design, and, therefore, a believer in the primacy of line over color, Poussin went so far as to fashion miniature statues in clay, arranging them in three-dimensional dioramas in preparation for painting his history canvases.* (The Louvre, Paris. Photo: Erich Lessing/Art Resource, NY.)

TIMELINE **The Long Seventeenth Century**

Musical Events

1585–1612
Giovanni Gabrieli in Venice

1600
Artusi attacks Monteverdi in print; first surviving opera performed in Florence

1605
Monteverdi publishes Fifth Book of Madrigals, with *Cruda Amarilli* (NAWM 71)

Galileo's telescope

1611
Gesualdo's last book of madrigals published

1613
Parthenia, collection of works for virginal, published

Gentileschi, *Young Woman with a Violin*

1580

Historical Events

1590
Guarini's pastoral drama *Il pastor fido*

1602
Dutch East India Company chartered

1607
First English colony in Virginia at Jamestown

1609
Kepler sets forth his astronomical laws

1616
Shakespeare dies

1618–1648
Thirty Years' War (religious wars in Germany)

ca. 1620
Artemisia Gentileschi, *Judith Slaying Holofernes* (Figure III.6)

1623–1624
Bernini, *David* (Figure III.4)

1632
Galileo charged with heresy for claiming the Earth revolves around the sun

The Musical Baroque

Design vs. color

Along with painting and poetry, music became one of the sister arts when it allied itself inseparably with words during the Renaissance. As such, it participated in the various aesthetic debates that characterize the seventeenth century. Chief among these was the quarrel between the "ancients" and the "moderns," or between conservatives and innovators. For example, in painting, particularly in France, the traditionalists upheld the superiority of design over color and championed the artist Nicolas Poussin, who modeled the figures on his canvases after antique sculpture (Figure III.7) The partisans of color, the modernists, rallied around Peter Paul Rubens, questioning the supremacy of ancient sculpture and arguing that color, light, and shade could produce a more compelling imitation of nature than could drawing alone (Figure III.8).

First and second practices

At the heart of the debate between conservatives and moderns in music was the subject of text expression. With the publication of Claudio Monteverdi's Fifth Book of Madrigals in 1605, the composer distinguished between a *prima pratica* and a *seconda pratica*, or a first and second "practice," or compositional method (see Vignette, page 184). By the first, Monteverdi meant the received rules of counterpoint, the style of vocal polyphony codified by Zarlino in the

1637
First public opera house opens in Venice

ca. 1675–1684
Amati and Stradivari perfect the art of violin making

1678
Hamburg opera house opens

1679
Alessandro Scarlatti's first opera in Rome

Bernini, *Ecstasy of Saint Theresa*

1685
Births of J. S. Bach and Handel

1686
Lully, *Armide*

1689
Purcell, *Dido and Aeneas*

1700
Corelli, Op. 5 violin sonatas

1707
Death of Buxtehude

1711–1759
Handel in London

1723–1750
Bach in Leipzig

1750
J.S. Bach dies

1750

1637
Descartes, *Discourse on Method*

1643–1715
Reign of Louis XIV in France

1645–1652
Bernini, *Ecstasy of Saint Teresa* (Figure 11.4)

1667
Milton, *Paradise Lost*

1687
Newton, *Principia mathematica*

1727–1760
George II rules England

1740
Frederick the Great becomes king of Prussia

Rembrandt, self-portrait with turban

Figure III.8 Detail from Peter Paul Rubens (1577–1640), The Rape of the Sabine Women, ca. 1635–1640. Of Flemish origin, Rubens achieved enormous success as both painter and diplomat at the courts of Italy, the Netherlands, England, and Spain. The followers of Rubens challenged the supremacy of ancient sculpture and argued in favor of color, light, and shade, which they believed could produce a more convincing imitation of nature than could drawing alone. (Scala/Art Resource, NY.)

ARTS & IDEAS

Science and Philosophy

German astronomer Johannes Kepler (1571–1630) helped to establish the validity of the sun-centered Copernican system by his application of the laws of physics to the motion of heavenly bodies. His *Commentaries on the Motion of Mars* and *Harmony of the Worlds* were published in 1609 and 1619, respectively.

Galileo Galilei (1564–1642), the Italian astronomer, physicist, and philosopher known simply as Galileo, was the son of humanist musician and theorist Vincenzo Galilei (see Chapter 10), whose interest in the mathematics of tuning systems helped to inspire his son's career. A staunch advocate of Copernicus, Galileo was harassed and denounced by the Church after publishing his *Dialogue on the Great World Systems* (the first scientific treatise written in Italian, 1632), although he was acclaimed and revered in other circles, as much for his accomplishments in physics and mathematics as for his astronomical theories.

René Descartes (1590–1650), French mathematician and philosopher, divided the universe into mutually exclusive but interacting spirit and matter, the spirit being subject to reason and the matter being subject to mechanical laws. His treatise *The Passions of the Soul* (1650) helps to explain the Baroque theory of the affections. In *Discourse on Method* (1637), he subjected all received opinions to his challenge of "methodical doubt," arguing from the principle *Cogito, ergo sum* ("I think, therefore I am"), which he held to be a model of certainty. (See Figure 12.17.)

The "Einstein of his day," Isaac Newton (1642–1727) was an English mathematician and natural philosopher whose accomplishments include laying the foundation for modern calculus, discovering the composition of light, and developing the law of universal gravitation. His major work, *Principia mathematica* (1687), which presented his method of reasoning from physical events, signified the beginning of a new era of scientific investigation.

Literature

Italian author Giambattista Guarini (1538–1612) was the poet most responsible for the pastoral vogue that swept Europe in the seventeenth century. His famous verse play *Il pastor fido* (The Faithful Shepherd, 1590) inaugurated the hybrid literary genre of tragicomedy. Its lyrics provided the text for hundreds of madrigal settings, among them *Cruda Amarilli*, and its dramatic action set the stage for opera.

As a soldier, Spanish author Miguel de Cervantes (1547–1616) fought in several battles, was captured by Turks, and was ransomed from slavery in Algiers. His taste for adventure informs his greatest work, *Don Quixote* (in two parts, 1605 and 1615), in which he portrays the interaction between the visionary idealist (the title character) and the undisguised realist (the squire Sancho Panza), and details their fantastic misadventures. Overflowing with vitality, the work won immediate success in Spain and was quickly translated into English, French, and Italian, which helps explain its enormous influence on the modern novel.

English actor, poet, and playwright of enduring fame, William Shakespeare (1564–1616) penned 154 sonnets of intense feeling and verse plays that included tragedies (such as *Hamlet* and *Othello*), comedies (such as *The Merchant of Venice* and *Twelfth Night*), and histories (such as *Henry IV*). His great gift for character portrayal and his virtuosity with language make him the most widely known author in all English literature.

Creator of the classic French farce, Molière (Jean-Baptiste Poquelin, 1622–1673) established and starred in his own acting troupe, which became a favorite at court. His plays — among them *The Bourgeois Gentleman, The Wise Women, The Phony Doctor,* and *The Hypochondriac* (a role he was playing, ironically, when he died) — wittily satirize human behavior and often feature conflict between the sexes or social classes and rivalry between young and old. (See Figure 13.9.)

---

mid-sixteenth century and cultivated by Palestrina. By the second, he meant the adventurous style of the modern Italians: Rore, Marenzio, and himself among others. In the first practice, according to Monteverdi, the music prevailed over the words, while in the second practice the text dominated and dictated its musical setting. Just as the advocates of color over design in painting thought they could achieve a more convincing representation of nature, Monteverdi

John Milton (1608–1674), English poet, writer, and supporter of the Puritan cause against the monarchy, as well as a humanist and lover of music and literature (author of the masque *Comus*), is one of the most respected figures in English literature. His masterpiece *Paradise Lost* (1667), a national epic in twelve books, followed by *Paradise Regained* (1671), explores themes of temptation and sin.

French dramatist Jean Racine (1639–1699) specialized in tragedies of passion in which his characters, many of whom became subjects of opera, are portrayed with unrivaled psychological depth. His plays (including *Iphigénie*, *Phèdre*, and *Athalie*) adhere to classical values and explore moral issues with subjects such as revenge, jealousy, the agony of guilt, and the renunciation of love for duty.

Art

The foremost Flemish painter of the seventeenth century, Peter Paul Rubens (1577–1640) spent his apprentice years in Italy, where he learned the newest techniques of color, light, and shade. Back in Antwerp, his reputation flourished, and he received commissions from the French court as well as from British and Spanish royalty. He mastered all genres, including portrait, landscape, religious, history, and allegory, and his work was championed by the "moderns" in part because of its use of the visual to appeal to the emotions. (See Figure III.8.)

Artemisia Gentileschi (1593–ca. 1653), Tuscan painter and pupil of her father, Orazio, was the first Italian woman whose accomplishments not only were praised by her contemporaries but also influenced other artists. She worked in Rome, Florence, Genoa, and Naples, and refused to limit herself to the genres of portraiture and devotional pictures deemed suitable for women; she also tackled powerful historical subjects. (See Figure III.6.)

Considered by his contemporaries the greatest of living painters, Nicolas Poussin (1594–1665), although French, spent most of his time in Rome surrounded by ancient art, which he emulated in his own work. His methods became the basis of French classical art and were taught at the French Academy of Painting and Sculpture, established in Paris in 1648. His work was intended to appeal to reason and intellect, rather than arousing a response through the senses. (See Figures III.7 and 12.11.)

Appointed architect of Saint Peter's church in 1629, Gian Lorenzo Bernini (1598–1680) left his mark especially on modern Rome by virtue of the commissions he received from cardinals and popes to design churches, chapels, fountains, monuments, tombs, and statues. The astonishing virtuosity of his marble works, characterized by their semblance of exuberant motion and dramatic action, makes him the dominant figure of the Italian Baroque. (See Figures III.2, III.4, 11.4, and 11.5.)

Diego Velázquez (1599–1660), the most celebrated Spanish painter of the seventeenth century, enjoyed the close friendship of King Philip IV, who appointed him to positions at court — including administrator of the royal galleries — that often interfered with his freedom to paint. His subtle portraits of the royal family and other members of the court combine a deep psychological intensity with a sense of serene dignity, and his treatment of more ordinary subjects illustrates his interest in naturalism. (See Figure III.9.)

The greatest master among Dutch artists of the time, Rembrandt van Rijn (1606–1669) was renowned as the painter, etcher, and draftsman of a prodigious number of works. His use of dramatic contrasts of light and shade, and the warm brown and gold hues of his canvases reveal the influence of Italian painters. But the greatest appeal of his work lies in its profound humanity, notable in his frequent portraits of the old and the poor.

believed that his modern (second) practice—with its use of unorthodox dissonances and unexpected harmonic progressions (see Chapter 10)—would make his music more affecting.

The 1600s was a century of classifications—of naming and ordering everything from the passions of the soul (as in Descartes' treatise) to the various musical styles and functions that emerged early in the century. Although not a

Classifications

theorist, Monteverdi enumerated a staggering array of options available to the composer: first and second practices; distinct musical languages appropriate to music's differing functions (church, chamber, theater, and dance); styles implying categories or types of affections (relaxed, moderate, or excited); and more. The century witnessed similar tendencies in instrumental music: the ordering of dances into suites and suites into tonal cycles; the symmetrical arrangement of movements (slow–fast–slow–fast) into sonatas and the grouping of sonatas into collections for church or chamber (see Chapter 12). There were centripetal forces that held pieces together, such as ostinato basses, underlying harmonic patterns, and recurring tutti sections; and centrifugal forces that pushed them apart, such as the improvisational impulse behind a stream of fantasy-like sections of a toccata or the expansion of such divergent sections into separate, contrasting movements. Eventually, these movements became codified into pairs of contrasting pieces: prelude and fugue, allemande and courante, recitative and aria.

Order and disorder

The tension between order and disorder, control and freedom, is also mirrored in the century's drama and architecture. On the one hand, in the façade and formal gardens of the royal palace of Versailles may be seen the rhythm and order of classicism, with its symmetrically positioned forms and repetitive, fixed modules (see Figure III.10). On the other hand, the plan of one of the Baroque churches (see Figure III.11) designed by Bernini's colleague in Rome, the architect Francesco Borromini (1599–1667), is a complex structure of asymmetrical, irregular shapes that are neither cross, octagon, oval, nor rectangle. This duality between control and freedom also appeared in England, where the playwright Ben Jonson wrote both court masques and antimasques. Masques were musical plays that portrayed a world of ideal abstractions, whereas antimasques were antic or grotesque interludes that introduced disintegrating forces and resorted to comedy and satire. Antimasque elements

Figure III.9 Diego Velázquez (1599–1660), Three Musicians, *ca. 1618, from among his works that portray a world of subheroic characters—in this case, a boy holding a guitar, a blind vihuela player, and a violinist. Note the monkey behind the boy's back—a symbol of baseness or ignorance.*
(Bildarchiv Preussischer Kulturbesitz/Art Resource, NY.)

Figure III.10 *Garden façade of the palace of Versailles, built 1661–1690. The columns and arches echo classical architecture, and the gardens display the repetitive forms and symmetrical arrangements so characteristic of French rationalism.*
(Rudy Sulgan/Corbis)

continued to influence the English stage, as the witches in Henry Purcell's opera *Dido and Aeneas* (1689) attest (see Chapter 13). Indeed, in most Baroque music there is a constant creative tension between control and freedom or between composition and improvisation.

It was in the very nature of Baroque expression to place the arts on an equal footing with each other as valid interpreters of human experience and to foster their association in seventeenth-century Europe. Their combined powers immeasurably enhanced their individual effect, as exemplified by the integration of sculpture, architecture, and lighting in Bernini's chapel (Figures 11.4 and 11.5), or of music, poetry, and theater in a Monteverdi opera (see Chapter 10). All the arts in the seventeenth century sought to move the affections, and that goal licensed painters, sculptors, poets, and musicians to transcend previously established limits to imitate and penetrate the invisible realm of the soul.

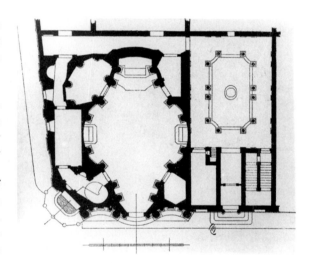

Figure III.11 *Francesco Borromini's plan for San Carlo alle Quattro Fontane, Rome, begun 1638, revealing the basic irregularity of Baroque design.*
(Scala/Art Resource, NY.)

Vocal Music of the Early Baroque and the Invention of Opera

PRELUDE

As with other epochs, boundary dates for the Baroque period are only approximations. Many general characteristics of Baroque music appeared before 1600, and many were declining by the 1730s. But within the chronological limits of 1600 to 1750—the long seventeenth century—composers adhered to an innovative set of conventions for organizing music and adopted certain ideas about how music should sound. Most important, they believed that music, by acting on the emotions, should move the listener.

Italian musicians living around 1600 knew they were inventing new ways of making music. They devised new idioms (such as basso continuo, monody, and recitative); new styles (marked by unprepared dissonance and greater focus on the solo voice or instrument directed by a supporting bass line); and new genres (including opera). This generation saw the most deliberate cultivation of the new in music since the Ars Nova in the early 1300s (see Chapter 4).

Italian trends continued to dominate musical fashions during the seventeenth and early eighteenth centuries, and by 1750 the international language of European music had acquired a distinct Italian accent. Despite its political fragmentation, Italy remained the most influential region of Europe in musical matters during this period. Several Italian cities loomed disproportionately larger on the musical map than their real size or political power suggested. Florence, for example, hosted a brilliant period of musico-theatrical innovation at the dawn of the seventeenth century that led to the flowering of early opera. Rome continued to influence sacred music and for a time became an important center of opera, several types of vocal chamber music, and instrumental music. Venice, a leading musical city throughout the seventeenth century, nurtured the development of opera, as did Naples in the eighteenth century. Generations of composers centered at Saint Mark's church in Venice wielded a mighty influence on Baroque choral and instrumental music as well.

In this chapter, we will discuss the general characteristics of Baroque music before exploring their application in specific genres. The rise of opera, the newest and most quintessential art form of the Baroque era, will occupy the rest of the chapter. New genres of chamber and church music that became prominent in the early seventeenth century will be introduced in the next chapter.

General Characteristics of Baroque Music

Baroque composers were united by a common goal: to express or represent a wide range of feelings vividly and vigorously, continuing the efforts begun in the late sixteenth-century madrigal. They sought musical means to excite or arouse the affections. Rather than express their personal feelings, composers, like painters, wanted to represent universal emotions in a general way.

One musical tool for expression was dissonance, for which there were established rules (see A Closer Look, page 193). As discussed in the introduction, Claudio Monteverdi (1567–1643; see Biography, page 194) referred to these rules as part of the first practice, the compositional method that prevailed in the sixteenth century. He deliberately broke the rules governing the handling of dissonance in some of the madrigals in his Fifth Book to express the text more forcefully, inaugurating what he later called a new, second practice, better suited to moving the affections. The madrigal *Cruda Amarilli* (Cruel Amaryllis, NAWM 71), a lover's complaint from Guarini's *Pastor fido*, is a good example. To dramatize the harsh sound and meaning of the opening word (*cruda*, or cruel), Monteverdi introduced and resolved dissonances "incorrectly" in measures 2

The second practice

Full 🔊   Concise 🔊

Example 10.1 Claudio Monteverdi, Cruda Amarilli

Cruel Amaryllis, who with your very name [teach bitterly] of love, alas . . .

VIGNETTE Monteverdi's Reply to Artusi, 1605

In his Fifth Book of Madrigals (1605), Monteverdi included a brief preface asserting that there is a "different way" of treating consonance and dissonance in his modern second practice. Here the composer sought to defend his work against the criticisms of Artusi, who championed the older, or first, contrapuntal practice. In response to Artusi, Monteverdi deliberately gave the offending work, Cruda Amarilli *(NAWM 71), primacy of place in the collection. Two years later, his brother Giulio Cesare further explained that in the second practice the music serves the expression of the text rather than following its own rules as taught by Zarlino in the first practice. The text was the "mistress of the harmony," the dominant factor in the partnership of words and music, and, therefore, the one that called the tune.*

Don't be surprised that I am giving these madrigals to the press without first replying to the objections that Artusi made against some very minute portions of them. Being in the service of His Serene Highness of Mantua, I am not master of the time I would require. Nevertheless I wrote a reply to let it be known that I do not do things by chance, and as soon as it is rewritten it will see the light under the title, *Seconda pratica overo Perfettione della moderna musica* [Second Practice, or the Perfection of Modern Music]. Some will wonder at this, not believing that there is any other practice than that taught by Zarlino. But let them be assured concerning consonances and dissonances that there is a different way of considering them from that already determined, which defends the modern manner of composition with the assent of the reason and the senses. I wanted to say this both so that the expression *seconda pratica* would not be appropriated by others and so that men of intellect might meanwhile consider other second thoughts concerning harmony. And have faith that the modern composer builds on foundations of truth.

Live happily.

C. V. Palisca, "The Artusi-Monteverdi Controversy," in *The New Monteverdi Companion*, ed. Denis Arnold and Nigel Fortune (London: Faber & Faber, 1985), pp. 151–152.

and 6, in both the bass and the upper voices (see Example 10.1, where the offending notes are marked with asterisks). Similarly, at "ahi lasso" (alas) in measure 13, the canto sings a descending phrase, evoking a sigh, in which two successive notes create unprepared dissonances with the bass.

Artusi-Monteverdi controversy   Although *Cruda Amarilli* was not printed until it appeared in the Fifth Book of Madrigals in 1605, it must have been in circulation before 1600. In that year, the theorist Giovanni Maria Artusi published his scathing commentary, *L'Artusi overo delle imperfettioni della moderna musica* (The Artusi; or, Concerning the Imperfections of Modern Music), which vehemently criticized Monteverdi for the grating dissonances and contrapuntal liberties in this and other madrigals later published in the Fifth Book. Monteverdi defended himself in a brief response (see Vignette, above), justifying his new practice on the grounds that expressing the text through striking musical means was more important than following the traditionl rules of counterpoint.

Rhythm and texture   In contrast to the rhythmically unvaried flow of Renaissance polyphony, music during the Baroque period was either very free or very metric. Composers used flexible, speechlike rhythms for vocal recitative (see below) and for improvisatory solo instrumental pieces like toccatas and preludes (see Chapter 12). For other music they deployed regular rhythms, such as those found in dances, that were conventional ways to arouse a particular affection. Bar lines became common for the first time (see Figure 10.2) and eventually indicated recurring patterns of strong and weak beats. Along with the active bass lines and propulsive harmonic motion of much Baroque music, the pervasiveness of these rhythmic patterns parallels the dynamic movement so characteristic of the painting and sculpture of the seventeenth century. The two types of rhythm, flexible and metric, were often used in succession to provide contrast, as we will discover in the pairing of recitative and aria or toccata and fugue.

The prevailing texture of Renaissance music is a polyphony of independent voices, all similar in motion and nearly equal in importance. By contrast, the new texture of seventeenth-century music is homophonic, typically consisting of a firm bass and a florid treble, held together by unobtrusive harmonies. A single melody line supported by accompanying parts was not in itself new—something like it appears in earlier vocal genres and was frequently used, for example, in the performance of sixteenth-century chansons and madrigals (see In Performance, page 138). What was new around 1600 was the contrast between bass and treble that emphasized these two essential lines of the texture and subordinated the inner parts. Significantly, when three voices were used, a second treble line was introduced rather than an alto part, further highlighting the contrast between top and bottom.

Related to this polarity between treble and bass was the system of notation called thorough bass or basso continuo (Italian for "continuous bass"). In this system, the composer wrote only the melody and bass, leaving it to the performers to fill in the appropriate chords or inner parts. Moreover, the notation appeared in score format rather than in parts, which gave music an entirely new look on the page, as shown in Figure 10.2. The bass and chords were played on one or more continuo instruments, typically harpsichord, organ, lute, or theorbo (see Figure 10.1). By the later seventeenth century, the bass line was frequently reinforced by a viola da gamba, cello, bassoon, or other bass instrument that could sustain tones. When the chords to be played were not simply common triads in root position, or if nonchord tones (such as suspensions) or accidentals were needed, the composer usually added figures—numbers or flat or sharp signs—above or below the bass notes to indicate the precise pitches required, as in Figure 10.2. Such a bass line is called a figured bass. The realization—the actual playing—of such an accompaniment varied according to the type of piece and the skill and taste of the player, who had considerable room for improvisation (see In Performance, page 187).

The first collection of solo songs with basso continuo was composed by the singer Giulio Caccini (1551–1618) and published in 1601–1602 with the demonstrative title *Le nuove musiche* (New Pieces of Music; more correctly, Musical Pieces in a New Style). The songs divide into two distinct formal types in use by the fashionable poets of the day: madrigal and air. Caccini called those with strophic settings (many stanzas sung to the same music) arias (Italian for "airs"), which at that time denoted any written setting or improvised oral performance of strophic poetry. The others he called madrigals, which were through-composed like the polyphonic madrigals. In his foreword, Caccini boasted that his madrigal *Vedrò 'l mio sol* (I'll see my sun, NAWM 72 and Figure 10.2) had been greeted "with affectionate applause" in Bardi's Camerata (an informal academy sponsored by Caccini's patron, Count Giovanni de' Bardi; see below). Caccini set each line of poetry as a separate phrase ending in a cadence, shaping his melody in a declamatory style according to the natural accentuation

Figure 10.1 A theorbo, a type of lute with long, unstopped bass strings in addition to shorter strings across a fretted fingerboard, often used to accompany singers. The alternate Italian name, chitarrone (large kithara), reflects Italians' interest in ancient Greek music. The instrument's first known appearance was in the Florentine intermedi of 1589 (see page 189), whose theme was the power of Greek music; the theorbo may have been invented for the occasion. Detail from The Five Senses *by Theodoor Rombouts, ca. 1630.*
(Museum voor Schone Kunsten, Ghent. Scala/Art Resource, NY.)

Full 🔊   Concise 🔊

Figure 10.2 Giulio Caccini's madrigal Vedrò 'l mio sol *as printed in* Le nuove musiche *(Florence: Marescotti, 1601–1602). In this early example of thorough-bass notation, the bass is figured with the exact intervals to be sounded in the chords above it—for example, the dissonant eleventh resolving to the sharped tenth in the first measure. Compare to the partial transcription in Example 10.2.*

of the text. But he subverted the typical contrapuntal texture of the madrigal by not composing any parts except treble and bass so that the words and melody have a greater impact on the listener.

Caccini's ornaments

Although singers were expected to add embellishments in performance, Caccini occasionally wrote his own, sometimes newly devised ornaments into the music, hoping to teach his pupils how to execute them and where to place them so that they didn't distort the words. Faithful to the goals of the Camerata's humanists, he insisted that ornaments should be used sparingly and then only to enhance the message of the text, not merely to display vocal virtuosity. His foreword to *Le nuove musiche* includes descriptions of the vocal ornaments then in use and instructions about their execution, providing a valuable resource for scholars and singers. In his day, Caccini was much in demand as a teacher of the new style of solo singing and trained many of the singers who performed at court, where some participated in the first operas. In many ways this collection, with its lengthy and meticulous preface about the art of singing, was a monument to the deceased members of the Camerata who were his mentors as well as a legacy to his students, among whom were many members of his own family, including his composer daughter Francesca (see page 195).

The concertato medium

Another reason the texture of Baroque music sounds different from that of the Renaissance is that seventeenth-century composers frequently combined voices with instruments, assigning different roles to each, in contrast to the sixteenth-century preference for homogeneous ensembles. The result was the concertato medium (from Italian *concertare*, "to reach agreement"). In a concerto, contrasting forces are brought together in a harmonious ensemble. Today we think of concertos as pieces for soloists and orchestra, but the meaning was broader in the seventeenth century, embracing such genres as the concerted madrigal for one or more voices and continuo, and the sacred concerto, a sacred vocal work with instruments.

Chords and dissonance

Basso-continuo practice led composers to think of consonant sounds as vertical entities, or chords, rather than as discrete intervals over the bass. This notion eventually allowed a dissonance to be heard not as an interval between

In Performance   Realizing the Basso Continuo

The ability to realize a figured bass at sight is expected of any accompanist of Baroque music and requires considerable skill in improvisation. The performer might play only chords or add passing tones or melodic motives that echo ideas appearing in the treble or bass parts. Example 10.2 shows two possible realizations of the opening phrase of Caccini's madrigal for solo voice presented in Figure 10.2. The first merely adds the chords implied by the intervals between bass and treble, as well as those that are specified by the figures. The second is more active, using moving parts—with passing and neighbor tones and an embellished suspension—to fill out the texture. Whether one or another style is more appropriate in improvising a given performance would depend on a number of factors: the number and sustaining power of the accompanying instruments, the tempo chosen for the song, the size of the room and its audience. The written music remains the same; its realization varies from one performance to another. Modern editions of works with continuo may print an editor's realization in smaller notes to distinguish them from what the composer actually provided (compare Figure 10.2 with its realization in NAWM 72), but even those are only the editor's recommendations to the performer.

In choosing how to realize the bass, the continuo player (or players—some early seventeenth-century scores call for a miniature band of performers) had to be sensitive to the interpretation and style of the soloist, much as the rhythm-section players in a jazz combo interact with a singer or lead melody instrument. Many instruction manuals were published throughout the seventeenth and eighteenth centuries to guide organists and other keyboard players in the art of continuo playing. In addition to teaching the basic principles of chord realization, some suggest that the player should add passage work, especially when the singer holds or repeats a note; but others warn against a realization that is too "ornamental" and apt to detract from the song's expressivity. The author of one text distinguishes between those who play with "invention and variety, now with gentle strokes and repeating notes/chords, now with generous passage-work" and those with "technical facility but little learning" who play endless and unmusical runs.[1]

Such performance practices varied from nation to nation and from one generation to another. But what remained constant in Baroque music is the centrality of the performer and performance, not the composer and the work.

Example 10.2 Two possible continuo realizations for the opening of Vedrò 'l mio sol

a. Chordal style

Ve   drò'l___   mio   sol,

b. With figuration

Ve   drò'l___   mio   sol,

I'll see my sun

1. Agostino Agazzari, *Del sonare sopra il basso* [On Playing above the Bass], 1609.

two voices but rather as a note that does not fit into a chord. As a result, musicians and listeners tolerated a greater variety of intervals. Many dissonances remained ornamental and experimental, but by the mid-seventeenth century, conventions governed how they could be introduced and resolved. Chromaticism

Chromaticism

followed a similar development, from experimentation around the turn of the century to freedom within an orderly scheme by midcentury. Chromaticism expressed intense emotions in vocal works, suggested harmonic exploration in instrumental pieces, and created distinctive subjects for treatment in imitative counterpoint.

Cantus mollis and *durus*

While the features described above tend to characterize the entire Baroque period, one aspect of music that did change from the beginning of the Baroque to the end is harmonic organization. Musicians in the early seventeenth century still thought of themselves as working within the system of church modes, but they considered these to belong to one of two large affective areas, known as *cantus mollis* and *cantus durus* (literally, "soft song" and "hard song"). The first was indicated by a key signature of one flat and used chords belonging to the flatter regions of the tonal spectrum; it was deemed appropriate for the expression of subdued and pleasant emotions. The other had a key signature of no sharps or flats, and its harmonies explored the sharper regions (using accidentals where necessary); its use was reserved for harsher and more intense emotions. By the last third of the century, however, Corelli, Lully, and other composers were writing music that today we would unhesitatingly call tonal, operating within the system of major and minor keys familiar from music of the eighteenth and nineteenth centuries. But it wasn't until 1722 that Rameau's *Treatise on Harmony* offered the first complete theoretical formulation of the new system, which by then had existed in practice for over half a century.

Emergence of tonality

Like the modal system used in the Renaissance, then, tonality evolved gradually. The long-standing use of certain techniques—standard cadential progressions, bass movement by a fourth or fifth, conventional bass patterns, the use of suspensions and other dissonances to create forward motion—eventually bred a consistent set of procedures that could be codified in a theory. Although early Baroque works often point toward a tonal center, the mere presence of such techniques did not yet mean that the works were tonal. Still, figured bass was important in the development of tonality because its notation drew attention to the succession of chords. Indeed, figured bass became the link between counterpoint and homophony, bridging the gap between a linear-melodic concept of musical structure and a chordal-harmonic one.

Early Opera

An opera is a drama sung to continuous or nearly continuous music and staged with scenery, costumes, and action. It is composed to a libretto (Italian for "little book"), a play usually written in rhymed and unrhymed verse. The quintessential art form of the Baroque, combining as it did action and reaction, drama and spectacle, poetry, music, and the visual arts, opera was to become the most common path to fame and even, occasionally, fortune for many composers and performers of the era.

Forerunners

Although the earliest operas date from the very end of the sixteenth century, the association of music with drama goes back to ancient times. The choruses and principal lyric speeches in the plays of Euripides and Sophocles were sung (see NAWM 2), as were medieval liturgical dramas (see NAWM 6). Some Renaissance plays incorporated songs or sung choruses; others presented musical interludes, known as intermedi, between their acts. On important occasions at the Italian courts, such as the 1589 wedding in Florence of Grand Duke Ferdinand de' Medici and Christine of Lorraine, these intermedi became elaborate musical productions, with choruses, soloists, large instrumental ensembles, and spectacular costumes and stage effects (see Figure 10.3). The production of the 1589 Florentine intermedi called for the collaboration of artists, poets, composers, musicians, singers, and choreographers, many of whom were later involved in the earliest operas.

Florentine intermedi

Another source for early opera was the pastoral drama, a play in verse with incidental music. In a tradition derived from ancient Greece and Rome, pastoral poetry, whose intense lyricism had already appealed to the madrigalists, told of idyllic love in an imaginary world of fields, woods, and fountains, peopled by simple rustic youths and maidens. In this idealized setting, music was the sign of a special state of being, and song seemed the natural mode of expressing the joys and melancholies of love. By the end of the sixteenth century, pastoral plays were very much in vogue at Italian courts. The most popular was by the Ferrarese court poet Giovanni Battista (or Giambattista) Guarini; his *Il pastor fido* (The Faithful Shepherd, 1590) not only was performed as a theater piece, but also supplied lyrics for hundreds of madrigal settings, including Monteverdi's *Cruda Amarilli* (NAWM 71). The first operas also drew on the poetic and musical traditions of the pastoral.

Pastoral drama

Full 🔊   Concise 🔊

Despite these musical and theatrical precedents, however, opera might never have emerged without the interest in ancient Greek tragedy expressed by humanist scholars, poets, musicians, and patrons. They hoped to revive the legendary ethical powers attributed to ancient tragedy, which some believed was entirely sung, by creating modern works that were equally powerful in performance. In this respect, opera fulfilled a profoundly humanist agenda, paralleling in dramatic music the emulation of ancient Greek sculpture and architecture in art.

Greek tragedy as a model

Girolamo Mei

The prime mover behind the idea that the entire text of a Greek tragedy was performed in song was Girolamo Mei (1519–1594), a Florentine scholar who edited several Greek dramas. While working in Rome as a cardinal's secretary, Mei conducted a great deal of research on Greek music, particularly its role in the theater. After reading almost every Greek treatise on music that survived from the ancient world, he concluded that Greek music had consisted of a single melodic line, sung by a soloist or chorus, with or without accompaniment. Such a direct delivery of the text could evoke powerful emotional responses from the listener through the natural expressiveness of the voice via the register, rhythms, and contours of its utterance.

Mei communicated his ideas to colleagues in Florence, notably Count Giovanni de' Bardi (1534–1612) and Vincenzo Galilei (ca. 1520s–1591), a lute player, singer, composer, theorist, and father of the astronomer Galileo. From the early 1570s, Bardi hosted an informal academy at his palace in Florence, where

Figure 10.3 Costume designs for dancing women from the second of the 1589 Florentine intermedi in celebration of a Medici wedding. Drawing by Andrea Boscoli (1550–1606).
(Victoria & Albert Museum, London/Art Resource, NY.)

The Florentine
Camerata

scholars discussed literature, science, and the arts, and musicians performed new music. Bardi's young protégé, Giulio Caccini, later referred to this gathering as Bardi's "Camerata" (club or coterie). Mei's letters about Greek music often appeared on the agenda.

Vincenzo Galilei

If Mei was the elder statesman of Bardi's Camerata, Galilei was its trailblazer. In his *Dialogo della musica antica et della moderna* (Dialogue on Ancient and Modern Music, 1581), Galilei used Mei's ideas to criticize the theory and practice of vocal counterpoint and proposed a revival of the Greek ideal of the union of music and poetry through monody (or *monodia*, from the Greek *monos*, "alone"), the ancient style of solo singing. Like Mei, Galilei argued that the semantic and emotional message of the text was impaired by counterpoint: if, as in the fashionable madrigals and motets of the time, some voices were low and others high in register, some rose while simultaneously others descended, some moved in slow notes together with others in faster rhythms, then not only were the words distorted and the music's emotional message neutralized, but the resulting web of contradictory impressions confused the listener and served merely to show off the cleverness of the composer and the skillfulness of the performers.

Ancient versus modern

The debate over the relative merits of old and new implied in the title of Galilei's *Dialogo* conforms to one of the central concerns of seventeenth-century aesthetics, as we have seen. Like his contemporaries in the arts, Galilei equated "ancient" and "modern" with "old" (in the sense of "antique" or "classical" rather than "conservative") and "new" (in the sense of "au courant" or "fashionably modern"), and he championed the qualities of the old as worthy of adoption by new or modern composers, whose works he thought did not measure up to the ideals of Greek music. In this way, Galilei's and Bardi's generation privileged the "ancient" style over the "modern," perhaps for the first time in music history, just as Renaissance artists and sculptors had when they emulated the marble statues and architectural remains of antiquity. After the turn of the century, however, the "new" or modern style of music was redefined to include those composers who put into practice the reforms advocated by the older generation, either by modifying the rules of counterpoint to allow for a more expressive "second practice," as Monteverdi did, or by rejecting counterpoint altogether, as did Caccini and other composers of monody. Although it had roots in the oral tradition of improvised solo singing—which, by its very nature, focused on the performer—composed monody became the newest of the new musics.

The First Operas

Corsi's academy

After Bardi moved to Rome in 1592, discussions about ancient and modern music continued under the sponsorship of another nobleman and musician, Jacopo Corsi (1561–1602), who was a member of a different Florentine circle, the Accademia degli Alterati. Among the participants were two veterans of the 1589 intermedi, poet Ottavio Rinuccini (1562–1621) and composer Jacopo Peri (1561–1633), shown in Figure 10.4. Convinced that Greek tragedies were sung in their entirety, Corsi's group set out to re-create the ancient genre in modern form. They first experimented with Rinuccini's pastoral poem *Dafne*, performed privately for invited guests in Corsi's palace in Florence in 1598. Although only fragments of the music survive, this was the first opera: a staged drama set entirely to music, with a new kind of singing designed specifically for theatrical delivery. It was followed in October 1600 by Rinuccini's more ambitious drama *L'Euridice*, set to music by Peri and Caccini and performed during

L'Euridice

the court festivities celebrating the marriage of Maria de' Medici to Henry IV of

France. Because Caccini, who wanted to protect his position at court, would not allow his singers to perform Peri's music, the first performance consisted of a combination of both composers' settings. In their rivalry to claim credit for writing the "first" opera, both composers published their scores a few months later (though Caccini's work appeared slightly earlier than Peri's), and the status of the new theatrical genre was assured.

L'Euridice elaborated the well-known myth of Orpheus and Eurydice, giving it a happy ending to suit the joyous occasion. The story demonstrates music's power to move the emotions: through his singing, Orfeo (Orpheus) persuades the gods of the underworld to restore his bride, Euridice, to life. Peri and Caccini, both singers by profession, had similar approaches to theatrical music, but Caccini's setting is more melodious and lyrical, resembling the songs of *Le nuove musiche*, whereas Peri's is better suited to the drama because he found a new way to imitate speech and varied his musical style to suit the meaning of the text and developments in the plot (see NAWM 73).

Why was the imitation of speech so important to Peri and his librettist, Rinuccini? Galilei and other humanists had reinforced the ancient Greek idea that "how one speaks" the words reveals their underlying emotion. For a songwriter, it became a question of how to set the words musically to disclose their significance, allowing the melody hidden in the tonal and rhythmic shapes of the words themselves to suggest the contours, rhythms, and accents of the musical melody. If the composer succeeded in doing that, the meaning inherent in the words would be revealed and would, in turn, disclose the emotional state of the performer and ultimately influence or move the listeners to experience a similar state.

So Peri invented a new style of singing, soon known as recitative, for the dialogue portions of *L'Euridice*, and he wrote a detailed explanation of his procedure in the preface to the published score (see Vignette, page 192). There Peri reviewed the ancient Greek distinction between the "continuous" fluctuation or sliding pitches of speech and the intervallic, or "diastematic," motion of song. He sought a speech-song that was halfway between them, similar to the style scholars thought the Greeks used for reciting heroic poems. On the one hand, by writing long notes in the bass line and allowing the voice's shorter notes to pass through both consonances and dissonances—thereby imitating the continuous, sliding pronunciation of words—he freed the voice from the harmony enough so that it resembled the pitchless declamation of speech. On the other hand, where a syllable of text was stressed in speaking—in Peri's words, "intoned"—he formed a consonance with the bass. Thus, Peri conceived of recitative as a spontaneous-sounding, speechlike medium for imitating, expressing, and arousing the emotions, following the natural rhythmic patterns and pitch inflections of the voice (see A Closer Look, page 193).

Recitative, then, was an extreme form of monody and opera's most radical innovation because it sought not merely to imitate speech but to eradicate completely the distinction between speaking and singing, or between words and music. It did so by fusing the two elements into an inseparable whole, creating a new language that was more than speech but less than song—as Peri described it, a language able to communicate simultaneously to both the intellect and the emotions. Thus, although Peri and his associates knew they had not brought back Greek music, they believed they had created a speech-song that not only resembled what had been used in the ancient theater but also was compatible with modern musical practice.

The performance and publication of the *Euridice* operas attracted significant attention in the musical world, and within the decade Claudio Monteverdi tried his hand at the new genre—so successfully that his *Orfeo* (1607) became the first

Full 🔊

Imitation of speech

Figure 10.4 A sketch of Jacopo Peri, costumed as the legendary singer Arion, a role he played in the Florentine intermedi of 1589. Arion, returning from concerts in Corinth, sings an elaborate aria just before he plunges into the sea to escape his mutinous crew. The music was by Jacopo Peri and Christofano Malvezzi, the costume by Bernardo Buontalenti.

(Biblioteca Nazionale, Florence/MicroFoto.)

VIGNETTE Peri's Description of His Recitative Style

In the preface to his opera L'Euridice, *published in 1601, Jacopo Peri described his search for a new kind of musico-theatrical delivery partly adapted from his understanding of ancient Greek drama and partly based on his own analysis of the oral patterns of speech. This new style, known as recitative, became an essential component of the new genre of opera.*

Putting aside every other manner of singing heard up to now, I dedicated myself wholly to seeking the kind of imitation necessary for these poems. And I reflected that the sort of voice assigned by the ancients to singing, which they called diastematic (as if to say sustained and suspended), could at times be hastened and made to take an intermediate course between the slow sustained movements of song and the fluent and rapid ones of speech, and that it could be adapted to my purpose (just as the ancients, too, adapted the voice to reading poetry and heroic verses), and made to approach that other kind of speech, which they called continuous and which our moderns (though perhaps for another purpose) also used in their music.

I recognized likewise that in our speech some sounds are pronounced in such a way that a har-mony can be built upon them, and that in the course of speaking we pass through many others that are not so intoned, until we reach another that will support a progression to a new consonance. Keeping in mind those inflections and accents that serve us in our grief, in our joy and in similar states, I made the bass move in time to these, now more, now less [frequently], according to the affections. I held [the bass] firm through both dissonances and consonances until the voice of the speaker, having run through various notes, arrived at a syllable that, being intoned in ordinary speech, opened the way to a new harmony. I did this not only so that the flow of discourse might not offend the ear (as though stumbling over the repeated notes it encountered with more frequent consonant chords), but also so that the voice would not seem to dance to the movement of the bass, particularly in sad or solemn subjects, granted that other more joyful subjects would require more frequent movements [changes of harmony].

Jacopo Peri, *Le musiche sopra l'Euridice* (Florence, 1600), trans. in C. V. Palisca, *Humanism in Italian Renaissance Musical Thought* (New Haven: Yale University Press, 1985), pp. 428–432; adapted by B. R. Hanning.

Monteverdi's *Orfeo*

opera to achieve a permanent place in the repertory. Monteverdi patterned *Orfeo*, in its subject matter and its variety of styles, on the earlier works; but his concept of recitative, especially, is clearly derived from Peri's score, a copy of which he must have studied. Already an experienced composer of madrigals and church music (see Biography, page 194), Monteverdi drew on a rich palette of vocal and instrumental resources. Through careful tonal organization, his recitative achieves more continuity and a longer line than that of his predecessor although, like Peri's, it becomes intensely expressive at dramatic moments. Furthermore, Monteverdi and his librettist, Alessandro Striggio the younger, interspersed many solo airs, duets, madrigalesque ensembles, and dances, which, taken together, make up a larger proportion of the work than in Peri's opera and furnish a welcome contrast to the recitative. The ritornellos—recurring instrumental sections—and choruses help organize the scenes into schemes of almost ceremonial formality.

Many passages from *L'Orfeo* parallel those from *L'Euridice* (NAWM 73), but it becomes clear immediately that the proportions are very much expanded. Orfeo's strophic canzonet, *Vi ricorda, o boschi ombrosi* (Do you remember, O shady woods, NAWM 74a), is a simple dance song in which the bridegroom recalls how his unhappiness turned to joy as he won Euridice. The musical idiom is a traditional one: the hemiola rhythm is the same as in many frottole

A Closer Look Peri's Recitative

The speech in which Dafne (the Messenger) tells of Euridice's death (NAWM 73b) exemplifies the new recitative style, and Example 10.3 shows how Peri followed his own prescription for composing recitative (see Vignette, page 192). The vertical boxes identify the syllables that are sustained or accented in speech and support a consonant harmony; the horizontal boxes contain the syllables that are passed over quickly in speech and may be set by either dissonances (marked by asterisks) or consonances against the bass and its implied chords. The manner in which the dissonances are introduced and then left often violates the rules of counterpoint, as in measures 3, 4, and 5; the attempt to imitate speech exempts these notes from normal musical conventions. This combination of speechlike freedom and songlike, harmonized, accented syllables realized Peri's idea of a dramatic delivery halfway between speech and song. Note how Peri changes key signatures from *cantus mollis* to *durus* at the words "O bitter, angry fate" to signal the change in affect (see measure 5).

Example 10.3 Jacopo Peri, L'Euridice

But the lovely Eurydice
dancingly moved her feet on the green grass
when—O bitter, angry fate!—
a snake, cruel and merciless,
that lay hidden among flowers and grass
bit her foot . . .

Claudio Monteverdi (1567–1643)

Monteverdi stood out among his contemporaries as the most innovative and imaginative composer of his day, a distinction that caused his music to be attacked in public as too radical. His genius lay in creating vocal works—madrigals, operas, and sacred pieces—that brought music's expressive partnership with words to new heights.

Monteverdi was born in Cremona, in northern Italy, and was trained there by the cathedral's music director. He was a prodigy as a composer and had already published two collections each of madrigals and sacred music when, at age twenty-three, he took a position as a string player at the court of Vincenzo Gonzaga, duke of Mantua. He married a court singer, Claudia Cattaneo, and in 1601 was appointed court music director by the duke.

The Gonzagas commissioned Monteverdi's first operas, *L'Orfeo* (1607) and *L'Arianna* (1608; only the heroine's much-praised lament survives). Between the two premieres, Claudia died, leaving Monteverdi with two young sons. Overworked and poorly paid, Monteverdi suffered ill health, but he remained in Mantua under slightly better conditions until a new duke dismissed him in 1612. The following year he became maestro di cappella at Saint Mark's in Venice, the most prestigious musical post in Italy, where he remained until his death thirty years later. He wrote a great deal of sacred music for Saint Mark's and became a priest in 1632.

Throughout his career, however, Monteverdi reserved a special place in his work for the

Figure 10.5 Claudio Monteverdi, in a 1640 portrait by Bernardo Strozzi. (Landesmuseum Ferdinandeum, Innsbruck, Austria.)

madrigal, publishing no fewer than 250 in nine collections over five decades. He transformed the genre from the witty, polyphonic, a cappella part-songs of the late Renaissance to powerful explorations of the concertato medium and updated its language with emotionally charged dissonances and declamatory melodies in the new, dramatic, Baroque style.

His last works, two operas written in his seventies for the Venetian stage, were remarkably "modern" in style and technique. After his death in 1643, he was lauded in both poetry and music, and his influence, though not long-lived, spread via the circulation of his published works and the operas of his younger contemporaries.

Major works: 3 surviving operas—*L'Orfeo, Il ritorno d'Ulisse,* and *L'incoronazione di Poppea;* 9 books of madrigals; 3 other volumes of secular songs; *Vespro della Beata Vergine;* 3 masses; 4 collections of sacred music.

Full 🔊

written a hundred years earlier (see NAWM 55, for example), and the harmonization with root-position chords is also similar.

Full 🔊 Concise 🔊

Like Peri, Monteverdi reserves the most modern style for dramatic dialogue and impassioned speeches. The Messenger's narrative relating how Euridice perished from a snakebite, in NAWM 74c, beginning *In un fiorito prato* (In a flowery meadow), imitates the characteristics of Peri's recitative, but the harmonic movement and melodic contour are more broadly conceived. Orfeo's lament

Full 🔊 Concise 🔊

(NAWM 74d and Example 10.4) displays a new expressive force that leaves the first monodic experiments far behind. In the passage that begins "Tu se' morta" (You are dead), each phrase of music, like each phrase of text, builds on the preceding one and intensifies it through heightened pitch and quickened rhythm. The dissonances against sustained chords, marked with asterisks in the example, enhance the illusion of Orfeo's halting speech, and the rests, syncopations, and word repetitions in the melody suggest his state of shock. The raw passage from an E-major chord to a G-minor chord (measures 45–46) emphasizes his poignant

Example 10.4 Claudio Monteverdi, L'Orfeo, Tu se' morta

You are dead, my life, and I still breathe?
You have departed from me . . .

question: Why must I continue to live, when my bride—my "life"—is dead? The progress of the melody parallels Orfeo's changing mood—from his initial despair to his resolution to follow and rescue Euridice from the realm of death.

Despite the interest aroused by the first operas, only a few more were written and performed during the next thirty years. The Florentine court continued to prefer ballets, masques, and intermedi as a means of glamorizing state weddings and other events. When a Polish prince visited Florence in 1625, the court staged a combination of ballet and musical scenes—*La liberazione di Ruggiero dall'isola d'Alcina* (The Liberation of Ruggiero from the Island of Alcina) written by Francesca Caccini (1587–ca. 1645). Billed as a ballet, the work had all the trappings of opera: an opening sinfonia, a prologue, recitatives, arias, choruses, instrumental ritornellos, and elaborate staging (see Figure 10.6). Commissioned by the archduchess, *La liberazione* explores the theme of women and

Francesca Caccini

Figure 10.6 Stage design by Giulio Parigi for the second change of scene in Francesca Caccini's La liberazione di Ruggiero, *produced in 1625 at the Medici villa of Poggio Imperiale. The setting is the enchanted island of the sorceress Alcina, who holds the pagan knight Ruggiero captive there. The plot is based on an episode in Ludovico Ariosto's epic* Orlando furioso *(1532).*
(Engraving by Alfonso Parigi.)

power, with two sorceresses—one good and one evil—delineated by contrasting musical styles, contending over the young knight Ruggiero.

Francesca Caccini had a brilliant career as a singer, teacher, and composer, becoming the highest-paid musician employed by the grand duke of Tuscany. The daughter of Giulio Caccini, she performed frequently with her sister Settimia and stepmother, Margherita, in a *concerto delle donne* that rivaled the famous ensemble at Ferrara (see Chapter 7). She composed music for at least fourteen dramatic entertainments, making her among the most prolific composers of theater music at the time.

Opera in Rome and Venice

Rome

In the 1620s, the center for new developments in opera shifted to Rome, where wealthy prelates vied with each other in offering lavish entertainments. Subjects expanded from pastoral and mythological plots to include episodes from Italian epics; the lives of saints; and comedy. The most prolific librettist was Giulio Rospigliosi (later Pope Clement IX), who helped establish libretto writing as an independent craft. His most famous libretto, *Il Sant'Alessio* (1632), based on the life of the fifth-century Saint Alexius, was set to music by Stefano Landi (1587–1639). Because Baroque theater relied on the concept of *la meraviglia* (Italian for "wonderment") to arouse astonishment and inspire awe in audiences, operas often emphasized spectacular stage effects—showing the devils and demons in *Sant'Alessio* being consumed in flames, for example.

In Roman opera, solo singing increasingly fell into two clearly defined types—recitative and aria. The recitatives were more speechlike than Peri's or Monteverdi's, and the arias were melodious and mainly strophic. Because women were prohibited from the stage in Rome, female roles there were given to castrati (sing., castrato), males who were castrated before puberty to preserve their high vocal range, a practice in keeping with the cultural and commercial premium placed on high voices. Later in the seventeenth and in the eighteenth centuries, castrati also sang in operas outside Rome but almost always in male rather than female roles (see Chapter 14). Since women were also generally banned from singing in church, boys and castrati performed the higher parts in sacred polyphony throughout Italy.

Castrati

Venetian opera

A decisive step in the history of opera occurred in 1637 with the opening in Venice of the first public opera house, Teatro San Cassiano. Until then, musical theater had been supported by wealthy aristocratic patrons for courtly and elite audiences, but now it was presented for and attended by a paying public, with financial backing from wealthy and prominent families who rented boxes for the season. Venice was ideal for public opera. Although small in size, its reputation for freedom from religious and social constraints attracted thousands of visitors each year for Carnival, which ran for several weeks between the day after Christmas and the day before Lent (a penitential period leading to Easter during which public entertainments were banned). By the end of the century, there were nine theatrical stages competing for audiences, and more than 150 operas had been produced.

After Monteverdi moved to Venice in 1613 and became maestro di cappella at Saint Mark's church, he continued to write operas and other dramatic works in addition to composing church and vocal chamber music (discussed in Chapter 11). In his seventies, but still very much up on the latest musical trends, he composed three operas for the Venetian stage. Two survive: *Il ritorno d'Ulisse* (The Return of Ulysses, 1640), based on the last part of Homer's *Odyssey*, and *L'incoronazione di Poppea* (The Coronation of Poppea, 1642), a historical opera on

Monteverdi's
L'incoronazione di Poppea

the Roman emperor Nero's illicit affair with the ambitious Poppea, whom he eventually married. *Poppea*, often considered Monteverdi's masterpiece, lacks the varied instrumentation and stage effects of *Orfeo* because it was written for a commercial theater instead of a wealthy court presentation, but it surpasses *Orfeo* in its depiction of human character and passions. The love scene between Nero and Poppea in Act I, scene 3 (NAWM 75) demonstrates Monteverdi's nuanced language as he changes styles to reflect the characters' shifting feelings: expressive recitative inflected with dissonance and chromaticism as Poppea pleads with Nero not to leave her bedchamber after a night of lovemaking; calmer or more excited recitation for dialogue, as the situation warrants; aria styles with ritornellos, often in triple meter, for declarations of love; and passages that lie somewhere between recitative and aria style, called *arioso*, that often serve as

Figure 10.7 *A view of the Teatro San Giovanni Grisostomo, one of the first public opera houses in Venice, showing the stage with sets in place, the orchestra in front of the stage, and several tiers of boxes, which offered both a better view and greater prestige for audience members than seating on the main floor. Engraving from 1709.*
(Museo Correr, Venice, Italy.)

transitions between the two. Content more than poetic form, and heightened emotional expression rather than the wish to charm or dazzle determine the shifts from one level of musical expression to another. Thus the stylistic variety in *Poppea*, though even greater than in *Orfeo*, serves the same dramatic goals.

In modern performances of *Poppea*, the role of Nero is often sung by a tenor. However, Monteverdi originally cast Nero as a castrato, not only because of the fashionable obsession with high voices, but also for dramatic reasons: by sharing the same vocal range, Nero and Poppea's intertwining voices present a more convincing depiction of their physical union during their sensuous love scenes.

Among Monteverdi's successors in Venice were his pupil Pier Francesco Cavalli (1602–1676) and Antonio Cesti (1623–1669). Cavalli was a leading figure on the Venetian musical scene, composing for the theater during most of his working life. The most celebrated of his more than thirty operas was *Giasone* (Jason, 1649), which incorporates most of the conventions of the period, including complicated dramatic intrigue that mixes serious and comic elements, and a formal separation of recitative and aria based on dramatic function. Cesti was Cavalli's most serious competitor but spent much of his career abroad. His *Orontea*, written for Innsbruck in 1656, was one of the most frequently performed operas in the seventeenth century, appearing on stages all over Italy as well as in Austria. Typical for midcentury opera, most of the action unfolds in simple recitative, and a new lyrical idiom reigns in the arias, which are mainly in strophic form and crystallize the affective moments of the plot. The melody of *Intorno all' idol mio* (Around my idol, NAWM 76b), in which Orontea confesses her love for Alidoro, reveals smooth, mainly diatonic lines and flowing triple meter, characteristics gratifying to the singer and audience alike.

By the middle of the seventeenth century, Italian opera had acquired the main features it would retain without significant change essentially for the next two hundred years: (1) concentration on solo singing rather than ensembles and instrumental music; (2) the separation of recitative and aria; and (3) the

Pier Francesco Cavalli

Antonio Cesti

Full 🔊

Italian opera at midcentury

TIMELINE The Early Baroque Period: The Invention of Opera

Musical Events

ca. 1573–1587
Meetings of
Giovanni de' Bardi's
Camerata

1581
V. Galilei, *Dialogo
della musica antica
et della moderna*

1589
Intermedi for Medici
wedding, Florence

1594
Death of Palestrina
and Lassus

1598
Jacopo Peri, *Dafne*

1600
Artusi attacks
Monteverdi in print;
L'Euridice (NAWM 73)
by Peri and Caccini,
performed in Florence

1601–1602
Giulio Caccini, *Le
nuove musiche*
(NAWM 72)

1605
Claudio Monteverdi
publishes Fifth Book of
Madrigals
(NAWM 71)

1607
Monteverdi, *L'Orfeo*
(NAWM 74), in
Mantua

1611
Gesualdo's last book
of madrigals

1613
Monteverdi
appointed maestro
di cappella at Saint
Mark's, Venice

1625
Francesca Caccini,
*La liberazione di
Ruggiero*

1637
First public opera
house opens in
Venice

1642
Monteverdi,
*L'incoronazione di
Poppea* (NAWM
75), in Venice

1550		1650

Historical Events

1590
Guarini, *Il pastor fido*

1604
Shakespeare, *Othello*

1609
Kepler sets forth his astronomical
laws

1618–1648
Thirty Years' War (religious wars
in Germany)

1620
Mayflower brings first English
colonists to New England

1645–1652
Bernini, in Rome, *The Ecstasy of
Saint Teresa* (Figure 11.4)

introduction of distinctive styles and forms for the arias, which drew the most attention from composers and audiences. The Florentine view of music as the servant of poetry and drama had by now been reversed: the Venetians and their imitators saw the drama and poetry as scaffolding for the musical structures, yet their interest centered on the visual elements of scenery, costumes, and special effects and, most of all, on the arias and the stars who sang them (see Chapter 13).

POSTLUDE

Opera began as an effort to re-create ancient Greek ideals of drama, linking the new Baroque era with the earliest Western musical culture. Yet it also had sources in theatrical spectacles like intermedi and in various types of solo song.

These roots proved strong, and spectacular staging and solo singing soon became preeminent, emphasizing what might be called the theatrical side of opera at the expense of the dramatic. This tension between drama, spectacle, and vocal display has continued in all later opera and musical theater. Many operatic reform movements in the eighteenth and nineteenth centuries sought to restore the balance in favor of drama, once again looking back to Greek tragedies for inspiration. But love of the theatrical has been a constant theme, from the elaborate costumes and dances to the virtuosic singing and extravagant productions that emphasize everything from costumes to dancing over plot.

Most seventeenth-century operas lasted only a single season. Those that were revived two or three decades after their composition were exceptional. Almost inevitably, a new production brought new singers and revisions to the score, often by other hands. Historians and musicians have tended to value Monteverdi most highly for the way his music serves the drama and have devalued other early opera, which is rarely heard today. But the focus on solo singing, separation of recitative and aria, and use of varied styles that were characteristic by 1650 continued to dominate Italian opera for the next two centuries.

> Ⓢ Resources for study and review available at
> wwnorton.com/studyspace

Vocal Music for Chamber and Church in the Early Baroque

PRELUDE

The religious differences that had separated Protestant northern Europe from the Catholic south in the sixteenth century continued to echo in seventeenth-century music. Several new genres of sacred music emerged, such as the sacred vocal concerto and the oratorio; these were cultivated both in southern Europe, where Catholic sacred music flourished, and in northern Europe, where Lutheran church music spread through German-speaking lands and Scandinavia. Throughout Europe, instrumental music found its place in both religious and secular circles, expanding on genres that had their beginnings in the sixteenth century. This development will be explored in the next chapter, but many of the general characteristics of Baroque music that we will continue to examine in connection with vocal genres pertain to instrumental music as well.

The changes occurring in intellectual and artistic realms profoundly influenced the course of music history. While seventeenth-century thinkers discarded outmoded ways of viewing the world and proposed new explanations, musicians expanded their vocabulary to meet new expressive needs. As scientists such as Galileo and Newton developed new ideas within the framework of older methods, so composers—such as Claudio Monteverdi in his madrigals and Heinrich Schütz in his motets—poured more intense and more varied emotions into the musical genres they inherited from the Renaissance. Much early seventeenth-century music was truly experimental but by the middle of the century the new resources of harmony, tone color, and form had created a common language with a clear vocabulary, grammar, and syntax.

Vocal Chamber Music

Although by midcentury opera had become the focus of musical life in Venice, elsewhere it was still an uncommon event. Chamber music for mixed voices and instruments remained the standard fare for private music-making (see Figure 11.1). The concertato medium (the use of competing or contrasting

Figure 11.1 Le concert, *a painting by Nicholas Tournier from the early seventeenth century, illustrates the new concertato style of mixed voices and instruments—in this case, solo voice with bass viol, spinet, violin, and lute.* (Louvre, Paris, Réunion des Musées Nationaux/Art Resource, NY.)

forces), whether monody or other textures with basso continuo, permeated all genres of chamber and church music. Composers found new ways of organizing their works—including ritornellos (recurring instrumental interludes), strophic variations, repeating bass patterns, and contrasting styles and textures—to create large-scale forms and enrich their music's expressive resources.

From the beginning of the century, Italian composers turned out thousands of pieces for solo voice or small vocal ensemble with basso continuo. Following Caccini's *Le nuove musiche*, these pieces were published in numerous collections of madrigals, arias, dialogues, and duets, and some were more widely known than any opera. Several of the formal types that became crucial to opera were first perfected in solo song. An example is the strophic aria, which accommodated a variety of treatments. A composer might repeat the same melody, perhaps with minor rhythmic modifications, for each stanza of poetry; write a new melody over the same bass line for successive stanzas; or keep the same harmonic and melodic plan for all the stanzas, but vary the surface musical details. The last two procedures, known as strophic variations, were favorite techniques for instrumental as well as vocal composition (see Chapter 12).

Strophic arias

The importance of the concertato medium can be gauged by its impact on the madrigal. We can trace the change from the unaccompanied polyphonic madrigal to the concerted madrigal with instrumental accompaniment in Monteverdi's fifth through eighth books of madrigals. Beginning with the last six madrigals of his Fifth Book (1605), Monteverdi includes a basso continuo and sometimes calls for other instruments as well. Solos, duets, and trios are set against the full vocal ensemble, and there are instrumental introductions and ritornellos. Monteverdi entitled his Seventh Book *Concerto* (1619) and described it as containing "madrigals and other kinds of songs," without specifying that it includes strophic variations and canzonettas as well as through-composed madrigals.

Concerted madrigals

Monteverdi's Eighth Book, entitled *Madrigali guerrieri et amorosi* (Madrigals of War and Love, 1638), features a remarkable variety of concertato forms and

Madrigals of War and Love

types, including madrigals for five voices with continuo; solos, duets, and trios with continuo; and large works for chorus, soloists, and orchestra. The Eighth Book also contains two sung *balli* (dances or ballets) and the *Combattimento di Tancredi e Clorinda* (The Combat of Tancredi and Clorinda), a work blending mime and dramatic music that was first performed in 1624. Here Monteverdi set the portion of Tasso's *Gierusalemme liberata* (Jerusalem Delivered) that describes the armed confrontation between the crusader knight Tancredi and the pagan heroine Clorinda, ending with her death (see Figure 11.2). Monteverdi assigns the narrative text to a tenor, who delivers it in recitative. The brief dialogue between Tancredi and Clorinda is sung by characters who also mime the actions during the narrative. The instruments (strings with continuo) accompany the voices and play interludes that suggest the action—the galloping of horses, the clashing of swords, the excitement of combat. To convey anger and warlike affections and actions, Monteverdi devised what he called in the book's preface the *concitato genere* ("excited style"), characterized by rapid reiteration of a single note, whether on quickly spoken syllables or in a measured string tremolo. Other composers imitated this device, which became a widely used convention.

Many works used basso ostinato (Italian for "obstinate" or "persistent bass"; often called "ground bass" in English), a short pattern in the bass that repeats while the melody above it changes or, in some cases, elaborates a matching melodic outline. Most ostinato bass patterns were in triple or compound meter, usually two, four, or eight measures long. There was a well-established tradition in Spain and Italy of singing or playing popular songs and dances, composed or extemporized, to familiar ostinato basses such as *Guárdame las vacas* (see NAWM 68b); its close relative, the romanesca; and the *Ruggiero*. (Ruggiero was one of the heroes of Ariosto's epic, so the name betrays the pattern's origins in the Renaissance oral tradition of singing the stanzas of epic poetry to a repeating melodic formula with a standard harmonization.) Such patterns, which provided a ready-made, logical structure for composing or improvising a lengthy song or dance, underlie many vocal and instrumental works of the early seventeenth century (see Chapter 12).

Figure 11.2 The scene from Torquato Tasso's epic poem Gierusalemme liberata (1590), *in which Tancredi, after mortally wounding an enemy warrior in the Crusades, discovers on removing the Saracen's armor that it is his beloved, Clorinda. Monteverdi set their speeches to music in his* Combattimento di Tancredi e Clorinda. *Accompanied by two violins, a viola da braccio, and basso continuo, Clorinda sings, "The heavens open; I go in peace."*
(From *Tasso, La Gierusalemme liberata con le figure di Bernardo Castello* (Genoa, 1690). Beinecke Rare Book and Manuscript Library, Yale University.)

Certain patterns or musical gestures, such as the descending tetrachord (a stepwise descent spanning a fourth), became associated with particular affections. Throughout the Baroque period, especially in opera, composers used various forms of the descending tetrachord ostinato, with its falling contour and relentless repetition, to represent sorrowful affections such as lament.

Lament

A new genre of vocal chamber music developed from the strophic aria and the extended, quasi-dramatic madrigal (such as those in Monteverdi's Eighth Book): the cantata, meaning simply a piece that was "sung." By midcentury, the genre had established itself in Italy as a piece for voice and continuo on an intimate poetic text having several sections that included recitatives, arias, and arioso passages. Among leading cantata composers of the mid-seventeenth century were Luigi Rossi (1597–1653) and Giacomo Carissimi (1605–1674) in Rome—the first an opera composer, the second remembered chiefly for his oratorios (see page 208)—and Barbara Strozzi (1619–1677) in Venice (see Biography, below).

Cantata

Barbara Strozzi (1619–1677)

Strozzi was a rarity among Baroque composers in that she achieved notoriety as a singer and composer despite not having access, as a woman, to the realms of opera and church music. She sang her own music, the bulk of which was intended for intimate, private gatherings, and consequently became the central figure in an academy created in part to showcase her talents.

She was born in Venice, the adopted (and perhaps natural) daughter of poet and librettist Giulio Strozzi. Her father nurtured her ambitions as a composer and introduced her to the intellectual elite of Venice. From her teens, she sang at the Strozzi home for gatherings of poets and other writers, formalized in 1637 as the Academy of the Unisoni. She studied with Pier Francesco Cavalli, the leading Venetian opera composer and a student of Monteverdi's. She was supported financially by her father, by the noble patrons to whom she dedicated her publications, and probably by Giovanni Paolo Vidman, the apparent father of at least three of her four children.

Between 1644 and 1664, Strozzi published eight collections of music (one is now lost). Her publications contain over one hundred madrigals, arias, cantatas, and motets, placing her among the most prolific composers of vocal chamber music of the century. Indeed, she published more cantatas than any other composer of the time. Her choice to publish her music was unusual for a woman musician in the seventeenth century and may reflect the feminist sympathies of her father and his circle.

Figure 11.3 Female musician with viola da gamba, almost certainly a portrait of Barbara Strozzi around 1637, painted by Bernardo Strozzi (perhaps a relative). Her seductive costume, the flowers in her hair, and the musical attributes (instruments and songbook) suggest that the subject is a personification of La Musica, allegorized as an invitation to sensual love.

(State Art Archives, Dresden. Photo: Artothek.)

Major works: 3 collections of cantatas and arias, 2 of arias, and 1 each of madrigals and motets.

Example 11.1 Barbara Strozzi, Lagrime mie

a. opening

Tears of mine, [what holds you back] . . . ?

b. aria over a descending tetrachord ostinato

If it is true then, O God [that cruel fate thirsts only for my tears] . . .

Strozzi's chamber cantata

Full 🔊   Concise 🔊

Strozzi's *Lagrime mie* (NAWM 77), published in her *Diporti di Euterpe* (Pleasures of Euterpe, 1659), is representative of the solo chamber cantata in its successive sections of recitative, arioso, and aria, and of Strozzi in its emotional focus on unrequited love. The first section, which invokes the distraught lover's tears, begins with a stunningly doleful cry, which bursts upon the ear at the top of the vocal register and makes its way downward over a stationary harmony, faltering in its syncopated rhythms and prolonging the dissonances D♯, A, and F♯ to imitate the lover's wailing and lamentation (see Example 11.1a). The passage recurs several times like a refrain, helping to unify the rather loose poetic and musical structure of the rest of the work. The opening section has the rhythmic flexibility and harmonic language of the most expressive recitative; yet it is also marked by the word repetition and intervallic motion associated with aria. Throughout the cantata, Strozzi changes style and figuration frequently to capture the successive moods and images of the text with a fluidity that recalls Monteverdi's late operas. And near the end she employs the minor version of the descending tetrachord ostinato to capture the utter despair expressed in the text (see Example 11.1b). The effect, combining contrasting musical elements to represent shifting emotions, is typical of the concerted chamber style at midcentury.

Airs de cour

Although the Italian style of monody was imitated in other nations, composers outside Italy also produced songs of distinctly national character. In France, the most important genre of secular vocal music was the air de cour (court air), a homophonic, strophic song for four to five voices or for solo voice with lute accompaniment, written by composers associated with the French royal court and sung as independent vocal music or as part of a court ballet. Airs de cour are mostly syllabic with simple, diatonic, elegantly arching melodies, and tend to lack the melismas, sequences, motivic construction, chromaticism, and word-painting used by Italian composers. Furthermore, the French did not widely adopt basso continuo notation until the 1660s.

Catholic Sacred Music

Just as Bernini used theatrical effects in his religious sculpture and architecture (see In Context, page 206), so Catholic composers of the Baroque adopted the theatrical style for church music, setting religious texts as sacred concertos that made use of basso continuo, the concertato medium, monody, and operatic styles from recitative to aria. The goal was the same in both cases: to convey the Church's message in the most dramatically effective and, thus, persuasive way.

Yet sacred music did not abandon polyphony altogether. Composers were routinely trained to write in the old contrapuntal style associated with Palestrina (Chapter 9) and known as the *stile antico* ("old style"), which coexisted alongside the *stile moderno* ("modern style"). A composer might deploy both styles, sometimes in a single piece. Over time, the *stile antico* was modernized as composers added a basso continuo and dependence on church modes gradually gave way to major-minor tonality. At the end of the Baroque period, Johann Joseph Fux codified this quasi-Palestrinian counterpoint in his famous treatise *Gradus ad Parnassum* (Steps to Parnassus, 1725), which remained the most influential textbook on counterpoint for the next two centuries.

Stile antico

From before the time of Willaert (Chapter 9), composers in the Venetian region wrote for two choruses that sometimes echoed one another in antiphony, a style particularly suited to psalm settings. The medium of divided choirs (*cori spezzati*), which encouraged homophonic choral writing and spacious rhythmic organization, did not originate in Venice but found a congenial home there in the vast interior of Saint Mark's church (see Figure 12.4 and In Context, page 151). In the polychoral music of Giovanni Gabrieli—who served as organist and composer of ceremonial music at Saint Mark's—the performance forces grew to grand proportions (hence the modern term *grand concerto*). Two, three, four, or even five choruses, each with a different combination of high and low voices, mingled with instruments of diverse timbres, answered one another antiphonally, alternated with solo voices, and joined together in impressive walls of sound. Sometimes the choirs were separated spatially, with groups in the two organ lofts, one on each side of the altar, and another on the floor. In Chapter 8 we saw how Gabrieli's innovative instrumental works explored these resources (see NAWM 70). He also wrote ploychoral motets for St. Mark's in Venice that included two or more choirs, vocal soloists, and instrumental ensemble, and one or more organs playing continuo. One of his most spectacular large-scale sacred concertos is *In ecclesiis* (In churches; NAWM 78), written for an annual celebration in Venice and published posthumously in 1615. Here Gabrieli combined four vocal soloists, a four-part chorus, a six-part instrumental ensemble with parts assigned to specific instruments (a practice unusual at the time), and organs in a kaleidoscope of styles from modern arias and instrumental canzonas to Renaissance imitative polyphony. At the same time, Gabrieli carefully structured the alternating forces into contrasting sections unified by a refrain (Alleluia) while slowly building to a massive sonorous climax.

Large-scale sacred concerto

Polychoral motets

Full 🔊

Full 🔊 Concise 🔊

The small sacred concerto for few voices, in which one, two, or three solo voices sang to the accompaniment of an organ continuo, was much more familiar to the average churchgoer than the large-scale concerto, which was used to

Small sacred concerto

In Context The Ecstasy of Saint Teresa

By the mid-seventeenth century, the dramatic gestures and attitudes of the stage permeated sacred works, as we see in the music of Schütz and Carissimi. Nowhere is this more evident than in the church of Santa Maria della Vittoria in Rome, where Gian Lorenzo Bernini's marble sculpture *The Ecstasy of Saint Teresa* (see Figure 11.4) dominates the Cornaro Chapel. The Cornaro family commissioned Bernini, working in Rome, to design a side chapel within the church as their final resting place. The commission gave Bernini the opportunity not only to create a sculptural group for the chapel's altarpiece, but also to plan and decorate its entire setting. Perhaps at the family's request, he chose as his subject the popular Saint Teresa of Ávila.

Figure 11.5 Bernini, Cornaro Chapel, marble relief on side wall.
(Photo courtesy of the author.)

Saint Teresa (1515–1582), a Spanish nun, was one of the greatest mystics of the Catholic Church. In her autobiography, she describes how, in one of her many visions, an angel repeatedly pierces her heart with a golden arrow, her pain made bearable by the sweet sensation of her soul being caressed by God. With consummate skill, Bernini transformed Saint Teresa's words into action and reaction: the angel is frozen *in the act* of plunging the arrow into the saint's breast, bringing about her mystical union with Christ, the heavenly bridegroom. Saint Teresa *reacts* by swooning in an ecstatic trance, her limbs dangling, her head tipped back, her eyes half closed, and her mouth forming an almost audible moan. The pair is bathed in a warm and mysterious glow coming through the chapel's hidden window of yellow glass, architecturally contrived to throw a spotlight on the scene.

Bernini reinforces the theatricality of it all with his stunning treatment of the chapel's side walls: there, in pews that resemble theater boxes, he depicts the members of the Cornaro family in almost three-dimensional relief, as though they are witnessing the enactment of this dramatic mystery (see Figure 11.5). Because Bernini created the illusion of the Cornaro family sharing the same space in which we are moving, we feel as if they are among us. In this way, we, too, are drawn in, both physically and emotionally, to the Baroque world of Saint Teresa's vision; we become the audience at a command performance of this silent, sacred opera.

Figure 11.4 The Ecstasy of Saint Teresa, sculpted by Giovanni Bernini (1598–1680) for the Cornaro Chapel in the church of Santa Maria della Vittoria in Rome.
(Scala/Art Resource, NY.)

Discussion of the chapel and its sculpture is based on Rudolf Wittkower, *Gian Lorenzo Bernini: The Sculptor of the Roman Baroque*, 2nd ed. (London: Phaidon, 1966), pp. 24–26.

celebrate major feast days only in the wealthier churches. One of the first composers to exploit this smaller medium for church music was Lodovico Viadana (1560–1627), who in 1602 published a collection, *Cento concerti ecclesiastici* (One Hundred Sacred Concertos). These were intended for performance during Mass, replacing the older-style motet during the Offertory or Communion.

Where resources permitted, the grand concerto was combined with the concerto for few voices, as in Monteverdi's pioneering *Vespers* of 1610, which includes all varieties of solo, choral, and instrumental groupings. In these settings for the liturgical Office, Monteverdi also incorporated the traditional psalm tones while employing the new musical resources of the time—recitative, aria, and concerto.

Alessandro Grandi (1586–1630), Monteverdi's deputy at Saint Mark's in Venice in the 1620s, composed many solo motets that used the new styles of monody. His *O quam tu pulchra es* (NAWM 79), published in 1625, blends elements from recitative, solo madrigal, and lyric aria. The changing styles reflect the moods of the text, drawn from the Song of Songs, a book in the Hebrew Scriptures whose dialogue between two lovers was taken as a metaphor for God's love for the Church. As shown in Example 11.2a, the wonder of the opening exclamation, "Oh how beautiful you are," is captured in recitative style by a sustained note in the voice, a skip to a dissonance in the bass, and a quick descent to a resolution in the voice, while parts of the text suggesting motion are set in aria style in triple meter (Example 11.2b). The use of modern musical styles and the language of love parallels Bernini's sensuous depiction of St. Teresa in ecstasy (see In Context, page 206) in suggesting the intensity of communion with the divine. No doubt many more people encountered the modern vocal styles in church services and devotional music than in opera or in private concerts of secular vocal music.

In Rome, the dramatic impulse found an outlet in sacred dialogues, which combined elements of narrative, dialogue, and commentary. Toward midcentury, such

Full 🔊

Oratorio

Example 11.2 Contrasting styles in Grandi's O quam tu pulchra es

a. Recitative style

Oh how beautiful you are

b. Aria style

Arise, hasten, arise, my bride

works began to be called oratorios because they were most often performed during the Lenten season (the period of penitence before Easter) in the oratory, a building where groups of the faithful met to hear sermons and sing devotional songs, in keeping with the reforming spirit of the Council of Trent (see Chapter 9).

Oratorio versus opera

Like operas and chamber cantatas, oratorios used recitatives, arias, duets, and instrumental preludes and ritornellos. But oratorios differed from operas in several ways: their subject matter was religious; they were seldom, if ever, staged; action was described or suggested rather than mimed; there was often a narrator, called a *storicus* ("storyteller") or *testo* ("text"); and the chorus—usually an ensemble of several voices singing one to a part—could take various roles, from participating in the dramatic dialogue to meditating on or narrating events. Early oratorio librettos were in Latin or Italian.

Carissimi's *Jephte*

The leading composer of Latin oratorios was Giacomo Carissimi, one of several composers in Rome associated with Queen Christina of Sweden (see In Context, page 233). Carissimi's *Jephte* exemplifies the midcentury oratorio. The Latin libretto comes from the Book of Judges 11:29–40, with some paraphrasing and added material to emphasize the Lenten themes of obedience and suffering. The narrator introduces the story in recitative. Jephtha, leader of the Israelites, vows that if the Lord gives him victory over the Ammonites in the impending battle, he will sacrifice the first thing he sees on his return home. That turns out to be his beloved only daughter, who, along with her friends, welcomes Jephtha with songs of rejoicing (solo arias, duets, choruses). After a section of dialogue, in recitative, between father and daughter in which she learns of her father's vow and accepts her fate, the chorus relates how the daughter, still a virgin, goes away to the mountains with her companions to bewail her approaching untimely death. She then sings a lament, to which the chorus responds, as in a Greek tragedy (this final scene is in NAWM 80). The lament is a long, affecting recitative, sweetened, as was customary in sacred music, with moments of florid song and with arioso passages built on sequences. Two sopranos, representing the daughter's companions, echo some of her cadential phrases. The choral response, a moving six-voice lamentation, employs both polychoral and madrigalistic effects, including a descending tetrachord in the opening measures of the basso continuo.

Full 🔊   Concise 🔊

Lutheran Church Music

In German-speaking regions, composers in both the Catholic and Lutheran churches soon took up the new monodic and concertato techniques. Sacred music in Austria and Catholic southern Germany remained under strong Italian influence, with Italian composers particularly active in Munich, Salzburg, Prague, and Vienna. Composers in the Lutheran central and northern regions gradually began to employ the new media, sometimes using chorale tunes as melodic material. Alongside compositions in *stile moderno*, Lutheran composers continued to write polyphonic chorale motets as well as motets on biblical texts that did not use chorale melodies. Many were in the large-scale concerto medium, showing German musicians' admiration of the Venetian fashion.

Heinrich Schütz

The pioneering German composer Heinrich Schütz (1585–1672; see Biography, page 210), like many of his countrymen for centuries to come, completed his musical education in Italy. He studied in Venice with Giovanni Gabrieli from 1609 to 1612 and renewed his acquaintance with Italian music in 1628, when he found it much changed under Monteverdi's tenure at Saint Mark's.

Consequently, Venetian magnificence and color appear frequently in Schütz's music. His sacred works were published in a series of collections that show a remarkable variety. The first, *Psalmen Davids* (Psalms of David, 1619), combines sensitive treatment of German texts with the grandiosity of the Venetian large-scale concerto for two or more choruses, soloists, and instruments, following the model of Gabrieli. The first book of *Symphoniae sacrae* (Sacred Symphonies, 1629) presents concerted Latin motets for various small combinations of voices and instruments. Published in Venice during Schütz's second sojourn there, it shows the strong influences of Monteverdi and Grandi, combining recitative, aria, and concerted madrigal styles.

In 1636 and 1639, when the Thirty Years' War had reduced the number of musicians in the Dresden court chapel, Schütz published his *Kleine geistliche Konzerte* (Small Sacred Concertos), motets for one to five solo voices with continuo that again show his debt to the Italian monodic and concerted styles. But in 1648, Schütz published another collection of sacred choral music (Geistliche Chor-Musik) for five, six, and seven voices without basso continuo, "to be performed both vocally and instrumentally." Interestingly, in his preface to this volume, Schütz pleads with young German composers not to abandon the study of counterpoint (see Vignette, below). Then, in 1647 and 1650 two more books of *Symphoniae sacrae*, featuring sacred concertos in German, appeared. The last installment, published after the Thirty Years' War, used the full musical resources of the Dresden chapel, including continuo, now again available. Many of its pieces are laid out as dramatically conceived "scenes." One of the most stunning is the large-scale concerto *Saul, was verfolgst du mich* (NAWM 81), which calls for two choirs doubled by instruments, six solo voices, two violins, and continuo, and combines the polychoral style of Gabrieli with the dissonant rhetoric of Monteverdi. It brings to life the moment when Saul, a Jew on his way to Damascus to round up Christian prisoners, is stopped by a blinding flash of light and the voice of Christ calling to him: "Saul, why do you persecute me?" The

Sacred concertos

Schütz's *Symphoniae sacrae II* and *III*

Full 🔊   Concise 🔊

VIGNETTE Schütz Advocates a Balance of Old and New Styles

In his sixties, Schütz could look back with satisfaction on his early training in Venice and over his many years in charge of the Dresden court chapel. Here, in the Preface to his collection of Geistliche Chor-Musik *(Sacred Choral Pieces, 1648), he makes the case for striking a balance between the contrapuntal and basso continuo styles of composition, which he had been able successfully to synthesize during his productive career as a church composer.*

As everyone knows, since the concertizing style of composition over a basso continuo came from Italy to the attention of us Germans, it has been most successful and popular here. In fact, it has gained more followers than any other style we ever had. The varied musical works now scattered hither and yon in the book shops of Germany offer sufficient evidence for this. By no means do I find fault with such publications. . . .

On the other hand, no musician, not even those trained in a good school, can approach the most difficult study of counterpoint or any other well-regulated style of composition . . . unless he has previously gained sufficient skill in the style without the basso continuo and has mastered the necessary requisites for regular composition. These are (among others): orderly arrangement of the modes; simple, mixed, and inverted fugues; double counterpoint; differentiation of diverse styles in the art of music . . . and similar subjects on which the learned theorists write voluminously.

Heinrich Schütz, *Geistliche Chor-Musik*, Preface, translated in Ruth Halle Rowen, *Music Through Sources and Documents* (Englewood Cliffs, NJ: Prentice-Hall, 1979), pp. 159–161.

Heinrich Schütz (1585–1672)

The first German composer of international stature, Schütz is known especially for his church music and for his intellectual and emotional depth in conveying the meaning of words.

The son of an innkeeper, Schütz showed an early talent for music. Although his family did not want him to pursue music as a career, his singing at age twelve so impressed Moritz, landgrave of Hesse, that the nobleman insisted on bringing Schütz to Kassel and sponsoring his education in music and other subjects.

Moritz persuaded him to go to Venice in 1609 and study composition with Giovanni Gabrieli. After Gabrieli died in 1612, Schütz returned to Kassel as court organist, but the elector of Saxony pressured Moritz first to lend and ultimately to grant him the young musician, showing not only that Schütz was greatly esteemed as a musician but that musicians were essentially servants, not entirely free to decide their own destinies.

From 1615 to his death in 1672, Schütz was chapel master for the elector's court in Dresden,

although he took leaves to visit Italy, where he made Monteverdi's acquaintance, and to work briefly at other courts. Schütz wrote music for all major ceremonies at court, secular and sacred. The former included the first German opera (1627), several ballets, and other stage works, although almost none of this music survives. He apparently did not write independent instrumental music. What remains is a great quantity and variety of concerted church music. Some had personal resonance: his first sacred collection, *Psalmen Davids*, was published shortly before his 1619 wedding to Magdalena Wildeck, and her death in 1625 prompted simple four-part settings of a German Psalter (published 1628). His *Musikalische Exequien* (1636) was funeral music for a friend and patron. But most was simply service music, each piece perfectly suited to the text at hand and the musicians at his disposal.

At the end of his extraordinarily long career as chapel master of the Dresden court, Schütz made a formal request to be relieved of his duties, writing to the elector that he could no longer trust himself to serve "fittingly . . . nor uphold . . . the rather good name I gained in younger years: not only because of the ceaseless studying, traveling, writing, and other constant labors in which I have, in all modesty, been engaged since youth, but also because old age has now come upon me, and my sight and vital strength have waned."[1] Although relieved of his daily responsibilities, Schütz continued to compose and be involved intermittently in musical affairs at court until his death at age 87.

Major works: *Psalmen Davids* (polychoral psalm settings in German), *Cantiones sacrae* (Latin motets), *Symphoniae sacrae* (sacred symphonies, 3 volumes), *Musikalische Exequien* (funeral music), *Kleine geistliche Konzerte* (small sacred concertos, 2 volumes), *Geisthiche Chor-Musik* (sacred choral pieces), *The Seven Last Words of Christ, Christmas Story,* 3 Passions.

Figure 11.6 Heinrich Schütz at about age seventy (ca. 1655), in a portrait by Christoph Spetner.
(Bibliothek der Leipzig Universität. Lebrecht Music & Arts Library.)

1. Quoted in Piero Weiss (ed.), *Letters of Composers Through Six Centuries* (Philadelphia: Chilton Books, 1967), pp. 46–51.

TIMELINE   Vocal Music for Chamber and Church in the Early Baroque

Musical Events

1601–1602
Caccini, *Le nuove musiche*

1607
Monteverdi, *Orfeo*
(NAWM 74), in Mantua

1613
Monteverdi appointed
maestro di cappella
at Saint Mark's, Venice

1615
Gabrieli, *Sacrae sympho-
niae II*

1625
Grandi, *O quam tu
pulchra es* (NAWM 79)

1629
Schütz, *Symphoniae
sacrae I*

1636
Schütz, *Kleine geistliche
Konzerte*

1638
Monteverdi, *Madrigali
guerrieri et amorosi*

1642
Monteverdi, *L'incoronazione
di Poppea* (NAWM 75),
in Venice

1650
Schütz, *Symphoniae
sacrae III* (NAWM 81);
Carissimi, *Jephte*
(NAWM 80)

1659
Strozzi, *Lagrime mie*
(NAWM 77)

1600   **1650**

Historical Events

1590
Guarini, *Il pastor fido*

1609
Kepler sets forth his astronomical laws

1618–1648
Thirty Years' War
(religious wars in Germany)

1632
Galileo charged with heresy
for claiming Earth revolves
around the sun

1635–40
Poussin, *The Rape of the
Sabine Women* (Figure III. 7);
Rubens, *The Rape of the
Sabine Women* (Figure III. 8)

1637
Descartes, *Discourse on
Method*

1645–1652
Bernini, *The Ecstasy of Saint
Teresa* (Figure 11.4)

---

experience leads to his conversion and to his new career as the Apostle Paul, spreading the Gospel. Paired solo voices rising from the depths of the basses through the tenors to the sopranos and violins represent the flash of light and the voice leaping from the desert. Christ's question "Why do you persecute me?" is a mesh of dissonant anticipations and suspensions. Then the polychoral style takes over as the choruses and soloists together reverberate with echoes, suggesting the effect of Christ's voice bouncing off rocky peaks in the desert. This large-scale sacred concerto shows how well Schütz assimilated the bold dissonances and coloristic techniques of the Venetians.

Another prominent genre in the Lutheran tradition was the historia, a musi-   **Historia**
cal setting based on a biblical narrative. In *The Seven Last Words of Christ* (1650s?), Schütz set the narrative portions as solo recitative or for chorus with continuo, while the words of Jesus, in free, expressive monody, are accompanied by strings and continuo. The whole is introduced by a short chorus and instrumental sinfonia and ends with a repetition of the sinfonia and a closing chorus. His *Christmas Story* (1664) features recitatives for the narrative interspersed with scenes in the concertato medium, including arias and choruses with instrumental accompaniment.

The most common type of historia was a Passion, a musical setting of the   **Passions**
story of Jesus' crucifixion. Schütz wrote three in 1666, following the accounts of Matthew, Luke, and John. For these he used not concertato style but the older

Legacy

German tradition of treating the narrative in plainsong and the words of the disciples, the crowd, and other groups in polyphonic motet style.

During his lifetime, Schütz's music was known mainly in Lutheran areas of Germany, and after his death it faded from the repertory until it was revived in the nineteenth and twentieth centuries. Yet he helped to establish Germany as a central part of the European tradition rather than as a peripheral region. His synthesis of German and Italian elements, of counterpoint and basso continuo style, was essential in laying the foundation for later German composers, from Bach through Brahms.

POSTLUDE

The extraordinary burst of innovation in the early seventeenth century is as apparent in the chamber and church music of the time as it is in opera. Yet all drew deeply on sixteenth-century traditions as well, redefining existing genres and approaches by combining them with new styles and techniques. Monody and madrigal joined forces in the service of church music; form was achieved via the organization of the bass and the harmonies it supported, and through the systematic introduction of ritornellos, ostinato patterns, and variation techniques; and the typical basso-continuo texture—a florid treble supported by a firm bass—was varied by the use of the contrasts inherent in the concertato medium. By these means, composers enlarged and enriched the representational and emotional resources of music.

Like opera, new genres of composition such as oratorio, sacred vocal concerto, and cantata incorporated novel styles of writing such as recitative and aria. Choral textures also assimilated the new dramatic aesthetic. In both Catholic and Lutheran church music, composers availed themselves of a wide range of secular and religious styles to convey particular messages to their listeners. One especially noteworthy development of the period was the recognition that different styles were appropriate for different purposes. Thus, the older *stile antico* was preserved and practiced alongside newer styles; because of its associations with sacred music and with pedagogy, it was often deployed to evoke the solemnity and authority of tradition. At the same time, most styles could be used outside their original contexts for expressive ends, so that, as we have seen, theatrical styles were used in church. Nevertheless, because the primacy of the text and the persuasive delivery of its message were central to any vocal work of the period, rhetorical effectiveness was prized far above stylistic purity.

 Resources for study and review available at
wwnorton.com/studyspace

12

Instrumental Music in the Seventeenth Century

PRELUDE

The rise of instrumental music during the Renaissance and its coming of age in the Baroque era is evident in the cultivation of new instruments, new roles for instrumental music, new genres, and new styles, as well as in the growing supply of written music for instruments alone, including many published collections. The growth in music for instruments is partly an illusion; it simply means more was being written down. But that change in itself shows that music without voices was now more often deemed worthy of preservation and dissemination in written form. By the end of the seventeenth century, instrumental music had moved out of the long shadow cast by vocal music to gain independence and become the latter's equal in both quantity and quality.

At the same time, instrumental composers borrowed many elements typical of the new vocal idioms, including employment of the basso continuo, interest in moving the affections, focus on the soloist, and use of virtuosic embellishment and stylistic contrast. Even specific vocal styles such as recitative and aria made their mark on instrumental music, especially on works for violin, which rose to prominence in the seventeenth century partly because it was able to mimic the expressive and sensual qualities of the high solo voice.

Once instrumental music came into its own, composers had to make decisions about what instruments to use rather than simply what kind of piece to write. During the second half of the seventeenth century, the possibilities offered by modern organs, by double-manual harpsichords (instruments with two keyboards, each with the capability of a distinct sound), by improved wind instruments (see In Context, page 251) and particularly by the violin family inspired new idioms, genres, and formal structures. Because the sound and distinct characteristics of instruments were becoming more important, the second half of this chapter is organized around the two most prevalent types of instrumentation: music for solo lute and keyboard, which includes organ and harpsichord music; and ensemble music, which includes chamber and orchestral music for a variety of instrumental combinations, all employing the ever-present keyboard as a supporting, or continuo, instrument.

Among the keyboard instruments, the so-called Baroque organ (see Figures 12.5 and 12.7) is familiar to us from the many copies of instruments that exist today, modeled especially on those originally constructed by the skilled

German organ builders of the late seventeenth and early eighteenth centuries. They emulated the full French organ sound, with its colorful ranks of pipes, used to play solos and contrapuntal lines.

While organs were constructed mainly in churches, the keyboard instrument of choice for princely chambers and household use was the harpsichord, called *clavecin* in French (see Figure 12.8), which was easily adapted to solo or ensemble playing. Although the most prominent harpsichord makers were Flemish, like the Ruckers firm in Antwerp (see Figure 12.12), the most eminent composers for the instrument during the seventeenth century were French.

By about 1700, the French clavecinists and the north German organists had established distinct styles. But in the realm of instrumental chamber music, as in opera and cantata, Italians reigned as the undisputed masters and teachers. The seventeenth and early eighteenth centuries were the age of the great violin makers of Cremona—Nicolò Amati (1596–1684), Antonio Stradivari (1644–1737; see Innovations, page 229), and Bartolomeo Giuseppe Guarneri (1698–1744). It was also the age of great string music in Italy, as we will discover.

Within the newly flourishing instrumental repertory, certain basic compositional procedures divide the works into five broad categories. In some measure, these are extensions of the types listed in Chapter 8, although the ones based on vocal music recede in importance while the more abstract types of composition increase in number and significance; their order merely reflects the chronology of the examples chosen for study. To some extent, the classification into types is artificial because elements of one category often appear in works of another. Nevertheless, the categories are useful as an introduction to the main genres of instrumental music that prevailed throughout the Baroque era.

Variations
- A work that varies a preexisting melody, such as a chorale, called a set of variations, or partitas; or a work based on a traditional bass line or harmonic progression, called a partita, chaconne, or passacaglia

Abstract types
- Improvisatory works, such as keyboard or lute pieces, called toccatas, fantasias, or preludes
- Continuous works, such as pieces in imitative counterpoint, called ricercari, fantasias, fancies, capriccios, or fugues
- Sectional works, or pieces in contrasting sections and textures, some contrapuntal and some homophonic, called canzonas or sonatas

Dance music
- Dances (intended for dancing) and other pieces in stylized dance rhythms (unsuited for dancing), whether alone, paired, or grouped into a suite

Variations

The variation principle permeated many of the instrumental genres of the seventeenth century, although the term *variation* did not always appear in the title. Composers of the early seventeenth century often used the term *partite* ("divisions" or "parts") for sets of variations; later it was applied to dance suites as well.

Chaconne and passacaglia

New subjects for variation forms emerged in the seventeenth century and became "standards." Among these, the most popular were the chaconne and passacaglia, the first deriving from the *chacona*, a lively dance-song imported from Latin America, and the second from the Spanish *passacalle*, a ritornello improvised over a simple cadential progression and played before and between strophes of a song. Both were essentially bass or harmonic progressions rather than melodies. Although the earliest known keyboard variations on these forms are by an Italian composer, Girolamo Frescobaldi, the terms soon appeared in France, Germany, and elsewhere, to designate variations over a ground bass. Whether traditional or newly composed, these repeated progressions were usually four measures long, in triple meter and slow tempo. Chaconnes and passacaglias appeared in solo keyboard music, chamber music, and theatrical dance music. In later centuries, the distinctions between the two faded and the terms became interchangeable.

Abstract Instrumental Works

Improvisatory Genres

The toccata, from the Italian *toccare* ("to touch"), was the principal genre of lute and keyboard music in improvisatory style. Established in the sixteenth century as a kind of "warm-up" piece full of scalar and other florid passages that burst forth from the player's fingers at irregular intervals, the toccata continued to thrive in the seventeenth century. Toccatas could be played on the harpsichord (as chamber music) or the organ (as church music; see Figure 12.1).

Toccata

The most important composer of toccatas was Girolamo Frescobaldi (1583–1643; see Biography, page 216), organist at Saint Peter's in Rome. Toccata No. 3 from his first book of toccatas for harpsichord (1615; NAWM 82) is typical in featuring a succession of brief sections, each focused on a particular figure that is subtly varied. Some sections display virtuoso passage work, while others pass ideas between the hands. Each section ends with a cadence, weakened harmonically, rhythmically, or through continued movement in order to sustain momentum until the very end. According to the composer's preface, the various sections of these toccatas may be played separately, and the player may end the piece at any appropriate cadence, reminding us that in the Baroque era written music was a platform for performance, not a fixed text. Frescobaldi indicated that the tempo "must not be subject to the beat—just as we see in modern madrigals which, though difficult, are made more manageable by [altering] the beat,

Frescobaldi's toccatas

Full 🔊   Concise 🔊

Figure 12.1 Church musicians depicted on a carved lectern from Biecz, Poland, 1633. The organ, played by one person while another works the bellows, is mounted on lions' feet. A mustached singer reads from a partbook on the lower left, while a pair of string players complete the concertato ensemble. Compare this organ, which has no pedal rank, with the instruments shown in Figures 12.5 and 12.7.
(Edgor Film, ul. M. Konopnickiej 17, 38-300 Gorlice and courtesy Muzeum Ziemi Bieckiej, Biecz, Poland.)

Girolamo Frescobaldi (1583–1643)

As one of the first composers of international stature to focus primarily on instrumental music, Frescobaldi helped put it on a par with vocal music. He set the trend for every keyboard genre of his era and wrote vocal works and ensemble canzonas as well.

Born in Ferrara, Italy, Frescobaldi was trained there in organ and composition. In 1608, he became organist at Saint Peter's in Rome. He supplemented his income by serving noble patrons and teaching keyboard, which gave him an outlet for harpsichord and other chamber music. He published collections of keyboard works with dedications to various patrons. In 1628, he became organist to the grand duke of Tuscany in Florence, then returned to Rome and Saint Peter's in 1634 under the patronage of the Barberini family, nephews of the pope. By then, his music was celebrated in France, Flanders, and Germany.

From a French musician traveling in Italy we get a glimpse of Frescobaldi at the organ, "displaying a thousand kinds of inventions on his instrument while the organ stuck to the main tune. . . . Although his printed works give sufficient evidence of his skill, still, to get a true idea of his deep knowledge, one must hear him improvise toccatas full of admirable refinements and inventions."[1]

Figure 12.2 *Girolamo Frescobaldi in his forties, in a chalk drawing by Claude Mellan.* (Scala/Art Resource, NY.)

After his death, Frescobaldi remained widely admired across Europe. His keyboard music was a model for composers as late as J. S. and C. P. E. Bach, particularly his toccatas because of their bold harmonies and technical difficulty, and his ricercari and other contrapuntal works because of their learned style.

Major works: keyboard toccatas, fantasias, ricercari, canzonas, and partitas; *Fiori musicali*, with 3 organ masses; ensemble canzonas; madrigals, chamber arias, motets, and 2 masses.

1. André Maugars, *Response faite à un curieux sur le sentiment de la musique d'Italie, escrite à Rome la premier Octobre 1639,* trans. Walter H. Bishop, *Journal of the Viola da Gamba Society of America* 7 (1971).

making it now languid, now quick, and occasionally suspending it in mid-air, according to their *affetti* [affections], or the sense of the words."[1]

Fiori musicali   The role of the toccata as service music is illustrated by those in Frescobaldi's *Fiori musicali* (Musical Flowers, 1635), a set of three organ masses, each containing all the music an organist would play at Mass. All three include a toccata before Mass and another at the Elevation of the Host before communion, and two add another toccata before a ricercare. These toccatas are shorter than those he wrote for harpsichord but just as sectional, and they feature the sustained tones and harmonic surprises often found in organ toccatas.

Johann Jacob Froberger   Frescobaldi's most famous student was Johann Jacob Froberger (1616–1667), organist at the imperial court in Vienna. Froberger's toccatas tend to alternate improvisatory passages with sections in imitative counterpoint. His pieces were the model for the later merging of toccata and fugue, as in the works of Buxtehude (see NAWM 95), or their coupling, as in Bach's toccatas or preludes and fugues (see NAWM 100).

1. Frescobaldi, foreword to his *Capricci* (1624). Translation by Andrew Dell'Antonio.

Continuous Genres

The seventeenth-century ricercare was typically a serious composition for organ or harpsichord in which one subject, or theme, is developed continuously in imitation. The Ricercare after the Credo from Frescobaldi's *Mass for the Madonna* in *Fiori musicali* (NAWM 83) is remarkable for its skillful handling of chromatic lines and its subtle use of shifting harmonies and dissonance, revealing a quiet intensity that characterizes much of Frescobaldi's organ music.

In the early seventeenth century, some composers, especially in Germany, began to apply the term *fugue* (from the Italian *fuga*, "flight"), formerly used for the technique of imitation itself, to a genre of serious pieces that treat one theme in continuous imitation. As we will see in Chapter 14, fugues became increasingly important in the late seventeenth and early eighteenth centuries.

The keyboard fantasia, an imitative work on a larger scale than the ricercare, had a more complex formal organization. The leading fantasia composers in this period were the Dutch organist Jan Pieterszoon Sweelinck (1562–1621) and his German pupil Samuel Scheidt (1587–1654). Scheidt's *Tabulatura nova* (New Tablature, 1624) includes several monumental fantasias. He called it new because instead of using tablature notation, like most German organ music of the time, Scheidt adopted the modern Italian practice of writing out each part on a separate staff in the pitch notation used for vocal and ensemble music. The works of Scheidt, and his influence as a teacher, founded a remarkable development of north German organ music in the Baroque era.

In England, music for viol consort (see Figure 12.3) was a mainstay of social music-making in the home. The leading genre was the imitative fantasia, often called *fancy*, which treated one or more subjects in a fugal fashion. Structurally, it resembled the solo keyboard fugues or ricercari, but it was intended for ensemble performance. Popular composers included Alfonso Ferrabosco the Younger (ca. 1575–1628), son of an Italian musician active at Queen Elizabeth's court, and John Coprario (ca. 1575–1626), whose Italianized name (he was born Cooper) exemplifies the English fashion for things Italian.

Sectional Genres

The term *sonata* (Italian for "sounded") was often used early in the seventeenth century to refer broadly to any independent piece for instruments. It gradually came to designate a type of composition that resembled a canzona in form (see Chapter 8 and NAWM 70). Sonatas were often scored for one or two melody instruments, usually violins, with basso continuo, while the ensemble canzona was written in four or more parts and could be played without continuo. Sonatas

Ricercare and fugue

Full 🔊

Fugue

Fantasia

English consort fantasias

Sonata

Full 🔊

Figure 12.3 A viol consort, anonymous French, ca. 1625.
(DEA/G. Dayli Orti.)

often exploited the idiomatic possibilities offered by a particular instrument and imitated the modern expressive vocal style, while the typical canzona displayed more of the formal, abstract quality of Renaissance polyphony.

Ensemble sonatas

The Venetian sonata was a close relative of the canzona, consisting of a series of sections each based on a different subject or on variants of a single subject. Both canzonas and sonatas were used at Mass and Vespers as introductions or postludes, or to accompany significant rituals. The *Sonata pian' e forte* from Gabrieli's *Sacrae symphoniae* has earned a prominent place in music history because it is among the first instrumental ensemble pieces to designate specific instruments in its printed parts: in the first choir, cornett (a wooden wind instrument resembling a straight or curved trumpet—see Figure 8.5) and three sackbuts (early trombones); in the second, a violin and three sackbuts. Another innovation in the printed music was indicating passages as *pian* (*piano*, meaning "soft") or *forte* ("loud"), one of the earliest instances of dynamic markings in music. Through contrasts of one instrumental choir against the other, single choir against both together, loud versus soft, and slow homophonic passages versus faster motion and points of imitation, Gabrieli created a purely instrumental work with as much interest, variety, and depth of content as a madrigal or motet.

Figure 12.4 Interior of the eleventh-century church of Saint Mark (architecturally known as a basilica), where Venetian composers cultivated a style of composition and performance involving multiple antiphonal choirs (cori spezzati) *of voices, instruments, or a combination of the two.*

(Historical Picture Archive/Corbis.)

One of the earliest composers of sonatas for solo violin and continuo was Biagio Marini (1594–1663). Marini served as violinist at Saint Mark's under Monteverdi and then held various posts in Italy and Germany. His *Sonata IV per il violino per sonar con due corde*, from Op. 8 (NAWM 84), published in 1629, is an early example of what may be called "instrumental monody." Like the canzona, it has contrasting sections, but almost every one features idiomatic violin gestures, including large leaps, double stops, runs, trills, and embellishments. Marini's sonata opens with an expressive melody, shown in Example 12.1a, that recalls a solo madrigal before turning almost immediately to idiomatic sequential figures. The violin part in the next section (Example 12.1b) illustrates double stops and the influence of Caccini's vocabulary of *affetti* or ornaments. Rhapsodic and metrical sections alternate, resembling the contrasts between recitative and aria styles that were developing about this time.

By the middle of the seventeenth century, the canzona and sonata had merged, and the term sonata came to stand for both. However, styles for voice and for each family of instruments gradually diverged, eventually becoming so distinct that composers could purposefully evoke vocal idioms in instrumental

Biagio Marini

Full 🔊

Example 12.1 Biagio Marini, Sonata

a.

b.

Figure 12.5 Organ built in 1695 for Saint John's church in Hamburg, now in a church at Kassel. The elaborate carving of the chest encasing the pipes and the decorative angels are typical of the Baroque organ. The tall pipes in the center and around the sides of the upper half of the instrument produce the deepest notes, played by the pedals. Compare this instrument to the more modest one pictured in Figure 12.1.
(Photo courtesy of Martin Jean, Institute of Sacred Music, Yale University.)

Full 🔊   Concise 🔊

writing and vice versa. We will return to the development of sonata at the end of this chapter.

Music for Organ

Organ music enjoyed a golden age in the Lutheran areas of Germany between about 1650 and 1750. Dieterich Buxtehude (ca. 1637–1707), one of the best-known Lutheran composers of the late seventeenth century (see Figure 12.6), continued the tradition established by Sweelinck and powerfully influenced J. S. Bach, whose keyboard music will be discussed in Chapter 14. Buxtehude was organist at Saint Mary's Church in Lübeck, one of the most important and lucrative musical posts in northern Germany. He composed organ pieces as well as sacred concerted music, and he played organ solos as preludes to chorales and other parts of the service.

Most organ music written for Protestant churches served as a prelude to something else—a chorale, a scriptural reading, or a larger work. Such pieces were often chorale settings, or they were toccatas or preludes that contained fugues or culminated in them.

Buxtehude's toccatas typify those of seventeenth-century German composers in presenting a series of short sections in free style that alternate with longer ones in imitative counterpoint. In this respect, they bridge the gap between improvisatory and sectional genres. Filled with motion and climaxes, the toccatas display a great variety of figuration and take full advantage of the organ's idiomatic qualities. Their capricious, exuberant character made them ideal vehicles for virtuosic display at the keyboard and on the pedals.

The free sections simulate improvisation by contrasting irregular rhythm with an unceasing stream of sixteenth notes, by using phrases that are deliberately irregular or have inconclusive endings, and by featuring abrupt changes of texture, harmony, or melodic direction. Example 12.2 shows a passage that is typical of toccata style, from Buxtehude's Praeludium in E Major (NAWM 95). The virtuoso part for the pedals (the lowest staff in the score) includes long trills; when the pedal sustains a tone, the two hands erupt in rapid passage work with many unpredictable changes of speed, direction, and figuration. At the opposite extreme is a later, slow-paced free section marked by suspensions and many passing key changes.

Fugue

In the Praeludium in E, five such sections in toccata style frame four fugal sections, each featuring imitative counterpoint on a different "subject" and in a different meter or tempo. All four blend into the free sections that follow them.

In the eighteenth century, the two types of section, fugal and free, grew in length and became separate movements, so that the typical structure consisted of a long toccata or prelude in free style followed by a fugue. Composers wrote fugues both as independent pieces and as sections within preludes or toccatas. We will examine a masterful fugue by J. S. Bach in Chapter 14 (see page 278).

Chorale compositions

While toccatas, preludes, and fugues remained independent of vocal music, organ compositions based on chorales used the melodies in a number of differ-

Elisabeth-Claude Jacquet de La Guerre (1665–1729)

Women continued to play an active role in the music of the seventeenth century, from singers and composers to patrons of art and hostesses at private gatherings where music was actively cultivated. One such extraordinary woman was the French composer Elisabeth-Claude Jacquet de La Guerre, born into a family of musicians and instrument makers. Trained by her father, she was the original child prodigy in music. From the age of five, she sang and played the harpsichord at Louis XIV's court and was a favorite of the king's mistress. In 1677, the Paris journal *Mercure galant* gushed:

> There is a prodigy who has appeared here for the last four years. She sings at sight the most difficult music. She accompanies herself, and others who wish to sing, on the harpsichord, which she plays in an inimitable manner. She composes pieces and plays them in any key one suggests.

Some years later, the same writer called her "the marvel of our century."

In 1684, she married the organist Marin de La Guerre and moved permanently to Paris. There she taught harpsichord and gave concerts that won her wide renown. She enjoyed the patronage of Louis XIV and dedicated most of her works to him, including the first ballet (1691, now lost) and first opera (*Céphale et Procris*, 1694) written by a Frenchwoman.

Jacquet de La Guerre is best known for her two published collections of harpsichord pieces (1687 and 1707) and three books of cantatas.

Figure 12.9 A portrait by François de Troy (1645–1730) of Elisabeth-Claude Jacquet de La Guerre seated at a harpsichord and holding a quill pen and sheet of (music) paper, all attributes of her talents as a musician. (Wikimedia Commons.)

Her violin and trio sonatas show an interest in the Italian instrumental style. Her output was small but encompassed a wide variety of genres, and she was recognized by her contemporaries as one of the great talents of her time.

Major works: *Céphale et Procris* (opera), 3 books of cantatas, 2 books of *Pièces de clavecin*, 8 violin sonatas, 4 trio sonatas.

---

and François Couperin (1668–1733; see Chapter 14). All of them served Louis XIV in various capacities but are best known today for their printed collections of harpsichord music, marketed to a growing public of well-to-do amateur performers.

Lutenists systematically developed the use of agréments, ornaments designed to lend a charming and graceful quality and to emphasize important notes while giving the melody shape and character. Agréments became a fundamental element of all French music, and the proper use of ornaments was a sign of refined taste. Agréments were often left to the discretion of the player, especially in other countries, but French composers worked out precise ways of notating them. Figure 12.18 shows the table of agréments in D'Anglebert's *Pièces de clavecin* (Harpsichord Pieces, 1689), the most comprehensive of many such

Agréments

tables published in collections of harpsichord music. Some of these ornaments are discussed further on pages 234–235.

Lute style also strongly influenced the texture of harpsichord music. Since lutenists often struck only one note at a time, they sketched in the melody, bass, and harmony by sounding the appropriate tones—now in one register, now in another—and relying on the listener's imagination to supply the continuity of the various lines. This technique, sometimes described by the French phrase *style brisé* ("broken style"), was imitated by harpsichord composers and became an idiomatic part of French harpsichord style, as seen in Examples 12.3 and 12.4.

Style brisé

Dance Music

Lute dances

Dances formed the core of the lute and keyboard repertory, reflecting their importance in French life. Composers arranged ballet music for lute or harpsichord and composed original music in dance meters and forms. Most dance music for lute or keyboard was stylized, probably intended not for dancing but for the entertainment of the player or a small audience. Nevertheless, paired two- and four-measure phrases occur frequently in dance music, matching the patterns of many dance steps.

Binary form

Whereas earlier dances had assumed a variety of forms, such as the three repeated sections of the pavane or the repeating bass of the passamezzo, most seventeenth-century dances were in binary form: two roughly equal sections, each repeated, the first leading harmonically from the tonic to close on the dominant (or sometimes the relative major), the second returning to the tonic. This form was widely used for dance music and other instrumental genres over the next two centuries.

Denis Gaultier

Many of Denis Gaultier's dances for lute are contained in a sumptuous manuscript of his lute music titled *La Rhétorique des dieux* (The Rhetoric of the Gods, ca. 1650). Typical of his style is *La Coquette virtuose* (The Virtuous Coquette; NAWM 87), whose title may have been given by the compilers of the manuscript rather than by the composer himself. This is a courante, a dance in binary from in a moderate triple or compound meter (see discussion below and Figure 12.10). Example 12.3 shows the first section, which moves from tonic to dominant as expected. Gaultier did not write out any agréments, leaving them to the performer. Characteristic of the style brisé are the many

Full 🔊

Example 12.3 Gaultier, La Coquette virtuose

Dance type	Meter	Tempo	Character
Allemande (French for "German")	$\frac{4}{4}$	Moderate	Continuous, flowing rhythm; often starts on upbeat
Courante (French for "running")	triple or compound	Moderate	Often starts on upbeat
Sarabande	$\frac{3}{4}$ or $\frac{3}{2}$	Slow	Emphasizes second beat; dignified
Gigue (French for "jig")	$\frac{6}{8}$ or $\frac{12}{8}$	Fast	Nearly continuous eighth notes, often with dotted rhythm
Chaconne (typical only of French suite)	triple	Moderate	Opening theme recurs between contrasting sections; stately
Gavotte	duple	Moderate	All phrases begin on upbeat
Minuet	$\frac{3}{4}$	Moderate	Elegant

Figure 12.10 Baroque Dance Characteristics.

broken chords; whether simply arpeggiated (as in measures 3 and 7) or embellished by neighbor tones (as in the succession of chords in measures 5 and 6), each chord is presented in a different way, creating an irregular, unpredictable, and ever-changing surface for the underlying progression.

French composers often grouped a series of stylized dances into a suite, as did their German counterparts. The tempo and rhythm contributed to the character of each dance (see Figure 12.10). A look at excerpts from Jacquet de La Guerre's Suite No. 3 in A Minor from her *Pièces de clavecin* (1687, NAWM 88), shown in Example 12.4, illustrates both the structure of a typical suite and the most common types of dance. All but two movements, the prelude and a chaconne, are in binary form. Although none of the movements would have been used for dancing, the steps and associations of the dances were known to the listeners and influenced the rhythm and style of the music.

Many suites begin with a prelude in the style of a toccata or other abstract work. Here it is an unmeasured prelude, a distinctively French genre whose nonmetric notation allows great rhythmic freedom, as in an improvisation. In Example 12.4a, the whole notes indicate arpeggiated chords, the black notes show melodic passages, and the slurs show groupings or sustained notes.

The allemande, no longer danced in the seventeenth century and thus highly stylized, was usually in a moderately fast tempo. As shown in Example 12.4b, all voices participate in almost continuous movement, and agréments appear often. Signs of the style brisé include the opening arpeggiation of the tonic chord in the bass and staggered rhythms between the voices. The courante, in Example 12.4c, is in a moderate triple or compound meter ($\frac{3}{2}$ or $\frac{6}{4}$) or shifts between the two. The steps were dignified, with a bend of the knees on the upbeat and a rise on

Figure 12.11 Nicolas Poussin (1594–1665), Saint Cecilia *seated at a harpsichord in the company of angels (1627–1628). Images of the patron saint of music playing the harpsichord (rather than the organ, her original attribute) affirmed its suitability for young women and its popularity for domestic music-making. See also Figures 8.8 and 8.9.*

(The Prado, Madrid, Spain. Photo: Scala/Art Resource, NY.)

Example 12.4 Elisabeth-Claude Jacquet de la Guerre, Pièces de clavecin, *movements from Suite No. 3 in A Minor*

a. Prelude

b. Allemande

c. Courante

d. Sarabande

e. Gigue

f. Gavotte

Characteristic rhythm:

g. Minuet

Figure 12.12 Jan Vermeer (1632–1675), The Music Lesson. *This work, painted by the prominent Dutch master around 1665, belongs to a genre associating music with courtship that not only was popular during the seventeenth century but also emphasized the link between the harpsichord and domestic music-making, particularly by women. The meticulously rendered keyboard instrument at which the woman stands, her back to us, is exactly like the virginals made by the famous Ruckers firm in Antwerp. Its open lid reveals the inscription* Musica letitiae comes . . . medicina dolorum *("Music is the companion of joy and the cure for sorrow"). The viol and the empty chair in the foreground imply the possibility of a duet.*

(The Royal Collection, 2001, Her Majesty Queen Elizabeth II.)

the downbeat, often followed by a glide or step. The sarabande was originally a quick, lascivious dance song from Latin America. When it came to France through Spain and Italy, it was transformed into a slow, dignified dance in triple meter with an emphasis on the second beat, as in Example 12.4d. The melodic rhythm in the first measure is especially common. The gigue originated in the British Isles as a fast solo dance with rapid footwork. It became stylized as a movement in fast compound meter such as $\frac{6}{4}$ or $\frac{12}{8}$, with wide melodic leaps and continuous lively rhythms. Sections often begin with fugal or quasi-fugal imitation, as in Example 12.4e.

Numerous other dances could appear in suites. Jacquet de La Guerre's suite also includes a gavotte, a duple-meter dance with a half-measure anacrusis, as in Example 12.4f. It concludes with a minuet, an elegant couples dance in moderate triple meter, shown in Example 12.4g, that remained fashionable well into the eighteenth century.

Ensemble Music

In instrumental chamber music, as in opera and cantata, Italians remained the undisputed masters and teachers. Italians of the late seventeenth century and early eighteenth century were renowned not only as violin makers, but also as composers of great string music, of which the leading genres were the sonata and the instrumental concerto (see Figure 12.13).

Chamber Music: The Sonata

The word *sonata* appears regularly on Italian title pages throughout the seventeenth century. In the earlier decades of the century, the term (like the parallel

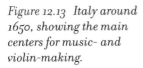

Figure 12.13 Italy around 1650, showing the main centers for music- and violin-making.

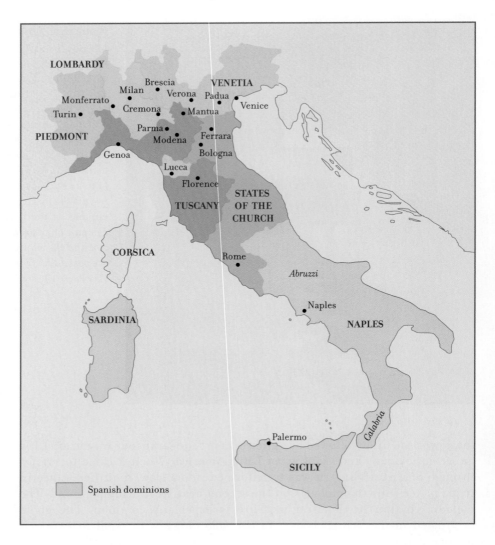

Development
of the sonata

word *sinfonia*) loosely designated any piece to be "sounded" on instruments, but especially a prelude or interlude in a predominantly vocal work. After 1630, the two terms were used more and more often to designate independent instrumental compositions.

Sonatas in the first half of the seventeenth century consisted of a number of small sections differentiated by musical material, texture, mood, character, and sometimes meter and tempo, as in the Marini sonata briefly discussed above (NAWM 84). As the genre developed, these sections gradually became longer and more self-contained. Finally, composers separated the sections into distinct movements, so that in time the sonata became a multimovement work with contrasts between movements. These contrasts were in keeping with the theory of the affections, which held that music stimulated the bodily humors and could keep them in balance by offering a diversity of moods. While some composers still maintained thematic similarities among movements, thematic independence of movements increasingly became the rule.

By about 1660, two main types of sonata had emerged. The sonata da camera, or chamber sonata, featured a series of stylized dances, often beginning with a prelude. The sonata da chiesa, or church sonata, contained mostly abstract movements, often including one or more that used dance rhythms or binary form but were not usually titled as dances. Church sonatas could substitute for

Innovations   **The Violin Workshop of Antonio Stradivari**

Just as Italian composers excelled in writing songs and arias for the solo voice from the beginning of the seventeenth century, so, too, it was the Italians who created new instrumental genres—solo sonata, trio sonata, and concerto—that called on the violin to imitate the sensuality, nuanced expressivity, and virtuosity of the singing voice. Thus, it is no surprise that it was also the Italians—specifically, a few families of instrument builders in Cremona—who elevated the art of violin making to a peak that has never been surpassed. During its heyday, the violin became the new agent of that artistic power which had previously resided only in the voice.

Antonio Stradivari (ca.1644–1737) was the most prominent member of his universally renowned family of instrument makers in the area of northern Italy famed for violin construction. He may have studied with Nicolò Amati, founder of another dynasty of violin makers. During his long life, Stradivari made or supervised the production of more than 1,100 instruments—including harps, guitars, violas, and cellos—about half of which survive and are still being used today by some of the world's leading string players. Figure 12.14 shows one of the few Stradivari violins that has been restored to its original form, with a shorter fingerboard and the neck angled back only slightly from the body. Thousands of violins were made in tribute to Stradivari and modeled on his superior design; with no intention to deceive, these instruments bear the label "Stradivarius," although they were produced neither by the master nor by his workshop, which, by the mid-eighteenth century, was engaged in a healthy rivalry with that of the Guarneri family.

Figure 12.14 Violin, 1693, by Antonio Stradivari, restored to its original Baroque form.
(The Metropolitan Museum of Art/Art Resource, NY.)

What was involved in making a "Strad," and why are these instruments so highly prized? First, Stradivari selected woods of the highest possible quality—pine for the front and sides, and maple for the back of the instrument. Then he proceeded to carve the pieces, taking care to get just the right degree of arching (because the body of the instrument is not flat but slightly rounded) and arrive at just the right thickness (because even the tiniest variation in the thickness of the wood affects the instrument's resonance). Next he cut the elegantly shaped f-holes into the front piece to optimize the vibrations and maximize the sound. Finally, he applied the varnish to protect the instrument from dirt and to stop it from absorbing moisture. In addition to its practical function, the varnish itself added greatly to the beauty of the instrument by giving it a radiant, orange-brown sheen and highlighting the grain patterns on the wood's surface. In an effort to explain the extraordinarily rich and powerful tone of a Stradivarius violin, a popular theory held that its varnish had some sort of magic ingredient. However, historical research has shown that the varnish is no different from that used by ordinary furniture makers when Stradivari was alive. Other theories have advanced the idea that the wood was first soaked in water and then specially seasoned before being carved, or that the grain of the wood used is tighter than that of modern woods. But so far, scientists have been unable to ascertain any measurable qualities that set these instruments apart. Even if such properties are discovered, the intrinsic superiority of a Stradivarius remains a matter not only of science but also of an apparently lost art.

Trio sonatas

certain musical items in church services, and both types were played for entertainment in private concerts.

The most common instrumentation after 1670 for both church and chamber sonatas was two treble instruments, usually violins, with basso continuo. Such a work is called a trio sonata because of its three-part texture but a performance generally features four or more players with more than one used for the basso continuo, such as a cello performing the bass line and a harpsichord, organ, or lute doubling the bass and filling in the chords. The texture we find in the trio sonata, with two high melody lines over basso continuo, was extremely popular from the mid-seventeenth century and served many other types of solo music, both vocal and instrumental. Its appeal undoubtedly lay in its ability to exploit the polarity between firm bass and florid treble while admitting the possibility of contrapuntal play between the treble parts.

Solo and ensemble sonatas

Solo sonatas, for violin or other instrument with continuo, were at first less popular than trio sonatas but gained in popularity after 1700. Composers also wrote sonatas for larger groups, up to eight instrumental parts with continuo, and a few for unaccompanied string or wind instruments.

Arcangelo Corelli's Sonatas

Unlike most of his countrymen, Arcangelo Corelli (1653–1713; see Biography, page 231) composed no vocal music; instead, he sang through the violin, the instrument that most nearly approaches the lyric quality of the human voice. Although fewer than ninety of his compositions survive, they served as models of form and style that composers followed for the next half century.

Trio sonatas

In his trio sonatas, Corelli emphasized lyricism over virtuosity. He rarely used extremely high or low notes, fast runs, or difficult double stops. The two violins, treated exactly alike, frequently cross and exchange ideas, interlocking in suspensions that give his works a decisive forward momentum. Example 12.5 shows a passage from the first movement of his Trio Sonata in D Major, Op. 3, No. 2 (NAWM 94) that features several typical traits of Corelli's style: a walking bass, with a steadily moving pattern of eighth notes, under free imitation between

Full 🔊   Concise 🔊

Example 12.5 Corelli, Trio Sonata, Op. 3, No. 2, first movement

Arcangelo Corelli (1653–1713)

Renowned as violinist, teacher, and composer, Corelli had an unparalleled influence on performers and composers alike. His solo and trio sonatas for one or two violins with continuo represent the crowning achievement in Italian chamber music of the late seventeenth century. Already in Sebastien de Brossard's *Dictionary of Musical Terms* (1701), the entry for "sonata" declares: "for models, see the works of Corelli."

Born into a well-to-do family in a small town in northern Italy, he studied violin and composition in Bologna beginning in 1666. By 1675, Corelli was living in Rome, where he quickly became a leading violinist and composer, enjoying the support of Queen Christina of Sweden and other patrons. As a violinist, teacher, and ensemble director, he helped to raise performance standards to a new level. His teaching was the foundation of most eighteenth-century schools of violin playing. Others may have surpassed him in bravura, but his playing was full of expression, as is suggested in this account from 1702: "His eyes will sometimes turn red as fire, his countenance will be distorted, his eyeballs roll as in agony, and he gives in so much to what he is doing that he does not look like the same man."

Figure 12.15 Portrait of Arcangelo Corelli, ca. 1700, by Hugh Howard.
(With permission of the Faculty of Music, University of Oxford.)

Beginning in 1681, Corelli published a series of collections of trio sonatas, violin sonatas, and concerti grossi that were disseminated across Europe, bringing him international fame.

Major works: 6 published collections known by opus (work) number—Op. 1 (1681), 12 trio sonatas (sonate da chiesa); Op. 2 (1685), 12 trio sonate da camera (one is a chaccone); Op. 3 (1689), 12 trio sonate da chiesa; Op. 4 (1695), 12 trio sonate da camera; Op. 5 (1700), 12 solo violin sonatas; Op. 6 (1714), 12 concerti grossi—6 other trio sonatas, and 3 quartets for three instruments and basso continuo.

the violins (measures 9–10); a chain of suspensions in the violins above a descending sequence in the bass (measures 11–12); and a dialogue between the violins as they leapfrog over each other to progressively higher peaks (measures 13–15).

Most of Corelli's church trio sonatas contain four movements, often in two pairs, in the order slow-fast-slow-fast. Although there are many exceptions to this pattern, it gradually became standard for Corelli and later composers. The first slow movement is typically contrapuntal with a majestic, solemn character. The Allegro that follows normally features fugal imitation, with the bass line fully participating in the contrapuntal texture. This movement is the musical center of gravity for the church sonata, and it retains elements of the canzona in two ways: its use of a subject with a marked rhythmic character presented in imitation and the presence of variation at later entrances of the subject. The subsequent slow movement most often resembles a flowing operatic duet in triple meter. The fast final movement usually features dancelike rhythms and often is in binary form. All of these traits appear in Op. 3, No. 2.

Corelli's chamber sonatas usually begin with a prelude, after which two or three dances may follow, as in the French suite. Often the first two movements resemble those of a church sonata, with a slow introduction and fugal Allegro. Some of the introductions feature dotted rhythms, like those of the French overture (see Chapter 13). The dance movements are almost always in binary

Church sonatas

Chamber sonatas

form, with each section repeated, the first section closing on the dominant or relative major and the second making its way back to the tonic. Rather than sharing an almost equal role in the texture as in the church sonatas, the bass line in the chamber sonatas is almost pure accompaniment to the upper parts.

Solo sonatas

Corelli's solo violin sonatas are also divided between church and chamber, following similar patterns of movements but allowing considerably more virtuosity. In the Allegro movements, the solo violin sometimes employs double and triple stops to simulate the rich three-part sonority of the trio sonata and the interplay of voices in a fugue. There are fast runs, arpeggios, extended perpetual-motion passages, and cadenzas—elaborate solo embellishments at cadences, either notated or improvised. The slow movements were notated simply but were meant to be ornamented freely and profusely (see In Performance, pages 234–235).

Thematic organization

In Corelli's sonatas, movements are thematically independent from each other (with rare exceptions) and tend to be based on a single subject stated at the outset. The music unfolds in a continuous expansion of the opening subject, with variations, sequences, brief modulations to nearby keys, and fascinating subtleties of phrasing. This steady spinning out of a single theme, in which the original idea seems to generate a spontaneous flow of musical thoughts, is highly characteristic of the late Baroque from about the 1680s on.

Tonal organization

Corelli's music is marked by the sense of direction or progression that, more than any other quality, distinguishes tonal music from modally influenced music. Example 12.5, for instance, features several series of chords whose roots move down the circle of fifths, falling by a fifth or rising by a fourth (see measures 8–10, 11–12, and 13–14). The forward motion associated with this progression characterizes tonal music. Moreover, Corelli often relies on chains of suspensions and on sequences to propel the harmony forward: measures 11–12 in Example 12.5 display both these devices. The increasing use, over the course of the seventeenth century, of directed progressions like Corelli's demonstrated the new functional harmony we call tonality.

Figure 12.16 Portrait of the string band of Grand Duke Ferdinand de' Medici, ca. 1685, by Antonio Domenico Gabbiani. In addition to the harpsichord, the instruments depicted are violins, alto and tenor violas, mandolin, and cello. An ensemble such as this could have performed the concerti grossi of Corelli's Opus 6.

(Galeria Palatina, Palazzo Pitti, Florence, Italy. Scala/Art Resource.)

In Context Queen Christina of Sweden and Her Circle

In 1681, Arcangelo Corelli dedicated his first opus, twelve trio sonatas (da chiesa), to Queen Christina of Sweden (1626–1689):

> If Your Majesty will have the generosity, as I hope, to both receive with favor and support these first fruits of my studies, it will renew my strength to continue with my other works, which are already in draft; and to make known to the world that perhaps I am not wrong to aspire to the glorious position of Your Majesty's servant. . . .

Who was this eminence whom Corelli hoped would become his patron?

Nearly thirty years earlier, Christina had abdicated her throne, left Sweden dressed as a man, converted to Catholicism, and in 1655 established her court-in-exile in Rome, where, until her death in 1689, she presided as an independent thinker, avid book collector, and beneficent if impetuous patron. In Rome, Christina founded at least two academies that attracted scholars and poets, theologians and philosophers, librettists and composers, as well as members of the Roman aristocracy. She encouraged open discussion of ethical and scientific questions at a time when Galileo's theories were still taboo. She supported theatrical and operatic performances around the city, right under the

nose of the reigning pope Innocent XI, who was oppressively hostile to the stage. And she regularly sponsored concerts at her palace, which became an important center in the city's musical life. Among others, Alessandro Scarlatti, who had just begun his long career as a composer of operas and cantatas (see Chapter 13), was employed by Christina. He described himself in 1680 as her maestro di capella, a position he held until his departure for Naples in 1684.

One of the foremost violinists in Rome, Arcangelo Corelli also became a protégé of Christina, as he had hoped in the dedication to his Opus 1, quoted above. After entering her service as a chamber musician, he attracted her attention by composing and performing sonatas for her academy. When Christina organized a huge concert at her palace in honor of the new English ambassador to the Holy See, she asked Corelli to conduct an orchestra of 150 string players and an ensemble of more than 100 singers and soloists lent by the pope. On this magnificent occasion, there were seats for 150 ladies, and the number of gentlemen who were left standing was even greater. In 1689, Corelli again directed a large group of performers in two solemn masses to celebrate Christina's apparent recovery from illness. Unfortunately, she died one month later.

Christina was among the most prominent intellectuals of her day, as suggested by the painting in which, surrounded by scholars and clerics, she engages the philosopher René Descartes (1596–1650) in animated discussion (see Figure 12.17).

Figure 12.17 This detail, from a seventeenth-century painting by Pierre Dumesnil, shows a youthful Queen Christina of Sweden (seated to the left of the table) presiding in the company of scholars, clerics, and others in her circle. Standing opposite her is René Descartes.

(Chateaux de Versailles et de Trianon, Versailles, France. Photo: Hervé Lewandowski/Réunion des Musées Nationaux/Art Resource, NY.)

In Performance **Baroque Ornamentation**

The word *ornament* now connotes something superficial, an added decoration that has no intrinsic merit; but for the Baroque musician, ornaments were the chief way of moving the affections. Musical ornamentation originated in improvisation—that is, it was applied spontaneously to make a performance more expressive; more wondrous; and, in the case of certain dissonant ornaments, to add a touch of spice that the notated music lacked. Even though it might later be written down or indicated with special symbols (as in Example 12.4 and Figure 12.18), ornamentation retained a degree of spontaneity.

Both vocalists and instrumentalists recognized two principal ways of ornamenting a melody. First, brief formulaic clusters of notes—such as trills, turns, appoggiaturas, and mordents—were added at certain points in the melody to highlight accents, emphasize some words over others, or decorate cadences and other significant events. Special signs sometimes indicated their placement, as discussed below. Second, more extended embellishments—such as passages (*passaggi*) of rapid scales, arpeg-

gios, and other types of flourishes—were added to create a free and elaborate paraphrase of the written line. This process—sometimes called division, diminution, or figuration—was especially appropriate for melodies in slow tempo, as in Figure 12.19. Performance practices relating to the interpretation and execution of ornaments varied from nation to nation and from one generation to another, but the tasteful and appropriate application of ornaments was always an essential part of the performer's training and skill. Although the task is complex and the results sometimes controversial, modern performers and scholars try to reconstruct these practices based on written treatises, descriptive accounts, and transcribed improvisations.

A number of "tutors," or practical treatises, were published in the seventeenth and eighteenth centuries. Most were written for a specific instrument such as lute or keyboard and tailored to the tastes of a certain region. One of the most important treatises in France was *L'Art de toucher le clavecin* (The Art of Playing the Harpsichord, 1716) by François Couperin (see Chapter 14). Sometimes, particu-

Figure 12.18 Table of ornaments from Pièces de clavecin *(1689) by Jean-Henry D'Anglebert, showing for each ornament its notation, name, and manner of performance.*

larly in France, composers included instructions for decoding their symbols right in their published works. Figure 12.7, the table of ornaments, or agréments (charming or graceful qualities), in D'Anglebert's *Pièces de clavecin* (Harpsichord Pieces, 1689), illustrates this practice. Abbreviations or signs for the most common ornaments are named and their proper execution suggested on the staff below. For example, the mordent (*pincé*, or "pinched" in French) appears at the beginning of the second row, followed by another (*autre*), longer version. Next comes a trill (*tremblement*, or "trembling") combined with a mordent. Ascending and descending appoggiaturas follow.

Skilled performers were expected to add even more extensive embellishments, especially to the slow movement of a work, which was often notated simply but meant to be ornamented elaborately and freely. In 1710, the Amsterdam publisher Estienne Roger reissued Corelli's solo sonatas, showing for the slow movements both the original solo parts and embellished versions that, Roger claimed, represented the way the composer himself played the sonatas, as in Figure 12.19. Although Corelli lived until 1713, he never publicly affirmed or denied that the embellishments were his. But they surely reflect the practice of his time and are believed by modern scholars to be authentic.

Figure 12.19 The Adagio of Corelli's Sonata Op. 5, No. 3, in the edition printed about 1711 for John Walsh, London, and based on a 1710 edition by Estienne Roger, Amsterdam. The violin part is given both as originally published and in an embellished version said to represent the way Corelli himself performed it.

(Yale University Music Library, New Haven.)

One of Corelli's students, Francesco Geminiani (1687–1762), published an important violin method, *The Art of Playing on the Violin* (1751), which, like Couperin's treatise for harpsichord, elucidates the performance practices of the age. Geminiani compares the performer to an orator, an idea that was widely held and often repeated in the Baroque, and one that helps to explain the central role of ornamentation: "The intention of musick is not only to please the ear but to express the sentiments, strike the imagination, affect the mind, and command the passions." He urges the violinist to use his instrument in a manner that rivals "the most perfect human voice" by imitating qualities of eloquent speech.

Performers were free not only to embellish a written score but also to change it in other ways. Singers often added cadenzas—elaborate passages decorating important cadences—to arias, and later these became a feature of solo instrumental works as well. Sections of variation sets and movements of suites were omitted or rearranged as desired. Title pages of ensemble collections encouraged players to choose which instruments and even how many to use for a performance. In every respect, the written music—whether published or not—was regarded as a script that could be adapted to suit the convenience and the varying tastes and habits of the performers. French musicians, for example, emphasized rhythmic freedom over the melodic ornamentation characteristic of Italian opera. Passages notated in equal values were typically played unequally, lengthening the first of every pair of eighth notes in a series, and shortening the second, resulting in a string of uneven, triplet-like rhythms called *notes inégales* ("unequal notes"). A related French practice is overdotting, in which a dotted note is prolonged beyond its notated value—according to the performer's taste—while the next note is necessarily shortened. These changes, which may be heard in the NAWM recording of Lully's opera overture (85a; see Chapter 13) emphasize the beats and sharpen the rhythmic profiles of the passages to which they are applied. But more important, they were thought to impart a certain stylish elegance to the performance, not unlike the "swing" effect in jazz.

Corelli's music is almost completely diatonic; beyond secondary dominants (as in measures 8 and 12 in Example 12.5), we find only a rare diminished-seventh chord or Neapolitan sixth at a cadence. His modulations within a movement—most often to the dominant or the relative minor or major—are always logical and straightforward. All movements of a sonata are either in the same key or, in major-key sonatas, the second slow movement is in the relative minor.

Influence and reputation

Composers all over Europe, especially Henry Purcell in England (see Chapter 13) and François Couperin in France (see Chapter 14), were greatly influenced by Italian trio sonatas, which were synonymous with the works of Corelli, and freely imitated or adapted them. The motivic techniques and principles of tonal architecture that Corelli helped to develop were extended by Vivaldi, Handel, Bach, and other composers of the next generation. Corelli has been called the first major composer whose reputation rests exclusively on instrumental music and the first to create instrumental works that became classics, continuing to be played and reprinted long after his death.

Music for Orchestra

Toward the end of the seventeenth century, musicians began to distinguish between music for chamber ensemble, with only one instrument for each melodic line, and music for orchestra, in which each string part was performed by two or more players. The French court had a string ensemble, essentially the first orchestra, with four to six players per part. By the 1670s, similar ensembles were formed in Rome and Bologna, followed by others in Venice, Milan, and elsewhere. For special occasions in Rome, Corelli often led a pick-up orchestra of forty or more, gathered from players employed by patrons throughout the city (see In Context, page 233). While some pieces, such as the overtures, dances, and interludes of Lully's operas (see Chapter 13), were clearly intended for orchestra, and others, such as Corelli's solo violin sonatas, could be played only as chamber music, a good deal of seventeenth- and early eighteenth-century music could be performed either way. For instance, on a festive occasion or in a large hall, each line of a trio sonata might be played by several performers. The natural result of these new opportunities was the instrumental concerto, which will be introduced in Chapter 14.

Ensemble music in Germany

The ensemble sonata and particularly the instrumental suite had a long life in Germany, where musical traditions frequently became part of everyday life. Most cities employed town musicians, called *Stadtpfeifer* ("town pipers"), who had the exclusive right to provide music in the city. They performed at public ceremonies, parades, weddings, and other festivities and supervised the training of apprentices. Figure 12.20 shows a small troupe in Nuremberg playing in the New Year. *Stadtpfeifer* were jacks-of-all-trades, proficient at numerous wind and string instruments, and typically won their posts through auditions or family connections. The system encouraged whole families to make music their trade, among them the Bach family, already prominent in the seventeenth century and about to reach new heights in the eighteenth. In some places, chorales or sonatas called *Turmsonaten* (tower sonatas) were played daily on wind instruments from the tower of the town hall or church. In Lutheran areas, church musicians were often employed directly by the town. Some Lutheran churches sponsored concerts and recitals, as well as having music during services.

Collegium musicum

Amateur music-making was a prominent part of social life. Many German towns had a collegium musicum, an association of amateurs from the educated middle class who gathered to play and sing together for their own pleasure or to hear professionals in private performances. Such groups were also organized in

Figure 12.20 Stadtpfeifer *in Nuremberg heralding the New Year. Detail of a drawing by an unknown sixteenth-century artist.*
(Berlin, Staatsbibliothek zu Berlin, Preissischer Kulturbesitz. Handschriftenabteilung.)

schools, and some drew their members primarily from university students. In the eighteenth century, some collegia gave public concerts (see Chapter 14).

POSTLUDE

The extraordinary burst of innovation associated with opera and vocal music in the seventeenth century is equally apparent in the instrumental music of the time, whether for soloist or ensemble, church or chamber.

The sixteenth century had seen the rise of instrumental music cultivated for its own sake, whether derived from dance music, related to vocal music, or conceived as abstract music independent of dance or song. Some genres of instrumental music continued into the Baroque era and beyond, including stylized dances, variations of sacred and secular tunes, and preludes or toccatas and fugues. Whereas composers of Renaissance polyphony had not differentiated between instrumental and vocal writing, to the point where almost any combination of voices and instruments was interchangeable, even the earliest music for solo lute, organ, or harpsichord manifested a quality peculiar, or idiomatic, to the instrument. The pursuit of such idioms fostered the increasing separation and independence of instrumental from vocal music. Then, too, the more prominent role of the soloist in the Baroque era—whether singer, violinist, or wind player—enticed composers to adapt their writing to take advantage of the particular attributes of one medium or the other. Famous teachers and practitioners of the art of singing promoted new standards of virtuosity and new expressive devices for moving the emotions that were then adapted to instruments. Once instrumental and vocal styles had sufficiently diverged and achieved their distinct idioms, composers could transfer these styles from

Musical Events

1585–1612
Gabrieli at Saint Mark's, Venice

1589
Arbeau, *Orchésographie* published

1597
Gabrieli publishes *Sacrae symphoniae* (NAWM 70)

1600
First surviving opera, *L'Euridice* (NAWM 73), performed

1602
Caccini publishes *Le nuove musiche*

1613
Parthenia published

1629
Marini, Sonatas for Violin and Continuo, Op. 8 (NAWM 84) published

1635
Frescobaldi publishes *Fiori musicali* (NAWM 83)

ca. 1650
Gaultier, *La Rhétorique des dieux* (NAWM 87)

1580

Historical Events

1590
Guarini, *Il pastor fido*

1594
Shakespeare, *Romeo and Juliet*

ca. 1601
Shakespeare, *Hamlet*

1610
Galileo publishes *Starry Messenger*

1618–1648
Thirty Years' War (religious wars in Germany)

1645–1652
Bernini, *The Ecstasy of Saint Teresa*

1655–1689
Queen Christina of Sweden in Rome

1658–1705
Leopold I reigns as Holy Roman emperor

vocal to instrumental works and vice versa, writing a violin melody that sighed like a voice or a vocal melody that blared like a trumpet.

Two types of instrumental music became prominent during the second half of the seventeenth century: (1) solo keyboard music, especially that written for the harpsichord in France and the great Baroque organs built in Germany; and (2) ensemble music, dominated by the violin, whose famous Italian makers flourished during this period. Important genres of keyboard music included toccata and fugue, a variety of chorale-based compositions cultivated by Lutheran composers, stylized dance suites, and all sorts of variations, especially the chaconne and passacaglia. Influential composers were Dieterich Buxtehude in Germany and Elisabeth-Claude Jacquet de La Guerre in France. Ensemble and solo sonatas for church and chamber emerged in Italian centers such as Rome, and then spread throughout Europe. Arcangelo Corelli brought the genre to its first heights of perfection. Meanwhile, soloists refined the art of ornamentation for expressive purposes as well as for virtuosic display.

1668
Buxtehude appointed organist
at Lübeck

1673
Buxtehude inaugurates
Abendmusik series

ca. 1675–1684
Amati and Stradivari perfect
the art of violin making

1685
J. S. Bach and Handel born

1687
Elisabeth-Claude Jacquet de
La Guerre, *Pièces de clavecin*
(NAWM 88) published

1689
Arcangelo Corelli, Op. 3,
Twelve Trio Sonate da chiesa
(NAWM 94) published

1700
Corelli, Op. 5 violin sonatas
published

1707
Buxtehude dies

1720

1677
Racine, *Phèdre*

1683
First coffeehouse opens in
Vienna

1687
Newton, *Principia
mathematica*

1688
Louis XIV invades Holy Roman
Empire

1692
Salem witchcraft trials in
Massachusetts

1715
Louis XIV dies

Even though instrumental music explored and exploited the independent idioms of organ, harpsichord, and violin, composers still aimed to move the affections. How was this possible in the absence of words? They borrowed and adapted the already rich harmonic, melodic, and rhythmic vocabulary of vocal music, dance, and theatrical music, with all of its affective associations. With this essentially international, Baroque language, Corelli on the violin could lament as effectively as any operatic heroine; Jacquet de La Guerre on the harpsichord could charm her listeners as elegantly as any singer of chamber cantatas; and Buxtehude on the organ could inspire awe as convincingly as a massive church choir.

 Resources for study and review available at
wwnorton.com/studyspace

Opera and Vocal Music in the Late Seventeenth Century

PRELUDE

Opera spread throughout Italy and to other countries during the second half of the seventeenth century. The principal Italian center remained Venice, whose opera houses were famous throughout Europe. Germany imported Venetian opera, which then fused with native styles into a national German opera. France resisted Italian influence and eventually developed its own operatic idiom—one that was largely determined by the court's penchant for ballet and the tastes of Louis XIV, who acquired his nickname le Roi Soleil ("the Sun King") after dancing in a court ballet costumed as Apollo (see Figure 13.6). The reception of opera in England, however, was different: there King Charles I was beheaded in 1649, and during the ensuing Commonwealth period the puritanical climate was hardly friendly to the cultivation of such an extravagant art form. Even after the restoration of the English king in 1660, the monarchy was too weak and its treasury too depleted to support opera on the grand scale of the French or the Italians.

Vocal music for chamber and church also flourished during this period. The Italian chamber cantata, as well as French, English, and German song and concerted church music, were all influenced by the language of opera—especially recitative and aria—and by its musical vocabulary of the affections. Despite borrowings across borders, however, distinctive national styles developed that were shaped in part by the politics and culture of their respective countries.

Italy

The birthplace of opera, Italy continued to be the stylistic source for composers of operas and chamber cantatas all over Europe. Both genres relied on recitative and aria, which developed a set of conventions that remained relatively unchanged throughout the century.

Opera

Venice's public opera houses remained famous all over Europe, but by the late seventeenth century, opera was also well established in Naples and Florence, and its importance was growing in Milan and other major cities. Leading composers included Alessandro Scarlatti (1660–1725; Figure 13.3), who held sway in Rome and Naples.

Opera houses continued to vie with one another to lure audiences to their productions. More than the drama or spectacle, it was the singers and arias that attracted the public. By offering high fees, impresarios competed for the most popular singers, who sometimes earned more than twice as much as composers (see Innovations, pages 242–243).

Singers

The singers' vehicle was the aria. While it was common in midcentury for an opera to include twenty-four arias, sixty became the norm by the 1670s. The favorite form at that time was the strophic song, in which every stanza of an aria was performed to the same music. An example of this type is *Intorno all'idol mio* (Around my idol) by Antonio Cesti from his Venetian opera *Orontea* (1656; see NAWM 76 and Chapter 10). Also common were ground-bass arias, short two-part arias in AB form, and three-part arias in ABB′, ABA, or ABA′ forms.

Aria types

Full 🔊

Arias typically reflected the meaning of the text in musical motives in the melody or accompaniment. For example, a composer might imitate trumpet figures or a march to portray martial or vehement affections, or use a lively gigue, a sultry sarabande, or other dance rhythm to suggest feelings or actions conventionally associated with those dance types.

By the end of the century, the most prevalent form was the da capo aria, essentially a large ABA structure, which provided for both repetition and contrast. The form takes its name from the words "Da capo" ("from the head") placed at the close of the second section, instructing the performers to return to the beginning of the aria and repeat the first section, producing an ABA form. The aria's text usually comprises two sentences. Typically, the A section is itself a small two-part form, with two different settings of the first sentence, each introduced by a brief instrumental ritornello. In some da capo arias, the first section closes with another (often partial) ritornello, or the opening ritornello is omitted when the first section repeats. The aria *In voler ció che tu brami* (In wanting that which you desire), from Scarlatti's last opera, *La Griselda* (1720–21; NAWM 93), exemplifies the rich contrasts the composer achieved in his later arias both between and within sections. The A section shows two sides of the protagonist's character as an obedient wife, combining dignity and strength with tenderness and love for her husband despite his public rejection of her, while in the B section, she adamantly insists that she will never stop loving him. For a diagram of the typical form of a da capo aria, see Figure 13.4.

Da capo aria

Full 🔊

Chamber Cantata

The cantata had become the leading form of vocal chamber music in Italy, and the center of cantata composition was Rome. There, wealthy prelates and diplomats sponsored regular private parties for the elite, where the entertainment often included a cantata written expressly for the occasion. Because cantatas were meant for performance before a small, discriminating audience in a room without a stage, scenery, or costumes, they invited elegance, refinement, and wit that would be lost in a spacious opera house. Moreover, the demand for a new cantata at frequent

From its very beginnings, opera was a complicated, costly, even extravagant affair requiring the collaboration of the librettist, the composer (who held a decidedly lower status than the librettist), and the artists whose performances engaged the audience directly. In addition, it demanded the services of a vast array of craftspeople who worked behind the scenes. Among these silent and unseen participants—including stage managers, carpenters, painters, costume designers, tailors, hairdressers, and copyists—none was more crucial than the impresario, who was roughly equivalent to the modern producer. (Transferred into English from the Italian, the word *impresario* acquired its distinctive meaning with the rise of Venetian opera.) The theater's owner, head of one of the noble families of Venice, entrusted the impresario with managing the theater successfully for one season at a time, which meant bringing in a profit after all the production expenses and artists' fees were paid. Naturally, the economic outcome depended in good

Figure 13.1b *Giuseppe Torelli's design for the final scene of Carlo Caproli's "Le nozze di Peleo e di Theti." Engraving by Israel Silvestre after François Francart, 1654.*
(Paris, Petit Bourbon.)

measure on the impresario's decisions about how many and which operas were to be performed in a given season. Competition was fierce, so the impresario also had to consider the financial risks involved in mounting spectacular scenic effects (Figures 13.1a and 13.1b) or hiring the most highly paid singers, and measure these costs against the potential gains of attracting larger audiences.

This volatile commercial atmosphere fostered, among other things, the phenomenon of the operatic diva (literally, goddess) or star. Impresarios went to great lengths and expense to secure effective performers because they realized that a singer could make or break an entire opera season no matter what work was being produced. Although singer power had been a theme in opera from its beginnings—think of Orfeo, whose legendary song persuaded supernatural forces to return his bride to life—that power now resided with the singers themselves rather than the characters they portrayed. Sopranos, especially those capable of virtuosic ornamentation and persuasive interpretation, quickly achieved stardom. Once having made it to the top, a diva could demand that composers and librettists alter roles to suit her particular vocal talents and range. In doing so, she not only exercised her star power but actually influenced the development of opera in ways that eventually affected its dramatic structure as well as its musical values.

The career of Anna Renzi, leading lady of the Venetian operatic stage in the 1640s, is a case in point and illustrates the rise in stature of the

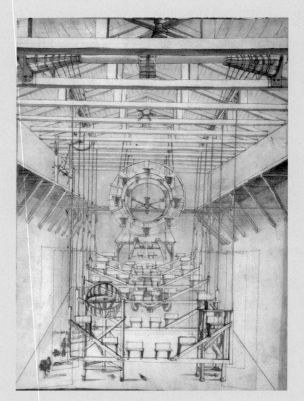

Figure 13.1a *Stage designers of Baroque opera specialized in rapidly moving scenery for their most dazzling effects. Shown here is the machinery for one such set; a drawing of the intended realization appears as Figure 13.1b.*
(Bibliothèque de l'Opéra, Paris. Photo: AKG Images.)

female singer. Renzi was only about twenty years old when her teacher brought her from Rome to Venice to perform the title role in the work that was scheduled to open the newest public opera house in that city—the Teatro Novissimo. The composer, Francesco Sacrati, undoubtedly tailored the role specifically to her in order to capitalize on her particular talents. That she played a woman pretending to be afflicted with madness on that occasion and then, a few years later, created the role of Nero's spurned empress Ottavia in Monteverdi's *Incoronazione di Poppea* speaks to her capabilities as an actress, one who could impart a certain dramatic intensity to her characters. Although her powers as a performer were by all accounts splendid, her meteoric ascent was at least in part a product of media hype. The librettist of her first Venetian opera, Giulio Strozzi, anxious to prove that public opera employed singers as divine as those of the wealthiest courts, published a special volume of adulatory poetry in her honor in 1644. The engraving of her likeness seen in Figure 13.2 comes from that volume.

In an introductory essay, Strozzi describes Renzi's stage presence and vocal qualities, stressing the apparently spontaneous nature of her movements and gestures: "Our Signora Anna is endowed with such lifelike expression that her responses and speeches seem not memorized but born at the very moment. In sum, she transforms herself completely into the person she represents." He goes on to praise her diction and vocal delivery, extolling her "fluent tongue, smooth pronunciation, not affected, not rapid, a full, sonorous voice, not harsh, not hoarse." He also remarks on her stamina and resilience, her ability to "bear the full weight of an opera no fewer than twenty-six times, repeating it virtually every evening . . . in the most perfect voice." Finally, Strozzi praises Renzi's offstage attributes and lauds her as a person of "great intellect, much imagination, and a good memory . . . ; of melancholy temperament by nature [she] is a woman of few words,

Intima si cantum simulat præcordia mulcet,
Ipsam animam serisim si canit Anna rapit.
Jacobus Pecinus Venetus fecit:et Uni:

Figure 13.2   The famous opera singer Anna Renzi, in an engraving from Giulio Strozzi's adulatory book The Glories of Signora Anna Renzi the Roman. *The elegiac couplet in Latin below her oval portrait reads: "When Anna merely pretends to sing, she delights the inmost heart; but when she truly sings, little by little she ravishes the very soul."*

(Ellen Rosand, *Opera in Seventeenth-Century Venice: The Creation of a Genre.* Berkeley: University of California Press, 1991.)

but those are appropriate, sensible, and worthy."[1] Although she did not have what might be called a "classic beauty," Renzi's qualities set the standard for the prima donna (Italian for "first lady," the lead soprano in an opera).

Divas became larger-than-life heroines with lucrative international careers. Following her memorable Venetian years, Renzi performed roles in other Italian cities and in Innsbruck, where Queen Christina of Sweden, who was then visiting the Austrian court, acknowledged her stunning skills by giving her the gift of her own medal and chain. Other prima donnas (and leading male singers) enjoyed similarly close relationships with patrons, composers, librettists, and impresarios in whose homes they sometimes lived when they were on the road. It is no surprise that they frequently exploited these ties by insinuating themselves into the creative process, exerting their influence on such matters as the selection of a plot, the number and length of arias written for their parts, and the casting of supporting roles. Occasionally a singer even refused to participate in a production unless a particular composer was commissioned to write the music.

Singer power and singer worship, then, significantly influenced the direction that opera took in the seventeenth century. But the story does not end there. After taking hold of the Venetian imagination, the glamorous world of opera and its stars went on to captivate all of Europe and eventually the Americas. Even today, the powerful personalities of divas and their equivalents outside of opera—rock stars and film icons, for example—are the driving force behind much of the entertainment industry.

1. Quotations from Giulio Strozzi are taken from Ellen Rosand, *Opera in Seventeenth-Century Venice: The Creation of a Genre* (Berkeley: University of California Press, 1991), pp. 228–235.

Figure 13.3 Alessandro Scarlatti, in an oil painting by an unknown artist. (Liceo Musicale, Bologna. The Art Archive/Corbis.)

intervals offered poets and composers regular work and chances to experiment.

Cantatas around 1650 featured many short, contrasting sections, as we saw in Barbara Strozzi's *Lagrime mie* (NAWM 77). By the 1660s, poets and composers settled on a pattern of separate and alternating recitatives and arias, normally two or three of each, making for a much longer work. Most cantatas were written for solo voice with continuo, although some featured two or more voices. The text, usually pastoral love poetry, took the form of a dramatic narrative or soliloquy.

The more than six hundred cantatas of Alessandro Scarlatti (1660–1725, see Figure 13.3) mark a high point in this repertory. His chamber cantata *Clori vezzosa, e bella* (Charming and pretty Clori), consisting of two recitative-aria pairs, is typical of the solo cantata around 1690–1710. The second recitative (NAWM 92a) exemplifies Scarlatti's mature style in using a wide harmonic range, chromaticism, and diminished-seventh chords, rare for the time, to convey strong emotions and to add bite to cadences.

Scarlatti's da capo arias

The most common form of aria in Scarlatti's operas and cantatas is the da capo aria. In Scarlatti's hands, it was the perfect vehicle for sustaining a lyrical moment through a musical design that expressed a single sentiment, often joined by a related or opposing one in the contrasting middle section.

Both arias in *Clori vezzosa, e bella* are da capo arias. The second, *Sì, sì ben mio* (Yes, yes my love; NAWM 92b), has this structure:

Section:	A					B	A repeats
	Ritornello	Sentence 1	Rit	Sentence 1		Sentence 2	Da capo
Key:	Dm	Dm→Gm	Gm	Gm→Dm		FM→Am	Dm
	i	i→iv	iv	iv→i		III→v	i

Figure 13.4 Plan of Sì, sì ben mio.

The da capo aria became the standard aria form in the eighteenth century for opera and cantata alike because it offered great flexibility in expression. The music of the B section could be as similar or contrasting as the poetry required, while the form guaranteed a contrast of key, a sense of departure and return, and harmonic and thematic closure. Singers typically introduced new embellishments on the repetition of the A section, the perfect opportunity to display their artistry.

France

Because of their country's strong cultural traditions of dance and spoken theater, French composers were slow to adopt Italian vocal styles. And when they did, the sound of the French language, with different rhythms and accents from Italian, required adjustments to the pace and flow of the music that produced very different results and some practices that were distinct from the Italian styles. However, while French composers shared the same goal as the Italians—the naturalistic expression of human emotions—some French critics could not conceal their distaste for what were perceived as opera's offenses against nature and reason (see Vignette, below).

Dance reinforced the state by offering a model of discipline, order, refinement, restraint, and subordination of the individual to a common enterprise. Requiring aristocrats to participate in social dancing and in ballet performances kept them busy and provided a ritualized demonstration of the social hierarchy, with the king at the top. It is no wonder that French Baroque music, so centered on dance, is marked by refinement, elegance, and restraint, in strong contrast to Italian music at the time, which allowed for a good deal of individuality and showmanship.

Opera

By around 1700, Italian opera was flourishing in every corner of western Europe except France. Having long opposed Italian opera on political and artistic grounds, the French finally established a national opera in the 1670s under the royal patronage of Louis XIV (r. 1643–1715; see Figure 13.5). Two powerful traditions influenced French opera: the sumptuous and colorful ballet, which had flourished at the royal court ever since the late sixteenth century; and the classical French tragedy, represented best by the works of Pierre Corneille (1606–1684) and Jean Racine (1639–1699). France's literary and theatrical culture insisted that poetry and drama be given priority on the stage. Meanwhile, the king's love of, and participation in, dancing ensured the ballet a prominent place in French opera (see Figures 13.6 and 13.7). The composer who succeeded in reconciling these demands of drama, music, and ballet was Jean-Baptiste

Ballet and tragedy

While French writers of the seventeenth and eighteenth centuries praised the "natural" in art and music, including the naturalistic representation of human emotions, some condemned operatic conventions as being contrary to nature and reason. Here, the courtier and wit Charles de Saint Évremond (ca. 1610–1703) forcefully reveals his complaints in a letter to the English Duke of Buckingham.

I am no great admirer of Comedies in music, such as nowadays are in request. I confess I am not displeased with their magnificence; the Machines have something that is surprising; the Music, in some places, is charming; the whole together seems wonderful: but it must be granted me also, that this Wonderful is very tedious; for where the mind has so little to do, there the Senses must of necessity languish. . . .

There is another thing in Operas so contrary to nature, that I cannot be reconciled to it; and that

is the singing of the whole piece, from beginning to end. . . .

Would you know what an Opera is? I'll tell you that it is an *odd medley of poetry and music, wherein the poet and musician, equally confined one by the other, take a world of pains to compose a wretched performance.* . . .

That which vexes me most at this our fondness for operas, is that they tend to ruin the finest thing we have, I mean *Tragedy,* than which nothing is more proper to elevate the soul, or more capable to form the mind. . . . The constitution of our operas cannot be more faulty than it is. But it is to be acknowledged at the same time, that no man can perform better than *Lully,* upon an ill-conceived subject, and that it is not easy to out-do Quinault in what belongs to his part.

John Hayward, ed., *The Letters of Saint Évremond,* trans. by Pierre Desmaizeaux (London: G. Routledge & Sons, Ltd., 1930).

Figure 13.5 *Louis XIV in his sixties, in a portrait by Hyacinthe Rigaud from around 1700. The king is surrounded by images that convey his grandeur: a red velvet curtain, multicolor stone column, an impressive wig, and an enormous ermine robe covered on one side with gold fleurs-de-lis, the symbol of French royalty. His crown is by his side, shadowed and partially obscured, as if he did not need to emphasize the sign of his power, even while his hand and staff draw the eye to it. His elongated, upright stature and exposed, perfectly shaped legs proclaim his physical strength and remind the viewer of his renown as a dancer.* (Musée du Louvre, Paris. Réunion des Musées Nationaux/Art Resource, NY.)

Lully (1632–1687; see Biography, 247). His new synthesis, *tragédie en musique*, later renamed *tragédie lyrique*, persisted for a century.

When Lully, an Italian musician, came to Paris as an adolescent, he attracted the attention of the French king and spent the rest of his adult life in France. He remained Louis XIV's favorite musician for more than three decades. From 1653, as director of the smaller of the king's two string orchestras and eventually of the larger ensemble as well, Lully composed instrumental music and dance pieces for Italian operas produced at court. He also provided overtures, dances, and vocal numbers for court ballets, and he collaborated with comic playwright Molière to create a series of successful comédies-ballets that blended elements of ballet and opera (see Figure 13.9). Then, in 1672, with Louis XIV's support, Lully purchased a royal privilege granting him the exclusive right to produce sung drama in France and established the Académie Royale de Musique. The exercise of this monopoly not only made him a rich man but also made him the virtual dictator of music and musical taste in France as long as he lived and even perpetuated his influence for decades after his death.

Lully's librettist, the esteemed playwright Jean-Philippe Quinault, provided the composer with five-act dramas combining serious plots from ancient mythology or chivalric tales with frequent divertissements ("diversions"), long interludes of dancing and choral singing. He cleverly intermingled episodes of romance and adventure with adulation of the king, glorification of France, and moral reflection. His texts were overtly and covertly propagandistic, in tune with Louis's use of the arts. Each opera included a prologue, often singing the king's praises literally or through allegory. The plots depicted an orderly, disciplined society, and the mythological characters and settings reinforced the parallels Louis sought to draw between his regime and ancient Greece and Rome. The librettos also provided opportunities for spectacles to entertain the audience.

Figure 13.6 (left) *Eventually earning a reputation as a brilliant dancer, Louis XIV acquired his nickname le Roi Soleil (the Sun King) after dancing in a court ballet dressed in the golden-rayed costume of Apollo, shown here.* (Lebrecht Music & Arts Photo Library.)

Figure 13.7 (right) *At the end of the century, his reign in decline, the helios symbol appeared in this Protestant caricature, which depicts Louis as a persecuting Inquisitor.* (Time and Life Pictures/Getty Images.)

Jean-Baptiste Lully (1632–1687)

Lully was the most powerful force in French music in the seventeenth century, creating French opera, pioneering the French overture, and fostering the modern orchestra.

Born in Florence, Lully came to Paris at age fourteen as Italian tutor to a cousin of Louis XIV. In Paris, he completed his musical training and studied dance. His dancing so impressed Louis that in 1653 he appointed Lully court composer of instrumental music and director of the Petits Violons (the smaller of the king's two string ensembles). In 1661, Lully became Superintendent of Music for the King's Chamber, taking over the royal instrumental ensembles, and became a French citizen. His marriage the next summer to Madeline Lambert, daughter of composer Michel Lambert, was witnessed by the king and queen, showing how high Lully had risen at court.

Lully composed music for numerous court ballets and sacred music for the royal chapel. He turned to comédies-ballets in 1664, then in 1672 to opera, where he gained his greatest fame.

The discipline Lully imposed on his orchestra, enforcing uniform bowing and coordinated use of ornaments, won admiration, was widely imitated, and became the foundation for modern orchestral practice. Although Lully beat time with a six-foot pointed staff or cane instead of a baton, the tradition of dictatorial leadership that he introduced, modeled on the king's own absolute power, has been continued by later conductors.

Lully's close relationship with Louis XIV was clouded by scandal in 1685, when the king learned that Lully had seduced a young page. While the police removed the boy from Lully's house to con-

Figure 13.8 Jean-Baptiste Lully, in a bronze bust by Antoine Coyzevox placed on Lully's tomb in the church of Notre-Dame-des-Victoires, Paris. (Bridgeman Art Library.)

finement in a monastery, Lully remained rich and powerful but had to rely on patrons other than the king. Lully died in 1687 after he hit his foot with his staff while conducting, and the injury turned gangrenous. Although surgeons advised amputation, Lully declared that he would rather die in possession of both his feet.

Major works: *Alceste, Armide*, and 13 other operas; 14 comédies-ballets; 29 ballets (most in collaboration with other composers); numerous motets and other liturgical music.

Lully's music projected the formal splendor of Louis's court. Each opera began with an ouverture (French for "opening"), marking the entry of the king (when he was present) and welcoming him and the audience to the performance. Lully's French overtures, as they are now called, were appropriately grand and followed a format that he had already used in his ballets. There are two sections, each played twice. The first is homophonic and majestic, marked by dotted rhythms and anacrustic (upbeat) figures rushing toward the downbeats. The second section is faster and begins with a flurry of fugal imitation, sometimes returning at the end to the tempo and figuration of the first section. The overture to Lully's opera *Armide* (1686; NAWM 85a) exemplifies the genre.

A divertissement usually appeared at the center or end of every act, but its connection to the surrounding plot was often tenuous. These extended episodes, which directly continued the French ballet tradition, offered opportunities for

French overture

Full 🔊 Concise 🔊

Divertissements

Figure 13.9 An engraving representing the production of Molière's comedy Le Malade imaginaire *(The Hypochondriac) before Louis XIV at Versailles in 1673. Most of Molière's theatrical entertainments were presented at Louis's court.*

(Bibliothèque Nationale, Paris. Photo: Giraudon/Bridgeman Art Library.)

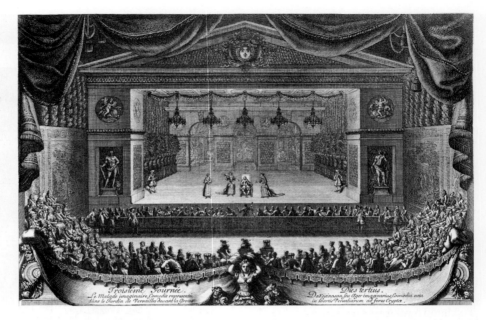

Full 🔊

spectacular choruses and a string of dances, each with colorful costumes and elaborate choreography (see NAWM 85b). The divertissements were especially appealing to the public. Dances from Lully's ballets and operas became so popular that they were arranged in independent instrumental suites, and many new suites were composed imitating his divertissements.

Adapting recitative to French

To project the dramatic dialogue, Lully adapted Italian recitative to French language and poetry. This was no simple task since the style of recitative typical in Italian opera of the time was not suited to the rhythms and accents of French. Lully is said to have solved the problem by listening to celebrated French actors and closely imitating their declamation. Certainly the timing, pauses, and inflections often resemble stage speech, but Lully did not aspire to create the illusion of ordinary speech (as Peri did in his recitatives; see Chapter 10). Also, the bass is often more rhythmic and the melody more songful than in Italian recitative.

Récitatif simple, récitatif mesuré, and air

In what would later be called *récitatif simple* ("simple recitative"), Lully followed the general contours of spoken French while shifting the metric notation between duple and triple to allow the most natural declamation of the words. This style was frequently interrupted by a more songlike, uniformly measured style, *récitatif mesuré* ("measured recitative"), which had more deliberate motion in the accompaniment. More lyrical moments were cast as airs—songs with a rhyming text and regular meter and phrasing, often featuring the meter and form of a dance. Far less elaborate and effusive than arias in Italian operas, airs were typically syllabic or nearly so, with a tuneful melody, little text repetition, and no virtuosic display.

Full 🔊   Concise 🔊

Armide's monologue in Act II, scene 5, of *Armide* (NAWM 85c and Figure 13.10) illustrates this mixture of styles. The scene begins with a tense orchestral prelude suffused with dotted rhythms. The sorceress, dagger in hand, leans over her captive, the sleeping warrior Renaud. In simple recitative, she speaks of her determination to kill him as revenge for freeing her captives, but she is prevented from acting because she has fallen in love with him. Measures of four, three, and two beats are intermixed, permitting the two accented syllables in each poetic line to fall on downbeats. Strong beats are almost always approached anacrustically, a direct result of the language's cadence, illustrated by the curved arrows in Example 13.1a Rests follow each line and are also used

Example 13.1 Jean-Baptiste Lully, monologue Enfin il est en ma puissance, *from* Armide

a. Simple recitative

What makes me hesitate? What in his favor does pity want to tell me? Let us strike . . .
Heavens! Who can stop me? Let us go on with it . . . I tremble! Let us avenge . . . I sigh!

b. Measured recitative

*Since he could not find my eyes charming enough, let him love me at least through my
sorcery, so that, if it's possible, I may hate him.*

Figure 13.10   In a painting by Nicolas Poussin dating from about 1630, Armide is torn between hate and love for the sleeping Renaud: her right hand, restrained by a miniature Cupid, clutches a knife, while her outstretched left hand caresses her prisoner's forehead. The scene is an exact parallel to Act II, scene 5 of Lully's Armide.
(Dulwich Picture Gallery, London/Bridgeman Art Library.)

dramatically, as when Armide vacillates between hesitation and resolve in the excerpt shown in Example 13.1a. When she finally decides to use sorcery to make Renaud love her, her new determination is reflected in measured recitative, in Example 13.1b. This leads to an air with the meter, rhythm, and character of a minuet (see Chapter 12), a dance associated with surrender to love. It is accompanied only by continuo, as are most of Lully's airs, but is introduced by an orchestral statement of the entire air, which would perhaps have been choreographed.

Lully's influence extended beyond the arena of opera and ballet. Elsewhere in France and in Germany, both composers and musicians admired the discipline with which he conducted his players and imitated his methods of scoring. The first large ensembles of the violin family, Lully's bands became the model for the modern orchestra. Louis's predecessor had established the Vingt-quatre Violons du Roi (Twenty-four Violins of the King), which typically played music in a five-part texture: six soprano violins, tuned like the modern violin, on the melody; twelve alto and tenor violins tuned like the modern viola, divided among three inner parts; and six bass violins, tuned a whole tone lower than the modern cello, on the bass line. In 1648, the Petits Violons, with eighteen strings, was created for Louis XIV's personal use. These two groups accompanied ballets, balls, the king's supper, and other court entertainments. By the 1670s, the term *orchestra* was used for such ensembles, after the area in front of the stage in a theater where the musicians were usually placed for opera and other entertainments.

String orchestras

Wind instruments

The numerous dances in Lully's operas were always written specifically for orchestral performance. In addition to the string ensembles, the French king kept a whole stable (literally) of wind, brass, and timpani players, who performed at military and other outdoor ceremonies and sometimes joined the chapel, chamber, or opera ensembles, adding instrumental color (see In Context, page 251).

Church Music

Until about 1650, French church music was dominated by the old style of Renaissance counterpoint. In the second half of the century, in sacred as in secular vocal music, French composers borrowed genres invented in Italy—notably the sacred concerto and oratorio—but wrote in distinctively French styles.

Petit motet and grand motet

Composers in the royal chapel produced numerous motets on Latin texts. These were of two main types: the *petit motet* ("small motet"), a sacred concerto for few voices with continuo, and the *grand motet* ("large motet") for soloists, double chorus, and orchestra, corresponding to the large-scale concertos of Gabrieli and Schütz. *Grands motets* featured several sections in different meters and tempos, encompassing preludes, vocal solos, ensembles, and choruses. Lully and Marc-Antoine Charpentier (1634–1704), a pupil of Carissimi,

In Context The Music of la Grande Écurie, or the Great Stable

Louis XIV's musicians of the Great Stable played at all manner of court events that took place outdoors: processions occasioned by royal weddings and funerals, fireworks displays commemorating royal births, visits by foreign dignitaries, military reviews, hunts, and other types of games and pageants. Like the uniformed trumpeters who always preceded the king's coach when he rode out from his palace, stable musicians often mounted horses, which helps to explain their association with what now seems an undignified place of lodging. In fact, the stable musicians were Louis XIV's best wind and brass players. They performed ceremonial music on fifes and drums, oboes and bassoons, cornetts and trumpets, all of which could easily be heard in the open air. Stable musicians were relatively well paid and sometimes enjoyed exemption from taxation or permission to pass their position onto their sons.

Because employment as a stable musician offered status and job security, the Great Stable became a proving ground for several important families of wind players. A member of one such family, Jean Hotteterre (ca. 1610–ca. 1692), not only had the opportunity to perfect his playing technique but also experimented with the construction of several kinds of wind instruments. Fashioning them out of wood, he sometimes included elegant ornamental details in ivory and ebony, signs that his instruments were highly prized and appreciated at court (see Figure 13.11). Hotteterre's newly refined wind instruments inspired Lully to include woodwinds in his opera orchestra and stimulated their makers and players to strive for a sweeter, more refined sound— one that merited a place alongside the Vingt-quatre Violons du Roi.

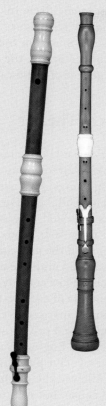

Figure 13.11 (left) Replica of a transverse flute in three sections, after those made by the Hotteterre family from ebony wood and carved ivory.
(Library of Congress, Music Division)

Figure 13.12 (right) A Baroque oboe, ca. 1700, made in three sections out of boxwood and ivory with brass keys and a freestanding reed (not shown).
(Museum of Fine Arts, Boston/Lebrecht.)

Wind players and instrument makers at the French court are generally believed to have created the Baroque oboe (see Figure 13.12). This instrument differed from its predecessor, the shawm, in having a fully freestanding reed (rather than a partially enclosed one) that allowed greater control of intonation and tone quality. Instead of being constructed out of a single piece of wood, the instrument had three sections that were fitted together to facilitate the most delicate adjustments in tuning. It also had an expanded, two-octave range, and its improved design and smaller finger holes allowed the player to produce more accurate chromatic pitches. Flutes were treated to similar modifications and improvements. Thus, despite its unpromising name, the Great Stable actually initiated the rise to prominence of woodwind instruments in today's orchestras.

wrote outstanding *grands motets*. Among the grandest is Lully's *Te Deum* (1677, conclusion in NAWM 86), scored for soloists, large and small choruses, full string orchestra, trumpets, and timpani, and performed by as many as 150 musicians. In the later years of his reign, Louis XIV's favorite sacred composer was Michel-Richard de Lalande (1657–1726), whose more than seventy motets reveal a masterly command of the resources of the *grand motet*: syllabic solos, homophonic and fugal choruses, and operatic airs and duets, with frequent contrasts of texture and mood.

England

English music drew inspiration from both Italy and France, in combination with native traditions. Royal patronage exercised a major influence, as in France, but music for the public grew increasingly important. Despite attempts to introduce opera, the English monarchy, aristocracy, and public preferred native genres of dramatic and ceremonial vocal music.

Musical Theater

Masques   A favorite court entertainment since the time of Henry VIII was the masque. Masques shared many features with opera, including instrumental music, dancing, songs, choruses, costumes, scenery, and stage machinery, but they were long, collaborative spectacles rather than unified dramas with music by a single composer. One such work was *The Triumph of Peace* (1634) by William Lawes (1602–1645) and others. This highly elaborate masque began with a procession of all the principal characters on horseback through the streets of London, featured multiple changes of scenery, and included several antimasques, or scenes of low comedy (see page 180 and Figure 13.13). The genre appealed to all segments of society, both as public spectacle and as private entertainment, and shorter masques were produced not only in aristocratic ballrooms but also in theaters and private schools.

Mixed genres   After the English Civil War (1642–1649), Cromwell's Puritan government prohibited stage plays but not concerts or private musical entertainments. This policy allowed the production of the first English "operas"—not operas in the Italian sense, but mixtures of elements from spoken drama and the masque,

Figure 13.13 Costume designs from about 1610 by Inigo Jones, probably intended for masque (left) and antimasque (right) characters.

(Left: Bridgeman Art Library. Right: Lebrecht Music & Arts.)

including dances, songs, recitatives, and choruses. After the Restoration in 1660, audiences eagerly returned to the theaters, where plays often included masques or similar musical episodes. Charles II had spent his exile in France, and French music and court ballet became increasingly influential in England after his return. But an attempt to introduce French opera in the 1670s failed, and there was little interest in dramas set to continuous music. Only two dramas sung throughout met any success, both composed for private audiences rather than for the public: John Blow's *Venus and Adonis* (ca. 1680) and Henry Purcell's *Dido and Aeneas* (ca. 1689).

Henry Purcell (1659–1695), England's leading composer and a royal favorite (see Biography, below), composed *Dido and Aeneas* in about 1689. The first known performance took place at an exclusive girl's boarding school in Chelsea, but the work may have been intended for performance at court. Purcell's score is a masterpiece of opera in miniature: there are only four principal roles, and the three acts take only about an hour to perform. Indebted in many ways to Blow's *Venus and Adonis*, the work masterfully incorporates elements of the English masque and of French and Italian opera.

Dido and Aeneas's overture and homophonic choruses in dance rhythms resemble those of Lully, and the typical scene structure also follows Lully's example, with solo singing and a chorus leading to a dance. The most notable Italian element is the presence of several arias, rare in French opera or English masque. Three arias are built entirely over ground basses, like many Italian

Purcell, Dido and Aeneas

French and Italian elements

Henry Purcell (1659–1695)

Celebrated after his death as "the British Orpheus," Purcell was favored by royal patronage throughout his career. His father, a member of the Chapel Royal, died just before the boy's fifth birthday. Purcell joined the Chapel Royal as a choirboy and proved to be a gifted prodigy as a composer, publishing his first song at the age of eight. When his voice broke, he was apprenticed to the keeper of the king's keyboard and wind instruments. In 1677, he became composer for the violins at court, and in 1679 he succeeded John Blow as organist of Westminster Abbey, a post he retained for the rest of his brief life, serving three different kings over twenty-five years. He died at the height of his career, at age thirty-six, and was buried next to the organ in Westminster Abbey. His epitaph describes him as "the many-sided master of his art, the brief delight and glory of his age." He was survived by his wife Frances, who published a number of his works after his death.

Purcell wrote enormous amounts of music in almost all genres. His primary focus was vocal music: he composed songs for home performance, choral music for Anglican services and

Figure 13.14 Henry Purcell in 1695, in a portrait by John Closterman. (National Portrait Gallery, London.)

royal ceremonies, chamber music for the growing London public concert scene, and music for the theater. He was invited by the newly formed Musical Society of London to be the first to compose an ode to celebrate the Festival of Saint Cecilia. Purcell's greatest achievement lay in consciously fashioning a viable English song that sounded at once natural and expressive.

Major works: *Dido and Aeneas* (opera); 5 semi-operas; incidental music for 43 plays; 65 anthems; 6 services; numerous odes, songs, and catches; and chamber and keyboard music.

Full 🔊   Concise 🔊

arias. The last of these, and one of the most moving arias in all opera, is Dido's lament, *When I am laid in earth* (NAWM 89b), which follows the Italian tradition of setting laments over a descending tetrachord (see Chapter 11), here altered chromatically. As shown by asterisks in Example 13.2 Purcell creates great tension by rearticulating suspended notes on strong beats, intensifying their dissonance.

English elements

Amid these foreign influences, English traits remain strong. The use of dance for dramatic purposes owes less to Lully than to the masque tradition. Many solos and choruses use the style of the English air: tuneful, diatonic, in the major mode, with simple, catchy rhythms. Others, like the closing chorus *With drooping wings* (NAWM 89c), convey a profound sense of sorrow. Descending minor-scale figures portray the "drooping wings" of cupids, and arresting pauses mark the words "never part."

Full 🔊

English recitatives

Full 🔊   Concise 🔊

In the recitatives, Purcell draws on English and French precedents to fashion melodies flexibly molded to the accents, pace, and emotions of the English text. Dido's final recitative, *Thy hand, Belinda* (NAWM 89a), is a miniature masterpiece that portrays the dying Dido through a slow, stepwise, meandering descent tinged with chromaticism (see Figure 13.15).

Dido and Aeneas had no successors because the English strongly preferred spoken drama. For public theaters, Purcell wrote incidental music for almost fifty plays, most in the last five years of his life. During this period, he also wrote the music for five works in the mixed genre called dramatic opera or semi-opera—a spoken play with an overture and four or more masques or substantial musical episodes—including *The Fairy Queen* (1692), based on Shakespeare's *A Midsummer Night's Dream*.

Semi-operas

England did not develop a native tradition of full-fledged opera until the late nineteenth century. Although Purcell died young, there is no sign that he would have inaugurated one had he lived. Without support for it from the monarchy,

Example 13.2 Henry Purcell, Dido and Aeneas, *Act III, Scene 2, Dido's lament*

Figure 13.15 In a painting by Andrea Sacchi (1599–1661) dating from the 1630s, the abandoned queen Dido holds her lover's sword, which is to be the instrument of her suicide, to her breast.
(Musée des Beaux-Arts, Caen, France.)

as in France, or from the public, as in Venice and other cities, there was no role for opera in English.

Ceremonial and Domestic Music for Voice

Vocal music outside the theater owed relatively little to foreign models. The royal family often commissioned large works for chorus, soloists, and orchestra for ceremonial or state occasions, such as royal birthdays, the king's return to London, or holidays. Purcell's magnificent *Ode for St. Cecilia's Day* (1692), with its elaborate choruses and declamatory solos—one of which was sung in its first performance by the composer himself "with incredible graces"—was a direct ancestor of Handel's English oratorios (see Chapter 14). In addition to hundreds of theater songs, Purcell wrote a large number of vocal solos, duets, and trios, all published for home performance. A specialty of Purcell and other English composers in this period was the catch, a round or canon with a humorous, often ribald text. Catches were sung unaccompanied by a convivial group of gentlemen, paralleling the bawdy songs and coarse jokes of other all-male gatherings.

Anthems and services remained the principal genres of Anglican church music after the Restoration. Since Charles II favored solo singing and orchestral accompaniments, Blow, Purcell, and their contemporaries produced many verse anthems for soloists with chorus. Coronation ceremonies inspired especially elaborate works. Purcell also set nonliturgical sacred texts for one or more voices with continuo, evidently for private devotional use.

Occasional music

Church music

The Public Concert

Perhaps more important in the long run than the music composed in seventeenth-century England was an institution pioneered there: the public concert. Although in Venice opera had become a commercial institution some thirty years

VIGNETTE The First Public Concerts

Concerts that anyone can attend for the price of a ticket are so much a part of modern musical life that it is hard to imagine they are only three centuries old. The public concert is an English invention, inspired by the presence in London of excellent musicians with inadequate salaries and of middle-class audiences eager to hear music but without means to employ their own musicians. The first concert series was advertised in the London Gazette in December 1672:

These are to give notice, That at Mr. *John Banisters* House (now called the Music-School) over against the *George Tavern* in *White Fryers*, this present Monday, will be Music performed by excellent Masters, beginning precisely at 4 of the clock in the afternoon, and every afternoon for the future, precisely at the same hour.

Roger North, a writer and critic, recalled the concerts:

But how and by what steps Music shot up into such request, as to crowd out from the stage even comedy itself, and to sit down in her place and become of such mighty value and price as we now know it to be, is worth inquiring after. The first attempt was

low: a project of old Banister, who was a good violin, and a theatrical composer. He opened an obscure room in a public house in Whitefriars, filled it with tables and seats, and made a side box with curtains for the music. 1ˢ [one shilling] apiece, call for what [food and drink] you please, pay the reckoning [the bill], and *Welcome gentlemen.*

Elsewhere, North noted that Banister was "one of the [King's] band of violins" whose "course of life was such as kept him poor" and who started the concert series "by way of project to get a little money." The performers, "the best hands in town," were

the mercenary teachers, chiefly foreigners, who attended for a *sportula* [a gift or share of the proceeds] at the time. Sometimes consort, sometimes solos, of the violin, flageolet (one of Banister's perfections), bass viol, lute, and song *all'Italiana*, and such varieties diverted the company, who paid at coming in.

John Wilson, ed., *Roger North on Music, Being a Selection from His Essays Written during the Years ca. 1698–1728* (London: Novello, 1959), pp. 302–3, 352 (spelling and punctuation modernized).

earlier, and was open to the paying public, in England and elsewhere all musical performances outside of church were private affairs, given for an invited audience by amateurs, by performers employed by a patron, or by learned academies. Then, in London in the 1670s, several factors came together: a middle class interested in listening to music, a large number of excellent musicians in the service of the royal court and the London theaters, and the inability of the king to pay his musicians well, which encouraged them to supplement their income elsewhere. Impresarios rented rooms in or attached to taverns, charged an entrance fee, and paid the performers out of the proceeds (see Vignette, above). Soon the first commercial concert halls were built, and modern concert life began. Public concerts gradually spread to the Continent, reaching Paris in 1725 and major German cities by the 1740s.

Germany

In German-speaking lands, as in England, composers blended elements from both French and Italian styles with native traditions. In opera, this resulted mostly in eclectic works; but in the case of sacred vocal music, German composers achieved a unique and enduring synthesis in the genre of sacred concerto, which blossomed into the chorale cantata in the eighteenth century.

Opera in Italian

Italian composers were welcomed at Austrian and German courts, where opera in Italian became central to musical life. Native composers took up the genre alongside Italian composers who made operatic careers in Germany. In the eighteenth century, several of the most successful composers of Italian opera were German, from Handel and Hasse to Gluck and Mozart (see Chapters 14, 15, and 16).

Opera in German

After scattered experiments, opera in German found a home in Hamburg with the 1678 opening of the first public opera house in Germany. In this prosperous commercial center, the opera house was a business venture designed to turn a profit through year-round productions of works that would appeal to the middle class. Local poets translated or adapted librettos from Venetian operas and wrote new ones that were similar in subject matter and general plan. Composers adopted the recitative style of Italian opera but were eclectic in their arias: in addition to Italianate arias, they occasionally wrote airs in the French style and in the rhythms of French dances. Also common in early German opera, especially for lower-class or comic characters, are short strophic songs in the popular style of northern Germany, displaying brisk, forthright melodies and rhythms. The foremost and most prolific of the early German opera composers was Reinhard Keiser (1674–1739), who wrote almost sixty works for the Hamburg stage. A slightly younger composer who directed the Hamburg Opera between 1722 until it closed in 1738, Georg Philipp Telemann (1681–1767), also wrote numerous works for it.

Georg Philipp Telemann

Although opera constituted only a tiny fraction of his output, Telemann was regarded by his contemporaries as one of the best composers of his era. He was also the most prolific, with over 3,000 vocal and instrumental works in every genre and style of the era spanning his long lifetime. The flexibility that allowed him to draw elements from various traditions and adapt or synthesize them to suit any purpose or audience—amateur or professional—gave his music broad appeal. Good examples lie in his so-called *Paris* Quartets (1730), also referred to as suites, sonatas, or concertos because of their versatility of structure and instrumentation. Written for three instruments and basso continuo (NAWM 99), the treble parts could be played by violins or flutes; and if performed only by strings—two violins, viola, and cello without basso continuo—the resulting texture would make them the earliest examples of the string quartet, a genre which was to dominate chamber music in the classical eighteenth century. In fact, Telemann became more widely published and more popular in his day than J. S. Bach, who was offered an important position in Leipzig only after Telemann had turned it down.

Full ⟫

Lutheran Vocal Music

After the ravages of the Thirty Years' War, churches in the Lutheran territories of Germany quickly restored their musical forces. However, two conflicting tendencies arising within the church inevitably affected the music. Orthodox Lutherans, holding to established doctrine and public forms of worship, favored using all available resources of choral and instrumental music in their services. In contrast, Pietists, or those who emphasized private devotions and Bible readings, distrusted formality and high art in worship, and preferred simple music and poetry that expressed the emotions of the individual believer. This division gave rise to two distinct genres: elaborate works for public worship and devotional songs intended for private use.

Chorales

Lutherans possessed a common heritage in the chorale, which formed the foundation for both private and public worship (see Chapter 9). New poems and

At the Time

In 1686, at the time of the premiere of Lully's *Armide* in Paris (see Figure 13.16):

- The artists who pioneered the visual Baroque—Rubens, Caravaggio, Gentileschi, Poussin, Bernini, and Rembrandt—are all dead.
- The French king, Louis XIV, is in the forty-third year of his reign and at the height of his power. He recently revoked the Edict of Nantes, which extended religious freedom to French Protestants, resulting in the return of fierce persecutions and massive migrations of Protestants to the New World and elsewhere. The previous year, Louis secretly married his longtime mistress, Madame de Maintenon, who then founded the first state-supported school for girls.
- Pope Innocent XI issues a bull condemning the extension of slavery to the French colonies.
- G. F. Leibniz describes integral calculus for the first time in print. Isaac Newton presents the manuscript of the first volume of his *Principia mathematica* to London's Royal Society, one of the oldest scientific institutions in Europe.
- Queen Christina of Sweden holds court in Rome, where Alessandro Scarlatti is composing chamber cantatas and operas (NAWM 92 and 93) and Arcangelo Corelli's trio sonatas are soon to be published (NAWM 94). In northern Italy, violin trade thrives under the family dynasties of Amati and Stradivari.
- James II wears the English crown, having suceeded Charles II the previous year, and enjoys masques and other entertainments at court, as well as service music in Westminster Abbey, by Henry Purcell and his contemporaries.
- Public opera in Germany at last has a home in the thriving commercial center of Hamburg, while Londoners enjoy performances of public concerts, now in their second decade.
- The croissant is invented, in the shape of the Turkish flag's crescent moon, to commemorate the long siege of Vienna and other cities by the Ottoman Turks, during which many citizens died of starvation.
- Georg Philipp Telemann, Johann Sebastian Bach, and George Frideric Handel, musical giants of the next century, all celebrate their first birthday.

Figure 13.16 Marie Le Rochois as Armide at the opera's premiere in 1686.
(Dulwich Picture Gallery, London/ Bridgeman Art Library.)

melodies continued to be composed, many of them intended not for congregational singing but for use in private devotions at home. At the same time, Orthodox Lutheran centers provided a favorable environment for developing the sacred concerto for public worship. The backbone was the concerted vocal ensemble singing a biblical text, as established by Schütz and others in the early and mid-seventeenth century. Of more recent vintage was the solo aria, normally in Italian style, on a strophic, nonbiblical text. The chorale was the most traditional and characteristically German ingredient, set either in the concertato style or in simple harmonies. Composers often drew on these elements in various combinations to create multimovement works. Today such works are usually referred to as cantatas, but their composers called them concertos, sacred concertos, or simply "the music" for a service.

Concerted church music

Dieterich Buxtehude and Johann Pachelbel (1653–1706) followed in Schütz's footsteps by writing sacred concertos for chorus, solo voices, and orchestra, with or without the use of chorale texts and melodies. The most famous in a long line of composers working in or near Nuremberg, Pachelbel frequently wrote for double chorus, like many composers in southern Germany, where Venetian influence remained powerful.

Pachelbel

Buxtehude, a northerner rooted in the native Lutheran tradition, was organist at the Marienkirche in Lübeck, where he composed and played much of his church music for the Abendmusiken, public concerts following the afternoon church services in Lübeck during the Advent season. These concerts were long, varied, quasi-dramatic affairs, on the order of loosely organized oratorios, incorporating recitatives, strophic arias, chorale settings, and polyphonic choruses, as well as organ and orchestral music. Among the vocal works composed for these concerts is a setting of *Wachet auf*, a sacred concerto consisting of a series of variations on the chorale. The Abendmusiken attracted musicians from all over Germany, including the twenty-year-old J. S. Bach, who made a kind of pilgrimage during the autumn of 1705 to Lübeck, traveling a distance of more than two hundred miles on foot, to hear the elderly Buxtehude play.

Buxtehude

POSTLUDE

Recitative and aria became the most characteristic styles of vocal music in the seventeenth century in all European nations. While Italian recitative spawned several different varieties, French recitative took another path, accommodating the sonic patterns of the French language. Among the aria types common in this period—strophic, ostinato, and da capo—perhaps the most important, and certainly the most ubiquitous, was the da capo aria. Its function was to epitomize and explore a particular affection, to portray and project a psychological state, in much the same way a film director dwells on the close-up or slow-motion camera shot to convey the emotional values of a particular scene. Not confined to amorous or heroic sentiments, the da capo aria was also suited to the expression of religious piety or fervor and so was eventually adopted by composers of church music, such as oratorios, and in many sacred works with dramatic elements.

Whereas Alessandro Scarlatti was among a host of competing Italian composers in representing the most forward-looking trends in Italy, Lully exercised a virtual monopoly over the musical stage in France. His *tragédies lyriques* were stylistically conservative and continued to be performed unchanged even after the death of Louis XIV in 1715. Across the Channel, Purcell synthesized French and Italian elements with native styles into a unique English operatic style, but it did not survive into the eighteenth century.

In German-speaking lands, composers drew deeply on both French and Italian styles, remaking the foreign elements to suit local tastes and blending them with homegrown traditions such as the Lutheran chorale. In doing so, they laid the foundations for the extraordinary developments of the eighteenth century, when German and Austrian composers would play key roles in forging a new international musical language.

 Resources for study and review available at
wwnorton.com/studyspace

14

Baroque Music in the Early Eighteenth Century

PRELUDE

The early eighteenth century—particularly between 1720 and 1750—was a period of stylistic change in music. Newer, Classic styles were emerging to compete with older, Baroque styles. This newer music sounded more songful and less contrapuntal, more natural and less artificial, more sentimental and less intensely emotional than its Baroque counterpart. We will explore these emerging styles in the next chapter, but their influence is already apparent in some of the later works by Vivaldi, Rameau, J. S. Bach, and Handel, the four masterful composers discussed in this chapter. Together with Couperin, Rameau's older contemporary, these composers summarize and, to some extent, synthesize the Baroque musical qualities and trends we have studied so far in Italy, France, Germany, and England. All of these figures were successful and eminent during their own time. All were aware of new currents in musical thought, each finding his own solution to the conflicts between counterpoint and homophony, older and more recent styles. All worked within the established genres of the late Baroque, one of which, the instrumental concerto, will be introduced in this chapter. Vivaldi excelled as a composer of concertos and operas. Couperin wrote stylish music, especially for keyboard, and advocated a synthesis of French and Italian styles. Rameau wrote opera and instrumental music in France and developed new ideas about harmony and tonality in his theoretical writings, some aspects of which were incorporated into later theory. J. S. Bach, somewhat isolated in Germany from the main European cultural centers, brought to consummation all forms of late Baroque music except opera. And Handel, who excelled in composing Italian opera, recognized the social changes in England that would create the perfect climate for a new kind of oratorio, one that long outlived the audiences for which it was intended.

Italy: The Rise of the Concerto

At the beginning of the eighteenth century, Venice, though declining in political power and headed for economic ruin, still remained the most glamorous city in Europe. It was full of tourists, tradespeople, intellectuals, prostitutes, artists, and musicians—all attracted to its colorful and exciting diversity.

Musicians sang on the streets and canals; gondoliers had their own repertory of songs; amateurs played and sang in private academies; and opera impresarios competed for the best singers and composers.

Venice

Public festivals, more numerous in Venice than elsewhere, remained occasions of musical splendor, and the musical establishment of Saint Mark's was still famous. The city had always taken pride in its musical greatness—as a center of music printing, church music, instrumental composition, and opera. Even in the eighteenth century, Venice never had fewer than six opera companies, which together played thirty-four weeks of the year. Between 1700 and 1750, the Venetian public heard ten new operas annually, and the count was even higher in the second half of the century.

Ospedali

In addition to these musical establishments, Venice nurtured a unique group of institutions that were actually state-run shelters for chronically ill, poor, or homeless children, including many who were illegitimate, orphaned, or otherwise abandoned. The Pio Ospedale della Pietà was one of four such "hospitals" that provided excellent music education for women outside the convent and that became famous as musical centers. Already in the seventeenth century, some ospedali were accepting nonresident girls and boarders who paid tuition. Educating the girls in music served several purposes: it occupied their time; it enhanced their prospects for marriage or prepared them for convent life; and it earned donations for the hospitals through regular performances, such as the concert pictured in Figure 14.1. Careers as instrumentalists or church musicians were not open to women, and, before the girls were allowed to leave, they had to promise never to perform in public again. Because they offered the only opportunity to see women performing, services with music at the Pietà and other institutions in Venice attracted large audiences. Travelers wrote of these occasions with enthusiasm and even amusement at the unusual sight of a choir and orchestra comprised mainly of teenage girls (see Vignette, page 263). Thus, like their counterparts, the boys' conservatories in Naples, the Venetian ospedali influenced the musical life of the entire peninsula, serving as premier laboratories for composers.

The instrumental concerto

The instrumental concerto was a new kind of orchestral composition, developed in the 1680s and 1690s and destined to become the most important type of

Figure 14.1 Women singers and string players (upper left), thought to be from the Venetian orphanages, perform a concert in Venice. Oil painting by Gabriele Bella (1730–1799).
(Galleria Querini-Stampalia, Venice, Bridgeman Art Library.)

Baroque instrumental music and to establish the orchestra as the leading instrumental ensemble. Like the vocal concerto, it united two contrasting forces into a harmonious whole in an instrumental version of the concertato medium. It combined this texture with other traits favored at the time: florid melody over a firm bass; musical organization based on tonality; and multiple movements with contrasting tempos, moods, and figuration. Concertos were closely related to sonatas and served many of the same purposes: they were played at public ceremonies, entertainments, and private musical gatherings, and they could substitute for elements of the mass.

By 1700, composers were writing three kinds of concertos. The first two types — concerto grosso and solo concerto — were more numerous and, in retrospect, more important. Both played on the sonic contrast between many instruments and one or only a few. The concerto grosso set a small ensemble (concertino) of solo instruments against a large ensemble (concerto grosso or ripieno, meaning full). The concertino normally comprised two violins, cello, and continuo, the same forces needed to play a trio sonata, although other solo string or wind instruments might be added or substituted. In the solo concerto a single instrument, most often a violin, contrasted with the large ensemble. The large group was almost always a string orchestra, usually divided into first and second violins, violas, and cellos, with basso continuo and bass viol either doubling the cellos or separate. The third type, the orchestral concerto, was a work in several movements that emphasized the first-violin part and the bass, distinguishing the concerto from the more contrapuntal texture of the sonata. Corelli (see Chapter 12) was an early composer of concerti grossi, and his approach was widely imitated by later composers in Italy, England, and Germany.

Giuseppe Torelli (1658–1709), a leading figure in the Bologna school, also composed solo and orchestra concertos, and concerti grossi, including the first

Types of concertos

Giuseppe Torelli

Tutti	Solo	Tutti	Solo	Tutti
Ritornello I	Solo I	Ritornello II	Solo II	Ritornello III

	Ritornello I	Solo I	Ritornello II	Solo II	Ritornello III
Motives:	a　　b		a　　b		a　　b
Key:	i　　i	v	III	iv　　V_7	i　　i

Figure 14.2　Master plan of a Torelli concerto, first movement.

concertos ever published (his Op. 5; 1692). In his concertos, we can see a new notion of the concerto develop; his master plan, detailed in Figure 14.2, became the basis for the later ritornello form. He wrote trumpet concertos for services in San Petronio, and his Op. 6 (1698) includes two solo violin concertos, perhaps the first by any composer. Six more violin concertos and six concerti grossi appeared as his Op. 8 (1709). Most of these works follow a three-movement

Three-movement structure

structure, taken over from the Italian opera overture: an opening fast movement; a slow movement in the same or a closely related key (relative minor, dominant, or subdominant); and a final fast movement in the tonic, often shorter and sprightlier than the first.

Ritornello form

In the fast movements of his violin concertos, Torelli often used a form that resembles and may have been modeled on the A section of a da capo aria (compare the scheme of Scarlatti's aria in Figure 13.4 with Figure 14.2). There are two extended passages for the soloist, framed by a ritornello that appears at the beginning and end of the movement and recurs, in abbreviated form and in a different key, between the two solo passages. The solos present entirely new material, often featuring the soloist's virtuosity, and modulate to closely related keys, providing contrast and variety. The return of the ritornello then offers stability and resolution.

Antonio Vivaldi

The best-known Italian composer of the early eighteenth century was Antonio Vivaldi (1678–1741), a native Venetian who spent most of his career there (see Biography, page 265). A virtuoso violinist, master teacher, and popular composer of opera, cantatas, and sacred music, he is known today primarily for his concertos, which number around five hundred.

The Pietà

From 1703 to 1740, Vivaldi was conductor, composer, teacher, and superintendent of musical instruments at the Pio Ospedale della Pietà. His job required him to maintain the string instruments, teach his students to play, and meet the public's demand for new music—there were no "classics" and few works of any kind survived more than two or three seasons. Such relentless pressure accounts both for the vast output of many eighteenth-century composers and for the phenomenal speed at which they worked. Vivaldi was expected to furnish new oratorios and concertos for every church holiday at the Pietà. Concertos were especially well suited for players of varying abilities because the best performers could show off their skill in the solo parts while those of lesser ability could play in the orchestra. Vivaldi's innovation of placing the performers in galleries, partly obscured from the audience's view, added to the women's appeal (see Figure 14.1).

Vivaldi's concertos

Vivaldi's concertos have a freshness of melody, rhythmic verve, skillful treatment of solo and orchestral color, and clarity of form that have made them perennial favorites. Working at the Pietà, having skilled performers at his disposal, and being required to produce music at a prodigious rate provided

Antonio Vivaldi (1678–1741)

Internationally renowned as a virtuoso violinist, Vivaldi was one of the most original and prolific composers of his time, and his influence on later composers was profound. Born in Venice, the eldest of nine children of a violinist at Saint Mark's, Vivaldi trained for both music and the priesthood, a combination that was not unusual at the time. His bright red hair earned him the nickname il Prete Rosso (the Red Priest).

In 1703, the year he was ordained, he became a music teacher at the Pio Ospedale della Pietà, a Venetian orphanage and school for girls. He was later appointed director of concerts, a position of greater responsibility, and he remained at the Pietà until 1740, with some breaks in service.

Like most of his contemporaries, Vivaldi composed every work for a definite occasion and for particular performers. For the Pietà, he composed oratorios, sacred music, and especially concertos. He also fulfilled forty-nine opera commissions, most for Venice and a few for elsewhere. Between 1713 and 1719, the theaters of Venice staged more works by him than by any other composer. Since he usually supervised the production of his operas in person, he was often absent from the Pietà for long periods. During a two-year sojourn in Rome (1723–1724), the Pietà's governors asked him to compose two new concertos a month for a fee, which he did for the next six years; this arrangement is one of the most direct signs of Vivaldi's value to them as a composer, distinct from his roles as teacher and performer.

In the 1720s, Vivaldi took the contralto Anna Girò as his singing pupil (and, some gossiped, his mistress, although he denied it). In 1737, he was censured for conduct unbecoming a priest. By then, his popularity with the Venetian public had dwindled, and he increasingly sought commissions elsewhere, traveling to Amsterdam in 1738 and Vienna in 1740. He earned enormous sums of money from his music but spent almost all of it, and when he died in Vienna in 1741, he was given a pauper's funeral.

Major works: About 500 concertos (including *The Four Seasons*), 16 sinfonias, 64 solo sonatas, 27 trio sonatas, 21 surviving operas, 38 cantatas, and about 60 sacred vocal works.

Figure 14.3 Portrait of Antonio Vivaldi, Italian School (18th century).
(Civico Museo Bibliografico Musicale/Alinari/The Bridgeman Art Library.)

Vivaldi with an ideal workshop for experimenting with the concerto. The secret of Vivaldi's success and of the profound influence he exercised on other composers was a simple but flexible recipe that allowed him to achieve extraordinary variety through ever-changing combinations of a few basic elements.

Vivaldi included a remarkable range of colors and sonorities through different groupings of solo and orchestral instruments. His orchestra at the Pietà probably consisted of twenty to twenty-five string instruments, with harpsichord or organ for the continuo. The strings were divided in what was becoming the standard arrangement: violins I and II, violas, cellos, and bass viols (usually doubling the cellos). This was always the core group, although in many concertos

Vivaldi's orchestra

Vivaldi also called for flutes, oboes, bassoons, or horns, any of which might be used as solo instruments or in the ensemble. He also used special coloristic effects, like pizzicato and muted strings especially in his oratorios, perhaps in an effort to compensate for their lack of costumes and scenery.

Instrumentation of the concertos

About 350 of Vivaldi's concertos are for orchestra and one solo instrument—mostly violin, but also bassoon, cello, oboe, flute, viola d'amore, recorder, and mandolin. The concertos for two violins give the soloists equal prominence, producing the texture of a duet for two high voices. The concertos that call for several solo instruments feature the same opposition between virtuoso soloists and orchestra that is found in Vivaldi's solo concertos.

Expanded ritornello form

Vivaldi expanded Torelli's basic ritornello form, shown in Figure 14.2, which is less a formal mold than it is an approach or a set of guidelines, and one that allows a great deal of variety:

- Orchestral ritornellos alternate with solo episodes.
- The opening ritornello is composed of several small units, typically two to four measures in length, some of which may be repeated or varied. These segments can be separated from each other or combined in new ways without losing their identity as the ritornello.
- Later statements of the ritornello are usually partial, comprising only one or some of the units, sometimes varied.
- The ritornellos are signposts to the tonal structure of the music, confirming the keys to which the music modulates. The first and last statements are in the tonic, at least one (usually the first in a new key) is in the dominant, and others are usually in closely related keys.
- The solo episodes are characterized by virtuosic, idiomatic playing, sometimes repeating or varying elements from the ritornello but often presenting scales, arpeggiations, or other figuration. Many episodes modulate to a new key, which is then confirmed by the following ritornello. Sometimes the soloist interrupts or plays some part of the closing ritornello.

Figure 14.4 A page from one of Vivaldi's manuscripts—a tutti section from the finale of the Concerto in A for solo violin and four-part string ensemble.

All these points are illustrated by the first Allegro movement of Vivaldi's Concerto for Violin and Orchestra in A Minor, Op. 3, No. 6 (NAWM 96). Example 14.1 shows the opening ritornello. Each of the segments, denoted by letter, has a strongly etched, individual character that makes it easy to remember. Each is a distinct harmonic unit, enabling Vivaldi to separate and recombine the segments later on. In both movements, later statements of the ritornello are only partial, and some vary motives from the original ritornello, as do some of the solo episodes. New figurations are introduced in the episodes, as shown in Example 14.2, providing even more variety within a clearly understood structure; one passage—Example 14.2c—exploits the open strings of the violin (tuned g–d'–a'–e", circled) for impressive leaps.

Vivaldi's Violin Concerto in A Minor

Full 🔊   Concise 🔊

Example 14.1 Antonio Vivaldi, Concerto in A Minor, Op. 3, No. 6, first movement

Example 14.2 Antonio Vivaldi, Concerto in A Minor, Op. 3, No. 6, first movement, examples of figuration in solo episodes

Figure 14.5 Antonio Vivaldi (1678–1741), "the Red Priest," drawn in Rome in 1723 by P. L. Ghezzi. It is the only authenticated portrait of the composer.
(Lebrecht Music & Arts Library.)

Typical of Vivaldi is that each movement has a small aberration that makes its form unique, yet the overall formal strategy is clearly the same from piece to piece. Far from following a textbook plan, Vivaldi's ritornello structures show almost infinite variety in form and content.

Vivaldi was the first concerto composer to make the slow movement as important as the fast ones. His slow movement is typically a long-breathed, expressive, cantabile melody, like an adagio operatic aria or arioso, to whose already rich figuration the performer was expected to add embellishments. Some slow movements are through-composed, and others use a simplified ritornello or two-part form.

Vivaldi once said he could compose a concerto faster than a copyist could write out the parts. One reason was that ritornello form allowed him to spin out relatively long movements from a small amount of material that he repeated, transposed, varied, and recombined. In both fast and slow movements, he frequently used sequences, generating several measures from a short motive while dramatizing a strong chord progression, as in the second segment (b) of Example 14.1 (indicated by brackets).

Despite Vivaldi's reliance on formulas, what is most striking about his concertos is their variety and range of expression. His works were known for their spontaneity of musical ideas, clear formal structures, driving harmonies, varied textures, and forceful rhythms. He established a dramatic tension between solo and tutti, not only giving the soloist contrasting figuration, as Torelli had already done, but also letting the soloist prevail as a dominating musical personality. Not surprisingly, Vivaldi was also a stellar composer of operas.

In addition to composing many of his concertos for the Pietà, Vivaldi also wrote on commission and earned money through publications. Nine collections of his concertos (Opp. 3–4 and Opp. 6–12) were published in Amsterdam, the last seven apparently printed at the publisher's expense instead of being subsidized by the composer or a patron, as was common. This shows Vivaldi's marketing value to his publisher and reflects the immense popularity of his concertos, especially in northern Europe. Several of these collections were given fanciful titles, in part to attract buyers: Op. 3, *L'estro armonico* (Harmonic Inspiration, 1711); Op. 4, *La stravaganza* (Extravagance, 1716); Op. 8, *Il cimento dell'armonia e dell'inventione* (The Contest between Harmony and Invention, 1725); and Op. 9, *La cetra* (The Kithara, 1727), evoking ancient Greek values. Some individual concertos were also given titles and even programs. Most famous are the first four concertos in Op. 8, known as *The Four Seasons*. Each of these is accompanied by a sonnet, perhaps written by Vivaldi himself, that describes the season, and the concertos cleverly depict the images in the poetry, taking advantage of the variety possible in ritornello forms.

Range of styles

Vivaldi's music reflects the stylistic changes of the first half of the eighteenth century. At the conservative extreme are his trio and solo sonatas, which emulate the style of Corelli. Most of his concertos were part of the stylistic mainstream, responding to and often creating contemporary trends. At the progressive extreme are the solo concerto finales, the orchestral concertos, and most of the sixteen sinfonias—works that establish Vivaldi as a founder of the Classic symphony (see Chapter 16).

France: Couperin and Rameau

While Italy had many cultural centers, France had only one, Paris, the capital and by far the largest city. Musicians in the provinces dreamed of careers in Paris, where patrons, publishers, and an eager public waited to hear and see the latest music. Only there could a composer achieve true success and a national reputation. Other cities had concert series in which amateurs could perform, but Paris was home to the most prestigious concert organizations like the Concert spirituel, a public concert series founded in 1725. The royal court of Louis XV (r. 1715–1774) continued to support musicians but no longer dominated musical life, as had the court of his great-grandfather, Louis XIV. In its place, a wider range of patrons and institutions supported musicians and composers.

Paris as musical center

Since the seventeenth century, Italian music in France was viewed as a foreign influence, welcomed by some and resisted by others. The latest Italian music could be heard in Paris, particularly the sonatas and concertos of Corelli, Vivaldi, and others, and the relative merits of French and Italian styles were discussed constantly in salons and in print. Many French composers sought to combine the two musical styles, especially in genres pioneered in Italy.

Reconciling French and Italian styles

François Couperin

Among the most active proponents of blending French and Italian tastes was François Couperin (1668–1733). His career reflects the growing diffusion of patronage in France: he was organist to the king and at the church of Saint Gervais in Paris, but he earned much of his money teaching harpsichord to members of the aristocracy and publishing his own music. His harpsichord *ordres*, or suites, published between 1713 and 1730, were loose aggregations of miniature pieces, usually in dance rhythms and binary form but highly stylized and refined, intended as recreation for amateur performers. Thoroughly French yet individual in style, most of these pieces carry evocative titles. Couperin's *Vingt-cinquième ordre* (Twenty-fifth Suite, 1730), for example, contains *La Visionaire* (The Dreamer; NAWM 97a), a whimsical French overture; *La Mistérieuse* (The Mysterious One), an allemande; *La Montflambert*, a tender gigue probably named after the wife of the king's wine merchant; *La Muse victorieuse* (The Victorious Muse; NAWM 97b), a fast dance in triple time; and others. Couperin's book *L'Art de toucher le clavecin* (The Art of Playing the Harpsichord, 1716) is one of the most important sources for performance practice of the French Baroque.

Keyboard suites

Full 🔊   Concise 🔊

Couperin's chamber music synthesized French with Italian styles. In his titles, prefaces, and choice of contents for his published collections, he proclaimed that the perfect music would be a union of the two national styles. He admired the music of both Lully and Corelli, and celebrated them in suites for two violins and harpsichord: *Parnassus; or, The Apotheosis of Corelli* (1724) and *The Apotheosis of Lully* (1725). In the second work, Lully is represented as joining Corelli on Mount Parnassus to perform a French overture and then a trio sonata. Couperin was the first and most important French composer of trio sonatas, beginning in 1692. His collection *Les Nations* (The Nations, 1726) contains four *ordres*, each consisting of a sonata da chiesa in several movements followed by a suite of dances, thus combining the most characteristic genres of

Chamber works

France and Italy in a single set. He also wrote twelve suites that he called "concerts" for harpsichord and various combinations of instruments, each consisting of a prelude and several dance movements. He entitled the first four *Concerts royaux* (Royal Concerts, published 1722) because they were played before Louis XIV. Couperin published the last eight in a collection entitled *Les Goûts-réünis* (The Reunited Tastes, 1724), signifying that they combined French and Italian styles.

Jean-Philippe Rameau

Jean-Philippe Rameau (1683–1764) had an unusual career, spending two decades as an organist in the provinces, winning recognition as a music theorist around the age of forty, and achieving fame as a composer in his fifties (see Biography, page 271). Attacked then as a radical, he was assailed twenty years later as a reactionary. His treatises founded the theory of tonal music, and his operas established him as Lully's most important successor.

When he settled in Paris in 1722, Rameau's prospects as a composer were poor: he had neither money nor influential friends nor the disposition to curry favor at court. Although he aspired to become a composer of operas—indeed, it was the only road to real fame—the monopoly of the Académie Royale de Musique thwarted that ambition. Seeking other opportunities, he wrote airs and dances for a few musical comedies, pieces with spoken dialogue performed at the popular theaters. He published some cantatas and several books of keyboard pieces. Meanwhile, his reputation as a teacher and organist began to attract students. Rameau's luck finally changed when, in 1732, he was appointed organist, conductor, and composer-in-residence to the wealthy tax collector Alexandre-Jean-Joseph le Riche de la Pouplinière (1693–1762), who supported an orchestra, sponsored concerts for the wealthy, and took pleasure in promoting the careers of obscure musicians. He maintained several residences in Paris as well as houses in the country nearby. His salon attracted a diverse company of aristocrats, writers (Voltaire and Rousseau), painters (van Loo—see Figure 14.15—and La Tour), adventurers (Casanova), and above all, musicians.

La Pouplinière helped Rameau make his name as an opera composer. He funded a production of *Hippolyte et Aricie*, which was performed privately in 1733 before being produced in Paris later that same year, winning both admiration and scorn. A string of successes followed, including the opera-ballet *Les Indes galantes* (The Gallant Indies, 1735) and the opera *Castor et Pollux* (1737), generally considered his masterpiece. After a relatively fallow period in the early 1740s came his most productive years—from the comedy *Platée* (1745) to the tragic opera *Zoroastre* (1749), the most important of Rameau's later works.

From their first performances, Rameau's operas stirred up a storm of critical controversy. The Paris intelligentsia divided into two noisy camps, one supporting Rameau and the other attacking him as a subverter of the good old French opera tradition of Lully. The Lullistes found Rameau's music difficult, forced, grotesque, thick, mechanical, and unnatural—in a word, Baroque. Rameau protested, in a foreword to his opera-ballet *Les Indes galantes*, that he had "sought to imitate Lully, not as a servile copyist but in taking, like him, nature herself—so beautiful and so simple—as a model."

Rameau's theater works resemble Lully's in several ways: both composers apply realistic declamation and precise rhythmic notation in the recitatives; both mix recitative with more tuneful, formally organized airs, choruses, and instrumental interludes; and both include long divertissements. But within this general framework, Rameau introduced many changes.

(marginal notes)

La Pouplinière

Operas

Lullistes versus Ramistes

Comparison with Lully

Jean-Philippe Rameau (1683–1764)

Practically unknown before the age of forty, Rameau became the leading composer in France because of the operas and ballets he turned out in his fifties and sixties. Possessing a strong intellect, he also emerged as the most significant music theorist of his era.

Rameau was born in Dijon, in Burgundy (east-central France), the seventh of eleven children. From his father, an organist, Rameau received his first and, as far as we know, only formal musical instruction. He attended a Jesuit school and was sent to study in Italy briefly as a teenager. After two decades as organist in various provincial French towns, he settled in Paris in 1722, seeking better opportunities. His pathbreaking *Traité de l'harmonie* (Treatise on Harmony), published that year, quickly won him renown as a theorist. He made a living teaching harmony and playing continuo but could not find a position as organist until 1732. In 1726, at age forty-two, he married a nineteen-year-old singer and harpsichordist, Marie-Louise Mangot, and over the next two decades they had four children.

Success as a composer came gradually and late. He published some cantatas and two books of harpsichord pieces in the 1720s. He found patrons who helped to support him, particularly Alexandre-Jean-Joseph le Riche de la Pouplinière. His first opera, *Hippolyte et Aricie* (1733), helped build his reputation as a composer, followed by four other operas and opera-ballets in the next six years. Rameau served la Pouplinière as organist and in various capacities until 1753, and members of his patron's circle became enthusiastic backers as well. In 1745, King Louis XV granted him an annual pension. The next few years were his most productive and successful, with eleven dramatic works by 1749. Given Rameau's late start, it is remarkable that over twenty-five of his ballets and operas were staged, more than any other French composer of the eighteenth century.

Polemical writings and theoretical essays occupied Rameau's last years. He died in Paris in 1764 at the age of eighty-one. Feisty to the end, he found strength even on his deathbed to reproach the priest administering the last rites for chanting poorly.

Major works: 4 *tragédies en musique* (*Hippolyte et Aricie*, *Castor et Pollux*, *Dardanus*, and *Zoroastre*); 6 other operas; *Les Indes galantes* and 6 other opera-ballets; 7 ballets; harpsichord pieces; trio sonatas; cantatas; and motets; *Traité de l'harmonie* and other theoretical writings.

Figure 14.6 Jean-Philippe Rameau, in a copy by Jacques Aved of a portrait by Jean-Baptiste-Siméon Chardin.
(Musée des Beaux-Arts de Dijon. Lebrecht Music & Arts Library.)

The melodic lines offer one notable contrast. Rameau the composer constantly practiced the doctrine of Rameau the theorist—that all melody is rooted in harmony (see A Closer Look, page 272). Many of his melodic phrases are plainly triadic, outlining the harmonic progressions that must support them. Orderly relationships within the tonal system of dominants, subdominants, and modulations govern the harmony. Rameau drew from a rich palette of chords and progressions, including chromatic ones, diversifying his style

Melodic and harmonic style

A Closer Look   Rameau's Theories

Theory—or the "science" of music, as it was called at the time—engaged Rameau throughout his life as he tried to derive the basic principles of harmony from the laws of acoustics. In his numerous writings, Rameau not only clarified the musical practice of his time but also influenced music theory for the next two hundred years. A synopsis of his most important ideas about tonal harmony follows:

Figure 14.7 *Jean-Philippe Rameau, seated near his harpsichord with pen and music paper in hand, occupies himself with writing, an activity suggestive of his status as a thinker as well as a composer.* (Musée Condé, Chantilly, France/Bridgeman Art Library.)

1. A chord is generated naturally when a string is divided into two, three, four, and five equal parts, which produces the octave, the fifth above it, the double octave, and the major third above that. (Rameau soon realized that the overtone series supports this theory.)
2. Triads and seventh chords are the primal elements of music, derived from the natural consonances of the perfect fifth, major third, and minor third. Chords are built over a fundamental tone (known today as the root). Motion from dissonance to consonance drives the music forward.
3. In a series of chords, the succession of fundamental tones becomes the *basse fondamentale*, or fundamental bass, the underlying or determining bass line of the progression. In modern terms, Rameau was asserting that a chord keeps its identity through all its inversions and that the harmony of a passage is defined by the root progression rather than by the lowest sounding notes.
4. He coined the terms *tonic, dominant*, and *subdominant* for the chords that became the pillars of tonality. By clarifying the relationship of chords to one another, Rameau formulated the hierarchies of functional harmony.
5. Modulation results from the change in function of a chord (in modern terminology, a pivot chord).

much more than Lully and achieving dramatic force through expressive, highly charged dissonances that propel the harmony forward.

Instrumental music   Rameau made his most original contributions in the instrumental sections of his operas—overtures, dances, and descriptive symphonies that accompany the stage action. The French valued music for its powers of depiction, and Rameau was their champion tone painter. His musical pictures range from graceful miniatures to broad representations of thunder (*Hippolyte et Aricie*, Act I) or earthquake (*Les Indes galantes*, Act II). The depiction is often enhanced by novel orchestration, especially independent woodwind parts.

Airs and choruses   In comparison to Italian composers, Rameau, like Lully and other French composers, minimized the contrast between recitative and air. He often moved smoothly between styles to suit the dramatic situation. Frequently, he achieved his most powerful effects by using a solo voice and chorus jointly. Choruses remained prominent in French operas long after they were no longer used in Italy, and they are numerous throughout Rameau's works.

The closing minutes of Act IV of *Hippolyte et Aricie* (NAWM 98) illustrate the high drama that Rameau could achieve by combining all these elements. A divertissement of hunters and huntresses is suddenly followed by tragedy; the change is so fast that the audience has little time to adjust. Throbbing strings depict a rough sea, while rushing scales in the flute and violins evoke high winds. A monster appears, and the chorus, singing over the orchestra, begs for aid from the goddess Diana. Hippolyte steps up to fight the monster as his beloved Aricie trembles in fear; they, too, sing over the orchestra, in a style of accompanied recitative borrowed from contemporary Italian opera. The monster breathes flame and smoke, then disappears, and the orchestra stops abruptly. When the smoke clears, Aricie mournfully sees that Hippolyte is gone, and the chorus comments on the tragedy in stirring, richly dissonant homophony. The rapid juxtaposition of styles continues as Phèdre, Hippolyte's stepmother, enters, hears the news from the chorus, and laments his death, for which she feels responsible. Although no full-fledged air appears—indeed, one would be inappropriate—short segments of airlike melody are intermixed with measured and unmeasured recitative, with and without the orchestra, over varying styles of accompaniment, each element perfectly placed for maximum dramatic effect.

Rameau's influence as a music theorist trumps his importance as a composer. Inspired by Descartes and Newton, he approached music as a subject to be studied empirically and explained according to rational principles. In the music of his contemporaries—especially Corelli—Rameau observed harmonic practices that he described and codified into universal laws. He recorded his methods in *Traité de l'harmonie* (Treatise on Harmony, 1722), one of the most influential theoretical works ever written. By the late eighteenth century, his concepts about music theory became the principal basis for teaching harmony.

Hippolyte et Aricie

Full | Concise

Rameau as theorist

Germany: Johann Sebastian Bach

Toward the middle of the eighteenth century, for the first time in history, the leading composers in Europe came from German-speaking lands. Telemann, Handel, members of the Bach family, Haydn, and Mozart all rose to prominence not by inventing new genres, as the Italians had in the two previous centuries, but by synthesizing elements from Italian, French, German, and other national traditions in new, rich ways. The German secret was a balance of tastes between native trends and foreign influences. No one exemplifies this better than Johann Sebastian Bach (1685–1750; see Biography, page 274).

In the eighteenth century, German-speaking central Europe remained divided among hundreds of political entities, from the large states of Austria, Saxony, and Brandenburg-Prussia to tiny principalities and independent cities. Each of these supported music. Some rulers followed Louis XIV's example of displaying their power and wealth through patronage of the arts, as did the Holy Roman emperors in Vienna and King Frederick II (the Great) of Prussia (r. 1740–1786) in Berlin. City governments also employed musicians, especially in Lutheran areas, where the town council was often responsible for hiring music directors for the churches.

German patrons

Lutheran environment

Compared to Vienna and Berlin or the exciting cosmopolitan centers of Venice and Paris, however, an eighteenth-century traveler would have found the world of Lutheran Germany—where Bach spent his entire career—very ordinary indeed. For example, one of its principal cities, Leipzig, had several prominent churches and one of Europe's oldest universities, but not one opera house

Johann Sebastian Bach (1685–1750)

Now considered one of the greatest composers in the Western musical tradition, Bach regarded himself more modestly—as a conscientious craftsman doing his job to the best of his ability. He was a virtuoso organist and keyboard player, a skilled violinist, and a prolific composer in almost every contemporary genre except opera.

Bach came from a large family of musicians from Thuringia, in central Germany. So synonymous was the family name with "musician" that in 1693 the local count urgently called for "a Bach" to fill a vacancy in his orchestra. But at that point, Johann Sebastian was still attending the Latin school in his birthplace, Eisenach, where he received a solid grounding in theology and humanistic studies. He must have learned violin from his father, a court and town musician who died just before Bach's tenth birthday. Johann Sebastian then lived and studied music with his older brother Johann Christoph Bach, organist in Ohrdruf. Bach spent 1700 to 1702 in school at Lüneburg, where he encountered the organist Georg Böhm and experienced the French repertoire and style of the local orchestra. (For cities important in Bach's career, see Figure 14.9.)

Bach's first positions were as a church organist, beginning at Arnstadt in 1703, when he was eighteen, and then at Mühlhausen in 1707. That year he married Maria Barbara Bach, his second cousin, with whom he had seven children before her death in 1720. His second wife, Anna Magdelena Wilcke, a court singer from a family of musicians, whom he married a year later, bore him thirteen children, seven of whom died in infancy.

Figure 14.8 Johann Sebastian Bach. Detail from the Bach monument at Leipzig. (Bettmann/Corbis.)

From his time at Mühlhausen to the end of his life, Bach tutored private students in performance and composition, including several of his own sons, and served as a consultant to organ builders.

In 1708, Bach became a court musician for the duke of Weimar, first as organist and later as concertmaster. He was appointed Kapellmeister (music director) at the court of Prince Leopold of Anhalt in Cöthen in 1717. After a stay of six years, Bach moved to Leipzig, a center of Lutheran church music, to become cantor of the Saint Thomas School and civic music director, one of the most prestigious positions in Germany.

After a lifetime of hard work, Bach's last two years were marked by disease (probably diabetes), vision problems, and severe eye pain. At his death after a stroke, he left a small estate, split among his nine surviving children and his wife, who died in poverty ten years later. Many of Bach's compositions became casualties of this division and hardship.

Bach's works are identified by their number in Wolfgang Schmieder's catalogue of his compositions, abbreviated BWV for Bach-Werke Verzeichnis (Bach Works Catalogue).

Major works: *Saint Matthew Passion, Saint John Passion,* Mass in B Minor, about 200 church cantatas and 30 secular cantatas, about 200 organ chorales and 70 other works for organ, *Brandenburg Concertos, Well-Tempered Clavier, Clavierübung, A Musical Offering, The Art of Fugue,* and numerous other keyboard, ensemble, orchestral, and sacred compositions.

Figure 14.9 Cities that figured in J. S. Bach's career are indicated in red on this map of modern Germany. In Bach's time, Germany comprised a number of duchies, bishoprics, principalities, and electorates of the Holy Roman Empire. For example, Leipzig and Dresden were in the electorate of Saxony, Lüneburg in that of Hanover, Berlin in that of Brandenburg. Hamburg and Lübeck belonged to the duchy of Holstein, and Anhalt-Cöthen and Weimar were themselves tiny dukedoms.

after 1729 nor any princes or bishops in residence. For the last twenty-five years of his life. Bach lived and worked in Leipzig, where he had to engage in petty disputes with town and university officials and to confront their apathy. Although he enjoyed a reputation in Protestant Germany as an organ virtuoso and skilled composer of contrapuntal works, he remained unknown in wider circles. Unlike Vivaldi, who traveled and was recognized throughout Europe, or Rameau, who rubbed shoulders with Parisian high society, Bach, though enormously learned, was essentially a working musician who composed to satisfy his superiors, to please and edify his fellow citizens, and to glorify God.

Bach composed in all the genres of his time with the exception of opera. He wrote primarily to meet the demands of the positions he held, and his works may be grouped accordingly. Thus, at Arnstadt (1703–1707), Mühlhausen (1707–1708), and the court and chapel of the duke of Weimar (1708–1717), where he was employed as an organist, he composed mostly for organ. At Cöthen (1717–1723), where he worked as music director for a princely court, he composed works for keyboard or instrumental ensembles as well as music for instruction and for domestic or court entertainment. He produced most of his cantatas and other church music during his years in Leipzig (1723–1750), where his final position

Cities where Bach worked

as cantor of Saint Thomas's School and music director at the churches of Saint Thomas and Saint Nicholas carried considerable prestige in the Lutheran world. Some of his most important mature compositions for organ or harpsichord also date from the Leipzig period, including teaching pieces for his many private students. Our survey of Bach's compositions corresponds approximately to his places of employment.

Bach at Arnstadt, Mühlhausen, and Weimar: The Organ Works

Bach was trained as a violinist and organist, and it was organ music that first attracted his interest as a composer. As a youth, he visited Hamburg to hear the organists there; and, while working in Arnstadt, he made a journey on foot to Lübeck—a distance of about 225 miles—to hear the famous Buxtehude, who was then almost seventy. There, the music of the older composer so fascinated him that he overstayed his leave and got into trouble with his employers.

As a church organist, Bach focused on the genres employed in Lutheran services: chorale settings, played before each chorale and sometimes to accompany the congregation's singing; and toccatas, fantasias, preludes, and fugues, featured as introductions or interludes at other points in the service and also as recital pieces (see Vignette, page 283).

Preludes and fugues

One of the favorite larger musical structures in this period was the combination of a prelude (or toccata or fantasia) and fugue (from Italian *fuga*, "flight"). Many of Bach's important compositions in this form are idiomatic for the organ and technically difficult, although they never parade empty virtuosity, and their well-defined themes, called fugue subjects, show remarkable inventiveness. His well-known Toccata in D Minor, BWV 565 (before 1708), recalls both the form established by Buxtehude, in which a prelude alternates sections of free fantasia with fugal sections of imitative counterpoint, and the exuberant spirit and length of Buxtehude's *Praeludium* (see NAWM 95).

Vivaldi's influence

While at Weimar, Bach became fascinated by the music of Vivaldi. He arranged several Vivaldi concertos for organ or harpsichord solo, writing out the ornaments and occasionally reinforcing the counterpoint or adding inner voices. As a consequence, Bach's own style began to change. From Vivaldi, he learned to write concise themes, to clarify the harmonic scheme, and to develop subjects into grandly proportioned formal structures based on the ritornello idea.

Bach's Prelude and Fugue in A Minor

Full 🔊

Bach's Prelude and Fugue in A Minor, BWV 543 (NAWM 100), demonstrates Vivaldi's influence particularly vividly. In the prelude, violinistic figuration resembling that of concerto solos, as in Example 14.3a, alternates with toccata sections. Contrasting textures, sequences, circle-of-fifth progressions, clear tonal structure, and returns of the opening material in new keys all recall Vivaldi's typical procedures. The fugue subject, shown in Example 14.3b, is also violinistic, featuring the rapid oscillation between a repeated note and a moving line that on a violin is accomplished by alternating strings. Typical of Bach fugues, the form closely resembles that of a concerto's fast movement because the fugue subject functions like a ritornello, returning in related keys as well as the tonic. Between these statements are episodes that have the character of solo sections, often marked by lighter texture, sequences, or a change of key. More will be said below about the structure of Bach's keyboard fugues.

Bach wrote over two hundred chorale settings for organ, encompassing all known types in a constant striving for variety. At Weimar, he compiled a manuscript collection, the *Orgelbüchlein* (Little Organ Book), containing forty-five short chorale preludes. These served in church as introductions before the congregation sang the chorale. But Bach also had a pedagogical aim, as is true for several of his other collections. The title page reads: "Little Organ Book, in which a beginning organist is given guidance in all sorts of ways of developing a chorale, as well as improving his pedal technique, since in these chorales the pedal is treated as completely obbligato [essential, not optional]." He added the words "To honor the Most High God alone, and for the instruction of my fellow men." In each prelude, the chorale tune is heard once through, but otherwise the settings vary greatly. The melody may be treated in canon, elaborately ornamented, or accompanied in any number of styles. Some preludes symbolize the visual images or underlying ideas of the chorale text through musical figures in a tradition extending back through Schütz to the Italian madrigalists. In *Durch Adams Fall* (Through Adam's fall), BWV 637 (NAWM 101), shown in Example 14.4, while the top line carries the chorale tune, jagged descending leaps in the bass depict Adam's fall from grace. Meanwhile, the twisting chromatic line in the alto portrays the sinuous writhing of the serpent in the Garden of Eden, and the downward-sliding tenor combines with both to suggest the pull of temptation and the sorrow of sin.

Bach conceived his later organ chorales in grander proportions. The settings are less intimate and subjective, replacing the vivid expressive details of the earlier works with a purely musical development of ideas.

Chorale settings

Full 🔊

Example 14.3 J. S. Bach, Prelude and Fugue in A Minor, BWV 543

a. Opening of prelude

b. Fugue subject

Example 14.4 J. S. Bach, Chorale Prelude on Durch Adams Fall, *BWV 637*

[Through Adam's fall are utterly corrupted]

Bach at Cöthen and Leipzig: The Harpsichord Music

Bach's music for harpsichord includes masterpieces in every contemporary genre: preludes, fantasies, and toccatas; fugues and other pieces in fugal style; suites; and sets of variations. In addition, there are early sonatas and capriccios, miscellaneous short works (including many teaching pieces), and concertos with orchestra. The harpsichord compositions, which were not bound to a local German tradition or liturgy as organ works were, reveal the international features of Bach's style—the intermingling of Italian, French, and German characteristics.

The Well-Tempered Clavier

Undoubtedly, Bach's best-known works for keyboard are found in the double cycle of preludes and fugues that he entitled *Das wohltemperirte Clavier* (The Well-Tempered Clavier—also called The Well-Tempered Keyboard—Books I and II, 1722 and ca. 1740, respectively). Each book consists of twenty-four preludes and fugues, paired in each of the twelve major and minor keys, arranged in rising chromatic order from C to B. Book I is more unified in style and purpose than Book II, which includes compositions from many different periods of Bach's life. Both sets were designed to explore the possibilities of playing in all keys on an instrument tuned in near-equal temperament, then still novel for keyboards (see A Closer Look, page 280).

Pedagogical aims

Full 🔊   Concise 🔊

But Bach had pedagogical aims as well. The typical prelude assigns the player a specific technical task, so that the piece functions as an étude. In addition, the preludes illustrate different types of keyboard performance conventions and compositional practices. For example, Nos. 2 and 21 of Book I are toccatas, No. 8 in E♭ minor (NAWM 102) resembles a sonata slow movement, No. 17 a concerto fast movement, and No. 24 a trio sonata. The fugues constitute a compendium of contrapuntal writing, from two to five voices and from archaic procedures to more modern techniques. As in the organ fugues, each one is based on a single idea, or subject, that unfolds throughout the piece in keeping with Baroque theories of the affections. This is in contrast to the ricercar, the fugue's ancestor, which often presented a series of sections each based on a different subject.

Fugue structure

Bach's fugue subjects always have a clearly defined melodic character and a prominent rhythmic profile. As in other contrapuntal genres, independent voices enter with the theme in turn; in a fugue, one complete set of these entries is called the exposition. Normally, the first voice states the subject in the tonic and the second "answers" at the dominant; together they define the main key of the piece and often hint at possibilities for its future harmonic activity. Subject and answer continue to alternate throughout the exposition, which usually concludes when all the voices have entered the texture.

Exposition

Full 🔊   Concise 🔊

In Bach's Fugue No. 8 in D♯ Minor (for three voices) from *The Well-Tempered Clavier*, Book I (NAWM 102), the middle voice states the subject alone, beginning on the tonic and emphasizing the dominant and subdominant before returning to the tonic. The answer then appears in the upper voice at the dominant (A♯) while the first voice continues in counterpoint (see Example 14.5). Note, however, that the answer in this case is not transposed exactly, but rather alters the subject's opening interval from a fifth to a fourth, to ensure that the fugue's exposition remains in D♯ minor. This type of answer is called tonal. (When the answer is an exact transposition of the subject, it is said to be "real.") After two measures of counterpoint serving to lead back to D♯, the third and final voice enters to present the subject in the bass, once again on the tonic. From this point on, there are virtually no breaks in the three-part texture and the almost continuous eighth-note rhythm propels the counterpoint relentlessly forward—features that make Bach's fugues difficult to play and demanding to hear.

Example 14.5 J. S. Bach Fugue No. 8 in D-Sharp Minor, from The Well-Tempered Clavier, *Book I*

Short episodes (passages in which the subject does not appear or appears only in fragments), sometimes characterized by lighter texture or sequences, usually separate the exposition from later full or partial restatements of the subject. Like the episodes separating the ritornellos in a concerto, these may modulate to various keys, which serve as temporary hosts for the subject's repetitions before its final statement in the tonic. The return of the subject to the tonic key is often intensified by devices such as pedal point, stretto (in which statements of the subject pile up in quick succession), or augmentation (in which the rhythmic values of the subject are doubled) as happens beginning in m. 62 in the bass, and again in the soprano in m. 77 of this fugue, leaving the impression that Bach applies the brakes as the composition draws to an end. He also uses the time-honored contrapuntal devices of canon, beginning in m. 19, and inversion, which appears most prominently in the bass in m. 44.

Episodes

Stretto and other devices

Bach's harpsichord suites show the influence of French and Italian as well as German models. He wrote three sets of six: the *English Suites*, the *French Suites*, and the Partitas. The designations "French" and "English" for the suites are not Bach's own, and both collections blend French and Italian qualities in a highly personal style. In line with German tradition, each suite contains the standard four dance movements—allemande, courante, sarabande, and gigue—with additional short movements following the sarabande. Each of the *English Suites* opens with a prelude in which Bach transferred Italian ensemble idioms to the keyboard. The prelude of the third *English Suite*, for example, simulates a concerto allegro movement with alternating mock tutti and solo sections. The dances in the *English Suites* are based on French models and include several examples of the *double*, or ornamented repetition of a movement.

Keyboard suites

Bach at Cöthen and Leipzig: Solo and Ensemble Music

At Cöthen, Bach wrote sonatas, partitas, and suites for unaccompanied violin, cello, and flute in which he created the illusion of a harmonic and contrapuntal texture. By requiring the string player to stop several strings at once and by writing solo melody lines that leap from one register to another and back, he suggested an interplay of independent voices. The incomparable chaconne from Bach's unaccompanied Violin Partita in D Minor illustrates this technique. Bach's chief compositions for chamber ensemble are his sonatas for violin, viola da gamba, or flute and harpsichord. Most of these works have four

✖ A Closer Look   The Well-Tempered Clavier

The title of Bach's *Well-Tempered Clavier*, his collection of forty-eight preludes and fugues in all the major and minor keys, requires some explanation. By using the generic term "clavier," Bach signaled that these pieces could be played on different types of keyboard instruments, leaving the decision to the performer's preference and common sense. A brilliant, toccata-like prelude, while playable on any keyboard instrument, might sound best on the sparkling harpsichord. The clavichord—whose sweet and intimate sound made the instrument a special favorite of Bach—seems more suitable for some of the gentler and more lyrical preludes (see Figure 14.10). And because of its greater sustaining power, the organ might be ideal for certain of the fugues in the cycle. Since Bach never intended the collection to be performed as a single work, it follows that no single instrument can do justice to all the pieces in both books, even though some pieces in the collection would sound equally good whether plucked (harpsichord), struck (clavichord), or blown (organ).

The other part of Bach's title ("well-tempered") refers to the keyboard's tuning. The temperament best known today is equal temperament, in which each semitone is exactly the same size. However, this was not the tuning preferred by Bach, as is sometimes assumed. Unlike the lute, where frets marked off twelve equal semitones in the octave, keyboard octaves in the sixteenth and seventeenth centuries were not usually so equally divided. The preference during the Renaissance was to keep fifths and thirds mathematically pure according to simple ratios (for example, a fifth was 3:2). However, this resulted in tunings in which notes such as G♯ and A♭, were different in pitch, causing problems for keyboards and fretted instruments and making it impossible for them to sound in tune in every key. As musicians increasingly used chromatic tones, compromise

tuning systems, or temperaments, evolved, in which pitches were adjusted to make most or all intervals usable, even if not mathematically correct. Bach's well temperament adjusted the fifths unevenly to allow for the best possible tuning in the greatest number of possible keys.

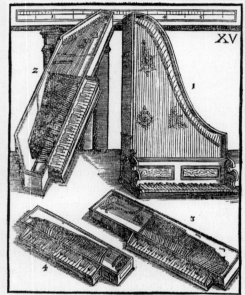

1. Clavicytherium. 2. Clavichordium , Italianischer Mensur.
2. Gemein Clavichord. 4. Octav Clavichordium.

Figure 14.10 A plate from Michael Praetorius's Syntagma musicum *(1619) showing (1) a clavicytherium, or upright harpsichord and (2, 3, and 4) several types of clavichord. The small size of the latter instrument is partly owing to the fact that it is fretted and has fewer strings than keys. Thus, different pitches are produced when keys strike a string at different points along its complete length. The instrument's popularity continued well into the eighteenth century, when Bach's son Carl Philipp Emanuel conceived some of his newly expressive keyboard music largely in terms of the sweet and delicate sound of the clavichord.*
(Lebrecht Music & Arts Photo Library.)

movements in slow-fast-slow-fast order, like the sonata da chiesa. Indeed, most of them are virtual trio sonatas because the right-hand harpsichord part is often written as a melodic line in counterpoint with the other instrument.

Orchestral suite   Impressed by the high standards of performance in Lully's orchestra and by the French musical style he cultivated, many German musicians sought to introduce these traits into their own country. One result of this effort was a fashion in Germany between about 1690 and 1740 for a new type of orchestral suite. The dances of these suites, patterned after those of Lully's ballets and operas, did not appear in any standard number or order. Because they were always introduced by a pair of movements in the form of a French overture, the word *ouverture* soon came to designate the suite itself. Among the early collections of orchestral suites was Georg Muffat's *Florilegium* (1695 and 1698), which includes an essay with musical examples about the French system of bowing, the correct performance of agréments, and similar matters. A host of other German composers, including Telemann, wrote overture suites for orchestra. Bach composed four of them, once again balancing Italian and French influences.

Bach's best-known orchestral works are the six *Brandenburg Concertos*, dedicated in 1721 to the Margrave of Brandenburg—who had requested some pieces—but composed during the previous ten or so years. For all but the first, Bach adopted the three-movement, fast-slow-fast order of the Italian concerto as well as its triadic themes, steady driving rhythms, ritornello forms, and overall style. The Third and Sixth are orchestral concertos without featured soloists; the others pit solo instruments in various combinations against the body of strings and continuo, and, hence, are concerti grossi. In typical Bach fashion, he also expanded on his model, introducing more ritornello material into the episodes, featuring dialogue between soloists and orchestra within episodes, and enlarging the form with devices such as the astonishingly long solo cadenza for the harpsichord (normally a continuo instrument) in the Fifth Concerto.

Brandenburg Concertos

Most of Bach's other orchestral music was written in the 1730s, when he directed the Leipzig collegium musicum, which was made up mostly of university students. By the early eighteenth century, such organizations often presented public concerts, like the one shown in Figure 14.11. Leipzig's collegium had done so since its founding by Telemann in 1704. Bach apparently wrote his two violin concertos and his Concerto in D Minor for Two Violins for such concerts. He was one of the first to write—or arrange—concertos for one or more harpsichords and orchestra, which he no doubt led in performance from the keyboard. The concerto for four harpsichords and orchestra is an arrangement of a Vivaldi concerto for four violins, and most or all of the others are arrangements of concertos by Bach himself or perhaps by other composers.

Collegium musicum

Figure 14.11 A collegium musicum gathering (in a coffeehouse?) with performers assembled around a harpsichord. Such gatherings were a feature of musical life in Germany from the sixteenth century on. Bach led a collegium in Leipzig in the 1730s. Anonymous eighteenth-century painting. (Germanisches Nationalmuseum, Nuremberg. Courtesy RCMI. Photo: AKG Images.)

Bach at Leipzig: The Vocal Music

Conditions in Leipzig

In 1723, when Bach was appointed cantor of Saint Thomas's School and Leipzig's director of music, he was not the first choice of the city councilmembers, who had hopes of hiring a more "modern" musician—Georg Philipp Telemann (1681–1767), then regarded as the greatest living composer after Handel. (Telemann turned the job down after using the offer to wangle a raise from his employer in Hamburg.) Saint Thomas's School was a long-established institution that took in both day and boarding pupils. It provided fifty-five scholarships for boys and youths chosen for their musical and scholastic abilities. In return, they sang or played in the services of four Leipzig churches and fulfilled other musical duties. As cantor of Saint Thomas's School, Bach was obliged to teach Latin and music four hours each day and also to compose, copy, and rehearse music for the services at Saint Thomas and Saint Nicholas. In addition, he had to promise to lead an exemplary Christian life and not to leave town without permission from the mayor. For all of his duties he was paid a comfortable middle-class salary and provided with an apartment for his family in one wing of the school, where his study was separated by only a thin partition from the homeroom of the second-year schoolboys.

The citizens of Leipzig spent a great deal of time in church—at daily services, special celebrations on festival days, and regular Sunday liturgies beginning at seven in the morning and lasting until about noon. At the Sunday services, the choir sang a motet, a Lutheran mass (Kyrie and Gloria only), hymns, and a multimovement cantata. Bach carefully wrote down the order of events on the back of one of his cantata scores (see Vignette, page 283).

Role of the church cantata

The church cantata figured prominently in the Lutheran liturgy of Leipzig. The subject matter was often linked to the content of the Gospel reading, which immediately preceded it. This suggests that Bach's role was like that of a musical preacher whose responsibility was to interpret and comment on the Gospel reading in the cantata and to bring its message forcefully home to the congregation. Singers and instrumentalists, however inadequate they may have been at times, were always at his disposal. Ideally, the choir Bach directed had a minimum of twelve singers, but we know from surviving performing parts that he sometimes had to make do with only four or eight singers total. The orchestra that accompanied them included strings with continuo, two or three oboes, and a couple of bassoons, sometimes augmented by flutes or, on festive occasions, trumpets and timpani.

Altogether, the Leipzig churches required fifty-eight cantatas each year, in addition to Passion music for Good Friday, Magnificats at Vespers for three festivals, a cantata for the annual installation of the city council, and occasional music such as funeral motets and wedding cantatas. Between 1723 and 1729,

Bach's church cantatas

Bach composed at least three and possibly four complete annual cycles of cantatas for use in church, each with about sixty cantatas. He apparently composed a fifth cycle during the 1730s and early 1740s, but many of those cantatas and some from the fourth cycle have not survived, leaving only three cycles extant in their entirety.

We have in existence, then, approximately two hundred cantatas by Bach, some newly written for Leipzig, others refashioned from earlier works. Under tremendous time pressure to produce this repertory, Bach sometimes reworked movements from his chamber and orchestral compositions and inserted them into his Leipzig cantatas. For example, a movement from one of the Brandenburg Concertos and no fewer than five movements from the solo harpsichord concertos found a niche in the cantatas. But given Bach's religious outlook, which offered even his secular art "to the glory of God," there is nothing incongruous or surprising about this accommodation. In the early cantatas, the composer responded to the changing affections and images of the text with music of intense dramatic expression and unexpectedly varied forms. By comparison, the later Leipzig cantatas are less subjective in feeling and more regular in structure but still powerfully effective.

Although no single example can suggest the breadth and variety of Bach's cantatas, *Nun komm, der Heiden Heiland*, BWV 62 (Now come, Savior of the heathens; NAWM 103), composed in 1724 for the first Sunday in Advent, illustrates many of his typical procedures. This work was part of his second cycle for Leipzig, which consisted of cantatas whose words and music were based on chorales. The unknown poet who wrote the texts of these cantatas used the first and last stanzas of a chorale for the opening and closing choruses, and paraphrased the middle stanzas in poetry suitable for recitatives and arias. Bach then based the opening chorus on the chorale melody, ended the work with a simple four-part harmonization of the chorale for its closing stanza, and set the middle movements as recitatives and arias in operatic style for the soloists, with few, if any, references to the chorale melody. For this cantata, Bach and the librettist used Luther's Advent chorale *Nun komm, der Heiden Heiland* (NAWM 46b).

As we often find in Bach's choral works, the opening chorus displays an ingenious mixture of genres—here, concerto and chorale motet. The orchestra begins with a sprightly ritornello that would be at home in a Vivaldi concerto, yet features the first phrase of the chorale as a cantus firmus in the bass. Repeated rising figures evoke the sense of welcome and anticipation in the chorale's text, which heralds the coming of the Savior. As in a concerto, this ritornello frames the movement, recurring three times in shortened or transposed form before its

Chorale cantatas

Full 🔊   Concise 🔊

Nun komm, der Heiden Heiland

VIGNETTE   Music in Lutheran Church Services

In his first year as cantor and music director in Leipzig, Bach wrote out the order of events, particularly the musical ones, for the main morning service on the first Sunday in Advent. The main musical item was the cantata, which Bach refers to here as "the principal composition." The subject for the cantata was usually linked to the Gospel reading that immediately preceded it, and the sermon would generally be on a similar theme. The choir also sang a motet and the Kyrie, the congregation sang chorales, and the organist (probably Bach himself) performed a prelude, often improvised, before each choral work.

1. Preluding
2. Motet
3. Preluding on the Kyrie, which is performed throughout in concerted manner
4. Intoning before the altar
5. Reading of the Epistle
6. Singing of the Litany

7. Preluding on [and singing of] the Chorale
8. Reading of the Gospel
9. Preluding on [and performance of] the principal music [cantata]
10. Singing of the Creed [Luther's Credo hymn]
11. The Sermon
12. After the Sermon, as usual, singing of several verses of a hymn
13. Words of Institution [of the Sacrament]
14. Preluding on [and performance of] the music [probably the second part of the cantata].

After the same, alternate preluding and singing of chorales until the end of the Communion, *et sic porrò* [and so on].

From Hans T. David and Arthur Mendel, eds., *The New Bach Reader: A Life of Johann Sebastian Bach in Letters and Documents*, rev. and expanded by Christoph Wolff (New York: Norton, 1999), p. 113, no. 113.

Figure 14.12 Johann Sebastian Bach in a portrait by Elias Gottlob Haussmann (a 1748 copy of a 1746 original). Shown in Bach's hand is the manuscript of his triple canon for six voices, BWV 1076.

(Courtesy William H. Scheide.)

Passions

Full 🔊

full reprise in the tonic at the end. But instead of episodes, Bach presents the four phrases of the chorale in the chorus, set in cantus firmus style: the sopranos, doubled by the horns, sing each phrase in long notes above imitative counterpoint in the other three parts, while the orchestra continues to develop motives from the ritornello. The first and fourth phrases are preceded by the lower voices in a point of imitation based on the chorale. Example 14.6 shows the fore-imitation and subsequent soprano entrance for the first chorale phrase. The mixture of secular and sacred models and of old-style counterpoint and cantus firmus with modern Italianate style is characteristic of Bach, creating deep meaning through references to many familiar types of music.

The four solo movements set sacred texts in operatic idioms. A da capo aria for tenor muses on the mystery of the Incarnation. As if to show Jesus's humanity, Bach wrote the aria in minuet style with predominantly four-measure phrasing, evoking the physical body through dance. Next are a recitative and aria for bass, praising the Savior as a hero who conquers evil. The recitative includes word painting, such as a run on "laufen" (to run). The aria follows the operatic conventions for heroic or martial arias, with the orchestra playing in octaves throughout and the figuration emphasizing rapid motion, large leaps, and jumping arpeggios. The soprano and alto join in an accompanied recitative, moving in sweet parallel thirds and sixths as they express awe at the Nativity scene. The closing chorale verse is a doxology, praising Father, Son, and Holy Spirit.

For performance at Vespers on Good Friday in Leipzig, Bach wrote five Passions, two of which survive; they tell the story of Jesus's crucifixion. Both the *Saint John Passion* (1724, later revised), based on John 18–19, and the *Saint Matthew Passion* (1727, revised 1736; NAWM 104), based on Matthew 26–27, employ recitatives, arias, ensembles, choruses, chorales sung by the chorus, and orchestral accompaniment. This type of Passion setting, drawing on elements from opera, cantata, and oratorio, had replaced the older type composed by Schütz and others, which combined plainsong narration with polyphony (see Chapter 11). In both Passions, a tenor narrates the biblical story in recitative, soloists play the parts of Jesus and other figures, and the chorus sings the words of the disciples, the crowd, and other groups. At other times, the chorus comments on events, like the chorus in a Greek drama, and also sings the huge opening and closing numbers. The interpolated recitatives, ariosos, and arias serve a similar purpose, reflecting on the story and relating its meaning to the individual worshipper.

Although now performed as works for large choir and orchestra, Bach's Passions were recently shown to have been intended for just four solo and four choral singers, who divided the roles among themselves and joined together for the choral movements.

Late Works

Goldberg Variations

In the 1740s, Bach produced a number of instrumental and vocal works that demonstrated all of the possible uses of a unifying musical idea. Variety marks the *Goldberg Variations* (1741), which raised the genre of keyboard variations to a new level of artfulness. All thirty variations preserve the bass and the harmonic structure of the set's theme, a sarabande. Every third variation is a

Example 14.6 J.S. Bach, Nun Komm, der Heiden Heiland, *BWV 62*

a. Fore-imitation

b. Cantus firmus in soprano

Now come, Savior of the heathens

canon, the first at the interval of a unison, the second at a second, and so on through the ninth. For the thirtieth and last variation, Bach wrote a quodlibet, a combination of two popular song melodies in counterpoint above the bass of the theme. The noncanonic variations take many forms, including fugue, French overture, slow aria, and sparkling bravura pieces for two manuals. The result is a unique work that draws on many existing types, like a summation of the music of his time.

Musical Offering and Art of Fugue

Musikalisches Opfer (A Musical Offering) is a collection of various kinds of pieces, all based on a theme proposed by Frederick the Great of Prussia (see Example 14.7). Bach had improvised on the theme while visiting the monarch at Potsdam in 1747, subsequently writing out the improvisations and later revising them. He then added a trio sonata in four movements for flute (King Frederick's instrument), violin, and continuo in which the theme also appears, had the set printed, and dedicated it to the king. A second collection, *Die Kunst der Fuge* (The Art of Fugue), composed in the final decade of Bach's life and apparently left unfinished at his death, systematically demonstrates all types of fugal writing. It consists of eighteen canons and fugues in the strictest style, all based on the same subject or one of its transformations and arranged in a general order of increasing complexity.

Example 14.7 J. S. Bach, theme from A Musical Offering, *BWV 1079*

Mass in B Minor

Bach assembled the Mass in B Minor, his only complete setting of the Catholic Mass Ordinary, between 1747 and 1749. He drew most of it from music he had composed much earlier. He had already presented the Kyrie and Gloria in 1733 to the Catholic elector of Saxony in hopes of getting an honorary appointment to the electoral chapel, which he did receive three years later. The Sanctus was first performed on Christmas Day 1724. He adapted some of the other sections from cantata movements composed between 1714 and 1735, replacing the German text with the Latin words of the Mass and reworking the music. Of the newly composed sections, the opening of the Credo and the Confiteor (a later passage of the Credo) are in *stile antico*, the Et incarnatus (also in the Credo) and Benedictus (from the Sanctus) in modern styles.

Throughout the work, Bach juxtaposed contrasting styles, making the Mass in B Minor a monumental compendium of approaches to church music. Since the mass was never performed as a whole during Bach's lifetime and is too long to function well as service music, he may have intended it as an anthology of movements, each a model of its type, that could be performed separately. As a collection of exemplary works, the Mass in B Minor stands with the *Well-Tempered Clavier, Art of Fugue*, and *Musical Offering* as witness to Bach's desire to create comprehensive cycles that take the potential of a medium or genre to its furthest limit.

Reception History

The history of Bach's music tells a story of burial and resurrection. Only a few pieces were published in his lifetime, almost all for keyboard; the rest remained only in handwritten copies. Bach's sons Carl Philipp Emanuel and Johann

Christian were influenced by him but went their own ways, and for a time their fame eclipsed his.

Musical tastes changed radically in the middle of the eighteenth century. The new style that emerged from the opera houses of Italy and invaded Germany and the rest of Europe made Bach's music sound old-fashioned. The composer-critic Johann Adolph Scheibe (1708–1776) considered Bach unsurpassable as an organist and keyboard composer, but he found the rest of Bach's music overly elaborate and confused (see Vignette, below), preferring the more tuneful and straightforward style of younger German composers such as Johann Adolf Hasse (1699–1783; see Chapter 15).

Bach's obscurity in the mid-eighteenth century was not total. In the second half of the century, some of the preludes and fugues from *The Well-Tempered Clavier* appeared in print, and the whole collection circulated in innumerable manuscript copies. Haydn owned a copy of the Mass in B Minor; Mozart knew *The Art of Fugue* and studied the motets on a visit to Leipzig in 1789. Citations from Bach's works appeared frequently in the musical literature of the time, and the important periodical, the *Allgemeine musikalische Zeitung*, opened its first issue (1798) with a Bach portrait. A fuller discovery of Bach began in the nineteenth century, with the publication of a biography by Johann Nikolaus Forkel in 1802. The revival of the *Saint Matthew Passion* by composer-conductor Carl Friedrich Zelter (1758–1832) and its 1829 performance at Berlin under Felix Mendelssohn's direction did much to inspire interest in Bach's music.

The establishment of the Bach-Gesellschaft (Bach Society), founded by Robert Schumann and others in 1850 to mark the centenary of Bach's death, led to the publication of the first collected edition of Bach's surviving works,

Changing tastes

Bach's influence

VIGNETTE A Critique of Bach's Style

The composer and critic Johann Adolph Scheibe (1708–1776) considered Bach unsurpassable as an organist and keyboard composer. However, he found much of the rest of Bach's music overly elaborate and confused, preferring the more tuneful and straightforward styles of younger composers such as Johann Adolph Hasse (see Chapter 15). Scheibe's critique is only one volley in the long argument between advocates of Baroque style and partisans of the new galant style.

This great man would be the admiration of whole nations if he had more amenity, if he did not take away the natural element in his pieces by giving them a turgid and confused style, and if he did not darken their beauty by an excess of art. Since he judges according to his own fingers, his pieces are extremely difficult to play; for he demands that singers and instrumentalists should be able to do with their throats and instruments whatever he can play on the clavier. But this is impossible. Every ornament, every little grace, and everything that one thinks of as belonging to the method of playing, he expresses completely in notes; and this not only takes away from his pieces the beauty of harmony but completely covers the melody throughout. All the voices must work with each other and be of equal difficulty, and none of them can be recognized as the principal voice. In short, he is in music what Mr. von Lohenstein was in poetry. Turgidity has led them both from the natural to the artificial, and from the lofty to the somber; and in both one admires the onerous labor and uncommon effort—which, however, are vainly employed, since they conflict with Nature.

From "An able traveling musician," letter, in Johann Adolph Scheibe, *Der critische Musikus* (May 14, 1737); trans. in Hans T. David and Arthur Mendel, eds., *The New Bach Reader: A Life of Johann Sebastian Bach in Letters and Documents*, rev. and expanded by Christoph Wolff (New York: Norton, 1998), p. 338, no. 343.

completed in sixty-one volumes by 1900. Today, there is a second complete edition (the Neue Bach-Ausgabe), and almost all of Bach's works have been recorded at least once. We realize the central position that Bach occupies in the history of Western music when we consider that, of the eight recordings of European classical music placed on *Voyager 1* and *2*, the first man-made objects to leave the solar system, no fewer than three were by Johann Sebastian Bach.

England: George Frideric Handel

Compared to Vivaldi, Rameau, and Bach, each thoroughly rooted in his own country, George Frideric Handel (1685–1759) moved comfortably among German-, Italian-, and English-speaking cities (see Biography, page 289). His German music teacher gave him a thorough education in organ, harpsichord, counterpoint, and current German and Italian idioms. As a young man, he spent three years at the Hamburg opera house and four years in Italy, where he laid the foundations of his style. He matured in England, the country then most hospitable to foreign composers. Moreover, England provided the choral tradition that made Handel's oratorios possible. Vivaldi's influence on the musical world was immediate, although he died almost totally forgotten; Rameau's was felt more slowly and then mainly in the fields of opera and music theory; and Bach's work lay in comparative obscurity until the nineteenth century. But Handel won international renown during his lifetime, and his music has been heard ever since, making him the first composer whose music has never ceased to be performed.

Popularity

Handel's music was enormously popular. When his *Music for the Royal Fireworks* was given a public rehearsal in 1749, it attracted an audience of over 12,000 people and stopped traffic in London for three hours. How could a composer gain such popularity, and why should it be Handel? The answer to the first question is that for virtually the first time, a composer was working for the public—not just for a church, a court, or a town council—and it is the public that bestows popularity. And why Handel? He was supremely adaptable, able to measure and serve the taste of the public because of his cosmopolitan and eclectic style, which drew on German, Italian, French, and English music.

Patrons

Although Handel achieved his greatest fame writing music for public performance, he was no freelancer. From his early years in Italy to the end of his life, he enjoyed the generous support of patrons. Their wishes often determined what he composed, yet their support also allowed him freedom to write operas and oratorios for the public. Handel's most important patrons were the British monarchs. In 1713, Queen Anne granted Handel a pension of £200 a year (roughly twice what Bach made in Leipzig). After she died in 1714 and the elector of Hanover (Handel's former employer) was crowned King George I, he doubled Handel's pension to £400, and after that it was raised again. But while he was closely identified with the royal house, most of his activities were in the public sphere, writing and producing operas and, later, oratorios, and composing for publication.

The Operas

Handel devoted thirty-six years to composing and directing operas, which contain much of his best music. In an age when opera was the main concern of ambitious musicians, Handel excelled among his contemporaries.

George Frideric Handel [Georg Friedrich Händel] (1685–1759)

Handel, recognized since his own time as the dominant figure in eighteenth-century English music, was a master of all types of vocal and instrumental composition. He is best known for his English oratorios, a genre he invented, and for his Italian operas.

Handel was born in Halle, Germany, the son of a barber-surgeon at the local court. His father wanted him to study law, but he practiced music secretly. His organ playing at the age of nine impressed the duke, who persuaded Handel's father to let him study with Friedrich Wilhelm Zachow, composer, organist, and church music director in Halle. Under Zachow, Handel excelled at organ and harpsichord, studied violin and oboe, mastered counterpoint, and learned the music of German and Italian composers by copying their scores. He entered the University of Halle in 1702 and was appointed cathedral organist. The following year, he abandoned both and moved to Hamburg, the center of German opera. There he played violin in the opera-house orchestra and wrote his own first opera, *Almira*, performed with great success in 1705, when he was just twenty.

The following year, Handel traveled to Italy, the homeland of opera, at the invitation of Prince Ferdinand de' Medici. Winning recognition as a promising young composer, he associated with the leading patrons and musicians of Florence, Rome, Naples, and Venice, and made the acquaintance of Corelli and Scarlatti, whose influence stamped his work. While in Italy, Handel wrote a large number of Italian cantatas, two oratorios, and the operas *Rodrigo* (1707) for Florence and *Agrippina* (1709) for Venice.

Following a brief period at the court in Hanover, Germany, Handel spent the rest of his life in London, where he served numerous aristocratic patrons and enjoyed the lifelong support of the British royal family. In the 1730s, after three decades of writing Italian operas for the London theaters, Handel turned to oratorios in English, mostly on sacred subjects. He also published a considerable amount of instrumental music, from solo and trio sonatas to concertos and orchestral suites, including *Water Music* and *Music for the Royal Fireworks*.

Handel never married. In Italy and London, he lived with various patrons until 1723, when he leased a house in an upper-class neighborhood, where he stayed the rest of his life. There were rumors of brief

Figure 14.13 George Frideric Handel at his composing desk, in a portrait by Philippe Mercier.
(The Art Archive/Corbis.)

affairs with sopranos, but none has been substantiated. Recently, scholars have noted that several of his patrons moved in social circles where same-sex desire was common and that the texts of the cantatas Handel wrote for these patrons often allude—in coded terms—to love between men. Whether Handel himself had intimate relationships with anyone of either sex remains open to question.

Handel's imperious, independent nature and cosmopolitan tastes made him a formidable presence, but the rougher sides of his personality were balanced by a sense of humor and redeemed by a generous and honorable approach to life. Experiencing both successes and failures, criticism and praise, Handel suffered physical ailments as he aged, notably a paralytic stroke in 1737 (from which he recovered) and blinding cataracts in his final years. By the end of his life, he ranked among the most revered figures in London, and some three thousand people attended his funeral at Westminster Abbey, where he is buried alongside kings and princes.

Major works: *Messiah, Saul, Samson, Israel in Egypt*, and about 20 other oratorios; *Giulio Cesare* and about 40 other Italian operas; numerous odes, anthems, and other sacred vocal music; about 100 Italian cantatas; about 45 concertos; 20 trio sonatas; 20 solo sonatas; numerous keyboard pieces; and about 6 orchestral suites.

International style

Handel's blending of national styles is evident from his first opera, *Almira* (1705), performed in Hamburg when he was twenty. He kept to the local fashion of setting the arias in Italian and the recitatives in German so the audience could follow the plot. Imitating Reinhard Keiser, the dominant opera composer in Hamburg, Handel patterned the overture and dance music on French models, composed most of the arias in the Italian manner, and incorporated German elements in the counterpoint and orchestration. In Italy, he learned from Scarlatti's cantatas and operas how to create supple, long-breathed, rhythmically varied melodies that seem naturally suited for the voice, amply demonstrated in Handel's *Agrippina* (Venice, 1709). Ever after, his operatic style was uniquely international, combining French overtures and dances, Italianate arias and recitatives, and German traits, notably the tendency to double the vocal line with one or more instruments.

London operas

Handel's *Rinaldo* (1711) was the first Italian opera composed for London. Its brilliant music and elaborate stage effects made it a sensation and helped establish Handel's public reputation in England. The arias were published by John Walsh, bringing Handel additional revenue. He wrote four more operas in the 1710s, and, with revivals of *Rinaldo*, a Handel opera was staged almost every season.

Royal Academy of Music

In 1718–1719, about sixty wealthy gentlemen, with the support of the king, established a joint stock company—called the Royal Academy of Music—for producing Italian operas. The operas were staged at the King's Theatre in the Haymarket, and Handel was engaged as the music director. He traveled to Germany to recruit singers, mostly Italians performing in Dresden and other courts. Perhaps his biggest catch was the arrogant but widely celebrated castrato Senesino. Giovanni Bononcini (1670–1747) was brought from Rome to compose operas and to play in the orchestra. Later, the eminent sopranos Francesca Cuzzoni (1696–1778) and Faustina Bordoni (1697–1781) joined the group (see Chapter 15). For this company, which flourished from 1720 to 1728, Handel composed some of his best operas, including *Radamisto* (1720), *Ottone* (1723), *Giulio Cesare* (Julius Caesar, 1724), *Rodelinda* (1725), and *Admeto* (1727).

Figure 14.14 A painting (by Antonio Longhi?) of a Baroque opera performance. The leading man (perhaps a castrato) seems to be comforting the prima donna while a third character, holding a sword, looks on. Offstage, people are seated or standing in various states of inattentiveness, which does not necessarily mean that they were not listening; portraying the audience in attitudes of conversation may have been the artist's way of suggesting that opera was often a topic of lively discussion.
(Museo Teatrale alla Scala, Milan. Photo: Scala/Art Resource, NY.)

Figure 14.15 Charles André (Carle) van Loo (1705–1765) painted The Grand Turk Giving a Concert for His Consort, *1727, as one among many pictures that borrowed exotic subjects, usually with Turkish or Spanish backgrounds. Touches of realism are provided by the legible music on the harpsichord, an aria from Handel's opera* Admeto *(1727), "Si caro, si" (Yes, dear, yes), and by the dog lying in the foreground, an age-old symbol of faithfulness. The painter's own wife was the model for the woman seated at the harpsichord.*
(Wallace Collection, Bridgeman Art Library.)

The subjects of Handel's operas were the usual ones of the time: episodes from the lives of Roman heroes freely adapted to include the maximum number of intense dramatic situations, or tales of magic and marvelous adventure revolving around the Crusades.

The action was developed through dialogue rendered in the two distinct types of recitative that emerged in Italian opera in the early eighteenth century. One type, accompanied by only basso continuo, set stretches of dialogue or monologue in as speechlike a fashion as possible. It would later be called *recitativo semplice*, or "simple recitative," and eventually *recitativo secco*, or "dry recitative." (As an example, see NAWM 92a from a cantata by Alessandro Scarlatti.) The other type, called *recitativo obbligato* and later *recitativo accompagnato*, or "accompanied recitative," used stirring and impressive orchestral outbursts to dramatize tense situations. These interjections reinforced the rapid changes of emotion in the dialogue and punctuated the singer's phrases. (See the discussion below about Handel's oratorio, *Saul*, page 295; and NAWM 106a.)

Solo da capo arias allowed the characters to respond lyrically to their situations. Each aria represented a single specific mood or affection, or sometimes two contrasting but related affections in the A and B sections. At the singers' insistence, the arias had to be allocated according to the importance of each member of the cast and had to display the scope of each singer's vocal and dramatic powers. Thus, the prima donna ("first lady"), the soprano singing the leading female role, normally demanded the greatest number of arias and the most impressive ones at that. In addition, Handel wrote for specific singers, seeking to show off their abilities.

Handel's scores are remarkable for their wide variety of aria types. They range from brilliant displays of florid ornamentation, known as coloratura, to sustained, sublimely expressive tender songs, such as *Se pietà* in *Giulio Cesare*. Arias of regal grandeur with rich contrapuntal and concertato accompaniments contrast with arias containing simple, folklike melodies or understated arias in which the strings play in unison with the voice throughout. The pastoral scenes are noteworthy examples of eighteenth-century nature painting. Some arias feature the tone color of a particular instrument to set the mood, as the French horn does in Caesar's aria *Va tacito e nascosto* ([The clever hunter] moves stealthily and hidden) from *Giulio Cesare*, in which both voice and instrument imitate a hunting horn.

Full 🔊

Arias

In Context The Voice of Farinelli

The castrato voice resulted from the same impulse that motivates today's athletes to take hormones and steroids: the desire to control and manipulate nature in order to enhance a performer's abilities. The ever-increasing demand by opera audiences for virtuosic superstars and the rise of certain castrato soloists stimulated the practice of castrating singers throughout Italy, especially among poor families who saw it as a possible way of improving their miserable circumstances. However, although thousands aspired to stardom, only a few ever achieved the fame of Farinelli, whose career took him from triumph to triumph in all the operatic capitals of Europe. He was legendary for his vocal range, spanning more than three octaves, and for his breath control, which enabled him to sustain a note for a full minute before having to inhale. Charles Burney, a keen eighteenth-century observer and author, helps us understand why Farinelli and other castrati were adored by audiences, swarmed by fans, coddled by composers, paid huge sums by producers—in short, treated very much like modern athletes:

He was seventeen when he left [Naples] to go to Rome, where, during the run of an opera, there was a struggle every night between him and a famous player on the trumpet, in a song accompanied by that instrument. . . . The audience began to interest themselves in the contest, and to take different sides: after severally swelling out a note, in which each manifested the power of his lungs, and tried to rival the other in brilliancy and force, they had both a swell and a shake [a crescendo and a trill] together, by thirds, which was continued so long, while the audience eagerly awaited the event, that both seemed to be exhausted, and, in fact, the trumpeter, wholly spent, gave it up, thinking, however, his antagonist as much tired as himself, and that it would be [considered a draw]; when Farinelli with a smile on his countenance, shewing he had only been sporting with him all this time, broke out all at once in the same breath, and with fresh vigour, and not only swelled and shook the note, but ran the most rapid and difficult divisions [passagework], and was at last silenced only by the acclamations of the audience. From this period may be dated that superiority which he ever maintained over all his contemporaries.[1]

The painting shown here depicts Farinelli (Carlo Broschi, 1705–1782) as he appeared in 1734, the year of his London debut with the Opera of the

---

Scene complexes

Handel sometimes combined one or both types of recitative with arias, ariosos, and orchestral passages to make larger scene complexes that recall the freedom of Monteverdi's operas and foreshadow the methods of later composers such as Gluck (see Chapter 15). Instead of presenting the scene as a static moment in recitative and aria with orchestral ritornellos, Handel interweaves these elements so that the plot continues to move forward, as in Cleopatra's da capo aria *V'adoro, pupille* (I adore you, pupils [eyes]) from *Giulio Cesare* (Act II, Scenes 1–2, NAWM 105). Caesar has been brought to a grove, where he will overhear Cleopatra singing. An orchestral sinfonia, essentially the opening ritornello, introduces the aria's principal motive. From his hiding place, Caesar unexpectedly breaks in, expressing awe at the beautiful strains in a brief recitative. Cleopatra sings the first and middle sections of the aria, then stops, as though waiting to see whether her charms are working. Caesar again comments in recitative, marveling at the melody's beauty. Only then does Cleopatra take up the repetition of the A section, now not just a conventional formal device but something more profound because she now knows (as do we) of Caesar's entrancement. Figure 14.16 compares in outline form the elements of this scene from Act II to the structure of a typical da capo aria of the period.

National elements

Throughout *Giulio Cesare*, one of Handel's most successful midcareer operas, his characteristic combination of national elements is apparent. Cleopatra's

Full Concise

Nobility—the company that rivaled Handel's own (see below)—led by Nicola Porpora, who had been Farinelli's teacher in Naples. The portrait gives us a good idea of the physical characteristics typical of castrati: somewhat effeminate facial features, including a smallish head and smooth pale skin with no beard; a large chest; well-rounded hips; and narrow shoulders. Contemporary writers also commented on castrati's fairly tall stature, which was unusual in the eighteenth century, and their tendency to be obese. In addition to illustrating these general characteristics, the portrait presents Farinelli, the singular virtuoso, as a commanding presence, exquisitely outfitted in brocade, fur-trimmed velvet, and lace, his right hand leaning on a harpsichord as if acknowledging what must have been the principal tool of his training. We may assume from his authoritative, even arrogant, pose that he had already reached the height of his powers. In fact, he retired from the stage only three years later, at age thirty-two, having been invited to Madrid, where he spent the next two decades in the service of the Spanish kings.

1. Charles Burney, *The Present State of Music in France and Italy*, vol. 1 of Percy A. Scholes, ed., *Dr. Burney's Musical Tours in Europe* (London: Oxford University Press, 1959), pp. 153–155.

Figure 14.17 Portrait in oils of Farinelli (Carlo Broschi), 1734, by Bartolommeo Nazari.
(Royal College of Music, London.)

aria uses a French sarabande rhythm, arousing the associations that dance carried with dignity, love, and seduction. Yet the da capo form of the aria is Italian, the voice is doubled by instruments in the German manner, and the orchestra is divided as in an Italian concerto grosso, with soloists (the concertino) accompanying the voice and the full orchestra offering punctuation.

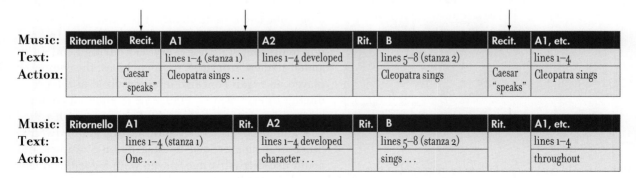

Music:	Ritornello	Recit.	A1	A2	Rit.	B	Recit.	A1, etc.
Text:			lines 1–4 (stanza 1)	lines 1–4 developed		lines 5–8 (stanza 2)		lines 1–4
Action:		Caesar "speaks"	Cleopatra sings ...			Cleopatra sings	Caesar "speaks"	Cleopatra sings

Music:	Ritornello	A1	Rit.	A2	Rit.	B	Rit.	A1, etc.
Text:		lines 1–4 (stanza 1)		lines 1–4 developed		lines 5–8 (stanza 2)		lines 1–4
Action:		One ...		character ...		sings ...		throughout

Figure 14.16 Structure of V'adoro, pupille *(above) compared to a typical da capo aria (below), with arrows indicating the main points of difference between them.*

Handel as impresario

Stressed by rising salaries for the singers and a scandalous dispute between the two sopranos Cuzzoni and Bordoni, the Royal Academy dissolved in 1729. Although the collapse has sometimes been linked to the popular success in 1728 of *The Beggar's Opera*, John Gay's English ballad opera (see Chapter 15), which satirized opera and the Academy, the main causes were financial. Handel and a partner took over the theater, formed a new company, and had several great successes with Senesino in the major roles. But Senesino found Handel dictatorial; he left in 1733 and soon joined a competing company, the Opera of the Nobility, which featured the Neapolitan composer Nicola Porpora (1686–1768) and the highest-priced singers in Europe, including Farinelli (see above). The two companies spent so much on singers and staging, and so completely divided the London public, that by 1737 both were nearly bankrupt, and the Opera of the Nobility closed that summer. Although Handel continued to write and produce operas until 1741, none matched his earlier successes.

The Oratorios

In the 1730s, Handel devised a new genre that would reward him as richly as opera had and create his greatest popularity: the English oratorio.

The Italian oratorio was essentially an opera on a sacred subject, presented in concert, usually in a religious building rather than onstage and including at most a few ensembles. But Handel's experience with choral music led him to give the chorus much more prominence in his oratorios. His early training had made him familiar with Lutheran choral music and with the south German combination of chorus with orchestra and soloists. He also drew from the strong English tradition of cathedral choirs, which had existed for centuries. The chorus in Handel's oratorios plays a variety of roles: participating in the action, narrating the story, and commenting on events like the chorus in Greek drama. Furthermore, the character of Handel's choral style, drawn from the English tradition, suits the oratorio's emphasis on communal rather than individual expression.

Prominent choruses

Handel's choruses show him to be a dramatist, a master of effects. Yet his style was simpler and less consistently contrapuntal than Bach's. He alternated passages in fugal texture with solid blocks of harmony and often set a melodic line in sustained notes against one in quicker rhythm. Everything lies comfortably for the voices, and the orchestra usually reinforces the vocal parts, making his choral music a pleasure to sing—one factor in its enduring popularity.

Handel and a collaborator leased a theater in London to present oratorios every year during Lent. As an added attraction at these performances, the composer played an organ concerto or improvised at the organ during intermissions. Figure 14.18 shows a contemporary sketch of an oratorio performance, with a chorus and orchestra each numbering about twenty. Since oratorios needed no staging or costumes and could use English singers, who were a good deal less expensive than Italian ones, it was much easier to turn a profit. Oratorios also appealed to a potentially large middle-class public that had never felt at home with the aristocratic entertainment of opera in Italian.

Figure 14.18 An oratorio performance, rendered in the satirical style of the English painter and engraver William Hogarth (1697–1764), a contemporary of Handel who was a keen observer and critic of social customs.
(Lebrecht Music & Arts Library.)

Oratorios were intended for the concert hall and were much closer to theatrical performances than to church services. But stories from the Hebrew Bible and Apocryphal books were well known to middle-class Protestant listeners, much more so than the historical or mythological plots of Italian opera. Therefore, most of Handel's oratorios were based on the Scriptures. Moreover, such subjects as *Saul* (1739), *Israel in Egypt* (1739), *Judas Maccabaeus* (1747), and *Joshua* (1748) had an appeal based on something beyond familiarity with the ancient sacred narratives: in an era of prosperity and expanding empire, English audiences felt a kinship with what they saw as the chosen people, whose heroes triumphed with the special blessing of God.

Handel's first oratorio in English was *Esther*, revised from a masque of about 1718. Like his operas but unlike oratorios in Italy, Handel's oratorios were usually performed in theaters. *Esther*, which premiered at the King's Theatre in 1732, was the first in a series of oratorios that Handel produced in almost every subsequent Lenten season as a way to extend his earnings from opera, which could not be staged during Lent. But the decisive move from opera to oratorio began when subscriptions to the 1738–1739 opera season were insufficient; so, instead of a new opera, Handel composed the oratorio *Saul* for a three-month season of choral works in early 1739.

The closing scene of Act II (NAWM 106) illustrates the blending of genres in Handel's oratorios. Saul, king of Israel, sees the young military hero David as a rival. In an accompanied recitative in martial style (NAWM 106a) Saul resolves to have David killed. Dialogue between Saul and his son Jonathan, David's beloved friend, is rendered in simple recitative (NAWM 106b). After these two numbers in styles borrowed from opera, Handel presents not an aria, but a chorus that reflects on the morality of the situation: *O fatal Consequence of Rage* (NAWM 106c). It comprises a series of three fugues, each ending with a majestic homorhythmic passage. In typical Handelian style, the chorus is filled with musical gestures that convey the meaning of the text. Here the falling tritone to express sorrow in the opening fugue subject and the use of rapid repeated notes to express rage both recall techniques first introduced by Monteverdi (see Chapter 10).

A new oratorio that premiered in Dublin, Ireland, *Messiah* (1741) was to become Handel's most famous work. Its libretto is unusual: instead of telling a story, it unfolds as a series of contemplations on the Christian idea of redemption using texts from the Bible, beginning with Old Testament prophecies and going through

First English oratorio

Saul

Full 🔊   Concise 🔊

Figure 14.19 Handel memorial in Westminster Abbey, London, sculpted in 1760 by Louis-François Roubiliac. The music shows the soprano aria I know that my Redeemer liveth *from* Messiah. (The Art Archive/Corbis.)

the life of Christ to his resurrection. However, the music of *Messiah* is typical of Handel, full of his characteristic charm, immediate appeal, and mixture of traditions—from the French overture to the Italianate recitatives and da capo arias, the Germanic choral fugues, and the English choral anthem style.

Borrowings

We have seen that Bach often borrowed and reworked his own or other composers' music. Although this practice was common at the time, Handel borrowed more than most. Three duets and eleven of the twenty-eight choruses of *Israel in Egypt*, for example, were taken in whole or in part from the music of others, while four choruses were arrangements from earlier works by Handel himself. When such instances of borrowing were discovered in the nineteenth century, Handel was charged with plagiarism because audiences and critics at that time valued originality and demanded original themes. In Handel's time, simply presenting another composer's work as one's own was condemned, but borrowing, transcribing, adapting, rearranging, and parodying were universal and accepted practices. When Handel borrowed, he more often than not repaid with interest, finding new potential in the borrowed material.

Instrumental Works

Although Handel made his reputation with vocal works, he wrote a great deal of instrumental music. Much of it was published by John Walsh in London, earning Handel extra income and keeping his name before a public that performed music at home. His keyboard works include two collections of harpsichord suites that contain not only the usual dance movements but also examples of most keyboard genres current at the time. Handel composed some twenty solo

Figure 14.20 Johann Zoffany, The Sharp Family's Boating Party on the Thames, *ca. 1781. On their barge, named the* Apollo, *the Sharps regularly gave outdoor concerts in which Handel's instrumental music was prominently featured.*
(The National Portrait Gallery, London/Bridgeman Art Library.)

TIMELINE　The Early Eighteenth Century

Musical Events

1703
Handel in Hamburg; Vivaldi appointed at the Pietà

1708
Bach in Weimar

1711
Vivaldi, Concertos, Op. 3 (*L'estro armonico*; NAWM 96)

ca. 1716
Bach, Chorale Prelude on *Durch Adams Fall* (NAWM 101)

1717
Bach in Cöthen

1722
Rameau, *Traité de l'harmonie*; Bach, *The Well-Tempered Clavier*, Book I (NAWM 102)

1723
Bach in Leipzig

1724
Handel, *Giulio Cesare* (NAWM 105)

1725
Vivaldi, *The Four Seasons*; Concert Spirituels begin in Paris

1727
Bach, *Saint Matthew Passion* (NAWM 104)

ca. 1730
Couperin, Keyboard Suites (NAWM 97)

1733
Rameau, *Hippolyte et Aricie* (NAWM 98)

1738
Handel, *Saul* (NAWM 106)

1741
Handel, *Messiah*

1747
Bach, *Musical Offering*

1750
Bach dies

1700　　　　　　　　　　　　　　　　　　　　　　　　　　　　　　**1750**

Historical Events

1702
First daily newspaper in England

1715–1774
Reign of Louis XV in France

1717–1718
Watteau, *The Music Party* (Figure IV.1)

1727
Quakers demand an end to slavery in British colonies

1727–1760
Reign of George II of England

1734
Voltaire, *Philosophical Letters*

1740
Frederick the Great of Prussia crowned

sonatas and almost as many trio sonatas for various instruments. Corelli's influence can be heard in these works, but the sophisticated harmonies and vivacious fast movements reflect a later Italian style.

Handel's most popular instrumental works are his two suites for orchestra or winds, both composed for the king and intended for outdoor performance. *Water Music* (1717) contains three suites for winds and strings, played for the king from a boat during a royal procession on the river Thames (see Figure 14.20). *Music for the Royal Fireworks* (1749), for winds (although Handel later included strings), was composed to accompany fireworks set off in a London park to celebrate the Peace of Aix-la-Chapelle.

Ensemble suites

Handel's concertos mix tradition and innovation but tend toward a retrospective style. His six Concerti Grossi, Op. 3 (published 1734), feature woodwind and string soloists in novel combinations. He invented the concerto for organ and orchestra, which he performed during the intermissions of his oratorios and published in three sets (1738, 1740, and 1761). His most significant concertos are the Twelve Grand Concertos, Op. 6, composed during one month in 1739 and published the next year. Instead of following Vivaldi's model, Handel adopted Corelli's conception of a sonata da chiesa for full orchestra (see Chapter 12), although he often added a movement or two to the conventional slow-fast-slow-fast pattern. The serious, dignified bearing and the prevailing

Concertos

Handel's reputation

full contrapuntal texture of these concertos hark back to the early part of the century, when Handel was forming his style in Italy.

The English came to regard Handel as a national institution—and with good reason. He spent all his mature life in London, becoming a naturalized British citizen in 1727, and wrote all his major works for British audiences. He was the most imposing figure in English music during his lifetime, and the English public nourished his genius and remained loyal to his memory (see Figure 14.19).

POSTLUDE

In this chapter, we have studied the lives and works of the eighteenth-century composers who represent, in many respects, both the radiant peak and the afterglow of the musical Baroque in Italy, France, Germany, and England. Each made lasting contributions.

Although Vivaldi was a complete master of opera, he is best remembered for his influence on instrumental music of the middle and later eighteenth century. His impact equaled that of Corelli a generation earlier, and his codification of ritornello form provided a model for later concerto composers. His successors admired and emulated his concise themes, clarity of form, rhythmic vitality, and logical flow of musical ideas. Among those who learned from Vivaldi was J. S. Bach, who made keyboard arrangements of at least nine of Vivaldi's concertos, including five from Op. 3. Later in the eighteenth century, concerto composers adopted and developed Vivaldi's dramatic conception of the soloist's role.

Couperin's harpsichord music was well known in his lifetime, in England and Germany as well as France, then slowly fell out of fashion. Rameau's work, dominated by his operas (which are especially noteworthy for their novel instrumental music), is characterized by the French traits of clarity, grace, moderation, elegance, and interest in pictorialism. In these respects, he may be compared to his contemporary, the painter Watteau (see Figure IV.1). Equally typical of his countrymen, Rameau thought of himself as a philosophe as well as a composer, an analyst as well as a creator. In short, he was one of the most complex and productive musical personalities of the eighteenth century.

Bach was an encyclopedic composer: he absorbed into his works all the genres, styles, and forms of his time and developed their potential to a degree never even imagined by others. In his music, the often conflicting demands of harmony and counterpoint, of melody and polyphony reached a tense but satisfying balance. The continuing vitality of his compositions cannot be explained in a few words, but among the qualities that stand out are his concentrated and distinctive themes, his ingenious counterpoint, his copious musical invention, the majestic formal proportions of his works, his imaginative musical representation of pictorial and symbolic ideas, and the careful attention he paid to every detail. A composer who spent most of his life teaching, Bach wrote challenging and rewarding pieces for students at every level, from beginning to advanced. He worked in positions that constantly demanded new music for immediate performance, embraced a wide variety of genres and approaches, and aspired to explore all the possibilities of every kind of music he encountered. It is no wonder that Bach achieved the central position he now occupies in the Western musical tradition.

Handel's greatness and historical significance rest largely on the fact that his compositions, especially the choral works, still command an eager audience. His music aged well because he embraced devices that became important in the new style of the mid-eighteenth century. Handel's emphasis on melody and harmony, as compared to the more strictly contrapuntal procedures of Bach, allied him with the fashions of his time. As a choral composer in the grand style he had no peer. He was a consummate master of contrast, not only in choral music but also in all types of composition. And in the oratorios, he deliberately appealed to a middle-class audience, recognizing social changes that had far-reaching effects on music.

Ⓢ Resources for study and review available at
wwnorton.com/studyspace

PART FOUR

The Eighteenth Century

PART CONTENTS

C ontinuities between the seventeenth and eighteenth centuries are stronger than any differences. Certainly there was not the kind of sudden stylistic revolution in the arts, fueled by aesthetic debates and controversy, that had occurred at the beginning of the Baroque age. Rather, the history of this century's music can be seen as a long, leisurely, albeit lively, argument about older and newer tastes and styles that was carried on in newspapers, journals, salons (gatherings held in private homes and usually hosted by aristocratic women), and coffeehouses. The "older" eighteenth century manifested itself in the late-Baroque styles of Bach, Handel, and their contemporaries, all of whom were discussed in Chapter 14. The "newer" eighteenth century, often called the Age of Reason or the Enlightenment, is also known in music history as the Classic era and is covered in Chapters 15 through 18.

The word *Classical* is applied to the mature styles of later eighteenth-century composers such as Haydn, Mozart, and Beethoven. Their music is classic—an adjective that also refers to the ancient Greeks and Romans—because it shares many attributes with the art and architecture of antiquity. At its best, Classical

Jean Antoine Watteau, The Foursome, *1712.*

(Album/Art Resource, NY.)

Figure IV.1 Jean Antoine Watteau, The Music Party *(ca. 1717–1718), one of his many fêtes galantes, a genre noted for flirtatious interaction. The central figure is a theorbist tuning his instrument, perhaps a metaphor for initiating gallant conversation. Watteau's style is distinguished by its restrained use of gesture and emotion, a quality associated with Classicism.*
(Wallace Collection, London. Bridgeman Art Library.)

music reached a consistently high standard and possessed the qualities of noble simplicity, balance, perfection of form, diversity within unity, seriousness of purpose, and restrained use of ornamentation. However, many different personal and regional styles thrived for generations before the three composers just named reached their peak, and all shared some of these qualities to a greater or lesser extent. Thus it is convenient and appropriate to call the years from approximately 1730 to 1815 the Classic era even though its boundaries overlap the preceding Baroque and subsequent Romantic periods.

Galant style

Other terms have also been coined to characterize the early phases of Classical style in the eighteenth century, among them *galant* and *empfindsam*. The French word *galant* was widely used during the eighteenth century to describe literature that was elegant and courtly, as well as paintings in which the subject matter was often bucolic and flirtatious, as shown in Figure IV.1. It was a catchword for everything that was considered modern, smart, chic, smooth, easy, and sophisticated. Contemporary music theorists distinguished between the learned or strict style of contrapuntal writing and the freer, more chordal, galant style, the latter marked by an emphasis on "naturalness"—simple melody with light accompaniment—which became stylish in the 1730s.

Empfindsam style

The German word *Empfindsamkeit* (noun) or *empfindsam* (adjective) derives from the verb *empfinden*, "to feel." *Empfindsamkeit*, which means "sentimentality" or "sensibility," is a quality associated with the intimate, sensitive, and subjective tendencies of some eighteenth-century literature and art. We will see how it is relevant to certain musical works during the Classic era—for example, some keyboard sonatas by C. P. E. Bach—in Chapter 16.

Europe in the Eighteenth Century

Realignment and revolution

In political and social terms, the eighteenth century moved from continuity with the past, through new currents, to radical change. When the century began, a balance of power was emerging in Europe among several strong, centralized states, each supported by a professional military and government bureaucracy. France had the biggest army, but the lavish domestic and foreign expenditures of

Louis XIV (r. 1643–1715) and, later, Louis XV (r. 1715–1774) depleted the treasury even before their expansionist ambitions were checked by other nations. England had the most powerful navy and used it to wrest India, Canada, and several Caribbean islands from France during the Seven Years' War (1756–1763). Austria took Hungary back from the Turks, and now, as the Austro-Hungarian Empire, its increasing influence was reflected by the emergence of its capital, Vienna, as the leading musical city in Europe. A new power arose when Prussia became a kingdom in 1701 and developed one of the Continent's largest and best-trained armies. Late in the century, Poland fell victim to the centralized states around it; Prussia, Russia, and Austria divided Poland's territories among themselves and erased it from the map for over a century. By then, the American Revolution (1775–1783) and the French Revolution (1789) were generating the winds of change that would remake the political culture of Europe and the Americas.

Economic expansion

The population of Europe expanded rapidly, especially after 1750. New methods of agriculture and new crops like the potato, introduced from the New World, met the growing demand for food. Roads improved, making travel faster and more comfortable; a hundred-mile trip that took four days in 1700 required only sixteen hours in 1800. The poor increasingly suffered dislocation from land and overcrowding in cities, becoming victims of the very progress that helped the well-born and the lucky. As manufacturing and trade increased, the middle class grew in size and economic clout, while the landed aristocracy became less important even though they still occupied the top rung of the social ladder. As the Continent became more urbanized, nature was increasingly idealized. Jean Antoine Watteau inaugurated a new genre of painting, the *fête galante*, which perfectly captured the nostalgia for an idyllic rural life (Figure IV.1), while the squalor of lower-class city life and the mores of high society were satirized in the paintings and engravings of William Hogarth.

Education and learning

Many new schools were founded, both for the elite—teaching the traditional Greek and Latin—and for the middle classes—providing more practical education. Frederick the Great of Prussia (r. 1740–1786; see Figure 16.5) and Empress Maria Theresa of Austria (r. 1740–1780; see Figure IV.2) sought to require

Figure IV.2 Friedrich Heinrich Füger (1751–1818), Maria Theresa of Austria Surrounded by Her Children. *At the right is Joseph II, who ruled jointly with Maria Theresa from 1765 until her death, whereupon he became the sole ruler until he died in 1790.*
(Österreichische Galerie Belvedere, Vienna. Erich Lessing/Art Resource, NY.)

TIMELINE The Eighteenth Century

Musical Events

1723
J. S. Bach becomes cantor in Leipzig

1725
Concert spirituel series begins in Paris

1732
Joseph Haydn born

1741
George Frideric Handel, *Messiah*

Eighteenth-century organ

1750
J. S. Bach dies

1759
Handel dies

1770
Ludwig van Beethoven born

1776–1789
Charles Burney, *A General History of Music*

Gainsborough, *The Blue Boy*

1700

Historical Events

1702
First daily newspaper in England

1717–1718
Jean Antoine Watteau, *The Music Party* (Figure IV.1)

1740
Frederick the Great crowned king of Prussia; Maria Theresa crowned Holy Roman empress

1748
Excavations of Pompeii begin

1751–1772
Publication of Denis Diderot's *Encyclopédie* in 28 volumes

1759
Voltaire, *Candide*

1762
Jean-Jacques Rousseau, *The Social Contract*

1765
Greuze, *Girl with a Dead Canary* (Figure IV. 8)

1770
Thomas Gainsborough, *The Blue Boy*

1775
Beaumarchais, *Barber of Seville*

1776
American Declaration of Independence

1781
Immanuel Kant, *Critique of Pure Reason*

---

primary school for every child. By 1800, half the male population of England and France was literate, and women, usually home-taught, were catching up. Daily newspapers began publishing in London in 1702 and quickly spread to other cities. More and more books were published, purchased, read, and circulated. At public coffeehouses, meetings of learned societies, and salons, people avidly discussed current events, ideas, literature, and music. Amid this broadening interest in learning, thinkers such as Voltaire and Jean-Jacques Rousseau sought to shed the institutions and ideas that had immersed the Continent in brutal religious and political conflicts and to renew hope in the perfectibility of the human condition through reason and science. Their new vision spawned the Enlightenment, the most vibrant intellectual movement of the century.

The Enlightenment

The Enlightenment embraced rationalism—the view that reason, combined with experience and knowledge, could solve problems, including scientific ones. In Germany, Immanuel Kant aimed to unite reason with experience, believing that using pure reason alone (as in traditional philosophy) leads merely to theoretical illusions. In France, the methodology of reason in accumulating and codifying knowledge led to the monumental *Encyclopédie* (1751–

Jane Austen

1791
Haydn makes first trip to
London; Mozart dies

1803
Beethoven, *Eroica* Symphony (NAWM 126)

1809
Haydn dies

1824–1826
Beethoven, Late string
quartets (NAWM 127)

1825

1784
Beaumarchais, *The Marriage of Figaro*

1789
The French Revolution begins

1792–1794
Reign of Terror in France

1793
Eli Whitney invents cotton gin; Louis
XVI and Marie Antoinette beheaded

1804
Napoleon crowns himself emperor

1805–1809
Napoleon's forces occupy Vienna

1806
Holy Roman Empire dissolved

1813
Jane Austen, *Pride and Prejudice*
published

1814–1815
Congress of Vienna

1815
Wellington defeats Napoleon at
Waterloo

1772), edited by Denis Diderot and Jean le Rond d'Alembert. In religion, the
Enlightenment valued individual faith and practical morality over the supernatural and the Church. In social behavior, naturalness was preferred to formality and to conventions that were seen as artificial.

The French leaders of the Enlightenment, known as philosophes, were social **The philosophes**
reformers more than philosophers. In response to the inequalities between the
condition of the common people and that of the privileged classes, they developed doctrines about individual human rights, some of which were incorporated
into the American Declaration of Independence and adopted by the framers of
the Constitution of the United States. Their sharp social criticism also helped set
the stage for the French Revolution and the downfall of the old political order.

Enlightened rulers such as Frederick the Great of Prussia, Catherine the **Humanitarianism**
Great of Russia, and Holy Roman Emperor Joseph II (Maria Theresa's son,
shown in Figure IV.2) not only patronized the arts and letters, but also promoted social change and improved the lives of their subjects. Some even subscribed to the teachings of the secret fraternal order of Masons, whose tenets
were based on humanitarianism and the idea of universal brotherhood.

Founded in London in the early eighteenth century, Freemasonry spread rapidly and numbered among its adherents statesmen (George Washington), poets (Johann Wolfgang von Goethe), and composers (Haydn and Mozart) as well as kings (Friderick the Great). Among other works, Mozart's opera *Die Zauberflöte* (The Magic Flute) and Schiller's *Ode to Joy* (set by Beethoven in the finale of his Ninth Symphony) reflect the eighteenth-century humanitarian movement.

The arts

The promise of a new political and economic order, in which the industrial revolution and middle-class entrepreneurship would eventually overtake the entrenched wealth of the landed aristocracy, was naturally echoed in the arts. The emergence of novels such as Henry Fielding's *Tom Jones* (1749) and Samuel Richardson's *Pamela* (1740–1741)—a genre that celebrates the lives of ordinary people—went hand in hand with the new concern for the individual. Similarly, some think that the symphony, which became an important focus for Classic-era composers and the chief vehicle for Haydn's enormous popularity, insofar as it depended upon the precise collaboration of orchestral forces, was an expression of communal sentiment and a reflection of new, democratic ideals.

Figaro

The fictional character who best symbolizes the challenge to the old order is Figaro, the rascally servant and protagonist of two French comedies by Beaumarchais: *The Barber of Seville* (1775) and *The Marriage of Figaro* (1784). It is no accident that both plays were almost immediately turned into operas, the latter in a brilliant setting by Mozart. Beaumarchais was briefly imprisoned for his audacious criticism of the ruling classes. An unsophisticated barber and jack-of-all-trades, Figaro is a clever and resourceful schemer who not only outwits his aristocratic master in romance, but makes him look ridiculous in the bargain. In short, he was the spokesperson and hero of the new age (see Figure IV.3).

While the French Revolution was inspired in part by the ideas of the Enlightenment, it also had other causes. The first phase of the Revolution (1789–1792) was reformist. Stimulated by King Louis XVI's ruinous fiscal policies and supported by popular uprisings like the assault on the Bastille, shown in Figure IV.4, a National Assembly of well-to-do citizens forced the king to accept a new constitution for France and set up elected local governments. But after Austria and Prussia attacked France in 1792, seeking to restore the old regime, a more radical group came to power, declared France a republic, and executed the king and his queen (Marie Antoinette). In this second phase (1792–1794), as French armies fought off attacks, the government maintained control by putting tens of thousands of political opponents to death during the Reign of Terror. In the third phase, the government adopted a more moderate constitution and sought to restore order, but opposition and economic hardship continued.

In 1799, Napoleon Bonaparte, an army general and war hero, became first consul of the republic. Ignoring the elected legislature, Bonaparte consolidated power and in 1804 crowned himself emperor in Notre Dame Cathedral. Through a series of military victories, he overran nearby countries, expanded French territories, ended the 840-year-old Holy Roman Empire, and created client states in Spain, Switzerland, and most of Germany and Italy, installing his own siblings as rulers. He introduced reform that made government more efficient, the legal system more uniform, and taxation less burdensome, carrying out some of the goals of the Revolution. But a disastrous military campaign against Russia led to Napoleon's defeat and abdication in 1814. As a congress of the major European powers met in Vienna to finalize a peace treaty, Napoleon escaped from exile and briefly resumed power, only to suffer final defeat in 1815 at Waterloo

Figure IV.3 An early nineteenth-century sketch by Massimo Gauci of the character of Figaro, as portrayed in a performance of Beaumarchais's Marriage of Figaro *at the King's Theatre in London in 1823.*
(City of Westminster Archive Centre, London. Bridgeman Art Library.)

Figure IV.4 Contemporary oil painting of the fall of the Bastille, July 14, 1789. The citizens of Paris stormed the old fortress, a symbol of royal authority, to obtain the guns and ammunition stored there and to protect the new municipal government from attack by the king's forces. The action cost almost one hundred lives but demonstrated the popular will for revolutionary change. The anniversary is now celebrated as Bastille Day, a French national holiday.
(Châteaux de Versailles et de Trianon, Versailles. Hervé Lewandowski/Réunion des Musées Nationaux/Art Resource, NY.)

in Belgium. Although the Revolution and Napoleon's wars of conquest ultimately failed, they changed European society utterly, giving rise to new cultural and political agendas in the nineteenth and early twentieth centuries.

From Baroque to Classic

If the aim of the Baroque arts was to move the emotions, the aim of Classicism was to construct an ideal vision of life and nature in tune with Enlightenment goals of realism, restraint, harmony, and order. Renewed study of the classical past was spurred by the writings of such figures as Johann Joachim Winckelmann and stimulated by the architectural discoveries of the ancient Roman ruins at Herculaneum (1738) and Pompeii (1748; see Figure IV.5). The culture of that earlier age was perceived as a worthy and achievable ideal, and attempts to recapture its style and subject matter were directed at the moral improvement of the viewer, giving art a socially beneficial role. Winckelmann's assertion in 1755 that "there is only one way for moderns to become great and, perhaps, unequalled: by imitating the Ancients" set the artistic agenda for the second half of the century.

In keeping with these goals, the painter Jacques-Louis David perfected a new type of history painting that featured morally uplifting themes from antiquity. Actively involved in Revolutionary politics, David portrayed Napoleon as a larger-than-life hero in the tradition of the Roman Caesars (see Figure IV.6). Contemporary sculpture followed Winckelmann's precepts of noble simplicity and calm grandeur. The semicircular plans and tiered seating of Greek and Roman amphitheaters were adapted for political assemblies and lecture halls (see Figure IV.7), promoting the educational aspirations of the era. In England, the influential portraitist Sir Joshua Reynolds became the first president of the newly founded Royal Academy of Art in London (1768); his series of classicizing discourses on art, delivered annually to the Academy, also raised the status of

Aim of Classicism

Realizations in the arts

Figure IV.5 A Roman courtyard in the excavated city of Pompeii on the Bay of Naples in southern Italy. It was buried along with Herculaneum by an eruption of nearby Mount Vesuvius in the year 79 C.E. and was rediscovered in the mid-eighteenth century.
(Scala/Art Resource, NY.)

the arts and artists in Britain to a new peak. On the Continent, Beethoven's so-called heroic, post-Revolutionary style actualized these classical ideals in music, thereby changing society's concept of music and of composers, and earning him universal acclaim (Chapter 18).

Strong as it was, the influence of rationalism in the eighteenth century was tempered by a deep vein of sentimentality that surfaced both in literature and in the arts. The word *sensibilité* ("sensibility") entered the vocabulary of criticism for the first time, along with the belief that sentiment or feeling is more important than reason in the apprehension of truth. For example, notwithstanding his involvement in the *Encyclopédie*, Rousseau celebrated nature and the emotions over culture and progress in his writings. His objections to the rules of classical art on the grounds that they constrained creative liberty, and his championing of the importance of educating the senses, allied him with the nineteenth-century Romantic movement. Rousseau's ideas about music were similarly antiestablishment—he promoted the notion that music and all artistic activity should be part of everyday life rather than the exclusive province of professionals.

These ideas found an echo in the new respect accorded the medium of genre painting, represented principally by Jean-Baptiste Greuze. The philosophe Diderot heaped praise upon Greuze's genre scenes, many of which concentrated on themes of ordinary family life, undoubtedly because the critic saw in them the visual equivalent of his own sentimental dramas. Greuze also frequently depicted moral or pathetic subjects, as illustrated by the idealized *Girl with a Dead Canary* (Figure IV.8). The world he created on canvas may find its musical equivalent in the *empfindsam* style of composers like C. P. E. Bach, to be discussed in Chapter 16; but its literary parallel is surely found in the novels of Jane Austen, whose complex and subtle view of human nature elevated a narrow world of unremarkable domestic relationships into a revealing microcosm of middle-class society. In fact, it is worth noting that the protagonists of *Sense and Sensibility*—two marriageable sisters

Figure IV.6 David's portrait of Napoleon I in imperial dress, 1805.
(Musée des Beaux-Arts, Caen, France.)

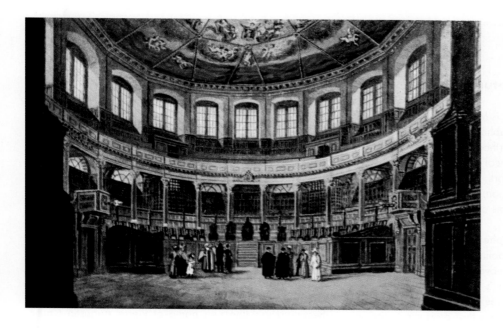

Figure IV.7 The Sheldonian Theatre, Oxford University. Designed by Christopher Wren in the 1660s, the building has the neoclassical shape of an amphitheater and is still used for concerts and ceremonial occasions. Haydn's Symphony No. 92 was performed there in 1791 as part of a three-day festival commemorating his receiving an honorary Doctor of Music degree.
(Lebrecht Music & Arts Photo Library.)

of opposite personalities, representing "sense" and "sensibility"—embody the two characteristic intellectual currents of the age: reason and sentiment.

The Place of Music in the Classic Era

As the pursuit of learning and the love of art became more widespread, particularly among the expanding middle class, a growing interest in hearing and making music spurred composers and publishers to address a general public beyond a select group of experts and connoisseurs. Amateur musicians bought music that they could understand and play, and most of the published music for keyboard, chamber ensemble, or voice and keyboard was designed for amateurs to perform at home for their own pleasure. The growing enthusiasm for music also encouraged connoisseurs, informed listeners who cultivated a taste for the best in music. Thus, C. P. E. Bach's keyboard works published in 1779 were entitled *Sonatas for Connoisseurs and Amateurs* (Chapter 16); and Mozart aimed at pleasing his Viennese audiences with a musical style that combined sophisticated art with appealing entertainment (Chapter 17).

Popular treatises were written with an eye to bringing culture within the reach of all, while what might be called "the Figaro factor"—depicting everyday people with everyday emotions—had far-reaching effects in the world of opera: comic opera or opera buffa encroached on and satirized the more staid opera seria, eventually setting a course for opera reform, both musically and dramatically (Chapter 15). As the musical public broadened, more people became interested in reading about music and discussing it. By midcentury, magazines devoted to musical news, reviews, and criticism began to appear, catering to both amateurs and connoisseurs. The public's curiosity about music extended to its origins and past styles,

Figure IV.8 Jean-Baptiste Greuze, Girl with a Dead Canary, *1765. Although Diderot analyzed the painting as symbolizing the loss of virginity, the superficial subject and its treatment are typical of the painter's sentimental style.*
(National Gallery of Scotland, Edinburgh/Bridgeman Art Library.)

ARTS & IDEAS

Philosophy and Literature

Voltaire (pen name of François-Marie Arouet, 1694–1778) was a French satirist, philosopher, historian, prolific writer, and irreverent wit whose unorthodox ideas were a constant source of irritation to the political and religious authorities of his time. His most famous work, *Candide* (1759), is a brilliant satire on the Age of Reason; it gives literary expression to his outrage against all forms of religion and privilege.

Swiss-born French philosopher Jean-Jacques Rousseau (1712–1778) was also a political theorist, writer, and composer. His essays and novels celebrate the "natural man" — one whose behavior is guided by human nature rather than by society's mores — oppose inequality and oppression, and reject the idea that progress in the sciences and arts increases one's happiness. His most influential work, *The Social Contract* (1762), is a treatise on government and the rights of citizens.

The philosophe Denis Diderot (1713–1772) compiled, coedited, and contributed to the monumental (28 volume) *Encyclopédie, ou Dictionnaire raisonné . . .* (1751–1772). His writings include novels, satire, art criticism, and philosophy in which he presents insights into the physical, moral, and social universe, including studies on how the senses work.

Johann Joachim Winckelmann (1717–1768) was a German art historian whose writings on the sculpture of ancient Greece and Rome provided a theoretical basis

for eighteenth-century Classicism. His *History of Ancient Art* (1764) considers how the political freedom of the ancient Greek city-states contributed to the flowering of its art, and his descriptions of ancient relief sculptures were widely quoted in travel books and art treatises. His work had a major impact on the discipline of art history.

In his *Critique of Pure Reason* (1781), the German philosopher and university professor Immanuel Kant (1724–1804) maintained that human knowledge about the real world must be subject to the experience of the senses. He also made room for the essentially irrational idea of genius within his investigations of pure and practical reason.

Beaumarchais (the pen name of Pierre Augustin Caron, 1732–1799) was a French dramatist, courtier, and watchmaker to Louis XV. He is best known for creating one of literature's cleverest servants, Figaro, and presenting Figaro's exploits in two comic masterpieces, *The Barber of Seville* (1775) and *The Marriage of Figaro* (1784). Both plays were transformed into operas, the latter composed by Mozart on a libretto by Lorenzo Da Ponte (see Figure 17.17) and the former by Gioachino Rossini, among others (see Chapter 21; and also Figure IV.3).

English novelist Jane Austen (1775–1817) was the seventh child of a country parson and spent her life almost entirely within her family circle, having no contact with London literary life. Out of the materials of such a narrow world

---

addressed in the first universal histories of music, among which was Charles Burney's *A General History of Music* (1776–1789; see Figure IV.9).

Public concerts

As wealth was redistributed in the new economy, private patronage declined and a modern audience for music emerged among the more affluent citizens of Europe. Public concerts competed with the older-style private concerts and academies. In Paris, the Concert spirituel series was founded in 1725, and other concert series began in cities all over Europe (see Innovations, pages 358–359). This increased concert activity created a favorable climate for instrumental music, which rivaled opera in popularity by the end of the century. Chamber or solo sonatas, symphonies, and concertos for pianoforte and other instruments became the new vehicles to fame for composers of the Classic period. The ceaseless demand for new music accounts for the vast output of many eighteenth-century composers and the phenomenal speed at which they worked.

Musical tastes and styles

Many musical styles coexisted in the eighteenth century, each supported by strong adherents and criticized by detractors. Every country had distinctive traditions and developed a national form of opera. Works in new styles, such as the operas of Pergolesi and Hasse (Chapter 15), were written at the same time as Rameau's operas, Handel's oratorios, and J. S. Bach's fugues, all representative

she completed six novels, among them *Emma, Mansfield Park, Pride and Prejudice,* and *Sense and Sensibility* (see portrait, page 305).

Art

The French painter Jean Antoine Watteau (1684–1721) created a distinctive pictorial world in which elegantly attired people are depicted in conversation or making music in a secluded, often bucolic setting. Known as *fêtes galantes,* these works are associated with the light, galant musical style, but their subjects are subtle and ambiguous, suggesting both psychological interaction and theatrical fantasy (see Figure IV.1).

William Hogarth (1697–1764), the influential founder of an English school of painting, is best remembered for his satirical engravings of low-life scenes of the period. By publishing engravings after his own paintings, he demonstrated that artists could become independent of wealthy patrons (see Figure 15.2).

The foremost portrait painter in eighteenth-century England, Sir Joshua Reynolds (1723–1792) executed more than 2,000 portraits of people whose poses were intended to invoke classic values and enhance their subjects' dignity. His influential *Discourses on Art,* propounding a rationalist view of the ideal of beauty, were delivered to the students and members of the Royal Academy between 1769 and 1790, and earned him a wide reputation as a man of letters (see Figure IV. 9).

Standing apart from the Classic style of his contemporaries is the work of French painter Jean-Baptiste Greuze (1725–1805), who became famous for his genre scenes of family life and his expressive heads (see Figure IV.8). A keen observer of detail in the tradition of seventeenth-century Dutch masters, he combined faithful realism with sentimental drama, often suggesting an underlying moral.

The English painter Thomas Gainsborough (1727–1788) was the contemporary and rival of Sir Joshua Reynolds. Known for his virtuosic landscapes and portraits, especially *The Blue Boy* (see page 304), he was also an accomplished musician and sophisticated intellectual. Rather than following an academic ideal of art, he grounded his style in the imagery of contemporary life (see Figure 16.7).

Jacques-Louis David (1748–1825), the foremost painter of the Napoleonic era, directed the Classic revival in French art. Like Beethoven, he adopted the ideals of Republicanism and placed his hopes in Napoleon. His grandly heroic paintings became a political manifesto about returning to the patriotic and moral values associated with republican Rome (see Figures IV.6 and V.4).

of the late Baroque. But despite the array of styles, leading writers in the middle and late eighteenth century articulated the prevailing view of what was most valued in music. Some affirmed the superiority of vocal music over instrumental music because it could appeal to both the intellect and the emotions, whereas instrumental music, without words, could only appeal to the emotions. Instead of the contrapuntal complexity and spun-out instrumental melody of Baroque music, audiences and critics preferred music that featured a vocally conceived melody in short phrases over spare accompaniment. Writers held that the language of music should be universal rather than limited by national boundaries and should appeal to all tastes at once, from the sophisticated to the untutored. The best music should be noble as well as entertaining, expressive within the limits of decorum, and "natural"—free of technical complications and capable of immediately pleasing any sensitive listener. The composers we will encounter in Chapters 15, 16, 17, and 18 shared most of these values. The best among them created works unprecedented in their individuality, dramatic power, wide appeal, and depth of interest.

Figure IV.9 Portrait by Sir Joshua Reynolds of Charles Burney, the first historian of music.

The Early Classic Period: Opera and Vocal Music

PRELUDE

Musical life in the early Classic period reflected the international culture that spread throughout Europe during the Enlightenment. German symphonic composers were active in Paris; Italian opera composers and singers worked in what are now Austria and Germany, as well as in Spain, England, Russia, and France. In a climate where shared humanity mattered more than national and linguistic differences, many believed that the ideal musical style was made up of the best features of music from all nations.

This universality of the new Classical style in music depended in part on its similarity to the logic of intelligible speech, which proceeds in any language through a series of words arranged to follow one another, with some repetitions, stops, and starts, forming units that make the ideas readily understood. Music was thought to be more or less "natural" to the extent that it emulated the flow of speech. According to leading critics of the time, educated people wanted music to communicate expression without artifice—that is, in a manner free of any complication that would hinder music's enjoyment and appeal. Writers distinguished between the learned or strict style of contrapuntal writing—associated particularly with the German Baroque—and the freer, more tuneful, homophonic writing that was becoming fashionable, particularly in Italy. Known at the time as the galant style, its values became the foundation for the musical idiom of the mid- to late eighteenth century that we call the Classical style.

This chapter will focus on developments in the early Classic period, roughly to 1770. We find the new characteristics enumerated below most evident in the music of Gluck, presented here, and Haydn and Mozart, who will be discussed later.

General Characteristics of the New Style

The focus on melody in the new styles led to a musical syntax quite different from the continuous motivic variation of earlier styles. J. S. Bach, for example, typically announced at the outset of a movement the musical idea, a melodic-rhythmic subject embodying the basic affection. This idea was then spun out, using sequential repetition, within a generally irregular phrase structure marked by relatively infrequent cadences.

In contrast, the newer styles were characterized by periodicity, in which frequent resting points break the melodic flow into segments that relate to each other as parts of a large whole. Musical ideas, rather than being persistently repeated, were articulated through distinct phrases, typically two or four measures in length (but also frequently three, five, or six measures). Two or more phrases were needed to form a period, a complete musical thought concluded by a cadence, and a composition was made up of two or more periods in succession. This technique creates a structure marked by frequent cadences and unified through small motivic correspondences.

Periodicity

The terminology of phrases and periods was borrowed from rhetoric, the art of oration. Eighteenth-century theorists frequently compared a melody to a sentence or a musical composition to a speech. The most thorough guide to melodic composition based on rhetorical principles was written by Heinrich Christoph Koch (1749–1816) in one of several treatises for amateurs who wished to learn how to compose. Here the student learns how to construct a melody by joining short melodic segments to form phrases, and phrases to form periods. Koch likens the components of a musical phrase to the subject and predicate in a sentence. He states that this kind of organization is necessary to make a melody intelligible and capable of moving our feelings, just as the sentences and clauses that break up a speech make it easier to follow the train of thought.

Musical rhetoric

The division of the melody into phrases and periods is supported by the harmony, and shaped by a series of weaker and stronger cadences, depending on whether they mark off a phrase, a period, or the end of a larger section. Because the harmony articulates the phrases rather than driving the musical flow continuously forward, harmonies tend to change less frequently than in the older Baroque style. To compensate for the slower harmonic rhythm, composers often animated the musical texture with pulsing chords or other rhythmic means. One of the most widely used devices in keyboard music was the Alberti bass, shown in Example 15.1. Named for the Italian composer Domenico Alberti (ca. 1710–1746), who used it frequently to accompany his galant-style melodies, this device arpeggiated each of the underlying chords into a simple repeating pattern of short notes that produced a light chordal background, setting the melody in relief.

Harmony

Alberti bass

Finally, the coherence of late-eighteenth-century music was made possible by the differentiation of musical material according to its function. Each segment of music was immediately recognizable as a beginning, middle, or ending statement. Just as an orator uses emphasis, inflections, and pauses to mark the beginnings and ends of sentences, paragraphs, sections, and entire speeches, so, too, does the composer assemble distinct musical segments into larger units, making it possible for an attentive listener to follow the logic of the entire form.

Form

One of the most striking characteristics of the Classical style resulted from a new view of human psychology. Descartes and others in the seventeenth

Emotional contrasts

Example 15.1 Domenico Alberti, VIII sonate per cembalo, Op. 1 (London, 1748), Sonata III, Allegro ma non tanto

century believed that once an emotion, such as anger or fear, was aroused, a person harbored that affection until moved by some stimulus to a different emotional state. Accordingly, composers in the Baroque era sought to convey a single mood in each movement, or at most to contrast conflicting moods in self-contained sections, such as the two parts of a da capo aria or the ritornello and episodes of a concerto movement. But greater knowledge of blood circulation, the nervous system, and other aspects of human physiology led to a new understanding that feelings were constantly in flux, jostled by associations that might take unpredictable turns.

Form and content

Reflecting the notion that emotions were not steady states, but were constantly changing and sometimes contradictory responses to one's experiences and thoughts, composers began to introduce contrasting moods in the various parts of a movement or even within the themes themselves. The possibilities for contrasts were broadened by the new music's many short phrases and its dependence on differences in function to articulate the form as a whole. But while composers desired individuality for each of their works, content had to be expressed within universally valid forms, whose principles will be discussed below.

Opera Buffa

Many of the stylistic traits associated with the Classic period had their origins in the first decades of the eighteenth century in Italian musical theater. Because tradition weighed less heavily on comic opera than on opera seria, the former was more hospitable to innovations. Emotions that were stereotyped in serious opera could be portrayed in more natural ways in comic opera. An Italian opera buffa at this time was a full-length work with six or more singing characters and, unlike comic opera in other countries, was sung throughout. It served a moral purpose by caricaturing the foibles of both aristocrats and commoners, vain ladies, miserly old men, cleverly scheming servants, deceitful husbands and wives, pedantic lawyers and notaries, bungling physicians, and pompous military commanders. These figures generally resemble the stock characters of the commedia dell'arte, a type of improvised theater popular in Italy since the sixteenth century. The comic characters often spoke or sang in dialect, as they did in some of the Venetian comedies, or the entire play might be in the local dialect, as in Naples. In opera buffa, the comic cast was often complemented by serious characters around whom the main plot revolved and who interacted with the comic characters, particularly in amorous intrigues. The dialogue was set in rapidly delivered recitative, often accompanied by keyboard only. The arias were typically in galant style, made up of short tuneful phrases, often repeated or varied, accompanied by simple harmonies and organized into tidy periods.

Another important type of Italian comic opera, the intermezzo, took the

Figure 15.1 Painting of a performance of an intermezzo, a short comic work given between the acts of an opera seria. Venetian school, eighteenth century.
(Museo Teatrale alla Scala, Milan.)

form of two or three musical interludes between the acts of a serious opera or spoken play. These intermezzi contrasted sharply with the grand and heroic manners of the principal drama, sometimes even parodying its excesses. The plots were mostly situation comedies involving a few ordinary people who sang, as in serious opera, alternating recitatives and arias.

Intermezzo

Giovanni Battista Pergolesi (1710–1736) was an early master of the comic intermezzo. One of the most original composers in the early classical style, he wrote *La serva padrona* (The Maid as Mistress) as an interlude to one of his own serious operas in 1733 in Naples. Its performance in Paris nearly twenty years later set off an aesthetic debate known as the *querelle des bouffons* or "quarrel of the comic actors" (see A Closer Look, page 323).

Pergolesi

In two brief acts, *La serva padrona* is lightly scored (for strings and continuo) and uses only three characters: Uberto (bass), a rich old bachelor; his maid, Serpina (soprano); and his mute valet, Vespone. Typical of comic opera, the social order is upended as Serpina manipulates her boss into proposing marriage by inventing a rival suitor (in fact, Vespone in disguise). The scene after Serpina tells Uberto that she will marry another (NAWM 107) displays the extraordinary aptness and nimbleness of Pergolesi's music. Serpina delivers the news in simple recitative, to which Uberto reacts first in an agitated, orchestrally accompanied recitative, then in a da capo aria. In serious opera, these styles were reserved for the most dramatic situations; knowing this convention, Pergolesi's audience understood the effect here as comic, elevating Uberto's bewilderment to high drama. Neither the main nor the middle section develops a single musical motive as in opera seria; rather, there are as many melodic ideas as there are shifting thoughts and moods in the text. The first line, in which Uberto exclaims in patter style how confused he is, repeats the same music three times, suggesting Uberto's mental paralysis (Example 15.2a). Then, realizing that something mysterious is stirring his heart (measure 15), Uberto waxes lyrical as he asks himself whether he is in love. But a sober voice within checks his ardor—he should think of himself, guard his interests and independence—and now the melody shifts to deliberate, brooding, drawn-out notes (Example 15.2b). The middle section, instead of presenting contrasting music, develops earlier material, based on some of the musical motives of the

La serva padrona

Full 🔊 Concise 🔊

Example 15.2 Giovanni Battista Pergolesi, Son imbrogliato già, *from* La serva padrona

a.

I am all mixed up! I have a certain something in my heart. Truly, I cannot tell [whether it's love or pity].

b.

[I hear a voice that tells me:] Uberto, think of yourself!

first section but in the minor mode. The stopping and starting in the musical flow of ideas and the abrupt shifting between motives suggest the comic actor's physical gestures and actions on stage, all mimicking his indecision and confusion.

Comic opera

Unlike opera seria, which maintained its character across national boundaries, comic opera took different forms in different countries. Although traveling Italian troupes of opera buffa players were much in demand and performed in Italian, home-grown comic opera librettos were always written in the national tongue, and the music itself tended to accentuate the national musical idiom. From humble beginnings the comic opera grew steadily in importance after 1760, and before the end of the century many of its characteristic features were absorbed into the mainstream of operatic composition. The historical significance of comic opera was twofold: it responded to the widespread demand for naturalness during the latter half of the eighteenth century, and it anticipated the trend toward musical nationalism, which became prominent during the nineteenth century.

French opéra comique

The French counterpart of opera buffa, known as opéra comique, began around 1710 as a lowly form of popular entertainment performed at parish fairs. Until the middle of the century, the music consisted almost entirely of popular tunes (vaudevilles) or simple melodies imitating such tunes. The visit of an Italian comic opera troupe to Paris in 1752 and the ensuing controversy stimulated the production of comic operas in which original airs (called ariettes) in a mixed Italian-French style were introduced alongside the old vaudevilles. Ariettes gradually replaced the vaudevilles until, by the end of the 1760s, they, too, were completely discarded and all the music was freshly composed. Christoph Willibald Gluck (see below), one of the composers exposed to the French opéra comique during this transitional decade, arranged and composed a number of such works for the entertainment of the Vienna court, and the French philosopher Jean-Jacques Rousseau (1712–1778) wrote a charming little comic opera in 1752, *Le Devin du village* (The Village Soothsayer) in response to the Italian productions.

The French opéra comique, like all the national variants of light opera except the Italian, used spoken dialogue instead of recitative. Following the European trend in the second half of the century, opéra comique sometimes used serious plots and dealt boldly with the social issues that were agitating France during the pre-Revolutionary years. The leading French opera composer of the time was Belgian-born André-Ernest-Modeste Grétry (1741–1813), whose masterpiece *Richard Coeur-de-Lion* (Richard the Lion-Hearted, 1784) inaugurated a vogue for "rescue" operas, in which the hero is saved from death through a friend's devoted loyalty.

English ballad opera

Ballad opera rose to popularity in England after the extraordinary success of *The Beggar's Opera* in 1728. This work broadly satirizes fashionable Italian opera; its music, like that of the early opéra comique, consists for the most part of popular tunes—ballads—set to new words and a few numbers that parody familiar operatic airs (see excerpts in NAWM 109). The immense popularity of ballad operas in the 1730s signaled a general reaction in England against foreign opera—that "exotic and irrational entertainment," as Dr. Samuel Johnson called it. As we have already seen, that reaction was one reason Handel turned his energies from opera to oratorio in the latter part of his life.

Full 🔊

German *Singspiel*

Although *Singspiel* had existed in Germany since the sixteenth century, the success of the ballad opera in the eighteenth century inspired its revival. At first, librettists adapted English ballad operas, but they soon turned to translating or arranging French comic operas, for which the German composers provided new music in a familiar and appealing melodic vein. Many of the

Figure 15.2 A ticket for a performance of The Beggar's Opera *at the Theatre Royal at Covent Garden in London. The evening's receipts were to be paid to Thomas Walker, the actor playing the central character, the notorious thief and murderer Macheath. In the engraving by renowned satirist William Hogarth (1697–1764), Polly and Lucy, both in love with Macheath, plead for his release from prison.*
(Lebrecht Music & Arts Photo Library.)

eighteenth-century *Singspiel* tunes found their way into German song collections and, in the course of time, have virtually become folk songs. The principal composer of *Singspiel* music during this period was Johann Adam Hiller (1728–1804) of Leipzig.

Opera Seria

The light and charming aria style of opera buffa soon invaded serious opera, which treated high-minded subjects without comic scenes or characters. Opera seria received its standard form from the Italian poet Pietro Metastasio (1698–1782), whose dramas many eighteenth-century composers set to music hundreds of times. Metastasio's success with librettos for Naples, Rome, and Venice led to his appointment in 1729 as court poet in Vienna. He remained in Vienna for the rest of his life, turning out a profusion of Italian librettos and many works for special occasions at the imperial court. His heroic operas, based on ancient Greek or Latin tales, present a conflict of human passions, often pitting love against duty. They were intended to promote morality through entertainment and to present models of merciful and enlightened rulers. The magnanimous tyrant—for example, Alexander the Great in *Alessandro nell'Indie* or Titus in *La clemenza di Tito*—is a favorite character. The librettos conventionally present two pairs of lovers and several subordinate personages. The action provides opportunities for introducing varied scenes—pastoral or martial episodes, solemn ceremonies, and the like. The resolution of the drama, which rarely has a tragic ending, often turns on a heroic deed or a sublime gesture of renunciation by one of the principal characters.

Metastasio

The three acts of an opera seria almost invariably consist of alternating recitatives and arias: recitatives promote the action through dialogue, while each aria is a dramatic soliloquy in which a principal actor gives vent to an overriding emotion or reaction to the preceding scene. Although there are occasional duets, a few larger ensembles, and rare, simple choruses, the main musical focus of the Italian opera seria is on the aria, which eighteenth-century composers created in astounding number and variety.

Arias

Demands of the singers

Turning the aria into the primary musical ingredient in opera opened the way to abuses. Singers, including the famed Italian castrati, made arbitrary demands on poets and composers, compelling them to alter, add, and substitute arias without respect for dramatic or musical appropriateness. Moreover, the melodic embellishments and cadenzas that singers added at will were often mere displays of vocal acrobatics having nothing to do with the aria's affective content (see In Performance, page 321).

New features of
da capo arias

Despite its shortcomings and abuses, the da capo aria continued to grow and evolve. Arias written in the first decades of the century had usually projected only one affection through the development of a single motive. Now composers started to express a succession of moods, using a variety of musical material that ranged from lighthearted to tragic. Furthermore, the aria's ritornello may introduce all the material sung later, thus resembling the orchestral exposition of a concerto (see page 334 and A Closer Look, below). In this way, vocal music began incorporating structural features of instrumental music—the sonata and concerto—a practice that remained throughout the eighteenth

---

 A Closer Look 　**The Da Capo Aria and the Abbreviated Da Capo**

The most frequently used form for vocal music in the first half of the century was the da capo aria, a basic ABA scheme that permitted enormous variation in detail. Metastasio's two-stanza aria texts set the standard for the full-blown da capo aria from the 1720s through the 1740s. The form, originally presented in Chapter 13, is now somewhat expanded and may be represented by the following outline (in which the keys, indicated by Roman numerals, are hypothetical).

Structure:	A					B	A (da capo)				
Music:	Rit 1	Solo 1	Rit 2	Solo 2	Rit 3	Solo 3	Rit 1	Solo 1	Rit 2	Solo 2	Rit 3
Text:		stanza 1		stanza 1 developed		stanza 2		stanza 1		stanza 1 developed	
Key:	I	mod	V	mod	I	vi	I	mod	V	mod	I

Figure 15.3 Structure of the da capo aria.

The ritornello structure is comparable to that of a Baroque concerto, but its expanded harmonic scheme and formal methods are closer to instrumental works of the Classic period. Often two keys are contrasted in the first main period (the first solo section); then the material in the second key is brought back in the tonic at the close of the second main period (the second solo section). (For an example of an aria that conforms to this outline, see NAWM 108.)

For some arias, composers shortened the repetition of the first section by omitting the opening ritornello, altering the instruction "da capo" (from the beginning) to "dal segno" (from the sign, which was placed so that only part of the first section is to be repeated), or writing out an abridged return (see the aria by Pergolesi, NAWM 107, for an example). Some arias lacked the contrasting second section (B) and instead followed a format like a da capo's first section, with two vocal statements framed by ritornellos.

In Context An Eighteenth-Century Diva, Faustina Bordoni

The career of Faustina Bordoni (1700–1781), leading lady of the operatic stage in the first half of the eighteenth century, illustrates the commanding stature of the diva. Bordoni established her reputation in Venice while still in her

Figure 15.4 Faustina Bordoni (1700–1781), universally admired as one of the great singer-actresses of her age. (Sächsische Landesbibliothek, Dresden. Deutsche Fotothek.)

teens and went on to have a lucrative international career that lasted into her fifties. She created several roles in Handel's London operas and enjoyed great successes in Munich and Vienna, where she became a favorite of the empress and sang duets with the empress's daughter Maria Theresa. Burney praised her fluent articulation, trills, improvised embellishments, and expressive power. He also emphasized her exceptional breath control, which allowed her to sustain a note longer, "in the opinion of the public," than any other singer. Universally admired as one of the great singer-actresses of her age, Bordoni married the composer Johann Adolf Hasse in 1730 and from then on was associated chiefly with his music. The next year they were hired by the Saxon court at Dresden, where she was a big hit in the title role of his *Cleofide* (see NAWM 108). She was paid 1,000 ducats as prima donna; he received only 500 as the composer. Hasse remained as Kapellmeister in Dresden for more than thirty years, and Bordoni sang in at least fifteen of his many opere serie before retiring from the stage. On one notorious occasion, egged on by her fans, she actually exchanged blows on stage with another great soprano, Francesca Cuzzoni, during a performance of an opera. She is shown here as Attilia in Hasse's *Attilio Regolo* in a costume designed for the original production at the Dresden court theater in 1750.

century. But the vocal melody still dominated the music and carried it forward, and the orchestra provided harmonic support to the singer, rather than adding independent contrapuntal lines. The melodies were usually presented in four-measure units, consisting of two-measure antecedent and consequent phrases. When a composer deviated from this formula, it was usually for a deliberately unbalancing effect. Handel employed this new idiom in his late operas such as *Alcina* (1735) and *Serse* (1738), as did Pergolesi and the German Johann Adolph Hasse (1699–1783).

Hasse (shown in Figure 15.5) was acknowledged by most of his contemporaries as the great master of the opera seria. For most of his life, he directed music and opera at the court of the elector of Saxony in Dresden, but he spent many years in Italy, married the celebrated Italian soprano Faustina Bordoni (see In Context, above), and became so thoroughly Italian in his musical style that the Italians nicknamed him "il caro Sassone" (the dear Saxon). His music is the perfect complement to Metastasio's poetry: the great majority of his eighty operas use Metastasio librettos, some of which he set two or even three times.

Figure 15.5 Johann Adolf Hasse, in a pastel portrait by Felicitas Hoffmann. (Dresden Gallery, Dresden.)

Hasse was the most popular and successful opera composer in Europe around the middle of the century, and the contemporary English music historian Charles Burney reveals the qualities that endeared him to the connoisseurs:

> the most natural, elegant, and judicious composer of vocal music . . . now alive; equally a friend to poetry and the voice, he discovers as much judgment as genius, in expressing words, as well as in accompanying those sweet and tender melodies, which he gives to the singer.[1]

Full 🔊

The famous da capo aria *Digli ch'io son fedele* (Tell him that I am faithful; NAWM 108) from Hasse's *Cleofide* (1731), his first opera for Dresden, illustrates the qualities that Burney admired (see In Performance, page 321).

Opera Reform

Certain Italian composers wanted to bring opera into harmony with the changing ideals of music and drama. They sought to make the entire design more "natural"—that is, more flexible in structure, more deeply expressive, less laden with coloratura, and more varied in other musical resources. They did not abandon the da capo aria but modified it and introduced other forms as well; they employed arias and recitatives less predictably in order to move the action forward more rapidly and realistically; they made greater use of obbligato recitative and ensembles, such as trios; they made the orchestra more important, both for its own sake and for adding harmonic depth to accompaniments; they reinstated choruses, long absent in Italian opera; and they stiffened their resistance to the arbitrary demands of solo singers.

Figure 15.6　Christoph Willibald Gluck, in a 1775 portrait by Joseph-Siffred Duplessis.
(Kunsthistorisches Museum, Vienna. Erich Lessing/Art Resource, NY.)

Two of the most important figures in the movement of reform were Nicolò Jommelli (1714–1774) and Tommaso Traetta (1727–1779). That these Italian composers worked at courts where French taste predominated—Jommelli in Stuttgart and Traetta in Parma—naturally influenced them to lean toward a cosmopolitan type of opera. As the composer of some one hundred stage works, Jommelli enjoyed great popularity. Traetta aimed to combine the best of French *tragédie lyrique* and Italian opera seria in his *Ippolito ed Aricia* (1759), adapted from the same libretto that Rameau had set (NAWM 98). He even utilized some of Rameau's dance music and descriptive symphonies, and, unusual for this time in Italy, included a number of choruses. In his own way, Traetta reconciled the two types of music drama—Italian and French—years before Gluck set out to do so.

Christoph Willibald Gluck (1714–1787; see Figure 15.6) achieved a synthesis of French and Italian opera that made him the man of the hour. Born in what is now Bavaria to Bohemian parents, Gluck studied with Sammartini in Italy (see page 330), visited London, toured in Germany as conductor of an opera troupe,

---

1. Charles Burney, *The Present State of Music in Germany. . . .* 2nd ed., 2 vols. (London, 1775), I, pp. 238–239.

In Performance Vocal Embellishment

An elaborated version of Hasse's da capo aria from *Cleofide* (NAWM 108) survives in the hand of amateur flutist and composer Frederick II, king of Prussia (r. 1740–1786), as sung by the castrato Antonio Uberi, known as Porporino. This version, written out above Hasse's melody in Example 15.3, is ablaze with trills (a), mordents (b), rapid turns (c), appoggiaturas (d), scales, triplets, and arpeggios. Scholars believe that such embellishments were added especially in the da capo repetition, where, after concentrating on the words and their dramatic message the first time through, the performer was expected to embroider the melody so as to enhance the aria's expression and display an impressive vocal technique. Indeed, the execution of such ornamentation required extraordinary vocal flexibility and dexterity, perfect intonation, careful breath control, and precise articulation. And, whether or not the singer was improvising the ornaments anew at every performance, the ability to remember the outline of the original melody was important, as were the training and imagination to know how to vary it tastefully. One of the great castrati of the age, Pier Francesco Tosi (ca. 1653–1732), wrote a singing treatise that reflects these practices (translated into English as *Observations on the Florid Song*).

Example 15.3 J. A. Hasse, Cleofide, *Act II, Scene 9,* Digli ch'io son fedele

Tell him that I am faithful,
tell him that he's my darling;
[Tell him] to love me; that I adore him;
that he not yet despair.

became court composer to Emperor Charles VI at Vienna, and triumphed in Paris under the patronage of Marie Antoinette. After writing operas in the conventional Italian style, he was strongly affected by the reform movement in the 1750s and collaborated with the poet Raniero de Calzabigi (1714–1795) to produce *Orfeo ed Euridice* (1762) and *Alceste* (1767) in Vienna. In his preface to *Alceste*, Gluck expressed his resolve to remove the abuses that had deformed Italian opera (see Vignette, below) and to confine music to its proper function—to serve the poetry and advance the plot. He wanted to accomplish this without regard to either the worn-out conventions of the da capo aria or the desire of singers to show off their skill in ornamental variation. He further aimed to make the overture an integral part of the opera, to adapt the orchestra to the drama, and to lessen the contrast between aria and recitative.

Gluck's *Orfeo*

That Gluck chose Orpheus, a figure from classical antiquity, as the subject of his first reform opera is undoubtedly significant; it suggested a new beginning, unhindered by the weight of accumulated tradition. Gluck aspired to write music of "a beautiful simplicity," which he realized in the celebrated aria *Che farò senza Euridice?* (What shall I do without Euridice?), Orfeo's restrained and noble lament, and elsewhere in the work. Throughout, Gluck molded the music to the drama, intermingling recitatives, arias, dance, and choruses in large, unified scenes. He also assigned an important role to the chorus, evident in the chorus of Furies in Act II (NAWM 110), which is integrated into the action. In

► GLUCK, *Orfeo ed Euridice*

this scene, Orfeo, accompanied by harp and plucked strings to imitate the sound of his lyre, pleads for the liberation of Euridice, but the Furies resist, provoking and challenging Orfeo.

Gluck's other operas

Gluck achieved his mature style in *Orfeo* and *Alceste,* amalgamating Italian melodic grace, German seriousness, and the stately magnificence of the French *tragédie lyrique.* The success of those two works was followed by the Paris production of *Iphigénie en Aulide* (Iphigenia in Aulis) in 1774 and a new setting of *Armide* (1777) to the same libretto that Lully had used in 1686. Having restored the balance between dramatic and musical interest, producing a total effect of classical tragic grandeur, Gluck's operas became models for the works of his

Influence

immediate followers in Paris. His influence on the form and spirit of opera was transmitted to the nineteenth century through composers such as Niccolò Piccinni (1728–1800), Luigi Cherubini (1760–1842), and Hector Berlioz (1803–1869).

VIGNETTE Gluck on the Reform of Opera

In his manifesto on operatic reform, published in Italian in the dedication of his score of Alceste *(1769), Christoph Willibald Gluck expounded ideals that were characteristic of the early Classic period.*

I sought to confine music to its true function of serving the poetry by expressing feelings and the situations of the story without interrupting and cooling off the action through useless and superfluous ornaments. I believed that music should join to poetry what the vividness of colors and well disposed lights and shadows contribute to a correct and well-composed design, animating the figures without altering their contours.

I further believed that the greater part of my task was to seek a beautiful simplicity, and I have avoided a display of difficulty at the expense of clarity. I assigned no value to the discovery of some novelty, unless it were naturally suggested by the situation and the expression. And there is no rule that I did not willingly consider sacrificing for the sake of an effect.

From Christoph Willibald Gluck, *Alceste* (Vienna, 1769), dedication.

The musical atmosphere of Paris was so charged that Gluck's *Iphigénie en Aulide* awakened extraordinary interest. Long-simmering critical opposition to the old-fashioned, state-subsidized French opera had erupted in 1753 in a pamphlet war known as the querelle des bouffons ("quarrel of the comic actors"). The immediate occasion for the dispute was the presence in Paris of an Italian opera company that for two seasons had enjoyed sensational success with its performances of Italian comic operas and intermezzi, particularly Pergolesi's *La serva padrona*, which was performed in 1752 between the acts of Lully's *Acis et Galatée*, thereby highlighting the contrast between the two works. Practically every intellectual and would-be intellectual in France took part in the debate over the relative merits of French and Italian opera. Jean-Jacques Rousseau, one of the leaders of the "Italian" faction, vehemently attacked the aristocratic opera of the late Baroque era for its artificial plots and complicated music. He published an article in which he praised Italian composers' emphasis on "nat-ural" melody, their use of "simple and pure harmony," and their "lively and brilliant accompaniments."[1] Rousseau and his friends represented enlightened opinion in Paris, and as a result of their campaign, the traditional French opera of Lully and Rameau soon lost favor. But nothing appeared to take its place until Gluck arrived on the scene. Gluck cleverly represented himself—or was represented by his supporters—as wanting to prove that a good opera could be written to French words: he claimed to want Rousseau's help in creating "a noble, sensitive, and natural melody . . . music suited to all nations, so as to abolish these ridiculous distinctions of national styles."[2] He thus appealed at the same time to the patriotism and to the curiosity of the French public.

1. Rousseau, *Letter on French Music* (1753), trans. William Strunk, Jr., and Oliver Strunk, in *Source Readings in Music History*, rev. ed. by Leo Treitler (New York: Norton, 1998), vol. 5, pp. 166–167.

2. Christoph Willibald Gluck, Letter to the Editor, *Mercure de France* (Feb. 1773).

The New World

Not surprisingly, opera was slow to gain a foothold in the New World. During the century after the first settlers arrived in North America, there was little time for entertainment. Resources were scarce and the population was scattered. More importantly, the Puritans brought with them their disdain for the theater, which extended to singing and displaying emotions in public, and their distrust of pleasure in general. The situation was different in the Spanish colonies, however, where theatrical productions at court carried on the traditions of the Old World. The first opera produced anywhere in the New World was staged in 1701 at the court of the viceroy of Peru in Lima to celebrate the accession to the Spanish throne of Philip V. This work, *La púrpura de la rosa* (The Blood of the Rose; NAWM 90) was composed by the maestro di capilla of Lima cathedral, Tomás de Torrejón y Velasco (1644–1728), then the most famous composer in the Americas.

Full

Much early American music grew out of the religious traditions of the settlers, who fled various forms of intolerance in Europe to find their own voices in the new land. Church musicians drew on their respective national styles: villancicos throughout the Spanish colonies, the Catholic music of France in Canada, and English hymns and anthems in the Anglican churches of British North America. Two groups were especially notable for their music: the Puritans of New England and the Moravians of Pennsylvania and North Carolina.

The Puritans who settled New England were Calvinist, and their worship music centered on metrical psalm singing. The original *Bay Psalm Book* (1640),

Puritans

TIMELINE The Early Classic Period: Opera and Vocal Music

Musical Events

1725
Concerts spirituels begins

1728
The Beggar's Opera
(NAWM 109)

1731
Hasse, *Cleofide* (NAWM 108)

1733
Pergolesi, *La serva padrona*
(NAWM 107) in Naples;
Rameau, *Hippolyte et Aricie*
(NAWM 98)

1750
J. S. Bach dies

1752
Pergolesi, *La serva padrona*
in Paris

1753
Outbreak of the
Querelle des bouffons

1762
Gluck, *Orfeo ed Euridice*
(NAWM 110)

1776–1789
Burney, *A General History
of Music*

1794
William Billings, *Continental
Harmony* (NAWM 112)
published

1700 | **1800**

Historical Events

1717–1718
Watteau, *The Music Party*
(Figure IV.1)

1740–1786
Reign of Frederick the Great
of Prussia

1740
Maria Theresa of Austria crowned
Holy Roman empress

1751
First volume of Denis Diderot's
Encyclopédie published

1759
Voltaire, *Candide*

1760–1820
Reign of George III of England

1762
Jean-Jacques Rousseau, *The Social
Contract*

1770
Gainsborough, *The Blue Boy*
(Figure 16.9)

1776
American Declaration of Independence

1781
Kant, *Critique of Pure Reason*

1789
The French Revolution begins

the first book of any kind published in North America, contained no music, but its ninth edition, published in 1698, furnished thirteen melodies for singing the psalms. Eventually, singing schools established during the eighteenth century trained a core of amateurs to sing psalms and anthems in parts. The availability of such singers became an invitation for composers to write new music.

William Billings (1746–1800), the most prominent of these composers, left a significant body of music and writings. His *New England Psalm Singer* (1770), shown in Figure 15.7, contained 108 psalms and hymn settings as well as 15 anthems and canons for chorus. He issued several more collections, including *The Continental Harmony* (1794), from which the fuging tune *Creation* provides a good example of his rugged style (NAWM 112). Fuging tunes generally feature a passage in free imitation, framed by opening and closing sections in straightforward four-part harmony. But Billings declared his independence from the standard rules of counterpoint by using numerous parallel octaves and fifths as well as open chords without thirds, spiced with unconventional dissonances. Not only did these purposely austere sounds match Billings's colorful and eccentric personality, they also led the way for a distinctive "yankee" idiom that stood apart from European styles.

In contrast, the Moravians cultivated the more sophisticated genres of the German-speaking Protestants from Moravia, Bohemia, and southern Germany. They embellished their church services with concerted arias and motets

Full 🔊

in current styles, whether imported from Europe or composed in America. Moravians also collected substantial libraries of music, both sacred and secular, and regularly performed chamber music and even symphonies by leading European composers.

POSTLUDE

The early Classic period explored a wealth of new genres, forms, and expressive means. Much of the innovation originated in opera, particularly comic opera. There, the urge to entertain and to reach a diverse audience led composers to simplify their approaches and strive for naturalness of expression. From the Italian theaters, the new styles spread through the cosmopolitan network of musicians, composers, and directors to other regions, stimulating new genres of opera that reached a wider public than ever before. Many practices spilled out of the theaters into the concert halls and private chambers. Seeking to serve the growing taste for a clear and universally appealing music, composers developed a spare, logically organized flow of musical ideas that could be grasped on first hearing.

The new styles were inspired by vocal music, yet they had a tremendous impact on instrumental music—the sonata, symphony, and concerto, as described in the next chapter. These genres profited from the new approach to melody and form because they could now be understood even without a text or a title. These changes laid the foundation for the increasing importance of instrumental music in the Classic period.

Figure 15.7 The frontispiece to William Billings's New England Psalm Singer *(1770).*
Surrounding the singers at the table is a canon for six voices with a ground bass to be sung "by three or four deep voices." Engraving by Paul Revere.
(Germanisches Nationalmuseum, Nuremberg, inv. #MIR 1097.)

 Resources for study and review available at wwnorton.com/studyspace

16

The Early Classic Period: Instrumental Music

PRELUDE

The new musical idiom of the mid-eighteenth century, developed primarily in opera, became pervasive in instrumental music. Periodic phrasing, songlike melodies, diverse material, contrasts of texture and style, and touches of drama, all typical of the galant style, made it easier to follow instrumental music and to be engaged by it. As an abstract play of gestures and moods, a drama without words, the music itself absorbed the listener's attention. Paradoxically, by borrowing from vocal music, instrumental music gained new independence, rising in the next two generations to unprecedented prominence.

Instrumental music was a form of entertainment for the players and for listeners. Pleasing the performers and appealing to a wide audience became paramount for composers. With its strong, nuanced tone, the piano replaced the harpsichord and clavichord as the favorite keyboard instrument, and new chamber ensembles, notably the string quartet of two violins, viola, and violon-cello, were developed for social music-making. The sonata (including similar works called by other names) became the leading genre for solo and chamber music, and the concerto and symphony dominated orchestral music. All these genres had deep roots in Baroque music, but the new melodic style brought novel forms to the individual movements, including sonata form. Other genres characteristic of Baroque instrumental music fell out of fashion in the Classic period, including preludes, toccatas, fugues, chorale settings, and dance suites. Composers continued to write variations, fantasias, and individual dances for keyboard, but the major genre became the keyboard sonata in three or four movements of contrasting mood and tempo. Similar multimovement works were also composed for a variety of chamber ensembles.

Sonata

In the Baroque era, *sonata* generally meant a multimovement work for a small group of instruments, most often in trio texture. In the Classic period, the word had different meanings for different composers. It also connoted a compositional procedure or form, first articulated by the German theorist Heinrich Christoph Koch. Koch describes sonata form as an expanded version of binary

Sections of music:	FIRST SECTION	SECOND SECTION	
	One Main Period	First Main Period	Second Main Period
Harmonic plan:	‖: I ——— V :‖:	V - mod - on V	I ——— I :‖

Figure 16.1 Eighteenth-century view of sonata form as expanded binary form.

form, which we have already encountered in the dances and dance suites of the Baroque period (see A Closer Look, page 328). Also called first-movement form, this was the most common plan for the first movement of a sonata, chamber work, or symphony in the Classic period. Taking his cue from the grammar and syntax of speech, Koch details two large sections, each of which is repeated (see Figure 16.1). The first section has one main period, moving from tonic to dominant (or relative major in a minor key), and presents the principal ideas organized into a series of smaller phrases. The second section has two main periods. The first of these periods often begins with the opening theme on the dominant before digressing harmonically and ending on the dominant chord in preparation for the return of the tonic. This coincides with the final period, which begins and ends on the tonic, although it typically parallels the first section and for the most part restates the same material.

Koch's first-movement form

Stimulated by the growing demand by amateurs for music that could be played at home and in private gatherings, composers of the middle and late eighteenth century produced great numbers of keyboard works, especially sonatas, which were widely regarded as the most challenging and rewarding genre for performers and listeners. Among the most prominent keyboard composers active in the middle decades of the century, the Italian Domenico Scarlatti (1685–1757; Figure 16.2) was also the most original and creative.

Keyboard sonata

Alessandro Scarlatti's son Domenico was born in the same year as Bach and Handel and left Italy in 1720 or 1721 to work as a musician for the king of Portugal. When his pupil, the infanta of Portugal, wed Prince Ferdinand of Spain in 1729, Scarlatti followed her to Madrid, where he remained for the rest of his life in the service of the Spanish court. Being so isolated from the musical mainstream of Europe (Italy), he seems to have created his own keyboard idiom virtually uninfluenced. He published his first collection of harpsichord sonatas (called on the title page *essercizi*, "exercises") in 1738, but most of his 555 sonatas are known to us through scribal copies from his time.

Figure 16.2 Domenico Scarlatti, in a portrait from about 1740 by Domingo Antonio de Velasco.

(Casa Museu dos Patudo, Alparca, Portugal.)

Scarlatti's sonatas are typically organized in balanced binary form, in which the closing part of the first section returns at the end of the second section, but in the tonic key. What is new in comparison to a keyboard piece by Handel or J. S. Bach is the sheer diversity of figuration. Scarlatti strings together short, repetitious phrases, each of which has a unique place in the compositional design. Some phrases function as openers—for example, by defining the key with an arpeggiated fanfare; others are unstable and introduce accidentals outside the key, serving as transitions; still others are cadential formulas, confirming an arrival. Although each phrase introduces a well-defined sometimes contrasting motivic idea, not all are equally important, and some have a clearer role to play in the piece's overall structure than others. Although Scarlatti's melodies are not vocally

A Closer Look Binary Forms

Simple

Many Classic forms originated in binary form, which features two sections, each repeated, the first usually moving from tonic to dominant or relative major and the second returning to the tonic. Several types of binary form were common during the Baroque period. In simple binary form, the two sections are roughly equal in length and feature musical material that is different or only loosely related. For example, most individual movements of the keyboard suites of Elisabeth-Claude Jacquet de la Guerre conform to simple binary form (NAWM 88).

Sections of music:	‖: A :‖: B :‖
Harmonic plan:	I – V V – I

Balanced

In the eighteenth century, composers tended to emphasize the return to the tonic in the second section. One common strategy, resulting in balanced binary form, was to introduce new material in the dominant near the end of the first section and to restate it in the tonic near the end of the second section (compare b's below), like a musical rhyme that confirms the return to the home key. Such an approach contrasts tonic and dominant by associating different musical ideas with each and then resolves the contradiction by restating in the tonic the same material that first appeared in another key. Balanced binary form is typical of Domenico Scarlatti's sonatas (NAWM 113), discussed below.

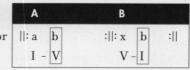

Sections of music:	A B A B
Harmonic plan:	‖: a b :‖: a b :‖ or ‖: a b :‖: x b :‖
	I – V V – I I – V V – I

Rounded

Another approach, known as rounded binary form, highlights the return to the tonic in the second section by repeating the material that opened the first section (compare a's below). The double return of the opening key and the opening material lends a strong sense of closure. Minuets, like the one in Jacquet de la Guerre's Suite in A Minor, often adhere to this form.

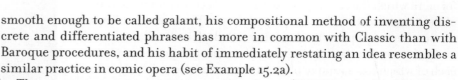

Sections of music:	A B
Harmonic plan:	‖: a b :‖: x a b :‖
	I – V mod I – I

smooth enough to be called galant, his compositional method of inventing discrete and differentiated phrases has more in common with Classic than with Baroque procedures, and his habit of immediately restating an idea resembles a similar practice in comic opera (see Example 15.2a).

The one-movement sonata written around 1749 (NAWM 113), identified by its number in Ralph Kirkpatrick's standard index as K. 119, illustrates Scarlatti's style and exhibits many of the genre's traits. It has two sections, each repeated. After a brilliant opening, several ideas are announced, each immediately restated. The first, a broken-chord motive spanning two octaves, introduces and asserts the tonic. The next bold theme (Example 16.1a), immediately repeated, never returns. The third (Example 16.1b) is purely cadential; the

Example 16.1 Domenico Scarlatti, Sonata K. 119, motives.

fourth (Example 16.1c), imitating the rhythm and effect of castanets, has a modulatory function here but comes back again to close each half of the sonata. Then the central idea arrives in the dominant minor (Example 16.1d). It is inspired by Spanish guitar music, with an almost constant a′ sounding like a strummed open string alongside fingered notes. This thematic element is developed throughout the piece: in the second section, it rises to a vigorous climax in which all the notes of the key but one are sounded together (Example 16.1e).

The majority of Scarlatti's sonatas after 1745 appear as pairs in the manuscripts. In effect, each pair may be seen as a sonata of two movements, always in the same key (though one may be major and the other minor), sometimes similar in mood, sometimes contrasted. Many eighteenth-century composers, from Alberti to Mozart, wrote sonatas in two movements, possibly under Italian influence, although there is no evidence that they borrowed the idea from Scarlatti. In fact, just as Scarlatti seems to have had no predecessors, he had no successors either, with the exception of a few Iberian composers, notably the Catalan Antonio Soler (1729–1783).

Paired sonatas

Symphony

Early symphonies

Sonatas and orchestral compositions of similar form during the early part of the eighteenth century adopted the overall shape of the Italian opera overture or sinfonia. About 1700, the overture had assumed a three-movement, fast-slow-fast, structure: an Allegro, a short lyrical Andante, and a finale in a dance rhythm such as a minuet or a gigue. Except insofar as such overtures incorporated contrast and drama into their musical rhetoric, they usually had no thematic connection with the operas they introduced and were played as independent pieces in concerts. It was a natural step, then, for Italian composers to begin writing concert symphonies using the general plan of opera overtures. The earliest of these, dating from around 1730, are equally indebted to the late Baroque concerto (see Figure 14.2 and NAWM 96), the orchestral suite (see page 280), and the trio sonata (see page 230 and NAWM 94) in details of structure, texture, and thematic style.

One of the early works in this genre, the Symphony in F Major, No. 32 (ca. 1740) by Giovanni Battista Sammartini (1701–1775) of Milan, is scored for two violins, viola, and a bass line, played by cellos, bass viol, and probably harpsichord and bassoon. There are three contrasting movements in the fast-slow-fast format, each relatively short. The opening Presto (NAWM 115) presents a variety of ideas in rapid succession, much like a Scarlatti keyboard sonata. It follows the first-movement form described by Koch (see Figure 16.1) in a concise thirty-eight measures. Each phrase of the form has one or two distinctive ideas, and their diversity helps to make the structure clear.

From Italy the symphony spread north to Germany, Austria, France, and England. Mannheim and Berlin were the principal German centers of symphonic composition after 1740. Under the leadership of Bohemian composer Johann Stamitz (1717–1757), the Mannheim orchestra became renowned all over Europe for its discipline and impeccable technique, prompting Charles Burney to call it "an army of generals." It was also famous for its astonishing and novel dynamic range—from the softest *pianissimo* to the loudest *fortissimo*—and for the thrilling sound of its crescendo, both effects that Stamitz exploited in his music.

Stamitz was the first symphony composer to use consistently what would later become the standard plan: four movements, with a minuet and trio as the third movement, and a very lively finale, often marked Presto (fast). He was also among the first to introduce a strongly contrasting, full-blown theme after the modulation to the dominant in the first section of an allegro movement, a practice that likewise became standard. The first movement of his Sinfonia in E♭ Major (NAWM 116), written in the mid-1750s, follows the usual plan outlined by Koch, but without the sectional repetitions of binary form and on a much larger scale than in Sammartini's symphony. To the four string parts, Stamitz adds two oboes and two horns, as was becoming customary. The transition to the dominant exploits the famous Mannheim crescendo, building excitement by means of string tremolos that progress from *piano* to *fortissimo*. After the arrival in the new key, a series of lyrical, graceful, and playful ideas provides a change of mood. The return of the tonic key is marked not with the opening phrases but with the series of ideas that were introduced on the dominant, as in the balanced binary form of Scarlatti (NAWM 113). The opening motives reappear at the end, in reverse order, to emphasize the tonic once again.

The principal symphonists of the Berlin, or north German, school clustered around Frederick the Great, who was himself a composer (see Figure 16.4); Johann Gottlieb Graun (1702/3–1771) and Carl Philipp Emanuel Bach (1714–1788) were two of its chief members. The north Germans were conservative, as is evident in their holding to the three-movement structure for the symphony and in their reluctance to introduce sharp thematic contrasts within a movement. But they were also forward-looking, often using thematic development within a dynamic, organically unified, serious, and quasi-dramatic style, as well as enriching the symphonic texture with contrapuntal elements.

Other centers of symphonic activity included Vienna and Paris. In Vienna, Georg Christoph Wagenseil (1715–1777) and others wrote symphonies that feature pleasant lyricism and good humor, as well as the contrasting first-movement theme groups that later became important characteristics of Mozart's

O rchestras in the eighteenth century had three main fields of activity: church, theater, and chamber (or concert room). The Italians, who had perfected the violin and other string instruments, were largely interested in church and theater music, where the orchestra served mainly to support the vocal medium and consisted essentially of strings, as in Sammartini's symphony (NAWM 115). The French, who had added many technical improvements to instruments of the wind family, were especially passionate about opera and ballet, and Lully and Rameau played an important role in the development of orchestral instruments and ensembles in France. As these composers and their counterparts elsewhere in Europe responded to the enhanced qualities and variety of instruments in every category, they began to devote more attention in their compositions to tone color. The result was the establishment of symphony orchestras as ensembles in their own right, independent of their function in church or theater. For the first time, orchestral music was distinguished from chamber music and became more forceful and varied in sound. By the middle of the eighteenth century, although all the essential musical material was still assigned to the strings, more attention was paid to the wind instruments (flutes, oboes, and bassoons) and the brass (horns and occasionally trumpets), which were regularly used for doubling the strings, reinforcing and coloring the melodic ideas, and filling out the harmonies. The clarinet, invented around 1710, took its place alongside the standard wind instruments by the 1780s. Court orchestras rose to special prominence in France and Germany. The French were fond of wind bands, ensembles comprising only two oboes and/or two clarinets with two horns and two bassons, as in Figure 16.3. Amateurs tended not to play wind instruments other than the flute and even that was thought unsuitable for women. As German composers took the lead in developing purely instrumental forms such as symphony and concerto, it was in German lands that some of the most renowned orchestras in Europe came into being.

Figure 16.3 A wind band consisting of two oboes, two clarinets, two horns, and two bassoons. Detail from an engraving of a company of grenadiers, published in London in 1753.

Figure 16.4 Frederick the Great playing the flute, accompanied by a small orchestra, with C. P. E. Bach at the harpsichord. Painting by Adolph von Menzel, 1852.
(Nationalgalerie, Berlin, Bildarchiv Preussischer Kulturbesitz/Art Resource, NY.)

music. In Paris, an important center of composition and publication in the mid-eighteenth century, symphonies flowed from the city's presses. Foreign composers flocked to the city, including Sammartini, Stamitz, and Wagenseil. The Belgian François-Joseph Gossec (1734–1829) came to Paris in 1751 and eventually established himself as one of France's leading composers of symphonies, string quartets, and comic operas. He became one of the most popular composers of the Revolutionary period and one of the first directors of the Paris Conservatoire.

The Empfindsam Style

Berlin was also a center of the *empfindsam*, or sentimental, style of composition (see page 302), which German composers began introducing into their instrumental music toward the middle of the century. Two of J. S. Bach's sons are important in this connection. The eldest, Wilhelm Friedemann (1710–1784), was a gifted organist and composer whose life ended in disappointment and poverty because he could not adjust to the demands of a successful musical career. Carl Philipp Emanuel, in contrast, was one of the most influential composers of his generation. Trained in music by his father, he served at the court of Frederick the Great in Berlin from 1740 to 1768 and then became music director of the five principal churches in Hamburg. His compositions include oratorios, songs, symphonies, concertos, and chamber music; but most numerous and important are his works for keyboard. In 1742, he published a set of six sonatas (the *Prussian* Sonatas) and, in 1744, another set of six (the *Württemberg* Sonatas). These sonatas were new in style and strongly influenced later composers. His favorite keyboard instrument was not the harpsichord but the softer, more intimate clavichord, which had a capacity for delicate dynamic shadings. The clavichord enjoyed a spell of renewed popularity in Germany around the middle of the eighteenth century before both it and the harpsichord were gradually supplanted by the pianoforte, invented around 1700 by the Italian Bartolomeo Cristofori. The last five sets of C. P. E. Bach's sonatas

Example 16.2 C. P. E. Bach, Sonata in A major, second movement

(1780–1787) were written with the pianoforte chiefly in mind, as were many of the later keyboard pieces of W. F. Bach. This instrument, ancestor of the modern piano and now commonly called the "fortepiano," permitted the player to vary the loudness from *piano* to *forte* by controlling through touch the impact the hammer makes as it strikes the string.

The main characteristics of *empfindsam* style, of which C. P. E. Bach was a leading exponent, are apparent in the second movement, Poco Adagio, of the fourth sonata of his *Sonaten für Kenner und Liebhaber* (Sonatas for Connoisseurs and Amateurs; composed in 1765 but not published until 1779; NAWM 114). It begins with a long melodic sigh, a singing motive ending in an appoggiatura and its resolution, followed by a rest, all in the first measure (Example 16.2). This opening gesture is decorated with a turn, Scotch snaps (the short-long dotted rhythms on beat 2), and a trill. The great variety of constantly changing rhythmic patterns—short dotted figures, triplets, asymmetrical flourishes of five and thirteen notes—and the unusual key of F-sharp minor give the music a restless, melancholy quality. The abundant ornaments serve expressive rather than merely decorative ends, characteristic of *Empfindsamkeit*.

C. P. E. Bach

Full 🔊   Concise 🔊

Figure 16.5 A private performance by a chamber ensemble consisting of a singer, two violins, viola, cello, and harpsichord. The presence of a woman at the keyboard and the similarity of dress and wigs worn by the musicians and listeners indicate that the performers were most likely skilled amateurs rather than professionals, who would have been dressed in servants' livery. Engraving of 1769 by Daniel Nicolaus Chodowiecki.

The *empfindsam* style of C. P. E. Bach and his contemporaries often exploited the element of surprise, with abrupt shifts of harmony, unconventional modulations, unusual turns of melody, suspenseful pauses, changes of texture, sudden *sforzando* accents, and the like. The subjective, emotional qualities of this *Empfindsamkeit* reached a climax during the 1760s and 1770s. The trend is

Sturm und Drang

sometimes described by the expression *Sturm und Drang*—"storm and stress"—a movement in German literature that relished tormented, gloomy, terrified, irrational feelings. Later, composers moderated this emotionalism, but its characteristics resurfaced in some instrumental music, to be discussed in the next chapter.

Concerto

Johann Christian Bach

An important composer in many genres, Johann Christian Bach (1735–1782; Figure 16.6), J. S. Bach's youngest son, was among the first to compose piano concertos. After being trained in music by his father and his elder brother C. P. E. Bach, Johann Christian made his way to Milan at the age of twenty. He studied with the celebrated theorist, teacher, and composer Padre Giovanni Battista Martini (1706–1784) of Bologna. Bach was appointed organist of the cathedral at Milan in 1760, by which time he had converted from Lutheranism to Roman Catholicism. Two years later, after two of his operas had been produced successfully in Naples, he moved to London, where he enjoyed a long career as composer, performer, teacher, and impresario. He had great success there with some forty keyboard concertos, written between 1763 and 1777. The title of his Op. 7 (ca. 1770), *Sei concerti per il cembalo o piano e forte* (Six Concertos for Harpsichord or Pianoforte), bears witness to his early adoption of the pianoforte for public performance. The eight-year-old Mozart spent a year in London (1764–1765), during which time he met Bach and was very much impressed with his music. Mozart later converted three of Bach's keyboard sonatas into concertos (K. 107/21b) and must have had Bach's models in mind when he wrote his first piano concerto (K. 175) in 1773.

The first movement of Bach's Concerto for Harpsichord or Piano and Strings in E, Op. 7, No. 5 (NAWM 117), illustrates many features typical of the concerto at this time. It retains elements of the ritornello structure and textural contrasts of the Baroque period but is imbued with the contrasts of key and thematic material characteristic of the sonata. To demonstrate these parallels, Figure 16.7 aligns the elements of ritornello form and sonata form with the first movement of Bach's concerto, outlined in the right-hand column. (The figure uses the nineteenth-century terminology for sonata form, although the sections match Koch's three periods; compare Figure 16.1.) The Baroque plan of alternating ritornellos and episodes is clearly reflected in Bach's concerto, yet the three solo "episodes," in which the soloist takes the lead and the orchestra provides accompaniment and punctuation, resemble the exposition, development, and recapitulation of sonata form. The only long ritornello is the first, which introduces most of the movement's material in the tonic. In some modern views of concerto first-movement form, this is called the "orchestral exposition," followed by the "solo exposition," while the second and third solos are compared to the "development" and "recapitulation" sections of the mature Classic sonata form (outlined in the second column of Figure 16.7 and further discussed in the next chapter). The later ritornellos can use any element from the first one, and here Bach mostly uses the closing theme.

Figure 16.6 Johann Christian Bach, J. S. Bach's youngest son, known as "the London Bach," in a painting by the famous English portrait artist Thomas Gainsborough.

(National Portrait Gallery, London. Scala/Art Resource, NY.)

Ritornello Form		Late-Eighteenth-Century Sonata Form		Form of J. C. Bach Movement	
SECTION	KEY	SECTION	KEY	SECTION	KEY
Ritornello	I			Ritornello ("Orchestral Exposition")	
				First theme	I
				Transition	I
				Second theme	I
				Closing theme	I
Episode	mod	Exposition		Solo ("Solo Exposition")	
		First theme	I	First theme	I
		Transition	mod	Transition, extended with new ideas	mod
		Second theme	V	Second theme	V
		Closing theme	V	Closing theme varied	V
Ritornello	V			Ritornello	
				Closing theme abbreviated	V
Episode	mod	Development	mod	Solo ("Development")	mod
Ritornello	X			(Ritornello)	
				Brief orchestral cadence	on V
Episode	mod	Recapitulation		Solo ("Recapitulation")	
		First theme	I	First theme	I
		Transition	mod	Transition, altered	I
		Second theme	I	Second theme	I
		Closing theme	I	Closing theme varied	I
				Cadenza	
Ritornello	I			Ritornello	
				Closing theme	I

Figure 16.7 Concerto first-movement form in J. C. Bach's Op. 7, No. 5, compared with ritornello and sonata forms.

By Bach's time, it had become traditional for the soloist to play a cadenza, usually improvised, just before the final orchestral ritornello. The cadenza developed from the trills and runs that singers inserted, particularly before the return of the opening section, in a da capo aria. By convention, concerto cadenzas are typically introduced by a weighty $^6_4$ chord, and the soloist signals the orchestra to reenter by playing a long trill over a dominant chord.

The parallels between this movement and Mozart's concerto, K. 488 (see Chapter 17) are striking though not surprising, since, by 1770, the main outlines of the first-movement form for the solo concerto were well established.

Cadenza

POSTLUDE

We saw in the sixteenth and seventeenth centuries how composers and performers of instrumental music imitated and adapted elements of vocal music, and in the process created works of greater expressivity, meaningfulness, interest, and independence than ever before. Musicians in the eighteenth century embraced

At the Time

In **1770,** at the time of Beethoven's birth to an obscure musician in the town of Bonn, Germany,

- Marie Antoinette, youngest daughter of empress Maria Theresa, ruler of the Holy Roman Empire (Figure IV.2), is sent from her home in Vienna to marry (at age 14) the future king Louis XVI in Paris. The pair will be beheaded before the end of the century in the aftermath of the French Revolution.
- Operas in Italian by Gluck and Hasse continue to meet the approval of audiences in Vienna and elsewhere.
- The Italian diva Francesca Cuzzoni, star of operas by Handel and Hasse whose fame once rivaled that of Faustina Bordoni (Figure 15.4), now in her seventies, lives in obscure poverty in Bologna, supporting herself by making buttons.
- In Paris, subscribers attend symphony concerts given by the newly founded Concert des Amateurs, soon to become one of Europe's finest orchestras. Among the violinists is the composer and swordsman Chevalier de Saint Georges, the son of a Guadeloupe planter and his African slave, who will make his debut as a soloist with the orchestra in a few years.
- The Enlightenment author and wit Voltaire writes: "If God did not exist it would be necessary to invent him."
- Captain James Cook first reaches Australia and claims it in the name of King George III of England.
- A leading figure in the musical life of London, Johann Christian Bach (Figure 16.6) publishes his Op. 7, a set of six concertos for keyboard and strings, and no doubt performs them himself at public concerts in the British capital. (NAWM 117)
- Britain's thirteen American colonies have an estimated population of 2.2 million people, an increase of more than half a million over the last decade. In Boston, Massachusetts, William Billings publishes the first collection of music by an American composer, his *New England Psalm Singer* (Figure 15.7). Although he will die in poverty, in part because there are not yet copyright laws to protect his most popular songs, which spread southward and westward through America, he will experience a revival and will be inducted into the Songwriters' Hall of Fame in two hundred years.
- The "Boston Massacre," in which British Army soldiers kill five civilians and injure six others, foreshadows the outbreak of the American Revolution.
- The English portrait artist Thomas Gainsborough completes his oil painting *The Blue Boy* (Figure 16.8), perhaps his most famous work, which will be purchased in 1921 by the American railway pioneer Henry Huntington for ca. $700,000; it will eventually hang in his collection at the Huntingdon Library in San Marino, California, and be worth approximately $7 million.

Figure 16.8 Thomas Gainsborough, The Blue Boy.
(Francis G. Mayer/Corbis.)

the same idea, bringing instrumental music to new heights. Composers absorbed the new styles pioneered in opera and vocal music and blended them with existing traditions within each instrumental repertory. New genres, including the piano sonata and symphony, as well as new forms like sonata form and first-movement concerto form, were consolidated and later became the basis for much instrumental music. Still, in all of them, melody was paramount.

The instrumental music of this era was designed to appeal to a wide variety of people, to be understood on first hearing, and above all to please its performers and listeners. The tremendous numbers of new pieces show that they found ready audiences among middle- and upper-class amateurs and concertgoers (see Innovations, pages 358–359). These numbers also confirm that consumers were eager for new music. Most of the vast quantities of instrumental music composed and published during this time passed from the stage fairly quickly, displaced by new works and styles, like popular music of later centuries.

Because of the way the history of music has been told, emphasizing Bach and Handel as paragons of Baroque music and Haydn and Mozart as masters of the Classical style, the music of the middle eighteenth century, by composers such as Domenico Scarlatti and C. P. E. Bach, is often seen merely as transitional. But this music was of great importance to its performers and listeners, as made evident by the flood of writings and discussions about music by everyone from professional musicians to merchants and monarchs. From their own perspective, musicians of the time were engaged in a vigorous argument about musical taste and style, and in a constant search to gratify their growing audiences.

 Resources for study and review available at wwnorton.com/studyspace

The Late Eighteenth Century: Haydn and Mozart

PRELUDE

Classicism, nurtured by the Enlightenment, reached its peak in the late eighteenth century. This was also the age of "enlightened" rulers like Joseph II (r. 1765–1790), who fostered the liberal atmosphere in cosmopolitan Vienna that continued to attract artists and musicians from all over Europe, among them (Franz) Joseph Haydn (1732–1809) and Wolfgang Amadeus Mozart (1756–1791), the two most remarkable composers of the late eighteenth century. Both men experienced the currents that led up to the French Revolution, and Haydn lived to see the changes that began to unfold in its wake. They were also personal friends even though Haydn was the elder by twenty-four years. They were both practicing musicians—Mozart a virtuoso pianist and highly skilled string player, Haydn a fine violinist who also conducted from the harpsichord—and each admired and was influenced by the music of the other. And, most important historically, they both composed prolifically and excelled at reaching a diverse audience.

Their lives and careers also diverged in many ways, which helps to explain some significant differences in their respective compositional styles and output. Haydn, born during J. S. Bach's lifetime, lived to the ripe old age of seventy-seven. Mozart, born in 1756, died in the prime of his life, at the age of thirty-five. Haydn's growth to artistic maturity was much slower than that of Mozart, a child prodigy whose star rose quickly and burned brightly for only a few decades. Haydn worked loyally during most of his career in the service of a noble Hungarian family; Mozart, craving the celebrity and adulation he had earned as a boy, gave up a steady job in his hometown of Salzburg to become a free agent in Vienna. Most importantly, Mozart traveled a great deal in his early years—to England, Italy, Germany, and France—and absorbed the many styles and practices current in these countries, whereas Haydn found his models within local traditions around Vienna.

Because Haydn remained in the same job for so long, his career does not easily divide itself into distinct periods. We will, therefore, discuss his works according to genre: first his instrumental music, where he made his most original contribution, and then his vocal works, which include operas, oratorios, and masses. By contrast, Mozart moved around a lot, and each new location brought new opportunities for composition. Therefore, we will discuss his works chronologically and geographically, grouping them generally into his years in Salzburg and then Vienna, even though he did not confine his activities solely to these cities.

(Franz) Joseph Haydn (1732–1809)

Haydn (see Biography, page 340) spent nearly thirty years at the court of Prince Paul Anton Eszterházy and his brother Nikolaus under circumstances that were ideal for his development as a composer. Although later in life he filled commissions from others and traveled extensively, his years at Eszterháza had a formative influence on his career.

The remote country estate of Eszterháza was designed to rival the splendor of the French court at Versailles; the palace and grounds boasted two theaters, one for opera and one for puppet plays, and two large and sumptuously decorated music rooms in the palace itself (see Figure 17.1). Haydn was required to compose whatever music the prince demanded, to conduct the performances, to train and supervise all the musical personnel, and to keep the instruments in repair (see Vignette, page 343). He built up the orchestra to about twenty-five players. Operas and concerts became weekly events, and almost every day in the prince's private apartments chamber music was heard. The prince himself usually played the baryton, an instrument resembling a large viola da gamba with an extra set of resonating metal strings (see Figure 17.3). Haydn wrote some 165 pieces for the baryton, mostly trios with viola and cello.

Music at Eszterháza

Figure 17.1 In this hall in the Eszterháza Palace, near Eisenstadt, where the Viennese court spent the summer, Haydn (from around 1768) conducted his symphonies while playing the first violin.
(Erich Lessing/Art Resource, NY.)

(Franz) Joseph Haydn (1732–1809)

HAYDN! Great Sovereign of the tuneful art!
Thy works alone supply an ample chart
Of all the mountains, seas, and fertile plains
Within the compass of its wide domains. —

So wrote the celebrated music historian Charles Burney in 1791 on Haydn's arrival in England. Indeed, Haydn was hailed in his time as the greatest composer alive. In public life, he exemplified the Enlightenment ideals of good character, piety, and kindness. He was also an ambitious entrepreneur and skillful businessman, capable of both seriousness and humor, and he devoted his enormous talent to satisfying his patrons and pleasing his audiences.

Born in Rohrau, a village about thirty miles southeast of Vienna, Haydn became a choirboy at age seven at Saint Stephen's Cathedral in Vienna, where he acquired practical experience in music and learned singing, harpsichord, and violin. Dismissed at seventeen when his voice changed, Haydn barely supported himself as a freelance musician, composer, and teacher. He mastered counterpoint using Fux's *Gradus ad Parnassum*, studied the music of other composers, and took composition lessons from Nicola Porpora, a famous Italian composer and singing teacher who had been Handel's rival in London.

Figure 17.2 Joseph Haydn, in an oil portrait by Thomas Hardy, painted in 1791–1792 during Haydn's first sojourn in London.
(Royal College of Music, London.)

Haydn became music director for Count Morzin in about 1757 and probably wrote his first symphonies for the count's orchestra. Three years later, he married a wigmaker's daughter, Maria Anna Keller, although he was really in love with her sister, who became a nun; his long marriage was unhappy, childless, and marked by extramarital affairs on both sides.

In 1761, Haydn entered the service of a Hungarian prince, Paul Anton Esterházy, and continued in the family's service for the rest of his life. For years, Haydn was responsible for composing on demand, presenting concerts or operas weekly, and assisting with almost daily chamber music. While the position forced him to compose at a prodigious rate, it also provided a laboratory in which he could try out new ideas. In Haydn's words,

> My prince was pleased with all my work, I received applause, and as conductor of an orchestra I could make experiments, observe what strengthened and what weakened an effect and thus improve, substitute, make cuts, and take risks; I was isolated from the world; no one in my vicinity could make me lose confidence in myself or bother me, and so I had to become original.[1]

The publication of Haydn's music brought him praise and fame throughout Europe and generated commissions from many other patrons. Between 1790 and 1795, he made two extended trips to London, where he had long been famous, to compose, give concerts, and teach. His triumphs in London raised his reputation at home, and he was invited to return to Vienna as court music director for Prince Nikolaus Esterházy II with minimal duties. During his last decade, his health declined and he composed very little. He died a rich man at age seventy-seven in 1809, at which time he was still universally admired.

Major works: 104 symphonies, 20 concertos, 68 string quartets, 29 keyboard trios, 126 baryton trios, 47 keyboard sonatas, 15 operas, 12 masses, *The Creation, The Seasons*, numerous other ensemble, keyboard, and vocal works.

1. Trans., Elaine Sisman, in "Haydn, Shakespeare, and the Rules of Originality," in Elaine Sisman, ed., *Haydn and His World* (Princeton: Princeton University Press, 1997), p. 3.

Figure 17.3 This baryton, shown leaning against its case, was owned by Prince Nikolaus Esterházy. The instrument, a favorite of the prince's, resembled a bass viol but had a set of sympathetic strings that could also be plucked simultaneously, creating additional notes and adding to its resonance. Haydn composed a baryton repertory of some 165 pieces so that the prince could participate in chamber music.

(Hungarian National Museum, Budapest.)

Although Eszterháza was isolated, Haydn kept abreast of current developments in the world of music through the constant stream of distinguished visitors and through occasional trips to Vienna, where he met Mozart around 1784. He had the double advantage of a devoted, highly skilled troupe of singers and players and an intelligent patron, who demanded a great deal but whose understanding of and enthusiasm for music were inspiring.

Haydn's Instrumental Works

Although Haydn's long career as a composer reflected the changing tastes of the times and his works explored a variety of genres, certain enduring traits stand out in his music.

Haydn's style drew on many sources—among them folk, galant, *empfindsam*, and learned Baroque styles—yet was recognized in his time as highly individual. He made his music appealing by following conventions for phrasing, form, and harmony, but also by introducing the unexpected. In this way, he forged a unique combination of simplicity and sophistication to which he sometimes added large doses of musical wit and humor or evocations of the sublime (see page 352). Furthermore, although Haydn's music may sound simple and natural, it was not produced without effort. According to his own report, he began a composition by improvising at the keyboard. After devising a satisfactory theme, he worked out the piece more fully and then committed it to paper, usually writing down only the main melody and harmony on one or two staves. Finally, he wrote out the completed score. This process combined spontaneity and calculation as Haydn first searched for something to say and then determined the most effective way to say it.

Haydn's style
and compositional
process

Symphonies

Overview of the
symphonies

Haydn has been called "the father of the symphony," not because he invented the genre but because his symphonies established the standard for later composers through their high quality, wide dissemination, and lasting appeal. Of his more than 100 symphonies, at least 92 were completed by 1789, most of them for Prince Esterházy's orchestra. Beginning about 1768, they were performed in the palatial concert room shown in Figure 17.1, with Haydn leading the orchestra while playing the violin. During the 1780s, he composed six symphonies (Nos. 82–87), now known as the *Paris* Symphonies, on commission for a concert series in the French capital. His last twelve, the *London* symphonies (Nos. 93–104), were written during the 1790s for a concert series organized by impresario and violinist Johann Peter Salomon in that city. Many of his symphonies that have acquired nicknames for one reason or another—few of them given by the composer himself—are among the best known.

Symphonic form

Most of Haydn's earliest symphonies were typically three-movement works (fast, slow, fast), a form derived from the Italian opera overture (sinfonia). Other symphonies from the early period are in four movements, all in the same key, recalling the slow-fast-slow-fast sequence of the sonata da chiesa. During the late 1760s, however, Haydn established the four-movement pattern described here as the standard for the Classic era: I—Allegro (a lively sonata-form movement, often with a slow introduction); II—Andante moderato (a slow movement); III—Minuet and Trio; IV—Allegro (a fast finale, usually in sonata or rondo form).

The typical symphony generally demanded the most attention from its audience in its first movement. The first-movement or sonata form described here is only an abstract design that matches symphonic first movements by Haydn to varying degrees. Its basic outline derives from the nineteenth-century view of the form as a three-part structure, which in turn is based on the eighteenth-century's expanded binary form, first presented as Figure 16.1. Their outlines are compared in Figure 17.4. The opening movement of Symphony No. 88 in G Major, composed in 1787 (NAWM 119), illustrates many of the most common features of sonata form discussed below.

First-movement form

A typical first-movement Allegro may be compared to a drama: it presents a set of sympathetic characters, involves them in an interesting plot (exposition), introduces some complications (development), and then resolves the resulting tension in a satisfying way (recapitulation). This musical drama unfolds

EIGHTEENTH-CENTURY VIEW; EXPANDED BINARY FORM

FIRST SECTION	SECOND SECTION	
One Main Period Key: ‖: I - V :‖	First Main Period ‖: V - on V	Second Main Period I - I :‖

NINETEENTH-CENTURY VIEW; TERNARY FORM (ABA')

EXPOSITION	DEVELOPMENT	RECAPITULATION
Key: ‖: I - V :‖	mod on V	I - I
Themes: 1T tr 2T CT		1T tr 2T CT

Figure 17.4 Views of first-movement form. In this diagram, 1T = first theme group, 2T = second theme group, tr = transitional material, and CT = closing theme.

VIGNETTE Haydn's Contract

When he entered the service of Prince Paul Anton Esterházy, Haydn was named Vice-Kapellmeister, allowing the elderly Kapellmeister to retain his title but giving Haydn sole direction of orchestral, chamber, and dramatic music. His contract, excerpted below, spells out his duties and his social standing as a house officer, higher than that of a servant yet still required to wear the court uniform. On the death of the Kapellmeister in 1766, Haydn succeeded to the title. The limits in clause 4 on circulating his music to others were later relaxed, and he earned both fame and money through performances and publications elsewhere.

2. The said Joseph Heyden [sic] shall be considered and treated as a member of the household. Therefore his Serene Highness is graciously pleased to place confidence in his conducting himself as becomes an honorable official of a princely house. He must be temperate, not showing himself overbearing toward his musicians, but mild and lenient, straightforward and composed. It is especially to be observed that when the orchestra shall be summoned to perform before company, the Vice-Capellmeister [namely, Haydn] and all the musicians shall appear in uniform, and the said Joseph Heyden shall take care that he and all the members of his orchestra follow the instructions given, and appear in white stockings, white linen, powdered, and with either a pigtail or a tiewig. . . .

4. The said Vice-Capellmeister shall be under obligation to compose such music as his Serene Highness may command, and neither to communicate such compositions to any other person, nor to allow them to be copied, but he shall retain them for the absolute use of his Highness, and not compose for any other person without the knowledge and permission of his Highness.

5. The said Joseph Heyden shall appear daily in the antechamber before and after midday, and inquire whether his Highness is pleased to order a performance of the orchestra. On receipt of his orders he shall communicate them to the other musicians, and take care to be punctual at the appointed time, and to ensure punctuality in his subordinates. . . .

7. The said Vice-Capellmeister shall take careful charge of all music and musical instruments, and be responsible for any injury that may occur to them from carelessness or neglect.

8. The said Joseph Heyden shall be obliged to instruct the female vocalists, in order that they may not forget in the country what they have been taught with much trouble and expense in Vienna, and, as the said Vice-Capellmeister is proficient on various instruments, he shall take care himself to practice on all that he is acquainted with.

Trans. in Karl Geiringer, *Haydn: A Creative Life in Music* (New York: Norton, 1946), pp. 52–53.

---

through a series of alternating stable and unstable periods. The stable periods—the statements of the first, second, and closing theme groups, which coincide with the establishment of a tonic and a second, closely related key—are usually presented in balanced four-measure phrases and are clearly set off by cadences, at least in the early symphonies. A combination of string and wind ensembles presents the thematic ideas. The unstable passages, mainly the transition and development, are often scored for full orchestra and are characterized by bustling rhythmic energy, sequences, modulatory twists and turns, overlapping phrases, and avoidance of cadences. Slow introductions, when they occur, are usually unstable from the outset and often create a solemn, suspenseful mood that makes the ensuing Allegro seem bright and energetic by comparison (see NAWM 119a).

In the exposition of a typical Allegro movement, Haydn reiterates the opening statement immediately but with some destabilizing turns of harmony or rhythm that steer the music in a new direction. A transition or bridge to the dominant or relative major follows. The transition is usually a loud passage with

Full 🔊   Concise 🔊

Exposition

dramatic, rushing figures, a perfect foil for the second thematic section, which is more lightly scored, melodically distinctive, and harmonically stable. In most of his symphonies of the 1770s and 1780s, Haydn clearly contrasted the secondary material (2T) with the opening idea (1T). But in some, as in No. 88 (NAWM 119a) and the later *London* symphonies, Haydn built the second thematic section on the opening material, albeit sometimes with significant alteration, resulting in a compact and sophisticated monothematic movement. The exposition usually ends with a closing section (CT) for full orchestra based on a cadential, repetitive, vigorous figure, sometimes harking back to the opening, as in No. 88, but usually distinct from the primary and secondary subjects. In some of the movements, the section in the second key is devoted entirely to the closing material.

Development

Haydn rarely introduced new thematic ideas after the exposition's closing double bar. The development, where most of the "complication" occurs, often begins with a restatement of the opening subject, or sometimes with transitional material or with one of the other subjects. Motives from the exposition are combined, superimposed, extended, and manipulated in many other ways. Abrupt changes of subject, digressions, and sudden silences are particularly characteristic of Haydn's developments. He also often enriched them through the use of counterpoint, which brought the older learned style into works of the more modern galant style. In the course of his career, Haydn increased the length and artfulness of the development section until it roughly equaled the other sections of the sonata form, providing an appropriate counterweight to them.

Recapitulation

We are usually well prepared for the recapitulation, often because its onset is dramatized by an extended dominant pedal, but Haydn sometimes disguises or plays down its arrival so that we may not immediately recognize that it has begun. Frequently, the opening statement is rescored or extended in new ways, such as by introducing counterpoint where there was none in the exposition. The recapitulation section reprises all of the material from the exposition in the tonic, although sometimes a theme originally in the major mode may return in the minor or vice versa. Also, instead of curtailing the transition because he does not need to modulate, Haydn likes to intensify and animate it by simulating a modulation. Furthermore, he sometimes emphasizes the secondary and closing themes in his recapitulations.

Second movement

The second movement of a Haydn symphony almost always offers an oasis of calm and gentle melody after the contrasts, drama, and complexity of the first movement. Many of the slow movements are in sonata form without repeats. In later works Haydn often used theme-and-variation form, as in the *Largo* of Symphony No. 88 (NAMW 119b), where Haydn surprises the listener by suddenly introducing trumpets and drums in one of the variations, instruments which have until now been silent in this symphony.

Minuet and trio

The third movement provides another type of contrast since it is shorter than either of the first two movements, it is in a more popular style, and its form is easy for listeners to follow. It comprises a pair of stylized minuets, with the first repeated after the second (the trio) to create an ABA form. The minuet itself is always in a two-part (binary or rounded binary) form—‖: a :‖: b (a′) :‖. The trio is built along similar lines; it is usually in the same key as the minuet (possibly with a change of mode), but it is shorter with lighter orchestration, sometimes reduced to a three-part texture, and it has its own thematic content—‖: c :‖: d (c′) :‖. After the trio, the minuet returns da capo, resulting in a three-section ABA form for the movement as a whole. The very directness of the form, however, allowed Haydn to introduce interest and humor. In Symphony No. 88, for example (NAWM 119c), the minuet is a boisterous affair, resembling a dance at a peasant wedding, with drums softly punctuating the end of each half. The rustic mood persists in the B section or Trio with its drone bass imitating the sound of bagpipes and its quirky, off-beat accents suggesting

Full 🔊 Concise 🔊

Full 🔊

Full 🔊

Example 17.1 Haydn, Symphony No. 88 in G Major, Trio

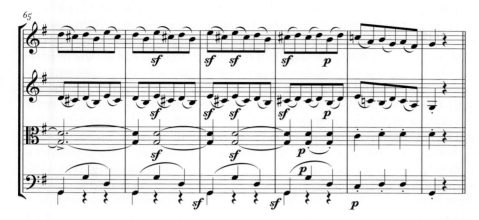

the missteps of awkward dancers (see Example 17.1). Haydn's minuet and trio movements contain some of his most charming music and are remarkable for their wealth of musical ideas, harmonic invention, and instrumental color—all happy traits in such a modest form.

After the easygoing minuet, the fourth and final movement closes the symphony with a new buildup of tension, a climax, and then a release. The finale is typically faster and shorter than the first movement, overflowing with high spirits and impish surprises. While many of Haydn's finales are in sonata form, in symphonies from the 1770s on, he favored rondo finales, a form in which the main theme, usually itself a small complete binary form, alternates with several contrasting thematic sections, often in the pattern ABACABA. Some are sonata-rondos, as is the finale of Symphony No. 88 (NAWM 119d), in which the A and B sections resemble the first and second theme groups in a sonata-form exposition, C is a modulatory development passage, and B returns near the end in the tonic.

Finale

Full 🔊

Haydn's Symphonic Compositions

The symphonies of 1768–1772 show Haydn as a composer with a mature technique and fertile imagination. No longer viewing the symphony as light entertainment or as a delightful overture to an opera, Haydn now regarded it as a serious work that demanded close listening. The deeply emotional and agitated character of some of these symphonies, particularly those in minor keys, has been associated with the literary movement known as *Sturm und Drang* ("storm and stress"). Many are longer, more rhythmically complex, more contrapuntal, and more dramatic than his earlier symphonies. They are marked by abrupt contrasts between loud and soft, with more crescendos and *sforzati*, all used to startling effect. The harmonic palette is richer than in the early symphonies, and modulations range more widely.

In the next group of symphonies, beginning around 1773, Haydn turned from minor keys and passionate accents to a more cheerful style, influenced by his comic operas. However, since audiences expected symphonies to be not only appealing and easy to understand but also serious, ambitious, stirring, and impressive, reflecting the esteem with which the genre was regarded in the 1770s, Haydn met these expectations with works like his Symphony No. 56 in C Major (1774), which is festive and brilliant. Like others in C major, No. 56 uses high trumpets and timpani but also encompasses a broad emotional range: the agitation characteristic of the *Sturm und Drang* style now contrasts with more stable, songlike phrases.

1768–1772

Sturm und Drang

1773–1788

Paris symphonies

In the 1780s, Haydn increasingly composed for the public, selling his symphonies to patrons or publishers abroad. The six *Paris* symphonies of 1785–1786, his grandest so far, were commissioned for the large orchestra of the Concerts de la Loge Olympique, consisting of flute, two oboes, two bassoons, two horns, and strings, occasionally augmented by trumpets and timpani. Queen Marie Antoinette is said to have loved especially Symphony No. 85, subsequently called *La Reine* (The Queen). After all six (Nos. 82–87) were performed again in 1787, this time at the Concert spirituel, a reviewer noted how "this great genius could draw such rich and varied developments from a single subject, so different from the sterile composers who pass continually from one idea to another."

Symphonies
No. 88–92

Symphonies No. 88 to 92, written in 1787 and 1788, were also composed on commission; the last of this group, No. 92, accompanied Haydn to Oxford University a few years later, when he was awarded an honorary degree. Like the *Paris* Symphonies, they offer deep expression combined with masterful technique, and a mixture of popular and learned styles that gave them wide, immediate, and lasting appeal.

London symphonies

Soon after Prince Nikolaus died in September 1790, the enterprising musician and impresario Johann Peter Salomon appeared on Haydn's doorstep, announcing, "I am Salomon of London and have come to fetch you." Thus began the greatest adventure of Haydn's life—two separate concert seasons of symphonies that Haydn composed and conducted for cosmopolitan London audiences. Hailed by the British as "the greatest composer in the world," he was determined to live up to expectations, and the twelve *London* Symphonies (Nos. 93–104) are indeed his crowning achievements. Everything he had learned in forty years went into them. While he did not depart radically from his previous works, he brought all the elements together on a grander scale, with more brilliant orchestration (now including trumpets, timpani, and clarinets), more daring harmonic conceptions, more intense rhythmic drive, and, especially, more memorable thematic inventions.

Special effects

Haydn's shrewd appraisal of London's musical tastes is evident. The sudden *fortissimo* crash on a weak beat in the slow movement of Symphony No. 94 has given this work its nickname, *Surprise*; it was put there because, as Haydn later acknowledged, he wanted something novel and startling to take people's minds off the rival concerts of his former pupil Ignaz Pleyel (1757–1831). The greater tunefulness may also have been prompted by this competition since Pleyel's strong suit was melody. Haydn turned to Slovenian, Croatian, and other peasant tunes that he remembered from his youth. Symphony No. 103 displays characteristic instances of folklike melodies, and the finale of Symphony No. 104, with its imitation of the bagpipe, suggests a peasant dance. Similar allusions are the "Turkish"-band effect (triangle, cymbals, bass drum) and the trumpet fanfare in the Allegretto of the *Military* Symphony (No. 100), and the ticking accompaniment in the Andante of Symphony No. 101 (the *Clock*). Haydn always aimed to please the casual music lover as well as the expert, and it is a measure of his greatness that he succeeded in delighting both.

The String Quartets

By the time Haydn was forty, his reputation as the first great master of the string quartet was assured. Unlike symphonies, which were often performed by professionals for a paying or invited audience, string quartets were primarily for amateurs to play for their own pleasure. Haydn's mature quartets are very much addressed to the players, who all share in the conversation among the instruments: the first violin plays the leading role, but the cello and inner parts often carry the melody or engage in dialogue. The evolution of Haydn's sixty-eight

Example 17.2 Joseph Haydn, String Quartet in G Major, Op. 33, No. 5, Scherzo

quartets parallels that of the symphonies in many respects—from early mastery, through increasing length and emotional depth, to completely individual late works.

Haydn tended to compose and publish his quartets in groups of six, which was common for printed collections in the eighteenth century. Opp. 9 (ca. 1770), 17 (1771), and 20 (1772) established for the quartet the same four-movement pattern as is found in the symphony, but with the minuet often before instead of after the slow movement. In the sonata-form movements, Haydn devised strategies unique to his quartets. After the first theme—almost always dominated by the first violin—he usually chose a looser texture in which the main motives pass from one instrument to another. In place of the passages for full orchestra that highlight the transitions in the symphonies, Haydn favored loud unisons or stark modulatory gestures. The development sections of the Op. 20 quartets are nearly equal in length to their expositions and recapitulations. Moreover, motives first presented in the exposition are developed over the entire movement, a procedure that Haydn followed throughout his career. Haydn systematically included at least one quartet in a minor key in each set of six, just as he used minor keys in the contemporary *Sturm und Drang* symphonies. Furthermore, three quartets from Op. 20 end with fugues, which suggests that Haydn was attempting to transcend the lighter, more galant style of writing for string quartet that had been fashionable in Paris during the 1760s.

Ten years went by before Haydn composed the six quartets of Op. 33 (1781) and advertised to potential subscribers that the works were written in a "quite new and special way." They are lighthearted, witty, and tuneful, perhaps influenced by Mozart's six quartets K. 168–173, which were published a few years earlier. One new feature is that the minuets, here entitled "Scherzo" (Italian for "joke" or "trick"), literally play tricks on the courtly dance by breaking the normal metrical pattern, as shown in Example 17.2.

Even apart from the Scherzos, Op. 33 contains some of Haydn's best strokes of wit and humor. One of three rondo finales in Op. 33 is the Presto of No. 2 (NAWM 118d), nicknamed *The Joke* because of enigmatic rests in a coda that "refuses" to end, and finally does so by using the same melodic gesture with which it began (see Example 17.3). But humor pervades the whole movement, as Haydn mischievously plays with the listener's expectations throughout. Not only are Haydn's themes playful in themselves, but the sparkling dialogue among players must have added merriment to the amateur-quartet evenings

Opp. 9, 17, and 20

Humor in Op. 33

Example 17.3 Joseph Haydn, String Quartet, Op. 33, No. 2, Presto, closing passage

that were held in cities such as London, Paris, and Vienna, in country houses of the nobility and upper classes, and even in monasteries (see Figure 17.5).

Later quartets   In his remaining years, Haydn composed another thirty-four quartets, of which the six of Op. 76 (1797) exemplify a new approach to the quartet as a genre for performance in concerts, alongside its traditional role in private music-making. As in his later symphonies, Haydn frequently began the second thematic area by repeating the first theme in the new key and used the closing section to inject contrast. He also expanded the harmonic frontiers, foreshadow-

Figure 17.5 Table for playing string quartets, from about 1790. With the tabletop (in the background) removed and the music racks raised (as shown here), the four players face one another, ideally positioned to listen to each other and engage in the "conversation" that string-quartet playing was thought to embody.

(Kunsthistorisches Museum, Vienna.)

ing Romantic harmony in his use of chromatic progressions and chords, enharmonic changes, and fanciful tonal shifts. The minuets of Op. 76, while less playful than those of Op. 33, are full of offbeat accents, "extra" measures, exaggerated leaps, and other satirical features such as the incongruous canon of No. 2 (Example 17.4), with its clumsy five- and six-bar phrases, that completely contradicts the graceful essence of this dignified dance. In contrast to such moments of drollery, however, is the beautiful theme and variations that constitute the slow movement of Op. 76, No. 3. Haydn composed the melody (Example 17.5) as a

Example 17.4 Joseph Haydn, String Quartet Op. 76, No. 2, Menuetto

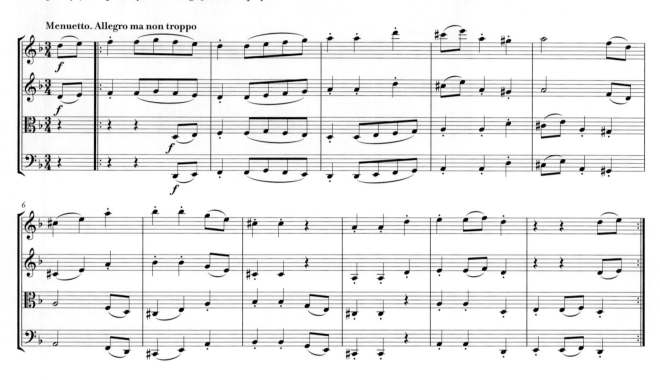

Example 17.5 Joseph Haydn, Gott erhalte Franz den Kaiser (hymn)

May God preserve Franz, the Kaiser/Our good Kaiser Franz!/Long may he live/in fortune's bright light!/The climbing laurel blooms for him/Bestowing him with wreaths of honor wherever he goes./May God preserve Franz, the Kaiser/Our good Kaiser Franz!

Figure 17.6 George, Earl of Cowper, with the Family of Charles Gore, *1775, by Johann Zoffany, showing a square piano and a cello. Such pianos were the main domestic musical instrument from the 1760s through the mid-nineteenth century.*
(Yale Center for British Art, Paul Mellon Collection/Bridgeman Art Library.)

birthday tribute to Kaiser Franz, but its memorable phrases later became the national anthem of the Austro-Hungarian Empire and serve to this day as the German national anthem. Like his late symphonies, then, Haydn's late quartets marvelously juxtapose the serious with the jocular, the artful with the folksy, and the complex with the simple.

Keyboard Sonatas

Haydn's early keyboard sonatas can be performed on a harpsichord, allowing for only certain changes in dynamics. His later sonatas, however, call for the performer to realize dynamic markings such as *sforzando* and *crescendo*, sudden accents, and other variations of touch that require a pianoforte. Haydn used a clavichord in his early years, but by 1780 he had a piano available. The authorized contemporary printed editions of the sonatas after 1780 give "fortepiano" or "pianoforte" as the first option, along with "clavicembalo" (usually meaning harpsichord).

Haydn's piano sonatas follow the same lines of development observed in the symphonies and quartets. Written for amateurs to play in private, they usually featured three movements in fast-slow-fast format and focused on the expression of intimate or sentimental feelings, befitting their private character and their intended middle class audience.

Haydn's Vocal Works

In a modest autobiographical sketch written for an Austrian encyclopedia in 1776, Haydn named his most successful works: three operas, an Italian oratorio, and his setting of the *Stabat Mater* (1767)—a work well known in Europe in the 1780s. He made no mention of the sixty-odd symphonies he had written by then and referred to his chamber music only to complain that the Berlin critics dealt with it too harshly. Haydn may have been reticent about the symphonies because they were little known outside Eszterháza. Also, as a child of the Baroque era, he believed that vocal music was more important than instrumental music. It was not until his symphonies and string quartets were so enthusiastically received in Paris and London during the 1780s and 1790s that he realized how highly regarded they were. By the early nineteenth century, Haydn's reputation rested primarily on his instrumental works.

Eszterháza was an international center for opera (see Figure 17.7), despite its remote location, and Haydn spent much of his time and energy on opera while he worked there. Between 1769 and 1790, he arranged, prepared, and conducted some seventy-five operas by other composers. Of his own fifteen or more Italian operas, most were comic, with music abounding in humor and high spirits. He also composed three serious operas, of which the most famous was the "heroic drama" *Armida* (1784), remarkable for its dramatic accompanied recitatives and arias on a grand scale. Although successful in their day, Haydn's operas are rarely produced now, having been eclipsed by the enduring appeal of his instrumental music and his oratorios (see below).

Operas

Among Haydn's best-known vocal works are his masses, especially the last six, which he composed for an Esterházy princess between 1796 and 1802. These are large-scale, festive works for chorus, full orchestra (including trumpets and timpani), and four vocal soloists, written in a style that blends traditional elements, such as choral fugues at the end of the Gloria and Credo movements, with modern operatic and symphonic elements. Haydn wrote his *Missa in tempore belli* (Mass in Time of War, 1796) and *Missa in angustiis* (Mass for

Masses

Figure 17.7 Eighteenth-century opera performance, perhaps at the Eszterháza opera house.
(Theater-Museum, Munich. Bridgeman Art Library.)

Figure 17.8 Performance of Haydn's The Creation *on March 27, 1808, in the banquet hall of the University of Vienna. Engraving after the watercolor by Balthasar Wigand.*
(Historisches Museum der Stadt Wien, Vienna.)

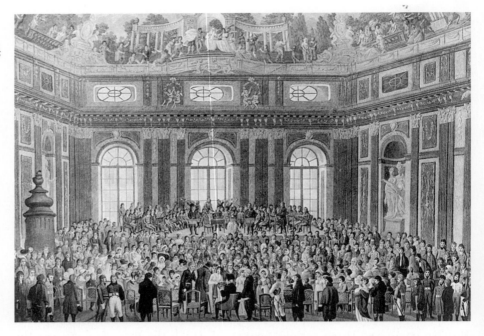

Troubled Times, 1798), also known as the *Lord Nelson Mass*, during the Napoleonic Wars. Like the masses of his contemporaries, Haydn's have a flamboyance that matches the ornate architecture of the Austrian Baroque churches in which they were performed. The occasional criticism that his sacred music was too cheerful prompted Haydn to respond that at the thought of God, his heart "leaped for joy," and he doubted that God would scold him for praising the Lord "with a cheerful heart."

Oratorios

During his stay in London, Haydn became better acquainted with Handel's oratorios. At Westminster Abbey in 1791, he was so deeply moved by the Hallelujah Chorus in a performance of *Messiah* that he burst into tears and exclaimed: "He is the master of us all." Haydn's appreciation for Handel inspired the choral parts of his late masses and especially his oratorios *The Creation* (completed 1798), on texts adapted from Genesis and Milton's *Paradise Lost*, and *The Seasons* (completed 1801). The German texts of both oratorios were written by Baron Gottfried van Swieten, the imperial court librarian in Vienna and a busy musical amateur, but they were issued simultaneously in German and English in acknowledgment both of Handel's influence and of the English public's delight in choral music.

Full 🔊

In both works Haydn's instrumental introductions and interludes are among the finest examples of pictorial depiction in music of the time. His "Depiction of Chaos" at the beginning of *The Creation* features confusing and disturbingly dissonant harmonies. The following recitative and chorus (NAWM 120) sets the opening words of the Bible in an unforgettable fashion. Darkness is depicted through the minor key, muted strings, and soft singing. Then suddenly, at the words "and there was Light," light streams forth with an awesome choral outburst on a radiant C-major chord backed by the full orchestra, including trumpets, trombones, and timpani. This moment made a profound impression on audiences and was extolled by contemporary writers as the supreme example of

The sublime

the sublime in music. Philosophers of the time distinguished between the sublime, which evoked awe and astonishment, and the beautiful, which afforded pleasure. This distinction helps to explain many passages in the music of Haydn, Mozart, and Beethoven, like this one in *The Creation*, that go beyond mere beauty to overwhelm the senses.

Wolfgang Amadeus Mozart
(1756–1791)

Wolfgang Amadeus Mozart was twenty-four years younger than Haydn but achieved wide renown earlier, as a touring child prodigy in the 1760s. Whereas Haydn worked contentedly for the Esterházy princes without having to worry about paying his bills, Mozart spent his mature years as a free agent in Vienna, enduring the hardships of an "irregular income" before finally securing a position at court (see Biography, page 354). Yet when he died at thirty-five, Mozart was seen by many (including Haydn) as the elder's equal, and the two have come to define the music of their era.

During his apprentice years until around 1773, Mozart was completely under the tutelage of his father in practical affairs and in most musical matters as well. Leopold was a composer of some ability and reputation, and the author of a celebrated treatise on violin playing published in 1756, the year of his son's birth. Thanks to his father's excellent teaching and to his own performing in dozens of cities during his formative years (see Figure 17.10) young Mozart was exposed to every kind of music written or heard in contemporary western Europe. In Paris, he became interested in the keyboard works of Johann Schobert (ca. 1735–1767), whose harpsichord writing sometimes simulated orchestral effects through rapid figuration and thick chordal textures, a technique Mozart later imitated (see Example 17.6). In London, he met J. C. Bach, whose music influenced his concertos. In Italy, he assimilated the traditions of opera seria, was influenced by Sammartini and other Italian symphonists, and studied counterpoint with Padre Giovanni Battista Martini. And in Vienna, he came into contact with Haydn's music, which became increasingly important in the young composer's creative life. He absorbed it all with uncanny aptitude, imitating others' works and synthesizing various national styles. The ideas that influenced him not only echoed in his youthful compositions but also continued to grow in his mind, sometimes bearing fruit many years later.

Mozart's teachers

Mozart's Salzburg Years

After touring Europe as a child prodigy with his father, Mozart lived chiefly in Salzburg, complaining frequently about the narrow provincial life and the lack of opportunities. In an effort to improve his situation, he undertook another journey in September 1777, this time with his mother, to Munich, Augsburg, Mannheim, and Paris. But all his hopes for a good position in Germany or France came to nothing. And, sadly, his mother took ill in Paris and died there in July 1778. He returned to Salzburg early the following year, more disconsolate and restless than ever. Nevertheless, he was steadily growing in stature as a composer and received a commission to compose an opera seria for Munich. He spent months there composing and supervising the production of *Idomeneo* (1781). The music for *Idomeneo* is dramatic and pictorial; in its numerous accompanied recitatives, its conspicuous use of the chorus, and its inclusion of the spectacular, the opera reveals the influence of Gluck and the French *tragédie lyrique*.

Idomeneo

Among the other important works of this period are thirteen piano sonatas and several sets of variations for piano, including those on the French melody *Ah, vous dirais-je maman*, K. 265 (300e), better known in English as *Twinkle,*

Piano sonatas

Wolfgang Amadeus Mozart (1756–1791)

Mozart composed prolifically from the age of six until his premature death at thirty-five. A master of every medium, he is widely considered one of the greatest musicians of the Western classical tradition. His mature works, mainstays of the repertory, epitomize the Classic style.

Mozart was born in Salzburg, an independent Austrian city ruled by a despotic archbishop. His father, Leopold, was a violinist and composer in the archbishop's service. When Wolfgang and his older sister Nannerl showed remarkable musical talent at an early age, Leopold trained them and took them throughout Europe, exhibiting their skills as child prodigies. Wolfgang was a phenomenon: by the age of three his perfect pitch was recognized; at five he was an accomplished harpsichord player; at six he was composing; at seven he could read at sight, harmonize melodies on first hearing, and improvise variations on any tune given to him. He composed at a stupendous rate, turning out thirty-four symphonies, sixteen quartets, five operas, and over one hundred other works before his eighteenth birthday. At age sixteen he was appointed third concertmaster in Salzburg, where his duties included composing church music; but Mozart was much more interested in opera and instrumental music, and he left the archbishop's service in 1781, over his father's objections, and settled in Vienna, convinced that he could make a living as a freelance musician. Indeed, he quickly became the darling of the Viennese public, establishing himself as a pianist and scoring a success with his singspiel *Die Entführung aus dem Serail*. With Leopold's grudging consent, he married Constanze Weber, a singer, in the summer of 1782. Their marriage was happy and affectionate. Four children died in infancy, but two sons lived into adulthood, the younger becoming a composer.

Composing at a prodigious pace, teaching private students, performing in public and private concerts, and selling his works to publishers brought Mozart a good income and impressed his father. At a quartet party in Mozart's home, Haydn told Leopold, "Before God and as an honest man I tell you that your son is the greatest composer known to me. . . . He has taste and, what is more, the most profound knowledge of composition."

In 1787, a few months after his father's death, Mozart finally received a salaried appointment as "imperial-court chamber music composer" to Joseph II and the public recognition that came with it; he was second only to the more senior Antonio Salieri, the court Kapellmeister. His musical pro-

Figure 17.9 Wolfgang Amadeus Mozart, in an unfinished portrait from about 1789 by his brother-in-law Joseph Lange.
(Lebrecht Music & Arts Photo Library.)

ductivity remained in high gear despite the discouraging economic conditions of the Austro-Turkish War of 1788–1790, which took the music-loving emperor away for long periods and dampened musical activity at court. When there were money problems, apparently due more to rising expenses than to declining income, the composer depended on friends for loans, confident that his future musical and monetary prospects were bright.

Mozart's death at the prime of his life prompted a variety of false rumors, including that he was poisoned, but it seems to have resulted from a sudden high fever. Unprepared for such an unexpected end, Constanze hastily arranged for Mozart to be buried in a pauper's grave, the actual position of which remains unknown to this day.

Mozart's almost six hundred compositions are listed and numbered chronologically in a thematic catalogue begun by the composer himself (see Figure 17.15), then compiled by Ludwig von Köchel in 1862, whose "K" numbers are used universally to identify Mozart's compositions.

Major works: *Die Entführung aus dem Serail, Le nozze di Figaro, Don Giovanni, Così fan tutte, Die Zauberflöte,* and 15 other operas and singspiels; 17 masses; Requiem; 55 symphonies; 23 piano concertos; 15 other concertos; 26 string quartets; 19 piano sonatas; numerous songs, arias, serenades, divertimenti, and dances.

Figure 17.10 The cities that were most important in Mozart's career are indicated in red. But his travels, particularly during his younger years, include all those in black as well.

twinkle, little star. The variations were probably intended for pupils, but the sonatas were part of Mozart's concert repertory. Before that time, he had improvised such pieces as needed, so that few solo piano compositions from the early years have survived.

The sonatas K. 279 through K. 284 were undoubtedly meant to be published together: there is one in each of the major keys on the circle of fifths from D down to E♭; and the six works show a wide variety of forms and content. K. 310 (300d), Mozart's first minor-key sonata, betrays the influence of Schobert (see above) in its full chordal accompaniments and stringlike tremolos (Example 17.6).

Example 17.6 Wolfgang Amadeus Mozart, Piano Sonata K. 310 (300d), Allegro maestoso

Sonata K. 331 (300i) is notable among the sonatas from the early 1780s for its first movement, which is in variation form, and for its finale. The latter, marked "alla turca," imitates the Janissary music of the Turkish military bands—then popular in Vienna—with their cymbals and triangles and exaggerated first beats. (Mozart also included "Turkish music" in his comic singspiel *Die Entführung aus dem Serail*, The Abduction from the Harem; see Vignette, page 367.)

Other instrumental music

Mozart also composed serenades and divertimenti in the 1770s and early 1780s for garden parties or other outdoor performances, for weddings and birthdays, and for concerts at the homes of friends and patrons. The most familiar of Mozart's serenades is *Eine kleine Nachtmusik* (A Little Night Music, K. 525; 1787), a work in four movements for string quintet but now usually played by a small string ensemble. Among the most notable compositions of Mozart's Salzburg period are the Violin Concertos K. 216, 218, and 219, in G, D, and A, respectively (all 1775), and the Piano Concerto in E♭ Major, K. 271 (1777), with its romantic slow movement in C minor. The three violin concertos are the last of Mozart's compositions in this genre. Piano Concerto K. 271, however, is but the first of a long series of engaging keyboard works that he wrote in hopes of captivating the Viennese public.

Mozart's Vienna Years

Figure 17.11 Three Mozarts making music: Leopold, violin; Amadeus, age seven, keyboard; and Marianne (Nannerl), age eleven, singing from a score. Engraving by Jean-Baptiste Delafosse, based on a watercolor of about 1764 by Louis Carrogis de Carmontelle.
(Musée Condé, Chantilly, France.)

By the middle of the eighteenth century, the largest and fastest-growing German-speaking city was Vienna (see In Context, page 363). When Mozart moved there in 1781, he convinced his father that, by taking a few pupils and playing in concerts, he could earn vastly more money than as a court musician in his hometown. He was right in thinking that no other city could give him so many opportunities; in the next five years, Mozart appeared as a soloist in at least seventy-one concerts, both private and public, which took place in the palaces of the nobility as well as in the city's theaters, restaurants, and public gardens. Leopold Mozart wrote approvingly to his daughter after hearing Mozart perform one of his own piano concertos in public: "A great many members of the aristocracy were present. Each person pays a gold sovereign or three ducats for these concerts. . . . Your brother . . . pays only half a gold sovereign each time he uses the hall."

Indeed, his first years in the imperial capital went well. His singspiel *Die Entführung aus dem Serail* was performed repeatedly. He had all the distinguished pupils he was willing to take, he was idolized by the

Freelance in Vienna

Viennese public both as pianist and composer, and he led the bustling life of a successful freelance musician. However, difficult times followed, coinciding with a period in Vienna that was marked by considerable economic and political instability. A war with the Turks in 1788–1790 led to a decline in musical patronage, cutting into Mozart's public appearances as a virtuoso pianist. And almost as soon as he achieved a salaried position at court as chamber composer to Joseph II, the emperor went off to wage war against the Ottoman Empire and all chamber concerts at court ceased. At the same time, Mozart's expenses increased as the result of a growing family, his passion for gambling, and his desire to pursue a lifestyle suitable for an imperial court composer. Nevertheless, he moved his family to cheaper quarters in 1788 and wrote begging letters to a merchant friend and brother Freemason, who always responded generously, apparently in the belief that Mozart's promising musical future would guarantee repayment.

Mozart composed most of the works that immortalized his name in Vienna between the ages of twenty-five and thirty-five, when the promise of his childhood and early youth came to fulfillment. In every kind of composition, he achieved a seemingly perfect synthesis of form and content, of the galant and learned styles, of polished charm and emotional depth. The principal influences on Mozart during these last ten years of his life came from his continuing study of the works of Haydn and his discovery of those of J. S. Bach and Handel. He was introduced to Bach's music by Baron Gottfried van Swieten, who during his years as Austrian ambassador to Berlin (1771–1778) had become an enthusiast for the music of north German composers. (He later wrote the librettos of Haydn's last two oratorios.) In weekly reading sessions at van Swieten's home during 1782, Mozart became acquainted with Bach's *Art of Fugue, Well-Tempered Clavier*, and other works. Bach's influence was deep and lasting, and may be seen in the more contrapuntal texture of Mozart's later works (for example, his last piano sonata, K. 576). It was probably also through van Swieten that Mozart became interested in Handel, whose *Messiah* Mozart reorchestrated in 1788–1790.

Baron van Swieten

Mozart's style at the beginning of his Vienna period is exemplified by the first movement of the Sonata in F Major, K. 332 (NAWM 121), one of three sonatas composed in 1781–1783 and published as a set in 1784 (K. 330–332). Especially characteristic of Mozart are his songlike themes, perhaps reflecting Italian influence, and his combination of heterogeneous styles. The movement, marked Allegro, clearly follows sonata form and employs the contrasts typical of the period to define formal sections, convey feelings, and provide variety. But Mozart's skill in using diverse styles—galant homophony, learned counterpoint, and intense *Sturm und Drang*—was unparalleled.

Solo piano works

Full 🔊

In 1785, Mozart published six string quartets dedicated to Joseph Haydn as a token of his gratitude for all that he had learned from the older composer. These quartets (K. 387, 421, 428, 458, 464, and 465) were, as Mozart said in his dedicatory letter, "the fruit of a long and laborious effort"; indeed, the manuscripts show an unusually large number of corrections and revisions for Mozart. As we have seen, Haydn's Op. 33 quartets (1781) had fully established the technique of pervasive thematic development with substantial equality among the four instruments. In Mozart's *Haydn* Quartets, although the themes remain characteristically Mozartean in their Italianate tunefulness, they are subjected to much more thorough development in an increasingly contrapuntal texture.

Chamber works

Many of Mozart's other chamber works are also classics, though composed for less standard ensembles. The String Quintets in C Major (K. 515) and in G Minor (K. 516) for two violins, two violas, and cello, composed in the spring of 1787, are comparable to the last two symphonies in the same keys. Another masterpiece,

Quintets

Innovations The Public Concert

During the eighteenth century, public concerts and concert series arose in many cities alongside the private concerts and academies that had long been presented by wealthy individual patrons and clubs. Private concerts were by invitation only, and the aristocratic patrons who sponsored them normally assumed all the costs. Public concerts, by contrast, were usually moneymaking ventures for which tickets were sold. Tickets were offered for an individual event or by subscription to a series, and anyone who could pay the price could attend. But ticket prices were not readily affordable for most people, so the audience for public concerts came mostly from the upper middle and wealthy leisure classes.

Concert halls and concert societies flourished in London starting in 1672 and especially after 1720. At pleasure gardens such as Vauxhall, shown in Figure 17.12, the public paid an entrance fee to enjoy music and other entertainment outdoors. A remarkable institution for the day was the Academy of Ancient Music, devoted to the performance of sixteenth- and seventeenth-century sacred music, madrigals, and other music of earlier times; its founding in 1726 inaugurated concerts of music from the past, which became increasingly popular over the next two centuries. By the second half of the eighteenth century, musical life in London centered around public concerts, including the annual subscription series put on by Johann Christian Bach and Carl Friedrich Abel from 1765 to 1781.

Paris had a very rich concert life throughout the eighteenth century. As in England, occasional out-

door celebrations drew a wider public, but it was not until after the French Revolution that entertainment for the masses developed in any significant way. In 1725, the composer and oboist Anne Danican Philidor founded the Concert spirituel series, which lasted until 1790 and became the century's most famous concert institution. Eventually the name was also used to describe a type of concert—one that included sacred music and took place during the Easter season. The repertory encompassed new music from France and other nations, with performers from across the Continent. The presentation of sonatas and concertos by Vivaldi and other Italians fostered a growing taste for Italian music in France, and from midcentury on, performances of symphonies by German and Austrian composers spurred French composers to cultivate the genre. Haydn's symphonies were heard beginning in 1777, and the following year Mozart's Symphony No. 31, K. 297 (300a), received its premiere at the Concert spirituel and is known for this reason as his *Paris Symphony*. Mozart's account of the event in a letter to his father reveals something of the audience's reaction and how much it meant to him:

> I had heard that final Allegros, here, must begin . . . [with] all the instruments playing together, mostly in unison. I began mine with nothing but the first and second violins playing softly for eight bars—then there is a sudden *forte*. Consequently, the listeners (just as I had anticipated) all went "Sh!" in the soft

Figure 17.12 Concert at Vauxhall Pleasure Gardens, where for a fee the public could enjoy music and other entertainment outdoors. Here, Mrs. Weischel sings from the "Moorish-Gothick" temple, accompanied by the orchestra behind her, while the writer Samuel Johnson and his companions eat in the supper box below. Watercolor ca. 1784, by Thomas Rowlandson.
(Victoria & Albert Museum, London/Art Resource, NY.)

Figure 17.13 An early example of a program for a public concert; this one lists pieces that were performed at a concert in Paris in 1781.
(Bibliothèque Nationale, Paris.)

passage—then came the sudden *forte*—and no sooner did they hear the *forte* than they all clapped their hands. I was so glad that, the minute the Symphony was finished, I went to the Palais Royal, ordered a good ice cream, said my Rosary as I had vowed to do, and went home.

The movement toward public concerts spread to German lands as well. Approximately a decade after Bach's death, J. A. Hiller began a concert series in Leipzig, which continued after 1781 in the new concert hall at the Gewandhaus (Clothiers' Exchange); the Gewandhaus Orchestra still exists and has become one of the most famous orchestras in the world. Similar concert organizations were founded in Vienna (1771) and in Berlin (1790).

Public concerts were advertised by word of mouth and through handbills, posters, notices in newspapers, and other printed media. Figure 17.13 is likely an early example of a program that was handed to concertgoers attending a 1781 Paris concert, which was sponsored by a private organization of amateurs. To judge from the program, it began "precisely at six o'clock" on March 25 and lasted about three hours, which was typical of the time. Rather than consisting of a single genre, it included a variety of vocal and instrumental genres. Only one composer is named, a Mr. Raymond, who directed the concert and received the profits. In some cases, the name given in the program was

that of the featured performer, which was of greater concern to the public than the composer. Listed ninth is "A Harpsichord Concerto, [performed] by an Amateur of this City." The unnamed amateur who played the keyboard was probably a woman, since women were not yet accepted as professional instrumentalists.

An eighteenth-century concert was a social occasion as well as an opportunity to hear music. Audience members could stroll around and converse, paying attention only to those pieces that interested them; the silent, motionless audience was an invention of the nineteenth century. The presence of women of the right social class was essential for making the event a success, so Raymond made sure they felt welcome by including a poem at the bottom of the poster:

TO THE LADIES,
Charming sex, whom I seek to please,
Come embellish the abode of our talents;
By your presence warm up my accents:
Just one of your glances enlivens and enlightens me.
Oh, what does it matter to me, this much-vaunted
  Laurel
With which genius is crowned,
This seal of immortality,
If it is not Beauty who bestows it.

the Clarinet Quintet in A Major (K. 581), was composed at about the same time as the opera buffa *Così fan tutte* and captures some of its comic spirit.

Symphonies

Like Haydn, Mozart approached the symphony in his maturity with great seriousness. He wrote only six in the last ten years of his life, having earlier produced nearly fifty, notwithstanding the traditional numbering of forty-one symphonies (introduced by a nineteenth-century publisher). The symphonies written before 1782 served most often as concert or theatrical "curtain raisers"; those composed after he settled in Vienna constituted the main feature on concert programs or at least shared billing with concertos and arias. The *Haffner* Symphony, K. 385, written in 1782 for the elevation to nobility of Mozart's childhood friend Sigmund Haffner, and the *Linz* Symphony, K. 425, written in 1783 for a performance in that city, typify the late symphonies in their ambitious dimensions, greater demands on performers (particularly wind players), harmonic and contrapuntal complexity, and climactic, rather than light, final movements. These symphonies are in every way as artful as the *London* Symphonies of Haydn, and some may indeed have served as models for the older composer. The other late symphonies—usually recognized as Mozart's greatest—are the *Prague* Symphony in D Major (K. 504) and the Symphonies in E♭ Major (K. 543), G Minor (K. 550), and C Major (K. 551, named *Jupiter* by an English publisher). The last three were composed within a six-week period during the summer of 1788.

From 1782 to 1788

Each of the six symphonies is a masterpiece with its own special character. Their opening gestures leave an indelible impression. Both the *Haffner* and the *Jupiter* begin with loud, forceful tutti statements in unison followed by delicately harmonized ensemble responses (Examples 17.7a and 17.8a). In both works, the disparate elements of the theme are immediately wedded through counterpoint (Examples 17.7b and 17.8b).

Opening gestures

Most unusual is the beginning of the Symphony in G Minor, which opens *piano*—rare in symphonies before this one—with a soft, undulating melody suffused with sighing gestures. Some of Mozart's symphonies are imbued with the spirit of his operas—for example, the comical element in the otherwise

Example 17.7 Wolfgang Amadeus Mozart, Haffner Symphony, K. 385, Allegro con spirito

Example 17.8 Wolfgang Amadeus Mozart, Jupiter *Symphony, K. 551, Allegro vivace*

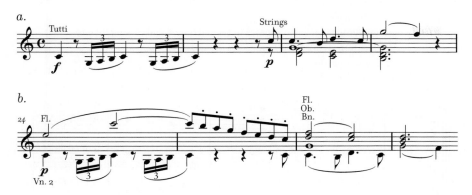

Example 17.9 Wolfgang Amadeus Mozart, Jupiter *Symphony, K. 551, Molto allegro*

heroic *Jupiter* Symphony. For the closing section of the first movement, Mozart borrowed the melody of a comic aria he had written. The repeated cadences in the symphony that follow this quotation are also from the world of comic opera.

The slow introductions to Symphonies K. 425, 504, and 543 are animated by the energy of the French overture, with its majestic double-dotted rhythms, intense harmony, and anacrustic figures. Rather than intimating subtly what is to come, as Haydn sometimes did, Mozart created suspense, tantalizingly wandering away from the key and making its return an important event.

As in Haydn's late symphonies, Mozart's finales do more than send an audience away in a cheerful frame of mind. They balance the serious and important opening movement with a highly crafted counterweight, fashioned with wit and humor. There is also a touch of bravura in the finale of the *Jupiter* Symphony, K. 551 (NAWM 123), which combines the sonata form and symphonic style of Mozart's day with learned counterpoint and fugue. The opening theme, shown in example 17.9, presents two contrasting ideas, as is Mozart's typical practice: a memorable motive in whole notes (a) and a more active response marked by repeated staccato notes and sweeping gestures (b). They have different functions and destinies. Motive a, drawn from a fugue subject in Fux's counterpoint treatise *Gradus ad Parnassum*, receives the full contrapuntal treatment prescribed in Fux's exercises, while b is presented solely as a melody in a homophonic texture. Other motives (c, d, e, and f), from the transition and second theme area, are introduced along the way. In a climactic tour de force, the coda then weaves all of the motives except b into a five-voice fugue, revealing that they all fit together in counterpoint (see Example 17.10). In this coda Mozart achieves a stunning integration of the galant style with the fugal style of the early eighteenth century, making us hear his themes in an entirely new context. The effect is sublime, inspiring awe and astonishment—not at Creation, as in Haydn's oratorio, but at human creativity and ingenuity.

Introductions

Finales

Full 🔊

Example 17.10 Wolfgang Amadeus Mozart, Jupiter *Symphony, K. 551, Allegro molto*

a = first theme, opening idea

c = first theme, concluding idea (also appears in second theme and closing theme)

d = figure from transition (also appears in second theme)

e = second theme, opening phrase

f = countersubject to second theme

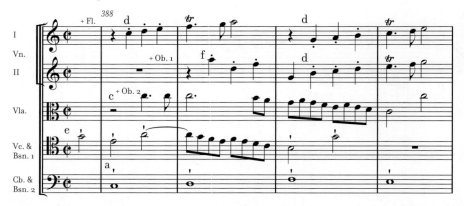

Piano Concertos

Seventeen concertos for piano occupy a central place in Mozart's output during the Vienna years. He wrote them primarily as vehicles for his own concerts and intended them to please a wide range of listeners. As he wrote to his father in 1782, the first three Vienna concertos, K. 413–415,

> strike a happy medium between what is too easy and too difficult . . . very brilliant, pleasing to the ear, and natural, without being vapid. There are passages here and there from which connoisseurs alone can derive satisfaction; but these passages are written in such a way that the less learned cannot fail to be pleased, though without knowing why.[1]

Concerto form

Mozart's concertos follow the traditional three-movement pattern in the sequence fast-slow-fast. The first movement blends elements of ritornello and sonata form, as do the concertos of J. C. Bach, Mozart's primary model for these keyboard works. Comparing the first movement of Mozart's Piano Concerto in A Major, K. 488 (NAWM 122), composed in 1786, to the J. C. Bach concerto (NAWM 117) outlined in Figure 16.7, we see the same general features:

First movement

- The solo sections resemble the exposition, development, and recapitulation of a sonata form, with the soloist accompanied by, and sometimes in dialogue with, the orchestra.
- The opening orchestral ritornello (the "orchestral exposition") introduces the movement's first theme, transitional material, sometimes the secondary theme, and usually the closing theme, but remains in the tonic.
- The ritornello returns, now in the new key and greatly abbreviated, to mark the end of the first solo and at the end of the movement.

Like his predecessors, Mozart typically punctuates the main themes with passages for full orchestra (tutti) that function as transitions or closing passages;

1. Wolfgang Amadeus Mozart, letter to Leopold Mozart, Dec. 23, 1782, trans. in Emily Anderson, ed., *The Letters of Mozart and His Family* (New York: Norton, 1989), p. 1242.

In Context Cosmopolitan Vienna

Eighteenth-century Vienna is a striking example of a cosmopolitan cultural center where conditions seem to have been ideal for music. Geographically, Vienna stood at the crossroads of four musical nations—Germany, Bohemia (now the Czech Republic), Hungary, and Italy—and, being the capital of the powerful Hapsburg Empire, it was also central in political terms. Between 1745 and 1765, the emperor was a Frenchman, Francis Stephen of Lorraine. The imperial court poet was the Italian Metastasio. A German, Johann Adolf Hasse, composed operas in Italian set to Metastasio's librettos, sometimes for state occasions. The manager of the court theaters was Count Giacomo Durazzo, a diplomat from Italy. An imported French company mounted a regular season of French comic operas. French-style ballets were also popular, though the music tended to be by local composers, among them Gluck, whose partner in oper-

atic reform was Raniero de Calzabigi, another Italian. The most influential musician in Vienna during the last quarter of the century was Antonio Salieri (1750–1825), who had been brought there from Venice at the age of fifteen. He eventually succeeded Florian Gassmann as imperial court composer and conductor of Italian opera, a post he held for thirty-six years. This mix of cultures underlay the phenomenon that has been called, not altogether appropriately, the "Viennese" Classical style.

Its most notable representatives were not actually Viennese but came there from other, smaller centers: Haydn from Rohrau, a village near the Hungarian border; Mozart from Salzburg, a town with a distinct Italian flavor, it being a hundred miles to the west and that much closer to the Italian peninsula; and Beethoven (see Chapter 18) from Bonn, in north-central Germany, not far from where the Bach family had originated.

Figure 17.14 Vienna—the capital of the Hapsburg Empire and geographically at the crossroads of Germany, Bohemia, Hungary, and Italy—was the magnet that drew Haydn, Mozart, and Beethoven.

Figure 17.15 Page from the catalogue of his own works, which Mozart began in 1784, listing four of his piano concertos and a piano quintet. The list became the basis of the Köchel catalogue by which we number and classify Mozart's works today.
(The British Library, London.)

these elements reappear, like partial or mini-ritornellos, in various keys throughout the movement. A diagram of the entire opening ritornello ("orchestral exposition") and first solo section ("solo exposition") of Mozart's K. 488 is shown in Figure 17.16. Notice that the modulation to the new key is not accomplished until the solo section gets under way. Therefore, in the opening orchestral ritornello, the passage (tr at measure 18) between the first and second theme groups (1T and 2T) merely serves as a connection between themes rather than as a real transition between keys (which is how it functions at measure 82).

Like J. C. Bach, Mozart includes a cadenza for the soloist, but his cadenza usually interrupts the final ritornello, as it does here. Both composers introduce new material at the beginning of the development, which becomes the focus of that section. The differences are in the details that make each first movement unique. The resulting form follows convention in most respects yet may surprise the listener with several individual features. This movement by Mozart is suffused with his characteristic wealth of melodic invention, diversity of figuration, and elegance.

Second and last movements

The second movement of a Mozart concerto resembles a lyrical aria. It is in the subdominant of the principal key or, less often, in the dominant or relative minor. Its form may vary but is most often a sonata form without development, a set of variations, or a rondo. The finale is typically a rondo or sonata-rondo on themes with a popular character. These are treated in scintillating virtuoso style with opportunities for one or more cadenzas.

Cadenzas

That Mozart put substance before fireworks may be seen in the cadenzas that he sketched or fully notated for his concertos. The cadenza had developed from

Figure 17.16 The exposition (sometimes called a "double exposition") of the first movement of Mozart's Piano Concerto in A Major, K. 488. In this diagram, 1T = first theme group, 2T = second theme group, CT = closing theme, and tr = transition.

Section:	EXPOSITION								
Tonal center:	Tonic						Dominant		
Instruments:	Orchestra				Solo with Orchestra				
Themes:	1T	tr	2T	CT	1T	tr	2T	CT	tr
Measure:	1	18	30	46	67	82	98	114	137

the trills and runs that singers inserted, particularly before the return of the opening section in the da capo aria. Mozart's early cadenzas similarly consisted of flourishes without thematic links to the movement, but after the 1780s they served to balance the longer modulatory or development sections. These cadenzas—almost second development sections—cast new light on familiar material in daring flights of technical wizardry.

Although the concertos were showpieces intended to dazzle an audience, Mozart never allowed display to gain the upper hand. He always maintained a healthy balance of musical interest between the orchestra and soloist, and his infallible ear regulated the myriad combinations of colors and textures that he drew from the interplay between the piano and orchestral instruments, especially the winds. Moreover, the goal of composing for an immediate public response did not keep him from expressing the most profound musical ideas.

Operas

Opera was still the most prestigious musical genre, and Mozart eagerly sought opportunities to compose for the stage. Once in Vienna, his fame was established by *Die Entführung aus dem Serail* (1782), with which he brought German Singspiel into the realm of great art without altering its established features. This work tells a romantic-comic story of adventure and rescue set in a Turkish harem. Such "oriental" settings and plots were popular, in part because they provided a taste of the exotic while making the Turks, long-standing enemies of Austria-Hungary, seem less threatening. Depicting the Turkish characters as humane and fully rounded, Mozart aimed to capture their temperaments and feelings in his music (see Vignette, page 367).

Mozart's next operas were three Italian comic operas: *Le nozze di Figaro* (The Marriage of Figaro, 1786), *Don Giovanni* (Don Juan, 1787), and *Così fan tutte* (All Women Behave That Way, 1790). All were set to librettos by Lorenzo Da Ponte (1749–1838), poet for the imperial court theater who later came to America and became a professor of Italian in New York (see Figure 17.17). Although *Figaro* followed the conventions of opera buffa (see Chapter 15), Da Ponte's libretto raised it to a higher level, giving greater depth to the characters, intensifying the social tensions between classes, and introducing moral issues. Mozart's psychological penetration and his genius for musical characterization similarly lent a greater seriousness to the genre. Character portrayal occurs not only in solo arias, but especially in duets, trios, and larger ensembles. The ensemble

Singspiel

Da Ponte operas

Le nozze di Figaro

Figure 17.17 Lorenzo Da Ponte, in a portrait by an unknown American artist. Best known as the librettist of Mozart's Marriage of Figaro, Don Giovanni, *and* Così fan tutte, *Da Ponte went to London in the 1790s and to America in 1805, where he was at various times a grocer, private teacher, bookdealer, translator, and eventually professor of Italian at Columbia University. He became an American citizen and sought to bring Italian culture to his new nation.*
(Columbia University, New York.)

Figure 17.18 Saint Michael's Square in Vienna. In the foreground is the Burgtheater, where Mozart performed several of his piano concertos in the mid-1780s and where the premieres of The Marriage of Figaro *and* Così fan tutte *took place.* (Historisches Museum der Stadt Wien, Austria/ Bridgeman Art Library.)

finales allow these characters to clash, combining realism with ongoing dramatic action and superbly unified musical form. Mozart's orchestration—particularly his use of winds—plays an important role in defining characters and situations.

Don Giovanni

Figaro enjoyed only moderate success in Vienna, but its enthusiastic reception in Prague led to the commission for *Don Giovanni*, premiered there the following year. The medieval legend of Don Juan, on which the plot is based, had been treated often in literature and music since the early seventeenth century. But Mozart, for the first time in opera, took the character of Don Juan seriously—not as an incongruous mixture of farcical figure, seducer, and horrible blasphemer, but as a romantic hero, a rebel against authority, a scorner of common morality, and a supreme individualist, bold and unrepentant to the last.

First scene

▶ MOZART, *Don Giovanni*

Don Giovanni incorporates opera-seria characters, situations, and styles into comic opera, effectively merging the two genres, as illustrated by the very first scene (NAWM 124). Alone on stage and waiting for his master to emerge from a nocturnal rendezvous, Don Giovanni's servant Leporello complains of his treatment by his master in an opera buffa–style aria, with aristocratic horn calls when he confesses his wish to live like a gentleman rather than a servant. He is interrupted by a clamor as Don Giovanni and Donna Anna emerge from her house, where he has tried to seduce her and perhaps succeeded. In furious pursuit, she sings in dramatic opera-seria style, and the Don replies in kind, while Leporello comments on the situation in buffo style from his hiding place. Donna Anna's father, the Commendatore, awakened by the commotion, rushes onto the stage and challenges Don Giovanni to fight. They do, and the Commendatore is mortally wounded—a shocking turn of events for a comedy. In a powerful trio, as the orchestra ticks away his last moments, the Commendatore weakly utters his dying words while the others comment, each in his own characteristic style. In the following recitative, master and servant instantly revert to the comic banter of opera buffa. All this takes place during a stream of continuous music and seamless dramatic action, and with a faultless sense of harmonic pacing that counts among Mozart's most original contributions to eighteenth-century opera. Moreover, the scene is preceded by an overture that,

VIGNETTE Mozart's Depiction of Character and Mood

In his operas, Mozart portrays the personalities of the characters and conveys their feelings so perfectly through his music that listeners can immediately understand them—sometimes better than the characters understand their own predicament. In a letter to his father, written while composing Die Entführung aus dem Serail, *Mozart described how he made the music of two arias fit the characters, the situation, and the singers who would premiere the roles.*

Osmin's rage will be rendered comical by the use of Turkish music. In composing the aria, I made [the singer] Fischer's beautiful deep tones really glisten. . . . The passage *Therefore, by the beard of the Prophet,* etc., is, to be sure, in the same tempo, but with quick notes—and as his anger increases more and more, the Allegro assai [a faster tempo]—which comes just when one thinks the aria is over—will produce an excellent Effect because it is in a different tempo and in a different key. A person who gets into such a violent rage transgresses every order, moderation, and limit; he no longer knows himself, in the same way the Music must no longer know itself. But because

passions, violent or not, must never be expressed to the point of disgust, and Music must never offend the ear, even in most horrendous situations, but must always be pleasing, in other words always remain Music, I have not chosen a key foreign to F, the key of the aria, but one that is friendly to it, not however its nearest relative in D minor, but the more remote A minor. Now about Bellmont's aria in A Major. "Oh how anxious, oh how passionate!" Do you know how I expressed it?—even expressing the loving, throbbing heart? With two violins playing in octaves. This is the favorite aria of everyone who has heard it—it's mine too. And it was written entirely for Adamberger's voice. One can see the trembling—faltering—one can see his heaving breast—which is expressed by a crescendo—one can hear the whispering and the sighing—which is expressed by the first violins with mutes and one flute playing in unison.

Wolfgang Amadeus Mozart, letter to Leopold Mozart, Sept. 26, 1781, in Robert Spaethling, ed. and trans., *Mozart's Letters, Mozart's Life* (New York: Norton, 2000), p. 286. Punctuation and spelling have been modernized.

---

instead of reaching an expected close, spills right into the introduction to Leporello's opening aria. And, true to the principles of Gluck's reform, Mozart uses the overture to set the dramatic tone of the opera, with its mixture of tragedy and farce.

Throughout *Don Giovanni*, as in the opening scenes, three different character types, each representing a distinct social class, interact: Donna Anna and other nobles, who emote in the elevated, dramatic tone of opera seria; Leporello and his peers, mostly lower-class, marked by the buffoonery of opera buffa (although they show both cleverness and wisdom); and Don Giovanni, who, as an opportunistic libertine, passes easily from one world to the other. All these types come together in the finale of Act I, where Mozart masterfully coordinates three onstage dance bands playing simultaneously: an elegant minuet for the nobles, a lively contredanse for Don Giovanni, and a rustic waltz for Leporello.

Figure 17.19 Don Giovanni about to meet his punishment at the hands of the Commendatore, or stone guest, whom the Don had boldly invited to dinner, in the final scene of Don Giovanni. *This is from the title page of an early edition (1801).* (Breitkopf & Härtel, Leipzig. Lebrecht Music & Arts Photo Library.)

TIMELINE The Late Eighteenth Century

Musical Events

1750
Death of J. S. Bach

1761
Haydn hired by Prince
Esterházy

1762
Gluck, *Orfeo ed Euridice*
(NAWM 110) in Vienna

1762–1773
Mozart tours as child prodigy

1772
Haydn, Op. 20 quartets;
Mozart concertmaster
at Salzburg

1781
Haydn, Op. 33 quartets
(NAWM 118); Mozart
freelances in Vienna

1784
Mozart writes six piano
concertos

1785
Mozart composes
Haydn Quartets

1787
Mozart, *Don Giovanni*
(NAWM 124) in Prague

1787
Haydn, Symphony No. 88
(NAWM 119)

1791
Mozart dies in Vienna; Haydn,
first *London* Symphonies

1798
Haydn, *The Creation*
(NAWM 120)

1750 | **1800**

Historical Events

1760–1820
Reign of George III of England

1765
Maria Theresa and Joseph II rule
Austria jointly

1775
Beaumarchais, *Barber of Seville*

1776
American Declaration
of Independence

1789–1794
French Revolution

1790
Leopold II becomes emperor

Così fan tutte

Così fan tutte is an opera buffa in the best Italian tradition, with a brilliant libretto glorified by some of Mozart's most melodious music. It is also a very moving drama about human frailty, exploring the themes of temptation, betrayal, and reconciliation.

Die Zauberflöte

Mozart wrote *Die Zauberflöte* (The Magic Flute, 1791) in the last year of his life. Although outwardly a Singspiel—with spoken dialogue instead of recitative and with some characters and scenes appropriate to popular comedy—its action is filled with symbolic meaning and its music is so rich and profound that it ranks as the first great German opera. The largely solemn mood of the score reflects the relationship between the opera and the teachings and ceremonies of Freemasonry. We know that Mozart valued his Masonic affiliation, not only from allusions in his letters but especially from the serious quality of the music he wrote for Masonic ceremonies in 1785 and in a Masonic cantata he composed in 1791 (K. 623), his last completed work. In *The Magic Flute*, Mozart interwove the threads of many eighteenth-century musical styles and traditions: the vocal opulence of Italian opera seria; the folk humor of the German Singspiel; the solo aria; the buffo ensemble, which is given new musical meaning; a novel kind of accompanied recitative applicable to German words; solemn choral scenes; and even (in the duet of the two armed men in Act II) a revival of the Baroque chorale-prelude technique, with contrapuntal accompaniment. The reconciliation of older and newer styles is summed up in the delicious overture, which combines sonata form with fugue.

Church Music

Since Mozart's father worked as a musician for the archbishop of Salzburg and Mozart himself served there as concertmaster and organist, it was natural for Mozart to compose church music from an early age. However, with notable exceptions—principally the Requiem—his settings of sacred texts are not counted among his major works. The Requiem, K. 626, was Mozart's last work, and the circumstances of its anonymous commission in July 1791, under conditions of absolute secrecy, are bizarre. It seems that a Viennese nobleman wished to pass the work off as his own. But Mozart, unaware of this fact and being ill and depressed, superstitiously conceived the idea that he was writing his own Requiem. Left unfinished at his death, it was completed by his pupil and collaborator Franz Xaver Süssmayr (1766–1803), who added some instrumental parts to Mozart's draft and set the Sanctus, Benedictus, and Agnus Dei, in part repeating music that Mozart had composed for an earlier section.

Requiem

POSTLUDE

This chapter about Haydn and Mozart does not presume to cover all the music of the late eighteenth century; these two composers shared the stage with a host of others. Some of their names may be familiar from the pages of this book—for example, Gluck. To those may be added dozens more, active in instrumental music as well as opera, each of whom contributed something unique to the period and each of whom deserves further study. But the music of Haydn and Mozart not only met with great success during the composers' lifetime, it also continued to be known and performed after their death. It provided models for Beethoven and many other composers of their own and succeeding generations. By the early nineteenth century, some of their compositions had become classics, part of the core group of works that cultured people were expected to know. Eventually, their music was dubbed "Classical," which, in turn, became the adjective most often applied to any work of the late eighteenth century. Yet, among the composers of their time, Haydn and Mozart excelled at composing complex and varied music, ranging over all the genres current in their day while maintaining that precarious balance between broad and deep appeal. Because of the unique merits of their music, only they managed to achieve such widespread and enduring fame.

 Resources for study and review available at wwnorton.com/studyspace

Ludwig van Beethoven
(1770–1827)

PRELUDE

In 1792, George Washington was president of the United States; Louis XVI and Marie Antoinette were imprisoned by the leaders of the new French Republic (they were executed the following year); Viennese life, not yet under Napoleonic rule, presented an atmosphere of frivolous gaiety, at least on the surface; Haydn was at the height of his fame; and Mozart had been dead since the previous December. Early in November 1792, the ambitious twenty-one-year-old composer and pianist Ludwig van Beethoven (see Biography, pages 372–373) traveled from the city of Bonn on the Rhine to Vienna, a five-hundred-mile journey that took a week by stagecoach. He ran short of money and for a while kept a detailed account of his finances. After he reached Vienna, one of the entries in his notebook records an expenditure of 25 groschen (pennies) for "coffee for Haidn and me."

The big city suited Beethoven perfectly. He soon established himself with the help of the contacts he maintained among members of the Austrian, Bohemian, and Hungarian aristocracy, who encouraged and supported him. The revolutions in France and America had brought far-reaching, even cataclysmic, changes to their world. The industrial revolution, which was well under way throughout Europe by this time—forging advances in medicine, science, and industry—was also leaving its mark on society, which soon came to regard invention and progress as the norm. Rather than placing their faith in authority and respecting only the past, people of the new industrial age believed in progress and cultivated an unprecedented enthusiasm for the future. Thus, Beethoven is said to have responded confidently to an uncomprehending critic of his works, "Oh, I have not written them for you, but for a later age."

Beethoven's total number of works is small by comparison to the output of Haydn and Mozart: 9 symphonies, for example, versus Haydn's 100-plus or Mozart's 50-plus. A partial explanation is that Beethoven's symphonies are longer and grander. But another reason is that Beethoven lacked the speed of Haydn and Mozart: he apparently wrote music with great deliberation and sometimes only after periods of intense struggle. We can see this struggle in his sketchbooks, which document the progress of a musical idea through various stages until it reached its final form. The sketches for the String Quartet in C♯ Minor, Op. 131, for example, are three times the length of the finished work.

Another glimpse into Beethoven's working habits reveals the extent to which he was guided by what the Romantics called "inspiration." A young composer he befriended recalled Beethoven saying:

> You will ask me whence I take my ideas? That I cannot say with any degree of certainty: they come to me uninvited, directly or indirectly. I could almost grasp them in my hands, out in Nature's open, in the woods, during my promenades, in the silence of the night, at the earliest dawn. They are roused by moods which in the poet's case are transmuted into words, and in mine into tones that sound, roar and storm until at last they take shape for me as notes.[1]

Scholars have customarily divided Beethoven's works into three periods on the basis of style and chronology. During the first period, to about 1802, Beethoven assimilated the musical language of his time and found his own voice as a composer. He wrote the six String Quartets Op. 18, the first ten piano sonatas (through Op. 14), the first three piano concertos, and the first two symphonies. The second period, in which his rugged individualism asserted itself, runs to about 1816 and includes the Symphonies Nos. 3 to 8, the incidental music to Goethe's drama *Egmont*, the *Coriolan* overture, the opera *Fidelio*, the last two piano concertos, the Violin Concerto, the String Quartets Opp. 59 (the *Rasumovsky* Quartets), 74, and 95, and the Piano Sonatas through Op. 90. The third period, in which Beethoven's music generally became more reflective and introspective, includes the last five piano sonatas, the *Diabelli Variations* for piano, the *Missa solemnis*, the Ninth Symphony, and the last great quartets.

Three periods

First Period, to ca. 1802

Beethoven's first decade in Vienna, where he quickly established himself as a pianist and composer, was relatively trouble-free. For a while, he had rooms in a house owned by Prince Karl von Lichnowsky, with whom he traveled to Prague for concerts in 1796 and who sponsored concerts in his palace in Vienna. Another patron, Prince Lobkowitz, kept a private orchestra that played in Vienna and at his Bohemian country estates; he bought rights to first performances of some of Beethoven's works. Lobkowitz, Prince Kinsky, and Archduke Rudolph—youngest brother of the reigning emperor Francis II and Beethoven's piano and composition student—joined in setting up an annuity for the composer so that he would stay in Austria when he got an attractive offer from Jérôme Bonaparte, king of Westphalia. Many of Beethoven's works of this and later periods are dedicated to these patrons. With their help and by selling a number of important works to a Leipzig publisher, performing as a pianist in concerts that he or others organized, and giving piano lessons, Beethoven was able to make a living outside of the church or court, granting him an independence Haydn and Mozart did not achieve until late in their careers.

Figure 18.1 Beethoven-Haus, the house in Bonn where Beethoven was born in 1770. It now contains a museum of Beethoven memorabilia and is open to the public.
(Beethoven Haus, Bonn.)

1. Alexander Wheelock Thayer, *Thayer's Life of Beethoven*, rev. and ed. Elliot Forbes (Princeton: Princeton University Press, 1967), vol. 2, p. 873.

Ludwig van Beethoven (1770–1827)

As the composer whose career and music best reflect the tumultuous changes in the decades around 1800, Beethoven became and remains the most familiar cultural icon of Western art music. His symphonies, concertos, string quartets, and piano sonatas are central to the repertory of classical music, and his influence has been virtually inescapable. His perseverance in the face of deafness, combined with the sense of struggle and triumph depicted in much of his music, made him a heroic figure. His individualism and self-expression appealed to middle-class audiences and served as a model for generations of composers.

Beethoven was born into a musical family in Bonn, a town on the Rhine in northwestern Germany. His father, Johann, was a court musician employed by the elector of Cologne, just downriver. He taught Ludwig piano and violin, and had every intention of turning the boy, who was small for his age, into a child prodigy. He took his son out of school at age eleven so that Ludwig could concentrate exclusively on music and placed his training in the hands of a reputable local composer, Christian Gottlob Neefe (1748–1798), an organist in the Baroque tradition of counterpoint and improvisation.

Beethoven visited Vienna in 1787 and probably met Mozart, who prophesied a bright future for him. After returning to Bonn, he also made the acquaintance of Haydn, who stopped there on his way to London in December 1790. On Haydn's recommendation, Beethoven went to Vienna for further study and settled there permanently in 1792. His lessons with Haydn began late that year and continued until the older composer left in 1794 on his second visit to London.

Unlike Mozart, Beethoven did not seek a court appointment in Vienna. He was able to live comfortably on commissions, sales of music (hand-copied as well as printed), public concerts, and support from aristocratic sponsors. Confident in his own worth as an artist, he treated his patrons with indifference and even occasional rudeness. His presumption of social equality led him repeatedly to fall in love with women of noble rank, whom he, as a commoner, could not marry (and some of whom were already married; see Figure 18.4 and In Context, page 385). Beethoven's lifestyle appeared poorer than it actually was. Moving from one apartment to another after arguments with his landlords, and with his social and professional life constantly in jeopardy after the onset of his deafness, he never succeeded in establishing a permanent home.

Around 1802, his gradual loss of hearing provoked a personal crisis, including thoughts of suicide, which he voiced in a letter called the Heiligenstadt Testament (see Vignette, page 375).

Piano sonatas

Like Mozart, Beethoven's success as a pianist depended in part on his writing works that not only showcased his talents, but also appealed to the amateur market. Indeed, the largest group of compositions written during his first decade in Vienna were sonatas, variations, and shorter works for piano. Beethoven dedicated his first three piano sonatas to Haydn; in them, he reveals his debt to the older composer's style by creating themes from brief motives that he then develops extensively. But these sonatas all have four movements, as in a symphony, instead of the usual three, and in the last two he replaced the minuet with a more dynamic scherzo. Like Mozart, Beethoven often used strong contrasts of style to delineate the form and broaden the expressive range.

Sonate pathétique

The title of Beethoven's eighth piano sonata, Sonate pathétique ("with pathos," a term used in rhetoric), Op. 13 (1799), indicates the composer's intention to evoke feelings of pity or compassion. In C minor, the outer movements have a stormy, passionate character that Beethoven's predecessors associated with that key. The first movement (NAWM 125) begins with a Grave introduction that is unusual for a piano sonata but common for a symphony. It immediately sets a

Full 🔊   Concise 🔊

But he emerged from his despair with new resolve to compose works of unprecedented scope and depth. The music of the next dozen years established him as the most popular and critically acclaimed composer alive. Through sales to publishers and support from patrons, notably a permanent stipend set up for him in 1809, he was able to devote himself entirely to composition and write at his own, very deliberate pace.

On his brother Caspar's death in 1815, Beethoven became guardian for his nephew Karl, giving Beethoven the family he had long desired but also bringing years of conflict with Karl's mother, Johanna. Growing deafness, bouts of illness, political upheavals, and the death or departure of many friends and patrons led to his increasing withdrawal from society. His music became more intense, concentrated, and difficult.

After years of ill health, Beethoven died at age fifty-six. Analysis of a lock of hair clipped after his death showed massive amounts of lead, suggesting that his illnesses were caused or aggravated by lead poisoning from his dishes or wine flasks. His funeral procession was witnessed by over 10,000 people, and his popularity and influence continue to this day.

Major works: 9 symphonies, 11 overtures, 5 piano concertos, 1 violin concerto, 16 string quartets,

Figure 18.2 Beethoven with a lyre, in a portrait from around 1804 by his friend Willibrord Joseph Mähler, an amateur painter. The composer kept this painting, suggestive of his status as a modern Orpheus, on his wall all his life.
(Historisches Museum der Stadt Wien. Photo: Fotostudio Otto.)

9 piano trios, 10 violin sonatas, 5 cello sonatas, 32 large piano sonatas, many piano variations, the opera *Fidelio*, the *Missa solemnis*, the Mass in C Major, as well as arias, songs, and numerous other works.

mood of drama and high seriousness, while its dense textures lend the sonata a symphonic grandeur. The opening measures of the introduction are recalled at symmetrically placed landmarks—namely, before the beginning of the development section and after the end of the recapitulation—and their sudden and unexpected recurrences deepen the pathos. The powerful Allegro that follows whips up a storm of excitement not heard before in Beethoven's or any other composer's piano sonatas. While the middle movement is a profoundly serene and songful Adagio in A♭ major, the sonata-rondo finale reverts to the serious intensity of the first movement, unlike the typically lighthearted rondos of Haydn and Mozart. Its theme recalls the second theme of the opening movement, and the key of its central episode echoes the A♭ of the slow movement, creating the sort of intermovement connections that mark many of Beethoven's later works.

Beethoven waited until he was well established in Vienna and confident in his craft before composing his first string quartets and symphonies. He knew that these were genres for which Haydn, then regarded as the greatest living composer, was famous, so that writing the same sorts of pieces would invite

String quartets and symphonies

VIGNETTE Beethoven's Playing and Improvising at the Piano

When, for several weeks in 1791, Beethoven's Bonn employer, the elector of Cologne, presided over a meeting of the Teutonic Order at Mergentheim in southern Germany, he took his musicians along. Carl Ludwig Junker, a composer and writer on music and art, came to hear them and published a glowing account of Beethoven's playing.

I have also heard one of the greatest of pianists—the dear, good Bethofen [sic]. . . . I heard him extemporize in private; yes, I was even invited to propose a theme for him to vary. The greatness of this amiable, light-hearted man as a virtuoso may, in my opinion, be safely judged from his almost inexhaustible wealth of ideas, the highly characteristic expressiveness of his playing, and the skill he displays in performance. I do not know that he lacks anything for the making of a great artist. I have often heard Vogler play by the hour on the pianoforte—of his organ playing I cannot speak, not having heard him on that instrument—and never failed to wonder at his astonishing ability. But Bethofen, in addition to skill, has greater clarity and profundity of ideas, and more expression—in short, he speaks to the heart. He is equally great at an *adagio* as at an *allegro*. Even the members of this remarkable orchestra are, without exception, his admirers, and are all ears when he plays. Yet he is exceedingly modest and free from all pretension. He, however, acknowledged to me that, upon the journeys which the Elector had enabled him to make, he had seldom found in the playing of the most distinguished virtuosi that excellence which he supposed he had a right to expect. His manner of treating his instrument is so different from the usual that he gives the impression of having attained his present supremacy through a path that he discovered himself.

From Heinrich Philipp Carl Bossler, *Musikalische Correspondenz* (Nov. 23, 1791), adapted from trans. by Henry Edward Krehbiel; in Alexander Wheelock Thayer, *Thayer's Life of Beethoven*, rev. and ed. Elliot Forbes (Princeton: Princeton University Press, 1967), vol. 1, p. 105.

people to compare him with his former teacher. For that very reason, Beethoven viewed these genres as a chance to prove himself as a composer.

Op. 18 string quartets

Beethoven's first six quartets, published in 1800 as Op. 18, are indebted to both Haydn and Mozart but are no mere imitations. Beethoven's individuality shines through in the character of his themes, frequent unexpected turns of phrase, unconventional modulations, and subtleties of form. Almost every movement is unique. The slow movement of No. 1, which Beethoven reportedly said was inspired by the tomb scene in *Romeo and Juliet*, is especially striking and was perhaps the most dramatic—even operatic—movement yet written for string quartet. The hilarious scherzo of No. 6 emphasizes offbeats so convincingly that the listener is continually befuddled about the meter. The finale is a rondo with a long, intense, slow introduction labeled *La malinconia* (Melancholy), which is recalled later in the movement. By simultaneously following and subverting tradition in these quartets and creating stark juxtapositions of opposing emotions and styles, Beethoven charts a new course for his later works.

First Symphony

Beethoven's Symphony No. 1 in C Major premiered in 1800 at a concert that offered, typically for its time, a potpourri of miscellaneous works (see Innovations, pages 358–359), including a septet and a piano concerto, also by Beethoven; a symphony by Mozart; an aria and duet from Haydn's oratorio *The Creation;* and improvisations at the piano by Beethoven himself. In his symphony, Beethoven sought to distinguish himself in certain details: the unusual prominence of the woodwinds, the frequent and carefully placed dynamic markings (one of the most essential traits of his early style), the scherzo-like character of the third movement, and long, meaningful codas in the other movements.

Second Period, ca. 1803–1816

Around 1803, Beethoven was acknowledged throughout Europe as the foremost pianist and composer for piano of his time and a symphonist on a par with Haydn and Mozart. His innovations were recognized, although they were sometimes dismissed as eccentricities. He was befriended by the most prominent families of Vienna and attracted devoted and generous patrons. He drove hard bargains with his publishers, getting them to bid against each other, and followed Haydn's lead in publishing works in several countries at once to preserve his rights and maximize his returns. Although he wrote on commission, he often dodged deadlines. He could afford, as he said, to "think and think," to revise and polish a work until it suited him.

In part because of his growing deafness, Beethoven carried around notebooks in which he scribbled bits of conversation. He also kept sketchbooks in which he jotted down themes and plans for compositions, worked out the continuity of each piece, and gradually filled in details. Figure 18.3 shows a page from the sketchbook for Beethoven's Third Symphony. Thanks to these sketchbooks, we can follow the progress of his ideas through various stages until they reached final form (see the commentary in NAWM 126). By composing in this deliberate way, Beethoven created music in which the relation of each part to the whole was remarkably sophisticated, satisfying one of the central tenets of nineteenth-century aesthetics.

Notebooks and sketchbooks

When Beethoven realized that his hearing loss was getting worse and that it would become permanent, he suffered a psychological crisis that he describes in a letter written from Heiligenstadt, a town outside Vienna where he was vacationing (see Vignette, below). After considering suicide, he emerged from his despair with a new resolve to continue composing, which may have translated into his music as a determination to say something new with each new piece. In fact, some have interpreted his compositions after 1802 as narratives or dramas

Personal crisis

VIGNETTE The Heiligenstadt Testament

The impression that Beethoven gave of being moody and unsociable had much to do with his increasing deafness. He began to lose his hearing around 1796, and by 1820 he was almost completely deaf. In the autumn of 1802, Beethoven wrote a letter, now known as the Heiligenstadt Testament, intended to be read by his brothers after his death. In it, he describes in moving terms how he suffered when he realized that his malady was incurable.

I must live almost alone like one who has been banished, I can mix with society only as much as true necessity demands. If I approach near to people a hot terror seizes upon me and I fear being exposed to the danger that my condition might be noticed. Thus it has been during the last six months which I have spent in the country. . . . What a humiliation for me when someone standing next to me heard a flute in the distance and *I heard nothing*, or someone heard a *shepherd singing* and again I heard nothing. Such incidents drove me almost to despair, a little more of that and I would have ended my life—it was only *my art* that held me back. Ah, it seemed to me impossible to leave the world until I had brought forth all that I felt was within me. . . . Oh Providence—grant me at last but one day of *pure joy*—it is so long since real joy echoed in my heart.

Alexander Wheelock Thayer, *Thayer's Life of Beethoven*, rev. and ed. Elliot Forbes (Princeton: Princeton University Press, 1967), vol. 1, pp. 304–306.

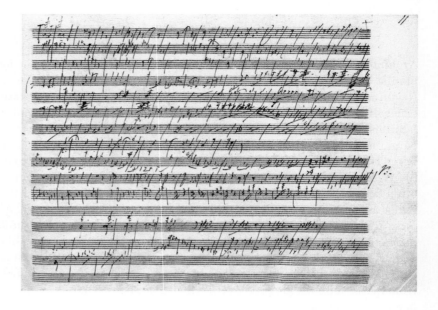

reflecting his own experience and feelings rather than the generalized and objectified emotions found in earlier music. Often, the thematic material assumes the character of a protagonist who struggles against great odds and eventually triumphs.

Eroica Symphony

The Symphony No. 3 in E♭ Major, Op. 55 (1803–1804), which Beethoven eventually named *Sinfonia Eroica* (Heroic Symphony), exemplifies his new approach. In fact, it marks a radical departure in Beethoven's symphonic writing because, beyond presenting conventional moods and abstract topics, as his first symphony had done, it has a subject—the celebration of a hero—and expresses in music the ideal of heroic greatness. It is also longer and more complex than any previous symphony, which made it difficult for audiences to grasp at first, although it was soon recognized as an important work.

First movement

Following the analogy drawn above, we may think of the first movement (NAWM 126)—a very large sonata form—as a story about challenge, struggle, and final victory, with its first theme as the main character. After two introductory chords, the theme (shown in Example 18.1a) emerges in the triadic shape of a fanfare, implying a heroic character, but sinks down suddenly to introduce an unexpected C♯, suggesting some inner conflict or flaw. Over the course of the movement, the theme undergoes a number of transformations: it is portrayed as striving, being opposed and subdued, but eventually triumphing. Most striking along the way is the recurrence of the syncopations first heard near the beginning, which culminate in the crashing, offbeat, dissonant chords of the terrifying climax of the development section (Example 18.1b).

One of the most suggestive reappearances of the main theme is in the horn, during the suspenseful dominant preparation for the recapitulation. The harmonic shock of the dominant-tonic conflict created by the premature return of the main theme in the horn convinced some early listeners that the horn player had mistakenly entered too soon. Carl Czerny, Beethoven's pupil, proposed this entrance be eliminated; the French composer and Beethoven-admirer Hector Berlioz even thought it was a copyist's mistake. But the sketches show that Beethoven contemplated this clever ploy from the very first draft.

Dedication to Napoleon

There is evidence that Beethoven intended to dedicate his third symphony to Napoleon, the enlightened hero who had promised to lead humanity into the new age of liberty, equality, and fraternity. According to his student Ferdinand Ries, when Beethoven heard that Napoleon had proclaimed himself emperor, he angrily tore up the title page containing the dedication, disappointed that his idol

Example 18.1 Ludwig van Beethoven, Symphony No. 3 in E♭ Major, first movement

a. Opening theme

b. Rhythmic climax near the end of the exposition

Example 18.2 Ludwig van Beethoven, Symphony No. 3 in E♭ Major, Funeral March

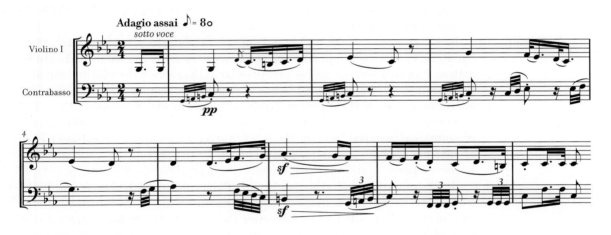

proved to be an ambitious ruler on the way to becoming a tyrant. The title page of a score containing Beethoven's corrections reveals that Bonaparte's name was violently scratched out, confirming the gist if not the details of the story. But Beethoven seems to have wavered in his opinion of the French Republic's leader because that August he wrote to his publisher that the symphony's title was "Bonaparte." When the symphony was first published in Vienna two years later, it bore the title "Sinfonia Eroica . . . composta per festeggiare il sovvenire di un grand Uomo" (Heroic Symphony . . . composed to celebrate the memory of a great man). Whatever his feelings toward Napoleon, Beethoven conducted the symphony in Vienna in 1809 at a concert that Bonaparte was to have attended.

It is the second movement—the *Funeral March*—more than anything else in the symphony that links the work with France, the republican experiment there, and Napoleon. Instead of the customary slow movement Beethoven composed a march in C minor, full of tragic grandeur and pathos, and a contrasting "trio" in C major, brimming with fanfares and celebratory lyricism, after which the march returns, broken up by rests suggestive of sighs at the end. Thirty-second-note upbeats in the strings imitate the roll of muffled drums used in the Revolutionary processions that accompanied French heroes to their final

Funeral March

Figure 18.4 An anonymous portrait of the Malfatti family, who originally came from Lucca, Italy. Giovanni, standing behind the piano with music in hand, moved to Vienna in 1795 and eventually became one of Beethoven's doctors. His niece, Therese, seated at the piano, inspired deep affection in Beethoven, who was profoundly hurt when the family refused his proposal of marriage in 1810. (Beethoven Haus, Bonn.)

resting places (Example 18.2), and one passage strikingly parallels a famous French revolutionary march by François-Joseph Gossec.

Fidelio

Beethoven began work on his only opera, *Fidelio*, almost immediately after finishing the Third Symphony, and the two works share a revolutionary atmosphere. Not only was the rescue plot popular at the turn of the century, but also the libretto itself was borrowed from a French Revolutionary–era opera, *Léonore; ou, L'Amour conjugal* (Leonore; or, Conjugal Love), in which Leonore, disguised as a man, rescues her husband from prison. Beethoven's music transforms this conventional material, making the chief character, Leonore, an idealized figure of sublime courage and self-denial. The whole last part of the opera glorifies Leonore's heroism and the great humanitarian ideals of the Revolution.

Beethoven struggled even more with Fidelio than he had with his other works. The first performances of the original three-act version, called *Leonore*, took place in November 1805, just after the French armies had marched into Vienna. Rearranged and shortened to two acts, the opera was brought out again the following March but immediately withdrawn. Finally, after still more extensive revisions, in 1814 a third version proved successful. In the course of all these changes, Beethoven wrote no fewer than four different overtures for the opera.

Chamber music

The chamber music of the middle period abounds in fresh explorations of each genre. Examples are the three string quartets of Op. 59, which are dedicated to the musical amateur Count Rasumovsky, the Russian ambassador to Vienna, who played second violin in a quartet that was said to be the finest in Europe. As a compliment to the count, Beethoven introduced a Russian melody as the principal theme for the finale of the first quartet and another in the third movement of the second quartet. These two quartets, composed in the summer and autumn of 1806, had such a new style that musicians were slow to accept them. When Count Rasumovsky's players first read through the Quartet No. 1 in F Major, they were convinced that Beethoven was playing a joke on them. The first movement is particularly peculiar in its use of single, double, and triple pedal points, frequent changes of texture, imitations of horns, unmelodious passages exploiting the extreme ranges of the instruments, fugues cropping up out of nowhere, and startling unison passages.

The Fourth, Fifth, and Sixth Symphonies were all composed between 1806 and 1808, a time of exceptional productivity. Beethoven worked on the Fourth and Fifth Symphonies at the same time; the first two movements of the Fifth, in fact, were already done before the Fourth was completed. The two works are very different, as though Beethoven wished to express polar feelings at the same time. Joviality and humor mark the Fourth Symphony in B♭ Major, while the Fifth in C Minor can be considered the musical projection of Beethoven's struggle with fate. The outcome of the struggle is suggested by the transition from C minor to C major just before the triumphant finale, likened to a grand expansion of the move from chaos to light in Haydn's *Creation* (see NAWM 120). The first movement is dominated by one of the best-known themes in all of Western music: the four-note anacrustic motive (♪♪♪♩) that is announced emphatically at the outset. The same rhythmic idea recurs in various forms in the other three movements. The transition from minor to major takes place in an inspired passage that begins with the timpani softly recalling the rhythmic motive and leading without a break from the Scherzo into the finale. Here, the entrance of the full orchestra with trombones on the C-major chord has an electrifying effect. The finale also adds a piccolo and a contrabassoon to the normal complement of strings, woodwinds, brass, and timpani.

The Sixth (*Pastoral*) Symphony in F Major was composed immediately after the Fifth, and the two were premiered on the same program in December 1808 at the Theater an der Wien, shown in Figure 18.5. Each of the *Pastoral*'s five movements bears a subtitle that suggests a scene from life in the country. Beethoven adapted his descriptive program to the normal sequence of movements, inserting an extra movement (*Storm*) to introduce the finale (*Thankful Feelings after the Storm*). In the coda of the Andante movement (*Scene by the Brook*), flute, oboe, and clarinet join harmoniously in imitating birdcalls—the nightingale, the quail, and the cuckoo. All these programmatic effects—which the composer himself warned against taking literally, calling the subtitles "expressions of feeling rather than depiction"—are subordinate to the expansive, leisurely form of the symphony as a whole.

Middle symphonies

Fifth Symphony

Full 🔊

Pastoral Symphony

Figure 18.5 An anonymous 1825 engraving of the Theater an der Wien. Beethoven's famous four-hour concert of December 22, 1808, took place in this bitterly cold hall. The program included the first public performances of the Fifth and Sixth Symphonies; the first Vienna performance of the Fourth Piano Concerto, with the composer as soloist; and, following some other pieces, the Choral Fantasy, Op. 80.
(Historisches Museum der Stadt, Wien.)

Symphonies No. 7 and 8

Symphonies No. 7 in A Major and No. 8 in F Major were both completed in 1812. Once again, Beethoven explored the diverse capabilities of a single genre by producing a pair of opposites: the Seventh is on a grand scale, the Eighth greatly condensed. They were well received at their premieres in late 1813 and early 1814, respectively, but even more thunderous applause greeted another work performed at both concerts: *Wellington's Victory* (1813), a descriptive symphony (see Chapter 19) that depicted the English defeat of Napoleon at Vittoria that summer, complete with the sound of 188 cannon shots provided by the bass drum and precisely written into the score.

Piano sonatas

Beethoven composed ten piano sonatas between 1800 and 1805. Among them are Op. 26 in A♭, with another funeral march, and Op. 27, Nos. 1 and 2, each designated "quasi una fantasia"—the second popularly known as the *Moonlight* Sonata. In Op. 31, No. 2, in D minor, the whole opening section of the first movement, with its rushing passages and abrupt punctuation, has the character of a recitative, anticipating the opening of the fourth movement of the Ninth Symphony (see page 387). The introductory *largo* arpeggio returns at the start of the development section and again at the beginning of the recapitulation, each time in expanded form and with new links to the surrounding music, its last appearance leading into an expressive recitative (see Example 18.3). The finale of this sonata is an exciting *moto perpetuo* in rondo form.

Waldstein and Appassionata sonatas

Also outstanding among the sonatas of this middle period are Op. 53 in C major (1804), called the *Waldstein* Sonata after the patron to whom it is dedicated, and Op. 57 in F minor (1805), known simply as the *Appassionata* (Impassioned). In the first movement of the *Waldstein*, Beethoven managed to make the

Example 18.3 Ludwig van Beethoven, Piano Sonata in D Minor, Op. 31, No. 2

a. Opening

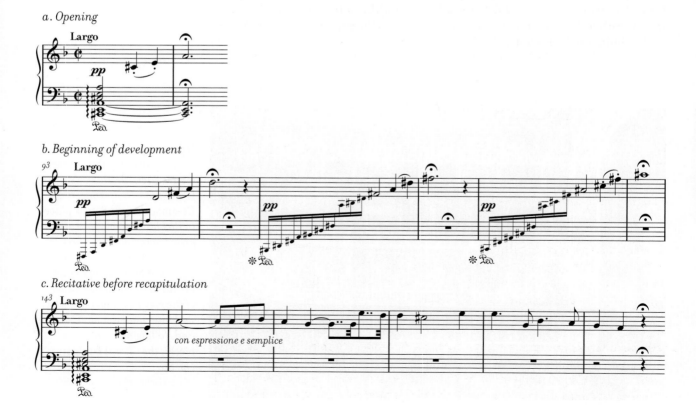

b. Beginning of development

c. Recitative before recapitulation

Example 18.4 Ludwig van Beethoven, Piano Sonata in C Major, Op. 53, Allegro con brio

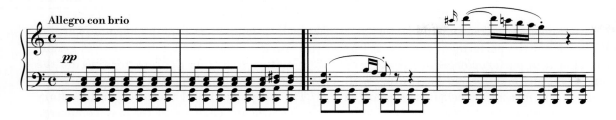

key of C major sound dark and brooding by means of the obstinate thundering of thick, low chords, to which a figure high in the right hand answers like a flash of lightning (Example 18.4). Then the storm clears, and a bright, chordally accompanied melody in E major glistens where a theme in the dominant is expected. The "normal" arrival of the dominant in the second part of the exposition is delayed until near the double bar, just in time to bring back the opening. In the recapitulation, the second theme is first heard in A major, and its restatement in C major is reserved for the coda. Through such unexpected and provocative relationships, together with unusual and evocative thematic ideas, Beethoven turned his sonatas into dramas of contrast, conflict, and resolution.

During his first decade in Vienna, Beethoven composed three piano concertos to play at his own concerts, following the custom of Mozart a decade earlier. But the concertos of his middle period are, like the symphonies, written on a grander scale. In the Piano Concerto No. 5 in E♭ Major, Op. 73 (*Emperor;* 1809), and the Violin Concerto in D Major, Op. 61 (1806), Beethoven greatly expanded the music's expressive range and dimensions. At times, the soloist seems pitted against the orchestra, as if playing the part of a lone hero contending with opposing forces. In the first movement of the *Emperor* Concerto, for example, the soloist enters with a (written-out) cadenza-like passage even before the orchestra's exposition begins. Such dramatic interplay between soloist and orchestra was to become a frequent feature of nineteenth-century concertos.

Piano concertos

Third Period, after 1816

The years up to 1815 were, on the whole, peaceful and prosperous for Beethoven. His music was played regularly in Vienna, and he was celebrated both at home and abroad. Thanks to the generosity of patrons and the steady demand from publishers for new works, his financial affairs were in good order. But his deafness posed a more and more serious challenge, and as it caused him to lose contact with others, he retreated into himself, becoming morose, irascible, and morbidly suspicious even of his friends. Family problems, ill health, and unfounded apprehensions of poverty also plagued Beethoven during his last decade, and it was only by a supreme effort of will that he continued composing.

Compounding these personal problems was the political and economic climate in Vienna. The final defeat of Napoleon in 1815 was followed by a disastrous postwar depression, making it difficult for Beethoven to produce large-scale public works. That same year saw the beginning of tremendous repression instituted by Count Metternich, head of the Austrian government under the emperor. Beethoven's sympathy with the ideals of republican government as it

Political climate in Vienna

In Performance **Beethoven's Tempo**

Written music was traditionally viewed as a vehicle for the performer, who was at liberty to alter it in performance—for instance, by adding embellishments. But beginning with Beethoven, the idea of strict adherence to the composer's score, as if it were a sacred text to be re-created with devotion and restraint, became a hallmark of the Classic era's performance tradition. This meant (as it does even today) that, rather than put forward their own personalities, interpreters must subordinate their understanding of the work to the composer's vision and dedicate their skill to bringing that vision into existence. For their part, composers began to assert more and more control over the performance by using frequent dynamic markings and other notational symbols, such as those for phrasing and articulation.

One particularly problematic area to establish with any precision was tempo. According to eighteenth-century convention, the correct tempo for any meter could be understood by studying courtly dance pieces. The assumption was that each dance had a certain fixed tempo, determined both by its meter and the note values chosen by the composer, who also assigned the piece an appropriate Italian tempo marking (Adagio, Andante, Allegro, and so forth) to match those characteristics. When transferred to a context other than dance, then, the same combination of tempo indication, meter, and note values created the expectation of a particular tempo. But the dances in question did not survive the disintegration of the aristocratic social order that prevailed in Europe before the French Revolution and the Napoleonic Wars; as the minuet, gavotte, and similar dances gradually disappeared from the repertory, so did the yardstick by which tempo had been measured.

The early decades of the nineteenth century saw significant changes in the way composers specified tempos. For one thing, they recognized the imprecise and subjective nature of conventional designations and began to insist on a precise tempo, recognizing that a well-chosen tempo is vital to the effective realization of a piece of music. For another, they worried that the enormous expansion of the amateur market for music publishing meant that their music would come into the hands of people with little or no knowledge of this difficult subject. In keeping with their efforts to exercise increasing control over the performance of their works, then, many nineteenth-century composers turned to the metronome, newly patented by Johann Nepomuk Maelzel around 1815, as a method for designating exact tempos (see Figure 18.6).

Beethoven took great care in assigning metronome designations to his music, even when it meant adding them to works he had composed earlier, before the widespread adoption of the device. Until the 1980s however, many turned a blind eye to Beethoven's indications, claiming that they were faulty or problematic, or ignoring them in favor of their own aesthetic preferences; and some musicians still regard it as their inalienable right to select their own tempo. In Beethoven's case, discrepancies occur particularly where the composer seems to have aimed for the fastest tempo at which a piece could be played

had developed in France was now seen as a threat to the state, and he was investigated and spied on by government security forces. During these years, he did not write politically suggestive works like *Fidelio*, or even the *Eroica* Symphony; the heroic style itself became psychologically inappropriate. In his last dozen years of life, Beethoven produced only two large public works, the *Missa solemnis* (1819–1823) and the Ninth Symphony (1822–1824), both completed only after the economy began to improve in the early 1820s. Otherwise, his major focus was on the last five piano sonatas (1816–1821), the *Diabelli Variations* for piano (1815–1822), and the last five string quartets (1824–1826), all in genres traditionally intended for private music-making.

Characteristics of late style

By now, Beethoven had resigned himself to living in a soundless world of tones that reverberated only in his mind. More and more of his compositions

without loss of essential detail. Indeed, Beethoven's apparent liking for extremely rapid tempos in certain types of movements caused consternation even among his contemporaries, and it is possible that he sometimes overestimated the capacity of mere mortal musicians. More recent scholarship,[1] however, and especially recordings by groups using period instruments—that is, those that approximate the qualities of eighteenth- and early nineteenth-century instruments—have vindicated many of Beethoven's supposedly problematic metronome marks.

1. See Clive Brown, *Classical and Romantic Performing Practice 1750–1900* (New York: Oxford University Press, 1999).

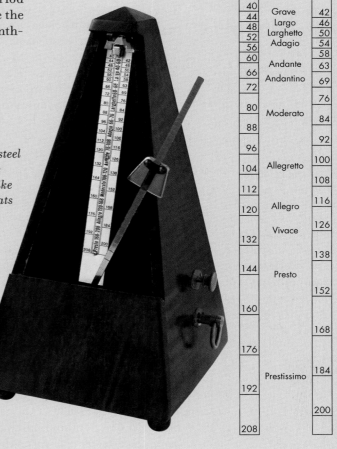

Figure 18.6 The metronome consists of a mounted steel pendulum that produces an audible measure of the passage of time, like the ticking of a clock; but, unlike a clock, its speed can be set between 40 and 200 beats per minute, depending on the position of the small weight attached to the pendulum. The inventor, Johann Nepomuk Maelzel, also published a metronome scale, linking tempo markings with specific speeds. The scale (shown at the right) has two sets of numbers, indicating a certain flexibility. For example, Andante could be anywhere in the range of 60 to 63 beats per minute and Presto between 144 and 152 beats per minute. Beethoven and others set the metronome marking by designating a particular note value and indicating how many times per minute it should be heard—for example, ♩ = 60.
(Photodisc Blue/Getty Images.)

were addressed to connoisseurs. The publication of his late quartets in score, as in Figure 18.7, in addition to the traditional parts format, shows that they were meant to be studied, not just played for the pleasure of the performers. The urgent sense of communication to a large public was replaced by a more introspective quality, and Beethoven's musical language became more concentrated, more abstract. Extremes met: the sublime and the grotesque in the mass and the Ninth Symphony, the profound and the apparently naïve in the last quartets. Classic forms remained, but resembled the features of a landscape after a geological upheaval—recognizable here and there under distorted contours, lying at strange angles beneath the new surface.

In his late compositions, Beethoven seems to have wanted to extract every bit of meaning latent in his themes and motives, as he had always done in his

Variations

Figure 18.7 Title page of Beethoven's String Quartet in C♯ Minor, Op. 131, published by Schott in 1827 and printed in score ("en partition"). Traditionally, quartets had been printed only in separate parts, since only parts were needed for performance. Printing this work in score made it possible for musical connoisseurs to examine the piece at leisure.
(Historisches Museum der Stadt, Wien.)

development sections. He adapted the technique of variation to this purpose. Variations appear within the slow movements of the Piano Sonata No. 29 in B♭ Major, Op. 106, and the String Quartet in A Minor, Op. 132, and in the finale of the Ninth Symphony (after the introduction), to mention a few examples. Although he composed only one independent set for piano during this period—the *Thirty-three Variations on a Waltz by Diabelli*, Op. 120, completed in 1823—it surpasses anything in this genre since Bach's *Goldberg Variations*. Rather than altering the theme in a fairly straightforward manner, Beethoven transformed the very character of the theme, thus setting these variations apart from earlier ones. Diabelli's commonplace little waltz expands surprisingly into a world of variegated moods—solemn, brilliant, capricious, mysterious—ordered with due regard for contrast, grouping, and climax. Each variation is built on motives derived from some part of the theme but altered in rhythm, tempo, dynamics, or context so as to produce a new design. In straying so far from the originally unpromising theme, the *Diabelli Variations* became the model for Schumann's *Symphonic Études*, Brahms's *Variations on a Theme of Handel*, and many other nineteenth-century works in this genre.

Another feature of Beethoven's late style is an emphasis on continuity. Within movements, he achieves continuity by intentionally blurring divisions between phrases or placing cadences on weak beats. Long harmonic arches and leisurely paced melodies communicate a feeling of vastness. Beethoven also emphasized continuity between movements, sometimes indicating that successive movements should be played without a pause.

The improvisatory character of some passages in his earlier piano sonatas (as in Example 18.3) may give us some idea of Beethoven's actual improvisations that so impressed his listeners (see Vignette, page 374). In his later piano sonatas, this compositional style becomes more prominent as Beethoven lingers over a phrase musingly or seems to lose himself in a detail—such as the trill that goes on for pages in the last movement of Piano Sonata No. 30 in E Major, Op. 109. Sometimes these reflective passages culminate in moments of instrumental recitative, as in the piano sonata shown in Example 18.3 from his middle period.

Beethoven's search for new expressive means in his late works gave rise to new sonorities, such as the widely spaced intervals at the end of the Piano Sonata Op. 110, or the simultaneous use in all four instruments of *pizzicato* or *sul ponticello* effects (playing on the bridge to produce a thin sound) in the Scherzo of the C♯-Minor Quartet. Some moments in Beethoven's scores almost require a miracle to make them "sound" in performance; the ideas seem too big for human capabilities. For this reason, early critics thought it was perhaps because of his deafness that Beethoven's musical conceptions sometimes demanded too much of the players. But we have no reason to believe that even a Beethoven with perfect hearing would have altered a single note, either to spare tender ears or to make life easier for performers. Such insistence on the composer's vision at the expense of the performer's freedom and the audience's comfort was to develop into an important strain in nineteenth- and twentieth-century music, with Beethoven becoming the model for later composers.

Counterpoint and fugue

Beethoven's late style is timeless in its prominent use of imitation and fugal texture. His attraction to these techniques undoubtedly came from a number of sources: his lifelong reverence for the music of J. S. Bach and Handel; his familiarity with works by Haydn and Mozart. But it was also perhaps

In Context The Immortal Beloved

My angel, my all, my very self—Only a few words today and at that with pencil (with yours)—Not till tomorrow will my lodgings be definitely determined upon—what a useless waste of time—Why this deep sorrow when necessity speaks—can our love endure except through sacrifices, through not demanding everything from one another; can you change the fact that you are not wholly mine, I not wholly thine. . . .

In the summer of 1812, Beethoven wrote this impassioned letter to a woman whom he addressed as the Immortal Beloved, and whose identity posed a baffling riddle for generations of Beethoven biographers. Whether the letter was ever delivered was also a matter of speculation; dated July 6 but with no year, it was found among the composer's effects after his death. Although Beethoven had several close friendships with women, he never married; in fact, even his most serious romantic attachments were short-lived. Who, then, was his secret, undying love?

Many candidates have been proposed, but one credible though controversial theory was advanced in a biography published 150 years after the composer's death by Maynard Solomon. He attempts to unravel the mystery of Beethoven's Immortal Beloved by reconstructing a powerful web of circumstantial evidence from contemporaneous documents. He proposes that the woman was Antonie Brentano, a beautiful Viennese matron with four children whom Beethoven met in 1810, when she was thirty. (See her miniature portrait, painted on ivory, also found among Beethoven's possessions when he died—Figure 18.8.) Her husband was Franz Brentano, a merchant from Frankfurt who had obtained her father's permission to marry her when she was eighteen years old. The couple resided far from Vienna in his native city, where Antonie missed her family and suffered periods of depression and mysterious physical ailments. During her father's illness and death in 1809, they moved back to Vienna and lived in her family's mansion. She persuaded her husband to open a

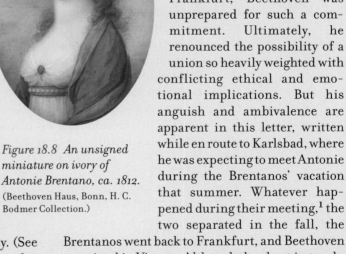

Figure 18.8 An unsigned miniature on ivory of Antonie Brentano, ca. 1812. (Beethoven Haus, Bonn, H. C. Bodmer Collection.)

branch of his business there and remained in Vienna for three years while she settled her father's affairs and disposed of his estate.

During this period (1810–1812), Beethoven was a regular visitor to the Brentano household, where he attended the quartet concerts that were performed there and often played the piano himself. He dedicated several compositions to Antonie and, during her periods of gloomy withdrawal when she would admit no one else to her company, consoled her with his piano improvisations. At some point, their attachment transformed itself into love, despite the looming prospect of Antonie's fated return to Frankfurt with her husband. It is probably no accident, then, that the letter to the Immortal Beloved—which eventually raises the issue of their living together—was written shortly after the final auction of her father's possessions.

If Antonie was willing to leave her husband and remain in Vienna rather than return to Frankfurt, Beethoven was unprepared for such a commitment. Ultimately, he renounced the possibility of a union so heavily weighted with conflicting ethical and emotional implications. But his anguish and ambivalence are apparent in this letter, written while en route to Karlsbad, where he was expecting to meet Antonie during the Brentanos' vacation that summer. Whatever happened during their meeting,[1] the two separated in the fall, the Brentanos went back to Frankfurt, and Beethoven remained in Vienna. Although they kept in touch, they probably never saw each other again.

1. The planned climactic meeting in Karlsbad was at the center of the 1994 film *Immortal Beloved*, in which the event was aborted by fate. The film, however, so distorted the facts as we know them that the encounter, had it taken place, would have reunited Beethoven with his sister-in-law (widow of his deceased brother), whom the script outrageously hypothesized as Beethoven's true Immortal Beloved. Despite such liberties, the film's portrayal of Beethoven (played by Gary Oldman) and his music is very moving.

For further information, see Maynard Solomon, *Beethoven*, 2nd ed. (New York: Schirmer, 1998), esp. pp. 207–246.

Figure 18.9 Beethoven at age forty-eight. Chalk drawing by August von Klöber, 1818.
(Beethoven Haus, Bonn.)

a by-product of the meditative quality of his late style. We find numerous canons and learned contrapuntal devices in all the late works, particularly in the fugatos so central to development sections. Many movements are predominantly fugal—for example, the finales of the Piano Sonatas, Opp. 106 and 110; the first movement of the String Quartet in C♯ Minor, Op. 131 (NAWM 127a); the gigantic *Grosse Fuge* for String Quartet Op. 133; and the two double fugues in the finale of the Ninth Symphony.

As with texture and sonority, so too with form in the instrumental works of Beethoven's third period: on a larger scale, his quest for new means of expression led him to reconceive the number and arrangement of movements. Each of the last five piano sonatas has a unique succession of movement types and tempos, often linked without pause. Two of the late quartets have four movements, but the others have five, six, and—in the case of the String Quartet in C♯ Minor, Op. 131—seven movements, played without breaks between them (the first two are in NAWM 127). The arrangement of forms, keys, and tempos in this quartet illustrates how Beethoven simultaneously invokes and departs from tradition in his late works (see Figure 18.10).

Novel as this arrangement seems, it still contains the elements of the traditional four-movement quartet, much transformed: we may imagine movements 1 and 2 as an introduction and first movement, 3 and 4 as an introduction and slow movement, 5 as a traditionally placed Scherzo, and 6 and 7 as an introduction and finale. Beethoven's concern for integrating the movements is clearly paramount; in addition to blurring the divisions between them, he also unifies them through subtle motivic and key relationships. For example, the most prominent notes in the fugue subject (marked with asterisks in Example 18.5) forecast the keys of the principal movements of the rest of the work; and two motives from the first theme group of the finale (only one is shown in Example 18.5) also echo the fugue subject.

Like all of Beethoven's late sonatas and quartets, Op. 131 is a piece for connoisseurs. Although it appeals to listeners on many levels—it is dramatic, emotionally rich, even funny in the Scherzo—only those "in the know" are likely to notice the clever combination of tradition and innovation or appreciate the complex relationships between the whole and the individual parts.

Mvt.	Form	Key	Tempo	Time Sig.
1	Fugue	C♯ minor	Adagio ma non troppo e molto espressivo	¢
2	Sonata-rondo	D major	Allegretto molto vivace	$\frac{6}{8}$
3	Brief recitative and transition	B minor to V of A major	Allegro moderato— Adagio	c
4	Variations	A major	Andante	$\frac{2}{4}$
5	Scherzo	E major	Presto	¢ $\frac{3}{4}$
6	Brief rounded binary	G♯ minor	Adagio quasi un poco andante	$\frac{3}{4}$
7	Sonata form	C♯ minor	Allegro	¢

Figure 18.10 Overall plan of Beethoven's String Quartet in C♯ Minor, Op. 131.

Example 18.5 Ludwig van Beethoven, String Quartet in C♯ Minor, Op. 131

a. First movement

b. Finale

* = prominent notes that appear as the tonic of a later movement.

Missa solemnis

The most imposing public works of the last period are the *Missa solemnis* and the Ninth Symphony; and, like his late sonatas and quartets, both reexamine the traditions of their respective genres. Beethoven regarded the mass as his greatest work—a deeply personal yet universal confession of faith, full of erudite musical references and liturgical symbols. Originally intended to celebrate the elevation of Archduke Rudolph to archbishop of Olmütz in 1820, the work grew too long and elaborate for liturgical use; instead, like Bach's B-Minor Mass, it became an encyclopedic, idealized treatment of a well-loved text.

The choral writing owes something to Handel, whose music Beethoven revered. But a Handel oratorio was a string of independent numbers, whereas Beethoven shaped his setting of the Kyrie, Gloria, Credo, Sanctus, and Agnus Dei as a unified five-movement symphony with voices. As in the late masses of Haydn, choruses and ensembles of soloists freely combine and alternate within each movement. Beethoven's attention to musical form led him to take liberties with the liturgical text, such as the rondo-like recurrences of the word "Credo," with its musical motive in the third movement.

Ninth Symphony

The Ninth Symphony was first performed on May 7, 1824, on a program with one of Beethoven's overtures and three movements of his mass. Beethoven, though deaf, was conducting. The large and distinguished audience applauded vociferously after a portion of the symphony, but Beethoven did not turn around to acknowledge the applause because he could not hear it: one of the soloists tugged at his sleeve and directed his attention to the clapping hands and the waving hats and handkerchiefs, whereupon he finally realized the audience's reaction and bowed. The receipts at the concert were large, but so little remained after expenses that Beethoven accused his friends who had managed the affair of cheating him. A repetition two weeks later before a half-full house resulted in a deficit. Thus was the Ninth Symphony launched into the world.

The work's most striking innovation remains its use of solo voices and chorus in the finale. Beethoven had thought as early as 1792 of setting Schiller's *Ode to Joy*, but more than thirty years went by before he decided to work this text into his Ninth Symphony. Consistent with his humanitarian ideals and religious faith, he selected stanzas that emphasize universal fellowship through joy and its basis in the love of an eternal heavenly father. The apparent incongruity of introducing voices at the climax of a long instrumental symphony posed an aesthetic problem, and Beethoven's solution determined the finale's unusual form:

- tumultuous introduction, inspired by the operatic genre of accompanied recitative

TIMELINE The Beethoven Years

Musical Events

1770
Beethoven born

1787
Mozart, *Don Giovanni*
(NAWM 124) in Prague

1791
Mozart dies

1792
Beethoven moves to Vienna

1797–1798
Beethoven, *Sonate pathétique*
(NAWM 125)

1802
Beethoven, Heiligenstadt
Testament

1803
Beethoven, *Eroica* Symphony
(NAWM 126)

1805
Beethoven, *Fidelio* premieres
unsuccessfully

1808
Premiere of Beethoven's Fifth
and Sixth Symphonies

1809
Haydn dies; Beethoven
receives lifetime annuity

1812
Beethoven, letter to the
Immortal Beloved

ca. 1815
Invention of the metronome

1824
Beethoven, Ninth Symphony

1824–1826
Beethoven, late string quartets

1827
Beethoven dies

1775   **1825**

Historical Events

1776
American Declaration
of Independence

1781
Immanuel Kant, *Critique of Pure
Reason*

1789
French Revolution begins

1804
Napoleon crowns himself emperor

1805–1815
Napoleon's forces intermittently
occupy Vienna

1806
Holy Roman Empire dissolves

1813
Jane Austen, *Pride and Prejudice*

1814–1815
Congress of Vienna

1815
Wellington defeats Napoleon
at Waterloo

- review and rejection (by instrumental recitatives) of the themes of the three preceding movements; proposal and joyful acceptance of the "joy" theme
- orchestral exposition of the theme in four stanzas
- return of the tumultuous opening
- bass recitative: "O Freunde, nicht diese Töne! sondern lasst uns angenehmere anstimmen und freudenvollere" (O friends, not these tones! Rather let us sing more pleasant and joyful ones)
- choral-orchestral exposition of the joy theme, "Freude, schöner Gotterfunken" (Beautiful joy, divine spark), in four stanzas, varied (including a Turkish march), and a long orchestral interlude (double fugue) followed by a repetition of the first stanza
- new theme, for orchestra and chorus: "Seid umschlungen, Millionen!" (Be embraced, O millions!)
- double fugue on the two themes
- brilliant *prestissimo* choral coda, bringing back the Turkish percussion, in which the joy theme is repeated in strains of matchless sublimity

Everything here builds on tradition, but the whole is unprecedented. This combination of innovation with reverence for the past, of disparate styles, and of supreme compositional control with profound emotional expression is characteristic of Beethoven's last period and has been seen as a measure of his greatness.

POSTLUDE

Having often celebrated heroism in his music, Beethoven himself became a cultural hero, one whose reputation grew throughout the nineteenth century. His life story helped to define the Romantic view of the creative artist as a social outsider who suffers courageously to bring humanity a glimpse of the divine through art.

Only a few of Beethoven's contemporaries understood his late works, which in any event were so personal that they could hardly be imitated. His influence on later composers stemmed mostly from the works of the middle period, especially the *Rasumovsky* Quartets, the Fifth, Sixth, and Seventh Symphonies, and the piano sonatas. Even in these works, it was not the Classic element in Beethoven's style, but the revolutionary element—the free, impulsive, mysterious, demonic spirit, the underlying conception of music as a mode of self-expression—that fascinated the Romantic generation. As E. T. A. Hoffmann wrote: "Beethoven's music sets in motion the lever of fear, of awe, of horror, of suffering, and awakens just that infinite longing which is the essence of romanticism. He is accordingly a completely romantic composer."[1] But since Hoffmann also realized the importance of structure and control in Beethoven's music and in the works of Haydn and Mozart, whom he called "romantic" as well, perhaps he used the word as a general term of commendation. Romantic or not, Beethoven was one of the great disruptive forces in the history of music in that no subsequent composer could view the symphony—or, indeed, any instrumental genre—the way it had been seen before.

 Resources for study and review available at
wwnorton.com/studyspace

1. E. T. A. Hoffmann, "Beethoven's Instrumental Music" (1813), trans. Oliver Strunk; in Oliver Strunk, ed., *Source Readings in Music History*, rev. ed. by Leo Treitler, (New York: Norton, 1997), vol. 6, p. 153.

PART FIVE

The Nineteenth Century: The Age of Romanticism

PART CONTENTS

The word *romantic* derives from the medieval romance, a narrative in verse or prose about the adventures of heroic figures such as King Arthur, which often took place in mysterious or exotic settings. It connoted something distant, legendary, and fantastic, an imaginary or ideal world far from everyday reality. In the nineteenth century, especially in German-speaking lands, the term was applied first to literature, then to music and art. In contrast to Classic poetry, which was deemed objectively beautiful, limited in scope and theme, and universally valid, Romantic poetry transgressed rules and limits, expressing insatiable longing and the richness of nature. Like the political liberalism espoused by such authors as Charles Dickens and Victor Hugo or the idealist philosophy of Friedrich Nietzsche,

Stage design for the final scene of Richard Wagner's Götterdämmerung.
(BPK/Berlin/Art Resource.)

391

Romantic art focused on the individual and on self-expression. By the mid-nineteenth century, the works of Haydn and Mozart were seen as Classic—that is, elegant, natural, simple, clear, formally closed, and universally appealing—while Romantic music was identified with a search for the original, interesting, evocative, expressive, or extreme. But the two designations were not necessarily mutually exclusive. Consequently, employing the terms *Classic* and *Romantic* to describe opposite qualities can be misleading because the continuity between these two style periods is more essential than the contrast between them; Romantic traits are found in some eighteenth-century music, and many Classic characteristics persisted throughout the nineteenth century. Beethoven's music, especially, was regarded as possessing all the qualities of both worlds and exercised an enormous influence throughout the nineteenth century (see pages 481–482). To the extent that composers emulated his works, they saw themselves as guardians of classical traditions as well as innovators.

From Classic to Romantic

Perhaps the best way to understand Romanticism is as a reaction—or, more precisely, a multitude of reactions—to the rationalist ideals of the eighteenth-century Enlightenment. The belief in the perfectability of society based on logical principles unraveled during the events of the late eighteenth century: first a terrible reign of terror in the aftermath of the French Revolution, and then a period of war all over Europe that ended only in 1815. Some people, their confidence in reason undermined, reacted by turning away from civilization to contemplation of the natural world, leading to the great outburst of nature poetry that reached its peak in the lyrics of Lord Byron, Percy Bysshe Shelley, and John Keats, and to the ambitious landscape paint-

Figure V.1 In Rain, Steam and Speed: The Great Western Railway *(1844), J. M. W. Turner explores light and color in depicting the effects of nature. He also ironically suggests the limits of technology by including a hare running ahead of the train.*

(National Gallery, London. Photo: Erich Lessing/Art Resource, NY.)

ings of John Constable and J. M. W. Turner (see Figure V.1). Others favored retreat into the supernatural worlds of spiritualism, mysticism, or even fantasy, as can be seen in the more visionary works of Henry Fuseli (see Figure V.2). Another form of retreat was found in the revival of past traditions, such as those of the Middle Ages, by artists like Edward Burne-Jones and his circle, evident in Figure V.3, and in the music dramas of Richard Wagner (see Chapter 20). Still another was the exploration of unknown and exotic worlds, either real or imagined, by writers like E. T. A. Hoffmann and artists such as Eugène Delacroix, whose painting *The Death of Sardanapalus*, based on a tragedy by Lord Byron, is discussed below.

Among the most telling visual signs of Romantic style is color, which was explored for its optical effects as well as for its symbolic associations. Many artists associated with Romanticism (Delacroix and Turner, among others) were interested in color theory, and even Goethe, known today mainly for his literary works, wrote a book about it. Concern with color led most Romantic theorists to view painting, as opposed to sculpture, as the quintessential visual art. Sculpture, they argued, with its emphasis on form, was essentially Classic, whereas painting, with its emphasis on color and illusion, was essentially Romantic. This has obvious parallels in music, as when some Romantic composers and critics seemingly prized colorful orchestration over formal design in a symphony, for example.

Romanticism first appeared in painting then, as a way of opposing academic and classical tendencies. But Classicism was cultivated during a period of Neoclassical revival at the end of the eighteenth century in France,

Figure V.2 Henry Fuseli's The Nightmare *(ca. 1790–91), foreshadows the kind of fantastic scene—exploiting terror, violence, eroticism, and the macabre— that attracted some nineteenth-century artists.*
(Goethe House and Museum, Frankfurt am Main, Germany. Photo: Snark/Art Resource, NY.)

Figure V.3 Edward Burne-Jones painted Le Chant d'amour *(1868–1877) on a subject that borrowed themes from medieval tapestry design and early Renaissance painting, demonstrating the interest shared by many Romantic artists in a "simpler" past.*
(© The Metropolitan Museum of Art/Art Resouce, NY.)

where Jacques-Louis David emerged as the leading painter. Years of study in Rome visiting its ruins and ancient monuments prompted the Romantic David to adopt a "classical" style and to use subject matter derived from antiquity, as seen in Figure V.4 In *The Love of Paris and Helen*, David represents the fabled pair of lovers from Greek legend as the perfection of manhood and the epitome of womanly beauty, like Renaissance statues suddenly brought to life. This same classicizing tendency underlies the heroic scale and epic quality of much Romantic music, including not only many symphonies but also, for example, Hector Berlioz's monumental five-act opera *Les Troyens* (The Trojans).

Romanticism in painting

Challenges to this restrained, predominantly Classic style in painting arose in France among Romantic artists who employed a colorful, painterly style that contrasted with the severity of the Classic mode. In general, they treated two types of subjects: modern life, often at its darkest and most harrowing; and exotic historical themes, sometimes bordering on the fantastic. (Again, Berlioz provides a revealing musical parallel in his quasi-autobiographical *Symphonie fantastique;* see Chapter 19). A good example of the first type is *Raft of "The Medusa"* by Théodore Géricault, shown in Figure V.5. The subject represents in the exalted language of monumental art an event that had caused a huge stir in France. The painting shows the victims of a catastrophic shipwreck, having been shamefully abandoned by the crew and left to drift for weeks, caught in the dramatic moment between hope and despair as they attempt to signal their rescuers. Géricault depicts the sordid and tense narrative with muted colors and dramatic gestures, suggesting the antiheroic and desperate plight of man's struggle against the forces of nature.

The second type of subject that appealed to Romantic painters is illustrated by Delacroix's *Death of Sardanapalus* (see Figure V.6), which became as important a manifesto for Romantic painting as Victor Hugo's works were for literature. Sardanapalus was a legendary Assyrian monarch who lived in great luxury but who died, after having set fire to his palace, in a conflagration that consumed his entire court. Delacroix's treatment combines Byronic exoticism with the use of vivid color to convey sensation. The same painterly application of color is also evident in his subdued but nonetheless intense portrait of Fryderyk Chopin (see Figure 19.12).

Figure V.5 Raft of "The Medusa" *by Théodore Géricault (1819) dramatically portrays a sensational contemporary tragedy, underlining the realist and antiheroic qualities of some Romantic art.*
(Louvre, Paris. Photo: Erich Lessing/Art Resource, NY.)

Figure V.6 Eugène Delacroix's Death of Sardanapalus *(1827) illustrates the Romantic use of color to suggest emotion, as well as the attraction to sensational and exotic subjects.*
(Louvre, Paris. Photo: Erich Lessing/Art Resource, NY.)

Europe in the Nineteenth Century

The new order

The upheavals of 1789–1815 changed the European political landscape. The French Revolution made peasants and workers into citizens instead of subjects. Napoleon's wars swept away old political boundaries and spread the Revolutionary ideals of liberty, equality, fraternity or brotherhood, and national identity across Europe. In 1814–1815, the Congress of Vienna drew a new map, shown in Figure V.7, made up of far fewer states on the European continent than before. Although Italy and German-speaking lands were still partitioned, the inhabitants of each felt increasingly strong national ties because of language and culture. So did the people in lands that recently lost independence, such as Poland, or that long endured foreign domination, such as Hungary and Bohemia: to them, the independent nation-state seemed an ideal worth fighting for. The largely unsuccessful series of popular uprisings that took place against repressive governments in western and central Europe is known as the Revolution of 1848. The initial revolt, which occurred in Paris, formed the basis of Victor Hugo's *Les Misérables*. Although reactionary forces prevailed, the revolution yielded significant social and cultural change,

Figure V.7 Map of Europe, 1815–1848.

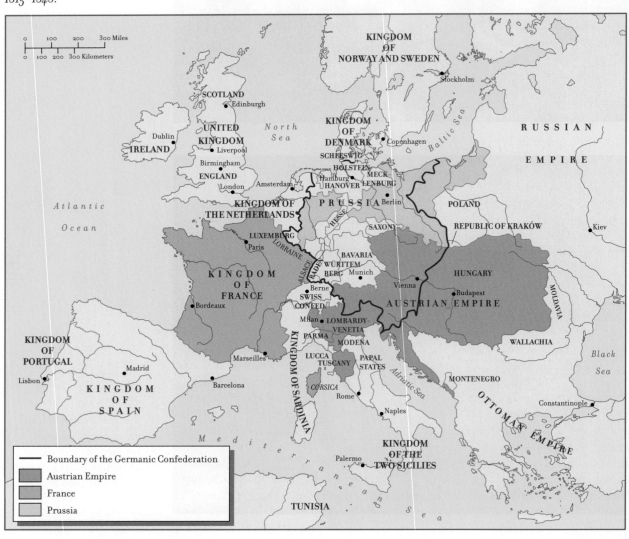

especially in stimulating awareness of national cultural identity. Composers began incorporating national traits in song, instrumental music, and opera. The eighteenth-century cosmopolitan ideal was replaced by the expectation that composers write music true to their national identities.

The Americas saw equally radical change. After the American and French Revolutions, the United States expanded west and south through purchase, treaties, and wars. Native Americans in many areas fought to retain control, but settlers moved west in increasing numbers. The United States began to create its own cultural identity in the tales of Washington Irving and Nathaniel Hawthorne, the novels of James Fenimore Cooper, and the songs of Stephen Foster. In Canada, French and British provinces were officially united in 1841, although the two sides continued to clash until the Canadian Confederation was established in 1867.

The Americas

The Industrial Revolution gradually transformed the economy, bringing people from the countryside to the cities and creating a society based on mass production and distribution. The result was a large and influential middle class and new ideological movements, such as socialism and Marxism (so named after the ideas of Karl Marx), which challenged the established order. The philosopher Arthur Schopenhauer emphasized the individual will as an impelling force, at the same time recognizing that conflicting wills cause continual strife and frustration, which can be eased only by philosophy and the arts. Thus, the artist became the new visionary of the Romantic era, and among the arts, music was accorded a new respect, taken more seriously than ever before. At the same time, scientific and technological innovations brought about profound changes in people's daily lives. Scientists like Louis Pasteur introduced vaccines, pasteurization, and other advances that contributed to an enormous increase in the population of the world's industrialized countries, while the construction of railroads altered travel and commerce by moving people and goods more efficiently.

Economic and social changes

The changed economic and political order in Europe dramatically affected musicians' lives. War and inflation impoverished the aristocracy and the elimination of over one hundred small states drastically reduced the number of courts supporting the arts. More and more musicians worked for the public—playing in orchestras, giving concerts, composing on commission and for publication, or teaching amateurs. While princely patrons had expected their employees to play several instruments and, like Bach and Haydn, to compose in most genres, many nineteenth-century musicians achieved success through specialization. Among the most prominent musicians of the age were virtuosos—performers such as violinist Niccolò Paganini and pianist Franz Liszt (see Chapter 21) who dazzled audiences with their technical mastery of only one instrument. Some composers also specialized in writing music for only one medium, such as Fryderyk Chopin in piano music and Giuseppe Verdi in opera.

Decline of patronage

As the urban middle class grew in size and influence, more people had the money and leisure to purchase instruments and learn to play them, and amateur music-making became an important social outlet and home diversion. Instruments themselves became more affordable as a result of mechanized production and other advances (see Innovations, pages 406–407). At the center of home music-making was the piano, and square pianos like that in Figure V.8, small enough for parlors, found their way into many homes on both sides of the Atlantic. Women, particularly, played piano, continuing a tradition of women at the keyboard that stretched back to the sixteenth century. Pianist-composers such as Chopin and Liszt supported themselves in part by giving lessons to well-to-do women. Although there were some professional women pianists in the first half of

Middle-class music-making

TIMELINE   The Nineteenth Century

Musical Events

Lord Byron

1827
Beethoven dies

1830
Berlioz, *Symphonie fantastique*
(NAWM 138)

Queen Victoria

1839–1847
Liszt tours Europe as a virtuoso
pianist

1840
Schumann, *Dichterliebe*
(NAWM 130)

1850
London firm of Broadwood
making 2,000 pianos a year

1800

Historical Events

1804
Napoleon crowns himself
emperor of France

1812–1818
Byron, *Childe Harold's
Pilgrimage*

1815
Napoleon defeated at
Waterloo; Congress of Vienna
redefines European boundaries

1819
Schopenhauer, *The World as
Will and Representation*

1825
First railway begins operating
in England

1827
Delacroix, *Death of
Sardanapalus* (Figure V.6)

1831
Goethe, *Faust*, Part II

1837
Victoria crowned queen of
England

1844
Turner, *Rain, Steam, and
Speed: The Great Western
Railway* (Figure V.1)

1848
Marx and Engels, *Manifesto
of the Communist Party*;
beginning of women's suffrage
movement

1848–1849
Unsuccessful revolutions
throughout Europe

Figure V.8 Family
Concert in Basle *(1849)
by Sebastian Gutzwiller
shows a typical domestic
scene of music-making:
a woman performs on a
square piano while
various other family
members play violin and
flute or engage in different
activities.*
(Öffentliche Kunstsammlung,
Kunstmuseum Basel.)

left: National Trust/Art Resource, NY.
center: Victoria & Albert Museum, London. Photo:
Victoria & Albert Museum, London/Art Resource, NY.
right: Tretyakov Gallery, Moscow, Russia. Photo: Scala/
Art Resource NY.

1859
Wagner, *Tristan und Isolde* (NAWM 149)

1865
Premiere of Schubert's *Unfinished* Symphony

Yuon, *Cupolas and Swallows*

1874
Verdi, Requiem; Musorgsky, *Pictures at an Exhibition*

1897
Brahms dies

1900

1852–1870
Second French Empire under Napoleon III

1859
Darwin, *On the Origin of Species by Natural Selection*

1860s
Bismarck unites Prussia with other states to forge German Empire

1861
Victor Emmanuel II becomes king of a united Italy; Serfdom abolished in Russia

1862
Hugo, *Les Misérables*

1867
Austrian Empire reorganized as Austro-Hungarian monarchy

1869
Opening of the Suez Canal; Tolstoy, *War and Peace*

1870–1871
Franco-Prussian War; France defeated and Germany unified

1877
Edison invents the phonograph

1888
Pasteur Institute founded in Paris

the nineteenth century, most women considered music an accomplishment designed to attract a spouse and entertain family and friends, rather than a career.

All these amateurs needed music to play, creating a boom in music publishing with catalogues of tens of thousands of pieces for sale. Again, technology proved crucial: newly invented lithographic processes enabled publishers to print music cheaply and with elaborate illustrations that helped it sell. Composers in turn were motivated to supply publishers with works that appealed to amateur performers by having tuneful melodies, attractive accompaniments, minimal counterpoint, strong musical and extramusical imagery, evocative titles, familiar chord progressions interspersed with dramatic or colorful harmonic contrasts, and relatively little technical difficulty. The most successful music offered something novel and individual that made it stand out from the crowd. However, originality was now marked not by how composers treated conventional material, as in the Classic era, but by the innovative qualities of the material itself: new descriptive genres, unexpected progressions, chromatic chords and voice leading, distant modulations, and tonal ambiguity. The new idiom, born of the constellation of factors just described and focused on beautiful melody, colorful harmony and orchestrations, emotion, novelty, individuality, and in some instances ethnicity, paralleled Romanticism in literature and art and came to be called Romantic music.

Market for music and the new idiom

ARTS & IDEAS

Science and Philosophy

German philosopher Arthur Schopenhauer (1788–1860) wrote *The World as Will and Representation* (1819), which held, among other things, that music was unique among the arts because it could express the will directly. His emphasis on the will as a motivating force influenced Nietzsche and the psychology of Freud; his impact on Wagner is discussed in Chapter 20.

German economist, philosopher, and socialist Karl Marx (1818–1883) promoted the idea that the state throughout history has been a device for the exploitation of the masses by a dominant class; that class struggle has been the main agent of historical change; and that the capitalist system, containing the seeds of its own decay, will be superseded by a socialist order and a classless society. His major works are the *Manifesto of the Communist Party* (1848), written for the Communist League, and *Das Kapital* (1867).

Louis Pasteur (1822–1895) was a French chemist and microbiologist whose work demonstrated that many diseases are caused by microorganisms. He developed some vaccines as well as pasteurization, a technique for killing harmful bacteria in fluids such as milk by heating the liquid for a specific amount of time. He was the first director of the Pasteur Institute, founded in Paris in 1888 to continue his research on virulent and contagious diseases.

Friedrich Wilhelm Nietzsche (1844–1900), German philosopher, emphasized the "will to power" as the chief motivating force of both the individual and society. He rejected Western bourgeois civilization and looked to the *Übermensch* (superman) to create a new heroic morality that would exist beyond the conventional standards of good and evil. Among his works are *The Birth of Tragedy* (1872) and *Thus Spake Zarathustra* (1883–1891), which inspired a tone poem by Richard Strauss.

Literature

Johann Wolfgang von Goethe (1749–1832), German poet, dramatist, and prose writer, was a modern Renaissance man. Influenced by Greco-Roman civilization, Homer, and Shakespeare, he was a classical humanist with Romantic leanings whose works were tremendously admired throughout the nineteenth century and inspired many musical treatments. His *Faust* (1790–1832), a play about the legendary German doctor who sold his soul to the devil in exchange for youth, knowledge, and magical powers, exemplifies the darker aspects of Romanticism.

E. T. A. Hoffmann (1776–1822), German author of novels, short stories, and criticism, was also an opera composer and set designer. His sometimes bizarre fiction helped to establish the grotesque vein that became popular in some nineteenth-century literature and art. (See Vignette, page 427.)

English poet George Gordon, Lord Byron (1788–1824) became famous throughout Europe as the embodiment of Romanticism with his quasi-autobiographical *Childe Harold's Pilgrimage*, which he dubbed a "romance" (meaning a narrative of adventure). The work introduced the century's "Byronic hero" — alienated, gloomy, passionate, mysterious — a figure who had countless descendants in life and art. Byron's legendary status was aided by his good looks, lameness (he had a club foot), flamboyant lifestyle, and exile from England.

Alexander Sergeyevich Pushkin (1799–1837) was a Russian poet and dramatist whose works inspired operas by Glinka, Musorgsky, Tchaikovsky, and others. Under the

Romanticism in Music

Even more than a collection of style traits, however, Romanticism in music is a state of mind that enabled composers to seek individual paths for expressing intense feelings — for example, melancholy, yearning, or joy. Composers respected the conventions of form and tonal relations up to a point, but their imaginations drove them past limits that once seemed reasonable and to explore new realms of sound such as instrumental color, harmony, and dynamics.

influence of Shakespeare and Byron, Pushkin blended Western and Russian culture and had an enormous impact on subsequent Russian literature, despite his death at a young age after being wounded in a duel over his wife.

French poet, playwright, and novelist Victor Hugo (1802–1885) was a leader of the Romantic movement in Paris. He is best known for the humanity and compassion of his novels *Les Misérables* and *Notre-Dame de Paris*. Several of his plays served as the basis for librettos of operas by Verdi and others, including the modern musical *Les Misérables*, with music by Claude-Michel Schönberg, which has been translated into twenty-one languages and made into a Hollywood film.

The prolific English novelist Charles Dickens (1812–1870) depicted life at all levels of society in Victorian England, attacked injustice and social hypocrisy, and created a host of characters with such vividness that their names became household words. His novels include *A Christmas Carol, David Copperfield, Great Expectations,* and *A Tale of Two Cities.*

The sisters Charlotte Brontë (1816–1855) and Emily Brontë (1818–1848) wrote, respectively, the classic English novels *Jane Eyre* and *Wuthering Heights*. Among other romantic themes such as the supernatural and the lure of the exotic, they articulated in their works the need of women for both love and independence.

Russian writer Count Leo Tolstoy (1828–1910) set his titanic novel *War and Peace* (1862–1869) against the backdrop of the Napoleonic invasion of Russia in 1812. The novel views history as a force marching to its own ends in which human characters play only an accidental role. His compelling psychological novel *Anna Karenina* concerns the tragedy of a wife consumed by an illicit passion.

Art

The works of Anglo-Swiss painter Henry Fuseli (1741–1825) reveal his Romantic fascination with terrifying and weird subjects. He was a great stimulus to a younger generation of artists who adopted the Romantic concept of the artist as prophet and visionary. (See Figure V.2.)

The English painter J. W. M. Turner (1775–1851) took Romantic landscape painting to its height, mastering both dramatic scenes of disasters and quiet moments of intense lyricism. He explored the effects of nature in his paintings, in which he achieved transcendent, almost abstract effects with color. (See Figure V.1.)

Théodore Géricault (1791–1824), arguably the greatest painter of the first half of the nineteenth century despite his premature death, began his career by celebrating the heroism of Napoleonic France but turned to representing antiheroic subjects, such as the monumental *Raft of "The Medusa."* (See Figure V.5.)

Eugène Delacroix (1798–1863), a close friend of Fryderyk Chopin and George Sand, had a tremendous influence on the later Romantics as a colorist. He favored turbulent scenes inspired by mythology, literature (especially Byron and Shakespeare), and history. (See Figures V.6 and 19.12.)

English painter and decorative artist Sir Edward Burne-Jones (1833–1898) was a leading figure in the Pre-Raphaelite movement, which took its inspiration from the early Renaissance. His paintings of subjects from medieval legend and classical mythology vividly illustrate the late nineteenth-century fantasy of a medieval Golden Age that so attracted Wagner. (See Figure V.3.)

Some nineteenth-century writers (Schopenhauer and Liszt, for example) considered instrumental music the ideal Romantic art because it was free from concrete words and images, and thus could evoke impressions, thoughts, and feelings that are beyond the power of words to express. Moreover, writers such as E. T. A. Hoffman (see Vignette, page 427) saw instrumental music as an autonomous art, free from earlier notions that music must serve the words of a madrigal or opera, convey an appropriate affect, or fulfill a particular social role, whether as entertainment or as accompaniment to a religious ritual or dinner party. This autonomy paralleled composers' own freedom of expression

Music as autonomous

and independent status outside the old patronage system. Musicians were no longer part of the servant class as Haydn and earlier composers had been. The autonomy of music as an art symbolized the individualism and economic independence so valued by the nineteenth-century middle class.

Although composers held instrumental music in the highest regard, poetry and literature occupied a central place in their thoughts and careers. A number of Romantic composers were also extraordinarily literary. Berlioz, Schumann, and, later, Liszt wrote distinguished essays on music. Schubert and Schumann attained a new and intimate union between music and poetry, and the lyrical spirit of their songs imbued even their instrumental music.

Program music vs. absolute music

Ultimately, the ideal of instrumental music as the premier mode of expression and the strong literary orientation of nineteenth-century composers converged in program music. The term *program music* referred to instrumental music associated with poetic, descriptive, or narrative subject matter, and came to be viewed as the opposite of absolute music, which purportedly had no such extramusical associations. Whether the program was outlined in detail or merely suggested, the music usually transcended its subject and could be understood and appreciated on its own. The program did not necessarily inspire or even precede the music; sometimes it was imposed as an afterthought.

Organicism

The esteem for instrumental music was reflected in a new concept of organic musical form. Eighteenth-century writers conceived of musical works as rhetorical, shaped like a speech and intended to have a certain effect on the listener (see Chapter 15). This metaphor for music can be traced back at least to the Renaissance and continued to echo throughout the nineteenth century and into the twentieth. But Goethe argued in a study of plant metamorphosis that, just as all the parts of a plant are adaptations of the same basic shape, so too artists should shape their works so that all the parts are unified by being derived from a common source. Applying this view to music, the organic relationship of the themes, sections, movements, and other parts of the whole (and to each other) becomes more important than rhetorical structure or persuasive force. In the metaphor of organicism, motivic links can contribute more to a work's unity than its harmonic plan or its use of a conventional form.

Cultivating extremes

Nevertheless, Romantic composers were also intent on testing the limits of musical expression, which meant pushing to extremes such elements as dynamic shadings, harmonic logic, formal boundaries, and even the physical capabilities of performers. One pair of opposites they explored with equal enthusiasm was the monumental and the miniature; at the same time as orchestras became larger and more colorful, matching the grandeur and boldness of some French history paintings, nineteenth-century composers cultivated many intimate genres for solo piano, solo voice, and chamber ensemble. In addition to writing hundreds of imposing works for orchestra, they produced thousands of pieces on a smaller scale—for piano solo, various chamber combinations, and voice—among which

Characteristic music

are the characteristic (or descriptive) miniatures that portray a mood or communicate a sentiment in a matter of minutes.

The next four chapters are devoted to the music of the nineteenth century. The extent to which these composers shared traits of Classicism or Romanticism, cultivated absolute or program music, and composed large-scale or miniature works varies with each individual and remains to be explored. Chapters 19 and 21 present representative composers and their works from the first and second halves of the century. Chapter 20 gives an overview of opera and related genres throughout the century and, therefore, covers the same chronological period as the other two chapters. Finally, Chapter 22 traces the last bloom of Romanticism in the closing decades of the nineteenth and the beginning of the twentieth centuries and paves the way for understanding musical modernism.

The Early Romantics

PRELUDE

The first generation of Romantic composers found new ways to engage the established musical genres of the eighteenth century: orchestral music and other large-scale works such as concerto and oratorio, as well as song, solo piano music, chamber music, and opera. As we survey representative composers to about 1850, we shall examine their contributions where relevant to the first four genres, postponing a discussion of opera until Chapter 20.

A principal tenet of Romanticism was that instrumental music could communicate pure emotion without using words. So the orchestra, with its infinite variety of colors and textures, became the medium par excellence of Romantic music. Most nineteenth-century composers we will study mastered the orchestra and proved themselves in symphonic composition. Moreover, they came to terms with how the towering figure of Beethoven had transformed the symphony.

The orchestra was central to public concert life, and the audience in the nineteenth century was increasingly made up of the middle class. Court orchestras in the eighteenth century had played to mixed audiences of nobility and city people, but now, public concerts—such as those arranged to benefit various causes or sponsored by individual entrepreneurs—became more popular. Even with these expanded opportunities, the experience of hearing a symphony orchestra was still a relatively rare event for a music lover of any class. Among the composers discussed in this chapter who conducted orchestral concerts, including their own music, are Berlioz, Mendelssohn, and Schumann. Although the prominence given to the symphony in this book is out of proportion to the place symphonic music actually occupied in the activities of composers, musicians, and the public in this period, such prominence reflects the importance accorded it by audiences, critics, and the composers themselves, who increasingly used it as a means of communication with a new middle-class audience.

Song—particularly the German art song, or Lied (plural: Lieder)—became a favorite outlet for intense personal feelings. In the works of Franz Schubert, for example, the Lied was the perfect foil to the "heavenly length" of his symphonies. At once the most suitable medium for the literary and lyrical tendencies of Romanticism, the Lied enjoyed a brilliant flowering in the nineteenth century—one that has never since been matched.

Lieder composers often grouped their songs into collections with a unifying characteristic, such as texts by a single poet or a focus on a common theme. Such a collection is called a song cycle, in which all the songs are to be performed in order as movements of a multimovement vocal work. This format brought about the possibility of telling a story through a succession of songs. The song cycle became especially common in the nineteenth century, providing a balance between small and large forms, lyric and narrative content, and unity and variety, qualities strongly valued at the time.

The piano, much enlarged and strengthened since Mozart's day (see Innovations, pages 406–407), became the perfect instrument for conveying repertory from either end of the compositional spectrum: concertos of grandiose proportions or brief statements of fleeting impressions. It was capable of producing a full, firm tone at any dynamic level and of responding in every way to demands for both expressiveness and virtuosity. Composers developed new ways of writing for the instrument, such as splitting the accompaniment between two hands, reinforcing the melody by simulating the orchestral technique of doubling, and calling for extended legato effects with the help of the damper pedal. For all these reasons, many Romantic composers of orchestral music—Schubert, Mendelssohn, and Robert Schumann, whom we will meet in this chapter, Liszt and Brahms in Chapter 21—also devoted their energy to writing solo music for piano, while others—like Chopin—made it the sole focus of their creative activity.

The medium of chamber music was not as attractive to some Romantic composers. It lacked the improvisational spontaneity and virtuosic glamour of the solo piano or the solo voice on the one hand, and the glowing colors and powerful sound of the orchestra on the other. So it is not surprising that the arch-Romantics Berlioz, Liszt, and Wagner contributed almost nothing to the repertory of chamber music, nor that the best nineteenth-century chamber works came from composers like Schubert, Brahms, Mendelssohn, and Schumann, who, being chamber-music players themselves, felt closest to the Classic tradition.

In this chapter, we will survey six of the most important composers of the first Romantic generation: Franz Schubert, Robert Schumann, Clara Wieck Schumann, Felix Mendelssohn, Fanny Mendelssohn Hensel, Fryderyk Chopin, and Hector Berlioz. And before moving on, we will have a glimpse of two of their contemporaries in the United States.

Franz Schubert (1797–1828)

The first great master of the Romantic Lied, Schubert also made substantial contributions to symphonic, solo-piano, and chamber-music repertoires, which we shall explore below (see Biography, page 408).

Lieder

The characteristics of the Romantic Lied are exemplified in Schubert's over six hundred songs, many of which were first performed for friends in home gatherings known as Schubertiads (see Figure 19.5). Many of his songs have the simple, artless quality of folk song and suggest uncomplicated feelings (for example, *Heidenröslein*, Example 19.1; and *Der Lindenbaum*, NAWM 129). Others are suffused with sweetness and melancholy (*Am Meer* and *Der Wanderer*). Still others are declamatory, intense, and dramatic (*Aufenthalt* and *Der Atlas*, Example 19.2). Every mood or nuance of feeling finds expression in Schubert's apparently effortless melody, which flows equally well in his songs and instrumental works, for few composers have possessed so fully Schubert's gift for creating beautiful melodies.

Melody

Example 19.1 Franz Schubert, Heidenröslein

A boy saw a rosebud standing, a rosebud on the heath

Example 19.2 Franz Schubert, Der Atlas

I, the unlucky Atlas!

Along with a genius for melody, Schubert possessed a strong sense of harmonic color. His complex modulations, sometimes embodied in long passages in which the tonality is kept in suspense, powerfully underline the dramatic qualities of his song texts. Striking examples of harmonic boldness may be found in *Gruppe aus dem Tartarus* and *Das Heimweh*, a song that also illustrates Schubert's trademark technique of alternating between major and minor forms of a triad. Masterly use of chromatic coloring within a prevailing diatonic sound is another Schubert characteristic (*Am Meer* and *Lob der Thränen*). His modulations typically move from the tonic toward flat keys, and chromatic mediants are favorite destinations, illustrating his penchant for modulation by third rather than by fifth. Such unconventional relationships reflect Schubert's use of harmony as an expressive device, a practice that greatly influenced later composers.

Schubert set poetry by many writers, often dwelling on a single poet for some time. Some of Schubert's finest Lieder are found in his two song cycles on poems by Wilhelm Müller, *Die schöne Müllerin* (The Pretty Miller-Maid, 1823) and *Winterreise* (A Winter's Journey, 1827). In these as in all his songs, Schubert strove to make the music the equal of the words, not merely their frame. Through melody, harmony, accompaniment, and form, he sought to embody the characters, describe the scene, and convey the situation and emotions being expressed.

Schubert always chose forms that suited the shape and meaning of the text. When a poem sustains a single image or mood, Schubert typically uses strophic form, with the same music for each stanza, as in *Heidenröslein* (Little Heath Rose, 1815) and *Das Wandern* (Wandering), the first song in *Die schöne Müllerin*.

Harmony

Texts

Form

Innovations The Industrial Revolution and Music-Instrument Manufacture

The Industrial Revolution was not a single event, but a series of inventions and applications that together radically changed the way goods were manufactured. Items that had been made by hand for centuries—the word *manufacture* itself originally denoted handcrafting—could now be mass-produced by machine, allowing them to be much more widely available and less costly. In addition, existing products were improved, and new ones developed in a continuous stream of innovation.

Musical-instrument manufacture was just one of many revolutionized industries. A profound change was in the sheer quantity of instruments that could be produced. In the 1770s, the output of even the largest piano-making firms in Europe was only about 20 pianos a year, because every piece of each instrument needed to be made by hand. Around 1800, the firm of John Broadwood & Sons of London was manufacturing about 400

pianos a year by employing a large and specialized workforce. However, by 1850 the firm was using steam power and mass-production techniques to make over 2,000 pianos a year, turning out each one a hundred times faster than before. Many were grand pianos, but most were the smaller square pianos (see Figure 19.1) more suitable for a domestic setting. Because they were produced in such quantity, pianos became inexpensive enough for middle-class families to afford.

The design of the piano was also improved through a number of innovations. The damper pedal raised all the dampers off the strings, letting tones continue to sound even after the keys were released and allowing greater resonance, closer imitation of orchestral sound, and new pianistic effects. The metal frame, introduced in England during the 1820s, allowed for instruments with higher string tension and thus greater volume,

Figure 19.1 The Duet *by George Goodwin Kilburne, a painting from the late nineteenth century showing domestic music-making with performers playing harp and square piano. Haynes Fine Art Gallery, Worcester, England.*
(Fine Art Photographic Library/Corbis.)

Figure 19.2 Boehm-system flute (1856) by Theobald Boehm.
(Bate Collection, Oxford, England.)

wider dynamic range, longer sustain, and better legato. By 1850, the piano's range was extended to seven octaves (from the six of Beethoven's day), and double-escapement action permitted more rapid repetition of notes, in turn enabling a new level of virtuosity. All of these new capabilities were exploited by performers and composers, and the piano became the indispensable instrument for home music-making as well as for public concerts.

Other instruments benefited from the same spirit of innovation. Paris had been the center of the harp industry at the close of the eighteenth century largely because Queen Marie Antoinette, herself a harpist, popularized the instrument for domestic use. Just before the French Revolution, Paris had as many as fifty-eight harp teachers and a great many harp makers, including Sébastien Érard, who moved his firm to London after the Revolution and registered the first British patent ever granted for a harp. Érard's firm, which also produced pianos, was instrumental in overcoming the technical problems of the older pedal harp, such as its instability of pitch, frequently breaking strings, and limited modulation. His most remarkable improvement was a new fork mechanism, still operated by a set of pedals, but one which allowed the strings to be temporarily shortened, raising the pitch by one half-step. Eventually, Érard patented a harp that could be played in any key because each string could be adjusted almost instantaneously to produce any of three notes, including the semitones above and below the string's original pitch. By 1820, the firm had sold 3,500 of these instruments, whose principles are still in use by modern pedal-harp makers.

Still other instruments profited from a combination of new technologies, enterprising innovators, and improved methods of manufacture. For example, Theobald Boehm, a goldsmith and musician with experience in the steel industry, established a successful flute factory in Munich in 1828. He experimented with a number of designs for mechanisms that would achieve a uniform tone production, superior sound volume, and better control of tuning. By 1849, he had created the modern Boehm-system flute, an all-metal instrument with large holes that were closed not by bare fingers but by padded keys, linked with each other by a series of rods and axles to facilitate accuracy and speed (see Figure 19.2). Others applied Boehm's ideas to the clarinet and the saxophone, a new wind instrument invented by Adolphe Sax about 1840.

Brass instrument makers applied the valve technology of the steam engine—in which valves controlled the flow of steam, water, or air—to the manufacture of trumpets and horns, enabling these instruments to produce all the notes of the chromatic scale. The valves allow a player to open one or more lengths of pipe to extend the sounding length of the air column and thus lower the pitch by one or more semitones (see Figure 19.3). Many new brass instruments were created as well, including the tuba, which became the bass of the orchestral brass section.

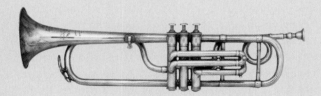

Figure 19.3 Trumpet with piston valves (ca. 1865) by Antoine Courtois of Paris.
(The Metropolitan Museum of Art, Purchase, Bequest of Robert Alonzo Lehman, by exchange, 2001 (2001.187a-1). Photo © 2001 The Metropolitan Museum of Art.)

Similar mechanical innovations brought about by the Industrial Revolution—such as interlocking rods, gears, and screws—also improved the construction and tuning of the timpani in the early nineteenth century. By the late nineteenth century, the piano, the harp, and the wind, brass, and percussion instruments of the orchestra had almost reached their modern form, thanks to the inventors and industrialists who applied the century's new technologies to music.

Franz Schubert (1797–1828)

Homely, humble, and hidden in Beethoven's shadow, Franz Schubert was nevertheless the first great Romantic song writer and an astoundingly prolific composer in all genres. In addition to composing more than 600 Lieder, he made important contributions to the piano, chamber, and symphonic repertories.

The son of a schoolteacher, Schubert grew up in cosmopolitan Vienna. After studying theory and performance, and taking composition lessons from court music director Antonio Salieri, he displayed sufficient musical talent to win a free, first-class education at a prestigious Vienna boarding school. Educated to follow his father's profession, he worked as a schoolteacher for three years before devoting himself entirely to writing music. He composed with astonishing speed and fluency; in 1815 alone (having just turned eighteen and even while teaching) he wrote 144 songs. By 1821, Schubert's music was being widely performed in Vienna and he was earning substantial sums from publishers.

Although Schubert never married, he had a large circle of friends in Vienna. Not physically handsome, he was nicknamed *Schwammerl*, which means "mushroom" but probably connoted something like "Fatso." His close friendships with men and veiled references made by his friends have suggested to some scholars that he was homosexual, although others dispute this conclusion. One member of his circle noted that Schubert's "character was a mixture of tenderness and coarseness, sensuality and candor, sociability and melancholy."[1] These and similar remarks suggest that he may have suffered from bipolar disorder. Others report that his behavior was sometimes dangerously hedonistic or even self-destructive. He apparently contracted syphilis by January 1823, and the last years of his life were clouded by illness. When he died at the age of thirty-one, his tombstone was inscribed "Music has here buried a rich treasure but still fairer hopes." Given the brevity of Schubert's

Figure 19.4 Franz Schubert, in a watercolor portrait from 1825 by Wilhelm August Rieder.
(Gesellschaft der Musikfreunde, Vienna, Austria. Photo: Erich Lessing/Art Resource, NY.)

career, his output of almost one thousand works is truly amazing.

Major works: two song cycles, *Die schöne Müllerin* and *Winterreise*, as well as hundreds of individual songs; 9 symphonies, notably No. 8 in B Minor (*Unfinished*) and No. 9 in C Major (*Great*); about 35 chamber works, including Piano Quintet in A Major (*Trout*), String Quartet in D Minor (*Death and the Maiden*), and String Quintet in C Major; 22 piano sonatas; many short piano pieces; 17 operas and singspiels; 6 masses; and 200 other choral works.

1. Johann Mayrhofer, quoted in Christopher H. Gibbs, *The Life of Schubert* (New York: Cambridge University Press, 2000), p. 96.

Contrast or change is often depicted in modified strophic form, in which some strophes repeat the same music but others vary it or use new music; an example is *Der Lindenbaum* (The Linden Tree) from *Winterreise*, described below. Some songs are in ternary form (ABA or ABA'), as in *Der Atlas* (Atlas), or bar form (AAB), as in *Ständchen* (Serenade), both from *Schwanengesang* (Swan Song,

1828). Longer narrative songs, called ballads, may be through-composed, with new music for each stanza, like *Erlkönig* (The Erlking, 1815), or combine declamatory and arioso styles as in an operatic scene, like *Der Wanderer* (The Wanderer, 1816); in either case, recurring themes and a carefully planned tonal scheme lend unity.

Schubert designed his piano accompaniments to depict and enhance the mood and imagery of the song. The accompaniment of *Gretchen am Spinnrade* (Gretchen at the Spinning Wheel, NAWM 128)—one of the earliest (1814) and most famous of the Lieder, on an excerpt from Goethe's famous play *Faust*—suggests not only the whir of the spinning wheel by a constant rising and falling sixteenth-note figure in the right hand and the perpetual motion of the treadle in the left hand, but also Gretchen's agitation as she thinks of her beloved. Similarly, in *Erlkönig*, one of Schubert's relatively few ballads—on a text by Goethe—the pounding octave triplets in the accompaniment depict at once the galloping of the horse and the frantic anxiety of the father as he rides "through night and wind" with his sick, frightened child clasped in his arms. The delirious boy imagines that he sees the legendary Erlking enticing him to a land where he will be comforted by the swaying, dancing, and singing of the Erlking's daughters. Schubert has characterized in an unforgettable manner the three actors in the drama: the concerned father, the bewitching Erlking, and the increasingly terrified child.

Schubert's mastery of all these elements is evident in *Der Lindenbaum* (NAWM 129) from *Winterreise*, Müller's cycle of twenty-four poems that expresses the nostalgia of a lover revisiting in winter the haunts of a failed summer romance. In this poem, he recalls lying under a linden tree dreaming of his love. Now, as he passes the tree, a chilly wind rustles the branches, which seem to call him back to find rest—or death. The modified strophic form marks the progress of the story: the first strophe, remembering summer love, is in the major mode; the second changes to minor to suggest the chill of winter; the third heralds the cold wind with a new, declamatory melody; and the fourth returns to the major mode and the original melody, now sounding more threatening than comforting. The subtle ways in which the music interprets the poem, and the progress of the poem reinterprets musical elements heard previously, demonstrate how well Schubert conveys meanings through music that deepens our experience of the words.

Gretchen am Spinnrade

Full 🔊 Concise 🔊

Erlkönig

Der Lindenbaum

Full 🔊 Concise 🔊

Figure 19.5 Schubert at the piano accompanying a singer in the home of Joseph von Spaun. Although the sepia drawing by Moritz von Schwind (1868) conveys the intensely emotional engagement with music that was characteristic of the age, it depicts an idealized gathering rather than an actual event.
(Historisches Museum der Stadt Wien. Photo: Erich Lessing/Art Resource, NY.)

Figure 19.6 Caspar David Friedrich, Wanderer above the Sea of Fog. *The figure of the lone wanderer captivated the Romantic imagination because it embodied, among other things, the era's esteem for solitude and the individual in the face of industrialization and mass society.* (Hamburger Kunsthalle, Hamburg, Germany. Bildarchiv Preussischer Kulturbesitz/Art Resource.)

Solo Music for Piano

During the nineteenth century, the piano emerged as the quintessential instrument of the salon, or living room, creating a steady demand for music that amateurs and professionals could play in a domestic setting. This was particularly important to freelance composers like Schubert and Chopin. Among Schubert's works suitable for amateurs are dozens of marches, waltzes, and other dances, as well as several short pieces that became for piano literature what his Lieder are to the vocal repertory. These include six *Moments musicaux* (Musical Moments, 1823–1828) and eight Impromptus (1827), each of which creates a distinctive mood. These works set a standard for every subsequent Romantic composer of intimate piano pieces.

Schubert's most important larger works for the piano are his eleven completed sonatas and the *Wanderer Fantasie* (1822), whose virtuosity and unusual form fascinated later composers. The fantasy's four movements are played without breaks, and they combine the general shape of a four-movement sonata—a fast movement in a truncated sonata form without recapitulation, a slow theme and variations, a scherzo and trio, and a brilliant finale—with constant variation of a rhythmic figure taken from a phrase in Schubert's song *Der Wanderer*, which is quoted explicitly at the beginning of the second movement. Drawing the movements together through musical continuity and common material lent the work an organic unity. The overall key scheme reflects Schubert's interest in harmonic relationships of a third: the movements are in C, E, A♭, and C major respectively (although the second movement begins in the relative minor of E, C♯). Schubert was the first to use such a complete circle of major thirds around the octave, an idea later adopted by Liszt (see Chapter 21) and many other composers.

In his piano sonatas, Schubert departs in subtle ways from the standard Classic patterns, often introducing three keys instead of two in his expositions (for example, tonic for the first theme, mediant for the second, and dominant for the closing theme). His last three piano sonatas (all composed in 1828), show a strong awareness of Beethoven's works, as in the stormy first movement of the Sonata in C Minor.

Chamber Music

Schubert modeled his first quartets on works by Mozart and Haydn, and wrote them primarily for his friends to enjoy. The most popular work from his earlier period is the *Trout* Quintet for piano, violin, viola, cello, and bass (1819), so called because of the Andantino variations, inserted between the scherzo and the finale, on his own song *Die Forelle* (The Trout). But his most important chamber works came in his last five years of life: the Quartets in A Minor (1824), in D Minor (1824–1826, *Death and the Maiden*), and in G Major (1826), and the String Quintet in C Major (1828). In mood, difficulty, style, and conception, Schubert's late chamber works are more dramatic pieces of concert music than entertaining diversions for amateur players.

Example 19.3 Franz Schubert, String Quintet in C Major, first movement

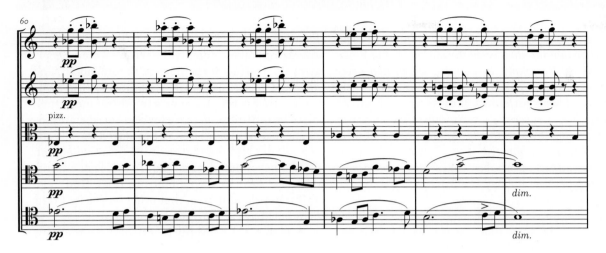

Schubert wrote his masterpiece of chamber music, the String Quintet in C Major (NAWM 141), just two months before his death. The added instrument is a second cello, providing an unusually deep range that was particularly appealing to Romantic sensibilities in its lushness. Schubert obtained exquisite effects and constantly varying textures from this combination. The ideas are set forth and developed in the first movement in a truly symphonic way, but with Schubert's typical approach to sonata form—including a three-key exposition, in which the second theme appears in E♭ before the key of the dominant is reached. The beautiful E♭-major melody of the second theme, shown in Example 19.3, appears first in the cellos in parallel thirds before it reaches the first violin. Its recapitulation in A♭, a third down from the tonic (just as E♭ is a third up), completes a tonal scheme that became popular in the nineteenth century.

String Quintet

Full

Orchestral Music

Schubert's *Unfinished* Symphony (No. 8, 1822, in only two movements) has been called the first truly Romantic symphony by virtue of its songlike melodies, its adventurous harmonic excursions, and its innovative colors and textures. Originally planned as a four-movement work, this was his first attempt at a large-scale symphony. The listener is struck immediately by its haunting opening in B minor. After this brief but unusual introduction, Schubert's first theme begins with a quietly stirring figure in the low strings that then combines with a plaintive melody that is quite different from the typical first themes of his predecessors and less easily fragmented into motives for symphonic development. After an extremely brief transition (only four measures) that modulates to the surprising key of G major, Schubert presents the relaxed second theme in the cellos, accompanied by syncopated figures in the violas and clarinets over the pizzicato of the double basses. Instead of centering the development section and coda on these two themes, as Haydn or Beethoven might have done, Schubert focuses on the introductory subject. In this way, he followed the custom for symphonic development while devoting the main thematic areas to the presentation of memorable, seductive melodies like those of

Unfinished Symphony

VIGNETTE Schumann on Schubert's Symphony in C Major

When he visited Schubert's brother Ferdinand in 1839, Robert Schumann discovered the manuscript of Schubert's Great *Symphony in C Major, which had never been performed in public. Through Schumann's intercession, it was performed that same year at the Gewandhaus Concerts in Leipzig under the direction of Mendelssohn. In a review of the piece the following year, Schumann praised it as revealing both an unknown aspect of Schubert's musicality and a new approach to the symphony.*

I must say at once that anyone who is not yet acquainted with this symphony knows very little about Schubert. When we consider all that he has given to art, this praise may strike many as exaggerated, partly, no doubt, because composers have so often been advised, to their chagrin, that it is better for them—after Beethoven—"to abstain from the symphonic form." . . .

On hearing Schubert's symphony and its bright, flowery, romantic life, the city [of Vienna] crystallizes before me, and I realize how such works could be born in these very surroundings. . . .

Everyone must acknowledge that the outer world—sparkling today, gloomy tomorrow—often deeply stirs the feeling of the poet or the musician; and all must recognize, while listening to this symphony, that it reveals to us something more than mere beautiful song, mere joy and sorrow, such as music has ever expressed in a hundred ways, leading us into regions that, to our best recollection, we had never before explored. To understand this, one must hear this symphony. Here we find . . . a suffusing romanticism that other works by Franz Schubert have already made known to us.

And then the heavenly length of the symphony, like that of a thick novel in four volumes. . . . How this refreshes, this feeling of abundance, so contrary to our experience with others when we always dread to be disillusioned at the end and are often saddened through disappointment.

From *Neue Zeitschrift für Musik* 12 (1840): 82–83, after the translation, by Paul Rosenfeld, in Robert Schumann, *On Music and Musicians*, ed. Konrad Wolff (New York: Norton, 1946), pp. 108–111.

---

his songs. This practice, to maintain the outward form of the symphony while infusing it with more lyrical context, was a solution adopted by many Romantic composers.

Great Symphony in C Major

Schubert's *Great* Symphony in C Major (No. 9, composed in 1828—the last year of his life—and first performed in 1839) received that nickname because of its "heavenly length," much admired by Robert Schumann (see Vignette, above). Schumann appreciated Schubert's expansion of the form to accommodate his appealing melodies and orchestral effects and, having thus far avoided writing a symphony himself, was inspired to follow Schubert's example. In fact, Schubert's Symphony in C Major provided an important model for younger composers by blending Beethovenian drama and his own Romantic lyricism within an expanded Classic form.

Influence

Schubert's ability to capture the mood and character of a poem and make the music its equal in emotive and descriptive power, along with the sheer beauty of his music and the pleasure it gives to those who perform it, have endeared the composer both to his contemporaries and to generations of singers, players, and listeners. His Lieder set the standard that later song composers strove to match. His lyricism—the melody-centered style of the songs and piano music—affected every other genre of the nineteenth century. Never before or since were symphonies, chamber works, and piano music so full of songlike melodies.

Robert Schumann (1810–1856)

Robert Schumann (see Biography, pages 414–415), like Schubert, composed in all the major genres of the nineteenth century, but he concentrated on one at a time—piano music until 1840, then songs in that year, symphonies in 1841, chamber music in 1842–1843, and dramatic music in 1847–1848. During his last decade Schumann, troubled by illness, was not enormously productive.

Piano Music

Schumann was a master of the miniature form, as his contributions to piano and song literature testify. The bulk of his piano compositions are short character pieces—descriptive works that depict a mood, personality, or scene, usually indicated in the title. These are often grouped into colorfully named sets: *Papillons* (Butterflies); *Carnaval* (NAWM 132); *Fantasiestücke* (Fantasy Pieces); *Kinderszenen* (Scenes from Childhood); and *Nachtstücke* (Night Pieces). Appealing little pieces for children are gathered in the *Album für die Jugend* (Album for the Young).

Schumann's titles are evocative, meant to stimulate players' and listeners' imaginations and to suggest possible meanings for the unusual effects and striking contrasts in his music. In *Carnaval* (1834–35), for instance, Schumann conjures up a masquerade ball in carnival season through twenty short pieces with dance rhythms, each named for a dance, a costumed figure or acquaintance at the ball (including Clara), or an interaction between revelers, such as flirtation or recognition. Among the guests are characters he had used in his literary writings to embody different facets of his own personality: the impulsive revolutionary Florestan (named after the hero of Beethoven's *Fidelio*) and the visionary dreamer Eusebius (after a fourth-century pope). The movement titles evoke strongly contrasting visual and emotional images that are paralleled in the music. *Eusebius* (NAWM 132a), shown in Example 19.4a, is a dreamy

Character pieces

Full | Concise

Titles and meanings in *Carnaval*

Full | Concise

Example 19.4 Schumann, Carnaval

a. *Eusebius*

b. *Florestan*

Robert Schumann (1810–1856)
Clara Schumann (1819–1896)

One of the most significant marriages in the history of music was that of Robert and Clara Schumann. He was an influential music critic and outstanding composer, especially of piano music, songs, chamber music, and symphonies, and she was among the foremost pianists of her day and a distinguished composer and teacher. Their careers intertwined, so that one is difficult to describe without the other.

Robert Schumann studied piano from age seven and soon began to compose. After pursuing a law degree, he dedicated himself to becoming a concert pianist, studying in Leipzig with Friedrich Wieck, his future father-in-law. An injury to his right hand, caused or aggravated by a finger-strengthening device, cut short his career. As the son of a writer and book dealer, Schumann had always had an intense interest in literature. So he turned to composition and criticism, founding and editing a magazine in Leipzig, the *Neue Zeitschrift für Musik* (New Journal of Music) from 1834 to 1844. It quickly became the most important journal of its kind and is still published today. His essays and reviews provided strong leadership for the Romantic movement: he opposed empty virtuosity, urged the study of older music, and was among the first to praise Berlioz's *Symphonie fantastique*, to advocate the music of Chopin and Brahms when they were still virtually unknown, and to champion the instrumental music of Schubert (see Vignette, page 412).

Meanwhile, Friedrich Wieck was training his daughter Clara to become a concert pianist. Recognized as a child prodigy from her first public appearance at age nine, she toured Europe and earned the praise of Goethe, Mendelssohn, Chopin, and Paganini. By the age of twenty, she was one of the leading pianists in Europe, with many published works to her credit. She and Robert became engaged, but Wieck opposed the relationship, and it took a lawsuit to permit their wedding in 1840.

Most of Robert Schumann's important piano compositions were written before 1840. In that year—the year of his engagement and marriage—he devoted his energies exclusively to songwriting; not until the following year, 1841, did he begin composing symphonies and then chamber music. He and Clara concertized throughout Europe, with Robert conducting and Clara at the piano. In 1850, he became municipal music director in Düsseldorf, his only salaried position as a musician, but increasing signs of mental

Full 🔊   Concise 🔊

fantasy with a slow, undancelike, chromatic bass under a curving melody in septuplets. By contrast, *Florestan* (NAWM 132b), in Example 19.4b is a fast, impassioned waltz full of angular melodies, pulsating dissonances, and offbeat *sforzandos*. The waltz rapidly shifts ideas but always returns to the opening figure, never finding a satisfactory cadence. Each of these movements, like many of Schumann's songs and piano pieces, lacks a clear harmonic conclusion and remains open to extension, as if it captured a momentary thought or experience while implying that there may be more to the story. The next movement, *Coquette* (NAWM 132c), presents a new contrast, still a waltz, like *Florestan*, but now all lilt and charm.

Full 🔊

One could view the music of *Carnaval* as fulfilling a program suggested by the titles. But it is truer to Schumann's intent to see the titles as a way to call attention to the special features of each piece and make each one more intriguing and memorable. Indeed, Schumann claimed that he did not always know the title of a piece until the music was written, making clear that the title is itself part of the composition, an invitation to both player and listener to enter the composer's musical world.

Ciphers and motives, unity and diversity

Another window into the music's meaning is Schumann's use of musical ciphers, representing names with notes. In *Carnaval,* many of the movements

instability forced him to resign in 1853. His last years were troubled by depression and melancholy; he suffered hallucinations and tried to commit suicide early in 1854. He spent the remaining two years of his life in a private asylum near Bonn, where, in keeping with medical practice of the time, his family was not permitted to visit.

Although Clara Schumann curbed her concert touring after marrying Robert and while bearing eight children, she continued to perform and compose. After his death, she performed and taught but ceased composing, instead promoting and editing her husband's music. She continued to play concerts, of her own and others' works, until 1891 and to teach until her death in 1896.

Major works (Robert Schumann): more than 300 piano pieces, including *Papillons* (Op. 2), *Carnaval* (Op. 9), *Fantasiestücke* (Op. 12), *Kreisleriana* (Op. 16), and *Album for the Young* (Op. 68); about 300 songs, including two cycles: *Dichterliebe* (A Poet's Love) and *Frauenliebe und -leben* (A Woman's Love and Life); one opera (*Genoveva*); several oratorios; 4 symphonies; a piano concerto; and various chamber works.

Major works (Clara Schumann): Piano Trio, Op. 17; piano concerto; many piano pieces; and several collections of Lieder.

Figure 19.7 Robert and Clara Schumann in 1850. Daguerreotype (early photograph) by Johann Anton Vollner.

(Musée d'Orsay, Paris. Photo: Hervé Lewandowski/Réunion des Musées Nationaux/Art Resource, NY.)

feature melodies based on motives that spell Asch, the home town of Schumann's then-fiancée Ernestine von Fricken: A–E♭–C–B♮ (in German, A–Es–C–H) and A♭–C–B♮ (As–C–H). The first of these is prominent in *Florestan* and *Coquette* and is more subtly present in *Eusebius,* as shown in Example 19.4. While inviting extramusical interpretation, these motives also give unity to the entire work, an organic connection between movements that underlies their surface diversity.

Songs

Among Lied composers, Schumann was the first important successor to Schubert, although their styles are very different: whereas Schubert's songs nearly always maintain a certain Classical serenity and poise, Schumann's are restless and intense. After some years of publishing only piano music, Schumann wrote more than 120 songs in 1840, which he called his "year of song." He concentrated on love songs, including the song cycles *Dichterliebe* (A Poet's Love) and *Frauenliebe und -leben* (A Woman's Love and Life). Inspired in part by his impending marriage to Clara Wieck, a renowned pianist and composer,

Schumann turned to song to express the passions and frustrations of love, to make money from publications in a lucrative genre, and to synthesize his two great interests—music and poetry.

Music and poetry

Schumann believed that music should capture a poem's essence in its own terms and that voice and piano should be equal partners in this effort. He often gave the piano a relatively long commentary at the beginning or, more frequently, at the end of a song, showing that the instrument is no mere accompaniment. Like Schubert, he typically used a single figuration throughout to convey the central emotion or idea of the poem. For his cycle *Dichterliebe,* Schumann chose sixteen poems from Heinrich Heine's *Lyrical Intermezzo* (1823) and arranged them to suggest the various stages of a relationship—from longing to initial fulfillment, abandonment, dreams of reconciliation, and, finally, resignation.

Dichterliebe

In the first song, *Im wunderschönen Monat Mai* (In the marvelous month of May, NAWM 130), the poet confesses a newborn love. The tonal ambiguity of the opening and the tension between voice and piano express his tentative feelings and reflect the pessimistic outlook of the cycle as a whole. The appoggiaturas and suspensions that begin almost every other measure underline the poet's longing and desire; and the music's refusal to settle into a key, ending the song on a dominant seventh, betrays his bittersweet anxiety about whether his love will be returned. These added layers of meaning demonstrate Schumann's success in making the piano accompaniment as important as the vocal melody, the music as significant as the words, and the composer an equal partner with the poet.

[Full 🔊] [Concise 🔊]

Symphony and Chamber Music

Symphonies

The prestigious status that Beethoven had conferred on the symphony made it a rite of passage to full recognition for any composer. Thus, in 1841, Schumann embarked on his "symphony year." After several starts, the composer completed his First Symphony in B♭ Major and drafted another that was to become his fourth in 1851. In addition to Beethoven, his primary orchestral models were Schubert's *Great* Symphony in C Major and the symphonies and concertos of Mendelssohn (see page 418), which showed how songlike themes could be integrated into developmental forms. Two of Schumann's four symphonies bear descriptive titles: No. 1, *Spring,* is a hymn to nature; and No. 3, *Rhenish,* dwells on the majesty of the Rhineland countryside, including the grand cathedral at Cologne.

Fourth Symphony

Symphony No. 4 in D Minor (NAWM 140) represents Schumann's most radical rethinking of the symphony. He conceived it as a work in one continuous flow—as if in a single movement—that contains within it the four standard movements of a symphony. There was precedent for linking movements in Beethoven's Fifth Symphony and String Quartet in C♯ Minor, whose seven movements are played without pause (NAWM 127). But Schumann's most important model was Schubert's *Wanderer Fantasy* for piano; in both works, four movements are played without breaks and are based on similar material.

[Full 🔊]

Cyclic structure

Each movement of the Fourth Symphony includes themes related to the main melody of the slow introduction, and themes from the first movement return in modified form in the second and fourth movements, making the entire work an integrated, organically unified cycle. The result is a symphonic fantasia that combines traditional forms with a continuous process of variation.

Like the melodies in *Dichterliebe* and *Carnaval,* Schumann's symphonic themes typically dwell on one rhythmic figure rather than embracing contrasting motives as in most Classic-era themes. In place of the balance of opposing elements within a theme, Schumann creates variety through constantly changing presentations of the theme, providing a dynamic experience for the listener.

Schumann followed his "Lieder year" and his "symphony year" with a "chamber-music year" in 1842–1843. After studying the quartets of Haydn and Mozart, he composed three string quartets (Op. 41), a piano quartet, and a piano quintet in rapid succession. In his critical writings, he had argued that string quartets should resemble a four-way conversation, and he took care to meet this ideal by spreading the material among all the parts. In 1847, after studying Bach, Schumann introduced a new, more polyphonic approach to chamber music with his Piano Trios No. 1 in D Minor, Op. 63, and No. 2 in F Major, Op. 80. These were his most influential chamber works, especially on Brahms and other German composers.

Chamber works

Clara Schumann (1819–1896)

Clara Wieck Schumann had a remarkably long career as a pianist, composer, and teacher (see Biography, pages 414–415); in her day, she was more famous as a performer than her husband Robert was as a composer. Women composers were discouraged from tackling large-scale works like symphonies, but Clara Wieck did compose a concerto, whose opening is shown on the piano stand in Figure 19.8. As a prominent pianist, Clara showcased her husband's works as well as her own, which include polonaises, waltzes, variations, preludes and fugues, a sonata, and character pieces. She also wrote several collections of Lieder, including one coauthored with Robert. The Schumanns had a similar approach to song setting, which involved capturing each poem's mood in long preludes and postludes, maintaining a particular figuration throughout, and making the voice and piano equal partners in conveying the images and feelings of the poem.

After Robert's death in 1856, Clara stopped composing; but she went on performing and teaching for another forty years, promoting Robert's music along with her own. Later in life she edited the first complete edition of his works with the help of Johannes Brahms, who had become a devoted friend. Her interpretations of the sonatas and concertos of Beethoven and of works by Bach, Chopin, and others attracted critics for her poetic sensitivity and masterful technique with none of the ostentatious display associated with other virtuosi. Because of her reputation and longevity as a solemn "priestess" of her art, she greatly influenced piano playing and concert life in the nineteenth century.

Clara Schumann regarded her Piano Trio in G Minor, Op. 17 (1846), as her best work; indeed, it may have inspired the trios her husband composed in the following year. The sonata-form first and last movements combine traits from Baroque, Classic, and Romantic models: memorable songlike themes; rich polyphonic treatment; development through motivic fragmentation and imitation; fugue; and rousing codas. The second movement is in minuet tempo but is labeled "Scherzo" to highlight its subtle rhythmic tricks. The slow, third movement (NAWM 142) is outwardly simple in form—a modified ABA with a melancholy first section resembling a nocturne and a more animated B section. But the effect is enriched by constantly changing textures. The opening melody

Figure 19.8 Clara Wieck at the piano in 1835.
(Color lithograph by F. Giere. Lebrecht Music and Arts Photo Library/Colouriser AL.)

appears three times, each time in a different instrument (piano, violin, and cello, respectively) and with ever more complex accompanying figuration.

The music of Clara Schumann disappeared for more than a hundred years until it was revived in the late twentieth century, when musicians sought out deserving pieces by women composers.

Felix Mendelssohn (1809–1847)

Mendelssohn's works, compared with those of Berlioz written during the same period, sound more Classical in style. This is because they exhibit a mastery of sonata and concerto form showing the influence of Mozart and Beethoven, and a command of counterpoint and fugue resulting from study of Bach and Handel. Together with the Romantic traits of colorful orchestration and the frequent use of pictorial depiction, these qualities helped to determine Mendelssohn's personal style, which combined elements of both Classicism and Romanticism. Although Mendelssohn composed in a variety of genres, we will concentrate on his works with orchestra, including the violin concerto and an oratorio.

Orchestral Works

Symphonies

Mendelssohn's symphonies, overtures, and violin concerto all follow Classic models, with departures that show the strong influence of Romanticism. For example, his two most important symphonies carry geographical subtitles—the *Italian* (No. 4, 1833) and the *Scottish* (No. 3, 1842)—in keeping with the literary and descriptive aspects of Romanticism. They preserve impressions he gained of sounds and landscapes on trips to Italy and the British Isles, which he also recorded in drawings and paintings like the one in Figure 19.9.

Overtures

As befitted the son of a well-to-do family, Mendelssohn was well traveled. His affinity for depicting musical landscapes of places he had seen is evident in his overtures *The Hebrides* (also called *Fingal's Cave*, 1832), on a Scottish topic, and *Meerestille und glückliche Fahrt* (Becalmed Sea and Prosperous Voyage, 1828–1832). His masterpiece in the genre is the *Midsummer Night's Dream Overture*, written in 1826 when he was seventeen, which set the standard for all subsequent concert overtures. A picture of the fairies in Shakespeare's famous play, it is a brilliant example of perpetual motion for a full orchestra trained to tiptoe like a chamber ensemble. The Classic structure of sonata form is perfectly clear, but the listener's attention is drawn to Mendelssohn's imaginative use of musical figuration and orchestral color to evoke everything from fairy dust to the braying of Bottom after his head is magically transformed into that of a jackass. Seventeen years later, Mendelssohn wrote additional incidental music, including the famous *Wedding March*, for a production of the play.

Violin concerto

Mendelssohn, a virtuoso pianist, wrote several concertos for his own performances. Unlike the showpieces composed by most virtuosos of the time, Mendelssohn's concertos emphasized the musical content, striking a balance between audience appeal and sophistication that connoisseurs praised in the concertos of Mozart. The same may be said for Mendelssohn's Violin Concerto in E Minor (1844, NAWM 139). The three movements are linked by thematic content and connecting passages; a transition leads from the opening Allegro molto appassionato to the lyrical Andante, and an introduction to the last movement alludes to the first movement's opening theme. In the first movement, Mendelssohn skips the orchestral exposition that was usual in the Classic concerto

Full 🔊   Concise 🔊

Figure 19.9 Watercolor by Felix Mendelssohn, entitled Amalfi in May 1831, *a view of the Gulf of Salerno from Amalfi, near Naples, in southern Italy. Mendelssohn sketched, drew, and painted throughout his journeys in Italy and Britain.*
(Bodleian Library, Oxford University.)

and instead has the soloist state the main theme at the outset; he also places the cadenza just before rather than after the recapitulation, allowing him to omit the closing ritornello. Essentially, he reworked the concerto form into a variant of sonata form with a featured soloist, a reformulation that is typical of Mendelssohn and of his age in finding new ways to interpret yet continue tradition. The middle movement, in ABA' form, is a romance for violin and orchestra driven by a slowly unfolding melody. The sonata-rondo finale has the lightness of a scherzo. Although there are plenty of opportunities for the soloist to show off, the concerto always seems motivated by a greater expressive purpose. The violin and orchestra share equally in the finale, where the leading melodies move seamlessly from soloist to orchestra and back.

Oratorios

Mendelssohn's involvement with music of the past along with the proliferation of amateur choral societies in Germany prompted him to write two successful oratorios, *St. Paul* (1836) and *Elijah* (1846), which have become standards of the choral repertory. Both were composed for choral festivals, events where large amateur choruses from across a geographical region gathered to perform, on the model of festivals begun in England that centered on Handel's oratorios. Like Handel's, Mendelssohn's oratorios treated biblical subjects and received great acclaim. In *Elijah,* Mendelssohn deployed a wide variety of choral styles and textures, including that of Bach's chorales; at the same time, he used unifying motives and links between movements to integrate them into a cohesive whole, following the practice of his own time.

The final chorus of *Elijah* (NAWM 143) is Handelian in spirit, with a powerful homorhythmic opening, a vigorous fugue with a culminating statement in chordal harmony, and a contrapuntal Amen, while contrasts of major and minor and touches of chromaticism draw on more recent styles. The fugue lends an appropriate solemnity to the close of the oratorio through the use of an old, familiar form.

Elijah

Full 🔊

Felix Mendelssohn (1809–1847)

As a child prodigy, Mendelssohn equaled or even surpassed Mozart's precocious musical talent. A renowned pianist, organist, and conductor, and one of the most prominent composers of his generation, Mendelssohn wrote music that combines Romantic expressivity with Classic forms and techniques.

Felix was the grandson of Moses Mendelssohn (1729–1786), the leading Jewish philosopher of the Enlightenment in Germany. Although Jews were slowly gaining legal rights, his family converted to Protestantism when Mendelssohn was a child, adding Bartholdy to the family's surname. (He later acknowledged his Lutheran faith in his *Reformation Symphony,* 1840, in which he quotes one of Luther's chorales.) His family was at the center of Berlin's intellectual life. His father, a wealthy banker, and his mother, an amateur pianist, encouraged their children's musical interests, and both Felix and his sister, Fanny, were trained from an early age by excellent teachers. A good amateur artist, he painted watercolors and sketched many of the places he visited when, after his schooldays were over, his father topped off his education by sending him on a Grand Tour of Europe, which also introduced him to the larger musical world.

As a boy, Mendelssohn showed astounding musical talent, composing a polished octet for strings at the age of sixteen and, in the following year, a brilliant concert overture for orchestra, inspired by his reading of Shakespeare's *A Midsummer Night's Dream.* At age twenty, he conducted a performance of the *Saint Matthew Passion* in Berlin that helped spark a revival of interest in Bach's music. He composed at an astonishing rate throughout his life, marked by frequent travel, concert tours as pianist and conductor, and positions as music director in Düsseldorf, music director and conductor of the Gewandhaus Orchestra in Leipzig (1835–1840 and 1845–1847),

Figure 19.10   Felix Mendelssohn at age twenty. Watercolor portrait by Warren Childe (1829).
(Staatsbibliothek zu Berlin, Berlin, Germany. Photo: BPK/Art Resource, NY.)

and in various capacities in Berlin (1840–1844). In 1843, he founded the Leipzig Conservatory, whose faculty included both Robert and Clara Schumann. Mendelssohn was also a great favorite in England, where his popularity took him often, prompting the composition of his oratorio *Elijah,* in the tradition of Handel. Queen Victoria, who graciously consented to receive the dedication of his *Scottish* Symphony, loved to pass musical afternoons in his company. He died at the age of thirty-eight, after a series of strokes.

Major works: 5 symphonies, a violin concerto, 2 piano concertos, 4 overtures, incidental music to *A Midsummer Night's Dream*, 2 oratorios, numerous chamber works, pieces for piano and organ, choral works, and songs.

Fanny Mendelssohn Hensel (1805–1847)

In contrast to Clara Schumann, pianist-composer Fanny Mendelssohn Hensel (1805–1847), who was Felix Mendelssohn's sister, did not pursue a public career. While she was equally well trained in music and almost as precocious and talented as her brother Felix, a musical career was considered inappropriate for a woman of her social class. After marrying painter Wilhelm Hensel, she led a salon, a regular gathering of friends and invited guests, where she played piano and presented her compositions. The salon met in a large music room in the Hensel home that could accommodate up to two hundred people and was attended by bankers, merchants, politicians, writers, artists, and musicians such as Franz Liszt and Clara Schumann. Hensel wrote more than four hundred works, mostly in the small genres suitable for home music-making; among them are at least 250 songs and 125 piano pieces. Her masterpiece is *Das Jahr* (The Year, 1841), a series of character pieces for piano on the twelve months, inspired by an extended trip to Italy in 1839–1840. The last of these pieces, *December* (NAWM 133), exploits the piano's wide range and colorful potential while presenting technically challenging passages such as trills in parallel thirds, and rapid scales and leaps in parallel octaves. After a transition that modulates via a series of third-related chords from the opening key of C minor to C major, a quiet middle section references the Christmas season by quoting a popular German carol based on Luther's chorale *Von Himmel hoch, da komm ich her* (From heaven above to earth I come). The piece ends with a "majestic" and "exultant" paraphrase of the familiar tune (marked in the score).

Full 📶

Hensel's husband encouraged her to publish her music, but she died suddenly of a stroke less than a year after her first publication appeared (Op. 1, six songs) in 1846. Only in recent decades has she become more than "Mendelssohn's sister," as scholars have discovered a trove of her works and realized the importance of her salon.

Fryderyk Chopin (1810–1849)

Unlike many of his contemporaries who wrote in all the standard genres of the early nineteenth century, Fryderyk Chopin concentrated almost exclusively on works for solo piano, and he composed some 200 pieces in this genre (see Biography, page 424). These are enjoyed by connoisseurs and amateurs alike because his idiomatic writing and his genius for maximizing the sonorous possibilities of the piano make them as gratifying to play as they are to hear.

Among Chopin's solo works, the dances stand out for their sheer beauty and sensuality. His waltzes evoke the ballrooms of Vienna, but his polonaises and mazurkas are suffused with the spirit of Poland. Polonaises (the word means "Polish" in French) are dances in $\frac{3}{4}$ meter often marked by a rhythmic figure of an eighth and two sixteenths on the first beat. Chopin's go beyond the stylized polonaises of Bach's time to assert a vigorous, sometimes militaristic, national identity. The mazurka was originally a Polish folk dance that became popular in the ballrooms of high society. Its stately triple meter with an accented second or third beat, frequent dotted rhythms, and unusual ornaments and modal effects make it sound rather like an exotic minuet—sometimes playful, sometimes brooding. The Mazurka in B♭ Major, Op. 7, No. 1 (NAWM 134), illustrates the genre. (See also In Performance, page 422.)

Dances

Full 📶 Concise 📶

The nocturnes, impromptus, and preludes are Chopin's most soulful and introspective works. He got both the name and the general idea of the nocturnes—descriptive pieces that evoke the quiet and fretful dreaminess of night—from the Irish pianist and composer John Field (1782–1837), who invented the genre, and Polish pianist-composer Maria Szymanowska (1789–1831), both of whom were active in St. Petersburg, the capital of Russia. Chopin's

Nocturnes

In Performance Tempo Rubato

Most of Chopin's pieces are introspective and, within clearly defined formal outlines, give the impression of an improvised or spontaneous flow of ideas. In this respect, a certain apparent (though controlled) freedom of delivery is appropriate in performance, as with recitative, which imitates the flexibility of speech rhythms. Such freedom is inherent in the tempo marking *rubato,* an effect most strongly associated with Chopin's mazurkas. (Some 75 percent of the written appearances of the term in Chopin's work occur in his mazurkas, where it is used as a tempo marking that governs the entire piece. In other types of pieces, it might be indicated as an expression mark governing only a few measures.) In Italian, tempo rubato means "stolen time," or time extended, slowed down, or stretched beyond its literal duration, implying some distortion of the strict tempo that may be applied to a few notes or to entire phrases. Chopin described it as a slight pushing or holding back of the right-hand melody while the accompaniment continues in strict time, although he is also known to have used this expressive device in both hands at once. A glossary of Italian musical terms published in a French magazine (*Le pianiste,* 1834) names Chopin as the composer most closely identified with tempo rubato.

Chopin himself was not theatrically overwhelming as a pianist (as Franz Liszt was; see Chapter 21), and other virtuosos have emphasized the heroic side of his music more than he himself could or would have. According to one critic, he had a small sound, though his playing was "elegant, relaxed, and graceful; . . . marked by both brilliance and clarity." But his own rhythmically inflected manner of performing was unique and nearly impossible to reproduce—perhaps even completely impossible if one had not heard him play. Contemporary critics recognized that, since no arrangement of known note values can accurately express rubato, it was elusive at best and the undoing of amateurs at worst. Indeed, the desire to apply rubato still renders even the simplest mazurkas somewhat treacherous to play.

Like the damper pedal, rubato can also be used in places where it is not marked, and nineteenth-century performers availed themselves of both devices freely for expressive purposes. Although Chopin's works are certainly gratifying to perform, many of them demand of the pianist not only a flawless technique and a sensitive touch but also an imaginative use of the pedals and a subtle execution of tempo rubato.

Figure 19.11 Autograph score of a mazurka dated Paris 1834 and signed by Chopin.
(Lebrecht Music and Arts Photo Library.)

lyrical lines, as in the D♭ Nocturne, Op. 27, No. 2 (NAWM 135), draw on the *bel canto* vocal style of Bellini's opera arias (see Chapter 20 and NAWM 146), as does the cadenzalike passage in the right hand.

> Chopin composed his preludes at a time when he was deeply immersed in the music of Bach, and indeed they belong to a tradition of improvising at the keyboard that goes back to the Baroque era. Like the preludes in *The Well-Tempered Clavier,* these brief, sharply defined mood pictures utilize all the major and minor keys, although the circle of fifths determines their succession— C major, A minor, G major, E minor, and so on—whereas Bach's were arranged in rising chromatic steps—C major, C minor, C♯ major, C♯ minor, and so on. The astounding inventiveness of Chopin's figuration may be seen in Example 19.5. Prelude No. 1 (19.5a) wraps arpeggiated chords around a tenor-range melody echoed an octave above; No. 2 (19.5b) alternates wide two-note intervals in the left hand; No. 3 (19.5c) has a sweeping sixteenth-note pattern; and No. 4 (19.5d) features pulsating chords that sink chromatically through nonfunctional sonorities on their way to more stable chords. Such rich chromatic harmonies and modulations influenced many later composers, as did the varied textures of Chopin's piano writing.

> Chopin projected his ideas onto a larger canvas in his ballades and scherzos. He was one of the first to use the name *ballade* (which originally denoted a long, narrative strophic poem) for an instrumental piece. His works in this genre—especially Op. 23 in G Minor and Op. 52 in F Minor—capture the mood

Preludes

Ballades and scherzos

Example 19.5 Chopin, Preludes, Op. 28

a. No. 1 in C Major

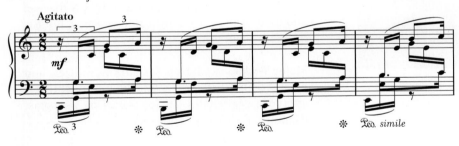

b. No. 2 in A Minor   *c. No. 3 in G Major*

d. No. 4 in E Minor

Fryderyk Chopin (1810–1849)

Chopin was the Romantic composer most closely identified with the piano. His solo piano music won him enormous popularity during his lifetime and, through its enduring appeal, has occupied a central place in the repertory ever since.

Chopin was born near Warsaw to a French father and a Polish mother in a section of Poland that was then under Russian domination. After he received early training at the Warsaw Conservatory, his talent as a pianist, improviser, and composer of unmistakably Polish music assured

Figure 19.12 Portrait of Fryderyk Chopin by Eugène Delacroix (1838).
(Musée de Louvre, Paris. Photo: Erich Lessing/Art Resource NY.)

him a strong following in his native country. In search of an international reputation, however, he left Poland in 1830 to tour Vienna and Germany, where Robert Schumann called the public's attention to him with the words "Hats off, gentlemen, a genius!" When Chopin learned of the failed Polish revolt against Russia that November, instead of returning to Poland he journeyed to Paris, where he settled in 1831, never to see his homeland again.

In Paris, Chopin soon gained entry into the most elite social circles, where he met artists, writers, and other musicians, including Berlioz, Rossini, and Liszt. He became the most fashionable piano teacher for wealthy students, whose fees meant that he could give up concertizing, although he still played at private concerts and in salons. He also earned considerable sums from his publications. He never married but had a tempestuous nine-year affair with the novelist George Sand (see In Context, page 425). During their stay in Majorca, he was diagnosed with tuberculosis and suffered with it for ten years. The 1848 revolution in Paris disrupted his teaching and forced a grueling tour of England and Scotland. By then, he was ravaged by his disease and died in 1849. He was buried in Paris, but his heart was sent to Warsaw and was interred there.

Major Works: 110 dances (mazurkas, waltzes, and polonaises), 4 ballades, 4 scherzos, 10 nocturnes, 27 études, 25 preludes, 2 piano concertos, 3 sonatas, 5 chamber works, and 20 songs.

swings of narrative ballads by contemporary poets (see page 409), which are filled with romantic adventures and supernatural incidents. The principal scherzos are his Op. 20 in B minor and Op. 39 in C♯ minor. Although these pieces are not joking or playful like their Classic counterparts, they are tricky and quirky (which the term *scherzo* also implies), particularly in their thematic material and rhythm. They are also serious, vigorous, and passionate works, organized—as are the ballades—in forms that grow organically from the musical ideas.

Études 　　　Chopin's twenty-seven études—twelve in each of Opp. 10 and 25, and three without opus number—are important landmarks in defining the piano idiom. Because études are intended primarily to develop technique, each one as a rule addresses a specific technical skill pursued through repetition of a single figure. Among the technical challenges in Opus 25 are parallel diatonic and chromatic

In Context A Ballad of Love

The novelist George Sand (Aurore Dudevant, 1804–1876) adopted her male pseudonym after she left her husband and moved to Paris, where she eventually met Fryderyk Chopin. She was forward and freethinking; he was fastidious and frail. She was a single mother who smoked cigars and wore men's clothing; he suffered from tuberculosis and required solitude and mothering, although he enjoyed the company of aristocratic friends. Despite their differences in age and experience—she was six years older than he and immensely more worldly—they developed a romantic relationship that coincided with his most productive years as a composer.

A prolific correspondent and diarist, Sand described Chopin's creative process as a combination of effortless improvisation and painstaking revisions:

> His musical composition was spontaneous and miraculous. [Ideas] would come to him unexpectedly and without effort. They simply burst forth out of his piano, sublime and complete. . . . But then began the most heartbreaking labor I have ever seen, consisting of a succession of struggles, uncertainties, and impatience to recapture certain details of the theme he had heard. What he had conceived as a whole he analyzed too much in trying to write down, and his dismay at not being able to capture it exactly again threw him into a kind of despair. He would shut himself up in his room for whole days at a time, weeping, pacing back and forth, smashing his pens, repeating or changing one measure a hundred times. . . . He sometimes spent six weeks on one page, only to finish by writing it exactly as he had sketched it at the first draft.[1]

Chopin's manuscripts show no sign of such extraordinary efforts, but the changes Chopin made from one edition of his works to another give evidence of his concern for details.

The couple's liaison lasted nine years, during which time they lived partly in Parisian society and partly at Nohant, the quiet country estate that Sand had inherited. Their holiday escape to

Figure 19.13 Anonymous nineteenth-century portrait of George Sand.
(Frederick Chopin Museum, Warsaw. The Art Archive/Corbis.)

Majorca during the winter of 1838–1839 turned into a terrible ordeal. Although Chopin managed to complete his Twenty-four Preludes (Op. 28) there, his health was permanently damaged by the bad weather and primitive living conditions. Nevertheless, they spent several more peaceful and productive years together after returning to France. Then, overwhelmed by intrigues involving a rivalry between Sand's two grown children, the lovers' affection for one another gradually dwindled, and by 1847 they were separated. Alone and physically ailing, Chopin lost all interest in composing and died two years later at the age of thirty-nine.

1. George Sand, *Histoire de ma vie* . . . , 20 vols. (1854); repr. (Paris: Calmann-Lévy, 1928–1932?), vol. 4, p. 470; adapted from the translation by William G. Atwood, *The Lioness and the Little One: The Liaison of George Sand and Frédéric Chopin* (New York: Columbia University Press, 1980), pp. 136–137.

Example 19.6 Fryderyk Chopin, Étude, Op. 25, No. 11

thirds (No. 6), parallel sixths in the right hand (No. 8), and chromatic octaves in both hands (No. 10). In No. 11, a brilliant yet highly evocative étude, the right hand spins out a perpetual filigree of sixteenth notes against a vigorous march theme in the left hand (see Example 19.6). Chopin's études are not only intensely concentrated technical studies but also transcendent poetic statements, successfully combining virtuosity with significant artistic content. In this respect, Liszt and Brahms followed Chopin's lead.

Hector Berlioz (1803–1869)

Symphonie fantastique

Full 🔊   Concise 🔊

If Hector Berlioz had been a character in a Romantic novel, we would surely describe him as a Byronic hero (see Biography, page 428). Because his imagination tended to run in parallel literary and musical channels, Berlioz subtitled his first symphony and most famous work, *Symphonie fantastique*, "Episode in the Life of an Artist" and provided it with an autobiographical program (given in NAWM 138). This work inaugurated the era of programmatic Romanticism, in which the symphony was reconceived as a narrative or sequence of events, often spelled out in an accompanying text called a program. Composed in 1830, only three years after Beethoven's death (indeed, Beethoven had pointed the way toward the program symphony), Berlioz's symphony is "fantastic" in the sense that it is a psychological fantasy, a product of the imagination—in this case, a musical drama without words. As Berlioz wrote, "The program should be regarded in the same way as the spoken words of an opera, serving to introduce the musical numbers by describing the situation that evokes the particular mood and expressive character of each." The literary influences in the program are too numerous to detail, although Goethe's *Faust* is conspicuous among them, and the fantasized situations are depicted in the passionate prose of a young and sensitive artist. Yet the symphony's narrative or sequence of events makes sense even without the program, illustrating E. T. A. Hoffmann's concept of music as an autonomous art (see Vignette, page 427).

Idée fixe

Berlioz unifies all five movements with the recurrence of the idée fixe, or the obsessive image of the hero's beloved, according to the program. In each movement the transformations of the idée fixe help to tell the story as they assume a wide range of contrasting attributes. The first movement, "Dreams and Passions," features a slow introduction followed by an Allegro that has the outward characteristics of sonata form. The idée fixe, a melody with the long, arching line of an operatic aria, serves as the first theme, accompanied by an irregular pumping figure that imitates the hero's racing heartbeat when he first sees his beloved. Example 19.7a shows the first phrase of the theme in its original form. For the second movement, "A Ball," Berlioz replaced the Classic minuet with a waltz, enacting a scene at a Ball where the hero catches a glimpse of his beloved, embodied in the waltzlike version of the idée fixe. The slow third movement, "Scene in the Country," sets a pastoral scene: as the hero walks in the country, phrases of the theme appear alternating with phrases of instrumental recitative as he thinks of his beloved and worries about her feelings for him. In the fourth movement, "March to the Scafffold," the hero dreams of his own execution in a macabre orchestral tour de force. Near its ending, only the opening of the idée fixe appears, as the hero envisions his beloved just before the guillotine falls. The fifth and final movement (NAWM 138) depicts a "Dream of a Witches' Sabbath," presenting a grotesque caricature of the idée

Full 🔊   Concise 🔊

Example 19.7 Hector Berlioz, Symphonie fantastique, *Op. 14*

a. *First movement, "Dreams and Passions"*

b. *Fifth movement: "Dream of a Witches' Sabbath"*

Hector Berlioz (1803–1869)

Hector Berlioz was something new in music: not only a radically original composer but also a well-known music critic and one of the first people to have a career as an orchestral conductor. He is especially remembered for his achievement in writing symphonies, operas, and choral works, which was remarkable for the time considering that he was neither a concert pianist nor a ranking performer on any instrument.

Berlioz was born in southeastern France near the Alps, the son of a well-to-do doctor and a pious mother. Well educated and well read in the classics, he developed a fascination with music, taught himself harmony from textbooks (including Rameau's *Traité de l'harmonie*), and began to compose in his teens. When Berlioz was seventeen, his parents sent him to medical school in Paris, but his interest in music frequently lured him to the opera, where he heard works by Gluck and Rossini, among others. He studied composition at the Paris Conservatory and eventually abandoned medicine to make his mark as the first important French composer since Rameau.

By the time Berlioz produced his first major work, he had become enchanted by Beethoven's symphonies, Shakespeare's plays, and the English actress Harriet Smithson, whose performance in *Hamlet* as Ophelia (Figure 19.15) led him to pursue her obsessively. When she rejected his advances, he began to sketch out his extraordinary *Symphonie fantastique*, which served as a kind of musical

Figure 19.15 Berlioz's wife, Harriet Smithson, as Ophelia in Shakespeare's Hamlet.
(Lebrecht Music & Arts Photo Library/Colouriser AL.)

autobiography, monumentalizing his feelings. After a rocky courtship, Berlioz and Smithson finally married and had a son, to whom Berlioz remained devoted even after his infatuation faded and the couple split up. After she died in 1864, he married the singer Marie Recio, with whom he had long had an affair. In his final years, Berlioz grew ill and disillusioned about his music's failure to gain acceptance, especially in France. He died at age sixty-five, having outlived two wives, his son, and most of his family and friends.

Berlioz was one of the most literary of composers; not only did he write music criticism, his own memoirs, and the first modern treatise on orchestration, but he emulated the authors he most admired—Virgil, Shakespeare, and Goethe—in his own musical compositions: the opera *Les Troyens* (The Trojans), adapted from the *Aeneid* (discussed in Chapter 20); *Beatrice and Benedict*, an opera based on Shakespeare's *Much Ado about Nothing*; and his dramatic symphonies, *Romeo and Juliet* and *The Damnation of Faust*, the latter inspired by Goethe's epic poem. Even his very first opera, which includes the *Roman Carnival* scene that gave rise to his popular overture, was based on the memoirs of the Italian sculptor Benvenuto Cellini. He also wrote the *Grande messe des morts* (a huge Requiem), an orchestral song cycle *Les Nuits d'été* (Summer Nights), and other songs with orchestra or piano accompaniment.

Figure 19.14 Hector Berlioz in a portrait by Émile Signol painted in 1832 during Berlioz's stay in Rome.
(Villa Medici, Rome, Italy. Photo: Scala/Art Resource, NY.)

fixe (Example 19.7b), implying the beloved's depravity. One of the other themes in this movement is the chant sequence *Dies irae*, part of the Mass for the Dead; this movement began a long tradition of using the *Dies irae* as a symbol of death, the macabre, or the diabolical.

The *Symphonie fantastique* is original not only in bending the symphonic genre to serve narrative and autobiographical purposes but also in Berlioz's dazzling musical vocabulary and astounding ability to express the many shifting moods and emotional content of his drama. The effort to find a musical effect able to express an idea or program undoubtedly led to Berlioz's innovations in harmony, melody, and instrumentation. Because of his colorful orchestral sonorities, we can say that Berlioz was to music what Delacroix was to painting in the nineteenth century (see Figure V.6); it is no wonder that Berlioz's treatise on orchestration became the bible for generations of nineteenth-century composers. Furthermore, by introducing a recurring theme and by developing the dramatic idea through all of the five movements, Berlioz was the first composer to unify the symphony, extending procedures Beethoven had used in his Fifth, Sixth, and Ninth Symphonies.

Berlioz's second symphony, *Harold en Italie* (1834; title suggested by Lord Byron's *Childe Harold's Pilgrimage*), is a set of four scenes inspired by the composer's recollections of an Italian sojourn. Each movement is connected by a recurring theme, played by solo viola. The instrument is featured throughout, though less prominently than in a solo concerto; for this reason, the great virtuoso violinist Niccolò Paganini (1782–1840), who commissioned the work from Berlioz, refused to play it.

Harold en Italie

Five years after *Harold en Italie*, Berlioz produced his "dramatic symphony" *Roméo et Juliette*, in seven movements, for orchestra, soloists, and chorus, departing even further from the traditional model. In adding choral parts to the orchestra, he was again following Beethoven's example; but in this work the voices enter in the prologue and are used in three of the symphonic movements as well.

Roméo et Juliette

The tension between Romantic musical energy, at times so flamboyant, and sacred themes was a problem for composers of church music in the nineteenth century. Berlioz composed two large-scale choral works—the *Grande Messe des morts* (Requiem, 1837) and the *Te Deum* (1855)—that were intended for special occasions. They are dramatic symphonies for orchestra and voices using poetically inspiring texts that happen to be liturgical. They belong not to an ecclesiastical but to a secular and patriotic tradition inspired by the great musical festivals of the French Revolution. Both works are of huge dimensions, not only in length and in the number of performers they require but also in grandeur of conception. For example, Berlioz's Requiem calls for a massive choir and an orchestra of 140 players, including 4 brass choirs, 4 tam-tams, 10 pairs of cymbals, and 16 kettledrums to accompany the chorus at "Tuba mirum" in the *Dies irae*, representing the thunderous clamor of the Day of Judgment.

Church music

Berlioz's first three symphonies, especially the *Symphonie fantastique*, made him the first leader of the Romantic movement's radical wing. All subsequent composers of program music—including Strauss (see Chapter 22) and Debussy (see Chapter 23)—were indebted to him. Berlioz's orchestration initiated a new era: he enriched orchestral music with new resources of harmony, color, expression, and form; and his use of the idée fixe in different movements (as in the *Symphonie fantastique* and *Harold en Italie*) was an important impulse toward the development of the cyclical symphonic forms of the later nineteenth century. By example and precept, he was also the founder of modern orchestration and conducting. (See A Closer Look, page 430.)

Berlioz's influence

In the 1780s, Haydn's orchestra at Eszterháza consisted of fewer than 25 instruments: a core of strings (10 violins, 2 violas, 2 cellos, and 2 basses) plus 2 oboes, 2 bassoons, 2 horns, and keyboard. Sometimes a performer would double on another instrument; for example, the first oboist might be called upon to play flute in one movement. The court orchestra in Mozart's Vienna was marginally bigger: it used a few more strings and 2 flutes in addition to the other winds. But, only forty years later, Beethoven's Ninth Symphony was premiered in Vienna by a force of 61 players plus a large chorus. In addition to the strings (without keyboard, which was no longer necessary as a foundation for the orchestra), it called for a piccolo; pairs of flutes, oboes, clarinets, and bassoons; a contrabassoon; four horns, two trumpets; three trombones; and percussion. By the 1830s, orchestras in Paris, too, had grown enormously and typically employed between 70 and 80 players, including some 50 strings (usually 24, 8, 10, 8). Berlioz scored his *Symphonie fantastique* for 2 flutes (one doubling piccolo), 2 oboes (one doubling English horn), 2 clarinets, 4 bassoons, 4 horns, 2 cornets, 2 trumpets, 3 trombones, and 2 ophicleides (large, keyed brass instruments, eventually replaced by tubas), as well as a variety of percussion instruments (including bells) and 2 harps.

Figure 19.17 Musicians in the Orchestra, *painted in 1868 by Edgar Degas, shows a few members of the woodwind section crowded against the string players in a pit orchestra, while above their heads are ballet dancers on stage.*
(Musée d'Orsay. Photo: Réunion des Musées Nationaux/Art Resource, NY.)

In addition to the increase in numbers, changes in the construction of instruments greatly enhanced the power of the strings and the efficiency of the winds (see Innovations, pages 406–407). At the same time, the expansion in the orchestra's size created a need for a permanent, baton-wielding conductor as well as larger concert halls, many of which were built in the late 1800s in such cities as Vienna, London, New York, and Boston.

As orchestras became fuller and richer in texture and timbre, audiences at first condemned their "noisiness"; listeners complained that Beethoven's symphonies, for example, had too many notes. But when nineteenth-century ears became accustomed to the new complexity and volume of orchestral sound, Mozart's scores were considered too empty! The Romantic taste for monumentality and expressivity demanded still more volume, more brilliance, more color, and more variety. By the end of the nineteenth century, the Vienna Philharmonic regularly had more than one hundred players, and many composers were aiming to keep them all occupied.

The question arises: did the developing orchestra, like some gigantic machine, drive the composers to write bigger scores, or was it the composers themselves who pioneered the increasingly massive sonority of the symphony orchestra?

Figure 19.16 Court musicians from the eighteenth century. The anonymous painter suggests that the conductor is a menacing tyrant who will not tolerate any wrong notes.
(Courtesy Bärenreiter.)

Two Americans: Foster and Gottschalk

During the nineteenth century, Europeans who migrated to the United States brought with them various national musical traditions. Many American families had a piano in their living room, which became the center of home music-making (see Figure 19.19). Schubert's Lieder thrived alongside "parlor songs," some imported from the British Isles and some by American composers. Parlor songs are usually strophic or in stanza-refrain form, with piano introductions and codas based on phrases from the tune. Their expressivity lies almost entirely in the vocal melody, while the piano typically supports the singer with conventional figuration rather than dramatizing or interpreting the text as it does in many German Lieder.

The leading American song composer of the nineteenth century was Stephen Foster (1826–1864), shown in Figure 19.18. Growing up in Pittsburgh, Foster heard German, Italian, and Irish music. He taught himself to play several instruments, but had no formal training in composition. After his 1848 song *Oh! Susannah* achieved great success, he signed a contract with a New York publisher and became the first American to earn a living solely as a composer. Foster combined elements of British ballads, minstrel songs from the American stage, German lieder, Italian opera, and Irish folk songs. Seeking—and finding—wide popularity, he made his music easy to perform and remember. One of his best-known parlor songs, *Jeanie with the Light Brown Hair* (1853, NAWM 131)—with its diatonic, mostly stepwise melody, simple accompaniment, and clear, four-bar phrases—illustrates the features that made his music so appealing and memorable.

Song was the most popular medium of the nineteenth century, but piano music ran a close second. The first American composer to achieve an international reputation was the globe-trotting Louis Moreau Gottschalk (1829–1869),

Figure 19.18 Photograph of the American songwriter Stephen Collins Foster with his most recognizable attributes—a piano and a piece of sheet music.

(Bettman/Corbis.)

Full 🔊

Louis Moreau Gottschalk

Figure 19.19 An American painter with impressionist leanings, Thomas Eakins (1844–1916) portrayed the parlor song in this work, entitled The Pathetic Song *(1881).*

(Corcoran Gallery of Art, Washington, D.C., museum purchase, Callery Fund. 19.26.)

At the Time

In 1840, when Robert Schumann and Clara Wieck are finally able to marry after her father's impeding their union for three years:

- Queen Victoria, in the third year of her reign, marries her cousin, Prince Albert of Saxe-Coburg and Gotha, and continues to rule for another sixty years.
- Railroads begin to spread across Europe and the United States. In 1840 a British locomotive designer builds the Firefly, the most powerful locomotive of its time, reaching average speeds of 50 miles per hour.
- J.M.W. Turner paints *The Slave Ship* (Figure 19.20), in part to help hasten the abolition of the slave trade. Consistent with the Romantic emphasis on color, the central focus is on the interaction of its colors rather than on the objects depicted—the ship, the gathering storm, and the bodies thrown overboard.
- Anton Schindler, Beethoven's secretary, publishes his biography of the composer, which greatly influences the Romantic view of Beethoven as the lonely artist-hero suffering for his art.
- Campaign songs enter American politics for the first time, with one popular hit being "Tippecanoe and Tyler Too." It is a time of deep economic depression in the United States and the sitting president, Martin van Buren, is nicknamed by his adversaries Martin van Ruin.
- Samuel Morse patents his electromagnetic telegraph, but Congress does not appropriate the money for him to demonstrate it successfully until four years later.
- Photography is in its infancy, but by the end of the century it will have a huge impact on art and society (Figure 19.18).
- The world's first adhesive postage stamp, the "penny black," is introduced in England.
- Robert Schumann composes more than 120 songs during this year, among them two song cycles. As one of many entries in his diary, he writes "A new ballade by Chopin has been published, dedicated to me, which gives me greater joy than if I had received a commission from some ruler."

Figure 19.20 J. M. W. Turner, The Slave Ship, *1840.*
(Museum of Fine Arts, Boston/Wikimedia Commons.)

a pianist in the nineteenth-century tradition who was celebrated for his audacity and showmanship. Born in New Orleans, Gottschalk completed his training in Paris, where Chopin heard him and predicted his fame. In addition to touring Europe, he performed throughout the United States, the Caribbean islands, and South America, playing largely his own compositions. The publication of pieces based on melodies and rhythms from his mother's West Indian heritage solidified his reputation as a composer. He incorporated American sounds and rhythms into piano music for the European market, and through his works European composers came to know and at times imitate the dance rhythms and syncopations of the New World. His *Souvenir de Porto Rico* (NAWM 137) uses a theme derived from a Puerto Rican song and features Afro-Caribbean rhythms. It is a perfect example of nineteenth-century piano music designed to appeal to middle-class audiences, combining an exotic subject, novel melodic and rhythmic material, virtuosic showmanship, and rewards for the amateur performer.

Full 🔊

POSTLUDE

The first Romantic composers explored new realms of expression in all mediums—orchestral, chamber, and solo music—giving particular prominence in the smaller forms to voice and piano. They reveled in pushing sounds to extreme limits, moving in the space of a few measures from the most bombastic fortissimo to the most delicate pianissimo, from the greatest possible dramatic turbulence to the simplest lyric serenity, from calculated chaos to cool calm. They indulged equally in luxurious length and tantalizing brevity, making symphonies longer and miniature forms shorter. They accomplished these effects by manipulating instrumentation, harmony, dynamics, and other elements in original ways, inventing new tempo markings to articulate their urgent moods, and new narrative strategies to achieve greater formal freedom as well as greater coherence.

20

Opera and Music Drama in the Nineteenth Century

PRELUDE

While purely instrumental music gained prestige, opera continued to be a central part of musical life in the nineteenth century, especially in France, Italy, and Germany. Opera served as elite entertainment, but its music was popular with audiences of all classes and professions. Composers followed national trends, even while they developed new forms and approaches and borrowed ideas across national boundaries.

Nationalism, both political and musical, brought new themes into opera during the nineteenth century. Subjects and settings varied widely, from grand historical epics to folktales, and from plots with strong political overtones to stories that centered on private emotions and personal relationships. Librettists spoke to the broader audience that was now attending operas primarily by addressing issues of concern to them: how to balance love with loyalty to family or nation, the influence of women in the domestic and public sphere, the struggle for freedom, and the fear of evil. Also, over the course of the century, librettists increasingly cast middle-class characters in their operatic works.

Although librettos and spectacular stage effects continued to be significant factors in an opera's success, in some quarters the music itself became the most important element. Star singers were still paid more than composers, but the composer was increasingly the dominant force. New operas by the leading composers became major events, and successful ones were performed numerous times and restaged in many cities. By 1850, a permanent repertory of operas began to emerge, paralleling the classical repertory in the concert hall. At the center of this repertory were operas by Rossini, Bellini, Meyerbeer, and Weber alongside the late operas of Mozart. In the second half of the century, Verdi and Wagner dominated Italian and German opera, respectively, while composers in France, Bohemia, Russia, and elsewhere developed new national styles (to be explored in Chapter 22).

During the first half of the nineteenth century, in the aftermath of the French Revolution and because of the success of Gluck and his followers, Paris became the operatic capital of Europe. Following Napoleon's defeat at Waterloo, the French monarchy was restored in 1815. Many who fled the city returned, and musical life flourished once more. A new theater for French opera was built in 1821 and, after it was destroyed by fire in 1873, was replaced by another, the Palais Garnier, which still stands (see Figure 20.1). The government continued to subsidize opera and concerts, and the royal family contributed informally to

Figure 20.1 Théâtre de l'Opéra, Paris. Inaugurated on January 5, 1875, and known also as the Palais Garnier (after its architect, Charles Garnier), it became the main opera house in Paris and remained so for most of the twentieth century. Wagner's operas were performed there in French in the 1890s.
(The Art Archive/Corbis.)

opera and benefit concerts. But with the increasingly large and powerful middle class thronging the opera theaters in search of excitement and entertainment, a new kind of opera came into being, designed to appeal to audiences of all classes and professions. French *grand opera*, as this genre came to be called, was still as much spectacle as music, consistent with the fashion that had prevailed in France since the time of Lully, but newly infused with Romantic elements, such as rescue plots and huge choral scenes.

Italian opera in the nineteenth century grew out of an established tradition, healthily grounded in the life of the nation. Moreover, because opera was the most important musical outlet in Italy during this period, the genre experienced a new golden age there and was exported all over western Europe and even to the New World. While opera's entrenchment in Italy tended to encourage a conservative attitude there, composers such as Rossini, Bellini, and especially Verdi created a distinctly Italian genre of Romantic opera that eventually dominated the field.

As a composite art form, opera integrated music and literature. This interaction, so typical of nineteenth-century Romanticism, was developed most fully by composers in the German-speaking lands, in opera as well as song and instrumental music. At the root of German Romantic opera was the singspiel, exemplified at its best by Mozart's *Die Zauberflöte* (The Magic Flute; see Chapter 17). In the early nineteenth century German composers of singspiel soaked up Romantic elements from French opera, while keeping and even intensifying singspiel's specific national features. Both trends culminated in Richard Wagner—one of the crucial figures in nineteenth-century music—and in the music drama, the new fusion of music, poetry, and theater that he forged to rival traditional opera.

French Grand (and Not So Grand) Opera

French grand opera occupied a place in nineteenth-century culture roughly equivalent to that of the Hollywood film epic in the twentieth and twenty-first centuries. Its leaders were the librettist Eugène Scribe (1791–1861) and the composer Giacomo Meyerbeer (1791–1864), who created the mix of spectacle and historical, political, and religious themes that defined the new genre. Together they exploited every possible occasion for special effects that could be

Meyerbeer

produced with the help of elaborate stage machinery, ballets, choruses, and crowd scenes, while catering to the middle classes by painting aristocrats as wicked and their opponents as virtuous. Two of their operas established the main features of the genre: *Robert le diable* (Robert the Devil, 1831) and *Les Huguenots* (The Huguenots, 1836). (The Huguenots were a French Protestant sect persecuted by the French monarchy and the Catholic nobility.)

Les Huguenots

Based on the Saint Bartholomew Massacre in France during the sixteenth century, *Les Huguenots* relates the tragic fate of a pair of lovers—one Protestant, one Catholic. It has five long acts, an enormous cast, a ballet, and dramatic scenery and lighting effects. Meyerbeer manipulates the solo, choral, and orchestral forces with broad strokes of extraordinary drama, combining lyrical highpoints such as an intimate love duet with thrilling pageantry and public ceremony. For example, during the closing scene of Act II (NAWM 147), in the middle of a crowd scene, the militant Protestant character Marcel defiantly booms out the Lutheran chorale *Ein feste Burg ist unser Gott* (A Mighty Fortress Is Our God), which, as an emblem of the Protestant struggle, was guaranteed to prick the sensibility of the largely French Catholic audience. It also gave *Les Huguenots* an unusual political-religious flavor (see Figure 20.2).

Full 🔊

Other grand operas

Grand-opera elements were admired and emulated by many composers, Italian and German as well as French. Two early examples were Rossini's *Guillaume Tell* (1829), featuring an onstage lake across which the folk hero rows to safety, and *La Muette de Portici* (The Mute Girl of Portici, 1828), which ends with the eruption of the volcano Vesuvius—and ironically has a title role that is danced, not sung, since the character is mute. Both operas explored rebellion against foreign repression.

Berlioz, *Les Troyens*

Hector Berlioz's great five-act opera *Les Troyens* (1856–58, partial premiere in 1863) drew on grand opera but also on the older French opera tradition of Lully,

Figure 20.2 Illustration of the final scene from Meyerbeer's grand opera Les Huguenots *(1836), a fictitious tale of personal tragedy in a historical setting of political and religious turmoil.*
(Lebrecht Music & Arts Photo Library.)

Rameau, and Gluck. The text, by Berlioz himself, is based on the second and fourth books of Virgil's *Aeneid*. Berlioz condensed the narrative in a series of powerful scenes and used appropriate occasions to introduce ballets, processions, and other musical numbers. Like Meyerbeer's *Huguenots, Les Troyens* can be classified as an "epic opera"—a work in which the story of a nation competes with the passions and emotions of individual characters. The style is severe, almost ascetic by comparison with Berlioz's earlier works, recalling the evocation of antiquity in some of the works of French painter Jacques-Louis David (see Figure V.4).

The French ideal of grand opera stayed alive to some extent throughout Europe in the nineteenth century, influencing the work of Bellini, Verdi, and Wagner. The grand-opera tradition also survives in such twentieth-century works as Giacomo Puccini's *Turandot*, Darius Milhaud's *Christophe Colomb*, Samuel Barber's *Antony and Cleopatra*, and John Corigliano's *The Ghosts of Versailles*.

Opéra comique

Side by side with grand opera, the opéra comique continued to be fashionable. As in the eighteenth century, the technical distinction between the two was that opéra comique used spoken dialogue instead of recitative. Apart from this, the differences were primarily those of size and subject matter. Opéra comique was less pretentious than grand opera and required fewer singers and players. Its plots, as a rule, presented straightforward comedy or semiserious drama instead of the historical pageantry typical of grand opera. Examples of opéra comique include works by Daniel-François Auber, who in *Fra Diavolo* (Brother Devil, 1830) and other comic operas mingled humorous and Romantic elements in tuneful music of considerable originality.

Opéra bouffe

Another strain of French light opera appeared around midcentury, during the reign of Napoleon's nephew Louis, who proclaimed himself Emperor Napoleon III in 1851. While censorship controlled the serious theaters, the opéra bouffe could freely satirize the society of the Second Empire by resorting to fictional character types. This new genre emphasized the smart, witty, and satirical elements of comic opera. Its founder was Jacques Offenbach (1819–1880), who even managed to introduce a cancan for the gods in his opéra bouffe *Orphée aux enfers* (Orpheus in the Underworld, 1858). His work influenced developments in comic opera in England (Gilbert and Sullivan, NAWM 154), Vienna, the United States, and elsewhere. The perennial charm of Offenbach's music owes much to its spontaneous melody and rhythm, its simple textures and harmonies, and its conventional formal patterns. But the deceptively naive quality often clothes a rapier wit, satirizing operatic as well as social conventions.

Full 🔊

Lyric opera

Still another type of French opera during this period might best be termed *lyric opera*, which lies somewhere between opéra comique and grand opera. Like that of the opéra comique, its main appeal is through melody. The subject matter is usually romantic drama or fantasy, and its general scale is larger than that of opéra comique, although not so huge as that of the typical grand opera. The most famous example of this genre is *Faust* by Charles Gounod (1818–1893), the most frequently performed opera in the last third of the nineteenth century. First staged in 1859 as an opéra comique, with spoken dialogue, it was later arranged by the composer in its now familiar form with recitatives. Gounod restricted himself to Part I of Goethe's drama, which focuses on the tragic love affair of Faust and Gretchen. The result is a well-proportioned work in an elegant lyric style, with appealing melodies that balance Classic and Romantic expressive qualities.

Gounod's *Faust*

Bizet's *Carmen*

A landmark in the history of French opera is *Carmen* by Georges Bizet (1838–1875), first performed at Paris in 1875. Like the original version of *Faust*,

In Context The Musical Attraction of "the Other"

Western Europe has often succumbed to the allure of exoticism, the seductive appeal of "otherness," of foreign cultures and customs. Certain Baroque dances, such as the sarabande and chaconne, were cultivated by European musicians precisely because of their non-European origin. By the eighteenth century, some operas—for example, Rameau's *Les Indes galantes* (The Gallant Indies, 1735) and Handel's *Giulio Cesare* (1724)—featured novel, exotic instrumental music for particular situations and characters. In the fourth act of Rameau's opera-ballet, the composer characterized in a "peace-pipe dance" the singing and dancing of two North American Indians he had seen perform in Paris; and Handel portrayed Cleopatra's allure by accompanying one of her arias with an unusual ensemble of strings (including muted violins), oboe, bassoon, harp, and theorbo (see page 292 and NAWM 105).

Of all the exotic cultures that became part of the European popular consciousness during the eighteenth century, none was so prevalent as that of the Turkish, or Ottoman, Empire. Both Haydn and Mozart occasionally imitated in their instrumental music the sound of its Janissary, or military, bands, which used colorful percussion instruments (see the commentary on *Rondo alla turca* from Mozart's Sonata K. 331, page 356); and,

on the stage, Mozart's singspiel *Die Entführung aus dem Serail* (The Abduction from the Seraglio [or Harem], 1782) was probably Rossini's inspiration, a generation later, for his opera *L'Italiana in Algeri* (The Italian Woman in Algiers, 1813), which similarly mocks Turkish music and customs. The turbaned instrumentalists accompanying a Handel aria in Carle van Loo's 1727 painting *The Grand Turk Giving a Concert for His Consort* (see Figure 14.15) testify to the cultural exchange promoted by the presence of Ottoman envoys and embassies in various European cities.

Later, some composers blurred the boundaries between different cultures, and musical characteristics first associated with Turkey were applied indiscriminately to Hungarian and Gypsy music alike or were used to represent barbarity in general. Other composers, like Beethoven and Schubert, may have identified with the plight of the downtrodden Viennese Gypsies, who were outcasts from polite society, and used the "Hungarian style" to express their own personal feelings. Some of Schubert's chamber music, as well as the second movement of his *Great* Symphony in C Major, deploy typical Gypsy themes and characteristic rhythms. Even Liszt, a native of Hungary and the greatest exponent of the *style hongrois* (Hungarian style), acknowledged that Beethoven,

Carmen was classified as an opéra comique because it contains spoken dialogue (later set in recitative by another composer) and despite its stark, realistic drama, which ends with a tragic murder. Bizet's rejection of a sentimental or mythological plot signaled an important move toward realism. Set in Spain and using Spanish rhythms and tunes, however, *Carmen* typifies exoticism, a vein running through the entire nineteenth century and evident in some other French operas and ballets of the period (see In Context, above).

The Spanish flavor is personified by Carmen (see Figure 20.3), a brazen Gypsy who works in a cigarette factory and lives only for the pleasures of the moment. Her suggestive costume and behavior, her provocative sexuality and language, and Bizet's music combine to characterize her as the Other, a creature living outside the conventions of normal society, making her both dangerous and enticing—in short, a *femme fatale*. Bizet borrowed three authentic Spanish melodies, including Carmen's famous habanera *L'Amour est un oiseau rebelle* (Love is a rebellious bird), set to the rhythm of a Cuban dance. But most of the Spanish-sounding music is Bizet's own invention, blending elements associated with Gypsy or Spanish music with the modern French style. As shown in Example 20.1, a motive linked to Carmen's fate emphasizes augmented seconds,

"after having himself tasted the dregs of the chalice of human suffering, seemed . . . to have more than once remembered Gypsy art in his later works."[1]

In the nineteenth century, opera composers of one country often imitated the local color of another without negativity or condescension (as in Bizet's *Carmen*, written in French but set in Spain, about a sultry, working-class Spanish Gypsy woman, smugglers, soldiers, and bull-fighters; see Figure 20.3). At least two more works by composers mentioned in this chapter are associated with France and the type of exoticism known as "musical Orientalism," which was generally fostered by French grand opera: Giacomo Meyerbeer's *L'Africaine* (1865), about a female slave purchased by the Portuguese explorer Vasco da Gama, has two of its five acts set in Africa; and, first performed in Cairo, Verdi's *Aida* (1871) was based on a scenario by a French Egyptologist. *Aida* is set entirely in Egypt and, within the standard forms and expressive conventions of Italian opera, frequently alludes to the exotic locale by means of harmony and orchestration. Giacomo Puccini (1858–1924), whose operas *Madama Butterfly* (set in Japan) and *Turandot* (in China) are mentioned in Chapter 22, carried this tradition of operatic Orientalism into the twentieth century.

Figure 20.3 Carmen dancing for Don José. Illustration by Paul Telemann for the cover of a 1930s piano score of the opera.
(Lebrecht Music & Arts Photo Library.)

1. Quoted by Jonathan Bellman, ed., *The Exotic in Western Music* (Boston: Northeastern University Press, 1998), p. 100. Several of the essays in Bellman's collection provided useful material for this discussion.

considered a hallmark of Gypsy music, and a variant of the same motive accompanies Carmen's first entrance. She seduces Don José, a naïve army corporal, by singing a seguidilla (NAWM 152), a type of Spanish song in fast triple time. The accompaniment pattern imitates the strumming of a guitar, the vocal melody features melismas and grace notes, and the harmony suggests the Phrygian mode—all features conventionally linked to Spanish music.

▶ **BIZET,** *Carmen*

Because *Carmen* violated the normal expectations at the Opéra-Comique, where productions were aimed at family-oriented bourgeois audiences, the opera provoked outrage among some at the premiere; one critic wrote that Bizet "had sunk to the sewers of society" to create his heroine. Even before the premiere, the director of the Opéra-Comique resigned, and prominent singers

Example 20.1 Georges Bizet, Carmen

refused to perform the title role. But while the opera plays on fears of the Other, its ultimate acceptance and success as one of the most popular operas of all time may lie in its reflecting many of the anxieties that still trouble audiences, as well as in the extraordinary vitality of its music. Bizet did not live to see its success; he died three months after the premiere.

Italian Opera

Rossini

If asked who was the most famous and important living composer, many people in Europe around 1825 would have answered not Beethoven but rather Gioachino Rossini (see Biography, page 441). He is best known today for his comic masterpiece *Il barbiere di Siviglia* (The Barber of Seville; Rome, 1816), composed and produced a decade before Beethoven's death and ranked among the supreme examples of Italian comic opera. Yet Rossini's reputation during his lifetime rested as much on his serious operas such as *Otello* and *Guillaume Tell*. He was the most popular and influential opera composer of his generation, in part because he blended aspects of opera buffa and opera seria into both his comic and serious operas, making them all more varied, more appealing, and more true to human character. The new conventions that he established for Italian opera were to endure for over half a century.

Bel canto

Rossini helped create a style of Italian opera known as *bel canto*, or "beautiful singing." The term refers to singing characterized by seemingly effortless technique, an equally beautiful tone throughout the singer's entire range, as well as agility, flexibility, and control. Rossini used the term only in retrospect to contrast the Italian singing style of his operas with the heavier dramatic style that dominated by midcentury. In bel canto operas, the most important element is the voice—even more important than the story, the orchestra, and the staging. Rosina's entrance aria from *Il barbiere*, *Una voce poco fa* (A voice a short while ago [resounded here in my heart]; NAWM 145), seems to acknowledge that fact, not only with its music but also with its opening words as she confesses to having been swept off her feet by Lindoro's tuneful serenade. Yet some of the most amusing and captivating moments in Rossini's comic operas are not bel canto, but in the style typical of the patter arias of buffo characters such as Figaro himself (the "barber" of the title, and the same character as in Beaumarchais's plays and Mozart's opera). These numbers specialize in rapidly delivered clever lines, sometimes mixed with nonsense syllables, that are repeated often and must be sung with incredible speed and precision. (An early example of the type is Uberto's aria from Pergolesi's *La Serva padrona*, NAWM 107.)

▶ ROSSINI, *Il barbiere di siviglia*

A combination of bel canto and comic patter appears in *Una voce poco fa*. In this witty two-section or "double" aria (called a *cavatina* in this case because it is Rosina's entrance aria), Rossini suggests action by changing tempo and style; the various sections portray Rosina's complicated situation—wooed by her guardian, who wants her money, but in love with a poor soldier—and the different facets of her character—part docile lady, part scheming vixen (as suggested by the caricature shown in Figure 20.4). In typical fashion, Rossini juxtaposes two separate lyrical sections—an opening *cantabile* and a faster, more brilliant conclusion, called a *cabaletta* (see A Closer Look, page 447). These are further divided through changes of style, as shown in Example 20.2.

There is no opening recitative, but the first section of the cantabile—as Rosina narrates being serenaded by and falling in love with Lindoro—is broken into small phrases punctuated by orchestral chords, a style appropriate to narration (Example 20.2a). When she swears to outwit her guardian, the style briefly

Figure 20.4 Caricature of Italian soprano Adelina Patti (1843–1919) in the role of Rosina from Rossini's Il barbiere di Siviglia.
(Opera News (March 2005). Metropolitan Opera Archives, New York.)

Gioachino Rossini (1792–1868)

Rossini had a meteoric career as an opera composer: beginning at the age of eighteen, he wrote almost forty operas in half as many years and then, at the height of his fame and fortune, far short of his fortieth birthday, he suddenly and mysteriously disappeared from the operatic scene.

Born in Pesaro on the Adriatic coast of Italy to musical parents, he enrolled in the Bologna Conservatory, where his studies of counterpoint and the music of Haydn and Mozart had a permanent impact on his style. An able singer himself, Rossini perfectly understood the singing voice. He wrote his first opera for Venice in 1813 but earned an international reputation by the age of twenty-one. He went on to compose numerous operas for Naples and other cities. Because copyright protection did not exist in Italy, he could earn money from operas only when he participated in the performances. As a result, he constantly had to produce new works, composing very rapidly (sometimes writing an opera in a month or less) and often borrowing or reworking overtures and arias from his own previous works. He always wrote for particular singers, creating music to suit their talents.

In 1822, Rossini married the soprano Isabella Colbran (Figure 20.6), with whom he had worked

Figure 20.5 *Gioachino Rossini around 1816, the year he composed* Il barbiere di Siviglia. *Painting by Vincenzo Camuccini.*
(Museo Teatrale alla Scalla, Milan.)

as musical director of the Teatro San Carlo in Naples. Eventually they traveled to London and then settled in Paris, where he became director of the Théâtre Italien. His last and greatest opera, *Guillaume Tell* (William Tell, 1829), written in French for Parisian audiences, combines Italian lyricism with French grand opera.

The remaining forty years of his life were marred by illness—some say hypochondria, others bipolar disorder—but he was financially comfortable, entertaining in his villa outside Paris, composing some sacred music and witty piano pieces and songs, eating to excess, and inventing recipes that he exchanged with some of the most famous chefs in Europe. He died in 1868, known best for music written four decades earlier.

Major works: 39 operas, including *Tancredi*, *L'Italiana in Algeri* (The Italian Woman in Algiers), *Il barbiere di Siviglia* (The Barber of Seville), *Otello*, *La Cenerentola* (Cinderella), *Mosè in Egitto* (Moses in Egypt), *Semiramide*, and *Guillaume Tell*; (William Tell); Stabat Mater, *Petite Messe solennelle*, and other sacred works; and smaller vocal and instrumental pieces collected in *Soirées musicales* and *Péchés de vieillesse* (Sins of Old Age).

Figure 20.6 *Spanish soprano Isabella Colbran (Rossini's wife) holding a lyre, an emblem of her Orphic status as a singer.*
(The Art Archive/Corbis.)

Example 20.2 *Gioachino Rossini*, Il barbiere di Siviglia, Una voce poco fa

a. Cantabile

A voice a short while ago here in my heart resounded.

b. Patter song

The guardian I shall refuse, I shall sharpen my wits.

changes to a comic patter song (Example 20.2b). Similarly, Rossini uses the cabaletta to reveal both sides of Rosina's personality: loving and obedient, singing a bel canto melody (Example 20.2c); but also a scheming trickster, showing off her sudden vocal leaps and rapid passage work in buffo style (Example 20.2d). The whole monologue reveals her control of the situation in Rossini's masterful combination of bel canto melody, wit, and comic description.

Rossini's style combines an irrepressible melody with animated rhythms, clear phrase structure, and well-shaped though sometimes unconventional musical periods. His spare texture and orchestration support rather than compete with the voice, while featuring individual instruments, especially winds, for color. His harmonic schemes are not complex but are often original, and he shares a fondness for juxtaposing third-related keys with other early nineteenth-century composers. Another important aspect of comic opera is the quickly paced ensemble scene, and Rossini manages this feature with sparkle and gusto. In these scenes he frequently uses a simple but effective device, the crescendo—building up excitement by repeating a phrase, louder each time and often at a higher pitch, sometimes giving the impression of a world about to spin out of control. The crescendo, also a prominent feature of many of Rossini's popular overtures, became his trademark.

c. Cabaletta, lyrical opening

I am docile, I am respectful . . .

d. Cabaletta, contrasting comic style

But if they touch my weaker side, I can be a viper . . .

Vincenzo Bellini (1801–1835) was a younger contemporary of Rossini who came to prominence after the elder had retired from opera composition. Bellini preferred dramas of passion with fast, gripping action. Of his ten operas, all serious, the most important are *La sonnambula* (The Sleepwalker, 1831), *Norma* (1831), and *I Puritani* (The Puritans, 1835). Bellini is known for long, sweeping, highly embellished, intensely emotional melodies that have a breadth, a flexibility of form, and a tinge of sadness that we associate with the nocturnes of Chopin (who was, incidentally, a great fan of Bellini's operas).

Among Bellini's most famous arias is Norma's cavatina, or entrance aria, *Casta diva* (Chaste goddess) from *Norma* (NAWM 146), shown in Example 20.3. The opera, set in ancient Gaul after its conquest by the Romans, reflected both the Romantic fascination with distant times and places and Italian yearnings for freedom from foreign domination, especially acute after the Austrians suppressed revolts in northern Italy in 1830–1831. When Norma, high priestess of the Druids, prays to the moon (the chaste goddess) for peace with the Romans, her vocal line is in constant motion, creating a deeply expressive and unpredictable melody. The secret of such melodies is that a simple underlying structure, often stepwise in motion (A—G—F in the first phrase, A—Bb in the second), is embellished with ever-changing figuration that draws our attention

Bellini

Norma's aria

Full 🔊

Example 20.3 Bellini, Norma, Casta diva

Chaste goddess, who plates with silver [these sacred ancient plants]

and plays with our expectations. The scene follows the double aria pattern (see *A Closer Look*, page 447). Compared to Rossini, Bellini makes much more frequent use of the chorus. Here, it plays an important role, alternately responding to Norma's pleas for peace and demanding revenge on the Romans. Meanwhile, Norma is secretly in love with the Roman proconsul and longs for their reunion. The complexity of the scene, showing the different sides of the situation and the emotions aroused, illustrates the power of Italian opera.

Giuseppe Verdi (1813–1901)

For the entire second half of the nineteenth century Giuseppe Verdi (see Biography, pages 448–449) was the ruling presence in Italian music, which continued to be dominated by the stage. The first of his twenty-six operas was produced in 1839, when he was twenty-six years old, the last in 1893, when he was eighty. His approach to dramatic structure and musical style evolved during these years, and he enjoyed many successes at each stage of his career.

Opera and nationalism   In contrast to developments farther north, where opera competed with other genres and where native and foreign composers vied with each other for the public's approval, Italy had a long, indigenous operatic tradition that was unchallenged by, for example, the symphony. Italians loved opera first and foremost. The Romantic issue that most affected their music at this time was nationalism, and here Verdi was uncompromising: he firmly believed that each nation should cultivate its own native music. He deplored the influence of foreign (especially German) ideas in the work of his younger compatriots and cultivated a personal musical style that remained resolutely independent. Except for his loyalty to the traditions of Italian opera, Verdi's work is rarely overtly nationalistic. Yet he supported and became identified with the Risorgimento ("resurgence"), a movement that aimed to liberate Italy from foreign rule, reunite its various regions, and reclaim the leading role it had played in Roman antiquity and the Renaissance. A few of his early operas contain choruses that

Figure 20.7 Teatro alla Scala (La Scala) in Milan, where many of Verdi's operas were first produced. It was built in the late eighteenth century by the Empress Maria Theresa. (The Art Archive/Corbis.)

some heard as thinly disguised appeals against foreign domination. By 1859, his name had become a patriotic symbol and rallying cry: "Viva VERDI!" to Italian patriots stood for "**Viva V**ittorio **E**manuele **R**e **d'I**talia!"—Long live Victor Emanuel, King of Italy.

Verdi's treatment of opera as human drama (in contrast to the Germans' emphasis on romanticized nature and mythology; see page 450) linked him to his Italian predecessors. He usually chose the opera's story himself, stating his preference for "subjects that are novel, big, beautiful, varied and bold—as bold as can be." He wanted librettos with fast action, striking contrasts, unusual characters, and strong emotional situations—and, indeed, those qualities describe most of his operas. Collaborating closely with his librettist, Verdi planned the sequence of musical forms to make sure each singer had opportunities for arias, dramatic duets, and larger ensembles.

Once the libretto was complete, Verdi wrote out a draft with the vocal melodies and essential accompaniment, then a skeleton score with more of the elements filled in. The final step was the orchestration, usually completed after the rehearsals had begun and he heard how the singers sounded in the theater. Verdi's involvement even extended to his rehearsing, directing, and sometimes conducting the opera's premiere. He could afford to take more time than his predecessors because he was better paid for each new opera and, thanks to improved copyright laws, could count on income from royalties and from sales of the published scores. He used that time to calculate the most effective setting to enhance the opera's dramatic impact on the audience. His strategy worked: although he wrote far fewer operas than Rossini or Donizetti, Verdi's have been far more frequently performed than theirs ever since.

To produce the dramatic impact that he sought, Verdi's primary medium was vocal melody (in contrast to the orchestral and choral luxuriance of French grand opera). The secret of his popularity was his ability to capture character, feeling, and situation in memorable melodies that sound both fresh and familiar. Many use a simple form that makes them easy to follow, and they combine regular phrasing and plain harmony with an intriguing rhythmic and melodic

Approach to opera

Working methods

Verdi's style

motive that catches the listener's attention. So aware was Verdi of the appeal of his melodies that he strove to keep a new opera's best tunes from being leaked to the public before the premiere. But his craft did not stop at melody. He had a wide knowledge of the music of his predecessors and revered Beethoven above all. He respected the conventions of Rossini's musical scene structure (see A Closer Look, page 447), and the impact of Bellini's emotional intensity, and learned much from the harmony and orchestration of Meyerbeer. But after absorbing any stylistic influence, he fully assimilated it and made it part of his own language.

Early operas

▶ **VERDI,** *Rigoletto*

Verdi's work falls roughly into three periods, the first culminating in 1853 with *Il trovatore* and *La traviata*. During this early period, many of his operas, such as *Luisa Miller*, told intimate stories of personal tragedy and were influenced by French culture. *Rigoletto* and *La traviata* were adapted from plays by Victor Hugo (*Le Roi s'amuse*, The King Enjoys Himself) and Alexandre Dumas the Younger (*La Dame aux camélias*, The Lady of the Camellias), respectively.

La traviata

▶ **VERDI,** *La traviata*

Many features of Verdi's mature works appear in *La traviata*, an opera about love and death or, as Verdi put it, "a subject of the times." In fact, *La traviata* was one of the first tragic operas to be set in the present rather than the historical past. Both its setting and its subject—a woman trapped between her livelihood as a courtesan, her desire to escape that life and be loved, the social forces that keep her in her place, and the tuberculosis that threatens her life—link the opera to the contemporary trend of realism in literature and art. The resources Verdi commanded are evident in the final act in which Violetta, the "fallen woman" of the title, and her lover Alfredo reconcile after she had left him to spare his family's reputation (NAWM 150). The scene follows the structure Rossini had standardized for duets (see Figure 20.8), yet it features a new kind of melody—more tuneful than recitative in some sections and more declamatory than outright song in others—a style that Verdi developed still further in his late operas. After the *scena* between Violetta and her maid, Alfredo's entrance launches the *tempo d'attacco*, or first movement, a tuneful song in which Alfredo and Violetta alternate phrases. The following slow *cantabile* (Andante mosso), in which they look forward to life together as she recovers her health in the country, is almost as simple and direct as a popular song (see Example 20.4). The *tempo di mezzo* offers a series of startling changes in mood and style as Violetta collapses, insists nothing is wrong, collapses again, and finally despairs that her illness will overtake her just as happiness is so near. These emotions intensify in the *cabaletta*; it brings the scene to a rousing conclusion, which allows Verdi to end on an emotional climax. Throughout the scene, he uses stark contrasts, strong emotions, and catchy melodies while keeping the action moving in an almost perfect marriage of drama and music.

Example 20.4 Verdi La traviata, *Act IV*

Paris, my dear, we shall forsake; our life, united, we shall pass together.

A Closer Look · Typical Scene Structure of Nineteenth-Century Italian Opera

In eighteenth-century operas, the dramatic action was confined to dry recitative passages (*recitativo secco*), and the emotional reactions were explored in static arias, sung with little or no change of mood or tempo. In the early nineteenth century, Rossini and his librettists established a very specific structure for an extended aria or duet that accommodated new developments in the story line and reflected the changing moods of the characters. This formula might be thought of as an expansion of the double-aria structure illustrated by Rossini's *Una voce poco fa* (NAWM 145).

I. Aria (so-called double aria)			
Scena recitative	1. *Primo tempo:* 1st mvmt. slow, cantabile, andante, etc.	2. *Tempo di mezzo:* mid. mvmt. ensemble, chorus, transition	3. *Cabaletta* often fast

II. Duet				
Scena recitative	1. *Tempo d'attacco* opening mvmt.	2. Slow mvmt.	3. *Tempo di mezzo*	4. *Cabaletta* often fast
action		stasis	action	stasis

Figure 20.8 Integration of action into nineteenth-century aria and duet types.

A typical Rossinian scene structure begins with an orchestral introduction and recitative section (called *scena*) that sets the scene. Thereafter, the sections or movements differ, as does the terminology, depending on whether the piece is a solo aria (indicated as I in Figure 20.8) or an ensemble such as a duet (indicated as II). The latter is more complex and allows for at least the possibility of more contrasts in tempo and mood as the situation develops. In an aria, after the introduction, the character launches into a formal song known as the *primo tempo*, or first movement (I.1; see the aria from Bellini's *Norma*, NAWM 146). In a duet, there are two movements in the first phase of the piece: the somewhat dialogue-like *tempo d'attacco* (II.1) and then a more formal song that the two characters sing—either in alternating phrases or simultaneously in harmony. (See the excerpt from Verdi's *La traviata*, NAWM 150). After I.1 (or, in a *duet*, II.2), an interlude usually follows—a *tempo di mezzo*, or middle movement (I.2 or II.3), which may be a transition or interruption by an ensemble or chorus, and in which something happens to provoke a change in the situation or mood. This section leads to the final movement, or *cabaletta* (I.3 or II.4), a lively and brilliant solo or duet in the same key, part or all of which is literally repeated, though perhaps with improvised embellishments. The successive parts of a typical Rossinian scene complex, then, allowed lyrical highpoints (or moments of stasis) to alternate with dramatic action. The structure also gave the singers a chance, usually during the repeat of the cabaletta, to show off their virtuosity and bring the scene to a rousing conclusion. Verdi adapted this scene structure for many of the solos, duets, and ensembles in his operas.

Giuseppe Verdi (1813–1901)

Verdi's long career dominates the history of Italian music in the second half of the nineteenth century. Today his operas remain among the most frequently performed works on the international stage.

"My youth was hard," Verdi recalled. His father was a tavern keeper and grocer in a hamlet near Busseto in northern Italy, an area that was oppressed alternately by the French and the Austrians. As a child, Verdi played the organ in church and studied music locally. When he took the entrance exam for the Milan Conservatory, he was evaluated as a promising composer with "genuine imagination" but was refused admission for lack of accomplishment in counterpoint. Rejected and humiliated, Verdi returned to Busseto to become the town's *maestro di musica*. In 1836, he married Margherita Barezzi, the daughter of a local merchant and patron who had sponsored his early musical education, and they had two children, both of whom died before their first birthday. When, in 1840, his wife also died, Verdi was left alone and despondent in Milan, where he had brought his family in hopes of having a career as an opera composer; he was then not even twenty-seven years old.

After several discouraging years writing for Milan's opera house, La Scala (see Figure 20.7), Verdi's luck began to change. He scored a huge success with his biblical opera *Nabucco* (Nebuchadnezzar, 1842), initiating a time of enormous productivity that the composer later referred to as "my galley-slave period": nineteen operas in fifteen years for theaters in Milan, Venice, Rome, Naples, Florence, London, Paris, and Trieste. His greatest hits among these works are still his most popular: *Rigoletto* (1851), *Il trovatore* (1853), and *La traviata* (1853).

Verdi met the soprano Giuseppina Strepponi (see Figure 20.10) when she, singing the leading female role in *Nabucco*, helped to launch his career. She provided the tempering, stabilizing influence he needed, and the two formed a lifelong partnership; they lived together openly as lovers for many years before marrying in 1859. Their relationship was the object of much gossip, about which Verdi rebuked his former father-in-law in a letter:

Figure 20.9 Portrait of Giuseppe Verdi
(DeA Picture Library/Art Resource, NY.)

Middle period

Now famous and well off, Verdi could afford to slow his pace and wrote only six new operas in the next two decades. In these operas, the action is more continuous; solos, ensembles, and choruses are more freely combined; harmonies become more daring; and the orchestra is treated with great originality. Verdi still used traditional forms but often reshaped them to suit the dramatic situation. An important influence was French grand opera, especially Meyerbeer. Verdi wrote *Les vêpres siciliennes* (The Sicilian Vespers, 1855) as a grand opera, for Paris, to a libretto by Meyerbeer's collaborator Eugène Scribe, blending French and Italian elements. This return to historical subjects with political ramifications coincided with renewed interest in Italian unification. He introduced comic roles in *Un ballo in maschera* (A Masked Ball; Rome, 1859) and in *La forza del destino* (The Force of Destiny, 1862, revised 1869), composed for the

I have nothing to hide. In my house there lives a lady, free, independent, a lover of solitude, as I am. . . . Neither I nor she owes to anyone at all any account of our actions. . . . I demand liberty of action for myself . . . since my nature rebels against conformity.[1]

After *La traviata*, Verdi took more time with each opera, writing only six in the sixteen years from *Les Vêpres siciliennes* (1855) to *Aida* (1871). Then he retired from the stage, focusing on the farm he had purchased near his birthplace and living off royalties from his music for another fifteen years. Eventually his publisher, Giulio Ricordi, persuaded him to write two final operas. In his seventies and after much deliberation, Verdi produced his crowning achievements: *Otello* (1887) and *Falstaff* (1893), one a tragedy, the other a comedy, both on Shakespearean subjects.

Verdi supported the Risorgimento and, despite having little tolerance for political machinations, became a reluctant deputy in the first Italian Parliament (1861–1865). But his lack of participation was unimportant; he had already served the cause of Italian unification through his operas, some of which were subtle appeals against foreign domination. When he died at eighty-eight, he had become a national institution. Escorted by a procession of nearly 300,000 mourners, his remains—along with Strepponi's—were interred in Milan at the home for retired musicians he had helped to found and which he had called "my last and best work." The funeral itself, in keeping with his wishes, was a very quiet affair, "without music or singing."

Figure 20.10 Italian soprano Giuseppina Strepponi (1815–1897), Verdi's second wife. (DeA Picture Library/Art Resource, NY.)

Major works: 26 operas, including *Nabucco, Rigoletto, Il trovatore, La traviata, Les Vêpres siciliennes, Simon Boccanegra, Un ballo in maschera, La forza del destino, Don Carlos, Aida, Otello, Falstaff*; Requiem and other Latin sacred works.

1. From a letter Verdi wrote to his father-in-law and one-time patron, Antonio Barezzi; quoted by Andrew Porter, "Verdi," in *The New Grove Dictionary of Music and Musicians*, ed. Stanley Sadie. (London and New York: Macmillan, 1980), vol. 19, p. 650.

imperial Russian opera in St. Petersburg. At crucial points in both these operas, Verdi brought back distinctive themes or motives introduced earlier in the score. Such reminiscence motives, already common in the works of other composers and previously used in *Rigoletto*, helped unify the work both dramatically and musically. All the traits of his mature style appear in *Aida* (1871), which combines the heroic quality of grand opera with vivid character delineation, pathos, and a wealth of melodic, harmonic, and orchestral color. Commissioned for the Cairo opera, *Aida* took Egypt as its setting, giving Verdi opportunity to introduce exotic color and spectacle.

Another decade elapsed before Verdi's publisher, Giulio Ricordi, was able to coax him out of retirement with the proposal that he set a new libretto based on *Othello*, a play by his favorite dramatist, Shakespeare. During that decade, a

Reminiscence motives

Late works

number of important works had joined the musical canon—among them his own Requiem (1874), Bizet's *Carmen*, all four of Brahms's symphonies (discussed in Chapter 21), and Wagner's huge cycle of operas on the *Ring* (see page 453)—and Ricordi was eager to see Verdi give Italian opera a boost. The poet and composer Arrigo Boito (1842–1918) wrote the libretto, which presents a powerful human drama that the music intensifies at every turn.

Otello

Another seven years passed before *Otello* was finally produced in Milan in 1887. The time and care Verdi took in creating the new opera clearly reflected his response to the evolving musical situation; despite his deliberate isolation, he was responsive to new trends. More than ever before, Verdi strove for continuity in music and action: "If in the opera there were no cavatinas, duets, trios, choruses, finales, etc., and if the whole work consisted, so to speak, of a single number, I should find that all the more right and proper."[1] In his late operas, he realized this ideal most completely, through reminiscence motives in the orchestra and in the unbroken flow of music within each act. The traditional scheme of declamatory and lyrical solos, duets, ensembles, and choruses is often present, but Verdi arranges these units in larger scene complexes so that the lyrical highpoints are connected by long transitions rather than abruptly set off as separate pieces. Instead of the "number opera" typical of the eighteenth century or the "scene opera" of Verdi's earlier style, we can now speak about "act opera," in which the musical units are neither individual arias nor separate scenes, but entire acts. Each act has a musical continuity that reinforces the inexorable sweep of its dramatic content. We find ourselves holding our collective breath (and our applause) until the curtain comes down at the end of the act; only then may we exhale and express (or withhold) our approval.

Falstaff

Two years after the premiere of *Otello*, Verdi's librettist, Boito, suggested an opera on scenes from Shakespeare's *The Merry Wives of Windsor* and *Henry IV* involving the character Falstaff. If *Otello* was the consummation of Italian tragic opera, *Falstaff* holds a parallel place in comic opera: as *Otello* reshaped dramatic lyrical melody, so *Falstaff* transformed the characteristic element of opera buffa—the ensemble. Carried along over a nimble, endlessly varied orchestral background, the comedy speeds to its climaxes in the grand finales of the second and third acts. At times, Verdi seems to be satirizing the entire Romantic century, himself included. The last scene culminates in a fugue on the words "Tutto nel mondo è burla. / L'uom è nato burlone" (All the world's a joke. We are all born fools).

German Romantic Opera

The interaction between music and literature, so typical of nineteenth-century Romanticism, was developed most fully by composers in German-speaking lands, in opera as well as song and instrumental music. At the root of German opera was Singspiel, whose composers in the early nineteenth century soaked up Romantic elements from French opera while intensifying the genre's national features. German opera also leans toward increasingly chromatic harmony, the use of orchestral color for dramatic expression, and an emphasis on the inner voices of the texture in contrast to the Italian stress on melody.

The work that established German Romantic opera was *Der Freischütz* (The Magic Rifleman) by Carl Maria von Weber (1786–1826; see Figure 20.11), first

Figure 20.11 Carl Maria von Weber, in a portrait by Caroline Bardua.
(Lebrecht Music & Arts Photo Library.)

---

1. From a letter Verdi wrote to his librettist for *Il trovatore*; quoted by Roger Parker, "Verdi," in *The New Grove Dictionary of Music and Musicians*, ed. Stanley Sadie. (New York: Oxford University Press).

Figure 20.12 Set by Carl Wilhelm Holdermann for the Wolf's Glen scene in Weber's Der Freischütz *(Weimar production of 1822). As the bullets are being cast, the hero looks around with growing alarm, while "night birds crowd around the fire" and the "cracking of whips and the sound of galloping horses [are] heard."*
(Staatliche Kunstsammlungen, Schlossmuseum, Weimar. Photo: Lebrecht Music & Arts Photo Library.)

performed in Berlin in 1821. Written and premiered while Beethoven was still alive, Weber's work set the pace for German opera for the rest of the century. Its unusual harmonies and orchestral effects are especially daring. The libretto characteristically involves ordinary folk caught up in supernatural events against a background of wilderness and mystery. This and other plots often resemble fairy tales: mortals act not merely as individuals, but as agents of superhuman forces, whether good or evil. In emphasizing folklore, nature, and supernatural elements, Weber's opera differs sharply from contemporary French and Italian opera. While his musical styles and forms draw directly from those other countries, his use of simple folklike melodies introduces a distinctly national element. Also, in the Wolf's Glen Scene (NAWM 148) he incorporates elements of melodrama, a genre of musical theater that combines spoken dialogue with background music.

Full 🔊

In his music for the scene, Weber ingeniously exploited the orchestra to depict the eerie natural setting (see Figure 20.12) and underline its spectacular effects. Harmonically, the scene also emphasizes the tritone relationship, F♯–C, to suggest the diabolical forces at play in the plot. The immense popularity of *Der Freischütz,* based both on its appeal to national sentiment and on the beauty of its music was not matched by Weber's later works *Euryuanthe* (1823) or *Oberon* (1826), but his harmonic and orchestral innovations exercised an enormous influence on later composers of opera.

Richard Wagner and the Music Drama

For Richard Wagner the outstanding composer of German opera and one of the crucial figures in nineteenth-century culture (see Biography, pages 452–453), music's purpose was to serve the goals of dramatic expression. Consequently,

Goals and writings

Richard Wagner (1813–1883)

Wagner was a crusader for reform in opera and created a visionary ideal for musical theater—a *Gesamtkunstwerk*—which he saw as a ritual, with himself as high priest or chief wizard controlling all of its elements. His emphasis on music as the driving force of the drama, his use of leitmotives as an organizing principle, and his creative manipulation of chromatic harmony had a profound and far-reaching impact on many later composers. He was, as he saw himself, the Beethoven of his age.

Wagner was born in Leipzig, the ninth child of a police clerk who died shortly after his son's birth. Wagner's stepfather was an actor, a poet, and a portrait painter who evidently cultivated Richard's intellectual gifts. His early passions were theater and music, and he was particularly inspired by Weber's operas and Beethoven's symphonies. By the age of twenty he was writing librettos, composing operas, and working as a conductor for various regional opera companies. After he married the soprano Minna Planer in 1836, the couple spent several unhappy years in Paris, where Wagner worked as a music journalist while trying, unsuccessfully, to get his works performed. After returning to Germany, he scored his first triumphs in 1842 and 1843 with his early operas *Rienzi* and *Der fliegende Holländer*. Their success led to his appointment as second Kapellmeister for the king of Saxony in Dresden, directing the opera, conducting the orchestra, and composing for court occasions.

Wagner supported the 1848 revolution and fled Germany after a warrant was issued for his arrest. He escaped to Switzerland, where, during his dozen years in exile, he found the leisure to formulate his theories about opera and to publish them in a series of essays. There he also composed *Das Rheingold*, the first of his massive cycle of four music dramas about a cursed golden ring, *Der Ring des Nibelungen*. But with no regular income he complained, "I too am plagued by the need for gold!" Eventually, he found a patron in the young King Ludwig II of Bavaria, who became a fanatical fan, paid his debts (Wagner was a habitual gambler), granted him an annual pension, and sponsored the production of *Tristan und Isolde*, *Die Meistersinger*, and the first two operas in the *Ring* cycle.

Wagner's personal life was beset by stormy relationships—with King Ludwig and other

all of his important compositions are for theater. He presented his ideas in a series of essays, including *The Artwork of the Future* (1850) and *Opera and Drama* (1851, revised 1868). He believed that Beethoven had done everything that could be done in instrumental music and had shown in his Ninth Symphony the path to the future by joining music to words (see Vignette, page 455). Wagner saw himself—not composers of symphonies and string quartets—as Beethoven's true successor.

Gesamtkunstwerk   Wagner believed in the absolute oneness of drama and music—that the two are organically connected expressions of a single dramatic idea. Poetry, scenic design, staging, action, and music work together to form what he called a *Gesamtkunstwerk* (*Gesamt*, meaning "complete" or "united"; *Kunst*, meaning "art"; *Werk*, meaning "work"; thus, a "united artwork"). His vision of a new union of music and dramatic text has been called *music drama*, although he rejected that term; instead he called his works operas, dramas, or *Bühnenfestspielen* (festival stage plays), and in one essay suggested the phrase "acts of music made visible."

The last of these terms is revealing, because for Wagner the core of the drama is really in the music, and the other arts make it apparent. The orchestra conveys the inner aspect of the drama, while the sung words articulate the outer aspect—the events and situations that further the action and give names to the feelings and experiences suggested by the music. In a similar way, the traditional hierarchy of voice and orchestra is reversed. The orchestral web is the chief factor in the music, and the vocal lines are part of the musical texture. In most opera, especially the Italian variety, the voices lead and the

patrons—and he channeled the energy from his disastrous love affair with Mathilde Wesendonck, the wife of one of his patrons, into his sensuous opera about Tristan and Isolde, legendary victims of a forbidden love that could not be consummated in life. His second love affair was with Cosima, by whom he had three children out of wedlock. The daughter of Franz Liszt through his liaison with Countess Marie d'Agoult, Cosima was the wife of the conductor Hans von Bülow, another of Wagner's ardent admirers and promoters of his work. Wagner finally married Cosima in 1870, a month after her divorce.

Wagner dreamed of a permanent festival of his operas in his specially designed theater in Bayreuth, Germany (see Figure 20.16), begun in 1872. The first festival was held there in 1876, during which the complete *Ring* cycle was launched, and the second in 1882, with performances of his last opera, *Parsifal*. The following year Wagner died of a heart attack. His grave lies in the garden at Bayreuth, where his operas are still performed.

Figure 20.13 *Richard Wagner, in a portrait by Franz von Lenbach.*
(Lebrecht Music & Arts Photo Library.)

Major works: 13 operas, including *Rienzi, Der fliegender Holländer, Tannhäuser, Lohengrin, Tristan und Isolde, Die Meistersinger von Nürnberg, Das Rheingold, Die Walküre, Siegfried, Götterdämmerung, Parsifal.*

orchestra supports, punctuates, and comments; in a Wagner drama, the dramatic thread is in the music itself, led by the orchestra, and the voices give it definition and precision through words. As Wagner wrote in *Opera and Drama*, the dramatic singer's verse-melody is like a boat borne upon the sounding surges of the orchestra.

Wagner's published writings address not only music but also literature, drama, and even political and moral topics. He believed that the *Gesamtkunstwerk* could help reform society and that art should not be undertaken for profit. He argued for vegetarianism and against animal experimentation. More controversial were his views on nationalism, including anti-Semitism (see In Context, page 456).

Before formulating his conception of the *Gesamtkunstwerk*, Wagner composed several operas that drew directly on his predecessors: *Rienzi*, a grand opera in the Meyerbeer mold (Dresden, 1842); *Der fliegende Holländer* (The Flying Dutchman, Dresden, 1843), a Romantic opera in the tradition of Weber; and *Tannhäuser* (Dresden, 1845) and *Lohengrin* (Weimar, 1850), both adapted from Germanic legends about sin and redemption. In the last two works Wagner introduced a new kind of flexible, semi-declamatory vocal line that became his standard method of setting text.

Wagner's most colossal achievement is *Der Ring des Nibelungen*, a four-opera cycle for which he wrote the librettos himself. The plots are woven out of stories from medieval German epic poems and Norse legends featuring giants and dwarves, gods and mortals. Nearly thirty years in the making, it consists of

Other writings

Early operas

The *Ring* cycle

Figure 20.14 Photograph of singers portraying the Rhine maidens in the 1876 Bayreuth premiere of the Ring cycle. They were each held up and moved about by a machine, operated by several stagehands, giving the illusion that they were swimming in the Rhine.
(Lebrecht Music & Arts Photo Library.)

Leitmotives

about nineteen hours of music that Wagner intended to be performed over four consecutive evenings, although it is possible—in fact, even usual—to attend a production of only one of the four operas in a given season. All are linked by a common set of characters and musical motives, or leitmotives (see below). The "ring" of the title refers to a ring that the gnome Alberich fashioned out of the gold he stole from the river Rhine, where it was guarded by Rhine maidens. Wagner's stunning evocation of the watery riverbed at the opening of the first opera, *Das Rheingold*—by prolonging the tonic chord for 136 measures—is but one of the brilliant special effects of his orchestral palette and was matched by the watery stage effects shown in Figure 20.14. Wotan, ruler of the gods (see Figure 20.15), tricks Alberich into giving up the ring and also captures a hoard of gold, which he uses to pay the giants for building his new castle, Valhalla. But Alberich has put a curse on the ring that will bring its wearer misery and death. In the course of the mega-opera, the curse is fulfilled: Wotan's doomed empire comes to a fiery end, with more special effects, in the last drama of the cycle, *Götterdämmerung* (The Twilight of the Gods); and the Rhine maidens reclaim the ring. Despite its fantastical setting, the *Ring's* themes—love, greed, power, innocence, passion, and betrayal, to name a few—are as universally relevant now as then.

The music of all four operas in the cycle is organized around a network of motives, each of which is associated with a particular character, object, event, or emotion. Wagner referred to these motives as the work's principal themes, the same term one uses in describing a symphony. But analysts since Wagner's time have labeled each one individually with the general term *leitmotive* (leading motive), and have given them specific names as well (such as the Ring, Valhalla, the Curse), in accord with their meaning in the drama. Often the significance of a leitmotive can be recognized from the words to which it is first sung or from its being played by the orchestra at the first appearance or mention of the subject, and by its repetition during subsequent appearances or references. But a leitmotive becomes more than just a musical label through its symphonic treatment in the music drama: it accumulates significance as it recurs in new contexts; it may serve to recall an object in situations where the object is not present; it may be varied, developed, or transformed as the plot develops; and similar motives may suggest a connection between things, especially if one leitmotive morphs into another (see A Closer Look, pages 458–459).

The mutability of Wagner's leitmotives distinguishes them from the reminiscence motives of operas by Verdi and his predecessors and of Wagner's own earlier works. He uses them not once in a while but constantly, in intimate alliance with every step of the action. In principle, there is a complete correspondence between the symphonic web of leitmotives and the unfolding of the dramatic action; but leitmotives also serve to unify a scene or opera just as recurrent themes unify a symphony. In this way, moreover, they create a seamless flow of music, unbroken by the stops and restarts of Classic musical syntax, and give the impression of what some commentators have described as "endless melody." For this reason, they also furthered Wagner's goal to purge opera of arias and other artificial set pieces that he believed impeded the drama.

Wagner's mature music dramas, beginning in the 1850s with *Tristan und Isolde*, were influenced by the philosopher Arthur Schopenhauer (1788–1860), whose pessimistic views gained prominence after the failed revolutions of 1848. In *The World as Will and Representation*, Schopenhauer argued that music was the one art that embodied the deepest reality of all human experience—our emotions and drives—and could, therefore, give immediate expression to these universal feelings and

Figure 20.15 One of the superheroes of Germanic mythology, the warrior Wotan was also known as Woden, for whom Wednesday is named (Woden's day).
(Lebrecht Music & Arts Photo Library.)

VIGNETTE The Artwork of the Future

In The Artwork of the Future *(1850), Richard Wagner argued that Beethoven strove to discover the full potential of music and found it in his Ninth Symphony by rooting his music in the word. Thus, for Wagner, purely instrumental music after Beethoven was sterile ("the last symphony had already been* written*"), and only the artwork that combined all the arts was worthwhile.*

This *last symphony* of Beethoven's is the redemption of music out of its own element as a *universal art*. It is the *human* gospel of the art of the future. Beyond it there can be no *progress*, for there can follow on it immediately only the completed artwork of the future, *the universal drama*, to which Beethoven has forged for us the artistic key.

Thus from within itself music accomplished what no one of the other arts was capable of in isolation . . . to offer to its sister arts a redeeming hand. . . .

Man as artist can be fully satisfied only in the union of all the art varieties in the *collective* artwork [*Gesamtkunstwerk*]; in every *individualization*

of his artistic capacities he is *unfree*, not wholly that which he can be; in the collective artwork he is *free*, wholly that which he can be. . . .

The highest collective artwork is the *drama;* it is present in its *ultimate completeness* only when *each art variety, in its ultimate completeness*, is present in it.

True drama can be conceived only as resulting from the *collective impulse of all the arts* to communicate in the most immediate way with a *collective public;* each individual art variety can reveal itself as *fully understandable* to this collective public only through collective communication, together with the other art varieties, in the drama, for the aim of each individual art variety is fully attained only in the mutually understanding and understandable cooperation of all the art varieties.

From Richard Wagner, *Das Kunstwerk der Zukunft: Sämtliche Schriften und Dichtungen*, 6th ed. (Leipzig, 1912–1914); trans. Oliver Strunk, in Oliver Strunk, ed., *Source Readings in Music History*, rev. ed. by Leo Treitler (New York: Norton, 1998), vol. 6, pp. 66–67 and 70.

In Context Wagner's Reception, Nationalism, and Anti-Semitism

The reception of Wagner's work in the twentieth century was affected by political, ethnic, and religious policies and issues. Moreover, as a published writer, Wagner made his views known not only about music but also about literature, drama, and even political and moral topics. The National Socialist (Nazi) movement in Germany appropriated his music as a symbol of the best of Aryan and German culture. The abhorrent anti-Semitism expressed in his essay *Das Judentum in der Musik* (Judaism in Music), which appeared under a pseudonym in 1850 and under Wagner's name in 1869, has alienated some listeners and musicians from his music dramas.

What drove Wagner to write this, he explained to Liszt, was his dislike of Meyerbeer, whose music he once admired and who had used his influence to help Wagner. But Wagner turned against the elder composer when critics wrote how much Meyerbeer had influenced his own music. Seeking to establish his independence, Wagner attacked Meyerbeer's music, arguing that it was weak because he was Jewish and therefore lacked national roots, without which a composer could not have an "authentic" style. In his essay, Wagner applied to music an emerging view of nationalism: the idea that only people who shared the same ethnicity could truly be part of a nation—for example, that Jews could never be German, no matter how many generations their families had lived in Germany, spoken German, and participated in German culture. Thus Wagner's ideas provided momentum to an anti-Semitic undercurrent in German culture.

For a well-documented review of this issue, see Jacob Katz, *The Darker Side of Genius: Richard Wagner's Anti-Semitism* (Hanover, N.H.: University Press of New England, 1986).

impulses in concrete, definite form without the intervention of words. Words and ideas were the product of reason, which governed only "Appearance," whereas emotions resided in the "Will," which Schopenhauer deemed the dominant and ultimate reality. Wagner described his reading of Schopenhauer's work as the most important event of his life. In *Tristan und Isolde*, with a libretto adapted by the composer from a thirteenth-century romance by Gottfried von Strassburg, Wagner depicts the raw, vital force of the Will in the passion of two lovers whose ardor can be consummated only in death, a fate they willingly accept.

Tristan und Isolde

The title characters' desire is evoked from the very beginning of the Prelude (NAWM 149a), shown in Example 20.5, as Wagner used chromatic harmony and delayed resolutions to convey an almost inexpressible yearning. Tonal music is based on our desire for dissonance to resolve to consonance, and for the dominant to resolve to the tonic. That desire is intensified when resolution is delayed, cadences are evaded, or the moment of resolution introduces a new dissonance, all of which Wagner does here.

Prelude

Full 🔊

Tristan chord

The opening motive, a rising sixth followed by a chromatic descent, suggests longing. The first chord, F–B–D♯–G♯, a striking sonority whose resolution is uncertain, is used throughout the opera. Instantly recognizable whenever it appears, this chord has become known as "the Tristan chord." Its resolution contains four dissonant sonorities in a row, each of which "resolves" the previous one without itself resolving to consonance. It is hard to imagine a three-measure phrase more effective in creating a sense of yearning in the listener. Desire and yearning are communicated unmistakably by repeatedly evoking and evading traditional harmonic expectations.

Act I

Motives and extended passages from the Prelude return in Act I and acquire significance as leitmotives through association with the words. The action takes

Example 20.5 Wagner, Tristan und Isolde, *Prelude with leitmotives labeled*

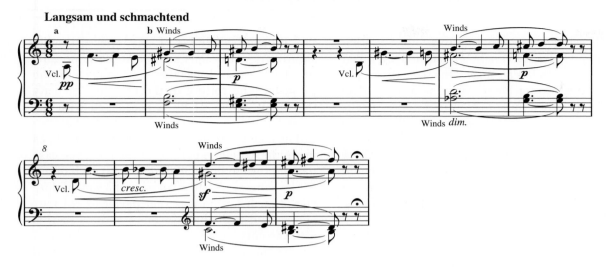

place aboard a ship on which the knight Tristan is transporting the reluctant Isolde from Ireland to Cornwall, where she will become King Mark's bride. But instead, in the final scene (concluding in NAWM 149b), the doomed pair unintentionally fall in love by drinking a magical love potion. From that moment, they are caught up in a drama that presents sexual love as the dominant force in life (the Will), a force that transcends duty, loyalty, and family ties (all aspects of Appearance). The rest of the scene demonstrates the effective intertwining of action, scenery, and musical forces: as the sailors on the ship drop anchor and prepare to greet King Mark, a castle comes into view atop a nearby cliff; but Tristan and Isolde, having drunk the potion, remain lost in mutual contemplation, unaware of what is taking place around them. The leitmotives signal the interior drama as the two gradually realize the import of their action and recognize the feelings that begin to overwhelm them.

▶ **WAGNER,** *Tristan and Isolde*

Figure 20.16 The Bayreuth Festival Theater, designed by Otto Brückwald, incorporated Wagner's ideals for the production of his operas. Here he was able to produce the Ring *cycle in its entirely for the first time in August 1876. Parisfal (1882) was written for this theater, which continues to be the stage for the Bayreuth Festival today.* (Bettmann/Corbis.)

A Closer Look Leitmotives in the *Ring* Cycle

The relationship of leitmotives to one another and to drama can be illustrated by a few examples from *Das Rheingold*, the first of the operas in the *Ring* tetralogy. Near the beginning of the opera, when one of the Rhine maidens tells Alberich that whoever fashions the Rhine gold into a ring can gain limitless power, the motive under the bracket in Example 20.6a descends by thirds through a half-diminished seventh chord (E–C–A–F♯) and rises again. Its very contour suggests the circularity of a ring throughout the four-opera cycle.

The motive's identification with the ring is confirmed by several repetitions and, by the time it is recalled in the orchestral interlude between scenes one and two, in the new rhythmic form seen in Example 20.6b, the motive's identity is firmly established.

The Valhalla leitmotive, introduced at the beginning of scene two (Example 20.6c), begins with a diatonic variant of the ring leitmotive, linking the two in our minds even before we learn that their fates are intertwined: the ring will pay for the castle, which will be doomed by Alberich's curse on the ring.

Alberich's curse is pronounced in the fourth scene, after Wotan tricks him into surrendering the ring. The curse motive reverses the notes of the ring motive F♯–A–C–E), as if perverting its significance (Example 20.6d). At the same time the strong dissonances that are formed with the F♯ pedal tone rolling in the timpani intensify the threat and foreboding associated with the curse leitmotive.

The melodic relationships among the motives make the dramatic point that the ring, the castle, and the curse are bound up with each other. At the same time, they are part of a web of dozens of such leitmotives that permeate all four operas and link them to one another. In this way, the entire course of the plot is determined by the music, exemplifying Wagner's concept that the actual drama plays itself out in the music while the words, scenery, and stage action do their part to make it visible.

The elemental quality of some of Wagner's leitmotives and the fact that they draw on codes of meaning that stretch back to Renaissance madrigals and Baroque operas (such as the expressive value of dissonance and consonance, of ascending and descending intervals, and of diatonic and chromatic harmonies) are what make them readily comprehensible and dramatically apt. Their stark, brief, and effective deployment to depict character and mood has had an enduring influence on later opera, film, and television scores.

Leitmotives in *Tristan*

Example 20.7 shows the leitmotives in Act I that are derived from the opening measures of the Prelude (compare Example 20.6). The motive in Example 20.7b, for instance, is identified with the intense longing that Tristan and Isolde feel for each other after drinking the love potion, whose leitmotive is Example 20.7a. The cause-and-effect relationship between the potion and the resulting passion is signaled by the enharmonic equivalence of the last chord of Example 20.7a to the first chord of 20.7b. The rising chromatic line characterizes Tristan and Isolde's yearning, particularly as it ends on its highest pitch over the unresolved dominant-seventh chord in A minor, as in the Prelude. Later in the scene, however, Wagner expands and intensifies the motive over the same dominant-seventh chord (20.7c), but this time the progression resolves deceptively to the chord on the sixth degree, indicating that the longing is destined to remain unfulfilled.

Wagner's influence

Few works in the history of Western music have so deeply impacted succeeding generations of composers as *Tristan und Isolde*. Especially in its harmony, we see the culmination of a personal style that, influenced by the chromatic idiom of Weber and the organic tendencies of music by Berlioz and others, went on to

Example 20.6 Wagner, Das Rheingold, *Leitmotives*

a. The ring leitmotive's first appearance, as the Rhine maiden refers to the ring

Der Welt Er - be ge - wän-ne zu ei - gen, wer aus dem Rhein - gold schü-fe den Ring,

Inheritance of the world would be won as his own by he who from the Rhine gold
could fashion the ring [that would endow him with limitless power].

b. The ring leitmotive in definitive form

c. Beginning of the Valhalla leitmotive

d. The first appearance of the curse leitmotive

Wie durch Fluch er mir ge - riet, ver - flucht sei die-ser Ring!

As through a curse it came to me, cursed be this ring!

Example 20.7 Richard Wagner, Tristan und Isolde, *leitmotives introduced in the Prelude*

a.

b.

c.

"Ich trink' sie dir!"
(I drink to you!)

(after she has drunk)

(they look fixedly at each other with longing)

I:"Tris - tan!"   T:"I - sol-de!"

I:"Treu - lo-ser Hol-der!"
(Trai - tor-ous lov - er!)

[A: V⁷ ———→ VI]

TIMELINE Nineteenth-Century Opera

Musical Events		
1816 Rossini, *Il barbiere di Siviglia* (NAWM 145)	**1836** Meyerbeer, *Les Huguenots* (NAWM 147)	**1876** Premiere of Wagner's *Der Ring des Nibelungen* at Bayreuth
1821 Weber, *Der Freischütz* (NAWM 148)	**1853** Verdi, *La traviata* (NAWM 150)	**1879** Gilbert and Sullivan, *The Pirates of Penzance* (NAWM 154)
1827 Beethoven dies	**1859** Wagner, *Tristan und Isolde* (NAWM 149)	**1883** Wagner dies; Metropolitan Opera opens in New York
1831 Bellini, *Norma* (NAWM 146)	**1875** Bizet, *Carmen* (NAWM 152)	**1901** Verdi dies

1800   **1900**

Historical Events		
1819 Schopenhauer, *The World as Will and Representation*	**1848** Marx and Engels, *Manifesto of the Communist Party*	**1879** Edison perfects the electric lightbulb
	1848–1849 Unsuccessful revolutions throughout Europe	**1889** Paris World's Fair
	1861 Victor Emmanuel crowned king of Italy	

forge a new vocabulary—one that stretched traditional tonal language almost to the breaking point. Some composers after Wagner, particularly those of German origin, understandably wondered whether tonal music had anything left to say. Others, especially among the French, rejected what they perceived as Wagner's overbearing orchestral rhetoric. In fact, more has been written about Wagner—both pro and con—than about any other musician. His own collected writings span sixteen volumes (excluding letters), and these, together with his music dramas, regained for dramatic and representational music the prestige that some had argued belonged to absolute music alone. His extraordinary vision of opera as a *Gesamtkunstwerk* affected virtually all later composers of opera, not to mention modern filmmakers, whose works necessarily involve the synthesis of disparate elements such as scenography, acting, special effects, and music. Also, as one of the first great conductors and a master of orchestration, Wagner left an example that inspired composers for generations to come.

POSTLUDE

Although French composers contributed significantly to opera in the Romantic century, and some works such as Gounod's *Faust* and Bizet's *Carmen* entered the permanent repertory, the two giants of nineteenth-century opera were Verdi and Wagner. However different in their compositional styles, together they transformed opera once more into drama. Having absorbed the innovations of French grand opera, each went on to cultivate his own national style and to represent the quintessential expression of opera in his respective country.

Verdi's relation to the Romantic movement was complex. Contrary to the prevailing winds, which exalted instrumental music over vocal, he concentrated on the expression of human emotion through the voice. Furthermore, his attitude toward nature was rather neutral for a Romantic composer: while he respected nature, he did not sentimentalize or mystify it in his music, as Wagner and other German composers did. Instead he depicted natural settings and phenomena—the storm music in *Rigoletto* and *Otello*, for example, or the exotic atmosphere in *Aida*—in a concise, though convincing, way. And though he remained a Classicist in many ways, adhering to traditional forms of arias, ensembles, and set pieces, he also tried to surpass these old conventions so that the action of an opera might be expressed in a piece of unbroken music.

Wagner's signficance is threefold: he brought German Romantic opera to its consummation; by fusing operatic and symphonic idioms, he created a new genre, the music drama, in which all elements contributed to the complete work of art (*Gesamtkunstwerk*); and, by so thoroughly exploiting harmony and chromaticism for expressive purposes, particularly in *Tristan*, he forged a hyperextended tonal idiom that hastened the dissolution of tonality. Composers after Wagner found there was no turning back. His music remains overwhelmingly powerful and arouses in its listeners that all-embracing state of ecstasy, at once sensuous and mystical, toward which all Romantic art had been striving.

The Later Romantics

PRELUDE

During the second half of the nineteenth century, the Western musical world diversified as the audience for music broadened. Several factors combined to create this greater diversity. By 1850, orchestral, chamber, choral, and other concerts increasingly focused on a repertory of musical classics, which eventually became known as "classical music." With each decade the proportion of old works to new grew so that, by the late nineteenth century, the variety of styles available to performers and audiences was greater than it had ever been and was rapidly forming an increasingly crowded permanent repertory.

As interest in music of the past intensified, the new discipline of musicology was established, and scholars unearthed, published, and studied music by Palestrina and Lasso, Schütz and Bach (whose complete works were issued, many for the first time, between 1851 and 1899), Handel and Mozart, and, of course, Beethoven, whose sketches provided a whole new field for scholars to mine. Since many of these scholars were German, it was only natural that they took a special interest in German composers, linking the revival of past music to nationalism (see Chapter 22).

The mixture of old and new music had wide-ranging consequences for programming and posed new problems for living composers. How were they to appeal to audiences who were accustomed to hearing only works already familiar to them, most of which were composed a generation or more ago? The composers that we will encounter in this chapter and the next responded in varying ways. Some, like Brahms, competed with the Classic masters on their own ground, writing symphonies and chamber works worthy of comparison with Beethoven's, and songs and piano pieces that rival the achievements of Schubert and Chopin. Others, like Wagner and Liszt, thought the legacy of Beethoven pointed in a different direction, toward new genres such as the music drama and symphonic poem. (The Postlude to this chapter will review and summarize Beethoven's influence on nineteenth-century musicians—performers as well as composers.) In German-speaking lands, these differing aesthetic attitudes polarized around Brahms and Wagner and around the dichotomies between absolute music and program music, and between tradition and innovation. Advocates of absolute music—music understood on its own terms, as an abstract play of sound and form—sided with the critic Eduard Hanslick (1825–1904), whose essay *On the Musically Beautiful* (1854) appeared in response to the writings of Wagner and Liszt. Hanslick challenged the principles of program music and the whole late Romantic notion that music's expressive value was enhanced by its association with the other arts, and he championed Brahms for upholding the great, absolutist tradition of German Classic instrumental music. (These opposing views are expressed in the Vignette below.)

The composers presented in this chapter include some of the most successful of the later Romantic generations: Franz Liszt, Anton Bruckner, Johannes Brahms, Piotr Il'yich Tchaikovsky, Bedřich Smetana, and Antonín Dvořák. They have been chosen in part because, among them, they adopted a wide range of strategies for meeting the challenges of their time.

VIGNETTE   Absolute and Program Music

The most articulate proponent of absolute music was music critic Eduard Hanslick (1825–1904). He claimed that music should be understood and appreciated on its own terms rather than for its ties to anything outside music.

What kind of beauty is the beauty of a musical composition?

It is a specifically musical kind of beauty. By this we understand a beauty that is self-contained and in no need of content from outside itself, that consists simply and solely of tones and their artistic combination. . . .

Nothing could be more misguided and prevalent than the view which distinguishes between beautiful music which possesses ideal content and beautiful music which does not. This view has a much too narrow conception of the beautiful in music, representing both the elaborately constructed form and the ideal content with which the form is filled as self-sufficient. Consequently this view divides all compositions into two categories, the full and the empty, like champagne bottles. Musical champagne, however, has the peculiarity that it grows along with the bottle.

Eduard Hanslick, *On the Musically Beautiful*, trans. and ed. Geoffrey Payzant (Indianapolis: Hackett, 1986), 32, in Oliver Strunk, ed., *Source Readings in Music History*, rev. ed. by Leo Treitler (New York: Norton, 1998), vol. 6, p. 161.

Liszt, on the other hand, argued in defending Berlioz's Harold in Italy *that a program could clarify the composer's intentions.*

The program asks only acknowledgment for the possibility of precise definition of the psychological moment which prompts the composer to create his work and of the thought to which he gives outward form. If it is on the one hand childish, idle, sometimes even mistaken, to outline programs after the event, and thus to dispel the magic, to profane the feeling, and to tear to pieces with words the soul's most delicate web, in an attempt to *explain* the feeling of an instrumental poem which took this shape precisely because its content could not be expressed in words, images, and ideas; so on the other hand the master is also master of his work and can create it under the influence of definite impressions which he wishes to bring to a full and complete realization in the listener. The specifically musical symphonist carries his listeners with him into ideal regions, whose shaping and ornamenting he relinquishes to their individual imaginations; in such cases it is extremely dangerous to wish to impose on one's neighbor the same scenes or successions of ideas into which our imagination feels itself transported. The painter-symphonist, however, setting himself the task of reproducing with equal clarity a picture clearly present in his mind, of developing a series of emotional states which are unequivocally and definitely latent in his consciousness—why may he not, through a program, strive to make himself fully intelligible? . . .

Through song there have always been *combinations* of music with literary or quasi-literary works; the present time seeks a *union* of the two which promises to become a more intimate one than any that have offered themselves thus far.

Franz Liszt (with Carolyne von Sayn-Wittgenstein). "Berlioz und seine Haroldsymphonie," *Neue Zeitschrift für Musik* 43 (1855): 49–50 and 77. Trans. Oliver Strunk, in Oliver Strunk, ed., *Source Readings in Music History*, rev. ed. by Leo Treitler (New York: Norton, 1998), vol. 6, pp. 126–127 and 129.

Franz Liszt (1811–1886)

Style

The cosmopolitan career of Franz Liszt is manifested in his eclectic style, the result of many factors and influences (see Biography, page 465). Those of his compositions based on or inspired by national melodies reflect his Hungarian roots, which perhaps also informed his colorful, extroverted personality. Superimposed on his ethnicity were his early Viennese training and a strong strain of French literary Romanticism, with its ideal of program music as represented by the works of Berlioz (many of Liszt's pieces have explicit programmatic titles). He modeled his piano style after several impressive Viennese and Parisian virtuosos, adding his own vocabulary of stunning effects to theirs. He adopted as well Chopin's lyricism of melodic line, his rubato rhythmic license, and his harmonic innovations, again amplifying and enhancing them.

Liszt and the Piano

In Paris, Liszt came under the spell of the great Italian violinist Niccolò Paganini (1782–1840), one of the most hypnotic artists of the nineteenth century (see Figure 21.1). Stimulated by Paganini's fabulous technical virtuosity as well as by the gift of a new grand piano manufactured by Erard with a double-escapement action, Liszt resolved to accomplish similar miracles on the piano and succeeded early in his career in becoming the greatest pianist of his time. He pushed the instrument to its furthest limits both in his own playing and in his compositions, which are technically beyond the ability of most amateurs. He directly imitated the violin master in his six *Études d'exécution transcendante d'après Paganini* (Transcendental Technical Studies Based on Paganini, 1851), transcribing four of Paganini's solo violin Caprices, Op. 1, and his *La Campanella* (The Bell) from the Violin Concerto No. 2 in B Minor.

As a young man, Liszt cut a dashing figure, but as a performer he was absolutely galvanizing, "subjugating his hearers with a power that none could withstand. For him there were no difficulties of execution, the most incredible seeming child's play under his fingers."[1] In fact, Liszt's unusually long and tapered fingers gave him an enormous reach and allowed him to play rapid consecutive tenths as easily as most pianists could play octaves. He was as showy as Chopin was understated and used his virtuosity very purposefully to cultivate a following. In fact, he is credited not only with having invented the modern piano recital—an entire program executed by one artist rather than by a variety of soloists offering a potpourri of selections—but also with the idea of

Figure 21.1 Contemporary satirical print showing Niccolò Paganini playing the violin as astonished musicians look on. (Bibliothèque Nationale, Paris. Photo: Erich Lessing/Art Resource, NY.)

THE MODERN ORPHEUS.
Opera House - June 3ª 1831.
Sketches of the Musical World N 50 to be continued

---

1. Charles Hallé, *Life and Letters of Sir Charles Hallé*, ed. C. E. Hallé and M. Hallé (London, 1896). Hallé, an accomplished pianist, first heard Liszt perform in Paris in 1836.

Franz Liszt (1811–1886)

Liszt stands out among his peers as an arch-Romantic, a tone poet who reconceived the language of music as an independent system of communication and claimed for it a world of its own. His accomplishments were broad and far-reaching: as a conductor he championed the music of the future while simultaneously honoring that of the past; as a performer he devised new playing techniques and transported his audiences to new heights; and as a composer he made the piano sound like an orchestra and strove to make his orchestral works sound like poetry.

One of the most intriguing musical personalities of his day, Liszt was born in Hungary, the son of an official in the service of Prince Miklos Esterházy. He studied piano with Carl Czerny in Vienna and theory and counterpoint with Antonio Salieri. At the age of eleven, Liszt played several public concerts, inaugurating a dazzling career as a virtuoso. The family subsequently moved to Paris, where Liszt studied theory and composition with private teachers and, after his father's death in 1827, earned a regular income by teaching piano to wealthy pupils and as a traveling virtuoso. But he left the concert stage in 1848, at the height of his career, and devoted the rest of his life to composing, conducting, and teaching.

From 1848 to 1861, Liszt was court music director at Weimar, where he encouraged new music by conducting performances of many important works, among them the premiere of Wagner's opera *Lohengrin* in 1850. Several well-publicized love affairs with women of elevated social status as well as honors showered upon him all over Europe added glamour to his fame. His relationship with the countess Marie d'Agoult resulted in three children, one of whom, Cosima, married Richard Wagner. A man of enormous contradictions, Liszt abandoned his life of pleasure and moved to Rome in 1861 where, in his mid-fifties, he joined the lowest ranks of Catholic clergy and became known as Abbé Liszt (see Figure 21.3).

Major works: 13 symphonic or tone poems for orchestra (*Les Préludes, Orpheus, Hamlet*), 2 symphonies (*Faust* and *Dante*), hundreds of large- and small-scale pieces for piano (Sonata in B Minor, *Années de pélerinage, Transcendental Études,* 19 Hungarian rhapsodies, transcriptions of orchestral and operatic works and of Paganini's violin pieces), 3 piano concertos and other works for piano and orchestra (*Totentanz* [Dance of Death], *Fantasia on Hungarian Folk Melodies*), 4 masses, and other choral works, organ pieces, chamber music, and songs.

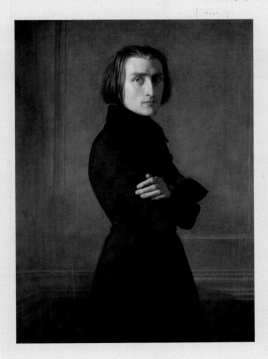

Figure 21.2 (left) Franz Liszt in a portrait by Henri Charles Lehmann, painted in 1838. Note how Liszt's long, tapered fingers are highlighted against his black sleeve.
(Musée de la Ville de Paris, Musee Carnavalet, Paris. Photo: Erich Lessing/Art Resource, NY.)

Figure 21.3 (right) Liszt-L'Abbé in a caricature by Spy (English artist Leslie Ward) that appeared in Vanity Fair *a few months before Liszt's death in 1886.*
(Lebrecht Music & Arts Photo Library/Colouriser AL.)

Figure 21.4 Liszt piano recital in Berlin, as depicted in an 1842 book by Adolph Brennglas on the city. The adulation of the audience, suggested by the excited gestures of the onlookers—one woman actually faints—is supported by many contemporary accounts. But another aspect of the picture is misleading: Liszt normally played from memory, and insisted on a silent audience, both innovative customs that became standard practice. (Lebrecht Music & Arts Photo Library.)

placing the piano sideways on the stage so as to display his elegant profile and imposing hands to the audience. He was the high priest of the piano in his time (see Figure 21.4 and Vignette, below).

Liszt aimed his *Trois études de concert* (Three Concert Études, 1849) at particular technical problems. In *Un sospiro* (A Sigh, NAWM 136), for example, a slower-moving melody must be projected outside or within rapid broken-chord figurations (Example 21.1). The pedal makes this possible by sustaining harmonies while the two hands brave treacherous leaps over each other to pick out a floating pentatonic tune. The notation makes it look as though the pianist needs three hands, but the bottom staff is played with the left hand, the middle with the right, and the top with whichever hand is free at the time.

Liszt's technical innovations served both to display his skill and to allow him a vast range of expression and pictorial effects. The breadth of his poetic imagination is evident in numerous character pieces, one of the most innovative genres of the Romantics. His Sonata in B Minor (1853), modeled on Schubert's *Wanderer Fantasy*, is a masterpiece of formal innovation, using four main themes in one extended movement subdivided into three sections analogous to the movements of a Classic-era sonata. The themes are transformed and combined in a free rhapsodic order, in keeping with the Romantic ideal of organicism.

Much of Liszt's piano music consists of arrangements: transcriptions and paraphrases of Schubert songs, Berlioz and Beethoven symphonies, Bach organ fugues, excerpts from Wagner music dramas, and fantasies on operatic arias. These pieces were useful in their day for bringing important works to a wide audience unacquainted with the originals. By transferring orchestral idioms to the piano, Liszt demonstrated new possibilities for that instrument. He also wrote piano music that makes free use of national elements. Chief among these are the nineteen *Hungarian Rhapsodies*, based on traditional Hungarian melodies and ornamentation styles.

VIGNETTE Liszt the Conqueror

Liszt's first concert in Vienna as a mature artist (1838) created a sensation comparable to the one Paganini had made a decade earlier. The review by the correspondent from Germany's leading music journal, the Allgemeine musikalische Zeitung, *ended with this extravagant description.*

After the concert, he stands there like a conqueror on the field of battle, like a hero in the lists; vanquished pianos lie about him, broken strings flutter as trophies and flags of truce, frightened instruments flee in their terror into distant corners, the hearers look at each other in mute astonishment as after a storm from a clear sky, as after thunder and lightning mingled with a shower of blossoms and buds and dazzling rainbows; and he the Prometheus, who creates a form from every note, a magnetizer who conjures the electric fluid from every key, a gnome, an amiable monster, who now treats his beloved, the piano, tenderly, then tyrannically; . . . he stands there, bowing his head, leaning languidly on a chair, with a strange smile, like an exclamation mark after the outburst of universal admiration: this is Franz Liszt!

From Piero Weiss and Richard Taruskin, eds., *Music in the Western World: A History in Documents* (New York: Schirmer, 1984), p. 365.

Example 21.1 Liszt, Un sospiro

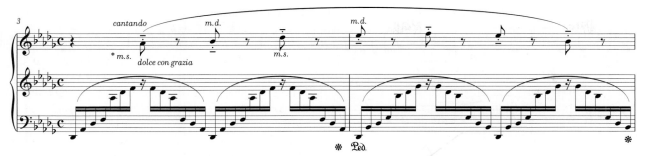

*Stems downward, left hand (*m.s.* = mano sinistra); stems upward, right hand (*m.d.* = mano destra).

Orchestral Music

In 1848, Liszt retired from his career as a touring pianist, became court music director at Weimar, and focused increasingly on composition. After Berlioz, he was the foremost proponent of program music, writing twelve symphonic poems between 1848 and 1858 and a thirteenth in 1881–1882. Liszt's term *symphonic poem* is significant: each is a one-movement programmatic work with sections contrasting in character and tempo presenting a few themes that are developed, repeated, varied, or transformed. These pieces are "poems" by analogy to literary poems, yet they are symphonic in sound, weight, and developmental procedures. Often the form has vestiges of traditional structures such as a sonata form or the contrasts in mood and tempo found in a four-movement symphony.

The content and form of symphonic poems were usually suggested by a picture, statue, play, poem, scene, personality, or something else identified by the title and often by a program. So, for example, Liszt's *Prometheus* (1850–55) relates to the myth and to a poem by Herder, *Mazeppa* (1852–54) to a poem by Victor Hugo, and *Orpheus* (1853–54) to Gluck's opera *Orfeo ed Euridice* and to an Ertuscan vase in the Louvre Museum depicting Orpheus singing to the lyre. The two works that Liszt called symphonies—the *Faust* Symphony (1854) and *Dante* Symphony (1856)—are also programmatic but in more than one movement, essentially consisting of a linked series of symphonic poems.

Liszt devised a method of providing unity, variety, and narrative-like logic to a composition by transforming the thematic material to reflect the diverse moods needed to portray a programmatic subject, following the lead of Berlioz's *Symphonie fantastique* (see Chapter 19 and Example 19.7). In his symphonic poem *Les Préludes* (1854), he applied this method, known as *thematic transformation*, with notable artistic success. We can see how this works in Example 21.2. A three-note motive that has both a rhythmic and a melodic shape (Example 21.2a) is modified and expanded to take on different characters: amorphous, like a prelude (Example 21.2b); resolute (c); lyrical (d and e); stormy (f and g); excited (h); and martial (i). Another version (e) serves as a contrasting theme and is itself transformed. (Asterisks in Example 21.2e show its relationship to the basic three-note motive.) Liszt linked *Les Préludes* to a poem of that title by Alfonse-Marie de Lamartine, following the same sequence of moods. He also used thematic transformation in works without an overt program. The four movements of his Piano Concerto No. 1 in E♭ Major (1855), for example, are linked by themes that are transformed within and between movements.

Symphonic poems

Thematic transformation

Example 21.2 Franz Liszt, Les Préludes, *thematic transformation*

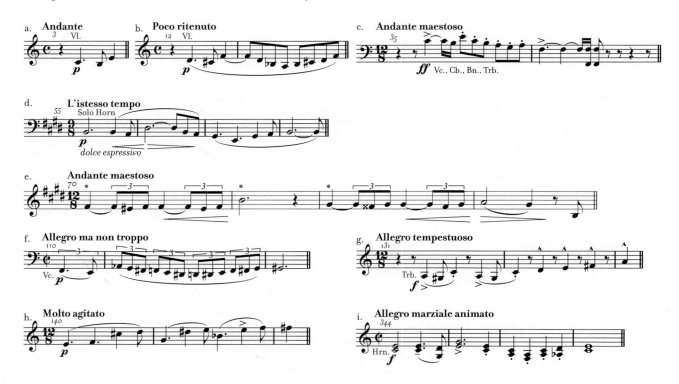

Choral Music

Liszt's choral works offer an accommodation between past and present. Most important are the two oratorios, *St. Elisabeth* (1857–62), on St. Elisabeth of Hungary, and *Christus* (1866–72), on the life of Christ. Both derive much of their thematic material from melodies of plainchants related to their subjects, paraphrased and treated in a modern style.

Liszt's influence   Liszt was perhaps even more influential as a composer than he was as a virtuoso. The symphonic poem was taken up by many composers, including Smetana, Franck, Saint-Saëns, Tchaikovsky, Rimsky-Korsakov, Richard Strauss, and Ives. Liszt's chromatic harmonies helped to form Wagner's style after 1854, and his interest in even divisions of the octave, such as the augmented triad, had a strong impact on Russian and French composers. His practice of thematic transformation had parallels in Wagner's treatment of leitmotives and Brahms's developing variation and had many later echoes in the late nineteenth and twentieth centuries.

Anton Bruckner (1824–1896)

If Liszt with his thematic transformation showed how to compose purely orchestral music in a Wagnerian spirit, Anton Bruckner, shown in Figure 21.5, tried the more daunting tasks of absorbing Wagner's style and ethos into the traditional symphony and of writing church music that united the technical resources of nineteenth-century music with a reverent, liturgical approach to the sacred texts. A devout Catholic, Bruckner was thoroughly schooled in counterpoint and served as organist of the cathedral at Linz, and as court organist in

Vienna from 1867 to his death. He was internationally renowned as an organ virtuoso, taught at the Vienna Conservatory, and later lectured at the University of Vienna.

Symphonies

Bruckner wrote nine numbered symphonies and two early unnumbered ones. He frequently revised them, often in response to criticism from friends and colleagues, and as a result most exist in two or three versions. All are in the conventional four movements, and none is explicitly programmatic.

Bruckner looked to Beethoven's Ninth Symphony as a model for procedure, purpose, grandiose proportions, and religious spirit. Beethoven's first movement, in which the theme emerges from inchoate intervals and rhythms, suggested an opening gambit, while Beethoven's fourth-movement hymn served as a model for the chorale-like themes in most of Bruckner's finales, although he never used voices. As in Beethoven's Ninth, Bruckner's finales often recycle subjects from earlier movements. Bruckner's debt to Wagner is evident in large-scale structures, the great length of the symphonies, lush harmonies, and sequential repetition of entire passages. Bruckner's experience as an organist informed his orchestration, in which instruments or groups are brought in, opposed, and combined, just like the contrasting keyboards of an organ are, and the massive blocks of sound, piled one on top of the other, suggest an organist's improvisation.

Figure 21.5 Anton Bruckner in 1891, around the time he was awarded an honorary Doctor of Philosophy degree by the University of Vienna. Bronzed plaster of Paris sculpture by Viktor Tilgner. (Museen der Stadt Wien.)

Choral Music

Bruckner's religious choral music blends modern elements with influences from the Cecilian movement, which promoted a revival of the sixteenth-century a cappella style. His motets for unaccompanied chorus reflect these Cecilian ideals, yet their harmonic palette ranges from the strictly modal *Os justi* to the quickly modulating harmonies of *Virga Jesse* (NAWM 157). His Mass No. 2 in E Minor (1866) is a unique neo-medieval work for eight-part chorus and fifteen wind instruments (paired oboes, clarinets, bassoons, and trumpets, four horns, and three trombones). Bruckner designed his sacred music to function equally well as part of the liturgy or as concert music and to project a sense of timelessness while incorporating up-to-date harmony, balancing these competing requirements perhaps better than any of his contemporaries.

Full 🔊

Johannes Brahms (1833–1897)

Johannes Brahms matured as a composer just as the classical repertory came to dominate concert life (see Biography, page 472). By the time he was twenty, three-fifths of the music played in orchestral concerts was by dead composers, and by the time he was forty, that proportion had risen beyond three-quarters. Brahms fully understood what it meant to compose for audiences whose tastes were formed by the classical masterpieces of the last two centuries: his own compositions had to embrace the past yet be different enough to offer something new and appealing. In practice, that meant applying the principles of sonata form and adhering to the traditional genres of instrumental music (sonata, string quartet, symphony, concerto, and so on) while synthesizing their formal conventions with current classical and folk idioms to create a unique personal style. At the same time, his erudition was balanced by a deeply Romantic sensibility, so that his music appealed at once to casual listeners drawn to its lyrical beauty and sincere expressivity as well as to connoisseurs who admired its integrity and elegant craft.

Piano Music

Trained as a keyboard player, Brahms developed a highly individual piano style characterized by full sonorities and rich textures, often employing broken-chord figuration and imaginative cross-rhythms. As a young man in 1852–1853, he wrote virtuoso music for his own use, including three large sonatas in the tradition of Beethoven that also incorporate the chromatic harmony of Chopin and Liszt and the songlike style of Schumann's character pieces. In his twenties and thirties, Brahms focused on variation form, culminating in the *Variations and Fugue on a Theme of Handel*, Op. 24 (1861), and the difficult, étude-like *Variations on a Theme of Paganini*, Op. 35 (1863). While his models included Bach's *Goldberg Variations* and Beethoven's *Diabelli Variations*, his twenty-five variations on Handel's theme are actually a series of short character pieces, without titles, evoking by turns Chopin and Mozart, a Hungarian rhapsody, an Italian siciliana, a French musette, a scherzo, a march, a fugue, and so on. In this way, he succeeded in breathing new life into one of the oldest instrumental genres.

Short piano works

In his last two decades, Brahms issued six collections of shorter pieces that are perhaps his greatest contribution to keyboard literature. Typical of Brahms, they avoid descriptive or programmatic titles in favor of generic names such as *intermezzo, cappriccio,* and *rhapsody*. Most are in ABA′ form and have songlike melodies, resembling songs without words or character pieces. The varied textures, surprising harmonies, and deft counterpoint in these pieces show Brahms's familiarity with keyboard music from Bach to his own time, while the pianistic idiom remains within reach of the amateur player, and the attractive melodies delight the listener.

Chamber Music

In chamber music as in orchestral music (to be discussed below), Brahms was the true successor of Beethoven. Not only is the quantity of his production impressive—twenty-four works in all—but the quality as well, including at least a half-dozen masterpieces. Perhaps as a result of his erudition, there are echoes of earlier composers integrated into music that could only have been written by Brahms.

Full 🔊

Seven of Brahms's chamber works feature piano with strings, including three piano trios and three piano quartets. Most popular is his Quintet for Piano and Strings in F Minor, Op. 34 (1864). The first movement (NAWM 156) is a powerful, closely knit Allegro in sonata form. Brahms's treatment of the opening idea (see Example 21.3a) illustrates a method, prevalent throughout his works, of continuously building on a germinal idea that Arnold Schoenberg later called *developing variation*. In diminution, the theme becomes a piano figure against string chords (b), and is then woven into a lyrical melody in the first violin (c). Then, with note values doubled, the piano introduces a variant of the second measure before it is imitated by the strings (d). The three ideas in Example 21.3b, c, and d have little in common, yet all derive from the same germ motive.

Developing variation

Example 21.3 Brahms, Piano Quintet in F Minor, Op. 34, first movement

Symphonies

Brahms's symphonies demonstrate his concern to position his music alongside the classical masterworks. He worked slowly and was severely self-critical, knowing that his works would have to withstand comparison with those of Beethoven; ultimately, he wrote only four symphonies.

Already in his forties, Brahms finished his Symphony No. 1 in C Minor, Op. 68, in 1876, after laboring over it on and off for more than twenty years. It has the conventional sequence of movements—fast, slow, a light movement, and fast—the first and last having slow introductions. Yet the third movement is not a scherzo, as was typical of Beethoven, but a lyrical intermezzo, a substitution that Brahms repeated in his other symphonies. The key scheme of the symphony (C minor–E major–A♭ major/B major–C minor/major) is characteristic of Schubert, Liszt, and later composers in its use of the major-third relation and the shifts between minor and major. As in Beethoven's Fifth, the initial C minor gives way to a triumphant major at the end of the last movement. The main theme of the finale is a hymnlike melody that suggests a parallel to the finale of Beethoven's Ninth Symphony. Yet there are no voices, as if to say that for Brahms, Beethoven's recourse to words is not necessary.

First Symphony

Brahms wrote his Symphony No. 4 in E Minor in 1884–1885 and conducted its premiere by the court orchestra in Meiningen, Germany. As it was an instant success, the composer took the orchestra on tour with the piece throughout western Germany and the Netherlands before publishing it in 1886. The work has the traditional four movements of a symphony in the usual arrangement of

Fourth Symphony

Johannes Brahms (1833–1897)

Brahms was the leading German composer of his time in every field but opera and an important influence on twentieth-century music.

Like Beethoven, Brahms was from a northern German city (Hamburg) but chose, as Beethoven had done, to spend his adult life in Vienna. He was highly regarded as a keyboard player and, as a young man, formed a traveling duo with a Hungarian violinist; he retained a lifelong taste for Hungarian-Gypsy music, which he cultivated in many compositions. He also developed a love for music of the great composers of the past and

Figure 21.6 Portrait of Johannes Brahms in middle age, by Léo B. Eichhorn.
(Private collection, Roger-Viollet, Paris/The Bridgeman Art Library.)

edited works by C. P. E. Bach, François Couperin, and others.

Brahms first met the Schumanns when he was twenty years old, and the couple quickly became his strongest supporters. Schumann praised Brahms in print, launching his career, and helped him secure a publisher. After Schumann's suicide attempt and during his confinement for mental illness, Brahms remained close to the family while Clara returned to her life as a performer. Although he loved her, it is not known whether she reciprocated his feelings, even after Schumann's death in 1856. But they became devoted friends for life and Brahms chose to remain a bachelor.

Brahms made his living by concertizing as a pianist and conductor and by selling his music to publishers. From 1872 to 1875, he directed the chorus and orchestra of the Gesellschaft der Musikfreunde (Society of the Friends of Music) and programmed mostly German works from the sixteenth century through his own day. In his last two decades, he traveled widely as a conductor, performing mainly his own works, and was awarded numerous honors. He died of liver cancer less than one year after Clara Schumann's death and was buried in Vienna's Central Cemetery near Beethoven and Schubert.

Major works: 4 symphonies, 2 piano concertos, a violin concerto, 2 overtures, 2 serenades, 3 string quartets, 21 other chamber works, 3 piano sonatas, numerous piano pieces (rhapsodies, intermezzi, variation sets), *A German Requiem*, works for chorus and other vocal ensembles, and about 200 Lieder.

tempos: *Allegro non troppo* (not too fast), *Andante, Allegro giocoso* (merrily fast) and *Allegro energico e passionato* (energetically and passionately fast). Brahms himself characterized the work as "sad," and there is a certain brooding, almost elegiac quality about some of the movements.

First movement

The first movement begins by setting out a chain of thirds in which all the notes of the E harmonic-minor scale are sounded in turn before any is repeated (see Example 21.4) The first violins continue this thematic statement with a similar series, this time rising from the tonic, to complete an eight-measure phrase. Another series of thirds accompanies the melodious second subject, and at the start of the recapitulation Brahms unfolds the initial series of thirds in augmentation.

The finale of Brahms's Fourth Symphony (NAWM 155) is a chaconne, a seventeenth-century form that reflects Brahms's fascination with Baroque music. It is a set of variations on an ostinato bass as well as on a harmonic pattern. Brahms adapted the bass from the final chorus of Bach's Cantata 150, *Nach dir, Herr, verlanget mich* ("For thee, O Lord, I long"), adding a crucial chromatic note which intensifies the highpoint of the theme just before the cadence. (See Example 21.5 for a comparison of the two ostinatos.) Brahms may have had other models in mind as well, such as Buxtehude's Ciacona in E Minor. Ending the symphony with a set of variations recalls Beethoven's *Eroica*, one of the few symphonies to feature such a finale, and like Beethoven, Brahms first presents his bass line as a melody in the upper register and then works it into the bass only after several variations. All three variation finales (by Bach, Beethoven, and Brahms) are laid out in a broad three-part form with a contrasting middle section.

Apart from its structure, the chaconne illustrates three frequently occurring characteristics in Brahms's music: wide melodic spans, as in variation 5 (see Example 21.6a); ambiguity between duple ($\frac{6}{4}$) and triple ($\frac{3}{2}$) meter, where the notated triple meter is contradicted in variation 14 by a duple rhythmic motive (Example 21.6b); and juxtaposition of simple and compound subdivisions, as in variation 24, which serves as the beginning of a recapitulation of the first four variations (Example 21.6c). Throughout, Brahms constantly varies the theme through figuration and registral placement and by giving each variation a distinctive accompaniment. Yet, all ultimately derive from the germinal motives at the opening, illustrating the concept of developing variation that was discussed in connection with the first movement of the Quintet in F Minor. Despite the movement's pithy theme, its affect is extremely varied. This can be heard in the many contrasts signaled by the combination of Brahms's overall tempo indication, *Allegro energetico e passionato* (energetically and passionately fast) and interior sections marked *dolce* (sweetly), *ben marcato* well emphasized), and the *più allegro* of the coda. Although this is not a program symphony, it is interesting that the original text of the Bach cantata's chaconne theme, which Brahms must have seen if that work was indeed his source, is "Meine

Example 21.4 Johannes Brahms, Symphony No. 4 in E Minor, Op. 98, first movement

Example 21.5 Comparison of Bach's and Brahms's ostinatos

a. Bach, Nach dir, Herr, verlanget mich, *BWV 150, final chorus*

b. Brahms, Symphony No. 4 in E Minor, Op. 98, fourth movement, Allegro energico e passionato

Example 21.6 Brahms, symphony No. 4 in E Minor, fourth movement

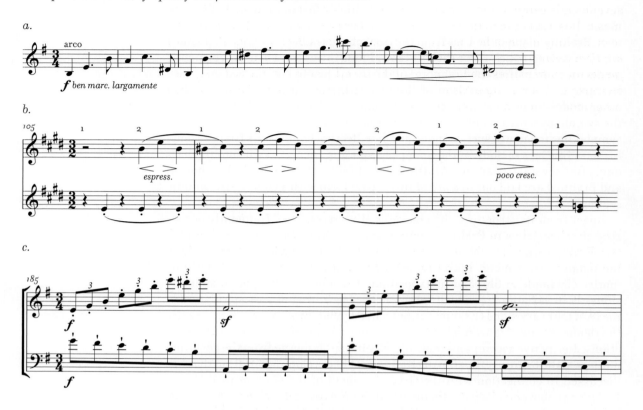

Tage in dem Leide/Endet Gott dennoch zur Freude" (My days spent in sorrow/ God nevertheless ends in joy), which helps to explain Brahms's characterization of the symphony as sad, as well as the almost plodding, relentless quality of the eight-measure theme repeated thirty-one times, the two chorale-like variations (15 and 16), and the movement's exciting coda, which builds to a stirring close.

Choral Works

Brahms's choral music was all composed for amateur performers. He arranged German folk songs for chorus and wrote many short, unaccompanied songs for women's, men's, or mixed voices, as well as larger pieces for chorus with orchestra.

A German Requiem　　His greatest choral work is *Ein deutsches Requiem* (A German Requiem, 1868), for soprano and baritone soloists, chorus, and orchestra. Performances of this piece across Europe won enthusiastic responses from audiences and critics and established Brahms as a major composer The text is not from the liturgy of the Latin Requiem (Mass for the Dead), but rather passages in German, chosen by the composer, from the Old Testament, Apocrypha, and New Testament. Brahms's music draws on Schütz and Bach in its use of counterpoint and expressive text-setting and echoes their concern with mortality and the hope for salvation. In the *German Requiem,* these solemn thoughts are clothed in opulent colors of nineteenth-century harmony, regulated by spacious formal architecture and guided by Brahms's unerring judgment for choral and orchestral effect.

Brahms's place　　Brahms's critics labeled him a conservative, especially in contrast to Wagner, but one of the most radical composers of the twentieth century, Arnold

Schoenberg, hailed him as a progressive. Although neither classification is accurate by itself, both are true to some degree. Brahms was among the first to view the entire range of music of the past and present as material to draw upon in composing his own new and highly individual music—a stance that we will see repeatedly in composers of the twentieth century. By introducing new elements into traditional forms and trying to meet the master composers on their own ground, he was arguably pursuing a more difficult course than those who simply made their mark through innovation.

Piotr Il'yich Tchaikovsky (1840–1893)

When Russian Czar Alexander II emancipated the serfs in 1861, he did so as part of a broader effort to modernize Russia and catch up to Western Europe. There were two main approaches to modernization: the nationalists, or "Slavophiles," idealized Russia's distinctiveness, while the internationalists, or "Westernizers," sought to adopt Western technology and education. However, all who composed operas, ballets, symphonies, or sonatas were adopting Western genres and approaches to some extent, whatever their style. But, while some pursued professional training in the Western mode, others opposed academic study as a threat to their originality. We shall meet the latter group, known as the Mighty Handful, in the next chapter.

Looking westward

Among the Westernizers, a key figure was Anton Rubinstein (1829–1894), virtuoso pianist and prolific composer who founded the Saint Petersburg Conservatory in 1862 with a program of training on the Western model. His pianist brother Nikolay Rubinstein (1835–1881) founded the Moscow Conservatory in 1866 along similar lines. Their work raised the standards of musicianship all over Russia and led to a strong tradition of Russian pianists, violinists, composers, and others that continues today.

Conservatories

The leading Russian composer of the nineteenth-century was Piotr Il'yich Tchaikovsky (see Biography, page 477), who sought to reconcile the nationalist and internationalist tendencies in Russian music. Since nineteenth-century Russia often looked to the West for its cultural models, particularly to France and the Austro-Hungarian Empire, it is not surprising that Tchaikovsky was drawn to writing for the ballet, a particularly French genre, or that he made the waltz, a dance associated with Viennese ballrooms as seen in Figure 21.7, the cornerstone of his ballet scores and elevated it to a new status in symphonic music. Tchaikovsky's three ballets—*Swan Lake* (1876), *The Sleeping Beauty* (1889), and *The Nutcracker* (1892)—include more than twenty waltz scenes, most of them strung together in a chain of several waltzes, to which he gave an entirely new range of character. Tchaikovsky won spectacular success with his ballets, outdoing the French on their own turf in terms of spectacular staging, a show of wealth and power by the Russian state. Tchaikovsky's are still perhaps the most famous and frequently performed works in the ballet repertory. For them, he created a style that combined memorable tunes, some of which suggest Russian folk melodies and rhythms, with wonderfully colorful orchestration perfectly suited to the fairy-tale atmosphere of the stories and to the gestures of classical ballet.

Ballets

Among Tchaikovsky's other works for the stage are a number of operas, two of which he based on works by the Russian author Alexander Pushkin (1799–1837). *Eugene Onegin* (1879) is notable for penetrating the passions of its

Operas

Figure 21.7 The
Viennese Ball, *a
painting by Wilhelm
Gause (1853–1916).*
(Historiches Museum der
Stadt, Vienna, Austria/The
Bridgeman Art Library.)

characters and for the way numerous themes are generated from a germ motive first announced in the orchestral prelude. In *The Queen of Spades* (1890), Tchaikovsky matched the ghoulish atmosphere of Pushkin's story and re-created the spirit of the eighteenth-century Russia of Catherine the Great by borrowing musical ideas from that period.

Fifth Symphony

Although Tchaikovsky's six completed symphonies broke no new formal ground, they are noteworthy for their lyricism, orchestration, and dramatic quality. Symphony No. 5 in E Minor (1888) builds on the cyclic method of some of his predecessors. The brooding motto announced in the introduction (see Example 21.7) recurs in all four movements: in the first movement's development section; before the coda of the lyrical Andante; as a coda to the third movement; and, greatly recast, as an introduction to the finale. The work as a whole demonstrates Tchaikovsky's mastery of orchestration, particularly in the sweeping effects he achieves in setting instrumental choirs against each other; in the Più mosso sections of the Andante, for example, we hear throbbing syncopations in the strings against a soaring melody in the winds. The usual scherzo is replaced by a waltz, a dance for which Tchaikovsky had great affinity.

Pathétique Symphony

The Sixth (and last) Symphony (*Pathétique*, 1893) had a private program that Tchaikovsky never specified but whose outline can be deduced from its unusual sequence of movements. Beginning with a somber slow introduction, the darkly passionate first movement in B minor features a first theme that seems to strive ever upward, only to fall back short of the goal, and a consoling, mostly pentatonic second theme. A brief quotation from the Russian Orthodox Requiem in the development intensifies the dark mood.

Example 21.7 Piotr Il'yich Tchaikovsky, Symphony No. 5 in E Minor, Op. 64, first movement

Piotr Il'yich Tchaikovsky (1840–1893)

The most prominent Russian composer of the nineteenth century, Tchaikovsky successfully reconciled his Russian musical heritage with influences from Italian opera, French ballet, and German symphony and song.

He was born in a distant province of Russia but moved with his family to Saint Petersburg, where he graduated from law school at age nineteen, destined for a career in government. After four years as a civil servant, Tchaikovsky enrolled as a student at the newly founded Saint Petersburg Conservatory, where he studied with the composer Anton Rubinstein and was among the first students to graduate. He quickly found a teaching

Figure 21.8 Photograph of Tchaikovsky in 1893, the last year of his life.
(Lebrecht Music & Arts Photo Library.)

position at the new Moscow Conservatory, where he remained for twelve years.

While Tchaikovsky's professional career was successful, his personal life was in disarray. Troubled by the growing confirmation of his homosexuality, he suffered bouts of depression and attempted suicide more than once. In 1877, he tried to escape into a hasty and disastrous marriage, after which, on the verge of a complete breakdown, he fled back to Saint Petersburg. Nadezhda von Meck, a wealthy widow who was enthralled by his music, became his financial supporter and intellectual correspondent, though the two took care never to meet. Their voluminous correspondence allows extraordinary glimpses into Tchaikovsky's thinking and personality. Her patronage enabled him to resign his teaching position in 1878 and devote himself entirely to composition.

Tchaikovsky traveled throughout Europe as a conductor and even made a brief tour of the United States, where, in 1891, he was invited to take part in the ceremonies inaugurating New York's Carnegie Hall. He was at the peak of his fame when he conducted the premiere of his Sixth Symphony in October 1893. Yet nine days later he died after a brief and unexplained illness, prompting some to see the symphony, later called the *Pathétique*, as a harbinger of his death. It is more likely that he conceived it as a kind of drama with a tragic arc, typical of many late-nineteenth-century operas.

Major works: 8 operas, including *Eugene Onegin* and *Pique Dame* (The Queen of Spades); 3 ballets: *Swan Lake*, *The Sleeping Beauty*, and *The Nutcracker*; 6 symphonies; 3 piano concertos; a violin concerto; symphonic poems and overtures, including *Romeo and Juliet* and the *1812 Overture*; and some chamber music and songs.

Instead of a minuet, Tchaikovsky used a waltz again in the second movement, but this time he changed the Viennese $\frac{3}{4}$ into a Russian $\frac{5}{4}$, as seen in Example 21.8. The third movement (NAWM 160) in G major begins with a light scherzando character and gradually evolves into a triumphant march. So far, the symphony has traced an emotional path from struggle to triumph, familiar from symphonies going back to Beethoven. But Tchaikovsky's *Pathétique* tells another story; it

Full

Example 21.8 Piotr Il'yich Tchaikovsky, Symphony No. 6 in B Minor (Pathétique), *Op. 29, second movement*

ends extraordinarily with a despairing slow movement, filled with lamenting figures, that fade away at the end over a low pulse in the strings, like the beating of a dying heart.

Bedřich Smetana (1824–1884) and Antonín Dvořák (1841–1904)

Bohemia Among the lands of central Europe, Bohemia (now part of the Czech Republic) had for centuries been politically attached to Austria and so, unlike Russia, had always been in the mainstream of European music. The two principal Bohemian or Czech composers of the nineteenth century were Bedřich Smetana and Antonín Dvořák (see Biography, page 479). Although they leaned toward nationalistic subjects in their program music and operas, their musical language was basically European. Like the Russians, Smetana and Dvořák are better known outside their native land for their instrumental music than for their operas, no doubt because instrumental music can leap over the language barrier.

Smetana Smetana sought to create a national music in his String Quartet No. 1, *From My Life* (1876), and in his cycle of six symphonic poems collectively entitled *Má vlast* (My Country, ca. 1872–1879). Of the latter, the best known is *The Moldau*, a picture of the river that winds through the Czech countryside on its way to Prague. But the most stirring is *Tábor*, named after the city where followers of radical religious reformer Jan Hus (ca. 1869–1415) built a fortress that became a symbol of Czech resistance to outside oppression. *Tábor* falls into two sections that resemble the slow introduction and Allegro of a symphonic first movement. In each half, fragments of a Hussite chorale are presented and developed until the entire chorale theme appears in full for the first time at the end. Smetana uses this process to embody the legend that the Hussite warriors will gather strength and emerge from their stronghold in the Czech people's time of need.

Dvořák Sometimes called "the Bohemian Brahms," Antonín Dvořák emulated Beethoven and Brahms in his cultivation of the symphony. Beethoven had transformed that genre from the realm of abstract ideas and forms into a medium capable of expressing individual heroism and communal feeling. As such, the symphony was a suitable vehicle for composers wishing to integrate nationalistic elements into their music.

Symphonies Dvořák's nine symphonies won him a place in the Viennese symphonic tradition and an international audience. His best-known symphony is No. 9 (*From the New World*), which Dvořák wrote in 1893 during his first sojourn in the United States, ostensibly to forge a path for a new breed of American composer. Believing that a truly national music could only derive from folk traditions, Dvořák

Antonín Dvořák (1841–1904)

While many of Dvořák's pieces are in an international style, he advocated musical nationalism and used elements from Czech traditional music to achieve a national idom.

He came from a peasant background (his father was an innkeeper) and, unlike some of his compatriots, resisted the idea of giving up the Czech countryside for life in Prague or Vienna. As a young man, he took a job playing viola in the Czech National Theater and eventually became a professor of composition at the Conservatory of Prague. Inspired by the older Czech composer Bedřich Smetana, he drew on dance rhythms and melodic inflections of rustic popular music in his instrumental works and composed operas based on Bohemian village life, Bohemian fairy tales, and Slavic history. His instrumental music was strongly influenced by Brahms, who persuaded his own publisher to accept Dvořák's works and urged the younger composer to leave Prague behind and come to "the big city"—Vienna. But although Dvořák was intellectually an international composer in the Viennese symphonic tradition, as many of his works demonstrate, his emotional allegiance remained with his native land.

Dvořák traveled frequently to England, where his choral works were very popular, and through his friendship with Tchaikovsky he paid a visit to Russia. But his most famous voyage was to America, when he was invited to become the artistic director of a new musical academy in New York (1892–1895). He was hired with the expectation that he would show the way to a new national style of art music for the United States. Although his sojourn provided inspiration for his own compositions (the *New World* Symphony, the *American* Quartet, and others), he could not be persuaded to stay long enough to establish a native school of composition. But in a magazine article written in 1895, a few months before he returned to Europe, Dvořák sounded this mildly encouraging note:

> Undoubtedly the germs for the best in music lie hidden among all the races that are commingled in this great country. The music of the people is like a rare flower growing amidst encroaching weeds. Thousands pass it, while others trample it under foot, and thus the chances are that it will perish before it is seen by the one discriminating spirit who will prize it above all else. The fact that no one has yet arisen to make the most of it does not prove that nothing is there. . . . The music of the people, sooner or later, will command attention and creep into the books of composers.[1]

Major works: 9 symphonies (notably No. 9, *From the New World*); four concertos (notably the Cello Concerto in B Minor); symphonic poems and other works for orchestra such as *Slavonic Rhapsodies* and *Slavonic Dances* (later orchestrated); 12 operas, including *Rusalka*; many chamber works, piano pieces, songs, and choral works.

Figure 21.9 Antonín Dvořák conducting at the 1893 World's Columbian Exposition in Chicago, in a painting by V. E. Nádherný.
(Lebrecht Music & Arts Photo Library.)

1. Antonín Dvořák, "Music in America," *Harper's* 90 (February 1895), as excerpted in Josiah Fisk, ed., *Composers on Music: Eight Centuries of Writings*, 2nd ed. (Boston: Northeastern University Press, 1997), p. 163.

TIMELINE The Romantic Century

Musical Events

1822 Schubert's *Unfinished* Symphony	**1861** Liszt moves to Rome	**1883** Wagner dies
1838 Liszt's piano performance in Vienna creates a sensation	**1864** Brahms, Piano Quintet (NAWM 156)	**1884–1885** Brahms, Fourth Symphony (NAWM 155)
1850 Bach-Gesellschaft (Society) founded	**1871–1879** Smetana, *Má vlast*	**1893** Tchaikovsky, Sixth Symphony (*Pathétique*; NAWM 160); Dvořák, *New World* Symphony
1854 Liszt, *Les Préludes*	**1876** Brahms, First Symphony	
	1878 Dvořák, *Slavonic Dances* (NAWM 161)	**1897** Brahms dies

1800   **1900**

Historical Events

1848 Marx and Engels, *Manifesto of the Communist Party*	**1860s** Bismarck unites Prussia with other states to forge German Empire	**1865** Lincoln assassinated
1859–1861 Victor Emmanuel II becomes king of a united Italy	**1864** Tolstoy, *War and Peace*	**1877** Edison invents the phonograph

looked to the music of Native Americans and African Americans. For the Ninth Symphony, the composer consciously used themes suggested by Native American melodies and, especially, by Negro spirituals that he heard sung in New York by an African American student, Harry T. Burleigh, who became a pioneer in arranging spirituals as art music for solo performance. Its two middle movements are loosely based on events in Henry Wadsworth Longfellow's epic poem *The Song of Hiawatha*. Similar sounds also suffuse Dvořák's String Quartet No. 12 in F Major (*American*), which was written in the summer of 1893 while the composer was vacationing with his family at a Czech settlement in Spillville, Iowa. As we will see soon, Americans differed on whether Dvořák's approach was the right one.

Operas   Opera was also an important force for nationalism, which is discussed more thoroughly in Chapter 22, and Dvořák wrote a dozen of these in Czech and on Czech themes, among them *Dmitrij* (1882, revised 1894), a historical music drama influenced by Meyerbeer and Wagner, and *Rusalka* (1900), a lyric fairy tale about a water nymph. In the second, he employs distinct musical styles to evoke and contrast the opera's two worlds—one inhabited by humans, and the other by the supernatural spirits of the Bohemian forest.

Slavonic Dances   In his *Slavonic Dances* for piano four hands or orchestra (1878 and 1886–1887), Dvořák used elements from Czech traditional music to achieve a national idiom. Yet he avoided quotation of Czech tunes, preferring to invoke national styles by using dance rhythms and his own folklike melodies. The first of the *Slavonic Dances* (NAWM 161) is in the rhythm and style of the *furiant*, a dance in triple meter that begins with hemiolas, as shown in Example 21.9. By choosing a furiant for the first dance in the set, Dvořák was highlighting his ethnicity: the furiant was one of the most widely known of Czech dances, popularized by Smetana's opera *The Bartered Bride*, and the dance starts with its idiosyncratic hemiolas.

Full 🔊

Example 21.9 Dvořák. Slavonic Dances. *Op. 46. No. 1*

POSTLUDE

In the three chapters about Romantic music so far, the number of times Beethoven or his influence has been mentioned is legion, indicating something of the enormous debt that nineteenth-century composers owed him. The extent to which they and other Romantic artists venerated him is captured in a painting by Josef Franz Danhauser (1805–1845), shown as Figure 21.10, in which an iconic bust of Beethoven hovers over the gathering from his perch against a window that looks out on a stormy sky. As we have seen, all nineteenth-century composers walked in his shadow to a certain extent, sometimes literally—if they lived in Vienna—but always figuratively. The end of the nineteenth century provides

Figure 21.10 Liszt at the piano in an 1840 painting by Josef Danhauser. From left to right: French novelist Alexandre Dumas the Elder, Berlioz, George Sand, Paganini, Rossini, Lord Byron (who died in 1824 and consequently appears only in the framed portrait on the wall), Liszt, and the countess Marie d'Agoult. Although Liszt is the central figure, Beethoven's spirit presides over the group in the form of a portrait bust at the extreme right of the painting.
(Neue Nationalgalerie, Berlin.)

a good vantage point from which to review how Beethoven's musical successors dealt with his gigantic impact and legacy.

To begin with the figures in Danhauser's painting, Berlioz felt licensed by Beethoven's Sixth (*Pastoral*) Symphony to shape a symphony's form around a set of feelings or passions and thus inaugurated the program symphony. Like the *Pastoral*, Berlioz's *Symphonie fantastique* is in five movements and explores a whole range of emotions, thoughts, and fantasies. Just as Beethoven had subjected the main theme in both his Third (*Eroica*) and Fifth Symphonies to a series of exciting adventures, Berlioz created a melody (the *idée fixe*) that he used in all five movements to represent the figure of his beloved.

As a performer and conductor, Beethoven had created expectations that were more than fulfilled by the virtuoso-composers of the nineteenth century; Paganini and Liszt (both visible in the painting) on their respective instruments demanded ever-newer sounds and increasingly spectacular technical feats. Conductors who made international reputations while leading their own and others' works in Beethoven's footsteps were Mendelssohn, Brahms, Tchaikovsky, Dvořák, Rossini, Verdi, and Wagner.

Beethoven's compositional achievements affected Brahms and Wagner in different ways. At the age of 37, Brahms exclaimed "I shall never compose a symphony! You have no idea how someone like me feels when he hears such a giant marching behind him all the time." And in fact, it wasn't until his forties that he brought out his First Symphony, unfairly dubbed "Beethoven's Tenth" at the time. In contrast, Wagner had no trouble wearing what he assumed was Beethoven's mantle; at the age of 37, he had completed *The Artwork of the Future*, in which he credited Beethoven with pointing the way to his own concept of a comprehensive work of art (*Gesamtkunstwerk*), and in his forties he was forging ahead with his "universal" music dramas, *Tristan und Isolde* and the Ring cycle.

In many respects, these two composers—Brahms and Wagner—together epitomize the second half of the century. Brahms was seen first as a conservative opposed to Wagner and Liszt, then as a cerebral composer of demanding music, but by his death in 1897 he was considered a classic—the third of the "three B's" after Bach and Beethoven—and the central figure of classical music in his time, outside of opera. But Wagner, too, however closely associated with opera, was deeply connected to the symphonic tradition through procedures of thematic presentation, development, transformation, and return. His writings and the success of his operas regained for dramatic and program music the prestige that some had argued belonged to absolute music alone.

From our perspective more than a century later, the dispute between the partisans of Brahms and those of Wagner seems like an argument among close relatives, for all traced their heritage back to Beethoven and the early Romantics and sought to add something of their own to an already rich common tradition.

22

Music in the Late Nineteenth Century: Nationalism, Romanticism, and Beyond

PRELUDE

In the eighteenth century, composers aspired to styles fashionable in other countries as well as their own. Handel, for example, wrote in a mixture of Italian, French, German, and English styles, depending on the genre and the intended audience of the music. The Viennese composers of the Classic period reflected the tastes of the Hapsburg rulers and the society around the imperial court, which included a fondness for Italian opera, French theater and ballet, Italian and German orchestral music, and the dance and popular music of Hungary, Poland, Bohemia, and Croatia. As we have seen, all this changed in the nineteenth century, when nationalism began to encourage an emphasis on native literary and linguistic traditions, an interest in folklore, an enthusiasm for patriotism, and a craving for independent identity. A sense of pride in language and native literature formed part of the national consciousness that led to German and Italian unification. How much national consciousness affected music—what and how composers wrote—has been suggested in previous chapters, especially for Smetana and Dvořák. In this chapter, we will discover that the rise of national trends prompted some composers to search for an independent, native voice, especially in Russia and the countries of eastern Europe, where the dominance of Austro-German styles and genres was felt as a threat to national cultural identity. At the same time, composers in the Austro-German tradition who had absorbed the styles of Wagner and Brahms sought new modes of expression that led to the emergence of Modernism in the closing years of the nineteenth century. Modernist composers looked both forward and backward, combining innovation with emulation of the past.

New currents in France, too, were sparked at least in part by nationalism, although these took many different paths. New trends also emerged in Italian opera in the late nineteenth century, involving more realistic librettos and greater naturalism. Finally, the Austro-German classical tradition was transplanted to the United States, where it flourished in conservatories and universities, even while competing with nationalist tendencies there.

The Austro-German Tradition

Wagner held an enormous fascination for European musicians in the last quarter of the nineteenth century. Many composers came under his spell, even as most struggled to find their own voices while making use of his innovations in harmony and orchestration. Composers in the Austro-German tradition continued to cultivate the solo song with piano accompaniment, the symphony and symphonic poem, and opera.

Hugo Wolf

Lieder

Hugo Wolf (1860–1903) is best known for adapting Wagner's methods to the German Lied. Wolf produced most of his 250 Lieder in short periods of intense creative activity between 1887 and 1897, when he was incapacitated by a mental breakdown. He published five principal collections of Lieder, each devoted to a single poet or group: Eduard Mörike (1889), Joseph Freiherr von Eichendorff (1889), Goethe (1890), and German translations of Spanish poems (1891) and Italian poems (1892 and 1896). By concentrating on one poet or group at a time and placing the poet's name above his own in the titles of his collections, Wolf indicated a new ideal of equality between words and music, derived from Wagner's music dramas. Wolf had little use for the folklike melody and strophic structures characteristic of Brahms. Instead, he judiciously applied Wagner's notion of a unified artwork to the Lied, achieving a fusion of poetry and music, and of voice and piano, without subordinating either to the other.

Beyond Wagner: Mahler and Strauss, and the Emergence of Modernism

The two most successful composers of their generation, Gustav Mahler and Richard Strauss both found ways to embrace and transform elements in their heritage to create music at once familiar and radically new. Thus they are among the first modernist composers in the Austro-German tradition to emerge in the wake of Wagner. Although they were born in the same decade and had similar careers as conductors and composers of orchestral music and song, Strauss burst onto the twentieth-century scene with a second career as an opera composer. He lived until the middle of the new century and therefore could even be discussed in the next chapter. However, for the sake of completeness, we will study all of his works here.

Gustav Mahler

Gustav Mahler (1860–1911) was the leading Austro-German composer of symphonies after Brahms and Bruckner, and one of the great masters of the song for voice and orchestra. Born to Jewish parents in Bohemia, Mahler went to Vienna in his teens to study piano and composition at the Conservatory and later attended classes at the University of Vienna. There he formed friendships with fellow student Hugo Wolf and with Anton Bruckner, who taught at the university. He became an avid Wagnerian, although he also respected and was influenced by Brahms.

Mahler made his living as a conductor, renowned for his dynamism, expressivity, and tyrannical precision—traits that are exaggerated in the caricature shown in Figure 22.1. After conducting at numerous opera houses, including Prague, Leipzig, Budapest, and Hamburg, he was appointed director of the Vienna opera in 1897, converting to Catholicism in order to be eligible for the post. Beginning in 1907 he spent most of each year in New York conducting German operas at the Metropolitan Opera until 1910 and leading the New York Philharmonic, which was reorganized as a full-time professional ensemble especially for him, from 1909 to 1911.

Composing mainly in the summers between busy seasons of conducting, Mahler completed nine symphonies, leaving a tenth unfinished, and five multimovement works for voice with orchestra or piano. He revised most of his works repeatedly, retouching the orchestration but not changing the substance of the music. Influenced by Berlioz, Schumann, Liszt, and Wagner, as well as by Viennese composers from Beethoven through Bruckner, Mahler, in turn, influenced the next generation of modernist Viennese composers, including Schoenberg, Berg, and Webern (see Chapter 23).

Mahler the symphonist cannot be separated from Mahler the song composer. Themes from his *Lieder eines fahrenden Gesellen* (Songs of a Wayfarer, 1883–1885,

Figure 22.1 Caricature of Gustav Mahler as conductor, by Hans Schliessmann, published in 1901. The face, glasses, haircut, stature, and gestures are all those of Mahler.
(Gesellschaft der Musikfreunde, Vienna, Austria.)

revised 1891–1896) appear in the First Symphony (1884–1888, revised 1893–1896 and 1906). Following the examples of Beethoven, Berlioz, and Liszt, Mahler used voices in four of his symphonies, most extensively in the Second (first performed in 1895) and Eighth (1906–1907). The Second, Third, and Fourth incorporate melodies and texts from his cycle of twelve songs, written between 1892 and 1898, on folk poems from the early nineteenth-century collection *Des Knaben Wunderhorn* (The Boy's Magic Horn).

Songs in the symphonies

Mahler extended Beethoven's concept of the symphony as a bold personal statement. He once observed that to write a symphony was to "construct a world," and his symphonies often convey a sense of life experience, as if telling a story or depicting a scene. For example, in the slow introduction to his First Symphony, the strings softly sustain the note A in seven octaves, producing an effect of vast space, filled in at times by ideas in other instruments—a melody in the winds, clarinets with hunting-horn calls, a trumpet fanfare, a cuckoo call, a Romantic horn theme in parallel thirds—like the sounds of humans and nature heard across a great landscape. In this and other works, he often drew on the styles and rhythms of Austrian folk songs and dances, using them at times to suggest his urban audience's nostalgia for rural scenes and simpler times. These traits also link his music with Austro-German nationalism.

Symphony as world

Mahler's instrumentation is highly unusual. His works typically require an enormous number of performers. The Second Symphony calls for a huge string section, 17 woodwinds, 25 brasses, 6 timpani and other percussion, 4 harps,

Instrumentation and sound

organ, soprano and alto soloists, and a large chorus; the Eighth demands an even larger array of players and singers, earning its nickname "Symphony of a Thousand." But the size of the orchestra tells only part of the story. Mahler showed great imagination in combining instruments, achieving effects ranging from the most delicate to the gigantic. He often selected only a few instruments from his vast palette of sounds to form different chamber groupings.

Programmatic content

In accord with Mahler's interest in presenting a world, his symphonies often imply a program. For the first four symphonies, he wrote detailed programs in the manner of Berlioz and Liszt but later suppressed them. No such clues exist for the Fifth, Sixth, and Seventh Symphonies (composed between 1901 and 1905), yet the presence of pictorial details, material borrowed from his own songs, and the overall plan of each work combine to suggest that the composer had extramusical ideas in mind like those ascribed to Beethoven's Third and Fifth Symphonies. Mahler's Fifth moves from a funereal opening march to triumph in the scherzo and a joyous finale. The Sixth is his "tragic" symphony, culminating in a colossal finale in which heroic struggle seems to end in defeat and death. The Ninth, Mahler's last completed symphony (1908–1909), conjures up a mood of resignation mixed with bitter satire, a strange and sad farewell to life.

Kindertotenlieder

Full 🔊 Concise 🔊

Irony haunts the *Kindertotenlieder* (Songs on the Death of Children, 1901–1904), an orchestral song cycle on poems of Friedrich Rückert. The first song, *Nun will die Sonn' so hell aufgeh'n* (NAWM 165), achieves the transparency of chamber music through its spare use of instruments. Mahler's characteristic post-Wagnerian harmony intensifies the emotion through stark contrasts of dissonance with consonance and of chromaticism with diatonicism. Thin textures and simple melodies and rhythms suggest understated restraint, ironic for a song about the death of one's child. An emotional mismatch between text and music heightens the irony: the opening line, "Now will the sun so brightly rise again," is sung to a woeful, descending, D-minor melody, while the next phrase rises chromatically to a sunny D major on the words "as if no misfortune occurred during the night."

Das Lied von der Erde

Das Lied von der Erde (The Song of the Earth, 1908) rivals the Ninth Symphony as the high point of Mahler's late works. It is a song cycle for tenor and alto soloists with orchestra, based on poems translated from Chinese. The texts alternate between frenzied grasping at the dreamlike whirl of life and sad resignation at having to part from all its joys and beauties. Just as Mahler called on the human voice in his symphonies to complete his musical thought with words, here he calls on the orchestra to sustain and supplement the singers, both in accompaniment and in extensive connecting interludes. The exotic atmosphere of the words is lightly suggested by instrumental color and the use of the pentatonic scale. In no other work did Mahler so perfectly define and balance the two sides of his personality, ecstatic pleasure and deadly foreboding.

Richard Strauss

Richard Strauss (1864–1949; see Figure 22.2) was a dominant figure in German musical life for most of his long career, which spread across two centuries and two different musical eras. Like Mahler, he mastered the medium of the orchestra and made his reputation as both a conductor and a composer. But unlike Mahler, who held essentially to the traditional, multimovement symphony even while imbuing it with programmatic elements, Strauss attached himself to the more radical Romantic genre—the symphonic poem, which he preferred to call a *tone poem*. He wrote most of his tone poems before 1900, after hearing Wagner's operas and absorbing the harmonic vocabulary of *Tristan und Isolde*. As a nineteenth-century composer, then, Strauss was the obvious heir to Berlioz, Liszt, and Wagner, and the last of the orchestral tone poets. As a twentieth-century composer, especially with the notoriety achieved by his operas written just after the turn of the century (see below), he allied himself with Viennese Modernism.

For his tone poems, Strauss's chief models were the programmatic works of Berlioz and Liszt, whose colorful orchestration, transformation of themes, and types of programs he emulated. Like theirs, some of Strauss's works are based on literature, including *Don Juan* (1888–1889), *Macbeth* (1888; revised 1891), *Also sprach Zarathustra* (Thus Spoke Zarathustra, 1896), and *Don Quixote* (1897). Others draw on his personal experience: *Tod und Verklärung* (Death and Transfiguration, 1888–1889) was inspired by Strauss's recovery from a life-threatening illness, and *Ein Heldenleben* (A Hero's Life, 1897–1898) is openly autobiographical, caricaturing his critics in cacophonous passages while glorifying his triumphs with quotations from his early works.

Don Juan is Strauss's first completely mature work, and its success established his reputation while still in his twenties. Events in Don Juan's career as a roving lover are pictured, including his wooing a new romantic interest, a rather graphic sexual climax followed by a search for his next conquest, and his death at the end. Yet most of the piece evokes general moods of activity, boldness, and romance, rather than narrating a specific plot.

Figure 22.2 A 1914 color lithograph of Richard Strauss, taken from an 1890s portrait painted at the peak of his career as a composer of symphonic poems.
(Private collection.)

Till Eulenspiegels lustige Streiche (Till Eulenspiegel's Merry Pranks, 1894–1895) is vividly representational, telling the comic tale of a trickster's exploits. The realistic details of Till's adventures are specified by marginal notes the composer added to the printed score. Two themes for Till are used and developed like leitmotives, changing to suggest his activities and situation. Yet the specific events are so thoroughly blended into the musical flow that the work could be heard simply as a character sketch of a particularly appealing rascal, or just as a piece of musical humor. This illustrates an important point about program music in the nineteenth and early twentieth centuries: as in opera, the suggestion of events and ideas outside music allows and explains the use of novel musical sounds, gestures, and forms, but in most cases the music still makes sense on its own terms, presenting, developing, and recalling themes and motives in ways that both parallel and diverge from the processes and forms of earlier music. Strauss indicated that the piece is "in rondo form." It is not a rondo in the classical sense, but rondo-like because the two Till themes keep recurring in a variety of guises, enlivened by shrewd touches of instrumentation. Rondo form is appropriate for Till, who remains the same fool after each prank.

Also sprach Zarathustra is a musical commentary on Nietzsche's long prose poem, which proclaimed that the Christian ethic should be replaced by the ideal of an *Übermensch* (superman) who is above good and evil. Although the general course of the program is philosophical, moments are directly representational. Zarathustra's address to the rising sun in the prologue inspired the splendid opening, with a deep C in the organ pedal and contrabassoon, a rising brass fanfare, opposing C-minor and C-major triads, thumping timpani, and a triumphant culmination for full orchestra. The passage became one of Strauss's

Till Eulenspiegels lustige Streiche

Also sprach Zarathustra

Figure 22.3 Page from the German translation of Miguel de Cervantes's Don Quixote, *first published in 1837 and reprinted in the 1890s, showing Don Quixote (right), who imagines himself to be a knight, with his servant, Sancho Panza, acting as his squire.*

(British Library, London.)

most famous when it was used in the soundtrack of the film *2001: A Space Odyssey* (1968) to accompany both the sunrise and a scene meant to suggest the birth of human reason.

Don Quixote

As the rondo suits *Till Eulenspiegel*, so variation form fits the adventures of the knight Don Quixote and his squire, Sancho Panza, shown in Figure 22.3, whose personalities are revealed in their frustrating experiences. We are no longer in a world of merry pranks but in one of split personalities and double meanings. The wry humor and cleverness in *Don Quixote* (see excerpt in NAWM 158) lie not so much in the apt depiction of real things as in the play with musical ideas. Much of this work has a chamber-music sound because it is conceived in contrapuntal lines, and its themes attach to particular solo instruments, notably the cello for Don Quixote and the bass clarinet, tenor tuba, and viola for Sancho Panza. Variation technique here does not mean preserving a melody or harmonic progression and its form through a number of statements. Rather, the themes of the two main characters are transformed, building on Liszt's idea of thematic transformation, so that the beginnings of the themes (shown in Example 22.1) sprout new melodic continuations.

Full 🔊　Concise 🔊

Example 22.1 Richard Strauss, Don Quixote, *Op. 35*

a. Don Quixote, the Knight of the Sorrowful Countenance

b. Sancho Panza

Having established himself in the 1880s and 1890s as the leading composer of symphonic poems after Liszt, Strauss turned to opera, seeking to inherit Wagner's mantle. In 1905, he scored a triumph with *Salome*, and from then on the powers of depiction and characterization that he had honed in his symphonic poems went almost exclusively into opera. His primary models were Wagner and Mozart, composers from the Austro-German tradition whose operas he enjoyed conducting and who—despite the great differences between them—were both adept at using contrasting styles to capture their characters' personalities, articulate their emotions, and convey the dramatic situation. But Strauss dealt with subjects, actions, and emotions stranger than any attempted before in opera. These stimulated him to forge harmonically complex and dissonant musical idioms that greatly influenced two later developments: the growth of musical expressionism (see Chapter 23) and the complete dissolution of tonality in German music.

Salome, a setting of a one-act Oscar Wilde play in German translation, is a case in point. In this decadent version of the biblical story, Salome, by performing her famous Dance of the Seven Veils, entices Herod to deliver the head of John the Baptist on a silver platter so that she can kiss his cold lips. In a passage just after Herod has reluctantly agreed to Salome's demand (NAWM 166), Strauss achieves blistering dissonance by superimposing ideas, using all twelve chromatic notes in quick succession and harmonies with up to seven notes. At times, the music seems to be in two keys at once. With these and similar devices, Strauss captures the macabre tone and atmosphere of the drama with great expressive force. Yet some passages in this opera sound as sweetly diatonic, consonant, and clearly key-centered as others are chromatic, dissonant, and ambiguous. The intense effect Strauss achieves here is predicated on our expectations that the dissonances will resolve. For his purposes of musical dramatization, Strauss needed the polarities inherent in tonal music between dissonance and consonance, chromaticism and diatonicism, instability and stability, tension and resolution.

With *Elektra* (1906–1908), Strauss began a long and fruitful collaboration with the Viennese playwright Hugo von Hofmannsthal (1874–1929) that resulted in seven operas. Adapted from a play by Sophocles, *Elektra* dwells on the emotions of insane hatred and revenge (see Figure 22.4). Accordingly, Strauss intensified the chromaticism, dissonance, and tonal instability at times even beyond *Salome*, offset at other times by serene, diatonic, and tonally stable passages.

The musical world was shocked by *Salome* and *Electra*, by the violence of their librettos and the tonal anarchy of their scores; and although both operas were vilified as lurid and blasphemous, that verdict generated enough publicity to ensure their subsequent success. Meanwhile, as if in reaction, Strauss and von Hofmannsthal wrote *Der Rosenkavalier* (The Knight of the Rose, 1909–1910). This opera takes us into a sunnier world of elegant, stylized eroticism and tender feeling in the aristocratic, powdered-wig milieu of eighteenth-century Vienna (see Figure 22.5). Here, deceptively simple diatonic music dominates while chromaticism, novel harmonic twists, unpredictably curving melodies, and magical orchestral colors suggest sensuality and enchantment. The whole score, with its mingling of sentiment and comedy, overflows with the lighthearted rhythms and melodies of Viennese waltzes—a witty anachronism, since the waltz craze did not begin until the early nineteenth century, and an ironic comment on Strauss's own culture in which the waltz had become merely a sentimental, bourgeois remnant of the Austro-Hungarian Empire.

Salome

Full

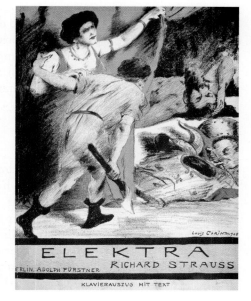

Figure 22.4 A 1908 cover design by Lovis Corinth for the piano score of Strauss's Elektra, *showing the vengeful heroine prompting her dutiful brother to murder their mother's lover after having already killed their mother, Clytemnestra.* (British Library, London/Bridgeman Art Library.)

Figure 22.5 Scene from Strauss's Der Rosenkavalier *at the Savonlinna Opera Festival 2002 (in Finland), showing the title character presenting the silver rose to the Countess.*
(Lebrecht Music & Arts Photo Library.)

Style and effect

Strauss's operas, different as they are from one another, all betray his cunning application of musical styles and his use of the polarities inherent in tonality to depict characters and convey the drama. Ultimately, his is a rhetorical art that seeks to engage the audience's emotions directly, as a film composer might do, and he deployed just as wide a range of style and effect.

National Trends Beyond Germany and Austria

The search for an independent, native voice — one important aspect of nationalism — was most pressing in Russia, France, England, Scandinavia, and the countries of eastern Europe whose composers wanted to be recognized as equals of their Austro-German counterparts. Employing native literature, folk songs, and dances, or imitating their musical character were among the strategies composers explored for developing a style that had ethnic identity. Individual composers in these countries took varying degrees of interest in a nationalist agenda. Thus, composers who were marginal nationalists will be included here alongside those who were more active nationalists.

Russia

When nationalism began to affect Russian artists, opera proved valuable as a genre in which a distinctive Russian identity could be proclaimed through subject matter, set design, costumes, and music. Ironically, while nationalism was a force for unification in Germany and Italy and for liberation struggles in Austria-Hungary, in Russia it was primarily a tool of propaganda for the absolutist government under the czar.

The Mighty Handful

Tchaikovsky was the most prominent Russian composer of his time (see Chapter 21), but others also found a place in the repertory. Standing against the professionalism of the conservatories established in Moscow and Saint

In a 1909 memoir, critic and composer César Cui recalled the gatherings almost fifty years earlier when the circle around Mily Balakirev met to pore over scores and argue about music. They opposed academic correctness, prized the most progressive composers of western Europe, and saw themselves as part of that international current.

We formed a close-knit circle of young composers. And since there was nowhere to study (the conservatory didn't exist) our *self-education* began. It consisted of playing through everything that had been written by all the greatest composers, and all works were subjected to criticism and analysis in all their technical and creative aspects.

We were young and our judgments were harsh. We were very disrespectful in our attitude toward Mozart and Mendelssohn; to the latter we opposed Schumann, who was then ignored by everyone. We were very enthusiastic about Liszt and Berlioz. We worshipped Chopin and Glinka. We carried on heated debates (in the course of which we would down as many as four or five glasses of tea with jam), we discussed musical form, program music, vocal music, and especially operatic form.

From César Cui, "Pervye kompozitorskie shagi Ts. A. Kiui," in *Izbrannye stat'I* (Leningrad: Muzgiz, 1952), p. 544; trans. Richard Taruskin in Richard Taruskin, *Defining Russia Musically: Historical and Hermeneutical Essays* (Princeton: Princeton University Press, 1997), p. xv.

Petersburg in the 1860s were five composers dubbed *moguchaya kuchka* (Mighty Handful or Mighty Five): Mily Balakirev (1837–1910), Aleksander Borodin (1833–1887), César Cui (1835–1918), Modest Musorgsky (1839–1881), and Nikolay Rimsky-Korsakov (1844–1908). Of these, Musorgsky and Rimsky-Korsakov are discussed below. Only Balakirev, who was their leader and informal teacher, had conventional training in music, but it would be wrong to call the others amateurs. They admired Western music but studied it on their own (see Vignette, above) outside the academic musical establishment, whose exercises and prizes they scorned. It was because of their enthusiasm for Schumann, Chopin, Liszt, Berlioz, and other progressive composers in the West that they sought a fresh approach in their own music. As part of that new approach, they incorporated aspects of Russian folk song, modal and exotic scales, and folk polyphony, but they also adopted traits from the Western composers they most admired.

Figure 22.6 Anonymous seventeenth-century portrait of Boris Godunov, the protagonist of Musorgsky's opera, based on Pushkin's play, in which Boris is suspected of murdering the young heir apparent to the throne in order to gain the crown for himself.
(Museum of History, Moscow, Russia. Photo: Bildarchiv Preussischer Kulturbesitz/Art Resource, NY.)

Modest Musorgsky

Widely considered the most original of the Mighty Handful, Musorgsky earned a living as a clerk in the civil service and received most of his musical training from Balakirev. His principal stage works were the operas *Boris Godunov* (1868–1869; revised 1871–1874), based on Pushkin's historical drama about the czar of Russia from 1598 to 1605 (see Figure 22.6); and *Khovanshchina* (The Khovansky Affair, 1872–1880, completed by Rimsky-Korsakov after Musorgsky's death). The realism so prominent in nineteenth-century Russian literature echoes especially in *Boris Godunov* in the way Musorgsky imitated Russian speech, in his lifelike musical depiction of gestures, and, in the choral scenes, the sound and stir of the crowds. Both realism and nationalism are reflected in a last portrait of the composer, shown in Figure 22.7.

Figure 22.7 Portrait of Modest Musorgsky by Ilya Repin, painted in early March 1881, only two weeks before the composer's death from complications of alcoholism. Artist and composer shared a devotion to nationalism, reflected in the peasant shirt Musorgsky wears, and to realism, evident in the unblinking depiction of his unkempt hair, watery eyes, and red nose.

(State Tretyakov Gallery, Moscow, Russia/Bridgeman Art Library.)

Musorgsky's individuality shines through every aspect of his music, as illustrated by the famous Coronation Scene from *Boris Godunov* (NAWM 153). Example 22.2 shows Boris's first statement in the scene, after he is hailed as the new czar. Musorgsky set the words naturalistically, following the rhythm and pacing of speech as closely as possible—almost always syllabic, with accented syllables on strong beats, often higher and louder than the surrounding notes. As a result, his vocal music tends to lack lyrical melodic lines and symmetrical phrasing, but at the same time he avoided the conventions of recitative. He sought a melodic profile closer to Russian folk songs, which typically move in a relatively narrow range, rise at the beginning of phrases and sink to cadences, and often repeat one or two melodic or rhythmic motives. All these characteristics are apparent here.

Musorgsky's harmony is essentially tonal, projecting a clear sense of the key, but in many respects it is highly original, even revolutionary. Some passages seem more modal than tonal. He often juxtaposes distantly related or coloristic harmonies, usually joined by a common tone. One example is the chord sequence of C minor–A♭ minor–G major (measures 114–115) in Example 22.2, which includes two chord pairings that became staples of eerie or gloomy movie music in the twentieth century. Those chord pairings are: two minor triads whose roots are a major third apart (C and A♭ minor, which share E♭), and a minor and a major triad with a common third degree (A♭ minor and G major share C♭/B). These types of chord progressions are not the result of naïve experimentation, as some have imputed to Musorgsky, but show his intellectual approach

Example 22.2 Modest Musorgsky, Boris Godunov, *Coronation Scene*

My soul is sad; a secret terror haunts me.

to composition and his familiarity with Liszt and other composers who had used such progressions. Here, the harmonies also paint a picture of Boris's ominous thoughts in contrast to the mostly major chords of the chorus's public celebration of his coronation.

Another trait that is characteristic of Musorgsky and of much Russian music is composition by the repetition and accumulation of large blocks of material rather than by continuous development. *Boris Godunov* is a series of episodes or tableaux held together by an epic thread and the central figure of the czar. Its dramatic structure is, therefore, enhanced by the score, which juxtaposes successive sections, each relatively consistent in style and figuration but strongly contrasting with one another. The opening section of the Coronation Scene, for example, elaborates on two chords with roots a tritone apart (A♭ and D). After twice building to a peak of intensity, this section yields to a new one (at measure 40), a kaleidoscope of different ideas culminating in the chorus singing a folk song in C major, accompanied by the first traditional harmony in the scene. Musorgsky rarely uses actual folk melodies; this tune adds an element of realism, as do the bells that ring constantly up to this point, like the church bells of Moscow.

Musorgsky's principal nonoperatic works are a symphonic fantasy, *Night on Bald Mountain* (1867); a set of piano pieces, *Pictures at an Exhibition* (1874; later orchestrated by Ravel); and song cycles. *Pictures at an Exhibition* is a suite of ten pieces inspired by an exhibition Musorgsky saw of over four hundred sketches, paintings, and designs by his late friend Viktor Hartmann, who shared with the composer an interest in finding a new artistic language that was uniquely Russian. Several of the paintings are rendered in character pieces, stitched together by interludes that vary a theme meant to represent the viewer walking through the gallery. Figure 22.8 shows Hartmann's design for a commemorative gate to be built at Kiev that combined classical columns, capitals, and arches with decoration modeled on Russian folk art. In Example 22.3, Musorgsky translates this image into a grand processional hymn that similarly combines Western and Russian elements, blending Classical procedures (rondo form) with a melody that resembles a Russian folk song and harmonies that suggest the modality and parallel motion of folk polyphony.

Figure 22.8 Design for the City Gate of Kiev, from a memorial exhibition held in Moscow in 1874 of Viktor Hartmann's works. The closing movement of Musorgsky's Pictures at an Exhibition, *a majestic rondo, is called* The Great Gate of Kiev *and is based on Hartmann's design—a massive stone structure that was never built.* (Novosti/Bridgeman Art Library.)

Pictures at an Exhibition

Example 22.3 Modest Musorgsky, Pictures at an Exhibition, The Great Gate of Kiev

Nikolay Rimsky-Korsakov

Another of the Mighty Handful, Nikolay Rimsky-Korsakov studied music with private teachers, including Balakirev, while pursuing a career in the Russian navy. In 1871, he became a professor at the Saint Petersburg Conservatory, abandoning the anti-academic stance of the Balakirev circle. Ironically, Rimsky-Korsakov's professionalism guaranteed the continuation of a distinctively Russian school. As a conductor, he championed Russian music; as an academic, he arranged and edited two collections of Russian folk songs (1875–1882) and wrote the harmony textbook most frequently used in Russia as well as a widely known manual on orchestration, a skill at which he was an acknowledged master. As a composer, he incorporated folk tunes and their melodic characteristics into his own compositions, and he completed and orchestrated works by the earlier Russian composer, Mikhail Glinka (1804–1857), Musorgsky, and others, helping to ensure their survival. He also taught some of the most important composers of the next generation, including Aleksander Glazunov and Igor Stravinsky.

Orchestral works   Rimsky-Korsakov is best known for his programmatic orchestral works, although he also wrote symphonies, chamber music, choruses, and songs, as well as operas. The symphonic suite *Sheherazade* (1888) displays his genius for orchestration and musical characterization. Based on tales from the *Arabian Nights*, it typifies exoticism. Its four movements, each on a different story, are woven together by the themes of the Sultan and his wife Sheherazade, the storyteller, portrayed by a solo violin.

Operas   It was through his operas that Rimsky-Korsakov proved his abiding interest in nationalism. Several of his fifteen operas draw on Russian history, plays, epics, or folktales. In many, including *The Golden Cockerel* (1906–1907), he alternates a diatonic, often modal style used for the everyday world with a lightly chromatic, "fantastic" style that suggests the world of supernatural beings and magical occurrences.

Russian influence   Tchaikovsky and the Mighty Handful developed musical styles that were strongly individual and markedly national, yet suffused with elements from the West. In turn, they influenced Western composers of the very late nineteenth and early twentieth centuries, who were especially drawn to the Russians' block construction, orchestral colors, use of modality, and new scales.

Other Countries

Grieg in Norway   At the same time that the Mighty Handful were forging a distinct Russian idiom and the Czech composers Smetana and Dvořák were integrating elements from their native Bohemia into their essentially Austro-German musical styles (see Chapter 21), Edvard Grieg (1843–1907) was writing a series of songs, short piano pieces, and orchestral suites that imitated the modal melodies and harmonies as well as the dance rhythms of his native Norway. An ethnic character emerges most clearly in his songs on Norwegian texts, his instrumental *Peer Gynt* Suite (1875), and especially the *Slåtter*, Norwegian peasant dances that Grieg arranged for the piano from transcripts of country fiddle playing. His piano style, with its delicate grace notes and mordents, owes something to Chopin as well as to the Germanic tradition of Mendelssohn and Schumann, whose music he studied in Leipzig. The Norwegian influence in his music is reflected in his modal turns of melody and harmony (Lydian raised fourth, Aeolian lowered seventh, mode mixture); frequent drones in the bass or middle register (suggested by the drone strings on Norwegian stringed instruments); and the fascinating combination of $\frac{3}{4}$ and $\frac{6}{8}$ rhythm in the *Slåtter*. Not all Grieg's music was nationalist; among his best-known pieces is the Piano Concerto in A Minor (1868; revised 1907), a bravura work that remains a favorite.

Edward Elgar (1857–1934) was the first English composer in more than two hundred years to enjoy wide international recognition. The English in the late nineteenth century did not strive for a distinctive national style, preferring to adopt the language of the classical tradition. Although Elgar's music is untouched by folk songs, it does link him to the national tradition of English cathedral choir festivals, for which he wrote several oratorios. He derived his harmonic style from Brahms and Wagner, and drew from Wagner the system of leitmotives in his oratorios. *The Dream of Gerontius* (1900), Elgar's oratorio on a poem by Catholic convert John Henry Newman and influenced by Wagner's *Parsifal*, gives the orchestra an expressive role as important as that of the chorus. His symphonic output includes the *Enigma Variations* (1899), the cello concerto, and two symphonies.

Figure 22.9 Statue of Edward Elgar and his bicycle outside of Hereford Cathedral, England. (Photononstop/SuperStock.)

New Currents in France and Italy

Throughout Italy, musical life continued to be dominated by the operatic repertory of Verdi and his successors. In France, Paris remained the center of musical life, for both concert music and opera. In keeping with a tradition that stretched back to royal control of music in the seventeenth century (see Chapter 13), French music remained linked to politics. Concert series, composers, and even musical styles were often associated with political movements or events. An enduring product of the Revolutionary era was the Paris Conservatoire, the first modern conservatory, founded by the government in 1795 as part of the new national system of education. It became the model for national and regional conservatories all over Europe and in the Americas, and has been a dominant force in French musical life ever since. Another product of political events, the Société Nationale de Musique (National Society of Music) was founded in 1871, when the government and the Parisian elite sought to reassert the vibrancy of French culture after the embarrassing defeat of the Franco-Prussian War. The society gave performances of works by French composers and set about reviving the great French music of the past through editions and performances of Rameau, Gluck, and sixteenth-century composers.

The growth in concert activity, proliferation of music schools, revival of past traditions, and encouragement of new music helped Paris regain a leading musical position. Two main strands in composition can be identified before the emergence of impressionism (discussed in Chapter 23): a cosmopolitan tradition, transmitted through César Franck (1822–1890) and his pupils, and a more nationalist, specifically French, tradition, embodied in the music of

Gabriel Fauré (1845–1924) and passed on to countless twentieth-century composers through his students, especially the famous pedagogue Nadia Boulanger (1887–1979).

Cosmopolitan Tradition in France

Franck

César Franck was born in Belgium, came to Paris to study at the Conservatoire, and became a professor of organ there in 1871. Working mainly in instrumental genres and oratorio, he achieved a distinctive style by blending traditional counterpoint and classical forms with Liszt's thematic transformation, Wagner's harmony, and the Romantic idea of cyclic unification through thematic return. Typical of Franck's approach is the *Prelude, Chorale, and Fugue* (1884) for piano, which emulates a Baroque toccata in the prelude, introduces a chorale-like melody in distant keys, presents a fugue on a chromatic subject that has been foreshadowed in both previous sections, and closes by combining the opening toccata texture with the chorale melody and fugue subject in counterpoint. It is a piece that could only have been written by someone who had absorbed the thematic and harmonic methods of Liszt and Wagner and also the organ music of Bach and the French Baroque.

Franck has been called the founder of modern French chamber music. His chief chamber works are a Piano Quintet in F Minor (1879), a String Quartet in D Major (1889), and the Violin Sonata in A Major (1886). All are cyclic, featuring themes that recur or are transformed in two or more movements. His Symphony in D Minor (1888), a model of cyclic form, is perhaps the most popular French symphony after Berlioz.

The French Tradition

The other tendency in French music drew primarily on earlier French composers from Couperin to Gounod and approached music with order and restraint, treating it more as sonorous form than as expression. Instead of emotional displays and musical or programmatic depiction, we hear subtle patterns of tones, rhythms, and colors. The music sounds more lyric or dancelike than epic or dramatic. It is economical, simple, and reserved rather than profuse, complex, or grandiloquent.

Figure 22.10 Gabriel Fauré in a portrait by John Singer Sargent (1889). (Bibliothèque du Conservatoire de Musique, Paris, France/ Bridgeman Art Library.)

The refined music of Gabriel Fauré (see Figure 22.10) embodies the qualities of the French tradition. He held various posts as an organist, and was a founder of the National Society for French Music. He became professor of composition at the Paris Conservatoire in 1896 and was its director from 1905 to 1920, when he resigned because of hearing loss. Fauré wrote some music in larger forms, including his best-known work, the Requiem (1887), and two operas. But he was primarily a composer of songs, of piano music—chiefly preludes, impromptus, nocturnes, and barcarolles—and of chamber music.

Fauré began by composing songs in the manner of Gounod, and lyrical melody, with no display of virtuosity, remained the basis of his style. But in his maturity, from about 1885, he developed a new style in which melodic lines are fragmented and harmony becomes much less directional. *Avant que tu ne t'en ailles* (Before you vanish; NAWM 160), from the song cycle *La bonne chanson* (The Good Song, 1892) to texts by the symbolist

Example 22.4 Gabriel Fauré, Avant que tu ne t'en ailles

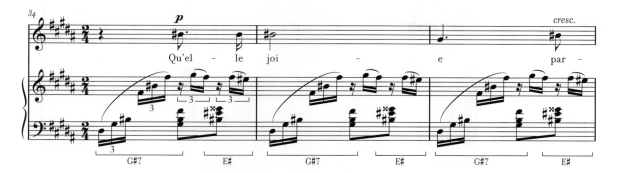

What joy [in the fields of ripe wheat].

poet Paul Verlaine, illustrates these characteristics. Each phrase of melody is a declamatory fragment in its own tonal world, joined to the others only by subtle motivic echoes. In the passage shown in Example 22.4, the chords consist mainly of dominant sevenths and ninths, as in Wagner's chromatic music, but the tension melts as one chord fades into another because Fauré links chords through common tones. In each of the first three measures, for example, the dominant-seventh chord on G♯ is succeeded by an E♯-major triad, which neutralizes the leading-tone tendency of the B♯ in the vocal line; instead of moving to C♯, the B♯ becomes the fifth of the new chord (E♯ major). The F♯, the seventh of the first chord in the piano part, is treated as an appoggiatura. Such harmonic successions dilute the need for resolution and undermine the pull of the tonic, creating a sense of repose or even stasis that is the opposite of the emotional unrest in Wagner's music. But the style is a fitting parallel to the transient images and nonnarrative qualities of Verlaine's poem.

New Currents in Italian Opera

By the late nineteenth century, Verdi was such a central figure in Italian opera that later composers struggled to escape his shadow. As opera houses increasingly performed works already in the repertory rather than new ones, few operas by composers after Verdi found a permanent place. Two operas that did enter the repertory are *Cavalleria rusticana* (Rustic Chivalry, 1890) by Pietro Mascagni (1863–1945) and *I pagliacci* (The Clowns, 1892) by Ruggero Leoncavallo (1858–1919), often paired with each other in performance. Both are examples of verismo (from Italian *vero*, "true"), an operatic parallel to realism in literature. Instead of treating historical figures or faraway places, verismo presents everyday people, especially the lower classes, in familiar situations, often depicting events that are brutal or sordid. Though short-lived, verismo had parallels and repercussions in France and Germany, and today the veristic impulse lives on in television reality shows and movie dramas.

The most successful Italian opera composer after Verdi was Giacomo Puccini (1858–1924), shown in Figure 22.11. The son of a church organist and composer, he was slated to

Figure 22.11 Photograph of Giacomo Puccini at Torre del Lago in 1909. (Private collection. Bettmann/Corbis.)

Figure 22.12 Cover by Leopoldo Metlicovitz for the 1906 vocal score of Giacomo Puccini's opera Madama Butterfly, *showing Butterfly waiting for her American husband Pinkerton to return.* (Lebrecht Music & Arts Photo Library.)

follow in his father's footsteps but chose instead to focus on opera. After studying at the conservatory in Milan, Puccini attracted attention with his first opera in 1884. His third opera, *Manon Lescaut* (1893), catapulted him to international fame and established him as one of the rising stars of his generation.

Puccini's highly personal style blends Verdi's focus on vocal melody with elements of Wagner's approach—notably the use of recurring melodies or leitmotives, less reliance on conventional operatic forms, and a greater role for the orchestra in creating musical continuity. Puccini often juxtaposed different styles and harmonic worlds to suggest his diverse characters, such as impoverished artists and other residents of the Parisian Latin Quarter in *La Bohème* (1896); the idealistic singer Tosca and the evil Scarpia in *Tosca* (1900); a Japanese woman and her American lover in *Madama Butterfly* (1904); or various levels of ancient Chinese society in *Turandot* (1926).

▶ **PUCCINI,** *La Bohème*

All of these characteristics of Puccini's style are evident in the scene of Butterfly's marriage to Pinkerton in *Madama Butterfly* (NAWM 151). The music moves seamlessly between dialogue and brief aria-like moments. The main continuity and many of the most important melodies are in the orchestra, which nonetheless always supports the singers. Puccini uses contrasting styles to convey the differences among the characters. In a private dialogue before the ceremony, Pinkerton sings in Puccini's normative, European style, unmarked by any special qualities. Butterfly responds in a hybrid style based on authentic Japanese melodies arranged to sound westernized, suggesting Butterfly's attempt to present herself in a manner that conforms to her lover's expectations. But at the point when she alludes to a darker side of Japanese culture by mentioning her father's ritual suicide at the emperor's command, we hear an unharmonized Japanese-style melody against a drone, marking the music as both primitive and foreign. Puccini's music balances exoticism with a very

▶ **PUCCINI,** *Madama Butterfly*

human portrait of Butterfly, captured also on the cover of a 1906 vocal score, shown in Figure 22.12. Through very simple means, Puccini responds directly to the text and the situation. His melody-centered, colorful, and emotionally direct style has won his operas a permanent place in the repertory and has exercised a strong influence on scoring for film and television.

The Classical Tradition in the United States

Beginning in the 1840s, crop failures and the 1848 revolution spurred many Germans to emigrate to the United States, following others who had come during the previous century. Many of the immigrants were musicians and music teachers strongly committed to classical music, and they contributed to an extraordinary growth in performing institutions, music schools, and university departments of music in the second half of the nineteenth century. German musicians filled positions in American orchestras, taught music at all levels, and—along with Americans who had studied in Germany—dominated the teaching of composition and music theory in American conservatories and universities. The new immigrants and the institutions that they helped to found fostered an increasingly sharp divide between classical music and popular music (discussed in Chapter 24). Not surprisingly, German tastes and styles dominated American music in the classical tradition until World War I.

German immigration

As classical music became well established, native-born composers were able to pursue careers that combined composition with performing and teaching, especially in the region from Boston to New York. Among them were John Knowles Paine (1889–1906), trained by a German immigrant, who became Harvard's first professor of music; George Whitefield Chadwick (1854–1931), who studied at the New England Conservatory in Boston and became its director; Chadwick's student Horatio Parker (1863–1919), who taught at Yale and was the first dean of its School of Music; and Edward MacDowell (1860–1908), a New Yorker who was the first professor of music at Columbia University. All studied in Germany as well as the United States, and all pursued styles deeply rooted in the German tradition.

German tradition in America

However, these composers had varying attitudes about nationalism. Parker believed American composers should simply write the best music they could; his Latin oratorio *Hora novissima* (1893), the piece that made his reputation, is modeled on German and English oratorios. Chadwick, in contrast, developed an idiom laced with American traits such as pentatonic melodies and characteristic rhythms from Protestant psalmody and African-Caribbean dances, used in his Symphony No. 2, in B♭ Major (1883–1885) and *Symphonic Sketches* (1895–1904). MacDowell opposed jingoistic nationalism, but like most Europeans saw national identity as an important aspect of any composer's claim to international attention. Among his overtly nationalist works is his Second (*Indian*) Suite for orchestra (1891–1895), based on Native American melodies.

Figure 22.13 Amy Beach in about 1903. (Corbis.)

Another Boston composer, Amy Marcy Beach (1867–1944), shown in Figure 22.13, could not study or teach at the top universities because they excluded women. A child prodigy, she studied piano, harmony, and counterpoint privately, then taught herself to compose by analyzing and playing works of composers she admired. Married to a wealthy physician, she was freed of financial concerns and devoted herself to composition. At the

TIMELINE Late Romanticism

Musical Events

1864
Brahms, Piano Quintet Op. 34
(NAWM 156)

1872–1879
Smetana, *Má vlast*

1874
Musorgsky, premiere of *Boris Godunov* (NAWM 153)

1876
Wagner, premiere of complete *Ring* cycle

1878
Dvořák, *Slavonic Dances* (NAWM 161)

1885
Brahms, Fourth Symphony

1887
Verdi, premiere of *Otello*

1888
Rimsky-Korsakov, *Sheherezade*

1889
Wolf, *Mörike Lieder*

1892
Fauré, *La bonne chanson* (NAWM 159)

1893
Tchaikovsky, Symphony No. 6 (*Pathétique*) (NAWM 160)

1897
Strauss, *Don Quixote* (NAWM 158)

1901–1904
Mahler, *Kindertotenlieder* (NAWM 165)

1904
Puccini, *Madama Butterfly* (NAWM 151)

1907
Beach, Piano Quintet Op. 67 (NAWM 162)

1907–1910
Mahler directs Metropolitan Opera in New York

1850 —— **1900**

Historical Events

1862
Hugo, *Les Misérables*

1870–1871
Franco-Prussian War

1877
Edison invents the phonograph

1879
Edison perfects the electric lightbulb

1888
Pasteur Institute founded in Paris

1889
Eiffel Tower erected

1898
Spanish-American War

1903
Wright brothers fly first successful airplane

1908
Ford begins manufacturing the Model T automobile

---

time, women were considered incapable of composing in longer forms. As if to prove them wrong, she wrote large-scale works such as her Mass in E♭ (1890), *Gaelic* Symphony (1894–1896), Piano Concerto (1899), and Piano Quintet (1907), all of them well received. She also wrote about 120 songs and dozens of piano and choral pieces, many of them very popular. Beach was internationally recognized as one of America's leading composers, and she inspired many women in later generations.

Some of Beach's music has an ethnic flavor—for example, the *Gaelic* Symphony on Irish tunes and the String Quartet (1929) on Native American melodies. But most of her works engage the traditions of the German classics. She based the themes of the first and third movements of her own Piano Quintet on a theme from Brahms's Piano Quintet Op. 34, which she had performed in 1900. Her individual voice emerges forcefully in the third and last movement (NAWM 162), going beyond the Brahmsian music of the first movement to embrace late nineteenth-century chromatic harmony, with unusual inversions, augmented triads, and colorful nonchord tones.

Full 🔊

POSTLUDE

By the end of the nineteenth century, what seemed to have been the main-stream of musical development in the late eighteenth century had broken into many smaller currents. Foremost among the Austro-Germans were Mahler and Strauss who were themselves representative of a national voice, albeit the dominant one of their era. A restless experimenter with wide-ranging inter-ests, Mahler expanded the symphony and the orchestral Lied; at the same time, he ushered in a new age of Modernism, influencing the Viennese composers of the next generation—Schoenberg, Berg, and Webern (see Chapter 25). Whereas Mahler essentially adhered to the traditional symphony and its musical archi-tecture, even while admitting many programmatic and operatic elements, Strauss cultivated the more radical Romantic genre of the symphonic poem and eventually even dared to write operas in the wake of Wagner's domination of that genre, forging new paths that link him to modernist composers of the twentieth century.

The rise of nationalism stimulated new bursts of native musical creativity in many European countries and in the United States, with Russia and France being among the most significant for later musical developments. In the United States, composers such as Amy Beach combined their training in the German classical tradition with original ideas that sometimes made reference to ethnic musical traditions. In Russia, Musorgsky emerged as the most original and influential of the group of five composers known as the Mighty Handful; but national flavor also helped composers of other lands to gain a niche in the per-manent repertoire. In France, a revival nurtured by several factors and tradi-tions, not least an awareness of the importance of its own musical past, produced a number of fine composers, including César Franck and Gabriel Fauré. France's musical renewal also deposited on the doorstep of the twentieth century a composer of the first rank—Claude Debussy—who, as we shall dis-cover, enabled composers of all nationalities to create new styles that turned away from the influence of Wagner and the Romantics.

This sampling of a few composers can give only a taste of the variety of national and individual styles in Europe and the United States in the second half of the nineteenth century. Composers often first found a niche for their music within a local, regional, or national performing tradition. A lucky few won a broader audience, often by capitalizing on their national identity, espe-cially when that nation was not yet represented in the international repertory. This remained true for composers in the early twentieth century, as we will see in the next chapter.

PART SIX

The Twentieth Century and Today

PART CONTENTS

Few eras have been as self-consciously "modern" as the early twentieth century. The pace of technological and social change was more rapid than in any previous era, prompting both an optimistic sense of progress and nostalgia for a simpler past.

The growth of industry continued to foster an expanding economy. As in the nineteenth century, people migrated from rural areas to cities, although not without regret; popular songs and Mahler symphonies alike expressed a yearning for home and the countryside. Economic inequalities prompted workers to organize in labor unions to fight for better conditions, inspired social reformers to work with the poor, and sparked revolutions in Russia and elsewhere. International trade continued to increase. European nations grew rich importing raw materials and then marketing manufactured goods to the world. The great powers—Britain, France, and the German, Austro-Hungarian, Russian,

Gustav Mahler conducting the Vienna Philharmonic in a 1935 painting by Max Oppenheimer
(Erich Lessing/Art Resource, NY.)

and Ottoman empires—competed for dominance, while the peoples of eastern Europe, from the Balkans to Finland, agitated for their own freedom. Increasing tensions and complex political issues culminated in World War I (1914–1918).

United States

During these years, the United States emerged as a world power. American industries and overseas trade expanded rapidly, growing to rival the industrial powerhouses of Britain and Germany. The United States' entrance into World War I in April 1917 on the side of Britain and France tipped the scales against Germany and Austria-Hungary, and President Woodrow Wilson played a leading role in negotiating the peace. After the war, while the nations of Europe were faced with war debt, crippling inflation, and a shattered infrastructure, the United States and Canada, which had suffered far fewer casualties, enjoyed a financial boom. But as in Europe, rapid economic development brought social conflict. Immigrants continued to stream into the United States, now increasingly from southern and eastern Europe, and their presence in cities caused strains with earlier immigrant groups. Looking for new opportunities, African Americans from the South moved to the large northern cities but, because of racist attitudes, settled into segregated neighborhoods, giving rise to a black urban culture in which music played a major role.

New nations and ideologies

World War I brought an end to the large European empires and yielded independence to Finland, Estonia, Poland, Czechoslovakia, and Hungary. In Russia the Bolsheviks—radical Marxist revolutionaries—seized power in late 1917 and set up a dictatorship, forming the Soviet Union. In several other nations, democratic governments gave way to totalitarian rule. Benito Mussolini and the fascists took over the Italian government in 1922, and the Spanish Civil War (1936–1939) brought Francisco Franco to power. In Germany the democracy formed after World War I, known as the Weimar Republic (for the city where the constitution was drafted), proved too weak to handle mounting economic problems. After the National Socialists (Nazis) won an electoral plurality, their leader, Adolf Hitler, was appointed chancellor in 1933 and soon established a dictatorship. In a fierce anti-Semitic campaign, the Nazis passed laws to deprive Gypsies, homosexuals, and especially Jews of their citizenship and all other rights, driving into exile countless writers, artists, composers, and scholars, many of whom settled in the United States.

Economic depression

In America, increased prosperity and leisure time helped make the post–World War I years a golden age for music, both popular and classical. American culture and music, especially jazz, profoundly influenced Europeans during the 1920s. But in October 1929, the New York stock market crashed, beginning a worldwide depression. Unemployment approached 50 percent in some areas, producing unprecedented turmoil. In response, governments in Europe and the Americas undertook public-works programs such as the New Deal in the United States.

World War II and after

The economies in most nations were still recovering when Germany invaded Poland in September 1939, thereby beginning World War II, the most global and destructive war the world had ever seen. The Axis powers, (Germany, Italy, and Japan) were defeated by the Allies (the United States, the Soviet Union, and Great Britain), but at great cost. Millions were dead: soldiers killed in action, civilians in bombing raids, and Jews and others in Nazi death camps. Much of Europe and the Far East lay in ruins, and many buildings, cultural institutions, and works of art were destroyed. The atrocities of the Holocaust and the use of nuclear weapons to end the war provoked a wide range of cultural reactions, from the French existentialist literature of Jean-Paul Sartre and Albert Camus to a growing fashion for horror and science-fiction films.

At war's end, the Soviet Union occupied most of eastern Europe. By 1948, it reabsorbed some countries that had been independent between the wars, such as Estonia, and installed communist regimes under its control in others, such as Poland, Czechoslovakia, and Hungary. Communist governments also took power in Yugoslavia, Albania, and China. Western nations attempted to contain the expansion of communism, and international relations for the next two generations were framed by a sustained state of political and military tension known as the Cold War that existed between the United States and its allies on the one hand and the Soviet Union and communist nations on the other. Figure VI.1 shows a map of postwar Europe, divided between the North Atlantic Treaty Organization (NATO) — an alliance of the United States, Canada, and European democracies — and the Soviet Union's parallel organization, the Warsaw Pact. Symbolic of this political conflict was the metaphor of the "Iron Curtain" drawn across Europe, and the reality of the division between a democratic, pro-Western government in West Germany and a communist government in East Germany was confirmed by the erection in 1961 of the Berlin Wall.

After 1945

The Cold War

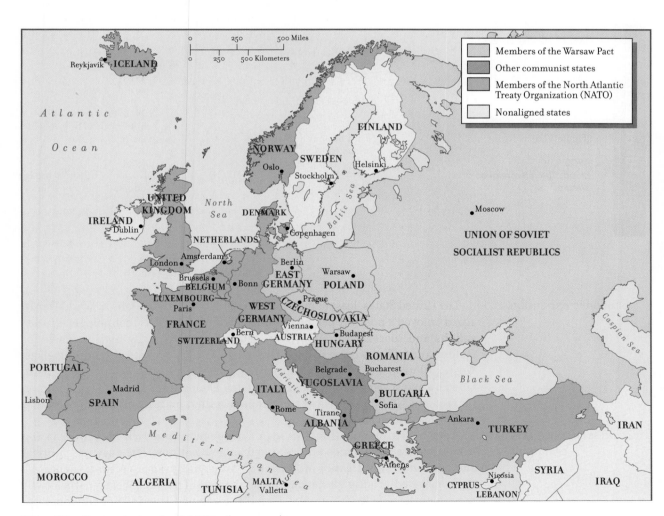

Figure VI.1 Europe during the Cold War (1945–1991).

TIMELINE The Twentieth Century and Today

Musical Events

Renoir, *Dance in the City*

Albert Einstein

1894
Debussy, *Prélude à L'Après-midi d'un faune*

1899
Joplin, *Maple Leaf Rag* (NAWM 164)

1913
Stravinsky, *The Rite of Spring* (NAWM 176)

1925
Electric microphones introduced

1927–1931
Ellington's band plays Cotton Club, Harlem

1933
Steiner, film score for *King Kong*

1890

Historical Events

1872
Monet, *Impression: Soleil levant* (Figure VI.2)

1889
Paris World's Fair

1893
Munch, *The Scream* (Figure VI.5)

1900
Freud, *The Interpretation of Dreams*

1903
The Wright brothers fly first successful airplane

1907
Braque and Picasso paint first cubist pictures (Figure VI.4)

1908
Ford designs the Model-T automobile

1914–1918
World War I

1916
Einstein proposes general theory of relativity

1917
Russian Revolution

1918–1919
Britain and U.S. give women the right to vote

1934
Doctrine of socialist realism adopted in Soviet Union

Economic expansion

The United States, least damaged among the combatant nations in World War II, again enjoyed a postwar period of rapid economic growth. Technological innovations and increased productivity resulted in historically high incomes for factory and office workers that lifted most Americans into the middle class. Western European countries and Japan underwent similar economic growth, aided by investments from the United States. Cooperation through the Common Market and NATO wove Western Europe together, making old nationalist tensions increasingly obsolete.

Independence and civil rights

Starting with British India in 1947, European colonies throughout Asia and Africa won independence and emerged as new nations. The growing political and economic significance of Asia and Africa encouraged cultural exchanges that generated a rising Western interest in music of the non-Western world. The nonviolent strategies Mohandas Gandhi developed to win independence for India were adopted by Martin Luther King, Jr. and others in the quest for equal civil rights for African Americans, a movement in which music unified and inspired the participants.

left: Musée d'Orsay. Photo: Réunion des Musées Nationaux/ Art Resources, NY.
middle: HIP/Art Resource, NY.
right: Cason del Buen Retiro, Madrid, Spain. Photo: Giraudon/ Art Resource, NY. © 2006 Estate of Pablo Picasso/Artists Rights Society (ARS), New York.

1940
Stravinsky and Bartók emigrate to the United States

1957–1958
Varèse, *Poeme electronique* (NAWM 206)

1960
Penderecki, *Threnody: To the Victims of Hiroshima* (NAWM 208)

Picasso, *Weeping Woman*

1966
Moog and Buchla synthesizers introduced

1970
Crumb, *Black Angels* (NAWM 205)

1981
Gubaidulina, *Rejoice!* (NAWM 213)

1995
Sheng, *Seven Tunes Heard in China* (NAWM 209)

2000
Saariaho, *L'Amour de loin* (NAWM 216)

2005
Adams, *Doctor Atomic* (NAWM 219)

2010

1939–1945
World War II leads to defeat of Italy, Germany, and Japan

1945–1991
Cold War between Soviet Union and United States

1960s
Emergence of pop art (Figure VI.8)

1963
John F. Kennedy assassinated

1964–1975
Vietnam War

1968
Martin Luther King, Jr. assassinated

1969
First humans set foot on the moon

1989
Berlin Wall torn down

1991
Soviet Union dissolves

2001
Terrorist attacks on World Trade Center and Pentagon

2003–2011
U.S. involvement in Iraq War

2009
Barack Obama becomes forty-fourth U.S. president

The late 1960s and 1970s brought a series of political and economic shocks to Western nations. Student protests signified a growing gulf between younger and older generations. In the United States, urban riots, growing discord over the Vietnam War, and the assassinations of Martin Luther King, Jr. and Robert F. Kennedy marked increasing social strife.

Meanwhile, Cold War tensions began to ease during the 1970s. Under the policy of *détente* (relaxation or easing of strained relations), the United States and the Soviet Union sought greater cultural contacts and signed treaties to reduce nuclear arms. European leaders reached across the East-West divide, while President Nixon initiated diplomatic relations with the communist government in China after years without formal contact.

Increasing communication with the West and the election of a Polish pope, the first from a communist country, helped to inspire movements for change in Eastern Europe. Beginning with the 1980 strike by the Solidarity movement in Poland and climaxing with the fall of the Berlin Wall in 1989 and the political reunion of East and West Germany the following year, the people of central and

Détente and democracy

Collapse of European communism

Eastern Europe freed themselves from Soviet domination with remarkably little bloodshed. In the Soviet Union itself, Mikhail Gorbachev's policies of *glasnost* (openness) and *perestroika* (restructuring) encouraged freer expression and a more entrepreneurial economy.

New conflicts

The Soviet Union's collapse ended the Cold War that had defined the postwar world. It did not end the fear of a nuclear attack, however, because of the spread of knowledge and technology for manufacturing nuclear weapons. In the post-Soviet era, regional conflicts from the Middle East to the Korean peninsula became more urgent, and civil wars proliferated, from the Balkans and Africa to the Philippines. Extremists increasingly turned to terror as a tactic, whether directed at their own government, as in the 1995 Oklahoma City bombing, or other lands, as in al-Qaeda's attack on the World Trade Center in New York City and the Pentagon in Washington, D.C., on September 11, 2001.

Global economy

In the economic realm, the end of the Cold War encouraged a trend toward integration across national boundaries. The Common Market became the European Union, absorbing new members from Eastern Europe and pursuing a unified European economic system, symbolized by the euro, a new international currency introduced in 2002. Asian countries enjoyed rapid growth, sustained by increasing trade with the rest of the world. Reductions in trade barriers and new technologies led to rising productivity in the Western democracies, producing an economic boom in the 1990s. By then, almost every country was part of an interwoven global economy, so that an economic crisis in one place had ripple effects around the world. The first decade of this century brought new economic problems to the United States, including the decline of the dollar, increased oil prices, stagnant household income, expensive wars in Iraq and Afghanistan, and the collapse of major corporations from airlines to banks following the financial crisis of 2007–2008 and the subsequent recession.

The Arts and the Modern Human Condition

New views on the human mind

With the advent of new technologies and increasing mechanization, psychologists raised questions about what it means to be human. Sigmund Freud developed psychoanalysis, theorizing that human behavior springs from unconscious desires that are repressed by cultural restraints and that dreams are windows into a person's internal conflicts. Ivan Pavlov showed that dogs accustomed to being fed after a bell was rung would salivate at the sound of the bell even if no food was present and that humans could likewise be conditioned to respond to stimuli in predictable ways. These approaches challenged the Romantic view of individuals as protagonists in their own dramas, instead portraying humans as subject to internal and social forces of which they were only dimly aware. Such changing views of human nature forcefully influenced literature and the other arts.

Sustained by Romantic notions of art as a window on the divine and of the artist as an enlightened visionary, artists increasingly regarded their work as an end in itself to be appreciated for its own sake. Success was measured not by wide popular appeal but by the esteem of intellectuals and fellow artists. Many artists searched for new and unusual content or techniques. Symbolist poets such as Paul Verlaine, Stéphane Mallarmé, Paul Valéry, and Stefan George, for example, used intense imagery, symbols, and disrupted syntax to evoke an indefinite, dreamlike state and to suggest feelings and experiences rather than describing them directly. Similarly, modernist novelists such as James Joyce and Marcel Proust broke with the Victorian aim of telling a story or expounding a moral; instead they aspired to discover what Proust called "a different self" by exploring the interaction of conscious and subconscious thought.

In the late nineteenth century, French painters known as impressionists — named after Claude Monet's painting *Impression: Soleil levant* (1872), shown in Figure VI.2 — inaugurated the first in a series of artistic movements that utterly changed styles and attitudes toward art. Rather than depicting things realistically, the impressionists sought to capture atmosphere and sensuous impressions from nature, adopting a stance of detached observation rather than direct emotional engagement. In Monet's paintings, objects and people are suggested by a few brush strokes, often of starkly contrasting colors, leaving it to the viewer's eyes and mind to blend the colors and fill in the missing details. The effect of light on an object is often as much the subject of a painting as is the object itself. Although impressionist paintings are widely popular today, they were at first poorly received, derided as lacking in artistic skill and opposed to traditional aesthetics. Such reactions also greeted other modern styles of painting and music.

Each impressionist painter had a highly individual style, and later artists extended their ideas in unique ways. Paul Cézanne depicted natural scenes and

Impressionism

Figure VI.2 Claude Monet, Impression: Soleil levant *(Sunrise; 1872). Monet entered this work and eight others in an exhibition he helped to organize in 1874. A disapproving critic headlined his mocking review "Exhibition of the Impressionists," picking up on Monet's title and coining a term that would define an entire artistic movement. Instead of mixing his colors on a palette, Monet juxtaposed them on the canvas to capture impressions of the early light of day. He and other impressionist painters popularized outdoor painting and specialized in representing sunlight and water, two of the most formless yet luminous aspects of nature.*

(Erich Lessing/Art Resource, NY.)

Figure VI.3 Paul Cézanne, Mont Sainte-Victoire *(1906). Cézanne painted many versions of this scene, which was visible from his house in Aix-en-Provence in southern France, rendering the massive mountain and the details of the town nestled in the countryside as blocks of color placed side by side in geometrical arrangements.*
(Erich Lessing/
Art Resource, NY.)

Figure VI.4 Pablo Picasso, The Treble Clef *(1912). This cubist painting includes a violin on the right, broken into its various components and planes, and a clarinet on the left, stylized as gray, blue, and brown bands, some with finger holes, and concentric circles with a cone to represent the instrument's bell.*
(Private Collection. © Photo Edimédia/Corbis. © 2006 Estate of Pablo Picasso/Artists Rights Society (ARS), New York.)

figures as orderly arrangements of geometrical forms and planes of color, as in his painting of Mont Sainte-Victoire (1906; Figure VI.3). Pablo Picasso and Georges Braque further abstracted this idea in cubism, a style in which three-dimensional objects are represented on a flat plane by breaking them down into geometrical shapes such as cubes and cones, and juxtaposing or overlapping them in an active, colorful design. Figure VI.4 shows an example, one of a series Picasso painted in 1912 that used two musical instruments as a subject.

The revolution begun by impressionism stimulated new ways of making, seeing, and thinking about paintings, giving birth to movements such as expressionism (discussed in Chapter 25), surrealism, and abstract art. In most of these new movements, artists and their approving critics no longer prized beauty, as had painters from the Renaissance to the Romantic era. Instead, they sought a deeper engagement, demanding that the viewer work to understand and interpret the image. Surrealist painters like Salvador Dalí and René Magritte explored the dreamlike world of the unconscious opened up by Freud; and artists associated with the expressionist movement, like the Norwegian Edvard Munch, whose work is shown in Figure VI.5, and the composer Arnold Schoenberg, one of whose self-portraits is shown in Figure VI.6, gave vent to feelings of anxiety and alienation that seemed to pervade modern society. Other artists sought to objectify the horrors of warfare, as

Figure VI.5 Edvard Munch, The Scream *(1893). Munch's work was especially concerned with the expressive representation of emotions, particularly anguish, despair, fear, and melancholy. Here, the swirling colors, eerie shapes, and featureless face all combine to symbolize a dreamlike, soundless scream.*
(Munch Museum, Oslo, Norway. Photo: Erich Lessing/Art Resource, NY. © 2006 The Munch Museum/The Munch-Ellingsen Group/Artists Rights Society (ARS), New York.)

Picasso did in *Guernica*, painted after the bombing of civilians during the Spanish Civil War.

Disillusionment with modern society also showed itself in literature: T. S. Eliot's *The Waste Land*, with its many references to literature of the past; James Joyce's stream-of-consciousness novel *Ulysses*; Marcel Proust's multivolume novel of time and memory, *Remembrance of Things Past*; the politically engaged plays of Bertolt Brecht; and the feminist novels and essays of Virginia Woolf. Impelled by the worldwide depression of the 1930s, many artists reexamined their role and sought to make their work relevant to the economic and social problems of the time. Artists such as Diego Rivera in Mexico (see Figure 26.9) and Thomas Hart Benton in the United States pictured social conditions in assertive, direct styles that offered a muscular alternative to European modernism, as shown in Figure VI.7. Many classical composers likewise sought to write music that was accessible to all, hoping to catch the imaginations of ordinary working people.

After World War II, the center of the art world shifted from Paris to New York with the emergence of abstract expressionism, the first specifically American movement to become influential internationally. Abstract expressionism, typified by Jackson Pollock dripping paint onto a canvas laid on the floor of his studio, combined the emotional intensity of German expressionism with the anti-representational aesthetic of European abstract schools such as surrealism, and emphasized spontaneity and subconscious creation. In reaction, the late 1950s and 1960s spawned

Figure VI.6 Arnold Schoenberg, Self-Portrait *(ca. 1911). By depicting the subject walking away, his back to the viewer, the painting links Schoenberg with the quintessential modernist theme of alienation.*
(Arnold Schönberg Institute/Lebrecht Music & Arts Photo Library. © 2006 Artists Rights Society (ARS), New York/VBK, Vienna.)

a new movement known as pop art, whose leading figure was the prolific and versatile Andy Warhol. Pop art employed aspects of mass culture, such as advertising, comic books, and objects of everyday life (see Figure VI.8). In so doing, it helped bridge the perceived gap between "high" and "low" art and even between life and art in general. At about the same time, composers such as John Cage were experimenting with blurring the distinctions between music and its environment, as we shall see in Chapter 27.

The Technological Revolution

One symbol of progress in the modern age was the electrification of industry, businesses, and homes. Electric lighting increasingly replaced gas lighting, and electrical appliances were produced for the home market. Another symbol was the internal combustion engine fueled by petroleum, which gradually replaced coal engines in steamships and factories (see Figure VI.7). By streamlining production and distribution, Henry Ford made his Model T the first widely affordable automobile, launching the modern world's love affair with the car. Wilbur and Orville Wright flew the first working airplane in 1903, and by the end of the next decade airplanes were used for both military and commercial purposes.

The rise of a music industry

The rapid growth of diverse musical styles between the world wars was also due in part to new technologies (see Innovations, pages 540–541). Recordings, radio broadcasting, and the introduction of sound to motion pictures enabled the preservation and rapid distribution of music in performance, not just in score. Now a musical performance, formerly as impermanent as a moment in time, could be preserved, admired, and replayed many times. This change created a new mass market and new commercial possibilities, allowed performers to share in the benefits of mass distribution, and vaulted some performers—whether of classical music, popular music, or jazz—to international stardom.

Figure VI.7 Electric Power, Motor-Cars, Steel *is the title of this panel from the murals by American painter Thomas Hart Benton for the Indiana Hall at the 1933 World's Fair in Chicago. It shows workers and designers in the steel mills of northwest Indiana, electric-power generation, and the automobile industry, thus celebrating the industries that helped lift the country out of the Great Depression of the 1930s.* (Courtesy Indiana University Archives.)

The popular music industry had revolved around sheet music from the 1890s through the 1910s, but after the war publishers realized that recordings offered a market of potentially unlimited size. Songwriters and bandleaders also turned to recordings, often tailoring their pieces to fit the three- to four-minute limit of a 78-rpm record side. Musicians also profited from exposure via radio broadcasting since music was a good way of filling large periods of airtime. Recordings were still too poor in quality to be played successfully over the radio, so stations relied primarily on live performers in their own studios and on regional or national transmissions of live shows. Stations in Europe and the Americas sponsored orchestras, such as the BBC Symphony Orchestra (founded 1930) in London and the NBC Symphony Orchestra (1937) in New York. Dance bands, such as the one led by Benny Goodman, also made use of the new medium to gain wider exposure.

Figure VI.8 Andy Warhol's *Heinz Tomato Ketchup Box* (1964), *Brillo Box* (1964), *Campbell's Tomato Juice Box* (1964), *and Campbell's Soup Cans* (1962) on display at the High Museum of Art in Atlanta.
(AP Photo/David Goldman.)

After 1945

In the years following the Second World War, television and radio increasingly brought entertainment and music into the home. The invention of the transistor led to miniature portable radios that could be taken anywhere, bringing broadcast music into cars and the outdoors. Disc jockeys played recordings of popular songs on the radio, replacing most of the live music shows of previous decades. Tape recorders, invented during the 1930s and widely available from the 1950s on, made it possible for individuals to preserve and manipulate sounds, thereby enabling the entire field of electronic music.

Global arts

News, entertainment, and the arts became global as well. The spread of communications satellites and cable television, and the advent in the 1980s and 1990s of personal computers, fax machines, cell phones, and the Internet put people around the world in immediate touch with one another. Improved communications and travel also fostered a global market for the arts. Many forms of entertainment—from Hollywood movies to touring groups of traditional artists such as the Bulgarian Women's Choir and Tuvan throat-singers from Outer Mongolia—now reach audiences all over the world. Asians, including Japanese-born Seiji Ozawa (formerly long-time conductor of the Boston Symphony Orchestra) and Chinese-born musician Bright Sheng (composer of *Seven Tunes Heard in China,* NAWM 209), have become prominent as musicians in the Western classical tradition. At the same time, some Americans and Europeans have become proficient performers of Indian, Javanese, and other Asian musics. Music from around the world is now easily accessible through recordings, MP3 files, online streaming, and live performances. The diversity of the world's music has brought a growing awareness in Europe and the Americas that each musician's work is but one strand in a global tapestry.

Full 🔊

ARTS & IDEAS

Science and Technology

U.S. inventor Thomas Alva Edison (1847–1931) patented more than a thousand devices, including the phonograph and the incandescent lightbulb.

Sigmund Freud (1856–1939), Austrian psychiatrist and founder of modern psychoanalysis, inspired one of the great intellectual movements of the twentieth century. His writings transformed modern culture's attitudes toward human sexuality, religion, and childhood development, and identified the unconscious and its influence on behavior. *The Interpretation of Dreams* (1900), *The Ego and the Id* (1923), and *Civilization and Its Discontents* (1930) are among his major works.

Originally a machinist and engineer with the Edison Company, American industrialist Henry Ford (1863–1947) launched his own firm in Detroit, Michigan, in the first decade of the century. By cutting production costs, adapting conveyor-belt and assembly-line methods to car manufacturing, and featuring an inexpensive, standardized car, he outdistanced his competitors and became the largest automobile producer in the world, regarded by many as the apostle of mass production.

Wilbur (1867–1912) and Orville Wright (1871–1948), American airplane inventors and brothers, experimented with aircraft design and achieved the first controlled and sustained flight in 1903.

Literature

Stéphane Mallarmé (1842–1898) believed that poetry should evoke thoughts through suggestion rather than description and that it should approach the abstraction of music. One of his best-known poems, *L'Après-midi d'un faune* (1876; The Afternoon of a Faun), inspired a symphonic poem by Debussy, which in turn was choreographed as a sensuous ballet by Vaslav Nijinsky (see Figure 23.1).

French author Marcel Proust (1871–1922) transformed the novel with his monumental work *À la recherche du temps perdu* (Remembrance of Things Past; originally in 16 volumes, 1913–1927), a semiautobiographical cycle that is less a story than an interior monologue. His vision and technique were vital to the development of modernism in that he raised artistic endeavor almost to the status of a religion.

James Joyce (1882–1941), Irish writer of novels, short stories, and poems, is known for his revolutionary innovations in narrative techniques, making extensive use of the interior monologue or stream of consciousness. His unique and inventive use of the English language at first caused his books (*Ulysses*, 1914–1921; and *Finnegans Wake*, 1912–1939) to be misunderstood by the public and denounced by critics as unintelligible, nonsensical, and obscene. In that respect, they embody a frequent theme of the modernist novel — the difficulty of communicating.

English author Virginia Woolf (1882–1941) advocated cultural and intellectual independence for women in her novels (*To the Lighthouse*, 1927; *Orlando*, 1928) and essays (*A Room of One's Own*, 1929). Her works are noted for their psychological penetration, sensitive style, and evocation of place and mood. Depressed by the war and fearful of recurring mental breakdowns, she committed suicide.

T. S. Eliot (1888–1965), a Harvard-educated American poet and critic who migrated to England, won the 1948

The Changing World of Music

Music was directly affected by the expanding economy, new technologies, the devastation of World War I, the emergence of the United States on the world stage, the role of African American urban culture in fostering new musical styles, new thinking about human nature, and new artistic movements.

Modernism   In the closing years of the nineteenth century and before World War I, as we have seen, a younger group of composers carried out a more radical break from the musical language of the past than their predecessors or contemporaries,

Nobel Prize in literature. His most famous poem, *The Waste Land* (1922), broke with nineteenth-century poetic tradition by employing complex allusions and dense imagery, influenced by the French Symbolists. In his hands, modernist poetry became a particularly exalted and sophisticated form of cultural criticism.

French existential philosopher, playwright, and novelist Jean-Paul Sartre (1905–1980) subscribed to a radical individualism that saw humans as responsible but lonely beings who must continually struggle against an unfavorable environment in order to achieve any degree of authenticity. His philosophy was partly a response to the Second World War and to the struggle of the Free French against Nazism, as was his monumental work *Being and Nothingness* (1943).

Art

The forerunner of modernism in painting, Paul Cézanne (1839–1906) articulated revolutionary principles that became fundamental to twentieth-century art. Among them was the idea that art is a harmony not derived from nature but existing in and for itself. His belief that a painting "should represent nothing but color" is evident in his many versions of *Mont Sainte-Victoire* (Figure VI.3).

Claude Monet (1840–1926), one of the foremost painters of landscape in the history of art, was a founder of impressionism. His work explores light and color in different atmospheric conditions and at various times of the day, as illustrated in his *Impressions: Soleil levant* (Sunrise, 1872), shown in Figure VI.2, the work that gave the French movement its name.

Norwegian artist Edvard Munch (1863–1944) took the lead among artists in exploring the borders between the conscious and unconscious, thereby paving the way for German expressionism. "Inside us are worlds," he wrote. His most famous work, *The Scream* (1893), shown in Figure VI.5, exemplifies his emotionally charged style.

Spanish-born Pablo Picasso (1881–1973) was a painter, sculptor, printmaker, decorative artist, and writer. Although he was active mainly in France, he dominated twentieth-century European art, initiating or influencing most of the artistic dialogues that took place during his long lifetime. Together with Georges Braque, he was responsible for cubism, one of the most radical explanations of how a work of art constructs its meaning (see Figure VI.4). Because of his enormous versatility, technical virtuosity, prolific output, and unquestionable originality, he became the very image of the modern artist.

Mexican painter Diego Rivera (1886–1957) won international acclaim for his vast public murals, in which he created a new style based on socialist ideals and on the native and popular heritage of Mexican culture. His images use symbols drawn from Christian and Aztec cultures, exalt the peasant and working classes, and had a worldwide influence on public art (see Figure 26.9).

Andy Warhol (1928–1987), a controversial American artist, explored the relationship between artistic expression, celebrity culture, and advertising imagery, and in the 1960s created a style known as pop art (Figure VI.8). In his own words, "Art is what you can get away with." Though reviled by some, his works presented a challenge to traditions of fine art and include some of the most expensive paintings ever sold.

while maintaining strong ties to tradition. These composers, known as *modernists*, reassessed inherited conventions as profoundly as the modernists in art who pioneered expressionism, cubism, and abstract art. Modernists in both art and music did not aim to please viewers or listeners at first sight or first hearing, an attribute that had always been considered essential. Instead, they sought to challenge audience perceptions and capacities, providing an experience that would be impossible through traditional means. Modernists offered an implicit critique of mass culture and easily digested art, and their writings often show it. These composers saw no contradiction in claiming the masters of the past as models. In fact, they saw their own work as continuing what the pathbreaking classical composers had started, not as overthrowing that tradition. The paradox of all modern classical music—that it must partake of tradition yet offer something new—is especially acute in the work of modernist composers, who are often most radical in the ways they interpret and remake the past.

Stylistic diversification

　　The period between World Wars I and II saw remarkable changes in musical life and continued diversification in musical styles. Recordings and radio brought about widespread dissemination of the classical repertory from Bach to Bartók as well as less well-known music from the remote past to the present. Classical concert music and opera remained the most prestigious musical traditions, but popular music was better known and usually more lucrative. Especially prominent were trends from the United States, notably jazz. Music, always an accompaniment to "silent" movies, became an integral part of sound films, and many composers of opera, classical concert music, musicals, and popular songs found a place in the movie industry. Composers of art music went in numerous directions, sharing less common ground as they explored new possibilities. A few composers, such as Igor Stravinsky and Aaron Copland, were able to support themselves with commissions, royalties, and income from conducting or performances. Other composers sought patronage, but without the kings and aristocracy of earlier times, it had to come from new sources.

New forms of patronage

　　In Europe, composers were supported by the state, through radio stations, annual subsidies, grants, arts agencies, and educational institutions. In the United States and Canada, many composers taught in universities, colleges, and conservatories; employment that gave them time to compose, a ready audience, and access to performing organizations, including ensembles created specifically to present new music. Since colleges and universities prize academic freedom, the music coming from academic composers has been diverse, varying from traditional styles to avant-garde and experimental. Indeed, the safety of tenure and the ivory tower tended to isolate composers from the public and make them independent of its support. Among many refugees from Europe, Arnold Schoenberg taught at the University of California at Los Angeles, Darius Milhaud at Mills College in Oakland, California, and Paul Hindemith at Yale. More recently, urban centers and the Internet have played a role in allowing musicians to find small but devoted audiences that support specialized types of music, creating niche markets in which everything from early-music groups to avant-garde rock bands can thrive.

　　Of the dizzying number and variety of trends in this century, we will explore some of the most important and distinctive. Chapter 23 surveys the first modernist generation of composers in Europe, among them Claude Debussy, and the variety of tonal, atonal, and post-tonal approaches that they devised. Other composers, especially those who identified with a particular national heritage, are also represented. Chapter 24 surveys the variety of vernacular musics in America, including jazz. The next chapter is devoted to six of the most prodigious and influential modernist composers of the century. In Chapter 26 we look at the interwar period and at the effects of political disruptions and government policies on music, particularly in Nazi Germany and the Soviet Union. In the final chapters, we identify some of the myriad trends in European and American classical music since the Second World War, linking individual composers with one or more of the styles that most closely define their music. Many other composers and styles remain to be explored, from a perspective that will undoubtedly look very different to the next generation of teachers and students.

23

Classical Modernism

PRELUDE

By the turn of the twentieth century, an established repertory of musical classics dominated almost every field of concert music. The change was enormous: in the eighteenth century, performers and listeners demanded a constant stream of new music and considered anything written more than twenty years earlier to be "ancient"; but in the early 1900s they expected most concert music would be at least a generation old, and they judged new music by the standards of the classics already established in the repertory. In essence, concert halls and opera houses had become museums, displaying the musical artworks of the past. Living composers increasingly found themselves in competition with the established repertory. They had to write music that would fit comfortably into that repertory yet was different enough from other pieces to attract attention—a tricky balancing act. This became the great theme of modernism in the classical tradition, especially in the first half of the century.

Writers on music have used the word *modernism* with more than one meaning. Some reserve it for composers who break radically from the musical language of the past, like those we will meet in Chapter 25. Here we use it more broadly, to encompass the entire range of composers in the late nineteenth and early twentieth centuries whose music is marked by the quest for a place beside the classics of the past, whatever style they adopted in their efforts to combine innovation with tradition. Faced with common problems, composers devised highly individual solutions, differing in what they valued most in their nationalist traditions, in what they discarded, and in what innovations they introduced. Most continued to use tonality, but many wrote music that diverged from the common-practice tonal language in use since the time of Bach. Among the composers who moved beyond tonality, each developed a personal musical language that followed its own rules, resulting in the post-tonal practices to be discussed. As a result of these varied solutions, music became increasingly diverse in style and approach, a process that accelerated throughout the twentieth century.

Our exploration of musical modernism will not be confined to the composers discussed in this chapter. Rather, we will continue to refer to the term in connection with many of the most prominent composers of the twentieth century to be studied in the following chapters—Igor Stravinsky, Béla Bartók, and the American Charles Ives, among others. All developed unique combinations of nationalism and modernism that won them a central place in the world of modern music.

The First Generation of Modernists

We have already seen how the careers and music of Mahler and Strauss exemplify the search by those in the first generation of modernist composers for a personal style that absorbed what was useful from the past, and was true to their national identity, yet was distinctive and individual. This search continued with Claude Debussy, the premier modernist in France.

Claude Debussy

While Mahler and Strauss extended Wagnerian harmony to new levels of rhetorical intensity, their French contemporary Claude Debussy (1862–1918; see Biography, page 522) took it in a different direction, toward rhetorical understatement and emotional reserve. In general, French modernists sought greater independence from German music by drawing elements from their own musical past dating back to the seventeenth and eighteenth centuries, elements marked by refined taste and restraint. So, while Debussy admired Wagner's works, especially *Tristan* and *Parsifal,* he deliberately abandoned Wagner's sense of urgency and the desire for resolution that underlies all tonal music, especially German Romantic music. Instead, Debussy promoted a modernism that focused on what he regarded as the traditionally French values of decoration, beauty, and pleasure. In his music, we are content to enjoy each moment as it comes. Debussy admired particularly his older contemporary Emmanuel Chabrier (1841–1894) and found new ideas in Russian composers, especially Rimsky-Korsakov and Musorgsky; in medieval music, notably parallel organum; and in music from Asia. He was fascinated by the Javanese gamelan, which he encountered at the Paris World's Fair in 1889. Blending these and other influences, he produced works of striking individuality that had a profound impact on almost all later composers.

Style   Debussy's music is often called impressionist by analogy to the impressionist painters (see page 509), but it also shares qualities with the Symbolist poets by evoking a mood through suggestion, connotation, and indirection. This stylistic connection was reinforced by Debussy's friendships with Symbolist poets and his use of their texts for songs and dramatic works. As in their poetry, the normal syntax in Debussy's music is often disrupted, so that the chord progressions of common-practice harmony are avoided or attenuated. Our attention is drawn instead to individual musical ideas or images that carry the work's structure and meaning. Debussy creates these musical images through motives, harmony, exotic scales (such as the whole-tone, octatonic, and pentatonic scales), instrumental timbre, and other elements, which he then assembles into a composition. Motives need not develop but may repeat with small changes, like an object viewed from different perspectives; dissonances need not resolve; sonorities may move in parallel motion; contrasts of scale type underlie the articulation of phrases and sections; and instrumental timbres are intrinsic to the musical content rather than simply coloration. Indeed, Debussy's mature works are shaped more by contrasts of timbre and texture than by traditional formal devices or tonal function.

Piano music   These traits are evident in the passage from Debussy's piano piece *L'Isle joyeuse* (The Joyous Isle, 1903–1904) in Example 23.1. Each motive is associated with a particular figuration, scale type, dynamic level, or range on the piano, producing a succession of images that remain distinct from one another even as

Example 23.1 Claude Debussy, L'Isle joyeuse

each flows into the next: (a) a rising major-third motive (F–A) in a whole-tone environment D♯–C♯–B–A–B–C♯–D♯, etc.); (b) an upward pentatonic sweep of three D octaves; (c) a partially chromatic motive based on undulating thirds; (d) a pentatonic filigree comprising the five notes B–C♯–E–F♯–A; and (e) chromatic lines in contrary motion over an A pedal, combined with motive (c). In the motion from one segment to the next, some notes remain the same and some change in a leisurely harmonic progression.

As in most of his music, Debussy maintains a tonal focus—a kind of key center, here A—but he defies conventional tonal relationships between chords and allows each chord a degree of independence. This changed attitude toward harmony, inviting us to take pleasure in each event rather than yearn for resolution, gives his music a feeling of detached observation. Debussy once said of his music, "There is no theory. You merely have to listen. Pleasure is the law." Of course, pleasure can lead to exuberance or even ecstasy, as it does in the climactic conclusion of this piece, so it should not be imagined that Debussy's music is without emotion.

Many of Debussy's other piano pieces also have evocative titles, often suggesting a visual image, like *Estampes* (Engravings, or Prints, 1903) and the two sets of *Images* (1901–1905 and 1907). *Children's Corner* (1906–1908), inspired by Debussy's daughter, depicts a child's world, including a sly poke at a prominent pedagogue's piano exercises in *Dr. Gradus ad Parnassum*. The last piece in the set, Golliwogg's *Cake-Walk*, imitates Scott Joplin's ragtime style (see chapter 24) and satirically quotes the opening of Wagner's *Tristan* Prelude. The twenty-four Preludes (two books, 1909–1910 and 1911–1913) are character pieces whose

Harmony

picturesque titles are placed at the end rather than the beginning of each piece to allow performers and listeners to form their own associations. Other works are relatively abstract, although unmistakably in Debussy's style: *Suite bergamasque* (ca. 1890) and *Pour le piano* (1894–1901) update the French tradition of the keyboard suite, and the late *Études* (1915) explore pianistic timbre as well as technique in the tradition of Chopin.

Orchestral music

Debussy's orchestral music shows the same characteristics as his piano works, with the added element of instrumental timbre. Often a particular instrument is associated with a certain motive, and different musical layers are separated through tone color. His works require a large orchestra, which is seldom used to make a loud sound but instead offers a great variety of tone colors and textures. Even more than Mahler, Debussy treated music as an art of timbre and reveled in the wide range of sounds available in the orchestra.

Debussy based his celebrated *Prélude à "L'Après-midi d'un faune"* (Prelude to "The Afternoon of a Faun," 1891–1894) on a Symbolist poem by Mallarmé, and he treated the subject, the sensual experiences of a forest god who is half human and half goat, with the same detachment and delicacy that French Symbolist poets did (see Figure 23.1). At the same time, he shared the impressionist painters' fascination with atmosphere, color, and light—qualities that are evident in his masterful orchestral technique. The variety of his orchestral palette is well represented in the three *Nocturnes* (1897–1899): we find subdued, imagist instrumentation in *Nuages* (Clouds), the brilliance of the full ensemble in *Fêtes* (Festivals), and the blending of orchestra with a wordless female chorus in *Sirènes* (the Sirens of Greek mythology). *La Mer* (The Sea, 1903–1905), subtitled "three symphonic sketches," in which the orchestra captures the undulating and unpredictable movements of the sea, betrays Debussy's self-declared "sincere devotion to the sea." The Japanese print pictured in Figure 23.2 hung in his study and inspired him while he was composing the work.

Figure 23.1 Costume sketch for the faun by Léon Bakst (1866–1924), who also designed the stage set for Sergei Diaghilev's ballet (1912) based on Debussy's Prélude. (Erich Lessing/Art Resource, NY.)

Nuages (NAWM 167) from *Nocturnes* exemplifies the interaction of timbre with motive, scale type, and other elements to create a musical image. The piece begins with an oscillating pattern of fifths and thirds—adapted from a Musorgsky song—that conveys an impression of movement but no harmonic direction, an apt analogy for slowly drifting clouds. Each time the pattern appears, it features different tone colors or pitches or both, sometimes changing into a series of parallel triads or seventh or ninth chords. Near the end the pattern practically disappears, giving the impression of dispersing clouds. Contrasting with this figure's inconstancy is one that changes little: an English-horn motive that quickly rises and slowly falls through a segment of the octatonic scale. The English horn sometimes omits or repeats some of its final notes, but the motive is never developed, transposed, or given to another instrument, and the English horn never plays anything else; there is complete identification between timbre and motive. It is not clear what, if anything, these musical gestures represent: they are themselves, lending coherence to the music and helping to convey a sense of stillness and contemplation.

Debussy's lifelong engagement with texts—he was also a music critic—made him particularly interested in the

Figure 23.2 Original cover for Debussy's orchestral score of La Mer, *first published in 1905. The design, based on a popular print by the Japanese artist Katsushika Hokusai (1760–1849) from his renowned series* Thirty-six Views of Mount Fuji, *reflects the nineteenth-century French enthusiasm for the arts of East Asia.*
(Bibliothèque Nationale, Paris.)

written word. Notable among his songs are settings of several major French poets, including Charles Baudelaire, Paul Verlaine, and the ballades of fifteenth-century poet François Villon. He repeatedly sought out dramatic projects, such as incidental music for Gabriele D'Annunzio's mystery play *The Martyrdom of Saint Sebastian* (1910–1911) and the ballet *Jeux* (1912–1913), and several unfinished works. His only completed opera, *Pelléas et Mélisande* (1893–1902), which was his response to Wagner's *Tristan und Isolde,* made his reputation when it premiered at the Paris Opéra-Comique. The veiled allusions and images of the text—a Symbolist play by Maurice Maeterlinck—are matched by the strange, often modal harmonies, subdued colors, and restrained expressiveness of the music. The voices, set in fluent recitative that matches the flow of the French language, are supported but never dominated by a continuous orchestral background, while the instrumental interludes connecting the scenes carry on the mysterious inner drama.

The changes that Debussy introduced in harmony and orchestration made him one of the seminal forces in the history of music. Nearly every distinguished composer of the early and middle twentieth century came under his influence at one time or another, from Ravel, Messiaen, and Boulez in France to Puccini, Janáček, Strauss, Scriabin, Ives, Falla, Bartók, Stravinsky, Berg, and others from many national traditions, as well as American jazz and popular musicians. His emphasis on sound itself as an element of music opened doors to new possibilities later explored by Varèse, Cage, and many postwar composers.

Influence

Claude Debussy (1862–1918)

Claimed by some as a major source of modern music, Debussy's evocative style introduced a new aesthetic of suggestive sounds and delicate colors. Not surprisingly, he numbered among his friends as many poets and painters as musicians.

Born in a suburb of Paris to a middle-class family, Debussy began studying at the Conservatoire in Paris at the age of ten, first piano and then composition. In the early 1880s, he worked for Tchaikovsky's patron Nadezhda von Meck and twice traveled to Russia, where he heard the recent works of Rimsky-Korsakov and others that deeply influenced his style and orchestration. In 1884, he won the coveted Prix de Rome and spent two years in Italy. Returning to Paris in 1887, he cultivated friendships with several Symbolist poets and other artists. Although he dutifully made the pilgrimage to Bayreuth to hear Wagner's operas in 1888 and 1889, he came away having recognized both the power of the music and his own need to avoid being overly influenced by it.

In the 1890s, Debussy lived with his lover, Gabrielle Dupont, in Montmartre, the "Bohemian" neighborhood in Paris that had become a center for the new artistic movements. He found his own voice in composing a series of songs, his early piano music, his *Prelude to "The Afternoon of a Faun,"* and, especially, his opera *Pelléas et Mélisande,* whose 1902 premiere made him a star overnight. He made a living through his work as a music critic and by publishing his music.

In 1898, Debussy left Dupont for Lilly Texier, whom he married the next year. But in 1904, he fell in love with Emma Bardac, with whom he had a child in 1905 and whom he married in 1908 after they had both divorced their spouses. By then, he was well established as France's leading

modern composer, producing orchestral works like *La Mer* and *Images* and piano pieces that soon entered the standard repertory. Although depressed by World War I and a diagnosis of cancer in 1914, he soon regained his productivity and composed his Études and three chamber sonatas before his death in 1918.

Major works: *Pelléas et Mélisande* (opera); *Jeux* (ballet); *Prelude to "The Afternoon of a Faun," Nocturnes, La Mer, Images,* and other orchestral works; Preludes, Études, *Images, Children's Corner,* and many other piano pieces; about 90 songs; string quartet, sonatas, and other chamber works.

Figure 23.3 Portrait of Claude Debussy by Jacques-Émile Blanche, completed in 1902.
(Lebrecht Music and Arts Photo Library. © 2006 Artists Rights Society (ARS), New York/ADAGP, Paris.)

Maurice Ravel

Maurice Ravel (1875–1937; see Figure 23.4) is often grouped with Debussy as an impressionist, and some of his works seem to fit the label. But he might better be called an assimilationist because his music encompasses a variety of influences while carrying his distinctive stamp marked by consummate craftsmanship, traditional forms, diatonic melodies, and complex harmonies within an essentially tonal language.

Varied influences

The descriptive piano piece *Jeux d'eau* (Fountains, 1901), the sets *Miroirs* (Mirrors, 1904–1905) and *Gaspard de la nuit* (Gaspard of the Night, 1908), the orchestral suite *Rapsodie espagnole* (Spanish Rhapsody, 1907–1908), and the ballet *Daphnis et Chloé* (1909–1912) invoke impressionism in their strong musical imagery, brilliant instrumental technique, and colorful harmonies. But Ravel also absorbed ideas from older French music and from the eighteenth-century Classic style. His interest in classical forms is clear in works such as the String Quartet in F (1902–1903) and the Violin Sonata (1923–1927). He borrowed from the French tradition of stylized dances and suites in his piano pieces, *Menuet antique* (1895), *Pavane pour une infante défunte* (Pavane for a Dead Princess, 1899), and *Le Tombeau de Couperin* (Memorial for Couperin, 1914–1917), all of which he later orchestrated.

Le Tombeau de Couperin, a suite of six movements in eighteenth-century genres, was an early example of neoclassicism, which was to become the prevailing trend in France during and after World War I. Although the term has many shades of meaning, it has come to represent a broad movement from the 1910s to the 1950s in which composers revived, imitated, or evoked the styles, genres, and forms of pre-Romantic music, especially those of the eighteenth century, then called Classic. ("Baroque" as a term for early eighteenth-century music became widely used only after 1940.) Neoclassicism originated in France as a rejection of German Romanticism, whose associations with intense emotions, irrationality, yearning, individualism, and nationalism became increasingly suspect in the wake of the wanton destruction of the war.

Neoclassicism

The link to the war is especially poignant in *Le Tombeau de Couperin*, as each movement is dedicated to the memory of a friend of Ravel's who died while serving in the French military during the war. The title invokes the seventeenth-century tradition of the *tombeau*, a piece (usually an allemande) composed in memory of a deceased colleague, and François Couperin, the greatest of the French keyboard composers of the seventeenth and eighteenth centuries (see chapter 14). Like French keyboard suites of that era, *Le Tombeau de Couperin* includes a prelude and several dances—here a forlane, rigaudon, and menuet (minuet).

Le Tombeau de Couperin

The Menuet (NAWM 168) from the orchestral version of the suite exemplifies Ravel's brand of neoclassicism. The trick in writing neoclassical music is to make it sound both classic and new at the same time. The classical traits are clear: a lilting minuet rhythm, a melodic style and ornaments reminiscent of

Full 🔊

Figure 23.4 Maurice Ravel at the piano in an undated photograph.
(Lebrecht Music & Arts Photo Library.)

Couperin, the minuet and trio form (though with some varied repetitions and a coda), four-measure phrases, a simple harmonic plan with motion to the dominant and parallel minor, dominant-to-tonic cadences in the minuet, and in the trio drones and repeating figures on an open fifth imitating the drone bass of an eighteenth-century musette. But from the opening measures, where seventh and ninth chords outnumber the triads, it is clear no eighteenth-century composer could have written this music. Unexpected harmonies abound, and the entire trio presents its melody clothed in parallel triads, virtually an impressionist trademark. At the reprise of the minuet, the themes of the minuet and trio are combined in counterpoint, which recalls the contrapuntal feats of Bach. The combination of classic and new traits is quintessentially neoclassical. Especially in the colorful orchestral version, with its varied timbres and special effects from string harmonics to muted brass, the blend of elements is also characteristic of Ravel.

Ravel also looked to popular traditions outside France, using Viennese waltz rhythms, Gypsy-style melodies, blues, and jazz elements, the last of these especially in the Piano Concerto for the Left Hand (1929–1930), composed for pianist Paul Wittgenstein, who had lost his right arm in World War I. Many works feature Spanish idioms, including *Bolero* (1928), an orchestral rumination on a single theme that is varied by changes of instrumentation and gradually increasing and then decreasing dynamics. Beyond impressionist and neoclassical traits, Ravel borrowed ideas from many kinds of music to enrich his own.

Modernism and National Traditions

Figure 23.5 Serge Rachmaninoff in a 1940 portrait by Boris Chaliapin.
(Courtesy B.P.K., Berlin.)

The careers and music of Debussy and Ravel, and of Mahler and Strauss (discussed in the previous chapter), exemplify the search by members of the first generation of modernist composers for a personal style that absorbed what was useful from the past and was true to their national identities, yet was distinctive and individual. As we survey a number of major composers from other nations across Europe, we will also see this interplay between tradition and innovation and between national identity and personal style at work.

Russia: Serge Rachmaninoff and Alexander Scriabin

The works of Rachmaninoff and Scriabin illustrate the wide variety of personal styles in this period. Classmates at the Moscow Conservatory, each developed an individual idiom that drew both on Russian traditions and on the cosmopolitan heritage of the virtuoso pianist-composer.

Serge Rachmaninoff (1873–1943), shown in Figure 23.5, made his living primarily as a pianist, especially after leaving Russia in 1917 in the wake of the Russian Revolution and making his home in the United States. His notable works include three symphonies, the symphonic poem *The Isle of the Dead* (1907), and the choral symphony *The Bells* (1913). But his most characteristic music is for piano, especially the twenty-four preludes (1892–1910) and two sets of *Études-Tableaux* (1911 and 1916–1917) for piano solo, four piano concertos, and his *Rhapsody on a Theme of Paganini* for piano and orchestra (1934), a salute from one great virtuoso to another.

Rachmaninoff's Prelude for Piano in G Minor, Op. 23, No. 5 (1901, NAWM 169), illustrates the composer's ability to create innovative textures and melodies within traditional harmonies and ABA′ form. At the opening of this work, Rachmaninoff immediately commands our attention by elaborating a simple G-minor triad in a new and distinctive way, using a pattern of energetic, marchlike rhythms and alternating registers that continues with variation throughout the A section.

Rachmaninoff, like Tchaikovsky, cultivated a passionate, melodious idiom. Some have dismissed his music as old-fashioned; but, like other composers of his generation, he sought a way to appeal to listeners enamored of the classics by offering something new and individual yet steeped in tradition. Rather than introduce innovations in harmony, as did Strauss, Debussy, and Scriabin—which would have violated both his temperament and the demands of the audience for touring virtuosos—he focused on other elements of the Romantic tradition, creating melodies and textures that sound both fresh and familiar. As in the best popular music or long-standing traditions such as Italian opera, Rachmaninoff made his mark by using conventions in a way no one had done before.

Alexander Scriabin (1872–1915; caricatured in Figure 23.6) traveled a different path. He began by writing nocturnes, preludes, études, and mazurkas in the manner of Chopin, then gradually absorbed the chromaticism of Liszt and Wagner; the octatonic scale (alternating half and whole steps) and other exotic elements from Rimsky-Korsakov; and the juxtapositions of texture, scale, and figuration from Debussy and from fellow Russian composers. He gradually evolved a complex harmonic vocabulary all his own. Skirting conventional tonal harmony, he chose a referential chord for each work that serves as a kind of tonic and as the source of the work's melodies and harmonies. The chord typically contains one or two tritones derived from an octatonic scale (see Example 23.2a). These source chords resemble Wagner's *Tristan* chord (see Chapter 20), yet they are treated as static objects and do not produce the desire for resolution that Wagner sought to evoke; instead they suggest a transcendence of desire, which can be seen as erotic or mystic. Scriabin creates a sense of harmonic progression by transposing and altering the referential chord, enlivening the texture with vigorous figuration, until the chord returns at the end.

Scriabin's *Vers la flamme* (Toward the Flame), Op. 72 (1914; NAWM 170), a one-movement "poem" for piano, illustrates this process. The opening

Figure 23.6 Caricature of Alexander Scriabin by John Minnion.
(John Minnion/Lebrecht Music & Arts Photo Library.)

Vers la flamme

Full | Concise

Example 23.2 Scriabin. Vers la flamme

a. Octatonic scale on E–F

b. Opening

(Example 23.2b) establishes a referential sonority of two tritones, E–A♯ and G♯–D, but instead of resolving as in tonal music—inward to a third or outward to a sixth—both tritones "resolve" over the course of the movement to form the perfect fifths E–B and G♯–D♯, a harmonic embodiment of the journey toward transcendence implied by the title. The predominant figuration changes from section to section, producing an effect of static, juxtaposed blocks of sound, as in music by Musorgsky or Debussy.

Besides piano music, Scriabin wrote symphonies and other orchestral works, notably *Poem of Ecstasy* (1908) and *Prometheus* (1910). During performances of *Prometheus,* the composer asked for the concert hall to be flooded with changing colored light. His own sense perceptions caused him to link particular pitches to colors, and he aspired to a synthesis of all the arts with the aim of inducing states of mystic rapture. For Scriabin, music was a means to transcend daily existence and offer a glimpse of the divine, an otherworldly truth, an experience of ecstasy.

Tonal or Post-Tonal?

Of all the composers surveyed in this chapter, Scriabin traveled the furthest from common-practice tonal harmony, Rachmaninoff the least far. Yet both came from a similar heritage as virtuoso pianist-composers in the Russian tradition. Their differences exemplify the range of choices open to modernist composers and the variety of paths they pursued.

Spain: Manuel de Falla

French, Russian, and other composers had often used Spanish elements to create an exotic atmosphere. In the early twentieth century, Spanish composers sought to reclaim their national tradition, using authentic native materials to appeal to their own people and to gain a foothold in the international repertoire. The principal Spanish composer of the time, Manuel de Falla (1876–1946), developed a nationalism that resisted the merely exotic. He collected and arranged national folk songs, introducing a wider public to the variety in the Spanish folk tradition. His earlier works—such as the opera *La Vida breve* (Life Is Short, 1904–1913) and the ballets *El Amor brujo* (Love, the Sorcerer, 1915) and *El Sombrero de tres picos* (The Three-Cornered Hat, 1916–1919)—are imbued with the melodic and rhythmic qualities of Spanish popular music. His finest mature works are *El Retablo de maese Pedro* (Master Pedro's Puppet Show, 1919–1923), based on an episode from the great Spanish novel *Don Quixote,* and the Concerto for Harpsichord with Five Solo Instruments (1923–1926), which harks back to the Spanish Baroque. Both works combine specific national elements with the neoclassical approach that was popular after World War I. Yet for Falla the assertion of national identity was as much directed against the potentially overwhelming influence of French music as Ravel's was marked by resistance to German music.

Figure 23.7 Photo portrait of Ralph Vaughan Williams, ca. 1951, by Norman Parkinson. (Bettmann/Corbis.)

England: Ralph Vaughan Williams

The English musical renaissance begun by Elgar (see Chapter 22) took a nationalist turn in the twentieth century, when composers sought a distinctive voice for English art music after centuries of domination by foreign styles. Cecil Sharp (1859–1924), Ralph Vaughan Williams (1872–1958; see Figure 23.7), and others collected and published hundreds of folk songs, leading to the use of these melodies in compositions such as Vaughan Williams's *Norfolk Rhapsodies* (1905–1906) and *Five Variants of*

"Dives and Lazarus" (1939). Along with Gustav Holst (1874–1934), his close friend and classmate at the Royal Conservatory of Music, Vaughan Williams became a leader of a new English school.

Vaughan Williams cultivated a national style in his works, which include nine symphonies and other orchestral pieces, film scores, works for band, songs, operas, and many choral pieces. He drew inspiration not only from folk song but also from English hymnody and the music of earlier English composers such as Thomas Tallis and Henry Purcell. He also studied with Ravel and was strongly influenced by Debussy, Bach, and Handel. Vaughan Williams exemplified a trait common to several modern English composers: he wrote both art music and practical, or utilitarian, music, using elements from each tradition in the other. He gained a profound knowledge of hymnody as musical editor of the *English Hymnal* in 1904–1906, writing later that "two years of close association with some of the best (as well as some of the worst) tunes in the world was a better musical education than any amount of sonatas and fugues." Throughout his long career, he conducted local amateur singers and players, for whom he wrote a number of pieces. Such links with amateur music-making kept Vaughan Williams and other English composers from cultivating an esoteric style addressed only to educated listeners.

The national quality of Vaughan Williams's music comes from his incorporation or imitation of British folk tunes and his assimilation of the modal harmony of sixteenth-century English composers. One of his most popular works, *Fantasia on a Theme of Thomas Tallis* (1910) for double string orchestra and string quartet, is based on a Tallis psalm setting in the Phrygian mode that Vaughan Williams had revived for the *English Hymnal*. The piece introduces fragments of the tune, states it simply once, and develops motives from it in a free fantasy, using antiphonal sonorities and triads in parallel motion in a modal framework. Like his teacher Ravel, Vaughan Williams found ways to write varied music that was at the same time national and recognizably individual in style.

Figure 23.8 Cover of Leoš Janáček's Moravian Folk Songs, *illustrated by Karel Svolinsky and published in Prague in 1947.*
(British Library/Bridgeman Art Library.)

Czechoslovakia: Leoš Janáček

Spain and Britain were independent nations for whom nationalism was primarily a cultural issue. But for the peoples of Eastern Europe under the Austro-Hungarian and Russian empires, it was also an urgent political concern. Music that reflected a people's language and traditions was valuable at home as an assertion of an independent national identity and abroad as an appeal for international recognition as a nation.

The leading twentieth-century Czech composer, Leoš Janáček (1854–1928), cultivated genres of Western art music, especially opera, but sought a specifically national style. Beginning in the 1880s, he collected and edited folk music from his native region of Moravia (see Figure 23.8), studied the rhythms and inflections of peasant speech and song, and devised a highly personal idiom based on them. He asserted his independence from Austria not only in melodic style but also in his

characteristic procedures. His music relies on contrasting sonorities, harmonies, motives, and tone colors, and it proceeds primarily by repeating and juxtaposing ideas in a manner akin to Musorgsky or Debussy rather than by developing them, as in the Germanic tradition.

Janáček's operas

After winning local renown for his folk song and dance collections, Janáček gained wider prominence in his sixties, when his opera *Jenůfa*, based on a Moravian subject and premiered in Brno in 1904, was performed in Prague twelve years later and again in Vienna in 1918, the year that Czechoslovakia gained independence after the dissolution of Austria-Hungary. With new confidence from both personal and political triumphs, in his last decade Janáček produced a string of operas that dominated the Czech stage between the world wars and later became part of the international repertory, including *Kát'a Kabanová* (1921), *The Cunning Little Vixen* (1924), *The Makropulos Affair* (1925), and *From the House of the Dead* (1928). In his operas, strongly contrasting ideas are used to delineate diverse characters and situations. His instrumental works, such as the flashy orchestral *Sinfonietta* (1926) and two late string quartets (1923 and 1928), depend on similar contrasts.

Finland: Jean Sibelius

Much like his peer Janáček, Finnish composer Jean Sibelius (1865–1957) was deeply moved by the spirit of nationalism. Sibelius expressed his fervent patriotic sentiments by incorporating themes of national identity into his compositions, even after Finland achieved its independence from Russia following the Revolution of 1917. He became fascinated with the Finnish national epic, the *Kalevala*, which he mined for texts to set in his vocal works and for subjects to treat in his symphonic poems.

Sibelius established his reputation as Finland's leading composer in the 1890s with a series of symphonic poems, including *Kullervo* (in five movements with soloists and chorus), *The Swan of Tuonela*, and his most famous (and political), *Finlandia*. From 1897 to the end of his life, he was supported by the Finnish government as a national artist. He turned toward an international audience around 1900 with publication and performances of his symphonic poems and with his first two symphonies (1899 and 1901–1902) and Violin Concerto (1903–1904), followed by five more symphonies through 1924. Sibelius devised a personal style marked by modal melodies, simple rythms, insistent repetition of brief motives, pedal points, and strong contrasts of orchestral timbres and textures, all designed to create a distinctive sound and musial discourse far removed from the nineteeth-century academic tradition in which he had been trained. Sibelius's search to reconcile his status as an outsider with the classical heritage, to blend nationalism with international appeal, and to balance innovative with traditional elements reveals many of the fault lines in twentieth-century music.

The Avant-Garde

While modernist composers were devising ways to say something new within the classical tradition, the years before World War I also brought the first stirrings of a movement that directly challenged that tradition and was to grow in importance over the course of the century: the avant-garde. Originally a French military term, it described an advance group that prepared the way for the main army. The term was then adopted in the mid-nineteenth century for and by

French artists who saw themselves as a vanguard exploring new territory. In music, the term gained currency around the time of the First World War.

Although sometimes applied to anyone who departs from convention or to modernists such as Schoenberg (see Chapter 25), the term *avant-garde* is most helpful when used more narrowly for art that is iconoclastic, irreverent, antagonistic, and nihilistic—seeking to overthrow accepted aesthetics and start afresh. Rather than attempt to write music suited for the classical repertoire, avant-garde composers have challenged the very concept of deathless classics, asking their listeners to focus instead on what is happening in the present. Their movement is marked not by shared elements of style but by shared attitudes, particularly an unrelenting opposition to the status quo.

Erik Satie

One aspect of the avant-garde is exemplified by the music of the French composer Erik Satie (1866–1925), which wittily upends conventional ideas. Satie was a French nationalist in a similar vein to Debussy and Ravel, but made a more radical break with the entire classical tradition. His set of three *Gymnopédies* (1888) for piano, for example, challenged the Romantic notions of expressivity and individuality. Instead of offering variety, as expected in a set of pieces, they are all ostentatiously plain and unemotional, using the same slow tempo, the same accompanimental pattern, virtually the same melodic rhythm, and similar modal harmonies and puzzling dynamics. Satie's use of modal and unresolved chords opened new possibilities for Debussy and Ravel, who applied them to different ends but did not follow his avant-garde tendencies.

Between 1900 and 1915, Satie wrote several sets of piano pieces with surrealistic titles like *Three Pieces in the Form of a Pear* (1903, which actually includes seven pieces; see Figure 23.9) and *Automatic Descriptions* (1913). Most had running commentary and tongue-in-cheek directions to the player, such as "withdraw your hand and put it in your pocket," "that's wonderful!" or "heavy as a sow." These phrases satirized the titles and expressive directions of Debussy and other composers of descriptive and programmatic music. Moreover, by printing the commentary on the music rather than in a program, so that only the player was aware of it, Satie critiqued the idea of concert music and reclaimed the fading tradition of music for the player's own enjoyment. But the comic and critical spirit resides also in the music itself, which is spare, dry, capricious, brief, repetitive, parodistic, and witty in the highest degree. The classical masterworks are a particular target: the second of three pieces in *Embryons desséchés* (Dessicated Embryos, 1913) pokes fun at Chopin's famous funeral march—the score is marked "they all begin to cry"—and the third (NAWM 171) satirizes Wagner's leitmotives and ends with a long "obligatory cadenza" that pounds on the tonic repeatedly, a jibe at the similar passages that close several Beethoven symphonies. Clearly, Satie was not out to create masterpieces that would take their place in the great tradition; rather, he was challenging the very assumptions of that tradition.

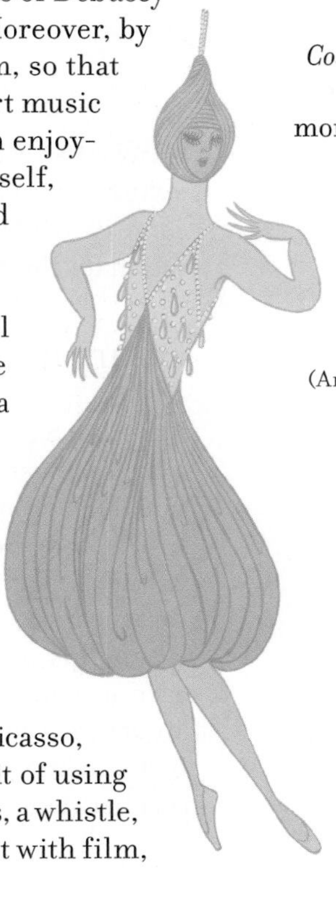

In his larger pieces, Satie sought to create music that would fix our attention on the present. His "realistic ballet" *Parade* (1916–1917), featuring a scenario by the writer Jean Cocteau, choreography by Léonide Massine, and scenery and costumes by Picasso, introduced cubism (see page 510) to the stage, In the cubist spirit of using fragments of everyday life, Satie's score incorporated jazz elements, a whistle, a siren, and a typewriter. It caused a scandal, as did his later ballet with film,

*Figure 23.9
Costume for a ballet on
Erik Satie's* Trois
morceaux en forme de
poire *(Three Pieces
in the Form of a
Pear. 1890–1903),
actually seven
pieces for piano
for four hands.*
(Archives de la Foundation
Erik Satie, Paris.)

TIMELINE Classical Modernism

Musical Events

1897
Strauss, *Don Quixote* (NAWM 158)

1897–1899
Debussy, *Nocturnes* (NAWM 167)

1901
Ravel, *Jeux d'eau*

1901
Rachmaninoff, Prelude in G Minor (NAWM 169)

1901–1904
Mahler, *Kindertotenlieder* (NAWM 165)

1905
Strauss, *Salome* (NAWM 166)

1907–1910
Mahler directs Metropolitan Opera in New York

1910
Ralph Vaughan Williams, *Fantasia on a Theme of Thomas Tallis*

1913
Futurist manifesto, *The Art of Noises*

1914
Alexander Scriabin, *Vers la flamme* (NAWM 170)

1914–1917
Ravel, *Le Tombeau de Couperin* (NAWM 168)

1915
Falla, *El amor brujo*

1916–1917
Satie, *Parade*

1925
Janáček, *The Mahropulos Affair*

1934
Rachmaninoff, *Rhapsody on a Theme of Paganini*

1900   **1950**

Historical Events

1872
Monet, *Impression: Soleil levant* (Figure VI.2)

1889
Erection of the Eiffel Tower for the Paris World's Fair

1900
Freud, *The Interpretation of Dreams*

1903
Wright brothers fly first successful airplane

1905
Einstein's first paper on the theory of relativity

1906
Cézanne, *Mont Sainte-Victoire* (Figure VI.3)

1907
Braque and Picasso paint first cubist pictures (Figure VI.4)

1908
Ford designs the Model T automobile

1914–1918
World War I

1917
Russian Revolution brings Bolsheviks to power

1929
New York stock market crash begins Great Depression

1933
Hitler comes to power in Germany

1938
Germany absorbs Austria

1939–1945
World War II

Relâche (No Show Tonight, 1924). His biting, antisentimental spirit, economical textures, and severe harmony and melody influenced the music of his younger compatriots Milhaud and Poulenc, among others, and he was a significant inspiration for the American avant-garde, notably John Cage (see Chapter 27).

Futurism

Although Satie questioned traditional assumptions about expressivity, individuality, seriousness, masterworks, and the very purpose of music, he used traditional instruments and musical pitches. The Italian futurists rejected even those. In *The Art of Noises: Futurist Manifesto* (1913; see Vignette, page 531), the futurist painter Luigi Russolo earnestly argued that musical sounds had become stale and that the modern world of machines required a new kind of music based on noise. He and his colleagues built new instruments called *intonarumori* (noisemakers), each capable of producing a particular kind of noise over a range of at least an octave and a half (see Figure 23.10). The composers wrote pieces for these instruments, alone or with traditional instruments, and presented them in concert between 1913 and 1921 in Italy, London, and Paris.

VIGNETTE The Art of Noises

Futurism began in 1909 as a literary and artistic movement in Italy celebrating the dynamism, speed, machines, and violence of the twentieth century. Luigi Russolo (1885–1947) was a futurist painter who turned his attention to music in 1913. In The Art of Noises: A Futurist Manifesto, Russolo laid out his argument for music based on noise rather than musical pitches.

The art of music at first sought and achieved purity and sweetness of sound; later, it blended diverse sounds, but always with intent to caress the ear with suave harmonics. Today, growing ever more complicated, it seeks those combinations of sounds that fall most dissonantly, strangely, and harshly upon the ear. We thus approach nearer and nearer to the *music of noise*.

This musical evolution parallels the growing multiplicity of machines, which everywhere are assisting mankind. Not only amid the clamor of great cities but even in the countryside, which until yesterday was ordinarily quiet, the machine today has created so many varieties and combinations of noise that pure musical sound—with its poverty and monotony—no longer awakens any emotion in the hearer. . . .

We must break out of this narrow circle of pure musical sounds, and conquer the infinite variety of noise-sounds.

Everyone will recognize that every musical sound carries with it an incrustation of familiar and stale sense associations, which predispose the hearer to boredom, despite all the efforts of innovating musicians. We futurists have all deeply loved the music of the great composers. Beethoven and Wagner for many years wrung our hearts. But now we are satiated with them and derive much greater pleasure from ideally combining the noises of street-cars, internal-combustion engines, automobiles, and busy crowds than from re-hearing, for example, the "Eroica" or the "Pastorale." . . .

We are convinced, therefore, that by selecting, co-ordinating, and controlling noises we shall enrich mankind with a new and unsuspected source of pleasure.

From Luigi Russolo. *The Art of Noises: A Futurist Manifesto*, translated by Stephen Somervell, in Nicolas Slominisky, *Music since 1900*, 4th ed. (New York: Scribner, 1971). pp. 1299–1301; repr. in Oliver Strunk, ed., *Source Readings in Music History*, rev. ed. by Leo Treitler (New York: Norton, 1998), vol. 7, pp. 60–62.

Figure 23.10 Luigi Russolo and his collaborator Ugo Piatti with futuristic noise instruments.
(Hulton Archive/Getty Images.)

In opposition to the constant recycling of classics in the concert halls, futurist music was impermanent, perhaps deliberately so; only one fragment of Russolo's music survives in a recording by Russolo's brother, and the instruments were destroyed during World War II. But the movement continued in various forms in Italy, France, and Russia during the 1920s and 1930s, and it anticipated or stimulated many later developments, including electronic music, microtonal composition, and the pursuit of new instrumental timbres. As different as futurist music was from Satie's, they shared a focus on the experience of listening in the present moment and an iconoclastic rejection of the music and aesthetics of the past, attributes that remained central to avant-garde music throughout the twentieth century.

POSTLUDE

The music of early twentieth-century composers in the classical tradition was remarkably diverse, and its reception has been equally varied. These composers' position between the lions of late Romanticism, discussed in Chapters 21 and 22, and the more radical composers discussed in Chapter 25 can make their music difficult to classify. Some music historians have treated Debussy as a late Romantic figure; others regard him as a seminal force in modern music. Similarly, composers like Mahler and Strauss have been grouped with the late Romantics while other writers have positioned them among the modernists. In truth, all the composers of this generation have aspects of both eras, combining nineteenth-century traits with twentieth-century sensibilities. Perhaps that is why much of their music—especially that of Mahler, Strauss, Debussy, Ravel, Vaughan Williams, and Rachmaninoff—has proven extremely popular with listeners.

Critical disputes about what is most valuable in music were especially acute in the twenteeth century, and as a result, critical esteem for these composers has changed over time, often dramatically. For example, when critics and scholars increasingly came to view tonality as old-fashioned, appreciation of Strauss and Sibelius declined, only to be revived later in the century when their innovations became better understood and when increasing numbers of living composers reclaimed the sounds and methods of tonal music. While some music by composers of this generation may sound late Romantic in spirit or technique, what makes all of it modernist is this overwhelming sense of measuring oneself against the past.

Vernacular Music in America

PRELUDE

The impact of prosperity and technology on music, and the growing importance of the United States and especially African Americans, are apparent in the varied and vibrant musical traditions outside the concert hall and opera house. These traditions are sometimes referred to as vernacular music, since they are intended to reach a broad musical public in a widely understood language, rather than appeal to a smaller number of concertgoers. Vernacular traditions assume greater significance in histories of twentieth-century music than in earlier centuries because recordings have enabled much more vernacular music to be preserved. Moreover, recordings and other mass media disseminate forms of popular music that otherwise would remain completely local. Then, too, much vernacular music of the twentieth century has achieved a permanence rivaling that of classical music: Sousa marches, African American spirituals, some popular songs, Broadway shows, film scores, band pieces, piano rags, jazz performances, and other music that will be discussed in this chapter. Some of these works became classics in their own tradition, widely played and in many cases more familiar a century later than the classical pieces of the same era. Important in their own right, some are also notable as influences on composers in the classical tradition, as we shall see in subsequent chapters. Finally, it was in the realm of vernacular music that the United States became the leading exporter of music to the world, matching in music its impact in industry and world affairs.

Vernacular Styles and Genres

In the nineteenth century, the search for a national cultural identity for the United States was complicated by the country's ethnic diversity and by the rapidly growing distinctions among classical, popular, and folk music. Among the many trends that emerged from the variety of musical traditions brought by settlers and immigrants to America, we will look at three: band music, which was strongly affected by a growing split between classical and popular music; popular song; and African American music, drawing on oral traditions but becoming a significant factor in both popular and classical music.

Band Music

The earliest American bands were attached to military units, but in the nineteenth century, local bands became common everywhere as amateur bands were formed in communities across the country. They played indoors or outdoors, seated or on parade, in concerts but also at dances, holiday celebrations, fairs, picnics, parties, ball games, political rallies, store openings, sales events, weddings, funerals, and other public and private gatherings. The Civil War was called the most musical war in history because almost every regiment on both sides had its own band, which entertained the troops, led marches, performed in parades, and played during battles to hearten the soldiers. After the war, community bands continued to proliferate, becoming such a fixture of American life that by the 1880s there were some ten thousand bands that performed at every opportunity.

John Philip Sousa

The period between the Civil War and World War I was the heyday of professional bands. The most successful bandmaster was John Philip Sousa (1854–1932), whose years conducting the United States Marine Band (1880–1892) raised it to national prominence through tours and savvy promotion. In 1892, he organized his own band, shown in Figure 24.1, which made annual tours of the United States, several European tours, and a world tour.

Repertory

Nineteenth-century band repertory consisted of marches; quicksteps (fast marches); dances, including two-steps, waltzes, polkas, galops, and schottisches; arrangements of opera arias and songs, including medleys; transcriptions of pieces by classical composers from Rossini to Wagner; and virtuosic display pieces often featuring famous soloists. Sousa's programming was especially astute. After every selesction listed on the program, the band played an encore, usually a light, quick piece guaranteed to please. Yet Sousa also performed the European classics from Bach to Richard Strauss, and he, more than anyone else, introduced Wagner's music to Americans. Sousa himself composed for band, and his music varies from programmatic fantasias to more than a hundred marches, including his most famous march, *The Stars and Stripes Forever* (1897; NAWM 163). Not limited to a single genre or medium, Sousa also

Full 🔊

Figure 24.1 John Philip Sousa with the Sousa Band at a fashionable outdoor concert.
(Brown Brothers, Sterling, PA.)

wrote more than a dozen operettas and some seventy songs, but his ever-popular marches earned him the nickname "the March King."

Brass bands were one of the main training grounds for African American musicians, along with black churches and dance orchestras. During the late nineteenth and early twentieth centuries, black bands occupied an important place in both black and white social life in many big cities. These bands performed from notation and did relatively little improvising, but they played with a swinging and syncopated style that distinguished them from white bands.

Music of African Americans

Africans were the one immigrant group that was brought to the United States unwillingly. Imported as slaves under inhuman conditions, they came from many ethnicities, each having different languages and customs. Mixed together on plantations or as domestic servants, they would have had a difficult time preserving their languages and cultures even if their owners had not actively worked to prevent it. But elements of their music were easier to preserve because they had been widely shared among African societies and because white slave owners did not consider singing a threat. Indeed, work songs were actively encouraged as a way to keep up the slaves' productivity and spirits.

Among the many traits of African American music that have been traced back to Africa are:

- alternating short phrases between leader and group, called *call and response*
- improvisation based on a simple formula that allows wide-ranging variation
- syncopation
- repetition of short rhythmic or melodic patterns
- multiple layers of rhythm, with beats in some instruments (or hand clapping or foot stomping) and offbeats in others
- bending pitches or sliding from one pitch to another
- moans, shouts, and other vocalizations
- instruments like the banjo, based on a west African stringed instrument

We will see these and other traits in ragtime, blues, jazz, and other twentieth-century genres based on African American traditions.

The African American form of music with the greatest impact in the nineteenth century was the spiritual, a religious song of southern slaves, passed down through oral tradition. The texts were usually based on images or stories from the Bible, but they often carried hidden meanings of the slaves' yearning for freedom or messages to escape. The first to appear in print was *Go Down, Moses,* which uses the story of Israel's deliverance from Egypt as a symbol for the liberation of the slaves. The song was published in 1861, during the first year of the Civil War, after a missionary heard it sung by refugee slaves.

The first publications of spirituals in the late nineteenth century tried to document the songs as former slaves sang them, though the editors admitted that they could not notate the bent pitches and other aspects of performance. But soon dozens of spirituals were arranged as songs with piano accompaniment that anyone could play or in four-part harmony for choirs. The Fisk Jubilee Singers, depicted in Figure 24.2, popularized spirituals in the 1870s through polished performances in concert tours on both sides of the Atlantic. By the end of the nineteenth century, spirituals served simultaneously as folk music for those who had learned them from oral tradition, as popular songs for those who bought them as sheet music or heard them in popular venues, and as a source of melodic material for classical composers.

Figure 24.2 *The original Fisk Jubilee Singers, photographed in 1873 in London during their European tour. Founded at Fisk University in Nashville, Tennessee, the group consisted of black student musicians who performed spirituals and other songs in four-part harmony.*
(Schomberg Center, The New York Public Library, Astor, Lenox, and Tilden Foundations.)

Ragtime

Among the dances played by both brass and concert bands were pieces in ragtime, a style popular from the 1890s through the 1910s that featured syncopated (or "ragged") rhythm against a regular, marchlike bass. This syncopation apparently derived from the patting (or pattin') juba of American blacks, a survival of African drumming and hand clapping. The emphasis on offbeats in one rhythmic layer against steady beats in another reflects the complex cross-rhythms common in African music.

The leading ragtime composer was Scott Joplin (1868–1917; Figure 24.3). Son of a former slave, he studied music in his hometown of Texarkana, Texas, and worked in Sedalia and St. Louis, Missouri, before moving to New York in 1907. His most ambitious work was the opera *Treemonisha,* completed in 1910 though not staged until 1972. But he was best known for his piano rags, especially *Maple Leaf Rag* (1899; NAWM 164). Like most rags, it is in $\frac{2}{4}$ meter and follows the form of a march, with a series of sixteen-measure strains, each repeated. The second strain, excerpted in Example 24.1, shows several rhythmic features typical of ragtime. The left hand keeps up a steady pulse in eighth notes, alternating between doubled bass notes and chords, while the right-hand figures syncopate both within and across the beat. The notes in octaves, which receive extra stress, occur every three sixteenth notes, momentarily creating the impression of $\frac{3}{16}$ meter in the right hand against $\frac{2}{4}$ in the left. Essentially the same rhythmic idea appears in each two-measure unit. Such repetition of a short rhythmic pattern, like syncopation and multiple rhythmic layers, is a characteristic of African-American music that can be traced back to Africa. So while the form, left-hand pattern, harmony, and chromatic motion all ultimately derive from European sources, the rhythmic elements have African roots, and the resulting mixture is quintessentially African American.

Figure 24.3 *Scott Joplin in a photograph printed on the cover of his rag The Cascades (1904).*
(John Edward Hasse.)

Example 24.1 Scott Joplin, Maple Leaf Rag

Popular Song and American Musical Theater

While bands embraced a wide repertory from marches to classics, the world of song also reflected the diverging tastes and needs of the American public. During the first half of the nineteenth century, Schubert's Lieder as well as parlor songs by American composers such as Stephen Foster (see Chapter 19) served similar purposes, intended primarily for home music-making and occasional performance in concerts.

Later in the century, we find a widening gulf between art song and popular song, a split that modernism intensified. While Foster's *Jeanie* had emulated Schubert's strophic, more folklike Lieder, combined with elements from British and American ballad traditions, some art songs, such as those of Fauré and Wolf, were meant to engage listeners on a sophisticated plane, and required high professional standards of both pianist and singer. Composers of popular song sought instead to entertain their audiences, accommodate amateur performers, and sell as many copies of sheet music as possible. For this type of song, immediate appeal and a catchy quality that made for easy recollection were the most important attributes.

Topics for popular songs included love, heartbreak, birth, death, racial and ethnic satire, new inventions like the bicycle and telephone, sentimental thoughts of mother and the old family home, and America's favorite pastime, baseball. This large variety of songs was pressed into service for every possible cause: abolition, the Civil War, temperance (the campaign against drunkenness), labor organizing, political campaigns, and evangelism, as with gospel songs such as *In the Sweet Bye and Bye.*

Popular art depends on the interplay of convention and novelty, and both are evident in the best popular songs. The standard form remained verse and refrain, with one or more verses followed by a thirty-two measure refrain in a pattern similar to AABA. Often the refrain was scored in parts for chorus (or four solo singers), so that *chorus* came to be used as a term for refrain. The focus was increasingly on the chorus, where songwriters placed their catchiest rhythms and melodic ideas.

The chorus of Charles K. Harris's *After the Ball* (1892), shown in Example 24.2 begins with a catchy phrase, sometimes called a hook, which is simple yet intriguing enough to grab the listener's attention. The phrase avoids starting or ending on the tonic note and has its high point early on an unstressed beat and syllable, which conveys the impression of being off balance, especially as it is repeated with variations many times in succession. Together with the waltz rhythm, which suits the words, these features suggest the intoxication of dancing at a ball.

Harris's song was enormously popular, selling millions of copies and—since he had published it himself—making him rich. It typifies the products of Tin Pan Alley, the jocular name for a district on West 28th Street in New York City where,

Art song versus popular song

Subjects

Conventions

Tin Pan Alley

Example 24.2 Charles K. Harris, After the Ball

Af – ter the ball is o – ver, af – ter the break of morn.

Af – ter the dan – cers' leav – ing: af – ter the stars are gone;

Man – y a heart is ach – ing, if you could read them all:

Man – y the hopes that have van – ished af – ter the ball.

beginning in the 1880s, numerous publishers specializing in popular songs were located. A songwriter's typical strategy for promoting the song was to pay a singer to introduce the song in a show; when it became a hit with audiences, people went out in droves to buy a copy of the sheet music. The link between success on stage and sales of printed music remained important even in the twentieth century.

The period between the two world wars, and especially the 1920s, was a rich time for American popular music. Music for stage shows of all kinds enjoyed great popularity: vaudeville troupes (including singers and dancers) toured the Continent, and operettas, variety shows, and musicals attracted large audiences. Popular songs from Tin Pan Alley also proliferated. The period roughly from 1920 to 1955—before the advent of rock and roll and the demise of the sheet-music industry—is known as the "golden age" of Tin Pan Alley.

In the 1920s, as in the previous two decades, popular song and music for theater were inextricably linked. In large part, it was the attractiveness of the songs that drove the popularity of a musical and its composer. Many of the best-known songs, made familiar in hit shows, were then sold as sheet music, often with a picture of the performer who introduced the song on the cover. But changes in the popular-song industry began to occur as publishers and songwriters increasingly counted on recordings to spread their tunes (see Innovations, pages 540–541). And with the arrival of sound technology for films in the late 1920s, the Hollywood musical was born, creating another important venue for songwriters. The most successful songwriters of this period—including Irving Berlin (1888–1989), Jerome Kern (1885–1945), and George Gershwin (1898–1937)—were equally at home writing music for Tin Pan Alley, musical theater, and Hollywood musicals.

Irving Berlin

Irving Berlin's lengthy career and prodigious output position him as one of America's most prolific and best-loved popular songwriters. Widely known for his sentimental and patriotic tunes that seem to capture the American spirit, like *God Bless America* and *White Christmas*, Berlin mastered all current popular song genres, often writing the lyrics himself, and was involved in every aspect of the music business. It was said that America could not fight a war or celebrate a holiday without a song from this Russian-born son of a Jewish cantor.

Musical theater

A significant new genre, the musical comedy, or musical, featured songs and dance numbers in styles drawn from popular music in the context of a spoken play with a comic or romantic plot. George M. Cohan inaugurated a distinctive style of American musical with his *Little Johnny Jones* (1904), which brought together American subject matter and the vernacular sounds of vaudeville and Tin Pan Alley with the romantic plots and European styles of comic opera and operetta. That show included two of the most famous and enduring popular songs of the era, *Give My Regards to Broadway* and *The Yankee Doodle Boy* (whose chorus begins "I'm a Yankee Doodle Dandy"). From these roots soon grew the musicals of Jerome Kern, Irving Berlin, George Gershwin, Rodgers and

Hammerstein, Stephen Sondheim, and Andrew Lloyd Webber, among many others.

Like all forms of musical theater, musicals were complex collaborations, with different artists responsible for the music, lyrics (the words to the songs), book (the spoken words of the play), choreography, staging, lights, sets, costumes, and often orchestration. Some musicals were primarily vehicles for star entertainers, featuring new popular songs that were framed by a loose plot, a structure reminiscent of the singer-centered and aria-focused Italian opera of the Baroque stage. Others were more integrated shows in which the musical numbers were closely related to a story that was plot-driven rather than focused on the performers. Like reform opera of the late eighteenth century (see Chapter 15), such musicals were valued for their dramatic impact in addition to their appeal as entertaining spectacle.

Figure 24.4 Sheet-music cover of the hit song Ol' Man River *from Jerome Kern's musical* Show Boat *(1927).*
(Lebrecht Music & Arts Photo Library.)

Jerome Kern's masterpiece *Show Boat* (1927), with book and lyrics by Oscar Hammerstein II, best exemplifies this new, integrated approach. *Show Boat* brings together a number of traditions (opera, operetta, musical comedy, revues, vaudeville) and musical styles (ragtime, spirituals, sentimental ballads, marches), but the multiple styles all serve dramatic ends. The score is operatic in scope, with interwoven referential themes and motives, much like the operas of Richard Wagner (whose music dramas Kern greatly admired). Based on a novel by Edna Ferber, *Show Boat* dealt with serious social issues, such as racism and miscegenation, and captured recent historic events, such as the 1893 World's Columbian Exposition in Chicago. It was a tremendous success, toured the country after its Broadway run, enjoyed numerous revivals, and sold sheet-music arrangements of its hit songs, including *Ol' Man River,* in huge numbers (see Figure 24.4).

Integrated musicals

George Gershwin, seen in Figure 24.5, was both a composer of classical music (see Chapter 26) and a writer of popular songs and musicals. Most of

George Gershwin

Figure 24.5 George Gershwin at the piano in 1937, during rehearsals for the film Shall We Dance. *His brother, lyricist Ira Gershwin, is to his left. Seated, to his right, are the actors and dance team Fred Astaire and Ginger Rogers.*
(Bettmann/Corbis.)

Innovations Recorded Sound and Its Impact

The advent of recording technology had the most significant impact on musical culture of any innovation since the printing press. It completely revolutionized the way we experience and share music as listeners, performers, or composers. When Thomas Edison made the first sound recording in his laboratory in Menlo Park, New Jersey, in 1877, using his tinfoil cylinder phonograph shown in Figure 24.6, he intended his new device as a dictation machine for offices. He had no idea that his invention would catapult some musicians to fame and fortune, deliver their product to huge audiences, and spawn a multibillion-dollar industry.

Early recordings featured famous artists, such as the great Italian tenor Enrico Caruso (1873–1921), who cut his first disc in 1902. Because he became one of the recording industry's earliest superstars, it has been said that "Caruso made the phonograph and it made him." His recordings also preserved his performances beyond the grave. The new technology allowed performers to achieve for the first time the kind of immortality previously available only to composers.

Edison's phonograph recorded sound by a mechanical process. Mechanical recording was well suited for voices, but the limited range of frequencies that it could reproduce made orchestra music sound tinny. For years, the only symphony available was Beethoven's Fifth, recorded in 1913 by the Berlin Philharmonic for His Master's Voice (Figure 24.7). Because it was such a long piece, the company had to issue it on eight discs gathered into an "album," which became the standard format for longer works. In the 1920s, new methods of recording and reproduction using electricity—including the electric microphone—allowed a great increase in frequency range, dynamic variation, and fidelity, making the medium still more attractive to musicians and music lovers.

Figure 24.6 The design of Thomas Edison's first "talking machine," a cylinder phonograph built in 1877. To record, a person spoke into the mouthpiece while cranking the handle.
(Bridgeman Art Library.)

his best-known songs feature lyrics by his brother, Ira Gershwin. Like Irving Berlin, Gershwin got his start writing for the stage, but moved increasingly toward integrated musicals throughout the 1920s, even venturing into social satire with a few of his shows. *Strike Up the Band* (1927) satirized war and big business and *Of Thee I Sing* (1931), a spoof of the American presidential election process, was the first musical to win the Pulitzer Prize for drama. Gershwin's musicals catapulted several new performers to fame; *Lady, Be Good!* (1924) featured the singing and dancing brother-and-sister team of Fred and Adele Astaire, while *Girl Crazy* (1930) made stars of Ethel Merman and Ginger Rogers.

I Got Rhythm

Full 🔊 Concise 🔊

In *Girl Crazy*, Ethel Merman sang the song *I Got Rhythm* (NAWM 181), which became an instant hit. Like most Tin Pan Alley and Broadway songs of the 1920s

Figure 24.7 The "Trademark Model" of the phonograph by His Master's Voice, available beginning in 1898. The firm's name and the dog's pose implied that the device reproduced sound so faithfully that a dog would recognize a recording of its owner's voice.
(Bettmann/Corbis.)

Encouraged by competition, companies continued to develop improvements. In 1948, Columbia Records introduced the long-playing record, or LP, which rotated at 33 1/3 revolutions per minute instead of 78, used smaller grooves, and thus allowed twenty-three minutes of music per side instead of four. Music lovers bought the LPs by the millions and got rid of their old 78s. High-fidelity and stereophonic records were introduced in the 1950s, which also saw the debut of an entirely new recording technology: magnetic tape. Philips introduced cassette tapes in 1963, and by the 1970s tape sales were rivaling those of records, especially among consumers who valued portability more than faithful sound reproduction. Then, in 1983, Philips and Sony unveiled the compact disc, or CD, which stored recorded sound in digital code etched

onto a 4-inch plastic disc and read by a laser. Even as listeners were replacing all their LPs with CDs, new technologies were being developed that now make it possible to download music from the Internet onto a personal computer or portable device.

Recordings irrevocably altered the way people listen to music. No longer did they have to get themselves to a concert hall or gather around a bandstand. They could now sit in their homes and order up a favorite singer or an entire orchestra at their convenience. The visual element of music-making suddenly disappeared; listeners heard performers without seeing them, and musicians played in recording studios for invisible audiences. Listening to recordings often replaced amateur music-making at home, with the paradoxical effect that people devoted less time and effort to engaging actively with music as participants. For many people, listening to music became no longer a communal activity but a largely solitary pursuit. People increasingly used recorded music as a background to other activities, rather than listening with focused concentration.

Along with performers and listeners, composers, too, have been influenced by the new technologies, being able to avail themselves of musical styles and ideas outside of their ordinary experience. Music from Africa, India, Asia, and elsewhere became available via recording without the hardships or expense of travel, as did the entire history of Western music, from the singing of plainchant by monks in a faraway monastery to the most recent pop tune. Furthermore, composers since the 1940s have used recorded sounds to make new music, incorporating an unprecedented variety of sounds.

and 1930s, it has only one verse, shifting the main interest to the chorus, which is in the typical AABA form. Example 24.3 shows the vocal melody of the opening A section. Like Harris's *After the Ball* (Example 24.2), it starts with a catchy phrase, marked by a striking rhythm and pleasing melodic contour; but it is

Example 24.3 Gershwin, I Got Rhythm

much more syncopated, drawing on the rhythms of ragtime and producing interesting cross-accents against the underlying duple meter. Both the style and the energy of *I Got Rhythm* attracted jazz musicians, who used the song as a vehicle for jazz improvisation. The chorus's harmonic progression (in jazz terminology, its *changes*) was adopted for so many new jazz tunes that this progression itself came to be known simply as "rhythm changes" (see page 550 and NAWM 184 and 197)

(see page 550 and NAWM 184 and 197)

Oklahoma!

Rodgers and Hammerstein produced some of Broadway's best-loved shows, including *Oklahoma!* (1943), *Carousel* (1945), *South Pacific* (1949), *The King and I* (1951), and *The Sound of Music* (1959). Their first collaboration, *Oklahoma!* not only enjoyed a record-breaking run of over 2,000 performances but also marked a pivotal moment in the development of the integrated musical. Set in the Oklahoma Territory around 1900, the story is richly textured, filled with both dramatic and comedic subplots. The characters, seen in Figure 24.8 as portrayed by the original cast, are developed not only through dialogue but also through song. Dance, choreographed by famed dancer Agnes de Mille, also played a crucial dramatic role. The story's emphasis on American folk history and the simple pleasures of rural life appealed greatly to Americans during wartime and the early postwar years.

Leonard Bernstein

Leonard Bernstein (1918–1990; Figure 24.9) was a major presence both on Broadway and in classical music. Initially known as a classical composer, he became an overnight celebrity in 1944 after brilliantly conducting the New York Philharmonic as a last-minute replacement. That same year, his Broadway musical *On the Town* opened for a run of 463 performances. In addition to his career as a conductor and composer of symphonies and vocal music, Bernstein enjoyed enormous success with his musical *West Side Story* (1957), with lyrics by Stephen Sondheim (b. 1930) and book by Arthur Laurents. Set in a gang-ridden New York City of the 1950s, *West Side Story* retells Shakespeare's *Romeo and Juliet*, substituting rival gangs from different ethnic groups for the warring Renaissance families of the original. The setting provided Bernstein with rich opportunities for embracing a variety of musical styles, including Afro-Caribbean dance styles, jazz, and soaring melodies in Tin Pan Alley AABA formulas. Bernstein called the work "an out-and-out plea for racial tolerance."

The music's principal function throughout the show is to suggest the emotional states of the gangs' members, using styles and gestures drawn from jazz, Latin music, and modernist classical music. In "Cool" (NAWM 198), the Jets' leader, Riff, attempts to calm his group before the upcoming fight with their rival gang, the Puerto-Rican Sharks, urging his members away from the disjointed, angular bebop style of the introduction toward the cool-jazz sounds of his song, which advises them to keep their cool. Riff's song is followed by a dance for the Jets, for which Bernstein wrote a fugue on a subject full of half-steps and large leaps, with entrances and answers at minor-third intervals rather than at fifths and fourths. He thereby avoided the normal tonal associations of a fugue while at the same time cultivating the mounting tension characteristic of fugal counterpoint as the voices pile up.

Figure 24.8 A publicity photo of the original cast of Rodgers and Hammerstein's Broadway musical Oklahoma! *(1943).* (Bettmann/Corbis.)

Figure 24.9 Leonard Bernstein conducting, 1975.
(Lebrecht Music & Arts Photo Library.)

The Birth of Film Music

In the same way that recordings and radio fostered the explosive growth of popular song, new technologies transformed film music. In the late 1920s, methods were invented to synchronize recorded sound with film, opening up new possibilities for the use of music as part of a film, not merely as live accompaniment to it. The first "talking picture" (so called because it featured recorded dialogue) was *The Jazz Singer* (1927), starring Al Jolson and including scenes of Jolson singing and other scenes in which music was used to accompany the action, as in earlier silent films. These two types of scene exemplify the two categories of music in film that have continued to the present:

Sound in film

1. music that is heard or performed by the characters themselves, known as *diegetic music* or *source music*
2. background music that conveys to the viewer a mood or other aspects of a scene or character, known as *nondiegetic music* or *underscoring*

Beginning in 1929, Hollywood studios produced numerous musicals composed for film. During the 1930s, considered the "golden age" of the Hollywood musical, many of Broadway's best-known composers wrote music for movie musicals, including George Gershwin (*Delicious* and *Shall We Dance?*), Irving Berlin (*Top Hat*), Jerome Kern (*Swing Time*), and Cole Porter (*Born to Dance*). The spectacular choreography of Busby Berkeley enlivened *Gold Diggers of 1933* and many other films, and the singing and dancing of Bing Crosby, Fred Astaire, and Ginger Rogers in many film musicals made them international stars. Movie musicals were enormously popular; they offered escape from the Great Depression, they featured extraordinary talent, and ticket prices were inexpensive compared to Broadway shows.

Movie musicals

Hollywood studios also fostered the rise of film scores that were fully integrated into the dramatic action, like the music for an opera—"opera without singing," in the memorable phrase of composer Erich Wolfgang Korngold. Many of the composers working in Hollywood were European immigrants, and they applied the language of Wagner and his successors to music for film. Max

Steiner (1888–1971), an immigrant from Vienna who had worked on Broadway for fifteen years as an arranger, orchestrator, and composer, established the model for the Hollywood film score with his music for *King Kong* (1933). The movie, whose poster is shown in Figure 24.10, centered on a giant gorilla discovered in Africa and brought to New York, where it threatens the city. Steiner's score is organized around leitmotives for characters and ideas, as in a Wagner opera, and coordinates the music with actions on screen, often marking particular movements with musical effects. The music conveys mood, character, and place through styles with strong associations, from primitivism for the African setting to orchestral Romanticism for dramatic moments, and it uses modernist techniques when appropriate, such as intense dissonance for fright and other extreme emotions. All of these traits became characteristic of film scoring. Steiner continued writing film scores through the 1960s, including *Gone with the Wind* (1939) and *Casablanca* (1943).

The Jazz Age

Musicals and Tin Pan Alley songs continued traditions that had been imported from Europe or arose among Americans of European descent. But African American music and musicians played an increasingly influential role in American musical life, and in the 1920s two related traditions of African American origin gained wide currency: blues and jazz. Indeed, the 1920s became known as "the Jazz Age," and jazz became the emblematic music for that period when a new generation was cultivating a spirit of social liberation.

Figure 24.10 Poster for the original film King Kong *(1933), whose score by Max Steiner established a high standard for Hollywood film music.*
(Swim Ink 2, LLC/Corbis.)

Blues

One of the most influential musical genres to come out of early twentieth-century America was the blues. The origin of the blues is obscure, likely stemming from a combination of rural work songs and other African American oral traditions. The lyrics typically speak of disappointment, mistreatment, or other troubles that produce the state of mind known since the early nineteenth century as "the blues." Yet the words also convey defiance and a will to survive abandonment by a faithless lover, a lost job, oppression, or disaster. Often, touches of humor suggest the narrow separation between sorrow and laughter, tragedy and comedy. The music reflects the feelings implied by the words through melodic contours, freely syncopated rhythms, and distinctive vocal or instrumental effects (such as a slide, rasp, or growl) that evoke the sound of a person expressing pain, sorrow, or frustration. Blues often feature flatted or bent (slightly lowered or sliding) notes, sometimes called *blue notes,* on the third, fifth, and seventh scale degrees, which add to the emotional intensity. Besides expressing feeling, the blues allows performers to display their artistry in a musical parallel to the defiance implied in the lyrics. Ultimately, the blues are not about *having* the blues, but about *conquering* them through a kind of catharsis embodied in the music.

The classic blues singers joined aspects of oral tradition with elements of popular song, thanks in part to W. C. Handy (1873–1958), known as the "Father of the Blues." Handy did not invent the blues, but, as a publisher, he introduced blues songs in sheet-music form as early as 1912, thus taking advantage of both the genre's new popularity and the booming sheet-music industry. With his

W. C. Handy

Example 24.4 Bessie Smith, Back Water Blues

1. When it rains____ five days and the skies____ turn dark____ as night,____ when it rains____

Basic progression: I   IV   I   I

____ five days____ and the skies____ turn dark____ as night,____ then

IV   IV   I   I

trou-ble's tak-in' place in the low-lands____ at night. 2. I woke up____

V   IV   I   I

publications, Handy solidified what we now think of as standard twelve-bar blues form. In this form, illustrated by Bessie Smith's *Back Water Blues* (1927, NAWM 182) in Example 24.4, each poetic stanza has three lines; the second line typically restates the first, and the third completes the thought. Each line of text is sung to four measures of music over a set harmonic pattern, in which the first four-measure phrase remains on the tonic chord; the second phrase begins on the subdominant and ends on the tonic; and the third phrase starts on the dominant and moves back to the tonic, as illustrated in Figure 24.11.

Twelve-bar blues

Measure:	1	2	3	4	5	6	7	8	9	10	11	12
Harmony:	I	I(IV)	I	I	IV	IV	I	I	V	V(IV)	I	I
Poetic structure:	A				A				B			

Figure 24.11 Twelve-bar blues form.

After a brief piano introduction, each of the seven stanzas of *Back Water Blues* follows the same form and general melodic outline. The form may be simple, but in Smith's recorded performance, the musical possibilities seem infinite. Known in the 1920s as "Empress of the Blues" (see Figure 24.11), she enlivens each stanza with unique timbres, phrasing, and melodic sensibility.

Figure 24.12 Bessie Smith (1894–1937), "Empress of the Blues," in the mid-1920s, when she was the most successful and prominent African American musician of the decade.

(Lebrecht Music & Arts Photo Library.)

Jazz

Jazz, another type of music from African American roots, evolved into a diverse genre encompassing many styles and social functions but seems to have begun as a mixture of ragtime and dance music with elements of the blues. Jazz was already established and growing in popularity during the late 1910s. The essence of 1920s jazz was syncopated rhythm combined with novel vocal and instrumental sounds and an unbridled spirit that seemed to mock earlier social and musical properties. Improvisation was an important element of jazz, but often melodies in the style of an improvisation were worked out in rehearsals, played from memory, or written down and played from notation. Jazz was very much a player's art, so the rise of the recording industry and of radio played a key role in fostering its growth and dissemination.

Figure 24.13 King Oliver's Creole Jazz Band in a 1923 publicity photo. King Oliver plays cornet in the center back; Louis Armstrong (kneeling), the slide trumpet; Lillian Hardin (later Armstrong's wife), piano.
(Courtesy of the Hogan Jazz Archives, Tulane University.)

Full 🔊

New Orleans jazz

King Oliver and Louis Armstrong

Full 🔊   Concise 🔊

Jazz differed from ragtime particularly in the way it was performed. Instead of playing the music "straight," observing the rhythms and textures of a fully notated piece, players extemporized arrangements that distinguished one performer or performance from another. A 1938 recording of early jazz pianist, composer, and New Orleans native Jelly Roll Morton (1890–1941) playing Joplin's *Maple Leaf Rag* (NAWM 164b) demonstrates the differences: the anticipations of beats; the swinging, uneven rendering of successions of equal note values so that notes on the beat are longer than those on offbeats; the many added grace notes; the enriched harmony; and the weaving of ragtime's brief motivic units into a more continuous line.

The leading style of jazz in the period just after World War I is now known as *New Orleans jazz*. This style, named after the city where it originated, centers on group variation of a given tune, either improvised or in the same spontaneous style as improvisation. The result is a counterpoint of melodic lines, alternating with solos during which the rest of the ensemble provides a rhythmic and harmonic background. New Orleans jazz incorporates the African idiom of call and response, as well as the ecstatic outpourings of the African American gospel tradition. The development of the style in New Orleans was enhanced by the healthy rivalry between musically literate Creoles and musically untutored African Americans, who possessed great improvisational skill. Leading musicians, including cornettist Joe "King" Oliver (1885–1938), trumpeter Louis Armstrong (1901–1971), and pianist Jelly Roll Morton, developed the style playing in clubs in Storyville, the city's red-light district. In the late 1910s, many New Orleans jazz performers left the city when professional opportunities elsewhere in the country beckoned, spreading the style to other regions.

Louis Armstrong initially played in King Oliver's Creole Jazz Band (shown in Figure 24.13) but soon assembled his own group, calling it the Hot Five or Hot Seven, depending on the number of musicians. The recordings of both Oliver's and Armstrong's bands embody the classic New Orleans style. Armstrong's recording of Oliver's tune *West End Blues* (NAWM 183), made with the Hot Five in Chicago in 1928, exemplifies the conventions of that style. The small ensemble is divided into two groups: the "front line" of melodic instruments, including trumpet, clarinet, and trombone—and the rhythm section that keeps the beat and fills in the background—comprising drums, piano, and banjo. New Orleans jazz typically takes twelve-bar blues, a sixteen-measure strain from ragtime, or a thirty-two-bar popular song form (usually AABA) as a starting point. A tune is presented at the beginning over a particular harmonic progression; then that same progression repeats several times, while various soloists or combinations of instruments play over it. Each such repetition is called a *chorus* (not to be confused with the chorus in a song with verse and chorus). Typically, each chorus features different instruments and some new musical ideas, producing a kind of theme-and-variation form (see In Performance, pages 548–549).

Although Armstrong's feats as a soloist inspired virtuosity in other jazz musicians, the main function of jazz was to accompany dancing. A fashion for larger bands began in the 1920s, propelled partly by the availability of larger performance spaces for jazz, including supper clubs, ballrooms, auditoriums, and theaters. African American bandleaders such as Armstrong, Fletcher Henderson, Duke Ellington (see page 549), and Count Basie, as well as white musicians—Paul Whiteman and Benny Goodman, for example—organized big bands. By 1930, the typical dance band was divided into three sections: brass, reeds, and a rhythm section consisting of piano, drums, guitar (replacing the banjo), and double bass (see Figure 24.14). These sections interacted as units and alternated with soloists, providing a great variety of sounds. Although solos might still be improvised, the piece was written down by an arranger, who was sometimes the leader (as in the case of Ellington) but more often a member of the band or a skilled orchestrator. Successful arrangers captured in notation the spontaneous spirit of improvised playing while making possible a wider variety of planned effects. With the creation of fully or largely notated jazz

Big bands

Arrangers and composers

Figure 24.14 Duke Ellington's big band in 1943, with the composer/ arranger/band leader at the piano. (Bettmann/Corbis.)

In Performance Jazz Improvisation

A crucial element of the musical language of jazz is improvisation over a given melody or set of chord "changes." This technique is illustrated in NAWM 183b, which presents a transcription of a recorded performance in 1928 by Louis Armstrong and His Hot Five in which the group varies an original tune by King Oliver. As the title suggests, *West End Blues* is built on a twelve-bar blues form. The published sheet music (NAWM 183a) adapts the blues formula to Tin Pan Alley verse-refrain form. The blues progression (I–IV–I–V7–I) appears once in its entirety in the verse, shown in Example 24.5, and twice more in the refrain. But the recorded performance dispenses with the piano introduction, the words, and their verse-refrain structure, and instead follows the conventions of jazz, presenting a series of improvised instrumental variations, or choruses (in this case, five), of the twelve-bar blues progression, in which members of the group take turns playing solos that are either spontaneously improvised or performed in the style of improvisation.

After a blazing trumpet solo by Armstrong that replaces the piano introduction of the original piece, the entire ensemble plays the first chorus together, with Armstrong taking the lead. He varies the published melody, as shown in Example 24.5 (which, unlike the NAWM score, is transposed to concert pitch), progressing from a fairly straight performance to increasingly fanciful acrobatics as he embellishes the tune both rhythmically, with triplet eighth and sixteenth notes, and melodically, with neighboring and chromatic passing tones. For example, in measure 7, he approaches every note of the E♭ triad from its upper neighbor. In the next measure, he uses six tones from the E♭ scale, omitting the A♭ until the beginning of measure 9, where the dominant harmony is introduced (A♭ being the seventh of the dominant chord). However, over the rest of the ensemble's dominant-seventh harmony (measures 9–10), Armstrong continues using the notes of the I chord, now inflecting them with chromatic passing tones. When the blues progression returns to the tonic chord at measure 11, he introduces a fanfare-like arpeggiation of F-minor7 (a passing ii chord) in the military-style marching-band tradition that Armstrong had heard in his native New Orleans.

In the second chorus, the trombonist plays off the first half of the published refrain and freely improvises over the rest. The third chorus features the clarinet alternating in call and response with Armstrong, who puts down his trumpet and sings in the novel vocal style that he popularized, scat—that is, singing nonsense syllables to an improvised melody, making his voice sound like an instrument. The pianist takes the solo in the fourth chorus, alternating between elaborate figurations in the right hand and syncopated chordal decorations of the melody. The entire ensemble returns for the fifth and final chorus, with Armstrong once again assuming the lead.

pieces, jazz composers who made their own arrangements came increasingly to resemble their counterparts in the classical music world. They also borrowed sounds from modern classical music, especially extended chords (such as ninth, eleventh, and thirteenth chords and added sixth chords) and the chromatic harmonies of their classical contemporaries and predecessors.

Much of the big-band repertory comprised popular songs in which the band both accompanied a singer and elaborated on the song through clever, harmonically adventurous arrangements that highlighted one or another of the band's sections. The combination of stylish, well-executed arrangements with

Swing

hard-driving jazz rhythms produced a music that became known as *swing.* Swing was an immediate hit with the American public, igniting a dance craze across the country. The number of swing bands exploded during the 1930s, boosted by new white bands entering the jazz world, especially those led by Tommy Dorsey and Glenn Miller.

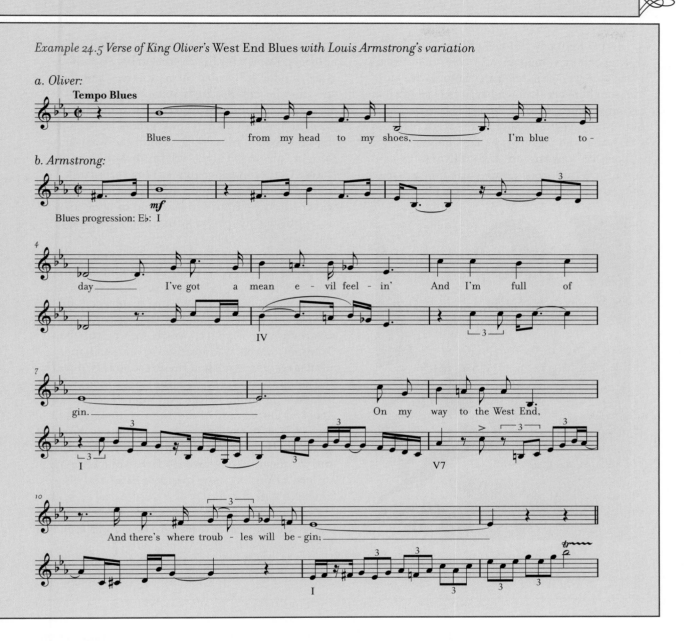

Example 24.5 Verse of King Oliver's West End Blues *with Louis Armstrong's variation*

Duke Ellington

One of the leading composers of the Jazz Age and after, and one of the most influential American composers ever, was Duke Ellington (see Biography, page 550). Ellington developed his individual style and began to garner national attention from 1927 to 1931, when his group was house band at the Cotton Club in Harlem, the vibrant and famous African American area in New York City. The Cotton Club period was crucial to the development of Ellington's sound. Because his was the house band, meaning that its personnel was relatively stable and had time to rehearse, Ellington could use the band as a workshop to try out new pieces and new effects, testing the unusual timbres and voicings that became his trademark. He started experimenting with longer jazz works, such as *Creole Rhapsody* and *Reminiscing in Tempo.* Rather than relying primarily on improvisation, the group moved more and more to arrangements worked out in advance

Cotton Club years

Duke Ellington (1899–1974)

Edward Kennedy ("Duke") Ellington, the most important composer of jazz to date, was an innovator who expanded the boundaries of jazz and sought to break down barriers between it and art music. He admired the great jazz musicians, but his favorite composers were Debussy, Gershwin, and Stravinsky (See Chapter 25).

Born in Washington, D.C., Ellington was the son of a White House butler. He studied piano, including ragtime, from the age of seven and received a good education in music and other subjects. Known for his regal bearing and sartorial splendor, he earned the nickname "Duke" by the time he entered high school. By the age of seventeen, Ellington was playing throughout the Washington area with his own group. In 1923, he moved to New York with his band, the Washingtonians, playing at clubs on Broadway and at the Cotton Club in Harlem and making recordings.

During the 1930s and early 1940s, Ellington was the leading figure in jazz, and in later years he continued to play a prominent role, especially in efforts to have jazz recognized as a kind of art music, not merely as entertainment. He and his band made several international tours in the 1950s and 1960s, sponsored by the State Department and intended to create good will toward the United States. By the 1960s, he was regarded as a national treasure. He won thirteen Grammy awards, was awarded seventeen honorary degrees, was granted the Presidential Medal of Honor in 1969, and in the early 1970s was named a member of the National Institute of Arts and Letters and of the Swedish Royal Academy of Music, the first jazz musician to be so honored. He played and toured with his band until his death at age seventy-five, when his son, Mercer Ellington, took over the band and continued to tour.

Figure 24.15 Duke Ellington at the piano.
(Lebrecht Music & Arts Photo Library)

Major works: *East St. Louis Toodle-oo; Black and Tan Fantasy; Mood Indigo; Creole Rhapsody; Concerto for Cootie; Ko-Ko; Cotton Tail; Black, Brown and Beige;* and more than 1,300 other compositions.

that contrasted ensemble passages with solos, whether scored or improvised. He wrote specifically for, or in collaboration with, the players, emphasizing their individual sounds, as in *Black and Tan Fantasy* (1927), which featured his trumpeter, and *Mood Indigo* (1930) for his clarinet and saxophone players, giving each a little piece of the limelight.

The 1940s

[Full 🔊] [Concise 🔊]

[Full 🔊] [Concise 🔊]

The early 1940s is widely considered the peak of Ellington's creative abilities and of the performing rapport among the band members. Ellington took advantage of their talents, writing a number of new pieces to display their gifts. *Cotton Tail* (1940, NAWM 184) illustrates Ellington's music from this era. It follows the typical form for jazz performances, with a tune at the beginning followed by a series of choruses over the same chord progression. *Cotton Tail* might be called a *contrafact*, a new tune composed over a harmonic progression borrowed from a particular song—in this case rhythm changes, the chorus of Gershwin's *I Got Rhythm* (NAWM 181). Ellington's melody—fast, angular, highly syncopated, and full of unexpected twists—is nothing like Gershwin's, even

Example 24.6 Ellington, Cotton Tail

though the harmonic progression is the same. The first two choruses featured solos by Ben Webster playing tenor saxophone, accompanied by the rhythm section with occasional punctuation from the rest of the band. Example 24.6 compares the opening measures of Ellington's tune with those of Webster's choruses. The solo follows the same chord progression as the tune but does not vary or develop the tune; rather, the music at each chorus presents new ideas and may or may not use melodic or rhythmic motives from earlier in the piece. The remaining three choruses feature various combinations of instruments playing together or in call-and-response fashion, and the first eight bars of Ellington's tune return to bring the piece to a close.

Throughout his career, Ellington rejected the label "jazz composer," preferring to consider his music (and all good music) "beyond category." He believed that jazz could serve not only as dance or entertainment music but also as art music, listened to for its own sake. He frequently pushed against the boundaries of technology and convention, composing unconventionally long pieces that, before the introduction of long-playing records in the late 1940s, had to be recorded on multiple record sides, making them more difficult to market. Later in his career, he composed suites, such as *Black, Brown and Beige* (1943), *Harlem* (1950), and *Suite Thursday* (1960), and collaborated with Billy Strayhorn in rescoring for jazz band classical favorites such as Tchaikovsky's *Nutcracker Suite* and Grieg's *Peer Gynt Suite.* In asserting the value of jazz as an art music, he was declaring it worthy of attentive listening and of a permanent place in American culture. In both respects, his view has prevailed.

"Beyond category"

POSTLUDE

The twentieth century witnessed a reversal in the direction of musical influences between Europe and America: after absorbing European styles and trends through colonization and immigration during the preceding centuries, American popular music, jazz, and film music spread outward and made a huge impact on other countries. Jazz in particular spread quickly in the 1920s throughout North America, Latin America, and Europe, and became a frequent topic in European literature and arts. European musicians and music lovers encountered American jazz through imported recordings, sheet music, and traveling jazz ensembles. African American musician-soldiers serving in Europe during World War I helped to introduce the new style. By the 1920s, jazz groups were forming in Europe, and a European jazz tradition was well established by the 1930s.

TIMELINE Vernacular Music in America

Musical Events

1877
Edison makes first sound recording

1897
Sousa, *Stars and Stripes Forever* (NAWM 163)

1899
Joplin, *Maple Leaf Rag* (NAWM 164)

1904
Cohan, *Little Johnny Jones*

1913
Berlin Philharmonic records Beethoven's Fifth Symphony

1922
King Oliver forms the Creole Jazz Band

1925
Electric microphones introduced

1927
Kern, *Show Boat*; Bessie Smith, *Back Water Blues* (NAWM 182)

1927–1931
Ellington's band at the Cotton Club

1928
Armstrong and His Hot Five record *West End Blues* (NAWM 183)

1930
Gershwin, *I Got Rhythm* from *Girl Crazy* (NAWM 181)

1933
Steiner, film score for *King Kong*

1940
Ellington, *Cotton Tail* (NAWM 184)

1943
Rodgers and Hammerstein, *Oklahoma!*

1948
LP records introduced

1983
Philips and Sony unveil the CD

1900 ———————————————————————————————— **1950**

Historical Events

1900
Freud, *The Interpretation of Dreams*

1903
Wright brothers fly first successful airplane

1907
Braque and Picasso paint first cubist pictures

1908
Ford designs the Model T automobile

1914–1918
World War I

1917
United States enters World War I; Russian Revolution

1918–1919
Britain and United States give women right to vote

1920
First sponsored radio broadcast in the United States

1922
Eliot, *The Waste Land*; Fascists take over government in Italy

1929
New York stock market crash begins world-wide depression

1933
Hitler comes to power in Germany

1939
Steinbeck, *The Grapes of Wrath*

1939–1945
World War II

1945
Cold War begins

1968
Reverend Martin Luther King, Jr. assassinated

1969
First humans set foot on the moon

Through the new technologies of recordings, radio, and sound on film, American vernacular styles reached audiences throughout the Western world. Music could now be preserved and enjoyed year after year for decades to come. As a result, much of this music maintained its popularity, and within a generation or two many American works achieved the status of classics: widely known, heard and reheard, and highly valued. Today, in addition to recordings and movies, live ensembles perform Tin Pan Alley songs, Broadway musicals, blues, New Orleans jazz, swing, big-band jazz, and even movie scores from the 1920s and 1930s. This music is admired both for its original value as entertainment and because it is considered artful, worthy of attentive listening, and capable of offering musical experiences available nowhere else—the same reasons that music of earlier generations was preserved and revived in the nineteenth century.

 Resources for study and review available at
wwnorton.com/studyspace

Radical Modernism

PRELUDE

The first wave of modernist composers discussed in Chapter 23 secured an enduring place in the classical repertory by combining elements from the classical tradition with something original to create an individual and distinctive body of music. In the years just before and after World War I, a younger group of modernist composers carried out a more radical break from the musical language of the past than their predecessors while still maintaining strong links to the earlier tradition. These composers reassessed inherited conventions as profoundly as the modernists in art who pioneered expressionism, cubism, and abstract art. Rather than please viewers or listeners on first sight or first hearing, an attribute that had always been considered essential in both art and music, radical modernists sought to challenge audience perceptions and capacities, providing an experience that would be impossible through traditional means. As their writings often show, they offered an implicit critique of mass culture and easily digested art. Yet these composers saw no contradiction in claiming the masters of the past as models. In fact, they viewed their own work as continuing what the pathbreaking classical composers had started, not as overthrowing that tradition, and their music is often most radical in the ways they interpret and remake the past.

That it was still possible to compose tonal music in the twentieth century is clear from the careers of Strauss, Ravel, Vaughan Williams, Rachmaninoff, and many younger composers active through the 1930s and beyond who found new flavors and possibilities within tonality but never abandoned it. Yet other composers, including Debussy, Falla, Janáček, and Scriabin, moved beyond tonal practice in the early 1900s as each developed a personal musical language that followed its own rules. Even when a tonal center can be identified in one of their works—whether a single pitch as in Debussy's *L'Isle joyeuse* or a chord complex as in Scriabin's *Vers la flamme*—it no longer makes sense to describe the music as tonal, because the harmonic language diverges too far from common practice. The most general term for such music is *post-tonal,* which embraces all the new ways composers found to organize pitch, from atonality to neotonality. The new possibilities of post-tonal idioms were part of the marvelous diversity of twentieth-century music in the classical tradition, as were the individual approaches to tonality.

In this chapter we will discuss six modernist composers who are among the best known and most influential of the century. Born between 1874 and 1885, all six began by writing tonal music in late Romantic styles, then devised new and distinctive post-tonal idioms that won them a central place in the world of modern music. Their paths developed in individual directions, yet they faced common concerns. They all lived through two world wars, and each was uniquely affected by politics, nationalism, and modernism.

Arnold Schoenberg (1874–1951)

Arnold Schoenberg (see Biography, page 555) was committed to continuing the German classical tradition, and for that reason felt compelled to move beyond tonality to atonality—a term for music that avoids establishing a tonal center—and then to a compositional process known as the twelve-tone method, based on systematic orderings of the twelve notes of the chromatic scale. His innovations made him famous in some quarters and—because the resulting music was both dissonant and difficult to follow—notorious in others.

Tonal Works

Like other modernists of his generation, Schoenberg began by writing tonal music in a late Romantic style. The chromatic idiom of his first important work, a tone poem for string sextet entitled *Verklärte Nacht* (Transfigured Night, 1899), derived from that of Wagner's *Tristan und Isolde,* while the symphonic poem *Pelleas und Melisande* (1902–1903) draws on Mahler and Strauss. The huge cantata *Gurrelieder* (Songs of Gurre, 1900–1901, orchestration completed 1911) outdoes Wagner in emotional fervor, and Mahler and Strauss in the complexity of its scoring.

Developing variation

Schoenberg soon turned away from late Romantic gigantism and toward chamber music. He found in Brahms the principle of developing variation (see Chapter 21) and applied it in his own works, such as the String Quartet No. 1 in D Minor, Op. 7. All the themes in that composition and most of the subsidiary voices evolve from a few germinal motives through variation and combination. A one-movement work combining an enlarged sonata form with the four standard movements of a quartet, it owes much to Liszt's Piano Sonata in B Minor, demonstrating Schoenberg's willingness to blend influences in order to create something new.

Nonrepetition

The quartet exemplifies Schoenberg's twin goals for his music: to continue the tradition and to say something that had never been said before (see Vignette, page 556). He asked of each work that it not simply repeat but build on the past. Remarkably, he required the same *within* each piece: except for marked repeats in binary forms, nothing should repeat exactly. As he wrote, "With me, variation almost completely takes the place of repetition." This principle of nonrepetition between and within pieces helps explain how Schoenberg's musical style evolved.

Atonal Music

In 1908, Schoenberg began to compose pieces that avoided establishing any note as a tonal center. Others called such music *atonal,* although Schoenberg disliked the term. He felt compelled to abandon tonality in part because the heightened chromaticism, distant modulations, and prolonged dissonances of late nineteenth-century music had weakened the pull of the tonic, making its declaration at the end of a piece seem increasingly arbitrary. Instead, he

Arnold Schoenberg (1874–1951)

Perhaps the most self-consciously modernist composer of his generation, Arnold Schoenberg was a product of Europe's musical hothouse—the Vienna of Brahms and Mahler. He emerged from that intense environment to become one of the truly influential composers of the twentieth century, best known for his atonal and twelve-tone music.

Schoenberg came by his musical heritage honestly. He was born in Vienna, the son of a Jewish shopkeeper. He began violin lessons at age eight, then taught himself to compose by imitating the music he played. When his father died in 1891, Schoenberg had to leave school and work as a bank clerk. His instruction in theory and composition was minimal, although the composer Alexander von Zemlinsky served for a time as sounding board and teacher.

Schoenberg married Zemlinsky's sister, Mathilde, in 1901, and they moved to Berlin, where he worked at a cabaret until Richard Strauss got him a job teaching composition. Two years later he returned to Vienna and taught privately, attracting his two most famous students, Alban Berg and Anton von Webern. He had the support of Mahler and other progressive musicians, but his works met with resistance, especially after he adopted atonality in 1908. He took up painting in an expressionist style (see In Context, page 558) and developed friendships with several expressionist painters (one of whom—Richard Gerstl—committed suicide when Mathilde, with whom he had an affair,

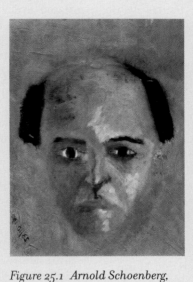

Figure 25.1 Arnold Schoenberg, Self-Portrait *(1910), showing his interest in expressionism in painting.*
(Arnold Schönberg Institute/Lebrecht Music & Arts Photo Library. © 2006 Artists Rights Society (ARS), New York/ VBK, Vienna.)

returned to Schoenberg for the sake of her two children).

After World War I, Schoenberg founded and directed the Society for Private Musical Performances in Vienna, which between 1919 and 1921 gave about 350 performances of music by him and his students and colleagues. After a creative impasse, he formulated the twelve-tone method used in the Piano Suite (1921–1923) and most of his later works.

After Mathilde died in 1923, Schoenberg married Gertrud Kolisch, with whom he had three more children and moved back to Berlin. But the Nazi government considered music by Schoenberg and other modernist composers to be "degenerate," and when it decided to remove all Jewish instructors from faculty appointments, Schoenberg fled with his family to France. He then traveled on to the United States, finally arriving in Los Angeles in 1934. He was appointed to a professorship at UCLA and retired in 1944 at age seventy. He died in Los Angeles in 1951 on July 13, having always feared the number 13.

Major works: 4 operas (*Erwartung, Die glückliche Hand, Von Heute auf Morgen,* and *Moses und Aron*); *Pierrot lunaire, Gurrelieder,* and numerous songs and choral works; 2 chamber symphonies, Five Orchestral Pieces, Variations for Orchestra, and other orchestral works; 5 string quartets, *Verklärte Nacht,* Wind Quintet, and other chamber works; Piano Suite and several sets of piano pieces.

cultivated a kind of *pantonality*, conceiving of each pitch and dissonance as autonomous. After all, in music with such complex chromatic chords, which notes are the dissonant ones that have to resolve? The ambiguities led Schoenberg to what he called "the emancipation of the dissonance"—freeing dissonance from its need to resolve to consonance, so that any combination of tones could serve as a stable chord that did not require resolution.

VIGNETTE New Music and Tradition

Arnold Schoenberg saw no contradiction between tradition and innovation. For him, the tradition of classical music was a legacy of innovation, and it was his job as a composer to weave threads from the past and the present into something truly new. He returned to this theme constantly in his writings.

In higher art, only that is worth being presented which has never before been presented. There is no great work of art which does not convey a new message to humanity; there is no great artist who fails in this respect. This is the code of honor of all the great in art, and consequently in all great works of the great we will find that newness which never perishes, whether it be of Josquin des Prez, of Bach or Haydn, or of any other great master.

Because: Art means New Art.

My teachers were primarily Bach and Mozart, and secondarily Beethoven, Brahms, and Wagner. . . .

I also learned much from Schubert and Mahler, Strauss and Reger too. I shut myself off from no one, and so I could say of myself:

My originality comes from this: I immediately imitated everything I saw that was good, even when I had not first seen it in someone else's work.

And I may say: often enough I saw it first in myself. For if I saw something I did not leave it at that; I acquired it, in order to possess it; I worked on it and extended it, and it led me to something new.

I am convinced that eventually people will recognize how immediately this "something new" is linked to the loftiest models that have been granted us. I venture to credit myself with having written truly new music which, being based on tradition, is destined to become tradition.

From Arnold Schoenberg, "New Music, Outmoded Music, Style and Idea" and "National Music (2)," in *Style and Idea: Selected Writings of Arnold Schoenberg*, ed. Leonard Stein, trans. Leo Black (London: Faber, 1975), pp. 114–115 and 173–174.

Coherence in atonal music

Without a tonal backbone, how was music to be organized? Schoenberg relied on three methods: developing variation, the integration of harmony and melody, and chromatic saturation. In addition, when writing vocal music, Schoenberg relied on the text and its structure. All had been used in tonal music, but now he drew on them more fully to provide coherence. Moreover, he often used gestures from tonal music, forging links to tradition and making his music easier to follow. One of Schoenberg's first entirely atonal pieces, dating from March 1908, is *The Book of the Hanging Gardens,* a cycle of fifteen songs on texts by Symbolist poet Stefan George (Op. 15, 1908–1909). The sense of floating in a sonic space created by music that does not gravitate to a tonic is perfectly suited to the vague eroticism of the poetry, which expresses, through outward symbols, the inner dynamics of a love affair.

Compositional process

Schoenberg integrated melody and harmony through a process he called "composing with the tones of a motive," which springs directly from developing variation. In this process, he manipulated a motive's collection of notes and intervals to create chords and new melodies. One way this worked was to treat the notes of a motive containing three or more pitches as though it were a triad or other tonal chord: as a collection of pitches that could be transposed, inverted, and arranged in any order and register to generate melodies and harmonies. By using a limited number of motives, along with their transpositions and inversions, Schoenberg gave his music a consistent sound. He tended to use strong dissonances because dissonant harmonies are most distinctive and, therefore, easier to follow as the music unfolds. This integration of melody and harmony harks back to music of earlier eras.

Atonal music can also be shaped through chromatic saturation, the appearance of all twelve pitch-classes within a segment of music. In an atonal context, the appearance of a note that has not recently been sounded gives a sense of moving forward harmonically. Once the twelfth chromatic note appears, there is also a sense of fullness and completion. Through these means, Schoenberg sought to write atonal music that was as logical as tonal music.

In addition to *The Book of the Hanging Gardens*, Schoenberg's works from this period include Three Piano Pieces, Op. 11; Five Orchestral Pieces, Op. 16; and *Erwartung* (Expectation), Op. 17, a one-character opera for soprano. In the works with orchestra, he followed Mahler in treating instruments soloistically and in swiftly alternating timbres to produce a great variety of colors. *Erwartung*, the height of expressionism in music, uses exaggerated gestures, angular melodies, and unrelenting dissonance to convey the tortured emotions of the protagonist (see In Context, page 558). In this opera, Schoenberg pushed nonrepetition to an extreme: not only is the work atonal, it has no themes or motives that return and lacks any reference to traditional forms. The fluid, constantly changing music suits the nightmarish text.

Another expressionist work that incorporates some of these devices combined with a return to a more traditional use of motives, themes, and long-range repetition is *Pierrot lunaire* (Moonstruck Pierrot, 1912), a cycle of twenty-one songs drawn from a larger poetic cycle by the Belgian Symbolist poet Albert Giraud. Schoenberg scored the text, translated into German, for a woman's voice with a chamber ensemble of five performers who play nine different instruments. In keeping with the principle of nonrepetition, the combination of instruments in each movement is unique. The voice declaims the text in a style known as *Sprechstimme* ("speaking voice"), also called *Sprechgesang* ("speech-song"), approximating the written pitches in the gliding tones of speech, while following the notated rhythm exactly—an innovative idea that blends traditional notions of song and melodrama. The inexact pitches evoke an eerie atmosphere for the Symbolist text, in which the clown Pierrot suffers gruesome visions provoked by a moonbeam that takes many shapes.

Expressionist features of the work aside, Schoenberg highlights many traditional elements. Each thirteen-line poem has two refrain lines in the pattern ABcd efAB ghijA, and Schoenberg typically sets the repeated lines with a variant of their original music at the original pitch level, thereby creating a sense of departure and return, as in tonal music. We find varied repetition at all levels, from motives and chords to themes and sections. One entire song—No. 7, *Der kranke Mond* ("The Sick Moon")—is recast as an instrumental epilogue heard at the end of No. 13, *Enthauptung* (Beheading, NAWM 172b). The cycle features several traditional forms and genres, including a waltz, a serenade, a barcarole (a boating song of Venetian gondoliers), and an aria over a walking bass, reminiscent of Bach. Schoenberg called No. 8, *Nacht* (Night, NAWM 172a), a passacaglia because the unifying motive—a rising minor third followed by a descending major third—is constantly repeated, with some rhythmic variation, in all parts and is often treated in canon. The omnipresence of this motive, whose notated contour in original and inverted forms resembles wings, fittingly illustrates Pierrot's obsession with the giant moths that enclose him in a frightening trap and shut out the sun. Even *Enthauptung*, which appears to abandon thematic development for anarchic improvisation,

Chromatic saturation

Expressionist characteristics

Pierrot lunaire

Sprechstimme

Full 🔊   Concise 🔊

Full 🔊   Concise 🔊

In Context Expressionism

In the early twentieth century, several groups of German and Austrian painters embraced an international movement called *expressionism,* which also extended to literature, music, dance, theater, and architecture. Expressionism developed from the subjectivity of Romanticism but differed from it in the introspective experience that it aimed to portray and how it chose to portray it.

Expressionist painters such as Ernst Ludwig Kirchner and Oskar Kokoschka rejected traditional Western aesthetic values by representing real objects or people in grossly distorted ways, characterized by an intensely expressive use of pure colors and dynamic brushstrokes, as in Kokoschka's poster for his own expressionist play *Mörder, Hoffnung der Frauen* (Murderer, Hope of Women, 1909) in Figure 25.2. These artists and others drew on contemporary themes involving the dark side of city life, in which people lived under extreme psychological pressure, as well as bright scenes from the circus and music halls that masked a more gloomy reality. They aspired to represent inner experience, to explore the hidden world of the psyche, and to render visible the stressful, emotional life of the modern person—isolated, helpless in the grip of poorly understood forces, prey to inner conflict, tension, anxiety, and fear, and tormented by elemental, irrational drives, including an eroticism that often had morbid overtones. That is also how the Viennese doctor Sigmund Freud, founder of psychoanalysis, described the deepest level of memory and emotional activity in his *Interpretation of Dreams* (1900). In short, expressionism sought to capture the human condition as it was perceived in the early twentieth century.

Arnold Schoenberg and his pupil Alban Berg were two leading exponents of expressionism in music, which paralleled expressionist art by adopting a similarly desperate and revolutionary style. Its characteristics are evident in Schoenberg's *Erwartung,* an opera in which a lone protagonist—emblematic of the artist's alienation from society and its conventions—gives voice to what the composer described as a dream of Angst, an overwhelming feeling of dread or anxiety. Its distorted melodies and fragmented rhythms, violently graphic musical images, and discordant harmonies create the quasi-hysterical atmosphere typical of the style. In none of

Figure 25.2 Oskar Kokoschka, poster for Mörder, Hoffnung der Frauen (Murderer, Hope of Women), *from 1909, the same year as Schoenberg's* Erwartung.
(© ARS, NY. Photo: Erich Lessing/Art Resource, NY.)

Schoenberg's expressionist pieces nor in Berg's opera *Wozzeck* did these composers try to create music that is pretty or naturalistic (as the impressionists did); rather, they deployed the most direct—even drastic—means, no matter how unappealing, to convey extreme and irrational states of mind.

Schoenberg was also an amateur painter and took lessons from Richard Gerstl, one of the foremost expressionist artists in Austria. Schoenberg's most striking pictures, a series of "gazes" in the form of faces, not only emphasize the act of looking but also suggest the same feelings of claustrophobia and angst as those portrayed in *Erwartung.* With other Viennese expressionists, Schoenberg shared an interest in producing self-portraits (see Figure 25.1 and Figure VI.6). They indicate, perhaps, his constant questioning, both of his own identity and of the human condition.

unfolds by constantly varying the initial ideas to capture the images and feelings in the text.

Twelve-Tone Method

Schoenberg still faced a problem: using his atonal methods, he could not match the formal coherence of tonal music and had to rely on a text to sustain pieces of any length. He formulated a solution in his twelve-tone method, which he described as a "method of composing with twelve tones that are related only to one another" (rather than to a tonic) in the early 1920s, after several years during which he published no music. The basis of a twelve-tone composition is called a *row,* or *series,* which consists of the twelve pitch-classes arranged in an order chosen by the composer and producing a particular sequence of intervals. The tones of the series may be used both successively, as melody, and simultaneously, as harmony or counterpoint, in any octave and with any desired rhythm. The row may be used not only in its original, or prime, form but also in inversion, in retrograde order (backward), and in retrograde inversion, and may appear in all twelve possible transpositions of any of the four forms (see Figure 25.3). The twelve-note series is often broken into segments of three to six notes, which are then used to create melodic motives and chords. As a rule, the composer states all twelve pitches of the series before going on to use the series in any of its forms again (unless two or more statements occur simultaneously). In this way, Schoenberg simulated the structural functions of tonality, using the transposition of his rows as an analogue to modulation in tonal music.

After focusing on vocal works in his atonal period, Schoenberg turned to traditional instrumental forms, as if to demonstrate the power of his method to reconstitute tonal forms in a new musical language. Among these works, composed between 1921 and 1949, are the Piano Suite, Op. 25, modeled on the keyboard suites of Bach; Variations for Orchestra, Op. 31; Third and Fourth String

Return to instrumental forms

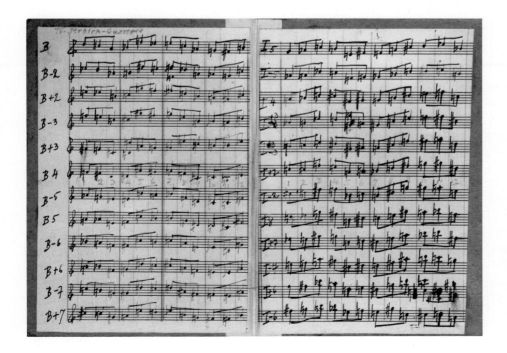

Figure 25.3 Schoenberg's tone-row chart from his Fourth String Quartet (1937), illustrating the various transpositions and inversions of the work's basic series of tones.

(Arnold Schönberg Center, Vienna.)

The Piano Suite (excerpted in NAWM 173) illustrates some of Schoenberg's methods of composing with twelve tones. Throughout the work, the row appears in only eight forms (shown in Example 25.1a): the untransposed prime form (P-0); the prime transposed up six semitones (P-6); the inversion in the same two transpositions (I-0 and I-6); and their retrogrades (R-0, R-6, RI-0, and RI-6). Schoenberg designed the row so that each of these forms begins and ends on either E or B♭, and all the primes and inversions have G and D♭ as their second pair of notes (see the box in Example 25.1a). The recurrence of E, B♭, G, and D♭ in the same places creates a consistency that Schoenberg saw as analogous to staying in a single key, the normal practice in a Baroque keyboard suite, although it is much more difficult for a listener to hear. The first four notes of R-0 give a nod to Schoenberg's model, J. S. Bach, by spelling his name: B♭-A-C-B♮ (B-A-C-H, in German nomenclature).

Example 25.1b shows the rows deployed at the beginning of the Prelude (NAWM 173a). P-0 is in the right hand as melody, divided into motives of four notes each (in brown, blue, and green circles

Example 25.1 Arnold Schoenberg, Piano Suite Op. 25

a. Row forms

Quartets, Opp. 30 and 37; Violin Concerto, Op. 36; and Piano Concerto, Op. 42. In these pieces, motives and themes are presented and developed, using the tonal forms and genres of Classic and Romantic music, but twelve-tone rows stand in for the keys (see A Closer Look, above).

Schoenberg as modernist

We have discussed Schoenberg's music at some length not only because of its complexity and its enormous influence on others, but also because the problems he chose to address as a modern composer and the way he faced them did much to shape the course of musical practice in the twentieth century. His desire to match the achievements of his forebears pressed him both backward—to reclaim the genres, forms, procedures, and gestures of the past—and forward toward a new musical language.

The Second Viennese school

Schoenberg attracted many devoted students. The two most notable, Alban Berg and Anton von Webern, were both natives of Vienna and are often grouped with Schoenberg as members of the second Viennese school, implying a connection to the first Viennese threesome, Haydn, Mozart, and Beethoven.

respectively). Twelve-tone theorists call such groups of four consecutive notes from the row *tetrachords,* using the ancient Greek term in a new sense (see Chapter 1). In the left hand, as accompaniment, we find P-6, using the same division into tetrachords and presenting the last two simultaneously. There is also a canon between the pitches of each hand, recalling Bach's contrapuntal practice. At the end of measure 3, I-6 begins, presenting its three tetrachords simultaneously, each in its own rhythm. The last two notes of its first tetrachord overlap the statement of R-6 in measure 5; that is, pitches 3 and 4 of I-6 (in the brown circle) are the same as pitches 9 and 10 of R-6 (in the next brown circle). The row-form R-6 also presents the tetrachords simultaneously, but here the texture is less contrapuntal and more chordal than it was in the preceding measure.

Typical for a piece in this style, all the movements use the same eight row forms, which was, in Schoenberg's mind, comparable to establishing unity through tonality.

b. Prelude

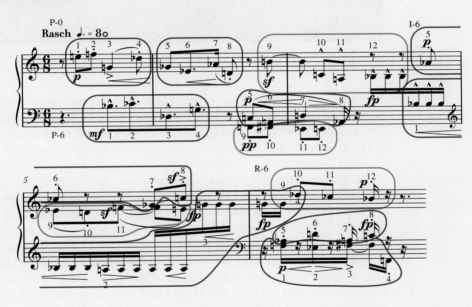

Alban Berg (1885–1935)

Alban Berg, shown in Figure 25.5, began studies with Schoenberg in 1904 at age nineteen. Although he adopted his teacher's atonal and twelve-tone methods, listeners found his music more approachable. Berg achieved much greater popular success than his teacher, especially with his opera *Wozzeck,* which premiered in 1925. His secret lay in infusing his post-tonal idiom not only with the forms and procedures of tonal music, as Schoenberg had done, but also with its expressive gestures, characteristic styles, and other elements that quickly conveyed meanings and feelings to his hearers. In this respect he was a direct heir of Mahler and Strauss.

Wozzeck is the outstanding example of expressionist opera. The libretto, arranged by Berg from a fragmentary play by Georg Büchner (1813–1837), presents the soldier Wozzeck as a hapless victim of his environment, despised by

Wozzeck

Figure 25.4 Scene from Alban Berg's Wozzeck, *showing the Captain and Wozzeck against a stark set in one of their bizarre interactions.*
(Robert Eric/Corbis Sygma.)

his fellow men, forced by poverty to submit to a doctor's experiments, betrayed in love, and driven finally to murder and suicide (see Figure 25.4). The music is atonal, not twelve-tone, and includes *Sprechstimme* in some scenes. Each of the three acts has continuous music, with the changing scenes (five in each act) linked by orchestral interludes.

Structure of *Wozzeck*

Berg highlights the drama and organizes the music by using leitmotives identified with the main characters and traditional forms that wryly comment on the characters and situation. Wozzeck's outburst in the first scene, "Wir arme Leut!" (We poor people!), shown in Example 25.2a, is one of his leitmotives and contains his characteristic tetrachord. The first act includes a Baroque suite, suggesting the formality of Wozzeck's captain; a rhapsody, suiting Wozzeck's fantastic visions; a march and lullaby for a scene with his common-law wife, Marie, and their child; a passacaglia for the doctor's constant prattling about his theory; and a rondo for Marie's seduction by a rival suitor, who tries repeatedly until she gives in. The second act, the heart of the drama, is a symphony in five movements, including a sonata form, a fantasia and fugue, a ternary slow movement, a scherzo, and a rondo. The third act presents six inventions, each on a single idea: a theme (seven variations and a fugue), a note (B), a rhythm, a chord, a key, and a duration (the eighth note). Together they reflect Wozzeck's growing obsessions, and they illustrate Berg's approach that combines atonal organization with allusions to tonality.

▶ **BERG**, *Wozzeck*

The invention on a rhythm in Act III, Scene 3 (NAWM 174b), illustrates Berg's approach. Just after murdering Marie, Wozzeck sits in a tavern drinking and singing, then dances briefly with Marie's friend Margret; she sits on his lap and sings a song, but when she spies blood on his hand, Wozzeck becomes agitated and rushes out. The scene begins with an onstage, out-of-tune tavern piano that is playing a wild polka, shown in Example 25.2b. The music is atonal—the notes in the first two measures comprise the tetrachord associated with Wozzeck (see Example 25.2a)—but it instantly conveys the impression of a popular dance tune, through triadic accompaniment under a melody that moves by step and by skip. Just as the singers on stage are acting their parts, so, too, the atonal music is acting the part of tonal music, and its meaning is immediately clear. The melody lays out the rhythmic theme for the scene, which is then obsessively reiterated at various levels of augmentation and diminution, so that it is almost always present. By constantly repeating the rhythm, Berg unifies the scene through developing variation and also reveals Wozzeck's preoccupation with his guilt, which he cannot escape. When Wozzeck sings a folk song and Margret a popular song with piano accompaniment, Berg imitates recognizable tonal styles in an atonal idiom. The almost constant references to tonality and to familiar styles and genres help to keep listeners engaged, while the atonality heightens the dramatic impact.

Soon after *Wozzeck* was premiered, Berg adopted twelve-tone methods, turning them to his own ends. He often chose rows that allowed for tonal-sounding chords and chord progressions, connecting the new style with the past and investing his music with immediate emotional impact. His chief twelve-tone works are his *Lyric Suite* for string quartet (1925–1926), his Violin Concerto (1935), and a second opera, *Lulu* (1928–1935), whose orchestration was not quite complete when he died.

Berg designed the row of his Violin Concerto with four interlocking minor and major triads, marked with square brackets in Example 25.3a, which permits frequent references to tonal chords while using twelve-tone procedures. The piece includes evocations of a violin tuning its open strings (using notes 1,

Twelve-tone works

Violin concerto

Example 25.2 Berg, Wozzeck

a. Wozzeck's leitmotive and characteristic tetrachord, from Act I, scene 1

b. Tavern piano in Act III, scene 3, with rhythmic pattern and Wozzeck's tetrachord

* The pitches E, G, and B in Wozzeck's tetrachord are 1, 4, and 8 semitones, respectively, above D♯ (and below G♯ in the inverted form).

Example 25.3 Row from Berg's Violin Concerto and Bach's Es ist genug!

a. Berg's row   *b. Bach's chorale setting*

3, 5, and 7 of the row), tonal chord progressions, Viennese waltzes, a folk song, and a Bach chorale. The last of these, *Es ist genug!* (It is enough!) alludes to the death of the young woman to whose memory Berg dedicated the concerto. As shown in Example 25.3b, the chorale melody begins with three rising whole steps, like the last four notes of Berg's row, and Bach's harmonization includes two four-note chords that appear in transposition within Berg's row. Thus the quotation of the chorale is not something foreign, but stems directly from the row itself.

Berg's concerto can be understood on first hearing by anyone familiar with tonal music, yet its structure is wholly determined by twelve-tone procedures. Thus his music accommodates innovation within tradition, its inner structure transformed just as radically as in Schoenberg's music, but with more familiar sounds and gestures kept on the surface.

Anton Webern (1883–1945)

Anton Webern (shown in Figure 25.5) began lessons with Schoenberg in 1904, at the same time as Berg. He was already studying musicology at the University of Vienna, where he received a Ph.D. in 1906 and absorbed ideas about music history that influenced his own (and perhaps also Schoenberg's) development.

View of music history

Webern believed that music involves the presentation of ideas that can be expressed in no other way; that it operates according to rules of order based on natural law rather than taste; that great art does what is necessary, not arbitrary; that evolution in art is also necessary; and that history—and thus musical idioms and practices—can move only forward, never backward. After Schoenberg had formulated, and Webern and Berg had adopted, the twelve-tone method, Webern argued in a series of lectures published posthumously as *The Path to the New Music* that twelve-tone music was the inevitable result of music's evolution because it combined the most advanced approaches to pitch (using all twelve chromatic notes), musical space (integrating the melodic and harmonic dimensions), and the presentation of musical ideas (combining Classic forms with polyphonic procedures and unity with variety, deriving every element from the thematic material). With his view of history, Webern regarded each step along the way, from tonality to atonality to twelve-tone music, as an act of discovery, not invention. This gave him—and Schoenberg, to whom he was completely devoted—total confidence in their own work, despite the incomprehension and opposition they encountered from performers and listeners. Webern's concept of the composer as an artist expressing new ideas, yet also as a researcher making new discoveries, sprang from his training in musicology, and it became enormously influential in the mid- to late twentieth century.

Figure 25.5 Anton Webern (right) with Alban Berg in 1912.
(Lebrecht Music & Arts Photo Library.)

Webern, like Schoenberg and Berg, passed through the stages of late Romantic chromaticism, atonality, and twelve-tone organization, the last beginning in 1925 with the three songs of Op. 17. His works, about equally divided between instrumental and vocal, are mostly for small chamber ensembles.

At heart a Romantic and a lover of nature, Webern sought to write deeply expressive music. Yet because he believed great art should do only what is necessary, his music is extremely concentrated. When writing his Six Bagatelles for String Quartet, Op. 9 (1911–1913), he remarked that once he had incorporated all twelve notes, he often felt that the piece was finished. Another atonal work, No. 4 of his Five Pieces for Orchestra, Op. 10 (1911–1913), runs to only six measures, and the last of his Three Little Pieces for Cello and Piano, Op. 11 (1914), to just twenty notes. Even larger works, like the Symphony, Op. 21 (1927–1928) and the String Quartet, Op. 28 (1936–1938), are only eight or nine minutes long, and Webern's entire mature output takes less than four hours to play. The dynamics are understated as well; specified down to the finest gradations, they seldom rise above *forte.* Perhaps influenced by his musicological studies—for his dissertation he edited a volume of sixteenth-century mass movements by Heinrich Isaac—Webern often used techniques of Renaissance polyphony, including canons in inversion or retrograde. Unlike Berg, he avoided using harmonies or rows with tonal implications.

Economy of means

The first movement of the Symphony, Op. 21 (NAWM 175) illustrates Webern's use of twelve-tone procedures, canons, instrumentation, and form. The entire movement is a double canon in inversion. Example 25.4 shows the beginning, with canon 1 in the upper two staves and canon 2 on the bottom. Instead of separating the canonic lines by making each a continuous melody with a distinctive timbre and range, Webern deliberately integrates them. Each line is filled with rests, changes timbre frequently, and weaves back and forth through the same three-octave range. The succession of timbres is as much part of the melody as are the pitches and rhythms, a concept known as *Klangfarbenmelodie* ("tone-color melody"), in which changes of tone color are perceived as parallel to changing pitches in a melody.

Symphony, Op. 21

Full 🔊

Klangfarbenmelodie

Although Webern received little acclaim during his lifetime and has never gained wide popularity, recognition of his work among scholars and composers—especially of his tone-row pieces—grew steadily in the years after World War II. His music had an abiding influence on some composers in Germany, France, Italy, and the United States, especially in the first two decades after the war.

Influence

Example 25.4 Anton Webern, Symphony, Op. 21, first movement

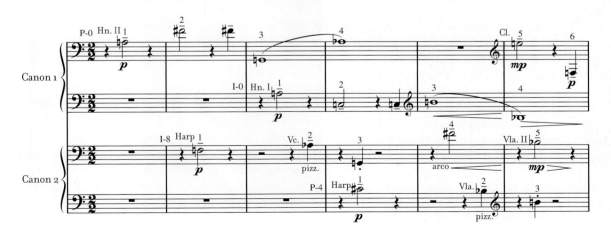

Igor Stravinsky (1882–1971)

While Schoenberg, Berg, and Webern worked inside the Austro-German tradition, Igor Stravinsky (see Biography, below) began his musical career as a Russian nationalist and became a cosmopolitan—and arguably the most important composer of his time. He created an individual voice by developing several distinctive trademarks, most derived from Russian traditions:

Igor Stravinsky (1882–1971)

Like Picasso in art, Stravinsky was the very icon of the twentieth-century composer, with his multiple stylistic transformations reflecting in some ways the cataclysmic upheavals of two world wars. Like Picasso, too, he was active in the foreground of every major stylistic trend of the century, spearheading some but participating in all.

Stravinsky was born in Orianienbaum, near Saint Petersburg in Russia, to a well-to-do musical family. He began piano lessons at age nine and studied music theory in his later teens but never attended the Conservatory. His most important teacher was Rimsky-Korsakov, with whom he studied composition and orchestration privately.

After demonstrating a command of his teacher's rich, colorful style, Stravinsky was asked by the impresario Sergei Diaghilev to compose for the Ballets Russes (Russian Ballet), a hotbed of artistic innovation in Paris from 1909 to 1929. For Diaghilev, Stravinsky wrote the ballets that made him famous and that are still his most popular works.

In 1906, Stravinsky married his cousin Catherine Nosenko, with whom he had four children. He moved to Paris in 1911, spent the war years in Switzerland, and, having realized that the Bolshevik Revolution meant permanent exile from Russia, returned to and settled in France in 1920. Commotion at the *Rite of Spring* premiere had bestowed on him a delicious notoriety; and because he performed tirelessly, first as a pianist and then as a conductor, Stravinsky was well known in 1920s Europe and America. He continued to work with the Ballets Russes, where one of his favorite collaborators was the choreographer George Balanchine, who later founded the New York City Ballet.

Catherine died in March 1939, after which Stravinsky moved to the United States, arriving just weeks after the outbreak of World War II. In March 1940, he married Vera Sudeikin, with whom he had a romantic liaison since the early 1920s. He settled in Hollywood, not far from Schoenberg and Rachmaninoff, and wrote several pieces that referred to American styles.

In 1948, Stravinsky met Robert Craft, who became his assistant. Craft was enthusiastic about the twelve-tone music of Schoenberg and Webern, and by the mid-1950s, Stravinsky had absorbed twelve-tone methods into his own idiom. Most of his late works are serial, and many are religious. Stravinsky and his wife moved to New York in 1969. He died there two years later and was buried in Venice.

Major works: *The Firebird, Petrushka, The Rite of Spring, L'Histoire du soldat, Symphonies of Wind Instruments, Les Noces*, Octet for Wind Instruments, *Oedipus rex, Symphony of Psalms*, Symphony in C, Symphony in Three Movements, *The Rake's Progress, Agon, Requiem Canticles*.

*Figure 25.6
Photograph of Igor Stravinsky in Paris in May 1913, the month of the premiere of* The Rite of Spring.
(Hulton-Deutsch Collection/Corbis.)

undermining meter through unpredictable accents and rests or through frequent changes of meter; pervasive ostinatos; layering and juxtaposition of static blocks of sound; discontinuity and interruption; dissonance based on diatonic, octatonic, and other collections of notes; and dry, antilyrical, but colorful use of instruments. He forged these traits during his early "Russian" period (to about 1918) and used them again in his later works. Through Stravinsky, elements of Russian music became part of a common international modernist practice.

Russian Period

Stravinsky wrote his most popular works early in his career: the ballets *The Firebird* (1910), *Petrushka* (1910–1911), and *Le Sacre du printemps* (The Rite of Spring, 1911–1913), all commissioned by Russian choreographer and impresario Sergei Diaghilev for the Ballets Russes in Paris. *The Firebird,* based on Russian folktales, stems from the Russian nationalist tradition and especially from the exoticism of Rimsky-Korsakov. Throughout, humans are characterized by diatonic music, while supernatural creatures and places inhabit octatonic or chromatic realms, following Rimsky's standard practice.

The Firebird

In *Petrushka,* Stravinsky introduced several stylistic traits that became closely identified with him. The opening scene of the ballet depicts a fair in St. Petersburg during carnival season. Here, we find Stravinsky's characteristic blocks of static harmony with repetitive melodic and rhythmic patterns as well as abrupt shifts from one block to another. Each group of dancers receives its distinctive music: a band of tipsy revelers, an organ grinder with a dancer, a music-box player with another dancer, the puppet theater where Petrushka stars. Seemingly unconnected musical events interrupt each other without transition, disappear, and then just as suddenly return, creating a kaleidoscope of diverse textures that has been compared to the cubism of Pablo Picasso (see Figure VI.4). The juxtaposition of contrasting blocks, which Stravinsky absorbed from the Russian practice of Musorgsky and Rimsky-Korsakov, is here linked to the changing visual effects of ballet.

Petrushka

Stravinsky enhanced the Russian elements and popular carnival atmosphere throughout the ballet by borrowing and elaborating several Russian folk tunes, a popular French song, and Viennese waltzes. Rather than integrating these borrowings into a musical continuity, Stravinsky preserved and heightened their stylistic differences to make each block of sound as distinctive as possible. The passage in Example 25.5, which accompanies drunken merrymakers, is based on a folk song from Rimsky-Korsakov's 1877 collection of traditional songs. But Stravinsky avoids the dominant-tonic harmony of Rimsky's version; instead, he places the melody in the bass and simulates folk harmony, in which voices sing in parallel fifths and octaves.

In contrast to the diatonic folk songs, Stravinsky uses octatonic music for supernatural elements. Because octatonic scales lack the strong gravitation

Octatonicism

Example 25.5 Igor Stravinsky, Petrushka

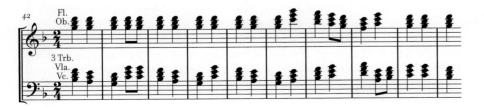

Example 25.6 "Petrushka" chord, with octatonic scale from which it derives

toward a tonic that is characteristic of diatonic scales, they are perfect for creating static blocks of sound and otherworldly effects. The puppet Petrushka, who has been brought to life by a magician, is characterized in the famous "Petrushka chord" that combines F♯-major and C-major triads, both part of the same octatonic scale, as shown in Example 25.6.

The Rite of Spring　　Stravinsky's distinctive style crystallized in *The Rite of Spring*. The subject was still Russian, but now it was an imagined fertility ritual set in prehistoric Russia, during which an adolescent girl is chosen for sacrifice and must dance herself to death. Stravinsky again borrowed folk melodies, while the scenario, choreography, and music are marked by primitivism—an evocation of the elemental, simple, and natural state believed to have been enjoyed by prehistoric peoples—and the sophistication and stylishness of modern life and trained artistry are cast aside. Figure 25.7 illustrates (a) a costume from the original production and (b) its modern re-creation. The audience at the premiere

Figure 25.7a (left)　"Painted maiden" costume designed by Nicholas Roerich for the original production of Stravinsky's ballet, The Rite of Spring, *1913. Compare Stravinsky's description of the adolescent girls as "knock-kneed and long-braided Lolitas."*
(Lebrecht Music & Arts Photo Library.)

Figure 25.7b (right)　Photograph of the actual costume, re-created for a 2003 production of The Rite of Spring *at the Royal Opera House in Covent Garden and worn by an artist of the Kirov Ballet Company.*
(Robbie Jack/Corbis.)

was utterly shocked by the ungainly choreography and provocative music, and some showed their disapproval by fomenting a riot (see Vignette, page 570 and A Closer Look, page 571). Eventually, the piece became one of the most frequently performed and universally appreciated compositions of its time.

The characteristics of Stravinsky's mature idiom can be heard in the first scene, *Danse des adolescentes* (Dance of the Adolescent Girls, NAWM 176a), whose opening measures are shown in Example 25.7. Despite the regular barring, each pulse in the first two measures is played with a downbow of the same strength, negating the hierarchy of strong and weak beats that is essential to meter. Then, accented chords, doubled by eight horns, create an unpredictable pattern of stresses that destroys any feeling of metrical regularity. Yet, while the listener is utterly disoriented by the repeated disruption of a steady pulse, the music is cleverly conceived for ballet; the passage makes an eight-measure period, and the dancers can count four-measure phrases. This reduction of meter to mere pulsation was the element that most strongly conveyed a sense of primitivism in the music, and the results were electrifying. In the final dance of the ballet, the *Danse sacrale* (Sacrificial Dance, NAWM 176b), Stravinsky adopted two additional strategies that reduce meter to pulse: rapidly changing meters and unpredictable alternation of notes with rests.

Example 25.7 Igor Stravinsky, The Rite of Spring, Danse des adolescentes

Ostinatos and juxtaposed blocks

The entire passage in Example 25.7 is built from ostinatos, including pounded or arpeggiated chords and the melodic ostinato in the English horn. Stravinsky uses these repeating figures to create static blocks of sound, which he places next to one another without transition. Here, one block is replaced by another, then returns. Within each block—and indeed, throughout the piece—there is no development of motives or themes as traditionally understood, but rather repetition and unpredictable variation. In typical Stravinsky fashion, the patterns within successive blocks are quite different, creating discontinuity. Yet the collection of pitches being used in each differs by only one note (C), lending a strong sense of continuity. Stravinsky offsets the obvious surface discontinuities of his music with more subtle connections. Here the dissonant chords in measures 1–8 combine an F♭-major triad in the lower strings with a first-inversion dominant-seventh chord on E♭ in the upper strings to produce a sonority that has all seven notes of the A♭ harmonic-minor scale.

Layering

Often Stravinsky builds up textures by layering two or more independent strands of music on top of one another. The material at measure 9 is composed of three layers distinguished by timbre (English horn, bassoons, and pizzicato cellos) and motivic figuration, with the top line also set off by register and pitch collection. Stravinsky often identified a musical idea with a particular timbre.

Timbre and orchestration

Here, the pounding chords are always in the strings with horn reinforcements, and the English-horn ostinato recurs only in that instrument throughout the first half of the dance. In the second half, it migrates through several other

---

VIGNETTE The Premiere of *The Rite of Spring*

The first performance of Igor Stravinsky's The Rite of Spring *on May 29, 1913, was greeted by a riot. As he told the story almost half a century later, Stravinsky was as shocked by the audience's reaction as some listeners were by the spectacle. Apparently, it was the choreography, more than the music, that provoked the audience, and ever since the piece has usually been performed in concert rather than as a ballet.*

That the first performance of *Le Sacre du printemps* was attended by a scandal must be known to everybody. Strange as it may seem, however, I was unprepared for the explosion myself. The reactions of the musicians who came to the orchestra rehearsals were without intimation of it and the stage spectacle did not appear likely to precipitate a riot. . . .

Mild protests against the music could be heard from the very beginning of the performance. Then, when the curtain opened on the group of knock-kneed and long-braided Lolitas jumping up and down [*Danses des adolescentes*], the storm

broke. Cries of "Ta gueule" [Shut up!] came from behind me. I heard Florent Schmitt shout "Taisez-vous garces du seizième" [Be quiet, you bitches of the sixteenth]; the "garces" of the sixteenth arrondissement [the most fashionable residential district of Paris] were, of course, the most elegant ladies in Paris. The uproar continued, however, and a few minutes later I left the hall in a rage; I was sitting on the right near the orchestra, and I remember slamming the door. I have never again been that angry. The music was so familiar to me; I loved it, and I could not understand why people who had not yet heard it wanted to protest in advance. I arrived in a fury backstage, where I saw Diaghilev flicking the house lights in a last effort to quiet the hall. For the rest of the performance I stood in the wings behind Nijinsky holding the tails of his *frac*, while he stood on a chair shouting numbers to the dancers, like a coxswain.

From Igor Stravinsky and Robert Craft, *Expositions and Developments* (Garden City, N.Y.: Doubleday, 1962), pp. 59–164.

instruments. In music without motivic development, such changes of timbre are one way to provide variety, a technique Stravinsky learned from Russian composers before him. His preference for dry rather than lush or resonant timbres is reflected in the pizzicato cellos; in the staccato English horn and bassoons; and in the staccato string chords.

Having developed these techniques, Stravinsky continued to use them throughout his career. During World War I, the wartime economy forced Stravinsky to turn away from the large orchestra of his early ballets toward small combinations of instruments to accompany stage works. For *L'Histoire du soldat* (The Soldier's Tale, 1918), he called for six solo instruments in pairs

Small-ensemble works

 A Closer Look **Stravinsky's Notorious Ballet**

A handsome Russian dancer and choreographer, Vaslav Nijinsky (1888–1950), in collaboration with Diaghilev and Stravinsky, burst colorfully upon the sedate, pastel world of classical ballet in Paris during the second decade of the twentieth century. In 1912, the year before the notorious premiere of Stravinsky's *Rite of Spring*, audiences had been scandalized by Nijinsky's first choreographed ballet, set to Debussy's symphonic poem *Prélude à "L'Après-midi d'un faune"* (see Figure 23.1). In that work, Nijinsky himself danced the role of the faun, a mythological creature half man, half goat. The ballet was shockingly original in its sensuous atmosphere and sexually suggestive movements, portraying the faun's visions of ethereal nymphs.

The next year, encouraged by Diaghilev and intent on pursuing his own unique course, Nijinsky created the perfect counterpart on stage to Stravinsky's galvanizing score of *The Rite*. According to an account by one of the dancers, Nijinsky was bent on reproducing every note of the music in his choreography, thereby emphasizing the jarring impact of the orchestra's explosive rhythms and unpredictable harmonies. The effect was further enhanced by the set and costume designs of the Russian-born painter Nicholas Roerich, who transformed his ideas about the prehistory of his native land and its primitive cultures into bold colors and exotic forms (see Figure 25.8). The costumes were loose-fitting garments and headbands, hand-painted with geometric shapes that were repeated in the steps and angular movements of the dancers (see Figure 25.7). Nijinsky's choreography was similarly bold and unorthodox, completely defying the audience's expectations and the graceful poses of classical ballet. As Stravinsky himself revealed in his graphic description of the first performance (see Vignette, page 570), not only did the dancers representing the "Lolitas" or tribal maidens wear long pigtails, but they also were intentionally awkward, moving in "knock-kneed" fashion with their toes turned in (the opposite of first position in classical ballet). At one point, according to an account by one of the dancers, they stalked across the stage in such exaggerated frontal poses that their silhouettes resembled a row of clumsy storks.

Figure 25.8 Tableau with dancers. Painting by Nicholas Roerich of one of his set designs for the original production of Stravinsky's The Rite of Spring.
(The State Russian Museum, St. Petersburg, Russia. Photo courtesy of the Nicholas Roerich Museum, New York.)

Figure 25.9 Title page designed by Picasso for Stravinsky's piano arrangement of Ragtime, *published by J. & W. Chester Ltd., London, 1919.* (Courtesy Swann Auction Galleries.)

(violin and double bass, clarinet and bassoon, cornet and trombone) and one percussionist to play interludes in a spoken narration and dialogue. In the marches, tango, waltz, and ragtime movements of *L'Histoire,* and in *Ragtime* (1917–1918; see Figure 25.9). Stravinsky discovered ways to imitate familiar styles while using the devices that had become his trademarks. Stranded in western Europe by the war and then by the Bolshevik Revolution in his home country, he began to move away from Russian topics while retaining the distinctive traits that stemmed largely from his Russian training.

Neoclassical Period

In 1919, Diaghilev asked Stravinsky to orchestrate pieces by the eighteenth-century composer Pergolesi (including music erroneously attributed to him) to accompany a new ballet, *Pulcinella.* Stravinsky applied his distinctive stylistic traits to the music, reworking a number of pieces so that they retained the original music faithfully yet sounded more like Stravinsky than Pergolesi. He later spoke of this experience as his "discovery of the past, the epiphany through which the whole of my late work became possible."

Thus was launched Stravinsky's neoclassical period, a new stage in his career. Although he was not the first to compose neoclassical music (see Chapter 23), Stravinsky was the most prominent composer of the neoclassical movement. His neoclassical period, from 1919 to 1951, marks a turn away from Russian folk music and toward earlier Western art music as a source for imitation, quotation, or allusion.

This step was timely because the fashion in the West for Russian nationalism was beginning to fade, in part because the political and cultural ties between France and Russia had dissolved after the Bolshevik Revolution. In addition to giving Stravinsky new subject matter, neoclassicism also addressed the dilemma of establishing a place in the crowded classical repertory. Stravinsky had already solved the problem of creating an individual style. He now used his distinctive idiom, forged in the Russian traditions, to establish fresh links to the Western classical tradition, just as Schoenberg used his modernist twelve-tone procedures to resurrect the forms and genres of the classical past. Yet even as Stravinsky became thoroughly cosmopolitan, he always remained something of an outsider in Western Europe, and instead of Schoenberg's agonized expressionism, we find in Stravinsky's music an emotional detachment. Thus his neoclassical style adopts an anti-Romantic tone, reflecting a preference for balance, coolness, objectivity, and absolute (as opposed to program) music.

Stravinsky's neoclassicism and its continuity with his earlier style are both evident in his *Symphony of Psalms* (1930) for mixed chorus and orchestra, based on psalms from the Latin Vulgate Bible. Stravinsky said he used Latin because the ritualistic language left him free to concentrate on its phonetic qualities, but its use also refers back to the long tradition of Latin texts in Western church music. Baroque features of the Symphony include almost perpetual motion, frequent ostinatos (also a Stravinsky trademark), and a fully developed fugue in the second movement. Stravinsky avoids a Romantic orchestral sound,

Uses of neoclassicism

Symphony of Psalms

emphasizing instead what he called an "objective" rather than emotional sound palette by omitting violins, violas, and clarinets.

In the first movement (NAWM 177), traditional elements are reinterpreted in new ways, and Stravinsky's personal idiom is much in evidence: changing meters, unexpected rests, and the alternation of contrasting sound blocks that are related through similar pitch collections. At the first vocal entrance (Example 25.8a), the melody is restricted to two pitches, E and F, suggesting a simple psalm tone. It is accompanied by three layers of ostinatos sounding the full octatonic scale (Example 25.8b). The scoring for double-reed instruments alone evokes a Renaissance consort. Later, the opening E-minor triad returns in a diatonic rather than octatonic context. Although E is emphasized as a tonal center, it is established simply through assertion and repetition, in both harmonic and melodic contexts. Such assertion of a tonal center through reiteration is very different from Schoenberg's atonality. Yet this music cannot be described as tonal, since it does not follow the rules of traditional harmony. Such music, characterized by the composer's finding new ways to establish a single pitch as a tonal center, is called *neotonal*.

Partly because Stravinsky's music was based on tonal centers—sometimes more than one in a given piece—as well as on recognizable genres and styles, performers and audiences found his neoclassical works easier to play and to follow than Schoenberg's twelve-tone compositions. Both composers attracted supporters, who argued about music's need to adhere to tradition versus the need to find new methods, echoing the Brahms–Wagner disputes of the nineteenth century. In recent decades, musicians and scholars have come to see how much in common the two composers had, especially in their music of the 1920s through the 1940s, when both sought to revive traditional forms in an entirely new and personal musical language.

Full 🔊

Neotonality

Schoenberg and Stravinsky

Example 25.8 Igor Stravinsky, Symphony of Psalms

a. Vocal entrance

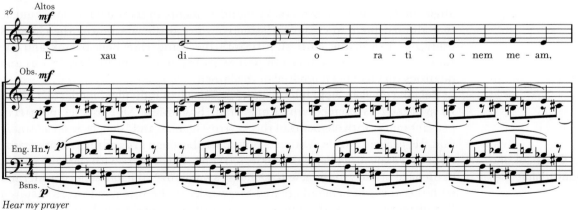

Hear my prayer

b. Octatonic scale

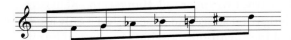

Serial Period

After Schoenberg's death in 1951, the twelve-tone methods he had pioneered were as much a part of history as sonata form. They were also becoming popular with younger composers, who extended the serial principle to elements other than pitch, such as rhythm and timbre (see Chapter 27). Such music, no longer simply twelve-tone, became known as serial music, a term that has also been applied retrospectively to Schoenberg and his students.

In part to encompass yet another branch of the classical tradition and in part to keep up with the times, Stravinsky—already in his seventies—adapted serial techniques in his music from about 1953 on. His best-known serial works include the song cycle *In memoriam Dylan Thomas* (1954); *Threni* (1957–1958), for voices and orchestra on texts from the Lamentations of Jeremiah; and *Movements* (1958–1959), for piano and orchestra. All of them show his characteristic idiom of juxtaposed blocks, disrupted meter, and his other signature traits.

Stravinsky's particular genius lay in finding stylistic markers, derived from Russian sources yet distinctly his own, that proved so recognizable and adaptable that he could assimilate or allude to any style while putting his personal stamp on the music. By drawing on everything from early music to the serial music of his time, he claimed the entire tradition as his own.

Influence

Stravinsky's impact on other composers was in a league with that of Wagner and Debussy. Through Stravinsky, elements that had been nurtured in Russian music and traits he had introduced became commonplaces of modern music, used by composers employing many different styles. Stravinsky popularized neoclassicism, setting an example that many others imitated. His serial music was less well known, but his support for serialism helped it gain a strong following among composers and academics. His willingness to change styles encouraged others to do the same, though few if any matched his ability to project a single personality in any style he adopted.

Béla Bartók (1881–1945)

Modernists other than Stravinsky found elements in their own national music that allowed them to create a distinctive voice while continuing the classical tradition. Two of the most significant—the Hungarian Béla Bartók and the American Charles Ives did so in part by incorporating musical traditions and qualities that had been ignored or disdained.

Béla Bartók (see Biography, page 575) created an individual modernist idiom by synthesizing elements of Hungarian, Romanian, Slovak, and Bulgarian peasant music with elements of the Austro-German and French classical tradition. He arrived at this synthesis only after thorough grounding in both traditions and exposure to several modern trends. Encounters with the tone poems of Richard Strauss in 1902, with Debussy's music over the following decade, and with the works of Schoenberg and Stravinsky in the 1910s and 1920s inspired Bartók to write music that emulated and ultimately absorbed their idioms.

Classical and
modern influences

Peasant music

Bartók's search for an innately Hungarian music led him to collect and study peasant music, often in collaboration with fellow composer Zoltán Kodály (1882–1967). Bartók published nearly two thousand Hungarian, Romanian, Slovak, Croatian, Serbian, and Bulgarian songs and dance tunes—only a small part of the music he had collected in expeditions ranging over central Europe,

Béla Bartók (1881–1945)

A virtuoso pianist, educator, musicologist, and composer, Béla Bartók pursued multiple careers. He was also one of the outstanding nationalist composers of the twentieth century and left a body of work that matches or exceeds that of any nineteenth-century composer of a nationalist bent.

Bartók was born in the Austro-Hungarian Empire in a small Hungarian city now in Romania. His parents were teachers and amateur musicians, and he took piano lessons from age five and composed from age nine. He studied piano and composition at the Hungarian Royal Academy of Music in Budapest, returning there in 1907 to teach piano. As a virtuoso pianist, he performed all over Europe and edited the keyboard music of Bach, Scarlatti, Haydn, Mozart, Beethoven, and others.

Figure 25.10   Caricature by Aline Fruhauf of Béla Bartók at the piano (December 1927). The caption reads: "An impression of Béla Bartók, the mild-mannered Revolutionist who plays in New York this week." Presumably, it was the dissonant and angular style of his music that prompted the epithet "Revolutionist."
(Lebrecht Music & Arts Photo Library.)

In 1904, Bartók overheard the singing of a woman from Transylvania (a region then in Hungary and now in Romania), which sparked a life-long interest in the folk music of Hungary, Romania, and nearby lands. He collected thousands of songs and dances, edited them in collections, and wrote books and essays about folk music. He arranged many folk tunes, wrote pieces based on them, and borrowed elements from various folk traditions for use in his concert music.

In 1909 Bartók married his student Márta Ziegler, who assisted him in his work. Their son was born in 1910. In 1923 he divorced Márta and married Ditta Pásztory, with whom he had a second son the next year.

In 1934 Bartók left the Academy of Music and moved to a full-time position as ethnomusicologist at the Academy of Sciences, where he joined Zoltán Kodály and others in preparing a critical edition of Hungarian folk music. His compositions over the next five years, including the last two string quartets and *Music for Strings, Percussion and Celesta*, marked the high point of his career. When the rise of the Nazis in Germany and their 1938 takeover of Austria brought the threat of fascism to Hungary, Bartók arranged to send his manuscripts to the United States. He followed with his family in 1940, settling in New York, where his last years were difficult both financially and physically. Friends procured jobs and commissions for him, sometimes without his knowledge, but he was already suffering from leukemia, which took his life in 1945.

Major works: *Bluebeard's Castle, The Miraculous Mandarin, Dance Suite,* Concerto for Orchestra, *Music for Strings, Percussion and Celesta,* 3 piano concertos, 2 violin concertos, 6 string quartets, 2 violin sonatas, 1 piano sonata, *Mikrokosmos,* numerous other works for piano, songs, choral works, and folk-song arrangements.

Turkey, and North Africa. He used the new technology of audio recording (Figure 25.11), which preserved the unique and unfamiliar characteristics of each folksinger and style far better than the older method of transcribing music by ear into conventional notation. He then analyzed the collected specimens with

Figure 25.11. Béla Bartók in 1907, recording Slovakian folk songs on an acoustic cylinder machine in the Hungarian village of Zobordarázs.
(Collection of Ferenc Bónis.)

techniques developed in the new discipline of ethnomusicology, and he edited collections and wrote commentaries that established him as the leading scholar of this music.

Works   Bartók first achieved a distinctive personal style around 1908, with compositions such as the First String Quartet and the one-act opera *Bluebeard's Castle*, composed in 1911 and premiered in 1918, which combines Hungarian folk elements with influences from Debussy's *Pelléas et Mélisande*. His *Allegro barbaro* (1911) and other piano works introduced a new approach to the piano, treating it more as a percussion instrument than as a medium for cantabile melodies and resonant accompaniments. In his compositions from the decade after World War I, he explored the limits of dissonance and tonal ambiguity, reaching the furthest point with his two violin sonatas of 1921 and 1922. Other works of this decade include the expressionist pantomime *The Miraculous Mandarin* and the Third and Fourth String Quartets. His later works, which seem in comparison more accessible to a broad audience, have become the most widely known, including the Fifth and Sixth Quartets, *Music for Strings, Percussion and Celesta* (1936), and the Concerto for Orchestra (1943).

Bartók's synthesis   In synthesizing peasant with classical music, Bartók emphasized what the traditions have in common and, at the same time, what is most distinctive about each. In both traditions, pieces typically have a single pitch center, use diatonic or other scales, and feature melodies built from motives that are repeated and varied. Then, from the classical tradition, Bartók retained certain contrapuntal and formal procedures, such as fugue and sonata form. From the peasant tradition, he drew rhythmic complexity and irregular meters, common especially in Bulgarian music; modal scales and mixed modes; and specific types of melodic structure and ornamentation. His *Mikrokosmos* (1929–1939)—153 piano pieces in six books of graded difficulty—is a work of great pedagogical value that summarizes Bartók's style and exemplifies his synthesis. For example, *Staccato and Legato* (NAWM 178) is like a Bach two-part invention, with a canon between the hands, inversion and invertible counterpoint, and a tonal structure reminiscent

Mikrokosmos

Full 🔊   Concise 🔊

of Bach. Yet the shape of the melody adapts the structure of many Hungarian songs, built from a short phrase that rises and falls within the span of a fourth, repeats transposed up a fifth, is varied, and finally falls back to the tonic. Many elements, from its mixture of diatonic and chromatic motion to its ornamentation, draw from both traditions.

Music for Strings, Percussion and Celesta also illustrates Bartók's synthesis as well as several characteristics of his personal style. He uses neotonality in combining peasant and classical elements to create a modernist idiom. Each of the four movements establishes a tonal center by methods analogous to the modal melodies of folk song and to the chordal motion and tonic-dominant polarities of classical music, while avoiding common-practice harmony. The tonal center of the first and last movements is A, with an important secondary center at the tritone E♭/D♯, a post-tonal analogue to the conventional dominant E. The second movement is in C, with a similar tritone pole, as shown in Figure 25.12. The slow third movement (NAWM 179) has the opposite arrangement, centering on F♯ with C as the competing pole. Some of the principal themes of the four movements and all of the final cadences clearly bring out this tritone relationship, as shown in Example 25.9. In addition, the cadences evoke standard procedures in tonal music, from counterpoint in contrary motion (Example 25.9a) to a mock dominant-tonic cadence (Example 25.9c). There are also strong similarities to peasant melodies, which often rise from and return to a tonal center or circle around a central tone, as in the second movement theme (Example 25.9b); or descend to the tonal center from its upper octave, as in the finale (Example 25.9e). Here the synthesis of the two traditions to create a modernist idiom is rich in allusions to music in both traditions.

Bartók creates each theme by varying small motives, a typical procedure both in classical music—from Bach and Haydn to Schoenberg and Stravinsky—and in the peasant music of central and southeastern Europe. Many Hungarian tunes use short phrases and repeated motives with slight variations, while Bulgarian dance tunes typically spin out a rhythmic-melodic motive, as in the finale's theme (Example 25.9e). The latter is diatonic, like many classical themes, but clearly in the Lydian mode, which is used in some peasant songs. Hungarian songs can mix modes, an effect Bartók borrows at the end of the second-movement theme (Example 25.9b), where the melodic rise and fall suggests Lydian, then Phrygian, modes.

Bartók's complex forms and contrapuntal procedures come strictly from the classical tradition. The first movement is an elaborate fugue, with entrances that successively rise and fall around the circle of fifths in both directions from A, meeting in a climax at the opposite pole of E♭. The second movement is a sonata form; the third movement a modified arch form (ABCB'A') in which the phrases of the first-movement fugue theme are embedded; and the finale a rondo that includes a modified reprise of the fugue theme. Such thematic references to the first movement recall the cyclic symphonies of Berlioz and Tchaikovsky, among others. Each movement includes canon and imitation,

Music for Strings, Percussion and Celesta

Full 🔊   Concise 🔊

Melodic structure

Form and counterpoint

Movement:	1	2	3	4
Tonal Center:	A	C	F♯	A
Tritone pole:	E♭/D♯	F♯	C	E♭/D♯

Figure 25.12 Tonal centers in Bartók's Music for Strings, Percussion and Celesta.

Example 25.9 Béla Bartók, Music for Strings, Percussion and Celesta

a. Final cadence of first movement

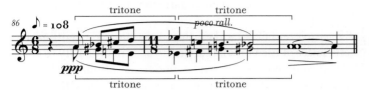

b. Second-movement theme

c. Final cadence of second movement   *d. Final cadence of third movement*

e. Fourth-movement theme

f. Final cadence

often in inversion. Bartók was very fond of symmetries and palindromes, as we can see in the mirror counterpoint at the end of the first movement (Example 25.9a).

Peasant elements

Formal and rhythmic elements from traditional peasant styles are also evident. Bulgarian dance meters feature long and short beats rather than strong and weak beats, with the longs half again as long as the short. In Western notation, this translates into irregular groupings of twos and threes as, for example, 2 + 3, 3 + 2 + 2, or 2 + 2 + 2 + 3. Bartók adopts this effect in the fourth movement theme (Example 25.9e), which exhibits the pattern 2 + 3 + 3. The heavily ornamented, partly chromatic type of Serbo-Croatian song in Example 25.10a,

Example 25.10 Béla Bartók, Music for Strings, Percussion and Celesta

a. Serbo-Croatian song

b. Passage near beginning of third movement

which Bartók described as *parlando-rubato* ("speechlike, in free tempo"), is echoed near the beginning of the third movement, shown in Example 25.10b. Melodies over drones, as in this example, are also a feature of peasant music. String glissandi, snapped pizzicati, percussive chords laced with dissonant seconds, and other characteristics of Bartók's personal style do not derive directly from peasant music but can convey a rough, vibrant effect that suggests a source other than art music.

Like his fellow modernists, Bartók aspired to create masterpieces resembling those of the classical masters he took as models. He both emulated their music and sought new methods and materials in order to distinguish his music from that of other modern composers. The new elements he found were those of another tradition—the peasant music of his and other nations. Through his synthesis of both traditions, he created new works with a strong personal identity and a rich connection to the music of the past.

Bartók as modernist

Charles Ives (1874–1954)

Like his European counterparts, Charles Ives, the first modernist American composer, synthesized international and regional musical traditions to create a distinctive personal idiom that successfully combines modernism with Americanism. Ives (see Biography, page 580) was fluent in four distinct spheres: American vernacular music, Protestant church music, European classical music, and experimental music (see below), of which he was the first major exponent. In his mature music, he combined elements from all four, using the multiplicity of styles as a rhetorical device to convey rich musical meanings.

Charles Ives (1874–1954)

Like the archetypal artist in countless movies, Ives worked in comfortable obscurity for most of his career but lived to be recognized as one of the most significant classical composers of his generation.

Ives was born in Danbury, a small city in Connecticut where his father was a bandmaster, church musician, and music teacher. Ives studied piano and organ, showing prodigious talent—at age fourteen he became the youngest professional church organist in the state. His father taught him theory and composition, and encouraged an experimental approach to sound.

At Yale, he took liberal-arts courses and studied music theory and composition with composer, teacher, and organist Horatio Parker. While in college, Ives wrote marches and songs for his fraternity brothers and church music for Center Church in New Haven, where he was organist.

After graduating in 1898, he settled in New York, where he worked as a church organist, got a job in the insurance business, and lived with fellow Yale graduates in an apartment they called "Poverty Flat." When his cantata *The Celestial Country* failed to garner strongly positive reviews, Ives quit his organist position and focused on insurance. His firm, Ives & Myrick, became one of the most successful agencies in the nation, as Ives pioneered the training of agents (his classes are one inspiration for the modern business school) and the idea of estate planning.

His courtship with Harmony Twichell, whom he married in 1908, inspired a new confidence, and the next decade brought an outpouring of music, including most of the pieces that later made Ives's reputation. Composing evenings and weekends, he prepared finished copies of his less radical pieces, such as the first three symphonies and the violin sonatas, but published nothing and left many works in sketch or partial score.

After trying in vain for over a decade to interest performers and publishers in his music, Ives was spurred in 1918 by a health crisis to edit and self-publish *114 Songs* and his Second Piano Sonata (*Concord, Mass., 1840–60*), which was accompanied by a book, *Essays before a Sonata.* He devoted the 1920s to completing several large pieces. The remaining three decades of his life saw the premieres and publication of most of his major works. Although accused—despite his thorough musical training—of amateurism because he was a businessman, Ives won a number of advocates among younger composers, performers, and conductors, who promoted his music. By the time of his death at age seventy-nine, he was widely regarded as the first to create a distinctly American body of art music, and his reputation has continued to grow.

Figure 25.13 Charles Ives in an undated photograph.
(Lebrecht Music & Arts Photo Library.)

Major works: 4 symphonies, *Holidays Symphony, Three Places in New England, The Unanswered Question,* 2 string quartets, 4 violin sonatas, 2 piano sonatas, about 200 songs.

Vernacular music   Ives grew up surrounded by American vernacular music (see Chapter 24), from parlor songs and minstrel show tunes to the marches and cornet solos his father performed as leader of the town band. In his teens, Ives wrote numerous marches and parlor songs in the styles of the day, and during his college years at Yale he composed partsongs for the glee club and stage music for fraternity shows. As a young church organist (1888–1902), he improvised organ preludes and postludes, and composed solo songs and sacred choral works representing all the styles then prominent in American Protestantism—from simple hymnody to the cultivated manner of his composition teacher at Yale, Horatio Parker. With Parker he intensified his study of art music, writing exercises in counterpoint, fugue, and orchestration, and composing in genres from art song to symphony. His First Symphony, which he began during his last year in college, was directly modeled on Dvořák's *New World* Symphony, with elements from Schubert, Beethoven, and Tchaikovsky.

In his experimental music, Ives's typical approach was to preserve most of the traditional rules but change others to see what would happen. As a youth, he practiced drumming on the piano, devising dissonant chords that would suggest the sound of drums. He wrote several pieces in his teens that were polytonal, with the melody in one key and the accompaniment in another, or with four imitative voices, each in its own key. "If you can play a tune in one key," he asked, "why can't a feller, if he feels like [it], play one in two keys?" Polytonality was later developed independently by other composers, but Ives was the first to use it systematically. Like many of his experiments, his polytonal pieces introduced unprecedented levels of dissonance and rhythmic complexity, although they usually preserved the idea of a tonal center.

None of Ives's experimental pieces was published or performed in public until long after they were written; they were essentially ways of trying out ideas. But one experimental work became one of Ives's best-known pieces because his novel means fit the inspired program so perfectly: *The Unanswered Question* (1908). Slowly moving strings in G major represent "the silences of the Druids—who know, see and hear nothing," while over them a trumpet poses "the perennial question of existence" and four flutes attempt ever more energetic and dissonant answers until they give up in frustration, leaving the question to sound once more, unanswered. The trumpet and flute parts are atonal, making Ives one of the first composers to use atonality (roughly contemporary with Schoenberg but independent of him) and the first to combine tonal and atonal layers in the same piece.

From 1902 on, Ives wrote only in classical genres, but he brought the styles and sounds of the other traditions that he knew into his music. Typically, he employed them to suggest extramusical meanings, whether in a character piece or in a programmatic work. Doing so was a radical act; although classical audiences welcomed folk melodies as sources for concert works, they tended to regard the hymn tunes and popular songs that Ives used as beneath notice and entirely out of place in the concert hall.

Ives's Third Symphony, four violin sonatas, and First Piano Sonata all feature movements based on American hymn tunes. Here Ives uses procedures of thematic fragmentation and development from European sonata forms and symphonies, but reverses the normal course of events so that the development happens first and the themes appear in their entirety only at the end. This procedure has been called *cumulative form.* While not overtly programmatic, these instrumental works suggest the coming together of individual voices and the fervent spirit of hymn-singing at the camp-meeting revivals of the composer's youth. Thus, Ives is not only a musical nationalist in these works, but he is also asserting the universal value of his country's music by making a place for American melody within the European tradition (see Vignette, page 583).

Many of Ives's later pieces are programmatic, celebrating aspects of American life. *Three Places in New England* presents orchestral pictures of the first African American regiment in the Civil War, a band playing at a Fourth of July picnic, and the composer's walk by a river with his wife during their honeymoon. Other

Marginal notes

Church music

Classical music

Experimental works

Polytonality

The Unanswered Question

Syntheses

Cumulative form

Programs

Figure 25.14 General William Booth (1829–1912), founder and first General of the Salvation Army.
(Lebrecht Music & Arts Photo Library.)

General Booth Enters into Heaven

works are more philosophical, such as the Fourth Symphony, an extraordinary, complex work that poses and seeks to answer "the searching questions of What? and Why?" In all of these, Ives references American tunes or musical styles, from Stephen Foster to ragtime, to suggest the meanings that he wanted to convey. In some pieces, he uses a collage technique, quoting multiple tunes and layering them on top of each other, weaving them together like a patchwork quilt, to invoke the way experiences are recalled in memory. He also uses techniques developed in his experimental music, often to represent certain kinds of sounds or motions, such as exploding fireworks or mists over a river.

With such a wide range of styles at his command, Ives frequently mixed them—whether traditional or newly invented—within a single piece. This variety of styles allowed Ives to evoke a wide range of extramusical references and also to articulate musical form, distinguishing each phrase, section, or passage from the next through stylistic contrast. He also used style, alongside timbre, rhythm, figuration, register, and other more traditional means, to differentiate layers heard simultaneously, as in *The Unanswered Question.*

Ives synthesized all four traditions his music encompassed in his song *General William Booth Enters into Heaven* (1914, NAWM 180), on a poem by Vachel Lindsay that pictures the founder of the Salvation Army (see Figure 25.14) leading the poor and downtrodden into heaven. It is an art song, but the musical content is drawn primarily from American vernacular music, church music, and experimental music. At the opening, shown in Example 25.11, Ives evokes Booth's bass

Example 25.11 Charles Ives, General William Booth Enters into Heaven

VIGNETTE Americanism in Music

Dvořák had advised American composers to use African American or American Indian music as sources for a distinctively national music, and many did so. Charles Ives felt that for himself, as a white New Englander, a more appropriate source was the music regularly heard and sung by people in his own region, from hymns to popular song. No matter what sources are used, he argued, the composer must understand the music from the inside and know what it meant to the people who heard and performed it.

If a man finds that the cadences of an Apache war dance come nearest to his soul—provided he has taken pains to know enough other cadences, for eclecticism is part of his duty; sorting potatoes means a better crop next year—let him assimilate whatever he finds highest of the Indian ideal so that he can use it with the cadences, fervently, transcendentally, inevitably, furiously, in his symphonies, in his operas, in his whistlings on the way to work, so that he can paint his house with them, make them a part of his prayer-book—this is all possible and necessary, if he is confident that they have a part in his spiritual consciousness. With this assurance, his music will have everything it should of sincerity, nobility, strength, and beauty, no matter how it sounds; and if, with this, he is true to none but the highest of American ideals (that is, the ideals only that coincide with his spiritual consciousness), his music will be true to itself and incidentally American, and it will be so even after it is proved that all our Indians came from Asia.

The man "born down to Babbitt's Corners" may find a deep appeal in the simple but acute Gospel hymns of the New England "camp meetin'" of a generation or so ago. . . . If the Yankee can reflect the fervency with which "his gospels" were sung—the fervency of "Aunt Sarah," who scrubbed her life away for her brother's ten orphans, the fervency with which this woman, after a fourteen-hour work day on the farm, would hitch up and drive five miles through the mud and rain to "prayer meetin'," her one articulate outlet for the fullness of her unselfish soul—if he can reflect the fervency of such a spirit, he may find there a local color that will do all the world good. If his music can but catch that spirit by being a part with itself, it will come somewhere near his ideal—and it will be American too—perhaps nearer so than that of the devotee of Indian or negro melody. In other words, if local color, national color, any color, is a true pigment of the universal color, it is a divine quality, it is a part of substance in art—not of manner.

From Charles Ives, *Essays before a Sonata, The Majority, and Other Writings,* ed. Howard Boatwright (New York: Norton, 1970), pp. 79–81.

---

drum through the experimental technique of piano-drumming, using a standard rhythmic pattern of American drummers, and derives the vocal line from the hymn *There Is a Fountain Filled with Blood.* Each group of Booth's followers described in the poem receives a different musical characterization, using polytonality, novel chord structures, dissonant ostinatos, and other techniques that Ives first explored in his experimental works. Thus, Ives combines the art-song framework with the American vernacular tradition, church music (hymn tune), and experimental techniques to convey the experience of the poem.

Ives was isolated as a composer. Among his contemporaries, he was influenced by the music of Strauss, Debussy, and Scriabin, but he encountered that of Stravinsky only late in his career, after arriving independently at similar methods, and that of Schoenberg and other modernists only after he had ceased to compose. Nor did they know his music; except for some early vernacular and church works, most of his pieces were performed and published only long after he had written them. Thus, his direct influence was felt mostly after World War II, when his departures from convention were taken as an example by postwar composers, encouraging them to experiment and providing models for some novel procedures. He can justifiably be called the founder of the

Ives's place

At the Time

In 1913, at the time of the premiere in Paris of Igor Stravinsky's *Rite of Spring*, which provokes audiences to riot with its evocation of primitive ritual, shocking choreography, and compelling modernist score:

- The New York Armory show introduces Pablo Picasso's works to the American public.
- Charles Ives, a mature composer residing in New York, is writing his second String Quartet, in three movements titled "Discussions," "Arguments," and "The Call of the Mountains."
- Suffragettes demonstrate in London and Washington, D.C. for women's right to vote, not granted until 1920 (in the United States) and 1928 (in the United Kingdom).
- Hungarian pianist-composer Béla Bartók, disenchanted with the musical establishment in Budapest, collects folk songs among Romanians in Hungary and the Berbers in North Africa (in a region now in Algeria).
- Mohandes (Mahatma) K. Ghandi is arrested for leading Indian miners in a protest march in South Africa.
- The Ford Motor Company introduces a continuously moving assembly line to mass-produce its Model T, allowing each car to be manufactured in two hours and forty minutes.
- The Futurist Manifesto, *The Art of Noises*, published in Italy, declares that the modern world of machines calls for a new type of music based on noise (see Figure 25.15).
- A concert in Vienna, conducted by Arnold Schoenberg and featuring modernist works by Schoenberg, Anton Webern, Gustav Mahler, and Alban Berg, becomes a notorious event; the performance of Berg's new songs cause a riot of such proportions that the police are called in and the concert cannot be finished.
- Charlie Chaplin begins his film career at Keystone Studios, earning $150 per week.
- A Swedish immigrant in Hoboken, New Jersey, patents the zipper.

Figure 25.15 Music *(1911) by futurist painter Luigi Russolo, author of* The Art of Noises.
(Private collection. Photo: © DeA Picture Library/Art Resource, NY.)

experimental-music tradition in the United States and, as such, his work was incalculably important to younger generations of American musicians.

POSTLUDE

Of the six composers surveyed in this chapter, Arnold Schoenberg and Igor Stravinsky were leaders of two very different branches of musical modernism. Schoenberg's students Alban Berg and Anton Webern took their teacher's ideas in individual directions, while Béla Bartók and Charles Ives, like Stravinsky, developed unique combinations of nationalism and modernism within the classical tradition. Their music intensified the split between popular and classical music that had grown wide in the nineteenth century because, like that of many other modernist composers, it was directed at connoisseurs—those willing to study it, hear it repeatedly, and explore its rich structure and references to other music. The works studied here have a central place in the musical canon but on the whole they are more admired by critics, composers, and scholars than they are loved by audience members, who tend to prefer their less radical contemporaries such as Strauss and Rachmaninoff.

Yet the dissonances, atonality, multiple layers, sudden juxtapositions, unpredictability, and startling stylistic contrasts that offended audiences generations ago are now familiar from repeated performances and recordings, and from their use in more recent music, especially music for films. Bartok's *Music for Strings, Percussion and Celesta* turns up in *The Shining*, Webern's *Five Pieces for Orchestra* in *The Exorcist*, and Ives's *The Unanswered Question* in *The Thin Red Line*, and many more film scores use sounds and techniques pioneered by these six composers in an effort to exploit their strong emotional effects.

 Resources for study and review available at wwnorton.com/studyspace

26

Music between the Two World Wars

PRELUDE

Music has been linked to politics since the days of Plato and Aristotle, who wrote about its place in the ideal society (see Chapter 1). But in the nineteenth century, some writers claimed that classical music was an autonomous art that transcended politics and should be composed, performed, experienced, and admired for its own sake, separate from political or social concerns. The new "science" of musicology that emerged during the nineteenth century reinforced this view, focusing more on the styles and procedures of past music than on its social functions. To some extent, treating music on its own terms was an admirable ideal, allowing many listeners to enjoy music for its own sake and as a respite from the concerns of the day. But in other respects, from its cultivation by the economic and social elite to its association with nationalism, classical music never fully escaped politics.

The period between the world wars brought new links between music and politics. In democracies such as Britain, France, Germany under the Weimar Republic, and the United States, economic troubles and political conflicts led many composers to believe art that set itself apart from social needs was in danger of becoming irrelevant to society at large. As the gap widened between the unfamiliar sounds of modernist music and the ability of listeners to understand it, composers tried to bring contemporary music closer to the general public by crafting widely accessible concert works or by writing music for films, theater, and dance. Convinced that music performed by amateurs and school groups was as important as art music, some composers wrote works that were within the capabilities of amateurs and rewarding to perform yet modern in style. Others used music, especially musical theater, to engage current social, political, and economic issues. Nationalism continued as a strong force in most countries, exemplified in the musical styles of individual composers and in efforts to edit, publish, and perform music of the nation, including both folk music and the written music of earlier times.

Most governments sponsored musical activities directly, and public schools increasingly included music in the curriculum. Throughout most of Europe, radio was controlled by the government and was a major employer of composers and performers. Totalitarian governments insisted that music under their regimes support the state and its ideologies. Although musical styles were often identified with particular ideologies, these links were contingent on the unique political situation in each nation; the same style, even the same piece, could be seen as progressive or socialist in one place and conservative or fascist in another.

This chapter will begin by surveying some avant-garde composers and then move to a discussion of how modernist and experimental (or ultramodernist) composers in Europe and the Americas dealt with various political movements, the disruptions caused by two world wars, and the ideological forces for change through the middle of the twentieth century.

France

World War I and its aftermath brought a new wave of anti-German sentiment and a renewed opposition to German influences in French culture. During and after the war, nationalists asserted that French music was intrinsically Classic as opposed to the Romanticism of the Germans. Thus neoclassicism—the use of classical genres and forms, tonal centers, and common-practice or neotonal harmonies, allied with emotional restraint and a rejection of Romantic excess—became the prevailing trend in France after the war, one associated with patriotism. But exactly how the "Classic" was to be defined became a point of contention. Conservatives identified it with balance, order, discipline, and tradition, in contrast to the irrationality and individualism of Romanticism. More progressive composers, like Ravel (see Chapter 23), saw the Classic as encompassing the universal and not merely the national.

Notions of classicism

Les Six

A younger group of composers absorbed the strong influence of neoclassicism but sought to escape old political dichotomies. Arthur Honegger (1892–1955), Darius Milhaud (1892–1974), Francis Poulenc (1899–1963), Germaine Tailleferre (1892–1983), Georges Auric (1899–1983), and Louis Durey (1888–1979) were dubbed "Les Six" (The Six), in a parallel to the Mighty Handful in Russia (see Chapter 22), by a French journalist who saw them as seeking to free French music from foreign domination. They drew inspiration from Satie (see Chapter 23) and were hailed by the writer Jean Cocteau, who called for new music that would be fully French and anti-Romantic in its clarity, accessibility, and emotional restraint.

The group, pictured in Figure 26.1, collaborated in joint concerts and other projects but did not remain together long. Instead of conforming to Cocteau's program, each wrote highly individual works that drew on a wide range of influences, including but not limited to neoclassicism. Tailleferre was the most in tune with neoclassical ideals, drawing on Couperin and Rameau (see Chapter 14) in her Piano Concerto (1923–1924) and other works. Auric was the most taken with Satie's avant-garde approach. But the most individual were Honegger, Milhaud, and Poulenc, who achieved success

Figure 26.1 Jacques-Émile Blanche, Les Six (Hommage à Satie) *(The Group of Six [Homage to Satie]) (1922–1923). This group portrait, from about 1921, shows five of the six composers and three of their collaborators. Clockwise from the bottom left are Germaine Tailleferre, Darius Milhaud, Arthur Honegger, conductor Jean Wiener, pianist Marcelle Mayer (in the center), Francis Poulenc, writer Jean Cocteau, and Georges Auric.*

(Musée des Beaux-Arts, Rouen, France. Photo: Bridgeman Art Library. © 2006 Artists Rights Society (ARS), New York/ADAGP, Paris.)

independent of the group and found ways to make their music distinctive within the broad outlines of neoclassicism.

Arthur Honegger

Arthur Honegger excelled in music of dynamic action and graphic gesture, expressed in short-breathed melodies, strong ostinato rhythms, bold colors, and dissonant harmonies. His symphonic movement *Pacific 231* (1923), a translation into music of the visual and physical impression of a speeding locomotive, was hailed as a sensational piece of modernist descriptive music. Honegger won an international reputation in 1923 with his oratorio *King David,* which combined the tradition of music for amateur chorus with allusions to styles from Gregorian chant to Baroque polyphony to jazz. The evocations of pre-Romantic styles, use of traditional forms and procedures, and prevailing diatonic language all reveal the impact of neoclassicism.

Darius Milhaud

Darius Milhaud produced an immense quantity of music, including piano pieces, chamber music, suites, sonatas, symphonies, film music, ballets, songs, cantatas, operas, and music for children. His works are diverse in style and approach, ranging from the comic frivolity of the ballet *Le Boeuf sur le toit* (The Ox on the Roof, 1919) to the earnestness of the opera-oratorio *Christophe Colomb* (1928) and the religious devotion of the *Sacred Service* (1947), which reflects Milhaud's Jewish heritage. He was especially open to sounds and styles from the Americas. Saxophone, ragtime syncopations, and elements of the blues (see Chapter 24) find their way into his ballet *La Création du monde* (The Creation of the World, 1923; NAWM 185). These elements are synthesized with neoclassic and other modernist traits, including fugue, polytonality, and polyrhythms.

La Création du monde

Full 🔊

Brazilian folk melodies and rhythms appear in *Le Boeuf sur le toit* and in the suite of dances *Saudades do Brasil* (Souvenirs of Brazil, 1920–1921) illustrated in Example 26.1. In addition to the syncopated rhythms and diatonic melodies of Brazilian dance, the latter uses polytonality, in which two lines of melody and planes of harmony, each in a distinct and different key, sound simultaneously—here, B major in the upper register over G major in the accompaniment. This procedure would become associated with Milhaud, although many used it before and since. In all his music, Milhaud blended ingenuity, freshness, and variety with the clarity and logical form he had absorbed from neoclassicism. Yet his openness to foreign influences, from jazz to Schoenberg, was a far cry from the program of nationalist classical purity initially adopted by Les Six.

Francis Poulenc

Francis Poulenc drew especially on the Parisian popular chanson tradition sustained in cabarets and revues. This too, violated the strictures of neoclassicism, which rejected influence from "lower" forms of music. Poulenc's compositions revel in an ingratiating harmonic idiom, draw grace and wit from popular styles, and combine sharp satire with pleasing melody, as in his surrealist comic opera *Les Mamelles de Tirésias* (The Breasts of Tiresias, 1940).

Example 26.1 Darius Milhaud. Saudados do Brasil, *I. No. 4,* Copacabaña

Germany

Germany under the Weimar Republic (1919–1933) was a hotbed of political contention, which echoed in the musical world. After the Nazis came to power in 1933, they attacked most modern music as decadent, banned the political Left and Jews from participating in public life, and persecuted Jews and other minorities. As a result, many leading musicians took refuge abroad.

New Objectivity

In opposition to the emotional intensity of the late Romantics and the expressionism of Schoenberg and Berg, a new trend emerged in the 1920s under the slogan "Neue Sachlichkeit," meaning New Objectivity, New Realism, or "New Matter-of-Factness." The phrase was first used in art criticism and quickly adopted by musicians. As articulated by the composer Ernst Krenek (1900–1991) and others, the New Objectivity opposed complexity and promoted the use of familiar elements, borrowing from popular music and jazz or from Classic and Baroque procedures. In their view, music should be objective in its expression, as in the Baroque concept of the affections (see Chapter 10), rather than subjective or extreme. The notion of music as autonomous was rejected. Instead, it should be widely accessible, communicate clearly, and draw connections to the events and concerns of the time.

Krenek's *Jonny spielt auf* (Jonny Strikes Up the Band), premiered in Leipzig in 1927, was the embodiment of these ideals, an opera set in the present time that used the interaction of a European composer and an African American jazz musician to examine dichotomies between contemplation and pleasure and between a seemingly exhausted and inward-looking European tradition and a new and energetic American one. The music drew on jazz and on a simplified harmonic language. The opera, an immediate success, was produced on more than seventy stages during the next three years, and established Krenek's reputation. But almost from the start it was vociferously attacked by the Nazis as "degenerate" for its use of African American elements. Krenek later adopted the twelve-tone method and emigrated to the United States after Nazi Germany absorbed his native Austria in 1938.

Ernst Krenek

Kurt Weill (1900–1950), an opera composer in Berlin, was also an exponent of the New Objectivity. Sympathetic to the political Left, he sought to offer social commentary and to entertain everyday people rather than the intellectual elite. Weill collaborated with the playwright Bertolt Brecht on the allegorical opera *Aufstieg und Fall der Stadt Mahagonny* (Rise and Fall of the City of Mahagonny, 1930). In the opera, fugitives from justice build a town dedicated to pleasure, free of legal or moral taboos, but soon find that they have created a hell rather than a paradise on earth. Weill's score incorporates elements of popular music and jazz, and makes witty references to a variety of styles. The pit orchestra includes instruments typical of jazz bands—two saxophones, piano, banjo, and bass guitar—as well as winds and timpani, while three saxophones, zither, bandoneon (a kind of accordion), strings, and brass play in the stage orchestra. Through satire in both libretto and music, Brecht and Weill sought to expose what they regarded as the failures of capitalism, which the city of Mahagonny exemplified.

Kurt Weill

Mahagonny

The most famous collaboration between Weill and Brecht was *Die Dreigroschenoper* (The Threepenny Opera, premiered 1928). Brecht based the libretto on *The Beggar's Opera* by John Gay (see Chapter 15 and NAWM 109), although

The Threepenny Opera

Full ⤵

Figure 26.2. Lotte Lenya as Jenny in the 1931 film version of Kurt Weill's The Threepenny Opera.
(Kurt Weill Foundation/Lebrecht Music & Arts Photo Library.)

Paul Hindemith

Weill borrowed only one air from the score. The cast included Lotte Lenya (Figure 26.2), whom Weill had married in 1926; she became his favorite interpreter and, after his death, a champion of his work. The music parodied rather than imitated American hit songs, then the rage in Europe. In a surreal manner, Weill juxtaposed the eighteenth-century ballad texts, European dance music, and American jazz. The opening song, "Die Moritat von Mackie Messer" (The Ballad of Mack the Knife, NAWM 186), lists the murderous deeds of Macheath, the central character, a gang leader in London. The lilting melody belies the brutal imagery, conveying Macheath's easygoing charm, and creating a disturbing sense that we are meant to sympathize with the criminal underclass rather than with the establishment. The original Berlin production ran for over two years, and within five years *The Threepenny Opera* enjoyed more than ten thousand performances in nineteen languages. The Nazis banned it in 1933, when Weill and Lenya left for Paris and then for the United States.

In New York, Weill began his second career as a composer for Broadway musicals. The most successful were *Knickerbocker Holiday* (1938), *Lady in the Dark* (1940), and the musical tragedy *Lost in the Stars* (1948), about apartheid in South Africa. The spirit of the New Objectivity lived on in these works, crafted by a classically trained modernist yet addressed to a broad musical public and meant to be immediately grasped by mind and heart.

Paul Hindemith (1895–1963) was among the most prolific composers of the century. At the Berlin School of Music (1927–1937), Yale University (1940–1953), and the University of Zurich (1951–1957), he taught two generations of musicians (see Figure 26.3). He thought of himself primarily as a practicing musician, performing professionally as violinist, violist, and conductor, and able to play many other instruments. The experience of performance became central to his music, whether it was intended for amateurs or professionals.

In the fragmented world of new music between the wars, Hindemith changed his approach several times. He began composing in a late Romantic style, then developed an individual expressionist language in works like the one-act opera *Murderer, Hope of Women* (1919), based an Oskar Kokoschka's play (see Figure 25.2). Soon he adopted the aesthetic stance later dubbed the New Objectivity, which in his music was exemplified by an avoidance of Romantic expressivity and a focus on purely musical procedures, especially motivic development and a polyphony of independent lines.

Figure 26.3. Paul Hindemith teaching a composition class at the Yale University School of Music, 1953.
(The Paul Hindemith Collection, Yale University Music Library.)

By the late 1920s, Hindemith was disturbed by the widening gulf between modern composers and an increasingly passive public. In response, he began composing what was known as *Gebrauchsmusik*—"music for use," as distinguished from music for its own sake. His goal was to attract young or amateur performers with works that were of high quality, modern in style, and challenging yet rewarding to perform. An example in his musical play for children, *Wir bauen eine Stadt* (We Build a Town, 1930).

When the Nazis came to power, they attacked Hindemith in the press and banned much of his music as "cultural Bolshevism." He began to examine the role of the artist in relation to politics and power, and from his questioning emerged the opera *Mathis der Maler* (Matthias the Painter, 1934–1935;

premiered 1938 in Zurich) and *Symphony Mathis der Maler* (1933–1934), his best-known work, composed while he was writing the libretto for the opera. The opera is based on the life of Matthias Grünewald, painter of the famous Isenheim Altarpiece shown in Figure 26.4. Mathis, the opera's main character, leaves his calling as a painter to join the peasants in their rebellion against the nobles during the Peasants' War of 1525. In despair after their defeat, he comes to realize that by abandoning his art he betrayed his gift and his true obligation to society, which is to paint. Yet Hindemith does not portray art as entirely autonomous since Mathis's experiences inform his moral vision. The opera can be read as an allegory for Hindemith's own career.

For *Mathis* and his other works from the 1930s on, Hindemith developed a more accessible neo-Romantic style, with less dissonant linear counterpoint and more systematic tonal organization. He devised a new harmonic method that he called *harmonic fluctuation*: fairly consonant chords progress toward combinations containing greater tension and dissonance, especially involving parallel fourths and seconds, which are then resolved either suddenly or by slowly moderating the tension until consonance is again reached. We can hear this technique in the beginning of the second movement of the symphony (NAWM 187), representing Mathis's painting of the entombment of Christ, shown in the lower panel in Figure 26.4.

Because the Nazi government forbade performances of Hindemith's music from 1936, *Mathis der Maler* had to be premiered in Switzerland, and Hindemith moved there in 1938. He emigrated to the United States in 1940 after the outbreak

Mathis der Maler

Harmonic fluctuation

Full 🔊

Later works

Figure 26.4. Three panels from the Isenheim Altarpiece, painted by Matthias Grünewald between 1512 and 1516 for the chapel of a hospital and monastery. On the top right is the Nativity, *with Mary holding the infant Jesus; on the left is the* Concert of Angels, *the inspiration for the first movement of Hindemith's* Symphony "Mathis der Maler," *and below is the* Entombment, *evoked in the second movement. Both movements were reused in the opera* Mathis der Maler, *about Grünewald's life.*
(Erich Lessing/
Art Resource, NY.)

of World War II and stayed for over a decade, returning to Switzerland in 1953. Having found his mature style in *Mathis,* he applied it to a series of sonatas for almost every orchestral instrument (1935–1955). *Ludus tonalis* (Tonal Play, 1942) for piano evokes the model of Bach's *Well-Tempered Clavier* with twelve fugues, each based on a different note in the chromatic scale, linked by modulating interludes and framed by a prelude (modulating from C to F♯) and postlude (F♯ to C). Other notable later works include *Symphonic Metamorphosis after Themes of Carl Maria von Weber* (1943) and the Symphony in B♭ for band (1951).

Music under the Nazis

Schoenberg, Krenek, Weill, and Hindemith all fled to the United States, but other composers stayed in Germany during the Nazi era. The Nazis established a Reich Chamber of Culture under Joseph Goebbels, which included a State Music Bureau to which all musicians had to belong. Richard Strauss, the grand old man of German music, was appointed its first president, but was soon forced to resign when he continued to collaborate on operas with a Jewish librettist, Stefan Zweig.

"Degenerate" music

The Nazis' requirements for music were mostly expressed in negatives: music must not be dissonant, atonal, twelve-tone, "chaotic," intellectual, Jewish, jazz-influenced, or left wing, which excluded most modernist music. Composers had to cooperate with the regime in order to have their music performed, and most did. But many German composers continued to write in personal idioms influenced by Schoenberg, Stravinsky, Hindemith, or Weill, whose music the Nazis had attacked as degenerate or banned outright. As a result, no coherent Nazi style of new music emerged. Rather, the government focused more on performance than on composition, exploiting the great German composers of the nineteenth century from Beethoven to Bruckner as symbols of the alleged superiority of the German people. They especially fostered a cult of Wagner, whose anti-Semitic views supported their own and whose *Ring* cycle embodied a German mythology they could embrace (see Chapter 20).

Carl Orff

The one German composer who won an international reputation during the Nazi era was Carl Orff (1895–1982), who was far from sympathetic to the regime but, perhaps naively, believed that music was autonomous from politics and stayed in Germany when others had left. His best-known work, *Carmina burana* (1936), for chorus and orchestra, set medieval poems akin to goliard songs (see Chapter 2) in an attractive, deceptively simple neomodal idiom. Drawing on Stravinsky, folk songs, chant, and medieval secular song, Orff created a monumental pseudo-antique style based on drones, ostinatos, harmonic stasis, and strophic repetition. His *Carmina burana* is distinctive yet immediately comprehensible and has been much imitated, especially by composers for film and television. Orff also developed methods and materials for teaching music in schools, calling for movement, singing, and playing on percussion and other instruments, leading children in a natural way to experience a great variety of scales and rhythms and to arrive at a broad understanding of music.

The Soviet Union

In the Soviet Union, the government controlled the arts along with every other realm of life. The arts were seen as ways to indoctrinate the people in Marxist-Leninist ideology, enhance their patriotism, and venerate their leaders. Soon after the 1917 revolution, theaters, conservatories, concert halls, performing ensembles, publishers, and other musical institutions were all nationalized, and concert programming and the opera and ballet repertories were strictly regulated.

Civil war in 1918–1920 and an economic crisis through the early 1920s preoccupied the government and forced some relaxation of state control over the arts. During this period of relative freedom, divergent tendencies emerged among composers and crystallized in two organizations founded in 1923. The Association for Contemporary Music sought to continue the modernist trends established by Scriabin and others before the First World War and promoted contacts with the West, sponsoring performances of music by Stravinsky, Schoenberg, Hindemith, and others. In contrast, the Russian Association of Proletarian Musicians considered such music elitist and instead encouraged simple tonal music with wide appeal, especially "mass songs" (songs for group unison singing) to socialist texts. After Joseph Stalin gained total power in 1929, dissent was quashed. The competing composers' groups were replaced in 1933 by a single new organization, the Union of Soviet Composers.

> Composers' organizations

A 1934 writers' congress promulgated socialist realism as the ideal for Soviet arts. In literature, drama, film, and painting, this doctrine called for using a realistic style (as opposed to abstraction, expressionism, or symbolism) in works that portrayed socialism in a positive light, showing signs of progress for the people under the Soviet state and celebrating revolutionary ideology and its heroes. For music this meant the use of a relatively simple, accessible language, centered on melody, often drawing on folk or folklike styles that promoted patriotic or inspirational subject matter. Interest in music for its own sake or in modernist styles was condemned as "formalism."

> Socialist realism versus formalism

But the definitions of socialist realism and formalism were so vague and arbitrary that composers, including Sergey Prokofiev and Dmitri Shostakovich, the two leading Soviet composers of the time, often ran afoul of the authorities.

Prokofiev (1891–1953), shown in Figure 26.5, made his reputation before 1918 as a radical modernist, combining striking dissonance with motoric rhythms. He left Russia after the Revolution and spent almost two decades residing and touring in North America and Western Europe, composing solo piano works and concertos for himself to play and fulfilling commissions for larger compositions, among them an opera. *The Love for Three Oranges* (1921), as well as ballets for Sergei Diaghilev's Ballets Russes in Paris.

His career at a low ebb, Prokofiev succumbed to promises from the Soviet regime of commissions and performances. He returned to Russia permanently in 1936, having already fulfilled Soviet commissions for the film *Lieutenant Kijé* (1933), later arranged as a concert suite, and for the ballet *Romeo and Juliet* (1935–1936; see Figure 26.6). Both became favorites and entered the standard repertory, as did his symphonic fairy tale for narrator and orchestra, *Peter and the Wolf* (1936)—one of many pieces he wrote in response to the Soviet demand for high-quality music for children—and his music for the film *Alexander Nevsky* (1938) became one of the most celebrated film scores of the era. Prokofiev's pieces for state occasions, like his cantatas for the twentieth and

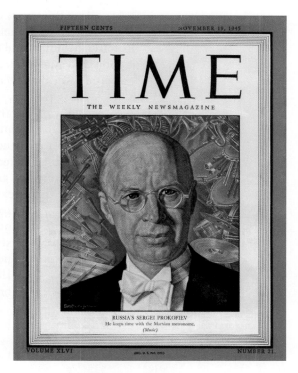

Figure 26.5 Sergey Prokofiev on the cover of Time *magazine, November 19, 1945. The unflattering caption reads, "He keeps time with the Marxian metronome."*

(Time Life Pictures. Getty Images.)

Figure 26.6 A scene from a 2005 London performance of Prokofiev's ballet Romeo and Juliet *by the Kirov Ballet Company. The work was first performed in Czechoslovakia in 1938.*
(Laurie Lewis/Lebrecht Music & Arts Photo Library.)

thirtieth anniversaries of the Russian Revolution, were less successful and were ignored outside of the Soviet Union.

Full 🔊   Concise 🔊

In 1939, Prokofiev adapted his cantata *Alexander Nevsky* from the music for the film. The fourth movement (NAWM 188), drawn from a scene in which the people of Russia are called to take up arms against German invaders, works well as film music; it includes stirring choral melodies in folklike style, mostly diatonic melodies, and accessible harmonies. The modal melodies and orchestration convey a Russian sound, including clanging bells and prominent brass and percussion that recall the Coronation scene from Musorgsky's *Boris Godunov*

Full 🔊

(NAWM 153).

World War II again brought a relaxation of government control, and Prokofiev turned to absolute music in classical genres, notably the Piano Sonatas Nos. 6–8 (1939–1944) and the Fifth Symphony (1944). These works are largely tonal, with the unexpected harmonic juxtapositions and the alternation of acerbic dryness, lyricism, and motoric rhythms that had been features of his personal style since the 1910s. But after the war, the authorities again cracked down in a 1948 resolution that condemned the works of Prokofiev and other leading composers as "formalist." He tried to write more simply, but never recovered the balance between wit and feeling nor between convention and surprise that marks his best music. He died in 1953—ironically, on the same day as Stalin, whose brutal regime had so circumscribed his freedom.

Figure 26.7 Soviet postage stamp commemorating the death of Dmitri Shostakovich in 1975.
(Lebrecht Music & Arts Photo Library.)

Dmitri Shostakovich (1906–1975; Figure 26.7) received his education and spent his entire career within the Soviet system. He studied at the Conservatory in Petrograd (later Leningrad, now St. Petersburg), cultivating a combination of traditionalism and experimentation. In the 1920s, he was more aligned with the modernists than with the proletarian wing in Russia. The premiere of his First Symphony in 1926, when he was nineteen, and subsequent performances in the West rocketed him to international prominence.

Shostakovich's opera *Lady Macbeth of the Mtsensk District* was premiered in 1934 in both Leningrad and Moscow, and scored a great success, with subsequent performances throughout the Soviet Union and abroad. But when Stalin saw it in January 1936, he was angered by its discordant modernist music and surrealistic, often grotesque, portrayal of violence and sex (see Figure 26.8). Shortly thereafter, the newspaper *Pravda* printed an unsigned article attacking the opera as "chaos instead of music" (see Vignette, page 596). In its wake, the production was closed down and the opera withdrawn. Shostakovich temporarily lost his favored status and may have feared for his life: the previous year, Stalin had begun a campaign of repression known as the Purges, during which many political figures, intellectuals, and artists were executed or banished to prison camps.

It is difficult not to see the Fifth Symphony, written and premiered to great acclaim in 1937, as Shostakovich's response to the criticism of his opera; indeed, he endorsed a description of the work as "a Soviet artist's reply to just criticism." The symphony embodies a new approach Shostakovich had been developing, inspired by close study of Mahler's symphonies, that encompassed a wide range of styles and moods—from lyricism to dynamism and from deep feeling and high tragedy to bombast and the grotesque. It is framed as a heroic symphony in the grand manner of Beethoven and Tchaikovsky and in the traditional four movements. A dynamic opening movement in sonata form, suggestive of struggle, is followed by a scherzo-like Allegretto (NAWM 189), an intensely sad slow movement, and a boisterous finale. The symphony outwardly conformed to the tenets of socialist realism, infusing the most prestigious nineteenth-century instrumental genre with an optimistic, populist outlook and adopting a clear, easily understood tonal language. For those reasons, it provided the vehicle for Shostakovich's rehabilitation with the state. Yet it was also possible to hear in it messages of bitterness and mourning in the face of totalitarian repression. The Allegretto adopts the jarring contrasts of a Mahler scherzo, juxtaposing passages that evoke a variety of popular styles from waltz to fanfare. The sorrowful slow movement evokes traditional Russian funeral music; it prompted open tears at the premiere and has been

Lady Macbeth of the Mtsensk District

Fifth Symphony

Full 🔊

Figure 26.8. Scene from Shostakovich's opera Lady Macbeth of the Mtsensk District, *in a 1992 production by the English National Opera.* (Lebrecht Music & Arts Photo Library.)

After Shostakovich's opera Lady Macbeth of the Mtsensk District *had been performed widely to great acclaim, Stalin's government singled it out for censure with a negative review in* Pravda (Truth), *the Communist Party newspaper. Through this attack on the nation's leading composer, it signaled a crackdown on composers' artistic freedoms.*

From the first minute, the listener is shocked by deliberate dissonance, by a confused stream of sounds. Snatches of melody, the beginnings of a musical phrase, are drowned, emerge again, and disappear in a grinding and squealing roar. To follow this "music" is most difficult; to remember it, impossible.

Thus it goes practically throughout the entire opera. The singing on the stage is replaced by shrieks. If the composer chances to come on the path of a clear and simple melody, then immediately, as though frightened at this misfortune, he

throws himself back into a wilderness of musical chaos—in places becoming cacophony. The expression which the listener demands is supplanted by wild rhythm. Passion is here supposed to be expressed by musical noise. All this is not due to lack of talent, or to lack of ability to depict simple and strong emotions in music. Here is music turned deliberately inside out in order that nothing will be reminiscent of classical opera, or have anything in common with symphonic music or with simple and popular musical language accessible to all. . . . The power of good music to infect the masses has been sacrificed to a petty-bourgeois, "formalist" attempt to create originality through cheap clowning. It is a game of clever ingenuity that may end very badly.

From "Chaos Instead of Music," as translated in Victor Seroff, *Dmitri Shostakovich: The Life and Background of a Soviet Composer* (New York: Knopf, 1943), pp. 204–205; repr. Oliver Strunk, ed., *Source Readings in Music History*, rev. ed. by Leo Treitler (New York: Norton, 1998), vol. 6, pp. 127–128.

seen by some as expressing sorrow at the Purges. The triumphalism of the final movement could also be interpreted as false enthusiasm. Such double meanings do not suggest that Shostakovich was a dissident—there was no room for dissidence under Stalin—but that by composing multivalent music, he could at once please the party bosses and release emotions that had to remain unspoken.

All of Shostakovich's works were created in a politicized context, and the search for double meanings has been widespread in the West and in Russia since the fall of the Soviet Union. But the Seventh Symphony, which premiered in bombed-out Leningrad in 1941, at the peak of that city's siege by the Nazis, had a special significance for the people: it was broadcast across the USSR during the Soviets' darkest hour and both galvanized and comforted them during their resistance. The symphony, subtitled *Leningrad,* deals programmatically with the heroic defense of the city against Hitler's armies, although some hear in its depiction of the totalitarian invaders a complaint against Stalin's repression as well. It was performed in London and New York in 1942 and immediately became a symbol of the war against Nazi Germany, in which the United States, Britain, and the Soviet Union were allies.

Seventh Symphony

Later works

In the 1948 crackdown, Shostakovich was denounced along with Prokofiev and others, and he had to write patriotic film scores and choral paeans to the regime to gain rehabilitation. He wrote some of his music "for the drawer"— with no expectation of performance until the political atmosphere changed.

The ambivalence in Shostakovich's music reflects the accommodations he had to make to survive in a state where people could never say precisely what they felt, and thus where the arts—especially music—offered an outlet for what was otherwise inexpressible. The relative accessibility of his music combined with its impression of giving voice to inner feelings has won Shostakovitch many devoted listeners not only in Russia but throughout the world.

The Americas

In the New World, the interwar period saw the emergence of composers who gained prominence in their own countries and recognition in Europe, placing their homelands on the international stage for the first time. As with composers in the "peripheral" nations of Europe, these composers of the Americas found that creating a distinctive national style was often the only way to gain attention from an international audience. Their nationalism was sometimes infused with national politics, but it was always linked to the cultural politics of securing for themselves and their countries a niche in the repertory of performed classics.

Canada had a thriving musical life that developed along patterns similar to those in the United States. In both nations, performance of the European classical repertory was far more central than playing music of homegrown composers in the classical tradition. Performing spaces, concert societies, bands, professional chamber ensembles, choral societies, and conservatories all emerged in Canada during the nineteenth century, and the twentieth century brought the founding of orchestras in most large cities, beginning with Quebec (1903) and Toronto (1906).

Canada

The first Canadian composer to achieve an international reputation was Claude Champagne (1891–1965). He learned French-Canadian fiddle music and dance tunes in his youth, then as a young man was deeply influenced by Russian composers, from Musorgsky to Scriabin. During studies in Paris from 1921 to 1928, he encountered Renaissance polyphony, Fauré, and Debussy, and saw in their modal practice links to the folk tunes of Canada. He developed a distinctive nationalist style in his *Suite canadienne* (Canadian Suite, 1927) for chorus and orchestra, blending elements from French-Canadian folk music and polyphonic French chansons with the symphonic tradition. His best-known piece, *Danse villageoise* (Village Dance, 1929), evokes both French-Canadian and Irish folk styles, acknowledging another ethnic strain in Canada and in his own heritage.

Claude Champagne

The most important Brazilian composer was Heitor Villa-Lobos (1887–1959), who drew together traditional Brazilian elements with modernist techniques. He spent the years 1923 to 1930 mostly in Paris, where performances of his music won widespread praise and established him as the most prominent Latin American composer. He returned to Brazil in 1930 and, with government support, instituted a national effort to promote music in the schools and through choral singing. He was criticized for his collaboration with Brazil's nationalist dictatorship, akin to the totalitarian regimes of Europe at the time, but it is not clear whether he shared its ideology.

Brazil

A series of nine *Bachianas brasileiras* (1930–1945) pays tribute to Bach and thus to neoclassicism. Each of the *Bachianas* is a suite of two to four movements combining elements of Baroque harmony, counterpoint, genres, and styles with Brazilian folk elements and long, lyrical melodic lines. This unique blend is exemplified in Villa-Lobos's most famous work, *Bachianas brasileiras No. 5* for solo soprano and an orchestra of cellos. The first movement (NAWM 190) invokes the spirit of a Bach aria, spinning out a long-breathed cantabile melody from a few initial motives, and alludes to the typical da capo form of Baroque

Bachianas brasileiras

Full 🔊   Concise 🔊

Figure 26.9 The Corn Harvest, *a mural by Mexican artist Diego Rivera (1886–1957), painted on the south wall of the Ministry of Public Education in Mexico City in 1923–1924. It depicts a traditional scene of native life in a style that draws on pre-Columbian art and offers an uncomplicated alternative to European modernism.* (Secretaría de Educación Pública, Mexico City, D.F., Mexico. Photo: Schalkwijk/Art Resource, NY.)

arias through a modified ABA structure and the suggestion of an instrumental ritornello. At the same time, it draws on styles of improvisation in Brazilian popular song and on vocal embellishment in Italian opera, a tradition that was as strong in Brazil as in Europe. The result, simultaneously neoclassical and national, exemplifies how the Western musical tradition has become a transatlantic culture.

Beginning in 1921, the Mexican government supported bringing the arts to a wide public and promoted a new nationalism that drew on native cultures, especially from before the Spanish conquest. As part of this effort, Diego Rivera and other artists were commissioned to paint murals in public buildings that illustrated Mexican life, such as the fresco shown in Figure 26.9.

One composer associated with the new nationalism, Silvestre Revueltas (1899–1940) studied in Mexico and then in the United States before returning to assume the post of assistant conductor of Mexico's first professional orchestra. His compositions do not use folk songs but combine melodies modeled on Mexican folk and popular music with a modernist idiom. Characteristic is his *Homenaje a Federico García Lorca* (Homage to Federico García Lorca, 1936), written in memory of one of Spain's most important poets and playwrights, killed by a Nationalist militia in the early days of the Spanish Civil War (1936–1939). In the first movement, *Baile* (Dance, NAWM 191), Revueltas begins and ends with a slow, recitative-like melody on a muted trumpet that evokes the style of *cante jondo*, a Spanish flamenco song tradition Lorca celebrated in his poetry. The main body of the movement is a lively dance that recalls popular Mexican band music in its overall sound, instrumental timbres, melodic structure, strophic form, characteristic rhythms, and parallel thirds. At the same time, modernist elements, including strong dissonance, parallel dissonant sonorities, glissandos, and grotesque combinations of instruments, make clear that this is concert music about popular culture rather than popular entertainment itself.

The United States

American composers and performers developed new links with Europe between the wars, due in part to the immigration of many of Europe's leading composers for political or professional reasons. By the early 1940s, these refugees included Rachmaninoff, Schoenberg, Stravinsky, Bartók, Milhaud, and others. Americans had studied in Germany since the mid-nineteenth century, but World War I helped to foster a reorientation of American music away from Germany and toward France. Starting in the early 1920s, a steady stream of Americans went to France to study with Nadia Boulanger (1887–1979), renowned pedagogue and promoter of Fauré and Stravinsky, who taught classes in Paris and Fontainebleau until her death. Among her pupils were Americans Aaron Copland, (discussed below) and Elliott Carter (see Chapter 27).

The interwar period also saw several new currents among American composers. Two of the most salient were an experimentalist or ultramodernist
trend, focused on developing new musical resources, and an Americanist trend
that incorporated national styles and sounds into European genres. The former
group included Edgard Varèse, Henry Cowell, and Ruth Crawford, and the latter
encompassed George Gershwin, Aaron Copland, William Grant Still, Cowell's
later works, and many others. Both currents asserted independence from
Europe while still drawing on the European tradition. In order to secure performances for their music in a concert culture that focused on European masterworks, American composers formed their own organizations, including the
International Composers Guild, cofounded by Varèse, and the League of Composers, headed by Claire Reis; for similar reasons, Cowell established the print
journal *New Music.*

Among the experimentalists, the French-born Edgard Varèse (1883–1965)
had a brief career in Paris and Berlin as a composer and as a conductor of early
and contemporary music before moving to New York in 1915 and setting the pace
there for the early modernist scene. Varèse celebrated his adopted country in
his first major work, *Amériques* (1918–1921). Its fragmentary melodies and loose
structure betray links to Debussy. He was also influenced by Schoenberg, notably in the use of strong dissonance and chromatic saturation, and by Stravinsky, especially in his avoidance of linear development, his associating a musical
idea with a particular instrumental color, and the juxtaposition of disparate
elements through layering and interruption.

Next came a series of works that laid down a new agenda: *Offrandes* (1921),
Hyperprism (1922–1923), *Octandre* (1923), *Intégrales* (1924–1925), *Ionisation* (for
percussion only, 1929–1931), and *Ecuatorial* (1932–1934). In these works, Varèse
aimed to liberate composition from conventional melody, harmony, meter,
regular pulse, recurrent beat, and traditional orchestration. For Varèse, sounds
as such were the essential structural components of music, which he defined as
"organized sound," and he considered all sounds acceptable as raw material. He
imagined music as spatial, akin to an aural ballet in which what he called *sound
masses* moved through musical space, changing and interacting. A sound mass
is a body of sounds characterized by a particular timbre, register, rhythm, and
melodic gesture, which may be stable or may gradually be transformed. In
Varèse's compositions, these sound masses collide, intersect, speed up, slow
down, combine, separate, diffuse, expand, and contract in range, volume, and
timbre. A great variety of percussion instruments—some drawn from non-
Western cultures and others (such as the siren) from city life—play key roles,
acting independently as equals to the winds and strings. For Varèse, form was
not the starting point but the result of working with the invented material.
Typically, his pieces are organized as a series of sections, each centered around
a few sound masses, some of which may carry over to later sections.

The passage from *Hyperprism* (NAWM 192) in Example 26.2 illustrates how

pitch, instrumental color, gesture, and rhythm interact to suggest sound masses
colliding and changing. The tenor trombone has introduced and embellished the
pitch C♯, and in the first measure the horns take it up with flutter-tonguing (fast
tongue motions) and *sforzandos,* both effects that produce brassy sounds excluded
from traditional music. The tenor trombone returns, decorating the C♯ with
glissandos (another nontraditional effect), and exchanges short gestures with
the horns. The horns ultimately take over the note and the glissando, as if the
sound mass has gradually changed timbre. Meanwhile a low D in the bass trombone, a strong dissonance against the C♯, swells and fades in alternation with a
siren, forming another sound mass that changes color. In the percussion, similarly competing gestures alternate, producing two distinct sound masses. Every

Example 26.2 Varèse, Hyperprism

combination of sounds is unusual, so that the music is heard as a block of sound rather than as melody, harmony, or accompaniment.

Influence

In Varèse's entirely new conception of music, the listener must put aside expectations that music will be rhetorical or will develop organically, as in earlier styles, and must simply observe the interaction of "intelligent bodies of sound moving in space." His ideas and his music had an enormous influence on younger composers, both in the United States and in Europe (see Chapter 27).

Electronic music

Since his music depended on sound itself, especially unusual ones, Varèse sought new instruments from the 1920s on. Only after World War II did the new resources of electronic sound generation and the tape recorder (discussed in Chapter 27) make possible the realization of the sounds he heard in his mind in his *Déserts* (1950–1954) for winds, percussion, and tape and in the tape piece *Poème électronique* (1957–1958; NAWM 206, discussed in Chapter 27).

Henry Cowell

California-born Henry Cowell (1897–1965) began composing as a teenager with little training in European music, and from the start he pioneered new resources. Many of his early pieces are experimental, designed to try out new techniques. *The Tides of Manaunaun* (ca. 1917) uses tone clusters—chords of diatonic or chromatic seconds produced by pressing the keys with the fist or forearm, as shown in Figure 26.10—to represent the tides moved by Manaunaun, the legendary Irish sea god. In *The Aeolian Harp* (1923), the player strums the piano strings while holding down three- and four-note chords on the keyboard, as if playing a grand autoharp. In *The Banshee* (1925; NAWM 193), an assistant holds the damper pedal down so that the strings can resonate freely while the pianist strums the strings, plucks some, and rubs along the length of the lower, wire-wound strings with the fingertips to create an eerie, voice-like howl similar to that of a banshee, a spirit in Irish legend. Besides new playing techniques, Cowell also explored new textures and procedures, such as giving each voice or instrument a different subdivision of the meter. He summarized his new ideas in his book *New Musical Resources* (1930).

Throughout his career, Cowell was interested in non-Western musics. He took an eclectic approach to composition, trying out everything that interested him rather than developing a single identifiable style. During and after the 1930s, Cowell turned from experimentalism to a more accessible language, often incorporating American, Irish, or Asian elements. He wrote a series of works called *Hymn and Fuguing Tune* for band or for orchestra, modeled on the style of William Billings and his contemporaries, alongside symphonies and other traditional genres. In the years after World War II, several pieces show his interest in Asian music and incorporate instruments such as the Indian tabla and the Japanese koto.

Cowell promoted music by his contemporaries as well as his own through concerts and through the periodical *New Music*, in which he published scores by Ives, Schoenberg, and other modernist and ultramodernist composers. His adventurous search for new resources and his interest in non-Western music heavily influenced younger composers, especially in the United States.

Among the composers whose works Cowell published was Ruth Crawford Seeger (1901–1953), shown in Figure 26.11, the first woman to win a Guggenheim Fellowship in music. She was most active as a composer in Chicago between 1924 and 1929 and in New York between 1929 and 1933. In New York, she studied composition with the composer and musicologist Charles Seeger, whom she married in 1932. Charles had developed theories about dissonant counterpoint, rhythmic freedom between contrapuntal voices, and other modern techniques that Ruth helped to refine and then applied in her own music. In her New York period, she experimented with serial techniques, including their application to parameters other than pitch. Influenced by the New Deal, she became convinced that preserving folk songs would be a greater contribution to the nation's musical life than writing modernist works that few would hear or appreciate. She collaborated with writer Carl Sandburg and folklorists John and Alan Lomax, editing American folk songs from field recordings. She also published many transcriptions and arrangements in which she sought to be faithful to the songs' native contexts. Crawford Seeger stands out for her advocacy in preserving American traditional music and for being one of the very few women in the ultramodernist group.

Crawford Seeger's best-known work is the String Quartet (1931), composed while in Europe on a Guggenheim Fellowship. Each movement

Figure 26.10 Henry Cowell at the piano, playing clusters with his fist and forearm.
(Bettmann/Corbis.)

Figure 26.11 Ruth Crawford Seeger in a 1920s photograph by Fernand de Gueldre.
(Photo Courtesy Judith Tick.)

Example 26.3 Crawford Seeger, String Quartet, finale

a. Opening

b. Approaching the midpoint

Full 🔊   Concise 🔊

is organized differently, embodying her constant search for new procedures. The finale (NAWM 194), excerpted in Example 26.3, is written in two-part counterpoint, pitting the first violin against the three other instruments playing in parallel octaves with mutes. At the beginning of the movement, shown in Example 26.3a, the first violin plays a single note, then two, then three, four, and so on, adding one note with each phrase (not shown in the example) until it reaches twenty-one (beginning in measure 55, Example 26.3b), gradually becoming softer. Punctuating the first violin's utterances, the other instruments play rapid eighth-note groups that decrease in number from twenty (Example 26.3a, measures 3–4) to one (by measure 57, as shown in 26.3b), gradually getting louder, so that the density and dynamics of both voices move in opposite directions. At the end of this process, by which point the two lines have completely exchanged roles, each part sustains its last tone (shown at the end of 26.3b), and then the entire musical fabric is repeated in retrograde, transposed up a semitone, to create a nearly perfect palindromic structure. Thus Crawford Seeger simultaneously embraces the tradition of the string quartet and satisfies the ultramodernist desire for something truly new.

George Gershwin

George Gershwin (1897–1938) first made his reputation as a composer of popular songs and Broadway shows (see chapter 24), but in the late 1920s and 1930s he also established himself as the most famous and frequently performed American composer in classical genres. For Gershwin, this was no contradiction, because he saw no firm line between popular and classical music. He always had a foot in both camps: he studied classical piano as a teenager, including works of Chopin, Liszt, and Debussy; took private lessons in harmony, counterpoint, form, and orchestration from 1915 to 1921; and later studied composition with several teachers, including Cowell. Gershwin recognized the potential of jazz and blues to add new dimensions to art music, and he used his familiarity with those traditions to create a distinctively American modernist style.

Gershwin's most famous piece, *Rhapsody in Blue* (1924), billed as a "jazz concerto," had its premiere as the centerpiece of an extravagant concert organized by bandleader Paul Whiteman as "An Experiment in Modern Music." Scored for solo piano and jazz ensemble, and incorporating stylized popular song forms, blue notes, and other elements of jazz and blues, the *Rhapsody* met with immediate approval. Along with Milhaud's *La création du monde* from the year before, Gershwin's *Rhapsody* pointed the way for other composers to incorporate jazz, blues, and popular music into their art music, suggesting that such a blend could produce music that was at once truly modern, truly American, and broadly appealing.

Rhapsody in Blue

Gershwin himself continued to fuse the seemingly disparate traditions, producing compositions like the three Preludes for Piano (1926), which bring elements of blues, jazz, and Latin dance rhythms into preludes influenced by Chopin and Debussy. Gershwin's *Porgy and Bess* (1935), which he called a folk opera, has been produced both as an opera and as a musical, and it draws from both genres. The music is continuous and features recurring motives like those in Verdi or Wagner operas. Yet in part because the characters are all African American, the musical style is heavily influenced by African American idioms such as spirituals, blues, and jazz. This blending of traditions is part of Gershwin's appeal, and it makes his music especially rich in reference and in meaning. Because of his early death from a brain tumor, his output of classical works was relatively small, but he remains the most familiar American composer of the century.

Porgy and Bess

Aaron Copland (1900–1990), shown in Figure 26.12, moved from stringent dissonance in the 1920s to a streamlined style in the 1930s and 1940s that combined modernism with national American idioms. Copland's Jewish faith, homosexuality, and leftist politics made him something of an outsider, yet he became the most important American composer of his generation through his own compositions and his work for the cause of American music. He organized concert series and composer groups, and promoted works of his predecessors and contemporaries, including Ives. Through encouragement and counsel, and by example, he influenced many younger American composers, among them Leonard Bernstein, Elliott Carter, and David Del Tredici.

Figure 26.12 Aaron Copland in the 1930s, composing in his studio. (Courtesy New York Public Library, Astor, Lenox, and Tilden Foundations.)

Growing up in a Jewish immigrant family in Brooklyn, Copland was exposed to ragtime and popular music from a young age, while studying piano, theory, and composition in the European tradition. He was the first of many American composers to study in France with Nadia Boulanger, from whom he learned to write music that was clear, logical, and elegant. Jazz elements and strong dissonances figure prominently in his early works, such as *Music for the Theatre* (1925) and the Piano Concerto (1927).

Recognizing the growing number of radio and record listeners, Copland sought to appeal to a larger audience. At the same time, the depression had deepened his belief in socialism, and he turned to writing music in a language that the broad masses of people could understand and on subjects that were relevant to their lives and concerns. He developed a new style that combined his modernist technique with simple textures and diatonic melodies and harmonies. He incorporated Mexican folk songs in the orchestral suite *El Salón México* (1932–1936) and cowboy songs in the ballets *Billy the Kid* (1938) and *Rodeo* (1942), which reflected the American frontier experience. His opera *The Second Hurricane* (1936)—written for schools—and his scores for a number of films including *Our Town* (1940) represent music composed specifically "for use."

Appalachian Spring

Full 🔊 Concise 🔊

Copland's Americanist idiom is exemplified in *Appalachian Spring* (1943–1944), first written as a ballet with an ensemble of thirteen instruments but better known in its arrangement as an orchestral suite (excerpt in NAWM 195). The work incorporates variations on the Shaker hymn *'Tis the Gift to Be Simple*. Example 26.4 shows two variations on the hymn's third phrase. The song is subtly transfigured and its essence is absorbed in music that simply and sincerely expresses the spirit of rural life in American terms. Copland's use of transparent, widely spaced sonorities, empty octaves and fifths, and diatonic dissonances creates a distinctive sound that has been frequently imitated and has become the quintessential musical emblem of America, especially in music for film and television.

William Grant Still

William Grant Still (1895–1978), shown in Figure 26.13, also incorporated specifically American idioms into art music. He drew on a diverse musical background, including composition studies with George Whitefield Chadwick and Edgard Varèse, and work as an arranger for W. C. Handy's dance band. Still's success as a composer, when blacks were still largely excluded from the field of classical music, earned him the sobriquet "Dean of Afro-American Composers." He broke numerous racial barriers and became the first African American to conduct a major symphony orchestra in the United States (the Los Angeles Philharmonic, 1936); the first to have an opera produced by a major company in the United States (*Troubled Island* at New York's City Center, 1949); and the first to have an opera televised over a national

Example 26.4 Aaron Copland, Appalachian Spring, *variations*

a.

b.

Figure 26.13 *William Grant Still in an undated photograph.*
(Courtesy of Special Collections, University of Arkansas Libraries, Fayetteville.)

network. His compositions, numbering over 150, include operas, ballets, symphonies, chamber works, choral pieces, and solo vocal works.

Still established his reputation with the *Afro-American Symphony* (1930), which encompasses African American musical elements within the traditional framework of a European four-movement symphony. The opening movement (NAWM 196) is in sonata form, with a first theme in twelve-bar blues structure and a second theme that suggests a spiritual. It also features numerous other traits from African American traditions: call and response, syncopation, varied repetition of short melodic or rhythmic ideas, jazz harmonies, dialogue between groups of instruments as in a jazz arrangement, and instrumental timbres common in jazz, such as trumpets and trombones played with mutes.

Afro-American Symphony

Full 🔊   Concise 🔊

In addition to composers who forged new paths using experimental techniques or American idioms, other Americans emerged to write in styles ranging from the neoclassical to the Romantic. The astonishing variety of American idioms that emerged in the first half of the twentieth century illustrates the general point about modernist composers in the classical tradition, no matter what their stripe. Most sought a place in the crowded classical repertoire by writing music that was individual and distinctive yet drew on past traditions and genres. Meanwhile, each of the most radical composers—like Varèse, Cowell, and Crawford Seeger—forged a new concept of music. For them, the best solution to the problem of competing with the past was to ignore it and focus on creating something fundamentally new, or ultramodernist.

Diversity of styles

POSTLUDE

The interwar period witnessed the creation of some of the most widely performed art music of the twentieth century. By now, listeners and musicians have largely forgotten the political circumstances under which most of this

TIMELINE Between the Wars

Musical Events

1917
Satie, *Parade*

1917–1921
Berg, *Wozzeck* (NAWM 174)

1922–1923
Varèse, *Hyperprism*
(NAWM 192)

1923
Milhaud, *La Création du monde* (NAWM 185)

1924
Gershwin, *Rhapsody in Blue*

1925
Cowell, *The Banshee*
(NAWM 193)

1927
Champagne, *Suite canadienne*

1927–1931
Ellington's band at
the Cotton Club

1928
Weill, *The Threepenny Opera*
(NAWM 186)

1930
Still, *Afro–American Symphony*
(NAWM 196)

1931
Crawford Seeger, String
Quartet (NAWM 194)

1933
Union of Soviet Composers
founded

1933–1934
Hindemith, *Symphony Mathis
der Maler* (NAWM 187)

1936
Shostakovich's opera *Lady
Macbeth* attacked in Soviet
press

1936
Orff, *Carmina burana*

1936
Revueltas, *Homenaje a
Federico García Lorca*
(NAWM 191)

1937
Shostakovich, Fifth Symphony
(NAWM 189)

1938
Prokofiev, music for the film
Alexander Nevsky

1940
Stravinsky and Bartók
emigrate to the United States

1943–44
Copland, *Appalachian Spring*
(NAWM 195)

1948
Soviet Union cracks
down on Prokofiev,
Shostakovich, and
"formalist" composers

1914 ———————————————————————————————— **1945**

Historical Events

1914–18
World War I

1917
Russian Revolution

1919
Women win right to vote in
United States

1922
Fascists take over government
in Italy

1929
New York stock market crash
begins worldwide depression

1933
Hitler comes to power in
Germany

1933
Roosevelt institutes New Deal
in United States

1934
Doctrine of socialist realism
adopted in Soviet Union

1936–1939
Spanish Civil War

1938
Germany absorbs Austria

1939–1945
World War II

music was created. Audiences enjoy Poulenc's operas, Orff's *Carmina burana*, Shostakovich's Fifth Symphony, and Copland's Americanist ballets without regard to the politics or circumstances that shaped their creation. Indeed, the insistence on immediate wide appeal by authorities in totalitarian states seems to have helped the popularity of some works such as Prokofiev's *Romeo and Juliet* and *Peter and the Wolf*, which lack the dissonance and satire of his pieces composed in the West. Today Milhaud, Poulenc, and Weill are admired for their wit and clarity, Hindemith for his summation of the German tradition from Bach through Brahms in a novel musical language, Shostakovich and Prokofiev for their highly emotional and passionate symphonic styles, and composers in the Americas for giving their nations a place in neoclassical tradition—all with little thought to the ideologies that swirled around these composers and the constraints under which they labored. Yet politics still shapes the reception of some of this music—as shown, for example, by a continuing controversy in scholarly circles about whether Shostakovich meant his music to convey a dissident message.

The postwar depoliticizing of art music composed between the wars resulted in part from the idea that classical music is a thing apart, an idealized, autonomous art, a notion that continues today but has come under increasing scrutiny from historians and musicians. With historical distance comes a greater focus on the music itself and fading memories of the circumstances under which it was born. In the long run, what seems most important about classical music of the first half of the twentieth century, including that of the composers discussed in Chapters 23 and 25, is its great variety. Most composers still sought a place in the permanent concert repertory and tried to secure it by combining elements from the classical tradition with individual and innovative traits that distinguished their music from that of their peers. The varied styles that emerged resulted in part from different views of what was valuable in the past classics and in part from composers' differing circumstances. They transformed their ways of thinking, from the political to the personal, into music of unprecedented diversity. Among their works are riches for every taste.

Resources for study and review available at
wwnorton.com/studyspace

The Changing World of Postwar Music

PRELUDE

The postwar years brought a significant expansion in music-making. Audiences grew, government support in many nations rose, schools of music expanded, and music education in primary and secondary schools increased in quality and quantity.

Among jazz musicians, new styles arose, including bebop and free jazz, both of which featured small ensembles and emphasized the virtuosity of the performers. Simultaneously, a body of jazz classics, paralleling the classical concert repertory, began to form and was reinforced through performances, jazz education, and recordings.

Meanwhile, composers who saw themselves as participants in the classical tradition shared less and less common ground, with little consensus on style, aesthetic, or purpose. Some composers sought to preserve and extend particular aspects of the tradition, from audience appeal to modernist complexity, while others focused on the new. In every nation there was a diversity of styles and approaches, and ideas that began in one place were often imitated elsewhere.

Developments in Jazz

In the years immediately following the end of World War II, financial support for big bands declined sharply. More musicians now joined smaller groups, called combos. The styles they played differed from region to region and group to group. A new style of jazz built around virtuosic soloists fronting small combos, known as bebop, or bop, emerged in the early 1940s during the waning years of the swing craze.

Bebop was rooted in standards from the swing era, in blues progressions, and in other popular sources for contrafacts, but it was newly infused with extreme virtuosity, harmonic ingenuity, unusual dissonances, chromaticism, complicated rhythms, and a focus on solo voices and improvisation. A typical bebop combo featured a rhythm section of piano, drums, bass, and one or more melody instruments, such as trumpet, alto or tenor saxophone, or trombone. In contrast to big-band music, bebop was meant not for dancing but for attentive listening. The focus was on the star performers and their prowess as improvisers.

Performances in which one of the players was essentially the composer are preserved on recordings that have become classics, listened to over and over again, analyzed, and reviewed in critical essays.

A characteristic example of bebop is *Anthropology* (NAWM 197), by alto saxophonist Charlie Parker (1920–1955, nicknamed "Bird") and trumpeter Dizzy Gillespie (1917–1993), who are shown in Figure 27.1. Like many other bebop standards. *Anthropology* is a contrafact on the "rhythm changes"—that is, it features a new melody over the chord progression for Gershwin's *I Got Rhythm* (see NAWM 181 and 184). A bebop performance normally begins with an introduction and then the primary tune, known as the head, played in unison or octaves by the melody instruments. Players perform from an abbreviated score called a lead sheet (shown in NAWM 197a), which includes only the head and chord symbols indicating the harmony. The tune for *Anthropology* is typical of bebop in consisting of short, rapid bursts of notes separated by surprising rests, creating a jagged, unpredictable melody. The head is followed by several choruses (solo improvisations over the harmony), and the piece ends with a final statement of the head. In the classic recording of *Anthropology*. Parker plays a sizzling solo of unusual length (transcribed in NAWM 197b), taking up three choruses and surrounding the chord changes with a flurry of chromatic alterations.

Figure 27.1 Alto saxophonist Charlie Parker and trumpeter Dizzy Gillespie on stage at Birdland, the legendary jazz club in New York City, ca. 1950. (RA/Lebrecht Music & Arts Photo Library.)

Musicians like Parker, Gillespie, and Miles Davis (1926–1991) pioneered new jazz styles in the 1950s, seeking paths for individual expression by extending the methods and ideas of bebop. Some employed techniques borrowed from classical music: nonchordal dissonance, chromaticism, irregular phrase structures, modality, atonality, and unusual instrumental effects. Davis was behind a series of innovations, beginning with his album *Birth of the Cool* (1949–1950). Its softer timbres, more relaxed pace, and rhythmic subtleties inaugurated the trend that became known as *cool jazz*, soon taken up by the Modern Jazz Quartet, Dave Brubeck (1920–2012), and many others. Later, in *Kind of Blue* (1959), Davis explored yet another new style, *modal jazz*, which featured slowly unfolding melodies over stable, relatively static modal harmonies.

In the 1960s, Ornette Coleman (b. 1930, see Figure 27.2) and his quartet introduced a more radically new jazz language called free jazz, named after their landmark album *Free Jazz* (1960). This experimental style moved away from jazz standards and familiar tunes, turning instead to a language built of melodic and harmonic gestures, innovative sounds, atonality, and free forms using improvisation that was carried on outside the strictures of standard jazz forms. John Coltrane (1926–1967) developed a personal avant-garde style based on very fast playing, motivic development, new sonorities, and greater dissonance and density of sound. Like avant-garde composers in the classical

Figure 27.2 Columbia University President Lee C. Bollinger presents Ornette Coleman with the 2007 Pulitzer Prize in Music. (Eileen Barroso/Columbia University.)

tradition, creators of free jazz and other avant-garde jazz styles questioned some of the basic assumptions of the tradition yet clearly drew from it, wanting to say something new in a distinctive style that remained rooted in the tradition.

Third stream

In the 1950s and 1960s, as jazz was being taken more and more seriously, some American composers who were conversant with both jazz and classical music sought consciously to merge the two. One of the most successful of these, Gunther Schuller (b. 1925), called this combination "third stream." In his *Transformation* (1957), a pointillistic twelve-tone context with elements of Webern's *Klangfarbenmelodie* is transformed into a full-blown modern jazz piece.

Jazz as a classical music

While some jazz performers were pursuing new alternatives, others maintained older styles, reviving ragtime and New Orleans jazz or continuing to play swing. In a striking parallel to the rise of the classical concert repertory over a century earlier, by 1970 the jazz world had developed its own roster of classics that were treasured on recordings and kept alive in performance. A sense of history was inculcated by written histories and recorded anthologies of jazz. As younger listeners turned to the latest pop styles and other new trends, jazz increasingly became music for the well-informed listener. Jazz critics and historians began to describe jazz as a kind of classical music. Jazz ensembles were formed at many schools, colleges, and universities beginning in the 1950s and 1960s, and jazz history became part of the curriculum. Jazz is now respected as art music, as evidenced by Ornette Coleman's receipt of the 2007 Pulitzer Prize in Music for his composition *Sound Grammar*. However, it still retains some of the aura of the rebellious popular music it had been half a century earlier.

Heirs to the Classical Tradition

Although critical discussion of twentieth-century music has often focused on new sounds and techniques, many postwar composers used traditional media. Like their forebears, they sought an individual voice within the classical tradition.

Olivier Messiaen

Olivier Messiaen (1908–1992), shown in Figure 27.3, was the most important French composer born in the twentieth century. A native of Avignon in southern France, he studied organ and composition at the Paris Conservatoire, served as organist at Sainte Trinitée church in Paris from 1931 on, and became professor of harmony at the Conservatory in 1941. After the war, he taught many important composers of the younger generation, including his fellow Frenchman Pierre Boulez (b. 1925) and the German Karlheinz Stockhausen (1928–2007). It is a tribute to the quality and impartiality of Messiaen's teaching that each of these pupils went his own way.

A devout Catholic, Messiaen composed many pieces on religious subjects, such as the *Quatuor pour la fin du temps* (Quartet for the End of Time) for violin, clarinet, cello, and piano, written at a German military prison camp in 1941 for performance by the composer and three fellow prisoners; *Vingt regards sur l'Enfant-Jésus* (Twenty Looks at the Infant Jesus, 1944) for piano; his opera *Saint Francis of Assisi* (1975–1983); and numerous works for his own instrument, the organ. Other principal compositions include *Turangalîla-symphonie* (1946–1948) and *Catalogue d'oiseaux* (Catalogue of Birds, 1956–1958) for piano.

Figure 27.3 Olivier Messiaen photographed in 1972 at the organ in Trinité Church, Paris, where he played services until his death in 1992.
(George Tames/The New York Times/Redux.)

Messiaen sought to embody in music an aesthetic of ecstatic contemplation. His works typically present an experience of concentrated meditation on limited material, like a musical mantra. Rather than develop themes, he juxtaposes static ideas, showing his heritage from Debussy and Stravinsky. Messiaen used several characteristic devices, described in his book *The Technique of My Musical Language* (1944), that helped him achieve his goal of writing meditative music. The opening movement of the *Quatuor pour la fin du temps*, entitled *Liturgie de cristal* (Crystal Liturgy, NAWM 201), illustrates several of them, as shown in Example 27.1. Both the violin and clarinet play figures that suggest birdcalls, which Messiaen frequently used to convey a sense of contemplating the gifts of nature and the divine. The cello notes are all from a single whole-tone scale, in a repeating sequence of five notes (C–E–D–F♯–B♭, bracketed in Example 27.1), another device that enables Messiaen's music to suggest contemplation and a negation of desire. Messiaen's harmony also avoids moving forward to a resolution. Rather, chord series are simply repeated to create a sense of stasis or meditation. In this movement, the piano plays a succession of twenty-nine chords six times (the last incomplete); the second statement begins in measure 8 (marked by an arrow below the score). Such a repeating pattern is similar to the color in a medieval isorhythmic piece (see Chapter 4).

Messiaen treats rhythm as a matter of duration, not meter. In Example 27.1 and throughout the movement, both piano and cello play a repeating series of durations that resembles the talea, or rhythmic pattern, of medieval isorhythm. The piano features a string of seventeen durations (numbered in the example) played ten times, of which the first two statements appear in the example. Because such repeating pitch and rhythmic series create cyclic repetition, and because they preserve their identity outside the propulsive force of regular meter, they seem to float in time, once again inviting contemplation.

Finally, Messiaen preferred beautiful timbres and colorful harmonies. Here, the cello plays in high harmonics (sounding two octaves above the notated pitches), creating an ethereal sound, augmented by the gentle birdcalls in the high violin and clarinet over soft dissonances in the piano. Messiaen invites us to meditate on these sonorous objects as they recombine in new ways yet remain the same, like colorful shapes in a kaleidoscope.

Music as contemplation

Quartet for the End of Time

| Full 🔊 | Concise 🔊 |

Harmonic stasis

Rhythmic stasis

Ethereal sounds

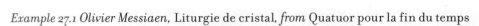

Example 27.1 Olivier Messiaen, Liturgie de cristal, *from* Quatuor pour la fin du temps

Glissando bref: id. aux passages similaires.

Benjamin Britten

While Messiaen focused on music of contemplation, English composer Benjamin Britten (1913–1976) was concerned primarily with communication. After studying privately and at the Royal College of Music, Britten spent several years in the late 1930s writing music for films, an experience that shaped his style by teaching him to communicate by the simplest means. Like Copland, he tempered modernism with simplicity to achieve a clear and widely appealing idiom. Maturing in the 1930s, he was deeply influenced by humanitarian concerns and ideals of public service, manifest in his interest in writing music for children and amateurs, his allegorical pleas for tolerance, and his pacifism.

Britten was a homosexual, and his lifelong partner was the tenor Peter Pears (1910–1986). Shown in Figure 27.4, the two met in 1936 and lived together until Britten's death five decades later. Britten wrote most of his tenor roles for Pears, and the two collaborated as performers and as producers of the annual music festival at Aldeburgh in England. Several of Britten's operas have themes that relate to homosexuality, including *Billy Budd* (1950–1951) and *Death in Venice* (1971–1974).

Peter Grimes (1944–1945), which established Britten's reputation and became the first English opera since Purcell to enter the international repertory, centers on a fisherman who is disliked by the other residents of his village, pursued by mobs, and ultimately driven to suicide (see Figure 27.5). The theme of the individual persecuted by the crowd can be read as an allegory for the condition of homosexuals in a hostile society. Tellingly, Grimes is not a sympathetic character; we are meant to see ourselves not in him, but in the ugly crowd that unthinkingly persecutes outsiders on the basis of suspicions and misinformation, forcing a poignant catharsis in the final tragedy. In the last scene (NAWM 200), as a search party pursues him calling his name, Grimes raves and mocks them in an unmeasured recitative, until his friend urges him to sail his boat out to sea and sink it. The opera ends with a stunning depiction of the uncaring sea and equally uncaring townsfolk in a most successful application of bitonality: strings, harp, and winds arpeggiate thirds that encompass all the notes of the

Figure 27.4 Benjamin Britten (right) and Peter Pears, ca. 1944, when Britten was working on his opera Peter Grimes.
(Enid Slater. Courtesy of the Britten-Pears Library, Aldeburgh.)

▶ **BRITTEN,** *Peter Grimes*

Figure 27.5. A scene from the 1995 production of Peter Grimes *at the Royal Opera House in London, with Ben Heppner (left) singing the role of Grimes's friend, Balstrode.*
(Wladmir Polak/Lebrecht Music & Arts Photo Library.)

C-major scale, depicting the shimmering sea, as the town's citizens go about their business, singing a slow hymn to the sea in A major. The entire scene displays the eloquent dramatic effects Britten creates out of simple means.

War Requiem

Britten's pacifism—his conscientious objection to war in any form—is expressed in his choral masterpiece, *War Requiem* (1961–1962). Commissioned for the consecration of the new cathedral at Coventry, a city destroyed in a German bombing raid during World War II, the work weaves together the Latin text of the Requiem Mass with verses by Wilfred Owen, an English soldier and poet killed in France in 1918 just days before the end of World War I. Britten's commitment—to pacifism, to tolerance, to including all ages and talents in music-making—gives his music a quality of social engagement that has attracted many performers and listeners, and has inspired later composers.

Tonal Traditionalism

Many twentieth-century composers developed individual styles without departing radically from the past. Tonality or neotonality often, though not necessarily, characterizes their music, along with identifiable themes, readily audible forms, and programmatic subjects or titles. (See also neo-Romanticism on page 641.)

Samuel Barber

Of the American composers who remained committed to tonality, one of the most successful was Samuel Barber (1910–1981). His tonal romanticism is fully expressed in his best-known work, *Adagio for Strings* (arranged from the slow movement of his String Quartet, 1936), and in his Violin Concerto (1939) and Piano Concerto (1962). He often incorporated modernist resources into his tonal music—for example, his Piano Sonata (1949), which uses twelve-tone rows in a tonal framework. Barber was renowned for his vocal music, including *Dover Beach* (1931) for voice and string quartet, *Knoxville: Summer of 1915* (1950) for voice and orchestra, and three operas.

The Avant-Garde

As noted in our discussion of Satie and futurism in Chapter 24, avant-garde composers have a variety of motivations: they challenge accepted aesthetics, dismiss the concept of permanent classics, and invite listeners to focus on what is happening in the present.

John Cage

Figure 27.6 John Cage, called by one writer "the genial emperor of the avant-garde," in a photograph taken in 1987.
(Richard S. Schulman/Corbis.)

The leading composer and philosopher of the postwar avant-garde was John Cage (1912–1992), shown in Figure 27.6. Over the course of a long and influential career, Cage sought to bring into music sounds, approaches, and ideas that previously had been excluded, repeatedly challenging the core concepts of music itself. Building on the work of his teacher Henry Cowell, Cage used novel sounds in his music during the late 1930s and 1940s. He wrote numerous works for percussion ensemble, using both traditional instruments and untraditional ones, such as tin cans of varying size and pitch. Cage's experimentation with timbre culminated in his invention of the prepared piano, in

Music in the Present Moment

John Cage articulated his views about music in a series of lectures given at Darmstadt, Germany, in 1958 and published in his first book of writings, Silence *(1961). The lecture "Changes," from which the following is excerpted, was interleaved in its presentation with excerpts from Cage's* Music of Changes.

[In my recent works,] the view taken is not of an activity the purpose of which is to integrate the opposites, but rather of an activity characterized by process and essentially purposeless. The mind, though stripped of its right to control, is still present. What does it do, having nothing to do? And what happens to a piece of music when it is purposelessly made?

What happens, for instance, to silence? That is, how does the mind's perception of it change? Formerly, silence was the time lapse between sounds, useful towards a variety of ends, among them that of tasteful arrangement, where by separating two sounds or two groups of sounds their differences or relationships might receive emphasis; or that of expressivity, where silences in a musical discourse might provide pause or punctuation; or again, that of architecture, where the introduction or interruption of silence might give definition either to a predetermined structure or to an organically developing one. Where none of these or other goals is present, silence becomes something else—not silence at all, but sounds, the ambient sounds. The nature of these is unpredictable and changing. These sounds (which are called silence only because they do not form part of a musical intention) may be depended upon to exist. The world teems with them, and is, in fact, at no point free of them. He who has entered an anechoic chamber, a room made as silent as technologically possible, has heard there two sounds, one high, one low—the high the listener's nervous system in operation, the low his blood circulation. There are, demonstrably, sounds to be heard and forever, given ears to hear. Where these ears are in connection with a mind that has nothing to do, that mind is free to enter into the act of listening, hearing each sound just as it is, not as a phenomenon more or less approximating a preconception. . . .

The early works have beginnings, middles, and endings. The later ones do not. They begin anywhere, last any length of time, and involve more or fewer instruments and players. They are therefore not preconceived objects, and to approach them as objects is to utterly miss the point. They are occasions for experience. . . . The mind may be used either to ignore ambient sounds, pitches other than the eighty-eight [keys on a piano], durations which are not counted, timbres which are unmusical or distasteful, and in general to control and understand an available experience. Or the mind may give up its desire to improve on creation and function as a faithful receiver of experience.

From John Cage, "Changes," in *Silence: Lectures and Writings* (Middletown, Conn.: Wesleyan University Press, 1961), pp. 22–23 and 31–32.

which various objects—such as pennies, bolts, screws, pieces of wood, rubber, plastic, weather stripping, or slit bamboo—are inserted between the strings, resulting in delicate, complex percussive sounds when the piano is played from the keyboard. Essentially, the prepared piano is a one-person percussion ensemble, with sounds that resemble drums, woodblocks, gongs, and other standard or unusual instruments. Cage's *Sonatas and Interludes* (1946–1948) is his best-known work for prepared piano, consisting of twenty-six "sonatas"—movements in two repeated parts, as in a Scarlatti sonata, but without thematic returns—and four interludes. The pianist prepares the piano in advance, following detailed instructions concerning what objects to place between the strings and where to put them. Each movement explores a different set of timbres and figurations. Sonata V (NAWM 203) illustrates the contrasts Cage achieves between wood, drum, gong, and unal-

Sonatas and Interludes

Figure 27.7 *The score of Cage's three-movement work 4′33″, published by Edition Peters. "Tacet" means "Be silent."*
(Lebrecht Music & Arts Photo Library.)

tered piano sounds, and the interactions he creates between the content—the succession of sounds—and the durational structure, or units of time determined by binary and square root forms.

Cage turned in the 1950s and 1960s to ever more radical reconceptions of music. In his writings, he strongly opposed the museumlike preservation of music from the past and argued for music that focused the listener's attention on the present moment. He did not seek to write works that expressed emotions, conveyed images, developed material, revealed a coherent structure, or unfolded a logical series of events, as music had done for centuries. Instead, influenced by Zen Buddhism, he created opportunities for experiencing sounds as themselves, not as vehicles for the composer's intentions (see Vignette, page 615). His three main strategies for accomplishing this were chance, indeterminacy, and the blurring of boundaries between music, art, and life.

By leaving some of the decisions normally made by a composer to chance, Cage created pieces in which the sounds did not convey his intentions, but simply existed. His approach varied from piece to piece but typically involved choosing a variety of elements to be included, planning how they were to be selected, and then using chance operations to make the selection. *Music of Changes* for piano (Book I, 1951; NAWM 204) took its name from the ancient Chinese book of prophecy *I-Ching* (Book of Changes), which offers a method of divination by tossing coins. For *Music of Changes*, Cage devised charts of possible sounds (half were silences), dynamics, durations, and tempos, and used the method from the *I-Ching* to select which were to be used, filling in a formal structure based on units of time. The result is a piece in which sounds occur (and may recur) randomly and at random volumes, durations, and speeds.

Chance is a way to determine certain aspects of the music without recourse to the composer's intentions. Another approach Cage pioneered is what he called *indeterminacy*, in which the composer relinquishes control not to chance operations but by leaving certain aspects of the music to the performer or even to the audience. Cage's *Concert* for piano and orchestra (1957–1958) is intended to be realized by the players according to instructions in the score; the exact sounds produced vary considerably from one performance to another. Cage's most extreme indeterminate work—and his most famous piece—was *4′33″* (Four Minutes Thirty-three Seconds, 1952), in which the performer or performers sit silently at or with their instruments of choice for a span of time specified in the title (subdivided into three "movements"; see Figure 27.7), while whatever noises that can be heard in the concert hall or from outside constitute the music. The piece implies that silence is simply openness to ambient sound and that there are always environmental sounds worth contemplating.

In chance music, elements are specified as determined by chance; in indeterminate music, they are left unspecified by the composer. In both, Cage invites the listener simply to hear sounds as sounds, whether notated in the music or not, whether generated by the performers or occurring as part of the ambience, experiencing each sound as it comes along, not trying to connect it to what precedes or follows it, not expecting the

Figure 27.8 *Jackson Pollock,* Untitled *(ca. 1950). Compare the score of Earle Brown's* December 1952 *(Figure 27.9).*
(ARS, NY. © The Metropolitan Museum of Art. Image: Art Resource, NY.)

In Performance Indeterminacy

One by-product of indeterminacy is a variety of new kinds of notation. Scores range all the way from fragments of conventional staff to purely graphic suggestions of melodic curves, dynamic ranges, and rhythms to even more slippery and meager directives. An example is *December 1952* (Figure 27.9) by Earle Brown (1926–2002), a piece in graphic notation in which nothing is specified. The score offers lines and rectangles of various sizes, some vertical and others horizontal, and Brown explains in a note

that the score can be placed in any orientation, read in any direction, and performed for any length of time by any number of instruments or sound-makers. It is up to the performers to determine how to translate the signs on the page into sounds.

Inspired by the mobiles of Alexander Calder, Brown took another approach to indeterminacy in his "open form" pieces *Available Forms I* (1961) for eighteen players and *Available Forms II* (1962) for large orchestra, in which the musicians play completely scored fragments—with some leeway in the choice of pitches—in the order and tempo determined by the conductor. In such works the piece will vary considerably from performance to performance, while its overall character remains within a certain range.

Another consequence of indeterminacy is that no two performances of a piece are identical. In effect, a composition does not exist independently, but only as a performance or as the sum of possible performances. Through the reconsideration of "the musical work" that indeterminacy and related notions stimulated, musicians in the later twentieth century became increasingly aware of the openness of earlier music as well, coming to understand that a medieval song or a Baroque aria is also a platform for performance open to a variety of choices within a stylistically appropriate range, not a rigidly defined, unchanging work.

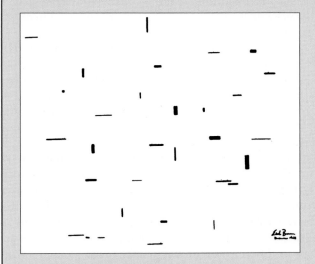

Figure 27.9 Earle Brown, December 1952.
(Lebrecht Music & Arts Photo Library.)

music to communicate feelings or meanings of any kind, but listening as intently as we would listen to any art music. Thus, as we learn to extend our attention beyond music to the world itself, value judgments become irrelevant.

Beginning in the late 1950s, Cage moved toward complete openness in every aspect of composition and performance. *Variations IV* (1963), for instance, uses both indeterminacy and chance (pages of transparent plastic with lines, dots, and other symbols are superimposed randomly and then read as graphic notation) to create a piece "for any number of players, any sounds or combinations of sounds produced by any means, with or without other activities." The "other activities" might include speech, theater, dance, and activities of daily life. Accordingly, these "musical" works blurred the boundaries between music, other arts, and the rest of life. *Musicircus* (1967) is an open-ended "happening," consisting of any number of musicians and ensembles, each performing different music, all playing at once in a large space while the audience wanders freely. Through such events, Cage sought to focus our attention on whatever is happening in the present, experiencing it without prejudice.

"Happenings"

Indeterminacy in Works of Other Composers

Cage was inspired to use indeterminacy in part because of his association with Morton Feldman (1926–1987), a like-minded musician also based in New York. Feldman was closely associated with New York abstract expressionist painters, including Jackson Pollock (see Figure 27.8), who inspired him to trust instinct, reject compositional systems and traditional forms of expression, and compose in a manner analogous to flat, abstract images. His *Projection I* for solo cello uses boxes rather than noteheads to indicate approximate register, leaving the specific pitches up to the player. But timbre and rhythm are specified and the pattern of sounds and silences and of changing timbres and densities of attack will be the same no matter what pitches are chosen. By deemphasizing pitch, Feldman focuses attention on other aspects of the music.

Many other composers adopted indeterminacy in some form under the influence of Cage or his associates. Another member of the New York group around Cage and Feldman was Earle Brown (1926–2002). For a discussion of his work, see In Performance, page 617.

Serial and Nonserial Complexity

After World War II. Young composers in Germany and elsewhere embraced music that the Nazi regime had condemned, especially that of Schoenberg and Webern. By the early 1950s, many composers had adopted twelve-tone methods, adapting them to their own purposes. We have seen that established composers like Stravinsky took up serialism, but it had its most profound impact on the generation of composers who were just beginning their careers at the end of the war. Their interest was partly musical, reflecting enthusiasm for new possibilities, and partly political, expressing a rejection of the Nazi and communist ideologies that had opposed such dissonant and esoteric music.

Politics and institutional support

The new developments were encouraged by government-sponsored musical institutions, such as the courses for new music held in Darmstadt, West Germany, each summer beginning in 1946 (with the secret assistance of the United States' occupying forces). At a memorial concert of his works at Darmstadt in 1953, Webern was hailed as the father of a new movement. In the United States, serialism was adopted by many university composers and others, even Copland, as a way to achieve a music free of nationalist, fascist, or leftist ideology and thus escape the taint of politics many styles had acquired during the 1930s and early 1940s. Government and university support was crucial since there was never a large or enthusiastic audience for serial music. Some saw that as a virtue, allowing music to advance on its own terms, like physics, without having to please the untutored listener (see Vignette, page 621).

The Darmstadt school

The anationalist ideas fostered at Darmstadt and other centers for new music inspired experiments by composers in many countries. But every composer worked independently, striking out in new directions, cultivating a personal language and style. Pierre Boulez of Paris and Karlheinz Stockhausen of Cologne, both pupils of Messiaen, became the two principal composers of the Darmstadt group, and Milton Babbitt (1916–2011) became the leading serial composer and theorist in the United States.

Extensions of Serialism

Beginning in the late 1940s, composers applied the principle of Schoenberg's tone rows to musical parameters other than pitch, giving rise to what has been called total serialism. If the twelve notes of the chromatic scale could be serialized, so could durations, intensities, timbres, and other elements, at least hypothetically, although typically only some nonpitch elements are treated serially, and the rest are used to highlight the serial structure.

In Babbitt's Three Compositions for Piano (1947), the first piece to apply serial principles to duration, he used a four-number durational row in addition to a pitch row, manipulating both by the usual operations of inversion and retrograde. His music quickly grew more complex, as he went beyond the practices of Schoenberg and his circle to realize new potentials of serialism. Babbitt once commented, "I want a piece of music to be literally as much as possible," and he pursued this goal by making the relationships between notes as numerous and intricate as possible.

Milton Babbitt

Composers in Europe explored similar ideas, independent of Babbitt. Inspired by Messiaen's repeating cycles of pitch and rhythm, Boulez and Stockhausen wrote the first European works of total serialism. Karlheinz Stockhausen (1928–2007; Figure 27.10) heard Messiaen's work at Darmstadt in 1951 and composed his *Kreuzspiel* (Cross-Play) for piano, oboe, bass clarinet, and percussion that fall. The work uses complex serial processes to control permutations of pitch, duration, dynamics, and register. They all cross at precisely the same point in the middle, hence the title *Kreuzspiel*.

Karlheinz Stockhausen

Stockhausen continued to develop serial procedures in *Kontra-Punkte* (1952–53) and other works, but also moved in many other directions, combining serialism with other methods while creating a very diverse body of work. Stockhausen was also one of the pioneers of electronic music (discussed on page 623).

Pierre Boulez (see Figure 27.11) was also inspired by some of the methods of his teacher, Messiaen, to apply serialism to both pitch and duration. In *Structures* (1951–52) for two pianos, pitches and durations are both serial while dynamics and articulation are used to distinguish rows from one another. Boulez soon relaxed the rigidity of total serialism. In his best-known piece, *Le*

Pierre Boulez

Figure 27.10 Karlheinz Stockhausen.
(Clive Barda/ArenaPAL/Topham/The Image Works.)

Figure 27.11 Pierre Boulez conducting in the 1970s.
(SW Lauterwasser/Lebrecht Music & Arts Photo Library.)

Marteau sans maître (The Hammer without a Master, 1953–1955), he fused the pointillist style—featuring a very spare texture with only a few notes at once—and the serial method with sensitive musical realization of the text. This work, in nine short movements, sets verses from a cycle of surrealist poems by René Char, alternating them with instrumental movements that comment on the vocal ones by realizing the same material in different ways. The ensemble—a different combination in each movement, as in Schoenberg's *Pierrot lunaire*—produces a translucent scrim of sound, all in the middle and high registers, with effects often suggestive of Balinese gamelan music. The contralto vocal line is characterized by wide melodic intervals, glissandos, and occasional *Sprechstimme*.

A totally serial composition—such as the sixth movement of *Le Marteau sans maître*, Boulez's setting of Char's *Bourreaux de solitude* (NAWM 202)—may give a listener an impression of randomness because music based on these principles typically lacks readily perceived themes, a distinct rhythmic pulse, and a sense of progression toward points of climax. Instead, the listener hears only unrepeated and unpredictable musical events. To be sure, the totality of these events does form a logical pattern, but it is inevitably unique, likely resembling nothing the listener has heard before, and, therefore, difficult to perceive. As a result, postwar serial music has enjoyed an enduring unpopularity, appealing principally to a small set of enthusiasts. At the same time, some composers maintained their right to be indifferent to the public's likes and dislikes. Milton Babbitt expressed this attitude in a 1958 essay entitled (by a magazine editor) "Who Cares If You Listen?" (see Vignette, page 621).

The New Virtuosity

Champion performers

The music of total serialism was extraordinarily difficult to perform. For the structure to be clear in a work like Boulez's *Le Marteau sans maître*, not only must the pitches and rhythms be absolutely accurate, but the dynamics must be exact—*ff* must be distinct from *f* and *fff*. In the postwar years, a new generation of technically proficient performers emerged who were capable of playing such works and who made careers as champions of the newest music. Their presence encouraged composers to write pieces to challenge the skills of these new virtuosos. Much of this new music was not serial, but drew on sounds and textures like those explored in serial music.

Luciano Berio

The new virtuosity is well represented by the series of works by Italian composer Luciano Berio (1925–2003) entitled *Sequenza*, each for an unaccompanied solo instrument from flute (1958) to accordion (1995–1996) and each composed for a specific performer. *Sequenza III* (1965–1966) emphasizes vocal virtuosity. It is mostly in graphic notation, rather than precise staff notation, to convey vocal sounds from singing to humming, whispering, muttering, laughing, coughing, gasping, and clicking the tongue. Out of these primal sounds come vowels, consonants, syllables, and occasionally words and phrases, all heard as sounds rather than as carriers of meaning. The indeterminate aspects of the piece derive in part from Cage, the sound qualities from treating the voice like an instrument, and the virtuosity from the singer for whom he wrote it, his former wife Cathy Berberian.

VIGNETTE Composition as Research

Milton Babbitt, professor of music and of mathematics at Princeton University, argued that composers, like scientists, engage in research that advances knowledge and should be supported for that work, even if it lies beyond most people's comprehension. His view extends in new terms the nineteenth-century view of music as an autonomous art to be pursued for its own sake. This excerpt is from an essay he wrote under the title "The Composer as Specialist," changed by an editor at the magazine where it first appeared to the more provocative "Who Cares If You Listen?"

Why should the layman be other than bored and puzzled by what he is unable to understand, music or anything else? It is only the translation of this boredom and puzzlement into resentment and denunciation that seems to me indefensible. After all, the public does have its own music, its ubiquitous music: music to eat by, to read by, to dance by, and to be impressed by. Why refuse to recognize the possibility that contemporary music has reached a stage long since attained by other forms of activity? The time has passed when the normally well-educated man without special preparation can understand the most advanced work in, for example, mathematics, philosophy, and physics. Advanced music, to the extent that it reflects the knowledge and originality of the informed composer, scarcely can be expected to appear more intelligible than these arts and sciences to the person whose musical education usually has been even less extensive than his background in other fields.

But to this, a double standard is invoked, with the words "music is music," implying also that "music is just music." Why not, then, equate the activities of the radio repairman with those of the theoretical physicist, on the basis of the dictum that "physics is physics"? . . .

I dare suggest that the composer would do himself and his music an immediate and eventual service by total, resolute, and voluntary withdrawal from this public world to one of private performance and electronic media, with its very real possibility of complete elimination of the public and social aspects of musical composition. By so doing, the separation between the domains would be defined beyond any possibility of confusion of categories, and the composer would be free to pursue a private life of professional achievement, as opposed to a public life of unprofessional compromise and exhibitionism.

But how, it may be asked, will this serve to secure the means of survival for the composer and his music? One answer is that after all such a private life is what the university provides the scholar and the scientist. It is only proper that the university, which—significantly—has provided so many contemporary composers with their professional training and general education, should provide a home for the "complex," "difficult," and "problematical" in music.

From Milton Babbitt, "Who Cares If You Listen?" *High Fidelity* 8, no. 2 (February 1958): pp. 39–40; repr. in Oliver Strunk, ed., *Source Readings in Music History*, rev. ed. by Leo Treitler (New York: Norton, 1998). vol. 6, pp. 38–40.

The prolific American Elliott Carter (1908–2012), who composed right up until his death at the age of 103, also wrote for virtuoso performers, using a complex style characterized by innovations in rhythm and form. Beginning with his Cello Sonata (1948), Carter developed what he called "metric modulation," in which proportional tempo changes at different layers of the music create a kind of rhythmic polyphony. This technique, which became highly influential, was inspired in part by the multilayered textures in the music of Ives and Stravinsky, whom Carter knew in his youth. His late piano work *Caténaires* (2006, NAWM 218) requires another kind of virtuosity, one that resembles in its uninterrupted energy the linearly conceived keyboard toccatas of J.S. Bach or Chopin's scintillating piano pieces. Commissioned, premiered, and recorded by the French pianist Pierre-Laurent Aimard, *Caténaires* is, in the composer's own words, "a fast one line piece with no chords . . . a continuous chain of notes using different spacings, accents, and colorings, to produce a

Elliott Carter

Caténaires

Full 🔊

wide variety of expression." The score is appropriately marked "jaillissant" (gushing forth). The work's title suggests the U-shaped catenary curve produced by suspending a cable between two fixed points and therefore aptly describes the garlands of notes that spill across the pages of the printed score.

The difficulties of performing works like these have meant that they are seldom played and are known mainly through recordings. Yet, like nineteenth-century virtuoso showpieces, the best of these pieces attract some of the top performers and are likely to endure.

New Sounds and Textures

One prominent strand in twentieth-century music was the exploration of new musical resources, including new sounds and new conceptions of music. In the postwar period, the search for new resources intensified. Among all the variety, at least four overlapping trends can be identified: the use of new instruments, sounds, and scales; incorporation of non-Western sounds and instruments; electronic music; and music of texture and process.

New Instruments, Sounds, and Scales

In their efforts to offer something new and distinctive in art music, many composers sought new sounds, sometimes building new instruments or reconfiguring traditional ones, and some explored scales featuring intervals smaller than a semitone.

Figure 27.12 Harry Partch playing the gourd tree, one of the instruments he invented to realize his music based on a forty-three-note untempered scale.
(The Sousa Archives and Center for American Music.)

One composer who combined the exploration of new instrumental sounds with a new approach to pitch was Harry Partch (1901–1974), the sometime hobo who undertook an individualistic, single-minded search for new sonic media. He repudiated equal temperament and Western harmony and counterpoint to seek a wholly new system inspired partly by Chinese, Native American, Jewish, Christian, African, and rural American music. His writings speak of a "monophonic" musical ideal, harking back to the ancient Greeks. Partch devised a new scale with forty-three notes to the octave based on just intonation, in which notes relate to each other through pure intervals from the harmonic series. He then built new instruments that could play in this scale, including modified guitars, marimbas, tuned cloud-chamber bowls (large glass containers used in early particle physics), a large string instrument like the ancient Greek kithara, and the gourd tree (Figure 27.12). In his multimedia works of the 1950s and 1960s, these instruments accompany speaking and chanting voices and dancing by singer-actor-dancers. In much of his work, in particular *Oedipus — a Music-Dance Drama* (1951) and *Revelation in the Courthouse Park* (1962), based on Euripides' *The Bacchae*, Partch aspired to the ideal of Greek tragedy.

Taking a path similar to Partch, George Crumb (b. 1929) has been most imaginative in coaxing new sounds out of ordinary instruments and objects. In *Ancient Voices of Children* (1970), a cycle of four songs on poems by Federico García Lorca with two instrumental interludes, his unconventional sound sources include toy piano, musical saw, harmonica, mandolin, Tibetan prayer stones, Japanese temple bells, and electric piano. He obtained special effects from conventional instruments as well: for example, players must bend the pitch of the piano by applying a chisel to the strings, thread paper through the harp strings, and tune the mandolin a quarter tone flat. In *Black Angels* (1970, NAWM 205), a string quartet is electronically amplified to produce surrealistic, dreamlike juxtapositions. The composer explored unusual means of bowing, such as striking the strings near the pegs with the bow and bowing between the left-hand fingers and the pegs. The new and unusual effects in Crumb's music always have a musical purpose, providing material for juxtaposition and variation; they usually evoke extramusical associations as well. Here, they help to express his reactions to the Vietnam conflict, the social unrest in the United States, and the horrors of war. Crumb's works also often reflect on music of the past; in this case, *Black Angels* quotes the chant *Dies irae* and Schubert's *Death and the Maiden* Quartet for their affective associations.

Black Angels

Full 🔊 Concise 🔊

Non-Western Styles and Instruments

Growing sensitivity to the perspectives of other cultures led to an exploration of their music with respect for its uniqueness, rather than invoking the "foreign" for its sheer otherness, as in nineteenth-century exoticism. Several Western composers became fascinated with Asian instruments, sounds, and textures. While Partch drew on ideas from Asian music, Canadian-American composer Colin McPhee (1900–1964) studied music in Bali in the 1930s, transcribed gamelan music for Western instruments, and composed *Tabuh-tabuhan* (1936) for orchestra and many other pieces that drew on Balinese materials. Henry Cowell, the California-born pioneer of cluster chords, had a life-long interest in Asian music (see Chapter 26). After World War II, his travels to Iran, India, and Japan led to several works that blended Asian and Western elements, including *Persian Set* (1957) for chamber orchestra, Symphony No. 13 (*Madras*) (1956–1958), *Ongaku* (1957) for orchestra, and two concertos for the Japanese koto (a plucked string instrument) and orchestra (1961–1962 and 1965). Cowell's student and friend Lou Harrison (1917–2003) combined his interest in just intonation and his penchant for inventing new instruments—inspired by Partch—with enthusiasm for the music of Asia. After visiting Korea and Taiwan in 1961–1962, Harrison wrote several works that combine Western and Asian instruments, including *Pacifika Rondo* (1963) and *La Koro Sutro* (1972), and beginning in the 1970s he celebrated the sound of the traditional Javanese gamelan in dozens of his pieces.

Colin McPhee

Henry Cowell

Lou Harrison

Electronic Music

As new technologies developed, musicians explored their potential for new sounds and compositional techniques. No technology promised more far-reaching changes for music than the electronic recording, production, and transformation of sounds. These technologies were first exploited in art music but ultimately became more significant for popular music, especially after 1970.

One approach was to work with recorded sounds, taking the entire world of sound as potential material for music, manipulating the chosen sounds through

Musique concrète

mechanical and electronic means, and assembling them into collages. Pierre Schaeffer (1910–1995), who pioneered music of this type at Radiodiffusion Française (French Radio) in Paris in the 1940s, named it *musique concrète* because the composer worked concretely with sound itself rather than with music notation. He and his collaborator, Pierre Henry, created the first major work of musique concrète, *Symphonie pour un homme seul* (Symphony for One Man), premiered in a 1950 radio broadcast. Tape recorders, which became widely available around that year, made it possible to record, amplify, and transform sounds, then superimpose, juxtapose, fragment, and arrange them as desired to produce pieces of music.

Electronic sound

Another source was electronic production of new sounds. Most electronic sounds were created by oscillators, invented in 1915. The first successful electronic instrument was the theremin, invented around 1920 by Lev Termen, which changed pitch according to the distance between the instrument's antenna and the performer's hand. The ondes martenot, invented in 1928 by Maurice Martenot, was controlled by a wire, ribbon, or keyboard. Both instruments produced only one note at a time, were capable of glissandos along the entire pitch continuum, and projected a haunting, almost voice-like sound. Featured in some orchestral works, they became common in film scores like Hitchcock's *Spellbound*, where they lent an eerie or futuristic effect, but they

Electronic music studios

were not used in electronic music itself. Between 1951 and 1953, studios to create electronic music were founded at Columbia University in New York and at radio stations in Cologne, Milan, and Tokyo, followed by many others across Europe and the Americas. At most studios, composers focused on produced sounds electronically and manipulating them through electronic devices and on tape. A new realm of possible sounds became available, including sounds not produced by any "natural" means.

Karlheinz Stockhausen was one of the pioneers of electronic music composition. He and others often used recorded sounds alongside electronic ones, as in his *Gesang der Jünglinge* (Song of the Youths, 1955–1956), which incorporated a boy's voice. This was the first major electronic piece to use multiple tracks, played in concert through several loudspeakers placed in various positions relative to the audience, thereby creating a sense of the music coming from numerous directions and moving through space.

Edgard Varèse (see Chapter 26) also combined electronic sounds with recorded ones. His *Poème électronique* (Electronic Poem, 1957–1958; NAWM 206), incorporating pure electronic sounds with nontraditional sounds such as sirens and traditional ones such as voice (though altered by electronic means), represents the height of his concept of spatial music. Commissioned by the Philips Radio Corporation for the Brussels World's Fair in 1958, the eight-minute piece was projected by approximately 350 speakers arranged all about the interior space of a pavilion (designed by Le Corbusier and shown in Figure 27.13) and was accompanied by moving colored lights and projected images. By recording the sounds on three separate tracks and splitting them into the many speakers, Varèse controlled not only what sounds were heard but also in which specific spaces they were heard. Thus, unlike a piece for ensemble played in a concert hall, *Poème électronique* was

Figure 27.13 The Philips Pavilion at the 1958 World's Fair in Brussels, Belgium. Edgard Varèse collaborated with the architect Le Corbusier and the architect and composer Xenakis to fill this building with the sound of his Poème électronique.
(akg-images/Paul Almasy.)

part of a structure that realized its own music. Fifteen thousand people each day experienced this multimedia work over a six-month period during the World's Fair, so it was probably heard "live" by more people than any other serious work of electronic music.

Poème électronique has no score and no time signature, tempo, or metronome markings. Instead, the musical events are measured in seconds. For example, 405 seconds into the piece a female voice sings a textless line that grows gradually softer and higher until it is overtaken by a choir of male voices. Unlike musical cues written to accompany actions in a film or video, these sounds are entirely without associative meaning because Varèse was asked to compose his electronic poem without knowing what visuals would be shown. From sketches the composer made in preparation for turning his ideas into the medium of recorded sound, it is evident that he conceived of these sounds as continuous moving entities (as opposed to fixed pitches) that collide and either merge with or are repulsed by one another. In this way, he created a work defined not by melody, harmony, or counterpoint, but by a more-or-less continuous flow of organized sound.

Electronic music was at first produced by combining, modifying, and controlling in various ways the output of oscillators, then recording these sounds on tape. The composer had to splice the tapes and mix their output, sometimes in combination with recorded sounds of physical objects in motion or of musicians, speakers, or singers. Electronic sound synthesizers were developed to make the process much easier. The composer could call on pitches from a music keyboard and, with switches and knobs, control harmonics, waveform (which determines timbre), resonance, and location of the sound sources. The RCA Mark II Electronic Music Synthesizer, shown in Figure 27.14, was developed at the Columbia-Princeton Electronic Music Center in the late 1950s and used by many composers from the United States and abroad.

In the mid-1960s, Robert Moog and Donald Buchla each developed far simpler and more compact synthesizers based on voltage-controlled oscillators. When these became commercially available in 1966, they were adopted by electronic music studios and individual composers around the world. One of the early works created on the Buchla synthesizer was *Silver Apples of the Moon* (1967) by Morton Subotnick (b. 1933), the first electronic piece to be commissioned by a record company, designed to fill two sides of an LP and to be played at home rather than in concert. The new synthesizers were also adopted by popular artists such as the Beatles, and electronic synthesizers soon became a familiar sound in pop music.

The electronic medium gave composers complete, unmediated control over their compositions. Much of the new music already demanded complex rhythms and minute shadings of pitch, intensity, and timbre that could barely be realized by human performers, but in the electronic studio, every detail could be accurately calculated and recorded. Yet the absence of performers hindered the acceptance of purely electronic music since audiences expected to be able to watch and respond to live performers. Furthermore, performers' lack of involvement was detrimental on another level because performers are the main promoters and advocates for

Poème électronique

Synthesizers

Figure 27.14 American composer Milton Babbitt at the console of the RCA Mark II Electronic Music Synthesizer at the Columbia-Princeton Electronic Music Center in New York, ca. 1960. (Image courtesy EMF Archives.)

new music. Recognizing these factors, composers soon began to create works that combined prerecorded tape with live performers.

Philomel

Full 🔊   Concise 🔊

One of the most moving early examples was Milton Babbitt's *Philomel* (1964, NAWM 207), for soprano soloist with a tape that includes a distorted echo of the soloist's voice together with electronic sounds. The live voice and the voice on tape engage in dialogue, accompanied by synthesized sounds, all worked out according to Babbitt's usual serial procedures. The poem is based on a story from Ovid's *Metamorphoses* involving betrayal, pain, revenge, and lament. After Philomel is violated by her brother-in-law, her tongue is cut out to prevent her from disclosing the crime. Only after being transformed into a nightingale does Philomel regain her voice, at which point the sung text begins. In fear and confusion, she runs through the forest seeking counsel from a thrush, a hawk, an owl, and a gull, all represented on the tape by recorded birdsong.

Music of Texture and Process

Varèse's conception of music as spatial, with sonic masses moving through musical space and interacting with each other like an abstract ballet in sound, opened the door to music that centered not on melody, harmony, or counterpoint, but on sound itself. Moreover, the exploration of electronic sounds stimulated the invention of new sound effects obtainable from conventional instruments and voices, often imitating electronic music. Composers now wrote pieces whose material consists primarily of striking sound combinations that create interesting and novel textures, organized by gradual or sudden processes of change.

Iannis Xenakis

One of the first to write such music for acoustic instruments was Iannis Xenakis (1922–2001). A Greek who spent most of his career in France, Xenakis was an engineer and architect as well as a composer. Like the ancient Greeks, he saw mathematics as fundamental to both music and architecture, so he based his music on mathematical concepts. In *Metastaseis* (1953–1954), he gave each string player in the orchestra a unique part to play. In many sections of the work, each player has a glissando, moving slowly or quickly in comparison to the other parts. In Figure 27.15, Xenakis plotted out the glissandos as straight

Figure 27.15 Iannis Xenakis's graph for a passage in Metastaseis, *with pitch as the vertical axis and time as the horizontal axis. The lower half of the graph represents the lower strings attacking a chromatic cluster together, then curving upward as the lowest pitches in the cluster rise in rapid glissandi and the higher ones move progressively more slowly. Toward the end of the passage, groups of strings enter on the same note one after another, each successively rising in a faster glissando until all end together in a chromatic cluster.*

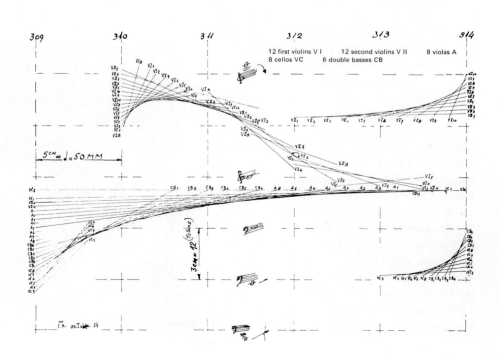

lines on a graph that add up to create an effect of curves in musical space. He then transferred the lines to standard musical notation. The resulting motions—of a chromatic cluster gradually closing to a unison or a unison expanding to a cluster—resemble changes achievable in electronic music through the use of pitch filters. The overall effect is very strongly visual, although the materials are musical. Indeed, Xenakis later applied the same idea of straight lines creating a curving effect in the design for the Philips Pavilion (see Figure 27.13), on which he worked with Le Corbusier.

One of the best-known pieces based on texture and process is *Threnody for the Victims of Hiroshima* (1960, NAWM 208) for fifty-two string instruments by Polish composer Krzysztof Penderecki (b. 1933; see Figure 27.16). The score gives few definite pulses or note values, instead measuring time in seconds. Each section focuses on a particular kind of sound, using newly invented notation that shows the effect graphically but not imprecisely. At the beginning, four to six instruments enter at a time, each playing its highest possible note, like a scream of very high clusters. The players then choose one of four patterns, they may move at different speeds (each as fast as possible), and the exact sounds each produces are indeterminate, but the overall effect is essentially the same in each performance, creating a prickly, interesting texture. The entire pitched and unpitched world, animate and inanimate, wailing and weeping at once, often in polychoral and antiphonal calls and responses, seems to mourn in this dirge. Remarkably, Penderecki originally conceived the work as a purely abstract play of sound and called it *8'37"* (its timing); the evocative final title has won it a much larger audience than it would otherwise have had, by connecting the new musical resources it uses to the tradition of expressive instrumental music extending back to the eighteenth century.

Penderecki used similar techniques in many other pieces, including the *St. Luke Passion* (1963–1966) and his opera *The Devils of Loudon* (1968), which show how the new resources can be used dramatically. But in these works he already began to incorporate elements of more traditional styles, and in the mid-1970s he turned to a personal style of neo-Romanticism.

Interest in texture and process gave rise in the late-twentieth century to a compositional movement known as spectralism, which emphasized timbre

Threnody

Spectralism

Figure 27.16 Krzysztof Penderecki, Polish composer and conductor, leads the Warsaw Symphony Orchestra in a concert on December 2, 2001, in memory of the victims of the 9/11 terrorist attack on the World Trade Center in New York.
(Lebrecht Music & Arts Photo Library.)

TIMELINE The Postwar Years

Musical Events

1940
Stravinsky and Bartók emigrate to the United States

1940–1941
Messiaen, *Quartet for the End of Time* (NAWM 201)

1944–1945
Britten, *Peter Grimes* (NAWM 200)

1946
Darmstadt school founded

1950
First piece of musique concrète

1951
Cage, *Music of Changes* (NAWM 204)

1953–1955
Boulez, *Le Marteau sans maître* (NAWM 202)

1954
Ives dies

1957–1858
Varèse, *Poème électronique* (NAWM 206)

1960
Penderecki, *Threnody* (NAWM 208)

1964
Babbitt, *Philomel* (NAWM 207)

1970
Crumb, *Black Angels* (NAWM 205)

1971
Stravinsky dies

1940   **1970**

Historical Events

1939–1945
World War II

1950–1953
Korean War

1950
Jackson Pollock, *Untitled* (Figure 27.7)

1958
World's Fair in Brussels

1963
John F. Kennedy assassinated

1964–1975
Vietnam War

1966
Moog and Buchla synthesizers introduced

1968
Students riot in Paris, antiwar protests in the United States

1969
First humans set foot on the moon

Kaija Saariaho

L'Amour de loin

Full 🔊   Concise 🔊

(often electronically produced) over pitch (or tonality) as a large-scale structural feature. One proponent of spectralism is Finnish composer Kaija Saariaho (b. 1952), who remarked that her music "is all about color and light." After working at Pierre Boulez's IRCAM electronic-music studio in the 1980s, Saariaho remained in Paris, where she also came under the influence of Olivier Messiaen. Her first opera, *L'Amour de loin* (2000, Love from Afar), was inspired by Messiaen's opera based on the life of Saint Francis of Assisi. Like Messiaen, Saariaho chose a historical figure as her subject—the twelfth-century troubadour Jaufré Rudel, who embodied the ideal of courtly love (*fine amour*) in his legendary long-distance desire for and devotion to the Countess of Tripoli (see Figure 2.16).

In Act IV of *L'Amour de loin* (whose title phrase comes from a poem by Jaufré), the troubadour sets sail from southern France to Tripoli (in North Africa) but encounters a storm at sea—a metaphor for his turbulent emotions—and falls gravely ill. Jaufré's impassioned "complainte" in the third scene of Act IV (NAWM 216) is in the tradition of the lament as found both in the troubadour and trouvère repertories (see NAWM 8 and 9) and in early Baroque opera (see NAWM 74c–e and 89b). Saariaho's vocal lines evoke the style of declamation characteristic of laments in their repetition of formulaic phrases and gestures, while the undulating and shimmering sonorities of the orchestra are consistent with the spectralists' emphasis on timbre.

Whether with new instruments, traditional instruments, modified instruments (such as an amplified string quartet), non-Western instruments, electronic instruments, or tape, composers using new sounds had to hope that listeners would forgo traditional expectations for melody, harmony, and form, and engage each work instead as an experience of sound itself. These pieces demand new thinking about music from their listeners as much as from their composers, and the questions and new insights they stimulate are part of what many have valued in these works.

New thinking

POSTLUDE

Perhaps like no other time in music history, the postwar years spawned a multitude of musical styles as composers explored the potential of new sounds, technologies, and ideas. With so many options available, we should not be surprised that composers created widely divergent sounds and aimed to reach radically different audiences. While Boulez continued to explore the implications of earlier modernist music, producing ever-more complex serial pieces, Varèse experimented with new technology, Penderecki found new potential in traditional instruments, and Cage challenged conceptions of music itself. Yet while the era saw an unprecedented diversity of styles, new communications technologies and a distrust of nationalism rendered national boundaries insignificant, as musicians around the world responded to the radically changing musical landscape.

 Resources for study and review available at wwnorton.com/studyspace

Into the Twenty-First Century

PRELUDE

The end of the twentieth century and the beginning of the twenty-first brought unprecedented technological innovation and global interconnectedness, advances which continue to impact composers, performers, and listeners. The digital revolution radically changed electronic music, as composers explored new ways of using samples taken from earlier music, and portable devices made live performances of electronic music possible for the first time. Minimalist composers challenged the aesthetic of modernism by constructing works from small, repeating fragments, while other musicians broke down barriers between Western and non-Western music, and between art and vernacular music, as nearly anything could potentially influence contemporary music.

Digital Technologies

Since the 1970s, new technologies have once again altered the ways musicians work with music and listeners consume it. Among the most important new inventions are the digital synthesis, recording, and reproduction of sound, which have given creators of music new tools and listeners new flexibility (see A Closer Look, page 631).

One significant technique, called *sampling*, is a process of creating new compositions by patching together digital chunks of previously recorded music. Although sampling raises copyright concerns, it has been used extensively in various types of pop music as well as in experimental, avant-garde, and classical concert music.

Advances in computing and the miniaturization of the computer have offered many new possibilities, explored by composers whose music is part experimentation with technology and part sound sculpture. One of the pioneers of computer music is Charles Dodge (b. 1942), whose *Speech Songs* (1972) features computer-synthesized vocal sounds, mixing life-like imitations of speech with transformations that change vowels into noise or natural inflections into melodies to create a word-based music well suited to the surrealistic poetry he uses as a text. Paul Lansky (b. 1944) developed his own software to create computer works. He manipulates recorded sounds, such as speech in *Six Fantasies on a Poem by Thomas*

Campion (1979) and *Smalltalk* (1988) or highway traffic noises in *Night Traffic* (1990), transforming them beyond immediate recognition and using them as a kind of pitched percussion. Despite the unusual sound sources, his music draws on pop traditions, with tonal harmonies, regular meter, propulsive beat, and layered syncopated rhythms. A very different aesthetic is pursued at the Institut de Recherche et Coordination Acoustique/Musique (Institute for Acoustic and Musical Research and Coordination, usually referred to by its French acronym, IRCAM) in Paris, one of the premier centers for computer music in Europe, founded by Pierre Boulez. In *Inharmonique* (1977) and other works written during his time as director of the IRCAM computer music department, Jean-Claude Risset (b. 1938) has used the computer to mediate between live voices or acoustic instruments and synthesized or electronically processed sound. He has continued to design new sounds, exploring the interaction of sound waves, harmonics, timbre, and other basic elements of sound. Meanwhile, portable computers made live performances of electronic music, either exclusively on computers or with acoustic instruments, possible for the first time (see Figure 28.1).

Figure 28.1 The Princeton Laptop Orchestra performs on laptop computers connected to six-channel speakers.
(© Evelyn Tu.)

A Closer Look Digital Technologies

In the 1970s and early 1980s, music joined the digital revolution. Inventors devised a method for translating sound into a coded series of on-off digital pulses, or ones and zeros, in the same way that computers stored and transmitted data. Soon digital processes were replacing older, analog ones, which relied on creating an analogue of the sound waves, as in the undulations in the groove of a phonograph record.

By the 1980s, musicians were using digital synthesizers (see Figure 28.2) instead of the older analog devices. Because digital processes produced and recorded sounds as streams of numbers, musical sounds could be reproduced and controlled precisely. Electronic keyboards combined with computers made synthesized music accessible to musicians everywhere. Through computers, composers could control all the parameters of pitch, timbre, dynamics, and rhythm, and the characteristics thus digitally encoded could be translated directly into music through MIDI (musical instrument digital interface).

Some musicians combined live performers with synthesized or computer-generated music into a performance medium that is now commonplace. Using software that responds to music, the composer devises formulas that are then played on a synthesizer, digital piano, or acoustic instrument. In this way, a musician can generate imitative or nonimitative polyphony, rhythmic or melodic ostinatos, heterophony, and a variety of other textures by playing on a synthesizer keyboard in "real time"—that is, as actually played and heard, rather than laboriously prepared in advance and tape-recorded.

The way composers, performers, and listeners interact with music is still being transformed by digital technology, bringing changes that are hard to predict.

Figure 28.2 Keyboard console of the Synclavier II digital synthesizer from 1981.
(Courtesy Yaking Cat Music Studio.)

Minimalism and Postminimalism

One of the most prominent new trends since the 1960s is minimalism, in which materials are reduced to a minimum and procedures simplified so that what is going on in the music is immediately apparent. Minimalism began as an avant-garde aesthetic focused on the musical processes themselves but over time became a widely used, popular technique, capable of a wide range of expressive content. In the world of art, painters such as Andy Warhol (see Figure VI. 8) and Frank Stella (see Figure 28.3) led the way by using mundane objects and repetitive forms while focusing attention on small-scale changes of detail. Composers of minimalist music employed similar techniques while at the same time absorbing influences from rock, African music, Asian music, tonality, and finally Romanticism to create what has been called the leading musical style of the late twentieth century.

One of the pioneers of musical minimalism was La Monte Young (b. 1935), whose *The Tortoise: His Dreams and Journeys* (1964) is an improvisation in which instrumentalists and singers come in and out on various harmonics over a fundamental tone played as a drone by a synthesizer. Terry Riley (b. 1935), who once performed in Young's ensemble, experimented with tape loops, short segments of magnetic tape spliced into loops that, when fed through a tape recorder, play the same recorded sounds again and again. His tape piece *Mescalin Mix* (1962–1963) piled up many such loops, each repeating a short phrase, over a regular pulse. His most famous work, *In C* (1964), uses a similar procedure with live instruments. It can be performed by any number of instruments, each playing the same series of brief repeated figures over a quickly pulsing octave C, with the number of repetitions in each part and the coordination of parts left indeterminate. The resulting sound combines a steady pulsation with a process of slow change from consonance to diatonic dissonance and back. The concept and materials are simple and the process immediately audible, but the multilayered texture is complex and different in each performance.

Figure 28.3 Hyena Stomp *(1962) by Frank Stella (b. 1936). Stella reduced painting to its fundamentals, intending his work to be understood as only a play of form and color, not as an expression of feelings. The title, from a jazz piece by Jelly Roll Morton, reflects Stella's interest in translating syncopation into visual form.*

(Tate Gallery/Art Resource, NY. © 2006 Frank Stella/Artists Rights (ARS), New York.)

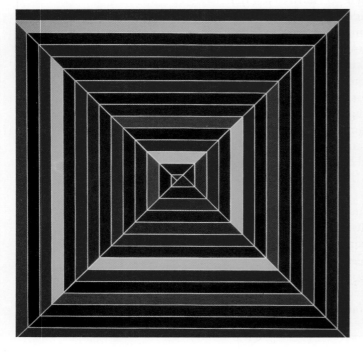

From Avant-Garde to Widespread Appeal

While Young remained an avant-garde experimentalist and Riley moved toward rock music, three other Americans brought minimalist procedures into art music intended for a broad audience.

Steve Reich (b. 1936), shown in Figure 28.4, developed a quasi-canonic procedure in which musicans play the same material out of phase with each other. Like Riley, he began in the electronic studio, superimposing tape loops of the same spoken phrase in such a way that one loop was slightly shorter and thus gradually moved ahead of the other, an effect called *phasing*. In *Piano Phase* (1967), shown in Example 28.1, Reich applied a similar idea to a work for two pianos. Both pianists repeat the same twelve-note figure in unison several times, then one gradually pulls ahead until the two are

Figure 28.4 Steve Reich, one of the pioneers of minimalism, playing the xylophone at his home studio in New York in 1997. (Lebrecht Music & Arts Photo Library.)

Piano Phase

exactly one sixteenth-note apart, and they repeat the figure several times in rhythmic synchronization but melodically out of phase. This process is repeated twelve times, producing a different series of harmonic combinations each time the parts slip into synchrony, until the two parts are again in melodic unison; then the same process is used for a figure of eight notes and then one of four notes. The fascination with music like this lies in observing gradual changes and the many possible permutations of very simple ideas. The processes that underlie the composition are revealed for every listener to hear and experience (see Vignette, page 634).

Reich formed his own ensemble and was able to make a living by performing, touring, and recording his works. Much of his music in the 1970s was percussive, superimposing layers of figuration in ways that parallel African drumming, one source of his inspiration. He attracted a wide range of listeners, drawing audiences accustomed to jazz, rock, and pop music as well as classical, as the diatonic material and rapid pulsation gave his music wide appeal.

By the 1980s, he no longer fully subscribed to a minimalist aesthetic, instead using minimalist techniques to create large-scale works with significant emotional content, often drawing on his Jewish heritage. *Tehillim* (1981) is a setting

Tehillim

Example 28.1 Steve Reich, Piano Phase

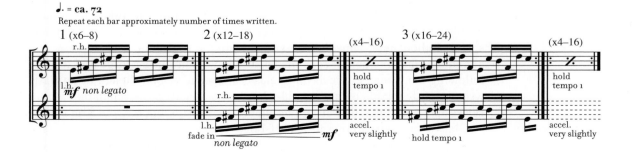

VIGNETTE Music as a Gradual Process

In his 1968 essay, Music as a Gradual Process, *Steve Reich describes his compositional philosophy, in which every composition consists of an audible process with a predetermined course that has been set in motion by the composer. The text excerpted here was influential in defining the work of Reich and other minimalist composers.*

I do not mean the process of composition, but rather pieces of music that are, literally, processes.

The distinctive thing about musical processes is that they determine all the note-to-note (sound-to-sound) details and the over all form simultaneously. (Think of a round or infinite canon.)

I am interested in perceptible processes. I want to be able to hear the process happening throughout the sounding music.

To facilitate closely detailed listening a musical process should happen extremely gradually.

Performing and listening to a gradual musical process resembles:

pulling back a swing, releasing it, and observing it gradually come to rest;

turning over an hour glass and watching the sand slowly run through to the bottom;

placing your feet in the sand by the ocean's edge and watching, feeling, and listening to the waves gradually bury them.

Though I may have the pleasure of discovering musical processes and composing the musical material to run through them, once the process is set up and loaded it runs by itself.

Steve Reich, *Writings about Music* (New York: New York University Press, 1974); in Oliver Strunk, ed., *Source Readings in Music History*, rev. ed. by Leo Treitler (New York: Norton, 1998), vol. 6, pp. 115–116.

of psalm texts in the original Hebrew for four singers and orchestra, using rhythmic and melodic canons at the unison in constantly changing meters over pulsing percussion and sustained diatonic but dissonant harmonies. Each of the first three sections uses different procedures, and the fourth section (NAWM 210) combines all these techniques, adding layers and building to a climactic conclusion. The texture in each section gradually becomes more complex, with all four soloists singing the same melody in close succession. As it becomes harder to follow a single part, we can shift our focus to hear just the salient points of each.

Full 🔊

Postminimalism
While a piece as rich and complex as this can hardly be called minimalist, it shows the application of minimalist techniques in the realm of art music. For this reason, Reich's music since 1980 is sometimes called postminimalist, reflecting the influence of minimalist procedures while moving beyond the original minimalist aesthetic to include traditional methods such as more harmonic motion, varied material, and renewed expressivity.

Philip Glass
Philip Glass (b. 1937) had published twenty works by the time he completed degrees at the University of Chicago and the Juilliard School and finished studies with Nadia Boulanger, but withdrew all of them after working with the Indian sitarist Ravi Shankar in Paris. Glass's works since the mid-1960s have been deeply influenced by the rhythmic organization of Indian music. They emphasize melodiousness, consonance, and the simple harmonic progressions and abundant amplification of rock music, and have won Glass a large and diverse following from rock enthusiasts to classical listeners. Like Reich, he initially wrote mainly for his own ensemble, but he has secured his reputation with a series of major works, including symphonies, concertos, operas, and film scores.

Einstein on the Beach
Glass's one-act, four-and-a-half-hour opera *Einstein on the Beach* (see Figure 28.5), which premiered at the Metropolitan Opera House in 1976, was

Figure 28.5 Scene from the 2012 revival of Robert Wilson's production of Einstein on the Beach. (© Jack Vartoogian.)

a collaboration with avant-garde director Robert Wilson, who wrote the scenario. The opera avoids narrative, has no sung text other than solfège syllables, and involves mostly nonsensical stage action. The music consists primarily of repeated figures, mostly arpeggiated triads, performed by an orchestra of electronic keyboard instruments, woodwinds, and a solo violinist. Other operas followed, including *Satyagraha* (1980), about Gandhi's nonviolent struggle for Indian independence, and *Akhnaten* (1984), about an Egyptian pharoah martyred for his monotheistic worship of the sun god. *The Voyage* (1992), commissioned by the Metropolitan Opera to commemorate the five-hundredth anniversary of Columbus's voyage to the New World, blends Glass's signature style of multilayered ostinatos, rapid pulse, and slowly changing tonal or modal harmonies with the orchestra, recitatives, and arias of the operatic tradition.

John Adams (b. 1947; Figure 28.6), has traced a path from minimalism to a personal postminimalist style that blends minimalist techniques with a variety of other approaches. His *Phrygian Gates* for piano (1977–1978) is representative of the period when minimalism was moving beyond its avant-garde origins to become a style rather than an aesthetic. Except for a middle section of shifting sustained chords, this twenty-four-minute piece relies almost entirely on quick repetitive figurations, primarily in diatonic modes. The music goes through what Adams calls "gates," changing from one set of notes to another: from the Lydian scale on A to the Phrygian scale on A, as shown in Example 28.2, then the Lydian and Phrygian scales on E, and so on. These changes give the work its title, and they convey the sense of a journey through a gradually changing environment.

Figure 28.6 American composer and conductor John Adams conducting the BBC Symphony Orchestra in London, five days before the 9/11 attack on the World Trade Center in New York. (Nigel Luckhurst/Lebrecht Music & Arts Photo Library.)

Example 28.2 John Adams. Phrygian Gates

Adams continued to use minimalist techniques in his later works, but also embraced elements from popular and classical music. *Harmonielehre* (Theory of Harmony, 1985), a symphonic poem that draws on Romantic and modernist styles, was greeted by one news magazine with the enthusiastic headline "The Heart Is Back in the Game." Adams's opera *Nixon in China* (1987), on Nixon's 1972 trip to China to open relations with the communist regime, treats its up-to-date subject with the formality of a Baroque historical opera while applying minimalist techniques. Typical of this postminimalist idiom from the 1980s is the orchestral fanfare *Short Ride in a Fast Machine* (1986; NAWM 211), which has become one of Adams's most frequently played pieces. A sense of harmonic progression, activated by ostinatos and repeating chords, moves the music forward, and wide-ranging melodies emerge to dominate the texture.

Short Ride in a Fast Machine

Full

Over time, Adams has relied less on minimalist techniques and more on traditional harmonic, melodic, and contrapuntal means. He has also embraced a wide range of topics, from celebrating Jesus' Nativity in the oratorio *El Niño* (1999–2000), to mourning the deaths in the 2001 terrorist attack on the World Trade Center in *On the Transmigration of Souls* (2002), which won the Pulitzer Prize in 2003, to the tests leading up to the dropping of the atomic bomb in the summer of 1945 in his opera *Dr. Atomic* (2005; see Figure 28.7). The diversity and depth of both his style and his subject matter have won Adams a broad and enthusiastic audience.

▶ **ADAMS,** *Doctor Atomic*

The title character of Adams's *Doctor Atomic*, the physicist J. Robert Oppenheimer, led America's effort to develop an atomic bomb as director of the Manhattan Project during World War II. Most of the opera takes place in the hours just before a prototype was tested in July 1945. Alone with his anguished thoughts in the closing scene of Act 1, Oppenheimer sings the soul-searching aria *Batter my heart* (NAWM 219). Set to one of the Holy Sonnets by the seventeenth-century English poet John Donne, the aria invokes the "three-person'd God." In fact, the physicist was deeply conflicted about unleashing the atom's awesome power of destruction and had dubbed the test site "Trinity" with this poem in mind.

Like much of Adams's instrumental music, the orchestral introduction to *Batter my heart* is characterized by rapid, continuous motion, ostinato, gradual accretion of dissonance, and subtle changes of texture. Irregular syncopations create an agitated effect, suggesting Oppenheimer's apprehension about the impending test. The orchestra's restless activity suddenly stops in preparation for the entrance of the voice, conveying a sense that time stands still. Oppenheimer's lyrical melody creates a chain of dissonances that underline the alliteration of the words "break, blow, break, blow, break, burn." In its tunefulness and emotional intensity, *Batter my heart* echoes the operatic style of nineteenth-century composers like Giuseppe Verdi who, like Adams,

Figure 28.7 A scene from John Adams's opera Dr. Atomic *showing baritone Gerald Finley in the role of physicist J. Robert Oppenheimer, one of the creators of the atomic bomb. Photograph from the Metropolitan Opera's production of 2008–2009.* (Ken Howard.)

sought to express the inner conflicts and psychological complexity of the characters in their music.

Since the music of Reich, Glass, and Adams achieved popularity in the 1970s and 1980s, minimalist techniques have grown increasingly common in popular music and film music, leading some to claim that minimalism is the common musical language of the late twentieth and early twenty-first centuries. Many composers in the classical tradition have adopted some elements of minimalism, such as repetition, drones, gradual processes of change, reduction in complexity, or modal harmonies, while rejecting others. For some, the greatest impact of minimalism was the permission it gave to write music that was comprehensible and appealing. By refuting (or simply ignoring) the nineteenth-century idea of progress in musical style—a notion that underlay the strand of modernism that led from the New German School through Schoenberg to Babbitt, Boulez, and Stockhausen—minimalism helped to create an atmosphere in which anything was possible.

Influence of minimalism

Interactions with Non-Western Musics

Minimalism was only one of many currents in Western music to be inspired by the musics of Asia and Africa. Some composers drew directly on Asian musics. Bright Sheng (b. 1955; Figure 28.8), born and trained in China, moved to New York in 1982 for further study and has made his career in the United States. He integrates elements of Asian and Western music while respecting the integrity of each, inspired by the attempts of Bartók to do the same with Eastern European folk and Western classical music. In the solo cello suite *Seven Tunes Heard in China* (1995; NAWM 209), Sheng joins the European tradition of the Bach

Bright Sheng

Full

Figure 28.8 Chinese-born composer Bright Sheng in a photograph taken in Los Angeles in 1998.
(Lebrecht Music & Arts Photo Library.)

cello suites—with sequences, double stops, and implied polyphony—to the playing style of Chinese bowed string instruments, marked by grace notes, glissandos, sudden dynamic changes, and flexible rhythm. The mostly pentatonic Chinese tune used as a source is fragmented and spun out using both Baroque and modernist methods, including polytonality. The result blends together fundamental aspects of Chinese, Western classical, and modern music.

In the final analysis, Sheng's work is quintessentially Western, representing another example of the centuries-old capacity of European music to absorb foreign elements and arrive at a new synthesis, as in the merging of French, Italian, and English traditions in the late Baroque era (see Chapter 14) or of various styles and habits into the cosmopolitan idiom of the Classic era (see Chapters 15–18). But recent works go beyond nineteenth-century exoticism in the respect they show for the intrinsic value of the non-Western traditions on which they draw.

Postmodernism and Other Trends

In the late twentieth century, composers in the classical tradition faced a new reality. While they were able to make a living teaching at universities or conservatories, obtaining performances for their music was increasingly difficult. It was often easier to win a commission for a new piece than to secure a second or third performance of an existing work. Few compositions entered the standard repertory, and few listeners heard a piece more than once. In some respects, the situation was like that of the eighteenth century, when a concerto or symphony was seldom heard twice by the same listeners. Moreover, at a time when music was growing more plentiful and easy to access, the audience for classical music seemed to be shrinking.

One strategy for reaching a wider audience was to evoke familiar idioms by earlier composers, from Bach and Handel to modernists like Schoenberg, Ives, and Stravinsky. Such blending of earlier and modern styles in music has been compared to the architecture of Philip Johnson, Robert Venturi, César Pelli, and others, who left behind the bare glass façades of mid-twentieth-century modernism by incorporating elements of earlier styles into essentially modern designs, as in Figure 28.9, a mixture that came to be called postmodernism. A central aspect of postmodernism is a turning away from the belief, crucial to modernist thought, that history progresses irreversibly in one direction. In music, this idea means abandoning the notion that musical idioms develop continuously, as if according to a plan or some inner necessity. To the postmodernist, history gives the artist more freedom than that; the styles of all epochs and cultures are equally available as musical material, to be employed as the composer sees fit. By the end of the twentieth century, postmodernism was the prevailing aesthetic in the concert hall.

Composers used a variety of approaches, often in tandem, to make their modernist idiom more accessible: radically simplifying their material and procedures, quoting from and alluding to past styles, resurrecting nineteenth-century tonal Romanticism, and invoking extramusical meanings and imagery.

Accessible Modernism and Radical Simplification

Like the minimalists, some composers writing in a modernist idiom have made their music accessible by keeping the ideas and procedures relatively simple and easy to grasp.

Hungarian composer György Ligeti (1923–2006) achieved renown through Stanley Kubrick's science fiction film *2001: A Space Odyssey*, which uses excerpts from three of his works: *Atmosphères* (1961), *Requiem* (1963–1965), and *Luxaeterna* (1966). This music is in constant motion because of the composer's manipulation of dissonant textures and changing sonorities; yet it is static both harmonically and melodically. In a later work, a series of études for solo piano (1985–2001), Ligeti combined elements of his earlier music with the virtuoso tradition of the nineteenth century and a simplicity of material—a combination that could appeal to a much wider audience. In *Vertige* (Vertigo, 1990; NAWM 212), his Étude No. 9, the constant repetition of simple material reflects the influence of minimalism. The piece is novel, thoroughly modernist, and consistent with Ligeti's previous work, but at the same time it is dramatic, emotionally expressive, and immediately comprehensible.

Estonian composer Arvo Pärt (b. 1935) forged a highly individual, instantly recognizable style using the simplest materials. Following early neoclassical and serial works and others that contrasted modernist with Baroque styles, he turned to a study of Gregorian chant and early polyphony. In the 1970s, he devised a method he called "tintinnabuli," after the bell-like sonorities it produced. Its essence lies in counterpoint between a pitch-centered, mostly stepwise diatonic melody and one or more other voices that sound only notes of the tonic triad, with the placement of each note determined by a preset system. The technique is exemplified in Pärt's *Seven Magnificat Antiphons* (1988, rev. 1991; NAWM 215) and illustrated in Example 28.3, which shows the opening of No. 6, *O König aller Völker*. The second tenor (the lower part on the tenor staff) presents a plain modal tune that is centered on A and that moves no more than a fourth away in either direction. Its rhythm is restricted to quarter and half notes, and measures change length to fit the text accentuation. The tenor melody is echoed by the second soprano to form an augmentation canon. The altos recite the text, phrase by phrase, on D. The other parts sound notes of the D-minor triad, following strict but simple rules reminiscent of early polyphony (see Chapter 3). The resulting texture alternates between consonance and diatonic dissonance, allowing for variety and dramatic climaxes within a stripped-down, pitch-centered style.

Figure 28.9 The AT&T Building in New York City, renamed the Sony Building. The architect, Philip Johnson, blends elements from the past, such as columns and arches, with modern elements of glass and concrete in his design. The resulting composite style, sometimes called postmodernism, rejects the stark glass walls and undecorated façades of many mid-twentieth-century buildings. (Alan Schein Photography/Corbis.)

Magnificat Antiphons

Full 🔊

Quotation, Collage, and Polystylism

One composer who quoted from and borrowed past styles effectively was Alfred Schnittke (1934–1998). He worked in the Soviet Union, where he was known chiefly for his film music, before moving to Germany in 1990. The Soviet

Alfred Schnittke

Example 28.3 Arvo Pärt, Magnificat Antiphons. *No.6* O König aller Völker

O king of all peoples, their expectation [and hope]

government began to relax its control over culture in the 1960s under Nikita Khrushchev, exposing Schnittke and other young composers to Western trends such as serial, chance, and electronic music. After writing several works based on serialism, indeterminacy, and new instrumental sounds, Schnittke turned to what he called "polystylism," a combination of new and older styles created through quotation or stylistic allusion. His Symphony No. 1 (1969–1972) incorporates passages from works by Haydn, Beethoven, Chopin, Tchaikovsky, Grieg, Johann Strauss, and Schnittke himself. For listeners familiar with works of these composers, such music embodies a contrast not only of styles, but of historical periods.

John Corigliano   Like Schnittke, the American composer John Corigliano (b. 1938) frequently juxtaposes styles to convey meanings, drawing on a stylistic continuum from Baroque and Classic to avant-garde. His opera *The Ghosts of Versailles* (1987) centers around ghosts in the French royal palace, including Marie Antoinette and others slain during the Revolution, and a play staged for their entertainment; the ghosts are rendered with modern serial music and timbral effects, while the play is set in a style based on Mozart operas. Corigliano's Symphony No. 1 (1989), a memorial to friends who died of AIDS, incorporates quotations from some of their favorite pieces framed by deeply expressive, often angry or tragic music drawing on a variety of modern techniques. In his Academy-Award-winning score for the film *The Red Violin* (1998), which follows a violin from its maker through a series of owners to the present, Corigliano created a leitmotive for the violin and developed it into a series of pieces representing the era and musical style of each owner.

Music based on quotation can carry many meanings, but often it gives the audience something familiar to grasp—either the quoted piece itself or the style or type of piece it represents—and provides a new experience drawing on what the listener already knows. As a result, many listeners find it much more approachable than the unfamiliar sounds of serialism, electronic music, the avant-garde, and other postwar trends. For some composers, using borrowed material has been a way to rediscover styles and methods of the past, including tonality. This is one origin for the late twentieth-century trend of neo-Romanticism.

Neo-Romanticism

In their search for expressive tools that connect directly with listeners, some composers adopted the familiar tonal idiom of nineteenth-century Romanticism or incorporated its sounds and gestures, a trend known as neo-Romanticism.

Having turned from serialism to quotation in the 1960s, American composer George Rochberg (1918–2005) moved on in the 1970s to use Romantic and early modernist styles for their expressive potential. His String Quartet No. 5 (1978) is neo-Romantic in three of its five movements. Each movement is written in a consistent style, but the styles differ considerably between movements. The first movement is a sprightly sonata form in A major reminiscent of late Beethoven or Schubert; the second, a sad E♭-minor slow movement whose canons and loosely dissonant harmonies recall early Bartók; the third, a Beethovenian scherzo in A minor with a Mahlerian trio; the fourth, an atonal serenade that resembles works of Schoenberg or Berg; and the finale, an energetic, constantly developing, rapidly modulating yet tonal rondo in late Romantic style, akin to Schoenberg's First Quartet. The mixture of idioms challenged the traditional expectation that music be stylistically uniform; but even more radical was Rochberg's choice to reclaim styles of the past and use them in a wholehearted effort to make their resources his own without the distancing effects notable in Stravinsky's neoclassicism (see Chapter 25) or Schnittke's polystylism.

California-born David Del Tredici (b. 1937) embraced neo-Romanticism for a different reason. After using atonal and serial methods in the 1960s, he changed his style radically when he set excerpts from Lewis Carroll's stories for children, feeling that their whimsy called for a direct, comprehensible presentation. *Final Alice* (1975), to a text from the final chapters of Carroll's *Alice's Adventures in Wonderland,* is scored for amplified soprano and orchestra, with a "folk group" of banjo, mandolin, accordion, and two soprano saxophones. The soprano narrates, plays all the parts, and sings a series of arias. The central motive of the piece, a rising major sixth introduced by the saxophones, is taken up by other instruments and becomes the fundamental interval of "The Accusation," sung by the White Rabbit, and shown in Example 28.4; a greater concentration of rising sixths in a melody is hard to imagine. Through this and other arias, the orchestra and folk group accompany in a kind of nonsense tonality, with slightly off-kilter dance rhythms and multiple layers in differing tempos. Most of the music is tonal, ranging from folklike episodes to an idiom reminiscent of Richard Strauss. But when Alice begins to grow larger, Del Tredici suggests the strange occurrence with atonal music, a twelve-tone motive, and the electronic sounds of the theremin. By using tonal and atonal styles side by side for their expressive effect, Del Tredici renounced the modernist ideology of progress. In its place, he returned to eighteenth- and

George Rochberg

David Del Tredici

Example 28.4 David Del Tredici. The Accusation, *from* Final Alice

David Del Tredici's Final Alice *won immediate praise from listeners, as noted in the reviews of its premiere in October 1976.*

When the last stroke of *Final Alice* died away at the Chicago Symphony concert, the audience broke into sustained applause which quickly grew into a standing ovation. Cheers and bravos mingled with the handclaps. . . . It was the most enthusiastic reception of a new work that I have ever heard at a symphony concert.
Thomas Willis, *Chicago Tribune*, October 9, 1976.

But some of his fellow composers viewed the piece as a betrayal of the tenets of modernism, and Del Tredici found himself having to defend his success.

About halfway through [composing] the piece, I thought, "Oh my God, if I just leave it like this, my colleagues will think I'm crazy." But then I thought, "What else can I do? If nothing else occurs to me I can't go against my instincts." But I was terrified my colleagues would think I was an idiot. . . . People think now that I wanted to be tonal and have a big audience. But that was just not true. I didn't want to be tonal. My world was my colleagues — my composing friends. . . . The success of *Final Alice* was very defining as to who my real friends were. I think many composers regard success as a kind of threat. It's really better, they think, if nobody has any success, to be all in one boat. Composers now are beginning to realize that if a piece excites an audience, that doesn't mean it's terrible. For my generation, it is considered vulgar to have an audience really, really like a piece on a first hearing. But why are we writing music except to move people and to be expressive? To have what has moved us move somebody else?

Right now, audiences just reject contemporary music. But if they start to like one thing, then they begin to have perspective. That will make a difference, it always has in the past. The sleeping giant is the audience.

From John Rockwell's interview with David Del Tredici, *New York Times*, October 26, 1980, sect. D, pp. 23, 28.

nineteenth-century ideals of music, mixing diverse styles in a coherent whole that is comprehensible on first hearing to an untrained listener yet holds hidden delights for the connoisseur (see Vignette, above).

Extramusical Imagery and Meanings

Composers using various styles invoked extramusical meanings and imagery, hoping that listeners would accept unusual sounds if their meanings were clear. Spirituality was a frequent theme, continuing music's long association with religion and the transcendent.

Sofia Gubaidulina
Despite the official atheism of her native Soviet Union, almost all the works of Sofia Gubaidulina (b. 1931; Figure 28.10) have a spiritual dimension, often suggested in the title. The five movements of her sonata for violin and cello, *Rejoice!* (1981), were inspired by eighteenth-century devotional texts. According to the composer, the sonata expresses the transcendence from ordinary reality to a state of joy and relies particularly on the passage from a fundamental note to its harmonics to embody this journey of consciousness. The fifth movement (NAWM 213), inscribed with the text "Listen to the still small voice within," is a study in chromatics, tremolos, and harmonics, particularly glissandos from low fundamental notes in the cello to their higher harmonics.

Concise 🔊   Full 🔊

R. Murray Schafer
R. Murray Schafer (b. 1933), the leading Canadian composer of the era, traversed a wide variety of styles from neoclassical to avant-garde, yet most of his

pieces are based on extramusical inspirations. His orchestral works *Dream Rainbow Dream Thunder* (1986) and *Manitou* (1995), for example, reflect ideas from the culture of the Inuits, natives of Canada. His most striking innovation is what he calls "environmental music," pieces that break out of the concert hall and require more than passive attention from listeners. *Music for Wilderness Lake* (1979) is to be performed at sunrise and sunset at a small lake away from human settlements, with twelve trombonists positioned around its shores playing meditative melodies to one another across the water, cued by a conductor on a raft, and joined by animal sounds. Ideally, listeners would partici-

Figure 28.10 Russian composer Sofia Gubaidulina, seated at the piano, playing an African drum in Moscow. (Lebrecht Music & Arts Photo Library.)

Full 🔊

pate in the event by experiencing the lake, its stillness, its sounds, and its surrounding wilderness as the music is performed; in fact, most can only watch the event on film.

Pulitzer-prize-winning American composer Jennifer Higdon (b. 1962) might well be grouped with the neo-Romantics, and her works might also be discussed as an example of accessible modernism. But her orchestral piece *blue cathedral* (2000, NAWM 220) has a spiritual dimension and extramusical associations that invite comparison with her older contemporaries Gubaidulina and Schafer. In a program note, Higdon describes her colorfully orchestrated work as a "journey through a glass cathedral in the sky" during which stained-glass figures magically spring to life and sing "heavenly music." For Higdon, the cathedral is a spiritual portal into and out of this world, and the color blue evokes images of the sky, of infinite potential, of journeys through space and time. Most poignantly, it recalls the composer's younger brother, Andrew Blue Higdon, whom *blue cathedral* memorializes.

The musical journey opens quietly with bell-like percussion and strings, which soon divide and expand, providing a rich tonal backdrop for flute and clarinet solos. (Higdon is a self-taught flutist; her brother played the clarinet.) As the interweaving solo lines gradually spiral upward, the musical tension builds and the melody reaches its highpoint, creating an aural image of the listener's ascent toward the immense glass dome of the cathedral. Then, suddenly, the melody falls back on itself, the sumptuous texture thins, and the tension subsides. The emotional directness of Higdon's musical language and its firm grounding in tonality have given *blue cathedral* wide appeal with audiences, and performances of the work already number in the hundreds.

Evoking Popular Musics

Another way composers have sought to connect to listeners directly while creating a distinctive musical personality is to incorporate elements from popular music. This approach is akin to neo-Romanticism, which incorporates the most popular idiom in the classical tradition, and to Third Stream music, which combines jazz with classical styles (see Chapter 27).

Argentine composer Ástor Piazzolla (1921–1992) combined the Argentine tradition of the tango with elements of jazz and classical music to create a new style, *nuevo tango* (new tango). He encountered jazz during his childhood in New

Ástor Piazzolla

York, became a professional tango musician in Argentina, and studied composition with Alberto Ginastera and Nadia Boulanger, so he was well schooled in all three traditions. His *nuevo tango* incorporated improvisation from jazz and drew several elements from the classical tradition, including the Baroque procedures of counterpoint, fugue, and passacaglia; modernist chromaticism, dissonance, and angular melodies; and the ideas of extended forms and of music worth listening to for its own sake. After developing the new style while playing with his ensemble in his club in Buenos Aires, Piazzolla moved in 1974 to Rome, writing more ambitious pieces like *Libertango* (1974), the three-movement *La Camorra* (1989), and *Five Tango Sensations* (1991). Like Gershwin in his *Rhapsody in Blue* and *Porgy and Bess*, Piazzolla drew on a living popular tradition to create music now performed by classical ensembles.

Osvaldo Golijov (b. 1960) grew up in an Argentine Jewish family hearing classical music, Piazzolla's *nuevo tango*, synagogue music, and klezmer (a European Jewish popular style), and has drawn on all of them and more in his music. After studying with George Crumb, he has made his career in the United States. In *La Pasión según San Marcos* (The Passion according to Saint Mark, 2000; NAWM 217), commissioned for a festival in Germany commemorating the 250th anniversary of J.S. Bach's death, Golijov combines the Baroque genre of the Passion (see NAWM 104) with elements of Latin-American popular music, including dances such as Brazilian samba, Afro-Cuban salsa, Spanish flamenco, and Argentine tango. The composer's desire to present Jesus as an indigenous person of color, rather than (in his words) "a pale European," led him to tell the story of the crucifixion through voices and movement suggestive of religious street processions of Latin America and the Caribbean. In addition to soloists and double chorus, the score calls for dancers and a small orchestra, including guitar, accordion, and a kaleidoscopic array of percussion instruments (see Figure 28.11). The polyglot musical vocabulary is matched by the texts Golijov assembled from an equally wide range of sources, sung in Spanish, Aramaic, Latin, and Galician. For example, in Peter's denial of Christ and his anguished repentance (NAWM 217), Golijov departs from the biblical text to express the disciple's tears in the form of a moving soprano aria, set to words by a nineteenth-century Galician poet, which has the simple, haunting character of a folk song. In this way the composer exploits both the internal and external drama of the Passion story.

Osvaldo Golijov

Full 🔊

Full 🔊

Figure 28.11 A 2012 performance of Golijov's Pasión según San Marcos *with the orchestra of the State of São and the Schola Cantorum de Venezuela.*
(Ricardo Maldonado Rozo/epa/Corbis.)

TIMELINE The End of the Millennium

Musical Events

1970
Crumb, *Black Angels*
(NAWM 205)

1971
Stravinsky dies

1975
Del Tredici, *Final Alice*

1981
Gubaidulina, *Rejoice!*
(NAWM 213)

1986
Adams, *Short Ride in a Fast Machine* (NAWM 211)

1988
Pärt, *Seven Magnificat Antiphons* (NAWM 215)

1995
Sheng, *Seven Tunes Heard in China* (NAWM 209)

1998
Corigliano, *The Red Violin* film score

2000
Saariaho, *L'Amour de loin* (NAWM 216); Golijov, *La Pasión según San Marcos* (NAWM 217)

2005
Adams, *Doctor Atomic* (NAWM 219)

2006
Carter, *Caténaires* (NAWM 218)

1970	2015

Historical Events

1969
First humans set foot on the moon

1972
Nixon visits China

1973
Embargo forces oil prices to rise

1974
Resignation of Nixon following Watergate scandal

1978
John Paul II becomes first Polish pope

1980
Successful solidarity strikes in Poland

1981
AIDS first described

1989
Berlin Wall torn down

1991
Soviet Union dissolves, ending Cold War

2001
Terrorist attacks on World Trade Center and Pentagon

2002
Euro introduced as new currency in European Union

2003–2011
United States involvement in Iraq War

2009
Barack Obama inaugurated as first African American president

2011
Osama Bin Laden killed

2013
Francis becomes first Jesuit pope

By incorporating elements of popular styles, composers like Golijov offer listeners something familiar that carries vivid associations, then create new sounds and meanings by reshaping the popular material with modernist procedures.

The pieces discussed in this chapter represent only a few of the many strategies composers have devised to communicate directly with listeners. By the new millennium, most composers sought to write music that nonspecialist audiences could grasp, by employing familiar idioms, gestures, and other elements drawn from the entire range of music history, popular styles, and musics of the world. These familiar elements were often juxtaposed or blended in unprecedented ways in order to provide a new experience and achieve a distinctive profile. Thus, composers sought to uphold the high value placed on individuality since the nineteenth century while seeking to reclaim the immediate appeal that many felt had been lost in the modernist era.

Direct communication

POSTLUDE

It is too early to know what music from the late twentieth or early twenty-first century will be remembered, performed, and listened to in the future or will influence later music. Trends change too quickly to give a balanced or complete overview of recent music. But it seems clear that there is a continuing tension in all types of music between finding a niche of committed listeners whose support will endure and finding a wide audience. Other than *Happy Birthday*, there are probably few pieces that everyone knows; perhaps national anthems and film music come closest to providing the shared musical experiences that seem to have been more common in the past. The immediate success and enduring place enjoyed by Beethoven in orchestral music, Verdi in opera, or Duke Ellington in jazz no longer seem possible because the audience is so divided that such unanimity of opinion is unlikely to be achieved.

Yet, the relative lack of dominant figures may be a good thing. Music of the past and of the entire world is more available now than ever. Thanks to radio, recordings, and marketing, most of the music we have studied is heard by more people each year today than it was during the composer's lifetime. There is no need to focus our interest on a few great composers when there is so much variety to enjoy. The choices we have for music to hear and perform have become almost limitless. So, too, are the possibilities for new music. With new computer software and the collage approach found in both classical and popular music, it is now possible for all of us with access to technology to make our own music without training. In some respects, we are surrounded by more music than we can ever consume. But perhaps we are also returning to something akin to the condition of music long ago, when every singer sang his or her own song.

Ⓢ Resources for study and review available at wwnorton.com/studyspace

FURTHER READING

A rich source of information, interpretation, and bibliography for all periods and styles of music history is the *New Grove Dictionary of Music and Musicians*, available at www.oxfordmusiconline.com.

Part One: The Ancient and Medieval Worlds

Aubrey, Elizabeth. *The Music of the Troubadours.* Bloomington: Indiana University Press, 1996.

Busse Berger, Anna Maria. *Medieval Music and the Art of Memory.* Berkeley: University of California Press, 2005.

Fassler, Margot. *Music in the Medieval West.* New York: Norton, 2013.

Hiley, David. *Western Plainchant: A Handbook.* New York: Oxford University Press, 1993.

Hoppin, Richard H. *Medieval Music.* New York: Norton, 1978.

Levy, Kenneth. *Gregorian Chant and the Carolingians.* Princeton, NJ: Princeton University Press, 1998.

Long, Michael. "Trecento Italy." In *Antiquity and the Middle Ages.* Ed. James W. McKinnon. Englewood Cliffs, NJ: Prentice Hall, 1991.

McKinnon, James, ed. *Antiquity and the Middle Ages.* Englewood Cliffs, NJ: Prentice Hall, 1991.

———, ed. *Music in Early Christian Literature.* New York: Cambridge University Press, 1987.

Mathiesen, Thomas J. *Apollo's Lyre: Greek Music and Music Theory in Antiquity and the Early Middle Ages.* Lincoln: University of Nebraska Press, 1999.

Page, Christopher. *Voices and Instruments of the Middle Ages: Instrumental Practice and Songs in France, 1100–1300.* Berkeley: University of California Press, 1986.

Robertson, Anne Walters. *Guillaume de Machaut and Reims: Context and Meaning in His Musical Works.* New York: Cambridge University Press, 2002.

Rosenberg, Samuel N., Margaret Switten, and Gerard Le Vot, eds. *Songs of the Troubadours and Trouvères: An Anthology of Poems and Melodies.* New York: Garland, 1998.

Strunk, Oliver, ed. *Source Readings in Music History.* Rev. ed. Leo Treitler. Vol. 1: *Greek Views of Music.* Ed. Thomas J. Mathiesen. New York: Norton, 1998.

Switten, Margaret L. *The Medieval Lyric.* South Hadley, MA: Mount Holyoke College, 1987–.

Treitler, Leo. *With Voice and Pen: Coming to Know Medieval Song and How It Was Made.* New York: Oxford University Press, 2003.

Wright, Craig. *Music and Ceremony at Nôtre Dame of Paris: 500–1500.* New York: Cambridge University Press, 1989.

Part Two: The Age of the Renaissance

Atlas, Allan. *Renaissance Music: Music in Western Europe, 1400–1600*. New York: Norton, 1998.

Brown, Christopher Boyd. *Singing the Gospel: Lutheran Hymns and the Success of the Reformation*. Cambridge: Harvard University Press, 2005.

Brown, Howard M. and Louise Stein. *Music in the Renaissance*. Rev. ed. Upper Saddle River, NJ: Prentice Hall, 1999.

Cumming, Julie E. *The Motet in the Age of Du Fay*. New York: Cambridge University Press, 1999.

Cummings, Anthony M. *The Maecenas and the Madrigalist: Patrons, Patronage, and the Origins of the Italian Madrigal*. Philadelphia: American Philosophical Society, 2004.

Duffin, Ross. *How Equal Temperament Ruined Harmony (And Why You Should Care)*. New York: Norton, 2007.

Fenlon, Iain. *Music and Culture in Late Renaissance Italy*. New York: Oxford University Press, 2002.

Freedman, Richard. *Music in the Renaissance*. New York: Norton, 2013.

Herl, Joseph. *Worship Wars in Early Lutheranism: Choir, Congregation, and Three Centuries of Conflict*. Oxford: Oxford University Press, 2004.

Kite-Powell, Jeffery T., ed. *A Performer's Guide to Renaissance Music*. New York: Schirmer, 1994.

LeHuray, Peter. *Music and the Reformation in England, 1549–1660*. New York: Cambridge University Press, 1967, 1978.

Merkley, Paul A. "Josquin at Ferrara." *Journal of Musicology* 18 (2001): 544–83.

Oettinger, Rebecca. *Music as Propaganda in the German Reformation*. Aldershot: Ashgate, 2001.

Palisca, Claude V. *Music and Ideas in the Sixteenth and Seventeenth Centuries*. Champaign: University of Illinois Press, 2006.

Perkins, Leeman. *Music in the Age of the Renaissance*. New York: Norton, 1998.

Roche, Jerome. *The Madrigal*. 2nd ed. New York: Oxford University Press, 1990.

Sherr, Richard, ed. *The Josquin Companion*. New York: Oxford University Press, 2000.

Silbiger, Alexander, ed. *Keyboard Music before 1700*. 2nd ed. New York: Routledge, 2004.

Sparks, Edgar H. *Cantus Firmus in Mass and Motet, 1420–1520*. Berkeley: University of California Press, 1963.

Strohm, Reinhard. *The Rise of European Music, 1380–1500*. New York: Cambridge University Press, 1993.

van Orden, Kate. *Music, Discipline, and Arms in Early Modern France*. Chicago: The University of Chicago Press, 2005.

Wright, Craig. *Music at the Court of Burgundy, 1364–1419: A Documentary History*. Henryville, PA: Institute of Medieval Music, 1979.

Part Three: The Long Seventeenth Century

THE SEVENTEENTH CENTURY

Anthony, James R. *French Baroque Music from Beaujoyeaulx to Rameau*. Rev. ed. Portland, OR: Amadeus Press, 1997.

Arnold, Denis and Nigel Fortune, eds. *The New Monteverdi Companion*. London: Faber & Faber, 1985.

———, et al. *The New Grove Italian Baroque Masters: Monteverdi, Frescobaldi, Cavalli, Corelli, A. Scarlatti, Vivaldi, D. Scarlatti*. New York: Norton, 1984.

Buelow, George J. *A History of Baroque Music*. Bloomington: Indiana University Press, 2004.

Carter, Stewart, ed. *A Performer's Guide to Seventeenth-Century Music*. New York: Schirmer, 1997.

Carter, Tim. *Music in Late Renaissance and Early Baroque Italy*. Portland, OR: Amadeus Press, 1992.

——— and John Butt, eds. *The Cambridge History of Seventeenth-Century Music*. New York: Cambridge University Press, 2005.

Cowart, Georgia. *The Triumph of Pleasure: Louis XIV and the Politics of Spectacle.* Chicago: University of Chicago Press, 2008.

Freitas, Roger. *Portrait of a Castrato: Politics, Patronage, and Music in the Life of Atto Melani.* Cambridge: Cambridge University Press, 2009.

Heller, Wendy. *Music in the Baroque.* New York: Norton, 2013.

Hill, John Walter. *Baroque Music: Music in Western Europe, 1580–1750.* New York: Norton, 2005.

McClary, Susan. *Desire and Pleasure in Seventeenth-Century Music.* Berkeley: University of California Press, 2012.

Neumann, Frederick. *Ornamentation in Baroque and Post-Baroque Music, with Special Emphasis on J. S. Bach.* 3rd ed. Princeton: Princeton University Press, 1983.

New Grove Dictionary of Opera. 4 vols. New York: Grove's Dictionaries of Music, 1992.

Ossi, Massimo. *Divining the Oracle: Monteverdi's Seconda Prattica.* Chicago: The University of Chicago Press, 2003.

Pagano, Robert. *Alessandro and Domenico Scarlatti.* Hillside, NY: Pendragon Press, 2006.

Palisca, Claude V. *Baroque Music.* 3rd ed. Englewood Ciffs, NJ: Prentice Hall, 1991.

——. *Music and Ideas in the Sixteenth and Seventeenth Centuries.* Champaign: University of Illinois Press, 2006.

Rifkin, Joshua, et al. *The New Grove North European Masters: Schütz, Froberger, Buxtehude, Purcell, Telemann.* New York: Norton, 1985.

Rosand, Ellen. *Opera in Seventeenth-Century Venice: The Creation of a Genre.* Berkeley: University of California Press, 1991.

——. *Monteverdi's Last Operas: A Venetian Trilogy.* Berkeley: University of California Press, 2007.

Spitzer, John and Neal Zaslaw. *The Birth of the Orchestra: History of an Institution, 1650–1815.* New York: Oxford University Press, 2004.

Stauffer, George, ed. *The World of Baroque Music: New Perspectives.* Bloomington: Indiana University Press, 2006.

Tomlinson, Gary. *Monteverdi and the End of the Renaissance.* Berkeley: University of California Press, 1987.

Wood, Caroline. *Music and Drama in the tragédie en musique, 1673–1715: Jean Baptiste Lully and His Successors.* New York: Garland, 1996.

THE LATE BAROQUE IN THE EARLY EIGHTEENTH CENTURY

Burrows, Donald. *Handel.* New York: Oxford University Press, 1996.

Christensen, Thomas. *Rameau and Musical Thought in the Enlightenment.* New York: Cambridge University Press, 1993.

David, Hans T. and Arthur Mendel. *The New Bach Reader: A Life of Johann Sebastian Bach in Letters and Documents.* Rev. and enl. by Christoph Wolff. New York: Norton, 1998.

Dill, Charles William. *Monstrous Opera: Rameau and the Tragic Tradition.* Princeton: Princeton University Press, 1998.

Harris, Ellen T. *Handel and the Pastoral Tradition.* London: Oxford University Press, 1980.

——. *Handel as Orpheus: Voice and Desire in the Chamber Cantatas.* Cambridge: Harvard University Press, 2001.

Marshall, Robert L. *The Music of Johann Sebastian Bach: The Sources, the Style, the Significance.* New York: Schirmer, 1989.

Robbins Landon, H. C. *Handel and His World.* London: Weidenfeld & Nicolson, 1984.

——. *Vivaldi: Voice of the Baroque.* New York: Thames and Hudson, 1993.

Smith, Ruth. *Handel's Oratorios and Eighteenth-Century Thought.* New York: Cambridge University Press, 1995.

Strohm, Reinhard. *Essays on Handel and Italian Opera.* New York: Cambridge University Press, 1985.

Talbot, Michael. *Vivaldi.* New York: Oxford University Press, 2000.

Tunley, David. *François Couperin and the "Perfection of Music."* Aldershot: Ashgate, 2003.

Wolff, Christoph. *Johann Sebastian Bach: The Learned Musician.* New York: Norton, 2000.

——, et al. *The New Grove Bach Family.* New York: Norton, 1983.

Part Four: The Eighteenth Century

Abert, Hermann. *W. A. Mozart*. Trans. Stewart Spencer, ed. Cliff Eisen. New Haven: Yale University Press, 2007.

Brown, A. Peter. *The First Golden Age of the Viennese Symphony: Haydn, Mozart, Beethoven, and Schubert*. Bloomington: Indiana University Press, 2002.

Brown, Clive. *Classical and Romantic Performance Practice 1750–1900*. New York: Oxford University Press, 1999.

Burnham, Scott and Michael P. Steinberg, eds. *Beethoven and His World*. Princeton: Princeton University Press, 2000.

Carew, Derek. *The Mechanical Muse: The Piano, Pianism and Piano Music, c. 1760–1850*. Aldershot: Ashgate, 2007.

Downs, Philip G. *Classical Music: The Era of Haydn, Mozart, and Beethoven*. New York: Norton, 1992.

Feldman, Martha. *Opera and Sovereignty: Transforming Myths in Eighteenth-Century Italy*. Chicago: University of Chicago Press, 2007.

Geiringer, Karl. *Haydn: A Creative Life in Music*. 3rd rev. and enl. ed. Berkeley: University of California Press, 1982.

Gutman, Robert W. *Mozart: A Cultural Biography*. New York: Harcourt Brace, 1999.

Heartz, Daniel. *Haydn, Mozart, and the Viennese School, 1740–1780*. New York: Norton, 1995.

———, *Mozart, Haydn, and Early Beethoven, 1781–1802*. New York: Norton, 2009.

———. *Music in European Capitals: The Galant Style, 1720–1780*. New York: Norton, 2003.

Hepokoski, James A. and Warren Darcy. *Elements of Sonata Theory: Norms, Types, and Deformations in the Late-Eighteenth-Century Sonata*. New York: Oxford University Press, 2006.

Howard, Patricia. *Gluck: An Eighteenth-Century Portrait in Letters and Documents*. Oxford: Clarendon, 1995.

Keefe, Simon P. *Mozart's Viennese Instrumental Music: A Study of Stylistic Re-Invention*. Woodbridge: Boydell, 2007.

Lockwood, Lewis. *Beethoven: The Music and the Life*. New York: Norton, 2003.

McKay, David P. and Richard Crawford. *William Billings of Boston: Eighteenth-Century Composer*. Princeton: Princeton University Press, 1975.

Mozart's Letters, Mozart's Life: Selected Letters. Ed. and trans. Robert Spaethling. New York: Norton, 2000.

Pagano, Robert. *Alessandro and Domenico Scarlatti*. Hillside, NY: Pendragon Press, 2006.

Parker, Mara. *The String Quartet, 1750–1797: Four Types of Musical Conversation*. Aldershot: Ashgate, 2002.

Rice, John. *Music in the Eighteenth Century*. New York: Norton, 2013.

Robbins Landon, H. C. *Essays on the Viennese Classical Style: Gluck, Haydn, Mozart, Beethoven*. New York: Macmilllan, 1970.

———, ed. *The Mozart Compendium: A Guide to Mozart's Life and Music*. London: Thames & Hudson, 1999.

Rosen, Charles. *The Classical Style: Haydn, Mozart, Beethoven*. Expanded ed. New York: Norton, 1997.

———. *Sonata Forms*. Rev. ed. New York: Norton, 1988.

Sisman, Elaine, ed. *Haydn and His World*. Princeton: Princeton University Press, 1997.

Solomon, Maynard. *Beethoven*. 2nd rev. ed. New York: Schirmer, 1998.

———. *Late Beethoven: Music, Thought, Imagination*. Berkeley: University of California Press, 2003.

Stanley, Glenn, ed. *The Cambridge Companion to Beethoven*. New York: Cambridge University Press, 2000.

Stevens, Jane R. *The Bach Family and the Keyboard Concerto: The Evolution of a Genre*. Warren, MI: Harmonie Park, 2001.

Walden, Edward. *Beethoven's Immortal Beloved: Solving the Mystery*. Lanham, MD: The Scarecrow Press, 2011.

Webster, James and Georg Feder. *The New Grove Haydn*. New York: Palgrave, 2002.

Wolff, Christoph. *Mozart at the Gateway to His Fortune*. New York: Norton, 2012.

Zaslaw, Neal, ed. *The Classical Era: From the 1740s to the End of the Eighteenth Century*. Englewood Cliffs, NJ: Prentice Hall, 1989.

———, with William Cowdery. *The Compleat Mozart: A Guide to the Musical Works of Wolfgang Amadeus Mozart*. New York: Norton, 1990.

Part Five: The Nineteenth Century

Abraham, Gerald and David Brown, et al. *The New Grove Russian Masters.* 2 vols. New York: Norton, 1986.

Barham, Jeremy. *The Cambridge Companion to Mahler.* Cambridge: Cambridge University Press, 2007.

Beckerman, Michael, ed. *Dvořák and His World.* Princeton: Princeton University Press, 1993.

——— *New Worlds of Dvořák: Searching in America for the Composer's Inner Life.* New York: Norton, 2003.

Bohlman, Philip. *The Music of European Nationalism: Cultural Identity and Modern History.* Santa Barbara: ABC-CLIO, 2004.

Bonds, Mark Evan. *After Beethoven: The Imperative of Originality in the Symphony.* Cambridge: Harvard University Press, 1997.

Brown, A. Peter. *The Symphonic Repertoire,* vol. 4, *The Second Golden Age of the Viennese Symphony: Brahms, Bruckner, Dvořák, Mahler, and Selected Contemporaries.* Bloomington: Indiana University Press, 2003.

Budden, Julian. *Verdi.* 3rd ed. Oxford: Oxford University Press, 2008.

———. *Puccini: His Life and Works.* Oxford and New York: Oxford University Press, 2002.

Cairns, David. *Berlioz,* vol. 1, *The Making of an Artist, 1803–1832.* Berkeley: University of California Press, 2000.

———. *Berlioz,* vol. 2, *Servitude and Greatness.* Berkeley: University of California Press, 2003.

Charlton, David, ed. *The Cambridge Companion to Grand Opera.* New York: Cambridge University Press, 2003.

The Complete Correspondence of Clara and Robert Schumann. Ed. Eva Weissweiler, trans. Hildegard Fritsch and Ronald L. Crawford. New York: P. Lang, 1994–.

Cooper, Martin. *French Music from the Death of Berlioz to the Death of Fauré.* New York: Oxford University Press, 1951.

Daverio, John. *Nineteenth-Century Music and the German Romantic Ideology.* New York: Schirmer, 1993.

———. *Crossing Paths: Schubert, Schumann, and Brahms.* New York: Oxford University Press, 2002.

Deathridge, John. *Wagner Beyond Good and Evil.* Berkeley: University of California Press, 2008.

Dent, Edward J. *The Rise of Romantic Opera.* Ed. Winton Dean. New York: Cambridge University Press, 1976.

Donelan, James H. *Poetry and the Romantic Musical Aesthetic.* Cambridge: Cambridge University Press, 2008.

Finson, Jon W. *Robert Schumann: The Book of Songs.* Cambridge: Harvard University Press, 2008.

Frisch, Walter. *Music in the Nineteenth Century.* New York: Norton, 2013.

Frolova-Walker, Marina. *Russian Music and Nationalism: From Glinka to Stalin.* New Haven: Yale University Press, 2008.

Garden, Edward. *Tchaikovsky.* New York: Oxford University Press, 2000.

Gilliam, Bryan, ed. *Richard Strauss and His World.* Princeton: Princeton University Press, 1992.

Gooley, Dana. *The Virtuoso Liszt.* New York: Cambridge University Press, 2004.

Gossett, Philip. *Divas and Scholars: Performing Italian Opera.* Chicago: University of Chicago Press, 2006.

Hamilton, Kenneth. *After the Golden Age: Romantic Pianism and Modern Performance.* New York: Oxford University Press, 2007.

Hefling, Stephen E., ed. *Nineteenth-Century Chamber Music.* New York: Routledge, 2004.

Holomon, D. Kern, ed. *The Nineteenth-Century Symphony.* New York: Schirmer, 1997.

Kramer, Lawrence. *Opera and Modern Culture: Wagner and Strauss.* Berkeley: University of California Press, 2004.

Kramer, Richard. *Distant Cycles: Schubert and the Conceiving of Song.* Chicago: University of Chicago Press, 1994.

The Memoirs of Berlioz. Trans. and ed. David Cairns. New York: Knopf, 2002.

Millington, Barry, ed. *The New Grove Wagner.* New York: Grove, 2002.

Musgrave, Michael, ed. *A Brahms Reader.* New Haven: Yale University Press, 2000.

Osborne, Richard. *Rossini*. 2nd ed. New York: Oxford University Press, 2007.

Pistone, Danièle. *Nineteenth-Century Italian Opera from Rossini to Puccini*. Trans. E. Thomas Glasow. Portland, OR: Amadeus Press, 1995.

Plantinga, Leon. *Romantic Music*. New York: Norton, 1984.

Reich, Nancy B. *Clara Schumann: The Artist and the Woman*. Rev. ed. Ithaca, NY: Cornell University Press, 2001.

Rosen, Charles. *Romantic Poets, Critics, and Other Madmen*. Cambridge: Harvard University Press, 1998.

———. *The Romantic Generation*. Cambridge: Harvard University Press, 1995.

Sadie, Stanley, ed. *Wagner and His Operas*. New York: St. Martin's, 2000.

Saffle, Michael and Rossana Dalmonte, eds. *Liszt and the Birth of Modern Europe: Music as a Mirror of Religious, Political, Cultural and Aesthetic Transformation*. Hillsdale, NY: Pendragon Press, 2003.

Samson, Jim. *Chopin*. New York: Oxford University Press, 1996.

Szulc, Tad. *Chopin in Paris: The Life and Times of the Romantic Composer*. New York: Da Capo, 2000.

Taruskin, Richard. *Defining Russia Musically: Historical and Hermeneutical Essays*. Princeton: Princeton University Press, 1997.

Tchaikovsky: A Self Portrait. Comp. Alexandra Orlova, trans. R. M. Davison. Oxford: Oxford University Press, 1990.

Todd, R. Larry. *Mendelssohn: A Life in Music*. New York: Oxford University Press, 2003.

Tyrell, John, et al. *The New Grove Turn of the Century Masters: Janáček, Mahler, Strauss, Sibelius*. New York: Norton, 1985.

Warrack, John Hamilton. *German Opera: From the Beginnings to Wagner*. Cambridge: Cambridge University Press, 2001.

Weaver, William and Martin Chusid, eds. *The Verdi Companion*. New York: Norton, 1979.

Weber, William. *Music and the Middle Class: The Social Structure of Concert Life in London, Paris, and Vienna between 1830 and 1848*. 2nd ed. Aldershot: Ashgate, 2004.

Youmans, Charles: *Richard Strauss's Orchestral Music and the German Intellectual Tradition: The Philosophical Roots of Musical Modernism*. Bloomington: Indiana University Press, 2005.

Part Six: The Twentieth Century and Today

Albright, Daniel, ed. *Modernism and Music: An Anthology of Sources*. Chicago: University of Chicago Press, 2004.

Auner, Joseph. *Music in the Twentieth and Twenty-First Centuries*. New York: Norton, 2013.

Bayley, Amanda, ed. *The Cambridge Companion to Bartók*. New York: Cambridge University Press, 2001.

Cook, Nicholas and Anthony Pople, eds. *The Cambridge History of Twentieth-Century Music*. New York: Cambridge University Press, 2004.

Crawford, Richard and Larry Hamberlin. *An Introduction to America's Music*. 2nd ed. New York: Norton, 2013.

Cross, Jonathan, ed. *The Cambridge Companion to Stravinsky*. New York: Cambridge University Press, 2003.

d'Escrivan, Julio and Nick Collins, eds. *The Cambridge Companion to Electronic Music*. Cambridge: Cambridge University Press, 2007.

Edmunds, Neil, ed. *Soviet Music and Society under Lenin and Stalin: The Baton and the Sickle*. New York: RoutledgeCurzon, 2004.

Hamm, Charles. *Music in the New World*. New York: Norton, 1983.

Haimo, Ethan. *Schoenberg's Transformation of Musical Language*. Cambridge: Cambridge University Press, 2006.

Hasse, John Edward. *Beyond Category: The Life and Genius of Duke Ellington*. New York: Simon & Schuster, 1993.

Hitchcock, H. Wiley. *Music in the United States: A Historical Introduction*. 3rd ed. Englewood Cliffs, NJ: Prentice Hall, 1988.

Horowitz, Joseph. *Classical Music in America: A History of Its Rise and Fall*. New York: Norton, 2005.

Kater, Michael H. and Albrecht Riethmüller, eds. *Music and Nazism: Art under Tyrrany, 1933–1945*. Laaber: Laaber, 2003.

Lampert, Vera, et al. *The New Grove Modern Masters: Bartók, Stravinsky, Hindemith*. New York: Norton, 1984.

Lester, Joel. *Analytic Approaches to Twentieth-Century Music*. New York: Norton, 1989.

McVeagh, Diana, et al. *The New Grove Twentieth-Century English Masters: Elgar, Delius, Vaughan Williams, Holst, Walton, Tippett, Britten*. New York: Norton, 1986.

Morgan, Robert P., ed. *Modern Times: From World War I to the Present*. Englewood Cliffs, NJ: Prentice Hall, 1993.

———. *Twentieth-Century Music: A History of Musical Style in Modern Europe and America*. New York: Norton, 1991.

Nectoux, Jean-Michel, et al. *The New Grove Twentieth-Century French Masters: Fauré, Debussy, Satie, Ravel, Poulenc, Messiaen, Boulez*. New York: Norton, 1986.

Pollack, Howard. *George Gershwin: His Life and Work*. Berkeley: University of California Press, 2006.

Potter, Keith. *Four Musical Minimalists: La Monte Young, Terry Riley, Steve Reich, Philip Glass*. Rev. ed. Cambridge: Cambridge University Press, 2002.

Reich, Willi. *Schoenberg: A Critical Biography*. Trans. Leo Black. 1971; repr. New York: Da Capo, 1981.

Ross, Alex. *The Rest Is Noise: Listening to the Twentieth Century*. Farrar, Straus and Giroux, 2007.

Salzman, Eric. *Twentieth-Century Music: An Introduction*. 3rd ed. Englewood Cliffs, NJ: Prentice Hall, 1988.

Schwarz, Boris. *Music and Musical Life in Soviet Russia, Enlarged Edition, 1917–1981*. Bloomington: Indiana University Press, 1983.

Simms, Bryan R. *Music of the Twentieth Century: Style and Structure*. 2nd ed. New York: Schirmer, 1996.

———, ed. *Schoenberg, Berg, and Webern: A Companion to the Second Viennese School*. Westport, CT: Greenwood Press, 1999.

Smith, Joan A. *Schoenberg and His Circle: A Viennese Portrait*. New York: Schirmer, 1986.

Southern, Eileen. *The Music of Black Americans: A History*. 3rd ed. New York: Norton, 1997.

Straus, Joseph N. *Remaking the Past: Musical Modernism and the Influence of the Tonal Tradition*. Cambridge: Harvard University Press, 1990.

Swafford, Jan. *Charles Ives: A Life with Music*. New York: Norton. 1996.

Swain, Joseph. *The Broadway Musical: A Critical and Musical Survey*. 2nd ed. Lanham, MD: Scarecrow, 2002.

Taruskin, Richard. *Stravinsky and the Russian Traditions: A Biography of the Works through Mavra*. Berkeley: University of California Press, 1996.

Tawa, Nicholas E. *The Coming of Age of American Art Music: New England's Classical Romanticists*. New York: Greenwood Press, 1991.

Tirro, Frank. *Jazz: A History*. 2nd ed. New York: Norton, 1993.

Watkins, Glenn. *Soundings: Music in the Twentieth Century*. New York: Schirmer, 1988.

———. *Pyramids at the Louvre: Music, Culture, and Collage from Stravinsky to the Postmodernists*. Cambridge: Harvard University Press, 1994.

GLOSSARY

Within a definition, terms that are themselves defined in this glossary are printed in SMALL CAPITALS. Pronunciation of foreign words is approximate; "nh" stands for a final "n" in French, which nasalizes the preceding vowel (as in "chanson," rendered here as "shanh-SONH").

Abgesang (pronounced AHP-ge-zong) See BAR FORM.

absolute music Music that is independent of words, drama, visual images, or any kind of representation.

a cappella (Italian, "in chapel style") Manner of choral singing without instrumental accompaniment.

accidental Sign that calls for altering the pitch of a NOTE: a sharp (♯) raises the pitch a semitone, a flat (♭) lowers it a semitone, and a natural (♮) cancels a previous accidental.

accompanied recitative RECITATIVE that uses ORCHESTRAL accompaniment to punctuate and reinforce the message of the text.

act Main division of an OPERA. Most operas have two to five acts, although some have only one.

affections Objectified or archetypal emotions or states of mind, such as sadness, joy, fear, or wonder; one goal of much BAROQUE music was to arouse the affections or move the emotions.

Agnus Dei (Latin, "Lamb of God") Of the five major musical prayers in the MASS ORDINARY, the fifth, based on a litany.

agrément (French, "charm"; pronounced ah-gray-MANH) ORNAMENT in French music, usually indicated by a sign.

air English or French song for solo voice with instrumental accompaniment, setting rhymed poetry, often STROPHIC, and usually in the METER of a dance.

air de cour (French, "court air") Type of song for voice and accompaniment, prominent in France from about 1580 through the seventeenth century.

Alberti bass Broken-CHORD accompaniment common in the second half of the eighteenth century and named after Domenico Alberti, who used it frequently.

Alleluia Prayer from the MASS PROPER, sung just before the Gospel reading, comprising a RESPOND with the text "Alleluia," a verse, and a repetition of the respond. CHANT alleluias are normally MELISMATIC in style and sung in a RESPONSORIAL manner, one or more soloists alternating with the CHOIR.

allemande (French for "German") Highly stylized DANCE in BINARY FORM, in moderately fast quadruple METER with almost continuous movement, beginning with an upbeat. Popular during the RENAISSANCE and BAROQUE; appearing often as the first dance in a SUITE.

alto (from ALTUS) (1) Relatively low female voice, or high male voice. (2) Part for such a voice in an ENSEMBLE work.

altus (Latin, "high") In fifteenth- and sixteenth-century POLYPHONY, a part in a range between the TENOR and the SUPERIUS; originally CONTRATENOR ALTUS.

Ambrosian chant A repertory of ecclesiastical CHANT used in Milan.

anacrusis (1) The NOTE or group of notes preceding a downbeat. (2) In poetry, a line of VERSE that begins with an unstressed syllable or group of syllables is said to be anacrustic.

answer In the EXPOSITION of a FUGUE, the second entry of the SUBJECT, normally on the DOMINANT if the subject was on the TONIC, and vice versa. Also refers to subsequent answers to the subject.

anthem A POLYPHONIC sacred work in English for Anglican religious services.

antiphon (1) A LITURGICAL CHANT that precedes and follows a PSALM or CANTICLE in the OFFICE. (2) In the MASS, a chant originally associated with ANTIPHONAL PSALMODY; specifically, the COMMUNION and the first and final portion of the INTROIT.

antiphonal Adjective describing a manner of performance in which two or more groups alternate.

Aquitanian polyphony Style of POLYPHONY from the twelfth century, encompassing both DISCANT and FLORID ORGANUM.

aria (Italian, "air") (1) In the late sixteenth and early seventeenth centuries, any setting of an Italian STROPHIC poem for a solo singer. (2) Lyrical monologue in an OPERA or other vocal work such as CANTATA and ORATORIO.

arioso (1) RECITATIVO ARIOSO. (2) Short, ARIA-like passage. (3) Style of vocal writing that approaches the lyricism of an ARIA but is freer in form.

arpeggio (from Italian *arpa*, "harp") Broken-CHORD figure.

Ars Nova (Latin, "new art") Style of POLYPHONY from fourteenth-century France, distinguished from earlier styles by a new system of rhythmic NOTATION that allowed duple or triple division of NOTE values, SYNCOPATION, and great rhythmic flexibility.

Ars Subtilior (Latin, "the subtler art") Style of POLYPHONY from the late fourteenth or very early fifteenth centuries in southern France and northern Italy, distinguished by extreme complexity in rhythm and NOTATION.

art music Music that is (or is meant to be) listened to attentively, for its own sake. Compare POPULAR MUSIC.

art song A song intended to be appreciated as an artistic statement rather than as entertainment, featuring precisely notated music, usually THROUGH-COMPOSED, and requiring professional standards of performance. Compare POPULAR SONG.

atonal, atonality Terms for music that avoids establishing a central pitch or tonal center (such as the TONIC in TONAL music).

aulos Ancient Greek reed instrument, usually played in pairs.

authentic mode A MODE (2) in which the RANGE normally extends from a STEP below the FINAL to an octave above it, as in modes 1, 3, 5, and 7. See also PLAGAL MODE.

avant-garde Term for music (and art) that is iconoclastic, irreverent, antagonistic, and nihilistic, seeking to overthrow established aesthetics.

balanced binary form BINARY FORM in which the latter part of the first section returns at the end of the second section, but in the TONIC.

ballad (1) Long narrative poem, or musical setting of such a poem. (2) Late-eighteenth-century German poetic form that imitated the folk ballad of England and Scotland and was set to music by German composers. The ballad expanded the LIED in both FORM and emotional content.

ballad opera GENRE of eighteenth-century English comic play featuring songs in which new words are set to borrowed tunes.

ballade (1) French FORME FIXE, normally in three stanzas, in which each stanza has the musical FORM aab and ends with a REFRAIN, C. (2) Instrumental piece inspired by the GENRE of narrative poetry.

ballata (from Italian *ballare*, "to dance"; pl. *ballate*) Fourteenth-century Italian song GENRE with the FORM AbbaA, in which A is the *ripresa* or REFRAIN, and the single stanza consists of two *piedi* (bb) and a *volta* (a) sung to the music of the ripresa.

ballet In sixteenth- and seventeenth-century France, an entertainment in which both professionals and guests danced; later, a stage work danced by professionals.

balletto, ballett (Italian, "little dance") Sixteenth-century Italian (and later English) song GENRE in a simple, dancelike, HOMOPHONIC style with repeated sections and "fa-la-la" refrains.

band Large ENSEMBLE of winds, brass, and percussion instruments, or of brass and percussion instruments without winds.

bar form Song FORM in which the first section of MELODY is sung twice with different texts (the two Stollen) and the remainder (the Abgesang) is sung once.

bard Medieval poet-singer, especially of epics.

Baroque period (from Portuguese *barroco*, "a misshapen pearl") PERIOD of music history from about 1600 to about 1750, overlapping the late RENAISSANCE and early CLASSIC periods.

bas (French, "low"; pronounced BAH) In the fourteenth through sixteenth centuries, term for soft instruments such as VIELLES and HARPS. See HAUT.

bass (from BASSUS) (1) The lowest part in an ENSEMBLE work. (2) Low male voice. (3) Low instrument, especially the string bass or bass VIOL.

basse danse (French, "low dance") Type of stately couple DANCE of the fifteenth and early sixteenth centuries.

basso continuo (Italian, "continuous bass") (1) System of NOTATION and performance practice, used in the BAROQUE PERIOD, in which an instrumental BASS line is written out and one or more players of keyboard, LUTE, or similar instruments fill in the HARMONY with appropriate CHORDS or IMPROVISED MELODIC lines. (2) The bass line itself.

basso ostinato (Italian, "persistent bass") or **ground bass** A pattern in the BASS that repeats while the MELODY above it changes.

bassus (Latin, "low") In fifteenth- and sixteenth-century POLYPHONY, the lowest part; originally CONTRATENOR BASSUS.

bebop, bop A style of JAZZ appearing in New York in the 1940s that developed an enriched HARMONIC vocabulary and required an increased level of technical and IMPROVISATIONAL skill to play rapid melodies and complicated rhythms.

bel canto (Italian, "beautiful song") Elegant Italian vocal style of the early nineteenth century marked by lyrical, embellished, and florid melodies that show off the beauty, agility, and fluency of the singer's voice.

big band Type of large JAZZ ENSEMBLE popular between the World Wars, featuring brass, reeds, and RHYTHM SECTIONS, and playing prepared arrangements that included rhythmic unisons and coordinated dialogue between sections and soloists.

binary form A FORM comprised of two complementary sections, each of which is repeated. The first section usually ends on the DOMINANT or the relative major, and the second section returns to the tonic. See also BALANCED, ROUNDED, and SIMPLE BINARY FORM.

blue note Slight drop or slide in pitch on the third, fifth, or seventh degree of a MAJOR SCALE, common in BLUES and JAZZ.

blues (1) African-American vocal GENRE that is based on a simple repetitive formula and characterized by a distinctive style of performance. (2) TWELVE-BAR BLUES.

bop See BEBOP.

branle gay RENAISSANCE DANCE in a lively triple METER based on a sideways swaying step.

breve (from Latin *brevis*, "short") In medieval and RENAISSANCE systems of RHYTHMIC NOTATION, a NOTE that is normally equal to half or a third of a LONG.

burden In the English CAROL, the REFRAIN.

Byzantine chant The repertory of ecclesiastical CHANT used in the Byzantine RITE and in the modern Greek Orthodox Church.

cabaletta In the operatic scene structure of the nineteenth century, the last part of an ARIA or ENSEMBLE, which was lively and brilliant and expressed active feelings, such as joy or despair. See also CANTABILE, TEMPO DI MEZZO, and TEMPO D'ATTACCO.

cabaret Type of nightclub, first introduced in nineteenth-century Paris, that offered serious or comic sketches, dances, songs, and poetry.

caccia (Italian, "hunt"; pronouced CAH-cha; pl. *cacce*) Fourteenth-century Italian song GENRE featuring two voices in CANON over a free untexted TENOR.

cadence MELODIC or HARMONIC succession that closes a musical PHRASE, PERIOD, section, or COMPOSITION.

cadenza (Italian, "cadence") Highly embellished passage, often IMPROVISED, at an important CADENCE, usually occurring just before the end of a piece or section.

call and response Alternation of short PHRASES between a leader and a group; used especially for music in the African-American tradition.

cambiata (Italian, "changed") Figure in sixteenth-century POLYPHONY in which a voice skips down from a DISSONANCE to a CONSONANCE instead of resolving by STEP, then moves to the expected NOTE of resolution.

Camerata (Italian, "circle" or "association") Circle of intellectuals and amateurs of the arts that met in Florence, Italy, in the 1570s and 1580s.

canon (Latin, "rule") (1) Rule for performing music, particularly for deriving more than one voice from a single line of notated music, as when several voices sing the same MELODY, entering at specified intervals of time or singing at different speeds simultaneously. (2) COMPOSITION in which the voices enter successively at determined pitch and time intervals, all performing the same MELODY.

cantabile (Italian, "songlike") (1) Songful, lyrical, in a songlike style. (2) In the operatic scene structure developed by Gioachino Rossini in the early nineteenth century, the first section of an ARIA or ENSEMBLE, somewhat slow and expressing a relatively calm mood. See also CABALETTA, TEMPO DI MEZZO, and TEMPO D'ATTACCO.

cantata (Italian, "sung") (1) In the seventeenth and eighteenth centuries, a vocal chamber work with CONTINUO, usually for solo voice, consisting of several sections or MOVEMENTS that include RECITATIVES and ARIAS and setting a lyrical or quasi-dramatic text. (2) Genre of Lutheran church music in the eighteenth century, combining poetic texts with texts drawn from CHORALES or the Bible, and including RECITATIVES, ARIAS, chorale settings, and usually one or more CHORUSES. (3) In later eras, a work for soloists, CHORUS, and ORCHESTRA in several MOVEMENTS but smaller than an ORATORIO.

canticle HYMN-like or PSALM-like passage from a part of the Bible other than the Book of Psalms.

cantiga Medieval MONOPHONIC song in Spanish or Portuguese.

cantor In Jewish synagogue music, the main solo singer. In the medieval Christian church, the leader of the CHOIR.

cantus (Latin, "melody") In POLYPHONY of the fourteenth through sixteenth centuries, the highest voice, especially the texted voice in a polyphonic song.

cantus durus (Latin, "hard song") Of the two large tonal areas commonly used in the early seventeenth century, the one characterized by a key signature of no sharps or flats that used chords containing (accidental) sharps to connote harsh or strident emotions. See also CANTUS MOLLIS.

cantus firmus (Latin, "fixed melody") An existing MELODY, often taken from a GREGORIAN CHANT, on which a new POLYPHONIC work is based; used especially for MELODIES presented in long NOTES.

cantus-firmus mass POLYPHONIC MASS in which the same CANTUS FIRMUS is used in each MOVEMENT, normally in the TENOR.

cantus-firmus variations Instrumental GENRE of the late 1500s and early 1600s, comprising a set of VARIATIONS in which the MELODY repeats with little change but is surrounded by different CONTRAPUNTAL material in each variation.

cantus mollis (Latin, "soft song") Of the two large tonal areas commonly used in the early seventeenth century, the one characterized by a key signature of one flat that used chords belonging to the flatter regions of the tonal spectrum to connote subdued and pleasant emotions. See also CANTUS DURUS.

canzona (canzon) (Italian, "song") (1) Sixteenth-century Italian GENRE, an instrumental work adapted from a CHANSON or composed in a similar style. (2) In the late sixteenth and early seventeenth centuries, an instrumental work in several contrasting sections, of which the first and some of the others are in IMITATIVE COUNTERPOINT.

canzonetta, canzonet (Italian, "little song") Sixteenth-century Italian (and later English) song GENRE in a simple, mostly HOMO-PHONIC style. Diminutive of CANZONA.

capriccio (Italian, "whim") (1) In the BAROQUE PERIOD, a FUGAL piece in continuous IMITATIVE COUNTERPOINT. (2) In the nineteenth century, a short COMPOSITION in free FORM, usually for PIANO.

carol English song, usually on a religious subject, with several stanzas and a BURDEN, or REFRAIN. From the fifteenth century on, most carols are POLYPHONIC.

castrati (sing. *castrato*) Male singers who were castrated before puberty to preserve their high vocal RANGE, prominent in the seventeenth and early eighteenth centuries, especially in OPERA.

catch English GENRE of CANON, usually with a humorous or ribald text.

cauda (Latin, "tail"; pl. *caudae*) MELISMATIC passage in a POLYPHONIC CONDUCTUS.

chacona (Italian, ciaccona) A vivacious dance-song imported from Latin America into Spain and then into Italy, popular during the seventeenth century; usually in triple meter and employing some type of variation technique.

chaconne (or ciaccona) BAROQUE GENRE derived from the CHACONA, consisting of VARIATIONS over a BASSO CONTINUO.

chamber sonata See SONATA DA CAMERA.

chance Approach to composing music pioneered by John Cage, in which some of the decisions normally made by the composer are instead determined through random procedures, such as tossing coins. Chance differs from INDETERMINACY but shares with it the result that the sounds in the music do not convey an intention and are therefore to be experienced only as pure sound.

chanson (French, "song"; pronounced shanh-SONH) Secular song with French words; used especially for POLYPHONIC songs of the fourteenth through sixteenth centuries.

chanson de geste (French, "song of deeds") Type of medieval French epic recounting the deeds of national heros, sung to MELODIC formulas.

chansonnier (French, "songbook") Manuscript collection of secular songs with French words; used both for collections of MONOPHONIC TROUBADOUR and TROUVÈRE songs and for collections of POLYPHONIC songs.

chant (1) Unison unaccompanied song, particularly that of the Latin LITURGY (also called PLAINCHANT). (2) The repertory of unaccompanied liturgical songs of a particular RITE.

chant dialect One of the repertories of ecclesiastical CHANT, including GREGORIAN, BYZANTINE, AMBROSIAN, and OLD ROMAN CHANT.

chapel A group of salaried musicians and clerics employed by a ruler, nobleman, church official, or other patron, who officiate at and furnish music for religious services.

character piece A piece of CHARACTERISTIC MUSIC, especially one for PIANO.

characteristic (or descriptive) **music** Instrumental music that depicts or suggests a mood, personality, or scene, usually indicated in its title.

choir A group of singers who perform together, singing either in unison or in parts. Used especially for the group that sings in a religious service.

choral society Amateur CHORUS whose members sing for their own enjoyment and may pay dues to purchase music, pay the CONDUCTOR, and meet other expenses.

chorale (pronounced ko-RAL) STROPHIC HYMN in the Lutheran tradition, intended to be sung by the congregation in German.

chorale motet CHORALE setting in the style of a sixteenth-century MOTET.

chorale prelude Relatively short setting for organ of a CHORALE MELODY, used as an introduction for congregational singing or as an interlude in a Lutheran church service.

chorale variations   A set of VARIATIONS on a CHORALE MELODY.

chord   Three or more simultaneous NOTES heard as a single entity. In TONAL music, three or more notes that can be arranged as a succession of thirds, such as a TRIAD.

chorus   (1) Group of singers who perform together, usually with several singers on each part. (2) A MOVEMENT or passage for such a group in an ORATORIO, OPERA, or other multimovement work. (3) The REFRAIN of a POPULAR SONG. (4) In JAZZ, a statement of the HARMONIC PROGRESSION of the opening tune, over which one or more instruments play variants or new musical ideas.

chromatic   (from Greek *chroma*, "color")   (1) In ancient Greek music, adjective describing a TETRACHORD comprising a minor third and two SEMITONES, or a MELODY that uses such tetrachords. (2) Adjective describing a melody that uses two or more successive semitones in the same direction, a SCALE consisting exclusively of semitones, an INTERVAL or CHORD that draws NOTES from more than one DIATONIC scale, or music that uses many such melodies or chords.

chromatic saturation   The appearance of all twelve PITCH-CLASSES within a segment of music.

chromaticism   The use of many NOTES from the CHROMATIC SCALE in a passage or piece.

church calendar   In a Christian RITE, the schedule of days commemorating special events, individuals, or times of year.

church sonata   See SONATA DA CHIESA.

ciaccona   See CHACONA.

Classic period   In music history, the era from about 1730 to about 1815, between and overlapping the BAROQUE and ROMANTIC periods.

classical music   (1) Common term for ART MUSIC of all PERIODS, as distinct from POPULAR MUSIC OR FOLK MUSIC. (2) Music in the tradition of the repertory of musical masterworks that formed in the nineteenth century, including lesser works in the same GENRES (such as OPERA, ORATORIO, SYMPHONY, SONATA, STRING QUARTET, and ART SONG) or for the same performing forces and newly composed works intended as part of the same tradition. (3) Music in the CLASSIC PERIOD.

classical style   Musical idiom of the eighteenth century, generally characterized by an emphasis on MELODY over relatively light accompaniment; simple, clearly articulated HARMONIC plans; PERIODIC phrasing; clearly delineated FORMS based on contrast between THEMES, between KEYS, between stable and unstable passages, and between sections with different functions; and contrasts of mood, style, and figuration within MOVEMENTS as well as between them.

clausula   (Latin, "clause," pl. *clausulae*)   In NOTRE DAME POLYPHONY, a self-contained section of an ORGANUM that closes with a CADENCE.

clavecin   French term for HARPSICHORD. A person who performs on or composes works for the clavecin is known as a clavecinist.

clavichord   A small keyboard string instrument producing a sweet, soft, and expressive sound, developed during the RENAISSANCE and used mostly for private music-making until the eighteenth century. The tone, which is produced by a brass disk striking the string, is under the direct control of the player.

clos   See OPEN AND CLOSED ENDINGS.

coda   (Italian, "tail")   A supplementary ending to a COMPOSITION or MOVEMENT; a concluding section that lies outside the FORM as usually described.

collage   Work or passage that uses multiple QUOTATIONS without following a standard procedure for doing so, such as QUODLIBET or medley.

collegium musicum   An association of amateurs, popular during the BAROQUE PERIOD, who gathered to play and sing together for their own pleasure. Today, an ensemble of university students that usually performs early music.

color   (Latin rhetorical term for ornament, particularly repetition, pronounced KOH-lor)   In an ISORHYTHMIC COMPOSITION, a repeated MELODIC pattern, as opposed to a repeating rhythmic pattern (the TALEA).

coloratura   Florid vocal ORNAMENTATION.

Communion   Item in the MASS PROPER, originally sung during communion, comprising an ANTIPHON without verses.

composition   The act or process of creating new pieces of music, or a piece that results from this process and is substantially similar each time it is performed; usually distinguished from IMPROVISATION and performance.

concert band   Large ENSEMBLE of winds, brass, and percussion instruments that performs seated in concert halls, like an ORCHESTRA.

concert étude   See ÉTUDE

concertato medium   (from Italian *concertare*, "to reach agreement")   In seventeenth-century music, the combination of voices with one or more instruments, where the instruments do not simply double the voices but play independent parts.

concerted madrigal   Early-seventeenth-century type of MADRIGAL for one or more voices accompanied by BASSO CONTINUO and in some cases by other instruments.

concerto   (1) Beginning in the seventeenth century, ENSEMBLE of instruments or of voices with one or more instruments, or a work for such an ensemble. (2) COMPOSITION in which one or more solo instruments (or instrumental group) contrasts with an ORCHESTRAL ENSEMBLE. See also SOLO CONCERTO, CONCERTO GROSSO, and ORCHESTRAL CONCERTO.

concerto grosso   Instrumental work that exploits the contrast in sonority between a small ENSEMBLE of solo instruments (*concertino*), usually the same forces that appeared in the TRIO SONATA, and a large ENSEMBLE (RIPIENO or *concerto grosso*).

concitato   See STILE CONCITATO.

conductor   A person who leads a performance, especially for an ORCHESTRA, BAND, CHORUS, or other large ENSEMBLE, by means of gestures.

conductus   A serious medieval song, often of a processional nature, MONOPHONIC or POLYPHONIC, setting a rhymed, rhythmic Latin poem.

conjunct   Adjective describing a MELODY, consisting mostly of STEPS.

conservatory   School that specializes in teaching music performance or composition.

consonance   INTERVAL or CHORD that has a stable, harmonious sound. Compare DISSONANCE.

consort   English name (current ca. 1575–1700) for a group of instruments, either all of one type (called a *full consort*), such as a consort of VIOLS, or of different types (called a *broken consort*).

consort song   RENAISSANCE English GENRE of song for voice accompanied by a CONSORT of VIOLS.

contenance angloise   (French, "English quality")   Characteristic quality of early-fifteenth-century English music, marked by pervasive CONSONANCE with frequent use of HARMONIC thirds and sixths, often in parallel motion.

continuo   BASSO CONTINUO.

continuo instruments   Instruments used to REALIZE a BASSO CONTINUO, such as HARPSICHORD, organ, LUTE, or THEORBO.

contrafact   In JAZZ, a new MELODY composed over a HARMONIC PROGRESSION borrowed from another song.

contrafactum   (Latin, "counterfeit"; pl. *contrafacta*)   The practice of replacing the text of a vocal work with a new text while the music remains essentially the same; or the resulting piece.

contrapuntal   Employing COUNTERPOINT, or two or more simultaneous MELODIC lines.

contratenor   (Latin, "against the tenor")   In fourteenth- and fifteenth-century POLYPHONY, voice composed after or in conjunction with the TENOR and in about the same RANGE, helping to form the work's foundation.

contratenor altus, contratenor bassus (Latin) In fifteenth-century POLYPHONY, CONTRATENOR parts that lie relatively high (ALTUS) or low (BASSUS) in comparison to the TENOR. Often simply written as "altus" or "bassus," these are the ancestors of the vocal ranges ALTO and BASS.

cornett Wind instrument of hollowed-out wood or ivory, with finger holes and a cup mouthpiece, blown like a brass instrument.

counterpoint The combination of two or more simultaneous MELODIC lines according to a set of rules.

couplet In a RONDO or seventeenth- or eighteenth-century RONDEAU, one of several PERIODS or passages that alternates with the REFRAIN.

courante A DANCE in BINARY FORM, in triple METER at a moderate tempo and with an upbeat, featured as a standard MOVEMENT of the Baroque DANCE SUITE.

court ballet Seventeenth-century French GENRE, an extensive musical-dramatic work with costumes, scenery, poetry, and dance that featured members of the court as well as professional dancers.

courtly love See FINE AMOUR.

Credo (Latin, "I believe") Third of the five major musical prayers in the MASS ORDINARY, a creed or statement of faith.

cumulative form FORM used by Charles Ives and others in which the principal THEME appears in its entirety only at the end of a work, preceded by its DEVELOPMENT.

cycle A group of related works, comprising MOVEMENTS of a single larger entity. Examples include cycles of CHANTS for the MASS ORDINARY, consisting of one setting each of the KYRIE, GLORIA, CREDO, SANCTUS, and AGNUS DEI (and sometimes also *Ite, missa est*); the POLYPHONIC MASS cycle of the fifteenth through seventeenth centuries; and the SONG CYCLE of the nineteenth century.

da capo aria ARIA FORM with two sections. The first section is repeated after the second section's close, which carries the instruction *da capo* (Italian, "from the head"), creating an ABA FORM.

dances Pieces used for dancing or in stylized dance rhythms, whether independent, paired, or linked together in a SUITE.

descriptive music See CHARACTERISTIC MUSIC.

developing variation Term coined by Arnold Schoenberg for the process of deriving new THEMES, accompaniments, and other ideas throughout a piece through variations of a germinal idea.

development (1) The process of reworking, recombining, fragmenting, and varying given THEMES or other material. (2) In SONATA FORM, the section after the EXPOSITION, which MODULATES through a variety of KEYS and in which THEMES from the exposition are fragmented and presented in new ways.

diastematic Having to do with INTERVALS. In diastematic motion, the voice glides between pitches that are separated by discrete intervals; in diastematic NOTATION, the approximate intervals are indicated by relative height (see HEIGHTENED NEUMES).

diatonic (1) In ancient Greek music, adjective describing a TETRACHORD with two WHOLE TONES and one SEMITONE. (2) Name for a SCALE that includes five whole tones and two semitones, where the semitones are separated by two or three whole tones. (3) Adjective describing a MELODY, CHORD, or passage based exclusively on a single diatonic scale.

diegetic music or **source music** In film, music that is heard or performed by the characters themselves.

digital Relating to methods for producing or recording musical sounds by translating them into a coded series of on-off pulses, in the same way that computers store and transmit data.

diminution (1) Uniform reduction of NOTE values in a MELODY or PHRASE. (2) Type of IMPROVISED ORNAMENTATION in the sixteenth and seventeenth centuries, in which relatively long notes are replaced with SCALES or other FIGURES composed of short notes.

direct Pertaining to a manner of performing CHANT without alternation between groups (see ANTIPHONAL) or between soloist and group (see RESPONSORIAL).

discant (Latin, "singing apart") (1) Twelfth-century style of POLYPHONY in which the upper voice or voices have about one to three NOTES for each note of the lower voice. (2) TREBLE part.

disjunct Adjective describing MELODY consisting mostly of skips (thirds) and leaps (larger INTERVALS) rather than STEPS.

dissonance (1) Two or more NOTES sounding together to produce a discord, or a sound that is unstable and "needs" to be resolved to a CONSONANCE. (2) A NOTE that does not belong to the CHORD that sounds simultaneously with it; a nonchord TONE.

diva A leading and successful female OPERA singer. See also PRIMA DONNA.

divertissement In TRAGÉDIE EN MUSIQUE, a long interlude of BALLET, solo AIRS, choral singing, and spectacle, intended as entertainment.

division See DIMINUTION (2).

dominant In TONAL music, the NOTE and CHORD a perfect fifth above the TONIC.

double leading-tone cadence CADENCE popular in the fourteenth and fifteenth centuries, in which the bottom voice moves down a WHOLE TONE and the upper voices move up a SEMITONE, forming a major third and major sixth expanding to an open fifth and octave.

double motet Thirteenth-century MOTET in three parts, with different texts in the DUPLUM and TRIPLUM.

Doxology A formula of praise to the Trinity used in GREGORIAN CHANT.

drone NOTE or notes sustained throughout an entire piece or section.

duplum (from Latin *duplus*, "double") In POLYPHONY of the late twelfth through fourteenth centuries, second voice from the bottom in a three- or four-voice TEXTURE, above the TENOR.

dynamics Level of loudness or softness, or intensity.

electronic music Music based on sounds that are produced or modified through electronic means.

empfindsam style (German, "sensitive style" or "sentimental style") Close relative of the GALANT style, but featuring surprising turns of HARMONY, CHROMATICISM, nervous RHYTHMS, and speechlike MELODIES.

enharmonic (1) In ancient Greek music, adjective describing a TETRACHORD comprising a major third and two quartertones, or a MELODY that uses such tetrachords. (2) Adjective describing the relationship between two pitches that are notated differently but sound alike when played, such as G♯ and A♭.

ensemble (1) A group of singers or instrumentalists who perform together. (2) In an OPERA, a passage or piece for more than one singer.

episode (1) In a FUGUE, a passage of COUNTERPOINT between statements of the SUBJECT. (2) In RONDO FORM, a section between two statements of the main THEME. (3) A subsidiary passage between presentations of the main thematic material.

equal temperament A TEMPERAMENT in which the octave is divided into twelve equal SEMITONES. This is the most commonly used tuning for Western music today.

ethos (Greek, "character") (1) Moral and ethical character or way of being or behaving. (2) Character, mood, or emotional effect of a certain tonos, MODE, METER, or MELODY.

étude (French, "study") An instrumental piece designed to develop a particular skill or performing technique. Certain nineteenth-century études that contained significant artistic content and were played in concert were called concert études.

exoticism Nineteenth-century trend in which composers sought to evoke the perceived glamour and strangeness of distant lands and foreign cultures.

experimental music A trend in twentieth-century music that focused on the exploration of new musical sounds, techniques, and resources.

exposition (1) In a FUGUE, a set of entries of the SUBJECT. (2) In SONATA FORM, the first part of the MOVEMENT, in which the main THEMES are stated, beginning in the TONIC and usually closing in the DOMINANT (or relative major).

expressionism Early-twentieth-century term derived from art, in which music avoids all traditional forms of "beauty" in order to express deep personal feelings through exaggerated gestures, angular MELODIES, and extreme DISSONANCE.

fantasia (Italian, "fantasy"), **fantasy** (1) Instrumental COMPOSITION that resembles an IMPROVISATION or lacks a strict FORM. (2) IMITATIVE instrumental piece on a single subject.

fauxbourdon (pronounced FOH-boor-donh) Continental style of POLYPHONY in the early RENAISSANCE, in which two voices are written, moving mostly in parallel sixths and ending each PHRASE on an octave, while a third unwritten voice is sung in parallel perfect fourths below the upper voice.

figuration, figure MELODIC pattern made of commonplace materials such as SCALES or ARPEGGIOS, usually not distinctive enough to be considered a MOTIVE or THEME.

figured bass A form of BASSO CONTINUO in which the BASS line is supplied with numbers or flat or sharp signs to indicate the appropriate INTERVALS to be played above the bass.

final The main NOTE in a MODE; the normal closing note of a CHANT in that mode.

finale Last MOVEMENT of a work in three or more movements, or the closing portion of an ACT in an OPERA.

fine amour (French, "refined love"; pronounced FEEN ah-MOOR; also called courtly love) An idealized love for an unattainable woman who is admired from a distance. Chief subject of TROUBADOUR and TROUVÈRE poetry.

first practice See PRIMA PRATICA.

florid organum Twelfth-century style of two-voice POLYPHONY in which the lower voice sustains relatively long NOTES while the upper voice sings note-groups of varying length above each note of the lower voice.

folk music Music of unknown authorship from a particular region or people, transmitted through oral tradition.

form The shape or structure of a COMPOSITION or MOVEMENT.

formes fixes (French, "fixed forms"; pronounced form FEEX) Schemes of poetic and musical repetition, each featuring a REFRAIN, used in late medieval and fifteenth-century French CHANSONS; in particular, the BALLADE, RONDEAU, and VIRELAI.

Franconian notation System of NOTATION described by Franco of Cologne around 1280, using note shapes to indicate durations.

free jazz An experimental JAZZ style introduced in the 1960s by Ornette Coleman, using IMPROVISATION that disregards the standard forms and conventions of jazz.

free organum Style of ORGANUM in which the ORGANAL VOICE, having more rhythmic and melodic independence, moves in a free mixture of contrary, oblique, parallel, and similar motion against the CHANT (and usually above it).

French overture Type of OVERTURE used in TRAGÉDIE EN MUSIQUE and other GENRES that opens with a slow, HOMOPHONIC, and majestic section, followed by a faster second section that begins with IMITATION.

frottola (pl. *frottole*) Sixteenth-century GENRE of Italian POLYPHONIC song in mock-popular style, typically SYLLABIC, HOMOPHONIC, and

DIATONIC, with the MELODY in the upper voice and marked rhythmic patterns.

fugal Resembling a FUGUE; featuring fugue-like IMITATION.

fuging tune Eighteenth-century American type of PSALM or HYMN tune that features a passage in free IMITATION, usually preceded and followed by HOMOPHONIC sections.

fugue (from Italian *fuga*, "flight") COMPOSITION or section of a composition in strict IMITATIVE COUNTERPOINT that is based on a single SUBJECT and begins with successive statements of the subject at contrasting pitches, usually the first and fifth scale degrees.

full anthem ANTHEM for unaccompanied CHOIR in CONTRAPUNTAL style.

fundamental bass Term coined by Jean-Philippe Rameau to indicate the succession of the roots or fundamental tones in a series of CHORDS.

futurism, futurists Twentieth-century movement that created music based on noise.

galant (French, "elegant") Eighteenth-century musical style that features songlike MELODIES, short PHRASES, frequent CADENCES, and light accompaniment.

galliard Sixteenth-century dance in fast triple METER, often paired with the PAVANE and in the same FORM (AABBCC).

gamut The entire range of written pitches in the Middle Ages.

gavotte BAROQUE duple-time dance in BINARY FORM, with a half-measure ANACRUSIS and a characteristic rhythm of short-short-long.

Gebrauchsmusik (German "utilitarian music" or "music for use") Term from the 1920s to describe music that was socially relevant and useful, especially music for amateurs, children, or workers to play or sing.

genre Type or category of musical COMPOSITION, such as SONATA or SYMPHONY.

genus (Latin, "class"; pronounced GHEH-noos; pl. *genera*) In ancient Greek music, one of three forms of TETRACHORD: DIATONIC, CHROMATIC, and ENHARMONIC.

Gesamtkunstwerk (German, "complete artwork" or "united artwork") Term coined by Richard Wagner for a dramatic work in which poetry, scenic design, staging, action, and music are integrated into one artistic expression.

gigue (French for "jig") Stylized DANCE movement of a standard BAROQUE SUITE, in BINARY FORM, marked by fast compound METER such as $\frac{6}{4}$ or $\frac{12}{8}$ with wide MELODIC leaps and continuous triplets. Both sections usually begin with IMITATION.

Gloria (Latin, "Glory") Second of the five major musical prayers in the MASS ORDINARY.

goliard songs Medieval Latin songs associated with the goliards, who were wandering students and clerics.

Gradual (from Latin *gradus*, "stairstep") Prayer in the MASS PROPER, sung after the Epistle reading, comprising a RESPOND and VERSE. CHANT graduals are normally MELISMATIC in style and sung in a RESPONSORIAL manner, one or more soloists alternating with the CHOIR.

grand motet French version of the large-scale SACRED CONCERTO, for soloists, double CHORUS, and ORCHESTRA.

grand opera A serious form of OPERA popular during the ROMANTIC era that was sung throughout and included BALLETS, CHORUSES, and spectacular staging.

Gregorian chant The repertory of ecclesiastical CHANT used in the Roman Catholic Church.

ground bass see BASSO OSTINATO.

half step (or semitone) The smallest INTERVAL normally used in Western music, equivalent to the interval between any two successive NOTES on the PIANO keyboard; half the size of a WHOLE STEP.

harmonia (pl. *harmoniai*) Ancient Greek concept having multiple related meanings: (1) the union of parts in an orderly whole; (2) SCALE type.

harmonic progression A logical succession of CHORDS with a sense of direction; especially, the succession of chords used to accompany a MELODY or used as the basis for VARIATIONS.

harmony Aspect of music that pertains to simultaneous combinations of NOTES, the INTERVALS and CHORDS that result, and the customary succession of chords.

harp Plucked string instrument with a resonating soundbox, neck, and strings in roughly triangular shape. The strings rise perpendicular from the soundboard to the neck.

harpsichord Keyboard string instrument in use between the fifteenth and eighteenth centuries. It was distinguished from the CLAVICHORD and the PIANO by the fact that its strings were plucked (by a quill or jack set into motion by depressing a key), not struck.

haut (French, "high"; pronounced OH) In the fourteenth through sixteenth centuries, term for loud instruments such as CORNETTS and SACKBUTS. See BAS.

head motive Initial passage or MOTIVE of a piece or MOVEMENT; used especially for a motive or PHRASE that appears at the beginning of each movement of a MOTTO MASS or CANTUS-FIRMUS MASS.

heightened neumes In an early form of NOTATION, NEUMES arranged so that their relative height indicated higher or lower pitch. Also called DIASTEMATIC neumes.

hemiola (from Greek *hemiolios*, "one and a half") A metrical effect in which three duple units substitute for two triple ones, such as three successive quarter NOTES within a MEASURE of $\frac{6}{8}$, or three two-beat groupings in two measures of triple METER. Hemiola may occur between voices or in successive measures.

heterophony Music or musical TEXTURE in which a MELODY is performed by two or more parts simultaneously in more than one way, for example, one voice performing it simply, and the other with embellishments.

hexachord (from Greek, "six strings") (1) A set of six pitches. (2) In medieval and RENAISSANCE SOLMIZATION, the six NOTES represented by the syllables *ut, re, mi, fa, sol, la*, which could be transposed to three positions: the natural hexachord, C–D–E–F–G–A; the hard hexachord, G–A–B–C–D–E; and the soft hexachord, F–G–A–B♭–C–D. (3) In TWELVE-TONE theory, the first six or last six notes in the ROW.

historia In Lutheran music of the sixteenth to eighteenth centuries, a musical setting based on a biblical narrative. See PASSION.

hocket (French *hoquet*, "hiccup") In thirteenth- and fourteenth-century POLYPHONY, the device of alternating rapidly between two voices, each resting while the other sings, as if a single MELODY is split between them; or, a COMPOSITION based on this device.

homophony Musical TEXTURE in which all voices move together in essentially the same RHYTHM, as distinct from POLYPHONY and HETEROPHONY. See also MELODY AND ACCOMPANIMENT.

homorhythmic Having the same RHYTHM, as when several voices or parts move together.

humanism Movement in the RENAISSANCE to revive ancient Greek and Roman culture and to study things pertaining to human knowledge and experience through independent thought rather than reliance on authority.

hurdy-gurdy An instrument with MELODY and DRONE strings, bowed by a rotating wheel turned with a crank, with levers worked by a keyboard to change the pitch on the melody string(s).

hymn Song to or in honor of a god. In the Christian tradition, song of praise sung to God.

idée fixe (French, "fixed idea" or obsession) Term coined by Hector Berlioz for a MELODY that is used throughout a piece to represent a person, thing, or idea, transforming it to suit the mood and situation.

imitation (1) In POLYPHONIC music, the device of repeating (imitating) a MELODY or MOTIVE announced in one part in one or more other parts, often at a different pitch level and sometimes with minor MELODIC or rhythmic alterations. Usually the voices enter with the element that is imitated, although sometimes imitation happens within the middle of a segment of melody. (2) The act of patterning a new work after an existing work or style; especially, to borrow much of the existing work's material.

imitative counterpoint CONTRAPUNTAL TEXTURE marked by IMITATION between voices.

imperfect (or minor) division In medieval and RENAISSANCE NOTATION, a division of a NOTE value into two of the next smaller units (rather than three). See MODE, TIME, and PROLATION.

impressionism Late-nineteenth-century term derived from art, used for music that evokes moods and visual images through colorful HARMONY and instrumental TIMBRE.

impresario During the BAROQUE PERIOD, a businessman who managed and oversaw the production of OPERAS; today, someone who books and stages operas and other musical events.

improvisation Spontaneous invention of music while performing, including devising VARIATIONS, embellishments, or accompaniments for existing music.

indeterminacy An approach to composition, pioneered by John Cage, in which the composer leaves certain aspects of the music unspecified, as distinct from CHANCE.

instrumental family Set of instruments, all of the same type but of different sizes and RANGES, such as a VIOL CONSORT.

intabulation Arrangement of a vocal piece for LUTE or keyboard, typically written in TABLATURE, or the score of such a piece.

intermedio Musical interlude on a pastoral, allegorical, or mythological subject performed before, between, or after the acts of a spoken comedy or tragedy.

intermezzo Eighteenth-century GENRE of Italian comic OPERA, performed between acts of a serious OPERA or play.

interval Distance in pitch between two NOTES.

intonation The first NOTES of a CHANT, sung by a soloist to establish the pitch for the CHOIR, which joins the soloist to continue the chant.

Introit (from Latin *introitus*, "entrance") First prayer in the MASS PROPER, originally sung for the entrance procession, comprising an ANTIPHON, PSALM verse, DOXOLOGY, and reprise of the ANTIPHON.

inversion (1) In a MELODY or TWELVE-TONE ROW, reversing the upward or downward direction of each INTERVAL while maintaining its size; or the new melody or row form that results. (2) In HARMONY, a distribution of the NOTES in a CHORD so that a note other than the ROOT is the lowest note. (3) In COUNTERPOINT, reversing the relative position of two melodies, so that the one that had been lower is now above the other.

isorhythm (from Greek *iso-*, "equal," and *rhythm*) Repetition in a voice part (usually the TENOR) of an extended pattern of durations throughout a section or an entire COMPOSITION.

jazz A type of music developed mostly by African Americans in the early part of the twentieth century that combined elements of African, popular, and European musics, and that has evolved into a broad tradition encompassing many styles and featuring IMPROVISATION.

jongleur (French, "juggler") Itinerant medieval musician or street entertainer.

jubilus (Latin) In CHANT, an effusive MELISMA, particularly the melisma on "-ia" in an ALLELUIA.

just intonation A system of tuning NOTES in the SCALE, common in the RENAISSANCE, in which most (but not all) thirds, sixths, perfect fourths, and perfect fifths are in perfect tune.

key In TONAL music, the hierarchy of NOTES, CHORDS, and other pitch elements around a central note, the TONIC. There are two kinds of keys, major and minor.

kithara Ancient Greek string instrument, a large LYRE.

Klangfarbenmelodie (German, "tone-color melody") Term coined by Arnold Schoenberg to describe a succession of tone colors that is perceived as analogous to the changing pitches in a MELODY.

krummhorn RENAISSANCE wind instrument, with a double reed enclosed in a cap so the player's lips do not touch the reed.

Kyrie (Greek, "Lord") One of the five major musical prayers in the MASS ORDINARY, based on a BYZANTINE litany.

lauda (from Latin *laudare*, "to praise") Italian devotional song.

Leitmotiv, leitmotive (German, "leading motive") In an OPERA or MUSIC DRAMA, a MOTIVE, THEME, or musical idea associated with a person, thing, mood, or idea, which returns in original or altered form throughout.

libretto (Italian, "little book") Literary text for an OPERA or other musical stage work.

Lied (German, "song"; pl. *Lieder*) Art song with German words, whether MONOPHONIC, POLYPHONIC, or for voice with accompaniment; used especially for polyphonic songs in the RENAISSANCE and songs for voice and PIANO in the eighteenth and nineteenth centuries.

ligature NEUME-like noteshape used to indicate a short RHYTHMIC pattern in twelfth- to sixteenth-century NOTATION.

liturgical drama Dialogue on a sacred subject, set to music and usually performed with action, and linked to the LITURGY.

liturgy The prescribed body of texts to be spoken or sung and ritual actions to be performed in a religious service.

long In medieval and RENAISSANCE systems of RHYTHMIC NOTATION, a NOTE equal to two or three BREVES.

lute Plucked string instrument popular from the late Middle Ages through the BAROQUE PERIOD, typically pear- or almond-shaped with a rounded back, flat fingerboard, frets, and one single and five double strings.

lute song English GENRE of solo song with LUTE accompaniment.

lyre Plucked string instrument with a resonating sound box, two arms, crossbar, and strings that run parallel to the soundboard and attach to the crossbar.

lyric opera ROMANTIC OPERA that lies somewhere between light OPÉRA COMIQUE and GRAND OPERA.

madrigal (Italian *madrigale*, "song in the mother tongue") (1) Fourteenth-century Italian poetic form and its musical setting having two or three stanzas followed by a RITORNELLO. (2) Sixteenth-century Italian poem having any number of lines, each of seven or eleven syllables. (3) POLYPHONIC CONCERTATO, or MONODIC setting of such a poem or of a sonnet or other nonrepetitive VERSE form. (4) English polyphonic work imitating the Italian GENRE.

madrigal comedy, madrigal cycle In the late sixteenth and early seventeenth centuries, a series of MADRIGALS that share the same subject, or represent a succession of scenes or a simple plot.

madrigalism A particularly evocative—or, if used in a disparaging sense, a thoroughly conventional—instance of TEXT DEPICTION; so called because of the prominent role of word painting in MADRIGALS.

major scale DIATONIC succession of NOTES with a major third and major seventh above the TONIC.

march A piece in duple or **6/8** METER comprising an introduction and several STRAINS, each repeated. Typically, there are two strains in the initial key followed by a TRIO in a key a fourth higher; the opening strains may or may not repeat after the trio.

masque Seventeenth-century English entertainment involving poetry, music, DANCE, costumes, CHORUSES, and elaborate sets, akin to the French COURT BALLET.

Mass (from Latin *missa*) (1) The most important service in the Roman Church. (2) A musical work setting the texts of the ORDINARY of the Mass, typically KYRIE, GLORIA, CREDO, SANCTUS, and AGNUS DEI.

mazurka A type of Polish folk dance (and later ballroom dance) in triple METER, characterized by accents on the second or third beat and often by dotted figures on the first beat, or a stylized PIANO piece based on such a DANCE.

mean-tone temperament A type of TEMPERAMENT in which the fifths are tuned small so that the major thirds sound well; frequently used for keyboard instruments from the RENAISSANCE through the eighteenth century.

measure (1) A unit of musical time consisting of a given number of beats; the basic unit of METER. (2) Metrical unit set off by bar lines.

mediant In a PSALM TONE, the CADENCE that marks the middle of the PSALM verse.

Meistersinger (German, "master singer") Type of German amateur singer and poet-composer of the fourteenth through seventeenth centuries, who was a member of a guild that cultivated a style of MONOPHONIC song derived from MINNELIEDER.

melisma A long MELODIC passage sung to a single syllable of text.

melismatic Adjective describing a MELODY, having many MELISMAS.

melodrama A genre of musical theater that combined spoken dialogue with background music.

melody (1) Succession of tones perceived as a coherent line. (2) Tune. (3) Principal part accompanied by other parts or CHORDS.

melody and accompaniment A kind of HOMOPHONIC TEXTURE in which there is one main MELODY, accompanied by CHORDS or other FIGURATION.

mensuration canon A CANON in which voices move at different rates of speed by using different MENSURATION SIGNS.

mensuration signs In ARS NOVA and RENAISSANCE systems of rhythmic NOTATION, signs that indicate which combination of time and prolation to use (see MODE, TIME, AND PROLATION). The predecessors of TIME SIGNATURES.

meter Recurring patterns of strong and weak beats, dividing musical time into regularly recurring units of equal duration.

metrical psalm Metric, rhymed, and STROPHIC vernacular translation of a PSALM, sung to a relatively simple MELODY that repeats for each strophe.

minim In ARS NOVA and RENAISSANCE systems of rhythmic NOTATION, a NOTE that is equal to half or a third of a SEMIBREVE.

minimalism One of the leading musical styles of the late twentieth century, in which materials are reduced to a minimum and procedures simplified so that the musical content is immediately apparent. Often characterized by a constant pulse and many repetitions of simple RHYTHMIC, MELODIC, or HARMONIC patterns.

Minnelieder (German, "love songs") Songs of the MINNESINGER.

Minnesinger (German, "singer of love"; also pl.) A poet-composer of medieval Germany who wrote MONOPHONIC songs, particularly about love, in Middle High German.

minor scale DIATONIC SCALE that begins with a WHOLE STEP and HALF STEP, forming a minor third above the TONIC. The sixth and seventh above the tonic are also minor in the natural minor scale but one or both may be raised.

minstrel (from Latin *minister*, "servant") Thirteenth-century traveling musician, some of whom were also employed at a court or city.

minstrel show Popular form of musical theater in the United States during the mid-nineteenth century, in which white performers blackened their faces and impersonated African Americans in jokes, skits, songs, and dances.

minuet DANCE in moderate triple METER, two-measure units, and BINARY FORM.

minuet and trio form FORM that joins two BINARY-FORM MINUETS to create an ABA pattern, where A is the minuet and B the TRIO.

mixed media Trend of the late twentieth century that combines two or more of the arts, including music, to create a new kind of performance art or musical theater.

mixed parallel and oblique organum Early form of ORGANUM that combines parallel motion with oblique motion (in which the ORGANAL VOICE remains on the same NOTE while the PRINCIPAL VOICE moves) in order to avoid TRITONES.

modal Making use of a MODE. Compare TONAL.

mode (1) A SCALE or MELODY type, identified by the particular INTERVALLIC relationships among the NOTES in the mode. (2) In particular, one of the eight scale or melody types recognized by church musicians and theorists beginning in the Middle Ages, distinguished from one another by the arrangement of WHOLE TONES and SEMITONES around the FINAL, by the RANGE relative to the final, and by the position of the TENOR or RECITING TONE. (3) RHYTHMIC MODE. See also MODE, TIME, AND PROLATION.

mode, time, and prolation (Latin *modus, tempus, prolatio*) The three levels of rhythmic DIVISION in ARS NOVA NOTATION. Mode is the division of LONGS into BREVES; time the division of breves into SEMIBREVES; and prolation the division of semibreves into MINIMS.

modernists Twentieth-century composers who broke away from the musical language of their predecessors and contemporaries while maintaining strong links to tradition.

modified strophic form Variant of STROPHIC FORM in which the music for the first stanza is varied for later stanzas, or in which there is a change of KEY, RHYTHM, character, or material.

modulation In TONAL music, a gradual change from one KEY to another within a section of a MOVEMENT.

monody (1) An accompanied solo song. (2) The musical TEXTURE of solo singing accompanied by one or more instruments.

monophonic Consisting of a single unaccompanied MELODIC line.

monophony Music or musical TEXTURE consisting of unaccompanied MELODY.

motet (from French *mot*, "word") POLYPHONIC VOCAL COMPOSITION having two or more independent voices, often with a different text in Latin or French for each voice, usually above a CHANT TENOR. From the fifteenth century on, any polyphonic setting of a Latin text (other than a MASS); from the sixteenth century on, sacred compositions in any language.

motive Short MELODIC or RHYTHMIC idea that recurs in the same or altered form.

motto mass POLYPHONIC MASS in which the MOVEMENTS are linked primarily by sharing the same opening MOTIVE or PHRASE.

movement Self-contained unit of music, complete in itself, that can stand alone or be joined with others in a larger work. Some types of COMPOSITION typically consist of several movements (such as the four movements common in the SYMPHONY).

music drama Nineteenth-century GENRE created by Richard Wagner in which drama and music become so interdependent as to express a kind of absolute oneness. See also GESAMTKUNST-WERK.

music video Type of short film popularized in the early 1980s that provides a visual accompaniment to a POPULAR SONG.

musica ficta (Latin, "feigned music") (1) In early music, NOTES outside the standard GAMUT, which excluded all flatted and sharped notes except B♭. (2) In POLYPHONY of the fourteenth through sixteenth centuries, the practice of raising or lowering by a SEMITONE the pitch of a written note, particularly at a CADENCE, for the sake of smoother HARMONY or motion of the parts.

musica mundana, musica humana, musica instrumentalis (Latin, "music of the universe," "human music," and "instrumental music") Three kinds of music identified by Boethius (ca. 480–524), respectively the "music" or numerical relationships governing the movement of stars, planets, and the seasons; the "music" that harmonizes the human body and soul and their parts; and audible music produced by voices or instruments.

musical GENRE of musical theater that features songs and dance numbers in styles drawn from POPULAR MUSIC in the context of a spoken play with a comic or romantic plot.

musical figure In BAROQUE music, a MELODIC pattern or CONTRAPUNTAL effect conventionally employed to convey the meaning of a text.

musique concrète (French, "concrete music") Term coined by composers working in Paris in the 1940s for music composed by assembling and manipulating recorded sounds, working "concretely" with sound itself rather than with music NOTATION.

musique mesurée (French, "measured music") Late-sixteenth-century French style of text-setting, especially in CHANSONS, in which stressed syllables are given longer NOTES than unstressed syllables (usually twice as long).

nationalism (1) In politics and culture, an attempt to unify or represent a particular group of people by creating a national identity through characteristics such as common language, shared culture, historical traditions, and national institutions and rituals. (2) Nineteenth- and twentieth-century trend in music in which composers were eager to embrace elements in their music that claimed a national identity.

neoclassicism Trend in music from the 1910s to the 1950s in which composers revived, imitated, or evoked the styles, GENRES, and FORMS of pre-ROMANTIC music, especially those of the eighteenth century.

neo-Romanticism A trend of the late twentieth century in which composers adopted the familiar tonal idiom of nineteenth-century ROMANTIC music and incorporated its sounds and gestures.

neotonal Term for music since the early 1900s that establishes a single pitch as a tonal center, but does not follow the traditional rules of TONALITY.

neumatic In CHANT, having about one to six NOTES (or one NEUME) sung to each syllable of text.

neume A sign used in NOTATION of CHANT to indicate a certain number of NOTES and general MELODIC direction (in early forms of notation) or particular pitches (in later forms).

New Objectivity Term coined in the 1920s to describe a kind of new realism in music, in reaction to the emotional intensity of the late ROMANTICS and the EXPRESSIONISM of Schoenberg and Berg.

New Orleans jazz Leading style of JAZZ just after World War I, which centers on group VARIATION of a given tune, either IMPROVISED or in the style of improvisation.

nocturne Type of short PIANO piece popular during the ROMANTIC PERIOD, marked by highly embellished MELODY, sonorous accompaniments, and a contemplative mood.

nondiegetic music or **underscoring** In film, background music that conveys to the viewer a mood or other aspect of a scene or character but is not heard by the characters themselves. See also DIEGETIC MUSIC.

notation A system for writing down musical sounds, or the process of writing down music. The principal notation systems of European music use a staff of lines and signs that define the pitch, duration, and other qualities of sound.

note (1) A musical TONE. (2) A symbol denoting a musical tone.

notes inégales (French, "unequal notes"; pronounced NOTS an-ay-GALL) Seventeenth-century convention of performing

French music in which passages notated in short, even durations, such as a succession of eighth notes, are performed by alternating longer notes on the beat with shorter offbeats to produce a lilting rhythm.

Notre Dame polyphony Style of POLYPHONY from the late twelfth and thirteenth centuries, associated with the Cathedral of Notre Dame in Paris.

octatonic scale (or **octatonic collection**) A SCALE that alternates WHOLE and HALF STEPS.

Offertory Prayer in the MASS PROPER, sung while the Eucharist is prepared, comprising a RESPOND without VERSES.

Office (from Latin *officium*, "obligation" or "ceremony") A series of eight prayer services of the Roman Church, celebrated daily at specified times, especially in monasteries and convents; also, any one of those services.

Old Roman chant A repertory of ecclesiastical CHANT preserved in eleventh- and twelfth-century manuscripts from Rome representing a local tradition; a near relative of GREGORIAN CHANT.

open and closed endings (French, *ouvert* and *clos*) In a BALLADE or other medieval form, two different endings for a repeated section. The first ("open") closes on a pitch other than the FINAL, and the second ("closed") ends on the final.

opera (Italian, "work") Drama with continuous or nearly continuous music, staged with scenery, costumes, and action.

opéra bouffe ROMANTIC operatic GENRE in France that emphasized the smart, witty, and satirical elements of OPÉRA COMIQUE.

opera buffa (Italian, "comic opera") Eighteenth-century GENRE of Italian comic OPERA, sung throughout.

opéra comique (French, "comic opera") (1) In the eighteenth century, light French comic OPERA, which used spoken dialogue instead of RECITATIVES. (2) In nineteenth-century France, opera with spoken dialogue, whether comic or tragic.

opera seria (Italian, "serious opera") Eighteenth-century GENRE of Italian OPERA, on a serious subject but normally with a happy ending, usually without comic characters and scenes.

operetta Nineteenth-century kind of light OPERA with spoken dialogue, originating in OPÉRA BOUFFE.

opus (Latin, "work") Work or collection of works in the same GENRE, issued as a publication.

oratorio GENRE of dramatic music that originated in the seventeenth century, combining narrative, dialogue, and commentary through ARIAS, RECITATIVES, ENSEMBLES, CHORUSES, and instrumental music, like an unstaged OPERA. Usually on a religious or biblical subject.

orchestra ENSEMBLE whose core consists of strings with more than one player on a part, usually joined by woodwinds, brass, and percussion instruments.

orchestral concerto Orchestral GENRE in several MOVEMENTS, originating in the late seventeenth century, that emphasized the first VIOLIN part and the BASS, avoiding the more CONTRAPUNTAL TEXTURE of the SONATA.

orchestral suite Late-seventeenth-century German SUITE for ORCHESTRA patterned after the groups of DANCES in French BALLETS and OPERA.

Ordinary (from Latin *ordinarium*, "usual") Prayers of the MASS that remain the same on most or all days of the CHURCH CALENDAR, although their melodies may change.

organ mass Setting for organ of all sections of the MASS for which the organ would play, including ORGAN VERSES and other pieces.

organ verse Setting for organ of an existing MELODY from the Roman Catholic LITURGY.

organal voice (Latin, *vox organalis*) In an ORGANUM, the voice that is added above or below the original CHANT MELODY.

organic Adjective describing a musical work in which all the parts are derived from a common source and relate to one another and to the whole like the parts of a single organism.

organicism Belief that musical works should be ORGANIC.

organum (Latin; pronounced OR-guh-num) (1) One of several styles of early POLYPHONY from the ninth through thirteenth centuries, involving the addition of one or more voices to an existing CHANT. (2) A piece, whether IMPROVISED or written, in one of those styles, in which one voice is drawn from a CHANT. The plural is *organa*.

organum duplum In NOTRE DAME POLYPHONY, an ORGANUM in two voices.

ornament A brief, conventional formula, such as a TRILL or turn, written or IMPROVISED, that adds expression or charm to a MELODIC line.

ornamentation The addition of embellishments to a given MELODY, either during performance or as part of the act of COMPOSITION.

ostinato (Italian, "persistent" or "obstinate") Short musical pattern that is repeated persistently throughout a piece or section. See BASSO OSTINATO.

ouvert See OPEN AND CLOSED ENDINGS.

ouverture (French, "opening") (1) OVERTURE, especially FRENCH OVERTURE. (2) SUITE for ORCHESTRA, beginning with an OVERTURE.

overdotting Performing practice in French BAROQUE music in which a dotted NOTE is held longer than written, while the following short note is shortened.

overture (1) An ORCHESTRAL piece introducing an OPERA or other long work. (2) Independent ORCHESTRAL WORK in one movement, usually descriptive.

parallel organum Type of early POLYPHONY in which an added voice moves in exact parallel to a CHANT, normally a perfect fifth below it. Either voice may be doubled at the octave.

paraphrase Technique in which a CHANT or other MELODY is reworked, often by altering rhythms and adding NOTES, and placed in a POLYPHONIC setting.

paraphrase mass POLYPHONIC MASS in which each MOVEMENT is based on the same MONOPHONIC MELODY, normally a CHANT, which is PARAPHRASED in most or all voices rather than being used as a CANTUS FIRMUS in one voice.

parlor song Song for home music-making, sometimes performed in public concerts as well.

parody mass POLYPHONIC MASS in which each MOVEMENT is based on the same polyphonic model, normally a CHANSON or MOTET, and all voices of the model are used in the mass, but none is used as a CANTUS FIRMUS.

partbook A manuscript or printed book containing the music for one voice or instrumental part of a POLYPHONIC COMPOSITION (most often, an anthology of pieces); to perform any piece, a complete set of partbooks is needed, so that all the parts are represented.

partita BAROQUE term for a set of VARIATIONS on a MELODY or BASS line.

part-song (1) A song for more than one voice. (2) In the nineteenth century, a song for CHORUS, parallel in function and style to the LIED or PARLOR SONG.

passacaglia BAROQUE GENRE of VARIATIONS over a repeated BASS line or HARMONIC PROGRESSION in triple METER.

Passion A musical setting of one of the biblical accounts of Jesus' crucifixion, the most common type of HISTORIA.

pastoral drama Play in verse with incidental music and songs, normally set in idealized rural surroundings, often in ancient times; a source for the earliest OPERA LIBRETTOS.

pavane Sixteenth-century dance in slow duple METER with three repeated sections (AABBCC). Often followed by a GALLIARD.

perfect (or major) division In medieval and RENAISSANCE NOTATION, a division of a note value into three (rather than two) of the next smaller unit. See MODE, TIME, AND PROLATION.

perfection In medieval systems of NOTATION, a unit of duration equal to three TEMPORA, akin to a MEASURE of three beats.

performance practice Conventions of performance peculiar to different musical styles, eras, and repertories.

period (1) In music history, an era whose music is understood to have common attributes of style, conventions, approach, and function, in contrast to the previous and following eras. (2) In musical FORM, especially since the eighteenth century, a complete musical thought concluded by a CADENCE and normally containing at least two PHRASES.

periodic Organized in discrete PHRASES or PERIODS, often equal in length.

periodicity The quality of being PERIODIC, especially when this is emphasized through frequent resting points and articulations between PHRASES and PERIODS.

petit motet (French, "little motet") French version of the SMALL SACRED CONCERTO for one, two, or three voices and CONTINUO.

phrase A unit of MELODY or of an entire musical TEXTURE that has a distinct beginning and ending and is followed by a pause or other articulation but does not express a complete musical thought. See PERIOD (2).

Phrygian cadence CADENCE in which the bottom voice moves down a semitone and upper voices move up a whole tone to form a fifth and octave over the cadential NOTE.

piano or **pianoforte** A keyboard instrument invented around 1700 that uses a mechanism in which the strings are struck, rather than plucked as the HARPSICHORD was, and which allowed for crescendos, dimuendos, and other effects.

pipe and tabor Two instruments played by one player, respectively a high whistle fingered with one hand and a small drum beaten with a stick or mallet by the other.

pitch-class Any one of the twelve NOTES of the CHROMATIC SCALE, including its ENHARMONIC equivalents, in any octave.

plagal mode A MODE (2) in a which the RANGE normally extends from a fourth (or fifth) below the FINAL to a fifth or sixth above it, as in modes 2, 4, 6, and 8. See also AUTHENTIC MODE.

plainchant, plainsong A unison unaccompanied song, particularly a LITURGICAL song to a Latin text.

point of imitation In a POLYPHONIC WORK, the musical idea or motive that is the subject of IMITATION by the other voices.

polonaise A stately Polish processional DANCE in triple METER, or a stylized piece in the style of such a dance.

polychoral For more than one CHOIR.

polychoral motet MOTET for two or more choirs.

polyphony Music or musical TEXTURE consisting of two or more simultaneous lines of independent MELODY. See also COUNTERPOINT.

polystylism Term for a combination of newer and older musical styles created through QUOTATION or stylistic allusion.

polytonality The simultaneous use of two or more KEYS, each in a different layer of the music (such as MELODY and accompaniment).

popular music Music, primarily intended as entertainment, that is sold in printed or recorded form. It is distinguished from FOLK MUSIC by being written down and marketed as a commodity, and from CLASSICAL MUSIC by being centered on the performer and the performance, allowing great latitude in rearranging the notated music.

popular song Song that is intended primarily to entertain an audience, accommodate amateur performers, and sell as many copies as possible. Compare ART SONG.

portative organ Medieval or RENAISSANCE organ small enough to be carried; played by one hand while the other worked the bellows.

positive organ Organ from the medieval through BAROQUE PERIODS that was small enough to be moved, usually placed on a table.

postmodernism Trend in the late twentieth century that blurs the boundaries between high and popular art, and in which styles of all epochs and cultures are equally available for creating music.

post-tonal General term for music after 1900 that does not adhere to TONALITY but instead uses any of the new ways that composers found to organize pitch, from ATONAL to NEOTONAL methods.

prelude Introductory piece for solo instrument, often in the style of an IMPROVISATION, or introductory MOVEMENT in a multimovement work such as an OPERA or SUITE.

prepared piano An invention of John Cage in which various objects—such as pennies, bolts, screws, or pieces of wood, rubber, plastic, or slit bamboo—are inserted between the strings of a PIANO, resulting in complex percussive sounds when the piano is played from the keyboard.

prima donna (Italian, "first lady") A soprano singing the leading female role in an OPERA. See also DIVA.

prima pratica (Italian, "first practice") Claudio Monteverdi's term for the style and practice of sixteenth-century POLYPHONY, in contradistinction to the SECONDA PRATICA. Also called STILE ANTICO.

prime In TWELVE-TONE music based on a particular ROW, the original form of the row, transposed or untransposed, as opposed to the INVERSION, RETROGRADE, or RETROGRADE INVERSION.

primitivism Musical style that represents the primitive or elemental through pulsation, static repetition, unprepared and unresolved DISSONANCE, dry TIMBRES, and other techniques.

principal voice (Latin, *vox principalis*) In an ORGANUM, the original CHANT MELODY.

program Text to accompany an instrumental work of PROGRAM MUSIC, describing the sequence of events depicted in the music.

program music Instrumental music that tells a story or follows a narrative or other sequence of events, often spelled out in an accompanying text called a PROGRAM.

prolation See MODE, TIME, AND PROLATION.

Proper (from Latin *proprium*, "particular" or "appropriate") Texts of the MASS that are assigned to a particular day in the CHURCH CALENDAR, often commemorating a saint.

psalm A poem of praise to God, one of 150 in the Book of Psalms in the Hebrew Scriptures (the Christian Old Testament). Singing psalms is a central part of Jewish, Catholic, and Protestant worship.

psalm tone A MELODIC formula for singing PSALMS in the OFFICE. There is one psalm tone for each MODE.

psalmody The singing of PSALMS.

psalter A published collection of METRICAL PSALMS.

psaltery A plucked string instrument whose strings are attached to a frame over a wooden sounding board.

Pythagorean intonation A system of tuning NOTES in the SCALE, common in the Middle Ages, in which all perfect fourths and fifths are tuned according to the ratios 4:3 and 3:2.

quadruplum (Latin, "quadruple") (1) In POLYPHONY of the late twelfth through fourteenth centuries, fourth voice from the bottom in a four-voice TEXTURE, added to a TENOR, DUPLUM, and TRIPLUM. (2) In NOTRE DAME POLYPHONY, an ORGANUM in four voices.

quodlibet (Latin, "whatever you please") COMPOSITION or passage in which two or more existing MELODIES, or parts of melodies, are combined in COUNTERPOINT.

quotation Direct borrowing of one work in another, especially when the borrowed material is not reworked using a standard musical procedure (such as VARIATIONS, PARAPHRASE, or PARODY MASS) but is set off as a foreign element.

rag   Instrumental work in RAGTIME style, usually in the FORM of a MARCH.

ragtime   Musical style that features SYNCOPATED rhythm against a regular, marchlike BASS.

range   A span of NOTES, as in the range of a MELODY or of a MODE.

realization   Performing (or creating a performable edition of) music whose NOTATION is incomplete, as in playing a BASSO CONTINUO or completing a piece left unfinished by its composer.

recapitulation   In SONATA FORM, the third main section, which restates the material from the EXPOSITION, normally all in the TONIC.

recital   Term popularized by Franz Liszt for his solo piano performances and used today for any presentation given by a single performer or a small group.

récitatif mesuré (French, "measured recitative")   In French BAROQUE OPERA, RECITATIVE in a songlike, measured style, in a uniform METER, and with relatively steady motion in the accompaniment.

récitatif simple (French, "simple recitative")   In French BAROQUE OPERA, RECITATIVE that shifts frequently between duple and triple METER to allow the syllables of words that are naturally accented in speech to fall on the downbeats.

recitation formula   In CHANT, a simple MELODY whose outline is used for a variety of texts.

recitative   A passage or section in an OPERA, ORATORIO, CANTATA, or other vocal work in RECITATIVE STYLE.

recitative style (from Italian *stile recitativo*, "recitational style")   A type of vocal singing that approaches speech and follows the natural inflections of the text over a rhythmically stagnant bass.

recitativo arioso   A passage or selection in an OPERA or other vocal work in a style that lies somewhere between RECITATIVE STYLE and ARIA style.

reciting tone (also called TENOR)   The second most important NOTE in a MODE (after the FINAL), often emphasized in CHANT and used for reciting text in a PSALM TONE.

recorder   End-blown wind instrument with a whistle mouthpiece, usually made of wood.

refrain   In a song, a recurring line (or lines) of text set to a recurring MELODY.

reminiscence motive   In an OPERA, a MOTIVE, THEME, or MELODY that recurs in a later scene, in order to recall the events and feelings with which it was first associated. See also LEITMOTIVE.

Renaissance (French, "rebirth")   PERIOD of art, cultural, and music history between the Middle Ages and the BAROQUE PERIOD, marked by HUMANISM.

respond   The first part of a RESPONSORIAL CHANT, appearing before and sometimes repeated after the PSALM verse.

responsorial   Pertaining to a manner of performing CHANT in which a soloist alternates with a group.

responsory   RESPONSORIAL CHANT used in the OFFICE services such as Matins.

retrograde   Backward statement of a previously heard MELODY, passage, or TWELVE-TONE ROW.

retrograde inversion   Upside-down and backward statement of a MELODY or TWELVE-TONE ROW.

rhythm   (1) Music's movement in time. (2) A particular arrangement of short and long durations.

rhythm section   In a JAZZ ENSEMBLE, the group of instruments that keeps the beat and fills in the background, usually piano or guitar, bass, and drums.

rhythmic modes   System of six durational patterns (for example, mode 1, long-short) used in POLYPHONY of the late twelfth and thirteenth centuries, used as the basis of the rhythmic NOTATION of the Notre Dame singers.

ricercare (ricercar) (Italian, "to seek out" or "to attempt")   (1) In the early to mid-sixteenth century, a PRELUDE in the style of an IMPROVISATION. (2) From the late sixteenth century on, an instrumental piece that treats one or more SUBJECTS in IMITATION.

ripieno (Italian, "full")   In a SOLO CONCERTO or CONCERTO GROSSO, the full ORCHESTRA, or TUTTI.

rite   The set of practices that defines a particular Christian tradition, including a CHURCH CALENDAR, a LITURGY, and a repertory of CHANT.

ritornello (Italian, "refrain")   (1) In a fourteenth-century MADRIGAL, the closing section, in a different METER from the preceding verses. (2) In sixteenth- and seventeenth-century vocal music, the instrumental introduction or interlude between sung stanzas. (3) In an ARIA or similar piece, an instrumental passage that recurs several times. Typically, it is played at the beginning, as interludes (often in modified form), and again at the end, and it states the main THEME. (4) In a fast MOVEMENT of a CONCERTO, the recurring thematic material played at the beginning by the full ORCHESTRA and repeated, usually in varied form, throughout the movement and at the end.

ritornello form   Standard FORM for fast MOVEMENTS in CONCERTOS of the first half of the eighteenth century, featuring a RITORNELLO (4) for full ORCHESTRA that alternates with EPISODES characterized by virtuosic material played by one or more soloists.

rock and roll (or **rock**)   A musical style that emerged in the United States in the mid-1950s as a blend of black and white traditions of POPULAR MUSIC, primarily rhythm-and-blues, country music, pop music, and TIN PAN ALLEY.

Romantic   Term applied to music of the nineteenth century. Romantic music had looser and more extended FORMS, greater experimentation with HARMONY and TEXTURE, richly expressive and memorable MELODIES, improved musical instruments, an interest in musical NATIONALISM, and a view of music as a moral force, in which there was a link between the artists' inner lives and the world around them.

rondeau (pl. *rondeaux*)   (1) French FORME FIXE with a single stanza and the musical FORM ABaAabAB, with capital letters indicating lines of REFRAIN and lowercase letters indicating new text set to music from the refrain. (2) FORM in seventeenth- and eighteenth-century instrumental music in which a repeated STRAIN alternates with other strains, as in the pattern ABACA.

rondo   Piece or MOVEMENT in RONDO FORM.

rondo form   Musical FORM in which the first or main section recurs, usually in the TONIC, between subsidiary sections or EPISODES. See also RONDEAU.

root   The lowest NOTE in a CHORD when it is arranged as a succession of thirds.

rota   FORM of medieval English POLYPHONY in which two or more voices sing the same MELODY, entering at different times and repeating the melody until all stop together. See CANON.

rounded binary form   BINARY FORM in which the beginning or all of the first section returns in the TONIC in the latter part of the second section.

row   In TWELVE-TONE MUSIC, an ordering of all twelve PITCH-CLASSES that is used to generate the musical content.

rubato (from Italian *tempo rubato*, "stolen time")   Technique common in ROMANTIC music in which the performer holds back or hurries the written NOTE values, distorting the strict tempo for expressive purposes.

sackbut   RENAISSANCE brass instrument, an early form of the trombone.

sacred concerto   In the seventeenth century, a COMPOSITION on a sacred text for one or more singers and instrumental accompaniment.

sampling   A process of creating new COMPOSITIONS by patching together snippets of previously recorded music.

Sanctus (Latin, "Holy") Of the five major musical prayers in the MASS ORDINARY, the fourth one, based in part on Isaiah 6:3.

saraband (1) Originally a quick dance-song from Latin America. (2) In French BAROQUE music, a slow DANCE in BINARY FORM and in triple METER, often emphasizing the second beat; a standard MOVEMENT of a SUITE.

scale A series of three or more different pitches in ascending or descending order and arranged in a specific pattern.

scat singing Technique in JAZZ in which the performer sings non-sense syllables to an IMPROVISED or composed MELODY.

scherzo (Italian, "joke") A joking or particularly fast MOVEMENT in MINUET AND TRIO FORM.

scholasticism System of teaching predominant in the Middle Ages based chiefly upon the authority of the Church Fathers, as well as of Aristotle and his commentators.

score notation A type of NOTATION in which the different voices or parts are aligned vertically to show how they are coordinated with each other.

seconda pratica or **second practice** Monteverdi's term for a practice of COUNTERPOINT and COMPOSITION that allows the rules of sixteenth-century counterpoint (the PRIMA PRATICA) to be broken in order to express the text. Also called STILE MODERNO.

semibreve In ARS NOVA and RENAISSANCE systems of rhythmic NOTATION, a NOTE that is normally equal to half or a third of a BREVE.

semiminim In ARS NOVA and RENAISSANCE systems of rhythmic NOTATION, a NOTE that is equal to half of a MINIM.

semi-opera Modern term for a seventeenth-century English mixed GENRE of musical theater, a spoken play with an OVERTURE and four or more MASQUES or long musical interludes.

semitone (or half step) The smallest INTERVAL normally used in Western music; half of a TONE.

sequence (from Latin *sequentia*, "something that follows") (1) A category of Latin CHANT that follows the ALLELUIA in some MASSES. (2) Restatement of a pattern, either MELODIC or HARMONIC, on successive or different pitch levels.

serenade A semidramatic piece for several singers and small ORCHESTRA, usually written for a special occasion.

serial music Music composed in the TWELVE-TONE METHOD; used especially for music that extends the same general approach to SERIES in parameters other than pitch.

series (1) A ROW. (2) An ordering of specific durations, dynamic levels, or other non-pitch elements, used in SERIAL MUSIC.

service A setting of Anglican service music, encompassing specific portions of Matins, Holy Communion, and Evensong. A Great Service is a MELISMATIC, CONTRAPUNTAL setting of these texts; a Short Service sets the same text in SYLLABIC, CHORDAL style.

shawm Double-reed instrument, similar to the oboe, used in the medieval, RENAISSANCE, and BAROQUE PERIODS.

simple binary form BINARY FORM in which the two sections are roughly equal in length and feature musical material that is different or only loosely related. See also BALANCED and ROUNDED BINARY FORMS.

simple recitative Style of RECITATIVE scored for solo voice and BASSO CONTINUO, used for setting dialogue or monologue in as speechlike a fashion as possible, without dramatization.

sinfonia (1) Generic term used throughout the seventeenth century for an abstract ENSEMBLE piece, especially one that serves as an introduction to a vocal work. (2) Italian OPERA OVERTURE in the early eighteenth century. (3) Early SYMPHONY.

singspiel (German, "singing play") German GENRE of OPERA, featuring spoken dialogue interspersed with songs, CHORUSES, and instrumental music.

sketch General term for a compositional idea jotted down in a notebook, or an early draft of a work.

slow-movement sonata form Classic-era variant of SONATA FORM that omits the DEVELOPMENT.

small sacred concerto Seventeenth-century GENRE of sacred vocal music featuring one or more soloists accompanied by organ CONTINUO (or modest instrumental ENSEMBLE).

socialist realism A doctrine of the Soviet Union, begun in the 1930s, in which all the arts were required to use a realistic approach (as opposed to an abstract or symbolic one) that portrayed socialism in a positive light. In music this meant use of simple, accessible language, centered on MELODY, and patriotic subject matter.

solmization A method of assigning syllables to STEPS in a SCALE, used to make it easier to identify and sing the WHOLE TONES and SEMITONES in a MELODY.

solo concerto CONCERTO in which a single instrument, such as a VIOLIN, contrasts with an ORCHESTRA.

solo madrigal In the late sixteenth and early seventeenth centuries, a THROUGH-COMPOSED setting of a nonstrophic poem for solo voice with accompaniment, distinguished from an ARIA and from a MADRIGAL for several voices.

sonata (Italian, "sounded") (1) A piece to be played on one or more instruments. (2) BAROQUE instrumental piece with contrasting sections or MOVEMENTS, each based on different material or on variants of the same material. (3) GENRE in several movements for one or two solo instruments, often exploiting the idiomatic possibilities of a particular instrument.

sonata da camera or **chamber sonata** BAROQUE SONATA, usually a SUITE of stylized DANCES, scored for one or more TREBLE instruments and CONTINUO.

sonata da chiesa or **church sonata** BAROQUE instrumental work intended for performance in church; usually in four MOVEMENTS—slow—fast—slow—fast—and scored for one or more TREBLE instruments and CONTINUO.

sonata form FORM typically used in first MOVEMENTS of SONATAS, instrumental chamber works, and SYMPHONIES during the CLASSIC and ROMANTIC PERIODS. An expansion of ROUNDED BINARY FORM, it was described in the nineteenth century as consisting of an EXPOSITION, DEVELOPMENT, and RECAPITULATION based on a limited number of THEMES.

sonata-rondo A FORM that blends characteristics of SONATA FORM and RONDO FORM. One frequent structure is ABACABA, in which A and B correspond to the first and second THEMES of SONATA FORM and B appears first in the DOMINANT and returns in the TONIC.

song cycle A group of art songs performed in succession that tells or suggests a story.

soprano (from SUPERIUS) (1) High female voice. (2) Part for such a voice in a CHORUS (1) or ENSEMBLE work.

sound mass Term coined by Edgard Varèse for a body of sounds characterized by a particular TIMBRE, register, RHYTHM, or MELODIC gesture, which may remain stable or may be transformed as it recurs.

source music See DIEGETIC MUSIC.

spatial Pertaining to a conception of music as sounds moving through musical space, rather than as the presentation and VARIATION of THEMES or MOTIVES.

spectralism Late twentieth-century compositional movement emphasizing TIMBRE (often electronically produced) over pitch as a large-scale structural feature.

spiritual African American type of religious song that originated among southern slaves and was passed down through oral tradition, with texts often based on stories or images from the Bible.

Sprechstimme (German, "speaking voice") A vocal style developed by Arnold Schoenberg in which the performer approximates the written pitches in the gliding tones of speech, while following the notated rhythm.

Stadtpfeifer (German, "town pipers") Professional town musicians who had the exclusive right to provide music within city limits.

step INTERVAL between two adjacent pitches in a DIATONIC, CHROMATIC, OCTATONIC, or WHOLE-TONE SCALE; WHOLE STEP or HALF STEP.

stile antico (Italian, "old style") Style used in music written after 1600 in imitation of the old contrapuntal style of Palestrina, used especially for church music. See PRIMA PRATICA.

stile concitato (Italian, "excited style") Style devised by Claudio Monteverdi to portray anger and warlike actions, characterized by rapid reiteration of a single NOTE, whether on quickly spoken syllables or in a measured string tremolo.

stile moderno (Italian, "modern style") Seventeenth-century style that used BASSO CONTINUO and applied the rules of COUNTERPOINT freely. See SECONDA PRATICA.

Stollen See BAR FORM.

stop (1) Mechanism on an organ to turn on or off the sounding of certain sets of pipes. (2) The particular set of pipes controlled by such a mechanism.

string quartet (1) Standard chamber ENSEMBLE consisting of two VIOLINS, viola, and cello. (2) Multimovement COMPOSITION for this ENSEMBLE.

strain In a MARCH or RAG, a PERIOD, usually of sixteen or thirty-two measures.

strophic Of a poem, consisting of two or more stanzas that are equivalent in form and can each be sung to the same MELODY; of a vocal work, consisting of a strophic poem set to the same music for each stanza.

strophic variation Early seventeenth-century vocal GENRE, a setting of a STROPHIC poem, in which the MELODY of the first stanza is varied but the HARMONIC plan remains essentially the same, although the duration of harmonies may change to reflect the accentuation and meaning of the text.

style luthé (French, "lute style") or **style brisé** (French, "broken style") Broken or ARPEGGIATED TEXTURE in keyboard and LUTE music from seventeenth-century France. The technique originated with the lute, and the FIGURATION was transferred to the HARPSICHORD.

subdominant In TONAL music, the NOTE and CHORD a fifth below the TONIC.

subject THEME, used especially for the main MELODY used in a RICERCARE, FUGUE, or other IMITATIVE work.

sublime In literature and the arts, the evocation of awe and astonishment.

substitute clausula In NOTRE DAME POLYPHONY, a new CLAUSULA (usually in DISCANT style) designed to replace the original POLYPHONIC setting of a particular segment of a CHANT.

suite A set of pieces that are linked together into a single work. During the BAROQUE, a suite usually referred to a set of stylized DANCE pieces.

superius (Latin, "highest") In fifteenth- and sixteenth-century POLYPHONY, the highest part. See also CANTUS.

suspension DISSONANCE created when a NOTE is sustained while another voice moves to form a dissonance with it; the sustained voice descends a STEP to resolve the dissonance.

swing A style of JAZZ originating in the 1930s that was characterized by large ENSEMBLES and hard-driving jazz rhythms played by the RHYTHM SECTION.

syllabic Having (or tending to have) one NOTE sung to each syllable of text.

symphonic poem (or **tone poem**) Term coined by Franz Liszt for a one-movement work of PROGRAM MUSIC for orchestra that conveys a poetic idea, story, scene, or succession of moods by presenting THEMES that are repeated, varied, or transformed.

symphony Large work for ORCHESTRA, usually in four MOVEMENTS.

syncopation Temporary disruption of METER by beginning a long NOTE on an offbeat and sustaining it through the beginning of the next beat.

synthesizer Electronic instrument that generates and processes a wide variety of sounds.

tablature A system of NOTATION used for LUTE or other plucked string instruments that tells the player which strings to pluck and where to place the fingers on the strings, rather than indicating which NOTES will result. Tablature was also used for keyboard instruments until the seventeenth century.

tabor See PIPE AND TABOR.

talea (Latin, "cutting"; pronounced TAH-lay-ah) In an ISORHYTHMIC COMPOSITION, an extended rhythmic pattern repeated one or more times, usually in the TENOR. See also COLOR.

temperament Any system of tuning NOTES in the SCALE in which pitches are adjusted to make most or all INTERVALS sound well, though perhaps not in perfect tune.

tempo (Italian, "time") Speed of performance, or relative pace of the music.

tempo d'attacco (Italian, "movement of the opening") The first fast movement, following the RECITATIVE, in a nineteenth-century operatic ARIA or duet. It usually contains dialogue and action and leads to a more lyrical and static second movement or section. See also CANTABILE, TEMPO DI MEZZO, and CABALETTA.

tempo di mezzo (Italian, "middle movement") In the early nineteenth century, the middle section of an ARIA or ENSEMBLE, usually an interruption or a TRANSITION, that falls between the CANTABILE and the CABALETTA.

tempus (Latin, "time"; pl. *tempora*) In medieval systems of NOTATION, the basic time unit. See also MODE, TIME, AND PROLATION.

tenor (from Latin *tenere*, "to hold") (1) In a MODE or CHANT, the RECITING TONE. (2) In POLYPHONY of the twelfth and thirteenth centuries, the voice part that has the chant or other borrowed MELODY, often in long-held NOTES. (3) Male voice of a relatively high range.

tenor mass See CANTUS FIRMUS MASS.

termination In a PSALM TONE, the CADENCE that marks the end of the PSALM VERSE.

ternary form A FORM in three main sections, in which the first and third are identical or closely related and the middle section is contrasting, creating an ABA pattern.

tetrachord (from Greek, "four strings") (1) In Greek and medieval theory, a SCALE of four NOTES spanning a perfect fourth. (2) In modern theory, a set of four pitches or PITCH-CLASSES. (3) In TWELVE-TONE theory, the first four, middle four, or last four notes in the ROW.

text depiction Using musical gestures to reinforce or suggest images in a text, such as a rising gesture on the word "ascend."

text expression Conveying or suggesting through musical means the emotions expressed in a text.

texture The combination of elements in a piece or passage, such as the number and relationship of independent parts (as in MONOPHONY, HETEROPHONY, POLYPHONY, or HOMOPHONY), GROUPS (as in POLYCHORAL MUSIC), or musical events (as in relatively dense or transparent sonorities).

theme Musical subject of a COMPOSITION or section, or of a set of VARIATIONS.

thematic transformation A method devised by Franz Liszt to provide unity, variety, and a narrative-like logic to a composition by transforming the thematic material into new THEMES or other elements, in order to reflect the diverse moods needed to portray a PROGRAMMATIC subject.

theorbo Large LUTE with extra BASS strings, used especially in the seventeenth century for performing BASSO CONTINUO as accompaniment to singers or instruments.

thoroughbass See BASSO CONTINUO.

through-composed Composed throughout, as when each stanza or other unit of a poem is set to new music rather than in a STROPHIC manner to a single MELODY.

timbre or **tone color** Characteristic color or sound of an instrument or voice.

time signature Sign or numerical proportion, such as $\frac{3}{4}$, placed at the beginning of a piece, section, or MEASURE to indicated the METER.

Tin Pan Alley (1) Jocular name for a district in New York where numerous publishers specializing in POPULAR SONGS were located from the 1880s through the 1950s. (2) Styles of American popular song from that era.

toccata (Italian, "touched") Piece for keyboard instrument or LUTE resembling an IMPROVISATION that may include IMITATIVE sections or may serve as a PRELUDE to an independent FUGUE.

tonal Operating within the system of TONALITY.

tonality The system, common since the late seventeenth century, by which a piece of music is organized around a TONIC NOTE, CHORD, and KEY, to which all the other notes and keys in the piece are subordinate.

tone (1) A sound of definite pitch. (2) See WHOLE STEP.

tone cluster Term coined by Henry Cowell for a CHORD of DIATONIC or CHROMATIC seconds.

tone color See TIMBRE.

tone poem SYMPHONIC POEM, or a similar work for a medium other than ORCHESTRA.

tonic (1) The first and central NOTE of a MAJOR or MINOR SCALE. (2) The main KEY of a piece or MOVEMENT, in which the piece or movement begins and ends and to which all other keys are subordinate.

total serialism The application of the principles of the TWELVE-TONE METHOD to musical parameters other than pitch, including duration, intensities, and TIMBRES. See SERIAL MUSIC.

Tract (from Latin *tractus*, "drawn out") Item in the MASS PROPER, comprising a series of PSALM VERSES, that replaces the ALLELUIA in Lent.

tragédie en musique (French, "tragedy in music"; later tragédie lyrique, "lyric tragedy") French seventeenth- and eighteenth-century form of OPERA, pioneered by Jean-Baptiste Lully, that combined the French classic drama and BALLET traditions with music, DANCES, and spectacles.

transcription (1) Arrangement of a piece for an instrumental medium different from the original, such as a reduction of an ORCHESTRAL score for PIANO. (2) In JAZZ, the notation of an improvised solo or other section of a sounding work, generally from a recording.

transition (1) In the EXPOSITION of a MOVEMENT in SONATA FORM, the passage between the first and second THEMES that effects the MODULATION to a new KEY. (2) More generally, a passage between two MOVEMENTS or SECTIONS of a work.

transverse flute Flute blown across a hole in the side of the pipe and held to one side of the player; used for medieval, RENAISSANCE, and BAROQUE forms of the flute to distinguish it from the RECORDER, which is blown in one end and held in front.

treble (French, "triple") (1) A high voice or a part written for high voice, especially the highest part in three-part POLYPHONY of the fourteenth and fifteenth centuries. (2) Pertaining to the highest voice.

treble-dominated style Style common in the fourteenth and fifteenth centuries, in which the main MELODY is in the CANTUS, the upper voice carrying the text, supported by a slower-moving TENOR and CONTRATENOR.

trecento (Italian, short for *mille trecento*, "one thousand three hundred"; pronounced treh-CHEN-toh) The 1300s (the fourteenth century), particularly with reference to Italian art, literature, and music of the time.

triad CHORD consisting of two successive thirds (for instance, C–E–G), or any INVERSION of such a chord.

trill Rapid alternation between a NOTE and another HALF STEP or WHOLE STEP above.

trio (1) Piece for three players or singers. (2) The second of two alternating DANCES, in the Classical-era MINUET AND TRIO FORM. (3) The second main section of a MARCH.

trio sonata Common instrumental GENRE during the BAROQUE PERIOD, a SONATA for two TREBLE instruments (usually VIOLINS) above a BASSO CONTINUO. A performance featured four or more players if more than one was used for the continuo part.

triple motet Thirteenth-century MOTET in four voices, with a different text in each voice above the TENOR.

triplum (from Latin *triplus*, "triple") (1) In POLYPHONY of the late twelfth through fourteenth centuries, third voice from the bottom in a three- or four-voice TEXTURE, added to a TENOR and DUPLUM. (2) In NOTRE DAME POLYPHONY, an ORGANUM in three voices.

tritone INTERVAL spanning three WHOLE TONES or six SEMITONES, such as F to B.

trobairitz (from Occitan *trobar*, "to compose a song") A female TROUBADOUR.

trope Addition to an existing CHANT, consisting of (1) words and MELODY; (2) a MELISMA; or (3) words only, set to an existing melisma or other melody.

troubadour (from Occitan *trobar*, "to compose a song") A poet-composer of southern France who wrote MONOPHONIC songs in Occitan (*langue d'oc*) in the twelfth or thirteenth century.

trouvère (from Old French *trover*, "to compose a song") A poet-composer of northern France who wrote MONOPHONIC songs in Old French (*langue d'oïl*) in the twelfth or thirteenth century.

tutti (Italian, "all") (1) In both the SOLO CONCERTO and the CONCERTO GROSSO, designates the full ORCHESTRA. Also called RIPIENO (Italian, "full"). (2) Instruction to an ENSEMBLE that all should play.

twelve-bar blues Standard formula for the BLUES, with a HARMONIC PROGRESSION in which the first four-measure PHRASE is on the TONIC, the second phrase begins on the SUBDOMINANT and ends on the tonic, and the third phrase starts on the DOMINANT and returns to the tonic.

twelve-tone method A form of ATONAL music based on the systematic ordering of the twelve notes of the CHROMATIC scale into a ROW that may be manipulated according to certain rules.

unmeasured prelude A French BAROQUE keyboard GENRE, usually the first MOVEMENT in a SUITE, whose nonmetric NOTATION gives a feeling of IMPROVISATION.

underscoring See NONDIEGETIC MUSIC.

variation The process of reworking a given MELODY, song, THEME, or other musical idea, or the resulting varied FORM of it.

variations (variations form) FORM that presents an uninterrupted series of variants (each called a VARIATION) on a THEME; the theme may be a MELODY, a BASS line, a HARMONIC plan, or other musical subject.

vaudeville In late-nineteenth- and early-twentieth-century America, a type of variety show including musical numbers.

verismo (Italian, "realism") Nineteenth-century operatic trend that presents everyday people in familiar situations, often depicting sordid or brutal events.

verse (1) Line of poetry. (2) Sentence of a psalm. (3) In GREGORIAN CHANT, a setting of a psalm verse or similar text, such as the verses that are part of the INTROIT, GRADUAL, and ALLELUIA.

verse anthem ANTHEM in which passages for solo voice(s) with accompaniment alternate with passages for full CHOIR doubled by instruments.

verse-refrain form   A FORM in vocal music in which two or more stanzas of poetry are each sung to the same music (the VERSE) and each is followed by the same REFRAIN.

vielle   Medieval bowed string instrument, early form of the fiddle and predecessor of the VIOLIN and VIOL.

vihuela   Spanish relative of the LUTE with a flat back and guitar-shaped body.

villancico (from Spanish *villano*, "peasant"; pronounced vee-yan-THEE-co)   Type of POLYPHONIC song in Spanish, with several stanzas framed by a REFRAIN; originally secular, the FORM was later used for sacred works, especially associated with Christmas or other important holy days.

villanella   Type of sixteenth-century Italian song, generally for three voices, in a rustic HOMOPHONIC style.

viol (viola da gamba)   Bowed, fretted string instrument popular from the mid-fifteenth to the early eighteenth centuries, held between the legs.

violin   Bowed, fretless string instrument tuned in fifths (*g-d′ -a′ -e″*).

virelai   French FORME FIXE in the pattern A bba A bba A bba A, in which a REFRAIN (A) alternates with stanzas with the musical FORM bba, the a using the same music as the refrain.

virginal   (1) English name for HARPSICHORD, used for all types until the seventeenth century. (2) Type of HARPSICHORD that is small enough to place on a table, with a single keyboard and strings running at right angles to the keys rather than parallel with them as in larger harpsichords.

virtuoso   Performer who dazzles audiences with his or her technical prowess in singing or playing an instrument.

walking bass   BASS line in BAROQUE music—and later in JAZZ—that moves steadily and continuously, often stepwise.

waltz   Type of couple dance in triple meter, popular in the late eighteenth and nineteenth centuries, or a short, stylized work for the PIANO in the style of such a dance.

whole step (or **whole tone**)   An interval equivalent to two SEMITONES.

whole-tone scale (or **whole-tone collection**)   A SCALE consisting of only WHOLE STEPS.

wind ensemble   Large ENSEMBLE of winds, brass, and percussion instruments, mostly with one player per part, dedicated solely to serious music, rather than to the mix of MARCHES and other fare typically played by BANDS.

word painting   See TEXT DEPICTION.

MUSIC CREDITS

INDEX